THE
JOHN
LENNON
ENCYCLOPEDIA

INTRODUCTION

As with this book's sister volume, *The Beatles Encyclopedia*, I have used a huge variety of sources in my research. Naturally, these include my own memories of art school days with John, which led on to the *Mersey Beat* magazine and scene, and our friendship, which lasted until John left to make his home in New York. In London, I regularly met John in clubs such as the Scotch Of St James and Bag O' Nails. I was also a regular visitor to Apple, and it was at an Apple Christmas Party that John first introduced me to Yoko. Several times, whilst at the Speakeasy Club, he would offer my wife Virginia and me a lift in his car as he and Yoko travelled on to the Bag O' Nails.

Obviously, the hundreds of interviews I have conducted over the past 40 years have been utilised – and they have included every member of the Beatles, Brian Epstein, Neil Aspinall, and a wide range of characters from John's life. More recent interviewees have included Stan Parkes, Rod Davis, Charlie Lennon, Len Garry and Nigel Walley. I also appreciate the help of numerous Beatles enthusiasts such as Bill Logan, and the wealth of information in publications such as *Beatlefan, Beatles Now, Beatles Unlimited* and *Good Day Sunshine*.

I have long been a hoarder of clippings relating to John and the Beatles, in addition to collecting magazines, fanzines, newspapers and books, all of which have proved valuable research tools – as has the world of the web!

Personally I look at John's life as B.Y. and A.Y. – before Yoko and after Yoko. From a personal perspective, I experienced much of the B.Y. period and little of the A.Y. one. We can only speculate what John might have created had he not met Yoko. We would have had solely the genius of John Lennon, rather than the splitting of his abilities to merge with – and perhaps be submerged by – the avant garde theories of Yoko. Did John merely become a funnel through which Yoko could channel her own creative ideas?

The A.Y. period is well documented – indeed, exhaustively chronicled – because John and Yoko made so many films, recordings and documentations of their love affair. So was it the romance of the century, or was it merely an obsessive love?

Since John's death, most of what we see about John on film and TV is of the A.Y. period because Yoko, as executrix of his estate, has complete control and the 28 years before he met Yoko are clearly of less interest to her.

Certainly, though, the ideas and desires of Yoko seemed to predominate the famous relationship. Her own recordings were used on John's releases (some fans regarded *Double Fantasy* as merely a John Lennon EP), the couple settled in New York, which was basically Yoko's home, and John became a house-husband – allegedly a prior condition insisted on by Yoko before she agreed to have Sean.

Camille Paglia on *The South Bank Show* described John as 'An innocent in Yoko's clutches,' and added that Yoko 'crushed John's originality with the moralism and political correctness that she imposed on him'. She concluded that in his time with Yoko, Lennon may have been a happier person, but he was a lesser artist.

On the other hand, it is unfair that Yoko has been the subject of as much hate as love from Lennon fans. The problem has been that much of John's personal quotes about the relationship are disingenuous. John had a tendency to rewrite elements of the relationship and create an often inaccurate picture of certain events. His own depictions of his love were not reliable. Witnesses to certain events contradict many of the things John said.

Whatever. This is a controversy that will run and run. John Lennon left a unique legacy in music and popular culture, and Yoko is a vital and essential figure in that legacy.

Finally, I would like to thank Ian Gittins, Mel Harrison, Kirstie Addis, Andrew Armitage and all at Virgin for helping to make this book a reality.

Bill Harry
London, April 2000

A Ultima Entrevista De John Lennon

A record containing excerpts from an interview John taped for RKO Radio on the morning of the day he was killed. The seven-inch record was available free with a special tribute edition of the Brazilian music paper *Somtres*, called 'John Lennon Documento', in 1981.

Aalborg

A town in the Jutland area of Denmark. Tony Cox (Yoko Ono's second husband) and his daughter Kyoko had moved to a remote farmhouse an hour's drive from Aalborg in Denmark, together with Melinda, Cox's new wife, a rich blonde-haired, bespectacled Texan he'd met in New York in the spring of 1968. The two had married in the summer of 1969 at Bellport, Long Island. A Danish friend, Aage Rosendal Nielsen, had found the couple work lecturing at Norden Fjord World University and they had moved into the remote farmhouse. Yoko wanted to see Kyoko, and John and Yoko were invited to join the Coxes and left London on 19 December 1969. As Cox had ceased to use tobacco, alcohol and drugs, he objected to Kyoko's being exposed to the Lennons, as he believed they used all three.

Cox was to write,

John and Yoko seemed to really be looking for the truth when they came out to the farm. And they did a lot of symbolic things. They burned their cigarettes in the snow outside the farmhouse and they cut their hair off. They were also determined that we should heal our relationship. They had literally shown up in tears and said they regretted the trouble they had caused us. They offered me a film project to help make up for some of my losses. They also offered me Allen Klein's job [as their manager]; their first contract with him was just ending then. But I said I couldn't do that. I'd committed myself to finding God. There was still a certain amount of tension between us, John invited [the comedian] Dick Gregory to join us. When Dick got there he said that the answer to our problems was to fast and pray together and so we went on a fourteen-day fast.

A young hairdresser, Aase Haukrogh, was invited to the farmhouse. She was asked to cut Kyoko's long hair in a very short style. Yoko began to cry; John encouraged her to get her hair cut too. In all, Haukrogh spent four hours cutting the hair of Kyoko, John, Yoko, Tony and Melinda.

John was to say, 'I just felt like shedding all that hair because a new haircut might enable me to move about anonymously.'

The house was fitted throughout with video cameras – in every room including the bathroom, bedroom and toilet – as Cox wanted to make a visual diary. He was later to use a video of John and Kyoko having a bath together in a future court case.

Tony's wife had been a member of a California cult called the Harbingers, based in Harbinger Springs, near San Francisco. Dr Don Hamrick ran it. The Coxes invited him over to try to hypnotise John into giving up smoking.

John and Yoko had been in negotiations to appear at a Peace Festival in Canada organised by John Brower and Ritchie York. John had contacted Brower and asked him to prepare a file on Allen Klein and demanded they bring the information to him. They consulted a number of people who had dealings with Klein, prepared the file and flew out to Denmark, booking into the White House Hotel in Aalborg, where they also encountered Hamrick.

When they visited John in the farmhouse he asked for the file. They were then shocked to see that John had also invited Klein to the meeting.

John then told Brower that he wanted Hamrick and his colleagues to be involved in the festival and he immediately came up with talk of contact with extraterrestrials and opening the festival with an 'air car' that could fly without fuel. Then John demanded that the festival be free of charge, despite the fact that Brower pointed out that, with the huge costs involved, there would need to be a minimum charge of $20. Brower and York, realising a free festival would be impractical and, reckoning that the Harbingers' ideas were too way out, flew back to American disconsolate.

John and Yoko returned to London on 25 January with their hair in a white plastic box, having decided to offer it to a charity.

John also remembered a phrase that Melinda Cox had been using, 'Instant Karma', and he was inspired to write a song with that title.

Abbey Road

Although *Let It Be* was released at a later date, *Abbey Road* turned out to be the last complete set of recordings by the Beatles. It was recorded at the request of Paul, who approached the producer George Martin and said, 'Let's get back and record like we used to. Would you produce an album like you used to?' It was also an album in which, during most of the recordings, the individual members weren't in the studio at the same time, although it isn't apparent when you listen to the end product. Three recording studios were used – Abbey Road, Trident and Olympic – and the recordings were made from 22 February to 19 August 1969. It was released in the UK on 26 September 1969, and topped the charts for eighteen weeks; and it was issued in the US on 1 October 1969, where it topped the charts for eleven weeks.

George Martin regarded it as his favourite Beatles album, although John was to say, 'It was a competent album, like *Rubber Soul*. It was together in that way, but *Abbey Road* had no life in it.'

John's compositions on the album were 'Come Together', 'I Want You (She's So Heavy)', 'Because', 'Sun King' and 'Polythene Pam'.

Accordion

The first musical instrument John ever learned to play. As a child he was given an accordion and he learned to play tunes such as 'Greensleeves', 'Moulin Rouge' and 'Swedish Rhapsody' on it.

Acorns

In April 1969, following their Amsterdam 'bed-in', John and Yoko decided to use acorns as a symbol of peace. They devised their 'Acorns For Peace' campaign in which they arranged to send acorns to the heads of state of various countries with a request that they plant them as a symbol of peace.

John commented, 'Yoko and I plan to send one of these envelopes containing two acorns to the head of state of every country in the world. We want them to plant them for peace.'

Yoko said, 'If they want us to, we would go to the countries and plant them ourselves.'

John added, 'I think this will be the most positive move for peace yet. It would be much better than all that phoney smiling and shaking hands you see in the papers.'

Only two heads of state planted the acorns – Golda Meir of Israel and Pierre Trudeau of Canada.

John and Yoko had also used acorns creatively the previous year in their 'Acorn Event' of Saturday 15 June 1968, when they planted two acorns outside Coventry Cathedral as part of the National Sculpture Exhibition. They explained that the planting was to symbolise 'the uniting and growth of our two cultures'.

In December 1997 a reader had written to the *Daily Express* saying, 'On June 15, 1968, John Lennon and Yoko Ono planted two "acorns for peace" outside Coventry Cathedral as part of the National Sculpture Exhibition. Have they blossomed into trees?'

The Revd Lawrence Mortimer of Coventry Cathedral replied. He wrote, 'John and Yoko's controversial contribution to the National Sculpture Exhibition at Coventry Cathedral Ruins, part of the June 1968 Peoples and Cities Conference, was not welcomed by the eminent artists involved, including Barbara Hepworth, but Canon Stephen Verney backed the decision to include it on Unity Lawn.

'Entitled *Yoko By John, John By Yoko – This Is What Happens When Two Clouds Meet*, the work consisted of a circular wrought-iron bench with two acorns buried at its centre.

'Viewers were encouraged to sit and contemplate the acorns growing and the exhibit was insured for £4,000.

'The acorns went missing within a month and various myths surround them. The present cathedral verger, Mary Wickens, a young girl at the time, says souvenir hunters stole them, while retired press officer Connie Downes believes they were still present when the bench was moved to gardens at the west end of the ruins.

'Lennon was clearly dissatisfied with Coventry's treatment of his opus, complaining that the acorns hadn't been planted in an east–west orientation. Retired clerk of works Jack West recalls him turning up a month after the exhibition "in a chauffeur-driven heap with a trailer attached. He piled the seat on board and that was the last we saw of it." '

Across the River
A home demo John recorded early in 1980. He made a ten-minute recording of a medley of songs that included 'Beautiful Boy', 'Memories' and 'Across The River'.

Across the Universe
The inspiration for the song came when John woke up at seven o'clock one morning with the words 'pools of sorrow, waves of joy' spinning around in his head. He couldn't get back to sleep and began writing the song.

Evidence of the influence of the Maharishi Mahesh Yogi is contained in the chorus phrase 'Jai Guru de va Om', which refers to the Maharishi's teacher, Guru Deva. George Martin produced the first version of the song on Sunday 4 February 1968.

During the session it was decided that some female voices were needed to sing the line 'nothing's going to change my world'.

Paul found two girls outside the studio and brought them in on the session. Thus Gayleen Pease and Lizzie Bravo found their own piece of immortality. Lizzie was sixteen and from Brazil and Gayleen was seventeen.

The song was originally considered as the A-side of a Beatles single, but 'Lady Madonna' was chosen instead; it was also considered as a flip side, and as an EP cut, but was left aside and the number lay on the shelf for some time.

John was to say, 'It's one of the best lyrics I've written; in fact it could be *the* best. It's good poetry, or whatever you call it. The ones I like are the ones that stand as words without melody.'

The comedian Spike Milligan had suggested to the World Wildlife Fund (now the World Wide Fund for Nature) that they issue an album, with the proceeds going to the charity. 'Across the Universe' was donated by the Beatles.

The album was called *No One's Gonna Change Our World*, and was issued on EMI Star Line SRS 5013 (LP) on 12 December 1969. Other artists featured on the album included Cilla Black, Rolf Harris, the Hollies, Spike Milligan, the Bee Gees, Lulu, Dave Dee, Dozy, Beaky Mick and Tich, Cliff Richard and the Shadows, Bruce Forsyth and Harry Secombe.

When Phil Spector was called in to work on a number of Beatles tapes, he completely altered 'Across the Universe', removing the vocals by Paul and the two girls and introducing his 'wall of sound' and the famous 'Spector overkill'. This version wound up on the *Let It Be* album.

The song also appeared on *The Beatles 1967–1970* LP issued in April 1973, and in the boxed set of albums, *The Beatles Collection*, issued in December 1968 on the album *Rarities*. It also found its way onto *Past Masters Volume II* and the *Anthology 2* CDs.

Rarities itself was issued as a separate album in October 1979.

David Bowie featured the number on his *Young Americans* album and John played on the track with him. The song was also performed by the Beatles in the film *Let it Be*.

Action for the Crippled Child
The name of a charity for which John donated one of his drawings to be used as a Christmas card in 1966.

Adams, Maude
Swedish actress who appeared in two Bond films, *The Man With the Golden Gun* and *Octopussy*.

Immediately following the recording of the *Double Fantasy*

album, the producer Jack Douglas's girlfriend Christine Desautels heard that John fancied Maude Adams. As Maude had been a close friend of Ringo Starr's ex-girlfriend, Nancy Andrews, Christine phoned her and told her that Lennon was interested in meeting Maude. Nancy told the actress, who travelled to New York to meet him, but nothing came of it.

Douglas had said, 'A request [from John] had gone out for a particular lady – Maude Adams. He was nuts about her. It was weird. He used to say "Do you think she'll like me?" '

Advertisements

John and Yoko were always conscious of the media and its power as a means of communication. Despite their access to the press, they occasionally paid for advertisements to convey a message they wished to get across. Their 'War Is Over' campaign, with its huge display posters, is an example of how they used advertising.

Another example occurred on John's fortieth birthday when Yoko hired a plane to fly past the Dakota Building in New York with the message SEAN AND YOKO LOVE YOU (Sean was John's second son). Not strictly an ad, but a striking way to make a point.

On 24 July 1967, Brian Epstein and the Beatles were among the signatories to a full-page advertisement in the London *Times*, in which they stated, 'The law against marijuana is immoral in principle and unworkable in practice.' They advocated the legalisation of this soft drug. On 8 November 1968 John and Yoko took out advertisements in the music press in support of the 'Peace Ship', an independent radio station aboard a ship in the Middle East that attempted to advocate peace between the Israelis and the Arabs.

One of their most famous advertisements appeared in Sunday newspapers in New York, London and Tokyo on 27 May 1979 under the headline: A LOVE LETTER FROM JOHN AND YOKO TO PEOPLE WHO ASK US WHAT, WHEN AND WHY?

A controversial aspect of advertisements is the television commercials, which use popular music hits to advertise their products. Many people feel this demeans the original song and once seen it is very difficult to dispel the image of a particular commercial whenever a person hears the song again.

'Help!' was used as an advertisement by Ford in 1985, leading Apple to state that actual recordings of the Beatles should not be used for commercial exploitation in advertising. Beatles fans throughout the world were in an uproar when Yoko gave her permission for the footwear manufacturer Nike to use the Beatles' 1968 recording 'Revolution' in their commercials, which began screening on Friday 27 March 1987. Although Yoko had given her agreement to the ads, Apple's attorney filed a lawsuit against Nike and Capitol Records on 18 July 1987 stating, 'The Beatles' position is that they don't sing jingles to peddle sneakers, beer, pantyhose or anything else. Their position is that they wrote and recorded these songs as artists and not as pitch men for any product – use of the Beatles' voices constitutes unauthorised exploitation of the Beatles' persona and good will.'

Despite this, Yoko approved further Nike commercials and on Friday 1 May 1992 their commercial included the music of John's original recording of 'Instant Karma!'. Once again, this infuriated fans of the artist. In February 1998 Johnson & Johnson used 'Love' in a TV commercial and in April 1999 Yoko also authorised the use of 'Instant Karma!' for British TV commercials advertising Walker's Crisps.

In 1992 'Beautiful Boy' was used as a television commercial in Japan to promote the Shiseido firm's Dungaree cosmetic products. Sean was featured in the ads.

A particularly interesting commercial television advertisement was screened on British television at the beginning of 1999. Chris Evans, the disc jockey and television personality, was featured in a commercial for One2One mobile phones. By some clever digital work he was featured on the bed with John and Yoko during their 1969 Amsterdam 'bed-in'. Yoko had authorised the use of the images of herself and John for a fee of $75,000 which she said she would donate to Help the Aged, a British charity.

Afterlife

When the Beatles were still together as a group they discussed life after death. Paul McCartney said they made a pact that, if one of them died, he would try to communicate with the others. They haven't so far heard from John. John believed in the afterlife and told his son Julian that, if he died, he would contact him. Julian recalled, 'He said if anything happened to him, he'd send a sign back to say he was OK. He said he'd make a feather float down the room.

'Ever since his death I've been waiting for that sign. Every time I'm alone in a room, I find myself staring round looking for a feather.'

Since John's death spiritualists from different parts of the world claim to have had communication with him. They allege that his spirit is still seeking to bring peace to a troubled world.

According to several spiritualists, John's spirit lingered on Earth for a short time before a group of spirit guides helped him to adjust to 'the other world'. A person who won't 'let go' after they are dead becomes a ghost who haunts the area of the tragedy. The guides persuaded him to join them in the spirit world and various mediums allegedly began receiving messages from him.

After John's death, a number of people claimed to have seen his ghost around the Dakota Building, including Joey Harrow, a musician, Shawn Robbins, a psychic, and Amanda Moores, a writer. Yoko Ono herself was reported to have seen John sitting at his white piano. He turned to her and said, 'Don't be afraid. I am still with you.'

Linda Deer Domnitz from California claims to have begun channelling conversations from the spirit of John four days after his death and taped over a thousand pages of messages, which she condensed and included in a book called *John Lennon Conversations*. For 26 months the medium claims she spoke to John, who disclosed to her that he is remaining close to the Earth in order to save the planet from destruction, working to further the cause of world peace and harmony. This is similar to messages about a white brotherhood of the spirit world, which John allegedly discussed with another medium.

Domnitz wrote to Bill Harry to report she was still receiving messages and advice, allegedly from John, which discuss the topics of a psychic and religious nature, with details of astral travel and life in the spirit world. There are also messages to Yoko Ono, Sean and Julian, Paul, George and Ringo.

To Ringo Starr he says, 'I want you to know that I am at peace, Ringo, and I am happy to be where I am. I have no regrets and no animosities towards anyone, so let that go and bear no grudges to anyone you think might have wronged me because I feel no such hatred or animosity.'

Part of the message to George Harrison said, 'I hope that you will emulate some of the things which I have taught you, especially in the peace movement, but that you will not be a clone for me any more than I was a clone for anyone else. I want your ideas to be original, and clear, and concise, and to the point, so that everyone hearing your music can understand exactly where you are coming from and where you've been. This is not John Lennon, but George Harrison, although there are some similarities. You are you, and I am me, but we can work together as we have in the past.'

To Paul, John conveys the message that he wishes him to continue to work through music to express some of the ideas for peace, which he had attempted in the 1970s. 'You can create a whole new type of music which has been somewhat alien to you in the past and which you considered my bag. I would like you to consider it now your bag, as I am transferring it to you and hope that you will understand what I am trying to tell you and how much you can be the focus for this type of new age music which will help bring us back together again as one family in the world of peace for all mankind.'

Domnitz even made a ninety-minute tape of her conversations available. Another medium who has issued tapes of conversations with John Lennon's spirit is Bill Tenuto of San Diego. He claims that his guide is a female spirit named Ellenore. Ellenore is English and was killed during an air raid on London in 1943.

In his messages through Ellenore, John claims that one of his best friends on 'the other side' is a Native American. He also related how he met his mother Julia again. 'She's so beautiful,' he said. He also alleges that he met Jesus: 'He's a spirit. He's a great person. He's a master.'

It also seems that parties are held on 'the other side'. John held a party in which a number of other personalities appeared, including Clark Gable and Carol Lombard. John's spirit said, '... and Carol Lombard was there, and I took to her. I want to tell you I really took to her. We are capable of having sex over here ... we do the same thing that you do except without the body. We love sex as much as anybody who's got a body. The sensations are a bit different, with an interplay of energies that take place when we have sex. We don't concern ourselves with Planned Parenthood since spirits can't propagate a baby spirit.'

Describing his murder, John said, 'I had flashes in my skin and then I was out.'

He admits to having contacted Yoko since his death and holds no rancour towards his killer, Mark Chapman, because his spirit was only evening up an old score. 'We had a past life together and you might say I did something not too nice to him. I shot him in the back.'

John remembers several previous incarnations. Directly before his birth in Liverpool he was living in 'the southwestern portion of China. I don't know what I was, a simple kind of person, perhaps a farmer or a merchant, but not a very wealthy one. I died quite early on.'

He also claims to have lived out a past life with Yoko. 'I was a very strict father to her. She was a rebellious and resentful type of daughter.'

John is also in league with the White Brotherhood, a group of highly advanced spirits who don't have to reincarnate any more.

John's spirit says, 'They've asked me to work with them, and I've agreed.' The work is to communicate the messages of the Masters to the rest of the world, particularly to political leaders. Other spirits who are helping John in this task include John Wayne, Harry Truman and Golda Meir.

Despite being discarnate, Tenuto also reported that John still enjoys sex. He told Tenuto that during a break between spiritualist sessions, 'I took up with a female energy-type spirit person and we went off and made it. It was a quickie. It was quite nice. It energised me.'

According to Domnitz, John has also revealed, 'I spent a great deal of time writing about my death and what it would be like. When these papers are discovered, it will be noted that I had no hesitancy about embracing death, although I loved life more dearly.'

Numerous other mediums from around the world have claimed to communicate with John's spirit, including the English spiritualist Rosemary Brown, who claimed John dictated songs to her.

There have also been several books published in which spiritualists have documented John's afterlife.

One such book is *Peace At Last: The After-Death Experiences of John Lennon*, in which the author, Jeremy Leen, quoted Lennon as saying: ' "As I felt the release of my physical body, I knew it was dead. A powerful surge of light filled the room, and the world I had known disappeared. I was being swept through a tunnel as bright as the sun itself." '

Leen goes on to say, 'After his journey through the tunnel of light, John is met by his mother Julia. She serves as his heavenly guide and teacher, introducing him to various angelic and etheric entities.' He then goes on to document the alleged after-life that John is experiencing.

Ai: Japan Through John Lennon's Eyes, a Personal Sketchbook

An unusual book originally published in Japan by Shagakukan in 1990 and issued in America in March 1992 by Cadence Books of San Francisco.

The 195-page publication contained 84 of John's line drawings from an exercise book he used in Japan while studying the Japanese language.

The book also featured a foreword by Yoko and a selection of photographs, which John took in Japan, reproduced in size. Yoko said that the book was named *Ai* (pronounced 'eye') because that was how John viewed and experienced Japan.

Ain't She Sweet

One of the tracks the Beatles recorded in 1961 under the name the Beat Brothers when they acted as a backing band for Tony Sheridan during some recording sessions in Hamburg.

Bert Kaempfert produced the sessions for Polydor Records and the group were able to record a couple of tracks without Sheridan. 'Ain't She Sweet' was one of them and it was the only track on which John was lead vocalist. Apart from being lead singer, John played rhythm guitar. George Harrison played lead guitar, Stuart Sutcliffe bass guitar and Pete Best drums, while Paul McCartney played rhythm guitar and provided back-up vocals.

The number was an 'oldie', like one or two others the group recorded at the time. Jack Yellen and Milton Ager had composed it in the 1920s. However, it was a song that had previously received rock 'n' roll treatment on record – by Gene Vincent and his Blue Caps in 1956 and Duffy Power in 1959.

'Ain't She Sweet' was issued on various Polydor albums and singles. At one stage in May 1964 it was a minor chart hit in Britain when it was issued as a single on Polydor NH 52-317 with 'If You Love Me, Baby' on the flip, reaching No. 24 in the *New Musical Express* charts. The flip side featured a Tony Sheridan vocal.

Ain't That a Shame

Song that Julia Lennon, John's mother, taught John to play on a banjo and that he later said was the first rock 'n' roll number he played. He featured the Fats Domino hit with his skiffle group the Quarry Men and also recorded it in March 1972 with Phil Spector and again in October 1974. It was featured on his *Rock 'n' Roll* album.

The song was originally written by Antoine 'Fats' Domino and Dave Bartholomew and had been a hit in Britain for Domino in 1957 when it reached No. 23 in the charts. Pat Boone's version reached No. 7 in the charts in 1955 and also achieved a No. 22 position when rereleased in Britain in 1957. It was also a hit for the Four Seasons in 1963, when they reached No. 38 in the British charts with the song.

Aisumasen (I'm sorry)

A track John included on the *Mind Games* album, recorded in August 1973. It was virtually a rewrite of a song called 'Call My Name', which he originally wrote as a home tape in May 1971. He recorded it in December 1971, considering it for his *Sometime in New York City* album. In the end he decided that the number, which was a man offering his girl a strong shoulder to rely on, didn't fit in with the politics of the album.

He rewrote the song with Yoko in mind when things were becoming tense between them. He also changed the name to 'Aisumasen', which means 'I'm sorry' in Japanese.

Alchemical Wedding, The

'The Alchemical Wedding: A Gathering of the Tribes' was the name of an event at London's Royal Albert Hall on 18 December 1968. London's 'Underground' scene held their

Christmas party at the hall and John and Yoko first introduced 'bagism' to the world.

The pair appeared on stage in a 'performance', moving about inside a huge, white linen bag. They had unfolded the sack, crawled inside and then began to wriggle, to the musical accompaniment of a flautist. Yoko declared that by entering the bag they would prevent the audience from being confused by their physical presence.

A girl in the audience was so impressed with the bag event that she stripped off her clothes and attempted to join them.

Aldridge, Alan

British artist who compiled both volumes of the popular books *The Beatles Illustrated Lyrics*.

Aldridge had taken a variety of jobs since the age of fifteen, ranging from barrow boy to insurance clerk, before deciding to become an artist at the age of twenty. He soon became one of the most commercially successful of the British illustrators in the 60s. Intrigued by the lyrics of the Beatles' songs, he interviewed Paul McCartney and the article 'The Beatles Sinister Songbook' was published in the Observer, together with Aldridge's illustrations. Because of the response, he decided to compile the books of illustrated lyrics.

The songs illustrated by Aldridge himself in Volume One were 'Nowhere Man', 'Sexy Sadie', 'Taxman', 'Tell Me What You See', 'There's A Place', 'Tomorrow Never Knows', 'What Goes On?' 'Yellow Submarine' and 'You Won't See Me'. In Volume Two he illustrated 'Instant Karma!', 'Across the Universe', 'Cold Turkey', 'I Don't Want to Spoil the Party' and 'I'm Happy Just to Dance with You'.

Aldridge began a portrait of John in 1965 and spent several years adding to the study, building it into a collage. He intended to auction it off for the Live Aid charity at an event in Los Angeles in March 1986 but the work, valued at £12,000, was stolen

Alexander, Arthur

One of John's seminal influences. Alexander was an R&B singer/songwriter born in Florence, Alabama, on 10 May 1940.

John introduced four of Alexander's songs into the Beatles'

repertoire and sang lead vocals on all of them. They were 'Anna (Go To Him)', 'Soldier of Love (Lay Down Your Arms)', 'A Shot of Rhythm & Blues' and 'Where Have You Been All My Life?'.

In addition to admiring Alexander's songs and singing style, John was also influenced by the singer's use of the word 'girl' in his songs. As a result he was to use the word on several of his Beatles compositions including 'Please Please Me', 'Thank You Girl', 'Eight Days a Week', 'Ticket to Ride', 'You're Gonna Lose That Girl' and several others.

Alexander died as a result of heart and respiratory problems on Wednesday 9 June 1993 at the age of 53.

Alexandra Palace

A huge building in the Wood Green area of London. It was originally built in 1875. In 1936 the BBC leased part of the building and broadcast the world's first public television service from the site in November of that year. The BBC moved out in 1949 and it became a site for exhibitions and conferences, having a large audience capacity. A benefit for *International Times* was held here on Saturday 29 April 1967 called the '14 Hour Technicolor Dream'. Ten thousand people attended, including John Lennon. Yoko Ono was one of the performers. A BBC team from *Look of the Week* filmed the event and a brief glimpse of John was seen when the programme was transmitted on 17 May 1867.

The venue also hosted 'The Art Spectrum' in its Great Hall from 11 to 30 August 1971, during which five short films by John and Yoko were screened daily.

The venue was virtually destroyed by fire in July 1980, but has been faithfully restored.

Alice Tully Hall

A concert hall situated in Lincoln Center in New York. On Monday 10 January 1972, Yoko, with the aid of John, performed at the venue. However, as John hadn't yet been granted an American work visa, the couple performed their act from their seats in the audience.

Ali, Tariq

Prominent political intellectual, born in Pakistan, who settled in England and was a major force in the anti-establishment movement of the late 60s, when he advocated direct political action by the people.

A campaigner, who led several anti-Vietnam War marches, he was the first person to interview John in depth about his political opinions, which were published in Ali's periodical, *The Red Mole*.

Entitled 'Power to the People: John Lennon and Yoko Ono talk to Robin Blackburn and Tariq Ali', the feature was published in the Monday 8 March 1971 edition. It was reprinted in America in the June issue of *Ramparts* magazine under the title 'The Working Class Hero Turns Red'.

Ali asked when John had begun to develop radical political views and the interview included John's thoughts about the English class system, Vietnam, the song 'Revolution', his family and the Communist party.

Typical of John's comments was, 'I think we must make the workers aware of the really unhappy position they are in, break the dream they are surrounded by. They think they are in a wonderful, free-speaking country, they've all got cars and tellies and they don't want to think there's anything more to life.'

The day after the interview, John phoned Tariq Ali and said, 'Look, I was so excited by the things we've talked about that I've written this song for the movement so you can sing it when you march.'

That song was 'Power to the People'. John was also to say that his political awareness began to develop because of Ali's influence.

Ali set up house in Hornsey, London, and continued to be politically active, and during the 80s began to work frequently on the Channel 4 TV network.

Allerton

The house at Quarry Bank School of which John was a member. It was also the name of a district of Liverpool. Boys at the school were placed in a house named after the district from which they came.

All I've Got To Do

A song penned by John in 1961 that was recorded on Wednesday 11 September 1963 at Abbey Road Studios and included on the *With the Beatles* album. John was to tell *Playboy* magazine, 'That's me trying to do Smokey Robinson again.' John was lead vocalist and played rhythm guitar. Paul was on bass guitar and harmony vocal, with George on lead guitar and Ringo on drums.

All Those Years Ago

George Harrison's tribute to John. The number originally saw life as a song George had written for a Ringo Starr album and Ringo recorded it in July 1980, although the lyrics were different then. The song wasn't included on Ringo's album and, after John's murder, George decided to pay tribute to John and changed the lyrics, making reference to the tragedy and recording his own vocal track for use on the original backing track on which Ringo had played drums. Paul and Linda McCartney, together with Denny Laine, recorded backing vocals at George's Friar Park studio and they were included on the final recording. The single then became the only post-Beatles number until that time to contain contributions from three of the former members of the group.

'All Those Years Ago' was issued in Britain on Dark Horse K17807 on 15 May 1981, with 'Writing's on the Wall' on the flip, where it reached No. 9 in the charts, providing George with his first Top 30 single for eight years. The single was issued in America on Dark Horse DRC 49725 on Friday 11 May 1981 where it reached No. 2 in the charts.

A press release at the time read: 'The three surviving Beatles – George Harrison, Ringo Starr and Paul McCartney – have made a new record together. The three of them can be heard on George Harrison's new single *All Those Years Ago*.

'Harrison sings and plays guitar, Ringo Starr is the drummer and Paul McCartney and his wife Linda take care of vocal harmonies in the background. According to friends of the Beatles it concerns a one-time event and it does not mean that the Beatles are back together again. It only means that they are still goods friends and will always try to help each other in making records.'

All You Need is Love

Song written by John for the *Our World* television spectacular, which the Beatles performed live on 25 June 1967. An estimated

400 million people in 24 countries saw the programme. George Harrison was to say, 'John has an amazing thing with his timing – he always comes across with very different time signatures, you know. For example, on "All You Need is Love" it just sort of skips a beat here and there and changes time. But when you question him as to what it is he's actually doing, he really doesn't know. He just does it naturally.'

The Beatles' manager, Brian Epstein, said, 'It is a wonderful, beautiful, spine-chilling record. It cannot be misinterpreted. It is a clear message saying that love is everything.'

The track was issued in Britain on 7 July 1967 and went straight to the top of the charts, where it remained for four weeks. It was issued in America on 17 July and also topped the charts there.

John provided vocal, harpsichord and banjo, Paul the harmony vocal, string bass and bass guitar, George the harmony vocal, violin and guitar and Ringo drums. George Martin played piano and the violinists were Sidney Sax, Patrick Halling, Eric Bowie and Jack Holmes. Trumpet players were Stanley Woods and David Mason while Evan Watkins and Harry Spain played trombones. Jack Emblow played accordion. The whole thing was conducted by Mike Vickers and voices in the chorus included Mick Jagger, Keith Richards, Marianne Faithfull, Jane Asher, Mike McCartney, Pattie Harrison, Eric Clapton, Graham Nash, Keith Moon and Gary Leeds.

The number was also included on the *Yellow Submarine* album.

Allsop, Kenneth

A respected British journalist whose advice to John proved to have a positive effect on his songwriting.

Allsop, who wrote for the *Daily Mail*, was 44 at the time he first met John at BBC's Lime Grove Studio on Monday 23 March 1964. He was conducting an interview with the 'literary Beatle' about his book *In His Own Write* for the television news programme *Tonight*. The actual interview lasted four minutes of screen time. In the green room he had a chat with John and advised him not to hide his feelings when he wrote his songs. Having read *In His Own Write*, Allsop suspected that John had the ability to produce lyrics of a more profound nature than the simple love songs associated with the Beatles at the time. He suggested that John use his own experience as a basis for his lyrics.

John met him again at a Foyles Literary Luncheon at the Dorchester Hotel.

As a result of Allsop's advice, John began to write songs such as 'I'm a Loser' and 'In My Life'.

Allsop also interviewed John on the last ever edition of the *Tonight* programme on Friday 18 June 1965, when they discussed John's second book, *A Spaniard in the Works*.

Allsop went on to present another TV programme series, *24 Hours*. He was found dead at his home, a victim of an overdose of painkillers, in May 1973.

Alomar, Carlos

A New York guitarist who was in the recording studio working on a David Bowie album in January 1975 when John dropped in on the session. John and Bowie heard Alomar playing a James Brown-style guitar riff and they both joined the guitarist in a jam session during which all three then developed the song 'Fame', which they then recorded. Alomar was later to work with Yoko Ono on her album *It's Alright*. He said that working with Yoko 'was funny, exciting and well paid'. He also appeared on Yoko's *My Man* video dressed up in a Japanese Kabuki costume. Alomar also worked with Paul McCartney.

American Songwriters' Hall of Fame

John received a posthumous award from this organisation. Yoko Ono accepted it on Monday 9 March 1987.

Amsterdam

Part of this track was recorded during John and Yoko's honeymoon in Amsterdam in March 1969. The title referred to 25 minutes of recordings from the time, which was then included on their *Wedding Album*. 'Amsterdam' covered one entire side of the album and began with John saying 'OK Yoko'. Yoko then sang 'John John (Let's Hope for Peace)'. An interview about their peace campaign followed which was recorded in London soon after their 'bed-in'. Yoko blames the world for the persecution of the Jews during World War Two and they then begin to discuss their ideas of political history and peace through the ages. John then says, 'I'm as violent as the next man. We're violent people. I prefer myself nonviolent. I prefer my friends when they're nonviolent. I prefer to live in peace.'

The track returns to Amsterdam with John strumming 'Day In Bed', the two of them awakening and saying 'Good morning'. John orders tea and toast and is given a dog as a present. He reads from some newspapers, answers some questions from journalists, sings 'Goodbye Amsterdam', followed by Yoko singing 'Stay in Bed – Grow Your Hair'. John says 'Goodnight, sleep tight' and Yoko says 'Beautiful day. Very tiring throughout.' Then the two of them chant 'Grow your hair. Bed peace. Hair peace.'

Amsterdam Hilton

The hotel that was the setting of the Lennons' first 'bed-in' for Peace.

The couple moved into the presidential suite of the luxury hotel at 138 Apollolaan, Amsterdam, on 26 March 1969 and decided to invite the world's press to visit them during their honeymoon 'bed-in'.

The two sat up in bed dressed in white pyjamas with the windows open so that they could hear the fans in the street, while over a hundred members of the international press filed through the suite over a period of days.

Said John, 'These guys were sweating to get in first because they thought we were going to be making love in bed – naked, bed, John and Yoko, *sex*!'

Flowers surrounded them and two notices by their bed head read: 'Bed Peace' and 'Hair Peace.'

John said, 'What we're really doing is sending out a message to the world protesting for peace or protesting against any form of violence.'

He was also to say, 'We sat in bed and talked to reporters for seven days. It was hilarious. In effect, we were doing a commercial for war.

'We were on the seventh floor of the Hilton, overlooking Amsterdam. It was very crazy: the press came expecting to see us fucking in bed; they all heard John and Yoko were going to fuck in front of the press for peace. So when they all walked in (about

50 or 60 reporters flew over from London, all sort of very edgy), we were just sitting in pyjamas saying "Peace Brother", and that was it.'

Although John and Yoko intended an uninterrupted stay in the bed for seven days, 'as a protest against war and violence in the world', on the second day of their stay they found they had to vacate the bed. The Portuguese maid, Maria de Soledade Alves, arrived with a pile of new linen to make the bed. Yoko, wearing a high-necked, old-fashioned white nightie had to sit in a chair until Maria had finished.

In 1980, when the management of the hotel heard the news of John's death, they turned out all the lights in the building as a mark of respect, with the exception of suite 902, which, from the seventh floor, shone like a beacon over the city.

At the time of John and Yoko's 'bed-in', the suite cost £25 per night. By the mid-80s it had escalated to £400 per night.

Although 80 per cent of the bookings for the suite are from honeymooners, the rest are from Beatles enthusiasts.

In the 80s the suite was re-created to exploit the John and Yoko week-long stay. Although the 'Hair Peace' and 'Bed Piece' signs that John and Yoko had pasted to the window are no longer there, drawings by the couple have been hung on the walls together with a photograph of their 'bed-in'. Also in the suite is a collection of records, videos and books about the Beatles and, through a hole in the wall, the guests can watch a twenty-minute slide presentation about the Beatles' life and career.

On the ceiling are the opening words to 'All You Need Is Love'.

And I Love Her

It was said that this was Paul's love song to Jane Asher, although Paul was to comment, 'It's just a love song; no, it wasn't for anyone.' John collaborated and wrote the middle eight. A track from the *A Hard Day's Night* album, it was issued as a single in America on 20 July 1964 and reached No. 12 in the charts.

And Your Bird Can Sing

A track from the *Revolver* album penned by John and recorded on Tuesday 26 April 1966, originally under the working title

'You Don't Get Me'. John was later to dismiss the song as 'a horror' and 'a throwaway'. The second tape from the recording session was eventually used on the Beatles *Anthology* 2 CDs. Paul Weller was to record it in 1980.

Anderson, Helen

A former Merseyside art student, Helen first became a friend with Cynthia Powell when she attended the Junior School of Art in Gambier Terrace. Later, the two girls entered the Liverpool College of Art and were both in the same class as John.

Helen had received publicity in the press because she'd painted a portrait of Lonnie Donegan and she and John became close friends, although the relationship was platonic. He also called her 'Heloon'.

Cynthia was jealous and realised she loved John when she noticed Helen stroking his hair one day.

During the first year at college John fancied a baggy, bright-yellow, cable-knit sweater Helen was wearing and asked if she'd give it to him. Helen was to say, 'I started off in the same class as John at Liverpool Art College in 1958. Somebody knitted the jumper for me and John coveted it. I said I'd swap it for one of his drawings and he gave me the book and said, "Here, take the lot." I have looked at them often over the years and they always make me laugh.'

The book was actually an exercise book from his Quarry Bank days with 22 caricatures of teachers and fellow pupils.

'Typical Hairy Hairless Smell-Type Smith' was Bill Smith, a classmate who was one of the first people recruited for John's skiffle group, the Quarry Men. 'His Hairy Hairless Highness Dr Mick Fishwick' was another fellow student, John Morris. 'Nick O'Teen, Irish Madman' was the Quarry Bank Latin master John Colvin and 'A Simple Soul On The Farm' was the school groundsman Albert Yoxhall. The caricature of John was labelled 'Simply A Simple Pimple Short-Sighted John Wimple Lennon'.

Helen tried to sell it at Sotheby's, London, on 14 September 1995 for a sum in excess of £120,000, but there were no buyers.

The twice-married former student is now a fashion designer living in Cheshire.

Angela

Title of a track on the *Sometime in New York City* album, produced by Phil Spector. The track also featured sax by Stan Bronstein and organ by Adam Ippolito. Yoko handled the main lead vocal.

John wrote the number early in 1972 and commented, 'We got a request, "Will you please write a song about Angela?" from the Angela Davis people. So there, how do you write a song about somebody you don't really know?'

Davis, a former UCLA lecturer and a member of the Black Panthers, was involved with George Jackson and the Soledad Brothers saga (*see* **Davis, Angela**). Apart from John's number, the incident was also immortalised in song by two other rock icons – in versions superior in their approach to John's. They were the Bob Dylan single 'George Jackson' and Mick Jagger's tribute to Davis, 'Sweet Black Angel', featured on the Rolling Stones' *Exile on Main Street*.

Angel Baby

A song originally recorded by Rosie and the Originals. Rosie Hamlin was the lead singer with the group who reached No. 5 in the American charts with the number in 1960. It was their only hit. John recorded the teen ballad with Phil Spector around October/November 1973 during his 'lost weekend' sessions for the proposed *Rock 'n' Roll* album. It was one of two tracks that were not included on the official Capitol release, although it had surfaced on the TV advertised *Roots* album on 8 February 1975. The track was also included on the *Menlove Avenue* album.

Anna (Go to Him)

A number by Arthur Alexander that was part of the Beatles' early repertoire. John was the Alexander enthusiast and always provided lead vocals on the Alexander numbers he chose for the Beatles to play. The group recorded the number on Monday 11 February 1963 during their marathon *Please Please Me* album session. The Beatles had included the number in their repertoire during 1962 and 1963. It had originally been recorded by Alexander and released in America on the Dot label on 17 September 1962.

Anthology

A four-CD box set released eighteen years after John's murder, containing outtakes, home demos, live recordings, alternative tracks from the albums *Plastic Ono Band*, *Imagine*, *Walls and Bridges* and *Double Fantasy*. Yoko Ono was executive producer of the package.

There were a hundred previously unreleased tracks in the set, which was issued simultaneously around the world on Tuesday November 3 1998. To promote the release, a 100-minute *Anthology* radio special was syndicated to American radio stations the previous day.

Yoko had added a message in her introduction to the set: 'I hope you enjoy the box. This is the John that I knew, not the John that you knew through the press, the records and the films. I am saying to you, here's my John. I wish to share my knowledge of him with you. It was an incredible honour for me to have been with him.'

Discussing the selections, Yoko said, 'John's catalogue is very important. The tracks on the set aren't all alternate takes for demos for songs that he included on his albums, but most of them are. There are some real rarities, of course, but I didn't want to just titillate people's curiosity. After all, those are the songs that John wanted to put out – and that's something I gave a lot of weight to. I wanted to deepen people's understanding of those songs, because they're the ones that John wanted you to know. I put a special emphasis on that. I hope that people see his train of thought – and how that train of thought influenced the world.' She added, 'This is a celebration of John's music – and not just for the fans who knew his music in the old days. I'm hoping there will be some new people who will hear this set and discover John's music.'

Each of the four discs had an individual title: *Ascot*, *New York City*, *The Lost Weekend* and *Dakota*.

Yoko had co-produced the package with Rob Stevens as chief engineer and there was an accompanying sixty-page booklet with John's artwork and writing, plus family photographs and a biographical text by Anthony DeCurtis.

Other people involved in the *Anthology* included the engineering and chief assistant Michael Rew, the assistant engineers Chris Habeck and Mike Anzelowitz, and the digital editor and processor Paul Goodrich. Quad and Merlin Studios were used and the mastering was by George Marino at Sterling Sound.

Stevens had worked with Yoko since 1986 and he took eighteen months to go through 2,000 hours of tapes. He also did new digital transfers of some of the material such as the *John Lennon/Plastic Ono Band* and *Double Fantasy* tapes. He used the Cedar system for declocking, decrackling and dehissing them. He was to tell *Billboard* magazine, 'The material came in all shapes and sizes. There was a fairly large cassette collection, the quality of which varied from tune to tune and from situation to situation. It was clear that when John set up the cassette deck, it wasn't to capture in full fidelity, it was to capture for himself, for ideas, for song development.'

Yoko also asked George Martin to work on the poor-quality demo cassette of 'Grow Old With Me', which had been used on *Milk and Honey*. Martin grafted an orchestral backing on it. He said, 'I didn't do the "Free As a Bird" translation, and I've always felt a little uncomfortable about people working with dead people. It wasn't a very good piece of tape, you know: it was pretty amateurish. So I decided the only way to treat it was to score it with classical overtones. And I took on the job of improving the sound and adding an orchestra to it.'

CD One: 'Working Class Hero' (a *Plastic Ono Band* outtake from 1970). 'God' (a *Plastic Ono Band* outtake from 1970). 'I Found Out' (a home demo from 1970). 'Hold On' (a *Plastic Ono Band* outtake from 1970). 'Isolation' (a *Plastic Ono Band* outtake from 1970). 'Love' (a *Plastic Ono Band* outtake from 1970). 'Mother' (a *Plastic Ono Band* outtake from 1970). 'Remember' (a *Plastic Ono Band* outtake from 1970). 'Imagine' (take 1 of an *Imagine* outtake from 1971). 'Fortunately' (dialogue from 1969). 'Baby Please Don't Go' (an *Imagine* outtake from 1971). 'Oh My Love' (an *Imagine* outtake from 1971. 'Jealous Guy' (an *Imagine* outtake from 1971). 'Maggie Mae' (a home demo from 1979). 'How Do You Sleep?' (an *Imagine* outtake from 1971). 'God Save Us' (a guide vocal for the Elastic Oz Band single in 1969). 'Do The Oz' (the B-side of the Elastic Oz Band single from 1971). 'I Don't Want To Be A Soldier' (an *Imagine* outtake from 1971). 'Give Peace a Chance' (a rehearsal for the single in 1969). 'Look At Me' (a *Plastic Ono Band* outtake from 1970). 'Long Lost John' (a *Plastic Ono Band* outtake from 1970).

CD Two: 'New York City' (a home demo from 1972). 'Attica State' (a live performance from 17 December 1971). 'Imagine' (a live performance from 17 November 1971). 'Bring On the Lucie' (a *Mind Games* outtake from 1973). 'Woman is the Nigger of the World' (a home demo from 1972). A Geraldo Rivera concert introduction from 30 August 1972. 'Woman is the Nigger of the World' (a live performance from 30 August 1972). 'It's So Hard' (a live performance from 30 August 1972). 'Come Together' (a live performance from 30 August 1972). 'Happy Xmas' (the rough mix of a single from 1971). 'Luck of the Irish' (a live performance from 10 December 1971). 'John Sinclair' (a live performance from 10 December 1971). Dialogue from *The David Frost Show* in 1972. 'I Promise' (a home demo from 1973). 'Make Love Not War' (a home demo from 1973). 'One Day at a Time' (a *Mind Games* outtake from 1973). 'I Know (I Know)' (a home demo from 1973). 'I'm The Greatest' (a guide vocal for Ringo Star from 1973). 'Goodnight Vienna' (a demo for Ringo Starr from 1973). Dialogue from a Jerry Lewis telethon in 1972. 'A Kiss Is Just a Kiss' (dialogue). 'Real Love' (a home demo from 1980). 'You Are Here' (a *Mind Games* outtake from 1973).

CD Three: 'What You Got' (a home demo from 1974). 'Nobody Loves You When You're Down And Out' (a *Walls and Bridges* outtake from 1974). 'Whatever Gets You Thru the Night' (a home demo from 1974). 'Whatever Gets You Thru the Night' (a *Walls and Bridges* outtake from 1974). 'Yesterday' (a parody from the *Walls and Bridges* sessions in 1974). 'Be-Bop-A-Lula' (a *Rock 'N' Roll* outtake from 1974). 'Rip It Up/Ready Teddy' (a *Rock 'n' Roll* outtake from 1974). 'Scared' (a *Walls and Bridges* outtake from 1974). 'Steel and Glass' (a *Walls and Bridges* outtake from 1974). 'Surprise, Surprise' (a *Walls and Bridges* outtake from 1974). 'Bless You' (a *Walls and Bridges* outtake from 1974). 'Going Down On Love' (dialogue from 1974). 'Move Over Ms L' (a *Walls and Bridges* outtake from 1974). 'Ain't She Sweet' (a parody from 1974). 'Slippin' And Slidin'' (a *Rock 'n' Roll* outtake from 1974). 'Peggy Sue' (a *Rock 'n' Roll* outtake from 1974). 'Bring It On Home to Me/Send Me Some Lovin'' (a *Rock 'n' Roll* outtake from 1974). 'Phil And John 1' (dialogue from 1973), 'Phil And John 2' (dialogue from 1973), 'Phil And John 3' (dialogue from 1973). 'When In Doubt, Fuck

It' (dialogue from 1973). 'Be My Baby' (a *Rock 'n' Roll* outtake from 1973). 'Stranger's Room' (a home demo from 1980). 'Old Dirt Road' (a *Walls and Bridges* outtake from 1974).

CD Four: 'I'm Losing You' (a *Double Fantasy* outtake from 1980). 'Sean's Little Help' (dialogue from 1979). 'Serve Yourself' (a home demo from 1980). 'My Life' (a home demo from 1980). 'Nobody Told Me' (a *Double Fantasy* outtake from 1980). 'Life Begins At Forty' (a home demo from 1980). 'I Don't Wanna Face It' (a *Double Fantasy* outtake from 1980). 'Woman' (a Bermuda demo from 1980). 'Dear Yoko' (a *Double Fantasy* outtake from 1980). 'Watching The Wheels' (a Bermuda demo from 1980). 'I'm Stepping Out' (a *Double Fantasy* outtake from 1980). 'Borrowed Time' (a Bermuda demo from 1980). 'The Rishikesh Song' (a home demo from 1980). 'Sean's Loud' (dialogue from 1979). 'Beautiful Boy' (a *Double Fantasy* outtake from 1980). 'Mr Hyde's Gone (Don't Be Afraid)' (a home demo from 1980). 'Only You' (a vocal guide for Ringo Starr from 1974). 'Grow Old With Me' (an orchestrated version of a home demo from 1980). 'Dear John' (a home demo from 1980). 'The Great Wok' (some comedy dialogue from 1979). 'Mucho Mungo' (a home recording from 1979). 'Satire 1 (Take This Make-up Off Me)' (a home recording from 1979). 'Satire 2' (a home recording from 1979). 'Satire 3' (a home recording from 1979). 'Sean's In The Sky' (dialogue from 1979). 'It's Real' (a home recording from 1979).

Anthony, Les

A former Welsh guardsman. John hired him as a chauffeur cum bodyguard in 1965 during his early days in Weybridge. When John moved into his new house, neither he nor his wife Cynthia could drive, so they had to have a car and chauffeur. Anthony worked for John for several years and observed his private life in its intimate details. He was with John when he met Yoko at the Indica Gallery and commented, 'Yoko took one look at John and attached herself to him like a limpet mine.' Apart from saying that Yoko clung to John until he fled, he added 'She came tripping after him into St James and begged to come along to the studio where we were going to record. A few days later she turned up at Abbey Road studio and was let in. John groaned about what a pest she was.'

Anthony revealed in the *News of the World*, 'One day Cynthia went up north. Yoko arrived at their home to talk to John about him sponsoring some art exhibition. It was supposed to be a business meeting. But she didn't go back until the morning and after that John couldn't leave her alone.' Anthony also claimed that John and Yoko made love in the back of the car within three weeks of their first meeting and not for the first time at Weybridge when they spent all night taping, as John and Yoko always maintained.

John sent Anthony to Poole to 'borrow' his MBE from Mimi Smith so that he could return it to Buckingham Palace on 25 November 1969. He also drove them in the white Rolls-Royce when John urged him to drive to Southampton and find a ship in which he and Yoko could get married. Anthony sold his story to the *News of the World* in May 1972.

Any Time at All

One of the songs John composed for the *A Hard Day's Night* soundtrack. It was recorded on Tuesday 2 June 1964, although John hadn't actually completed the song to his satisfaction when the recording began and he used a tea break in the afternoon to alter its middle section. John's written lyrics were sold at auction at Sotheby's, London, in April 1988 for £6,000.

Aos

Song by Yoko, which she performed at the Royal Albert Hall in London on Thursday 29 February 1968, with backing by Ornette Coleman, the jazz trumpeter. The other musicians who accompanied her were Edward Blackwell on drums and David Izenzon and Charles Haden on bass guitars. Contrary to rumour, John did not play guitar on the track.

The number, over seven minutes in length, was recorded during the rehearsals for the Albert Hall concert and was included on the *Yoko Ono/Plastic Ono Band* album issued at the end of the following year, on Friday 11 December 1970.

Apollo Theater

The famous theatre in Harlem, New York. On Friday 17 December 1971, John and Yoko appeared on a benefit concert held to raise funds for the dependants of the prisoners who had been shot in the Attica prison riots (see Attica State). It was John's second stage appearance in America in five years.

Fifteen hundred members of the audience listened as Livingston Wingate, the master of ceremonies, said, 'The black community will never forget that valiant brothers, who refused to remain ignored, brutalised and hopeless men, were murdered.'

After Aretha Franklin appeared on stage to sing, Wingate then announced that John and Yoko had 'written a new song that the world will never forget what happened'. They appeared on stage to perform the number 'Attica State'.

When they finished, John said, 'It's an honour – and a pleasure – to be here at the Apollo, and for the reasons we're all here.'

Yoko then sang 'Sisters, O Sisters', to be followed by John announcing, 'Some of you might wonder what I'm doing here with no drummers, nothing like that. Well, you might know I lost my old band or left it. I'm putting an electric band together, but it's not ready yet. Things like this keep coming up, so I have to just busk it. So I'm gonna sing a song you might know: it's called "Imagine".'

He then performed the number on acoustic guitar, without accompaniment.

Apotheosis (Balloon)

First of John and Yoko's films in which John took charge, investigating the possibilities of a feature-length colour film, although the finished movie is actually eighteen minutes in length.

Filming first began in the English countryside on a foggy September day in 1969. A balloonist was hired and together with the cameraman, Nick Knowland, John and Yoko set the project rolling at a deserted airfield near Basingstoke.

The movie starts with a slow-motion exploration of John and Yoko, the camera moving from their feet to above their heads into the sky. With Nick and the balloonist filming aerial scenes, John wanted to capture the sensation of flying as the camera was exploring the air in a hot-air balloon.

Derek Hill of the Institute of Contemporary Arts in London, where the film was premiered in October, 1969 suggested the actual title of the film. John was unhappy with the results of the initial filming and began work on *Apotheosis No. 2* at the village of Lavenham in Sussex.

Apple

The Beatles' Apple venture originally grew out of a suggestion from Clive Epstein, brother of Brian, who looked after their interests immediately following the death of his brother. He suggested that, unless they invested their money to offset taxes, they would be paying a large amount to the Inland Revenue. He revealed that they had £2 million to dispose of.

Epstein suggested that they enter the retail business and open some shops. Paul then suggested that they launch a department store in which everything that was sold would be white. 'We could have a department where they sell nothing but white clothes, another where you can buy white furniture – even a white grand piano – and still another where you can buy white pets,' he said.

It was decided that they should use the name Apple, and their business venture was launched as Apple Corps Ltd in February 1968. It was eventually to include an Apple Boutique, Apple Electronics Ltd, Apple Films Ltd, Apple Publishing, Apple Wholesale, Apple Retail, Apple Television and Apple Records.

Initially based at 95 Wigmore Street, it then moved to an impressive building in Savile Row. John and Paul flew to America to promote their venture on Saturday 11 May, holding a press conference at the St Regis Hotel in New York, organised by Derek Taylor, on Monday 13 May. They also appeared on *The Johnny Carson Show*. Carson was on holiday at the time and the host was Joe Garagiola, who gave John and Paul an unsympathetic reception, particularly as he couldn't control his other guest, the 66-year-old former movie star Tallulah Bankhead, who was antagonistic to them and attempted to ridicule the Apple venture. Despite this they got their message across to the audience of 11 million viewers that Apple would be offering new talents a unique opportunity to spread their wings without the usual hassle artists had to encounter when they sought financial backing, that they would be financing many enterprising projects in the fields of literature, science and music.

John was to say, 'The aim of the company isn't a stack of gold teeth in the bank. We'd done that bit. It's more of a trick to see if we can get artistic freedom within a business structure; to see if we can create things and sell them without charging three times our cost.'

One of the first ventures was a boutique in Baker Street, which was launched on Tuesday 5 December 1967 with a party attended by John and George. Both Paul and Ringo were on holiday at the time. They appointed a team of young designers, collectively called the Fool, but this turned out to be a disaster, with the designers proving to be so extravagant that the boutique began losing a fortune and cost the Beatles more than £100,000. The control over the boutique was also lax, with a great amount of theft going on. One member of staff actually admitted that she used regularly to help herself to £50 a week from the till. It was John who suggested that they close down the boutique, offering the public the remainder of the stock for free. However, according to Apple's Peter Brown, the night before the closure, 'Yoko Ono and John arrived at the shop. Before the amazed employees, Yoko spread large swatches of fabric out on the floor and began to pile merchandise into it waist high. Then she knotted the corners of the fabric hobo-style and dragged it out of the store on her back, like an Oriental Santa Claus, into John's Rolls-Royce.'

However, at least £20,000 worth of stock was given away to the public the following day.

It was discovered that three cars had been bought on behalf of the company – but no one knew who had bought them or where the cars had gone. Several advance payments to various people had to be written off – £1,000 to 'Magic' Alexis Mardas, £2,000 to John Dunbar and so on.

A furious John was to tell *Rolling Stone* magazine, 'People were robbing us and living on us. Eighteen or twenty thousand pounds a week was rolling out of Apple and nobody was doing anything about it. All our buddies that worked for us for 50 years were just living and drinking and eating like fucking Rome, and I suddenly realised it and said we're losing money at such a rate that we would have been broke, really broke.'

Vanishing almost daily from Apple were TV sets, hi-fi systems, electric typewriters, gold discs, cases of wine and numerous other items.

Although John was justifiably furious at the extravagance, he and the other members of the Beatles were partly at fault for allowing such indulgence. For instance, their kitchen was filled with the finest foods from Fortnum & Mason. John was in a rage when he discovered that there was no caviar when Yoko demanded it. He gave the instruction, 'If you know she is coming there should always be caviar for her,' and a messenger was sent to Fortnum's for a £40 jar of caviar every time Yoko was expected. If she didn't turn up, people just took it home with them.

Apple Records was the most successful division of the company, although much of this was due to the fact that the Beatles' own records were issued on the label. They signed up a host of acts, including Badfinger, James Taylor and Mary Hopkin, although a number of the other artists they signed failed to make any impact on the charts. John was to say, 'Apple was a manifestation of our collective naïveté. We got conned. We really didn't get approached by the best artists – we got all the bums.'

On 2 October 1969 John told *Record Mirror*, 'Far too much money is wasted on just running the company. It's fine as a company that just produces records. But all our other ideas have gone with the wind. Most of what I earn goes into Apple and never comes back.'

An Apple accountant, Stephen Maltz, resigned in October 1969, sending them a five-page letter informing them that they would be in great trouble if they didn't curb Apple's expenditure. 'Each of you has houses and cars,' he wrote; 'you also have tax cases pending. Your personal finances are in a mess. Apple is in a mess.'

John was to say, 'What we need is a big, big businessman to sort out the mess,' and he approached Lord Beeching, the man who had reorganised Britain's railway network, who turned down the offer of running Apple with the simple advice 'Get back to making records.'

John then gave an interview to Ray Coleman, editor of *Disc*, and told him, 'If Apple goes on losing money at this rate we'll all be broke in six months.' He also said that Apple was losing £20,000 a week owing to the profligacy of the hangers-on and said that he personally was down to his last £50,000.

Paul was furious at this and told Coleman, 'This is only a

small company and you're trying to wreck it. You know John shoots his mouth off and doesn't mean it.'

It was reputedly the comments John made to Coleman that convinced Allen Klein that the time was right for him to approach the Beatles, via John.

Despite John's statement, Apple Records gained $3.4 million in the first quarter of 1969 with a sales estimate for the year in question of $15 million, while John's royalties from his songs and recordings ensured that he had quite a substantial regular income.

Approximately Infinite Universe

Yoko's own double-album venture, produced by both her and John and recorded in late October and early November 1972 at the Record Plant in New York, although two of the tracks, 'Catman' and 'Winter Song', were recorded at the Butterfly Studio.

Yoko composed all of the 22 songs on the LP on which Elephant's Memory, the Endless Strings and choirboys backed her.

It was issued in America on Apple SVBB on Monday 8 January 1973 and in Britain on Apple SAPDO 1001 on Friday 16 February.

The album sleeve is a slight variation of the cover of John's *Mind Games* album, which featured Yoko's profile jutting horizontally from the horizon like a range of mountains. This time John's face replaces hers. The photographs on the gatefold sleeve were by Bob Gruen and the design was by Bettina Rossner.

The numbers on Side One are: 'Yang Yang', 'Death of Samantha', 'I Want My Love To Rest Tonight', 'What Did I Do!' and 'Have You Seen a Horizon Lately?'.

Side Two featured: 'Approximately Infinite Universe', 'Peter the Dealer', 'Song for John', 'Catman (The Roses Are Coming)', 'What a Bastard the World Is' and 'Waiting for the Sunrise'.

Tracks on Side Three are: 'I Felt Like Smashing My Face In a Clear Glass Window', 'Winter Song', 'Kite Song', 'What a Mess', 'Shirankatta (I Didn't Know); and 'Air Talk'. Side Four features: 'I Have a Woman Inside My Soul', 'Move On Fast', 'Now Or Never', 'Is Winter Here to Stay?' and 'Looking Over from My Hotel Window'.

John receives credit as co-producer and for his guitar work on 'Move On Fast', and 'Is Winter Here to Stay?' is credited to Joel Nohnn. This is an anagram of John Lennon, with one 'n' missing.

The double album received good reviews with the *New Musical Express* critic commenting, 'Yoko is an artist in the throes of creativity, forced to cope with the axe-grinding politics of reality. She won't quit. She'll work it all out and she'll tell the world "I have a woman inside my soul" and she does.'

Melody Maker commented, 'She can create a unique ambience with her voice – like that of a child on the edge of tears. And wistful.'

Aquarius

A television arts programme from London Weekend Television. There was an *Aquarius* special, directed by Tony Palmer, which was screened in Britain on Saturday 11 March 1972. It was 53 minutes in length and filmed in New York and Los Angeles. It covered the theme of 'The Pursuit of Happiness in Modern-Day America' and ranged over varied subjects including a female roller derby and an experimental theatre group.

A three-minute-thirteen-second sequence featured John and Yoko filmed at their Greenwich Village apartment on Monday 28 February. For one minute John played the song 'Attica State' on a steel guitar, then stopped playing because he said he'd forgotten the rest of it. He then said he had begun to believe that young people had become apathetic, explaining, 'Our job now is to tell them there is still hope and we still have things to do and we must get out now and change and change their heads and tell them it's OK. We can change! It isn't over just because flower power didn't work. It's only the beginning; we're just in the inception of revolution.'

He added, 'That's why we are going out on the road. All our shows we do will be for free. All the money will go to prisoners or to poor people, so we'll collect no money for the performance. We hope to start touring in America and then eventually go around the world and go possibly to China too. For instance, we'd go to, say, Chicago and then, in the Chicago prison, half or quarter of the money earned will go towards releasing the first five hundred people alphabetically who couldn't get bail to get out of prison. So, wherever we go, the show will arrive and we will release people in each town. So possibly when the Stones are touring America for money, we'll be touring for free!' He then looked into the camera, laughed and said, 'What are you going to do about that, Mick?'

Arnold, David

Chaplain to Liverpool Polytechnic. He was one of the speakers at the special memorial service for John in Liverpool town centre on Sunday 14 December 1980. He asked, 'Which do you think is the most powerful, a bullet or a song? I can tell you that a song is, because a bullet can kill one man, but a song can bring a thousand people to life.'

Around and About

One of the numerous literary works John gave to Bill Harry to publish in the magazine he founded, *Mersey Beat*. 'Around and About' was featured in the 14 September 1961 issue. The comic item was a satire on the club listings published in *Mersey Beat* and read:

'Reviving the old tradition of Judro Bathing is slowly but slowly dancing in Liddypool once more. Had you remembering these owld custard of Boldy Street blowing?

The Peer Hat is very popularce for sun eating and boots for nude brighter are handys when sailing.

We are not happy with her Queen Victorious Monologue, but Walky Through Gallery is goodly when the rain, and Sit Georgie House is black (and white from the little pilgrims flying from Hellsy College).

Talk Hall is very histerical with old things wot are fakes and King Anne never slept there I tell you.

Shout Airborne is handy for planes if you like (no longer government patrolled) and the L.C.C.C. (Liddypool Cha cha cha) are doing a great thing.

The Mersey Boat is selling another three copies to some go home foreigners who went home.

A little guide to entertain may be of some helpless, so here it is:

THE CASBIN – stricktly no members only.

THE SHEATES – the Bohernia of Liddypool.

THE JACKARANDY – Membrains only.
LA LOCANTRY – Next to La Grafty.
LA MATUMNA – For a cheap heal.
THE PHOELIX – Also Bohumbert.
EL CAMUNAL – Bald stream.
THE DODD SPOT – Watch out for details.

These are but to name a few of the few with so little for so many, we'll fight 'em in the streets, so to Speke. We've been engaged for 43 years and he still smokes. I am an unmurdered mother of 19 years, am I pensionable? My dog bites me when I bite it. There is a lot to do in Liddypool, but not all convenience.

A number of familiar Liverpool landmarks are referred to, including Bold Street, the Pier Head, New Brighton, Walker Art Gallery, St George's Hall, Helsby College, Speke Hall and Speke Airport.

When John writes 'boots for nude brighter are handys when sailing,' he is referring to the ferryboats crossing the Mersey to New Brighton. His mention of 'Mersey Boat' refers to the *Mersey Beat* paper.

There are also examples of the Liverpool trait for adding 'ie' or 'y' to names. Liverpudlians refer to the Cast Iron Shore as 'the cassie', a person called Walter is known as 'Wally'. It is in this context that John adds a 'y' to place names such as 'JACKARANDY' or 'LOCANTRY'.

An insight into John's style can be found by comparing his article with extracts from the actual entertainments guide published in *Mersey Beat*:

The Casbah. Haymans Green
Streates. Mount Pleasant.
The Jacaranda. Slater Street. Members only.
La Locanda. Duke Street.
La Cabala, Bold Street.
The Odd Spot. Bold Street.

The Casbin refers to the Casbah, the cellar coffee club that was the redecorated cellar of Pete Best's family home, which opened in 1958 with the Quarry Men as resident band. The Sheates refers to Streates, a coffee bar in Mount Pleasant where poetry readings were held – hence John's sly nod to the venue as 'the Bohernia of Liddypool'. This is the club that nurtured Mersey poets such as Roger McGough, Brian Patten and Adrian Henri.

The Jackarandy refers to the Jacaranda club run by Allan Williams. Because the club was restricted to members only, John refers to 'Membrains only'.

La Locantry refers to the Locarno, a large Mecca ballroom in West Derby Road, which is next door to another Mecca dance hall, the Grafton.

La Matumna is a pastiche of the many exotic names for Liverpool coffee clubs and restaurants at the time, where a cheap meal could be had – La Locanda, La Cabala, etc. Another coffee club popular with students was the Phoenix.

El Camunal refers to the various large coffee bars situated in Bold Street and the Dodd Spot refers to the Odd Spot club, also in Bold Street, whose actual *Mersey Beat* advertisements announced its forthcoming opening with the words 'Watch out for details.'

Art and Music of John Lennon, The

A book, published in Britain by Omnibus Press in 1990 and in America by Birch Lane Press the following year.

Its author, Peter Doggett, has used the pen name James Robertson.

The Art and Music of John Lennon is an ideal companion for a Lennon fan, cataloguing John's work as a musician, writer and artist with its listing of every known Lennon recording from 1960 to 1980. These include the officially released recordings, home demo recordings, composing tapes, studio outtakes, live recordings, interview records and collaborations with other artists, in addition to a complete British and American discography. There is also an appendix, which includes listings of his letters and interviews.

The work contains details of all of John's films, including documentaries and avant-garde work, his videos and promotional clips and background to all his literary output together with information on artwork, erotic lithographs and other drawings and paintings.

A useful guide to John's artistic works.

Art Spectrum

Event at the Alexandra Palace, London on Sunday 5 September 1971 that presented a series of five John and Yoko films. They were: *Cold Turkey, The Ballad of John and Yoko, Give Peace a Chance, Instant Karma!* – which was a clip from a *Top of the Pops* performance – and *Up Your Legs Forever.*

This was a few days after John and Yoko had left England and John was never to return.

Ashton, Peter

During the 1990s, the Liverpool radio station Radio City interviewed Pete Ashton, who claimed to have been a former member of the Quarry Men. He also claimed that the group was originally called the Union City Skiffle group. He said that their first song, which they performed at a church fête, was called 'Mama Don't Allow'.

A genuine former Quarry Man, Rod Davis, comments, 'There was a Pete Ashton who lived in Woolton Village. He was a bit of a tough nut whose family ran the local greengrocer's. I read somewhere that he claimed to have played the drums, but if it ever happened, it could only been once or twice, and I certainly don't remember it. The Pete Ashton story was pooh-poohed by Colin Hanton [Quarry Men drummer] some time ago. He said, "As for the Union City, this is all news to me!"'

Ask Me Why

A song written by John in 1962. It was part of the Beatles' stage repertoire in 1962 and 1963. At the time of writing it he was influenced by the style of Smokey Robinson. John first sang the number on the radio when he performed the song live on the BBC radio show *Here We Go* on Friday 15 June 1962. They also performed it on three other radios shows: *Here We Go* on Friday 25 January 1963, *The Talent Show* on Tuesday 29 January 1963 and *Pop Go the Beatles* on Thursday 24 October 1963. The number was also one of four songs the Beatles played on their EMI recording audition on Wednesday 6 June 1962 as a possible debut record. George Martin didn't consider the material strong enough. The group rerecorded 'Ask Me Why' on Monday 26 November 1962 at Abbey Road studios. When they performed the song as part of their stage repertoire at the Star Club, Hamburg, in December 1962, it was recorded by the Star Club stage manager Adrian Barber and was to appear on the album *The Beatles Live! At the Star Club In Hamburg, Germany, 1962* many years later, being only one of two original Beatles compositions that were recorded during their club performances.

The number also became the flip side of their second single, 'Please Please Me', released in Britain on Friday 11 January 1963 and in America on Saturday 23 February 1963, and it was also included on the *Please Please Me* album.

Aspen

An unusual American arts magazine. It took the form of a box with various sections, each a work of art in itself. It was sometimes referred to as 'the magazine in a box'.

Issue No. 7, the spring/summer 1969 edition, was referred to as 'The British Box' and Section 11 contained a flexi-disc by John and Yoko, together with a paper sheet with the song words printed on it.

Side One contained: 'Song For John by Yoko', plus 'Let's Go On Flying', 'Snow Is Falling All the Time', 'Mummy's Only Looking For Her Hand In the Snow' and 'No Bed For Beatle John'.

Side Two contained John's radio play, which lasted slightly more than eight minutes. 'No Bed For Beatle John' and radio play had previously appeared on the *Life With the Lions* album.

Section 9 of the magazine comprised a single sheet containing the lyrics to the John and Yoko songs. Section 8 of the magazine included a copy of a rare book by John, *The Lennon Diary 1969*.

Astaire, Fred

Famous screen song-and-dance man who died in 1987. He was one of more than seventy legendary figures selected to appear on the sleeve of the *Sergeant Pepper* album. Astaire was one of several American celebrities who provided a testimonial for John to the US immigration authorities. He was also one of the handful of celebrities who made a guest appearance in John's 1972 film *Imagine*. John and Yoko filmed him at the St Regis Hotel, where they were staying on Monday 6 September 1971.

Astor Towers Hotel

Hotel situated at 1300 North Ascot in Chicago. On Thursday 11 August 1966, when arriving in America for their final tour, the Beatles were driven straight from the airport to a press conference at the hotel.

The conference took place on the 28th floor and was primarily to express regret at the uproar in the United States following John's comments about the Beatles in relation to Jesus Christ in an interview with Maureen Cleave of the *London Evening Standard*.

Prior to the conference John had allegedly burst into tears and repeatedly apologised to Brian Epstein and his fellow Beatles for the situation he had got them into.

He was to tell the gathered media, 'I'm sorry I said what I said because of the mess it made. I suppose if I said television was more popular than Jesus, I would have got away with it. I am sorry I opened my mouth ... I'm not anti-God, anti-Christ, or anti-religion. I was not knocking it. I was not saying we were greater or better. I believe that what people call God is something in all of us. I believe that what Jesus and Mohammed and Buddha and all the rest said was right. It's just that the translations have gone wrong.

'I wasn't saying whatever they are saying I was saying. I'm sorry I said it, really. I apologise, if that will make them happy. I still don't know quite what I've done.

'I do believe Christianity is shrinking, that people are losing contact with it. But – we deplore this – I was worried stiff when I found out it had become so serious. I'm sorry for the mess it's made. There'll be no more words. I panicked when I first heard about the uproar. I said, "I'm not going to America at all." We could have hidden away, but we decided to come and try to straighten it out. That interview was with a friend of mine. It was a long one, in depth. And I wasn't thinking in terms of public relations.'

A reporter asked, 'Mr Lennon, we're now hearing a great deal of interpretations of your comment regarding the Beatles vis-à-vis Jesus Christ. Could you tell us what you really meant by that statement?'

John replied, 'I'll try and tell you. I was sort of deploring the attitude. I wasn't saying whatever they were saying I was saying, anyway. That's the main thing about it. I was just talking to a reporter; she also happens to be a friend of mine and the rest of us at home. It was a sort of in-depth series she was doing and so I really wasn't thinking in terms of PR or translating what I was saying. It was going on for a couple of hours and I just said it just to cover the subject, you know? And it really meant what ... you know, I didn't mean it the way it said it, that's the main thing. It's just so complicated it's got out of hand, you know. But I just meant it as that the Beatles ... I wasn't saying the Beatles are better than Jesus or God or Christianity: I was using the name Beatles because I can use them easier. Because I can talk about Beatles as a separate thing and use them as an example, especially to a close friend. But I could have said TV or cinema or anything else that's popular. Or motor cars are bigger than Jesus. But I just said Beatles because that's the easiest one for me. I just never thought of repercussions, I never really thought of it. I wasn't even thinking, even though I knew she was interviewing me, that she was gonna ... you know, that it meant anything.'

Another reporter asked, 'What's your reaction to the repercussions?' John replied, 'Well when I first heard it, I thought, it can't be true. It's just one of those things like bad eggs in Adelaide and things. And then when I realised it was serious, I was worried stiff. Because I knew how it would go on, and the more things that get said about it and all those miserable pictures of me looking like a cynic. And they'd go on and on and on and it would get out of hand and I couldn't control it, you know. I can't answer for it when it gets that big because it's nothing to do with me then.'

One reporter said, 'A disc jockey in Birmingham, Alabama, who really started most of the repercussions has demanded an apology from you.'

John answered, 'He can have it, you know. I apologise to him if he's upset and he really means it. You know, I'm sorry. I'm sorry I said it really for the mess it's made. But I never meant it as a lousy or anti-religious thing or anything. I can't say any more than that. There's nothing else to say, really, no more words. If an apology … if he wants one, he can have it. I apologise to him.'

Another reporter said, 'One of the newspapers pictured a caricature of the Beatles plus two priests and the priests were saying "I object to their holier-than-thou attitude." Why is it that the American journalists do not treat it in the same light?'

John said, 'I don't know. I think it's because when it came out in England it was a bit sort of, a bit of a blabbermouth saying anyway. A few people wrote in to the papers and a few wrote back saying, "So what, he said that? Who is he anyway?" Or they said, "So, he can have his own opinion", and then it just vanished. It was very small. But by the time it got over here and it gets put into a kids' magazine, and just parts of it or whatever was put in, it just loses its meaning or its context immediately. And even more so when it's miles away and everybody starts making their own versions of it. You know I think that's why, whatever you said.'

Another question was, 'Do you personally believe that Christianity will shrink?'

John answered, 'I think that, only from my views and from what I've read and observed of Christianity and what it was and what it has been or what it could be, it just seems to me to be shrinking. I'm not knocking it or saying its bad: I'm just saying it seems to be shrinking and losing contact.'

The Beatles were appearing at the International amphitheatre the following night, but didn't stay at the Astor Towers, although hundreds of girls milled around outside the hotel believing they were still there. They were booked in for the night at the Ascot Motel in South Michigan.

Attica State

A track on the *Sometime in New York City* album, which reflected John's concerns about recent events in America.

'Attica State' surrounded an incident that took place on Monday 13 September 1971 at the Attica Correctional Facility in upstate New York.

The majority of prisoners were black and 1,200 of the inmates rioted in D Yard and took fifty hostages. The prisoners let it be known that they had legitimate grievances and put forward a number of demands. The Black Muslim element wanted religious freedom, prisoners in general asked for a minimum wage for their prison work. They also requested competent medical care and more fresh fruit, and demanded that their reading material should be left uncensored.

The commissioner agreed to all the demands but two: he refused to grant an amnesty for any inmates accused of injuring guards and also refused to appoint a new warder.

Because of the stalemate, Governor Nelson Rockefeller was asked to intervene, but he refused. Instead, he sent in an attack group of 1,700 heavily armed men including state troopers, members of the National Guard and sheriff's deputies. Dumdum bullets were used in the onslaught and prisoners were left to bleed to death. Thirty-two prisoners were killed, along with ten guards, and eighty-five prisoners were wounded. It was later discovered that the National Guard had shot all ten hostages.

John and Yoko were outraged and on the evening of 9 October 1971, John's 31st birthday, they wrote the song 'Attica State'.

They composed it during the early part of a celebratory party for John's birthday with guests who included Ringo and his wife, Maureen, Phil Spector, Allen Ginsberg, Klaus Voormann (the former Manfred Mann bass player) and Jim Keltner.

Home demos of the song were recorded on Friday 12 November and on 10 December they performed the song at the *Ten For Two* concert. They performed it before a live audience once again on Friday 17 December at the Apollo Theater in Harlem in a special benefit for the dependants of the prisoners who had been killed. On Thursday 13 January 1972 they sang the song on *The David Frost Show* and performed it on *The Mike Douglas Show* the following month. John and Yoko recorded the number in March for their *Sometime in New York City* album.

John also wore a button, which read, 'Indict Rockefeller For Murder – Attica'.

Au

Last track on the *Sometime in New York City* album. It comprises Yoko uttering a vocal sound with feedback and electronics effects, originally recorded when John and Yoko were on stage with Frank Zappa at the Filmore East on Sunday 6 June

1971. Zappa also used the track on his *Playground Psychotics* release, naming it 'A Small Eternity With Yoko'.

Avri's Televizier

A Dutch programme on the Avro network. On Tuesday 16 December 1969 the show featured a three-minute interview with John and Yoko conducted by Jaap van Meekeren about the couple's action for peace in their 'War Is Over' campaign.

Baby It's You

A song written by Hal David, Burt Bacharach and Barney Williams. It provided the Shirelles with a chart hit following its release on the Scepter label on Monday 4 December 1961. The Beatles included it in their early repertoire, with John on lead vocals. The group recorded it during their *Please Please Me* album session on Monday 11 February 1963. The performance recorded live for the *Pop Go The Beatles* radio show was included on *The Beatles Live At the BBC* CDs in November 1994.

Baby's Heartbeat

Recorded in Queen's Charlotte Hospital in November 1968. Before Yoko suffered a miscarriage John taped a few seconds of the heartbeat of their unborn child. By utilising studio techniques he extended the sound by more than five minutes. The track was included on their album *Unfinished Music No. 2: Life With the Lions*.

Baby's In Black

A song that John and Paul co-wrote in the same room. It was the first track recorded for the *Beatles For Sale* album on 11 August 1964. And the Beatles included it in their live repertoire from 1964 until 1966.

Baby You're a Rich Man

A track originally intended for *Yellow Submarine* and the first number actually recorded for the project, although it wasn't used in *Yellow Submarine*, but included on the *Magical Mystery Tour* double EP instead. Recorded on Thursday 11 May 1967 at Olympic Sound Studios in Barnes, London, it was also issued in Britain as the flip side of 'All You Need Is Love' on 7 July 1967. It was issued in America on 17 July.

John commented, 'We just stuck two songs together for this one, the same as "A Day In The Life".'

In Ray Coleman's biography of Brian Epstein, he says that a source claimed John dedicated the song to Epstein, referring to it as 'Baby You're a Rich Fag Jew'.

Bacall, Lauren

A major Hollywood star of the 50s and former wife of Humphrey Bogart. Her second marriage was to the actor Jason Robards.

Bacall was a neighbour of John and Yoko in the Dakota Building, although it was no secret that the two women didn't get on.

In 1983 a minor feud was sparked off when Bacall's son, Sam Robards, came to visit his mother. As he got out of the lift he was confronted by two armed men who manhandled him. They were Yoko's bodyguards.

Another incident occurred on Yoko's fiftieth birthday, when fans gathered on the pavement outside the Dakota Building with a special cake for Yoko. Lauren told the security guards to clear them away as she was expecting guests. Yoko, hearing of this, sent for candles and the waiting throng broke into song, singing Beatles hits as the dinner-party guests struggled to get past them.

Bad Boy

A Larry Williams hit which the Beatles recorded on Monday 10 May 1965, with John on lead vocals. It was the first of two Williams numbers the Beatles recorded that day, the other being 'Dizzy Miss Lizzy'. 'Bad Boy' was recorded during the sessions for Side Two of the *Help!* album, but wasn't used on that release. It first emerged on Capitol's American album *Beatles VI*. Its first British outing was on *A Collection of Beatle Oldies* in

December 1966. It was also included on the British version of *Rarities*.

The original Williams single had been issued on 19 January 1959 and the Beatles included it in their repertoire during 1960, 1961 and 1962.

Bad To Me

Number penned by John for Billy J Kramer. John wrote it during the early part of April 1963 when he was on holiday in Spain with Brian Epstein. It was Kramer's second single and was issued in Britain on 26 July 1963 and in America on Liberty on 23 September 1963. The number topped the British charts while reaching No. 9 in America, and became a million-seller.

John recorded a demo disc with George Martin, which was then passed on to Kramer. The Beatles never recorded the song themselves.

Baez, Joan

American folk singer, born in New York on 9 January 1941. She had a number of hit records, including 'We Shall Overcome', 'There But For Fortune' and 'Farewell Angelina'. John once claimed they were lovers. However, she denied it in a *Rolling Stone* interview in 1983. She said that she went to bed with Lennon once in Los Angeles but both of them were tired and nothing happened.

Baez revealed that she travelled with the Beatles for four days at John's invitation and they ended up in a mansion in Los Angeles. Mentioning that there weren't enough master bedrooms for everyone, she said, 'John was stuck, having invited me and then not having anywhere to put me. So he offered me his room; it had a bed in it the size of a small swimming pool. I said, "Well, John, don't worry: I'm not fussy about these things. You just come in and use the other side of the bed when you're tired." ' Baez went to sleep and John returned in the middle of the night. She said that she thought John felt obliged to do something because he'd asked her along and then started to come on to her, but very unenthusiastically. She said to him, 'John, you know, I'm probably as tired as you are, and I don't want you to feel you have to perform on my behalf.' So they had a good laugh and went to sleep.

Bag One

The name John gave to his set of lithographs.

John and Yoko ran a company called Bag One Productions, which they had formed in order to market their creative product. The idea that John should attempt to express himself in lithographic drawings came from the art critic Anthony Fawcett in 1968.

Fawcett, who became personal assistant to John and Yoko, continued to encourage John to produce work in this field. It is to his credit that the actual lithographs saw the light of day.

A second set, based on the *I Ching*, was never completed.

From a large selection of sketches and drawings, John eventually chose a series of a dozen, half of which depicted scenes of his life with Yoko, such as their first 'bed-in' and wedding ceremony. The other half are quite explicit erotic scenes, including one of Yoko lying on her back with her legs apart and John making love to her from the rear. In one lithograph there are two images of John, one engaged in the art of cunnilingus, the other sucking her breast.

The finished work included a written sheet by John containing an A to Z of 'My story both humble and true'. Some of the items were:

'A is for Parrot which we can plainly see
'H is for England and (Heather)
'M is for Venezuela where the oranges come from
'T is for Tommy who won the war
'S is for pancake or whole wheat bread
'X is for Easter – have one yourself
'Y is a crooked letter and you can't straighten it.'

Bag One comprised fourteen separate prints, which were assembled into a limited edition of 300 sets. The lithographs were contained in a magnificent leather bag designed by the French clothes designer Ted Lapidus with the letters words 'Bag One' and John's signature printed in black.

The prints were taken to Canada, where John signed each one personally during his brief stay at Ronnie Hawkins' farm. Priced at £40 each or £550 per set, the lithographs were first exhibited at the London Art Gallery in January 1970, where eight of the prints were confiscated by the police as being obscene. The case was taken to court but was dismissed by the judge. The exhibition was moved on to the Lee Nordness Gallery in New York.

Bag One Arts
New York-based company set up by Yoko to exploit John's artwork. In 1998 they released a series of John's cartoons of animals, which he'd drawn specially for his second son Sean between 1975 and 1980 for use on cards, toys, plates, cups and saucers. Julian Lennon, in an interview that year in the *Washington Post*, accused Yoko of cheapening his father's legacy, saying, 'To be selling off his artwork in limited editions etched into marble and to take his other artwork which is on silk ties and mugs is not what he is about.'

Bag Productions Ltd
A company the Lennons formed on Tuesday 22 April 1969. The company was to take charge of John and Yoko's public relations, together with financing and co-ordination.

Bagism
A term invented by John and Yoko to describe a promotional 'happening', which they utilised between 1969 and 1971.

Actually, Yoko and her first husband Tony Cox invented a 'happening' called 'Bag Piece' in 1962. The two crawled inside a large black bag and undressed, then dressed again before emerging.

The first performance of 'bagism' by John and Yoko took place on Wednesday 18 December 1968 at the Alchemical Wedding at London's Royal Albert Hall. They next appeared inside a white bag at their press conference for their film *Rape* at the Sacher Hotel in Austria on 31 March 1969, announcing that 'bagism' was part of their peace drive. A few days later, on 1 April, they both appeared on television, being interviewed on the BBC's *Today* programme from inside a white bag labelled 'bagism.' At the Institute of Contemporary Arts in London on 10 September 1969 two people sat inside a white bag during the screening of films by John and Yoko – although it is doubtful whether they were the genuine articles. On 14 December 1969 another two people were contained inside a white bag labelled 'A silent protest for James Hanratty' at Speakers' Corner in London – again an arrangement by proxy.

Yoko herself appeared in a white bag on stage at the UNICEF concert at the Lyceum on Monday 15 December 1969 shouting, 'You killed Hanratty'.

Describing 'bagism' on a BBC TV's *24 Hours* programme in 1969, John said, 'We're all in a bag.' He pointed out that he had been in a 'pop bag' and Yoko in an 'avant-garde bag' He added, 'And if you ask us what "bagism" is, then we say "We're all in the same bag, baby." '

On Saturday 17 July 1971 on *Parkinson*, the BBC TV chat show hosted by Michael Parkinson, John and Yoko even managed to talk Parkinson into getting into the bag during the show. John explained to him, 'Hey, imagine if a black guy went for a job at the BBC and he had to wear a bag. They wouldn't know what colour people were and there'd be no prejudice, for a kick-off!'

Bahamas

John and Yoko had intended going to America to promote their peace campaign, with a particular emphasis on their opposition to the Vietnam War. Unfortunately, their visas were delayed, so they decided to travel to the Bahamas. John said, 'We'll go as near as we can to the states and do the Bed-In there for the American media. They won't mind flying out to see us.'

They selected Freeport as the ideal place for them to travel to and chose the Sheraton Oceanus Hotel, the best hotel in town, travelling there on Saturday 24 May 1969. However, when they arrived they found the people hostile to them and the heat oppressive; they thought the food was awful and they discovered there were only single beds in their suite – and they were concreted to the floor! The couple then decided to find another setting for their Bed-In and picked on the Queen Elizabeth Hotel in Toronto, Canada, and flew there the next day, Sunday 25 May. On their arrival in Toronto they were delayed for four hours before being cleared by immigration and customs officials.

Baird, Julia

One of John's half-sisters. She was the first daughter of Julia Lennon and John Dykins, born on 5 March 1947. Her parents didn't marry when they began to live together because Julia wasn't divorced from Freddie Lennon.

They went to live in Newcastle Road with 'Pop' Stanley, but, when he died two years after Julia was born, the family moved to a house on the Springwood Estate in Blomfield Road, where John began to visit them frequently. When he stayed overnight or for weekends, her younger sister Jacqui would move in with Julia while John slept in her room. The girls and their mother saw John perform for the first time when they were invited to watch the Quarry Men play at the street party in Rosebury Street on 22 June 1957.

Julia was only eleven years old when her mother was killed in a road accident, but the sisters weren't told about their mother's death at the time. They were taken to Scotland to spend six weeks with their Aunt Mater, having been told that their mother was ill. They were then boarded with their Aunt Harrie – and weren't even told of their mother's funeral. Their father couldn't cope with raising the two girls, but he moved to a house nearby to be close to them.

Once John had moved to London, Jackie visited Kenwood and was picked up at Heathrow Airport by a uniformed chauffeur in John's Phantom V Rolls-Royce. John's wife Cynthia took her shopping at Harrods and Harvey Nichols and she was taken to visit George Harrison at Kinfauns.

Julia remained in touch with John for a number of years, until he moved to America, and she never met Yoko Ono, although she talked to her on the telephone.

Julia commented, 'She never seemed particularly anxious to let us share John with her, as Cynthia had been. When John went to live with her in America he lost touch with the entire family.'

Julia originally considered travelling to Geneva to be an interpreter, but abandoned the idea. In 1965 she met Allen Baird. Julia was eighteen; Allen was living in Belfast studying psychology and they married three years later in 1969. After the birth of their first baby they moved to Liverpool and settled in a flat in Hope Street. The family didn't approve of their living there and gave them enough money to put down a deposit on a house. The couple settled in Cheshire, where Julia became a French teacher at Caldy Grammar School. Her teaching was interrupted by the birth of their third child. They then moved to another house in the area.

She'd been completely out of touch with John for five years. The last time they'd spoken was when Julia was in Ireland, having just given birth to her first child, and John phoned to congratulate her.

Once he'd left for America she lost touch. Then, in 1975, she received a call from her Aunt Elizabeth 'Mater' in Edinburgh saying that John had been trying to get hold of both her and her sister. He suddenly contacted her by phone, saying it was 'yer brudder John, uncle to yer kids'. He asked her to call him back 'by collect' (transfer-charge call), but she thought he'd said 'by Colette'. He continued to phone her every month for an eighteen-month period.

Jacqui didn't have a phone, but she'd come along to Julia's and they would both listen as John did most of the talking. He told them, 'I've been wanting a family, and I have had one all along.' He was eager to talk about their late mother and wanted to know all about the other members of the family and said he wanted to leave New York to visit Liverpool and then return to New York. He then asked them to send photographs

After John's death, there was no real relationship with Yoko. Julia recalled that at one time when her daughter needed some money, she let her have some letters from John, which she sold. Yoko then rang her up and berated her about it.

In 1986 Julia was interviewed by the *Liverpool Echo*, which then ran a series of articles on her life, which became the basis for a 59-page limited-edition book called *In His Own Youth, In My Own Words*, published the same year by River Women Press.

In 1988 her biography, *John Lennon, My Brother*, written in collaboration with Geoffrey Giuliano was published.

Still a teacher based in Chester, she lives with her new partner Roger and the two make trips to India, where they spend time helping needy children.

In the 1960s John bought a four-bedroom house in Gateacre Park Drive, Liverpool and gave it to his uncle and aunt, Norman and Harriet Birch, who had taken in Julia and Jacqui after their mother had died as security for his two half sisters. As the house remained part of the Lennon estate, after John's death, Yoko could do what she wanted with it legally. Rather than leave it in the hands of the family, as Julia says John intended, Yoko gave it to the Salvation Army in 1997 after Norman and Harriet had died – an action that Julia regards as unjust, commenting, 'The house was definitely for us. And the one in Poole was for all the family. I have a card from John talking about the house being for us. It is not the money we are interested in, it is the principle.'

The house referred to in Poole was the five-bedroom bungalow John bought for £250,000 in 1965, allegedly to be made available to other members of the family as well as his Aunt Mimi. John's cousin Stanley Parkes commented, 'Mimi got a terrible shock after John was killed. It was discovered that the house was not hers: the title deeds were owned by Yoko. Mimi was mortified. She said, 'To think I have been left beholden to Yoko. I really thought I'd have a little something to leave my family.' When Mimi died, Yoko sold the property for £410,000.

Baker, Barbara

John's first steady girlfriend and the one he lost his virginity to. They first met at Reynolds Park, near St Peter's Church in Woolton. John and his pal Len Garry were out walking and spotted two girls, Barbara and her friend Miranda. The two began to chat up the girls and asked whom Barbara would like to go out with. She was fourteen at the time and said she preferred Len and the two began dating. Then she began to go out with John and their young romance lasted for more than a year. The two were eventually forced to end the relationship because of parental pressure from Barbara's mum and John's Aunt Mimi.

Barbara was a member of St Peter's Sunday School and also attended Quarry Bank's sister school Calder High. John's friends remember her as a girl in school uniform with sandy-brown hair and huge breasts whom they'd see visiting John's house or sitting by the side of the football pitch when they were having a game of soccer.

Married and living in the Wirral, she refuses to discuss her romance with John.

Ballad of John & Yoko, The (book)

A collection of material, published in book form by Rolling Stone Press in 1982.

The items explore the life of John and his relationship with

Yoko in great thoroughness. The contents are a series of well-written, sometimes probing, sometimes critical, but always thought-provoking articles.

Yoko's childhood in Japan and John's early life in Liverpool are examined and there is a lengthy chronology.

The first *Rolling Stone* interview, which Jonathan Cott conducted in 1968, is reprinted, with various articles written between the years 1968 and 1976 by top rock journalists such as Ritchie York, Chet Flippo and Jann Wenner. Flippo also provides 'The Private Years', covering the period between 1976 and 1980, while Annie Leibovitz has contributed a portfolio of intimate pictures of John and Yoko at the Dakota Building in December 1980.

Mick Jagger and Harry Nilsson have recorded their memories of John in short articles in a section that also contains brief tributes from a range of people, including Gerry Marsden, Frank Sinatra, Ray Charles and Chuck Berry. The book includes critical analyses of John and Yoko's films and of Yoko's songs and conceptual happenings.

The eighty photographs, six of them in colour, are well selected and include many that are quite rare. Of particular interest are the childhood photographs of Yoko and a range of pictures of her conceptual creations.

Michael Joseph published the book in Britain. *Le Ballade de John & Yoko* was the title of the French edition published by Editions Denoel. A Swedish edition, *Balladen om John och Yoko*, was translated by Christian Douds and published by Askild och Karnekull Forlag in 1983.

Ballad of John & Yoko, The (musical)

A proposed Broadway musical, based on their life, which John and Yoko began planning in June 1978. Entitled, simply, *The Ballad of John and Yoko*, it was intended to be the story of their relationship, with songs such as 'Real Love', 'She Is a Friend of Dorothy's', 'Whatever Happened To …', 'Mirror Mirror On the Wall' and 'Free As a Bird' from John and numbers such as 'Every Man Has a Woman Who Loves Him' from Yoko.

John penned a lengthy piece, which he intended using as a basis for the programme of the show, but a script was never prepared. The programme notes appeared in the book

Skywriting By Word of Mouth under the title 'The Ballad of John and Yoko'.

Ballad of John and Yoko, The (single)

Penned by John, the recording featured only him and Paul McCartney. Paul played bass, maracas, piano and drums. George Harrison and Ringo Starr weren't in Britain at the time. Because of this there was a bit of friendly banter in the studio with John saying to Paul, 'Go a bit faster, Ringo' and Paul replying, 'OK, George.'

The number was recorded on 14 April 1969 and fully mixed within nine hours. The track was the first Beatles' release in stereo and chronicled events during the couple's marriage in Gibraltar and the honeymoon that followed. John actually bent the facts. The lyrics implied that they were turned back at Southampton as if it were some form of discrimination against them – but they had actually tried to get a ferry to France without having their passports with them. Released as a Beatles single, it topped the British charts on 4 June 1969 but reached only No. 8 in the States owing to the number of radio stations that wouldn't play it because of the use of the word 'Christ'. It was the last Beatles single to top the British charts. An example of its appeal is that it also topped the charts in Holland, West Germany, Denmark, Malaysia, Austria, Norway, Spain and Belgium. Its highest position in America was No. 8.

The song was included on *Past Masters Volume II*.

Ballad of Yoko and John

A BBC programme broadcast on Tuesday 6 January 1998. During the interview Yoko attacked Paul. She said, 'John did not make the phone calls. He was not on that level as a leader – he was on the level of a spiritual leader.

'He was the visionary and that is why the Beatles happened. Paul is put in the position of being a Salieri to a Mozart.'

She also said, 'Because John passed away, naturally people have this incredibly strong sentiment for him. Paul is encountering people not giving the same kind of compassion.'

Ballard, Arthur

A painter and teacher who was born in Liverpool in 1915. After attending local schools he won a scholarship to Liverpool

College of Art in 1930. Ballard spent most of his life in the city and taught at the college from 1947 to 1980.

He spent the World War Two in the Middle East and took part in the Battle of Eritrea.

His paintings attracted great interest in the late 1950s and early 1960s and were bought by the likes of Aldous Huxley, JB Priestley and Sam Wanamaker. However, his changing style and determination to remain in Liverpool impeded his chances of major success.

In 1957 he left for Paris for a short time to paint and study, and in 1958 had an exhibition at the New Shakespeare Gallery in Liverpool. His work was exhibited in the John Moore exhibitions at the Walker Art Gallery in 1950 and 1961.

Commenting on Ballard in his book *Art In a City*, the art critic John Willet wrote, 'He has great faith in Liverpool's individuality, which he thinks will assert itself in art sooner or later: we'll see something "better than the Beatles." He's proud of the efforts he's made to support individuals in the college, e.g., precisely, Lennon of the Beatles, whom the graphic design department were reluctant to accept. 'The boy was no good as an artist,' he claims, 'and an intolerable, rebellious nuisance. But he had character.'

As a teacher he took a personal interest in the fortunes of his pupils and aided them when in difficulties. His most talented student was Stuart Sutcliffe, who was to share Ballard's passion for the works of Nicholas da Stael.

Owing to Sutcliffe's reluctance to attend various classes at college, Ballard took it on himself to provide him with one-to-one tuition at Sutcliffe's flat in nearby Percy Street. He also took an interest in John Lennon and at one time prevented John's expulsion from the college. Ballard also used to meet students for discussions in the War Office of Ye Cracke pub in Rice Street.

Commenting on John, he said, 'He had a lot of talent as an illustrator and cartoonist, but the powers that be did not accept him as an illustrator. If I had my way he would never have been a Beatle. He would have been a professional artist.'

Ballard was married twice, the second time to Carol, one of his students. He had two sons and a daughter. On his retirement he moved to London for a while to live with his daughter, before settling down with one of his sons and his family in Wales. He died in Corwen Clyd on 25 November 1994.

His biographer, the art critic Peter Davies, prepared a touring exhibition of Ballard's work in 1996.

Ballou, Donald

Manager of a radio station in Ogdensberg in New York State. In 1966 following the *Datebook* magazine article, which took quotes from John's interview with Maureen Cleave out of context, he was one of the many radio executives to ban Beatles records. He said, 'I have personally read the article and do not appreciate my child listening to any group that would condemn Christianity. Neither would I allow my audience to listen to such a group.'

Bank Street (1051/2), Greenwich Village, New York

When John and Yoko moved to New York in September 1971 they rented a floor at the St Regis Hotel. On 1 November they moved into a two-roomed apartment in Bank Street, which was sparsely furnished, although they immediately had a piano moved in, and the couple slept on a mattress covered by an American flag. There was a large sitting room with a kitchen alcove *en suite* and a hall leading to a bedroom and bathroom.

One of their first guests was Bob Dylan and the couple also entertained a number of radicals and had lengthy political discussions with them, while Yoko provided her guests with macrobiotic food.

They bought the apartment from Joe Butler, former drummer with the Lovin' Spoonful. John and Yoko had bumped into Butler in Bank Street while they were visiting the avant-garde composer John Cage.

In addition, they also rented a loft in Soho.

John loved living in the West Village and commented, 'It's like a little Welsh village, with Jones the Fish and Jones the Milk, and everybody seems to know everybody.'

At one point the apartment bell rang and John opened the door to find two strange men, who then pushed their way into the flat and began taking away items, mumbling about 'collecting'. John protested, but they took a number of items away. He then realised that a drawer they'd taken contained his address book. Since the book had a number of sensitive contacts in it, John phoned Tom Basalari, a former narcotics agent who had become their chauffeur, and told him what had happened. A few hours later the address book was returned.

It emerged that Joe Butler had owed a gambling debt and the bookie concerned had sent along a couple of men to collect what they could.

A photograph of the apartment building is shown on the cover of the *Sometime in New York City* album.

Bardot, Brigitte

George, Paul and Ringo all cited Brigitte Bardot as their favourite actress in their biographical sheets in 1962, while John cited Juliet Greco and Sophia Lauren. Yet it was John who was BB's biggest fan.

The French sex kitten was a potent image in her time and John, in particular, was smitten to the point of obsession. His school chum Pete Shotton revealed that she was John's favourite fantasy figure when they were at Quarry Bank school in the early 1950s. He pointed out, 'For the next fifteen years, at least, Brigitte Bardot was to remain John's ideal girl.'

When the weekly news magazine *Reveille* ran a centre-page series, which built into a life-size image of Bardot in scanty lingerie, John collected the issues, assembled all the parts and taped them to the ceiling above his bed in Mendips.

He also favoured girls who styled themselves on the star. When Cynthia, his first wife, fell in love with him, John's friends told her she wouldn't make much of an impression on him because she didn't look like Brigitte. Once they started going steady she underwent a change. She was to say, 'John's perfect image of a woman was Brigitte Bardot. I found myself fast becoming moulded into her style of dress and haircut. I had only recently gone through my change from secretary-bird to bohemian when I met John, but under his influence another metamorphosis was taking place and this time the emphasis was on oomph! Long blonde hair (out with the Hiltone), tight black sweaters, tight short skirts, high-heeled pointed shoes, and to add the final touch, black fishnet stockings and suspenders.'

This obsession even found its way into his work. Helen Anderson, a student at Liverpool College of Art, pointed out, 'In his first six months at college, his paintings were very wild and aggressive. Every one he did incorporated the interior of a nightclub and they were very strongly drawn, very dark, and there was always a blonde girl at the bar looking like Brigitte Bardot.'

Astrid Kirchherr, Stuart Sutcliffe's fiancée, was to say, 'John always called me the German Brigitte Bardot and he admired my long blonde hair and small waist.'

Michael Braun, a journalist who accompanied the Beatles on their first trip to Paris, recalled that they'd made a specific request to their French record company that they'd like to meet up with Brigitte Bardot during their visit: 'All of the Beatles, apparently, shared a desire to meet Mlle Bardot. The following morning a large box of candy arrived in their suite. Accompanying it was a card of the director of their French record company. "Unfortunately," it read, "Brigitte Bardot is detained in Brazil. Let's hope that these sweets will make up for her."'

At one time the Beatles had the opportunity of co-starring in a movie with their favourite pin-up. The producer Walter Shenson suggested that they appear in a comedy version of *The Three Musketeers*, with Bardot as Milady De Winter. Nothing resulted of that particular casting, although the director Dick Lester later went ahead with the film, which starred Richard Chamberlain, Michael York, Oliver Reed and Frank Finlay, with Faye Dunaway as De Winter.

John used to have a framed photograph of Bardot on the wall of his house in Kenwood and he finally got to meet his dream girl in 1968. Pete Shotton recalled the historic moment, which had been arranged by longtime Beatles cohort Derek Taylor.

He wrote, 'Naturally I begged John to let me tag along; but since Brigitte had specified that she wasn't prepared to meet a crowd of strangers, only Derek was permitted to accompany him. He arrived home somewhat earlier than I'd expected, looking far more sullen than the occasion warranted.'

Shotton said that John told him, 'I was so nervous that I dropped some acid before we went in and got completely out of my head. The only thing I said to her all night was "Hello", when we went to shake hands with her. Then she spent the whole time talking in French with her friends, and I could never think of anything to say.'

Taylor had received a message at the Apple offices in Savile Row that Bardot was at the Mayfair Hotel and had requested a meeting with all four Beatles. When John arrived at the office, Taylor told him the news and John reminded him that Paul was in Scotland. Taylor phoned George and Ringo, but they declined the invitation.

John and Derek took some LSD and in the evening set off for the Mayfair in their chauffeur-driven car.

Although Derek had phoned earlier to explain that only John would be coming, communications hadn't been good and Bardot had a number of girls with her, presumably to balance out the party as she'd booked dinner at the fashionable Parkes in Beauchamp Place believing that all four Beatles were coming along.

John squatted in the middle of the room and lit a cigarette. Both he and Taylor felt that things weren't going too well and Bardot and her party weren't exactly fluent in English, while John couldn't speak any French at all.

A phone call was made to invite two young men to join the party for dinner so as not to make the male/female ratio too conspicuous. However, both John and Derek declined to join the dinner party and remained behind in the suite while a puzzled Bardot set off for Parkes.

Bardot and her friends returned in the early hours of the morning and she handed John a guitar and asked if he'd play some songs, which he did. Taylor had fallen asleep in her bedroom.

Later they said their goodbyes and left.

Be My Baby

A track John originally recorded with Phil Spector for the *Rock 'n' Roll* album. It was omitted from the original release, but included on the mail-order *Roots* album, issued on 8 February 1975. It was previously a hit for the Ronettes, also originally recorded by Phil Spector.

Bear Bar, The

A 200-year-old bar in Greenwich Village, New York, which John frequented. Other customers included Salvador Dali and Tom Waits.

Beatles, The

The group, who were to become the most popular pop musicians of the twentieth century, had their origins in a skiffle group formed at Quarry Bank School in the Woolton district of Liverpool.

Skiffle was a music phenomenon that had sprung up in Britain during the mid-1950s, although the word was actually a black American term used in the 1920s, and there was even a record called 'Hometown Skiffle' by Charlie Spanel in 1929.

The British boom began in 1953 and can directly be traced to a concert at the Royal Festival Hall. Performing were the Ken Colyer Band, who included in their act a turn by Lonnie Donegan and his skiffle group. He included in his programme an adaptation of 'Rock Island Line', a tune by Leadbelly, which Donegan issued as a single in 1955. This became a hit in both the British and American charts. 'Freight Train' by the Charles McDevitt Skiffle Group, with a vocal by Nancy Whiskey, also hit the American charts in 1957 and this was covered by American acts such as Margie Rayburn, Dick Jacobs and Rusty Draper. In 1958 Johnny Otis sought to capitalise on the British skiffle boom by composing 'Willie & the Hand Jive', a number that hit the American charts, but didn't make much impact in Britain.

Donegan was the prime influence who sparked off the British musical trend. The skiffle phenomenon, which he created, was aided by the fact that skiffle could be played on home-made instruments and, soon after he had topped the charts with 'Rock Island Line', skiffle groups began to spring up all over the country, at one time reaching the formidable figure of 5,000.

Many of the Liverpool music veterans credit the beginning of the Mersey boom with an appearance made by Lonnie Donegan at the Pavilion Theatre in Liverpool, a show attended by many of the embryonic local musicians. Then, when Donegan appeared at the Liverpool Empire, a fourteen-year-old Paul McCartney waited outside the theatre for his autograph while an even younger George Harrison sought out Donegan's lodgings and obtained his autograph there. George commented, 'Lonnie Donegan was the first music star to make a big impression on me. Donegan and skiffle music just seemed made for me.'

John Lennon was sixteen at the time and he bought the 78-r.p.m. disc of 'Rock Island Line' and played it until it was nearly worn. This inspired him to form a skiffle group of his own and included in the group's repertoire were a number of Donegan hits including 'Rock Island Line', 'Midnight Special', 'Railroad Bill', 'Cumberland Gap' and 'Worried Man Blues'.

John formed the group early in 1957 with schoolmates from Quarry Bank School and they decided to call themselves the Quarry Men. Over a period of time there were various changes in personnel. Initially there was John on guitar and vocals; Bill Smith on tea-chest bass – soon to be replaced by Ivan Vaughan, then Nigel Whalley, then Len Garry, until the tea chest was ditched in mid-1958; Eric Griffiths on guitar; Rod Davis on banjo; Colin Hanton on drums, and Pete Shotton on washboard.

Around that time in Liverpool there were scores of skiffle groups, usually playing in the particular districts of Liverpool where they originated. The Quarry Men spent a lot of time rehearsing in members' homes and playing at friends' parties, although there were a handful of paid gigs. Being from Woolton, they were appearing at venues such as Wilson Hall in Garston, St Barnabas Church Hall in Penny Lane, Holyoake Hall in Smithdown Road, and at various skiffle contests held at venues such as the Locarno and Grafton ballrooms in West Derby Road. They even appeared on the back of a lorry performing at a street party in Rosebery Street, Toxteth.

The most important date in their calendar was 6 July 1957 when they appeared at the St Peter's Church garden fête. This was the day that John was introduced to Paul McCartney for the first time. Paul was invited to join the group and accepted, although he did not appear with them at their Cavern Club debut on 7 August 1957.

The Cavern Club, which had opened that year, was strictly a jazz club. Its owner, Alan Sytner, had a strict policy at the club and rock 'n' roll music was banned. Skiffle groups were tolerated in between the jazz groups, who were the club's staple. When the Quarry Men appeared at the venue, John attempted to perform two Elvis Presley numbers, 'Hound Dog' and 'Blue Suede Shoes', which infuriated Sytner, who sent them a note on stage to 'cut the bloody rock'.

As it turned out, the Cavern became a latecomer on the Liverpool rock 'n' roll circuit and continued its policy of jazz as the local rock music grew in the numerous other venues around the city.

Another important member of the group was now in the line-up: George Harrison had replaced Eric Griffiths on lead guitar. However, by January 1959 they virtually ceased to exist and no longer performed, although John and Paul often got together and began writing songs at Paul's home in Forthlin Road, Allerton.

Since the Quarry Men had apparently folded, George joined a group called the Les Stewart Quartet. By this time the skiffle boom had faded. However, in Liverpool the majority of skiffle members didn't down instruments when the trend tailed off at the end of 1958 – they turned to rock 'n' roll.

The James Boys evolved into Kingsize Taylor and the Dominoes, the Raving Texans into Rory Storm and the Hurricanes, the Mars Bars became Gerry and the Pacemakers, the Gamblers Skiffle Group evolved into Karl Terry and the Cruisers and so on.

Another important date in the group's history took place on 29 August 1958. But for this particular date the Quarry Men would have ceased to exist and there never would have been a group called the Beatles.

A new coffee bar was due to open in the West Derby area of Liverpool. Launched by Mona Best, it was part of another British trend of the 1950s: the coffee club.

Coffee clubs had initially sprung up in London and then spread around the country. They were usually on tiny premises and served a limited fare with cappuccino and espresso being the main attraction, although, as in the case of a number of clubs such as the Casbah, the most popular drink turned out to be Coca-Cola.

Liverpool had numerous coffee bars. There were the professional establishments such as the Kardomah and El Cabala and there were the numerous little clubs set up by individual owners, usually in old shop fronts. In the heart of Liverpool centre these included the Kinkajoo, the Zodiac, the Studio Club and the Jacaranda, intimate places set up by enterprising young men such as Neil English and Allan Williams.

Mona Best decided to include entertainment at her new club and set her mind on hiring a resident group. George Harrison's girlfriend Ruth Morrison had heard about the imminent opening of the venue and mentioned it to Ken Brown, one of the guitarists with the Les Stewart Quartet. Brown convinced Best that his band were suitable to take up the residency.

However, prior to the opening, the group leader Les Stewart decided his band wouldn't play at the Casbah, angry at the fact that Brown had been missing rehearsals in order to help Best and her sons get the club decorated in time for the opening date. As a result, Ken Brown walked out and George joined him. They wanted to take up the residency at the club and George said he had two friends. He contacted John and Paul and the Quarry Men were reborn as a quartet with John, Paul, George and Brown.

Reporting on the event, the local paper commented, 'Four young men making a name for themselves in the world of skiffle and "pop" music are the Quarry Men, who played for many teenagers to dance at the opening of West Derby's "Kasbah" [sic] Club on Saturday evening.

'The club, where teenagers can meet their friends, dance and drink coffee, has been opened in the cellars of a house in Hayman's Green, West Derby. The Quarry Men, complete with a varied repertoire and their electric guitars, will play at the club each Saturday in the future.

'They are John Lennon, 251 Menlove Avenue, Woolton; Paul McCartney, 20 Forthlin Road, Allerton; George Harrison, 25 Upton Green, Speke; and Kenny Brown, 148a Storrington Avenue, Norris Green.'

The quartet, who felt they didn't need the services of a drummer, continued with their Saturday night residency until 10 October 1959, when they had a disagreement with Best over the fact that she had paid Brown, even though he was unable to play with them that evening. As a result they walked out on their residency and jettisoned Brown, deciding to continue as a trio.

However, owing to the fact that it saw the resurrection of the group and was the site of their first residency, the Casbah has often been referred to as 'the birthplace of the Beatles'.

Later that same month John, Paul and George appeared at the Empire Theatre, Liverpool, as part of the Carroll Levis *TV Star*

Search shows. For their appearances on the contest they used the name Johnny and the Moondogs. This was one of a number of name changes they underwent until they finally settled on the name the Beatles. These included the Beatals, the Silver Beats, the Silver Beetles and the Silver Beatles.

It was Casey Jones (a.k.a. Brian Casser), leader of a top Liverpool group Cass and the Cassanovas, who suggested they call themselves Long John and the Silver Men. They didn't like that name, but kept the 'silver'. They appeared only once as the Silver Beats, at a Lathom Hall gig for the promoter Brian Kelly. They then began a tour of Scotland calling themselves the Silver Beetles – although they weren't actually billed on the tour, promotional material merely referring to 'Johnny Gentle and his group'.

The suggestion of the inclusion of the word 'Beetles' in their name is generally acknowledged to be that of Stuart Sutcliffe, who had joined the group by that time. It came about because the group were playing a number of Buddy Holly numbers in their repertoire and they were looking for a name similar to that of Holly's backing group, the Crickets. They chose the name of an insect. It is then believed that John substituted the 'a', changing it to Silver Beatles.

There is absolutely no truth in the oft-quoted story that they got their name from the Marlon Brando film *The Wild One* in which a character played by Lee Marvin leads a motorcycle gang called the Beetles. British censors banned the film for fourteen years as they felt it was likely to incite violence among the young and it received its first ever showing in Britain in a London cinema on 15 February 1968.

John had left Quarry Bank and began attending the Liverpool College of Art in September 1957. Here Bill Harry, founder of *Mersey Beat* magazine, introduced him to Sutcliffe. Paul McCartney and George Harrison began attending Liverpool Institute next door to the art college and began rehearsing in the art college life rooms and also began performing at the college dances. Sutcliffe and Harry, being on the students' union committee, voted for union funds to pay for a PA system, which the 'college band' could use.

As students, Lennon, Sutcliffe, Harry and Rod Murray often used to hang around in a coffee bar in Slater Street called the

Jacaranda. Allan Williams, a former plumber, who also attempted one or two promotions under his Jacaranda Enterprises, ran the club.

Jacaranda Enterprises, in conjunction with the impresario Larry Parnes, presented a concert with Gene Vincent at Liverpool Stadium on Tuesday 3 May 1960. Williams booked a number of local groups such as Cass and the Cassanovas, Rory Storm and the Hurricanes and Gerry and the Pacemakers to appear.

Williams then attempted an equivalent of the Chelsea Arts Ball at St George's Hall and asked Sutcliffe to decorate some of the floats. He also had Sutcliffe and Murray paint some murals in the Jacaranda for him. However, he wasn't particularly interested in the group that John and Stuart were in.

John and Stuart had seen the Stadium show and Stuart was later to ask Williams why he hadn't booked his group on it. As the Liverpool bands had impressed Parnes the London impresario asked Williams to arrange an audition for a possible backing band for one of his stars, the Liverpool singer Billy Fury. Williams then told Stuart his band could appear at the audition.

By this time they had secured a drummer, Tommy Moore, on the recommendation of Casey Jones.

The audition took place at another club Williams was intending to open, the Wyvern Club, which he was later to convert into the Blue Angel. The bands appearing were Cass and the Cassanovas, Derry and the Seniors, Cliff Roberts and the Rockers and the Silver Beetles.

For setting up the auditions, Williams expected some fee from whichever group was selected. Who they were didn't matter.

When the Silver Beetles came to perform, Moore still hadn't arrived and Johnny Hutchinson of the Cassanovas deputised. Moore then turned up and completed the audition.

This became the subject of another myth. Williams asked Chenison Roland to take some photographs of the different groups at the audition. In one of the shots Sutcliffe is seen with his back to the photographer while tuning up. Years later, Williams was to allege that Stuart couldn't play and turned his back to Parnes during the audition. Yet in the other photographs of them playing, he is standing to the side and his hands and the guitar can be plainly seen, proving he wasn't performing with his back to anyone – photos of the Beatles performing in Hamburg also show him facing the audience. In the most famous photo of that Wyvern session, with Hutchinson sitting in with them, Stuart can clearly be seen playing his instrument.

Parnes himself also refuted Williams's allegation that the reason he had turned down the group as Billy Fury's backing band was due to Stuart's inability to play.

Three of the groups got work from Parnes. Cass and the Cassanovas were asked to back Billy Fury on tour, Derry and the Seniors to back Duffy Power and the Silver Beatles to back Lance Fortune.

Parnes declared that his only objection to the Silver Beetles was the fact that their drummer, Moore, turned up late, was dressed differently from the other members and was several years older than they were.

He decided to book some of the Liverpool groups to back artists of his and, because Williams had set up the audition, he was to get a cut from the three bands.

The Silver Beetles then went on the short tour of Scotland backing Johnny Gentle.

On their return Williams added them to the list of groups for whom he occasionally got local bookings and secured them a series of gigs with the promoter Les Dodd of Paramount Enterprises, from which he took a cut. He also booked them into a strip club run by a partner, Lord Woodbine, because they just happened to be around and were cheap, although he was to openly admit that he didn't think much of their music. These bookings between June and July 1960 were the only local bookings Williams ever got for the group (apart from a gig at the Grosvenor in 1961), acting purely as an agent, apart from a few bookings in his own Jacaranda, owing to the fact that his resident Caribbean Steel Band had left him.

In the meantime, Derry and the Seniors, who had turned professional to undertake a summer season backing one of Parnes's artists, saw the deal cancelled. Blaming Williams, Howie Casey, leader of the Seniors, went to the Wyvern and tackled Williams, who agreed to take the group down to London.

He drove them down to the 2 1's coffee bar in London, arranged for them to play – and by a stroke of pure good luck

Bruno Koschmider, a Hamburg club owner, was in the club seeking bands for his venue.

Williams had already allegedly been in touch with Koschmider. The story is a complicated one as it also involves claims from Casey Jones that he was the original person to contact Koschmider.

However, it resulted in Koschmider's booking Derry and the Seniors for his club, the Kaiserkeller, already having booked a group from London to precede them, the Jets (one of the members was Tony Sheridan).

The Seniors were very popular at the club and Koschmider contacted Williams to ask him to send over another group. Williams asked Rory Storm and the Hurricanes, but they were already booked for a summer season at Butlin's. He next approached Gerry and the Pacemakers, but they turned him down. Almost in desperation he turned to the Silver Beetles, who shortened their name to the Beatles prior to departure. Their drummer Tommy Moore had left them, but they had found another drummer, Norman Chapman. However, after appearing at three gigs with them he was called up for national service and had to leave. (He died in July 1995.) They then approached Pete Best, son of Mona Best, to join them.

Williams intended to travel to Hamburg with his wife, brother-in-law and his associate Lord Woodbine. His prime mission was to get Koschmider to agree to his becoming sole booking agent for British bands for the club. Since the impecunious Beatles didn't themselves have the cash to travel over, he hired a minivan to enable the entire party to travel together.

On arrival in Hamburg the Beatles were told that they wouldn't be playing at the Kaiserkeller. Koschmider had decided to turn a small strip club, the Indra, at the unfashionable end of the Grosse Freiheit into a music venue. The Beatles were to be the first group to perform there.

They were billeted in a dismal area to the rear of the Bambi-Filmkunstheater, a cinema owned by Koshmider, which had only three beds, although there were five in the band. The accommodation was so dire that they asked Williams to talk to Koshmider and do something about it, but he never did.

In the meantime, they began to play at the Indra on 17 August

1960, performing four and a half hours a night for a total of 48 nights.

Koshmider was pleased with Derry and the Seniors at the Kaiserkeller, who were packing them in. Derry Wilkie, a black Liverpool vocalist who fronted the group, was a dynamic performer. Pete Best was to call him 'a showman extraordinaire'. Koshmider wanted the Beatles to entertain the audience and be more active on stage, so he urged them to 'Mach schau' ('make show'), just as Wilkie did on stage.

The Kaiserkeller was doing so well that Koshmider decided to drop the interval where a jukebox played records and bring in an extra band, so he split up the Seniors and took Stuart from the Beatles to make up a third entity. The hybrid outfit comprised Howie Casey on sax, Stuart on bass, Stan Foster on piano and a German drummer.

Complaints to the police about the noise from the Indra obliged Koshmider to convert the club back to a strip joint and he moved the Beatles to the Kaiserkeller on 3 October, where he had them alternate with the Seniors. The Seniors then left and Rory Storm and the Hurricanes, fresh from their season at Butlin's, arrived to become the bill toppers.

Williams by this time had gone back to Liverpool, unsuccessful in his attempt to get Koschmider to give him sole booking rights for the club. He didn't have any further association with the Beatles, apart from a running argument in which he demanded an agency fee for the 1961 Top Ten season which they claimed to have arranged themselves.

The Williams episode is worth exploring because his claims of being their 'first manager' have passed into Beatle lore.

The Beatles historian Mark Lewisohn was nearer the truth in his book *The Beatles Live*, in which he wrote, 'Liverpudlian Allan Richard Williams, a stockily built opportunist who, from May 1960 until April 1961, became the group's occasional booking agent or, as he still claims, "their first manager". (Even now, more than twenty years on, the Beatles strongly dispute Williams' claim.)'

However, Lewisohn was wrong in stretching the period until 1961 because Williams had nothing to do with them after their return from Germany at the end of 1960 – apart from a Grosvenor Ballroom booking.

If Williams had been manager to the Beatles he would have booked them on his Liverpool Stadium event. They would have been his *first* choice for Hamburg, not this third, when Koschmider requested another group. If he had been their manager he would have looked after their interests in Hamburg when they requested better sleeping conditions. If he had been their manager how would he have allowed Rory Storm and the Hurricanes, whom he also booked into Hamburg, to have top billing, more money and better accommodation than the Beatles?

When the Hurricanes were at the Kaiserkeller Williams was impressed by the voice of Lu Walters of the Hurricanes and paid for a record of him singing at the Akustik Studio in Hamburg. Because of their vocal harmony, he wanted the Beatles to back Walters on a song, 'Summertime'. As the Hurricanes were so used to playing it, Ringo Starr provided the drumming, which is the first time all four of the future Beatles played together. The Hurricanes then backed Walters on two other numbers. The Beatles asked Williams if they could do some numbers, but he refused to pay.

If Williams had been their manager, why would he sooner pay to have a group other than his own make a record?

Over this period of time he did more for both Derry and the Seniors and Rory Storm and the Hurricanes than he did for the Beatles, but never claimed to have managed those bands.

The myth began to arise when a journalist, Bill Marshall, co-authored Allan's book *The Man Who Gave the Beatles Away*. Marshall freely admits to making up a large part of the book and more accent was given to the Beatles because the book was sold on their name.

On the first page of the book are the words 'I was the Beatles' first manager. I still have their contracts, ragged and burnt from being involved in a fire.' He omitted to mention that the contracts weren't management contracts: they were only the agency contracts booking the Beatles into the Kaiserkeller. They were actually slightly burned in a fire that destroyed his Liverpool Top Ten club venture.

Further evidence that Williams acted only in an agency and not a management capacity is found in the letter he sent to them in April 1961 in which he attempted to get a commission for their Top Ten season. He wrote,

> If you decide not to pay I promise that I shall have you out of Germany inside two weeks through several legal ways and don't you think I'm bluffing.
>
> I will also submit a full report of your behaviour to the Agency Members Association, of which I am a full member, and every Agent in England is a member, to protect Agents from Artists who misbehave and welsh out of agreements.

There you have it, in his own words, he was acting as agent, not manager.

While they were appearing at the Kaiserkeller, they made the acquaintance of a group of German youngsters they initially referred to as 'the Exis'. The term was applied to them because they were interested in Parisian intellectuals and existentialists in contrast to the 'rockers' who frequented the Kaiserkeller. One of 'exis', Klaus Voormann, had been attracted by the sounds of Rory Storm and the Hurricanes on stage when he'd been passing the Kaiserkeller and he was drawn inside. While there he also saw the Beatles, who impressed him even more. He persuaded his girlfriend Astrid Kirchherr and another friend, Jurgen Vollmer, to join him at the club. They began to frequent the Kaiserkeller, also joined by other friends.

The person who impressed them most was Stuart Sutcliffe – as a result of his influence, Voormann was later to become a bass guitarist and Kirchherr became his fiancée.

The Beatles had appeared at the Indra club from 14 August until 3 October and then appeared at the Kaiserkeller from 4 October until 30 November.

During this time another rock 'n' roll club had opened in the nearby Reeperbahn. This was a club that the Jets, with Tony Sheridan, had moved on to following their own stint at the Kaiserkeller. It had been named the Top Ten club on the suggestion of Sheridan, a former member of Vince Taylor's group – and Taylor had run a club in London's Soho called the Top Ten. The owner was Peter Eckhorn, who had also poached the Kaiserkeller's bouncer, Horst Fascher.

Situated at 136 Reeperbahn, it had formerly been a sex circus called the Hippodrome and the building had been given to Eckhorn by his father. The Beatles began to drift around the corner during their breaks to watch Sheridan and the Jets perform. They were soon getting up on stage and jamming with them.

This came to the notice of Koschmider, allegedly from Georg Sterner.

On their return to Liverpool, sans Stuart, they had no work lined up. Allan Williams had, in fact, intended to launch a new club, the Top Ten in Soho Street, and the Beatles were to follow Derry and the Seniors there. The club was the victim of arson and burned down, taking the Seniors' equipment with it and causing the group to break up. Pete Best's mother then stepped in to help the Beatles out and booked them into the Casbah on 17 December. Because of Stuart's absence, Best arranged for his former Blackjacks bass guitarist, Chas Newby, to join them. Newby was offered the opportunity to replace Sutcliffe as a permanent member of the band, but turned them down as he wished to continue his college studies. Like Chapman, he played only three gigs with them.

It was a local compere, Bob Wooler, who contacted the promoter Brian Kelly and talked him into booking the Beatles at Litherland Town Hall on 27 December 1960. This is generally regarded as the gig that set them on the road to their local fame. They'd been virtually unknown in Liverpool prior to this booking and were even advertised as 'direct from Germany', leaving some members of the audience believing they were a German group. Members of other Liverpool bands saw them that night and were startled by their dynamism. Kelly himself noted the sensational impact they had on the audience and posted bouncers on the dressing room door while he booked them for numerous appearances on his 'Beekay' promotions at Litherland Town Hall, Aintree Institute, Alexandra Hall and Lathom Hall. The only other promoter who squeezed his way into their dressing room was Dave Forshaw, who booked them for three appearances, beginning the next day. Mona Best also booked the group for more Casbah appearances, and also for her promotions at St John's Hall, Tuebrook. They then began to appear all over Merseyside on the numerous different 'jive hives'.

Their Litherland Town Hall appearance was described in a famous article by Wooler in *Mersey Beat*.

As this was another turning point in their career, it is appropriate to provide some background on the state of the Liverpool music landscape at the time.

It was a unique scene and an acknowledgement of its real contribution to the forging of the Beatles has not really been apparent in the many books that have been written about them.

In fact, the Hamburg scene has been given more prominence in the 'birth of the Beatles' story. However, there was no Hamburg scene when the Beatles arrived there in 1960. It wasn't a city like Liverpool, where thousands of youngsters were pouring into venues to listen to hundreds of bands. Rock 'n' roll hardly existed in Germany at the time and the only two bands to precede the Beatles were the Jets and Derry and the Seniors.

Their spell in Hamburg from August to December 1960 proved to be a real baptism of fire and made them a better group than they'd been previously, but it was their battles with the other bands in Liverpool over the following two years that gave them their edge. After all, even in Hamburg, the reason they were driven to 'make show' by Koschmider was because of the dynamic performances of the showman Derry Wilkie at the Kaiserkeller. In Liverpool their rivals included such great bands as the Big Three, Kingsize Taylor and the Dominoes, Rory Storm and the Hurricanes, the Remo Four and Gerry and the Pacemakers.

Basically, the Hamburg scene comprised only three clubs, all within walking distance of each other, although all were not operating at the same time. They were the Kaiserkeller, the Top Ten and the Star Club. As a rock venue the Kaiserkeller didn't last very long, leaving just two venues.

In contrast, Liverpool had far in excess of 300 venues where groups could play, including those such as the Tower and Locarno ballrooms, which were large enough to accommodate thousands of youngsters. However, these were not where the Mersey sound was originally forged.

In the late 1950s groups began to thrive in Liverpool in 'jive hives', the ballrooms and town halls booked by the enterprising local promoters such as Brian Kelly, Doug Martin, Wally Hill, Vic Anton Dave Foreshaw, Charlie McBain, Mona Best, Les Dodd and Sam Leach. They promoted frequently at venues such as the Grosvenor Ballroom, Wilson Hall, Hambleton Hall,

Aintree Institute, Blair Hall, Litherland Town Hall, St John's Hall, Alexandra Hall, Lathom Hall, Mossway Hall, Knotty Ash Village Hall and New Clubmoor Hall.

The three music venues in Hamburg were situated in the notorious red-light district of St Pauli, where audiences were generally composed of punters seeking 'adult entertainment' in clubs that actively encouraged their patrons to drink. In Liverpool it was the youth of Merseyside who crowded the venues, where only soft drinks were available. They went because they loved the music. The kids attended the venues throughout the area in their thousands in what was arguably the first major youth movement in the British Isles.

Between 1958 and 1964 there were probably around 500 different bands in the Merseyside area. The figure at any one time probably stood at 350. When Bob Wooler and Bill Harry originally compiled a list of groups for *Mersey Beat* that they were aware of, it ran to almost 300 names.

Among the Mersey bands and artists during this period were:

The Aarons, Abraham and His Lot, Adam and the Sinners, The Agents, The Alamos, The Alaskans, Alby and the Sorrals, Steve Aldo, Alfie Diamond and the Skiffle Kings, The Alibis, Tony Allen, The Alley Cats, The Almost Blues, The Alphas, The Ambassadors, The Anzacs, The Aristocrats, Arrow and the Archers, The Arrows, The Asteroids, The Atlantas, The Aztecs, Babs and Joan, The Bachelors, The Backbeats, Bags Blue Beats, The Banshees, The Beat Boys, The Beatcombers, The Beathovens, The Beatles, The Beatwoods, Bertis Collins and the Sundowners, The Big Three, Billy Forde and the Phantoms, The Black Cats, The Black Diamonds, The Blackjacks, The Black Knights, The Black Velvets, The Blackwells, The Blak Katz, The Blue Chips, The Blue Country Boys, The Blue Mountain Boys, The Blue Notes, The Blues System, Bob Evans and the Five Shillings, Bobby and the Bachelors, Bobby and the Halers, The Bobby Bell Rockers, Bob's Vegas Five, The Boleros, Amos Bonny, The Boot Hill Billies, The Boys, The Breakaways, The Brokers, Irene Brown, Bruce and the Cavaliers, Buddy Dean and the Teachers, The Buffaloes, The Bumblies, Billy Butler, Cadillac and the Playboys, The Cadillacs, The Calderstones, Carl Vincent and the Counts, Carol and the Corvettes, Irene Carroll, The Carrolls, Cass and the Cassanovas, The Casuals, The Cavaliers, The Cavemen, The Caverners, The

Centaurs, The Centremen, The Chain Gang, The Challengers, The Champions, The Chants, The Cheaters, The Cheetahs, Vicki Cheetham, The Chelseas, The Chessmen, Chick Graham and the Coasters, Chris and the Diamonds, Christine Ching, Tony Christian, The Cimarrons, The Cirques, The Citadels, The Citrons, The City Beats, The Clansmen, The Classics, Clay Ellis and the Raiders, The Clayton Squares, The Climbers, The Coins, Collage, The Collegians, The Columbians, The Comets, The Concords, The Connoisseurs, The Conquests, The Conspirators, The Contrasts, The Corals, The Cordelles, The Cordes, The Corsairs, The Corvettes, The Countdowns, The Country Four, The Creoles, The Crescendos, The Crestas, The Crossbeats, The Croupiers, The Cruisers, The Crusaders, The Cryin' Shames, Cy and the Cimmarons, Cy Tucker's Friars, The Dakotas, The Daleks, Danny and the Asteroids, Danny and the Escorts, Danny and the Hi-Cats, Danny Lee and the Stalkers, The Darktown Skiffle Group, The Dateliners, Dave and the Corvettes, Dave and the Rave-Ons, Dave Bell and the Bell Boys, The Daybreakers, The Dealers, Dean Fleming and the Flamingos, The Deans, Barbara Dee, Dee and the Pontiacs, The Dee Beats, Dee Fenton's Silhouettes, The Deepbeats, The Deerstalkers, The Defenders, The Defiants, The Delecardoes, The Delemeres, The Delltones, The Delmont Four, The Del Renas, The Demoiselles, The Demon Five, The Denems, Denis and the Newtowns, The Dennisons, Denny Seyton and the Sabres, The Deputies, Derry Wilkie and the Others, The Detonators, The Detours, The Diablos, The Diamonds, The Dimensions, Dino and the Wild Fires, The Diplomats, Dixie and the Daredevils, The Dominant Four, The Downbeats, The Drifting Cowboys, The Dynachords, The Dynamos, Earl Preston and the Realms, Earl Preston and the TTs, Earl Royce and the Olympics, The Earthlings Blues Band, The Easybeats, Eddie Dean and the Onlookers, Eddy Falcon and the Vampires, The Electrons, The Elektones, The Epics, The Escorts, The Everests, The Excelles, The Excheckers, The Executioners, The Explorers, The Expressions, The Eyes, The Factotums, The Falcons, The Fallons, Faron and the Burnettes, Faron and the Crossfires, Faron and the Tempest Tornadoes, Faron's Flamingos, The Fast Cats, The FBI, The Federal Five, The Feelgoods, The Few, The Fire-Flies, The Fix, The Flames, The Flintstones, The Flyaways, The Flyovers, The Foggy Mountain Ramblers, The

Fontanas, The Four Aces, The Four Aristokats, The Four Clefs, The Four Dimensions, The Four Gents, Four Hits and a Miss, The Four Jays, The Four Just Men, The Fourmost, The Four Musketeers, The Four Originals, Frank Knight and the Barons, Freddie Starr and the Delmonts, Freddie Starr and the Midnighters, Freddie Starr and the Ventures, The Fruit Eating Bears, The Futurists, The Galaxies with Doreen, The Galvanizers, Gary B Goode and the Hot Rods, The Gay Tones, Gee Gee and the Go Men, The Gems, Gene Day and the Django Beats, Geoff Stacey and the Wanderers, The George Nield Trio, The Georgians, Gerry and the Pacemakers, Gerry Bach and the Beathovens, Gerry De Ville and the City Kings, The Ghost Riders, The Gibsons, The Globetrotters, The G-Men, The Griff Parry Five, Barbara Grounds, Group One, Groups Inc, Gus Travis and the Midnighters, The Hailers, Hank and the Drifters, Hank Walters and the Dusty Road Ramblers, The Harlems, The Heralds, The Heartbeats, The Hellions, The Hi-Cats, The Hideaways, The Hi-Fi Three, The Hi-Hats, The Hi-Spots, The Hillsiders, Howie Casey and the Seniors, Rita Hughes, The Huntsmen, The Hustlers, The Hylites, Ian and the Zodiacs, The Illusions, The Impacts, The Incas, The Inmates, The Invaders, Irene and the Sante Fes, Jackie and Bridie, The Jackobeats, The Jaguars, The James Boys, The Jaybeats, The Jaywalkers, Jenny and the Tallboys, The Jensons, Jet and the Valiants, The Jets, Jimmy and the Jokers, Jimmy and the Midnighters, J.J. and the Hi-Lites, Joan and the Demons, Johnny Apollo and the Spartans, Johnny Gold and the Country Cousins, Johnny Marlowe and the Whip Chords, Johnny Martin and the Martinis, Johnny Paul and the Dee Jays, Johnny President and the Senators, Johnny Ringo and the Colts, Johnny Rocco and the Jets, Johnny Saint and the Travellers, Johnny Sandon and the Remo Four, Johnny Sandon and the Searchers, Johnny Tempest and the Tornadoes, The Jokers, Tommy Jordan, The Kandies, The Kansas City Five, The Karacters, Karina, Karl Terry and the Cruisers, Ken Dallas and the Silhouettes, Keoki and the Hawaiianeers, The Kingpins, Kingsize Taylor and the Dominoes, The Kinsleys, The Kirkbys, Kliff Hilton and the Merseys, The Knutrockers, The Kobras, The Koobas, The Kordas, The Kruzads, The Landslides, The Lawmen, Lee Castle and the Barons, Lee Crombie and the Sundowners, Lee Curtis and the All Stars, Lee Curtis and the Detours, Lee

Eddie and the Chevrons, The Lee Eddie Five, Lee Shondell and the Boys, Lee Shondell and the Capitols, The Leesiders, The Legends, Lenny and the Team Mates, Liam and the Invaders, Lilli Leyland, The L'il Three, The Lincolns, The Liverbirds, The Lonely Ones, The Long and the Short, Lottie and the Weimars, L'Ringo's, The Mafia, The Mailman, The Mal Craig Three, Joan Malloy, The Managers, The Maracas, The Marescas, The Markfour, Mark Swain and the Tornadoes, The Marlins, The Mars Bars, Jackie Martin, Jill Martin, The Masqueraders, The Masterminds, The Mastersounds, The Mavericks, The Megatones, The Memphis R&B Combo, The Memphis Three, The Merchants, The Merseybeats, The Mersey Bluebeats, The Mersey Four, The Mersey Five, The Mersey Men, The Mersey Monsters, The Mersey Sounds, The Meteors, The Method, The MGs, The Michael Allen Group, The M.I.5., The Mikados, Mike and the Explorers, Mike Byrne and the Thunderbirds, Mike Dee and the Detours, Mike Savage and the Wildcats, The Miller Brothers, The Minibeats, The Minutes, The Missouri Drifters, The Mojos, The Moments, The Morockans, The Mosquitos, The Motifs, The Musicians, The Music Students, The Mustangs, The Mystery Men, The Mystics, The Nameless Ones, The Nashpool Four, The Night Boppers, The Night Riders, The Night Walkers, The Nocturnes, The Nomads, The Notions, The Onlookers, The Others, The Outkasts, The Pacifics, The Page Boys, The Paladins, The Panthers, The Paragons, The Pathfinders, Paul and the Diamonds, Paul Francis and the Wanderers, The Pawns, The Pegasus Four, Peter Demos and his Demons, Pete Picasso and the Rock Sculptors, The Phantoms, Phil Brady and the Ranchers, Phil's Feelgoods, The Pikkins, The Pilgrims, The Plebs, The Plims, The Pontiacs, The Poppies, The Premiers, The Press Gang, The Pressmen, The Principles, The Profiles, The Prowlers, The Pulsators, The Pyramids, The Quarry Men, Tommy Quickly, The Quiet Ones, The Quintones, The Rainchecks, The Rainmakers, The Ramrods, The Ranchers, The Ravens, The Rebel Rousers, Reds Incorporated, The Remo Four, The Renegades, The Renicks, The Rent Collectors, Rhythm Amalgamated, Rhythm and Blues Incorporated, The Rhythm Quartet, Rick and the Delmonts, Ricky and the Dominant Four, Ricky Gleason and the Top Spots, Rikki and the Red Streaks, The Riot Squad, Rip Van Winkle and the Rip-It-Ups, Ritchie and the

Galvanisers, The Rivals, The Roadrunners, The Robettes, Robin and the Ravens, The Rockerfellers, The Rockin' Rivals, Rocky Stone and the Pebbles, Rogues Gallery, Rita Rogers, The Rondex, The Ron Pickard Combo, The Rontons, Rory and the Globe Trotters, Rory Storm and the Hurricanes, Roy and the Dions, Roy Montrose and the Midnights, The Runaways, St Louis Checks, The Sandgrounders, The Sandstorms, The Santones, The Sapphires, Savva and the Democrats, The Scaffold, The Schatz, The Screaming Skulls, The Searchers, The Secrets, The Seftons, The Seniors, The Senitors, The Sensations, The Sepias, The Set Up, The Shades, The Shakers, The Shimmy Shimmy Queens, The Silvertones, The Sinners, The Skeletons, The Skylarks, The Skyliners, The Sneakers, The Sobells, Some People, The Sonnets, Sonny Kaye and the Reds, The Soul Agents, The Soul Seekers, Sounds Plus One, The Spectres, The Spidermen, The Spinners, The Sportsmen, The Squad, The Statesmen, Steve and the Syndicate, Steve Day and the Drifters, The Strangers, The Strettons, The Subterranes, The Sundowners, The Swaydes, The Swinging Bluejeans, The Syndicate, The Tabs, Take Five, The Talismen, The Team-mates, The Teenbeats, The Tempos, The Tennessee Four, Terry and the Teen Aces, The Terry Hines Sextet, The Texans, That Group, Them Grimbles, The Three Bells, The Three Deuces, The Three of Diamonds, The Thrillers, The Thunderbirds, Tiffany's Dimensions, The T.J.s, The Tokens, Tom and Bernie, Tommy and the Metronomes, Tommy and the Olympics, Tommy and the Satellites, Tony and the Checkers, Tony and the Quandros, Tony Carlton and the Mersey Four, The Topics, The Tornadoes, The Traders, The Travellers, The Tremas, The Trends, The Trents, The Tributes, The Tudor Four, The Tudors, The Tuxedos, The Two Tones, The Undertakers, The Vaders, The Valkyries, The Vampires, Vance Williams and the Rhythm Four, The Ventures, The Verbs, The Vernons Girls, Vic and the TTs, The V.I.C.s, Vic Takes Four, The Vigilantes, The Vikings, Vikki Lane and the Moonlighters, Vince Earl and the Talismen, Vince Earl and the Zeroes, Vince Reno and the Sabres, Vinny and the Dukes, The V.I.P.s, The Walter Corless Combo, Wayne Calvert and the Cimmarons, Wayne Stevens and the Vikings, The Weeverbeats, Wells Fargo, The Wheels, Lorraine White, The Wild Harkes, The Willows, The Wranglers, Wump and His Werbles, The Young Ones, The Zenith Six, The Zephyrs

The most popular line-up was a quartet with three guitarists – lead, rhythm and bass – plus a drummer. The three guitarists up front would engage in vocal harmony. The Beatles were particularly adept at this as Paul McCartney, being left-handed, could also use the same microphone as John Lennon when they sang together – thus avoiding a clash of guitars and also producing a visual effect that many of the other groups couldn't imitate.

This basic line-up was the one generally referred to when people later talked of the Liverpool sound, and it was most apparent with groups such as the Beatles, the Searchers, Faron's Flamingos and the Swinging Bluejeans. However, this image tends to make people underestimate just how extensive the range of the music scene in Liverpool was: there were duo, trios, quintets and groups with pianos and saxophones in their line-ups.

Comedy outfits such as the Fourmost were parodying other artists long before Duke D'mond and the Barron Knights became famous for songs such as 'Call Up The Groups'.

There were folk groups, country music bands, vocal groups, girl rock bands – even speciality bands such as the Mersey Monsters.

Liverpool had been called the Nashville of the North because it had the largest country music scene in Europe. There were approximately forty C&W bands contemporary with the Beatles. They had their own clubs such as the Black Cat Club and Wells Fargo, their own Country Music Federation and they ran their 'Grand Ole Opry' annually at the Philharmonic Hall. Their attempt to revolutionise country music, just as the rock groups in Liverpool revolutionised rock 'n' roll, has never been properly acknowledged.

There were basically two forms of country band in Liverpool: the purists, who played in the traditional manner, parroting the American records and wearing stetsons and cowboy clothes; and the new wave, such as the Hillsiders, young bands with a fresh approach to the music, who didn't dress in country style, but provided a new and exciting beat to country sounds.

Unfortunately, this movement tended to be overshadowed by the Beatles and the Mersey sound, and the new revolution in country music didn't occur until the late 1980s, with young Nashville artists who gave the music a fresh image – but it was happening on the banks of the Mersey in the late 1950s!

There were also several all-girl rock 'n' roll groups in Liverpool, the most noted being the Liverbirds. The girls became so popular in Hamburg that they remained in Germany for several years, missing out on the *Mersey Beat* boom. But the fact remains that there were girl rock bands in Liverpool a decade before American groups such as Fanny.

In the field of folk music, Liverpool gave rise to the Spinners, who remained Britain's premier folk outfit for thirty years, until their retirement.

There was also a healthy black music scene on Merseyside. Apart from artists such as Derry Wilkie and Steve Aldo, there were several vocal outfits in the Liverpool 8 district such as the Chants, the Sobells, the Challengers and the Poppies. Only the Chants were to have a limited degree of success. It seemed that when Britain eventually accepted black artists into the charts – with the Motown acts and soul music – the black hit artists were almost exclusively American. Few black British artists made it until the 1970s. Strangely enough, the group to make the breakthrough and hit the top of the charts were the Real Thing, who included Eddie Amoo of the Chants. It had taken him fifteen years to achieve his success!

Coexisting with the rock, folk, country and black music scenes was the poetry scene. Local poets used to hold readings at clubs such as Streates. Three of the poets, Roger McGough, Adrian Henri and Brian Patten, established themselves as leading British poets of the decade, with major poetry readings at venues such as the Royal Albert Hall and bestselling books such as *The Mersey Sound* and *New Volume*.

Mersey Beat also reported on 'clubland', the thriving entertainment scene for an older generation. Over 300 clubs were affiliated to the Merseyside Clubs Association. There were social clubs for unions, stores and factories that provided live entertainment for their members – in addition to drinks at prices far below those in pubs.

It was on the clubland scene that many local comics, such as Ken Dodd and Jimmy Tarbuck, developed. Liverpool has always had a reputation for providing more than its fair share of comedians, including Tommy Handley, Ted Ray, Arthur Askey and Norman Vaughan.

Liverpool had already provided chart acts from this background in the 1950s, with artists such as Frankie Vaughan, Lita Roza and Michael Halliday.

Although clubland was the training ground for comedians, speciality acts and country bands, there was also work for numerous rock groups in the various clubs. Early gigs for groups with Gerry Marsden and Ringo Starr as members took place at Pitt Street Labour Club and a Quarry Men gig was held on behalf of the Speke Bus Depot Social Club.

Imagine groups taking the stage at cinemas in intervals between the films; performing in coffee bars; strutting their acts at swimming baths; performing at ice rinks; learning their craft in almost every youth club, church hall, synagogue and village hall in the Merseyside area; blasting their music from the stages of town halls; lugging their gear into the band rooms of the numerous ballrooms; performing before audiences of varying ages at social clubs; playing in the city-centre cellar clubs and pulling in the audiences by the thousand in the larger venues – no place in the world at that time had so many young groups performing virtually nightly in such a compact area. In 1961 Bill Harry dubbed Liverpool 'the Rocking City'.

Liverpool's maritime heritage had led the city to become a melting pot of cosmopolitan influences. As the main port during the days of the slave trade, its black population became established centuries ago. Ironically, the large mansions built by the slave traders became the abodes in the twentieth century of the black population, who mainly dwelt in the Liverpool 8, or Toxteth, district.

The city was also a main destination for the Irish fleeing the potato famine in the mid-nineteenth century and Liverpool boasts a huge Irish population – it's often jokingly referred to as the capital of Ireland. There is also a substantial Welsh intake and Liverpool had a Chinatown before San Francisco.

Different cultural influences also led to the development of a wide range of musical tastes and, from sea shanties to Irish folk songs, Liverpool danced to the music of the world for more than two centuries. Most specifically, pub singalongs were a standard form of Liverpool entertainment and the musical heritage was strong.

This is where the truth and myth part, for the maritime heritage had no direct influence on the development of the Mersey sound.

Writers in the 1970s began to suggest that the reason Liverpool groups were different from groups in other parts of the country was that 'Cunard Yanks' brought them records that couldn't be obtained elsewhere in Britain. 'Cunard Yanks' were the Liverpudlians who went to sea in the ocean liners and brought presents back to their families. The myth is that they brought American records for their younger brothers and sons, and this is how the Liverpool bands built up their repertoires.

There is no truth in it.

In the 1950s Liverpool was still a seaport and a number of Liverpool men still sailed the seas, but it was a feeble number compared with the prewar days and the turn of the century. One or two members of groups, such as John McNally of the Searchers, had brothers who went to sea and brought them records. However, the most important records in the Searchers' collection came from their drummer Chris Curtis, who gathered them on his trips around the record stores. Some of the country bands such as Hank Walters and the Dusty Road Ramblers, were able to obtain rare country albums from merchant seamen, but the 'Cunard Yank' theory remains a myth.

A study of the Beatles' repertoire from the time, laying aside the original Lennon and McCartney numbers, proves that every song they played was available on record in Britain through the normal channels.

The late Johnny Byrne, the noted Johnny Guitar of the legendary Rory Storm and the Hurricanes, confirmed: 'That's a myth about the groups receiving copies or having records from "Cunard Yanks". We certainly never got any material this way and I doubt that the Beatles did. Most group material was gleaned from the records (although some on limited release) that were issued at that particular time (1958–1961). Chuck Berry, Jerry Lee et cetera were available and groups took their material from these and lesser-known artists with material that we were able to play and adapt that suited all the groups' limited styles.'

Chris Huston of the Undertakers added, 'When Johnny Byrne says that Liverpool groups didn't get their material from sailors he's right. But he's only partly right about the rest. We spent hours searching through piles of records on the stalls at the flea markets every time we went down to London. They were apparently records that had come, mostly, from the PX stores on the

American Air force bases. In fact I got my first James Brown, Lonnie Mack, Major Lance and Joey Dee albums from market stalls.'

At the time when the Mersey scene began to flourish, the Cunard ships had long since been rerouted to Southampton. Cunard still had offices in Liverpool, but the days of liners coming to the port had ended more than a decade previously. Liverpool had been the centre of Atlantic trade and at one time was the main European port and second city of the Empire. Between 1900 and 1914 a tenth of the world's tonnage passed through Liverpool and the period of the great passenger liners was Liverpool's greatest era. But between 1920 and 1980 Liverpool's dockland steadily declined and, as ships got bigger, the docks became too small and the passenger liners no longer used the port.

The first major musical influence in Liverpool was a British artist, Lonnie Donegan, who sparked off the skiffle boom. When the boom began to wane, Liverpool groups turned to rock 'n' roll. Buddy Holly and the Crickets, Eddie Cochran, Elvis Presley, Chuck Berry, Little Richard, Ray Charles, the Everly Brothers, Gene Vincent, Carl Perkins, The Coasters, Arthur Alexander, Jerry Lee Lewis, The Olympics, Larry Williams, The Isley Brothers, Bobby Freeman, The Shirelles, Chan Romero, Lloyd Price, Bo Diddley, The Drifters and Fats Domino were their inspiration.

While rock 'n' roll bands were thriving in Liverpool, the music was encountering problems in America. Buddy Holly, the Big Bopper, and Ritchie Valens were killed in an air crash 'the day the music died'; Little Richard got religion; Eddie Cochran was to die in a car crash, while Carl Perkins' career suffered following his road accident; Chuck Berry was in jail; Elvis had joined the army; Jerry Lee Lewis was 'disgraced' for marrying an underage cousin. This was the opportunity media moguls had been waiting for – the chance to kill this devil's music! They titillated teenagers by saturating the airwaves with records by cleancut handsome white youngsters who sanitised the sound – Pat Boone, Bobby Rydell, Fabian, Ricky Nelson (although he turned out to be more influential than first thought), Dion, Tommy Roe, Tommy Sands, Frankie Avalon and Bobby Vinton.

Rock 'n' roll might have been safely caged in the States, but in

Liverpool bands began to adapt the music to their own style. What was also different about the Mersey groups was their age. They were actually teenagers, whereas the American rock 'n' roll giants were almost a decade older.

No one initially knew just how vast the music scene on Merseyside was until the publication of *Mersey Beat* in July 1961. Liverpool had been ignored by the media and, because of its position in the northwest, suffered from a degree of isolation. The two main Liverpool publications, the *Liverpool Echo* and the *Evening Express*, didn't cover the local music scene.

Historically, Liverpool had lost a great deal of power and prestige when the Manchester Ship Canal was built, allowing a lot of trade to bypass Liverpool and go straight to Manchester. Manchester became the capital of the north and was home to both Granada Television and the BBC studios, in addition to radio stations and the northern editions of the national newspapers. Most news on TV, radio and in the press had a Manchester bias. In comparison, Liverpool seemed to be almost a backwater. As a result, what was happening there developed without anyone realising it and without any outside interference.

This all changed with the appearance of *Mersey Beat*. The publication also had a bias – in favour of the Beatles. This is because its founder Bill Harry had been a close friend of John and Stuart at art college, which led to complaints from other groups who had dubbed it the *Mersey Beatle*.

Groups who had stayed in their own areas – Crosby, the Dingle, Wallasey, could now discover the promoters and venues in different parts of the city. Promoters began to be aware of just how big the scene was and promotion of venues increased and the local scene began to take on more of a profile.

What gave *Mersey Beat* the edge was 'the bulge', which Americans refer to as the 'baby boom', although it applied in a slightly different sense in Britain, which had been in the war a few years longer than America. The 'bulge' referred to the fact that there were more babies born in the few years towards the end of and immediately following World War Two than at any time in history, before or since. Those babies became teenagers in the 1950s.

In previous decades, there was no real awareness of 'teenagers' (a term that emerged in the 1950s). In Liverpool, for instance, youngsters were minireplicas of their parents. Fathers would look on with pleasure when their sons reached a certain age and started to accompany them to the local pub. Sons would also follow fathers into the business or union they belonged to, and youngsters would also dress exactly like their parents.

Suddenly, there was an awareness of being young, and young people wanted their own styles and their own music, just at the time they were beginning to earn money, which gave them spending power. *Mersey Beat* was their voice. It was a paper for them, crammed with photos and information about their own groups, which is why it also began to appeal to youngsters throughout Britain as its coverage extended to other areas.

The newspapers, television, theatres and radio were all run by people of a different generation who had no idea what youngsters wanted. For decades they had manipulated and controlled them (see the scene with George Harrison and Kenneth Haig in *A Hard Day's Night*); but now the youngsters wanted to create their own fashions.

This was Liverpool in 1961, the year in which the Beatles rose like cream to the top of the bottle and became a local phenomenon.

The Litherland Town Hall appearance began to make the Beatles hot. They'd arrived back in Liverpool broke and with hardly any work, apart from a single booking at the Grosvenor. Mona Best had stepped into the breach with Casbah appearances and Pete Best began to look after the bookings, which started to build up when Brian Kelly began to fill in their diary with dates at Litherland Town Hall, Lathom Hall and Aintree Institute.

Another turning point occurred on 21 February 1961, when they secured their first lunchtime session at the Cavern Club. Alan Sytner had sold the club to his former accountant Ray McFall in October 1959. McFall had continued the policy of presenting jazz, but it was becoming obvious that the audience for this type of music was waning. He decided to make a radical departure, cut down on the jazz and introduce the rock 'n' roll that was bringing in the kids to all the local 'jive hives'. He began giving groups such as the Swinging Blue Genes (later to become the Swinging Bluejeans) their own residency. By February 1961 he dispensed with modern jazz completely and decided to introduce lunchtime sessions.

The Beatles made their Cavern debut at the lunchtime session and the Cavern was to become part of musical history. One of the reasons why the Beatles were able to appear at lunchtime sessions was that they weren't working and were no longer students. Most other groups had their members at college, working as apprentices or employed in daytime jobs. Rory Storm, for example, couldn't get all his members to perform at lunchtime sessions at the nearby Iron Door Club, so he found other members for lunchtime gigs and called this band Rory Storm and the Wild Ones.

Although other promoters had pioneered the music on Merseyside, it was Ray McFall's vision with the Cavern, that makes him the most important Liverpool promoter of the Mersey Beat era.

Being in the city centre, the club was able to attract large crowds of working youngsters who were able to drop into the Cavern during their lunch hour. The atmosphere of the cellar club was also suited to the needs of the youngsters, who wanted their own clothes, fashions and music. Here was a place, with its arched brick walls and dark, damp atmosphere, that had the right ambience for the new teenage rock 'n' roll generation.

McFall was able to capitalise on the demand with not only his lunchtime and evening sessions, but all-night sessions, Saturday afternoon under-sixteens sessions and even promotions on the *Royal Iris*, the Mersey ferry.

The Beatles and other local rock groups initially appeared on bills with trad-jazz groups, but the jazz element then disappeared completely and Cavern bills became the major events on Merseyside.

The year was an important one. It was the year in which the group established themselves on their home territory; the year in which the Cavern became their home turf; the year in which the *Mersey Beat* paper was launched and built up their reputation; the year in which they found themselves a manager.

Mersey Beat made its debut on 5 July 1961 and featured the classic Beatles biography that its founder, Bill Harry, had commissioned John Lennon to write. The second issue, published on 21 July 1961, devoted the entire front cover to the group and succeeding issues were filled with Beatles material.

Brian Epstein, the manager of the Nems record store branch

in Whitechapel, saw the paper selling like the proverbial hot cakes in his store. With the second issue he ordered 144 copies. This was the issue in which the front page featured an Astrid Kirchherr photograph of the band and the story of their Polydor recording in Hamburg.

The story read,

Bert Kaempfert, who may be remembered for his golden record 'Wonderland By Night' which reached the top of the American hit parade, contracted the Beatles for Polydor, Germany's top recording company. Under the contract, they will make four records per year for the company.

At a recording session, the Beatles provided vocals and backing for three numbers for Tony Sheridan. Tony, a first-class songwriter, penned 'Why', a number familiar to readers through Gerry Marsden's excellent rendering. Apart from waxing 'Why', the Beatles recorded 'My Bonnie Lies Over the Ocean' opening in waltz-time, then breaking into a rock beat. Finally, the group provided good bass and drum backing to Sheridan for 'The Saints Go Marching In', a very popular number in Germany.

The Beatles recorded two further numbers for Kaempfert on their own. One side, an instrumental written by George Harrison, has not yet been named – probable titles include 'Cry For a Shadow' and 'Beatle Bop'. The other side, 'Ain't She Sweet', featured a vocal by John Lennon. The boys weren't quite satisfied with these two numbers, so they sold the rights to Polydor. Thus, in fact, under the contract, the Beatles still have four more records to make this year.

Bass guitarist Stuart Sutcliffe has remained in Hamburg and will shortly be marrying a German girl. At present he is studying at Hamburg Art College and has an English tutor. The group have no plans for taking on another guitarist, but have decided to remain a quartet.

Epstein began to ask Harry about the local rock 'n' roll scene and was particularly intrigued by the Beatles, who were featured so prominently. He began to write record reviews for the publication and then asked Harry if he could arrange for him to drop into the Cavern during a lunchtime session to see the Beatles. This occurred on Thursday 9 November 1961.

A few years later, Epstein recalled the event in a radio interview: 'It was pretty much an eye-opener, to go down into this darkened, dank, smoky cellar in the middle of the day, and to see crowds and crowds of kids watching these four young men on stage. They were rather scruffily dressed – in the nicest possible way or, I should say, in the most attractive way – black leather jackets and jeans, long hair of course. And they had a rather untidy stage presentation, not terribly aware, and not caring very much, what they looked like. I think they cared more even then for what they sounded like … I immediately liked what I heard. They were fresh and they were honest, and they had what I thought was a sort of presence and – this is a terribly vague term – star quality. Whatever that is, they had it, or I sensed that they had it.'

Further proof of Epstein's awareness of the Beatles can be found in the issue of *Mersey Beat* dated 31 August 1961 in a full-page feature on the Beatles, written by Bob Wooler. On the same page is an advertisement from Nems placed by Brian Epstein.

The article, entitled 'Well Now – Dig This', read,

Why do you think the Beatles are so popular? Many people many times have asked me this question since that fantastic night [Tuesday, 27 December 1960] at Litherland Town Hall, when the impact of the act was first felt on this side of the River. I consider myself privileged to have been associated with the launching of the group on that exciting occasion, and grateful for the opportunities of presenting them to fever-pitch audiences at practically all of the group's subsequent appearances prior to their last Hamburg trip.

Perhaps my close association with the group's activities, both earlier this year and since their recent re-appearance on the Merseyside scene, persuades people to think that I can produce a blueprint of the Beatles' Success Story. It figures, I suppose, and if, in attempting to explain the popularity of their act, the following analysis is at variance with other people's views, well that's just one of those things. The question is nevertheless thought-provoking.

Well, then how to answer it? First some obvious observations. The Beatles are the biggest thing to have hit the Liverpool rock 'n' roll set-up in years. They were, and still are, the hottest local property any Rock promoter is likely to encounter. To many of these gentlemen's ears, Beatle-brand noises are cacophonous on stage, but who can ignore the fact that the same sounds translate into the sweetest music this side of heaven at the box-office!

I think the Beatles are No. 1 because they resurrected original style rock 'n' roll music, the origins of which are to be found in American Negro singers. They hit the scene when it had been emasculated by figures like Cliff Richard and sounds like those electronic wonders, the Shadows and their many imitators. Gone was the drive that inflamed the emotions. This was studio set jungle music purveyed skilfully in a chartwise direction by arrangement with the A&R men.

The Beatles, therefore, exploded on a jaded scene. And to those people on the verge of quitting teendom – those who had experienced during their most impressionable years the impact of rhythm 'n' blues music (raw rock 'n' roll) – this was an experience, a process of regaining and reliving a style of sounds and associated feelings identifiable with their era.

Here again, in the Beatles, was the stuff that screams are made of. Here was the excitement – both physical and aural – that symbolised the rebellion of youth in the ennuied mid-1950s. This was the real thing. Here they were, first five and then four human dynamos generating a beat which was irresistible. Turning back the rock clock. Pounding out items from Chuck Berry, Little Richard, Carl Perkins, the Coasters and the other great etceteras of the era. Here they were, unmindful of uniformity of dress. Unkempt like long hair. Rugged yet romantic, appealing to both sexes. With calculated naiveté and an ingenious, throw-away approach to their music. Effecting indifference to audience response and yet always saying 'Thank you'. Reviving interest in, and commanding enthusiasm for numbers which descended the Charts way back.

Popularising (more than any other group) flip side items – example, 'Boys'. Compelling attention and influencing, wittingly or unwittingly, other groups in the style, choice and presentation of songs.

Essentially a vocal act, hardly ever instrumental (at least not in this country), here they were independently minded, playing what they liked for kicks, kudos and cash. Privileged in having gained prestige and experience from a residency at the Hamburg Top Ten Club during the autumn and winter of last year. Musically authoritative and physically magnetic, example the mean, moody magnificence of drummer Pete Best – a sort of teenage Jeff Chandler. A remarkable variety of talented voices which song-wise sound distinctive, but when speaking, possess the same naiveté of tone. Rhythmic revolutionaries. An act which from beginning to end is a succession of climaxes. A personality cult. Seemingly unambitious, yet fluctuating between the self-assured and the vulnerable. Truly a phenomenon – and also a predicament to promoters! Such are the fantastic Beatles. I don't think anything like them will happen again.

It's interesting to examine Brian Epstein's relationship to *Mersey Beat* at this stage because of an apocryphal story, which appeared in his autobiography, *A Cellarful of Noise*. He alleges that he had never heard of the Beatles until a youth called Raymond Jones came into his store at three o'clock on 18 October 1961 and asked for a copy of the record by the Beatles, the one mentioned in the 5 July issue of *Mersey Beat*. The only description of the youth was that he wore a black leather jacket. This tale forms the prologue of Epstein's book, ghost-written for him over a weekend by Derek Taylor.

The only significance this tale would have would be that Epstein had never heard of the Beatles before and this was the catalyst that sparked his interest.

However, he was already fully aware of their existence and actually making enquiries about them. The 5 July issue of *Mersey Beat*, with John Lennon's biography of the Beatles, sold out each time Epstein ordered copies of it. As we saw above, he specifically ordered 144 copies of issue No. 2, which contained the front cover story of the Beatles recording in Hamburg. If you consider it, for a small record store in the provinces to sell 144 copies of a single publication was unique. Average orders for the music publications he had from record companies were one dozen copies. He ordered 12 dozen copies because they were selling so well.

As we have seen, he wanted to review records for the paper. He wouldn't request to be reviewer, wouldn't pay for advertising space and wouldn't order so many copies if he never read the publication – and, reading it, he couldn't fail to notice all the major coverage of the Beatles, which had led to other groups, envious of such major publicity, nicknaming it the *Mersey Beatle*.

But even that is beside the point because he invited Harry up to his office on a regular basis to discuss the local music scene, which had begun to fascinate him.

He also asked about the Beatles, who, in addition to their regular coverage, were included in a personal poll of local groups by Bob Wooler, who placed them at No. 1. With Brian Epstein interested in the local scene and wanting to see what the groups were like, he obviously preferred to see the band lauded as No. 1 group in the pages of *Mersey Beat*.

George Harrison was to recall the visit Epstein made to the Cavern Club, arranged by Bill Harry: 'He started talking to us about the record that had created the demand. He came back several times and talked to us. We didn't know much about him but he seemed interested in us and also a little bit baffled.

'It seemed there was something he wanted to say, but he wouldn't come out with it. He just kind of watched us and studied what we were doing. One day he took us to the store and introduced us. We thought he looked rather red and embarrassed about it all.'

But let us return to the subject of the elusive Raymond Jones. In Paul McCartney's biography, *Many Years From Now*, he writes,

The story of how Brian Epstein visited the Cavern and was so entranced by the leather-clad boys cavorting on stage that he asked if he could manage them is well known. As Brian's autobiography *A Cellarful Of Noise* was ghosted for him by Derek Taylor at the height of Beatlemania and he hardly had time to read it, let alone correct any of the errors, it cannot be trusted on matters of detail. The account in the book about Brian being intrigued when three people in two days came into his record shop and asked for 'My Bonnie' by the Beatles, causing him to set out to find this elusive record by an unknown German group, is a good story – but it is not true.

Brian knew perfectly well who the Beatles were – they were on the front page of the second issue of *Mersey Beat*, the local music paper. Brian sold twelve dozen copies of this issue, so many that he invited the editor, Bill Harry, into his office for a drink to discuss why it was selling so well and to ask if he could write a record review column for it. He is unlikely to have missed the 'Beatles Sign Recording Contract' banner headline, reporting their session with Tony Sheridan for Bert Kaempfert, nor, with his penchant for rough boys, is it likely that he passed over the photograph of the leather-clad Beatles without giving them a second glance.

Not only had he been discussing them with Bill Harry and reading about them in *Mersey Beat*, the Beatles themselves were visiting his branch of Nems most lunchtimes in breaks from their Cavern sessions. Pete Best recalled, 'When we were at Nems we were very conscious of Brian, because whenever we went there there always used to be this guy who would flutter down the stairs, cast a furtive glance over to us, a look of disbelief – "Oh, it's them again." Then he'd disappear again up the stairs.'

In addition, Brian was selling tickets at Nems for a forthcoming Operation Big Beat promotion at the Tower Ballroom on 10 November, headlined by the Beatles. Nems displayed a large poster of the event and the Beatles' name was prominent. All this was before Raymond Jones allegedly turned up.

The point here is that it is irrelevant whether Raymond Jones existed or not. He had nothing to do with Epstein's discovering the Beatles because Brian already knew about them.

For many years people naturally assumed that such a person never existed because there seemed to be no evidence of him

apart from the mention in Epstein's book. Then Brian's assistant, Alistair Taylor, announced that Raymond Jones was a
myth. Taylor claimed that he had made Jones up in order to get
Brian to order the Beatles' record. Even this is irrelevant because
Taylor also knew them from *Mersey Beat*. In fact, he was the
one who took over Epstein's record review column in the publication.

During the 1990s Taylor even appeared at a Beatles event
advertising himself as Raymond Jones.

Even more bizarre is the fact that a Radio Merseyside disc
jockey, Spencer Leigh, said that he interviewed Jones in March
2000. If so, what credence is there to Taylor's story that he made
him up – and why pay such attention to a figure who had no real
relevance in the true story of the discovery of the Beatles?

If we take it that the most important elements in their career
to date was the relationship between John and Paul, which
resulted in their joint songwriting activities, and their trip to
Hamburg, which resulted in their act becoming more dynamic,
the next major step was having Brian Epstein as their manager.

There were no professional managers in Liverpool at the time.
The simple fact of having a telephone or transport would qualify
you to be the manager of a group, which merely meant hustling
the local promoter for gigs. Billy J Kramer's manager, Ted
Knibbs, for instance, was an old-age pensioner. Mona Best,
because her son Pete was in the group, was even promoting
extra dances in order to give the Beatles more work and was
writing to Granada Television requesting that they come and see
the group – she'd also contacted Ray McFall of the Cavern
asking for gigs on their behalf. Pete himself was arranging the
gigs, informing everyone of the dates, collecting the money and
handling most of the organisation.

Brian Epstein was a different kettle of fish. He had vision. He
had an intense belief in the group's talent and wasn't ashamed to
voice his conviction that they would become as big as Elvis
Presley. When he saw what was happening on the local scene
and realised the potential of the Beatles, he set out with a determination to make them into a major success. It's a pity that his
dream was tarnished by the Philip Norman allegation – in his
book *Shout!* – that he fell in love with John Lennon the minute
he saw him, with the implication that this is why he signed them

in the first place. This was a shoddy assertion, with no basis in fact, but one that many writers, using Norman's book as a guide, were to perpetuate.

There were many factors that stood in Epstein's favour. He was not only a record store manager, but a family member of wealthy store owners. He was well-to-do, professional, mature, had the backing of his family and was also able to contact record companies directly because of his position.

In other words, he wasn't a Mickey Mouse manager like many of the other managers of Liverpool groups. He was serious and dedicated.

It's true that he made many silly decisions during his years of management, which lost them money, and some of his deals defy explanation, yet in some ways he was a pioneer. He had no template on which to base his decisions. Sadly, it was dependency on drugs and gambling, specifically in the days when they finished touring, that made him surplus to their requirements and, when his contract was coming to an end, he was convinced that they would not be re-signing with him (he was correct in that assumption) and, without informing them, negotiated another contract with EMI that would have given him a percentage of their royalties for a dozen years after the expiry of his contract.

There were other things, too, that were in Epstein's favour. The time was right for such a home-grown talent to sweep Britain and he began to mould the group into one he considered would be acceptable to the media and the public. This meant smartening them up, jettisoning their black leather, fitting them out in mohair suits, teaching them to bow to audiences and generally taming what was a very exciting rock 'n' roll and R&B band. John Lennon never forgave him for that. He hated what the group became. From hours of playing on the stages of Hamburg and the cellars of Liverpool, they were reduced to twenty-minute spots with a small set repertoire on tours in which their music couldn't be heard anyway, which led John to say, 'Our best work was never recorded, you know. We were performing in Liverpool, Hamburg and around the dance halls, and what we generated was fantastic.'

The next important factor in their career was a series of incredibly fortunate pieces of good luck that came their way.

Epstein had been turned down by every major record company in Britain and was on the point of despair, with John, perhaps disdainful of Epstein's lack of success, commenting that he should try the Embassy label.

Decca Records had been interested enough in the group to send Mike Smith up to Liverpool to see them. Smith was impressed enough to book them for a recording audition at Decca's London studios. Brian Epstein decided on the numbers that they should play, which John disagreed with because he thought they should perform a typical Cavern set.

Decca turned them down, although the reason doesn't seem to have been because of their music. Smith was new to the A&R department of the company and he had auditioned another band, Brian Poole and the Tremeloes, that same day. As he was new, his boss Dick Rowe agreed to his taking on one new band. The decision to pick the Tremeloes seems to have been made simply on the fact that they were relatively local and could be in the studios within a short time, whereas the Beatles lived such a distance away – in a time before the motorways – that it took them several hours to travel to London.

This fairly rational decision led to Dick Rowe's being dubbed for the rest of his life 'the man who turned down the Beatles'. Not only was this untrue and unfair, but Brian Epstein in his biography quoted Rowe as saying, 'Groups with guitars are on the way out Mr Epstein – you really should stick to selling records in Liverpool.' Rowe denied saying that. It was a stigma that led even the Beatles to decry him with Paul saying, 'He must be kicking himself now' and John saying 'I hope he kicks himself to death.'

Decca had taken the trouble to send a man to Liverpool, to book the group into a recording studio – and finally also to hand over the tapes of their recording audition to them. This contrasted with EMI, Pye and the other companies who turned them down out of hand without even listening to them.

And now to the luck. It was Paul Murphy, a former member of Rory Storm and the Hurricanes, who met Brian in London and told him that no A&R man would listen to the Decca tapes, that he had to have acetates made. Murphy led him to the HMV shop in Oxford Street to have the acetates made. As a result Epstein was introduced to Syd Coleman of EMI's music arm,

Ardmore & Beechwood, who arranged for him to see George Martin, the only EMI A&R man who hadn't been approached regarding the group, mainly because his label didn't generally sign pop acts.

Purely by luck, Sid Bernstein, an agent in New York, was studying the British media at night school and came across the heavy coverage of the Beatles. He took the decision to book them for the Carnegie Hall in early 1964, despite the fact that they were unknown in America.

Coincidentally, the American talk-show host Ed Sullivan happened to be at London Airport when the Beatles were returning from Sweden. Impressed by the mobs of screaming teenagers, he booked them for his prestigious show early in 1964.

Purely by luck, a Washington disc jockey, Carroll James, obtained a copy of 'I Want To Hold Your Hand' from Britain and began playing it on his show. It proved such a success that it was picked up by other stations. As a result Capitol Records, who had finally decided to release a Beatles record, pushed up the release date, which resulted in the timing of its chart position at the right time early in 1964, when the other factors were coming together.

Purely by luck, America was seeking something to bring them out of their mourning for their recently assassinated President John F Kennedy.

All these factors came to a head in February 1964, when the Beatles made such an incredible impact in America. Also, owing to the fact that there were enough different Beatles singles available at that time to ensure for the group the unprecedented coup of the top five positions in the record charts in a single week.

By this time 'Beatlemania' was established in Britain and many other parts of the world. Shortly before they completed their first record, Pete Best was jettisoned and replaced by Ringo Starr. Pete improved tremendously as a musician in Hamburg, just as the other members did, and while there he developed what became known as 'the atom beat', a fierce drum sound that impressed the bands in Liverpool on the group's return. When they came to record at Abbey Road, it was usual for some A&R men to use session drummers. They felt that, while there was no problem with guitarists and singers, they needed a special drum sound in the studio and regularly booked session drummers including Clem Cattini and Alan White. Because Martin wanted a session drummer, the other members of the group were able to order Brian Epstein to sack Best. John admitted that they were cowards for not doing it themselves.

It's probable that he was sacked for reasons other than his drumming ability because Ron Richards, George Martin and Paul McCartney didn't like Ringo's drumming in the studio, either, and rebooked another session with Andy White.

Best was arguably the best-looking member of the group and he was certainly a favourite with fans, but it is likely that the reasons were that the others felt he was too taciturn and didn't have the same sense of humour or fit in as well as the drummer who replaced him.

Ringo was the drummer with Rory Storm and the Hurricanes, a group who were once bigger that the Beatles in Liverpool and who headlined above them in Hamburg. Oddly enough, some Beatles scribes think that the Beatles did not meet Ringo until Hamburg – yet he was well known to them in Liverpool prior to the Hamburg gig.

After Best was sacked and their EMI debut record 'Love Me Do' started to make inroads, they began touring on bills promoted by Arthur Howes. Rumours spread that Brian Epstein had bought 10,000 copies of 'Love Me Do' to help it into the charts and had them stashed away in a warehouse. Some Beatles books also treat this apocryphal story as a true one. For one thing, it would be totally useless to buy such a number of records for one shop, owing to the way that the charts were compiled in Britain at the time. Such a purchase by one person would not have an impact on the charts – and Epstein, being a record store manager, would be aware of this.

Tour followed tour and the Beatles made their final appearance at the Cavern on 3 August 1963. On 13 October they appeared on the biggest TV entertainment show in Britain, *Sunday Night at the London Palladium*, watched by 15 million viewers. Following their performance, the *Daily Mirror* headlined 'BEATLEMANIA!' – and the word was born. On 4 November they appeared on the Royal Variety Command Performance at the Prince of Wales Theatre, where John made his celebrated comment, 'On the next number I want you all to join in. Would those in the cheap seats clap their hands? The rest of you can rattle your jewellery.' They had now firmly established themselves, not only with the teenage population, but with the British public in general. They had, in a short time, become the biggest phenomenon in British entertainment history.

Bud Ornstein of United Artists, aware of the incredible record sales in Britain and Europe, saw that there would be a way for his company to acquire the Beatles on record – if they placed them in a cheap film, they would have a Beatles soundtrack. Yet, despite the extremely low budget, *A Hard Day's Night* became one of the classic musicals in cinema history, described by one critic as 'The *Citizen Kane* of Jukebox movies'. Signed to a three-picture deal, the group weren't too happy with *Help!* although it did have more innovations than they subsequently credited it with. Many other film offers came – *The Three Musketeers*, *A Talent For Loving*, *Shades of a Personality*, *Up Against It*, *Lord of the Rings* – although the Beatles as a group didn't really want to make any further movies.

It was only by chance that the animated *Yellow Submarine* was made and they initially weren't very interested in the project. However, the film that resulted will stand alongside *Fantasia* as one of the most acclaimed animated features ever made.

Their three-picture deal was completed by *Let It Be*, a venture that had originally begun as a TV documentary of the making of the *Get Back* album.

The group's first tour had been backing Johnny Gentle in 1960 in the latter part of May, followed by a brief tour of Scotland in January 1963 prior to their first major tour as part of the bill headlined by Helen Shapiro in February and March 1963. This was immediately followed, within a matter of days, by their inclusion on the bill of the Tommy Roe/Chris Montez tour, which continued throughout March, and they were then booked as co-headliners with Roy Orbison on a tour in May and June.

There was another mini-tour of Scotland in October and in the same month there was a short tour of Sweden, followed by their final tour of the year in November and December.

Their world tour took place in June 1964 covering Denmark, Hong Kong, Australia and New Zealand. August and

September saw them on their first American tour, followed by an autumn tour of Britain. They capped the year with a Christmas show at the Odeon, Hammersmith.

June and July 1965 saw them appearing on their European tour in France, Italy and Spain, followed by an American tour in August and a British tour in December. They toured Germany, Japan and the Philippines in June and July of 1966 and their final American tour – and the end of their touring days – came in August 1966.

From a musical perspective the Beatles never really enjoyed touring, because they just played by rote, mainly twenty-minute or half-hour spots, whatever sounds they created being swamped by screams from tens of thousands of throats. By 1966 touring had become a nightmare, which culminated in an unpleasant experience in Manila. They travelled to the Philippines, but hadn't been told that Imelda Marcos (wife of the President, Ferdinand Marcos) had invited them to the President's palace. When they didn't turn up, they were subjected to a campaign of hate and harassment with the television cameras showing the empty places at Malacanang Palace, where lots of children had been awaiting the Beatles' arrival.

Ringo commented, 'John and I were sharing a room, and the next morning we put the TV on and there was this horrific TV show of Madame Marcos screaming, "They've let me down!" and the camera tipped down on to these empty places and up on to these little kids' faces, all crying because the Beatles hadn't turned up.'

The Beatles and their entourage were literally forced to flee to the airport. George Harrison commented, 'There was about five real big funny-looking fellas with guns and all the rest of it. It was too obvious they'd arranged to give us the worst time possible.'

The Beatles' chauffeur Alf Bicknell was thrown down some stairs; Mal Evans was attacked by a group of thugs; the Beatles' gate money to their concerts was confiscated; their departure was delayed while a war of nerves was played out; and finally, when they were allowed to fly out, Brian Epstein, overcome by it all, became ill with the skin allergy hives and an ambulance was called to pick him up when the plane landed.

The Beatles really decided then that their touring days were over, although they had one more American tour to complete – and that also proved problematic. *Datebook* magazine printed excerpts from an interview John had given to Maureen Cleave of the *London Evening Standard* (see **Cleave, Maureen**), in which he compared the Beatles' popularity to that of Jesus Christ. This created a furore in the States, particularly in the Bible Belt regions. Beatle albums were consigned to bonfires, ministers threatened to excommunicate people who went to the Beatles' concerts. George was to say, 'The record burning was a real shock. I couldn't bear knowing I created another little piece of hate in the world. Especially with something as uncomplicated as people listening to records and enjoying what the Beatles are.'

John had to make a humiliating apology before a large press conference and their press officer Tony Barrow was to comment, 'It was the first time I had seen him really nervous at a press conference, probably because he didn't really know what to apologise for.'

In Memphis they were pelted with rotten fruit and there were reports of a bomb under the stage; at other concerts there were rumours of snipers.

Looking back at their touring years, George was to comment, 'It might have been fun for everybody else, but we never saw the Beatles. We're the only people who never got to see us.'

The next stage of their career was often referred to as 'the studio years'. This was the time when they spent more and more time in the studio and when George Martin became the most influential figure in their lives. By this time Brian Epstein had taken a back seat. With the group no longer touring and with them ensconced in the studio with Martin, he had very little to do.

The group began recording their masterpiece, the *Sergeant Pepper's Lonely Hearts Club Band* album; they adopted kaftans and hippie-style clothing, took LSD, began a course of Transcendental Meditation with the Maharishi Mahesh Yogi, and received the news of Brian Epstein's death by an accidental overdose.

It was Paul McCartney who seemed intent on making sure that the group didn't disintegrate and he came up with the idea of their filming *Magical Mystery Tour*. It was hammered by the critics following its screening on British television, which led to its cancellation by the US networks. It's hard to see why it received such a mauling: it is an interesting and charming, magical, zany, completely enjoyable film.

Had the critics not been so eager to castigate it, *Magical Mystery Tour* might have led to more intriguing rock music specials – at least it was completely different from the usual TV fare of just putting a stream of acts together with dancers in between.

Meanwhile, the long-time romance between Paul McCartney and Jane Asher ended; he fell in love with Linda Eastman and they got married. The marriage between Ringo and Maureen ended and he eventually married Barbara Bach. The marriage between George and Pattie ended and he eventually married Olivia Arias. And the marriage between John and Cynthia ended and he was eventually to marry Yoko Ono.

They had created a new company, Apple Corps, on the advice of Brian Epstein's brother Clive, who told them they had to offset their tax liabilities by launching a business venture. They began it on a high and then became despondent as it turned into a costly and unhappy venture.

Tensions within the group began and both Ringo and George walked out of recording sessions. The omnipresent Yoko Ono began attending all their recording sessions, much to the annoyance of Paul, George and Ringo. The members began to interest themselves in solo projects and John formed the Plastic Ono Band. John also said he would never work with the others again. And he said in an interview in *Rolling Stone* magazine that the Beatles were fed up with being sidemen for Paul.

The crunch came with the appearance of Allen Klein, who talked John, Ringo and George into appointing him their manager. Paul strongly opposed the appointment, but he was outvoted. Klein proved unable to gain control over Northern Songs or Nems Enterprises for them. When Klein called in Phil Spector to work on their *Let It Be* album and when Spector completely altered Paul's 'Long And Winding Road' without any consultation, Paul realised that the only way out for him would be the dissolution of the company.

Paul issued a writ in the Chancery Division of the High Court. David Hirst QC, acting for Paul, told the court of Allen Klein,

'He is a man of bad commercial reputation. Mr McCartney has never either accepted him as manager or trusted him. And on the evidence his attitude has been fully justified.'

On 13 March 1971 Mr Justice Stamp gave his ruling and, pending appeal, appointed James Douglas Spooner, a partner in a city firm of chartered accountants, as receiver and manager of the group's business interests, pending trial of the main action. In April John, George and Ringo abandoned their appeal and Spooner was immediately engaged as receiver.

The Beatles as a partnership had ceased to exist.

The members continued their individual pursuits over the years and in 1980 there was the tragic death of John. In the 1990s the three former members decided to get together again, along with Yoko Ono, executrix of John's estate, in producing their *Anthology* CDs, *Anthology* television series, *Anthology* home video set and two new Beatles singles, 'Free As a Bird' and 'Real Love', based on demo discs John had made.

In all the years that have passed, their appeal has not dimmed and at the end of the twentieth century the Beatles were dubbed 'the artists of the millennium' in a number of magazine and media polls.

Beatles, The (album)

The Beatles double album, often referred to as the 'white album' because of its white cover design. It was recorded between 30 May and 14 October 1968 and issued in the UK on 22 November 1968, where it topped the charts for nine weeks. It was issued in the US on 25 November 1968 and also topped the charts for nine weeks.

This album saw the beginning of a Beatles break-up. For one thing, despite the sheer volume of material, the songs were mainly compositions by either John or Paul, with each of them using the other members as backing musicians. In an interview, John was to observe, 'It's like if you took each track off it and made it all mine and all Paul's … [It] was just me and a backing group, Paul and a backing group, and I enjoyed it. We broke up then.'

Three of the numbers recorded for the album weren't actually used. They were John's 'What's the New Mary Jane?', Paul's 'Jubilee' and George's 'Not Guilty'.

During the sessions Ringo walked out, reputedly because Paul criticised his drumming. He returned after a short holiday. Further tension was created when John insisted Yoko be present at the sessions. The writer Ray Coleman observed, 'John broke a rigid, unwritten rule of the group: that their women would never be allowed in the studio. John perversely attended every session for the "White" album with Yoko at his side. His message, unspoken, was obvious to all: they were inseparable. She sat on the speakers, offering suggestions and, incredibly, criticism.'

A studio technician revealed that Yoko moved her bed into the studio and followed John everywhere, even into the toilet.

During the court case to dissolve the Beatles, John implied that the relationship between the members hadn't deteriorated during the making of the album. In his affidavit, he said, 'We were no more openly critical of each other's music in 1968, or later, than we had always been. I do not agree that after the touring ceased we began to drift apart socially and that the drift became more marked after Brian Epstein's death.' Yet this was quite different from the comments he made about the making of 'The White Album' in *Rolling Stone* magazine.

Most of the songs on the album had been written during the Beatles' stay in India at the Maharishi Mahesh Yogi's ashram. George Martin didn't like the idea of a double album and was later to comment, 'I tried to plead with them to be selective and make it a really good single album, but they wouldn't have it.'

John's compositions on the album were 'Dear Prudence', 'Glass Onion', 'The Continuing Story of Bungalow Bill', 'Happiness Is a Warm Gun', 'I'm So Tired', 'Julia', 'Yer Blues', 'Everybody's Got Something to Hide Except Me and My Monkey', 'Sexy Sadie', 'Revolution 1', 'Cry Baby Cry', 'Revolution 9', 'Good Night' and 'Don't Let Me Down'.

Beatles and Lennon: Marmalade and Dynamite

A fifty-page book in the Spanish language published by Nicolas Ediciones Casser S.I.

Beatles For Sale

The Beatles' third album, recorded at Abbey Road between 11 August and 26 October 1964 and released in the UK on 4 December 1964. In the US only eight songs from the British album were included, plus a track from the *A Hard Day's Night* album and both sides of a single to comprise *Beatles '65*, issued on 15 December 1964. John wrote 'No Reply, I'm a Loser', 'I Don't Want To Spoil the Party' and 'Yes It Is'. His collaborations with Paul were 'Baby's In Black', 'Eight Day's a Week', 'Every Little Thing', 'What You're Doing' and 'I'm Down'.

Beatty, Don

Beatty was responsible for first interesting John in Elvis Presley, an interest that steered his steps towards a life in music.

In 1965 both Don and John were in Form 4C of Quarry Bank Grammar School. Don was interested in records and showed John a copy of the *New Musical Express* and directed his attention to the chart position of 'Heartbreak Hotel'. John commented, 'Don said it was great, but I thought it sounded a bit phoney. We never listened to pop music in our house. Then one night I heard it on Radio Luxembourg. That was it. Nothing really affected me until Elvis.'

He was also to comment, 'It was Elvis who really got me interested in pop music and started me buying records. I thought that early stuff of his was great. The Bill Haley thing passed me by in a way.

'When his records came on the wireless my mother would start dancing around. She thought they were so good. I used to hear them, but they didn't do anything for me. It was Elvis who got me hooked on beat music. When I heard "Heartbreak Hotel" I thought, This is it, and I started to grow sideboards and all that gear.'

Beautiful Boy (Darling Boy)

Track from the *Double Fantasy* album. Written in 1979 as a lullaby to his second son, Sean.

John commented, 'I was with Sean in the kitchen with the bread. I kept thinking, Well, I ought to be inspired to write about Sean. I was going through a bit of that and when I finally gave up on thinking about writing a song about him, of course, the song came to me.'

A philosophical line, 'Life is what happens to you while you're busy making other plans', was said to have been suggested to him by the British astrologer Patric Walker, who died in 1998. Walker said he was having coffee one morning with john in New York and he told him that the essence of the line came from Sufism, an Islamic creed. John originally attempted to use the line in 'My Life', a song he wrote in 1979, but abandoned it.

Beautiful Boys

A track on the *Double Fantasy* album. The beautiful boys in question are John and Sean and this is Yoko's answer to John's 'Beautiful Boy' and in the song she addresses each of them in turn.

Be-Bop-A-Lula

A classic rock 'n' roll number from Gene Vincent. Vincent started writing the number while he was in hospital recovering from an accident, which had crushed his left leg. He was inspired by the comic strip *Little Lulu*. He recorded it in Nashville in 1955. The number reached No. 7 in the US charts. John Lennon first began singing the number on Saturday 6 July 1957, a historic date because it was the day John first met Paul McCartney. He was performing with his group the Quarry Men at the Walton Parish Church fête. Years later, John was to say, 'There's a picture on stage with the group before Paul had joined and I'm in a white jacket. That was the day, the first day I sang "Be-Bop-A-Lula" at a church fête with the Quarry Men. It was the day I met Paul and he was in the audience. A mutual friend had brought him.'

The group was performing it at Hamburg's Star Club when Adrian Barber began to record them. However, at the particular performance Barber recorded, it was Horst Fascher who took the stage to sing the number with the Beatles, a track that was to appear on the *Live At the Star Club, Hamburg* album.

John recorded the song as the first track on his *Rock 'n' Roll* album in October 1974 during his sessions with Phil Spector. When the album was first released in February 1974, 'Be-Bop-A-Lula' was the opening track. He recorded it again during his *Double Fantasy* sessions in September 1980.

Because

A song John wrote, which was the last one recorded for the *Abbey Road* album. It was cut on 1, 4 and 5 August 1969. The track featured three-part harmony from John, Paul and George and was based around a piano riff John said he'd found after Yoko had played Beethoven's piano sonata in C sharp minor, opus 27, number two, known as the 'Moonlight' sonata. After hearing her play it, he asked her to write out the chords backwards and then play it to him again in reverse.

He was later to say, 'This was a terrible arrangement. A bit like Beethoven's fifth [symphony] backwards.'

George Martin recorded the Bee Gees performing the number for the Robert Stigwood film *Sergeant Pepper's Lonely Hearts Club Band*.

John's handwritten lyrics to 'Because' were sold in auction at Sotheby's, New York on Saturday 10 June 1995 for $45,640.

Beef Jerky

A track from the *Walls and Bridges* album. John credited it to Booker Table and the Maître D's. It was one of the rare instrumental tracks John made and other musicians on the track include Jesse Ed Davis and the Little Big Horns featuring Bobby Keys.

B52s, The

An American group formed in 1976 comprising Cindy Wilson, guitar/vocals; Kate Pierson, organ/vocals; Ricky Wilson, guitar; Fred Schneider, keyboards/vocals; and Keith Strickland, drums. They were visually interesting as the stage act featured the girls wearing miniskirts, boots and outrageous bouffant hairstyles. They took their name from the hairstyles.

In 1978 they cut their first disc, 'Rock Lobster', for a private label. Island Records' boss Chris Blackwell heard the record and signed them up, and they hit the chart in America with a reissued version of 'Rock Lobster'.

John first heard the single when he went into the Forty Thieves disco in Hamilton, Bermuda, accompanied by Fred Seaman. He was so impressed with the number because it reminded him of Yoko's early style, particularly in the use of shrieks. John phoned her up the next day and played her the record as an example of how her early music was now being copied by new bands.

In interviews, John was to say that hearing the song inspired him to begin writing again after a writing block and that his phone call to Yoko also inspired her to begin writing new songs. However, it later became apparent that John had never ceased writing and made many home demo tapes during his 'house husband' period.

Ricky Wilson died of an AIDS-related disease in 1985. The B52s had a series of hits, which they recorded after Wilson's death. They included 'Give Me Back My Man', 'Future Generation', 'Rock Lobster/Planet Claire', 'Love Shack' and 'Candy'. Cindy Wilson left the group in 1990 and Julee Cruise replaced her. They also appeared in the movie *The Flintstones* in 1995.

Being For the Benefit of Mr Kite

On Tuesday 31 January 1967, while the Beatles were filming a promo for 'Strawberry Fields Forever' in Sevenoaks, Kent, John wandered into an antiques shop and was impressed with an old poster advertising a circus that took place on 14 February 1843. He bought it and the poster proved to be the inspiration for the song.

He said, 'Mr Kite was a straight lift. I had all the words staring me in the face one day when I was looking for a song. It was from this old poster I'd bought at an antique shop. We'd been down in Surrey or somewhere filming a piece. There was a break, I went into this shop and bought an old poster advertising a variety show, which starred Mr Kite. It said the Hendersons would also be there, late of Pablo Fanques Fair. There would be hoops and horses and someone going through a hogshead of real fire. Then there was Henry the Horse. The band would start at ten to six. All at Bishopsgate. Look, there's the bill, with Mr Kite topping it. I hardly made up a word, just connecting the lists together. Word for word, really.'

The track was recorded on 17 and 20 February and 28, 29 and 31 March 1961 and included on the *Sergeant Pepper* album.

It proved to be a complex recording. John told George Martin that he wanted to have the sound of an old-fashioned steam organ in the song. Unfortunately, one couldn't be found and Martin had to create a sound with a similar effect in the studio. Tapes of various old Victorian steam-organ noises were obtained; the tapes were then cut into pieces, thrown in the air and reassembled. It didn't work. The tapes were cut up once again and when the engineer, Geoff Emerick, stuck them back together, a desired effect was at last achieved.

George Martin was to say, 'John came to me with the request that the number had to have the smell of sawdust, just like in a real circus. He wondered how we could achieve that. He played the song for us on an acoustic guitar so that we could get an idea of it. We looked for a long time to get something new for the song. I knew that it had to be a strange kind of sound. That was clear to me. But not how. My first idea was to use the organ sound that you can also hear in the animated film *Snow White* but John thought that that sounded too tinny. It had to be the sound of a steam organ but there was not one to be found.

'Different organs were used for the recording and we also recorded the harmonica playing. With everything that we had, including a part of my organ playing that was recorded at a slower tempo to give an extra dimension to the sound, we had a pretty good working tape.'

When the album was released, some critics made out that there was a drug reference in the song. John commented, 'The story that Henry the Horse meant heroin was rubbish.'

Apart from the lead vocal, John played a Hammond organ to produce the main melody, Paul played lead and bass guitars, George Harrison, Ringo Starr, Mal Evans and Neil Aspinall all played harmonicas and George Martin played a Wurlitzer organ and piano.

The actual text of the original poster that John bought is as follows:

Pablo Fanque's Circus Royal, Town-Meadows, Rochdale. Grandest Night of the Season! And positively the LAST NIGHT BUT THREE! Being for the BENEFIT OF MR KITE (late of Wells's Circus)

And MR J HENDERSON, the celebrated Somerset thrower! Wire dancer, vaulter, rider, etc. On Tuesday Evening, February 14th, 1843. Messrs Kite & Henderson, in announcing the following Entertainment, assure the Public that this Night's Production will be one of the most Splendid ever produced in this Town, having been some days in preparation. Mr Kite will, for this Night only, introduce the celebrated HORSE, ZANTHUS! Well known to be one of the best Broke horses IN THE WORLD!!! Mr Henderson will undertake the arduous Task of THROWING TWENTY ONE SOMERSETS on the solid ground. Mr Kite will appear, for the first time this season, On the Tight rope, When Two Gentlemen amateurs of this town will perform for him. Mr Henderson will, for the first time in Rochdale, introduce his extraordinary TRAMPOLINE LEAPS and SOMERSETS! Over Men & Horses, through Hoops, over Garters, and lastly, through a hogshead of REAL FIRE! In this branch of the profession, Mr H. challenges THE WORLD!

The characters were brought to life in Robert Stigwood's 1974 film *Sergeant Pepper's Lonely Hearts Club Band*. The Bee Gees portrayed the Hendersons and George Burns played Mr Kite.

Bennett, Peter

An American promotions man (real name Peter Benedetto), who was an assistant to Allen Klein (of ABKCO). He had promoted artists such as Sam Cooke, the Rolling Stones, the Animals and Herman's Hermits. Bennett first began promoting Beatles records in the US in 1967 as an independent promotion man. When Klein took over the management of the Beatles, Bennett then worked for ABKCO and promoted their records in America. In the past he'd arranged for Bobby Vinton to sing at President Nixon's inaugural ball. When John and Yoko moved to New York, they became firm friends of Bennett and Bennett was to promote a number of John's records.

Bennett also promoted Apple Records in America, including the solo releases of artists such as James Taylor, Mary Hopkin and Billy Preston.

He worked hard on promoting all the discs, including ones he was unhappy about, such as John and Yoko's 'Woman is the Nigger of the World'. Bennett told John that he actually hated the record and wouldn't promote it, but John talked him into it. Despite his managing to get the record played, it went nowhere and John had to tell him, 'Pete, you were right.'

Bennett set up a television coup by arranging for John and Yoko to co-host *The Mike Douglas Show* on TV for a week and he also took George Harrison backstage at Madison Square Garden to meet Elvis Presley. Later, Bennett became executive producer of *The King of Rock 'n' Roll*, a film about Elvis.

In 1972, *Billboard* named Bennett as Best National Promotion Man.

Bennett was with John during his 'lost weekend' in Los Angeles, following the break-up with Yoko, and was present at the Troubadour club when the Smothers Brothers were appearing. Bennett later became a government witness in the trial against Allen Klein for tax evasion in both 1977 and 1978. He was also fined $2,200 and placed on a year's probation on a similar charge.

While appearing at Beatles conventions in the US in 1997, Bennett said he was writing a book about his Apple/ABKCO days.

Benny and the Jets

The title of a John Lennon collage from 1974 in which he superimposed Andy Warhol's head on a magazine cutting of three topless girls. It sold for $42,000 at an auction at Sotheby's, London, on Tuesday 21 August 1990.

Bentham, Ron

A former pupil of Quarry Bank School. Slightly older than John, Bentham formed the Quarry Bank Jazz Combo in 1956. John auditioned for the band, but was rejected.

In 1998, Bentham, a retired schoolteacher, remembered the time, commenting, 'He simply wasn't good enough to play with us. It was a joint decision, very democratic, because there were four or five of us involved in the band. A lot of people think it's pretty funny that we turned him down, and I guess it is, but we are talking about a pre-rock-'n'-roll era. We were playing a completely different style of music than he went on to play.'

Bermuda

British Caribbean island colony to which John took his four-year-old son Sean on holiday in June 1980 during his term as a househusband while Yoko remained in New York attending to business matters. During this holiday, while visiting the Botanical Gardens, he saw the Double Fantasy orchid and gained the inspiration to return to his career in music. The Agriculture Ministry explained that Double Fantasy was actually a hybrid of the freesia flower with a double bloom.

In September 1982 Yoko sent Sean on a fortnight's holiday to Bermuda accompanied by three bodyguards, but she herself remained in New York, once again to attend to business matters.

Bernstein, Sid

At the age of 38, Bernstein was an agent for GAC, who handled acts such as Dion, Fats Domino and Brenda Lee. He decided to enrol for evening courses in Max Lerner's political science class at New York's New School For Social Research. Whilst there he began to read British newspapers and noted the rise of Beatlemania. He decided he would try to independently gamble that they would be a success in America, found Brian Epstein's phone number and contacted Liverpool. Queenie Epstein answered the phone and passed it on to Brian, who listened to Bernstein's offers with interest.

This initiative was to result in the Beatles' appearances first at Carnegie Hall and then at two Shea Stadium concerts.

After the Beatles break-up Sid made several offers for the members to team-up again for special concerts, but he received no response.

Once John moved to New York, from February 1971 he began to bump into Bernstein regularly on the New York streets. Each time John met him he would introduce him to Yoko. She finally told him, 'John, I've met Sid a number of times. How often are you going to introduce me?'

When Bernstein presented Jimmy Cliff at Carnegie Hall for the first time, he intended to attend with his wife and three children, Then he got a call from John asking if he could have three tickets, to take May Pang and a friend. Sid asked his kids if they'd give up their seats for John, which they did.

John also rang him when he was with Harry Nilsson, asking for the name of a good Italian restaurant. Sid recommended Paolucci's on Mulberry Street. John took a party of twelve, who included Yoko, Alice Cooper, Nilsson and several others.

May Pang was actually Sid's babysitter, and used to babysit for his kids when she was a teenager.

Bernstein was asked to speak at the Central Park memorial service for John on December 14 1980. Two hundred thousand people were there. When ABC interviewed him for their *Eyewitness News,* he said, 'We are resting here where his ashes are resting and enrich this earth to pay tribute to a man who gave us so much.'

At one point Sid planned to organise a memorial concert for John with the aid of Cynthia Lennon, but this was upstaged by a huge venture organised by Yoko.

Berry, Chuck

A legendary American rock 'n' roll star, born in St Louis, Missouri, in 1931, who was one of the Beatles' seminal influences. They were impressed by the vitality of the songs he wrote, and recorded his 'Rock & Roll Music' for their *Beatles For Sale* album and 'Roll Over Beethoven' for their *With the Beatles* LP. His 'I'm Talkin' About You' and 'Little Queenie' are to be found on their Star Club performances in 1962, recorded by Adrian Barber and featured on several packages of a Star Club album.

John paid tribute to Berry when he composed 'Come Together', with a brief musical reference to Berry's 'You Can't Catch Me'. As a result he was sued by the publisher Morris Levy and as a measure of compensation agreed to perform some Berry numbers on his *Rock 'n' Roll* album, on which he played 'You Can't Catch Me' and 'Sweet Little Sixteen'.

In 1972 John achieved an ambition and actually performed with Chuck Berry. This occurred when John and Yoko were given a week's residency as hosts on the American TV programme *The Mike Douglas Show* with the option of selecting their own guests. John had Chuck Berry join him for the show on 16 February 1972 and the two jammed on 'Johnny B Goode' and 'Memphis, Tennessee', although Berry seemed quite distracted by Yoko screeching in the background.

Commenting on Berry, John was to say, 'When I hear good rock, the calibre of Chuck Berry, I just fall apart. I have no other interest in life. The world could be ending and I wouldn't care.'

On John's death, Berry stated, 'I feel as if I lost a little part of myself when John died.'

Berry, Mike

British singer, born in Hackney, east London, in 1943. At the time of his hit 'Tribute To Buddy Holly', Berry appeared on a bill with the Beatles at the Cavern. He was then booked to appear with them on their short tour of Scotland in October 1963, followed by their five-date mini-tour of Sweden. During the tour John offered to write a song for Berry, but he turned down the offer – and has regretted it ever since.

Best, Pete

Born in Madras, India, on 24 November 1941, Pete was to become the Beatles' drummer from August 1960 until August 1962.

His sacking from the band on the eve of their success caused great controversy. The fact that the Beatles got Brian Epstein to dismiss him, as they didn't have the nerve to do it themselves, led John to regret the way it was done and to say they were cowards when they did it.

During their time together, Pete shared better relations with John than he did with Paul and George and they often drank together and became quite friendly towards each other.

It was in the cellars of Pete's house in Hayman's Green, Liverpool – which had been converted into the Casbah club – that the Quarry Men re-formed and had their very first residency.

When they had the opportunity to go to Germany, they'd lost their drummer Tommy Moore and asked Pete to join them.

Following the group's return from their first trip to Hamburg, as they had no manager and had dispensed with Allan Williams's services as a part-time agent, Pete and his mother Mona Best were the ones getting bookings for the group, with Pete keeping the diary and organising transport to the gigs, eventually getting his close friend Neil Aspinall to become their road manager.

During their second trip to Hamburg, Pete and John tried to mug a sailor. The man had watched them on stage, loved the band and sent them over lots of beers. He then came over to them and invited them out to dinner. John, Pete, Paul and George joined him. After dinner, when he went to pay the bill the Beatles, who were inebriated by this time, noticed the wad of money he had and began to discuss the idea of mugging him. George and Paul would have none of it and left. John and Pete followed the man on his way to the station and then attacked him, but he pulled out a gas gun and they fled.

Pete and John were generally the tough characters of the Beatles and Pete could handle himself well in a fight. At one time, when Tony Sheridan seemed to resent the Beatles, he and Pete slugged it out between them, and then became friends. When Stuart Sutcliffe was attacked at Lathom Hall, it was Pete and John who went to his rescue.

Commenting on the rumours that John had copied Tony Sheridan, Pete was to say, 'People are wrong if they say that John copied his stance on stage from Sheridan. John had that stance before, even from the early days when I remember him. He always tended to have that little crouch. Sheridan always held his guitar quite high, but he wasn't as bent over as John.'

When they signed with Brian Epstein, they were aware that he was gay and Pete was to say, 'John was quite laid back about it, actually. At that stage, with typical Liverpool bravado, he said, "If he lays a finger on me I'll punch his lights out." '

Epstein wanted to smarten up the Beatles' image and make them more acceptable to a wider audience. He took them to see the Shadows at the Empire Theatre, Liverpool, and pointed out to them how the Shadows bowed to their audience at the end of their act. He had the group fitted out with mohair suits. Paul McCartney in particular was keen on the changes, but Pete and John hated the new image. Pete was to say, 'John and I hated going into suits. It was, I suppose, because we loved our leathers. We ate, slept, drank in them; that's what they were there for. We loved the image we had, the pseudo-macho thing. We didn't go round proclaiming, "This is the Beatles, this is the way we dress, these are the leather jackets, these are our Cuban heeled boots." But the outfits were readily identifiable. And we felt that the image was working: no one had said, "My God, these guys would look far better in suits." '

The aspersion was made that the Beatles got rid of Pete because he wasn't a good enough drummer. George Martin said at the time that he was surprised that they sacked him because he felt he was one of the group's main assets. At the time Martin preferred to use session drummers at recordings. He said that, while the instruments of the other members didn't worry him, he aimed for a particular drum sound in the studio. This was backed up by the fact that it was common practice for not only Martin but other A&R men, too, to use session drummers in their recordings.

Pete had actually gained a reputation in Liverpool for his drum style, which had been given the tag 'the atom beat'. When Ringo went to his first EMI recording session, George Martin, Ron Richards and even Paul McCartney weren't happy with his drum sound and the session had to be rebooked with a session drummer, Andy White.

Pete actually recorded with the Beatles in Germany with Bert Kaempfert as A&R man and in London at Decca's studios with Mike Smith recording, yet there were no complaints about his drumming on these occasions. They were to prove fortunate recordings for Pete owing to the fact that over thirty years after he recorded the tracks they were included on the Beatles' *Anthology* CDs and provided him with financial security for the rest of his life.

Bhaktivedanta, Swami AC (a.k.a. Srila Prabhupada)

The founder of the Hare Krishna movement. Together with a group of his followers, he recorded an album, *Krishna Consciousness*, in New York in December 1966. The Beatles ordered one hundred copies of the album, which contained the Hare Krishna mantra.

George Harrison was later to comment, 'I remember singing it. Just for days, John and I, with ukulele banjos, sailing through the Greek islands – Hare Krishna. Like, six hours we sang, because you couldn't stop once you got going.'

The swami had become more popularly known as Srila Prabhupada and during the antiwar riots in America in 1966 he wrote *The Peace Formula*, a tract advocating world peace. When John and Yoko were recording 'Give Peace A Chance' at the Queen Elizabeth Hotel, Montreal, members of the Hare Krishna movement participated. They had been in discussions with John for several days and John had told them, 'We want Krishna consciousness. We want peace, the same formula your spiritual master tells about.' He was referring to *The Peace Formula*, which possibly inspired his *Give Peace A Chance* campaign.

In September 1969 the swami was invited as a house guest to Tittenhurst Park. He gave public lectures three or four times a week in a tall building at the northern end of the property, a hundred yards from the main house, which accommodated John and Yoko.

The building where he gave the lectures had formerly been used as a hall for chamber-music recitals. Several of the swami's disciples, who resided with him in a block of guest houses on the property, installed a small deity altar and a podium for the swami. Although the building had never had a name before, it now became known as 'the temple'.

On Sunday 14 September, John, Yoko and George Harrison enjoyed an Indian vegetarian meal cooked by the disciples, then the three walked over to the swami's quarters for their first meeting. They then became involved in a long discussion with the swami, which became the basis for his book *Search for Liberation*, published in 1981.

Among the topics John and the swami discussed were Krishna, the Bhagavadgita (Sanskrit, meaning 'Song of the Lord'), reincarnation and mantras.

In April 1970 one of his disciples had written to him enquiring about a dream the swami had regarding John.

He replied, 'I dreamt that John was showing me a house in Calcutta, a big palatial building, which formerly belonged to a very rich man, who was also a famous musician. The fact is that John Lennon was previously that wealthy Indian musician and now he has taken birth in England.

'He has inherited his past musical talent, and because in his previous life he was very liberal and charitable he has now become very wealthy. Now in this life, if he utilises his talents for giving the world Krishna Consciousness, he will achieve the highest perfection of life.'

The Swami died on Thursday 17 November 1977, aged 81.

Bibliography
In His Own Write, John Lennon, Jonathan Cape, 1964.
A Spaniard in the Works, John Lennon, Jonathan Cape, 1965.
The Penguin John Lennon, 1966.

John Lennon: In His Own Write and *A Spaniard in the Works*, Signet, 1967.

In His Own Write: the Lennon Play, Adrienne Kennedy, Victor Spinetti, John Lennon, Jonathan Cape, 1968.

Lennon Remembers, Jann Wenner, Straight Arrow, 1971.

The Lennon Factor, Paul Young, Stein & Day.

The John Lennon Story, George Tremlett, Futura, 1975.

John Lennon: One Day at a Time, Anthony Fawcett, Grove Press, 1977.

A Twist Of Lennon, Cynthia Lennon, Star Books, 1978.

Strawberry Fields Forever: John Lennon Remembered, Vic Garbarini, Brian Cullman, Barbara Graustark, Delilah/Bantam, 1980.

John Lennon 1940–80: One Day at a Time, Anthony Fawcett, New English Library, 1980.

John Lennon: Death Of A Dream, George Carpozi Jr, Manor Books, 1980.

In His Own Write/A Spaniard in the Works, New American Library, 1980.

The Writings of John Lennon, Simon & Schuster, 1980.

Lennon: What Happened!, Timothy Green Buckley (ed.), Sunshine Publishing, 1980.

Lennon: Up Close and Personal, Timothy Green Buckley (ed.), Sunshine Publishing, 1980.

John Lennon In his Own Words, Miles (ed.), Omnibus Press, 1981.

John Lennon and the Beatles Forever, Ed Naha, Tower Books, 1981.

John Lennon 4Ever, Conrad Snell Crown Summit Books, 1981.

The John Lennon Story, John Swenson, Leisure Books, 1981.

Lennon '69: Search For Liberation, Jeff Long (ed.), the Bhaktivedanta Book Trust, 1981.

A Tribute To John Lennon 1940–1980, Lyn Lelanger, Michael Breder, Jo Kearns, Nicolas Locke and Mike Shatzhin (eds.), Proteus, 1981.

The Lennon Tapes, Andy Peebles, BBC Publications, 1981

John Lennon 1940–1980, compiled by Ernest E Schworck, ESE, 1981.

John Lennon: A Personal Pictorial Diary, Sportomatic Ltd, 1981.

John Lennon 1940–1980, Ray Connolly, Fontana, 1981

Pour John Lennon, Maurice Archard, Alain Moreau, 1981.

John Lennon's Secret, David Stuart Ryan, Kosmic Press, 1982.

The Legacy Of John Lennon: Charming Or Harming A Generation, Reverend David A Noebel, Thomas Nelson Publishing, 1982.

The 1972 John Lennon Interview, Lavinia Van Driver, privately printed, 1982.

Peace At Last: The After Death Experiences Of John Lennon, Jason Leen, Illumination Arts, 1982.

The Playboy Interview with John Lennon and Yoko Ono, David Sheff, Playboy Press, 1982.

The Ballad of John and Yoko, the Editors of *Rolling Stone*, Rolling Stone Press, 1982.

Loving John, May Pang and Henry Edwards, Warner Books, 1983.

Dakota Days, John Green, St Martin's Press, 1983.

John Lennon: Summer of 1980, Perigee Books, 1983.

John Lennon: A Family Album, Nishi F, Saimaru, 1983.

The Literary Lennon, James Sauceda, Pierian Press, 1983.

John Lennon: In My Life, Pete Shotton and Nicholas Schaftner, Stein & Day, 1983.

Give Peace a Chance: Music and the Struggle for Peace, Marianne Philbin, Chicago Review Press, 1983.

The Book of Lennon, Bill Harry, Aurum Press, 1984.

John Lennon: For the Record, Peter McCabe and Robert D Schonfeld, Bantam Books, 1984.

Come Together: John Lennon In His Time, Jon Wiener, Randon House, 1984.

Lennon: A Liverpool Echo Tribute, The Liverpool Echo, 1984.

John Winston Lennon 1940–1966, Ray Coleman, Sidgwick & Jackson, 1984.

John Ono Lennon 1967–1980, Ray Coleman, Sidgwick & Jackson, 1984.

John Lennon: An Illustrated Biography, Richard Wooton, Hodder & Stoughton, 1984.

Julian Lennon, Yolande Flesch, Running Press, 1985.

Listen To These Pictures: Photographs of John Lennon, Bob Gruen, William Morrow, 1985.

John Lennon Conversations, Linda Deer Domnitz, Coleman Publishing, 1985.

John Lennon, Dezo Hoffman, Columbus Press, 1985.

Lennon, Ray Coleman, McGraw-Hill, 1985.

The Faces of John Lennon, Dezo Hoffman, McGraw-Hill, 1986.

Julian Lennon, Kalia Lulow, Ballantine, 1986.

John Lennon/Julian Lennon, Nancie S, Martin, Avon Superstars, 1986.

Skywriting By Word of Mouth, John Lennon, Pan Books (UK), Harper & Row (USA).

In His Own Youth, In My Own Words, Julia Baird, River women Press, 1986.

Come Together: John Lennon In His Time, Jon Wiener, Faber, 1987.

The Lennon Companion, Elizabeth Thomson and David Gutman (eds.), Macmillan (UK), Schirmer Books (US), 1987.

Lennon, Carole Lynn Corbin, Franklin Watts Ltd, 1987.

John Lennon, Alan Posener, Rowohlt Taschenbuch Verlag, 1987.

The Lives of John Lennon, Albert Goldman, William Morris, 1988.

Imagine: John Lennon, Andrew Solt and Asam Egan, Macmillan, 1988.

Who Killed John Lennon? Fenton Bresler, St Martin's Press, 1989.

John Lennon: Vicendo Cantando, Racconti Arcana Editrice SRL, 1990.

John Lennon: Lennon Sense, Arcana Editrice SRL, 1990.

The Last Days Of John Lennon, Fred Seaman, Citadel Press, 1990.

John Lennon, Young Rock Star, Laurence Santrey, Troll Associates, 1990.

Ai: Japan Through John Lennon's Eyes, a Personal Sketchbook, Yoko Ono, Cadence Books, 1992.

The Immortal John Lennon, Michael Heatley, Octopus International, 1992.

Beatles and Lennon: Marmalade and Dynamite, Nicolas, Ediciones Casser SL.

John Lennon: Myths And Reality, VV Bokaryov, Klyton, Moscow, 1993.

The Anthology of Rock Music: John Lennon, Nikolay Endyanof, Klyton, 1993.

Let Me Take You Down: Inside the Mind of MDS, The Man Who Shot John Lennon, Jack Jones, Villard, 1993.

Candles for John Lennon: Philosophical Reflections on the Vision of a Pop Icon, Ralph Synning, Aardvark Books, 1993.

John Lennon In Heaven: Crossing the Borderlines of Being, Linda Keen, Pan, 1993.

The Illustrated John Lennon, Geoffrey Giuliano, Sunburst Books, 1994.

John Lennon, Miguel Martinez and Vicente Escudero, Jucar, Spain, November 1994.

John Lennon: Lennonsense, Arcana Editrice JRC, Milan, 1994.

Pop Culture Legends: John Lennon, Bruce W Conord, Chelsea House Publishers, 1994.

John Lennon, Miguel Martinez and Vicente, Luca Editorial SA, 1995.

John Lennon: Young Rock Star, Laurence Santrey, Troll Associates, 1995.

El Jouen Lennon, Jordi Sierra I Fabra, Ediciuones SM, 1995.

John Lennon, Zxeichnungen, Performance, Film, Wulf Herzogen Rath and Dorothea Hansen, Cantz Verlag, 1995.

They Died Too Young: John Lennon, Tom Stockdale, Paragon, 1995.

Imagine: A Celebration of John Lennon, Penguin, 1996.

John Lennon In Heaven: Crossing the Borderlines of Being, Linda Keen, Pan Publishing. 1996.

John Lennon – Lonely Heart, Satokuni Ishigamore, Shinpusha, 1996,

We All Shine On, Paul duNoyer, Carlton Books, 1997.

The Complete Guide to the Music of John Lennon, Johnny Rogan, Omnibus Press, 1997.

John, Paul and Me: Before the Beatles, Len Garry, CG Publishing, 1997.

Epic Moments and Secrets: John Lennon and the Beatles, At the Mirror of Man's Destiny, The Beatles Trilogy Part One, The Last Concerts, Richard Warren Lipack, Barrister Publishing, 1997.

The Lost Lennon Interviews, Geoffrey and Brenda Gouliano, Adams Media Corporation, 1997.

Birch, Harriet

The youngest of the five daughters of George and Annie Stanley, born in 1916. She was a student at Liverpool University and then met and married an Egyptian, Aki Hafez, and went to live in Cairo. Sadly, Ali died following a tooth extraction and Harrie, as she was known, returned to England with their daughter Leila. There were problems because Ali's parents followed her to Liverpool, seeking custody of Leila for themselves. As it was wartime, Harrie was suddenly declared an alien – owing to the fact that she had married an Egyptian. As a result she had to report to a local police station every day during the war.

Harrie's second marriage was to Norman Birch, and the couple had a son, David. When her sister Julia (John's mother) was killed in a road accident, her daughters Julia and Jacqui were sent to their Aunt Elizabeth's home in Scotland for six weeks. On their return they went to live with Harrie, because their father, John Dykins, was too distressed with the death of his wife and didn't think he could cope with bringing up two daughters. They initially lived in the Cottage, which was attached to the dairy farm that had been previously owned by George Smith, Mimi's husband (*see* **Smith, Mary Elizabeth**).

When John visited his aunt Harriet in March 1964 she revealed to him that he had another half-sister, Elizabeth. He hadn't been aware of it before and spent many years trying to trace her, without success.

In 1968, John, aware how cramped the Cottage was for five people, told his Aunt Harrie to go out and buy a new house and he would pay for it. She found a new place for the family in Woolton and John asked her to furnish and decorate it and send all the bills to him.

In 1970 when John and Yoko visited Liverpool, they visited Harrie and her family at their home.

She died in 1972.

Birch, Norman James

The second husband of Harriet 'Harrie' Stanley. He worked as a garage manager.

When Julia Lennon died in a car accident, her two daughters went to live in the Cottage, along with the Birch family. They still hadn't been told of their mother's death and it was Norman who eventually explained to them what had happened.

John told them that the Cottage was too small for the family and insisted that they find a larger house, which he would buy for them. As they understand it, he was buying it to assure them of their security, particularly his two half-sisters, Julia and Jacqui. Over the years, John was to confirm this on a number of occasions.

In 1969 when John and Yoko were taking Julian and Kyoko (Yoko's daughter by Anthony Cox) up to Scotland, they stopped at Norman and Harriet's house.

When the girls grew up and left the house, Harriet and Norman continued to live there as John had assured them it was their home. Harriet was later to die.

Norman became extremely concerned in 1991 when he received a letter from Yoko's New York attorney David WarmFlash, saying that Yoko was selling the house. He was given the opportunity of paying £120,000 for it or being evicted. Of course, he didn't have that sort of money and at his age could never raise a mortgage.

He was to tell the writer Geoffrey Giuliano, 'I read that Yoko was left with several hundred million dollars. What could possibly be her motivation for needing the few thousand pounds this place would buy?'

Norman sent several letters to Yoko, but all were returned unopened. He couldn't understand why she would want to evict one of John's relatives, who had lived in the house for so many years, when the price of her house wouldn't even pay for one of her fur coats. Reading that John had sometimes spent £500 a week on Polaroid film, that Sean had his own private plane, it seemed incredible that Yoko would take the time and trouble to evict an old man from his home.

Two days after the news that Yoko had been trying to evict him began to appear in the media, Yoko back-pedalled on her eviction plans. A spokesman then said, 'It is her wish that he remain there as long as he lives.'

However, soon after, Norman was killed in a hit-and-run car accident outside his home in Liverpool on Wednesday 30 October 1991. He was 77.

It appeared that neither of the two homes John had bought for his relatives – the Woolton home for his aunt, uncle, cousin and two half-sisters, and the one in Poole for his Aunt Mimi – was bought in their names. Perhaps for tax reasons, John's company had bought them.

Birthday

A collaborative effort between John and Paul. John said, ' "Birthday" was written in the studio. Just made up on the spot. I think Paul wanted to write a song like "Happy Birthday, Baby", the old fifties hit.' John was later to refer to the number as 'a piece of garbage'. The group took a break in the recording to rush to Paul's house in nearby Cavendish Avenue to watch the film *The Girl Can't Help It*. The song was included on the Beatles' 'White Album'.

Black Dwarf

A Marxist newspaper published in London during the 60s.

The publication began a series of attacks on the Beatles in its October 1968 issue. The publication was basically pro the Rolling Stones and anti the Beatles. Their attacks on the Beatles that issue included an item by one of their journalists in which he wrote, 'Although I've liked the Beatles in the past I hope that they get so fucked up with their money-making that they become as obscure as Cliff Richard.' More articles praising the Rolling Stones were featured in the following issue, which also included 'An Open Letter To John Lennon', written by John Hoyland who, in common with left-wingers in both Britain and America, considered *Revolution* to be an anti-left song. Hoyland ended his letter to John with the appeal, 'Come and join us.'

At the time the editor of the underground paper was Tariq Ali, who, following the publication of Hoyland's letter, said he received a phone call from the Beatle: 'It's John Lennon here. You've published these attacks on me.' Ali told him, 'They're not attacks. They're just friendly criticism, John, and you're very welcome to reply.'

'Oh, well, I will,' said John.

The next issue, dated January 1969, contained John's reply, in which he rebutted the accusations about Apple in the previous issue: 'We set up Apple with the money we as workers earned, so that we could control what we did productionwise.'

His general open letter attacked the *Black Dwarf* critics who had been attacking him: 'I don't worry about what you, the left, the middle, the right or any fucking boys club think. I'm not that bourgeois. I'm not only up against the establishment but you too.' He added, 'I'll tell you what's wrong with the world: people – so do you want to destroy them? Until you/we change our heads – there's no chance. Tell me of one successful revolution. Who fucked up Communism, Christianity, Capitalism, Buddhism, etc.? Sick heads, and nothing else.'

He ended his letter: 'You smash it – I'll build around it.'

Although the answer to John's letter printed in the same issue was credited to John Hoyland, an editorial committee wrote it. They analysed the letter in detail and then asked John to join the Left: 'The feeling I've got from songs like *A Day In The Life* is part of what has made me into the kind of socialist I am. But you suddenly went and kicked all that in the face with *Revolution*. That was why I wrote to you – to answer an attack you made on us, knowing that what you said would be listened to and respected by millions, whereas whatever reply we make here is read by only a few thousand.'

Black House, The

The name given to the premises at 95–99 Holloway Road, London N7, during the 1970s, when the building was used as the headquarters of black activist movements, led by Michael X.

Michael X, a.k.a. Michael Abdul Malik, received the patronage of John and Yoko. On 4 February 1970 they arrived at the Black House in order to generate some publicity for Malik's causes and their own peace campaign. The occasion was to spotlight the presentation of a bag containing John and Yoko's hair, recently cut short, which Malik could auction. In turn, Malik presented the couple with a pair of Muhammad Ali's boxing shorts, still stained with blood.

The swap took place on the roof of the building, although it didn't receive the anticipated publicity as the British media were beginning to tire of the series of stunts organised by the pair. Not one photograph of the presentation appeared in the press.

In 1989 the premises was converted into a public house.

Black Jacks, The

The name a sixteen-year-old John Lennon allegedly gave to the first skiffle group he formed in March 1957 shortly after his Aunt Mimi had bought him a guitar. The first member John enrolled was Pete Shotton on washboard. As they began to recruit members such as Bill Smith on tea-chest bass (soon replaced by Len Garry), Eric Griffiths on guitar and Rod Davis on banjo, the name changed to the Quarry Men.

It's said that the name the Black Jacks lasted little more than a week and that it was Shotton's idea to call the group the Quarry Men as most of the members came from Quarry Bank School.

While Pete Shotton says he doesn't remember the group ever being called the Black Jacks, Rod Davis commented, 'It is my distinct recollection that this was so. I feel that it came from the fact that we wore black jeans and white shirts and that the tea chest was painted black. I can't remember if we played any gigs as the Black Jacks, but the name certainly did not last very long, maybe a couple of weeks at the very most.'

Interestingly, Pete Best, later to become the Beatles' drummer, was also a member of a group called the Blackjacks.

Bless You

A love song to Yoko that John featured on his *Walls and Bridges* album. Ken Ascher played electric piano and mellotron on the track, with John crediting himself as Rev. Fred Ghurkin. He wrote it during his separation from Yoko and played it to his current lover May Pang, who told him, 'It's a beautiful song. She's going to love it.' The song was also included on his posthumous album *Menlove Avenue*.

Blomfield Road, No. 1

When Julia Lennon began living with John 'Bobby' Dykins and gave birth to a daughter, Julia, the family lodged with Julia's father George 'Pop' Stanley at 9 Newcastle Road in Wavertree.

The house was a rented one and when Pop died in 1949 the owner put it up for sale. Julia and Bobby couldn't afford to buy it and, as Julia was pregnant with their second daughter Jacquie, the council provided them with accommodation at Blomfield Road on the Springwood council estate in Garston, Liverpool L1. This was approximately two miles' distance from Menlove Avenue, where John was living with his Aunt Mimi. It was a corner council house semi with large gardens where children could play and an allotment (now gone) at the rear.

When John was in his teens he became reunited with his mother, visiting Blomfield Road frequently. Young Julia had a double bed, so whenever John stayed overnight, Jacqui would join her and John would sleep in Jacqui's room.

When the girls were in bed at night they said they could often hear John and their mother chatting and playing records downstairs when their father was working late. They recall they were mainly Elvis Presley records such as 'Hound Dog', 'Heartbreak Hotel' and 'Jailhouse Rock'. Elvis was such an influence on the household that they named their new cat Elvis – and then discovered their mistake when 'he' later gave birth to kittens!

On a number of occasions John would bring along Paul McCartney, George Harrison, Pete Shotton and Ivan Vaughan (one of the Quarry Men's tea-chest players) and they would rehearse crammed into the tiny bathroom.

At approximately 7 p.m. on 15 July 1958, after the family had had tea, young Julia, who was playing in the garden with friends, noticed her mother leave to visit Mimi. Her sister Jacquie was in bed and John and her father were in the kitchen chatting. It was John who opened the door when a policeman called later that evening to inform them that Julia had been killed in an accident. John said, 'It was awful, like some dreadful film where they ask you if you're the victim's son and all that. Well, I was, and I can tell you it was absolutely the worst night of my entire life.'

Dykins could no longer bear to live at Blomfield Road and rented off the property, while his daughters were taken away to live with their Aunt Harrie.

John paid a final visit to Blomfield Road in 1970 when he took Yoko on a nostalgic visit to his old haunts in Liverpool. They drove up to Blomfield Road in their white Rolls-Royce and were shown around the premises by Georgie Wood, who had taken over the lease from Dykins.

Blue Suede Shoes

John began performing this Carl Perkins number in his original group the Quarry Men. The Beatles also played it during the filming of *Let It Be* in 1969. John also performed it live with the Plastic Ono Band on 13 September 1969 at the Toronto Rock 'n' Roll Festival. During the performance Yoko crawled into a large white bag on the stage. The song is to be found on the album *Live Peace In Toronto 1969*, originally released in December 1969.

'Blue Suede Shoes' was the first number they performed in

Toronto, after the compere Kim Fowley announced, 'Get your matches ready. The Plastic Ono Band …' John said 'We're just going to do numbers we know because we've never played before.' And they began with 'Blue Suede Shoes'.

John was to explain, 'We just wrote the list. I hadn't even got the words to any of the songs. "Blue Suede Shoes" and a couple I hadn't done since Liverpool in the Cavern and that's all we could do. We went on and we were so nervous because we didn't know what we were doing.'

BMI Awards

Annual American awards from the music industry, which presents citations of achievement from Broadcast Music Inc. for the most performed songs of the year.

In 1981 John Lennon received three posthumous citations for 'Just Like Starting Over', 'Watching the Wheels' and 'Woman'.

He was also awarded a cumulative citation pin acknowledging a total of 62 awards over the years. George Harrison received an award at the same time for 'All Those Years Ago', his tribute to John.

Boat Song, The

Another rough demo by John of one of his many songs taped at home, but never recorded in a studio. He accompanied himself on acoustic guitar and the lyrics displayed some of John's goonish sense of humour – 'Burl Ives' brother in a cardboard box, Who wished his mum a pair of socks.'

The number received its first public hearing on the 150th edition of *The Lost Lennon Tapes* radio series.

Boldog Karacsonyt – Happy Christmas John Lennon

A book published in Hungary in 1991. It included lyrics to John's songs in both English and Hungarian, together with a discography and pictures of record covers.

BOMF

The name of the group who backed John on his appearance on the 'Salute to Sir Lew – The Master Showman' at the Hilton

Hotel, New York, on Friday 18 April 1975 (the Sir Lew being
Lew Grade, one of the pioneers of British commercial television). For that appearance they went under the name Etcetera.
They were dressed in red boiler suits when they backed him and
John had them wear masks, Janus-like, which gave them the
appearance of having two faces – a comment on John's feelings
about Grade.

BOMF are the initials of Brothers Of Mother Fuckers. They
had evolved from a group called Community Apple, which had
Joey Dambra on lead vocals. Joey had sung vocals on John's
'No. 9 Dream' as part of the 44th Street Fairies, along with
John, May Pang and Lon Burton. John suggested that they
change their name from BOMF to Dog Soldier.

Bony Moronie

John began recording this Larry Williams number late in 1973
during the sessions for his *Rock 'n' Roll* album, which was
released in February 1975. It was one of the songs he recorded
with Phil Spector in Los Angeles, but it was some time before he
was able to retrieve some of the tapes back from the producer
and was able to mix them himself. It's not an outstanding track,
but John recalled, 'I remember singing it the only time my
mother saw me perform.'

Bootlegs

John was an avid collector of bootlegs of his own and the
Beatles' recordings. In September 1974 he was to say, 'I collect
the memorabilia – why not? It's history, man, history! The
things I really want are the bootlegs; some of them are even
better than the final products that we released – like the *Beatles
In Sweden* bootleg.'

John's interest in collecting bootlegs saw him regularly buying
Beatles bootleg releases in New York record stores. He was also
known to exchange tapes of unreleased Beatles material to other
New York collectors.

Commenting to Andy Peebles in a BBC interview, he said, 'I
buy all the pirate records, file them away and … keep them.
Yeah, stuff from Sweden, things like that where there was good
live shows done.'

Bootleg recordings are usually made up of unreleased

material. This could derive from demo tapes, rehearsal tapes, alternate takes, studio outtakes and concert/radio/TV performances. They shouldn't be mistaken for pirate records, which are simply copies of original, authorised releases, albeit with different sleeves. Nor should they be mistaken for counterfeits, which are simply illegal copies of legitimate releases.

There have been a considerable number of bootleg releases of John Lennon material.

Born in a Prison

A ballad written by Yoko. It was included on the *Sometime In New York City* album, recorded in March 1972. John and Yoko also performed the number on stage at the One-To-One concert on 30 August of that year.

On the album there were songs written separately by John and Yoko and ones written jointly. *Born in a Prison* was Yoko's second song on the album in which she performed lead vocal, and John La Bosca on piano and Stan Bronstein on sax backed her on the track.

Written in a poetic style, the song contends that life itself is a prison into which we are born, struggle and die.

Borrowed Time

A song that John wrote while he was in Bermuda during the summer of 1980. At the time he was soaking in West Indian music and this song was inspired by a track from Bob Marley's album *Burnin'*, which was called *Hallelujah Time*.

The number was included on his posthumous album *Milk and Honey*. It was issued as a single in Britain on Saturday 10 March 1984 with Yoko's *Your Hands* on the flip and in the States on May 11.

Bowie, David

British solo superstar, born David Robert Jones in south London in 1947. Elizabeth Taylor first introduced him to John at her birthday party in Beverly Hills in March 1974. John was there with May Pang and Taylor asked Bowie if he had ever met John. He said, 'No, but I always wanted to meet him.' She then took him by the arm and approached John. May Pang was to say, 'When they met, you could really notice Bowie's admiration for Lennon.'

Although he had completed the recording of his album *Young Americans* in America in January 1975, Bowie asked John if he would work with him on a version of 'Across the Universe'.

John joined him at the Electric Ladyland studios in New York and, in addition to providing some vocal and guitar work on 'Across The Universe', he began a jam with Bowie and the guitarist Carlos Alomar. This resulted in a song 'Fame', credited to the three of them, which provided Bowie with his first No. 1 hit in America. The single was issued in Britain in July 1975 and reached No. 17 in the charts.

John was to say, 'David rang me and told me he was going to do a version of "Across the Universe" and I thought, Great, because I'd never done a good version of that song myself. It's one of my favourite songs, but I didn't like my version of it. So I went down and played rhythm on the track. Then he got this lick, so me and him put this together in another song called "Fame" – I had fun!'

When discussing his songwriting methods, John told Bowie, 'Look, it's very simple: say what you mean, make it rhyme and put a backbeat to it!'

Bowie was later to say, 'With John Lennon it was more the influence of having him in the studio that helped. There's always a lot of adrenaline flowing when John is around, but his chief addition to it all was the high-pitched singing of "Fame". The riff came from Carlos and the melody and most of the lyrics came from me, but it wouldn't have happened if John hadn't been there. He was the energy and that's why he's got a credit for writing it: he was the inspiration.'

At the Grammy awards in March 1975, when John and Yoko made their first public appearance together following their reunion, they were photographed with Bowie and Simon and Garfunkel.

On 8 December 1983, when Bowie was making his final appearance of the Serious Moonlight tour in Hong Kong, he decided to make an acknowledgement to John on the anniversary of his death.

He performed 'Fame' and then told the audience: 'I co-wrote that song with John Lennon. And I asked him one day, "How do you write your songs?" and he said: "It's easy, you just say what you mean and put a backbeat to it." I said, "What do you think about my kind of rock 'n' roll?" He said, "It's great, but it's just rock 'n' roll with lipstick on."

'The last time I saw John Lennon was in Hong Kong. We went to a Hong Kong market and there was a stall that sold clothes and there was a Beatles jacket on the stall and I did something that is not usual to my character – I asked him to put it on so that I could take a photograph. I took a picture and I've still got the photograph. The jacket doesn't fit properly: it looked like John has outgrown it.'

Bowie then said, 'On this day, December 8th, 1980, John Lennon was shot and killed outside his New York apartment.' Bowie then performed 'Imagine'.

Boyle, Peter

An American movie actor born in 1933. His films include *Joe*, *Young Frankenstein* and *Outland*. He first met John in a club in Los Angeles in 1974. Boyle was also among the several creative artists who appeared as witnesses and spoke on John's behalf during the court battles to obtain a green card (the permit that would allow him to work in the US).

He married a journalist, Loraine Alterman, who was on Yoko's 'friendly journalist' list following an interview she'd conducted with Yoko for *Rolling Stone* magazine.

The couple were among the handful of people favoured by being regular guests at John and Yoko's Dakota apartments and were also on the Christmas 'A' list, one of a select few dozen friends to whom John and Yoko sent expensive gift baskets.

Peter and Loraine were also invited by John and Yoko to spend time with them at their Palm Beach villa, El Solano, in February 1980.

Braun, Michael

The late author of *Love Me Do: The Beatles Progress*. In 1964 he'd been commissioned by the publisher Tom Maschler to write a book about the pop scene in Britain. He took some writings into Maschler's office one day, scribbles that had been written on hotel notepaper. Maschler said, 'I thought they were absolutely wonderful, but potential totally unsaleable.' Braun then told Maschler that they were by John Lennon.

Maschler then decided to commission John to collate his

writing for his publishing company, Jonathan Cape, resulting in *In His Own Write*, which sold almost a quarter of a million copies.

Bresler, Fenton
British criminologist and barrister educated at the Sorbonne and at London University, where he read law. Apart from being a practising barrister, he also works as a journalist, specialising in legal and criminal matters. He spent six years researching the circumstances of John's murder and came to the conclusion that it was a political assassination.

In his book *The Murder of John Lennon*, published in 1989, he maintains that John's death had been plotted and planned by the CIA for years and Mark Chapman had been programmed to fire the shots by undercover forces that controlled him. In other words, he was simply a cipher for the CIA, who imagined that Lennon was a representative of dangerous political subversion.

Bring It On Home to Me
This song, popularised by Sam Cooke, was one of John's all-time favourites. During the sessions for his *Rock 'n' Roll* album he recorded the number as part of a medley along with 'Send Me Some Lovin'', another Sam Cooke hit.

Bring On the Lucie (Freeda Peeple)
A track, part of which was originally recorded late in 1971. The complete version was recorded in August 1973 for the *Mind Games* album. It is one of John's political songs, with oblique references to Nixon and the war in Vietnam. The reference to '666' is obviously aimed at President Nixon, as it was John's nickname for him. He was to say, 'It was bell, book and candle against Mr 666 Nixon. We used magic, prayer and children to fight the good fight.'

Freeda Peeple is 'free the people'.

In addition to Jim Keltner on drums an extra drummer, Rick Marotta, was brought in and Sneaky Pete Kleinow was on pedal steel guitar.

Bron, Eleanor
London-born actress who appeared with the Beatles in the movie *Help!*.

John struck up a friendship with Bron and they used to spend time together drinking in hotel bars, discussing politics and philosophy.

When the Beatles were staying in Beverly Hills prior to their Hollywood Bowl concert, she visited John and spent a few hours with him. He was later to claim that she had been one of his conquests, but Bron denies that they were ever lovers.

Brown, Peter

Bebington-born friend of Brian Epstein who was one of a number of close associates invited by Epstein to join his organisation. Former manager of the record department at Lewis's department store in Liverpool, he replaced Brian at the Charlotte Street branch of NEMS and was later invited to join Brian in London at NEMS Enterprises.

In manner and tastes he was very similar to Brian and, following Brian's death, he became an executive at Apple. People were to refer to him as a 'Brian clone' and it was also suggested that he had ambitions of becoming the Beatles' manager, having had the experience of being Brian's personal assistant.

In his book *The Longest Cocktail Party*, Richard DiLello describes him as 'The impeccable Signor Suave of the Apple diplomatic corps and personal assistant and social coordinator to the Beatles.'

It was Brown who accompanied John and Yoko to Gibraltar and acted as best man at their wedding. John mentions Peter by name on his single, 'The Ballad of John and Yoko'.

Brown left Apple to join Robert Stigwood's organisation (he and Allen Klein were incompatible) and moved to America, where he enjoyed considerable success.

He was offered a very large advance payment to write what is known as a kiss-and-tell book about his days with Brian and the Beatles. Entitled *The Love You Make; An Insider's Story of The Beatles*, it was first published in America in January 1983 by McGraw-Hill.

The book was co-written with the music critic Stephen Gaines, and there are some highly controversial stories abounding in the work. Brown suggests that Yoko Ono was responsible for the Beatles' break-up and that she turned John into a heroin addict. He also said that John slept with more women than he could remember. As many people have noted, the book was riddled with inaccuracies, with one radio reporter annoying Brown during an interview by showing him a list of 100 inaccuracies he had found.

John died while Brown was still researching the book, but Yoko gave Gaines a five-and-a-half-hour interview in which he said she chain-smoked forty or fifty cigarettes and lined them up in careful order in an ashtray.

Brown, Rosemary

An elderly widow living in Wimbledon, London, who received considerable media attention because of her mediumistic abilities, in particular her claim that composers such as Liszt, Chopin and Beethoven, together with playwrights and philosophers such as George Bernard Shaw and Bertrand Russell, communicated regularly with her and channelled new works through her.

In this way she alleges she has 'brought over' 600 new pieces of music from composers such as Schubert, Bach, Brahms, Schumann, Debussy, Grieg, Berlioz, Rachmaninov and Delius. There have been recordings of the music issued commercially and a series of concerts in venues of repute such as the Queen Elizabeth Hall, the Purcell Room and Wigmore Hall.

Her books include *Unfinished Symphonies* and *Immortals At My Elbow*. She has also been the subject of a television documentary and numerous press features.

Look Beyond Today, her third book, was published in 1986 and in it she alleges contact with John Lennon, who she claims first arrived in spirit form in her living room in 1984 and has since dictated two dozen songs to her.

She says, 'He is taller than I always imagined him in this life. I seem to see him as he looked at the height of the Beatles' early success – he looks to be in his late 20s or so, is clean-shaven, fresh-faced, doesn't wear glasses.'

Brown also observed, 'What has most surprised John is that there is a continuing process of learning and evolving on the other side. He told me that the afterlife is very much a continuation of this life. You pick up where you left off. You don't suddenly change or know everything.'

He also told her that he still loves Cynthia, his first wife; that he wants Julian to record the songs he has dictated to Brown; and that he is now against the use of drugs.

The book also contains the lyrics to the songs she alleges John has written, using her as a guide, including 'Look Beyond Today', which became the book's title.

She did attempt to entice Julian Lennon to record the songs, but he refused.

The lyrics bear no great resemblance to anything John ever wrote, are composed as poems rather than songs, and the rhyming is too simplistic.

She writes, 'One of the songs I took from John does have a strong philosophical trait. It's called *Love Is All We Ever Need To Know*, and some of the lines go: "My thoughts reach out to find your soul ... on that transcendental plain." '

Brown, William

A literary character created by the writer Richmal Crompton. William was one of John's early heroes, a mischievous scamp with whom he identified. Crompton wrote forty books about the unruly English schoolboy between the years 1922 (when the first collection, *Just William*, was published) and 1970. There were also films and TV adventures featuring the character. The writer John Rowe Townsend, commenting on William – who remained eleven years old in all the books – wrote, 'Born at the age of eleven, he remained eleven for the forty-seven years of his life. Never did a boy's twelfth year hold so many birthdays, so many Christmases, so many unwilling visits to aunts, so many tales with beery tramps or eccentric spinsters, so many ingenious schemes gone so far awry, so many reluctant washings of so dirty a face.' In the leafy suburban area of Woolton, with its Calderstones Park and Strawberry Fields, accompanied by his own gang who included Pete Shotton, Ivan Vaughan and Nigel Walley, John could mentally live out the adventures of William Brown. When the Beatles were asked to submit a list of their heroes for the cover of the *Sergeant Pepper* album, Richmal Crompton was one of the names John put forward – although the author never appeared on the final list.

Browne, Tara

A 21-year-old heir of the Guinness family who was due to receive an inheritance of £1 million on his 25th birthday. For his 21st birthday he'd flown the Loving Spoonful to Ireland to play at his birthday party. He began to associate with a number of the leading pop music artists and had been present during some of the *Revolver* recording sessions.

Although married, he was estranged from his wife and dating a nineteen-year-old model, Suki Potier. On 18 December 1966 he'd been driving in the Chelsea area in his Lotus Elan when a Volvo saloon came out from a side street into their path. Browne swerved the car to avoid it, crashing into a van. His action saved the life of Suki but resulted in his own death.

The next day, at his home in Weybridge, John saw the story in the *Daily Mail* headed 'GUINNESS HEIR SAVED GIRL'S LIFE IN CRASH.' He began to compose a song about it on his piano. Part of this was allied to an unfinished song by Paul, which was to result in 'A Day In the Life'.

Built Around

John and Yoko's joint art venture took place in May 1968 at the Arts Laboratory in Drury Lane, which was the setting for Yoko's happening, 'Objects To Be Taken Apart Or Added To'.

Built Around was the title of a piece of sculpture made by John, which was on display at the lab. It was his first piece of sculpture to go on public display and was described by the *Observer* newspaper as 'a long low white plinth with two slats of wood angled upon it, encrusted with white, broken, plastic beakers and two porcelain doorknobs'.

Bulloch, Sally

A nanny whom Cynthia Lennon intended to hire to look after Julian when he was five years old. Cynthia first heard of Bulloch when she was dining with John at the comedian Peter Cook's home. Bulloch had been nanny to his two children. However, John prevented her hiring the nanny as he felt that a mother should care for a growing child.

Café La Fortuna

An Italian café at 69 West 71st Street. John visited this café almost every day from 1976 while he was living in the Dakota Building. It was a place where he went to relax, smoke his Gitanes and drink a cappuccino while he read the newspapers.

Calderstones Park

A park directly across from John's home in Menlove Avenue where John and Paul used to spend many hours in their youth. Paul and Len Garry (an old pal) also used to go there to watch girls playing tennis. 'Strawberry Fields Forever' originally had the title 'Calderstones Park'. In 1999 Paul planted a tree in the park in memory of his late wife Linda.

Cambridge 1969

The entire first side of the *Unfinished Music No. 2: Life With The Lions* album, lasting 26 minutes and 30 seconds. This had been recorded at Lady Mitchell Hall in Cambridge on Sunday 2 March 1969 before an audience of 500 people. At one point Yoko and John were backed by the American drummer John Stevens and the Danish saxophonist John Tchikai. The local Cambridge newspaper reported:

Miss Ono began with a fearsome siren note, as Japanese as a Noh Play Chant, and sustained it to the point of self torture. Lennon was squatting at her feet, back to the audience, holding, shaking, swinging electric guitars right up against a large speaker, or hitting the instrument against the speaker, to create ear-splitting feedbacks.

Cameron, Gordon

The head boy at Quarry Bank School when John was a pupil. Cameron considered that John was antisocial. During one incident, at a school cricket match, John was playing his guitar. The headmaster was annoyed at this and asked Cameron to confiscate the instrument. Cameron went over and asked John to stop playing, which he did. A short time later John resumed playing and Cameron then went over and confiscated the guitar.

In later years Cameron became an economics professor and a master of Fitzwilliam College, Cambridge.

Can't Buy Me Love

Mainly written by Paul, although John thinks he may have helped on the chorus. It was recorded at Pathé Marconi Studios, Paris, on 19 January 1964 and released in the UK on 20 March that year, and in the US on 16 March. It topped the charts on both sides of the Atlantic.

Capp, Al

A noted American cartoonist, creator of the famous *Li'l Abner* comic strip.

Capp was one of the numerous members of the media invited to attend the Lennons' 'bed-in' at the Reine Elizabeth Hotel in Montreal. His abrasive encounter with John and Yoko and the heated discussion they had was filmed at the time and later included in the 1988 documentary feature *Imagine: John Lennon*.

Capp, complete with his interview notes, seemed to take a hostile stance from the beginning. The debate covered John's antiwar attitude, the nude photos on the *Two Virgins* album sleeve, the lyrics to 'The Ballad of John and Yoko' and the fact that John maintained that he was a spokesman on behalf of people in general. The last incensed Capp to such an extent that

John had to explain, 'I'm a representative of the human race. – I'm speaking for us all.'

Capp retorted, 'Whatever race you're representative of, I ain't part of it. You belong to a race all your own. You don't represent me, and you don't write songs for me.'

Carricker, Tony

A member of John's small gang at Liverpool College of Art. Along with Geoff Mohammed and Jeff Cane, Carricker was in the same class as John and soon came under his influence. John, Carricker and Mohammed in particular caused regular disruption in the corridors of the art college with their pranks.

Carroll, Lewis

A major influence on both John's literary work and song lyrics.

Carroll was the pseudonym of the Victorian author Charles Lutwidge Dodgson, whose most famous works are *Alice's Adventures in Wonderland* and *Through the Looking Glass*. John was given the two books as a birthday present when he was a child and reread *Alice's Adventures in Wonderland* so many times he could recite parts from memory. As a youth he was not only enchanted by these books but by Carroll's surrealistic poems such as 'Jabberwocky'.

Many people sought hidden meanings in the Alice books, just as they did with various songs written by John, such as 'I Am The Walrus', his sole contribution to *The Magical Mystery Tour*, which was inspired by Carroll's poem 'The Walrus and the Carpenter'.

At the time he wrote it he hadn't realised that, of the two, the walrus was the villain because he was conscious of tricking the poor oysters into being eaten.

John said, 'To me it was a beautiful poem. It never occurred to me that Lewis Carroll was commenting on the capitalist and social system. I never went into that bit about what it really meant, like people are doing with Beatles work. Later I went back and looked at it and realised that the walrus was the bad guy in the story and the carpenter was the good guy. I thought, Oh shit, I picked the wrong guy.'

The carpenter isn't even mentioned in the song, but John explained, 'I should have said "I am the Carpenter" but that wouldn't have been the same, would it?'

In his song 'The Glass Onion', he also made the ambiguous statement, 'The walrus was Paul.'

During a radio interview to discuss *In His Own Write*, John admitted to only two influences in the work – Sir Arthur Conan Doyle (whose Sherlock Holmes inspired John's tale 'The Singularge Experience of Miss Anne Duffield') and Lewis Carroll.

He commented, 'I always admit to that because I love *Alice in Wonderland* and *Through the Looking Glass*, but I didn't even know he'd written anything else – I was that ignorant. I just had it as a birthday present as a child and I liked them.'

It has also been suggested that the Carroll influence is evident in 'Lucy in the Sky with Diamonds'.

The individual choices of the seventy-plus characters on the cover of the *Sergeant Pepper* album were made by Robert Fraser, Peter Blake, Paul McCartney, George Harrison and John, although they haven't all been attributed. It is more than likely that John selected Lewis Carroll to be represented as one of his all-time heroes.

Carter, Jimmy

A former American president. Once John had been given his green card, he and Yoko decided they wanted to attend President Jimmy Carter's inauguration. After some string pulling they flew to Washington where they were booked into the Watergate Hotel. They attended the event at the John F Kennedy Center for the Performing Arts on Wednesday 19 January 1977.

John wore a dress suit and a black cape lined with white satin while Yoko wore a white strapless gown, designed by Bill Blass. When they were presented to Jimmy Carter, John said, 'Maybe you'll remember me. I'm an ex-Beatle.'

There were numerous performers at the event, which was televised by CBS TV. However, although Stevie Wonder, Aretha Franklin, Paul Simon and Linda Rondstadt appeared in the televised show, John's appearance wasn't included.

Carter was the incumbent president when John was murdered and commented, 'John Lennon helped to create the music and spirit of our time. In the songs he composed, he leaves an extraordinary and permanent legacy. I know I speak for millions of Americans when I say I am saddened by his death and the senseless manner of it.'

Case of the Blues, A

A song, with psychedelic overtones, which John composed and made into a home demo tape in December 1968, prior to the *Let It Be* sessions. The number was featured on Episode 30 of the *Lost Lennon Tapes* radio series. John wrote it when he was beset by worries – over the miscarriage of his second wife Yoko Ono, being busted for drugs and the hostility of the press to his romance with Yoko.

Cast Iron Shore, The

In his song 'The Glass Onion', John mentions standing on the Cast Iron Shore. This is an area officially called the Dingle Shore, but more familiarly known to Liverpudlians as the Cast Iron Shore or the 'Cassie'.

One of the settings in Frankie Vaughan's 1958 film *These Dangerous Years* was the Cast Iron Shore.

In 1984 the area was transformed as part of the twenty-acre site for the Liverpool Garden Festival. The Cast Iron Shore was converted into a site where a special yellow submarine was constructed, submerged in a pool, near to a Beatle maze designed by Adrian Fisher. In the year 2000 the Yellow Submarine was moved to the Albert Dock.

Catcher in the Rye, The

A contemporary classic by JD Salinger, first published in the 50s.

The novel concerns a sixteen-year-old boy, Holden Caulfield, who hates 'phoneys' with an obsession. Lennon's assassin Mark Chapman read the book when he was sixteen and immediately identified himself with the character. Over the years he became so obsessed by the book that at one time he told his wife that he was thinking of changing his name to Holden Caulfield.

On Monday 8 December 1980, the day he shot John, Chapman walked into a bookshop and bought a copy of the red paperback Bantam edition of the book and in the street outside the shop wrote an inscription: 'To Holden Caulfield from Holden Caulfield. This is my statement.'

After he'd shot John and thrown away the gun, Chapman began reading *The Catcher in the Rye* as he stood outside the Dakota apartments.

When he was in prison he said, 'The reason I killed John Lennon was to gain prominence to promote the reading of JD Salinger's *The Catcher in the Rye*. I'm not saying I'm a messiah or anything like that. If you read the book and if you understand my past ... you will see I am indeed the Catcher in the Rye of this generation.'

Fenton Bresler in his book *The Murder of John Lennon*, theorises that *The Catcher in the Rye* was a *Manchurian Candidate*-style 'trigger' used by a brainwashed Chapman to commit the killing. Although this stretches credibility too far, there is no doubt that *The Catcher in the Rye* became an unhealthy obsession for Chapman, who even carried the book with him into court during his trial. When he was on the stand he quoted an extract from page 173 of the book and on Sunday 1 February 1981 he wrote a statement and sent it to the *New York Times*, who printed it eight days later.

The statement read: 'It is my sincere belief that presenting this written statement will not only stimulate the reading of J. D. Salinger's *The Catcher in the Rye* but will also help many to understand what has happened.

If you were about to view the actual copy of *The Catcher in the Rye* that was taken from me on the night of December 8, you could find it in the handwritten words 'This is my statement.'

Unfortunately I was unable to continue this stance and have since spoken openly with the police, doctors and others involved in this case. I now fully realise that this should not have been done for it removed the emphasis that I wanted to place on the book.

My wish is for all of you to some day read *The Catcher in the Rye*. All my efforts will now be devoted to this goal, for this extraordinary book holds many answers. My true hope is that in wanting to find these answers you will read *The Catcher in the Rye*. Thank you.

Mark David Chapman. The Catcher in the Rye.

Cats

In his early life, John had several cats as pets. When he lived in Mendips he had three cats – Tich, Tim and Sam. When he lived in Weybridge he had several cats, including one he called Aunt

Mimi. While living in the Dakota he had three Persian cats, Shasha, Misha and Charo.

When John went to live with May Pang in 1974, among their pets were two kittens, Major and Minor.

Cavett, Dick

American talk-show host. He invited John and Yoko onto his shows in 1971 and 1972 and said they could use the programme as a forum for their views on world peace. Cavett went to meet them in the St Regis Hotel to discuss their appearance and while he was there John took out a 16mm camera and said, 'Could I take a little thing of you?' As a result, Cavett appears in the *Imagine* movie.

Cavett also testified as a character witness on John's behalf during his fight with the US immigration authorities.

During prior discussions, John and Yoko said they'd like to perform the number 'Woman Is The Nigger of the World'. The network bosses refused. Cavett then went to fight on John's behalf for it to be included and eventually a compromise was reached whereby Cavett taped an insert, acknowledging that some people would find the song offensive but inviting the audience to make their own minds up.

A scene from one of Cavett's interviews with John was reconstructed for the film *Forrest Gump*.

CBC Weekend

Canadian television current-affairs and news programme. Broadcast from studios in Toronto by the Canadian Broadcasting Corporation, the show featured John on Saturday 20 December 1969. Lloyd Robertson interviewed both John and Rabbi Abraham Feinberg, who had appeared on the recording of 'Give Peace A Chance' at the Montreal 'bed-in'. During the broadcast, John advised youngsters not to become involved with drugs.

Chambers Street (112)

Address in Greenwich Village, New York, which was a loft rented as a studio by Yoko and her first husband, Toshi Ichiyanagi.

When Yoko first met Ichiyanagi, she persuaded him to give up his current girlfriend and then she moved in with him in his flat on West 8th Street. After the two were married they moved into a small flat at 426 Amsterdam Avenue and rented the studio in Chambers Street.

Yoko left Ichiyanagi and moved into the Chambers Street loft, where she had a series of lovers, beginning with the writer Michael Rumaker. She also presented several events and concerts for a group of artists called Fluxus at the attic flat.

Chapman, Mark David

John's assassin was born in Fort Worth, Texas, on 10 May 1955. His father was David Curtis Chapman; his mother was the former Diane Elizabeth Pease; and his younger sister was named Susan.

His father said that his son loved the Beatles: 'He collected every album they'd ever made since he was a little boy.'

When he was just a boy the family moved to Atlanta, Georgia. He was eight years old when the Beatles first made their impact in America and friends said that his room was like a shrine to the group, with photographs and clippings all over the walls and a record cabinet full of Beatles albums. Chapman graduated from Columbia High School in 1973, where fellow pupils regarding him as 'just a real, quiet normal guy'.

He experimented with LSD and at the age of fourteen ran away from home, repeating the action at another date.

While in the tenth grade he became a born-again Christian and other high school students called him a Jesus freak. He formed a rock band and wore metal-framed glasses, just like John.

For a short time Chapman worked as a YMCA camp counsellor and then applied for a job in the Lebanon. He left for Beirut in June 1975, but the civil war resulted in his return two weeks later. He then went to work at Fort Chaffee, a military reservation for Vietnamese refugees near Fort Smith in Arkansas, for around six months and then began a three-year relationship with a girl called Jessica Blenkinship. A friend, David Moore, commented, 'He was madly in love with her and she kind of straightened him around.' At her urging he enrolled at a Covenant College in Tennessee, but left after one semester.

After the affair ended he applied for the post of a security guard in Atlanta and took a training course to obtain a shooting permit. He moved to Hawaii, arriving in Honolulu in 1977, and at the age of 22 was employed at Castle Memorial Hospital on the island of Oahu, where he worked in the print shop from August 1977 until November 1979.

He was depressed about the ending of his affair with Blenkinship, the breakdown of his parents' marriage in 1978 and a nervous breakdown he had suffered recently. He took a round-the-world tour and proposed to Gloria Abe, a girl of Japanese descent who worked in the travel agency where he booked the tour. They married on 2 June 1979.

Despite fits of depression and two attempted suicides he successfully applied for a gun permit. He claimed that the apartment he shared with his wife had been burgled and, since he had no criminal record, the permit was granted. He bought a five-shot Charter Arms revolver with a two-inch barrel for $179 on 27 October. Nine days later he booked a round-trip ticket to New York. He had borrowed money from his mother and also $2,500 from the Castle Hospital credit union. On 23 October 1980, his last day as a security guard, he had signed himself out as 'John Lennon'.

In November he arrived in Atlanta, where he visited several old friends, but he didn't go and see his father. He returned to Hawaii but left again on 5 December. He arrived in New York on Saturday 6 December and checked into the Waldorf Astoria. The next night he moved to the West Side YMCA on 63rd Street at $16.50 per night. Chapman went to the Sheraton Center at 52nd Street and Seventh Avenue on Sunday 7 December 1980 and checked into an $82-a-day room. That same day he met Sean Lennon's babysitter and had a meal with her. He'd been hanging around the Dakota Building since he arrived in New York and returned there at 12.30 p.m. on Monday 8 December.

He walked up to Paul Goresh, a young photographer and asked, 'You waiting for Lennon?' Goresh told him he was and Chapman said he was from Hawaii.

At around 5 p.m. John and Yoko left the Dakota and Chapman held out a copy of their new album *Double Fantasy* and asked John to sign it, which he did. Goresh snapped a picture of it. John said, 'Is that OK? Is that what you want?'

When John left Chapman said to Goresh, 'Did I have my hat

on or off in the picture? I wanted my hat off. They'll never believe this in Hawaii.'

At around 7.45 p.m. Paul Goresh decided to leave and Chapman attempted to talk him into staying, saying, 'You never know: something might happen, you know. He could go to Spain or something tonight and you might never see him again.'

Goresh left.

After several hours at the Record Plant, John and Yoko returned to the Dakota.

Chapman stood in the shadow just inside the grand arch. As John and Yoko walked by he called, 'Mr Lennon'. He then dropped into a crouch, known as the 'combat position', and emptied his gun into John. Two shots hit John in the back, two in the shoulder. John staggered up six steps to the concierge's room at the end of the entrance. He said, 'I'm shot,' and fell face down. Yoko ran to him screaming and cradled his head in her arms crying, 'Help me.'

Chapman just stood there making no attempt to move, dropping his gun to his side and taking out a copy of JD Salinger's acclaimed novel *The Catcher in the Rye*. The doorman went up to him and said, 'Do you know what you just did?'

'I just shot John Lennon,' he said.

The doorman kicked the gun away. The elevator man picked it up for safekeeping. When the first two policemen arrived they found Chapman still there, reading his book.

One of the Lennons' neighbours, Ellen Chesler, was a witness to the killing. She said, 'Lennon's car left him off at the kerb and he walked into the courtyard. He turned right, to an office where he walks in to take the elevator to his part of the building. He was hit as he was turning to walk inside. The guy was sort of following him in. I watched the whole thing from my window. I was sitting in the rocking chair with my baby in my arms.

'I didn't hear any screams. He called out, "Mr Lennon", and he kept walking and he got it right in the back. I watched him fall down. I heard four shots. The shots echoed through the courtyard in the building.

'I saw people scurrying about and they were dragging his body in. The guy just stood there and dropped his gun and Yoko was there with John. The police were there within four minutes.

'It's just unbelievable. He very rarely went out. His son goes to nursery school with my son. It's very, very tragic. To the rest of the world it's John Lennon, but if you live in the building it's a neighbour.'

After the murder, Chapman was taken to the West 82nd Street station house, then on to the security section of the Criminal Court Building at 100 Centre Street, where an arraignment was made for the following day. At the ten-minute hearing the Assistant District Attorney, Kim Hogrefe, said, 'He committed a deliberate, premeditated execution of John Lennon and acted in a cool, calm and calculated manner in killing Mr Lennon by shooting him several times with a .38-calibre pistol.'

Chapman's possessions at the time of his arrest amounted to a copy of the Bible, JD Salinger's *The Catcher in the Rye*, fourteen hours of Beatles tapes, $2,000 and a gun.

Herbert J Alderberg had been appointed by the court as Chapman's attorney and said that his client had attempted suicide in Honolulu in 1977, after which he was institutionalised. He said that his client was 'not fully cognisant of what is going on in these proceedings'. The police said that during their questioning Chapman had said that he heard voices and claimed that the devil had motivated his acts.

Chapman was then ordered to Bellevue Hospital for sixty days for psychiatric examination and placed in a heavily guarded unit there where he soon began to claim that he had a 'bad side'. He was also placed on a round-the-clock 'suicide watch'.

'The bad side is very small, but it sometimes takes over and I do bad things,' he said. 'It is too complicated to explain.'

It appeared that he often convinced himself that he was John Lennon, that he wore a name tag above his own on his last job that read 'John Lennon' and he often signed his time sheet as John Lennon.

A Bellevue spokesman said, 'Signing John Lennon's name possibly meant that he somehow identified himself with Lennon. It is very strange and indicates that he was quite ill.'

Another spokesman said, 'He is not screaming crazy.'

Owing to fears of a revenge killing, on Saturday 13 December he was removed from Bellevue Hospital and taken to Rikers Island jail for thirty days of more psychiatric tests. A Correction Department spokesman said, 'The feeling is that he would be safer at Rikers; for one thing, there is only one bridge leading to Rikers and Bellevue is in the middle of Manhattan. It's just easier to keep people away from Rikers than from Bellevue.'

Alderberg, the court-appointed attorney, suddenly resigned from the case, saying, 'What's happened in the last few days had been beyond any proportion I believed it would be.' He added, 'It would be detrimental to the defendant if I stayed on the case.' There were rumours that he'd received death threats.

The case was then accepted by a 37-year-old attorney called Jonathan Marks, who claimed he was a long-term Beatles fan but felt that every citizen deserved a defence. He commented, 'Chapman appears to be a man desperately in need of a friend, and was grateful for someone at his side when the rest of the world was against him.'

Chapman pleaded guilty in court to the murder and the formal sentence of the court was, 'Mark David Chapman is sentenced to State Correctional Facility for a minimum gaol sentence of twenty years and a maximum gaol sentence of life.'

Many Beatles fanzines refuse to mention Chapman's name as they feel that such a thing would acknowledge that he achieved what he set out to do, achieve a degree of fame by killing John.

A detective at the time was to remark, 'It's an old rule. From now on, any time there is something with the name Lennon, it's got to have the name Chapman with it. The kind of killing brings names closer than marriage.'

Rolling Stone writer Dave Marsh, in his introduction to *Strawberry Fields Forever: John Lennon Remembered*, wrote that on hearing of John's murder he hoped they wouldn't release the name of the assassin: 'I hoped they'd leave him anonymous and not give him whatever solace or satisfaction might exist in fame. After all, I can't remember the name of every president of the U.S., but I know the name of Lee Harvey Oswald.'

In 1983 Chapman began to get death threats while he was interned in Attica State jail. A prison officer commented at the time, 'The cons hate his guts. Lennon was a hero to a lot of these guys – they grew up with his music and play it continually in their cells. There are men here doing two, maybe three life sentences with nothing left to lose. These are the ones ready to maim or kill him, if they ever get the chance.'

During his stint in prison Chapman has been the subject of

television interviews, a video documentary, even the front cover of a magazine.

In 1992 he was criticising people who treated him as a celebrity, refusing to answer requests for his autograph. 'This tells you something is truly sick in our society. I didn't kill John to become famous and I'm horrified by these people.'

Yoko Ono announced in 2000 that she was afraid for the safety of Sean (John's and her son) if Chapman were to be given parole at the end of the year. Beatles fans began petitions to plead that he not be allowed out on parole.

Chateau Champlain Hotel

A Canadian hotel in which John and Yoko held a press conference on Monday 22 December 1969. At the event John said, 'We think this was a positive decade, not a depressing one. This is just the beginning. What we've got to do is keep hope alive, because without it we'll sink.'

Cheap Trick

American band originally formed in Chicago in 1973. When the *John Lennon Anthology* was released late in 1998, a special video of 'Losing You' was made featuring Rick Nielsen and Bun E Carlos of Cheap Trick and the bass player Tony Levin of King Crimson backing John's vocal.

All three backed John on the original recording of the song in 1980.

Chelsea Town Hall

Venue, situated at 169–183 King's Road, London, where a press reception was held for the Plastic Ono Band launch of the 'Give Peace a Chance' single on Thursday 3 July 1969. However, John and Yoko were unable to attend, as they'd been involved in a motor accident in Golspie, Scotland, two days before. Ringo and Maureen Starr deputised for them. The Plastic Ono Band was represented at the reception by an abstract design of pieces of clear plastic and recording equipment.

Child of Nature

The second song about meditation that John wrote during his stay at the Maharishi's ashram in India. This was at a time when he was still under the Maharishi's influence. It was taped during some demo sessions in January 1969, but never used.

Some years later, John was to adapt the basic melody of the song for 'Jealous Guy'.

Christgau, Robert

American rock critic and writer of the new Left, who penned various features analysing the political nature of John's work. In the music magazine *Cheetah* he'd described *Sergeant Pepper's Lonely Hearts Club Band* as 'the best rock album ever made'. For the *Village Voice*, he often reviewed John's albums, commenting on *The Plastic Ono Band*: 'He needs continual reminders of his pop heritage, to balance his oedipal heritage and his class heritage.'

In September 1971 the *Village Voice* published his feature 'Now That We Can't Be Beatlefans Anymore', which considered the break-up of the Beatles and John and Yoko's relationship.

John and Yoko wrote to the editor: 'We have never read anything about us that was as observant as your article.' They then paid for Christgau to fly to Syracuse to attend the preview of Yoko's exhibition, *You Are Here*, and he was also a guest at John's 31st birthday party.

The couple then turned up at Christgau's East 8th apartment in New York. Christgau said, 'On Avenue 8 the limo attracted more attention than the star – one of the local youngsters thought I was the Beatle, while others didn't know what a Beatle was.'

Christgau continued writing about John's work and in *Newsday* magazine analysed the political aspects of it in a feature entitled 'The Political Power of Rock and Roll'.

Christianity
See Jesus Christ.

Cincinnati Pops Orchestra
Orchestra that performed at *A Tribute to John Lennon/A Concert In his Memory 1940–1980* at the New Haven Veterans' Memorial Coliseum on 9 December 1981.

The concert was organised in four sections. The first, 'A Symphonia Fantasia for Orchestra', arranged by Frank Proto, comprised abstract variations of John's music. Roberta Flack next appeared singing songs from the *Double Fantasy* album and numbers such as 'A Hard Day's Night'. Dr James Westwater then presented a slide show of pictures of John and Yoko with their music playing in the background. David Clayton-Thomas next appeared and the show ended with a singalong featuring Flack, Thomas, the orchestra and a four-piece rock group.

Clague, Eric

The driver who knocked down and killed John's mother Julia on 15 July 1958. The accident happened on Menlove Avenue. Clague was a police constable at the time of the accident and was unaccompanied in the car, although he hadn't yet passed his driving test. He said that he'd been unable to stop the car when Julia Baird stepped into the road without looking.

As a consequence of the accident he was suspended from the force and he later became a postman. Ironically, his round included Paul McCartney's house on Forthlin Road. As he had to deliver literally hundreds of letters to the address, he commented, 'I remember struggling up the path with them all. But of course they just reminded me of Lennon and his mother.'

He was also to say: 'I read later how his mother's death had affected John terribly. I feel desperately sorry about it.'

Although he felt he wasn't to blame, Clague decided not to contact the family. He said, 'I wanted to tell them how there was really nothing I could have done.'

The *Sunday Mirror* traced him and interviewed him in 1998. By that time he was 64 years old and he admitted he had been plagued by guilt for years because the constant media attention given to the Beatles kept reminding him of the accident.

Clapton, Eric

One of the world's premier rock guitarists, he was born Eric Patrick Clapp in Ripley, Surrey, on 30 March 1945. Clapton's first band was the Roosters, which he joined in January 1963, along with Tom McGuinness. After eight months Clapton and McGuinness left to join Casey Jones and the Engineers. Jones was the former leader of the Mersey Beat group Cass and the Cassanovas, but Clapton's stay lasted only a brief time, as he was then sought for the Yardbirds. While a member of the Yardbirds he gained the nickname 'Slowhand'.

With the Yardbirds, he appeared on the Beatles' Christmas show at the Odeon, Hammersmith. Eric recalled, 'The Yardbirds were on the bottom of the bill, but all of the acts in between were sort of music-hall – English rock 'n' roll groups. And the Yardbirds were an R&B band, or even a blues band, so there was a bit of, like, "What's this all about?" George was checking me out, and I was checking him out to see if he was a real guitar player. And I realised he was.'

When the Yardbirds aimed for a more commercial stance by recording 'For Your Love', Clapton felt they were deserting the blues and joined John Mayall's Bluesbreakers. His reputation grew as he moved on to Cream, regarded as one of the first of the British supergroups. It was while he was a member of the trio that Eric co-wrote 'Badge' with George Harrison, who adopted the pseudonym L'Angelo Mysterioso. George then decided to ask Eric to perform a guitar solo on the Beatles' recording of 'While My Guitar Gently Weeps'.

Eric was to say, 'George and I had become fast friends. This was during the 1967 era, the great age of psychedelia. And we were very good friends. We had a lot in common. We thought the same way musically. I think he was having a tough time convincing John and Paul that his songs were just as valid as theirs. I'm not sure, but I felt that he was calling me in to give him some moral support. And it ended up with me actually taking over the guitar playing for his song so that he could just be free to sing it.'

When John agreed to appear on the TV special *The Rolling Stones' Rock 'n' Roll Circus* on 11 and 12 December 1968 he performed an eight-minute version of 'Yer Blues', backed by Eric, Keith Richard and Mitch Mitchell.

When John received a phone call from the Canadian promoter John Brewer inviting him to attend the Toronto Rock 'n' Roll Festival, John surprised Brewer by saying that he'd form a band. It was George Harrison who originally approached Eric on John's behalf.

Unfortunately, on the day the group were to fly out to Canada, Eric couldn't be contacted at first. Terry Doran had tried to phone him at home, but there was no reply. He had been sleeping all day and Doran finally contacted him in the evening. John then decided to cancel, but Eric told him he had to go ahead and do it.

The actual organisation of the trip was bungled. Eric said, 'John just sits there and thinks up these things you wouldn't believe. I just had a phone call on the day we were to leave and he said that someone had asked him to do that concert and it was that night. So I have to make the airport in an hour.'

On Saturday 13 September 1969 John and Yoko, Eric, Klaus Voormann and the drummer Alan White, together with George Harrison's assistant, Terry Doran, and Jill and Dan Richter, who were filming John and Yoko, boarded a Boeing 707 for the trip to Toronto. During the flight the band rehearsed their numbers at the rear of the plane.

The next day they appeared before an audience of 27,000 at the Varsity Stadium at the University of Toronto and performed eight numbers.

John was vomiting and began to make excuses about not going on stage but Eric took him by the arm and led him out. After playing 'Blue Suede Shoes' and 'Dizzy Miss Lizzy', John looked at Eric and pleaded 'What next?' Eric told him, ' "Yer Blues"', which was then followed by 'Cold Turkey' and 'Give Peace A Chance'.

Then Yoko took over to perform 'Don't Worry Kyoko (Mummy's Only Looking For Her Hand In The Snow)' and a thirteen-minute version of 'John John (Let's Hope For Peace)'.

Eric was to comment, 'A few people started to boo, but it turned into howling along with Yoko. Yoko has the same effect on people as a high-pitched whistle has on a dog. Her voice is spine-chilling. Very weird. John and I played some feedback guitar while she was singing.'

After the show, a delighted Lennon told Eric that the Plastic Ono Band was to be his successor to the Beatles. He said that he wanted Eric, Klaus and Alan to go on tour with him.

For payment for his appearance at the Toronto show, John gave him five drawings, which Eric had framed.

That line-up was to play on the first Plastic Ono Band single, 'Cold Turkey', on Thursday 25 September 1969.

Delaney Bramlett and Bonnie Lynn, known simply as Delaney and Bonnie, were to tour Britain and asked Clapton to join them. George Harrison also joined them on tour. George, Eric, Keith Moon of the Who, Billy Preston and Delaney and Bonnie also turned up at the Lyceum Ballroom in the Strand on Monday

15 December 1969 to appear with John and Yoko. The occasion was the *Peace for Christmas* concert in aid of UNICEF and the musicians performed two numbers, 'Cold Turkey' and Yoko's 'Don't Worry Kyoko'.

In September 1971 John wrote to Eric saying that he wanted him to join him on a sea voyage in a big ship along with other musicians, recording engineers and their families. They would sail from Los Angeles to Tahiti and begin rehearsing, recording and filming. They'd relax for a while on Tahiti and then set sail again. The voyage never took place.

Eric was to continue his close association with George Harrison, which even survived the fact that George's wife Pattie left him for Eric and Eric then married her.

During the wedding party at Eric's mansion, there was a huge jam session in which Paul, George and Ringo played. When he heard about it, John phoned Eric from New York and said he would have been there if he'd known. It would have been the first time all members of the Beatles had played together since their split nine years before.

By 1987 Eric had parted from Pattie because of the affair with the Italian actress Lorry Del Santo, who bore him a son in August 1986.

Clark, Randy

An American singer/actor who has been involved in a number of John Lennon impressions.

He portrayed John in the Broadway run of *Beatlemania* and, when he was a member of the Beatles soundalike group Rain, he provided vocals for the TV movie *Birth of the Beatles*.

For a time he was also a member of another Beatles-style group, Imagine, who, like Rain, also performed at Beatles conventions.

He left the group to pursue a career as an actor.

Cleanup Time

A track from the *Double Fantasy* album, which John described as 'a piano lock, with words added'. Commenting in fuller detail, he said, 'I was talking to Jack Douglas [producer] on the phone from Bermuda. We were talking about the seventies and about people's getting out of drugs and alcohol and those kind of things. And he said, "Well, it's clean-up time, right?" And I said, "It sure is." That was the end of the conversation. I went straight to the piano and just started boogying and "Cleanup Time" came out. Then I had the music and thought, What is this about? I only had the title. So then I wrote the story on top of the music. It's sort of a description of John and Yoko in their palace, the Palace of Versailles, the Dakota: "The Queen is in the counting house, counting up the money; the king is in the kitchen ..." '

Cleave, Maureen

An Oxford-educated journalist who joined the *London Evening Standard* in the early 1960s as a staff writer, evolving into a highly respected interviewer.

It was Cleave who, in February 1963, gave the Beatles their first exposure in a large-circulation newspaper.

The *Evening Standard* was one of London's two evening papers at the time.

For the next three years she became a friend of the Beatles, particularly of John. She interviewed them frequently, covering their exploits in France and America by travelling on some of their jaunts abroad. She later said, 'If John hadn't liked me, I would never have dared to like him, but I had a nice pair of red boots that were considered outré at the time, and he fancied those.'

The most controversial item of all was sparked off by an interview Maureen conducted with John that was originally published in the *Evening Standard* in May 1966. The article covered John's life in Weybridge, his social activities and the cars he owned, details of his possessions, the books he read and his general lifestyle.

There were lots of fascinating little details such as the fact that he had five television sets, had his own gorilla suit which fitted him perfectly, read books such as *Curiosities of Natural History* and described himself as a Celt: 'I'm on Boadicea's side – all those bloody blue-eyed blondes chopping people up.'

A mere few paragraphs mentioned his feelings regarding the current state of Christianity, among them the sentences: 'Christianity will go. It will vanish and shrink. I needn't argue about that; I'm right and will be proved right. We're more popular that Jesus now; I don't know which will go first – rock and roll or Christianity. Jesus was all right but his disciples were thick and ordinary. It's them twisting it that ruins it for me.'

The comments didn't arouse any response in Britain at the time, but when an American magazine called *Datebook* printed excerpts from the interview in July on the eve of the Beatles' American tour the opinions about Christianity appeared out of context and sparked off a storm of protest in the United States.

Tommy Charles implored his listeners on the WAGY radio station in Birmingham, Alabama, to burn the Beatles' records and photographs. He said, 'We felt it was so absurdly blasphemous, that we just felt we had to do something to make it clear to the Beatles that they should keep out of this sort of thing.'

Another disc jockey, Betty Black of WAIM-WCWC, a station in Anderson, commented, 'We have been excluding Beatles from our programmes for months already, because we find them unacceptable to the lovers of good music. If he hadn't excluded them already, we would certainly have done so now.'

Not all disc jockeys thought that way. One in Salt Lake city commented, 'I'm not preaching their religious thoughts: I'm only playing their records.'

The controversy raged on with public burning of Beatles records, but there was also support from church leaders and fans who regarded John's comments as legitimate opinion.

The only other countries to react with a ban against Beatles records were South Africa and Spain.

Nat Weiss, Brian Epstein's American lawyer, contacted him to inform him that the American reaction was a serious problem. Despite having laryngitis, Epstein flew to New York and informed the press, 'Lennon didn't mean to boast about the Beatles' fame. He meant to point out that the Beatles' effect appeared to him to be a more immediate one upon, certainly, the younger generation. John is deeply concerned and regrets that people with certain religious beliefs should have been offended.'

Epstein decided that John would have to make a formal explanation. He held a press conference in America before the nineteen-day tour.

Maureen Cleave in the meantime had become quite upset at the furore caused by her article and said, 'John was certainly not comparing the Beatles to Christ. He was simply observing that so weak was the state of Christianity that the Beatles were to many people better known. He was deploring rather than approving this. Sections of the American public seem to have been given an impression of his views that is totally absurd.'

While sections of the American public took John's statements the wrong way and were incensed by them, the British public seemed to have accepted them as fair comment. The Catholic Church also understood what John was getting at and agreed with him. – The Vatican newspaper *L'Osservatore Romano* complimented John's social perception and said that his statements provided Christians with 'a well-placed kick where it was most needed'. *The Catholic Herald* in the UK stated, 'If a world-wide opinion poll could be taken, we should probably find that John Lennon was speaking the bare truth.' Some American voices also understood the essence of what had been said. The Revd Richard Pritchard of Westminster Presbyterian Church in Madison, Wisconsin, blamed the people who expressed outrage at Lennon's remarks for their validity, saying, 'Those people should take a look at their own standards and values. There is much validity in what Lennon said. To many people today, the golf course is also more popular than Jesus Christ.'

A number of music personalities made their own comments in the *Melody Maker*. Alan Price said, 'Lennon's got every right to say what he likes. But it's only because he's a Beatle that it's been picked up in the way it has.' Graham Nash commented, 'I, personally, don't believe the Beatles are too upset by the whole thing. I have the impression they are trying to cool things down for themselves – they want to be more independent and live a more comfortable life.' Dave Berry said, 'Lennon probably said all that for a laugh and didn't expect it to be taken so seriously. Anyway, people ought to look at the facts because what he said is probably true.'

Clive, John

An actor who was originally a compere for local bands in Liverpool. He provided the voice of John for the film *Yellow Submarine*. Clive pointed out that the director had told him that he and the other actors who were doing the voice-overs would have to change the voices and make them sound more American. He and the others refused, insisting that they were

going to remain as close to the real Beatles voices as possible –
and were prepared to lose their jobs if they weren't allowed to.
They won out in the end.

He went on to appear in a number of films, including *The
Italian Job* and *Revenge of the Pink Panther.*

Clock

One of the series of avant-garde films made by John and Yoko.
Clock was an hour-long movie showing the passage of time as
the camera concentrated on the face of the French clock in their
apartment at the St Regis Hotel in New York.

John and Yoko made the film in September 1971 and the
soundtrack included phone conversations by Yoko as she
discussed her forthcoming exhibition at the Everson Gallery,
together with the sound of John performing solo on his acoustic
guitar. The soundtrack was recorded in the St Regis Hotel on
Friday 10 September 1971 and John sang various numbers,
mainly songs by Buddy Holly and Carl Perkins, but also a version
of his song 'New York City'. Among the songs on the film's
soundtrack are 'Maybe Baby', 'Rave On', 'Not Fade Away', 'J.J.',
'Heartbeat', 'Peggy Sue Got Married', 'Peggy Sue', 'Send Me
Some Lovin'', 'Mailman Bring Me No More Blues', 'Shazam!',
'Honey Don't', 'Glad All Over' and 'Lend Me your Comb'.

The film was premiered on 9 October 1971.

Club Dakota

Name given by John to a 'private' club just for himself and his
friend Elliot Mintz. He suggested that they turn one of the
rooms in his Dakota Building apartments into a private club,
like an English gentleman's club. This was inspired by the Blues
Bar, a private club he'd heard of which was just for Dan
Aykroyd, John Belushi and their close friends.

He suggested they fit the room out and then surprise 'Mother'
with it. ('Mother' was the term by which he referred to Yoko.)
They bought 'naff' furniture – overstuffed couches with
crocheted doilies, cheap watercolour pictures of flamingos in
flight, standing ashtrays and the like. There was a jukebox with
records by Guy Mitchell, Frankie Laine and Bing Crosby. They
even had a Wurlitzer organ moved into the room, a present
Yoko had bought him for his 38th birthday, plus an electric

Yamaha piano, a present from Elton John. John would sit at the Yamaha and play some of Mintz's favourite songs for him – 'In My Life', 'As Time Goes By' and 'Dream Lover'.

On New Year's Eve 1979, they announced the official opening of Club Dakota, both dressed in second-hand coats with tails, with John also wearing his old school tie. A formal invitation to the opening was sent to Yoko on a silver serving tray. She decided to accept and arrived dressed in an elegant black gown. On the stroke of midnight the Wurlitzer began to play 'Auld Lang Syne' and John and Yoko danced together.

The following month, when Mintz returned to the Dakota, he learned that Club Dakota no longer existed and John had stripped the room and placed most of the items in storage.

Club Sandwich

The official Paul McCartney fan club magazine. This was published right up until the time of Linda's death, when Paul finally decide to suspend its publication. Following John's death, *Club Sandwich* issued a special issue that consisted entirely of photographs of John taken by Linda. There was also a dedication from Paul: 'I met John a long time ago at Woolton Village fête, and in all the years I knew him I saw a man of many faces, sometimes aggressive, sometimes warm and gentle. Linda and I hope that this special edition of *Club Sandwich* will keep alive the memory of a very special man who was loved by us all and who did so much to promote peace, love and understanding in a world that didn't always want to listen. We dedicate this issue to John, Yoko and their loved ones.'

Cogan, Alma

British singer, born in London on 19 May 1932, who had eighteen chart entries.

While at art college, John used to lampoon Cogan's 1958 hit 'Sugartime', pulling grotesque faces in imitation of her performance before his fellow students. Little did he know they would later become such great friends.

Just how friendly they would become is open to speculation. One of the hooks of the 1994 book *Elvis Meets the Beatles*, by Chris Hutchins and Peter Thompson, was 'How John Lennon fell in love with a cult British singer and only her untimely death threw him into the arms of Yoko Ono.' All is revealed in Chapter Ten, entitled 'Love Me Do, Alma Cogan', in which the authors contend that John was madly in love with the singer.

Chris Hutchins, a close friend and confidant of John at the time, said that John was totally smitten with Alma, who reminded him in some respects of his mother, Julia. He told Hutchins, 'Every time I'm with Alma, it feels right. Julia just couldn't cope with me, but Alma can read me like a book.' John nicknamed her Sarah Sequin.

In March 1966 she was diagnosed as having cancer and died of the disease on 26 October of that year at Middlesex Hospital in London. She was only 34 years old.

Cohen, Charles J
An American publicist based in Boston who was hired by John in July 1980 on a twenty-week trial basis.

Cold Turkey
John initially offered this song to the Beatles, but it was said that Paul refused to record it, so John decided to issue it as a Plastic Ono Band release. As a result of its being turned down as a Beatles single by Paul, John decided to dispense with the Lennon and McCartney credit and the number was solely attributed to him. The refusal of the others to record 'Cold Turkey' as a Beatles number also led to John's telling them that he wanted a 'divorce' from them.

The song did refer to drugs and John looked on the number as a warning against drug use. It had been inspired by the fact that after his use of LSD and marijuana, he had become addicted to heroin and late in 1968 both he and Yoko had decided to go 'cold turkey' and rid themselves of the habit. The phrase 'cold turkey' referred to a person withdrawing from drugs without medical supervision.

He'd originally made a home demo tape of the number early in September 1969 and recorded it at Abbey Road studios on 25 and 28 September, producing it himself with the aid of Tony Clark and Neil Richmond. John and Eric Clapton featured on lead guitars, with Klaus Voormann on bass and Ringo Starr on drums. There were 26 takes before John was satisfied with it.

John also began his policy of placing his B-sides in the hands of Yoko and the flip side of 'Cold Turkey' was 'Don't Worry Kyoko (Mummy's Only Looking for Her Hand In The Snow)'.

The disc was issued in America on Apple 1813 on 20 October 1969 and in Britain on Apple 1001 on 24 October. The song didn't make much of an impact compared with the Beatles' record sales but it reached No. 14 in the British charts and rose to No. 30 in the Billboard charts in America.

John then made his controversial move of sending a messenger to his Aunt Mimi's bungalow to retrieve his MBE from its place on top of her television set.

He next had it wrapped in brown paper and sent to the Queen at Buckingham Palace with the message: 'I am returning this MBE in protest against Britain's involvement in the Nigeria–Biafra thing, against our support of America in Vietnam and against *Cold Turkey* slipping down the charts. With love, John Lennon. Bag Productions, 3 Savile Row, London W1.'

He also sent an identical letter to the Prime Minister and to the Secretary of the Central Chancery.

The song was first performed in public at the Toronto Rock 'n' Roll Festival on 13 September 1969, in which John was supported by Eric Clapton, Klaus Voormann and Alan White. It was one of two songs performed by the Plastic Ono Band at the UNICEF Benefit Concert at the London Lyceum on 15 December 1969. For the occasion, the band became a supergroup with George Harrison, Keith Moon and the Delaney and Bonnie band adding to the line-up. John also performed the song at the One-To-One Concert at Madison Square Garden on 30 August 1972, backed by Elephant's Memory.

The Toronto performance had been recorded and a 'Cold Turkey' track appeared on the 1969 album *Plastic Ono Band/Live Peace At Toronto*. The UNICEF concert had also been recorded and a live track of 'Cold Turkey' from the Lyceum performance was included on the album *Sometime In New York City*. The studio version was also included on the *Shaved Fish* album compilation and on EMI's *The John Lennon Collection*, issued as a tribute on 1 November 1982.

Coleman, Ray

A British journalist who became editor of the music weekly *Disc* in the mid-1960s and interviewed the Beatles on several occasions.

One interview with John was for a *Disc* feature called *Treasure Chest*, in which John discussed various belongings to which he was attached.

They included his first Rickenbacker guitar, two Stuart Sutcliffe pictures, the boot used in the film *Help!*, books by Aldous Huxley, a record by the Singing Postman, a stone frog and four number plates displayed on his playroom wall.

In January 1969 John told Coleman his feelings about the state of Apple, commenting, 'Apple is losing money. If it carries on like this, we'll be broke in six months.' This was the story that inspired Allen Klein to make his attempt to take control of the Beatles' affairs.

Coleman left *Disc*, which later folded, to become editor of *Melody Maker*, a position he retained until the early 1980s when he became a freelance journalist and author. He immediately found success with his interviews with Yoko Ono, which he placed in several British national papers.

His most ambitious work was a two-volume work on John's life, first published in 1984. He also wrote a biography of Brian Epstein and a book devoted to Paul's song 'Yesterday'.

Coleman died of cancer at the age of 59 on 10 September 1996.

Collins, Phil

A British musician and singer, a former member of Genesis, who became a major solo star in his own right. As a teenager he appeared in *A Hard Day's Night*, one of the many extras gathered for the scene in the Scala Theatre. When he appeared on the CBS *This Morning* programme in America to comment on John on an anniversary of his death, he said, 'The other side of Lennon is I think he was a bit of a bastard, really. I don't think he was a very nice person.'

Come Together

One of John's personal favourites and a song he originally began during his week-long 'bed-in' in Montreal. One of his visitors was Timothy Leary, a leading light in the American 1960s counterculture, and Leary's wife asked John if he'd pen a campaign song for her husband's proposed idea of running for Governor of California against Ronald Reagan. John began writing a chantlike song based on Leary's campaign motto 'Come together and join the party'. That particular version was never completed as Leary was imprisoned for drug offences and Reagan made sure he was kept in Orange Country Jail on a marijuana charge for the duration of the election.

John rewrote the number, but the new version was to spark off some problems. His opening lines were a tribute to Chuck Berry's song 'You Can't Catch Me', and he also included part of Berry's lyric 'here come old flat top' in the song. This started a dispute involving the publisher and record-company executive Morris Levy, who claimed that both the melody and lyrics at the beginning of the song were taken directly from the Berry number.

John maintained that it was not plagiarism, merely a tribute, and agreed to settle the matter by recording two Chuck Berry songs, which led to further complications.

Phil Spector was to say that John had the Dennis Hopper character in *Easy Rider* in mind when he wrote 'Come Together'.

The number was also banned by the BBC because of the use of the words Coca-Cola.

'Come Together' was the last track recorded for the *Abbey Road* album and was also the first track on the LP, which was issued in 1969. The number was also used as the B-side of the single 'Something'.

John performed the song at the One-To-One Concert in August 1972 and it was included on the posthumous *Live In New York City* album, issued in February 1986.

He preferred the version he taped at Madison Square Garden in 1972.

The American band Aerosmith had a hit with 'Come Together' in 1978.

Connolly, Ray

Connolly was born in Liverpool and studied social anthropology at the London School of Economics before becoming a journalist on the *Liverpool Daily Post*. He joined the *London Evening Standard* in 1967 as a columnist and rock music writer. He became involved in the daily affairs of the Beatles and wrote many articles on John, Yoko and Paul.

He became a confidant and learned many of their secrets, the biggest of which was the story of John's intention to leave the Beatles.

Connolly respected John's wishes that he hold up the story. Four months later, Paul was able to make his own announcement to the press and John regretted that he had asked Connolly to keep the announcement on ice.

Ray also travelled to Toronto and stayed at Ronnie Hawkins's farm during John and Yoko's visit there. After John's period of being a househusband, Ray was one of the journalists invited to New York to interview him about his future plans.

His interview was set for 9 December 1980. On 8 December Yoko called Connolly to inform him of the tragedy of John's assassination.

He wrote his first screenplay, *That'll Be the Day*, in 1973. It starred Ringo Starr. His second movie script, *Stardust*, won him the Writers' Guild of Great Britain Award for best original screenplay. He was commissioned to write a screen biopic of John Lennon, which he completed. However, *Working Class Hero* was never filmed as Warner Bros opted for producing *Imagine* instead.

Connolly, who is married with three children, is also the author of the book *John Lennon 1940–1980*, published in 1981. In it, he has an illustration from one of the letters John sent him with a sketch of John, Yoko and Sean.

The book begins with a comment John made to him in December 1970: 'Have you written my obituary yet? I'd love to read it when you do.' In the biography Ray also makes the observation, 'Future historians will find the understanding of the sixties and seventies widened immeasurably by focusing on the life of John Lennon.'

In 1998, when there was a reference to John's being an adulterer, Ray commented in May of that year, 'Before he'd left her, Yoko said, John had been drinking a lot and was becoming very difficult to live with. For instance, they'd been to a party in Greenwich Village in New York, where a girl had begun coming on strongly to him. Flattered, he took her into a bedroom and began to make love to her on top of guest's coats. "It was very embarrassing," Yoko told me, because everyone could hear the noise John and the girl were making, but couldn't get their coats to go home until they'd finished having sex. So, I suppose, yes, he was an adulterer, unfaithful to his first wife Cynthia with Yoko and an eclectic assortment of others, and then unfaithful to Yoko in her turn.'

Continuing Story of Bungalow Bill, The

One of the several songs John composed during his stay at the Rishikesh ashram in India. He was to say, 'This was written about a guy in Maharishi's meditation camp who took a short break to go shoot a few poor tigers, and then came back to commune with God. There was a character called Jungle Jim and I combined him with Buffalo Bill. It's a sort of teenage social-comment song and a bit of a joke.'

The chap John referred to was a young American, Richard Cooke III, who came to Rishikesh to visit his mother, Nancy, who was studying at the ashram.

Both Cook and his mother went hunting and Cook shot a tiger. He later felt remorse and met up with the Maharishi to discuss it. John and Paul were also present.

The number was recorded on 8 October 1968 and was included on *The Beatles* double album. John sings lead vocal and plays an acoustic guitar and organ, while Yoko Ono sings one of the lines in the song, 'not when he looked so fierce'. Maureen Starkey also sings in the chorus with Yoko, and the engineer Chris Thomas comes in on mellotron at the end of the track.

Cook, Peter

A British humorist, satirist and TV personality who, in the 60s, was one half of a successful comedy duo with Dudley Moore.

The two appeared in films such as *Bedazzled* and had their own television series, *Not Only … But Also!* on BBC2. John guested on the first edition of their show in 1965 and appeared as a guest in their Boxing Day 1966 edition.

John and his first wife Cynthia were also guests of Cook and his wife at their Hampstead dinner parties. When Cynthia and John were dining at the Cook's home one day, the comedian mentioned Sally Bulloch, who had been nanny to his two children. Cynthia had been considering hiring a nanny to look after Julian, who was five years old, and decided to engage Sally.

However, John prevented her hiring the nanny as he felt that a mother should care for a growing child.

Cook died in 1995.

Cookin' (In the Kitchen of Love)

A song that John wrote for Ringo Starr's sixth album *Rotogravure*. Ringo commented, 'I asked John especially to write me a song ... and John came down to LA especially to work with me, 'cause he does that on all the records: he comes down, writes the song and plays.'

This was the third album by Ringo in succession for which John had provided an original song. He'd initially made a demo of the number, which he composed at home on the piano earlier in the year.

John recorded the track with Ringo in April 1976 and played piano on it. Other musicians featured on 'Cookin'' were Danny Kortchmar and Mac Rebennack on guitars, Will Lee on bass guitar, King Errisson on percussion and Dutch Helmer on backing vocals. Mac Rebennack also played organ.

Cooper-Hewitt Museum

The museum, situated at 2 East 91st Street, New York City, to which John and Yoko donated their 1965 Phantom V touring limousine with its psychedelic design, in 1977. The Rolls-Royce was displayed in an exhibition entitled *Ornament in the 20th Century*, which ran until 7 January 1979.

Corbett, Bill

A driver hired by John to become the chauffeur of his recently acquired £5,000 Rolls-Royce in 1964. Corbett had originally been an employee of a car-hire firm, which had assigned him to drive the Beatles around in an Aston Martin.

Cosell, Howard

One of America's most famous television sports commentators. Cosell was present in the audience of *The Ed Sullivan Show* when the Beatles made their debut. He later had John as his guest on his ABC Radio Network series, during which he said he wanted him to reunite the Beatles. But John told him it just wasn't possible. John told him he'd like to go to a Monday night football game so Cosell took him to Candlestick Park where he introduced him to Ronald Reagan. He took John to another Monday night game and also interviewed him on a live telecast.

On 12 September 1974 John videotaped a promotional appearance with Cosell for ABC's *Monday Night Football*, a one-and-a-half-minute excerpt of which was used later in the month.

When he received a call telling him that John had been killed, Cosell decided to open his *Monday Night Football* programme that night talking about John. As the programme was one with a massive audience, most Americans first learned of John's death through Cosell's announcement.

Commenting that the football game was of no consequence, he said, 'One of the great figures of the entire world, one of the great artists, was shot to death horribly at the Dakota apartments, 72nd Street and Central Park West, in New York City. John Lennon is dead. He was the most important member of the Beatles, and the Beatles, led by John Lennon, created much that touched the whole of civilisation. Not just people in Liverpool, where the group was born, but the people of the world.' He then discussed John's life and times.

Cott, Jonathan

An American author and journalist who conducted the first interview with John Lennon for *Rolling Stone* magazine on Tuesday 17 September 1968.

Jonathan was the magazine's European correspondent and Robert Fraser, owner of the Fraser Gallery, arranged the interview, which took place in London. John was holding an exhibition at the gallery at the time. At 5 p.m., Cott and a photographer, Ethan Russell, arrived at the Montague Square flat where John and Yoko were staying, although the initial session lasted only half an hour because John had to leave to record at Abbey Road studios. The conversation revolved around John's exhibition. The interview continued the next afternoon and revolved around John's songwriting techniques, the numbers he wrote himself and various aspects of songwriting composition. The interview was published in *Rolling Stone* on Saturday 23 November 1968.

Cott became an associate editor of *Rolling Stone* in 1967, has penned several books and co-wrote the text for *Get Back,* the lavish booklet issued with the original *Let It Be* album in Britain.

Apart from conducting the first *Rolling Stone* interview with John, Cott also conducted John's final *Rolling Stone* interview on the evening of Friday 5 December 1980 in Yoko Ono's office in the Dakota apartment. The main topic of discussion was the *Double Fantasy* album. The interview had been planned for *Rolling Stone*'s first issue of 1981, when John and Yoko were to be the cover stars. Owing to John's death the interview appeared in a special issue, published on 22 January 1981, which was devoted entirely to John's memory.

Several of Cott's articles about John are collected in the book *The Ballad of John and Yoko*, which he co-edited, and include 'John Lennon: How He Became Who He Was'; 'The First Rolling Stone Interview'; 'Daddy Has Gone Away Now: Let It Be'; 'Yoko Ono and Her Sixteen-Track Voice' and 'The Last Rolling Stone Interview'.

Cox, Anthony

Cox was a bespectacled saxophone player and former art student at Cooper Union when people began to tell him about Yoko Ono, who had left New York for Japan to join her husband Toshi. Cox went to Japan to seek her out and found her in hospital following a suicide attempt. He discovered that she was heavily drugged and felt she'd been given too high a dosage, and arranged her release from hospital. It was while he was having dinner with Yoko and Toshi that she told him her marriage had been over for some time and he soon moved in with them in a *ménage à trois*. He then became Yoko's second husband. The marriage did not work, although their baby daughter Kyoko was born in 1963, the same year as they were wed.

The couple apparently argued regularly, but soon settled down to a relationship that was more that of good friends than husband and wife. Apparently, Yoko became the dominant partner and in 1965 it was decided that she would concentrate on her career while Cox would stay at home with the baby. This was the same arrangement she insisted on between herself and John Lennon almost a decade later.

It was while Cox was in France that John invited Yoko to Weybridge in May 1968, and the two became lovers for the first time.

Cox, an erstwhile filmmaker, did not seem unduly worried that his wife had found another man, although he insisted on retaining care of Kyoko. Their divorce came through via the Virgin Islands on 2 February 1969 and Cox received £6,700 as a divorce settlement.

He began to live with a woman called Melinda, whom he later married. For a time, they moved to Aalborg, a small village in Denmark. John and Yoko joined them in December 1969 when Kyoko was ill. It was during this trip that Cox filmed John and the five-year-old Kyoko having a bath together, a film that he was to use in court during a custody hearing.

Yoko decided that she would like to have custody of Kyoko and travelled to Majorca, where Cox and Kyoko were staying. John and Yoko attempted to take the little girl from the island, but Cox alerted the police and Kyoko was reunited with her father.

Cox then realised that Yoko was determined to have the child and possessed the money and legal muscle to achieve her ends, so he fled the island. Yoko applied to the Virgin Islands for an order giving her custody of Kyoko. Cox, however, had resurfaced in Houston, Texas, and obtained a custody order in his favour.

By that time he'd changed Kyoko's name to Rosemary. John and Yoko arrived in America and insisted on having Kyoko stay with them over Christmas. Cox refused and was jailed for three days as a result. Yoko's high-powered lawyers went into action and managed to talk the court in Houston into giving custody of the child to Yoko, but by that time Tony, Melinda and Kyoko had fled again.

Cox, Kyoko

The daughter of Yoko Ono and her second husband Anthony Cox. She was born in Tokyo on Thursday 8 August 1963. Cox took his baby daughter to New York while Yoko remained in Tokyo. When Yoko did arrive in New York City and moved into Cox's small apartment, Kyoko was eighteen months old. The three later set off for England.

When Yoko began her affair with John, she was living with her husband and child in a Regents Park flat. A visiting friend observed, 'She was full of herself. I felt sympathy for Tony and Kyoko. Tony was functioning as mother *and* father. Funny thing was, Yoko talked about her own mother and how detached she was from her, how she had a sad childhood, and I felt Yoko was doing the same thing.'

The situation with Tony Cox deteriorated to such an extent that Cox moved with his daughter into a flat in Hanover Square in March 1968 while Yoko moved into a small hotel. Cox took Kyoko to Paris for a while. After their divorce in February 1969, Cox took custody of his daughter, although Yoko had access. In May 1969 Kyoko began travelling with John and Yoko, initially to their proposed 'bed-in' in the Bahamas, then to Toronto for the 'bed-in' and finally back to Britain, where they were joined by John's son Julian for a short holiday in Scotland.

A car crash brought the holiday to an abrupt halt and Yoko put Kyoko on a plane to New York to join her father. Kyoko was now six years old. Later that year Cox contacted Yoko to tell her that her daughter was ill, and on 29 December the Lennons flew to Aalborg in Denmark where Kyoko was living with Cox and his new wife Melinda.

It has been suggested that Yoko had a sudden desire to have custody of Kyoko following her first miscarriage with John's child.

Yoko wanted Kyoko back. A year after her trip to Denmark, Tony and Kyoko had apparently disappeared, so Yoko hired private detectives, who tracked them to Majorca, where they were attending a meditation course, taught by the Maharishi Mahesh Yogi. On 23 April John and Yoko travelled to the Spanish island, but when they took Kyoko, intending to fly back to Britain with her, they were accused of kidnapping the seven-year-old. Police quizzed the Lennons, who were ordered to appear in court. The court officials took Kyoko aside and asked her if she would prefer to go with her father or her mother. She opted for her father and Kyoko was returned to Cox. However, all parties were required to report to the magistrate twice a month while the kidnapping allegation was resolved.

Eventually, the judge dropped all charges. The Lennons had brought Allen Klein with them and he suggested to Cox that there should be joint custody. He said to the press, 'The Coxes were told that if Mr Cox does not agree, the Lennons would have to take the matter to the Virgin Islands, where Yoko's divorce took place and where, in all probability, Yoko would get complete custody.'

Cox and Kyoko disappeared again. The Lennons then spent several months pursuing the couple, even hiring private detectives to trace their whereabouts, and their search led them to Texas, New York and the American Virgin Islands in their attempts to gain custody of the child.

During the recording of *Imagine* at Tittenhurst Park, John and Yoko heard that Cox and Kyoko had been seen visiting his parents on Long Island. They immediately flew to New York, but Tony and the child had vanished once again. With their team of detectives and attorneys, the Lennons announced that they had already spent more than $100,000 trying to track the couple down.

In a *Playboy* interview conducted shortly before his death, John admitted that they had kidnapped Kyoko. However, when she was asked whom she'd prefer to live with, Kyoko opted for her father.

This echoed a similar experience in John's life when he was only five years old. His father had taken him to Blackpool and his mother turned up. John was asked whom he'd prefer to live with. His decision wasn't as clear cut as Kyoko's. John initially said he wanted to stay with his father, but when his mother walked away he ran after her.

As the divorce had taken place in the US Virgin Islands, the Lennons were advised to fly there and request custody from the courts. It was their determination to find Kyoko and gain custody that made the Lennons come to the decision to move permanently to the United States. However, initially John could obtain only a temporary visa. They hired a lawyer, Leon Wildes, who was to say that John didn't seem to have any desire to become a permanent resident. He commented, 'The interest was only in staying a couple of months so they could continue their efforts to find Kyoko; they were in the middle of some complicated custody proceedings.'

On Saturday 18 December 1971 they flew to Houston, Texas, in an effort to gain custody. Cox mentioned that throughout their marriage he'd lived in fear of Yoko, who had one time stabbed him with scissors and on another occasion trapped him in a bath for 45 minutes holding a broken bottle at his throat. He said he and his daughter had been harassed by the Lennons, who had hired private detectives to follow them everywhere. He said that Lennon had seduced his wife and got her on drugs and he then showed a home movie of a naked Lennon having a bath with his daughter when she was five years old. The judge awarded Cox and his wife temporary custody but allowed extensive visiting rights to Yoko. The court had ruled that Kyoko could spend Christmas with her mother, but when she arrived in Houston with John, Cox refused to let Yoko take her daughter and was placed in jail for five days for not allowing Yoko to visit the child. He was released on bail the next day and then disappeared with Kyoko once again.

During the immigration hearings when John was seeking to prevent himself being deported, he brought up the subject of the eight-year-old girl, pointing out that Yoko had been granted temporary custody by a second American court. The court had stipulated that Kyoko be raised in America. However, Kyoko could still not be found and Yoko wanted to remain in order to search for her. John pointed out that if he were deported, Yoko would be left with the difficult decision of having to decide between her husband and child.

The immigration service and FBI disagreed with this and said that the custody battle between John and Yoko and Tony Cox was a fraud, that the three had conspired together and were hiding Kyoko, saying they had planned 'to keep the child hidden as a tool to delay deportation proceedings'. When John said they couldn't find Kyoko they threatened to charge him with perjury.

In 1977 Tony Cox enrolled Kyoko at the Walter Reed Junior High School in North Hollywood and she studied there using the assumed name of Ruth Holman. Between 1972 and 1977 Tony and his daughter had sought refuge at the Church of the Living Word, also known as the Walk. Kyoko was later to become associate producer of her father's documentary film about his involvement in the Walk, which was called *Vain Glory*.

In 1979 Yoko received a call from Kyoko, who said she'd come and visit her at Christmas, but she never turned up.

In 1986 Cox was interviewed by *People* magazine and said

that he and Kyoko had left the Church of the Living Word in 1977, although his wife Melinda had remained. He was asked if Kyoko would be reunited with her mother and he said it was now up to Kyoko as she was 23 years old and an adult.

People magazine then got on to Yoko for her reaction and she wrote an open letter to her daughter:

Dear Kyoko,
    All these years there has not been one day I have not missed you. You are always in my heart. However, I will not make any attempt to find you now as I wish to respect your privacy. I wish you all the best in the world. If you ever wish to get in touch with me, know that I love you deeply and would be very happy to hear from you. But you should not feel guilty if you choose not to reach me. You have my respect, love and support forever.
                                                          Love, Mummy.

Yoko was to say that she was eventually reconciled with Kyoko in 1995. She said, 'She finally got in touch. We were getting calls from people all the time claiming "I'm your daughter", and there would be a photograph of some blonde, blue-eyed woman, but the first time I heard Kyoko's voice, I knew it was her.' Yoko mentioned that Kyoko was now a teacher.

Crawford, Michael

A British actor, born in 1942. He starred in *How I Won the War* in 1967, the film in which John made his solo movie-acting debut. During filming in Spain, Crawford and his wife Gabrielle shared a villa with John and Cynthia and they became the best of friends. It was John's first straight acting role and was coolly received, but it provided another vehicle for promoting his vision of a world free of war and nuclear weapons.

Crawford later recalled, 'He'd come in and sit cross-legged on the bed with his guitar or we'd take his Rolls to the beach.'

Crawford was later to concentrate his talents on the stage and television, in the hit TV series *Some Mothers Do 'Ave 'Em* and in the stage productions *Barnum* and *The Phantom of the Opera*.

Crazy John

A song about John written and recorded by Tom Paxton. It was issued in the States on Elektra 45667 in 1969. Paxton, who had involved himself in the peace movement, used the song to criticise John for his 'bed-ins' and 'War Is Over' campaign, contending that they were stunts that did not bring him close enough to the people he should have been communicating with. 'They never came near you, John – so how can you teach them?' he sang.

Paxton, born in Chicago on 31 October 1937, emerged as one of the leading American folk singers of the early 60s, although he never achieved the major commercial success of other folk artists such as Bob Dylan and Joan Baez.

Crenshaw, Marshall

An American singer born in 1954, who portrayed John in the American road show of *Beatlemania*.

Discussing his career, Crenshaw comments, 'I started playing in bands in school in the sixties when the Beatles came out, and when the Beatles made it in the US every little kid wanted a guitar. Most of them got them and a few of them learned to play.

'I played Lennon in *Beatlemania*, which was this terrible show in the United States; but the funny thing about it was it was a very big hit for quite a couple of years.

'It was running on Broadway for about a year and it was a touring company also, so it was really going strong after a while.

'It was a multimedia sort of show with a group of actors on stage who were supposed to look like the Beatles, and then there'd be all those films and different visual images going around from the sixties.

'They were trying to show how it was done in such a silly way that it made the whole thing look like a parody of itself. I did it because I was sick of playing in bar bands and I wanted to find a way of trying to break out.

'It was all live music and the music part of it was OK because I always liked the Beatles' music and it was fun to play and try to sound like them.

'I do sound like Lennon even when I don't try to – it just happens that way. But I don't really think I look like him. I used to think I did. I used to have really long hair and wear little wire glasses so I guess I used to look a bit like him.'

Crenshaw's debut album *Marshall Crenshaw* on Atlantic Records included the track 'Soldier of Love'.

Crippled Inside

A track on the *Imagine* album which John began recording in July 1971. He played guitar with Nicky Hopkins on piano, Klaus Voormann and Steve Brendell on upright basses, George Harrison on Dobro (a type of acoustic guitar named after its Czech-American inventors, the Dopera Brothers) and Ted Turner, Rod Linton and John Tout on acoustic guitars.

This was recorded at a time when John was incensed about Paul's *Ram* album, with its song '3 Legs', which John felt was an attack against him. *Imagine* contained the bitter attack on Paul, 'How Do You Sleep?'.

'Crippled Inside' is another song in which John accuses Paul of living a lie.

Cry Baby Cry

Song written by John and included on The Beatles' 'White Album'. Some years later he denounced the song, saying, 'Not me. A piece of rubbish.' Recording began at Abbey Road on 15 July 1968. John also played piano and organ on the track. With elements of nursery rhyme, the influence of Lewis Carroll can be detected in the lyrics.

Cry for a Shadow

The only known work crediting both John Lennon and George Harrison as composers, it was also the Beatles' first recorded instrumental.

George, who received some help from John, originally conceived the piece. It was recorded at the Friedrich Ebert Halle in Hamburg on Thursday and Friday 22 and 23 June 1961 during the Bert Kaempfert sessions. The title of the piece was said to have been inspired by the leading British instrumental group the Shadows, although an alternative title was 'Beatle Bop'. In fact it was suggested that George began composing the number after Rory Storm and the Hurricanes challenged him to write a Shadows-style instrumental.

The number was issued as a single by Polydor. The flip side, 'Ain't She Sweet', featured a vocal by John.

The recording session was the subject of the entire cover of *Mersey Beat* in June 1961, a story that first aroused Brian Epstein's interest in the Beatles.

Cuff, Nicky

A Liverpool midget who performed in various local groups, mainly of the showband variety. When Cuff was a member of the Sunnyside Skiffle Group, his outfit appeared at a number of venues on the same bill as the Quarry Men and one of his gimmicks was to stand on his tea-chest bass while he played it.

Nicky, at four foot six, was 19 when his group appeared on the *Carroll Levis Discovery Show* auditions at the Empire Theatre, Liverpool, on 9 June, 1957, and his group were said to have beaten the Quarry Men. The following year the group had changed their name to the Connaughts and in December they appeared at the Empire once again – they won the heat, also beating the Quarry Men, who were called Johnny and the Moondogs during the contests.

John once said that Cuff was his favourite comedian.

However, Rod Davis, a member of the Quarry Men at the time, has contradicted the reports regarding the Quarry Men's first appearance at the Carroll Levis show. He commented to the journalist Ian Forsyth, 'I've read in some books that we were beaten by a group with a midget called Nicky Cuff. This is absolutely untrue. Nicky Cuff was a bass player in a skiffle group who was mentioned by John in a later interview. Nicky, because of his size, stood on the bass and we saw him at the Silver Blades Ice Rink in Liverpool and John thought he was almost a goon show character. He certainly wasn't fascinated by midgets, as has been reported since. I don't think John was particularly fascinated by the grotesque, as has been stated. I think John just liked to put down the journalists.'

Rod recalls that they played 'Worried Man Blues' at the contest at the Empire, but were beaten by a group from Colwyn Bay, North Wales. He says the other skiffle group arrived in a coach with about fifty of their supporters and they gave a lively performance, with their bass player lying on his back on the stage while playing his instrument and with the other members jumping about. He says this was the Quarry Men's first glimpse of 'showmanship', as they just stood rather woodenly while they performed at the time.

Cult Heroes
A ten-part series on BBC Radio Five. The seventh programme was devoted to John and was broadcast on Tuesday 4 December.

Curran, Charles
In 1964, the Conservative Member of Parliament for Uxbridge. On 19 June that year he made a speech in Parliament during a debate on automation and brought up the subject of John's new book *In His Own Write*. He cited it as an example of the lack of education of less-gifted young people in Britain, who would be ill equipped to deal with the automated labour market.

In a rather patronising speech, part of which was reproduced in *The Times* the next day, he commented on the unsatisfactory education system in Britain and brought up the subject of John's book as a case in point – one of the consequences of people with inadequate skills. He said the book 'seemed to show a great deal about the kind of education Lennon received in Liverpool'. He added, 'He has a feeling for words and story telling and he is in a state of pathetic near-literacy.' He also said, 'It appeared that he had picked up pieces of Tennyson, Browning and Robert Louis Stevenson while listening with one ear to the football results on the wireless.'

After quoting three verses from 'Deaf Ted, Danoota and Me', Curran added that *In His Own Write* was a 'singularly pathetic and touching' testimony of what lay ahead for Britain.

Answering Curran, Norman Miscampbell, Conservative MP for Blackpool North, who had been born in Liverpool, said, 'I was interested in my honourable friend's mention of the Beatles. It is unfair to say that Lennon of the Beatles was not well educated. I cannot say which, but three of the four went to grammar school and as a group are highly intelligent, highly articulate and highly engaging.' He also pointed out that the emergence of so many music groups in the city had led to the disappearance of gangs, who were a deep-seated root of crime in Liverpool.

Curtis, King

A legendary saxophonist (real name Curtis Ousley), who was born in Fort Worth, Texas, on 7 February 1934. He was known as the 'King of the Tenor saxophone' and joined the Coasters in March 1958, recording the famous 'Yackety Yack', with its 'dirty' sax solo, the same year. His other hits with the Coasters included 'Charlie Brown', 'Poison Ivy' and 'The Chipmunks Song'. Curtis was later to form his own band, the King Curtis Band, who appeared on the bill of the Beatles American tour in 1965.

Lennon was an admirer of the Curtis sax sound and hired him to take part in the *Imagine* sessions on 4 July 1971 at the Record Plant in New York City. Curtis overdubbed saxophone on to two of the songs, 'It's So Hard' and 'I Don't Want To Be a Soldier'.

Tragically, scarcely six weeks later, on 13 August 1971, Curtis was stabbed to death outside his own New York apartment by a Puerto Rican youth, Juan Montanez, who stood trial for his murder. Curtis was only 37 years old.

Cut Piece

The title of one of Yoko's conceptual happenings. She sat in a chair and asked members of the audience to come on stage and snip off a piece of her clothing. At times she was left near naked. She performed 'Cut Piece' at her *Yoko Ono's Farewell Performance* at Sogetsu in Japan in 1964 and at the Carnegie Recital Hall in New York in March 1965.

Daily Howl

A collection of poems, stories and caricatures that John composed in an exercise book while at Quarry Bank School. A fellow pupil, Bill Turner, was to describe the book in *Mersey Beat*:

While we were at Quarry Bank School John produced a book called the *Daily Howl*. It was an exercise book filled with his stories, poems, drawings and cartoons.

He used to show his work to a bloke called Pete Shotton before he let anyone else see it. Pete was his best mate at Quarry Bank and I think John wrote the *Daily Howl* mainly for him.

I remember it was at the time Davy Crockett was all the rage and one of the poems was 'The Story Of Davy Crutch-Head'. He also took a current hit song called 'Suddenly There Was A Valley' and he incorporated this into a story which went: 'suddenly there was a valet who rode up riding …'

There were quick flashes in the book such as a weather report: 'Tomorrow will be Muggy, followed by Tuggy, Wuggy and Thuggy.'

He had an obsession for Wigan Pier. It kept cropping up,

mainly in a story called 'A Carrot In A Potato Mine', and the mine was at the end of Wigan Pier.

One of his favourite cartoons was a bus stop scene. I remember he wrote under the sign which said 'Bus Stop' – 'Why?' And he had a flying pancake at the top of the cartoon and below it there was a blind man wearing glasses leading along a blind dog – also wearing glasses.

At one time the *Daily Howl* was confiscated by one of the teachers and it went all round the staff before he got it back at the end of term.

John was to say, 'One of my earlier efforts at writing was a "newspaper" called the *Daily Howl*. I would write it at night, then take it to school and read it aloud to my friends. Looking at it now it seems strangely similar to *The Goon Show*! Even the title had "highly esteemed" before it!'

In the 1988 auction at Sotheby's in London, three pages of an original *Daily Howl* manuscript, which John had compiled in 1958, were sold for £12,000.

The first page had *Daily Howl* as the banner headline with 'Price 1d or McVicars Head' to the left and '?d to the Vicar' to the right. There was a drawing by John entitled *Our Vicar*, next to an item that read, 'The kindly Vicar of a parish, has kindly donated a kind donation, which he kindly decided to kindly donate to the Society for the Prevention of Standing on Toadstools. But it is found that the treasurer at the S.P.T.T has run away to Garston, he went on the bus.'

Below it is another piece: 'Talking of Vicars reminds us of the dreadful Gunpowder Plot. The gun powder plot was an awful thing, it is still done on the 5th Nov. Guy Fawkes chose the 5th Nov because it was Firework Day. Guy Mitchell, the singer claims direct descent from Guy Fawkes. His family tree is shown below.'

There is a drawing of a tree below it and to the left a drawing of a man with a bowl around his neck beneath the title: 'Have you got dandruff? Well, get a basin (basin) fitted of your head, it will stop the noise of the dandruff making you go deaf as it talk(s).'

There was, in fact, more than one exercise book. A pupil from the school tore out two of the poems and gave them to the

Mersey Beat magazine. Bill Harry published them, having obtained permission from John to publish any of his works he could trace. The poems were 'The Tales of Hermit Fred' and 'The Land of the Lunapots'.

THE TALES OF HERMIT FRED
The wandering Herman Fred am I
with candle stick bun
I nit spaghetti pie –
And crum do I have fun –
I peel old bagpipes for my wife
And cut all negroes' hair
As breathing is my very life
To stop I do not dare.

THE LAND OF THE LUNAPOTS.
T'was custard time and as I
Snuffed at the haggis pie pie
The noodles ran about my plunk
Which rode my wrytle uncle dunk
T'was Wilbur's graftiens graffen Bing
That makes black puddings want to sing
For them in music can be heard
Like the dying cough of a humming bird
The lowland chick astound agasted –
Wonder how long it lasted
In this land of Lunapots
I who sail the earth in paper yachts

Harry did trace another copy of the *Daily Howl*, which was in the possession of Rod Murray, who'd shared a flat in Gambier Terrace with John. John had left the book behind and Murray said he'd return it if he was reimbursed for the back rent that John had owed him. Rod eventually auctioned his copy off at Sotheby's.

Dakota Building

The Dakota was New York's first luxury apartment building. It was commissioned in 1884 by builder Edward Severin Clark and designed by architect Henry Janeway Hardenberg for

Edward S Clark, heir to the Singer sewing machine empire. It was given the name because the building was erected in a part of the city so far away from midtown Manhattan that it was referred to as Dakota Territory. It was also the first block of flats in New York City to incorporate a lift in the building. The nine-storey granite fronted block, which was used in the film *Rosemary's Baby,* is situated at the corner of Central Park West and 72nd Street, on the upper West Side of New York. It became known as 'the Dowager Queen Mother of apartment houses' and had a magnificent view of Central Park.

The Lennons acquired their first apartment there on the 17th floor in April 1973 from actor Robert Ryan, following the death of Ryan's wife from cancer. They moved in during May 1973.

Their dream was to buy up the whole of the Dakota. When asked about it, Yoko said, 'The thing is, John never had a house of his own.' The couple eventually bought five apartments, a total of 25 rooms.

The Dakota boasted a number of celebrity residents including Lauren Bacall, Shelley Winters, Roberta Flack and Leonard Bernstein.

In 1980 Random House published the book: *Life At The Dakota, New York's Most Peculiar Address,* by Stephen Birmingham.

Dakota Days

A book by John Green, the Lennons' tarot reader. St Martin's Press published it in America in June 1983 and Comet Books published it in the UK the following year, on Thursday 24 May. It was a slim 50,000-word volume, although the *Los Angeles Times* called it 'the most controversial pop biography since Albert Goldman's account of Elvis Presley', which is something of an exaggeration. A flavour of the book can be culled from the blurb, part of which read:

> In a room of the Dakota apartments overlooking Central Park, John Lennon brooded on his past and struggled to find his lost muse. His adviser, confidant and friend during those dark days was tarot reader John Green. In this poignant – but often hilarious – account of the Lennons' last five years together Green takes us inside a crazy world

where multi-million dollar business decisions are taken on the turn of a card and where life is lived by whim and superstition. John emerges as a lost soul kept sane only by his celebrated sense of humour, frequently locked in combat with Yoko while maintaining the myth of being a 'happy househusband'.

David Frost Show, The

David Frost had begun a weekly television series for syndication in America called *The David Frost Show*. John and Yoko appeared on it on 14 June 1969 in a taped appearance filmed at Stonebridge Park Studios, Wembley, before a studio audience. The duo were questioned about 'bagism' and their commitment to the peace movement. The interview was included when the show was broadcast in America on Thursday 10 July 1969.

Davis, Angela

A black American radical who had been fired from the faculty of UCLA after being named as a member of the Communist Party. Davis involved herself in a campaign to free three members of the Black Panther movement from a jail term in Soledad Prison, which they'd received for being involved in a petrol-station robbery. The trio, led by George Jackson, Angela's boyfriend, had become known as the Soledad Brothers.

In August 1970, Jonathan Jackson, George's younger brother, smuggled a carbine into Marin County Courthouse and together with two armed prisoners took the judge, the district attorney and a number of jurors hostage, intending to exchange them for the Soledad Brothers. During an attack by prison guards on the van in which the hostages were held, Jonathan Jackson, three black men and the judge were killed and the district attorney and the jurors were seriously wounded.

When it was discovered that Davis had supplied the guns, she was charged with kidnapping, conspiracy and murder. Despite trying to hide out, she was caught and arrested in December. Guards shot George Jackson to death the following August, claiming he was attempting to escape.

While Davis was in the county jail in San Jose, California, awaiting trial, John and Yoko decided to voice their solidarity with her in song and penned 'Angela', which was featured on their *Sometime In New York City* album. The cover, which was designed to look like a newspaper cover, also included a picture of Davis, together with the words of the lyrics, which called her a sister and named her as 'one of the millions of political prisoners in the world'.

Davis, Jesse Ed

John first met Jesse Ed Davis during the filming of *The Rolling Stones Rock 'n' Roll Circus* in December 1968.

Davis was a member of Taj Mahal, an American band the Stones had booked to appear on the show. Unfortunately, owing to Musicians' Union problems, they weren't allowed to play.

While the musicians were sitting backstage in a dressing room, John began to jam on a number of old rock 'n' roll songs and Davis began playing along with him. John was impressed by his expertise.

John's desire to have Davis record with him was satisfied when he hired Davis to play lead guitar on 'Beef Jerky' and 'Whatever Gets You Thru the Night'. He also performed on the *Walls and Bridges* and *Rock 'n' Roll* albums. Davis was also to appear on the Concert for Bangladesh and on George Harrison's albums *Concert for Bangladesh* and *Extra Texture*, in addition to appearing on Ringo Starr's albums *Goodnight Vienna* and *Rotogravure*.

Davis, who was a full-blooded Kiowa Indian with a BA in English literature from the University of Oklahoma, was living in Venice, California, with his girlfriend Patti and her son Billy when John embarked on his 'lost weekend' with May Pang. Davis became one of John's drinking buddies during this period, in addition to recording with him on the Phil Spector *Rock 'n' Roll* sessions. At one time, John and Jesse were so drunk they began to wrestle and John ended up knocking him out by hitting him over the head with a marble ashtray.

In 1974 John wrote a song called 'Mungo Macho', which he intended giving Jesse as a gift. He even made a demo on which he announces, 'Mucho Jesse!'. However, the number was given to Harry Nilsson for his *Pussy Cats* album, with the title altered to 'Mucho Mungo'.

Davis became addicted to drugs, although he made several attempts to cure himself of the habit. On Wednesday 22 June

1988, at the age of 43, he died of a suspected drug overdose at his home in Venice, the day after being released from a drug rehabilitation programme.

Davis, Rod

Born in Liverpool on 7 November 1941, Davis attended St Peter's Sunday School in Woolton, along with John, Pete Shotton, Nigel Walley and Ivan Vaughan, and knew John from the age of five. He also attended Quarry Bank School with John. He says, 'There was a group of us from Springwood Primary School who skipped a year and thus were younger than most of the other boys. Most of the classes had about thirty boys in them. At Quarry Bank I was part of a group of boys who took three or four GCEs at the end of year four and then started on A-level work in the fifth year.

'I had been in 4 Science for a month or two then changed to 4 Arts because I wanted to do Spanish and French. There was also a 4B and a 4C. I think that by this time John was in 4C but I could be wrong.

'When I joined the Quarry Men I was in a form which was called Lower Sixth Transitus Arts (what a mouthful that was) and I was never a member of a proper fifth-year form, but there were only about eight of us. I was already working on French and history A-level when I joined the Quarry Men. John and Pete were in 5C and Eric [Griffiths] in 5B or 5A.

'I'd been trying to get a banjo or a guitar for some time. I had tried plucking a violin but quickly realised this would get me nowhere. I tried to fix up an old ukulele but this was also useless. My father's elder brother George was quite a good violinist and he had played in a dance band in the Denbigh area some years before. His brother-in-law, Emrys Jones, played guitar and banjo and we discovered that Em was selling them both.

'By the time I got to see him in Denbigh, however, he'd already sold the guitar so we got the banjo for five pounds. I think this must have been on a Sunday. The following day I went into school and told Eric Griffiths that I had just got a banjo and he asked me if I wanted to be in a group with him, Lennon, Shotton and Bill Smith. I agreed. I knew I couldn't play it as I had only got it the previous day. When we practised he would shout the chord name at me and very soon I could play by ear. I later bought a banjo tutor and learned some chord inversions further up the neck, but John insisted I played the same ones as him and Eric.'

Incidentally, the banjo was called a Windsor World and Rod still has it in his possession.

The first rehearsal took place on the Thursday following his acquisition of the banjo and was at Griffiths' house at 96 Halewood Drive, Woolton.

Rod recalls various rehearsal sessions at several houses, including the garden of his own home. When they rehearsed at Colin Hanton's home there was a girl called Geraldine Davies, who lived next door, who recorded them on a Grundig tape recorder. They practised once or twice in the living room of John's Aunt Mimi's house, Eric Griffiths' house and John's mother's house in Springwood.

Rod had been tagged a 'purist' and commented, 'As for being a "purist" – I simply didn't like rock 'n' roll very much. I preferred skiffle and trad jazz. I argued with John on stage at the Cavern about his choice of rock rather than skiffle as I was concerned at the audience reaction to our playing rock in a jazz cellar.

'As soon as I left the Quarry Men I bought a guitar and got into folk music. As I stayed on at Quarry I became part of a jazz trio with a pianist called Gerald Greenwood and a drummer, Les Brough, both from Quarry. We appeared at the Prefects' Rag concert under the name the Elastic Band.

'I went to Cambridge University in 1960, where I joined the St Lawrence Folk Music Society and became president in my third year. I first heard bluegrass music here and was hooked. This was the real thing and skiffle had been only a pale imitation. I learned to play the mandolin, fiddle and concertina and became a bluegrass flatpicking guitarist, which I still am.

'I didn't *leave* the Quarry Men: I sort of drifted out. I don't remember Paul McCartney being invited to join the group, but in late July I clearly recall being at Mimi's (we almost never practised there) when Paul came in to hear us practise. This must have been several weeks after the St Peter's church fête [at which Lennon met McCartney]. It was the end of the fifth year at school and all the other guys left Quarry except for me. Eric went to be an engineering apprentice at English Electric. Peter went to the police cadets and John to art school. Colin was of course already working.

'In August I went camping to France with my family and by the time we came back we had all moved on to the rest of our lives. I was going to be very busy studying to get into university so I didn't worry too much about the Quarry Men. Shotton also left at the same time.'

In 1961, while at Cambridge, Rod made a record with a group called the Trad Czars and he was able to tell John when he met him in Liverpool the following year, 'I beat you onto record.' He told John that he played mandolin, fiddle, banjo, guitar, concertina and melodeon. John said, 'You don't play drums, do you? We need a drummer to take to Hamburg.' Rod's mother was to say, 'He's not going to Hamburg with that Lennon. He's taking his degree.'

Incidentally, Rod became head boy at Quarry Bank.

After graduating from Cambridge, Rod lived abroad for a number of years. He returned to England and became a tour guide in London and later got a job as a lecturer at a polytechnic in Uxbridge, where he still lives. Rod married, and had two children, although he now has a new partner and is in retirement.

He appears with the Quarry Men on their occasional appearances and is the one who arranges all their work permits and visas, saying 'It's very tedious being on the road, especially at our age. But it's fun.'

Dawson, Pat

A Liverpool barmaid who had a brief flirtation with John. She is nicknamed Polythene Pam because she believes John might have had her in mind when he wrote 'Polythene Pam', although, as she admits, 'It's not the kind of song you'd want dedicated to you if you listen to the lyrics.'

Day in the Life, A

Track on the *Sergeant Pepper* album recorded on 19 and 29 January; 3, 10 and 22 February and 21 April 1967. The number, which was one of John's favourites, was a collaboration between John and Paul. On the first day of recording the song was called 'In the Life Of'.

John had written the basic song, which included reference to the death of a friend, Tara Browne, in a car – which he read of in the *Daily Mail* on 17 January 1967 – and another item from the same newspaper, about the holes in the road in Blackburn, Lancashire. The brief item said, 'There are 4,000 holes in the road in Blackburn, Lancashire, or one twenty-sixth of a hole per person, according to a council survey.'

John was to say, 'I dug it. It was a good piece of work between Paul and me. I had the "I read the news today" bit, and it turned Paul on, because now and then we really turn each other on with a bit of song … it just sort of happened beautifully.' Basically, it was the merging of a Lennon song with no middle section and a McCartney middle eight that didn't have a beginning or end.

Commenting on his middle section of the number, Paul said, 'The next bit was another song altogether, but it happened to fit well with the first section. It was really only me remembering what it was like to run up the road to catch the school bus, having a smoke, and then going into class. We decided, "Bugger this: we're going to write a real turn-on song!" It was a reflection of my school days – I would have a Woodbine [cigarette] then, and somebody would speak and I would go into a dream. This was the only one on the album written as a deliberate provocation to people. But what we really wanted was to turn you on to the truth rather than just bloody pot!'

There were 41 musicians and then a whistle that only dogs could hear. It was also Paul's idea to use an orchestra, which he conducted with George Martin.

The huge orchestra was booked into the studio on 10 February and the plan was to make a film of the recording, so members of the orchestra were handed party pieces – false noses, funny hats and such. The record ended with a huge crescendo. Paul said, 'The orchestra crescendo and that was based on some of the ideas I'd been getting from Stockhausen and people like that.' The orchestra was instructed to race from the lowest to the highest note within a particular E-major chord inside twenty-four bars.

George Martin was to say, 'John wanted to start from nothing, increase in tension and build up to the most overpowering sound.'

John's voice effect was achieved with a tape echo and, in order to keep time, George Martin got Mal Evans to count each bar.

He says, 'And on the record you can still hear his voice as he stood by the piano counting "one, two, three, four". For a joke, Mal set an alarm clock to go off at the end of twenty-four hours and you can hear that too. We left it in because we couldn't get it off!'

The BBC banned the number because they declared that the line 'I'd love to turn you on' was a drug reference and that Paul's lyric about having a smoke and then going into a dream was about marijuana.

The noted composer and conductor Leonard Bernstein, who lived in the Dakota Building in New York, was to comment, 'Three bars of "A Day in the Life" still sustain me, rejuvenate me, inflame my sense and sensibilities.'

Day They Shot Lennon, The
A play presented at the NJ Theatre in Princeton, New York, on 19 January 1983. James McLure wrote it.

Day Tripper
Song written by John, although Paul helped with the verse. On the finished record, originally recorded on Saturday 16 October 1965, Paul sings the verses and John sings the chorus. It was released in Britain as a double-A-side on Parlophone R 5389 on 3 December 1965 with 'We Can Work It Out'. Although it was issued as a double-A-side, 'Day Tripper' was considered the stronger track and received top billing. This was reversed when it was issued Stateside on Capitol 5555 on 6 December 1965. It was also included on the American album *Yesterday and Today* in June 1966.

It was suggested that the title referred to 'a weekend hippie'. The track has been included in a number of other compilations, beginning with *A Collection of Beatles' Oldies (But Goldies)* in December 1965, *The Beatles 1962–1966* in April 1973, *The Beatles Box* in December 1980, *20 Greatest Hits* in October 1982 and *Past Masters Volume 2*.

Days in the Life: John Lennon Remembered
A book published by Century in Britain in 1990 to mark the tenth anniversary of John's death. It's primarily a picture book with some text by Philip Norman.

Dear Friend

A track on Paul McCartney's December 1971 album *Wild Life*, which was his answer to John's 'How Do You Sleep?'. This was basically a message to John that they should start patching up their relationship and become friends again. Paul said that when John slagged him off in public he had to think of a response. Instinctively he felt he shouldn't slag John back and was glad that he didn't.

Dear John

A song of which John made a home demo recording in November 1960. It was one of the last songs he began composing and it was unfinished. An introspective number about himself, based on the basic 'Dear John' theme – the letters received by soldiers in the World War Two when their girlfriends wrote to them ending their relationship.

John recorded the number with acoustic guitar, vocal and drum machine and he and Yoko intended it for a forthcoming album.

The song was included on the 'Lost Lennon Tapes' series, and also on a CD issued in Sweden with a new edition of *A Spaniard In The Works* in 1998.

Dear Prudence

Another of John's compositions from the sojourn in Rishikesh, which was to be used as a track on the album *The Beatles* (the 'White Album').

When the film actress Mia Farrow arrived at the ashram there was some excitement at the eminence of the celebrities gathered to study transcendental meditation under the master himself.

Her younger sister Prudence accompanied Mia. The girl seemed to spend all her time meditating and hardly ventured out of her hut. John was elected to persuade her to come out and join the others. She was an intense young thing who 'didn't come out to play'.

John was inspired to write 'Dear Prudence' despite his failure to persuade her to mix some more with the people around her.

The number was recorded on 28, 29 and 30 August 1968, while Ringo was temporarily absent from the group. Sean Lennon has also recorded and publicly performed it.

Dear Yoko

A song written by John when he was in Bermuda, which became the closing track on the *Double Fantasy* album. John was to mention it in his interview for *Playboy* magazine. 'It says it all,' he said. 'The track's a nice track and it happens to be about my wife, instead of Dear Sandra or some other person that another singer would sing about who may or may not exist.' There is a Buddy Holly influence evident.

Death of Samantha

Single written by Yoko Ono with performers' credits announced as Yoko Ono Plastic Ono Band with Elephant's Memory, the Endless Strings and choirboys. Co-produced by John during the *Approximate Infinite Universe* sessions in late October 1972.

The song was issued as a single in America on 26 February 1973 on Apple 1859 and in Britain on 4 May on Apple 47 with another Yoko number 'Yang Yang' on the flip.

DeMarino, Ron

A professional guitar technician. During the mid-1960s the former musician had begun to collect and repair musical instruments. He worked on instruments for a stream of musicians, including Jeff Beck and Alice Cooper, and also became John Lennon's personal guitar technician and consultant. An assistant of DeMarino's happened to be in Manny's Musical Instruments store on West 48th Street, Manhattan, in 1971 when John's road manager Claude came in asking if they had any old Fender Tweed twin amps. They hadn't, but Claude was given Ron's number and he called him a few days later.

Ron was then asked to meet John at his Bank Street apartment and was made his personal guitar technician and consultant. He oversaw the guitars at the One-To-One concert and also advised John on the guitars he bought – at times informing him which were forgeries. Ron saw that John had an extensive collection, which, apart from the Beatles' guitars, included a number of Martin acoustic guitars, a double-neck-lap steel guitar, a 1959 Cherry Sunburst Les Paul, a Les Paul Custom Black Beauty and a 1956 Les Paul Junior.

Ron was commissioned to work on repairing guitars in the

collection that had deteriorated, including John's original Rickenbacker 325.

Ron and his wife Joan also met the Lennons on a social basis, at home, in the studios and over dinner.

De Mesquita, Señor Bueno

A Commissioner for Oaths who, in a ceremony on the rooftop of Apple's Savile Row offices on Tuesday 22 April 1969, officially changed John's name by deed poll from John Winston Lennon to John Winston Ono Lennon (although he'd wanted to have 'Winston' removed and 'Ono' substituted). Yoko was now also called Ono Lennon.

The event took place the day after they'd formed Bag One Productions and that evening they went into the Abbey Road studios to begin a series of experimental recordings.

The idea for the name change came from John. Yoko had already made her feelings plain about the convention of a wife assuming her husband's surname and told him, 'I don't like being known as Mrs Lennon. How would you like it if you had to change your name upon marriage to Mr John Ono?'

When he told her he was to change his middle name officially, Yoko was pleased and commented, 'He hated being compared in any way to Winston Churchill. His incredible idea of having his middle name changed to Ono, to accommodate my request, made me feel good and amazed at the same time.'

On the day of the ceremony John was told that, while he could officially adopt the name Ono, he could not renounce the name Winston. John had come to hate the name Winston and protested, but to no avail, and the ceremony entitled him to legally be reregistered as John Winston Ono Lennon.

De Mesquita was a balding man with glasses and he wore a pinstriped suit for the brief ceremony.

Demonstrations

John aired his political views in interviews and on radio and television. He also supported what he considered worthy causes with cash. In addition, he took part in various demonstrations. On 29 Sunday March 1970 there was a gathering of 8,000 people in Victoria Park, Bethnal Green, assembled for a Campaign for Nuclear Disarmament (CND) rally. John sent a telephone message of support to them. On 11 August 1970 he joined a thousand demonstrators outside the Ulster Office in London, protesting about both the *Oz* trial and the internment of terrorists in Northern Ireland. On Saturday 5 February 1972 he joined 400 protesters outside the New York offices of British Overseas Airways Corporation supporting a boycott on British exports – in protest against British policy in Northern Ireland. He and Yoko sang 'Luck of the Irish' to the demonstrators. On Saturday 22 April 1972 he addressed the Natural Peace Rally in Duffy Square, New York, protesting against the bombing of North Vietnam. John and Yoko led the crowd in singing a chorus of 'Give Peace a Chance'.

Derlin, Bettina

A blonde, buxom *bierfrau* who attended the bar to the rear of the Star Club in Hamburg when the Beatles opened there in April 1962.

During that year the group played at the club for three short seasons and Bettina, known as Betty, was one of John's many girlfriends.

Displayed on the wall of her bar were photographs of the Liverpool bands. Among them were several pictures of John, including one to which a Preludin packet was attached – Bettina had added the slogan 'Prelly King'. (Preludin is a proprietary name for phenmetrazine, a compound related to amphetamine.)

According to the writer Albert Goldman, Bettina was slim when John first met her. He claims that she became pregnant and John forced her to have an illegal abortion, resulting in a glandular condition, which made her swell up like a balloon. Goldman also alleged that she became a prostitute.

Pete Best, who was the Beatles' drummer at the time, described the beehived barmaid as buxom from the outset. During their first appearance at the Star Club the Beatles would gather at her bar, where she would put her chin on the counter between her giant breasts – which she would then wrap around their ears!

She was later to work in the Herbertstrasse. She had a stroke in 1995, which left her partly paralysed.

Diaries, Notes and Sketches

A 1969 film by the Lithuanian-born experimental filmmaker Jonas Mekas. The movie was originally several hours long, but it was later divided into separate parts.

In the film, Mekas conducts a series of interviews with celebrities, intercut with a range of unusual images. Apart from John Lennon, the celebrities included Nico, the Velvet Underground, the Fugs, Allen Ginsberg and Andy Warhol.

Dick Cavett Show, The

An American television talk show on the ABC network, hosted by Dick Cavett. John and Yoko appeared on the programme on the evening of 22 September 1970, together with Dr Arthur Janov. They discussed primal therapy and the new converts were suitably enthusiastic about their experiences of undergoing it – and the effect it had on them.

Almost exactly a year later, on 21 September 1971, the pair were the only guests on the ninety-minute late-night show.

John began discussing his career as a Beatle, the film *A Hard Day's Night* and the group's break-up. He chatted about Yoko's book *Grapefruit*. Then May Pang, who was sitting inside a bag among the audience, was brought up on to the stage. Clips from the John and Yoko films *Fly* and *Erection* were shown, as were the promo films for 'Imagine' and 'Mrs Lennon'. The couple also appealed for Yoko's ex-husband Tony Cox to allow them to visit Yoko's daughter Kyoko. Cox had disappeared with Kyoko following the Lennons' attempts to take legal action to gain custody of the child.

John and Yoko next guested on the show on 4 April 1972. That appearance proved so successful that Cavett invited them to join him again on 11 May 1972, when they performed 'Woman is the Nigger of the World' and Yoko sang 'We're All Water'.

The network was concerned that the black community might be offended by the use of the word 'nigger'. They wanted Cavett to ban it. Cavett recalled the situation in an interview in 1983 and said, 'Every show is run before something called Network Standards and Practices before it's broadcast. I never could find out what their standards were, but I was all too familiar with their practices.'

He managed to persuade them to allow the song to be aired, but had to make a disclaimer: 'At this point in the show, which was taped a week ago, John and Yoko got into something, which ABC feels may develop into, in their words, "a highly controversial issue". It revolves around the song "Woman is the Nigger of the World", and the obvious fact that some members of our black audience will, or may, be offended by the use of that word. In the next segment, John Lennon gives his reasons for writing the song, and for using the word. I permitted this insertion into the show as the only alternative to full deletion by ABC of the segment. Watch it; let us know what you think.'

There was hardly any viewer objection to the song, main objections being relating to the fact that there had to be a disclaimer.

During the appearance John also revealed to the audience that he was under government surveillance and that his telephone was tapped.

On the day after the television show, John and Yoko attended a deportation hearing. Leon Wildes, representing the pair, called on a number of character witnesses. Cavett was one and his statement on the stand read, 'By their constant restless activity, testing themselves, fulfilling themselves in challenging artistic ways, they are an inspiration. Young people who are in danger of falling into apathy seem to be impressed by the example of the Lennons, as people who are concerned with what is valuable and true and the best way of expressing it.'

Cavett appeared in a cameo role in John and Yoko's *Imagine* film.

Dig a Pony

A number written by John and recorded by the Beatles on 30 January 1969. The song had originally been penned by John as two separate songs: 'All I Want Is You' and 'Dig a Pony'. It was first performed on the Apple rooftop on 30 January 1969 and was edited down for its inclusion on the *Let It Be* album. John referred to it as 'another piece of garbage'.

Disney World

The Walt Disney theme park set in Florida. John and May Pang took Julian to spend a day there on Friday 27 December 1974. Later that day John signed the papers that officially dissolved the Beatles' partnership. He was the last member of the group to do so.

Dissenters, The

A name coined by Bill Harry for a loose-knit group of friends (Harry, Stuart Sutcliffe, John Lennon, Rod Murray) at Liverpool College of Art when America's Beat Generation was popular with British students.

Harry felt that instead of being inspired by the poets of San Francisco, creative people in Liverpool should express their feelings about their own environment.

Liverpool had such character, history and individuality in music, verse and paintings that it could convey as romantic an image as America's West Coast. Harry first discussed this with Stuart Sutcliffe and the two intended preparing a book about Liverpool with Sutcliffe's illustrations and Harry's text.

Harry felt that they should form a group and attempt to portray what they felt was wrong with society in whatever form of creative work. Hence the term the Dissenters.

Discussions took place in Ye Cracke and in students' flats. Although the group didn't last very long, their ideals continued and they did achieve the aim of popularising Liverpool: John, beyond all expectations with his music, Stuart, in the short time he lived, with his paintings, and Harry by coining the phrase 'Mersey Beat' and founding a newspaper of that name.

Dizzy Miss Lizzy

A hit penned and performed by Larry Williams when it was originally released on the Specialty label in 1958.

The Beatles first included it in their repertoire in 1960.

The song, sung by John, was the closing track on the *Help!* album. It was included on the American release *Beatles VI*, and was also on the compilation *Rock 'n' Roll Music*. A live version of the number is also to be found on *The Beatles at the Hollywood Bowl* album, issued in 1977.

John performed 'Dizzy Miss Lizzy' at the Toronto Rock 'n' Roll concert and it is included on the *Live Peace in Toronto 1969* album.

Doctor Robert

A song John penned for the *Revolver* album, which contained the first reference to drugs on a Beatles composition. The song concerned a doctor who will prescribe something to pick a person up if they are down. Although the lyrics mention that Dr Robert works for the National Health, which would identify him as being British, the song was said to have been based on a New York doctor, Charles Roberts, who allegedly supplied hallucinogenic drugs to his friends.

John's friend Pete Shotton was to say, 'With "Doctor Robert", John paid sardonic tribute to an actual New York doctor – his real name was Charles Roberts, with an "s" – whose unorthodox prescriptions had made him a great favourite of Andy Warhol's entourage and, indeed, of the Beatles themselves, whenever they passed through town. When John first played me the acetate of "Doctor Robert", he seemed beside himself with glee at the prospect of millions of record buyers innocently singing along.'

Dogs

Cats were John's chief pets over the years. However, when he was a teenager, he had a pet dog called Sally. During his first year at art college, John was having various rows with his Aunt Mimi and would often spend a great deal of time at his mother Julia's house. Mimi became upset by this and in order to punish him got rid of Sally. He was heartbroken when he discovered that the dog was gone.

Doing Lennon

A science-fiction short story by Gregory Benford first published in the April 1975 issue of *Analog* magazine and also included in the anthology *Best Science Fiction of the Year 5*, published by Victor Gollancz in 1976.

In the story a wealthy man, obsessed by the Beatles and Lennon in particular, plans to be put into suspended animation and pretend that he is John Lennon when he is awakened in the 22nd century.

It was a charming story with several twists and a description of a revival of Beatlemania in the far future.

Donovan

A folk singer/songwriter who was born Donovan Leitch in Glasgow, Scotland on May 10 1946. His numerous hits included

'Sunshine Superman,' 'Mellow Yellow' and 'Hurdy Gurdy Man.'

Donovan first met the Beatles when he went to visit Bob Dylan at the Savoy Hotel. He entered the room, said, 'Hello,' and was invited to sit down. Then he realized that John, Paul, George and Ringo were also in the room. They were formally introduced, but didn't converse at the time.

Donovan became a good friend of the Beatles and even contributed the line "Sky of blue, sea of green" to 'Yellow Submarine'. He also joined them at the Maharishi Mahesh Yogi's ashram in India, where he taught John the finger-picking style he used on 'Julia,' 'Sun King' and 'Remember Love.'

In an interview with Scott Muni, Donovan was to claim, 'That finger style that John plays on the White Album is the one that I taught him. Just as I learned many things from the Beatles about song formation, George definitely picked up the style that I taught John. And the finger style that they had not known before led to some new songs.'

John commented, "Donovan is as important and influential as Bob Dylan and we are … listen, the man's a poet."

Don't Be Scared

Track by Yoko on the posthumous album release *Milk and Honey*.

Don't Let Me Down

A song that John originally began to write early in December 1968. He cut a demo and the song was recorded by the Beatles at Apple Studios on Monday 27 and Tuesday 28 January 1969. The group also performed it during their rooftop session on top of the Apple building on Thursday 30 January. John dedicated the song to Yoko.

'Don't Let Me Down' was featured on the B-side of the 'Get Back' single, issued in April 1969. The song, featured John singing a double-tracked lead vocal with Billy Preston featured on electric piano. The song was also included on *The Beatles 1967–1970* double album, issued in April 1973, the *Hey Jude* album in January 1979, the *Past Masters Volume 2* and *The Beatles Box*, issued in December 1980.

Don't Worry Kyoko (Mummy's Only Looking For Her Hand in the Snow)

A number by Yoko, which was issued as the flip side of 'Cold Turkey' in October 1969 and also appeared on the *Fly* album on December 1971. A live version from the *Toronto Rock 'n' Roll Revival* concert was included on the *Plastic Ono Band – Live Peace in Toronto 1969* album, issued in December 1969. A version performed live at the Lyceum Ballroom, London, was included on the *Sometime In New York City* album, issued in September 1972.

Dorinish Island

An island purchased by John on 17 March 1967 for £1,550 and he planned on building a holiday home there. The island consists of nineteen acres and is situated in Clew Bay, County Mayo, in the west of Ireland. Westport Harbour Commissioners formerly owned it.

In 1968 John and Yoko were visiting Ireland and during their trip they viewed Achill Island with Robert Shaw, the late actor. They had dinner at the Amethyst Hotel in Keel. They then visited Dorinish Island in the company of Ronan O'Rahilly, former head of the ship-based pirate radio station, Radio Caroline, who had become a member of the Apple staff. The party stayed at the Great Southern Hotel.

After John had bought the island, it became known as 'Beatle Island'. He was to describe it as 'the most peaceful place on earth'.

In 1983, Yoko said, 'It was a place where we thought we could escape the pressures and spend some undisturbed time together. We often discussed the idea of building a cottage there. It was so beautiful, so tranquil, yet so isolated it seemed a perfect place to get away from it all. But because of what happened our hopes never came to be.'

Although the couple bought Dorinish, they never visited it again following their brief picnic. A year later, in November 1969, a group of hippies led by Sid Rawle were given permission by John to set up a commune on the island. However, although the picturesque island was a miniature paradise during the summer months, it underwent a transformation in winter. Icy-cold weather and harsh gales from the Atlantic Ocean rendered it almost uninhabitable. The commune, unable to grow much of their own food on the sparsely vegetated island, just couldn't survive such chilling winters and left.

After John's death, Michael Cavanaugh, director of Ireland-West Tourism Organisation, sent a telegram to Yoko inviting her to scatter John's ashes on Dorinish Island. In the telegram he stated that the people of Mayo would regard it as a tremendous honour if she agreed. However, John's ashes were eventually scattered in New York's Central Park.

In November 1983, Yoko decided to sell the island with the proceeds going to an Irish orphanage. She commented, 'Putting Dorinish up for sale is an expression of the love we have for Ireland and its people. John would have wished the island to be returned to the Irish. John is still there is spirit. His grandfather was born in Dublin, and John always thought of himself as Irish.

'I have been surveying which charity to donate the proceeds to. Children's orphanages have come to mind, but I do not know which one.

'John was always very concerned about the Irish cause. He thought a lot about the Irish people and always associated sympathetically with their suffering. He was aware of how severe the Irish plight was. For John, buying the island was a bit like Jewish people buying a bit of Jerusalem.'

Yoko sold it in 1985 to the Gavin family in Murrisk, near Westport. They intended to use it for grazing purposes.

Double Fantasy *(album)*

Ironically, this album was to become the launching pad for John's return to music and was his first new album for six years.

After his period of looking after his son Sean, John decided to take the boy on a holiday to Bermuda in the spring of 1979. Yoko remained in New York City to carry on with the supervision of their various business activities.

It was while John was in a club listening to records that the inspiration came to him to take up music again. He was listening to the song 'Rock Lobster' by the B-52's, and suddenly thought that the record sounded just like one of Yoko's.

John said that he thought, 'It's time to get out the old axe and wake the wife up.'

Inspiration arrived almost immediately, and during the next

three weeks he wrote two dozen numbers and had decided on the title of the planned album.

He commented, 'I was walking in the botanical gardens in Bermuda, taking Sean and the nanny and the household, my little kitchen entourage. We all went to lunch and I looked down and there was this flower that said, "Double Fantasy". The flower was an orchid.'

On August 4, John was at New York's Hit Factory studios recording the new album with Jack Douglas, who was to share the producer credits with John and Yoko. A deal had been made with David Geffen, who had launched his own record label, Geffen Records.

The album was subtitled 'A Heart Play'. It was only half-Lennon, as seven of the 14 songs were by him and the others were by Yoko. It was said to be a male-female dialogue of their relationship over the years.

All the songs were intermingled and were not, as was once suggested, one side John and one side Yoko. There were also no co-compositions.

This arrangement led to disappointment for a lot of Lennon fans who had waited eagerly for its release. With half of the tracks by Yoko, they felt as if they were only getting a Lennon EP. Also, with the tracks being intermingled, rumours suggested that many of them played a Lennon track, then lifted the arm over the Yoko track onto the next Lennon one.

John told *Playboy* magazine that the album was, 'about very ordinary things between two people. The lyrics are direct. Simple and straight.'

According to co-producer Jack Douglas, the album was originally going to comprise all of John's new compositions, but it was Yoko who told Douglas that she'd recorded a number of demos with Elephant's Memory and insisted they be used on the album. 'When we started making *Double Fantasy* it was John who was going to make the album, not John and Yoko,' he said.

Musicians who recorded with John included bassist Tony Levin, drummer Andy Newmark, guitarists Hugh McCracken and Earl Slick, pianist George Small and percussionist Arthur Jenkins.

The album was issued in America on Monday 17 November 1980 on Geffen GHS-2001 and in Britain on Friday 21 November on Warner/Geffen Records K99131.

Titles were, Side One: *(Just Like) Starting Over. Kiss Kiss Kiss. Clean-Up Time. Give Me Something. I'm Losing You. I'm Moving On. Beautiful Boy (Darling Boy).* Side Two: *Watching The Wheels. I'm Your Angel. Woman. Beautiful Boys. Dear Yoko. Every Man Has A Woman Who Loves Him. Hard Times Are Over.*

In Britain the *Melody Maker* reviewed the album saying, 'The whole thing positively reeks of an indulgent sterility. It's a godawful yawn!'

Double Fantasy was voted Album Of The Year at the 1981 Grammy Awards in Los Angeles on Wednesday, February 24. Yoko collected the award to a standing ovation. In Canada it received the Juno Award, the Canadian equivalent of a Grammy.

In New York in 1998 the collectors shop *Moment In Time* announced they had the copy of *Double Fantasy* for sale that John had signed for Mark Chapman. It would cost any prospective buyer $1m. John had signed the sleeve 'John Lennon 1980' in blue ink. A fan, Philip Michael, found the album in a large flowerpot outside the Dakota after John had been shot. He handed it to the police for them to check the fingerprints. After Chapman had been jailed, the police returned the album to Michael. He kept it locked away in a vault for 18 years before deciding to auction it.

Inside the sleeve is the police number it was given and Chapman's dusted fingerprints, along with the signature of the police detective who catalogued the evidence.

Double Fantasy (video shoot)

The last known footage of John performing was taken during the *Double Fantasy* album sessions on Tuesday 19 August 1980. A mystery has surrounded this filming, of which only clips lasting for several seconds have been seen down the years in various documentaries. A researcher, Mike Corrothers, spent a great deal of time trying to discover what happened to the proposed music videos that were filmed that night at the Hit Factory in New York. The footage was directed by Jay Dubin and produced by John and Yoko.

Corrothers was actually able to track down Dubin by phone in Dublin in 1997. Dubin told him that he'd once been approached by the producer Jack Douglas to direct the film of a show Douglas had intended filming in Brazil. It never came off, but Douglas must have recommended him to John because Lennon phoned Dubin to commission him to film the shoot at the Hit Factory. When Corrothers asked Dubin what had happened to the videotapes, he was told, 'We turned them over to Yoko.' Apparently two guards came up to him and took the tapes personally.

Douglas, Jack

Co-producer of the *Double Fantasy* album.

Douglas was a producer/engineer noted for his work with Aerosmith and Cheap Trick. He'd also worked on the *Imagine* album. The album had been recorded at Tittenhurst Park, some of it on eight-track, some on two-track, and the tapes were brought to the Hit Factory in New York, where Douglas worked under Roy Cicala. Douglas was busy editing when John came into the room and said, 'How are you doing?' They'd first met earlier that day. He said, 'OK, OK.'

John started to smoke and Douglas said, 'I've been to Liverpool.' John said, 'Why the hell would you have been to Liverpool?' Then Douglas told him the story of how, as a young musician, he stowed away on a boat to Liverpool with a friend. They had been caught and the story had made the newspapers. John recalled reading the story and was amused by it. He asked Douglas what he was doing and then took him to a party. They continued their friendship during the 1970s and Douglas stayed with John in Los Angeles during the so-called 'lost weekend' while he was out there recording Alice Cooper.

Douglas recalled, 'We had just finished mixing a new tune for Yoko. In 1968 I was part of the smoke-dope, take-acid, riot-in-the-street-and-go-mad generation, and I was listening to that "White" album and I said, "God, what I really wanna do is produce records. That's really what I want and there's probably nothing more that I'd want to do than produce the Beatles, produce John Lennon." Then after a lot of hard work, being a janitor in the studio and finally becoming an engineer, then finally working with John in 1971, there was a communication, almost the kind of communication that a fan feels when he listens to a Beatles record. That was there when I met him.'

He said that it was Yoko Ono who contacted him first and

then John called him from Bermuda. When he asked John what the music was going to be like, John said, 'Oh, the same old commercial crap.' Douglas said that John then 'sent me a cassette that was really primitive, just his voice and guitar. I get better cassettes from groups out of Boise, Idaho. But it was beautiful. I listen to it every once in a while. It's a real prize.'

John and Yoko met with him on 31 July to ask him to co-produce *Double Fantasy* with him. Douglas had been the engineer on some of John and Yoko's recordings during the 1970s. He was reluctant at first as he felt he needed to be sole producer, but eventually agreed to share producing honours with them.

The initial meeting was very secretive. Douglas was told, 'Don't say anything to anyone – just go to 34th Street, get on a seaplane and come out.' He was flown to Glen Cove and landed on the beach there. The Lennons had a big house there and Yoko handed him an envelope with the words 'for Jack's eyes only' and said, 'John is going to call you in a few minutes. But I just want to tell you: he's going to ask you to do a record.'

Yoko then told him, 'But I'm going to have a few songs on it and John doesn't know yet.' She instructed him, 'You can't tell him.' Jack opened the envelope and there was a single cassette from John. Yoko then handed him a stack of her own songs. She'd been to the Record Plant studios with Elephant's Memory and cut a stack of dozens of songs on tape reels.

When John called, he told Douglas, 'I don't really think I have that much stuff, you know.' However, he decided to go ahead with the album and Douglas began to pick the musicians. He selected Hugh McCracken, because he'd played for John before, as had Andy Newmark. He also picked Earl Slick and asked the musicians to meet him at the corner of 72nd and Central Park West. When they met they looked at the Dakota Building and realised who they were going to record with.

John answered the door and invited them in and they began to rehearse. When John played 'Starting Over' to Douglas, Douglas said it had to be the first single and it was also the first number they recorded.

The sessions had to be very secretive because of John's uncertainty. He hadn't performed or recorded for such a long time and felt insecure. Douglas said, 'He thought he was too old – he just couldn't write, he couldn't sing, he couldn't play.'

Douglas contacted members of Cheap Trick because they were hot at the time and he thought they'd give John even more credibility. They were delighted and arrived to cut some tracks. John loved their backing him on 'Losing You' and told Douglas, 'Jack, these guys are great.'

Later, Yoko came up to Douglas and said, 'Who are these guys?' She then began to argue with him and said, again, 'Who are these guys? And why should they have a free ride on John's coat tails?'

Douglas explained, 'No, Yoko, it's not like that. If anything, because of where they're at in their career right now, it'll make John seem even hipper that he would know to have these guys come and work with him. It's, like, people will know that that was a good choice. I mean, listen to these tracks – they sound great.'

Yoko was furious and ensured that the tracks weren't used. Douglas said that John didn't want to argue with her over it.

Douglas then had to copy the Cheap Trick version with the studio band. He said, 'We played the other track, the Cheap Trick track, in their headphones and they played along with it. And that's how I recorded it.'

Douglas also revealed that Paul McCartney phoned the studio while they were recording. He'd heard from John that he and Paul were going to get together and write some material – but Yoko wouldn't allow the call to be put through to John and the opportunity was lost.

When he finished recording the *Double Fantasy* album, Douglas began recording with an RCA act and then received a call from John saying he wanted to go into the studio again and start work. He was also writing material for Ringo's album.

After some recording, John was leaving the studio and said to Douglas, 'I'll see you in the morning at 9 a.m.' Then 45 minutes later Douglas's wife came rushing in to tell him John had been shot.

Of John's death, he said, 'It was a disaster for me. Three or four days after it happened, Yoko and I went back into the studio and put together some collages with John's voice and music. It was almost like a funeral service. We teetered back and forth between hysteria and concentration. We did that for two nights. That seemed to provide some kind of therapy or release.'

Douglas was then to encounter great difficulties with Yoko. He waited patiently for three years for his royalties, but nothing was forthcoming. He then contacted Yoko to ask her when he was to receive some of the royalties and said, 'I got a nasty letter. Almost like "Fuck you, you're not getting anything." '

He also revealed, 'All kinds of nasty business went down after that, you know, being followed and having people offered money to say bad things about me.'

He was to say that all his gold and platinum records ended up in one of Yoko's closets.

With his requests for his promised share of royalties, Douglas found that Yoko was going to take him to court. He asked her not to go to court, but she went ahead and a jury trial took place.

Yoko brought on witnesses to denigrate Douglas. Jann Wenner, publisher of *Rolling Stone* magazine, took the stand and said that Douglas was a nobody and no one had heard of him. Wenner then had egg on his face when he was asked how many times Douglas had been mentioned in *Rolling Stone* magazine – which was a considerable amount.

In 1984 the verdict was announced on the case for royalties due. Jack Douglas was awarded $2,524,809, plus three years' interest due to him for royalties from *Double Fantasy*. He was to receive $75,000 plus 4 per cent of the gross receipts from the first 500,000 copies of *Double Fantasy* sold and 5 per cent of the gross over that number. Yoko claimed that she had orally agreed to pay 3 per cent and had signed the contract in excessive haste. She said the terms were obtained in fraud. She countersued Douglas for $750,000 advances and $225,000 in punitive damages. The jury found in Douglas's favour and added that Yoko must also pay a percentage of earnings on *Milk And Honey*.

A relieved Douglas commented, 'To have that kind of onus on you, that you were the guy who tried to defraud John Lennon, was a real horror. I feel a tremendous pressure was lifted off me.'

Douglas, Mike

American chat show host who invited John and Yoko to co-host a week of his shows in February 1972. He was to say, 'It was probably the most memorable week I did in all my twenty-something years on the air.'

Dovedale Road Primary School

Situated in Dovedale Road, Liverpool 18, three miles from Mendips, Dovedale Primary was the school John's Aunt Mimi picked for her nephew to attend. Some reports have hinted that he was expelled from his previous primary school, Mosspits Lane Infants' School, for bad behaviour, and there is some evidence to show that he proved unruly at the time. However, when he attended Mosspits he was living at Newcastle Road and it was the closest school to the Stanley household. When he moved in with his Aunt Mimi, Dovedale Road Primary was much closer to their home.

John was enrolled at his new infants' school on 6 May 1946. At a parents' meeting the headmaster told Mimi, 'There's no need to worry about him. He's as sharp as a needle. But he won't do anything he doesn't want to do.'

John admitted to being reasonably well behaved at Dovedale in comparison with his rebellious attitude at Quarry Bank School. He said, 'I'd been honest at Dovedale, if nothing else, always owning up. But I began to realise that I was foolish.'

However, he was also later to confess that at Dovedale he had a gang who indulged in shoplifting and 'pulling girls' knickers down'. He also said that the parents and even the teachers hated him.

Of other boys who tried to challenge him, he commented, 'I used to beat them up if they were small enough but I'd use long words and confuse them if they were bigger. What mattered was that I stayed in charge.'

Ivan Vaughan was among the friends he made at the school and another pupil at the time was Jimmy Tarbuck, who became a popular comedian. Tarbuck said that even when John was a child he was an oddball. Peter Harrison, one of George Harrison's elder brothers, was also in the same class as John. George himself attended Dovedale, but was three years behind John. In 1948 John transferred to the Junior Boys' School at Dovedale and remained there until his 11-plus examination in 1952.

From 1950–1952 John's teacher at Dovedale was Fred Bolt. Mr Bolt would take his pupils on an annual summer holiday to the Isle of Man. When he died on Monday 24 January 2000, one of his photographs was published in the *Daily Mail*. It showed

John, along with Jimmy Tarbuck and other youngsters from his class, playing on the beach at Port Erin.

Do You Want to Dance?

A million-selling hit in 1958 for Bobby Freeman, a former doo-wop singer from San Francisco, who also wrote the song. John recorded in for his *Rock 'n' Roll* album in October 1974 and the LP was issued in February 1975. An unauthorised mail-order version of tracks from the album had been issued by the publisher Morris Levy under the title *Roots* at the same time. The song was 2 minutes 53 seconds long on *Rock 'n' Roll* and 2:56 on *Roots*. It was also included on the 73-track, four-CD, boxed set *Lennon* issued on 30 October 1990 to commemorate what would have been John's fiftieth birthday.

John tried to introduce a reggae rhythm to the song, which had been covered by numerous other artists including Barbra Streisand, the Beach Boys and Cliff Richard.

Do You Want To Know A Secret?

John claimed that the inspiration for this number came from the memory of his mother singing a song for him from a Walt Disney film. The film is likely to have been *Snow White And The Seven Dwarfs*. In an early scene, when Snow White is working as a kitchen maid in the castle, she begins to sing to some doves, 'Wanna know a secret? Promise not to tell? We are standing by a wishing well.' This song was called 'Wishing Well' and was penned by Larry Morey and Frank Churchill.

John wrote 'Do You Want To Know A Secret?' at the flat at 36 Faulkner Street that Brian Epstein had loaned to him and Cynthia soon after they were married

He decided to give the song to George Harrison and so provide him with his first solo vocal with the Beatles. However, in the late 70s he rather ungenerously remarked, 'I thought it would be a good vehicle for him because it only had three notes, and he wasn't the best singer in the world.'

The recording was featured on the *Please Please Me* album (PCS 3042) and was also included on the 'Twist And Shout' EP, which rose to No 2 in the singles chart in Britain.

Vee Jay issued it in the US as the B side of *Thank You Girl* in 1964, when it reached No 2 and was eleven weeks in the chart.

Vee Jay released it again on August 10 1964, but it failed to chart.

Brian Epstein used the Lennon/McCartney catalogue to provide hits for other acts in his stable, and also to entice other acts to sign with him. He offered Shane Fenton 'Do You Want To Know A Secret?' as an incentive for Fenton to sign to him, but he wouldn't. Eventually, the number was given to Billy J. Kramer and the Dakotas.

John gave Billy the demo of the number he had made sitting on a toilet while playing an acoustic guitar. At the end of the demo is the sound of the toilet flushing.

Billy and the Dakotas had a No. 2 chart single in Britain when it was issued on Parlophone R 5023 on 26 April 1963. Kramer's version was also issued in the United States on 10 June on Liberty 55586.

Dragon

The name of a cross-Channel ferry. At Southampton docks John and Yoko had intended getting married on a ferry to France. John's full-time driver at the time was Les Anthony and he said that during a visit to his Aunt Mimi in Poole, Dorset, John asked him to see if they could get married that very day on a cross-Channel ferry. Anthony went to Southampton and talked to the skipper of the Dragon, who told them that marriages could no longer be performed aboard ferries. He told Anthony that the couple could get married on a Cunard ocean liner and that a round-the-world cruise was leaving that very day. Anthony immediately phoned John, but he had other ideas. They were also unable to take the ferry to Paris because Yoko had a passport problem.

Dream Is Over, The

A ballet choreographed by Christopher Bruce, which was originally premiered on London Weekend Television's arts programme the South Bank Show on 3 November 1986. It was performed by the Cullberg ballet of New York City and produced and directed by Daniel Wiles.

The ballet was based on John's 1970 album John Lennon/Plastic Ono Band and the South Bank Show presented a performance of the ballet, a 1968 interview with John and some newly discovered archival film.

During a performance of 'Well Well Well' the male dancers were dressed in red collarless jackets and were soothed by female dancers dressed in Japanese costumes. Other pieces featured in the ballet were performed to the music of 'Mother', 'Working Class Hero', 'I Found Out', 'Look At Me', 'God', 'Love', 'My Mummy's Dead', 'Imagine' and 'Instant Karma'.

The ballet received its world premiere on 24 April 1987 at Sadler's Wells in London.

Dreams

John's dreams included ones about weather, position, power, Beatles recording sessions and songwriting. Some dreams he said had been recurring, such as the one in which thousands of half-crown (12 pence) coins came falling around him. Another was of finding lots of money in old houses, which he'd ram into his pocket and into sacks, but he still couldn't carry away as much as he wanted. These dreams faded as he became famous.

In an interview with Alan Smith of the *New Musical Express* he revealed that he'd never had a nightmare in his life. He said, 'Some of my most vivid dreams were about me being on a plane, flying over a certain part of Liverpool. It was when I was at school. The plane used to fly over time and time again, all the while going higher and higher. There wasn't anything special about the plane, and I don't really remember anything about any other passengers. It was just the being up there. For a long time I didn't understand why I had this dream. It didn't seem to make any sense. Then it dawned on me. It was probably a subconscious urge to get above people, or out of a rut, or something. I used to mess around at school but I must have had ambition without realising it. Anyway, I got out of my rut; and I try not to fly any more!'

Driving

John first learned to drive at the age of 24. He took his driving test on 15 February 1965 at Weybridge, Surrey, after only seven hours of tuition. His driving instructor Paul Wilson commented, 'He was one of the most apt pupils I have had to teach in my thirty years' experience of driving instruction. He has done very well in such a short time. He has been very quick.'

After passing his test, he bought a black Mini Cooper, a black

Rolls-Royce and a black Ferrari. He sold the Ferrari soon after-wards and it was with the Rolls-Royce that he became mainly associated. He had one Rolls painted in psychedelic patterns and in 1970 paid £50,000 for the Rolls-Royce Phantom V that had been built specially for the Beatles in 1965.

He later donated the hand-painted Phantom to the Smithsonian Institution in Washington, DC. This was the car that was said to have inspired *Magical Mystery Tour*.

In 1982 Britain's glossy Sunday magazines displayed a special advertisement for Rolls-Royce – presenting a list of distin-guished past owners, including John and Brian Epstein. Every person mentioned in the list was dead.

Despite having passed his test, John preferred to leave the wheel in the capable hands of others and had a number of chauf-feurs, including Bill Corbett and Les Anthony. When John decided to handle a hired Austin Mini on a driving holiday in Scotland with Yoko, Julian and Kyoko he lost control of the vehicle. Everyone was taken to hospital and the car was a write-off. At Yoko's behest, John bought the damaged car and set it in a concrete plinth on the grounds of Tittenhurst Park as a piece of contemporary art.

After John's death, several of the cars he had previously owned began to attract buyers at various auctions, simply for the fact that he had once possessed them. For example, John's 1972 Chrysler station wagon, which originally sold at auction in 1984 for £7,700, was resold at a Sotheby's New York auction in June 1996 for $20,700. In 1986 there was some controversy regarding one of his cars. Mary Wilson of the Supremes had bought a white custom-built Mercedes from George Harrison for a five-figure sum in 1981. George had bought the car some years previously from John Lennon. As it was slightly damaged, Wilson put it into a garage for repair and storage and that was the last she saw of it – until it surfaced at a Sotheby's auction of rock memorabilia in London in 1985. She stopped the sale and a judge awarded her temporary custody pending a hearing to determine true ownership.

Drugs

Alcohol was John's first experience of a mind-altering substance. His first real soft-drug experience occurred in the Gambier

Terrace flat when the poet Royston Ellis was invited to stay for a few days. Ellis broke open a Vicks inhaler and showed John and other members of the Beatles the Benzedrine strips inside, which could be chewed and, being an amphetamine, produced the effect of stimulation.

John next became a user of Preludin (phenmetrazine, related to amphetamines but milder) while in Hamburg, was introduced to marijuana by Bob Dylan in America and was later to take more than 1,000 LSD trips.

Lots of people have assumed that particular songs of John's have been references to drugs. Although there was a drug-induced influence on some songs, there have been many misunderstandings. 'Lucy In the Sky With Diamonds' was not a clever reference to LSD, as many critics assumed. John always denied it, saying 'And once again, folks, this was Julian's title. It was nothing to do with LSD.' He also had to deny that the reference to 'Henry the Horse' in 'Being for the Benefit of Mr Kite' was about heroin. Of 'Happiness Is a Warm Gun', he pointed out, 'They all said it was about drugs, but it was more about rock 'n' roll than drugs. It's sort of a history of rock 'n' roll. The title came from an American gun magazine. I don't know why people said it was about the needle in heroin. I've only seen somebody do something with a needle once and I don't like to see it at all.'

'In *A Hard Day's Night* I was on pills – bigger drugs than pot. I started on pills when I was fifteen. The only way to survive in Hamburg for eight hours a night was to take polls. The waiters gave you pills and drink.'

In early January 1969 John and Yoko turned to heroin for the first time at a friend's flat – when he and Yoko were being hideously treated by friends and the British media. He said 'We took H because of what the Beatles and others were doing to us.' He also commented, 'Heroin? It wasn't too much fun. I never injected it or anything. We sniffed a little when we were in real pain. We were getting so much pain that we had to do something about it.'

When they were addicted to heroin the couple were booked into the London Clinic for four days for detoxification. They went on to methadone – a synthetic drug used in the treatment of addiction to heroin and other narcotics.

John was to say, 'I've always needed a drug to survive; the

others, too, but I always had more. I always took more pills, more of everything, because I'm crazy probably. I must have had a thousand trips. I used to just eat it all the time.'

In an interview on *CBC Weekend*, a television show in Toronto on 20 December 1969, John warned teenagers to stay away from drugs. He said that the time he was on drugs was when he had no hope. He said that when a person was on drugs it was harder to find hope.

John stopped taking drugs in order to become a father and Dr Hong, his acupuncturist, instructed him to take no more drugs or alcohol. The postmortem on John's body showed no signs of drugs in his system.

Dunbar, John

The man who is credited with introducing John to Yoko for the first time. This took place on 9 November 1966, the day before the opening of Yoko's exhibition *Unfinished Paintings and Objects* at the Indica Gallery.

Some years later, Dunbar was alleged to have said that if he had set out to destroy John, he couldn't have done better than by introducing him to Yoko.

The Indica Gallery and Bookshop in Mason's Ward, London was run by Dunbar, Peter Asher and (Barry) Miles. Indica had been partly financed by Dunbar's former school chum, Asher, and Paul McCartney had also invested £5,000 in the venture.

Dunbar enticed John along to the private viewing by telling him that a 'happening' was going to take place. John thought that he was referring to some sort of orgy.

Dunbar had been married to the singer Marianne Faithfull, but she left him when she became involved with the Rolling Stones. He now lived with his parents in Bentinck Street and during that summer John would arrive at the house in his Rolls Royce to pick Dunbar up and the pair would take LSD together.

They also spent a great deal of time at the Weybridge House, Kenwood, indulging in scores of LSD trips while Cynthia was abroad on holiday with Julian.

It was while John and Dunbar were on one of their acid trips at Weybridge that they saw a news item on the television about the 14 Hour Technicolor Dream party at the Alexandra Palace on 29 April 1967. John immediately called his driver and they were driven there. John was filmed at the event. Yoko Ono was one of the 41 performers. The two of then were then seen on BBC 2's *Man Alive* documentary about the event, screened on 17 May.

DuPont, Maurice

To give him his full title, Maurice DuPont, Agent Provocateur du Jour, R.E.T. – a fictional character created by John in the 70s. John was amused by his French spy character and would make tapes of stories concerning his adventures, which he sent to friends.

Dyansen Gallery

Situated at 122 Spring Street, SoHo, New York, a gallery that exhibited a number of drawings and lithographs by John during April 1986. Each lithograph had John's name embossed on it, with Yoko's countersignature and was also marked with a red seal with Japanese characters that John had made for himself in the 70s.

Dykins, Jacqueline Gertrude

One of John's half-sisters, who was born in Liverpool on 26 October 1949. Jacqui, who was a premature baby, was the second daughter of Julia Lennon and John Dykins.

When John resumed regular contact with his mother and stayed overnight at their house, he slept in Jacqui's bedroom, while Jacqui moved in with her sister Julia.

Jacqui attended Gateacre Comprehensive and later became an apprentice hairdresser. She lived for a while with Julia, and then moved in with her aunt Mimi in Poole. She then got a flat of her own before moving on to London to become a hairdresser.

Jacqui started using heroin in 1975 and was soon spending £20 per day on the habit. She said she was so far gone as a junkie that she wouldn't listen to John or other members of her family. She said, 'The family came round to my flat and tried to encourage me to stop, but I thought I knew better.'

She was still fighting her addiction after John's murder and, in desperation, contacted Yoko for help. 'I'm not close to Yoko but she did give me financial help. I have never asked for anything else,' she said. She began visiting a psychiatrist and became a registered addict. She left Liverpool and moved to a flat in a London suburb, working as a shop assistant.

In 1992, talking about the new life she has made for herself, she said, 'I don't want people to know. I can see a change physically come over their faces if they know John was my brother. They expect me to be very rich or something special – and I'm not.'

In 1995 she returned to Liverpool, fell in love with a student and settled down with her 11-year-old son John.

Dykins, John

John Dykins, who was born in 1918, was the man who lived with John's mother Julia, who bore him two daughters. Details of when the couple first met are disputed.

The writer Ray Coleman claims Dykins and Julia first began going out together in 1942, while the couple's daughter Julia claims they met shortly after the war at a café in Penny Lane where Julia worked in shifts as a waitress. The writer Albert Goldman claims they met in 1944 when Julia was dating a soldier, Taffy Williams, and they made up a foursome with Dykins and a girl called Ann Stout.

Julia had a baby to Williams, which was put up for adoption. She dropped Williams, Dykins dropped his regular girlfriend and the two began going out together, then moved into a one-room flat.

Julia also had her young son John living with them, much to the annoyance of her sister Mimi, who considered that Julia was living in sin. Julia never did marry Dykins – her husband never divorced her – but she wore his ring and called herself Mrs Dykins. Their two children didn't know their parents weren't married until after Dykins' death.

Mimi disapproved of the relationship so much, complaining that Julia was an unfit mother, that she brought a social worker around to the flat and demanded John be taken away from Julia and given to her. The social worker pointed out that a son should remain with his mother. However, when it was discovered that there was no bed for John and that he actually slept in the double bed with the couple it was decided that he had to move in with his Aunt Mimi until the couple found a bigger flat. They never did.

Their first daughter, Julia, was born in March 1947 and they moved in with Julia's father in Newcastle Road. When he died in 1949 they had to move out and as Julia was pregnant with their second daughter, Jacqui, they were given a council flat at 1 Blomfield Road in the Springwood Estate in Garston, fairly close to where John lived with Mimi.

Dykins was a tall, swarthy man with a moustache who was working as a wine steward at the Adelphi Hotel when he first met Julia. He worked long hours and moved to various different hotels, restaurants and pubs, mainly in the Liverpool area. At one time he ran the Bear's Paw public house, another time he worked at the Odd Spot Club.

John nicknamed Dykins, who was called Bobby by his wife, children and friends, 'Twitchy'. Eddie Porter, a colleague of Dykins, commented, 'John called him "Twitchy" because of a habit he had. He would press his nose back because it was badly scarred and needed a new bridge built.'

From the age of fifteen John began visiting Julia and Bobby in the Blomfield Road house. John's group the Quarry Men also used to rehearse there at times. Paul McCartney was to comment, 'Bobby was a good bloke and always seemed to enjoy seeing John. But I do know John had this sort of stepfather thing about him. He liked him all right but he couldn't associate him with his dad.'

On 15 July 1958 John was at the Blomfield Road house with Bobby while Julia went to visit Mimi. Later that evening a policeman knocked on the door and informed them that Julia had been killed in an accident. The two took a taxi to Sefton General Hospital. Dykins went to look at Julia's body while John waited in the lobby. When Dykins emerged he broke down and cried in John's arms.

Dykins couldn't cope with Julia's death and, since he also worked such long and unsociable hours that it would have proved difficult to bring up his daughters, Julia and Jacqui went to live with their Aunt Harriet. Bobby couldn't bear to remain alone in Blomfield Road and moved out a few weeks later. He lived only half a mile away from the girls and they visited each other frequently.

After a time Dykins met and married a woman called Rhona. Then, in 1966, another tragedy occurred. Bobby and Rhona had been visiting friends in Ruthin, North Wales, and drove back to Liverpool one rainy night. When they entered Penny Lane their car skidded and crashed into a lamppost. Rhona sustained minor injuries, but Bobby was taken to Sefton General Hospital, where he later died from his injuries. His daughter says the accident occurred in February, but Albert Goldman cites 1 June 1966 as the date.

Dylan, Bob

One of the major music figures of the 1960s. The singer/songwriter was born Robert Allen Zimmerman in Duluth, Minnesota, on 24 May 1941.

Dylan's influence was most obvious on John, more so than on the other Beatles – he had what was called his 'Dylan period' and even wore a Huck Finn cap similar to Dylan's. John turned to introspective lyrics after listening to Dylan and the influence is most apparent in 'I'll Cry Instead', 'I'm A Loser' and 'Norwegian Wood'. John was to say, 'I remember the early meetings with Dylan – he was always saying, "Listen to the words, man," and I said, "I can't be bothered. I listen to the sound of it, the overall sound." '

Commenting on the Beatles, Dylan said, 'They were doing things nobody was doing. Their chords were outrageous, and their harmonies made it all valid. I knew they were pointing to the direction where music had to go.'

In 1965, John told the journalist Chris Hutchins: 'We began admiring him during our visit to Paris in January of last year when we cadged a Dylan LP off a DJ who came to interview us. Paul had heard of him before but until we played that record, his name did not really mean anything to us. We went potty over the LP – I think it was *Freewheelin'* – and tried to get more of his records. Then when we were in New York during the American tour last summer somebody said, "Do you want to meet Dylan?" and we said, "Sure, if he wants to meet us." So he came up to the hotel room and we did nothing but laugh all night. He kept answering the phone saying, "This is Beatlemania here."

'It was ridiculous. He's got the same sense of humour as we have, and our tastes in music, though not the same, cross somewhere – you can tell that if you listen to his latest single, "Subterranean Blues".'

Incidentally, it was George Harrison who bought the copy of *Freewheelin'*.

Their meeting in the hotel room in which they were laughing all night was their first introduction to marijuana. On Friday 28 August 1964 at the Delmonico Hotel in New York, Al Aronowitz, a writer for the *Saturday Evening Post*, along with Dylan's road manager Victor Mamoudas, arrived with Dylan to meet the Beatles. They were brought into a room and introduced to Brian Epstein, Neil Aspinall, Mal Evans and the Beatles.

Asked what they'd like to drink, Dylan asked for cheap wine. Epstein said there was only champagne, French wines, Scotch and Coke, and Dylan said he'd drink whatever was available.

Dylan then suggested they smoke some marijuana. When they revealed they'd never smoked it before, Dylan was puzzled. He said, 'But what about your song, the one about getting high?'

They didn't know what he meant.

Dylan then sang it for them: '... and when I touch you I get high, I get high, I get high ...'.

John had to tell him that he'd been mistaken, that the words from 'I Want To Hold Your Hand' were 'I can't hide'.

Dylan then decided to induct them into the rituals of smoking pot and they spent half an hour preparing the suite, bolting the doors, getting towels from the bathroom to plug up gaps beneath the doors, closing the blinds and drawing the curtains. Dylan rolled the first joint and told them how to smoke it. He passed it to John, who took it, but didn't want to try it and passed it on to Ringo, calling him 'my royal taster'. Ringo finished the joint while Dylan rolled several others and they all smoked into the early hours.

In 1964 when Dylan was staying at the Savoy in London, John went to see him there late one night. At the time Dylan had been criticised in the media for staying at a plush hotel. John said, 'What's wrong with staying at the Savoy? Does starving in a garret make his points any more valid? They say that to be ethnic as a folker you must also be poor and act the part. Absolute rubbish! Especially when you consider that the people he's sometimes having a go at – politicians especially – are probably twice as well off, anyway. If you've got a lot to say, like Dylan has, and if you want to make it heard, you've just got to elevate yourself and make yourself famous so people will listen.

Earning a fortune's nothing to do with that side of it, but if he happens to do that as well good luck to him.'

On Friday 27 May 1966 Dylan and Lennon drove in John's limousine from his house in Weybridge to Dylan's hotel. This was filmed and used in the documentary *Eat the Document*.

John invited Dylan to dinner at Weybridge one evening. The two wrote a song together on a tape recorder. John said, 'We played a few records and talked. He's an interesting bloke with some good ideas. We swapped addresses and said we'd exchange ideas for songs, but it never happened. He said he sent me things, but he got the address wrong and it never arrived. Maybe that's why we get on well – we're both pretty disorganised blokes.'

Dylan was so impressed with John's 22-room house that as soon as he returned to America he bought a 31-room house.

John believed that Dylan's 'Fourth Time Around' was a take-off of Norwegian Wood and, when Dylan played it for him in London, John said he didn't like it. He admitted later that he'd been paranoid and, on reflection, thought the number was great.

John was said to have used 'Masters of War' as the inspiration for 'Working Class Hero' and in 'Yer Blues'. John wrote, 'Feel suicidal, just like Dylan's Mr Jones', referring to a character in 'Subterranean Homesick Blues', and he also mentioned Dylan in his number 'God'. When John produced an album for Harry Nilsson, he included a new arrangement of 'Subterranean Homesick Blues'. The Beatles were to perform five Dylan songs during their *Let It Be* sessions.

Despite the initial interest Dylan and Lennon had in each other, it was George Harrison who was to become most associated with the American artist. John asked him to appear on his 'Cold Turkey' single, but Dylan turned him down. On George Harrison's album *All Things Must Pass* there was the number 'I'll Have You Anytime', which was written by George and Dylan at Dylan's home in Woodstock; and 'If Not For You' was a number Dylan had written in 1968. Dylan appeared on George's *Concert for Bangladesh* and is featured on the album of the same name; and he later teamed up with George when George formed the Traveling Wilburys.

Eamonn Andrews Show, The

A programme hosted by the popular chat show host, the Irish-born Eamonn Andrews. John and Yoko appeared on this Thames Television production on Thursday 3 April 1969 when the show was broadcast from the fashionable Café Royal rather than its usual studio location. It was aired between 11 and 11.45 p.m. and other guests included Rolf Harris, Jack Benny, Yehudi Menuhin and the singer Gaynor Jones.

John and Yoko were interviewed by Andrews for seventeen minutes – and had appeared on another of his shows, *Today*, only a few days previously.

The Beatles had appeared on *The Eamonn Andrews Show* on 11 April 1965 when ABC TV produced the programme.

Eat the Document

A film of Bob Dylan's European tour of 1966, directed by DA Pennebaker, which includes a scene in which John and Dylan are pictured together. John makes some comments about Dylan in a strong Liverpool accent. John filmed the sequence on Friday 27 May 1966. They were being driven in John's limousine from Kenwood to Dylan's hotel and the filming in the back of the car lasted for twenty minutes. This sequence was edited down to three minutes in the finished film.

The ABC network in America had financed the movie, but they were unhappy with the finished result and didn't televise it.

That evening John and George Harrison attended Dylan's appearance with the Hawks (later to be known as the Band) at the Royal Albert Hall, where hecklers booed the use of electric instruments in Dylan's act.

Eat the Document was edited down to a length of 54 minutes and premiered in New York on 8 February 1967, although it was not generally released until 1972.

Echoes of Lennon

An instrumental album of John Lennon compositions by Morgan Fisher, issued by Global Pacific records in 1993. Yoko gave her blessing to the album and contributed her voice to the track 'Love'. Some of the receipts from the sale of the CD were donated to the Spirit Foundation.

Eight Days a Week

A song written by John and Paul, the title based on a comment Ringo made. They recorded it on 6 October 1964 for the *Beatles For Sale* album. John said, 'I think we wrote this when we were trying to write the title song for *Help!*. Because at one time they thought of calling the film *Eight Arms To Hold You* or something.' John didn't consider it a good song, although it is interesting to consider that it is one of the first songs to have a fade-in at the beginning rather than a fade-out at the end. It was considered as a potential Beatles single until John came up with 'I Feel Fine'.

Eleanor Rigby

A song generally attributed to Paul because he has detailed so much of the genesis of the song and how he wrote it. Yet John was to tell *Hit Parader* magazine that both of them wrote it, and 'I wrote a good lot of the lyrics, about 70 per cent.' He also told a *Playboy* interviewer, 'The first verse was his and the rest are basically mine.'

However, John was probably wrong in this instance. Paul first began writing the number in Wimpole Street and finished it in Cavendish Avenue. Paul's provenance of the number is so detailed that it is unlikely that John participated as much as he claimed, if at all. Even John's close friend Pete Shotton was to say, 'Though John was to take credit, in one of his last interviews, for most of the lyrics, my own recollection is that "Eleanor Rigby" was one Lennon and McCartney classic in which John's contribution was virtually nil.'

John also described Ray Charles's version of the number as 'fantastic'.

Electric Light Orchestra

Generally known as ELO, a band conceived by Roy Wood of the Move in 1970. Following their debut album in 1971 he lost interest, but the band continued under the leadership of Jeff Lynne and became hugely successful. Their strong orchestral melodies are reminiscent of the Beatles in their *Sergeant Pepper* period.

The group paid tribute to John during their American tour in the autumn of 1981 by performing 'Across the Universe' and 'A Day in the Life'.

John once called the band 'the Sons of the Beatles'.

Elephant's Memory

A New York band whose first claim to fame came when they had three tracks on the *Midnight Cowboy* film soundtrack, which resulted in their being awarded a Gold Disc. They'd been appearing at Max's Kansas City, on a regular basis and were building up a following.

John and Yoko had been looking for a band to back them on projects, but decided against reforming the Plastic Ono Band. Yoko commented, 'Rather than assemble the same musicians again, we decided to work with some people from the streets, used to performing together, part of the city. We had heard about this band called Elephant's Memory.'

It was, in fact, Jerry Rubin, an American radical who had the ear of the Lennons, who recommended the group.

The drummer, Rick Franks, was to comment, 'Elephant's Memory had two or three albums out and we had a good group of rockers together, but because nothing much was happening for us, we were sort of demoralised by this time. Then we got a note from Jerry Rubin telling me to call him at the Record Plant in New York. He said John Lennon might be interested in some musicians. Yeah, sure. I didn't believe him for a minute. But then John, Yoko and Phil Spector descended on our studio and met the band. We jammed on old Beatles tunes for two hours.'

The guitarist Wayne 'Tex' Gabriel remembered that first meeting: 'When we got to the studio John was there when we walked in. He was just as nervous as we were. He said, 'Are you *them*?' and we said, 'Are you *him*?' And we just stood there for a second and laughed and shook hands and introduced ourselves.'

Recording-wise, they appeared on the album *Sometime in New York City*, which was credited to 'John and Yoko/Plastic Ono Band with Elephant's Memory plus Invisible Strings'. Apart from John and Yoko, the other member of Plastic Ono was Jim Keltner, on drums and percussion. Elephant's Memory appeared on Record One of the double album.

They also appeared on Yoko Ono's *Approximately Infinite Universe* album and three Yoko singles, 'Now or Never', 'Death of Samantha' and 'Jose Joi Banzaie'. The band also recorded one album for Apple, which was produced by John and Yoko. Entitled simply *Elephant's Memory*, it was issued in America on Apple SMAS 3389 on 18 September 1972 and in Britain on Apple SAPCOR 22 on 10 November. The tracks were 'Liberation Special', 'Baddest of the Mean', 'Cryin' Blacksheep Blues', 'Gypsy Wolf', 'Madness', 'Life', 'Wind Ridge', 'Power Boogie' and 'Local Plastic Ono Band'.

From the album they had some single releases. In America 'Liberation Special' c/w 'Madness' was issued on Apple 1854 on 13 November 1972 and then reissued on 4 December with the same catalogue number, but with a new B-side, 'Power Boogie'. The British release on Apple 45 on 8 December was 'Power Boogie' c/w 'Liberation Special'.

Elephant's Memory worked with John and Yoko for approximately a year. As the Plastic Ono Elephant's Memory Band (POEM) they appeared on several TV shows with John and Yoko, including *The Dick Cavett Show* and *The Mike Douglas Show*.

Of their appearances on the latter, which took place between 14 and 18 February 1972, Rick Franks commented, 'We were very unprepared for the show. We did a loose rendition of everything we did. We went on with Chuck Berry, playing

"Memphis" in two different keys. Douglas and his people hated us. We were in completely different worlds from each other. There was a real "keep the animals in their cage" mentality surrounding us.'

The group appeared on stage with John and Yoko at Madison Square Garden on 30 August 1972. This event was in aid of the Willowbrook School, an institution in which mentally retarded children were given individual treatment, hence the name 'One-To-One Foundation', which raised money for the school. The concert was also known as the 'One To One Concert' and ABC TV in America televised excerpts on 14 December 1972.

Tex Gabriel recalls that the group had believed they would be touring with John and Yoko on a regular basis following the concert, but harassment from FBI agents put a damper on the proposed concert tour. Gabriel said, 'We'd go to dinner with John and we'd have FBI guys following us around. Agents were with us everywhere. They would keep in the background, but you knew they were there.'

The cancellation of the tour proved a major disappointment to the group. Gabriel says, 'Madison Square Garden was supposed to be the stepping stone for a worldwide tour. After it was over, he was so psyched up. He said, "God, it was so great to be back on stage again and performing again." But he couldn't get his visa cleared to go to work so that put an end to that.'

John had to tell the group to continue their career and not to hang around waiting to see if he could eventually tour again with Yoko. The group persevered for a number of years but by 1978 had been so unsuccessful that they were reduced to providing music for a porno film called *Take Off* and disbanded soon afterwards.

Early in 1986, an album and video of the One To One Concert were issued on both sides of the Atlantic. Called *John Lennon: Live in New York City*, the issue provoked a law suit from Adam Ippolito, former keyboards player with Elephant's Memory, who sued Yoko on the grounds that Elephant's Memory accepted no fee for the appearance, donating their services to the charity. However, as Yoko was to make money from the recording and video due to their release in 1986, he was suing her for $50 million.

He claimed that Yoko appeared to be playing keyboards next to John during the stage show. Her keyboards were not plugged into the PA system, he added, and he was the person actually playing the keyboards from an out-of-sight position backstage.

At the time of their collaboration with John and Yoko, the line-up and personnel of Elephant's Memory comprised Stan Bronstein, sax; Gary Van Scyoc, bass; Adam Ippolito, keyboards; Rick Frank, drums; and Wayne 'Tex' Gabriel, guitar.

Elliot, Bill

Newcastle-born singer who was picked by John to sing lead vocals on 'God Save Us', a number he'd written specially to help the magazine *Oz* in its obscenity trial. Elliot later teamed up with another friend from Newcastle, Bob Purvis, who wrote a song called 'Lonely Man' with Mal Evans, who had also helped John produce Elliot's single. Evans brought the two lads to the attention of George Harrison and under the name Splinter they recorded a number of singles and an album for George's Dark Horse label.

El Solano

A large house with an ocean view in West Palm Beach, Florida. John and Yoko hired it from the socialite Brownie McClean in March 1979. Julian (Lennon's son) was brought over from England to spend his sixteenth birthday there with his father. John's assistant, Fred Seaman, had also accompanied them. While there, John told Seaman, 'When the Nixon government was trying to deport me, the reason they couldn't pull it off was because Yoko knew beforehand every move they were going to make in court. Her psychics told us what the government lawyers were planning to do, so we were always one step ahead. We simply outmanoeuvred the other side since Yoko could anticipate their every move, you see. They never knew what hit them.' John also said that Yoko had even brought in a voodoo priestess to cast a spell on the judge.

Elsas, Dennis

A disc jockey who worked for the New York radio station WNEW-FM. On Saturday 28 September 1974, while he was on the air, Elsas received a call that John was in the lobby. It was around 3.30 p.m. He put on the longest record he could find, Chicago's 'Ballet For a Girl in Buchanan', which lasted for more than fourteen minutes, and went to join John, who then came back with him to the studio. John joined Elsas on his Saturday afternoon show, introducing himself as Doctor Winston O'Boogie, and went on the air from 4 until 6 p.m. He and Elsas discussed his career from its earliest days, his relationship with the other three ex-Beatles, his immigration problems and the Rolling Stones.

He'd brought along four of his favourite records. He told listeners that 'Day Tripper' was inspired by Bobby Park's 'Watch Your Step' and mentioned that the introduction to 'Instant Karma!' sounded similar to Ritchie Barret's 'What'd I Say'.

John then began announcing commercials and weather reports in his own inimitable way.

For one advertisement, he said: 'Tonight, at the Joint in the Woods – guess who's there! It's Ladies' Night, featuring the eight-piece all-female group Isis. All females admitted at half price. Oh, good! Well, Bowie can get in! Also dance and party with Lock, Stock and Barrel ... that probably is a group because it's in inverted commas. Coming next Wednesday October 2 to the Joint in the Woods. "There's nothing like a joint in the woods," said he, losing his green-card possibilities in one blow! T Rex on Friday. That's a good band. Buy a couple of his records ... he's getting fat with worry!'

At one point in the show they discussed the recent releases by EMI of the Beatles' greatest-hits compilations known as the *Blue* and *Red* albums.

Elsas: 'Many of these things have been remixed into stereo.'

John: 'Oh! It was awful.'

Elsas: 'I think the original monaural recordings are better.'

John: 'I didn't think it'd happen when they put out that package last year.'

Elsas: 'The *Blue* and *Red* albums?'

John: I just thought, or rather presumed, they'd just copy them off the masters and put them out. I didn't even listen to it until it was out and I took it back and listened to it and I played it and it was embarrassing! Some of the tracks survive but it was embarrassing. Some fool had tried to make it stereo and it didn't work.'

Elsas: 'People should stay with the mono.'

John: 'Yeah, because there's a difference between mono and stereo obviously, and if you mix something in mono and try to fake it, you lose the guts of it. The fast version of "Revolution" was destroyed! I mean it was a heavy record, but they made it into a piece of ice cream!'

John commented on a number of weather reports, at one time saying, 'We're not going to bother with the weather – just look out of the window! Oh, you want the weather? The degrees have changed ... Oh, this is a nice degree. The temperature is sixty-nine! ... The weather in Central Park is still there ... Tomorrow will be just the same as today, only different.'

John spoke for a full hour as a guest on the programme.

13 Emperor's Gate

Address in West Kensington, London, that provided a temporary home for John, Cynthia and Julian in 1964. Once it had been revealed publicly that John was married to Cynthia and was the father of a little boy, Julian, the family decided to find a place in which to live in London.

When John and Cynthia paid a visit to the photographer Bob Freeman and his wife they mentioned that they were looking for a flat. Freeman suggested that they could apply for the maisonette on the top floor of the building in which he lived, which was very central and just off the Cromwell Road.

Unfortunately, the premises proved unsuitable once Beatles fans had discovered the address soon after John and his family had moved in.

There were six flights of stairs and, as there was no lift, Cynthia had difficulty both arriving at and leaving the flat with a small boy, particularly as she was greeted by hordes of fans as she tried to leave. As the rear of the premises overlooked the Underground and a new air terminal, there was only one way into the flat – by the front door, which, at times, made Cynthia feel she was under siege.

There was also disturbance from the noise of the Underground to the rear of the premises. Opposite the flat was a students' hostel, whose occupants would always be trying to peek into the Lennons' premises or trying to attract their attention.

Empty Garden (Hey Hey Johnny)

Elton John's tribute to his friend. The number was featured on Elton's *Jump Up* album, issued in 1982 on Rocket Records, HISPD 127, and later issued as a single on PRES 77. He composed it with his lyricist Bernie Taupin and the single reached No. 51 in the British charts. Elton performed the number at Madison Square Garden in August 1982, with Yoko and the six-year-old Sean in the audience. Elton was dressed in a Prussian soldier's uniform and Sean was heard to say to Yoko, 'You mean that man in the silly suit playing the piano is Elton?'

As he was finishing the song 'Empty Garden', Yoko and Sean surprised Elton by walking on stage. A review stated, 'The concert reached its emotional peak about a third of the way through, when Yoko Ono and son Sean strode out on stage to thank [Elton] John for his performance of "Empty Garden". Teary-eyed, John pushed on at a pitch several notches more intense than the show had been up until then.'

When he performed the number, the 20,000-strong audience lit candles and matches in John Lennon's memory. The *New York Post* reported,

> Yoko Ono and son Sean Ono Lennon shocked Elton John by coming out on stage during his Madison Square Garden concert last night after his musical tribute to John Lennon. After the song ended and the applause swelled, a spotlight hit the side of the stage and out walked Ono with Sean at her side. 'I want to thank you,' she said. 'I really believe you are all my family.' Elton and Ono embraced and kissed. The emotional audience broke into five minutes of cheering. Elton, Sean's godfather, was still wiping tears from his eyes as he began the next number.

Entermedia Theater

An off-Broadway theatre on 2nd Avenue and 12th Street, New York, which presented a production of Bob Eaton's play *Lennon* in October 1982.

David Patrick Kelly portrayed the younger Lennon and Robert LuPone portrayed the elder. There was a cast of seven in the two-and-a-half-hour production, five males and two females, playing a variety of roles. Mitch Weissman, who was associated with the *Beatlemania* stage show, supervised the music.

Sid and Stanley Bernstein in association with Abe Margolis and Dennis Paget produced *Lennon*. Unfortunately, the play wasn't a success. There was a press opening on 5 October, but by 26 October the production closed.

Epstein, Brian

The Beatles' first manager was born in Liverpool on 19 September 1934.

Because he was homosexual at a time when being so was virtually a criminal offence, Brian's early life was quite traumatic.

In September 1956 he joined RADA (the Royal Academy of Dramatic Arts) with hopes of becoming an actor, but quit in July 1957.

By 1961 he had settled down in the family business and ran their record store in Whitechapel, Liverpool. In July 1961 he stocked a new local publication, *Mersey Beat*, and discovered the huge rock 'n' roll movement in Liverpool. He became record reviewer for the publication and asked *Mersey Beat* to arrange for him to go down to the Cavern and see the Beatles.

He decided he wanted to manage the group and asked for his family's approval and financial backing. They agreed on condition that he also take on his brother Clive to help him run the business.

Philip Norman in his book *Shout!* alleges that Brian Epstein fell in love with John the moment he saw him and this was one of his reasons for signing up the Beatles. This is completely untrue. Norman, who never met John, picked up this spurious piece of information from a gay friend of Brian's.

The Beatles were not the type of sexual partners Brian was interested in. He was genuinely intrigued by the Liverpool scene, was fascinated with what was going on in Liverpool and saw the potential of it. With such an exciting scene occurring virtually on his doorstep, he had the foresight to see that potential and wanted to become part of it. He decided on the Beatles because they appeared to be the most popular group in Liverpool, according to the publication that he wrote for.

Brian had meetings with the group and got them to sign a contract – although they were all underage and really needed their parents' consent. He did see each of their parents to assure them of his good intentions. Jim McCartney was initially suspicious of him and regarded him as a 'Jew boy', but soon realised the benefits he was bringing the group. When Epstein went to see John's Aunt Mimi, he said, 'I promise you, John will never suffer. He's the most important one.'

During the days of the Beatles' early success, John made positive comments about Brian. At other times he completely contradicted his earlier statements. For instance, when Brian changed the group's image by smartening them up and making them get rid of their leather gear, John was particularly upset, but didn't indicate this to the media at the time. He was to say, 'Epstein fronted for the Beatles and he played a great part in whatever we did. He was theatrical – that was for sure. And he believed in us. But he certainly didn't package us the way they say he packaged us. He was good at his job, but to an extent he wasn't the greatest businessman. He was theatrical and he believed.'

Later he was to say, 'He literally fuckin' cleaned us up and there were great fights between him and me over not wanting to dress up. In fact he and Paul had some kind of collusion to keep me straight because I kept spoiling the image.'

Later in his career he continually referred back to the fact that Brian had polished the group up. He said, 'The Beatles died then, as musicians. That's why we never improved as musicians. We killed ourselves trying to make it.'

He was also to say, 'Funnily enough, I tend to remember the times before the Beatles happened – Hamburg and the Cavern. In those days we weren't just doing an entertainment thing or whatever the hell it was we were supposed to be: that's when we played music.'

In her book *A Twist of Lennon*, John's first wife Cynthia was to recall that John said, 'Bloody hell, Brian, do we have to? I hate suits, Brian … They'll all think we're copying the Shadows.'

Recalling the early days before Brian smartened them up and changed their act, John said, 'Our best work was never recorded, you know. We were performing in Liverpool, Hamburg and around the dance halls, and what we generated was fantastic.'

It was obvious to Epstein that John was upset with certain of the changes. He'd taken them to see the Shadows and said they must dress similarly smartly and bow to the audience at the end of their act. He made meticulous notes informing them of what they could and could not do when performing – for instance, they were no longer to take requests from their fans, weren't to smoke or swear on stage and so on. He even told them to change their brand of cigarettes to Senior Service because Woodbines were too working class.

When they went for their Decca audition he told them not to perform a typical Cavern set, which John wanted to do, but to aim for less of an R&B and rock 'n' roll sound and include numbers such as 'Till There Was You'. John always thought this was a mistake.

As a result, Epstein felt John was pulling away from his influence. What Brian was effectively doing was changing the group from John's group to Paul's group, because Paul wholeheartedly welcomed all of Brian's changes, while John hated them.

When the Cavern crowd saw the Beatles change from their black leathers into mohair suits, they were surprised. Rod Punt, leader of Steve Day and the Drifters, was to comment, 'I remember talking to them in the Cavern band room when they first wore those dark suits with very narrow lapels. They had their arms in the air making sure there was enough room and they obviously felt uncomfortable. Yet, rebellious though John Lennon was, he still conformed to Epstein's demands! I could never understand how Brian got him to accept that outrageous behaviour and casual dress would not necessarily contribute to their success.

'There's no doubt about it: John was the leader, the boss man of the Beatles. Paul would fall into line. But, really, how Epstein ever persuaded Lennon to put on a suit I will never know.'

In order to recapture his rapport with John and explain to him that such changes were essential if they were to become a major international act, Epstein invited John to join him on a short holiday to Spain.

Cynthia was pregnant at the time, but John said, 'I wasn't going to let a baby get in the way. What a bastard I was!'

As a result of the trip, people insinuated that something had been going on between John and Brian. John denied that he and Epstein were lovers. 'We didn't have an affair. But I liked playing it a bit faggy, you know, and all that – it was quite enjoyable. There were big rumours in Liverpool. It was terrible, very embarrassing.'

Describing the trip in more detail, John said, 'I was on holiday in Spain where the rumours went around that he and I were having a love affair. Well, it was almost a love affair, but not quite. It was never consummated. But it was a pretty intense relationship. It was my first experience with a homosexual that I was conscious was homosexual.

'We used to sit in a café in Torremolinos looking at all the boys and I'd say, "Do you like that one? Do you like this one?" I was rather enjoying the experience, thinking like a writer all the time: I am experiencing this.'

Hearing of the Spanish holiday, a local disc jockey, Bob Wooler, made some remarks to John, hinting that he and Brian had been on 'honeymoon' together. John beat him savagely.

He said, 'The Beatles' first national coverage was me beating up Bob Wooler at Paul's 21st party because he intimated I was homosexual. I must have had a fear that maybe I was homosexual to attack him like that and it's very complicated reasoning. But I was very drunk and I hit him and I could have really killed somebody then. And that scared me.'

John often made cruel jibes at Brian and often ridiculed the fact that he was Jewish and a homosexual. For instance, when Brian was writing his biography *A Cellarful of Noise*, John told him it should be called *Queer Jew*, *A Cellarful of Boys* or *A Cellarful of Goys*.

Epstein's biographer Ray Coleman also noted the number of times John's barbed tongue was aimed in Brian's direction. When a reporter asked John where Brian was, John told him, 'In America, sorting himself out a new rhythm-and-Jews group.' When he was at Epstein's flat one night and a male friend of Brian's arrived, John said, 'Have you come to blackmail him? If not, you're the only bugger in London who hasn't.'

At another time he looked at Brian's passport and said, 'Oh look – he's a Jew and he's got a British passport!' He also aimed the song 'Baby, You're a Rich Man Too' at Brian, calling it 'Baby, You're a Rich Fag Jew'.

Once, when John was in Lionel Bart's flat with Epstein and others, he upset a German girl who was present by pointing to Brian and telling her, 'Your people killed six million of his relatives.'

When they were recording at Abbey Road and Epstein made

a comment about the music, John said, 'You stick to your percentages, Brian. We'll make the music.'

Brian actually admired John's talent and in his autobiography was to declare that John was the most dominant figure in the group and would have become famous even without the Beatles' or Epstein's participation. He wrote that John would have emerged from the mass of the population: 'He may not have been a singer or a guitarist, a writer or a painter, but he would most certainly have been a something. You cannot contain a talent like this.'

Despite the huge success of the Beatles and his other acts, and the huge wealth he had amassed in a few short years, Brian Epstein was heavily depressed, dependent on drugs, addicted to gambling, blackmailed by his male lovers and worried sick that the Beatles were not going to renew their contract with him.

He was found dead in his London home on Sunday 27 August 1967. At the time, the Beatles were in Wales with the Maharishi Mahesh Yogi.

When he heard the tragic news, John said, 'We were in Wales with the Maharishi. We had just gone down after seeing his lecture on the first night. We heard it then. I was stunned – we all were, I suppose – and the Maharishi, we went in to him, "What, he's dead," and all that, and he was sort of saying, "Oh, forget it, be happy." Like an idiot, like parents, smile, that's what the Maharishi said. And we did.

'I had that feeling that anybody has when somebody close to them dies: there is a sort of little hysterical sort of "hee-hee, I'm glad it's not me" or something in it, the funny feeling when somebody close to you dies.

'I knew we were in trouble then. I didn't really have any misconceptions about our ability to do anything other than play music and I was scared. I thought, We've fucking had it.

'I liked Brian and I had a very close relationship with him for years, because I'm not gonna have some stranger running things, that's all. I like to work with friends. I was the closest with Brian, as close as you can get to somebody who lives a sort of "fag" life, and you don't really know what they're doing on the side. But in the group I was closest to him. We had complete faith in him when he was running us. To us, he was the expert.

'I mean, originally he had a shop. Anybody who's got a shop

must be all right. He went round smarming and charming every-body. He had hellish tempers and fits and lock-outs and you know he'd vanish for days. He'd come to a crisis every now and then and the whole business would fucking stop 'cause he'd go on sleeping pills for days on end and wouldn't wake up. Or he'd be missing, you know. Beaten up by some old docker down the Old Kent Road. But we weren't too aware of it.

'It was later on we started finding out about these things. We'd never have made it without him and vice versa. Brian contributed as much as us in the early days, although we were the talent and he was the hustler. He wasn't strong enough to overbear us. Brian could never make us do what we didn't really want to do.'

Erection

A nineteen-minute film by John and Yoko, which was made in London during 1970 and 1971. When John had heard that the London International Hotel was to be built in Kensington, he sought permission to film its entire construction. Once he'd obtained it he contacted the photographer Iain MacMillan and asked him to take a series of photographs of the construction. MacMillan had a stills camera and filmed the erection of the hotel from a fixed position for a period of eighteen months.

The stills were presented in sequence in the film, which ended with a shot of the completed hotel where all the lights were then turned off, leaving a black screen.

On the soundtrack Yoko sang two songs, 'Airmale' and 'You', using tapes of recordings of Joe Jones Tone Deaf Music Co., which was, in fact, a number of toy percussion instruments that played themselves, a squeaky style of sound devised by a former associate of Yoko's Fluxus days, Joe Jones. (Fluxus was an experimental art movement.)

The hotel was situated at 147 Cromwell Road and later became the London Swallow Hotel.

Evans, Chris

British disc jockey and TV host of *TFI Friday*, who regards John Lennon as one of his major heroes. He participated in the TV ads for the mobile-phone company One2One, which featured stars revealing what they would ask their dead heroes if they had a chance to speak with them. The model Kate Moss had selected

Elvis Presley, while the footballer Ian Wright chose Martin Luther King and the comedian Vic Reeves chose Terry Thomas.

When Evans was approached he agreed to appear in his first telly advert so that he could star alongside his hero, John Lennon. He chose to speak to him during the famous Bed-In peace protest and viewers were able to see Evans taken back to Lennon's Amsterdam hotel bedroom in 1969.

At a secret location in Park Royal, west London, state-of-the-art computer graphics, together with a pair of lookalikes for John and Yoko, were able to re-create the scene. Evans was hoisted above the white bed in a winch. He was then dropped, landing between John and Yoko. Lying there, he began to act like a hippie, made a peace sign to John and said, 'Sorry, John. I can't believe I've done that. Peace, man.'

The commercial cost £500,000 and Evans donated his £200,000 fee to charity.

Evening with John and Yoko, An

The title of an event that took place at the newly opened ICA (Institute of Contemporary Arts) in Pall Mall, London, on 10 September 1969.

In addition to the world premier of *Self Portrait*, other films screened were the fifteen-minute version of *Two Virgins*, plus *Honeymoon*, *Smile* and *Folding*.

John and Yoko fooled the press by sending along a surrogate couple enclosed in a large bag who, when arriving in John's white Rolls-Royce, were taken to be John and Yoko. The pair were carried to the stage, where they remained in the white sack chanting 'Hare Krishna' throughout the show. A hidden infrared camera filmed the reaction of the audience.

Evening with John Lennon, An

A radio special transmitted on the London station Capital Radio on Thursday 10 April 1975. It was a prerecorded show in which John was interviewed in New York, primarily to promote his *Rock 'n' Roll* album.

Everett, Kenny

A zany British disc jockey and television personality, born Maurice James Christopher Cole in Liverpool. After working in an office and in a bakery, he joined the pirate ship Radio London and was the official pirate radio reporter invited to accompany the Beatles on their final US tour in August 1966.

On Saturday 20 May 1967 the BBC show *Where It's At* transmitted a prerecorded feature by Everett on *Sergeant Pepper's Lonely Hearts Club Band*, including interviews with John, Paul and Ringo. Another prerecorded interview by Everett, in which he talked to Paul McCartney and discussed 'All You Need Is Love', was transmitted on *Where It's At* on Saturday 1 July 1967.

On the edition of *Where It's At* on Saturday 25 November 1967, an eighteen-minute interview with John Lennon by Everett and Chris Denning was broadcast.

Everett, who used his real name, Maurice Cole, on the 1969 edition, edited the Beatles' fifth and final Christmas fan club recordings.

On Saturday 27 January 1968, Everett visited John at his home in Weybridge to record an interview for *The Kenny Everett Show*, which was broadcast on Radio 1 on 4 February.

Everett also visited the Beatles while they were recording at Abbey Road on Thursday 6 June 1968 and recorded an interview, which was broadcast on *The Kenny Everett Show* on Sunday 9 June.

On Thursday 14 August 1969, Everett again dropped by the Abbey Road studios while the Beatles were mixing some tracks and recorded an interview with John, which was broadcast in two parts on his *Everett Is Here* radio series on Saturday 20 and Saturday 27 September.

It wasn't merely the fact that Everett had the same Liverpool roots as the Beatles that led to his becoming such a personal friend of the group: he also had a wacky sense of humour that appealed to them, particularly to John. Kenny was also anarchic in his approach to his radio and television shows, another aspect of his talent that they liked.

His autobiography, *The Custard Stops at Hatfield*, published in October 1982, featured many anecdotes about his relationship with the Beatles.

One of the incidents he mentions tells of the time he bumped into John and Terry Doran when they were coming out of a club called the Speakeasy. While the two of them coped with some waiting fans, Kenny slipped into their car. They apparently didn't notice him. They arrived at John's house in Weybridge and Kenny made himself known, at which John made a comment that sounded like, 'Life is a bacon butty.'

Kenny died from an AIDS-related illness on 4 February 1994. He was 51 years old.

Every Little Thing
Number penned by John, which the Beatles recorded on 30 September 1964 for inclusion on their *Beatles For Sale* album. Yes covered the song in 1969.

Every Man Has a Woman Who Loves Him (album)
Album by Yoko Ono issued in America on Thursday 13 September 1984.

Every Man Has a Woman Who Loves Him (single)
A Yoko Ono composition, originally slated for the proposed Broadway musical *The Ballad of John and Yoko*, which was included on the *Double Fantasy* album. Released in Britain on 16 November 1984. Issued by Polydor as a seven-inch single on POSP 712 with Sean Lennon's version of 'It's Alright' on the flip. It was issued in America on Friday 5 October as the first single from the album on Polydor 881 378-7.

Everybody's Got Something To Hide Except Me and My Monkey
Song written by John, which was recorded on 26 and 27 June and 1 and 23 July 1968 and included on *The Beatles* double album.

John liked Fats Domino's version of the number.

Everybody Had a Hard Year
A number penned by John in December 1968 and recorded on an acoustic guitar as a home demo. It was basically an unfinished song, and was mixed with an also unfinished bluesy number by Paul called 'I've Got A Feeling'. It was recorded by the Beatles on the Apple rooftop on 30 January 1969 and included on the *Let It Be* album under the title 'I've Got A Feeling'.

Face – the Lives of John Lennon

A ballet by Anthony Sterago. It was performed at the town hall of Bremen, Germany, between 28 and 30 June 1995.

36 Falkner Street

Address of a private flat in the Liverpool L8 district, which Brian Epstein rented during 1961 and 1962. It was near to a flat occupied by his drama coach, Helen Lindsay. Epstein continued to live at home, but used the flat, which cost him £16 a month, for his private liaisons.

During John and Cynthia's wedding lunch at Reece's on 23 August 1962, Brian offered the newly married couple unlimited use of the luxuriously furnished ground-floor flat.

They were grateful for the use of the apartment, which was in complete contrast to the bedsit in Garmoyle Road, which Cynthia had been occupying.

In her autobiography *A Twist of Lennon*, Cynthia described how it took only a short time for the newly weds to settle into the flat, which extended the full length of the ground floor and even included a small, walled garden. She commented,

The only snag was that our bedroom was situated at the front of the house overlooking Falkner Street. Access to the rest of the flat was only by going through the main hall and past the front door which was used by all the other tenants of the building – very inconvenient when in need of the bathroom during the night. Anyone could wander in through the front door and walk from the street into our rooms if the door was open … It all made me very nervous at times, especially when John was away on tour.

She described one incident, which occurred at midnight when she'd gone to bed and John had just locked up. The front door-bell began to ring and, as no one answered it, John opened the door. There were two rough-looking characters who demanded to see someone named Carol. John told them no one of that name lived there. He closed the door and returned to the flat. A few minutes later someone began battering the flat door violently. The roughs began to shout, 'We know she's there, you dirty ponce. We'll bloody tear you apart when we get out hands on you. You bloody hand her over or else!'

Then Cynthia began screaming and shouted out that her name was Cynthia, there was no one named Carol in the flat and that she was three months pregnant. There was some mumbling from the other side of the door and the roughs left.

Cynthia was quite lonely there as John continued travelling with the group immediately after the wedding. However, it was while the couple were living in Falkner Street that John wrote 'Do You Want to Know A Secret?'.

He was to say, 'I was in the first apartment I'd ever had that wasn't shared by fourteen other students – gals and guys at art school.'

After several weeks, John took Cynthia on a visit to his Aunt Mimi's house. Mimi was concerned about the pregnant woman being alone in the flat while John was away on the road and invited her to move into Mendips.

Fame

A song that John recorded with David Bowie in January 1975.

Bowie had just completed his sessions for his *Young Americans* album at the Sigma Sound Studios in New York and his producer, Tony Visconti, had returned to Britain when John responded to a Bowie request that they record together, which they did, at the Electric Ladyland Studios.

John had always been unhappy about the Beatles' version of his song 'Across the Universe' and, when Bowie offered to record it, John attended and played at the session.

While they were in the studios, John began to jam with Bowie and the guitarist Carlos Alomar and the result was 'Fame'.

Alomar was to comment on the making of the track, which was recorded when John was 34, and during his 'lost weekend' with May Pang.

He said, 'Bowie was doing a song called "Footstompin'" on tour, which we really liked. So we went into the studio to record it at Electric Ladyland in New York. But it just didn't record well. It just sounded like a plain stupid old rock 'n' roll song. David didn't even like it. So what we did was just cut it up into blues changes, which is one-four-five-four, which is what "Fame" is. He cut it up so he just had drums, bass and that one guitar line, and while he was doing that he found out that Lennon was in town, so he invited him to come down.

They had some conversations, and I was basically waiting for him to stop talking to Lennon so we could get on with the damn thing.

'The next thing, Lennon is picking up one of my guitars and he's going into the recording booth to play a little acoustic on it. So we're playing everything and everything's cool. We finish the recording and play back the tape. Everyone's listening to it, and we keep hearing this thing on tape what we now know as the "Fame" noise. "What the hell is that?" David said. Lennon was playing acoustic guitar and it seems that he put his chin on the acoustic guitar when he played and just the breathing he did produced that funny noise. David thought he was saying "Fame".

'Then he and John left and I stayed with the engineer, Harry Maslin, to work out some overdubs and ideas for the song – going back to the whole James Brown period where you had four or five guitar players playing at a time and it was no big deal. I started laying down all these other guitar parts. David came back sometime later and I said, "Hey, David, you've got to hear this – it's cool." He heard it and said, "That's it, it's done, it's finished," and then he took it home, wrote the words and came back the next day and did the vocals.'

Musicians on both tracks were David Bowie, vocal/guitar;

John Lennon, vocal/guitar; Carlos Alomar, Earl Slick, guitars; Emir Kadasan, bass; Dennis Davis, drums; Ralph McDonald, Pablo Rosario, percussion; Jean Fineberg, Jean Millington, backing vocals.

'Fame' was issued as a single in Britain on RCA 2579 in July 1975 and reached No. 17 in the charts. It was released in America the following month and gave David Bowie his first American No. 1 single and remained at the top for two weeks, with a chart life of 27 weeks.

Commenting on the number in his *Playboy* interview, John said, ' "Fame" was an incredible bluff that worked. I'm really knocked out that people actually dance to my records, but let's be honest, my rhythm and blues are thoroughly plastic.'

Bowie's producer, Visconti, who had missed the recording sessions, said during interviews for the book *The Record Producers*, 'The first I heard of 'Fame' and 'Across the Universe' was when the record was released ... so I never heard 'Fame' until the public heard it, and I really wanted to record it.

'I'd met John Lennon the very same night that David had met him and the three of us stayed up until about ten o'clock in the morning and had a great time together. I wish I'd been in the studio with them, but David wasn't elbowing me – it really was spontaneous. I was in England and David was in New York with John, and that's exactly the way it happened.'

Family Album Blood Objects
An exhibition staged by Yoko Ono in 1994. The show featured bronze casts of John's bullet-riddled bloodstained shirt at $25,000 per cast and replicas of John's shattered spectacles at $18,000 each.

Farrow, Prudence
One of the actress Mia Farrow's sisters. It was Prudence who contacted Mia and told her about transcendental meditation and persuaded her to take a plane with her to Boston to see the Maharishi Mahesh Yogi. As a result the two were invited to study with him at his ashram in Rishikesh.

Prudence began meditating continuously and no longer turned up for meals. A plate had to be left outside her door. Finally, she reached the stage where she didn't even come outside her door at all. The Maharishi appointed 'team buddies' to look out for each other and John and George Harrison were assigned to Prudence. Every morning and most afternoons they would visit her in her room.

Prudence told her sister, 'I wanted to meditate as much as possible. It was a special time, and such a holy place. One night when I was meditating, George and John came into my room with their guitars, playing.'

John was to write the song 'Dear Prudence'.

Later, Prudence told her sister, 'I guess I thought it was really nice, but I didn't know they were going to put it on an album or anything. I didn't really think about it; it wasn't anything in my mind. Then much later, after India, I heard people saying there was a song. I was really grateful that it was something so nice.'

Fat Budgie, The

A cartoon that John drew and allowed the charity, Oxfam, to use as a Christmas card. John had received requests from several charities to provide them with illustrations for cards, but Oxfam was the only one he responded to.

On 19 September 1964, Oxfam printed a half million cards featuring his drawing of *The Fat Budgie*.

The illustration came from Page 16 of John's book *A Spaniard in the Works* in which the circular bird was the subject of one of John's intriguing poems. The Fat Budgie was a yellow pet called Jeffrey who ate scrambled eggs on toast.

Fawcett, Anthony

An art critic for the magazine *Art & Artists*, born in Hillingdon Heath, England, in 1948, who first met John in May 1968 at the Arts Laboratory in Drury Lane, London, where John and Yoko were celebrating their first arts venture together.

He'd met Yoko several times previously and was invited out to dinner by the couple, who then gave him a lift home. When they arrived at his house in Parsons Green, Fawcett invited them inside and John was surprised to find paintings by his former Liverpool College of Art friend Jonathan Hague in the hall. They had been stored there following his London exhibition, which had been sponsored by John and Paul.

Fawcett next arranged for them to be represented with their

acorn sculpture at the National Sculpture Exhibition and John and Yoko invited him to meet them at the Apple offices, where they offered him the post of personal assistant, in charge of the various art projects they were involved in.

Commenting about the offer in his book *John Lennon: One Day at a Time*, Fawcett wrote,

> My brain was deluged with thoughts and sensations. John and Yoko were such an amalgam of eccentricities – part genius, part egomaniac, part clown – that the thought of working for them and being intimately involved in their lives elated me. It wasn't just the thrill of who they were, or their lifestyle, it was the challenge of entering the unknown, the bizarre, where one never knew what to expect next.

He began working for them officially at the end of April 1968 and remained with them until May 1970, when they left for primal therapy in California. During this time Fawcett was involved in all aspects of the couple's life, dealing with their mail, meetings, travel arrangements and twenty or thirty projects that the Lennons had conceived. In 1968, one suggestion from Fawcett was that John should try his hand at lithography. This was to result in the Bag One erotic lithographs.

John nicknamed Fawcett 'Superchicken'.

Later in 1970, Fawcett became director of a company in London called APT Enterprises (Art and Pop on Television). He then moved to America, living in California for two years before settling in New York. *John Lennon: One Day at a Time* was first published in America in 1976 by Grove Press and by New English Library in Britain the following year.

Feliciano, Jose

Singer/songwriter, born in Puerto Rico on 10 September 1945. In July 1998, he told the *Liverpool Echo*, 'John was my hero in life. I actually worked on John's *Rock 'n' Roll* album sessions. Recently I was in my own recording studio and I wrote a song inspired by John called "It Came To Me In a Dream" and it was reminiscent of Beatle harmonies. I just loved the whole experience.'

Festival for Life

An event organised by the Campaign for Nuclear Disarmament on 29 March 1970 at Victoria Park, Bethnal Green. More than 5,000 people were gathered at the east London park to hear a programme of poetry, rock music, drama and speeches. John gave a telephone speech to the gathering in which he revealed that Yoko was expecting a baby. He told them, ' ... and if we are going to have a baby, we must have peace for it to survive.'

Unfortunately, Yoko miscarried later in the year.

Fieldsteel, Ira

Pressure from President Nixon's office and the FBI resulted in the Immigration and Naturalization Service seeking John and Yoko's deportation from America. The case against Yoko had to be dropped when it was discovered she'd received a green card several years before.

It was a New York judge, Ira Fieldsteel, who, on 23 March 1973, made a ruling that John would have to leave the United States or be deported.

John continued his battle to remain in America, despite the hostility of the Nixon administration, which kept applying pressure. There were various appeals and the New York State Supreme Court instructed the INS to reconsider John's case, stating, 'The court cannot condone selective deportation based upon secret political grounds.'

Fieldsteel, the judge who had ordered his deportation, finally awarded John his green card on 27 July 1976. Fieldsteel also informed him that he could apply for US citizenship in 1981.

Outside the courtroom, John commented, 'The Immigration Service has finally seen the light of day. It's been a long and slow road but I am not bitter. On the contrary, I can now go and see my relatives in Japan and elsewhere. I can travel now! Until today my attorney wouldn't even let me go to Hawaii for a vacation in case I couldn't get back. Whenever I flew to Los Angeles I was paranoid in case the plane was diverted to Tokyo on the way!'

Filmmakers' Fortnight Festival

Event at the annual Cannes Film Festival in France on 15 May 1971, which featured the world premier of two John and Yoko films, *Apotheosis (Balloon)*, an 18-minute movie produced by Nick Knowland and directed by John, and *Fly*, a 50-minute film, directed by Yoko.

Both John and Yoko travelled to Cannes for the occasion.

The audience booed *Apotheosis (Balloon)*.

Film No. 4 (Bottoms)

The controversial film that first brought Yoko Ono's name to the headlines in Britain. During her stay in London, over a two-day period, she filmed 365 pairs of buttocks belonging to a number of 'Swinging London' people, including celebrities of both sexes all shot from an identical position with comments from the participants on the soundtrack.

Made during the spring of 1967, the 80-minute film was a fuller version of her *Number 4* film made in New York in 1965, which featured twelve bare bottoms. When Yoko decided to make the film in Britain she threw out all the New York footage and placed an advertisement in *Stage* magazine. One of the first people to be filmed was the Beatles biographer Hunter Davies, then writing the Atticus column in the *Sunday Times*.

Yoko said that she was originally inspired to film people's bottoms after watching a housemaid polish a floor. She commented, 'People's behinds have right and left and top and bottom. And each part moves separately. I thought it would be visually interesting to film close up.'

The new film was not given a certificate by the British Board of Film Censors (BBFC) but the Greater London Council licensed it to be shown. John Trevelyan, the censor at the time, objected because 'other bits of the anatomy had crept into the footage'.

In protest at the censorship, Yoko and her supporters picketed the office of the BBFC in Soho Square, London, from 11 a.m. to 3 p.m. on Friday 10 March 1967.

In a story headlined 'BOTTOMLESS INDIGNATION OF MISS YOKO ONO' *The Times* ran a story in which it reported, 'Miss Ono turned out to be an attractive young woman with long black hair and a soft, shy voice. Her complaint was the board's refusal to grant a certificate to her latest film, which lasts an hour and a half and consists entirely of shots of human backsides.'

Yoko handed daffodils to passers-by. Commenting on her

seventh film, her first to be made in London, she said, 'The whole idea of the film is one of peace. It's quite harmless; there's no murder or violence in it. Why shouldn't it be given a certificate?' She was also angry at the fact that she'd been charged £57 for the censor's verdict.

Bottoms received its world premier at the Jacey Tatler cinema in west London in August 1967, and it was also to be screened for a season at the Times cinema in Baker Street. The movie was also shown at the 1967 Knokke-Le-Zoute avant-garde film festival held in Belgium.

Although she did not enter *Film No. 4* in the actual competition, Yoko, conscious of the value of attracting public attention, lay in the foyer of the cinema in a black bag for eight hours surrounded by signs stating; 'YOKO ONO IS NOT HERE'.

In an interview with the *Sunday Times*, she said, 'It's a social protest. It's signing a petition with your behind instead of your signature. We haven't just gone out in the street and snatched people's bottoms and given them a quick pound. All the people, most of them artists, writers and actors, have volunteered to do it for nothing.'

Two of the volunteers, the American art critic Mario Amaya and Robert Fraser, a gallery owner, were to die of AIDS.

John called the film *Many Happy Endings*.

Filmography

As a member of the Beatles John appeared in three feature films: *A Hard Day's Night*, *Help!* and *Let It Be*, and a TV special, *Magical Mystery Tour*. He had no participation in the animation picture *Yellow Submarine* apart from appearing briefly with his fellow Beatles at the end and penning some songs. John didn't even provide the voiceover for his own character: that was provided by John Clive.

A Hard Day's Night, despite a tiny budget, proved to be one of the best rock musicals ever made. The title itself is attributed to Ringo Starr, although, prior to the decision about the title, John's first book *In His Own Write*, had a story called 'Sad Michael' in which John wrote, 'He'd had a hard day's night that day, for Michael was a cocky watchtower.'

The inspiration for the film arguably came from a comment John made when the group embarked on a Scandinavian tour.

When asked to describe the Beatles' lot, John said, 'It was a room and a car and a car and a room and a room and a car.'

The quote so impressed the scriptwriter Alun Owen that he adapted it and had Wilfred Brambell saying, 'I thought I was going to get a change of scenery and so far I've been in a train and a room and a car and a room and a room and a room.'

Discussing the film, John said, 'We'd made it clear to Brian [Epstein] that we weren't interested in being stuck in one of those typical nobody-understands-our-music plots where the local dignitaries are trying to ban something as terrible as the Saturday night hop. The kind of thing where we'd just pop up a couple of times between the action ... all smiles and clean shirt collars to sing our latest record and once again at the end when the local mayor has been convinced that we're not all mass murderers or, worse still, about to start shagging some young Sunday school teacher in the town hall flower beds ... We all know that scene so well ... where he and a bunch of senile town councillors and the police chief start dancing around all over the place like those bloody *Thunderbirds* puppets ... Never mind all your pals – how could we have faced each other if we had allowed ourselves to be involved in that kind of movie?'

Despite the critical acclaim it received, John was not entirely happy with it, particularly with the dialogue by Alun Owen. He was to comment, 'Alun Owen was a bit phoney. He was like a professional Liverpool man, like a professional American. He stayed with us for two days and wrote the whole thing based on our characters then: mine witty; Ringo dumb and cute; George, this; Paul, that.'

Shortly after *A Hard Day's Night* was released, John was asked if the public could look forward to more Beatles films. 'There'll be more,' said John, 'but I don't know whether you could look forward to them or not.'

Their second feature, *Help!*, had double the budget of *A Hard Day's Night* and was also in colour. John was to describe it as 'bullshit'. He was to say, '*Help!* was a drag because we didn't know what was happening. In fact, Richard Lester [director of *A Hard Day's Night*] was a bit ahead of his time with the Batman thing but we were on pot by then and all the best stuff is on the cutting-room floor, with us breaking up and falling all over the place.'

John was also to say that because the film was crammed with so many British character actors, the Beatles felt like extras in their own movie. Lester concurred and commented, 'It was because they were put up against professional actors who were saying these bizarre lines better than they did. The Beatles made no real attempt at them because they were stoned throughout and probably thought, Oh, sod this! The Beatles used pot as a continuing device to amuse themselves because filmmaking didn't amuse them any longer. We had some wonderful times, but it had all become a bit of a giggle. The novelty of being around a film crew had obviously worn off and pot was there to alleviate the boredom of hanging around between takes.'

That was the last scripted feature they made. Numerous other movie scripts were rolled out – *The Three Musketeers*, *Shades of a Personality*, *Lord of the Rings*, *Up Against It*, *A Talent For Loving* – but all were rejected.

Within a week of completing the Beatles' last tour appearance at Candlestick Park in San Francisco, John began filming *How I Won The War*. At the time he was worried about having time on his hands and thought filming would occupy his interest. He flew out to Germany on Monday 5 September 1966 and immediately had his hair cut short for his part as Private Gripweed in this antiwar movie.

Michael Crawford was the star of the film.

After they'd begun filming, the director Richard Lester was to say, 'At one point while we were making the movie, I turned to John and said, "If you really wanted to you could either be a good serious or comic actor," and his reply was, "I know I probably could, but what a silly thing to do!"

'We were only into the first week of shooting, and I thought to myself, God, if he thinks it's silly, then how on earth am I going to get through the schedule?'

Once the film was released, Lester commented, 'I'm sorry in one way that John Lennon was in the film because it creates an imbalance. The part just seemed to fit John, though I didn't want to make a film with a Beatle in it.'

Despite turning down feature film proposals, the Beatles decided to write and direct their own television special, *Magical Mystery Tour*, which was basically an idea that Paul McCartney had come up with. John said, 'Paul would say, "Well, here's the segment, you write a little piece for that." And I thought, Fuckin' Ada! I've never made a film. What's he mean?'

Their final film also began life as a proposed television special, but developed into a full-scale feature film, which was to complete the three-picture deal they'd made with United Artists. It was a documentary account of them recording a new album and was directed by Michael Lindsay-Hogg. The sessions originally went under the name *Get Back* and they were chaotic. John was to comment, 'We didn't want to know. It's the first time since the first album that we didn't have anything to do with what was going on.'

This was because they actually abandoned getting a cohesive album together and eventually let Allen Klein place it in the hands of Phil Spector while they went away and recorded *Abbey Road*.

Commenting on the film itself, John said, 'Klein saw a rough cut of it and said he didn't want anyone else in the film but the Beatles, so everyone else who was in any shot at any time was taken out, the net result being that it got a bit difficult to watch after a while.'

John was also to say, 'I felt sad that film was set up by Paul. That's one of the main reasons the Beatles ended. I can't speak for George, but I pretty damn well know – we got fed up being sidemen for Paul. The camera work was set up to show Paul and not to show anybody else. And that's how I felt about it. As for the album? I'm fucked if I know. But, one of those versions that was put together when it was still *Get Back* was pretty damn good. It was the one that turned up as a bootleg and I got the blame. People reckon I was responsible for it. Maybe I was. I can't remember. They said it came from an acetate that I gave to someone who then went out and broadcast it as being an advance pressing or something. If that's true, then I suppose I am responsible.'

Apart from the above films John appeared in a brief excerpt in the DA Pennebaker documentary surrounding the Bob Dylan British tour of April/May 1966.

His most active involvement in films took place when he began making a series of shorts with Yoko Ono, although, in the making of avant-garde films, Paul McCartney had beaten him to the punch with two shorts, *The Defeat of the Dog* and *The Next Spring Then*.

Branching out into avant-garde films was primarily the wish of Yoko Ono. She had begun making minimalist films in New York as a member of a group of conceptual artists called Fluxus. In 1965 she exhibited her first revision of *Film No. 4* at the Fluxus film festival in addition to another five-minute short entitled simply *Number One*, which featured a slow-motion sequence of a match being struck.

Film No. 4 was the one that first brought her to the attention of the British press in 1967 after she'd moved to London. This was a more elaborate version of the film she had made in New York in 1965, which featured a dozen bare buttocks. In Britain the movie was commonly called *Bottoms* because she filmed 365 naked bottoms belonging to a number of Swinging London people, who included celebrities of both sexes.

John and Yoko's film partnership began in 1968. The first two films they made were shot in a single afternoon in the garden of John's house, Kenwood. Their first film was 51 minutes, directed by Yoko, called *No. 5*, but it has also been known as *Smile*. The idea was originally Yoko's, the initial concept being almost a facial version of her *Bottoms* film as she said she wanted to make a film 'which included a smiling-face snap of every single human in the world. But that had obvious technical difficulties.' She finally decided on a film of John's face smiling and said it would be available 'for people who'd like to have the film on their wall as a light portrait'.

It was shot with a high-speed camera able to take 20,000 frames per minute, in the garden of Kenwood. Originally a three-minute film, it was slowed down for public screening to last for 52 minutes. It showed John's facial expressions as he stuck out his tongue, wiggled his eyebrows and gave fleeting smiles.

The film was premiered at the Chicago Film Festival in 1968, together with *Two Virgins*, and was one of the films shown during the *An Evening with John and Yoko* film event at the New Cinema Club, London, in September 1969. She had originally considered making the movie four hours long, but even at 52 minutes it was considered overlong by most members of the audience in Chicago, and after thirty minutes more than half the audience had left the cinema.

The second film made that afternoon was *Two Virgins*. This nineteen-minute film was also in slow motion and ended with the couple kissing and embracing. John remarked, 'The idea of the film won't really be dug for another fifty or a hundred years probably.'

In November 1968 they launched one of their most ambitious ventures, a 75-minute mini-feature called *Rape*.

During 1969, John also appeared in a documentary film, *Diaries, Notes and Sketches*, by Jonas Mekas, another experimental filmmaker. The movie was originally several hours long but was later divided into several parts. In the film Mekas interviewed a number of celebrities with a range of unusual images. The celebrities involved, apart from John, were Nico, the Velvet Underground, the Fugs, Allen Ginsberg and Andy Warhol.

In 1969 DA Pennebaker filmed the Toronto Peace Festival. His 140-minute film was released in 1970. John and Yoko appeared with Eric Clapton, Klaus Voormann and Alan White as the Plastic Ono Band and during their performance in Toronto on 9 September. The film was re-edited and reissued the following year with the John, Yoko and Plastic Ono Band scenes missing because of legal complications. The movie was also retitled *Keep On Rockin'*.

John and Yoko were still involved with their own movies and produced *Honeymoon*, a sixty-minute short featuring scenes from one of their bed-ins, and *Self Portrait*, a controversial 42-minute film whose entire length centres on John's penis arising from a flaccid to an erect state in slow motion. It was premiered at the Institute of Contemporary Arts in London in September 1969. That year the couple also directed a 61-minute film called *Give Peace A Chance*.

In 1970 when John and Yoko were in New York they made two films, *Up Your Legs Forever* and *Fly*. The first took only two days to make because John and Yoko were keen to include some new material in a festival of their films that Jonas Mekas had arranged to be held at the Elgin Theatre. The film was eighty minutes long and featured over three hundred pairs of legs, photographed from the toes up to the top of the thighs. 'We asked everybody to donate their legs for peace,' said Yoko, and a host of celebrities obliged, including the film star George Segal, the rock singer Larry Rivers and the filmmaker DA Pennebaker.

Fly was only nineteen minutes long and it, too, took just two days to film, in a New York attic. Although only one person was filmed, in contrast with the 331 gathered for the *Legs* film, *Fly* was probably a more complicated project.

Apotheosis was the first of their films in which John took charge, investigating the possibilities of a feature-length colour film, although the actual finished movie is only eighteen minutes long. John was unhappy with the results of the initial filming and began work on *Apotheosis No. 2* at the village of Lavenham in Sussex. Both films were made in 1969.

Freedom Films were two sixty-second films, one directed by John, the other by Yoko in 1971. Other films that same year were: *Erection* (20 minutes), *Clock* (60 minutes) *Imagine* (70 minutes) and *Working Class Hero* (60 minutes).

The year 1972 saw *Ten for Two*, a film directed for them by Steve Gebhardt; *Hanratty* (40 minutes) and *One to One* (48 minutes), directed by Steve Gebhardt.

John and Yoko's major production of 1972 was their 81-minute colour film *Imagine*. The two of them were filmed together in various scenes, mainly set around Tittenhurst Park in Ascot. They also introduced a number of cameo guest appearances by various stars. The movie was first shown in a seventy-minute version on American television on Saturday 23 December 1972.

Imagine: John Lennon was a posthumous movie, made with the co-operation of Yoko, who gave access to her archives to Warner Bros in a film directed by Andre Solt.

First Sex, The

A feminist book by Elizabeth Gould Davis. Yoko gave the book to John and told him to read it. She had been slowly trying to instruct him on the position of women's roles and their relationships with men. The book saw women as being the oppressed sex and mentioned that in men's eyes there were only two kinds of woman: the sex object and the 'other'. 'Sex object' referred to wives and mistresses; 'other' referred to unmarried women over forty and to intellectual women. Regarding the latter, Davis wrote, 'To the masculist these women have no human rights, no reason for existence.'

John, apparently feeling guilty for his treatment of women during his life, wept when he read it.

Fluxfest

An event staged by the Fluxus Group Arts Festival, which ran during the months April, May and June 1970 at the Greenwich Village Store on Canal Street in New York's Greenwich Village. Although John and Yoko were in London, they sent along a number of contributions that began to appear weekly at the event. Their various displays were *Do-It Yourself* by John and Yoko; *Two Eggs* by John Lennon; *Tickets* by John and Yoko; *Measure* by John and Yoko; *Blue Room* by John and Yoko; *Three Rooms* by John Lennon; *Needle* by John Lennon; *Weight and Water* by John and Yoko; *Capsule* by John and Yoko; *Portrait of John Lennon as a Young Cloud*; *The Store* by John and Yoko; and *Exam* by John and Yoko.

An example of what the conceptual pieces were is *Portrait of John Lennon As A Young Cloud*. This consisted of a wall containing one hundred drawers, all but one of which were empty. The one drawer held 'John's smile'.

Fluxus

Fluxus was the name of an experimental art movement formed in New York early in the 1960s. Conceptual art, performance 'happenings' and minimalist work were all part of the art form whose exponents included John Cage, George Maciunas, Nam June Paik, Joe Jones, Tony Cox and Yoko Ono, who was the only female member of the movement.

The writer Francis Peeters considers that the avant-garde work by John and Yoko was mainly derivative of the other Fluxus artists. He points out that all the John and Yoko films were 'direct copies of earlier fluxfilms'. He also points out that the *Half Wind Show* by Yoko was literally taken from another flux artist who had exhibited various 'half' art works long before Yoko's show. He claims that the 'Bed-In' events were copied from Ben Vautier, who exposed himself for days in a shop window in a bed. He says the 'Bag' events were copies of Yoko's own 1967 'Stone Event' and that 'Two Minutes Silence' from the *Life With the Lions* album was taken from John Cage, who used to record longer periods of silence. 'John probably thought two minutes was more commercial,' he says.

Peeters also claims, 'The thought of John and Yoko's life being an event in its own right is literally the Fluxus philosophy.'

Fly

A film co-produced by John and Yoko in an attic in the Bowery area of New York in December 1970, although it was mainly Yoko's work. Her idea was basic: 'Let a fly walk on a woman's body from toe to head and fly out of the window.'

The pair hired the New York actress Virginia Lust and she had to lie down naked while a fly explored her body. A special macro lens had to be used for the filming, which needed to be refocused each couple of inches of the fly's movements.

The flies obviously couldn't be trained and approximately two hundred of them were used during the marathon filming session over a period of a day and a night.

John and Yoko sent a man out to find the flies at 25 cents each. He collected them all in the kitchen of a local cafeteria chain. All of the flies died after their performance.

Each fly had to be stunned with a special gas. The insect is seen at the woman's toes, then crawling all the way to her crotch, investigating her vagina, crawling up over her belly, on to her nipples, fingertips and face. Then two flies are seen converging on her stomach and four others on her hand.

The film ends with a long shot of her body covered with half a dozen flies, then the camera moves to the window and focuses on the sky to simulate the insect flying away.

Virginia Lust also had to be sedated during the filming.

Fly was one of three of John and Yoko's films premiered at the Elgin Theatre, New York, that month, although it was cut from 45 minutes to 19.

One reviewer wrote, 'The fly exhibited a degree of hammy exuberance, rubbing his forelegs and strutting about, that was astonishing in one so small.'

The film was also screened at the 1971 Cannes Film Festival, where Yoko commented, 'Everyone is that female, just lying down, just taking it.'

Yoko was also to compare it to a human liberation story, saying 'Everyone is that family, just lying down, just taking it. We don't live life, we just take it.'

The soundtrack of the film comprised 22 minutes and 43 seconds of Yoko soloing with a variety of vocal sounds, accompanied by John on electric guitar. The soundtrack was included on her album *Fly*, issued on 3 December 1971.

Yoko hummed in a varied-pitch style, which she learned in Japan. John strummed the guitar to produce a twang effect and then played the tape backwards.

Fonda, Peter

American actor, son of Henry Fonda and brother of Jane.

Peter starred in the cult 60s movie *Easy Rider*. Another film he starred in was called *The Trip*, and concerned the effect hallucinogenic drugs had on a group of characters.

In August 1965, when the Beatles were staying for five days at a house in Mulholland Drive in Los Angeles, Fonda, along with Roger McGuinn and David Crosby of the Byrds, was invited by Derek Taylor to join the Beatles at their house where they'd intended to take some LSD. It was the second time John and George had taken LSD.

Fonda was to recall to the journalist Bill De Young, 'I think George, along with John, had been dosed once before and it scared them.'

George and Fonda were sitting on the patio and George was on edge, saying that he felt like he was dying. Fonda said, 'Well, that's OK, that's what this is all about, not dying, but it's supposed to be letting go. Letting go of everything that you have thought of as your control factors. They're all being pulled away from you. You are not in control of the life, because you never were. This is putting you into reality.'

Then Fonda told him, 'Anyway, I know what it's like to be dead.'

George asked him what he meant.

Fonda explained, 'When I was a boy, just very young, I shot myself by accident. And I died on the operating table, three times. My heart stopped beating, and I died from loss of blood. So I know what it's like to be dead. It's nothing to worry about at all.'

John happened to be passing and heard part of the conversation. He said to George, 'What'd he say?' and George told him.

John looked at Fonda and said, 'Who put all that shit in your head? You know, you're making me feel like I've never been born.'

John was to say that Fonda kept repeating, 'I know what it's like to be dead. I know what it's like to be dead, man.' John got so fed up of hearing the sentence over and over again that he told Fonda to shut up.

However, he recalled the incident and based his song, 'She Said, She Said' on the experience.

(Forgive Me) My Little Flower Princess

A track on the *Milk and Honey* album, issued three years after John's death, in January 1984.

Forrest Gump

An award-winning 1994 film starring Tom Hanks and directed by Robert Zemeckis, who'd also directed the feature *I Want To Hold Your Hand*. One of the scenes, by the use of special effects and editing, teamed up John with Hanks, who played the dim-witted Gump. Having just become world ping-pong champion, Gump is interviewed on *The Dick Cavett Show*. The other guest is John Lennon and there is some dialogue between them. The scene was based on the actual interview John and Yoko gave to Dick Cavett on 9 September 1971. New footage of Hanks was used, placing him in the chair where Yoko was sitting. Cavett had extensive make-up to make him look twenty years younger. The words John used were his original ones, although his voice was rerecorded by the actor Joe Stefanelli.

Foyle's Literary Luncheon

A major event on the London literary calendar.

Christina Foyle owned the world's largest bookshop, Foyle's in Charing Cross Road, and held an annual prestigious literary luncheon. It was G Wren Howard, chairman of Jonathan Cape, the publishers of John's book *In His Own Write*, who suggested to Foyle that the 1964 luncheon be held in John's honour to celebrate *In His Own Write*. She agreed and it was officially announced on 23 March.

About 600 guests attended the function and the cartoonist Sir Osbert Lancaster had agreed to take the chair. The guests on the top table included Yehudi Menuhin, Mary Quant, Alma Cogan, Dora Bryan, Wilfred Brambell, Lionel Bart, Arthur Askey, Cicely Courtnidge, Giles, Harry Secombe, Victor Sylvester, Colin Wilson and Helen Shapiro.

Paul, George and Ringo were also invited, but they declined.

The event was held at the Dorchester Hotel on 23 April 1964 and Lancaster made his introductory speech.

He said, 'At John Lennon's request, I must pay tribute to his Beatles colleagues. I have only, alas, seen them through the medium of the television screen. In the Royal Variety Show they shone out like a good deed in a naughty world. They have re-established something pretty rare, something that has the same measure of success as the old English music hall: an accord between the stage and the audience. They represent, however different their methods may be, the genuine strength of English entertainment far more successfully than rows of ladies and gentlemen tramping with bustles and false whiskers. Therefore, it gives me great pleasure to propose the toast to one of the Beatles today – the one who has produced his first book. I find his book enormously provocative. Its message comes through straight and clear.'

John then half rose from his seat, muttered a five-second speech, 'Thank you and bless you,' and sat down. He later explained that he did not feel up to it, saying, 'Give me another fifteen years and I may make a speech. Anyway, I daren't today. I was scared stiff.'

Actually, John and Cynthia had spent the previous evening at the Ad Lib club and arrived at the Dorchester feeling a trifle under the weather.

Cynthia sat between the Earl of Arran and the singer Marty Wilde. John had to face a battery of TV cameras and press followers. After he had mumbled his few words, which some reports stated were 'Thank you all very much; you've got a lucky face,' he sat down.

The toastmaster then called on Brian Epstein to speak on John's behalf.

The writer Sandra Shevey comments, 'Brian Epstein publicly repudiated the book by saying that he had not encouraged John to write it, nor had he involved himself with its publication.'

Later, John signed copies of his book.

One woman stuck ten copies under his nose and said, 'Put your name clearly there,' then turned to a friend and said, 'I never thought I would stoop to asking for such an autograph.'

John told her, 'And I never thought I would be forced to sign my name for someone like you.'

A critic commented, 'Mr Osbert Lancaster, always clever and amusing and a brilliant speaker, was the chairman and made a scintillating speech. The author, who is of course one of the famous Beatles, sat next to him and refused to make a speech or even say a few words. The only other speakers were Mr Brian Epstein, to whom the Beatles owe so much of their tremendous success as he is their brilliant young manager, and another Liverpudlian, Mr Arthur Askey, who quickly had the whole room laughing.'

Frankenstein's monster

A creature created by the author Mary Shelley in the classic novel *Frankenstein*, which has become one of the most familiar of all monster stories.

In the animated film *Yellow Submarine*, Captain Fred sets out from Pepperland in a yellow submarine and travels to Liverpool to seek the help of the Beatles. He first encounters Ringo. The two then set out to gather the three remaining members of the group and Ringo and Captain Fred enter a room where a giant Frankenstein monster lies on a table, waiting to be revived. Despite Fred's protests, Ringo sets the machinery in motion and with much crackling of electricity and flashing of lights, the creature is animated and arises, towering above them. Then, in a speedy transformation, the creature metamorphoses into John, who then joins them on their mission.

Free As A Bird

John made a home demo of this number late in 1977, composing on piano. The next year, when he was planning a Broadway musical *The Ballad of John and Yoko*, he put the track aside as one of the compositions to be used in the show.

The demo was featured on Show No 78 of *The Lost Lennon Tapes* radio series in the late 1980s.

In 1993, Yoko Ono gave Paul McCartney a number of John's demo discs for the three surviving Beatles to consider as a potential single. The three considered 'Free As A Bird', 'Real Love' and 'Grow Old With Me', finally deciding on 'Free As A Bird' at the beginning of 1994.

The three remaining ex-Beatles took the incomplete 1980 Lennon tape and, with digital help from Jeff Lynne, finished the song which had been begun by John. The version Yoko gave to Paul has a second verse, a completed bridge and a different coda. Paul and George partially wrote their own bridge, ignored the third Lennon verse and included a slightly different melody and coda.

Yoko said, 'There are several versions of the song, and I selected the one that was best in terms of the quality of John's voice and performance for them to work with. I didn't know whether it was a good idea to take John's voice out of a tape and make something out of it like Natalie Cole did. Of course, 'Unforgettable' was a multi-track made in the studio, with Natalie Cole just putting her voice on it, which is very different from using a cassette work tape. I really had to go through a soul search about that. Then I finally found a tape that would probably work well, and it did.'

The so-called Threetles then began to work on the number at Paul's studio, the Mill, in Sussex. The recordings went on at various times over the next twelve months. Jeff Lynne, rather than George Martin, was selected as producer. George, who had worked with him when he produced the Traveling Wilburys, recommended him. The engineer was Geoff Emerick, who was assisted by John Jacobs.

The record only reached No 9 in the charts, with a chart life of 6 weeks. However, Yoko was to say, 'It's a beautiful song. I feel that the new production of 'Free As A Bird' was a great success, and it has given so much love, inspiration and excitement to people all over the world. It was a great thing that happened, and I know that Paul, George and Ringo really gave their best effort to it. I'm very happy about that.'

Free As A Bird *(video)*

This video was produced by Vincent Joller and directed by Joe Pytka. John Samerad blended archival footage with new material using computer technology. It was Pytka's idea to use references to the Beatles lives and music in the video and the clues were numerous, with almost 100 references.

These include a girl wearing a plastic mac ('Polythene Pam') while another whispers in her boyfriend's ear ('Do You Want to Know A Secret?'). Another woman carries a suitcase ('She's Leaving Home') and we see Penny Lane and Strawberry Fields.

A man at a typewriter is a 'Paperback Writer', kids in pig masks refer to 'Piggies' and there's a 'Blackbird' flying in the trees. Paul's dog Martha ('Martha My Dear') makes an appearance, and there are scores of other intriguing and arcane visual references.

Free Time

An American public-broadcast television show on which John and Yoko appeared on Thursday 14 October 1971. It was transmitted on the New York television station WNET TV.

Freedom Films

When John and Yoko were invited to submit work for inclusion in the Chicago Film Festival in 1971, they produced two sixty-second shorts especially for the event. John's contribution was simply the scratching of the word 'Freedom' directly on to film so that the word had an animated jerk.

John's electronic keyboard, playing two notes, which were repeated, provided the soundtrack to Yoko's one-minute venture, which consisted of a slow-motion shot of her taking off her bra and tossing it away.

Freeman, Robert

A photographer, born in England in 1936. Freeman became closely associated with the Beatles and travelled with them extensively from 1963 to 1966. He was first alerted to the group on the suggestion of Dick Fontaine, a Granada director who had filmed them at the Cavern.

Freeman contacted Brian Epstein, who asked him to send a selection of his work. He then received a message from Epstein, who arranged for Freeman to meet the Beatles at the Palace Hotel, Bournemouth, in August 1963. He met them and showed them his photographs. He was to say, 'The one who attracted my attention the most was John Lennon. He was the wittiest and his appeal was very strong.'

Within a few days he was asked to shoot the cover of their next album, *With the Beatles*, and he suggested a black-and-white shot, which he took in the dining room of the hotel with a telephoto lens during a half-hour session. Neil Aspinall had suggested that the Beatles wear black polo-neck sweaters.

Freeman was then invited to go to Sweden with the group and

during the five-day trip shared a hotel room with John. While they were in Stockholm he took the photograph that was to become the cover of their *Long Tall Sally* EP.

He next went with them to France during their short Olympia season and took the photos for their *A Hard Day's Night* album, creating a series of shots in the style of polyphotos. Epstein and the Beatles then discussed their next album cover, *Beatles For Sale*, with him and the decision was made for it to be in colour and at an outside location. They chose Hyde Park.

Altogether, Freeman was responsible for the pictures and design of five of their albums, the others being *Help!* and *Rubber Soul*.

The photographer also designed the final credit sequence for *A Hard Day's Night* and designed the letters of 'Help!' in the film, in addition to shooting the final sequence.

Freeman designed a circular montage of Beatles' faces for the *Revolver* album, but the group rejected it in favour of Klaus Voormann's design, ending Freeman's run of Beatles record sleeves.

Late in 1963 John and Cynthia were guests of Freeman and his wife in their Emperor's Gate flat. The couple mentioned that they were seeking a place to live in London. Freeman told them that the maisonette directly above him was free and made enquiries on their behalf. As a result, early in 1964 John, Cynthia and Julian moved into Flat 3, Emperor's Gate, Kensington. They used the pseudonym Hadley. Freeman considered the relationship between John and Cynthia a better one than that between John and Yoko.

He was also approached by the publishers Jonathan Cape to design the covers of *In His Own Write* and, the following year, *A Spaniard in the Works*.

Freeman had been taking many informal shots of the Beatles backstage, in addition to live action performances and professional sessions for record sleeves. In 1964, a compilation of his work, entitled *Beatles Ltd*, became the first published photographic book on the Beatles when it was issued by George Newnes.

He currently lives near Madrid, Spain.

Frees, Paul

An American actor who provided the voice of John for a series of 52 animation films of the Beatles, first screened by ABC TV in America in 1965.

Frees made no attempt to capture a Liverpool accent and the actual phoney British accent that he did use was one John found amusing.

Frees also provided the voice for George Harrison in the series.

From Hamburg to Hollywood

A deluxe limited-edition book of Jurgen Vollmer's photographs, including his early shots of the Beatles in Hamburg and the famous picture of John Lennon in a doorway that was to feature as the cover of the *Rock 'n' Roll* album. It was published by Genesis Publications in 1997. The edition was limited to 1,750 signed copies.

From Me To You

A collaboration by John and Paul which they wrote together in the back of a van on 28 February 1963 on their way from York to Shrewsbury. The title had been inspired by the readers' letters column in the *New Musical Express*, which was called 'From You To Us'. It was recorded on 5 March and released as the third Beatles single on 11 April, reaching No. 1 in the charts, a position it retained for six weeks. It was issued by Vee Jay in the US on 27 May 1963, but failed to chart, and was also unsuccessful when Vee Jay rereleased it on 10 August 1964.

John was to say, 'I think the first line was mine. I mean, I know it was mine. And then after that we took it from there. It was far bluesier than that when we wrote it.' He also commented, 'We nearly didn't record it because we thought it was too bluesy at first, but when we'd finished it and George Martin had scored it with harmonica, it was all right.'

Interestingly enough, Del Shannon recorded the song and issued it as a single in America on 3 June 1963, a week after the Beatles' version came out in the States.

From Them To Us

This Beatles Christmas album, issued on 18 December 1970, was a compilation of tracks from their fan club records previously released each December from 1963 to 1969. It includes material written by John, which he either sings or speaks.

The four items by John are: 'Gary Crimble', 'Old King Wenceslas', 'Jock and Yono' and 'Once Upon a Pooltable'.

'Gary Crimble' is a typical example of Lennon's fractured English style, of the type that appeared in his books: 'Gary Crimble to you, / Gary Mimple to you, / Getty Baybull dear Christmas, / Happy Birthday me too!'

'Old King Wenceslas' is in similar vein, a Lennonised version of the traditional carol 'Good King Wenceslas', with name checks for Henry Hall, David Lloyd and Betty Grable. 'Jock and Yono' is a piece John wrote as a defence against the attitude of Paul and George towards Yoko. He said, 'The only thing I did was write that piece about "some of our beast friends" in my usual way, because I was never honest enough. I always had to write in that gobbledegook.'

He refers to the lines in 'Jock and Yono' that say: 'But they battled on against overwhelming oddities / (Including some of their beast friends.)' Their 'beast friends' refers to Paul and George. 'Once Upon a Pooltable' is a four-verse nonsense poem.

Frost on Sunday

A London Weekend Television show, hosted by David Frost. John and Yoko were guests on the programme on Saturday 24 August 1968. This fourth edition of the show took place at Wembley Studios and was transmitted from 6.45 to 7.40 p.m. The couple were able to discuss their art, work and exhibitions. Other guests in the show were Blossom Dearie and Stan Freberg.

John was wearing a badge with the slogan 'You are here'. Frost asked him about the badge and John said, 'People read it and suddenly realise it's true. Yes, I'm here, they think. So are these other people. We're all here together. And that's where the vibrations start being exchanged. Good and bad ones according to who is sending out and how they feel.'

Frost Programme, The

On Friday 29 September 1967 John and George appeared on this evening Rediffusion chat show, taped earlier in the day at Wembley Studios. The duo discussed transcendental meditation with David Frost and the programme was aired at 10.30 p.m. The subject proved so fascination to the viewing audience that John and George returned to the studios on Wednesday 4 October to discuss it even further. The entire 45 minutes was devoted to the discussion in which questions were asked by the studio audience

Furlong, June

An artist's model at Liverpool College of Art during the years in which John attended.

Posing in the nude in front of a large class is usually a serious business, but Lennon often caused chaos. June remembers one incident in which he jumped from behind his easel as soon as the teacher left the room and sat on her knee and began groping her and necking with her. On another occasion he handed the teacher, Terry Griffiths, his drawing of June in the nude, which consisted solely of a sketch of her wristwatch.

June lent John some of her clothing when he appeared in an Art College pantomime of *Cinderella* in 1959. John was an ugly sister, together with his mate Geoff Mohammed, and the clothes June lent him included a pair of pink corsets, a dark-blue dress with white polka-dot decoration, a straw hat with pink and blue feather decoration and a pair of Victorian pinch-back earrings.

June put all of the items up for auction at the Eldon E Worrall sale in Liverpool in 1985.

The former Beatles agent Alan Williams acquired Stuart Sutcliffe's oil painting of June in the nude and sold it at auction in August 1998 for £2,500.

Gallagher, Liam and Noel

Leaders of the Manchester band Oasis. Liam, who is married to the film actress Patsy Kensit, had always rated John Lennon as one of his heroes and the couple named their first child, born in 1999, Lennon. They even received a handwritten note and sketch from Yoko Ono that read, 'To Lennon, welcome to the world. Love, love, love, Yoko.' The influence of the Beatles on the band is well documented and Liam's elder brother Noel, the songwriter of the group, told Tony Parsons in an interview for *GQ* magazine, 'All that screaming and shouting in bags – that's not me. John Lennon was probably clinically insane. I don't like much of his solo stuff, but I think musically he did it with the Beatles.'

Gallatone Champion

John's first guitar, which he obtained by mail order after seeing it advertised in *Reveille*. With a loan from his Aunt Mimi, he purchased the acoustic instrument for £10. There was a sticker inside the body, which announced 'Guaranteed not to split.' It arrived together with a Mills Music self-help book, *Play the Guitar*.

The Gallatone was the one John was playing when he first met Paul at the St Peter's village fête.

The guitar was sold at Sotheby's in an auction held in September 1999, where it raised £140,000.

3 Gambier Terrace

Gambier Terrace is a handsome Georgian terrace directly facing the Anglican cathedral in Liverpool. Situated less than a hundred yards from the Liverpool College of Art and Liverpool Institute, it also housed the junior art school and a nurses' home. Attendees at the junior art school included Cynthia Powell (later to marry John), Phyllis McKenzie, Helen Anderson, Bill Harry and Leslie Chadwick (who took photographs of the Beatles for *Mersey Beat* under the name Peter Kaye).

Two of John's schoolmates, Rod Murray and Stuart Sutcliffe, had both rented flats at No. 7 Percy Street, to the rear of Gambier Terrace.

Rod then leased No. 3 Gambier Terrace with his girlfriend Diz and another art student Margaret Duxbury. The flat comprised an entire floor of the building. Stuart and John were to move in. The first room was twenty foot square. There was a room at the back where Stuart originally slept in and was used as a studio. John moved in there with him. Diz and Margaret Duxbury had a small room, but they moved out and another student Rod Jones moved in after them. There was also a long corridor with a bathroom and kitchen at the end. The premises were quite large and John often had Cynthia stay with him, while Murray had just his girlfriend Diz as a fairly regular flatmate. Sutcliffe had no girl at the time and slept in a camp bed in the smallest of the rooms.

As students, they couldn't afford proper furniture and the elegance of the flat was often rendered tawdry by their erratic lifestyle and Stuart's painting equipment.

The Beatles sometimes rehearsed at the premises and they brought Royston Ellis, the beat poet, back to their flat after backing him at a 'Poetry-to-Beat' session at the Jacaranda. John Lennon once put Bill Harry and his girlfriend Virginia up in the bath overnight after a late-night chat session.

However, the premises were never as bad as those described in 'The Beatnik Horror' article in the *Sunday People* newspaper in the summer of 1960. The paper had decided to expose beatniks and deliberately angled stories to present beatniks as filthy layabouts.

The particular issue in which a photograph appeared of the main room in the Gambier terrace flat showed it to be in an appalling mess, with objects strewn about the floor. Among the five people lying around were Allan Williams and Stuart Sutcliffe.

This was a put-up job as the *Sunday People* reporters had been spending some time at the Jacaranda, and Allan Williams, ever helpful to the press, had decided to use John and Stuart's flat to facilitate the needs of the *Sunday People* story, deliberately roughing up the flat to provide the sort of picture they were after.

After the *Sunday People* exposé, they were asked to vacate the premises. Rod Jones moved to Jersey and as John and Stuart had left for Germany with the Beatles, Rod Murray was left alone in the flat.

When the Beatles left for Germany, Rod Murray was saddled with the entire rent bill, which he couldn't afford, so he had to move out. Mrs Sutcliffe collected Stuart's and John's possessions and Murray moved into a cheaper flat nearby. Among the items he'd taken with him from Gambier Terrace were copies of John's *Daily Howl*.

Gambier Terrace continues as a site for residential flats.

Garry, Len

Born 6 January 1942. His father was a printer, Henry Garry, who had married Phyllis Cartwright. They had two sons, Walter and Len.

Len Garry became a pupil at Liverpool Institute and used the same classroom as John's friends Ivan Vaughan and Bill Turner. As a result Len, who lived in the Penny Lane area, was introduced to John through Ivan Vaughan and became a member of his local gang.

When John formed the Quarry Men he and Pete Shotton made a bass instrument together out of a broom handle and an old tea chest. Initially they had a Quarry Bank schoolfriend, Bill Smith, play it, but he proved unreliable and they asked Len to take over. He joined the skiffle group in June 1957 and remained with them until January 1958.

Len and a fellow pupil, Bill Turner, bumped into John and Pete Shotton when they had a day off from the Institute and

John said, 'Why don't you come and join Quarry Bank? We've got a crazy art teacher. He won't know the difference.' So the two of them attended Quarry Bank for the afternoon as a prank.

He also recalls the Saturday night gatherings on the hill opposite the lake in Calderstones Park, where everyone used to congregate, most arriving on bikes. They'd all hang around chatting up the girls and would then get on their bikes and cycle down to the chip shop in Penny Lane.

Len and John began chatting up two girls and one of them, Barbara Baker, went out with Len and then began to date John, becoming his first serious girlfriend.

His career with the Quarry Men ended when, at the age of sixteen, he was struck down with tubercular meningitis and was taken to Fazakerley Hospital, where he was in a coma for a week. He was at the hospital for some time and remembers John and Paul visiting him and telling him that they'd changed the name of the group to the Silver Beatles.

Also in the hospital was Nigel Walley, who was suffering from pleurisy – and was a DJ on the hospital's radio.

Later, when John was at the art college, Len would accompany Paul and George from Liverpool Institute to Arthur Ballard's classroom during an occasional lunchtime to play for the students, with Len as one of the guitarists.

Len still lives in Liverpool, where he is a teacher, and occasionally takes time off to play with a revived Quarry Men.

Garwell, Barbara

Hull housewife who claimed she had been having premonitions in her dreams since the age of sixteen.

She said she had a dream in 1980 in which she saw John walking down some stairs with a stethoscope around his neck. She added: 'I was a patient lying in bed and John came into the room, still with the stethoscope around his neck. Suddenly I awoke from the dream and John's figure appeared to me at the bottom of my bed. I knew in that instant that something terrible had happened to him.'

The next morning she heard the announcements of John's death and later said, 'When the full facts became known I realised he'd died at more or less the same moment as he appeared to me in the bedroom.'

Gator Bowl

Venue in Jackson, Florida where the Beatles appeared on Friday 11 September 1964. When they were originally told that there would be a segregated audience they said they'd refuse to appear before segregated audiences, and the idea of segregation was dropped. John stated, 'We never play to segregated audiences and we're not going to start now. I'd sooner lose our appearance money.'

They also refused to tour South Africa for the same reason.

Gay Liberation Book, The

A book of homosexual writings published in America in the spring of 1972. John was invited to contribute and he penned a short limerick, together with a drawing of a male nude perched on a cloud.

His untitled limerick read:

Why make it so sad to be gay?
Doing your own thing is OK.
Our bodies are our own
So leave us alone.
Go play with yourself – today.

John signed the drawing and dated it 1972.

The limerick is the shortest poem John ever had published, in addition to its being his only published verse in this form.

Other contributors to *The Gay Liberation Book* included Alan Watts, Huey Newton, Gore Vidal, Allen Ginsberg and William Burroughs.

Gebhardt, Steve

An architect turned filmmaker from Ohio who was hired by John and Yoko during John's first visit to New York, when the couple were staying at the St Regis Hotel. Gebhardt was made a director of Joko Productions.

When they first met him he was working for Yoko's friend Jonas Mekas at the Anthology Film Archives in New York. They were looking for someone to help them produce two films, *Up Your Legs Forever* and *Fly*, and immediately hired Gebhardt.

Of the first movie, which was shot at the ABC television Studios in Manhattan, Gebhardt remembered they filmed the legs of numerous New York celebrities, standing them on a podium while John and Yoko sat in directors' chairs chain-smoking. He said their subjects included lots of people from Andy Warhol's group; John Cage; the painters Robert Rauschenberg and Jasper Johns; Jann Wenner, publisher of *Rolling Stone* magazine; Shirley Clarke and Jonas Mekas, who wouldn't take off his underpants!

They next moved into a loft in the Bowery to film *Fly*. Gebhardt, along with Dan Richter, painted a corner of the loft, brought in an Oriental rug and a bed and, together with Yoko, began to audition dozens of actresses until they decided on Virginia Lust.

The idea was that the actress would lie supine on the bed while a fly crawled across her naked body. He recalls, 'Yoko said put the fly on her pussy. I said the woman was having her period; there was a Tampax string there. She said, "Take it out." I told her to do it herself, and she did. Then we resumed filming.'

Gebhardt and Richter then produced and edited the film and delivered the prints to the Elgin Theatre scant hours before they were due to be screened. The two movies had been completed from scratch in only two weeks.

John and Yoko then asked Gebhardt to come to England, where he worked on the *Imagine* film, for which he was paid $100 a week by Allen Klein. He was responsible for editing 100,000 feet of film to 48 minutes.

Gebhardt was placed in charge of Joko Films in New York, working on the avant-garde movies, booking them into campuses across America, making the licensing deals and attending to the accounts.

Gebhardt then told them that he wanted to make a documentary on the Rolling Stones and John and Yoko told him to go ahead. The film was called *Ladies and Gentlemen, the Rolling Stones!*.

Altogether, Gebhardt worked on fourteen of John and Yoko's films, including the John Sinclair concert, *Ten For Two* and *Imagine*. His association was soured and resulted in his sacking when Yoko discovered that he had billed himself as director (which he was) of the Rolling Stones documentary. Although

Yoko wasn't present at either the filming or the editing, she felt that she should have been billed as director.

In 1984 Gebhardt contacted Yoko again and said he had an idea for a film documentary about John in which John's own voice would narrate the story of his life. Yoko expressed interest so he sent her a three-hour unfinished film, which still needed work, but which he felt would give Yoko an idea of what he had in mind.

Unfortunately, he used an excerpt from an interview John did with the disc jockey Andy Peebles shortly before John's death. Part of the original interview had John commenting, 'When I left England I still couldn't go on the street. We couldn't walk round the block, couldn't go in a restaurant, unless you wanted to go with the business of star-going-in-the-restaurant garbage.' He also said, 'When we first moved here, we lived in the Village, in Greenwich Village, which is a sort of arsty-fartsy section of town, for those who don't know, where all the students and would-be's live, you know? A few old poets and that. You know, people have lived here for years, still live here. [Yoko] told me that, "Yes, you can walk on the street." You know, she said, "You will be able to walk here." But I was walking around tense like, waiting for somebody to say something, or jump on me, and it took me two years to unwind.

'I can go right out this door now and go in a restaurant. You want to know what a treat that is? Or go to the movies? I mean, people come and ask for autographs, or say, "Hi", but they don't bug you, you know. They just, "Oh, hey. How you doin'? Like your record." '

Unfortunately for Gebhardt, he used only a small excerpt, with John saying 'She told me that, "Yes, you can walk on the street." You know, she said, "You will be able to walk here." '

As a result, Yoko thought that, because she encouraged John to walk the street, this was a form of blame, which actually wasn't Gebhardt's intention, but the film project never went through.

Gebhardt was also horrified in 1985 to see what Yoko had done to the film he'd made of the One To One concert, John's last major concert appearance. Gebhardt had edited the original film under John's supervision and it was originally broadcast in America on ABC TV on Thursday 14 December 1972.

However, the video release had completely altered the film. Yoko had completely re-edited the tapes, reducing John's presence and increasing her own. She abandoned John's powerful evening performance and replaced it with the afternoon performance, which John had regarded only as a 'rehearsal'.

Geffen, David

Born on Manhattan's Lower East Side in New York in 1943. He joined the mailroom of the William Morris Agency in 1964 and by 1967 had become one of the company's top agents.

He founded Asylum Records in 1971, which made stars of groups such as the Eagles, and sold the company to Warner in 1972 for $7 million. He created Geffen Records in 1980 and Yoko first met him on 19 September 1980 after first studying his astrological chart. During the meeting he agreed to release the *Double Fantasy* album. A contract with him was then signed on 22 September.

Yoko decided to split from Geffen Records in 1982 and under an agreement there was one final release, *The John Lennon Collection*, issued in America on 8 November 1982.

Geffen then went on to sign artists such as Elton John and Guns N' Roses and sold his company to MCA Records in 1989 for $550 million. In 1994 he founded Dreamworks with Steven Spielberg and Jeffrey Katzenberg and by the year 2000 his personal wealth was estimated at $3 billion.

Gentle, Johnny

Liverpool singer (real name John Askew), who was part of the Larry Parnes stable of acts. When Parnes auditioned a handful of Liverpool bands at the Wyvern Club in Liverpool on 10 May 1960, he decided on the Silver Beetles as the group to back Gentle on a short tour of Scotland from 20–28 May. They comprised John Lennon, Paul McCartney, George Harrison, Stuart Sutcliffe and Tommy Moore. On 21 May they appeared in Inverness. Gentle recalls that while they were staying at a hotel in Inverness he played a song he'd been writing to John and George. It was called 'I've Just Fallen For Someone'. He recalled he was having difficulty with the middle eight and says, 'John came up with something he had written which happened to fit this song I was writing. I had a middle eight but wasn't happy with it and John agreed and he started telling me what I needed. I was annoyed. I thought, Here's this upstart telling me how to write songs. But when he played me his middle eight I was impressed. I used it when I recorded the song a year later on Parlophone under the name Darren Young. It must be the first recorded work of John Lennon.'

When it was released, the record sold about 3,000 copies.

Getting Better

A song co-written by John and Paul. It was while Paul was walking his dog Martha that he saw the sun come up and thought, It's getting better. John arrived at Paul's Cavendish Avenue house to compose further material for the *Sergeant Pepper* album and Paul suggested that they work on a number called 'Getting Better'. They spent twelve hours writing the song, taking a break to have a meal. Paul commented, 'All I remember is that I said, "It's getting better all the time," and John contributed the legendary line, "It couldn't get much worse," which I thought was very good. Against the spirit of that song – which was all super-optimistic – then there's that lovely little sardonic line. Typical John.'

On 21 March 1967, when they were overdubbing the song, John began to feel weird. He'd taken LSD. He said, 'I suddenly got so scared on the mike. I thought I felt ill, and I thought I was going to crack. I said I must get some air.' He also said, 'They all took me upstairs on the roof, and George Martin was looking at me funny, and then it dawned on me I must have taken acid. I said, "Well, I can't go on – you'll have to do it, and I'll just stay and watch." You know I got very nervous just watching them all. I was saying, "Is it all right?" and they were saying "Yeah". They had all been very kind, and they carried on making the record.'

Paul then took him home and when they got there Paul took LSD to keep John company and it was the first time he had ever experienced the psychedelic drug.

Gibraltar

British colony in the Mediterranean, known as the Rock, with a population of less than 30,000.

John and Yoko decided to get married there after consulting Peter Brown. They were unsuccessful in arranging for their wedding to take place on a cross-Channel ferry as the captains of ferries no longer performed marriages. The couple's trip on a cross-Channel ferry was halted because of passport queries, so they flew to Paris. From Paris they phoned Peter Brown in London and asked him if he could discover a convenient place for them to have a speedy and secret wedding. He called them back to suggest Gibraltar.

John later said: 'We chose Gibraltar because it is quiet, British and friendly.'

Yoko's divorce from her second husband Anthony Cox had become final on 2 February and Paul and Linda had got married on 12 March. On 20 March 1969, John and Yoko, who were on holiday in Paris, flew in a chartered private plane to Gibraltar where they were met at the airport by Peter Brown and the photographer David Nutter, who were the only witnesses to the ceremony.

The jet, piloted by Captain Trevor Coppleston, landed in Gibraltar at 8.30 a.m. and the party arrived at the British consulate building at 9 a.m.

John and Yoko were in their 'white period' and Yoko was dressed in white knee socks, white linen minidress and white wide-brimmed hat. John wore a white jacket, white pullover and white trousers and both wore white tennis shoes.

John was to say, 'We are two love birds. Intellectually we didn't believe in getting married. But one doesn't love someone just intellectually. For two people, marriage still has the edge over just living together.'

The registrar, Cecil Wheeler, conducted the three-minute ceremony, during which John smoked a cigarette. The couple then flew by private jet to Paris, having spent a total of seventy minutes in Gibraltar. A few days later they were to hold press conferences at their honeymoon in Amsterdam.

Gibson, Gary

A singer from Preston who bears an uncanny resemblance to John. He began a show business career as guitarist/vocalist with a group called Cavern.

Discussing the number of fans who mistake him for a resurrected John, he says, 'I try to let them down lightly. I smile and say, "I'm not John Lennon at all – I'm Tom Jones!" '

Gibson was able to pursue a successful career as a John Lennon lookalike and was also featured on the TV show *Stars In Their Eyes*.

Gimme Some Truth

A track from the *Imagine* album, also known as 'Give Me Some Truth'. John had written the song in India and had originally rehearsed it during the *Let It Be* sessions, although the Beatles never recorded the song. When John began rehearsing the number in January 1969 it was still incomplete and two more years were to pass before he finished it.

'Gimme Some Truth' was finally recorded in July 1971. John played guitar on the track and George Harrison supported him on lead guitar, Nicky Hopkins on piano, Klaus Voormann on bass, Alan White on drums, with Rod Lynton and Andy Crosswell-Davis on acoustic guitars.

Gimme Some Truth (documentary)

A documentary on the making of the *Imagine* album, compiled by Yoko Ono and Andrew Solt, which was premiered in Cannes on 5 October 1999. The 56-minute film included previously unseen footage. It had been compiled by Yoko and Solt from hundreds of hours of 16mm footage taken at Tittenhurst Park during the making of the album in 1971. Solt produced and directed with Yoko credited as executive producer.

The 1971 footage, shot by Nick Knowland, includes sequences featured in Solt's 1988 film *Imagine: John Lennon*. There are also scenes of the band recording the album, with John and Nicky Hopkins on piano and a visit to the Ascot mansion by the *Red Mole* editors Tariq Ali and Robin Blackburn.

In addition to the Tittenhurst Park footage, there are scenes in New York featuring Andy Warhol and Jack Nicholson.

Gimme Some Truth also includes appearances by Phil Spector and Miles Davis and the film ends with a shot of John and Yoko walking towards the horizon on Staten Island. The documentary was aired on several TV stations internationally before being issued on DVD in the autumn of 2000 to tie in with celebrations to mark what would have been John's sixtieth birthday. The *Imagine* album was due to be issued on CD at the same time.

Girl

One of John's compositions featured on the *Rubber Soul* album, issued in December 1965. John said the song was about a dream girl, but there can be various interpretations for anyone studying the lyrics: they could refer to Cynthia, or they could refer to a woman whom he was seeking, but had yet to find – Yoko.

John was to comment, 'This was about a dream girl. When Paul and I wrote the lyrics in the old days we used to laugh about it like the Tin Pan Alley people would. And it was only later on that we tried to match the lyrics to the tune. I like this one. It was one of my best.'

There were two cover versions of the song, both of which entered the British charts. One was by the Manchester group St Louis Union, who reached No. 19 with the song, but it was their only hit. The other was by the duo Truth, and it reached No. 18.

The Beatles version was included on *The Beatles 1962–1966*, issued in April 1973, and on the *Love Songs* album from *The Beatles Collection* boxed set, issued in the autumn of 1977 and in *The Beatles Box*, issued in December 1980.

Give Me Something

A Yoko Ono track on the *Double Fantasy* album.

Give Peace a Chance

A song composed during John and Yoko's second Bed-In at the Queen Elizabeth Hotel, Montreal, Canada. The couple were staying in Room 1742, where John composed the song. He then ordered an eight-track mobile recording unit from the Andre Perry Studios, and the equipment was installed in the bedroom

On the evening of Sunday 1 June 1969, John and Yoko began recording their peace anthem in the company of a number of guests. Tommy Smothers joined John, playing guitar and singing. Yoko joined in, adding to the sound effects by banging on a wardrobe. Members of the chorus included the poet Allen Ginsberg, the LSD guru Timothy Leary and his wife Rosemary, the comedian Dick Gregory, the singer Petula Clark, Derek Taylor, Rabbi Geinsberg, a priest, members of the Canadian chapter of the Radha Krishna Temple and the disc jockeys Murray the K and Roger Scott. Additional voices on the chorus came from the film crew, journalists and members of the hotel staff.

In addition to the mantra-like repetition of the title, various names of people such as Norman Mailer and Tommy Cooper were added to the mélange.

There is a muffled double drum beat, which John explained with, 'My rhythm sense has always been a bit wild, and halfway through I got on the on beat instead of the backbeat, and it was hard because of all the non-musicians playing with us. So I had to put a lot of tape echo to keep a steady beat right through the record.'

He was also to point out that he had censored part of the song, commenting, 'The real word I used on the record was "masturbation", but I'd just got into trouble for "The Ballad of John and Yoko" and I didn't want any more fuss, so I put "mastication" in the written lyric. It was a cop-out, but the message about peace was more important to me than having a little laugh about a word.'

The song was the first recording to be credited to the Plastic Ono Band and the first solo single by a member of the Beatles. It was issued in Britain on Apple 13 on 4 July 1969 and in America on Apple 1809 on 7 July. The single sold over two million copies and reached No. 2 in the British charts and No. 14 in the American charts.

Perhaps through a sense of guilt, John issued the songwriting credit under the Lennon and McCartney banner.

The single also introduced another policy by John: that of presenting a Yoko Ono composition on the flip side of his recordings. The number was 'Remember Love', which Yoko had also composed and recorded during the Bed-In.

It had been John's desire to write a peace anthem that would take over from the song 'We Shall Overcome' – and he succeeded. On 15 November 1969 almost half a million people sang 'Give Peace a Chance' outside the White House in Washington and it became the main anti-Vietnam protest song.

On Monday 12 March 1984 EMI issued the number as a single, with 'Cold Turkey' on the flip as part of their series Golden 45s.

At the inset of the Gulf War, a special version of 'Give Peace a Chance' was issued as an antiwar song. Among the participants were Yoko Ono, Sean Lennon, Lennie Kravitz and a number of other artists, recording under the name the Peace Choir. The song was issued on Tuesday January 15 1991, but was banned by the BBC in Britain.

Kravitz, who was the person who originally suggested a new version of the song, had produced the number. He commented, 'I was quite nervous because you don't just ask someone to redo a Lennon song, but the minute Yoko Ono heard the idea, she said, "Let's do it, it sounds brilliant." '

It was released during the week beginning Monday 28 January and the initial pressing of 300,000 copies swiftly sold out. When it entered the billboard chart it became the first song hit recorded by two generations of the same family since Nat King Cole and Natalie Cole's recordings of 'When I Fall In Love'.

The full line-up of the Peace Choir who recorded the number was: Amina, Adam Ant, Sebastian Bach, Bros, Felix Cavallere, Terence Trent D'Arby, Flea, John Frusciante, Peter Gabriel, Kadeem Hardison, Ofra Haza, Joe Higgs, Bruce Hornsby, Lee Jaffe, Al Jarreau, Jazzle B, Davey Johnstone, Lenny Kravitz, Cyndi Lauper, Sean Lennon, Little Richard, LL Cool J, MC Hammer, Michael McDonald, Duff McKagan, Alannah Myles, New Voices of Freedom, Randy Newman, Yoko Ono, Tom Petty, Iggy Pop, Q-Tip, Bonnie Raitt, Run, Dave Stewart, Teena Marie, Little Steven Van Zandt, Don Was, Wendy and Lisa, Ahmet Zappa, Dweezil Zappa and Moon Zappa.

Give Peace a Chance (film)

A 61-minute film of John and Yoko's Bed-In, filmed in Montreal in 1969. Part of the film was edited down for the three-minute promo of the same title. Excerpts were also used in the 1988 film *Imagine: John Lennon*. A 75-minute version under the title *John and Yoko: the Bed-In*, was released on video in Britain in 1990.

Give Peace a Chance: Music and the Struggle for Peace

A 122-page book which also acted as a catalogue for the Chicago Peace Museum exhibition of John and Yoko's work, which was compiled with the aid of Yoko. There is an initial 24-page section concerning John and Yoko, illustrated with photographs by Bob Gruen.

There are also a number of essays concerning John and his peace efforts. They included an item from the *Los Angeles Times* on John's problems with the FBI, a *Rolling Stone* report on a John and Yoko peace conference and a feature by Jon Weiner called 'Give Me Some Truth: John Lennon and the Sixties'.

Give Peace a Chance (promo)

A film supervised and edited by Yoko as a promotional clip for the couple's version of 'Give Peace a Chance', recorded at the Reine Elizabeth Hotel in Montreal in 1969. Also known as *Bed Peace* or *Bed In*, it was edited down to three minutes by Yoko.

Originally, the entire week-long Bed-In at the hotel had been filmed for a projected feature-length movie to be called *The Way It Is*. Extracts from the footage, such as an encounter with the American cartoonist Al Capp, were included in the *Imagine: John Lennon* film in 1988. A video called *John and Yoko: the Bed-In* was also issued in 1990.

The film of the recording of 'Give Peace a Chance' was presented as a 16mm colour clip to various TV stations. A black-and-white version was screened on BBC TV's *Top of the Pops* on Thursday 10 July and Thursday 24 July 1969.

Glass Onion, The

Song featured on *The Beatles* (the 'White Album'). John also sings lead and plays acoustic guitar. Recording began on Wednesday 11 September 1968.

In the song, John makes reference to several Beatles tracks, such as 'Strawberry Fields Forever', 'I Am the Walrus', 'Lady Madonna', 'Fool on the Hill' and 'Fixing a Hole'. He also mentions an area called the Cast Iron Shore in the Dingle district of Liverpool.

Paul McCartney was to say, 'John wrote the tune "Glass Onion" – I mean he wrote it mainly, but I helped him on it, and when we were writing it we were thinking specifically of this whole idea of all these kind of people who write in and say "Who was the walrus?" or "Is Paul the walrus?"

'So John, I mean, he happened to have a line go "Oh yeah, the walrus was Paul," and we had a great giggle to say "Yeah, let's do that, let's put this line in, 'cause everybody's gonna read into it and go crackers," 'cause they all thought that John was the walrus – "I am the walrus," you know; and it goes kind of insane after a while. So eventually he said "Let's do this joke tune 'Glass Onion' where all kinds of answers to the universe are." But we thought it was a joke. Now someone the other night told me he'd met this feller who chartered a yacht and was going out into the middle of the ocean 'cause he knew the spot where to go through the glass onion. Now this feller hasn't been seen since!'

Some years later, John was to comment 'At that time I was still in my love cloud with Yoko, so I thought I'd just say something nice to Paul – you did a good job over these few years, holding us together. I thought, I've got Yoko, and you can have the credit.'

The number was recorded on 11, 12 and 13 September and 10 October 1968.

God

John recorded four acoustic-guitar demos on 26 July 1970 at Tittenhurst Park. Initially, it was suggested that he'd composed the number as a comment on George Harrison's involvement in religion. The iconoclasm came soon after he'd been exposed to primal therapy and reeks of pessimism. He'd originally begun composing one sentence, 'God is a concept by which we measure our pain.' This developed into a litany in which he denunciated a number of former idols, including Bob Dylan (whom he called by his real name, Zimmerman), Elvis and the Beatles.

The number was featured on his December 1970 album *John Lennon/Plastic Ono Band*. It was produced by Phil Spector and features Billy Preston on piano.

Describing the song, John was to say, 'A lot of the words, they just came out of me mouth. It started off like that. "God" was stuck together from three songs almost. I had the idea "God is a concept by which we measure pain", so when you have a word like that you just sit down and sing the first tune that comes into your head and the tune is simple because I like that kind of music.' He added, 'I don't know when I realised I was putting down all these things I didn't believe in. I could have gone on. It was like a Christmas card list. I thought, Where do you end? Churchill? And who have I missed out? I thought I had to stop. I was going to leave a gap and say, Just fill in your own and put whoever you don't believe in. It had just got out of hand.'

Among the many figures denied by John were the Beatles themselves. When asked about this, he said, 'I don't believe in the Beatles, that's all. I don't believe in the Beatles myth. "I don't believe in Beatles" – there is no other way of saying it, is there? I don't believe in them, whatever they were supposed to be in everybody's head, including our own heads, for a period. Beatles was the final thing because it's like I no longer believe in myth, and Beatles is another myth.'

Other figures dismissed by John include Bob Dylan, Jesus Christ, Buddha, the Kennedys and Elvis Presley.

He announces that 'the dream is over' but ends on a less pessimistic note by affirming that he believes in himself and Yoko.

God Save Us

A number written by John and Yoko to raise money and gain public sympathy for the British 'underground' magazine *Oz*, to which John was a subscriber. The notorious 'Schoolkids' issue of the magazine led to the principals, Felix Denis, Richard Neville and Jim Anderson, being charged with 'conspiracy to corrupt public morals'.

When the case went to trial, John testified on behalf of the magazine.

He decided to issue the single in order to raise funds for the *Oz* legal fees and the number was produced jointly by John, Yoko, Phil Spector and Mal Evans at John's studio in Ascot.

As John didn't want the single to be taken as the follow-up to 'Power to the People', he used as lead vocalist Bill Elliott, who came from Newcastle. John made a recording of the song and Elliott duplicated John's sound. The A-side was credited to Bill Elliot and the Elastic Oz Band, while the B-side, 'Do the Oz', was credited simply to the Elastic Oz Band, who were, in fact, the Plastic Ono Band. This side was produced by John and Mal Evans, and John was lead vocalist on the track and musicians who were involved in the recording of both tracks included Ringo Starr, drums; Klaus Voormann, bass guitar; Bobby Keyes, saxophone; and Charles Shaar Murray and John Lennon on acoustic guitars. Murray was a schoolboy at the time who had contributed to the notorious issue No. 28 of *Oz*, and he later became a prominent writer for *New Musical Express*.

The single was issued in Britain on 16 July 1971 on Apple 36 and in America on 7 July on Apple 1835. The blurb in the press advertisements for the record read,

> Every major country has a screw in its side, in England it's *Oz*. *Oz* is on trial for its life. John and Yoko have written and helped produce this record – the proceeds of which are going to *Oz* to help to pay their legal fee. The entire British underground is in trouble, it needs our help. Please listen – God Save *Oz*.

Going Down on Love

Song John wrote for his *Walls and Bridges* album, which he recorded at New York's Record Plant in August 1974. It was a plea to Yoko, emphasising his need for her.

The track, which opened the album, also featured Ken Ascher on electric piano and Nicky Hopkins on piano. For his guitar work on the track John credited himself as Dr Winston O'Ghurkin.

Goldman, Albert

Journalist and biographer who infuriated Lennon fans throughout the world with his iconoclastic book *The Lives of John Lennon*, first published in 1988. As feared, it exploited the negative aspects of John's life, enlarging on scandal in full kiss-and-tell style. Fans had been expecting such a slant ever since Goldman delivered a similar body blow to Elvis Presley's image in his Elvis biography in 1981.

Goldman grew up in Mt Lebanon, Pennsylvania, and in 1944 enrolled at the Carnegie Institute of Technology and later graduated from the University of Chicago with an MA in English Literature.

Between 1954 and 1963 he taught at three colleges of the New York City University and concluded his teaching career in 1972 as Adjunct Associate Professor of English and Comparative Literature.

He'd begun a career as a cultural journalist in 1959 and gradually saw his work accepted by mass-circulation magazines such as *New Yorker*, *Vogue* and *Penthouse*. During 1977–78, he was music critic for *Esquire* and contributing editor to *High Times*.

Among his hundreds of published articles are: 'Little Richard Beat the Beatles', *New York Times*, June 1968; 'The Beatles in Oil and Water', *Vogue*, October 1968; 'Beatles: Nostalgia, Irony', *Life*, November 1969; 'The Beatles Decide To Let It Be – Apart', *Life*, April 1970. His 'An Interview With John Lennon' was featured as a two-part series in *Charlie* magazine in June and July 1971.

Goldman was also author of several books including *Ladies and Gentlemen – Lenny Bruce!!!* and *Disco*.

He died of a heart attack on 28 March 1994.

Gollum

A rather repellent creature featured in JRR Tolkien's modern classic *Lord of the Rings*, which was one of the cult books of the 60s and a campus favourite.

Gollum is a pathetic creature whose mind had been warped by an elfin ring. The evil influence has completely corrupted him and possession of the ring becomes an obsession.

It was proposed that the Beatles should appear in a film adaptation of the book and it was mentioned that John would take the part of Gollum.

The other members would be the hobbit Frodo, played by Paul; his faithful servant Sam, played by Ringo and the white wizard Gandalf, played by George.

It was reported that after the announcement they began to seek film rights and found that the rights had been sold only a few days previously.

Gone From This Place

One of the songs that John had been working on shortly prior to his death. He had recorded a home demo of it, accompanying himself on acoustic guitar, in November 1980. One of the phrases in the song was 'I don't wanna die'. The demo was one of the numerous previously unreleased Lennon recordings featured on the American radio series *The Lost Lennon Tapes*.

Good Morning, Good Morning

A track on the *Sergeant Pepper* album, which John originally made as a home recording in January 1967.

The inspiration came when he was watching television and noticed a Kellogg's Cornflakes commercial with the phrase 'Good morning, good morning'.

He explained, 'I often sit at the piano working at songs with the telly on low in the background. If I'm a bit low and not getting much done, then the words on the telly come through. That's when I heard, "Good morning, good morning". It was a cornflakes advertisement.'

The track opens with the sound of a crowing cock and closes with the clucking of a chicken, with several cow and sheep sounds provided courtesy of George Martin's recording expertise and a sound-effects tape. John supplies the lead vocals, Paul has a guitar solo and the brass section is provided by Sounds Incorporated, while George Harrison plays lead guitar. The members of Sounds Incorporated playing on the track were the group's three saxophonists – Barrie Cameron, David Glyde and Alan Holmes.

John also makes a reference to the BBC TV sitcom, *Meet the Wife*.

The number was recorded on 8 and 16 February; and 13, 28 and 29 March 1967.

Good Night

Number that John wrote and Ringo recorded for *The Beatles* double album.

Goodnight Vienna

When Ringo asked John to provide him with some songs for his forthcoming album in 1974, John wrote two compositions. After completing the *Walls and Bridges* album, he flew to California with May Pang to join Ringo on his session.

One of the numbers, *Goodnight Vienna*, became the title track when the album was issued on Apple PCS 7169 in November 1974. John sang and played piano on the track, the title of which is reputed to be from a Liverpool expression meaning 'Let's get out of here'. Backing vocals were by Clyde King, the Blackberries and the Masst Abbots.

The album cover featured a photograph of the alien Klaatu and his robot Gort emerging from their flying saucer in the film *The Day the Earth Stood Still*, with Ringo's head replacing that of Michael Rennie's, the Klaatu character.

Goon Show Scripts, The

The Goons were an anarchic comedy trio who gained cult status in Britain after launching their radio series *The Goon Show* on BBC radio in May 1951. Spike Milligan, Peter Sellers and Harry Secombe were responsible for a surrealistic form of humour much enjoyed by Lennon. The show ran until January 1960, by which time the trio had become a quartet with the addition of Michael Bentine.

John was twelve years old when he first heard the Goons and listened avidly to their radio shows until he was sixteen. Their influence was evident in his books *In His Own Write* and *A Spaniard in the Works*, and it seemed appropriate that when St Martin's Press, New York, published *The Goon Show Scripts* by Spike Milligan in 1973, John was commissioned to review it for the *New York Times*.

The 700-word piece appeared in the Sunday 30 September 1973 edition and it was the only book review John had published.

In it he pointed out that 'the Goons influenced the Beatles (along with Lewis Carroll/Elvis Presley)' and he noted that the Beatles' record producer George Martin produced sessions with Milligan and Sellers prior to recording the Fab Four.

John mentioned the *Daily Howl*, how he wrote it at night, took it to school in the morning and read it out to his friends – ' … looking at it now it seems strangely similar to *The Goon Show*. Even the title had "highly esteemed" before it.'

He pointed out that when he played records of the shows to Yoko he had to explain to her that they were made in the days before *Monty Python's Flying Circus* and *Rowan and Martin's Laugh-In* and were madder than *Mad* magazine.

Commenting on the members of the Goons, he wrote that Spike Milligan was a genius, Peter Sellers had made all the money and Harry Secombe had got 'show biz'.

At the end of the article, *The Times* said of the author: 'John Lennon, the now and former Beatle, studied capitalisation in the Liverpool school system.'

Gordon, Jim

Drummer hired by John to play on tracks for the *Imagine* album. Gordon played on 'Jealous Guy', 'It's So Hard' and 'I Don't Want To Be A Soldier'. Gordon was also part of the personnel of the Plastic Ono Supergroup and appears on the *Sometime in New York City* album.

Gordon was reared in San Fernando Valley and his first band had been Frankie and the Jesters. He became a session drummer, married a go-go dancer and appeared regularly on the TV series *Shindig*. He joined Delaney and Bonnie, divorced his wife and took up with Rita Coolidge, although they broke up when he gave her a black eye.

George Harrison brought him to England to appear on the *All Things Must Pass* album, which led to his appearing on *Imagine*. A cocaine and heroin addict, he next married a girl called Renee, but it lasted only six months.

While Gordon was in England Eric Clapton asked him to join Derek and the Dominos and he co-wrote 'Layla' with him.

Gordon, a paranoid schizophrenic, began to hear 'voices' and entered a psychiatric hospital fourteen times, finally giving up drums in 1980. On 3 June 1983 he fatally stabbed his 72-year-old mother in the chest and was found guilty of second-degree murder and sentenced to 18 years in jail.

Goresh, Paul

In December 1980 Paul Goresh was a 21-year-old store detective from Jersey who had ambitions of becoming a police officer. In his spare time he was an amateur photographer and used to hang around outside the Dakota Building taking photographs of celebrities. On the afternoon of John's death he had already snapped pictures of Mia Farrow, Paul Simon and Lauren Bacall.

The previous year, when Goresh had been a college student in New Jersey, he'd begun to hang around the Dakota in an attempt to see John. At one time he posed as a TV repairman and obtained access to John's apartment. He bought a camera for $350 and began taking shots of John outside the building. John spotted him and demanded the film, which Goresh handed to him. Later on, John felt guilty about his action, realised that Goresh was a fan and not a journalist, and occasionally invited him on walks.

On the afternoon of John's death, Goresh began to chat to Mark Chapman, who was among the crowd of Lennon-watchers hanging around the outside of the building. John was talking to Goresh when Chapman came up and held out the *Double Fantasy* album. He didn't speak. John said, 'Do you want that signed?' and Chapman nodded. As John began to sign the album, Goresh took a number of shots. He told the writer Richard Buskin, 'In all, I shot seven or eight frames, and the last picture is of John's profile as he was getting into the limousine. That turned out to be the last picture of John alive.'

After the killing, Goresh phoned up the police twice to say that he believed he had a photograph of the man who killed Lennon. On both occasions they put the phone down on him. He felt so frustrated he called the *Daily News* and they paid him $10,000 for the photograph, which was soon appearing on the front pages of newspapers throughout the world.

The notoriety of that shot led Goresh to become a full-time photographer. He said, 'I was forced into it. People like the Beach Boys just started calling me to do assignments.'

A Goresh photograph of John and Yoko walking out of the Dakota was used on the picture sleeve for 'Watching the Wheels'.

Graham, Bill
The American rock promoter remembered for launching the famous Fillmore Auditorium in San Francisco. The venue was the major showcase for what became known as the West Coast Sound and featured a range of acts including Big Brother and the Holding Company, the Grateful Dead, Jefferson Airplane and Quicksilver Messenger Company. He then opened the Fillmore West and followed with a concert venue in New York he called the Fillmore East. On Saturday 4 April 1987 in New York, Yoko presented him with the first John Lennon New Age Award. Graham died in a helicopter crash on 25 October 1991.

Grammy Awards
Major American popular-music awards, presented annually by the National Academy of Recording Arts and Sciences with a fanfare of publicity.

John appeared at the awards as a guest presenter on Saturday 1 March 1975. Together with Andy Williams and Paul Simon he presented the award for 'Records of the Year – Artist and Producer'.

The three artists engaged in some scripted banter as they stood on the podium.

John began by saying, 'Thank you, Mother, thank you ... Hello, I'm John. I used to play with my partner Paul.'

Simon said, 'I'm Paul. I used to play with my partner Art.'

Andy Williams said, 'I'm Andy. I used to play with my partner Claudine.'

He turned to John and Paul and said, 'The music that you fellows wrote, though, really did influence my life. As a matter of fact, it helped tell the story of me and my partner.'

John asked, 'Any song in particular, Andy?'

Williams replied, 'Well, let's see. It started off with "I Want To Hold Your Hand" and finished off with "Bridge Over Troubled Water".'

John said, 'Touching, touching.' Then continued, 'Shall we get on with it? My God, so this is what dawn does, is it?'

Simon announced that Elton John was one of the nominees with 'Don't Let the Sun Go Down On Me'. Art Garfunkel arrived on stage to accept an award on behalf of Olivia Newton John for 'I Honestly Love You'. Tongue in cheek, John introduced him to Simon, his former partner, saying, 'Which one of you is Ringo?' Then adding, 'Are you guys getting back together again?' He sighed, and then said, 'Terrible, isn't it?'

Garfunkel asked Simon, 'Are you still writing?' and Paul replied, 'I'm trying my hand at a little acting, Art.'

John asked 'Where's Linda?' No one seemed to get the joke, so he said 'Oh well, too subtle that one.' And following Garfunkel's acceptance speech, said, 'You're so serious.'

After the event, John and Yoko attended a party with other guests, including David Bowie and Roberta Flack.

On Wednesday 24 March 1982, Yoko accepted the Album of the Year award for *Double Fantasy*, saying, 'I think John is here.' She went on to say, 'Both John and I were always very proud and happy that we were part of the human race who made good music for the earth and for the universe. Thank you.' Yoko and John also received awards for the album both as producers and writers and the co-producer Jack Douglas also received a Grammy.

On Wednesday 20 February 1991, John was granted a posthumous Lifetime Achievement award at the Grammy Awards held at Radio City Music Hall. To the sounds of the orchestra playing 'Oh Yoko', Yoko stepped forward and delivered a brief acceptance speech: 'I would like to thank the Academy for honouring John with this award. John would have been especially pleased to be acknowledged by the industry he had helped to expand. I would like us to take this opportunity and pray for the safety and health of this beautiful planet. John Lennon would have liked that. Thank you.'

Aerosmith performed 'Come Together' and Tracy Chapman sang 'Imagine'.

Grapefruit

Yoko Ono's small book of conceptual ideas, which had a profound effect on John. It was a small edition of pages five inches square and comprising a series of Zen-style exercises from between one and sixteen lines each.

Yoko said, 'Writing the book was like a cure for myself without knowing it. It was like saying, "Please accept me, I am mad." '

When she arrived in Britain, Yoko promoted it by wrapping copies in female panties and sending them off to reviewers – this gimmick was probably inspired by the fact that the cover had a drawing of a bare bottom on it.

Soon after they first met, Yoko had a copy delivered to John during the *Sergeant Pepper* sessions. He placed it on his bedside table and often read it at night. It had various conceptual pieces with titles such as 'Clock Piece, Fly Piece, Cut Piece' and 'Disappearing Piece', together with lists of 'instruction' and 'happenings,' such as 'Three Snow Pieces for Orchestra'. 'City Piece', for example, consisted of the instruction – 'Walk all over the city with an empty baby carriage.'

John was to comment, 'I used to read it sometimes and I'd get very annoyed at it. It would say things like "paint until you drop dead" and "bleed", and then sometimes I'd be very enlightened by it.'

When John and Yoko were living together, the publisher Peter Owen, who was issuing a British edition, visited the couple at the Apple offices in Savile Row, where John did a sketch of Yoko for Owen, to be included in the book, and also wrote a brief introduction: 'Hi! My name is John Lennon. I'd like you to meet Yoko Ono.'

The British edition included some additional items such as Yoko's '13 Days Do-It-Yourself Dance Festival', which she'd written in 1967 and 'Sky Event for John Lennon', which she'd penned the following year. Yoko reportedly wasn't comfortable with the fact that a selling point was John's involvement and his 'introduction', although it must be admitted that the book probably wouldn't have received as much attention without the association with John.

Wunternaum had printed the original 1964 issue in a limited edition of 500 copies in Japan. The same publisher also published it in a limited edition of 500 copies in American. The 1970 issue was published in a hard-bound edition by Simon & Schuster in America and Peter Owen in Britain and in Germany by Baermeier & Nikel, while in South America it was issued under the title *Un Libro de Instructions de Yoko Ono*. Sphere Books in Britain published a paperback edition in 1981.

Simon & Schuster also used John's two-line introduction in the American reprint in 1970.

In March 1970, while John and Yoko were in California, they recorded a thirty-minute session of readings from the book, intending to use it as a promotional record to send to American disc jockeys, but they never issued it.

The book inspired John and the title of his song 'Imagine' was derived from many of the book's exercises, which began: 'Imagine ...'

The book's cover featured a drawing of a bare bottom and John helped Yoko promote it at a special signing session at Selfridges store in London on 15 July 1971.

John was to suggest the name 'Grapefruit' for one of the bands signed to the Beatles' Apple Corps company.

Graustark, Barbara

On 17 September 1980, Barbara Graustark, an associate editor of *Newsweek* magazine, conducted the first interview John and Yoko had given together for almost five years.

Graustark had sought out John and Yoko through their photographer friend Bob Gruen, who had revealed that the couple were recording at the Hit Factory in New York.

Graustark visited the studio and made her request for an interview. She had to give her birthdate and address for Yoko to have checked out. The signs were obviously propitious and three days later Graustark found herself back at the Hit Factory to begin the interview.

She arrived while John was overdubbing a vocal on 'Cleanup Time' for the *Double Fantasy* album, which he and Yoko were recording. Graustark was able to comment, 'Whether we were munching eel, sipping Zen-blended coffee on West 57th Street, or limousining our way uptown, Lennon seemed eager to talk, self-assured and secure in his newly settled life.'

John told how he decided to devote five years of his life to rearing Sean personally. He described his daily routine; the dissolution of the Beatles; feminism; the loss of copyright of the Beatles' songs; his relationship with Yoko; his 'lost weekend' in Los Angeles; religion; the inspiration for *Double Fantasy*; Paul McCartney and other topics.

Eight days after the interview, John was recording at the Record Plant Studios and during a break tuned into a local radio station. Graustark was being interviewed about her interview with John and some extracts from the interview were played. He commented, 'What's it coming to when they interview the interviewer?'

Newsweek magazine rushed an edited version of the interview into their 29 September issue. John was unhappy about it. While acknowledging that the answers given by him and Yoko to various questions were accurate, he was annoyed that the actual questions had been rewritten after the event, which gave a different slant to the various responses.

The interview was also included in the paperback *Strawberry Fields Forever: John Lennon Remembered*, rush-released in December 1980 after John was shot. Graustark later interviewed Yoko for a feature, which was printed in the 1 October 1981 issue of *Rolling Stone* magazine.

She was also to direct, write and narrate the Yoko Ono documentary *Yoko Ono: Then and Now*.

Great Wok, The

A humorous sketch that John wrote to amuse his friend Elliott Mintz in December 1978.

Green, John

The former tarot-card reader for John and Yoko. The tarot comprises a pack of 78 cards, which are intended to supply answers to specific questions when the cards are shuffled, then placed down in certain patterns. With the tarot, business decisions would be read and every angle explored. This didn't mean that the cards had to be followed exactly. If there were a forthcoming meeting, then readings would take place in relation to everyone due at the meeting, with different scenarios on courses of action to take and what the ramifications would be. The information was also checked with other sources and professional advice from lawyers and accountants was also taken into consideration. Green would say that the decisions made were a cross between tarot advice, consensus and the random elements that occurred during the process.

It was Green who advised Yoko to break their contract with Allen Klein and devised a way for them to do so.

Green worked for the Lennons for six years at a salary of £13,000 per year and free accommodation. He first read the tarot cards for Yoko in May 1974, during her temporary split from John. He was initially employed at £50 per week to give regular readings. Green's relationship with the Lennons ended over an argument about money and he later sold some highly salacious gossip about the couple to a newspaper. One feature, published in the British tabloid the *Sun* in November 1981, was headlined 'SECRET SEX SESSIONS OF LOVE HUNGRY LENNON'. In it, Green claimed that Yoko hired prostitutes to satisfy John's cravings, that he called her Mummy, and that he insulted her mercilessly in public, picking on her nationality and sexuality.

Yoko denied Green's allegations, saying, 'John is dead and can't fight back. Those things that John Green said just aren't true.' She commented on each of the accusations Green had made, refuting them all.

In an interview with John Fielden of the *Sunday Mirror* headed 'THOSE FILTHY LIES ABOUT OUR SEX LIFE BY YOKO ONO', she said that sex with John was very ordinary. 'He was from England, I am from Japan, and we used to say to each other – and laugh about it – that we were both rather shy and rather ordinary in that way.

'I could not imagine John even knowing where a brothel *was* in New York.'

Nineteen eighty-three was the year of the kiss-and-tell books and Green's contribution was called *Dakota Days*. It was published in America by St Martin's Press on 6 July 1983 and was also serialised by *Penthouse* magazine.

John was to use the pseudonym J Green during a brief visit to Cape Town, South Africa, during 1980.

Greening of the World (concert in Japan)

A major tribute to John held in Tokyo at the Tokyo Dome Stadium on 21 and 22 December 1990. The first evening drew an audience of 35,000, while the second drew 43,000.

The first night's show lasted for three hours and forty minutes. Prior to the live performance a film of Yoko greeting the Japanese fans was followed by highlights from the Liverpool Lennon tribute the previous May. All the participants in the concert then came on to the stage to sing 'Power to the People'. Yoko and Sean then appeared on stage and Yoko said, 'Thank you very much for loving John. It's so emotive to hold this event here in Japan ... because John loved Japan and he loved you, Japanese people.'

Dave Edmunds performed 'Love Me Do' and 'All You Need Is Love'. Lenny Kravitz performed 'I Found Out' and 'Cold Turkey'. Linda Rondstadt and Peter Asher duetted on 'All I've Got To Do' and Rondstadt sang 'Good Night'. Natalie Cole duetted on 'Ticket To Ride' with Toshinobu Kubota and then performed 'Lucy in the Sky with Diamonds'. Miles Davis and Kenny Garrett performed 'Strawberry Fields Forever', Hall and Oates performed 'Julia' and 'Don't Let Me Down', and Sean sang 'You've Got To Hide Your Love Away'. A promo film for *Imagine* was shown and then all the performers, including Yoko and Sean, sang 'Give Peace a Chance'. Twelve Japanese artists were also on the bill.

On the second night the show lasted for four hours and twenty minutes. There were sixteen Japanese artists on the bill, apart from the original artists, who repeated their performances of the previous night.

Edmunds sang an extra song, 'A Day in the Life', and prior to the closing song, 'Happy Xmas', the gathered performers sang 'Give Peace a Chance'.

On 21 December, to coincide with the concert, a CD with five songs called *G.O.W. Special – Happy Birthday, John*, by Yoko and Sean, was issued by Pony Canyon Records. The tracks were 'Love '90' by Yoko; 'Asian Flowers' by Motoharu, Yoko and Sean; 'Dear Prudence' by Sean; 'Love '90', a new dub mix by Yoko; and 'Love '90', ambient mix by Yoko.

Gregory, Dick

A black American comedian and activist who became one of John and Yoko's closest friends.

Gregory, who was raised in St Louis, once went into a Southern restaurant and was told, 'We don't serve Negroes.' He said, 'That's all right, I don't eat Negroes.'

He penned an autobiography called *Nigger*, in which he wrote a dedication to his mother: 'Dear Momma, wherever you are, if ever you hear the word nigger, remember they are advertising my book.'

When John and Yoko were seeking to prevent Michael X from being executed in Trinidad, Gregory visited Michael in jail on their behalf. When he returned he was able to tell them that he considered there were a number of dubious aspects about the case that suggested to him that Michael X had been framed. He returned to Trinidad to meet with Michael X's local lawyer, but found he had been 'scared off', so Gregory picketed the jail before returning to New York.

Gregory was also a nutritionist and later began to specialise in New Age nutrition. When John had been ridding himself of drugs at Tittenhurst Park prior to his primal-therapy course, Gregory visited him at Ascot. He commented, 'Lennon had a lot of problems after he came out of the drug thing. He asked me to come and help. I came in to rebuild the body. My main concern was cleansing out the body and not doing it too fast. I was able to put him on the type of vitamin regimen that would replenish what the drugs had wiped out, and also fast him on a small scale.'

When the Lennons were staying at Ronnie Hawkins' farm in Canada, Gregory was also one of the guests and he was to become a member of the chorus of 'Give Peace a Chance' when it was recorded at the Queen Elizabeth Hotel in Montreal.

John, Yoko and Gregory had a lot in common – their quest for peace, their anti-Vietnam stance and fight against racism. Gregory even stood against Richard Nixon in the 1968 presidential election as the Candidate for Peace.

Gregson, John

The late, Liverpool-born screen actor, star of numerous British films, including the classic comedy of the 50s, *Genevieve*.

Cynthia Lennon related an anecdote concerning him in her autobiography, *A Twist of Lennon*. John saw the actor outside Ye Cracke pub in Rice Street, Liverpool, and wanted his autograph. He looked around for something unusual for the actor to sign and found an old boot and asked Gregson to autograph it for him, a gesture that quite amused the actor, who signed the offending article across the stitching.

Griffiths, Eric

When he was ten years old Griffiths moved to Woolton and later attended Quarry Bank School. He became good friends with John and the two of them went for a week's holiday at Eric's grandmother's cottage in Bodfari, North Wales.

Together with John and George Lee he was discussing skiffle and Lee suggested they form a group. But Lee didn't actually participate. John and Eric bought guitars and went to a guitar tutor in Hunts Cross. They left after two lessons, deciding it was boring. As John's mother, Julia, could play the banjo she retuned their guitar strings and they continued in that way until Paul McCartney joined.

The skiffle group they formed was to be called the Quarry Men with Pete Shotton, then Bill Smith came in on bass followed by Rod Davis and Colin Hanton, the last two having been introduced into the group by Griffiths.

Eric travelled on the same bus as Hanton and asked him if he could hear him play the drums. So Hanton invited him to his home, set up the drums, put on a record and played along with it. Eric invited him to meet the lads. Hanton went to Eric's house to see them and found himself a new member of the Quarry Men.

Eric was to say, 'Pete Shotton says that he and John decided to start a group, but I differ from that as John and I did try to learn the guitar for that purpose before any group was formed.'

Their first rehearsal took place at Eric's house in Halewood Drive and their first gig was at Lee Park Golf Club. They also played St Peter's Youth Club. They continued to rehearse at Eric's home. Other venues included St Barnabas Hall, the Locarno and Grafton ballrooms, and the Empire Theatre, where they appeared on the Carroll Levis talent show in October 1957. They also appeared at the Cavern three or four times.

Eric was a member of the Quarry Men from March 1957 until the middle of 1958. At times when he didn't turn up at rehearsals or couldn't make it to a gig, George Harrison deputised for him.

George eventually joined because he was a better guitarist. John wanted Eric to go on electric bass, but he wasn't too keen, so George replaced him. John finally said, 'You're out and George is in,' because Eric didn't want to play the bass – if he'd agreed he would have remained a member of the group, although Colin Hanton was the one appointed to tell him what John had said. Eric said that going on bass meant he'd have to buy a bass guitar and an amplifier and, as he didn't believe the group was going anywhere, he wouldn't take the risk. Eric later joined the Merchant Navy.

In later years he moved to Edinburgh, where he runs his own business, a small chain of dry-cleaning shops. He was to join the re-formed Quarry Men in 1997.

Gross, Dr Elliot M

The Chief Medical Examiner of New York City at the time of John's death. He said, after the autopsy, that John had died of shock and loss of blood and that nobody could have lived for more than a few minutes with such injuries.

Grow Old with Me

The number is allied with Yoko's song 'Let Me Count the Ways', which had its title taken from Elizabeth Barrett Browning's *Sonnets from the Portuguese*, in which the poet wrote, 'How do I love thee? Let me count the ways'. 'Grow Old with Me' takes the lines from 'Rabbi Ben Ezra', a poem written by Elizabeth Barrett Browning's husband Robert Browning, in which the poet wrote 'Grow old along with me! The best is yet to be'. The recording was taken from a home-made cassette because John never completed a studio version of the song. This was included on the *Milk and Honey* album.

Commenting on the song and 'Let Me Count the Ways', which preceded it on the album, Yoko said, 'To us, these two songs were the backbone of *Double Fantasy*, and we kept discussing how we would arrange them. For John, "Grow Old with Me" was one that would be a standard, the kind that they would play in church every time a couple gets married. It was horns-and-symphony time. But we were working against deadline for the Christmas release of the album [so we] kept holding "Grow Old with Me" to the end, and finally decided it was better to leave the song for "Milk and Honey".

'"Grow Old with Me" was a song John made several cassettes of, as we discussed the arrangements for it. Everybody around us knew how important these cassettes were. They were in safekeeping, some in our bedroom, some in our cassette file, and some in a vault. All of them disappeared since then, except the one on this record. It may be that it was meant to be this way, since the version that was left to us was John's last recording. The one John and I recorded together in our bedroom with a piano and a rhythm box.'

The home demo was recorded in November 1980 and Yoko says John wrote the number in Bermuda as an answer to her 'Let Me Count the Ways'.

John and Yoko did compare themselves to other great loving couples and could well have associated themselves with the Brownings.

'Grow Old with Me' was one of the four home demos by John, which Yoko gave to the three remaining Beatles as possible tracks to use for singles. It was mooted as the third single to be released following 'Free As a Bird' and 'Real Love', but it was decided not to release it then because the previous two singles hadn't topped the charts. Paul also mentioned that they weren't keen on the number.

Gruen, Bob

The American photographer most associated with the New York period of John's career.

Gruen began taking photographs at the age of eight; by the age of eleven he was selling his work (his first published

photograph was that of a fire for a local newspaper) and
turned professional in 1968. However, he had no formal
training.

He took photographs of John and Yoko backstage at an
Attica Benefit concert at the Apollo Theatre, Harlem, on 17
December 1971. John noticed him taking shots backstage and
said, 'Whatever happens to these photos? People are always
taking our picture and we never see them.' He told John that he
lived near to the Bank Street apartment where John and Yoko
were then living and would slip the pictures under the door. He
went to the apartment and the Lennon's friend Jerry Rubin
answered the door and Gruen gave him the photos.

A short time after that he met John and Yoko again when a
friend was interviewing them about their work with Elephant's
Memory. He took photographs of John and Yoko with the band
and the shots were used on the *Elephant's Memory* Apple album
cover.

A few weeks later he was asked to take photographs of the
pair on a regular basis, becoming, literally, their official photographer. He took pictures of John's sessions with Mick Jagger and
Elton John, was at the One To One benefit concert, the
Sometime in New York album sessions and even the *Double
Fantasy* recording sessions. He took the multiple-glasses shots of
John for the *Walls and Bridges* album cover and the passport
photo for John's green card, and was the first person to photograph the baby Sean. His last picture of John and Yoko together
was snapped on Forty 44th Street on 6 December 1978. He also
took the *Live in New York City* album cover.

Bob became an intimate associate of both John and Yoko and
took literally thousands of photographs at various concerts, TV
shows and at special events. He commented, 'Any business
transactions went through Yoko. She made the appointments; I
brought the finished prints to her. I was not on their staff, but
John and Yoko paid all my expenses ... I got paid by selling the
pictures to magazines and newspapers, sometimes to the record
company for an album cover.'

Bob's wife Nadya became a personal assistant to John and
Yoko for a few years, replacing Sara Segal.

A selection of 136 of Bob's best photographs of John
were published by the William Morrow Company Inc., in the

collection *Listen to These Pictures*, which also contains a fascinating and anecdotal text by Gruen. In 1991 a Japanese publisher issued *Bob Gruen's Works: John Lennon*, with a selection of colour and black-and-white shots by Gruen of John and Yoko during their years in New York and a limited-edition book, *Sometime in New York City*, was published by Genesis Publications in 1995.

Guardine, David

An American psychic who claimed that John sent a song to him at a seance. The song was called 'To Be One Again' and the lyrics were printed in the American weekly newspaper the *Examiner*, with the comment that it was 'John's last song'.

Hagel, Kristina

German girl who moved to Liverpool in 1994 and claimed she was John Lennon's secret daughter. She even convinced John's Uncle Charlie of her validity, producing a birth certificate to substantiate her claim. However, in September 1998 the certificate was exposed as a fraud. Hagel had typed John's details on a copy of her real certificate and used a colour photocopier to make a new document.

Her original birth certificate showed her real father to be Karl August Egon Hagel.

Hague, Jonathan

Born in Llandudno, Wales, Jonathan was educated at a public school in Lindisfarne before becoming a student at Liverpool Art College.

He comments, 'I was born and brought up in Wales and I think the country bumpkin upbringing helped my relationship with John, him being the tough city lad showing me the city life, teaching me to drink, etc.

'I spent the most time with John when we were both studying Intermediate in our second year. This was a course ending in an examination for the National Diploma in Design. We were split into separate classes for crafts. John and I did lettering, together with Cynthia and a girlfriend of hers called Phyllis McKenzie.

'John failed his Intermediate because of lettering, and at his second sitting he seemed to be beyond caring. I remember feeling very concerned because he was thinking of Hamburg. He once told me he would have finished college, but for Intermediate - and then what would have happened to the Beatles?!'

Jonathan has many memories of the art school days and says, 'I remember Arthur Ballard used to teach us every Monday morning in a small room where our pictures would be hung on a wall. This was the "Composition" homework and he would give us a big crit on them, discussing each one individually.

'They were the usual subjects for such studies: the railway station, a restaurant, the docks, roadworks, etc.

'For some reason John would get away with presenting one of his cartoon drawings each week. For instance, he would have hundreds of little dockers climbing over a boat. And his railway station was just a man's foot disappearing down a staircase.

'He was always the entertainer. The atmosphere in the life class when we drew from live models was always like that of a church. Everyone would sit in silence taking their drawing seriously.

'John would start by making the tiniest noise, then create a snigger which he'd let grow louder, bit by bit, until he had the whole room erupting in bursts of laughter.

'I remember the metalwork teacher took John outside the room into the passageway one day to give him a ticking off because John had cut out some monster-type figure.

'I heard the teacher saying, "What do you think you will end up doing?"

'John replied, "I want to be a pop star." The teacher groaned and said, "Be realistic!"'

Jonathan attained his ATD (Art Teachers Diploma). He says, 'After ATD I obtained a British Council scholarship to the Hague for about 18 months but stayed for three years. I took the scholarship as my last chance and worked every day - and held a number of private gallery exhibitions there, one at the Gemeentee Museum itself. I sent John a catalogue.'

Jonathan received a letter from John, thanking him for his

note: 'So there you are in Holland with all those clogs, eh? Glad you are now a FAMOUS PAINTER - just like Arthur Ballard said you would be!

The catalogue looked great, seems you've forgotten all about Bratby! I still can't paint - but still do, if you see what I mean, ANYWAY - I'm pleased to hear from you. My address is not so special - but here it is.

J. Lennon
Kenwood, St George's Hill
Cavendish Road
Weybridge
Surrey.

If you write - try and use a similar type of envelope to the one you sent - you know BROWN - or your letter might get lost in the happy fan mail.

See or hear you soon.
  Good Heavens.
John. A band (Lennon).'

Jonathan continues, 'After I left Holland, which I've always regretted, I did a two-week teaching job at both Coventry and Birmingham art schools for five years. I had a number of private gallery exhibitions as well, plus paintings in the Royal Academy etc, and started seeing Lennon again. Once again he showed me the Big City —this time it was London.'

When Jonathan was 29, John and Paul McCartney sponsored an exhibition of his work. He says: 'One day I took my paintings in a huge roll to John's house and we spread them all over his sitting room. He liked them, hence the exhibition. He dragged Paul in on it, but I don't think Paul was very keen, although he didn't mind putting up the money.'

The exhibition took place at the Royal Institute Gallery at 195 Piccadilly from 4 - 23 December, 1967 and there was a diverse selection of paintings whose subjects included the Beatles, Mick Jagger, Vincent van Gogh and the funeral of Sir Winston Churchill.

However, rather than boost Jonathan's career as a painter, it seemed to end it.

'After the exhibition, I gave up,' he says. 'I'm not sure why. I think I thought I was no good. So I drifted into antiques, which I still do for a living – it's better than teaching.'

Jonathan became an antiques dealer and settled in Leamington Spa in a house John bought for him for £4,000 while he was still teaching at Coventry Art College.

Hale House

A privately run institution set up to care for the children born to parents addicted to heroin, methadone and alcohol. When John heard about Hale House he located the director through the *Amsterdam News*. He then initiated a $10,000 annual gift to the organisation. On several occasions he also sent boxes and gifts and foodstuffs, which he and Yoko packed personally, to each child in the programme. They also sent Sean along to play with the children there.

On hearing of John's death, the founder, Dr Hale, said, 'We have lost a dear friend. John didn't just help my mother and me: he helped the children – black, and poor. As he touched us, we touched others.'

Half Wind Show

A Yoko Ono exhibition presented at London's Lisson Gallery in September 1967. John sponsored the exhibition, although he wanted it kept secret at the time and didn't even go and see it.

Yoko subtitled it 'Yoko Plus Me' in reference to John's support. The exhibition consisted of numerous everyday objects cut in half, painted white and displayed in their usual settings: objects such as chairs, washbasins and a toothbrush.

Hamrick, Don and Hollahan, Leonard

Two members of a Californian cult who visited John and Yoko in Aalborg, Denmark, on Monday 29 December 1969. They had been leaders of a psychic cult called the Harbingers, who were based at Harbinger Springs, near San Francisco.

Melinda Cox (the new wife of Tony Cox, who had been Yoko's second husband) had been a member of the cult. Dr Hamrick hypnotised the couple in an attempt to help them to give up smoking and also used the hypnotic sessions to see if they could discover who John and Yoko were in past lives. Hamrick and Hollahan said that they could fly John and Yoko to the planned Peace Festival in Canada in a psychic-powered 'cosmic craft' that would cost only $500 and never use any fuel.

They also believed that they could contact alien beings through the Beatles. It was Hamrick who told John and Yoko that Tony Cox and Kyoko (Yoko's and Tony's daughter) were with the Maharishi in Majorca in March 1971.

Hand in Pocket

Single by Alanis Morrissette, released in 1996. Her promotional video of the number featured an image of John Lennon passing by.

Handel Medallion

A special award presented by New York City to people who have distinguished themselves in the arts. John was awarded the medallion posthumously on Friday 22 May 1981 at a ceremony at the city hall. Mayor Ed Koch presented the medallion to Yoko. John became the 99th person to win the award, previous recipients having included Charlie Chaplin and Louis Armstrong.

Yoko said, 'I felt that, because of his love for the city, he would have been very happy to have received this award. This city meant a lot to him. This was our town, and it still is.'

Incidentally, when a Congressman, Koch worked hard to persuade the Immigration and Naturalization Service that John had contributed a great deal to music and the arts and should remain in America.

On hearing the news of John's death, Koch had said, 'John Lennon profoundly affected a generation. His music and that of the Beatles was worldwide in its impact. He was an international figure, and New York City became his home. That made us very proud. Every death by violence is a trauma to society. The death of someone of John Lennon's stature intensifies this trauma. We mourn his loss.'

Hanratty, James

Man hanged following the A6 murder case in Britain, a man whose name John wanted to try to clear.

On 22 August 1961 Michael John Gregson and Valerie Storie parked their car at a lovers' lane called Deadman's Hill. A man with a gun appeared and forced them to drive down the A6 and park at a lay-by. He then shot Gregson twice in the head, raped Storie and shot her several times.

James Hanratty was arrested a few months later, despite the fact that there was much conflicting evidence. Valerie Storie had originally described her attacker as having brown hair and brown eyes. Eight days later she completely changed her description and said he had staring blue eyes and fair hair.

The police had originally taken a man into custody named Peter Alphon who matched the Identikit description of the murderer. In the hotel room where he stayed on the night of the killing, cartridge cases from the murder gun were found. His alibi was proven to be false and a woman identified him in a line-up, saying that two weeks after the murder he had tried to rape her and shouted, 'I am the A6 killer.'

Hanratty was arrested. He had occupied the same hotel room the night before, but had never owned or used a gun and had never been involved in a sex crime. He was pronounced guilty and hanged in April 1963, three weeks after the end of the trial.

Before the execution Alphon had been telling newspapers that Hanratty was innocent. He gave a friend notes with his own confession to the killing. A year to the day after the execution he visited Hanratty's parents and offered them compensation for the death of their son. He also confessed to them. In 1967 he repeated his confession at a press conference in Paris and in 1968 wrote to the Home Secretary: 'I killed Gregson, the Establishment murdered Hanratty.'

In November 1969 Hanratty's parents were at the home of John Cunningham in Ascot. He was John Lennon's neighbour and John became interested in the Hanrattys' efforts to clear their son's name. After spending many hours with them, and also with witnesses and lawyers, John said, 'They convinced me there was a miscarriage of justice without a shadow of a doubt.'

On 16 December 1969 Hanratty's parents and Alphon visited John and Yoko at Apple. The following day the Apple press office issued the following statement to UPI, Reuters and the Press Association:

John and Yoko Lennon today announced from the Apple Headquarters, 3 Savile Row, London W1, that they plan to make a film about James Hanratty, the convicted A6 murderer. After discussion with Hanratty's parents, the Lennons were convinced that James Hanratty was innocent of the crime for which he was hung and said they are going to make a film that will insist that a new public enquiry be held and they themselves plan to reveal startling new facts about the case.

The next day, 11 December, John and Yoko attended the premier of *The Magic Christian* at the Odeon, Kensington. They alighted from their Rolls-Royce and unfurled banners announcing Hanratty's innocence.

Hanratty Snr had made a regular habit of appearing at Speakers' Corner in Hyde Park each Sunday gathering signatures requesting a public enquiry into the case. On 14 December the Lennons' Rolls-Royce drove up to Hyde Park and two men carried out a white sack, inside which were two wriggling occupants carrying out a silent protest for Hanratty.

At the Lyceum performance on 15 December, Yoko began her song 'Don't Worry Kyoko' with the scream, 'Britain, you killed Hanratty – you murderer!'

The Lennons' film was forty minutes long and in colour. It called for an enquiry into the case and was screened in the crypt of the church of St Martin in the Fields, London. The film, which John produced and directed, wasn't seen again for many years. It was discovered in the possession of Hanratty's brother and was screened by Channel 4 in Britain in 1992 as part of a programme concerning the A6 murder and the British system of justice.

Hanton, Colin

The drummer with the Quarry Men between 1957 and 1958. Colin attended a Catholic school, St Mary's in Horrocks Avenue, Garston. The first record he bought was Bill Haley's 'Rip It Up'.

Colin became interested in drumming and began to play on the furniture to the beat of jazz records. He became an apprentice upholsterer and then his parents said he could have a set of drums if he paid for them himself. He went to Frank Hessy's shop in Liverpool and bought a kit on hire purchase, putting down a deposit of ten shilling (50 pence), with payments of ten shillings a week for the £34 Broadway drum kit, with bass drum, snare drum, side drum and one cymbal, and began practising at home.

Colin used to travel on the same bus as Eric Griffiths and they became friends. One weekend he was visited by Eric, who told him he was in a group and asked if Colin would like to join. When Colin showed interest Eric told him that they were rehearsing at his house that day and asked him to come along. He took his drums to Eric's house, where he met John Lennon, Pete Shotton and Rod Davis and agreed to become a member of the skiffle group.

Colin's father was manager of a Co-operative Society store and the group often practised at Colin's house on Saturday afternoons.

Recalling George Harrison, Colin has stated that, contrary to what some people have said, George did not meet the group for the first time at Wilson Hall, Garston. He says that George met them at the Morgue Club in Old Swan, a small place run by Rory Storm. He recalls that George played a song to them in the back room. He thinks the song was 'Guitar Boogie'; others say it was 'Raunchy'. After George's performance, Nigel Walley, who was managing the group at the time, told him, 'George is joining; Eric is out.'

Colin was also with the group when they made the recording of 'In Spite of All the Danger' at Stan Phillips' studio in Kensington.

He was two years older than most of the other members, although he was small in stature and actually looked younger than they were. He was partial to 'black velvet', a mixture of Guinness and mild bitter, and always took his birth certificate around with him in case he was challenged about his age in pubs.

Colin recalls that they performed at a number of skiffle competitions, including one at the Empire Theatre, Liverpool, in June 1957. This was the Carroll Levis Discovery show. Colin's mother wouldn't let him attend a preliminary heat because it was on a Sunday and the others performed without him. They passed the heat and Colin appeared with them on the show, in which they played one number, 'Worried Man Blues'. He recalls that a group from North Wales won the heat. The Welsh group brought along a coachload of supporters – and naturally beat them on the applause meter. Colin felt that it was unfair on the Quarry Men because the other group were allowed an extra three minutes and were able to perform two numbers. He says that backstage Carroll Levis said to them, 'I might have been a bit unfair there, lads, but you were quite good so keep at it.'

His last performance with them took place at the Bus Drivers' Social Club in Finch Lane. George's father had booked them to appear there for a Saturday night dance. Harrison Snr, who also compered the show, told them that the manager of the Pavilion Theatre in Lodge Lane would be along to see them perform that night with a view to booking them on a regular basis. They had two sets to perform that evening. The first set went fine, but during the interval it was discovered that they could have free drinks at the bar. Paul and John in particular had too many pints and when they performed the second set the two of them began to take the mickey out of George, which embarrassed both his parents, who were in the audience. The manager of the Pavilion also noted their behaviour. He then followed them backstage and began to give them a lecture on professionalism. He told them that unless they learned to behave themselves he wouldn't book them in his theatre. John said to him, 'Oh, piss off.'

On the way home Colin had a big row on the bus with Pete Shotton and told them he wouldn't play with them again – he even got off the bus with his drums before he reached his stop.

He never performed with them again and they never contacted him or asked him back. He was to say that if they'd got in touch he would have returned, even though he was fed up with travelling with his drums by bus as they didn't have either a roadie or a van.

Colin finished his apprenticeship and established his own furniture and upholstery firm in Runcorn.

Married, with two grown-up daughters, he was invited to the fortieth anniversary of the Cavern Club, where he was to team up with other former members. He next performed with the Quarry Men at the fortieth anniversary of the famous St Peter's Church fête at which John and Paul first met. He still appears regularly with the group.

Happiness Is a Warm Gun

John had originally called this number 'Happiness Is a Warm Gun In Your Hand'.

Commenting on the inspiration, he said, 'A gun magazine was

sitting around, and the cover was the picture of a smoking gun. The title of the article, which I never read, was "Happiness Is a Warm Gun".' He also said, 'It was put together from bits and pieces of about three different songs and just seemed to run the gamut of many types of rock music.'

It was recorded on 23, 24 and 25 September 1968 and was included on *The Beatles* double album.

The BBC banned the record because they said it had sexual symbolism.

John considered it one of his best songs and further added, 'They all said it was about drugs but it was more about rock 'n' roll than drugs. It's sort of a history of rock 'n' roll. I don't know why people said it was about the needle in heroin. I've only seen somebody do something with a needle once, and I don't like to see it at all.'

The lines relating to 'Mother Superior' refer to Yoko Ono, as this is one of the names he called her. The reference to the man with the multicoloured mirrors on his boots refers to an actual man who had small mirrors inserted into the toe-caps of his boots to enable him to look up women's skirts.

A demo John made of the number was included on the Beatles' *Anthology 3* in October 1996. John had written a number of songs while at Rishikesh and some of them were unfinished; he used parts of two of them, 'I Need a Fix' and 'Mother Superior Jumped the Gun', to complete the song.

Happy Birthday, John

A song especially recorded by Ringo Starr to celebrate John's thirtieth birthday. The musicians he gathered on the unreleased record were Stephen Stills, Klaus Voormann and Billy Preston.

In 1970, Apple invited a number of musicians to compose a song to celebrate John's birthday, and several responded. Only one of the numbers was actually released as a single and this was George Harrison's 'It's Johnny's Birthday', which was featured on his album *All Things Must Pass*.

Other tributes included 'Happy Trails' from Janis Joplin and the Full Tilt Boogie Band, which was probably Joplin's last recording, as she was found dead a few days after cutting it. Another of the songs specially composed for the occasion was 'Here Comes The Threes' by Donovan.

Happy Birthday – John Lennon Remembered

A 55-minute MTV programme screened in America on 9 October 9 1988. It included clips of live performances and promos of John and was hosted by Adam Curry. The show also included interviews with David Bowie, Brian Wilson of the Beach Boys, Elton John and Bob Geldof. Some archive interviews were also presented with Paul McCartney, Julian Lennon and Yoko Ono.

Happy Xmas (War Is Over)

Having spent two years working on his peace campaign with 'War Is Over' posters displayed on prominent billboards, John decided he'd like to attempt writing a Christmas hit in which he could include his message about Christmas being the season of peace on earth and good will to all men.

He recorded the song on 28 and 29 October 1971 with the thirty-strong Harlem Community Choir. Yoko's 'Listen, the Snow is Falling' was on the B-side. The Plastic Ono Band included Nicky Hopkins playing chimes, piano and glockenspiel, Jim Keltner on drums and sleigh bells with John, Hugh McCracken and Klaus Voormann on guitars.

John, Yoko and Phil Spector produced the session at New York's Record Plant on West 44th Street. Spector, who had produced a superb Christmas album in 1963, *A Christmas Gift to You*, included several 'Christmassy' effects such as sleigh bells and chimes.

When John had initially played the number to Spector, his co-producer told him that the first line was a direct crib from the Paris Sisters' 'I Love How You Love Me', which Spector had produced. John said, 'I like quoting from old songs, but you get into such trouble with copyrights. It's a drag.' John was later to admit that he based his melody on the tune of the traditional folk song 'Stewball'.

The single was issued in America on Apple 1842 on 1 December 1971 but barely scraped into the Top 30.

There were legal problems surrounding its release in Britain, mainly to do with the fact that Yoko shared composing credits, which delayed release until November 1972, when it was issued on Apple R 5970 and reached No. 4 in the charts.

At the beginning of the number, John and Yoko can be heard whispering the names of their respective children, Julian and Kyoko.

The cover of the single featured a photograph of John and Yoko with the Harlem Community Choir, together with Phil and Ronnie Spector, Klaus Voormann, Jim Keltner and Hugh McCracken.

The number was released seasonally and was a big hit in 1981 and 1982.

Hard Day's Night, A (album)

John wrote the lion's share of songs on this album, ten of the thirteen tracks: 'A Hard Day's Night', 'I Should Have Known Better', 'If I Fell', 'I'm Happy Just to Dance with You', 'Tell Me Why', 'Any Time at All', 'I'll Cry Instead', 'When I Get Home', 'You Can't Do That' and 'I'll Be Back'.

Hard Day's Night, A (movie)

The Beatles' first feature film.

The most common story concerning the title attributes it to Ringo. Apparently he'd said 'It's been a hard day,' then looked at his watch and realised they'd been filming far longer than he'd imagined and added, 'I mean, a hard day's night.'

Yet the line 'a hard day's night' is to be found in 'Sad Michael', one of John's stories in the book *In His Own Write*, published during March 1964, the same month the group commenced filming and before they'd actually finalised the title.

The director, Dick Lester, was to say, 'The concept [for the film] came from John's reply to a question I asked him about a trip they'd made to Sweden.' When Lester asked him how did he like the trip, John replied, 'Oh, it was a room and a car and a room and a room and a car.'

The scriptwriter, Alun Owen, attempted to capture something of the personality of each of the Beatles. In one scene John is taking a bubble bath and he disappears beneath the foam. The plug is pulled out and the bath empties, with no indication as to where he has gone. This is a touch of surreal humour in the Lennon mould.

When asked by a reporter at the press conference, 'What's your philosophy of life?' John retorts, 'I'm torn between Zen and I'm-all-right-Jack!'

The dialogue seems to suit John, although he later said, 'We were a bit infuriated by the glibness and silliness of the dialogue and were always trying to get it more realistic, but they wouldn't have it. It ended up OK, but the next one was just bullshit because it really had nothing to do with the Beatles.'

Strangely enough there were solo scenes written for Paul, George and Ringo, but not for John. George had his own little piece set in an advertising studio. Ringo took a stroll by a canal bank, wandered into a pub and ended up in clink, and Paul had a scene with a young actress at a play rehearsal, but this was edited out of the final print.

John composed the title song for the film over a period of three days during filming breaks. It was recorded on 16 April 1964 and George Martin played piano on the session.

The film received a Royal World Charity Premier at the London Pavilion in Piccadilly Circus on 6 July 1964 and a northern premier took place at the Odeon Cinema, Liverpool, on 10 July. It was previewed in America at the Beacon Theater in New York on 14 July and was an international success, with one American critic dubbing it 'the *Citizen Kane* of jukebox movies'.

Hard Day's Night (single)

John was 23 when he wrote it and it was written, arranged, rehearsed and recorded within 24 hours. The Beatles went into the studio with it on 16 April 1964 and the single was released on 10 July 1964. It reached the top of the charts five days later and remained there for four weeks. It was issued as a single in the US on 13 July and topped the charts for two weeks. There have been two cover versions of the song, which have entered the British charts. The Peter Sellers version, which reached No. 15, and an instrumental version by the Ramsey Lewis Trio, which reached No. 30.

John was to comment, 'I was going home in the car and Dick Lester suggested the title "A Hard Day's Night" from something Ringo'd said. I had used it in *In His Own Write*, but it was an off-the-cuff remark by Ringo. You know, one of those mala-propisms. A Ringoism, where he said it not to be funny, just said it. So Dick Lester said "We are going to use that title," and the next morning I brought in the song. Because there was a little competition between Paul and I as to who got the A-side, who got the hit singles.'

The Beatles included the number in their repertoire during their concerts in 1964 and 1965.

Hard Times Are Over
A Yoko Ono number, which is the final track on the *Double Fantasy* album.

Harmonica
A type of mouth organ. In the summer of 1945 John was travelling to Edinburgh by bus on his own. He was due to spend his summer holidays with his Aunt Elizabeth, his Uncle Bertie and his cousin, Stan Parkes. During the journey, on a cheap mouth organ, he played 'The Happy Wanderer', a tune he'd learned, over and over. A student lodger at Mendips had given the mouth organ to him. The bus driver, impressed by John's determined playing of the ditty, told him to come the next day to the bus station at St Andrew Square in Edinburgh city centre. He said that someone had left a harmonica on his bus the previous week and John was welcome to it. The next day, accompanied by Stan, John turned up at the bus depot and collected the harmonica from the conductor. It was his first professional musical instrument.

John was later to comment, 'I can't remember why I took [the harmonica] up in the first place ... I know we used to take in students and one of them had a mouth organ and said he'd buy me one if I could learn a tune by the next morning – so I learned about two. I was somewhere between eight and twelve at the time – in short pants anyway.'

In 1960, when the Beatles were on their way to their first season in Hamburg, they stopped off at Arnhem. While there, John stole a harmonica from a shop and began playing it in the minivan during the rest of their journey.

Pete Best was to comment, 'John always used to stick it in his pocket, and during that first trip to Hamburg there'd be times when we'd be sitting in the band room at the back of the Bambi Kino, and he'd pull the old harmonica out and play. He'd stick it back in his pocket or throw it on his bed. It was always there. But I don't think that, at that stage, we had any intention of using it on stage. We were just saying, "Yeah, John, vamp on it, do it!" And he was having fun.'

John often referred to the harmonica as his harp and, in addition to its use on 'Love Me Do', it is also featured on 'I Should Have Known Better'.

Harmony

A magazine devoted to information on macrobiotic food and diets, which was sold in Greg's, a macrobiotic food store in London.

John was asked to contribute to the magazine and wrote 'A Short Essay on Macrobiotics' on 7 November 1968. This actually consisted of 38 words of text and eight small sketches. There was a sketch of John reading *Harmony* and the caption 'So I read this' was followed by a sketch of a naked John and Yoko residing on a cloud above a bright sun with them both commenting, 'Hi, Greg!'

Harrison, George

The Beatles' lead guitarist. He was born on 25 February 1943 at 12 Arnold Grove, Wavertree, Liverpool, to Harold and Louise Harrison. Harold was to comment, 'I remember tiptoeing up the stairs to see him after he was born. All I could think of was that he looked remarkably like me.'

George had a sister, Louise, born in 1931, and two brothers, Harold, born in 1934, and Peter, born in 1940.

He attended Dovedale Road Primary School, but was a few years below John Lennon and never met him there. George began attending Liverpool Institute in September 1954, which Paul McCartney had begun attending the previous year. He was to say, 'Paul went to school with me. I met him when I was twelve years old. I had this guitar, and Paul had a trumpet. His father, in his earlier days, had been involved in a little dance band. He was a piano player, so there was a lot of music in Paul's house, too.'

George and Paul began to frequent each other's company in 1956 and shared their interest in music. During the year George was able to buy a cheap guitar from a schoolmate for £3 10s (£3.50). He also formed a group called the Rebels, which included his brother Peter and best friend Arthur Kelly, but they performed only one gig, at the British Legion Club in Dam Wood Road, Speke.

Recalling the event, he was to say, 'I remember the Rebels had a tea chest with a lot of gnomes around it. One of my brothers had a five-shilling guitar, which had the back off. Apart from that it was all fine – just my brother, some mates and me.'

George's family had moved from 12 Arnold Grove, Wavertree, to 25 Upton Green, Speke, and George and Paul would get together in the Harrisons' front room to play some Lonnie Donegan numbers. George was to say, 'Paul was very good with the harder chords. After a time, we began playing real songs, like "Don't You Rock Me Daddy-O" and "Besame Mucho". Paul knocked me out with his singing, although I remember him being embarrassed – we were stuck in the middle of my parents' place with the whole family about.'

It was in 1957 that George acquired his first real guitar, a Hofner Futurama costing £30. He had obviously developed as a guitarist because Paul wanted him to join the Quarry Men and replace their current guitarist Eric Griffiths. George first saw the band perform at Wilson Hall, Garston, on Thursday 6 February 1958. He was to comment, 'I'd been invited to see them play several times by Paul, but for some reason never got round to it before. I remember being very impressed by John's big, thick sideboards and trendy Teddy Boy clothes. He was a terribly sarcastic bugger from day one, but I never backed down from him. In a way, all that emotional rough stuff was simply a way for him to help separate the men from the boys, I think. I was never intimidated by him. Whenever he had a go at me, I just gave him a little bit of his own right back.'

His actual introduction to the group, which was virtually an audition, took place at Rory Storm's club, the Morgue, in Broadgreen on Thursday 13 March that year. John was to recall that the decision to let George join the Quarry Men came then. He said, 'Paul introduced me to George, and Paul and I had to make the decision, or I had to make the decision, whether to let George in. I listened to George play and I said, "Play Raunchy" or whatever the old story is, and I let him in. I said "OK, you come in." '

The group were to cut their first record at a small studio in Kensington, Liverpool. They recorded only two numbers,

Buddy Holly's 'That'll Be the Day' and 'In Spite of All the Danger'. The latter was credited as having been composed by Paul McCartney and George Harrison.

The Quarry Men ceased performing for some months, so George joined another outfit called the Les Stewart Quartet, who had a residency at a club called Lowlands in West Derby. George's girlfriend Ruth Morrison mentioned that a new club was opening called the Casbah and they were also looking for a resident group.

They managed to secure the residency from Mona Best, owner of the coffee bar, but the group leader, Les Stewart, said he wouldn't play there.

George and his fellow guitarist Ken Brown walked out on Stewart and decided to take up the residency. George said to Mona Best, 'I know a couple of guys who say they've played in a band before. They're interested in coming down. Would you let them open?' She agreed and George contacted John and Paul and the Quarry Men were reborn as a quartet, sans a drummer. They made their debut at the Casbah on Saturday 29 August 1959 a month after George had left school.

On 10 October, following an appearance at the club, there was a dispute with Ken Brown because he'd been too ill to play that night, but had still got paid. And the group left the residency and continued as a trio, calling themselves Johnny and the Moondogs and appearing on the Carroll Levis *TV Star Search* talent show.

In January 1960 they were joined by Stuart Sutcliffe on bass guitar and in May, with the addition of a drummer, Tommy Moore, appeared on a brief tour of Scotland backing the singer Johnny Gentle. George paid tribute to his idol Carl Perkins by calling himself Carl Harrison during the tour. Moore left them soon after the tour and they recruited Pete Best as their drummer and left for a season in Hamburg on 17 August 1960.

Following appearances at the Indra and the Kaiserkeller, they had an offer to remain for a further season at a new club, the Top Ten, which incensed Bruno Koschmider, owner of the Kaiserkeller, who said that his contract with them precluded such an arrangement. Coincidentally, the police then came and informed George that they had discovered he was under age. At that time there was a curfew in place in the St Pauli district forbidding anyone under eighteen from being in the area. This meant that he wouldn't be able to play in the evening, and on 16 November 1960 he returned home, and was given a farewell at the train station by Stuart and his girlfriend Astrid Kirchherr.

The others returned soon after and, back in Liverpool, without Stuart, they appeared at the Casbah Club on Saturday 17 December and Litherland Town Hall on Tuesday 27 December. They had been billed as 'The Fabulous Beatles From Hamburg' and, as they were relatively unknown in their own home town, members of the audiences thought they were a German band. George was to say, 'We probably looked German as well. We looked very different from the other groups, with our leather trousers and cowboy boots. We looked funny and played differently.'

Their new dynamic style began to make a major impact locally and they performed their lunchtime debut at the Cavern Club on Thursday 9 February 1961 for a fee of £5. They made their first evening appearance at the club on Tuesday 21 March, which was when the club doorman, Pat Delaney, first noticed them. He was to comment, 'The first one I ever saw was George Harrison. In those days hairstyles were very strict and tidy, but George's hair was down to his collar. He was very scruffy. I remember him ambling down the middle of the street and, for a minute, I didn't think he was coming into the Cavern. I stopped him at the door and asked him if he was a member. He said no, he was with the Beatles. We'd heard a lot about the Beatles over the previous weeks and I knew they were on that particular night, so I let him in even though he was wearing blue jeans.'

The group returned to Hamburg on Saturday 1 April to appear at the Top Ten Club for the next 92 nights. During this time they made their first professional recordings for Bert Kaempfert backing the singer Tony Sheridan. However, Kaempfert also recorded them on two numbers without Sheridan: 'Ain't She Sweet' and 'Cry For a Shadow'. Kaempfert had actually asked them if they had any original numbers and George had penned the only one they recorded. 'Cry For a Shadow' was an instrumental, which had been composed when Rory Storm dared him to write a number in the style of the Shadows. George, therefore, became the first Beatle to have an original number professionally recorded for a record label.

In Liverpool they began to build up a tremendous local following and were promoted in every issue of the new local music paper *Mersey Beat*. The local music store manager, Brian Epstein, asked *Mersey Beat*'s editor, Bill Harry, if he could arrange for him to go down to the Cavern and see the Beatles one lunchtime, and this meeting occurred on 9 October 1961. He dropped into the band room for a chat and left a message with George that he would like to arrange a meeting with the Beatles to take place in his office.

After he signed the group, Brian sought a recording contract and managed to arrange an audition with Decca Records.

They performed fifteen numbers for their Decca audition with George taking lead vocal on 'The Sheik of Araby', 'Take Good Care Of My Baby', 'Three Cool Cats' and 'Crying, Waiting, Hoping'.

Among the other numbers that George used to sing during their appearances at Liverpool venues at that time were 'Everybody's Trying To Be My Baby', 'Glad All Over', 'I Forgot To Remember To Forget', 'Nothin' Shakin' (But The Leaves On The Trees)', 'So How Come (No One Loves Me)' and 'Youngblood'.

They set off for Germany once again to appear at the Top Ten Club. They ended their residency in July and returned to Liverpool, and in August that year they replaced their drummer, Pete Best, with Ringo Starr. George was probably the one who most encouraged the group to enlist Ringo, whom he liked. As a result, when they made their Cavern debut with Ringo, George was given a black eye by an angry Best fan – and was pictured with said shiner on the cover of *Mersey Beat* when the group flew down to London from Speke Airport to record at Parlophone.

In September 1963 George became the first member of the Beatles to visit America when he and his brother Peter visited their sister Louise in Benton, Illinois. During the trip George met up with the British singer Anthony Newley and played him some Beatles records. As a result, Newley recorded 'I Saw Her Standing There', which was released in America in October of that year.

When the Beatles were booked to appear on *The Ed Sullivan Show* in February 1964, George was sick on the flight over to America and was confined to bed when he reached the Plaza

Hotel. He didn't attend the rehearsal for the show and was nursed by his sister Louise, who described how the doctor almost prevented him appearing on the show itself. She said, 'The doctor almost said no, that he couldn't do it because he had a temperature of a hundred and four. But they pumped him with everything. The doctor wrote down this big list of stuff. He was thinking about getting a nurse to administer the medicine, every hour on the hour. Then the doctor suddenly realised that I was there and was his sister and he said to me, "Would you see to it?" He said, "It's probably just as well you're here because I don't think there's a single female in this city that isn't crazy about the Beatles. You'd probably be the only one who could function around him normally." '

On their return to Britain, the Beatles were to make their film debut with *A Hard Day's Night*. They began recording some tracks for it on 25 February 1964, George's 21st birthday. John had written the number 'I'm Happy Just To Dance With You' especially for George to sing in the film, although it seemed a backhanded compliment when he said, 'I would never have sung it myself.'

They began filming at the beginning of March. On Tuesday 3 March George met the model Pattie Boyd, who played the part of one of four schoolgirls they meet on a train. Pattie recalled, 'George hardly said hello, but the others came and chatted to us.

'When we started filming I could feel George looking at me and I was a bit embarrassed. Ringo seemed the nicest and easiest to talk to, and so was Paul. But I was terrified of John. After that first day's shooting, I asked them all for their autographs, except John. I was too scared.

'When I was asking George for his, I said could he sign it for my two sisters as well? He signed his name and put two kisses for each of them, but under mine he put seven kisses. I thought he must like me a little.'

George and Pattie began to live together and he proposed to her on Saturday 25 December 1965. They were married on 21 January 1966. Pattie said, 'We lived together for about a year before we got married. My mother knew, but she never mentioned it.'

On the eve of their world tour, Ringo became ill and had to be replaced by a temporary drummer, Jimmy Nicol. George said that he wanted the tour cancelled if Ringo wasn't with them. He commented, 'I was dead set against carrying on without Ringo. Imagine, the Beatles without Ringo Starr! Anyway, I bowed to the pressure and off we went, but I was none too pleased, even though Jimmy was actually quite a lovely guy.'

The group played their final tour date at the Candlestick Park, San Francisco, on 29 August 1966 and George was to remark, 'There was a certain amount of relief after the Candlestick Park concert. Before one of the last numbers, we actually set up this camera – I think it had a fisheye, a very wide-angle lens. We set it up on the amplifier and Ringo came off the drums, and we stood with our backs to the audience and posed for a photograph because we knew that was the last show.'

As they flew back to England, George was heard to say, 'Well, that's it. I'm not a Beatle any more.'

George was the first member of the Beatles to meet the Maharishi Mahesh Yogi and his future was to benefit from the influence of the Indian mystic, which led him to admire Indian music and philosophy and to gain his own teacher, Ravi Shankar.

The influence of the men from the East was to have a profound effect on both George's personal and professional life.

He also became involved in the Hare Krishna movement when they first came to England in 1968 and bought them a £500,000 Hertfordshire manor house to use as their first British temple. George claimed that the Hare Krishna chants saved him from death in a plane crash and persuaded him to become a full vegetarian and brought about his belief in reincarnation. He also chanted the Hare Krishna mantra for 23 hours nonstop while driving across Europe.

He was to say, 'I felt at home with Krishna, as if it was something that was with me from another birth.'

His spiritual master was AC Bhaktivedanta Swami Prabhupada. The swami encouraged George to give up drink and drugs, to follow Krishna's code of having no illicit sex, no intoxicants such as tea, coffee and tobacco and no gambling, meat, fish or eggs.

George said, 'A lot of religious prophets say, "I'm It. I'm the divine incarnation so let me hit you." But not Prabhupada. He told me, "I am a servant, we are all servants of God."

'Even though he was a great scholar, he spoke with childlike simplicity. He made me realise that we're not just physical bodies. We just happen to be in them but we really belong in the spiritual sky.'

George also began chanting 1,700 times a day and commented, 'Chanting is a form of meditating which helps me fix my mind on God. It doesn't stop you from being creative or productive. It actually helps you concentrate.'

By the beginning of the 1980s, George's passion for Hare Krishna had subdued and he was concentrating on being a gardener on his 36-acre estate, which includes a 200-foot scale model of the Matterhorn built in hundreds of tons of rock with catacombs, underground rivers and a temple for meditation.

He also became passionate about motor racing and was good friends with many drivers, including Jackie Stewart, who commented, 'If George's life had been different, he'd have loved to have been a racing driver.'

George became the first Beatle to issue material independently when he penned the soundtrack of *Wonderwall*, which reached No. 49 in the US charts in November 1968. George had been invited to compose the soundtrack for the film, which starred Jane Birkin, by his friend Joe Mussot, who directed.

In March 1968, just after Paul and Linda's wedding, George and Pattie were busted for possession of cannabis. George maintains that the 'evidence' was planted. A similar bust was made on John and Yoko that was to have far-reaching consequences when they attempted to settle in America.

George's next independent release was the album *Electronic Sounds*, issued in May 1969, which reached No. 191 in the American charts although, as with the soundtrack music from *Wonderwall*, it failed to find a placing in the British charts. He was experimenting with a Moog synthesiser and the album comprised only two tracks, the first side called 'Under the Mersey Wall', the second 'No Time or Space'.

He produced a number of Apple artists, including the Radha Krishna Temple who reached No. 12 in the British charts with 'Hare Krishna Mantra'.

In November 1969 his first and only Beatles A-side was released, 'Something', which topped the American charts and reached No. 4 in Britain. It was Allen Klein who decided that George's number should become the new Beatles single.

George had fought long and hard for every one of his compositions to appear on a Beatles recording, as John and Paul were the ones constantly jockeying for their songs to be used. George was also fed up with Paul making comments about how he should play and this came to a head on Friday 10 January 1969 following an argument while they were filming the *Let it Be* movie. George walked out and didn't return for a few days. The tensions are apparent in the film at a point when George turns to Paul and says, 'I always seem to be annoying you.' Paul also began to make suggestions as to how George should play and George said, 'All right, I'll play whatever you want me to play. Or I won't play at all if you don't want me to play.' George was to describe the *Let It Be* sessions as 'the low of all time'.

He also commented, 'To get a peaceful life I always let Paul have his own way, even when it meant that my songs weren't recorded. But I was having to record Paul's songs and put up with him telling me how to play my own guitar.'

The Beatles' press officer, Tony Barrow, once said of George, 'He came a very poor third in the pecking order, apart from his womanising. Often it seemed to me that Harrison was treated more like a hired studio session man than as an equal.

'I put his uncontrolled bouts of bad temper down to subconscious jealousy of John and Paul.'

As for John's attitude towards George, he was to say, 'George is ten years younger than me, or some shit like that. I couldn't be bothered with him when he first came around. He used to follow me around like a bloody kid, hanging around all the time. I couldn't be bothered. He was a kid who played guitar, and he was a friend of Paul's, which made it easier. It took me years to come around to him, to start considering him as an equal or anything.'

Around this time there were terrible tensions within the Beatles' camp, particularly since John was breaking their unwritten agreement that no wives or girlfriends should attend recording sessions by having Yoko permanently at his side at Abbey Road.

George's relationship with Yoko wasn't a good one and he initially considered that she was ruthless and ambitious, and was cold-bloodedly using John for her own ends. He tried to tell John, but John responded angrily and refused to speak to him for several weeks.

John was to say, 'Paul and George are the worst of the fuckin' lot. They're always making their cheap, snide little remarks about Yoko, always trying to do every little thing they can do to fuck up our love. Paul's even written a song about her. It's called "Get Back", and every time he sang the chorus in the studio I saw the way he looked at Yoko, like he was singing it to her. And I still can't believe the things George said to her, like he'd heard from New York that she'd got a bad vibe. I should have smacked him in the mouth but I still thought they would all come to love her once they knew her like I knew her.'

Songs by George that were recorded by the Beatles were 'Cry For a Shadow' (recorded by Bert Kaempfert in Hamburg); 'Don't Bother Me' (a track on the *With the Beatles* album); 'I Need You' and 'You Like Me Too Much' (tracks on the *Help!* album); 'Think For Yourself' and 'If I Needed Someone' (tracks on the *Rubber Soul* album); 'Taxman', 'Love You To' and 'I Want To Tell You' (tracks on the *Revolver* album); 'Within You, Without You' (a track on the *Sergeant Pepper's Lonely Hearts Club Band* album); 'Blue Jay Way' (a track on the *Magical Mystery Tour* EPS/album); 'The Inner Light' (flip side of 'Lady Madonna' and the first George Harrison composition to appear on a Beatles single); 'While My Guitar Gently Weeps', 'Piggies', 'Long, Long, Long' and 'Savoy Truffle' (tracks on *The Beatles* double album); 'Only a Northern Song' and 'It's All Too Much' (tracks on the *Yellow Submarine* soundtrack); 'Old Brown Shoe' (flip side of 'The Ballad of John and Yoko' and the second Beatles single with a composition by George); 'Something' and 'Here Comes the Sun' (tracks on the *Abbey Road* album); 'Something', the first George Harrison song to become a lead track on a Beatles single, 'I.Me.Mine' and 'For You Blue' (tracks on the *Let It Be* album). Considering the large number of Lennon and McCartney compositions on the Beatles' album and singles releases, it can be seen that George's original songs are few in proportion to those of his fellow songwriters in the group and he had to fight long and hard for those few tracks to be used in the first place.

In December 1969, along with his close friend Eric Clapton, he was playing concerts with Delaney and Bonnie. His triple album, *All Things Must Pass*, was released in December 1970, which also reached the position of the 'Something' single: No. 1

in the US and No. 4 in Britain. He became the first member of the Beatles to have a chart-topping solo album. This was to be his most successful one, and was co-produced by Phil Spector. Among the artists appearing on the album were Ringo Starr, Ginger Baker, Billy Preston, Badfinger and Derek and the Dominoes, with Eric Clapton. Bob Dylan also contributed two songs to the album, 'I'd Have You Anytime' and 'If Not For You'.

His single 'My Sweet Lord' topped both the British and American charts in January 1971, making him the first ex-Beatles to top the singles charts. In March of that year, Bright Tunes, a music-publishing company who owned the rights to the Ronnie Mack number 'He's So Fine', took legal action against George, claiming that 'My Sweet Lord' plagiarised 'He's So Fine'. As a result all royalties were frozen. George denied the plagiarism, claiming that his inspiration had been the Edwin Hawkins Singers' version of 'Oh Happy Day'.

His friend Ravi Shankar then approached George. He asked for his aid in suggesting ways in which money could be raised to help the refugees in war-torn Bangladesh. A million people had died of disease and starvation because of the civil war and there were countless orphaned children. Shankar's original idea had been a modest one, thinking that a concert could be organised that would raise about £25,000. George had a greater vision and suggested a major concert with international stars, which would provide a three-album set, a television special and a movie. His project eventually realised almost $13,000,000 for Bangladesh.

The concert took place on Sunday 1 August 1971 at Madison Square Garden in New York. Bob Dylan, Eric Clapton, Ravi Shankar, Badfinger and other artists had agreed to appear. George had hoped that John, Paul and Ringo would join him. Both John and Ringo agreed to appear and Paul considered it, but then felt that since the Beatles had officially split up it would be pointless if one of the first things they did was to re-form for a concert.

When John arrived, problems immediately loomed. John had seemed excited at the prospect of the concert and appearing with the cream of the world's musicians. Yoko had accompanied John and she insisted on taking part in the concert. When John asked George, 'Is there anything special you want Yoko to do?'

George replied, 'Yes, I'd like her to enjoy watching the show.' George took John aside and quietly explained that he wanted only John to appear and not Yoko. When she heard, Yoko went into a rage and there was a violent argument during which John's glasses were broken. Yoko engaged for nearly half an hour in a near-hysterical argument with the two of them. John then walked out and took the first flight back to Europe, ending up in Paris.

Despite the project being for a good cause, there were problems from the US Internal Revenue Service (IRS), who wanted their pound of flesh. George had expected all the proceeds to go to the struggling people of Bangladesh and, disgusted with the attitude of the taxmen, on Wednesday July 25 1973 he wrote out a personal cheque to the IRS for £1 million, commenting, 'And that's the last time I get involved in anything like that.'

The triple album *The Concert for Bangladesh*' reached No. 2 in the charts in January 1972. George's next album, *Living in the Material World*, also reached No. 2 in the charts in Britain and topped the American charts in June 1973. In the meantime, George had also guested on albums by Ringo Starr and Harry Nilsson.

Nineteen seventy-four saw the launch of George's own record label, Dark Horse. His first signing was Ravi Shankar. The label had a success with a group called Splinter, whose record, 'Costafine Town', reached No. 17 in the British charts and No. 77 in the US. However, it was the only hit on the label, apart from George's own recordings. During the year he embarked on a tour supported by Shankar and Billy Preston, although it wasn't a critical success. His next album, *Dark Horse*, released in December 1974, reached No. 4 in America but failed to chart in Britain. On the album was a version of 'Bye Bye Love' on which Pattie provided backing vocals. This was his way of saying goodbye to her as she'd recently left him to live with Eric Clapton.

His personal life seemed to be in ruins when his best friend fell in love with his wife.

Pattie had first met Eric Clapton at a party at Brian Epstein's house on 2 July 1967. She said, 'I was surprised by how alone Eric looked at that party. He was terribly reticent, he didn't talk to anybody or socialise.'

She told George she was going on a holiday to America to see her sister Jennie, then she joined Clapton on his American tour. When George heard he said, 'If she had to go off with someone, better Eric than some dope.'

George was to fall in love with Olivia Trinidad Arias, whom he met in 1974. George's health was in a bad state through depression caused by his marriage breakdown and he was suffering from serum hepatitis. Arias recommended an acupuncturist, who cured him. The two lived together in America for a while and then settled in George's mansion, Friar Park, in Henley-on-Thames, England. The couple had to wait until George's divorce from Pattie came through, and then set their wedding date for May 1978. However, this was postponed owing to the death of George's father. Their son Dhani was born on Tuesday 1 August 1978 and George and Olivia were married on Saturday 2 September 1978.

George's single 'Ding Dong' reached only No. 38 in the British charts and No. 36 in the American, although the 'Dark Horse' single reached No. 15 in the States.

During 1974, in an interview with Alan Freeman, George said, 'John Lennon is brilliant, a saint, he's great and I love him … but at the same time he's such a bastard!'

In October 1975 his album *Extra Texture (Read All About It)* was released, reaching No. 8 in the US charts and No. 16 in the UK. The following month EMI and Capitol decided to issue a compilation album, *The Best of George Harrison*, which reached No. 31 in the US charts and obviously affected the sales of George's official new album *Thirty-Three and a Third*, released the next month, which achieved only the No. 35 position in the UK and No. 11 in the US.

His single 'This Song' reached No. 25 in the American charts in January 1977.

George's next album, *Crackerjack Palace*, reached No. 19 in the American charts in March 1977.

In 1979 came the release of the eponymous album *George Harrison*, which reached No. 14 in America and No. 39 in Britain. The album indicated George's new passion, Formula One racing, as it included a track called 'Faster', which was inspired by the title of Jackie Stewart's book. A single from the album, 'Blow Away', reached No. 51 in the British chart and No. 14 in the American.

The year also saw George become involved in the world of movies. Peter Sellers had first introduced him to Denis O'Brien, an American lawyer and accountant, in 1973. In 1978 when EMI withdrew backing for the Monty Python film *The Life of Brian*, George stepped in and asked O'Brien to join him in saving the movie. They backed *The Life of Brian* with £2 million and used the profits to form Handmade Films, the company that underwrote other movies such as *The Long Good Friday* and *Time Bandits*.

George was particularly delighted with the success of *The Life of Brian*. He said, 'Let's face it, there are certain things in life which make it worth living and one of those things is Python. Especially to someone like me.

'When you've gone through so much in life and you're supposed to decide what's real and what isn't, you watch the television and see all this madness going on.

'Everyone is being serious and accepting it and you're ready to bang your head against the wall in despair. Then someone says, "And now for something completely different!" That saves the day. Laughter is the great release.'

In 1980 George's autobiography, *I.Me.Mine*, was published. The book incensed John, who is mentioned only eleven times in the entire work. He told *Playboy* magazine in one of his last interviews, 'I was hurt by it. By glaring omission in the book, my influence on his life is absolutely zilch and nil. Not mentioned. In his book, which is purportedly this clarity of vision of each song he wrote and its influences, he remembers every two-bit sax player or guitarist he met in subsequent years. I'm not in the book.'

He was also to give his opinion as to why he had been virtually left out of the book: 'George's relationship to me was one of younger follower and older guy. He's three or four years younger than me. It's a love–hate relationship and I think George still bears resentment towards me for being a daddy who left home.'

They were never to be reconciled as John was murdered soon after.

George was to receive the news of John's death from his sister Louise.

His album *Somewhere In England* was released in June 1981

and reached No. 11 in America and No. 13 in Britain. His single 'All Those Years Ago', dedicated to John, reached No. 2 in America and No. 13 in Britain around the same time, and also featured Paul and Ringo.

In November 1982 his next album, *Gone Troppo*, reached only No. 108 in America and the single from it, 'Wake Up My Love', reached No. 53 in the States the following month.

For the next three years George concentrated on Handmade Films – appearing in the film *Water*, along with Ringo Starr and Eric Clapton – and also established a second home in Australia.

During December 1985 he teamed up with Ringo and Eric again, together with other musicians, to appear in a special television tribute to his idol Carl Perkins; and the following year he contributed two tracks to a Duane Eddy comeback album, *Duane Eddy*. In 1987 he jammed with Bob Dylan, John Fogerty and Taj Mahal at the Palomino Club and in June of that year appeared on the Prince's Trust concert at Wembley Stadium with Ringo performing 'While My Guitar Gently Weeps' and 'Here Comes the Sun'.

He returned to the charts in November 1987 when his album *Cloud Nine* reached No. 10 in the British charts and his single 'Got My Mind Set On You' reached No. 2. The single then went on to top the American charts, with the album *Cloud Nine* also reaching No. 20 in the US in January 1988. A month later the single 'When We Was Fab' reached No. 23 in the US and No. 25 in the UK.

Other record releases from George included the single 'This Is Love' c/w 'Breathe Away From Heaven', which was released in the US on 2 May 1988 and in the UK on 13 June. A compilation album, *The Best of Dark Horse 1976–1989*, was released in the US on 17 October and in the UK on 23 October 1989. It reached only No. 132 in the US. George's single 'Cheer Down' c/w 'That's What It Takes' was issued in the States on 21 August 1989 and in the UK on 4 September.

His double album *Live In Japan* was released in the UK on 13 July and in the US on 14 July 1992.

On 10 January 1989 a Granada TV documentary, *The Movie Life of George*, about his career with Handmade Films, was screened.

George created the Traveling Wilburys in 1988. He was in Los

Angeles and needed an extra track for the B-side of a single from his *Cloud Nine* album. He called Jeff Lynne for a songwriting session. Then he called Bob Dylan, while Lynne brought in Roy Orbison, and George then invited Tom Petty. George began writing at Dylan's home and they all became involved. George said, 'I thought of the first line, then everyone was writing words, with Dylan saying some hysterical things. Then we thought, If Roy Orbison's coming along, we might as well have a lovely bit for him. So we wrote that, then just sang it. The next day we added electric guitar and bass, and mixed it. It was instant.'

The record company WEA considered the track 'Handle With Care' was too good for a B-side, so it was put on hold. George then thought of turning the collaboration into an album and the result was *The Traveling Wilburys Volume 1*. Roy Orbison died before the Wilburys got together again to record their second album and they decided not to find a replacement. Their second album was released in October 1990, entitled *The Traveling Wilburys Volume 3*. There never was a Volume 2.

From 1 to 17 December 1991 George toured Japan with Eric Clapton. He also performed at the Royal Albert Hall with Clapton on Monday 6 April 1992 in a concert in aid of the Natural Law Party.

Handmade Films was sold to Paragon Entertainment Corporation in Canada in May 1994.

The next year found George taking out a lawsuit against his former Handmade Films partner Denis O'Brien.

In May 1997 there was a US release for Ravi Shankar's *Chants of India* CD, which George had recorded at his own studios and on which he performed. The CD was released in the UK in September 1997.

During a visit to Toronto in March 1988 George was asked about the fact that Paul had recently said that he'd like to write some songs with him, and George commented, 'Yes, Paul has suggested that maybe he and me should write something again. I mean it's pretty funny really. I mean, I've only been there about thirty years in Paul's life and now he wants to write with me. But maybe it would be quite interesting to do that. There's a thing with Paul: one minute he says one thing and he's really charming and then next minute he's all uptight. We all go through that, good and bad stuff. But, by now, we've got to find the centre.'

In May 1998 George was the member of the Beatles elected to go to court and prevent the release on CD of the Hamburg tapes, recorded at the Star Club during their final appearance there. George was able to convince Mr Justice Neuberger in the High Court that they shouldn't be released as they were 'the crummiest recording ever made in the group's name'.

George also told the court that John Lennon was not the leader of the group. He said, 'I taught John the guitar. He had a little guitar with three strings tuned like a banjo. I had to show him all the chords.

'When I first met him I was very young, but so was he. He was seventeen and I was maybe fourteen or fifteen.

'But by the time we were in Hamburg I'd grown up a lot, and I could certainly hold my own against him.

'He was the loudest, the noisiest and the oldest. He could be wrong about something but try to win the argument just by being loud.'

In August 1998 it was announced that George had undergone treatment for throat cancer. He had a cancerous lump removed and underwent a course of radiation therapy. He was cleared of the disease, commenting, 'I'm not going to die on you folks just yet – I am very lucky.'

January 1999 saw him win a libel case against the publishers of *All Dressed Up: The Sixties and the Counter Culture*, by Jonathan Green, who claimed that George accepted sexual favours in exchange for a donation to charity.

The end of the millennium produced shock waves for Beatles enthusiasts throughout the world as George was almost killed. George and Olivia were in the bedroom of their 120-room gothic mansion on 30 December 1999 when they heard noises. George went to investigate and discovered an intruder who attacked him and plunged a six-inch knife into his chest. While he fought for his life, George called for help and Olivia rushed down to aid him, but was also stabbed by the intruder. She saved George's life by picking up a heavy table lamp and hitting the attacker on the head with it. Later, while in hospital, George made light of it, commenting, 'He wasn't a burglar and he definitely wasn't auditioning for the Traveling Wilburys.'

The assailant turned out to be from Liverpool. His name was Michael Abram and he was detained under the Mental Health Act.

No longer involved in the film world, George continues his passion for motor racing and frequently attends Grand Prix races throughout the world. He also continues his association and friendship with Ravi Shankar and has homes in Australia and Hawaii in addition to his beloved Friar Park. George intends to continue recording and the Traveling Wilburys will be revived.

Harrison, Peter

George Harrison's elder brother, who was in the same class as John at Dovedale Primary School. He was subsequently employed by George at his gothic mansion, Friar Park, supervising ten gardeners and a botanist to maintain the beauty of the extensive gardens.

Harrow, Joey

Musician who lived in close proximity to the Dakota Building in New York. In 1983 he claimed he saw John's ghost in the entrance doorway, the spot where he had been shot three years before.

'He was surrounded by an eerie light,' Harrow claimed. At the time of the sighting he was accompanied by a writer called Amanda Moores, who confirmed that she had also seen the ghost. 'I wanted to go up and talk to him, but something in the way he looked at me said no,' she said.

John's ghost had been reported by various other witnesses who claimed it had been haunting the Dakota. A psychic called Shawn Robbins said she saw John's ghost in the building and Yoko herself was reported to have seen John sitting at his white piano. He turned to her and said, 'Don't be afraid. I am still with you.'

Hart, Ian

Actor, born in Liverpool on 8 October 1964, who has portrayed John twice on the screen. He'd initially appeared at the Liverpool Playhouse and in the films *Zip* and *No Surrender*, before appearing in a number of TV dramas such as *The Monocled Mutineer*.

He first played John in 1992 in *The Hours and the Times* and received critical acclaim for his portrayed of John in the film *Backbeat*.

He is an actor much in demand and has since appeared in numerous films, including *Clockwork Mice*; *Land and Freedom*; *The Englishman Who Went Up a Hill, But Came Down A Mountain*; *All Our Fault*; *The Hollow Road* and *Michael Collins*.

Hartnell, Norman

A leading British fashion designer and dressmaker to the Queen. He was John and Yoko's nearest neighbour at Tittenhurst Park.

Harvey, Leila

John's cousin, who was four years older than him. Leila was born in Egypt in 1937, the daughter of John's aunt, Harriet, and her first husband Ali Hafez, who had gone to live in Cairo. When Ali died they returned to Liverpool.

The maternal side of the family was very close in the early years and Leila and John enjoyed a close relationship from the time he was two years old until he was fifteen. They'd always get together at Christmas and other holidays and used to play games together. When playing cowboys and Indians, Leila invariably had to take the role of the Indian.

She later went to Edinburgh University to study medicine and it was during a holiday, while she was working as a chalet maid at a Butlin's holiday camp, that she received a telegram: 'JUDY CAR ACCIDENT. DIED FRIDAY. FUNERAL TUESDAY.' John's mother Julia, known to the family as Judy, had died in a car crash, and Leila attended the funeral. When they got home, John put his head in her lap and they didn't say a word. Both were numb with shock.

Leila married, had three children and went to work in Germany as a consultant. She returned in 1968 and took a position as an anaesthetist at the Ear, Nose & Throat Hospital in Camden, London. While in London she dropped in at Apple to see John and was also invited along to a boardroom lunch there with aunt Mimi Smith. She also visited John at Kenwood in Weybridge.

John wrote to Leila after her mother died in 1972 and she

suspects he felt guilty about not attending his auntie's funeral. He then began to write to her on a semi-regular basis right until his death. A lot of the letters had been thrown away but one day, some years after John's death, Leila's daughter needed a little extra money and asked her mother if she could have one of the letters. She then auctioned it. Leila thought that John wouldn't have cared about such a thing, but she was surprised by the rude phone call she received from Yoko. Yoko apparently used some 'nasty language' and criticised Leila, who then told her, 'Look, Yoko, John was our *blood*. You were only married to him, and a second wife at that.'

One of Leila's letters was auctioned by Liverpool auctioneers Eldon E. Worrall, who commented, 'It seems that Leila gave this letter to a cousin, who sold it to a Beatles dealer, who offered it to us along with several other items of Beatles memorabilia.' It affords an insight into John's attitudes and state of mind in 1970. The letter, written in his inimitable style, with lower case letters and a casual attitude to punctuation, was dated 30 July 1970. It was in reply to a letter Leila had written to him, obviously about his heavy drinking and drug taking, in which she had called him a 'weak character.'

He began the letter by referring to her as 'Old Bossyboots,' which was a reference to the times they used to play together through the summers of the early 1960s when Leila would visit John at Menlove Avenue. Friends say they were inseparable in those days.

John wrote that he was no big drinker but that the previous year had been something 'special,' although he was now 'clean as a whistle.' He also wrote that he preferred mushrooms to drugs, 'a la aldous huxley,' and told her, 'It's a little naïve of you, dear cousin, to advise me about my private life.'

He admitted that he'd taken drugs in the past, but had overcome them and wrote, 'as a matter of fact I don't use any drugs including aspirin etc.'

John also wrote that he was thinking of taking piano lessons himself. 'I only play with one finger ... self taught and lousy. (mimi would never let me have a piano in the house ... said it was common).' He also said that Mimi still thought he 'got lucky' and had 'no talent.'

He declared he was going to learn to cook, that his diet was a healthy one with 'wholefood stuff ... pumpkin seeds etc vitamins ... fish ... meat ... but not always ... we try to avoid any 'junk' food especially SUGAR. I'm healthy as a bull ... I do yoga exercises (nearly) every day. I've been food-conscious for years ... quite an expert at revitalising a drug-crazed body ... I bet I live till a ripe old age.'

Another interesting topic he touched on referred to Julian. He said that Cynthia allowed him to visit him twice a year. Then he said that she insisted on coming along herself; 'She thought she could walk back in cos I wasn't with Yoko!' Then he said that since he was back with Yoko Cynthia had stopped Julian phoning him, as he had done the previous year, virtually once a week.

He also announced, 'oh yes the baby is due in November! Conceived feb 6.' He also referred to himself as 'a japangloamerican.'

In another letter to Leila, John wrote, 'Strange that you should think I was the one that lost touch with you ... I always thought it was the other way round ... didn't you leave first? Stranger still that my (our) family should always (nowadays) see me in terms of dollars and cents ... though before I guess they saw me in terms of a problem child ... or an orphan of sorts.'

Hastings, Jay

Hastings was a Beatles fan who became front-door clerk at the Dakota Building in 1978 and established a friendship with John and Yoko. They'd chat to him when they were entering or leaving the building and John would often say '*Bon soir*, Jay' to him.

The bearded doorman was 27 years old and was on duty the night John was shot. He rushed to John's aid when the singer collapsed in front of his office and placed his blue jacket over him.

He pressed the alarm alerting the police at the nearby 20th Precinct and then sought out the killer, but Mark Chapman was simply standing in the street reading a book.

When the police arrived they originally drew their guns on Hastings because his clothes were covered in blood, but a fellow doorman yelled out his identity to them.

Havadtoy, Sam

An interior designer, twenty years Yoko's junior. They first met when she went to a Fifth Avenue interior designer's soon after John's death and he decorated her New York apartment. Havadtoy was also to renovate Yoko's Palm Beach mansion in 1982. The press linked their names together romantically. Reports in October 1982 even suggested that a marriage was imminent and Havadtoy's friend and associate Kerry Westrookes told the press, 'Sam says the wedding is definitely on. He is more open about the relationship than Yoko, but she has changed her lifestyle completely since she has been with him.'

In 1981 Yoko visited Budapest, Hungary. When asked why, she said, 'My manager Sam Havadtoy is of Hungarian origin. We have been friends a long time and Sam always encouraged me to visit his native country.'

Rumours continued to spread and Havadtoy had to deny that he and Yoko were married. In 1990 he said, 'That's a state of mind. We're happy. We're living together, boyfriend and girl-friend, yes.'

In 1986, Yoko said, 'He has been very caring and he has been good for my son Sean. But we have no plans to get married at this stage.'

Have You Heard the Word?

A song that people have mistaken for a Beatles track. It came from a bootleg album of the same title and Steve Kipner and Steve Groves wrote the song. The bootleg cover attributed it to the Beatles, but the band was actually a soundalike outfit and the singer sounded so much like John that Yoko Ono mistakenly registered the song title for copyright protection on Friday 20 September 1985, when she registered 28 song titles. Two of the songs weren't by John: 'Have You Heard the Word?' and a number by Grapefruit called 'Lullaby'. During an interview on KHJ-FM in Los Angeles on the morning of Friday 27 September 1974 John was asked if the Beatles had ever recorded a song called 'Have You Heard the Word?' He answered, 'No, no ... I think they got that mixed up with "The Word", the Beatles song, "Word" on *Rubber Soul*, 'cause I know there's a bootleg on it, but there's no such song. It sounds like us. It's a good imitation.'

Hawkins, Ronnie

A rock singer born in Arkansas in 1935. He formed a group called the Hawks and moved to Canada in 1957. His backing group returned to the States, changed their name to the Band and backed Bob Dylan.

Hawkins settled down in Streetsville, near Toronto, with his wife Wanda. Their life was temporarily turned topsy-turvy in December 1969 when a rock journalist, Ritchie York, who also acted as press agent for Hawkins, arranged for John and Yoko with members of their entourage to stay for a short time on their ten-acre farm.

Several people accompanied them. These included their personal assistant Anthony Fawcett and the comedian Dick Gregory. Various journalists such as Ray Connolly and Ralph Ginsberg also turned up.

Extra phone lines were installed to enable John to call journalists and radio stations in different parts of the States on behalf of his Peace Campaign.

Hawkins was horrified some months later when he received the staggering phone bills, which amounted to $5,000 for the week John and Yoko had been present.

A huge white Christmas tree with a cage containing two doves arrived, together with a girl to do the washing up as the Lennons were into macrobiotic foods and had brought their macrobiotic cookbook with them.

They were at the farm for five days, during which John signed 3,000 copies of his erotic lithographs for his Bag One project.

Although the thought of paying the phone bills never entered John's head, he was obviously appreciative of the Hawkins' hospitality and recorded a special promotional message for his new single 'Down in the Alley'. A limited-edition single with John's spoken introduction on the A-side and a longer chat on the flip was sent along to radio stations throughout the US and Canada.

He Stands In a Desert Counting the Seconds of His Life

An avant-garde film directed by Jonas Mekas. The film features John and Yoko, Andy Warhol, Jackie Onassis and various people filmed in New York. A reviewer, Fred Camper, considered it 'one of the most intense, moving and beautiful examples of the tradition in the avant-garde film world to use the camera, not to show external events but for the exploration of the varieties of the private personas and inner visions of their makers'. Discussing the director, he said, 'He does not distinguish who is a celebrity and who is not.'

Heart Play – Unfinished Dialogue
Polydor album subtitled 'A Spoken Word documentary', which was issued in America on Polydor 817 238-1 Y-1 on Monday 5 December 1983 and in Britain on Polydor 817 238-1 on Friday 16 December 1983. It included a 42-minute extract from John's September 1980 *Playboy* interview. It reached No. 161 in the *Cash Box* album chart.

Heartbreak Hotel
Elvis Presley's famous hit and one of John's earliest influences. He said, 'It was Elvis who really got me interested in pop music and started me buying records. I thought that early stuff of his was great. The Bill Haley era passed me by in a way.

'When his records came on the wireless my mother would start dancing around, she thought they were so good. I used to hear them, but they didn't do anything for me. It was Elvis who got me hooked on beat music. When I heard "Heartbreak Hotel", I thought, This is it, and I started to grow sideboards and all that gear.'

Hello Little Girl
The song that John described as 'my first song'. He wrote it while he was sitting on the toilet when he was eighteen and was also to say that it was directly influenced by the music of Buddy Holly.

John sang lead vocals on the number with the Beatles until 1962 and performed it at the Decca audition sessions on 1 January 1962. It has since appeared on a number of bootleg albums such as *The Decca Tapes*, but was never issued as a Beatles single.

In 1963 Brian Epstein signed up another Mersey band, the Fourmost, who had appeared on numerous bills with the Beatles.

They didn't have any original material and a group member, Brian O'Hara, asked John if he had a song to give them. He said they could have 'Hello Little Girl'. The group recorded it as their debut disc on Parlophone R5056 in August 1963 and it reached No. 9 in the British charts. The Fourmost recording was also contained on the album *The Songs Lennon & McCartney Gave Away*, issued in Britain in April 1979 on EMI NUT 18.

In an interview with *Mersey Beat*, another group member, Billy Hatton, commented, 'We arranged to go to John Lennon's house, and they gave us a copy of the words. We hadn't heard the number before, and George and John gave us a rough idea of it by taping the tune. We received the tape at 4 o'clock on Monday morning.

'As we had to record on the following Wednesday, we had two days in which to make an arrangement good enough to put on disc. As a matter of fact, when we were recording, we were just learning the song as we went along and were tremendously encouraged by A&R man George Martin.'

Help! (album)

The Beatles' fourth album. It was released in the UK on 6 August 1965. The American album was issued on 13 August of that year and, as usual with American releases, was different from the British version. It contained the seven Beatles songs featured in the film, together with six orchestral numbers from the film by Ken Thorne. The Beatles had prevented the orchestral pieces from being included on their British release and were frustrated to find them included on the American record.

The songs written by John were 'Help!', 'You've Got To Hide Your Love Away', 'You're Going To Lose That Girl', 'Ticket To Ride', 'It's Only Love' and 'Day Tripper'. John and Paul collaborated on 'We Can Work It Out'.

Help! (single)

This was a song written to order. The Beatles' second film had undergone some title changes and one of the working titles, *Eight Arms To Hold You*, had now been changed to *Help!*. Both John and Paul were under pressure to come up with a theme song for the film and John won the race. Despite this, *Help!* was a very personal song, an autobiographical number in which

John attempted to express what he felt about himself. Many years later he said, 'I was fat and depressed and I was crying out for help.'

In 1970 he remarked, 'The only true songs I wrote were "Help!" and "Strawberry Fields". They were the ones I really wrote from experience and not projecting myself into a situation and writing a nice story about it, which I always found phoney. The lyric is as good now as it was then. It makes me feel secure to know that I was that sensible, aware of myself back then. But I don't like the recording that much: we did it too fast to try to be commercial.'

'Help!' was recorded on Tuesday 13 April 1965 in a very fast-paced version. John commented on this fact during a 1971 interview in which he said, 'I've thought of doing it again sometime and slowing it down.' He never did. Tina Turner recorded it as a tribute to John after his death, in a version sung in the style that John would have preferred.

Help Me to Help Myself

Another of the many songs that John wrote at the Dakota Building during his househusband period. As with his other compositions of the time, he made a home demo tape of the song, which eventually found an airing on Episode 180 of *The Lost Lennon Tapes* radio series.

On the track John sings and accompanies himself on piano, with lyrics such as 'They say the Lord helps those who help themselves.'

Helter Skelter

A Paul McCartney number included on *The Beatles* double album. John played bass and lead guitars and saxophone on the track. Charles Manson believed the title was the name for a coming apocalypse. John was to say that Manson's interpretation was absurd and that the killer had invented a message that simply didn't exist in the song.

Henri, Adrian

A prominent Liverpool poet/painter, who was a friend of John during the art college days. Henri featured the Beatles in one of his paintings *The Entry of Christ Into Liverpool*. His poem

'New York City Blues (For John Lennon)' was published by Allison & Busby in *Adrian Henri Collected Poems* in 1986.

He once related an anecdote about the time he was with John in the Liverpool pub Ye Cracke. He said John was lying on the floor pretending to swim when the proprietor's wife asked him to stop. 'I can't,' he said, 'I'll drown.'

Here Today

A track on Paul McCartney's 1983 album *Tug of War*, which was Paul's own tribute to John. Paul described the number as 'a song saying, well, if you were here today you'd probably say what I'm doing is crap. But you wouldn't mean it, 'cos you like me really. It's one of those "come out from behind your glasses, look at me" kind of things. It was a love song about my relationship with him. I was trying to exorcise the demons in my own head, because it's tough when you have somebody like John slagging you off in public.

'He was a major influence on my life, as I suppose I was on his. But the great thing about me and John was that it was me and John, end of story. Everyone else can say, "Well, he did this and so-and-so." But that's the nice thing that I can actually think, when we got in a little room it was me and John who wrote it, not any of these other people who think they all know about it. I was the one in the room with him.'

Here We Go Again

The only song that John co-composed with Phil Spector. John wrote the number and made a home tape performing it acoustically. He handed the tape to Spector when they were recording in Los Angeles in October 1973 and Spector arranged the composition.

'Here We Go Again' remained unreleased until 1986, when it was issued on the posthumous compilation, *Menlove Avenue*. A simple piano demo that John had made of the number was included on a CD issued in Sweden in 1998, along with an edition of John's book, *A Spaniard in the Works*.

Hey Bulldog

Recorded on Sunday 11 February 1968 and included on the *Yellow Submarine* soundtrack, this was the last song the Beatles recorded before they left for the Maharishi Mahesh Yogi's ashram in India. Other titles of 'Hey Bulldog' were 'Hey Bullfrog' and 'You Can Talk To Me'.

They began recording it with the title 'Hey Bullfrog' in mind, but Paul began to bark at the end of the song to make John laugh and they changed the title to 'Hey Bulldog', although such a canine is never mentioned in the lyrics.

Yoko Ono was present in the studio, attending a Beatles recording for the first time. She set the scene for future studio incursions, which annoyed the other members of the Beatles, by making comments about the songs they were recording. She was to say, 'I went to see the Beatles recording, and I said to John, "Why do you always use that beat all the time, the same beat? Why don't you do something more complex?" '

The song was left out of the American print of *Yellow Submarine*. Erich Segal, who wrote part of the screenplay for the animated movie, claimed that the song had been written for him and that the title was taken from the fact that the bulldog was the mascot of Yale University, where he was a lecturer – although this doesn't appear to be true.

Hey John

A song penned by Blossom Dearie and Jim Council, with Dearie providing the music and Council the lyrics. Dearie had appeared on the *Frost on Sunday* show with John and Yoko on Saturday 24 August 1968. John did an impression of her, which she liked, and she was so pleased that she decided to write this song.

Hey Jude

A song written by Paul. John was to comment, 'That's his best song. It started off as a song about my son Julian, because Paul was going to see him. Then he turned it into "Hey Jude". I always thought it was about me and Yoko but he said it wasn't.'

Hier En Nu

A Dutch television programme on the NCRV network, which transmitted a filmed five-minute interview with John and Yoko at the Amsterdam Hilton. The interview, conducted by Niek Heizenberg while the couple sat on their bed, was transmitted on Tuesday 25 March 1969.

Hill, Bernard

An actor who began his career by appearing as John in the Willy Russell play *John, Paul, George, Ringo and Bert*. He also starred as John in the BBC *Everyman* TV production, called 'John Lennon: A Journey In The Life', screened on Friday 6 December 1985. He was 40 years old at the time. Hill was to comment, 'From the start, I've always felt an affinity with Lennon and I get very depressed playing him now that he's dead.'

Hill, Mike

A boy who lived near to John during John's teenage years. Hill owned a huge collection of American records and, since he also lived close to Quarry Bank School, John was able to drop into his house with some friends, bringing along chips to eat and packets of five Senior Service cigarettes to smoke, while they listened to records. At that time John had recently discovered Elvis, who was his main idol. One day at Hill's house, he heard Little Richard for the first time when 'Long Tall Sally' was played. He was so impressed he was unable to speak. He recalls, 'Then someone said, "It's a nigger singing." I didn't know Negroes sang. So Elvis was white and little Richard was black. "Thank you, God," I said.'

Hippopotamus Club

A nightclub in New York. On Friday 20 December 1974 George Harrison held a party there to celebrate the end of his Dark Horse Tour following his final concert at Madison Square Garden. Hilary Gerrard, Ringo's manager, had taken John's son Julian along to the concert, but John hadn't attended. During that day he'd had a meeting with Lee Eastman to discuss the Beatles' final agreement. John and Yoko then attended the Hippopotamus party. After the party, John dropped by to see George in his hotel room and the two were interviewed separately by the Los Angeles radio station KHJ.

Discussing that night at a later time, John said, 'George and I are still good pals and we always will be, but I was supposed to sign this thing on the day of his concert. He was pretty weird because he was in the middle of that tour and we hadn't communicated for a while because he doesn't live here. I've seen Paul a bit because he comes to New York a lot, and I'm always seeing Ringo in Los Angeles. Anyway, I was a bit nervous about going on stage, but I agreed to because it would have been mean of me not to go on with George after I'd gone on with Elton. I didn't sign the document on that day because my astrologer told me it wasn't the right day.

'George was furious with me at the time because I hadn't signed it when I was supposed to, and somehow or other I was informed that I needn't bother to go to George's show. I was quite relieved in the end because there wasn't any time to rehearse and I didn't want it to be a case of just John jumping up and playing a few chords. I went to see him at Nassau and it was a good show. The band was great but Ravi [Shankar] wasn't there, so I didn't see the bit where the crowd is supposed to get restless. I just saw a good tight show. George's voice was shot but the atmosphere was good and the crowd was great. I saw George after the Garden show and we were friends again. But he was surrounded by the madhouse that's called "touring". I respect George but I think he made a mistake on the tour. Mistakes are easier to spot if you're not the person making them, so I don't want to come on like "I know better", 'cause I haven't done that – one of the basic mistakes seemed to be that the people wanted to hear old stuff. George wasn't prepared to do that, and I understand him. When I did that charity thing at Madison Square Garden, I was still riding high on "Imagine" so I was OK for material. But when I did "Come Together" the house came down, which gave me an indication of what people wanted to hear.'

Hoffman, Abbie

Political activist and antiwar protester who set up the radical movement of yuppies in America, together with Jerry Rubin.

He was to say, 'The effect of something like the *Sergeant Pepper* album on me and other activists, organisers and counterculture people around the world was one of incredible impact, like starting a fire in a fireworks factory.'

When John and Yoko moved to New York in 1971, Rubin contacted them and they went to meet Rubin, Hoffman and his wife Anita at Hoffman's lower eastside apartment, which had supposedly been bugged. They talked over their mutual aims during a five-hour meeting.

The FBI, who had been keeping their eye on the yuppies, also turned their attention to John and Yoko and many of their reports were allegedly fabricated.

For instance, on a meeting at Max's Kansas City in New York, an FBI report read, 'Over drinks, Lennon gave Hoffman and Rubin an envelope containing fifty $100 bills – $5,000 – for the cause.'

Hoffman and Rubin were members of the Chicago Seven, who had been accused of conspiracy by disrupting the Democratic National Convention in Chicago in 1968. Hoffman disappeared for a number of years, going underground after being discovered selling cocaine.

He was 52 years old when he committed suicide at his home in New Hope, Pennsylvania, on 12 April 1989.

Hoffmann, Dezo

Czech-born photographer who first met the Beatles in 1962. When he originally went up to Liverpool to take photos of the group, he took a shot of John when he was putting on a shirt at Paul's house. John didn't like it and told Hoffmann it made him look like a tramp. Hoffmann told him, 'Yes, but your face ... I never saw you look so human as on this picture.' John came to like the picture after that.

Hoffmann also pointed out that John didn't actually like being photographed.

When the Beatles were in Weston-super-Mare, Dezo wanted to take some shots for American magazines and felt that the pictures had to be something special, so he thought up the idea of dressing them in old-fashioned Victorian bathing suits. Both John and Brian Epstein were against the idea, but the session went ahead.

Between 1962 and 1964 he took more photographs of the Beatles than any other photographer, but the situation changed in 1964. He'd gone along to the Twickenham film studios where the group were making *A Hard Day's Night*. John was talking to a girl but as soon as he saw Dezo he turned on him because of a photograph that had been taken in Miami that Dezo had sold to *Titbits* magazine in which the wind had blown away his hair revealing his forehead. John berated Dezo in front of everyone and the photographer was to say, 'I felt so humiliated in front of all those people that I couldn't even answer him. I just turned my back on him and walked out. And I obviously finished with the Beatles also. In my imagination I had thought of myself as a father figure to them, and I couldn't believe that John could talk to me as if I were a six-year-old kid.'

When Dezo went along to the Prince of Wales Theatre, Derek Taylor approached him and said, 'Dezo, I feel so awkward because he doesn't want you at the press reception. He said he doesn't want to see you.'

The estrangement ended some years later when Dezo was in New York. He was staying at the Plaza hotel when he received a call from John asking him to come and see him. John began asking about London and mutual friends and Dezo noticed that Yoko was also in the room and it became obvious that the two weren't on speaking terms, so Dezo thought that John was using him as a middleman. However, they'd made up and, when Dezo left, John kissed him.

Dezo's book of photographs of John under the title *John Lennon* was published in Britain in 1985 and in America the following year as *The Faces of John Lennon*.

Hokey Pokey
Name by which John's aunt, Mimi Smith, sometimes referred to Yoko Ono.

Hold Me Tight
A number John co-wrote with Paul, although Paul was the main contributor.

Hold On
Track on the *John Lennon/Plastic Ono Band* album. A contrast to the mood of some of the other songs on the record, which was also known as the 'Primal Scream' album. (*The Primal Scream* was the title of a book by the psychiatrist Arthur Janov, to describe his 'primal therapy'.) John discussed it, commenting, 'I'm saying "Hold on, John" because I don't want to die … I don't want to be hurt and please don't hit me … Hold on now, we might have a cup of tea, we might get a moment's happiness any minute now. So that's what it's all about, just moment by moment. That's how we're living now, but really living like that and cherishing each day, and dreading it too. It might be your last.'

Holly, Ida

A dark-haired Liverpool girl who was 17 years old in 1963 when John began dating her. His marriage to Cynthia had been kept secret and Ida was unaware of it until her father found out and threatened to expose John in the press.

Ida attempted to appear as a compere at local beat-music events, such as the Mersey Beat Showboat and then moved to London, where she changed her name to Stevie Holly and attempted to find work as a model.

Hollywood Walk of Fame

The most famous sidewalk in the world, which displays hundreds of specially dedicated 'stars' to celebrities.

John Lennon was posthumously dedicated with Star No. 1,877 at 1750 Vine Street, in front of Capitol Records, on Friday 30 September 1988 at 12.30 p.m. Hosting the ceremony was Johnny Grant, honorary Mayor of Hollywood and chairman of the Walk of Fame, and Bill Welsh, Hollywood Chamber of Commerce president.

Accepting the honour of behalf of John was Yoko Ono, along with David J Wolper, producer of *Imagine: John Lennon*, a feature film released during the week of the ceremony.

Here is the full text of Johnny Grant's speech:

As honorary Mayor of Hollywood and chairman of the Walk of Fame Committee, I am very pleased to welcome all of you to the dedication of the 1,877th star on the world's most famous sidewalk. Today, ladies and gentlemen, we honour late Beatle, poet, philosopher, singer/songwriter, peace activist John Lennon for his many, many outstanding achievements in the recording industry.

Whenever a Beatles tune is heard or sung, the legacy of John Lennon lives on, for there is no doubt that John was one of the greatest singer/songwriters who ever lived.

John was born during an air raid in Liverpool, England, to Julia Stanley and Fred Lennon on October 9th, 1940. When his parents split up he went to live permanently with his Aunt Mimi.

John's interest in music began in the fifties when he first discovered Elvis Presley's 'Heartbreak Hotel'. He later credited Elvis as the influence that got him into rock and roll. In 1956 he formed his first group, the Quarry Men. His Aunt Mimi later bought him a guitar, but told him that he would never make a living out of it. Now that is a wrong prediction if I ever heard one!

A fourteen-year-old named Paul McCartney later joined the group as bass player, along with another young man named George Harrison.

The first song that John wrote was 'Hello Little Girl', which the Beatles later recorded for their audition at Decca Records. The Quarry Men later decided that they needed a catchier name and called themselves the Silver Beetles, later shortening it to just the Beatles. The band then acquired a new drummer named Ringo Starkey. Six months later the Beatles' first hit, 'Love Me Do', peaked on the British charts at Number Seventeen and later their first Number One album, *Please Please Me*, was released. A few months later their song, 'She Loves You' became the biggest-selling single in the history of Great Britain.

In 1964 Beatlemania overtook the US as the group appeared on two consecutive Ed Sullivan shows. They later that same year made their first feature film, *A Hard Day's Night*, and their song 'Can't Buy Me Love' topped the charts in Britain and America.

Some of the other popular songs that Lennon wrote include 'Love', 'Imagine', 'Oh Yoko' (named after his wife), 'Woman', '(Just Like) Starting Over'. The songs he wrote in collaboration with Paul McCartney include: 'I Want to Hold Your Hand', 'Nowhere Man', 'Strawberry Fields Forever', 'Lucy in the Sky with Diamonds', 'Revolution' and so many others we don't have the time to mention them all!

John along with his songwriting also wrote his own books. His first book, titled *In His Own Write*, was published and became an instant bestseller in 1964. His second book, *A Spaniard in the Works*, was published a year later.

John was also involved in the motion picture industry with films such as *A Hard Day's Night*, which I mentioned earlier. The others are *Help!* and *Magical Mystery Tour*.

John was also an active and dedicated supporter of many humanitarian causes such as performing a benefit concert along with Yoko for the families of inmates at Attica State Prison and a special performance for the One To One organisation, which collected funds to house mentally retarded children, and many others.

The great tragedy of John Lennon is a personal one. That he left a musical and artistic legacy to be valued and cherished is undoubted. His death at the age of forty stunned the world and left behind an unassailable sorrow.

Ladies and gentlemen, family and friends, please help me and the Hollywood Chamber of Commerce to extend a warm welcome to John's wife, Yoko Ono, as we unveil the star for Mr John Lennon, the man whose music will always stay in our hearts.

There were one or two inaccuracies in the speech, such as attributing 'Nowhere Man', 'Strawberry Fields Forever', 'Lucy in the Sky with Diamonds' and 'Revolution' as collaborations with Paul, and stating that John was born during an air-raid, which he wasn't.

Holt, Deziah
A clairvoyant who in 1980 warned Yoko that both she and John should beware of contact with strangers by the name of Bell, Richard or Mark.

Homenaje a John Lennon
Argentinian album of tribute songs recorded by various artists.

Honey Don't
A Carl Perkins number on which John had originally taken lead vocal during the Beatles early stage performances. However, when the group recorded the number on 26 October 1964, Ringo took over as lead vocalist and the song was included on their *Beatles For Sale* album.

Honeymoon
An hour-long film of highlights from the couple's honeymoon filmed between 25 and 31 March 1969. John and Yoko hired a

film crew to photograph their various activities, mainly shot using hand-held cameras. They instructed their assistants to film everything and then edited the material to produce the documentary *Honeymoon*.

The film received its British premier, along with *Two Virgins* and *Smile*, at the Edinburgh Film Festival in September 1969.

Hong, Dr

An acupuncturist/herbalist who helped John and Yoko regain the confidence that they could have a child. In 1972, on the advice of friends, the two approached Dr Hong seeking help because of their addiction to methadone and their poor sex life.

Hong was reputed to be between 65 and 90 years old at the time and was a kung fu master who gave lessons to the local police force. He lived in a small, pink stucco house in San Mateo County, San Francisco, and John and Yoko stayed there for a week, John kipping on the sofa in the living room. Hong immediately took them off methadone and used various treatments including acupuncture, vitamins, herbs and ginseng, making them renounce all drugs, except cigarettes and a moderate amount of alcohol.

While he was at the house John requested and was given some martial-arts lessons.

Yoko was 39 at the time and Dr Hong made her what he described as a 'magic potion' to increase her fertility, telling them they would have a child if they lived cleanly and healthily.

When Sean was born, John sent Dr Hong a Polaroid shot of the newborn child.

Hoover, J Edgar

Hoover was born in 1895 and became director of the Federal Bureau of Investigation for 48 years. He was a bigot, a fanatical anticommunist, who harassed black people and undermined their civil liberties, persecuted anyone with left-wing views and even blackmailed presidents and important politicians.

He decided to persecute John Lennon and have him deported from the country. He had John constantly spied on and amassed files of information about his activities. One of the files was two inches thick and had the words written across it in Hoover's handwriting: 'All extremists should be considered dangerous.'

His agents noted: 'Our source advises that Lennon appears to be radically oriented. However, he does not give the impression that he is a true revolutionary since he is constantly under the influence of narcotics.' Another reported: 'Lennon wanted an open society where free dope, free sex and free rock music abounded.'

Hoover hated Lennon and ordered the FBI to work hard to turn up anything that could help to have him deported. He also instructed that any information on Lennon's drug use was to be directed immediately to him. He wanted to prosecute John and Yoko under interstate law for transporting obscene material – the full-frontal nude photo on their *Two Virgins* album. However, his legal office advised him that the charge would not succeed in court.

Hoover was furious when John was allowed into America in the summer of 1970 when he declared he wanted to edit a film and also to attend a custody hearing in New York over Yoko's daughter Kyoko. He was granted a visa until September and then given an extension. Hoover then set the FBI on a Lennon hunt and memos began to sprout from his HQ: 'Every agent should remain alert for any activity on his part of a potentially illegal nature' and 'Lennon is a heavy user of narcotics. This information should be emphasized to local law enforcement agencies with regards to subject being arrested if at all possible on possession-of-narcotics charge.'

Hoover even had an obsession with anyone associated with John and another memo read:

Date: 23 April 1970

Subject: John Lennon, George Harrison, Patricia Harrison.

These individuals are affiliated with the Beatles musical group and Lennon will be traveling under the name of Chambers and the Harrisons are using the name Masters. They will remain in Los Angeles for business discussions with Capitol Records and other enterprises. They will travel to New York for further discussions. Waivers were granted by the Immigration and Naturalization service in view of the ineligibility of these three individuals to enter the US due to their reputations in England as narcotic users.

While Lennon and the Harrisons have shown no propensity to become involved in violent anti-war demonstrations, each recipient of this memo should remain alert for any information of such activity on their part or for information indicating they are using narcotics. Submit any pertinent information obtained for immediate dissemination.

Hoover failed in his efforts and died soon after, in 1972.

Hopkins, Nicky

Arguably, Britain's most famous session pianist. Hopkins was born in London on 24 February 1944. After leaving the Royal Academy of Music he joined Screamin' Lord Sutch's Savages, then Cyril Davies's All Stars. His career in live bands was inhibited by serious illness and he became a session musician in 1964, performing on Jeff Beck studio sessions. He also appeared on 'My Generation' by the Who and, after appearing on Beck's *Truth* album, joined Beck's band for a short time. He guested on Jefferson Airplane's *Volunteers* album and joined the Quicksilver Messenger Service for a while, settling in America, but commuting across the Atlantic for further session work.

Hopkins became associated with the Rolling Stones, appearing on 'Their Satanic Majesties Request' and various other Stones recordings. He played with the group at their Hyde Park concert in 1969 and was asked to remain with the band. He agreed, but became seriously ill again and had to drop the idea, although he did play with them on their American tour in 1972. In 1973 he recorded his solo debut 'The Tin Man Was A Dreamer' on which George Harrison performed on four tracks. Other musicians who guested on the album included Klaus Voormann and Mick Taylor. Hopkins returned to live in Britain in 1974 and, despite his frail condition, continued session work.

In 1968 he received a call from Laurie Gold at EMI inviting him up to the Abbey Road studios to play on the Beatles' 'Revolution' track. The invitation came at the instigation of John Lennon and Nicky overdubbed electric piano on the single.

John and Paul also participated in a Rolling Stones session at which Nicky also played in July 1967 at Olympic Sound Studios for the recording of 'We Love You'.

Nicky appeared on George Harrison's *Living in the Material World*, *Dark Horse* and *Extra Texture* albums and Ringo's *Ringo* and *Goodnight Vienna* albums.

John also invited him to Tittenhurst Park to take part in the recording of the *Imagine* album. Nicky played chimes, piano and glockenspiel on John's hit single 'Happy Xmas (War Is Over)'. He also contributed to the *Walls and Bridges* album.

Nicky moved to Nashville in 1994 and died in a local hospital on Tuesday 6 September of that year, suffering from abdominal and heart trouble.

Hotel Okura

Hotel in Tokyo where John and Yoko stayed during their four-month vacation in 1977. On Tuesday 4 October 1977 they held a 45-minute press conference at the hotel on the eve of their return to New York, at which initially John thanked the Japanese for respecting the couple's privacy. He also informed the press that he would be abandoning his creative pursuits to spent his time in the coming years to raising Sean.

Hound Dog

Elvis Presley's No. 1 hit, penned by Jerry Leiber and Mike Stoller, which John introduced into the Quarry Men's repertoire in 1957. John sang lead vocal on the number, which remained part of the Beatles' repertoire until 1961.

This was one of the songs John sang on stage at the Cavern Club on 7 August 1957 when the Quarry Men made their only appearance at the venue. The club was then strictly a jazz venue and skiffle groups were told to stick to skiffle music and not play rock 'n' roll. After John had sung two Presley numbers, 'Hound Dog' and 'Blue Suede Shoes', the Cavern owner, Alan Sytner, sent a message to the group on stage, 'Cut out the bloody rock!'

During his recording sessions with Phil Spector in March 1972, John performed the number during a jam session and he also performed the song on the One To One Concert at Madison Square Garden on 30 August 1972. During the song, John shouted out, 'I love you, Elvis!'

Hours and Times, The

A sixty-minute monochrome film directed, produced and written by Christopher Munch, who was also the cinematographer. The movie was released in 1991 and concerned the brief holiday John Lennon and Brian Epstein took in Spain in 1963.

Filmed at the Avenida Palace Hotel in Barcelona, *The Hours and Times* featured the actor Ian Hart as John and David Angus as Brian.

The synopsis for the Antarctic Pictures production read,

The friendship of Brian Epstein and John Lennon has been the subject of speculation and myth. To portray a sense of that generous, intense and ambiguous friendship is the intent of the film, a work of fiction taking place over just four days.

The story is set in a city of mythic beauty, Barcelona, where in the spring of 1963, following a gruelling winter of touring, Epstein and Lennon spent a memorable holiday. More than a holiday, it marked a crucial juncture in both men's lives: while six months had yet to elapse before Beatlemania would fully engulf Britain (nine months before America), Lennon's first child had just been born, and his marriage was beginning to stand the test of burgeoning stardom. At the time, Epstein, whose affection for Spain was to last up until his premature death in 1967, was poised before the immense dizzying potential that lay just ahead, his personal life an adventuresome whirlwind of exultation and despondency. Within this tense historical context the story unfolds.

The film was shot entirely on location in Barcelona amidst landmarks of the great Catalan architect, Antoni Gaudi. Much of the action occurs in the Hotel Avenida Palace, one of Europe's most majestic. Additional photography took place in Liverpool, once the most important port city of northern England, and birthplace of the Beatles.

The film's music consists of an adaptation of Narvaez' classic Catalan folk song, *Guardame Las Bacas*; a flamenco piece in the Malagueno style; and one of JS Bach's *Goldberg Variations*.

The Hours and Times was premiered in Britain on Saturday 13 June 1992 at Southampton University during the Southampton Film Festival as a special John Lennon Evening, which also featured a series of Yoko Ono films, *Number Four*, *Love*, *Love Love* and *Ai Love*, which was followed by a live debate about the film with David Angus, Ian Hart and Bill Harry on the panel.

Hoving, Thomas PF

One of several character witnesses called to testify on behalf of John at his second deportation hearing, which began on 12 May 1972.

Hoving had impressive credentials, which included a Princeton PhD in art history. He was also a director of the Metropolitan Museum of Art and a member of the New York State Council on the Arts.

When speaking on John's behalf, he declared, 'There are few people in the last period of this decade in all of the arts, whether it's painting or sculpture, or architecture, who have contributed so much and in such extremely deep and essential manner as Mr Lennon. And I would say my basic business in life, sir, as a person, is to recognise, exhibit, and teach about artistic qualities.'

He added, 'I would say that if he were a painting, he would be hanging in the Metropolitan Museum.'

How

A number that John included on the *Imagine* album. John played piano on the track, as did Nicky Hopkins, while Klaus Voormann played bass, Alan White drums and John Barham vibes. John originally composed the song at a home demo tape recording session in December 1970. The number harks back to his sense of loss of a normal family life as a child with lines such as, 'How can I go home when home is something I have never had?'

Its producer, Phil Spector, added strings to the track.

How Do You Sleep?

A track on the *Imagine* album that was fiercely critical of Paul McCartney. Paul's second solo album, *Ram*, had been issued four months previously and John believed that several of the tracks were criticisms aimed at him. He hated the material on *Ram* and decided to take his revenge. However, John wrote only half of the song: Yoko contributed most of the lyrics and Allen Klein also wrote a line of this particular vitriolic number.

The items on *Ram* that John took to be criticisms included a photo of a pair of beetles on the cover who appear to be 'screwing' each other, Paul opening the album with the words 'Piss off, yeah' and the mention in the song '3 Legs' of a friend who let him down.

The cover of *Ram* showed Paul holding a sheep. John lampooned this by having a photograph of himself in the same position holding a pig and included it as a postcard with the album. John implied that the only good song Paul wrote was 'Yesterday' and ridiculed Paul's latest single 'Another Day'. This was apparently the line suggested by Klein. Klein may have done this to prevent a possible libel action as the original line virtually accused Paul of plagiarising the tune of 'Yesterday'. In the song John also referred to Paul's music as 'Muzak'.

John was to say, 'You know, I wasn't really feeling that vicious at the time. But I was using my resentment towards Paul to create a song, let's put it that way. He saw that it pointedly refers to him, and people kept hounding him about it. But, you know, there were a few digs on his album before mine. He's so obscure other people didn't notice them, but I heard them. I thought, Well, I'm not obscure: I just get right down to the nitty-gritty. So he'd done it his way and I did it mine.'

When the song was being recorded at Tittenhurst Park, Felix Denis, one of the publishers of *Oz* magazine, was present. He observed that they were practically writing the song in the studio as they were recording it and Ringo was getting more and more upset until he finally said, 'That's enough, John.' Denis also declared that he actually observed Yoko writing most of the lyrics and running up to John waving the piece of paper to show him. The other musicians all seemed unhappy about the situation, but John didn't seem to care.

John also commented, 'The song isn't only about Paul: it's a song in its own right anyway, you know.' When he was informed that Paul had asked, 'How can he [Lennon] make the quarrel so public?' John answered, 'Oh hell's bells ... listen to *Ram*, folks!

The lyrics weren't printed – just listen to it. I'm answering *Ram*. When I heard *Ram*, I immediately sat down and wrote my song, which is an answer to *Ram*. It's as simple as that. It's also a moment's anger. But it was written down on paper and when I sang, I wasn't quite as angry as when I sang it in the studio, because it was four weeks later and we were all writing it, you know. It was like a joke, "Let's write this down." We didn't take it that seriously.'

John also comments about it in the *Imagine* film, saying, 'It's not about Paul: it's about me. I'm really attacking myself. But I regret the association – well, what's to regret? He lived through it. The only thing that matters is how he and I feel about these things and not what the writer or commentator thinks about it. Him and me are OK.'

Shortly before his death, John told the DJ Andy Peebles in a BBC interview, 'I used my resentment and withdrawing from Paul and the Beatles and the relationship with Paul to write "How Do You Sleep?". I don't really go round with those thoughts in my head all the time.'

The vindictiveness of the song was universally criticised and *Rolling Stone* magazine called it 'a song so spiteful and self-indulgent that it sanctified the victim and demeaned the accuser'.

Paul decided not to take the bait and did not retaliate in song, although he did comment, 'I think it's silly. So what if I live with straights? I like straights. I have straight babies. It doesn't affect him. He says the only thing I did was "Yesterday". He knows that's wrong. He knows and I know that's not true.'

How I Won the War (film)

John's first real solo venture – a film in which he made his first appearance minus his fellow Beatles in the role of Private Gripweed of the Third Troop of the Fourth Musketeers.

The part was specially written for John and filming took place between 5 September and 7 November 1966.

The film was an antiwar movie set in the Western Desert, Dunkirk, Dieppe, El Alamein and Arnhem, with newsreel shots linking parts of the film.

The movie was based on the novel by Patrick Ryan and the screenplay was written by Charles Wood, who was the author of *The Graduate*.

The part had been offered to John by Dick Lester, director of *A Hard Day's Night* and *Help!*, who produced and directed this film for United Artists, who also distributed the Beatles' films.

Location work in Germany and Almeria, Spain, began in September 1966 and a large corps of photographers were present at the Inn on the Heath hotel near Celle in Hanover, West Germany, when a German hairdresser, Klaus Baruck, gave John his short back and sides for the film. John also wore granny glasses in the film and they later became something of a trademark with him.

John's wife Cynthia said, 'When he was doing *How I Won the War* he was petrified. It was the first thing he'd done on his own, and it was like leaving the family nest. He went through hell.'

John explained, 'I did the film because I believed in it. There never had been a war film which showed war as it really is. A man fighting in a battle doesn't see the whole thing. He never meets the enemy until the day a man comes round the corner and sticks a bayonet in him and he can't quite believe it is happening.'

The film was premiered at the London Pavilion on 18 October 1967 and part of the *Sunday Times* review read 'John Lennon dies the death in Dick Lester's *How I Won The War*. A shell from a German tank catches him just below his ribs and he expires in a welter of well-photographed gore.'

Although the part of Gripweed was only a supporting role, the press dubbed it 'the film starring a Beatle' and 'John Lennon's film'.

Headlines were created at the premiere, which was attended by the Beatles and their wives, because of demonstrations by the right-wing political group the National Front.

They believed the film was an insult to the British dead of World War Two and a hundred of them mingled with the 1,200 members of the Pavilion audience and began to throw stink bombs and cause chaos. Eventually, fifty policemen had to be called in to control the situation.

There was a single called 'How I Won the War' issued in Britain on United Artists UP 1196 on 13 October 1967 with 'Aftermath' as the flip. Credited to Musketeer Gripweed and the Third Troop, it obviously had many fans thinking it was a special release from John as he portrayed Musketeer Gripweed in the film.

In fact, the only time John is on the record is when his voice is heard repeating a single line from the film soundtrack on the A-side of the record and the B-side is an instrumental by the Ken Thorne Orchestra.

The United Artists synopsis of the plot, issued on the film's release, read,

Lieutenant Ernest Goodbody (Michael Crawford) had a trying war. So did his men; mostly as a result of his trying.

He was young, inexperienced. The Third Troop of the Fourth Musketeers was his first command. He was keen, and saw war as a game, nobler even than his favourite sport of cricket.

He loved his men and cared for them, and the more he loved and cared for them, the more they hated him. It was no coincidence that his regimental number was 131313.

His Troop Sergeant Transom (Lee Montague), the regular soldier, the anchor man of the outfit, foresaw trouble the first time he clapped eyes on him. He was right ...

But somehow they staggered from campaign to campaign, until destiny led them to the Western Desert and their Finest Hour ...

In the end (which is the beginning) Goodbody was bound to get himself captured ... it was inevitable. Ostensibly leading his platoon on a night attack across the Rhine towards the end of the war, Goodbody finds himself alone in his rubber boat in the middle of the river. His men are nowhere to be seen. This does not surprise him unduly. It has happened before.

He bumps ashore by a bridge, the last intact across the Rhine. In the first few frightened minutes of capture he begins to remember how it all started.

His training as an officer, his meeting with that veteran of veterans, Lt Col Grapple (Michael Hordern), who impressed him immensely, and who keeps turning up throughout his career to re-inspire him with the rousing cry 'Bum on, young fella! Bum on!' – to the next place along the line ... Rome ... Paris ... Berlin ...

Moscow.

And then Egypt, and the days the jolly general puts an arm on his shoulder and murmurs softly, 'Would you like to do something for me? Get away from here? See some action, eh?

'I would like you,' said the general, 'to nip 300 miles behind the enemy lines and set up an advance cricket pitch ... so that when the battle is over and the Very Important Person drives through, he will see the men, straight from battle, happy, relaxed, enjoying themselves ... you do that for me? Good show!'

Goodbody makes the landing, but somehow his men, including Gripweed (John Lennon) and clapper (Roy Kinnear) do not ... and he wanders disconsolately around the desert, complaining that he is much too young to win the war on his own.

All these memories flood through Goodbody's mind in those first few moments of capture. He is taken before Odlebog, the bridge commandant (Karl Michael Vogler), and finds he can relax.

Odlebog has guarded the bridge throughout the war, and he loves it. Now the retiring German Army is going to blow it up, and he is sad.

Goodbody finds Odlebog is the first person he can talk to about the war, his men and why he is a soldier. They get on famously and Goodbody helps the German with his demolition charges.

They discuss their mutual experiences ... Goodbody remembers the desert, how he eventually found his men, the difficulty with morale, how he struggled through, had their cricket pitch roller stolen by Italians, how they failed to capture a German dump for much needed petrol and the triumphant moment when they shot down their first plane. The fact that it was British took the edge off that moment slightly ...

He remembers the death of Corporal Dooley (Ewan Hooper), of Private Drogue (James Cossins) and Private Spool (Ronald Lacey). And old soldier Juniper (Jack MacGowran) who raised morale by 'entertaining the troops' in the most unlikely way and most unlikely places

... and how he was going to recommend him for promotion ... until he found Juniper was going mad ... and how, after all their labours the Very Important Person drives through with barely a glance at their cricket pitch ...

Goodbody and Odlebog get very friendly ... Odlebog decided he cannot blow his bridge up ... he'll give it to Goodbody ...

Goodbody says he could not possibly accept ... but he will buy it. As the last remnants of the German army hurry past, they haggle over the price ...

Goodbody writes the cheque and buys the bridge, and Lt Col Grapple roars through in the leading tank.

'By courtesy of the Fourth Musketeers,' says Goodbody, with a graceful wave of the hand. 'Bum on, young fella,' roars Grapple. 'Bum on to Moscow.'

Many years later, in his little suburban semi-detached house, Goodbody attempts to hold a reunion. Only one man sits with the empty chairs around him ... the last of the Musketeers, the melancholy musketeer (Jack Hedley) who was a coward.

'I wanted to fight. I knew we had to fight. I really wanted to ... but I couldn't'.

'I know you did, I know you did,' says Goodbody soothingly, 'but I won the war.'

How Late It Is

A BBC2 television programme on which John and Yoko were interviewed on Friday 2 May 1969. The couple recorded it earlier in the day between 12.30 and 1 a.m. at Lime Grove Studios and the programme was broadcast that evening at 10.55 p.m. They were interviewed by Michael Wale and discussed their latest film *Rape*. An excerpt from the film lasting three minutes and 31 seconds was also shown.

Howitis – The John Lennon Anthology/Yoko Ono Interview

A CD set issued to promote sales of *The John Lennon Anthology* boxed set. It contained 24 questions put to Yoko, together with her answers. She said, 'I was already doing this project before the *Beatles Anthology* came out. And then it was nice, because I said, "Oh that's how we did the *Beatles Anthology*." And I felt that John's *Anthology* should be slightly different. And so I knew what not to do.'

She also explained that there were more recordings in the archives. 'I found that there were many more takes and stuff that really were very presentable. In the beginning I was thinking that this was going to be the ultimate John Lennon box. And I thought, No, we shouldn't call it ultimate, because there's so much more there. There are still more beautiful songs, but I couldn't fit them all in there. It's possible that this is not the last presentation of John's work.'

Hoylake Parish Church

A church in Trinity Road, Hoylake. Julian Lennon was christened there on 10 November 1963. Cynthia had attended Sunday School at the church when she was a child and it was opposite her home.

John was appearing on tour at the time, but Cynthia hadn't informed him of the christening. The ceremony proceeded quite smoothly, although nine-month-old Julian knocked the vicar's glasses off. They emerged from the church to find a waiting horde of photographers and pictures were featured in the newspapers the next day.

John was furious and phoned Cynthia, creating the first major argument of their marriage. He told her he hadn't wanted Julian to be baptised or christened. Cynthia told him that he needed some sort of religious belief, that it wouldn't do any harm.

Hughes, Howard

Eccentric American multimillionaire who was born in 1905. Hughes' life has been the subject of numerous books and films and Harold Robbins based his bestseller *The Carpetbaggers* on him. A womaniser and film mogul, he became a virtual recluse following a near-fatal air crash and took to living like a hermit in the penthouse suite of one of his hotels. Plagued with obsession and paranoia, he began tapping the phones of his employees to check for subversive behaviour and employed a group of Mormons to protect him. He'd lay down fresh toilet paper to walk on, handled everything with surgical gloves and eventually metamorphosed into an almost unrecognisable figure with talon-like fingernails and long hair and beard. When he died in 1976 there began to be numerous court cases revolving around his incredible fortune.

When the Beatles were in Las Vegas in 1964 John expressed a desire to see the outside of the building where Howard Hughes lived. He was told it would be impossible because of the thousands of fans outside their hotel. Irving Kandell, a programme seller, borrowed a doorman's uniform for John to wear, hired a catering van and smuggled him down the fire escape and through the kitchen into the van and showed him the building where Hughes lived like a recluse on the heavily curtained top floor of the Desert Inn Hotel. John was fascinated by the lifestyle of the eccentric hermit and said, 'That would suit me. In one place for ever instead of this constant travelling. Total privacy, nobody to bother you, scream at you, poke your hair or ask you what your favourite colour is.'

John continued to be fascinated by Hughes for the rest of his life and became a hermit-like figure himself in the Dakota Building. His friend Elliot Mintz gave him some books about Hughes and, for a laugh, he'd wear white gauze gloves and a white face mask when he entered John's bedroom. He also began calling John 'Mr Hughes'.

Hur Coat

A shaggy black coat that John began to wear in 1969. It was made by Fran Cooney from human hair taken from thirty Asian girls and backed by thin-knit wool as John refused to wear animal skins.

Hutchins, Chris

One of the important journalists during the British side of the Beatles' career as he worked for the *New Musical Express*, the music paper with the biggest circulation. He first met the Beatles in Hamburg in 1962 when he went to Germany to interview Little Richard.

It was at Hutchins' Chelsea flat following a Royal Albert Hall radio show that the romance between Paul McCartney and Jane Asher began.

Hutchins was the person who set up the meeting between the

Beatles and Elvis Presley, and he accompanied them on that historic occasion. Discussing it, he said, 'The meeting was tense. John Lennon didn't want to be there: Paul was ever the diplomat, George looked bored and Ringo played snooker with the Memphis mafia. "Be sure to tell the fans they had a great night together," the Colonel [Presley's manager] called to me as we got into the limousine for the drive back to the LA house the Beatles had rented. "Tell them the truth – it was crap," said John Lennon.'

In 1995, together with Peter Thompson, Hutchins authored the book *Elvis Meets the Beatles*. In it, there were various items about John, depicted in the book's blurb: 'How the meeting at Elvis's Bel Air mansion lit the touch paper for a dangerous feud between John Lennon, the anti-war idealist, and Elvis, the former tank corps sergeant'; 'How Elvis the drug-busting Federal agent plotted with the FBI to have John Lennon deported from the United States'; 'How John Lennon fell in love with a cult British singer and only her untimely death threw him into the arms of Yoko Ono'; 'How Elvis's one-time lover Jayne Mansfield set out to seduce John, but her tarot card reader intervened and foretold their violent deaths with terrifying accuracy.'

Hutchins was to meet up with John in New York in 1977 and said he was dressed in a smart three-piece suit, had long hair and more than a drop to drink. He greeted John, who asked why he hadn't phoned him. When Hutchins told him he didn't have his phone number, John said it was in the book. He told Hutchins, 'I just look after Sean and give my money away. I actually gave 25,000 dollars to a bloke the other day for a New York down-and-outs' hostel and it made me feel great.'

Huxley, Aldous

A British writer and philosopher, author of such contemporary classics as *Brave New World*, *Island* and *Crome Yellow*.

John was very influenced by his work, which he discovered in 1966. He was later to make the comment, 'I've always wondered what it was about politics and government that was wrong. Now, since reading some books by Aldous Huxley, I've suddenly found out what it's all about.'

When interviewed by Ray Coleman for the 26 March 1966 issue of *Disc*, John listed his prized possessions, quoting one of them as 'Aldous Huxley books. I've just started reading him because he's the new guvnor, it seems to me.'

Huxley also wrote *The Doors of Perception,* a book about the effects of psychedelic drugs on the mind, which, in some ways, could stimulate a person into experimenting with hallucinogenic drugs. It was this book that led Jim Morrison to call his band the Doors.

Huxley was one of the seventy-plus figures chosen by the Beatles to appear as cut-outs on their *Sergeant Pepper* sleeve and it is probable that Huxley may have been one of John's choices.

The writer died in 1963.

I Am Also A You
Title of a book by the American writer Jay Thompson. John
wrote an introduction to it.

I Am the Walrus
A track from the *Magical Mystery Tour,* recorded on 5, 6, 27, 28
and 29 September 1967.

John was obviously inspired by the work of Lewis Carroll, in
particular the tale of woe from *Alice's Adventures in Wonderland,*
in which a band of young oysters are lured by the charms of the
Walrus, who then begins to devour them.

A number of people have claimed that John was influenced in
his writing by the works of James Joyce, yet John said that he
had never read Joyce.

People then pointed to the phrase 'goo goo g'joob' in this song
and said that the phrase appeared in Joyce's *Finnegans Wake.*
However, it appears that both Joyce and John got the line from
the same source because it is the last line that Humpty Dumpty
speaks when he falls to his doom in *Alice's Adventures in
Wonderland.*

At times John said that it was written when he was on acid
trips; at other times he says he was inspired by the sound of a
police-car siren.

The track is replete with imagery and a couple of the lines – 'stupid bloody Tuesday' and 'waiting for the van to come' – were interpreted as references to the accident that supposedly killed Paul McCartney in the 'Paul is dead' saga (*see under* 'Strawberry Fields Forever').

Commenting on the track in 1970, John said; 'I was the Walrus, whatever that means. The Walrus was a big capitalist that ate all the fucking oysters, if you must know. I always had this image of the Walrus in the garden and I loved it, so I didn't ever check out what the Walrus was. But he's a fucking bastard – that's what he turns out to be. Everybody presumes that means something, that just because I said I am the Walrus, it must mean I am God or something, but it's just poetry.'

On the track sixteen members of the Mike Sammes singers were chanting 'Oompah, oompah, stick it up your jumper' and 'Got one, got one, everybody's got one'.

The Mike Sammes Singers provided their vocal backing on Wednesday 27 September. They comprised eight male and eight female vocalists: Peggie Allen, Wendy Horan, Pat Whitmore, Jill Utting, June Day, Sylvia King, Irene King and G Mallen. The male vocalists were Fred Lucas, Mike Redway, John O'Neill, F Dachtler, Allan Grant, D Griffiths, J Smith and J Fraser.

There was also an orchestral overdub made that day. The musicians were violinists Sidney Sax, Jack Rothstein, Ralph Elman, Andrew McGee, Jack Greene, Louis Stevens, John Jezzard, Jack Richards; cellists were Lionel Ross, Eldon Fix, Bram Martin and Terry Weil; clarinettist was Gordon Lewis and horn players were Neil Sanders, Tony Tunsall and Morris Miller.

On Friday 29 September, during the mixing, the tuning dial picked up a performance of Shakespeare's *King Lear* on the BBC Third Programme (now Radio 3). The production starred John Gielgud as King Lear and several lines from the drama were included on the record.

Commenting on this in his book '*Summer of Love*', Sir George Martin said, 'He took a leaf out of John Cage's book, who long before had used a radio broadcast to create a "happening". So we had a radio brought in, hooked it up to the recording console, and gave John the tuning knob to twiddle. In no time, he found what he wanted: a Shakespeare play, *King Lear*, in full flow, going out live. It was by then so late in the evening that we were probably the only people listening to Will's drama; but it went into the mix all the same, and is there now for ever.

At one time John rated this as his favourite Beatles song.

The original lyrics to the song were sold at auction in September 1999.

I Apologise

A one-sided twelve-inch disc by the Chicago record label Sterling Productions, run by Bill Bender and Barney Sterling, which was issued on Sterling Productions 8895-6481 in 1966. This was taken from the press conference recorded by the *Chicago Tribune* at the Astor Towers Hotel on 11 August 1966 when John had to apologise for comments about Jesus Christ, which had caused such a furore in America. As the entire conference was taped, it also includes comments from Paul, George and Ringo.

The disc was available only by mail order and came with a ten-by-eight-inch monochrome photograph of the Beatles at the press conference. By 1999 the disc was worth £150, plus an extra £20 with the photograph.

I Call Your Name

A song that John had written in Liverpool when he was sixteen. He completed the middle eight in 1963 to enable Billy J Kramer to record the song. It was used as the flip side of Kramer's hit 'Bad To Me', which John also wrote. Kramer and his backing band the Dakotas recorded the number at Abbey Road studios on 27 June 1963 and Paul McCartney attended their session.

John commented, 'That was my song when there was no Beatles and no group – I just had it around. It was my effort as a kind of blues, originally, and then I wrote the middle eight when it came out years later. The first part had been written before Hamburg, even.'

John later decided that the Beatles should record the number and they included it on their first Sunday recording session on 1 March 1964. 'I Call Your Name' was then featured on their fifth British EP, *Long Tall Sally*, issued in June 1964.

I Ching

Also known as *The Book of Changes*. An ancient Chinese oracle of wisdom and philosophy whose symbols have been used for consultations providing personal advice for the future for over 4,000 years. The system became popular in the West when studied by the psychologist Carl Jung.

There are 64 hexagrams, each with a text. Consultation of an individual nature is made with the use of either yarrow stalks or coins. Both John and Yoko used 'the oracle of change' and following the success of his Bag One lithographs John began to work on a second series of lithographs based on the *I Ching*. Unfortunately, he completed only three in the series.

I Don't Wanna Face It

Also known as 'I Don't Want To Face It'.

A song John wrote in Bermuda. John first made a home demo recording in late 1977. He attempted to record it during sessions at the Hit Factory in June 1980, but didn't seem to get it right. A demo was included on the posthumous *Milk and Honey* album.

John had intended it to be one of four songs he was giving to Ringo Starr for a forthcoming album.

I Don't Want To Be a Soldier, Mama, I Don't Want To Die

Track recorded at John's own studios in Tittenhurst Park – Ascot Sound Studios – in July 1971 for the *Imagine* album. Musicians on the track were: John Lennon, guitar; Nicky Hopkins, piano; Klaus Voormann, bass guitar; Jim Gordon, drums; George Harrison, slide guitar; King Curtis, saxophone; Joey Molland and Tom Evans of Badfinger, acoustic guitars; Steve Brendell, maracas; and Mike Pinder of the Moody Blues, tambourine.

It was a number expressing John's feeling of pacifism, and had also been the title of a popular working-class song during World War One.

John had barely escaped the end of national service. While still a schoolboy and dreading the possibility of being drafted, he'd imagined slipping off to Southern Ireland before any call-up papers were sent to him. He told *Red Mole* magazine that he had been brought up 'to despise the army as something that takes everybody away and leaves them dead somewhere'.

The influence of the nursery rhyme that goes 'Tinker, tailor, soldier, sailor, rich man, poor man, beggarman, thief' is evident.

I Don't Want To Spoil the Party

Song written by John that was recorded on 29 September 1964 and included on the *Beatles For Sale* album.

I Feel Fine

An inspiration for this number was said to be a guitar riff on Bobby Parker's 'Watch Your Step', a popular R&B number with Liverpool bands. The track opens with the sound of feedback, deliberately distorted by John, and an effect he was proud of.

Commenting on the piece, John said, 'I actually wrote the song around that riff that's going on in the background. I tried to get that effect into practically every song on the *Beatles For Sale* LP, but the others wouldn't have it! I told them I'd write a song specially for the riff, and one morning as we were going into the studio I said to Ringo, "I've written this song, but it's lousy." But we tried it, complete with the riff, and it sounded like an A-side, so we decided to release it just like that.'

The song was introduced by the sound of feedback and John was to say, 'I defy anybody to find a record – unless it's an old blues record in 1922 – that used feedback that way. I claim it for the Beatles. Before Hendrix, before The Who, before anybody. The first feedback on any record.'

The group began recording it on Sunday 18 October 1964 and it was issued as the Beatles' eighth single, gaining advance sales of over 750,000 in Britain by the time of its release on Parlophone R 5200 on 27 November 1964. It went straight to No. 1 and remained there for six weeks, and within weeks had become the Beatles' fifth consecutive million-selling British single. It was issued on Capitol 5327 in America on 23 November 1964 with a million sales during its first week of release and it remained in the No. 1 position for three weeks.

The track was also included on the *Past Masters* CDs.

I Found Out

One of the songs written directly as a result of John and Yoko's treatment at Arthur Janov's primal-therapy centre in Los Angeles.

On his return to England John began planning an album to express his post-therapy experience, the cathartic release of emotions in screaming and crying to expurgate the deep-rooted anxieties from his childhood, reputedly caused by lack of parental care.

'I Found Out' expressed some of this pain and he cut two demos in August 1970, backing himself on electric guitar. The song, with lines such as 'Now that I found out I know I can cry' and 'Can't do you no harm to feel your own pain', became one of the tracks on his *John Lennon/Plastic Ono Band* album, recorded in October 1970 with Ringo Starr and Klaus Voormann.

The lyrics to the song were printed on the sleeve, although one of the words was replaced with an asterisk. Another song, 'Working Class Hero' had two words replaced by asterisks as EMI said they wouldn't release the album if those particular words remained on the sleeve.

The song was partly an attack on the counterculture radicals who had sought to use John's fame to influence their causes. He was also to attack religion, venting his spleen on various creeds.

He was to tell *Rolling Stone* magazine, 'I'm sick of those aggressive hippies or whatever they are, the New Generation, sort of being very uptight with me, either on the street or anywhere, or on the phone, demanding my attention as if I owed them something. I'm not their fucking parents, that's what it is. They come to the door with a fucking peace symbol to just sort of march around the house or something like an old Beatles fan. They're under a delusion of awareness by having long hair and that's what I'm sick of. I'm sick of them, they frighten me, a lot of uptight maniacs going around wearing fucking peace symbols.'

I Know (I Know)

A acoustic ballad featured on the *Mind Games* album and another of John's love songs to Yoko.

I Read The News Today (The Social Drama of John Lennon's Death)

A 1995 book by Fred Fogo, published by Littlefield Adams Quality Paperbacks. A serious study of the social impact of

John's murder and its effect on people during the 1980s, with an analysis of the reaction of the media in newspapers, books and magazines.

I Saw Her Standing There

One of three songs John performed on stage with Elton John at Madison Square Garden. New York on 28 November 1974. The live recording was included on Lennon's boxed set issued in October 1990 on Parlophone CDS 79 5220 2.

When he announced the number on stage, John said, 'I'd like to thank Elton and the boys for having me tonight. We're trying to think of a number to finish off with so's I can get off here and be sick. And we thought we'd do a number of an old, estranged fiancé of mine called Paul. This is one I never sang – it's an old Beatles number and we just about know it.'

The number had appeared on their first album *Please Please Me*, and John commented, 'That's Paul doing his usual good job of producing what [the Beatles' producer] George Martin used to call a "pot-boiler". I helped with a couple of the lyrics.'

I Saw Her Standing There/Whatever Gets You Thru the Night/Lucy in the Sky with Diamonds

The three numbers John sang with Elton John during the 28 November 1974 Madison Square Garden concert, issued as a fifteen-minute single by DJM Records on DJS 10965 on 13 March 1981. The record reached No. 24 in the British charts.

The advertisement for the single read:

28th November 1974 ... was Thanksgiving Day as well as the date that an Elton John concert at New York's Madison Square Garden turned into a very special event. Towards the end of the evening Elton was joined onstage by close friend and fellow musician John Lennon. Together they performed three numbers – *Whatever Gets You Thru the Night, Lucy in the Sky with Diamonds* and *I Saw Her Standing There*. Lennon's performance of the last number surprised many, as he had never been known to sing a McCartney song before. This was the last concert appearance by John Lennon.

I Should Have Known Better

A composition by John recorded on 26 February 1964 for the soundtrack album *A Hard Day's Night*. The scene in the film in which the number was performed was in a train compartment, although it was actually filmed inside a van. Members of the film crew rocked the van to fake the motion of a train. It was issued as the flip side of 'A Hard Day's Night'. John plays harmonica on the track and George played his brand-new Rickenbacker guitar. It was covered by a group from Harlow called the Naturals, who had their only chart entry with it and got to No. 26 in the charts in 1964.

Ichiyanagi, Toshi

Yoko was first introduced to Toshi Ichiyanagi while she was at the Sarah Lawrence School. He was a young Japanese pianist-composer, studying in America at the Julliard music conservatory. She encouraged him to move into her New York flat with her, much to the disapproval of her parents, who regarded him as being of a lower status. The day after she brought him home she had a fierce argument with her parents.

They told her that he was unsuitable and that if she continued their relationship it would bring disgrace on their family.

Oddly enough, Yoko's father Eisuke had also been a concert pianist, but gave up his career in order to marry her mother. When Yoko brought this point up, it was argued that Eisuke had been willing to become a banker and abandon his music.

The rebellious Yoko left the family home, left college and moved into a small apartment with Toshi.

When Yoko's parents returned to Japan in May 1957 she immediately married Toshi. By all accounts she completely dominated him, but through his many friends in the creative arts, whom she met, she became involved in the avant-garde scene. They moved to West 89th Street before settling into a flat in Amsterdam Avenue, followed by a move to 112 Chambers Street on Manhattan's Lower West Side.

Yoko had several affairs that he was aware of, which caused him a great deal of unhappiness, but he seemed unable to do anything about them. Reportedly, she had a number of abortions and was to tell *Esquire* magazine in 1970, 'I was too neurotic to take precautions. I was always having trouble, messed up, always having abortions. I would go out and have an affair and come back and, oh, I'm in a mess, and my first husband was very kind.'

They agreed to split up early in 1961 and Toshi moved back to Japan to pursue his musical career. Yoko commented, 'He used to write Stravinsky-type material, but he gradually changed after we met and now he's the foremost avant-garde composer in Japan.'

In 1962 Yoko's parents requested that she return to Japan as her brother Keisuke was getting married. By that time Toshi had become known in the avant-garde community in Tokyo and she moved in with him on the eleventh floor of a high-rise. Yoko became suicidal, She said, 'In the middle of the night, I would wake up almost unconsciously and walk towards the window. I would try to jump off the window. Toshi would pull me back. This kept happening almost every night. He urged me to go see a doctor and I started thinking I should. I took an overdose of pills. I was feeling that I always wanted to die.' Yoko was then placed in an institute to prevent her from killing herself.

The filmmaker Tony Cox arrived in Tokyo specifically to see Yoko and managed to free her from the institution. He began to live with the married couple in a *ménage à trois*. It didn't work out and when Yoko became pregnant to Cox, Toshi and Yoko decided to split up and Yoko married Cox in Tokyo in November 1962. However, she was still married to Ichiyanagi at the time and was advised to divorce Tony, then divorce Toshi, and then remarry Tony, which she did.

Some years later, discussing his marriage to Yoko in a Japanese newspaper, Toshi said 'Yoko was never pleased unless she was treated like a queen.' He also accused her of being selfish and morbid and added, 'She was indeed an artist in the sense that she played and spent as she pleased.'

I Wanna Be Your Man
A number co-written by John and Paul, although John admits it was mainly written by Paul, commenting, 'I helped him finish it.'

I Want You (She's So Heavy)
John's love song to Yoko, featured on the *Abbey Road* album in 1969. The Beatles began recording the number on Saturday 22 February 1969 at Trident Studios.

The song was really the merging of two John wrote about Yoko, 'I Want You' and 'She's So Heavy'.

At over seven minutes in length, it was the longest number on the *Abbey Road* album, with John on lead vocal and an organ sound featured throughout the track.

I Watch Your Face

Working title of a home demo recorded by John in the autumn of 1977, which has a hillbilly flavour and a Buddy Holly influence. John played acoustic guitar on the tape, but the song never progressed to recording-studio stage and was eventually to be heard on *The Lost Lennon Tapes* radio series.

If I Fell

Recorded in fifteen takes on 27 February 1964. It was included on the *A Hard Day's Night* album issued in Britain on 10 July 1964 and in the US on 26 June 1964. It was also issued as the flip side of 'And I Love Her'.

It's actually a love song, which John claimed was semi-autobiographical. It concerned a man who was about to leave his wife for another woman, but was asking her if she would love him more than he'd ever been loved before. As there was no romantic interest in the film, he sings the song to Ringo. The two of them are in a television studio and Ringo is sulking, so John starts joking with him and then sings the song.

I'll Be Back

A composition written by John and recorded by the Beatles on 1 June 1964 with John on lead vocals. It was the final track on the *A Hard Day's Night* album and was also included on the *Beatles '65* and *Love Songs* compilations.

One source claims that it was a reworking of a Del Shannon song, but the most likely inspiration seems to be the meeting he had with his father Fred after a gap of almost twenty years.

John was to comment, 'A nice tune, though the middle is a bit tatty.'

I'll Cry Instead

Number John penned for the *A Hard Day's Night* soundtrack. During the recording sessions on 1 June 1964 the group found some difficulty recording it and divided it into two sections, which George Martin was then able to edit together. This also enabled the song to be extended for its release in America.

I'll Get You
Song jointly written by John and Paul, recorded on 1 July 1963, and issued as the B-side of 'She Loves You' on 23 August 1963. It was included on the *Past Masters* CDs.

Illustrated John Lennon, The
A large-format, 96-page book by Geoffrey Giuliano with an introduction by Charlie Lennon, which was published by Sunburst Books in 1993. As the title implies, it mainly comprises illustrations and there are more than a hundred photographs, mainly of a large size. Oddly enough, the majority of photos are from the John/Yoko period and pics of the first 28 years of his life are very sparse.

Imagine (album)
The recording of the *Imagine* album by Phil Spector was filmed, with Nick Knowland, Lennon's personal cameraman, as director, and Franco Rosso editing. The film was tentatively called *Working Class Hero* and 35 hours of colour film were produced featuring John working on the album at Tittenhurst Park. The film was shelved because Allen Klein had wanted a slick TV film for use in America.

Imagine was recorded in the summer of 1971 in the home recording studio at Tittenhurst Park, which John called Ascot Sound Studios. John invited Phil Spector to produce and also invited various musicians, including George Harrison, Klaus Voormann and Alan White. John, Yoko and Spector produced the album, with the strings credited as the Flux Fiddlers. The cover featured a photograph of John taken by Yoko.

Kieron Murphy, a photographer invited to the session, was to comment on the arrival of Spector, 'It was almost as if he'd come up out of the floor in a puff of smoke. He had a very heavy presence. He just seemed to arrive without coming into the room. And the interesting thing was that John looked almost as in awe of Spector as I was of John. He leapt up to give him his chair, fussed around him and got him tea or coffee. Everybody else was being a bunch of boisterous lads, swapping football stories and whatever, but Spector just sat there.

'Then Spector says to him, very quietly, "John, I think we should make a start." Whereupon John leapt to his feet and literally took the cups of tea out of people's hands, frogmarching them into the studio: "Phil wants us now!" I was amazed to see that John Lennon had to obey anybody.'

'Crippled Inside' was one of the tracks. It featured John on guitar with Nicky Hopkins on piano, Klaus Voormann and Steve Brendell on upright basses, George Harrison on Dobro (a type of acoustic guitar named after its Czech-American inventors, the Dopera brothers) and acoustic guitars played by Ted Turner, Rod Linton and John Tout. 'Jealous Guy' featured John on electric guitar with Klaus Voormann on bass guitar, Jim Gordon on drums, John Barham on harmonium and Alan White on vibes. 'It's So Hard' featured John on guitar, Klaus Voormann on bass guitar, Jim Gordon on drums and King Curtis on saxophone. 'I Don't Want To Be a Soldier' featured John on guitar, Nicky Hopkins on piano, Klaus Voormann on bass guitar, George Harrison on slide guitar, King Curtis on saxophone, Joey Molland and Tom Evans on acoustic guitars, Steve Brendell on maracas and Mike Pinder on tambourine. 'Give Me Some Truth' featured John on guitar, George Harrison on lead guitar, Nicky Hopkins on piano, Klaus Voormann on basses, Alan White on drums and Rod Linton and Andy Cresswell-Davis on acoustic guitars. 'Oh My Love' featured George Harrison on guitar, John on piano, Klaus Voormann on bass guitar, Alan White on drums and Tibetan cymbals and Nicky Hopkins on electric piano. 'How Do You Sleep?' featured John on guitar, Nicky Hopkins on piano, Alan White on drums and George Harrison on slide guitar. 'How' featured John and Nicky Hopkins on piano, Klaus Voormann on bass guitar, Alan White on drums and John Barham on vibes. 'Oh Yoko' featured John on guitar and mouth organ, Nicky Hopkins on piano, Klaus Voormann on bass guitar, Alan White on drums and Rod Linton and Andy Davis on acoustic guitars.

There was a degree of controversy about the album because of John's criticism of Paul McCartney found on the number 'How Do You Sleep?' and, possibly, 'Crippled Inside', together with a photograph of John with a pig, parodying Paul's photograph with a sheep on his *Ram* album, issued four months before.

Imagine topped the charts on both sides of the Atlantic following its release in America on 9 September and in Britain on 8 October 1971. It was issued in Britain on Apple SAPCOR 10004. After John's death it was re-released and charted again in January 1981, reaching No. 4.

The album was re-released in February 2000 after being digitally remastered and remixed with Yoko Ono spending much of the autumn of 1999 at Abbey Road studios in London supervising the project.

At the same time she was executive producer on a documentary film *Gimme Some Truth*, which documented the making of the original album. She commented, 'I am so grateful that EMI Records and Abbey Road Studios took so much time and care to bring this project to fruition. In Abbey Road Studios I found the engineers top notch and the studios were the latest and the best.'

The *Imagine* package didn't contain any bonus tracks or outtakes from the original session. Yoko Ono commented, '*Imagine* is such an incredibly important album. And I wanted to keep it as close as possible to the original.' While achieving this she also decided that the sound quality of the album needed to be upgraded, saying, 'Machinery has developed so much now. We can do so much more than in 1985 when *Imagine* was first issued on CD. I thought it would be much better to use the newest mechanical power to make sure that the sound is clean and in maximum good condition. People expect that now.'

The success of the *Yellow Submarine* soundtrack the previous year also affected her decision. She said, 'I wondered how people would take it. I listened to Sean, my son, and his friends to see what they had to say, and they were so surprised at how great the *Yellow Submarine* remix was. I thought, So that's how they're taking it. For them it's normal that the sound is the best we can get, but I was very careful, because, as well as making sure we got the best possible sound, I also wanted to make sure that the feeling of the remixes remained true to the original. I wanted to make it very faithful. That was very delicate to do. I feel that I was very careful about that. I think the technicians at Abbey Road studios have done an incredible job.'

The new release came with a booklet containing colour and

back-and-white photographs from the *Gimme Some Truth* video, together with lyrics and a song-by-song personnel line-up.

The CD-box release was a see-through inlay with a black-and-white photograph at the bottom.

Imagine – A Celebration of John Lennon

A slim hardback book published by Penguin Studio in 1995. Each line of the song is presented on a page of the book. The lyrics are accentuated with a selection of black-and-white photographs, a number of them taken at Tittenhurst Park in August 1971 by Tom Hanley.

Imagine (film)

Eighty-one-minute colour film directed and produced by John and Yoko featuring the tracks from the album *Imagine*. Released in 1972, the music from John, Yoko and the Plastic Ono Band provided a soundtrack for numerous scenes filmed in Ascot and New York, with guest appearances by George Harrison, Fred Astaire, Jack Palance, Phil Spector, Dick Cavett and Andy Warhol. The film was premiered on American television on Saturday 23 December 1972. It was dubbed 'the most expensive home movie of all time'. The couple had originally used 40,000 feet of film, which was originally to be edited down to provide promotional footage to accompany John's *Imagine* album and Yoko's *Fly* album, but both records had been issued prior to the release.

A sixty-minute version, which had edited out Yoko's tracks, was issued in Britain on home video by PMI (Picture Music International) in 1985.

Imagine: John Lennon (book)

Book by Andrew Solt and Sam Egan, published in Britain by Bloomsbury in 1988. A sumptuous publication issued as a companion to the Warner Bros film of the same name, produced by David L Wolper. Andrew Solt was the director and he wrote and edited the text with Sam Egan, which is drawn from the film's script and features excerpts from new interviews with those closest to John, including Cynthia, Yoko, Sean and Julian.

It was the most lavishly illustrated of the Lennon books

published up to that time with 225 photographs, more than 50 of them in colour by photographers such as Astrid Kirchherr, Jurgen Vollmer, Annie Leibowitz, Ethan Russell, Robert Freeman and Bob Gruen.

It's basically an illustrated history and that is where it succeeds.

Imagine: John Lennon (film)

A Warner Bros feature film, produced by David L Wolper and Andrew Solt, directed by Andrew Solt, written by Sam Egan and Andrew Solt and narrated by John Lennon.

Yoko Ono originally made contact with David Wolper while he was in New York producing the 1986 Liberty Weekend festivities. Wolper recalls, 'As chairman of Liberty Weekend I was on the phone, when my secretary brought me a note that Yoko Ono was on the line. My immediate thought was, What was her connection to Liberty Weekend?

'Yoko assured me that the call was about something else entirely: she wanted to get together and talk. I told her that I'd be delighted to.

'I found Yoko to be articulate, charming and full of purpose. She got right to the point. She felt it was time for a definitive theatrical documentary on John's life, and she wanted me to do it. I wondered, Why me? Yoko's answer impressed me. "I want someone tough. Someone I can't push around." Her only admonition was that the movie had to be honest. She went on to say that she had some two hundred hours of film and videotape – much of it unseen by the public – covering every aspect of John's life.

'We talked at length about what other elements might be involved. I thanked Yoko for her gracious offer and told her I wanted to think about it. My concern was simply that I wanted to be sure that we could assemble the material in such a way that we could reveal not just John Lennon's music, but John Lennon – the man behind the myth. When I began viewing the available footage, my fears were quickly put to rest.'

Wolper told Yoko that he had to have total creative control over the project if it were to proceed and that she would have no approvals of the project at any point in its editorial assemblage, nor would she have a say in the final picture.

Yoko agreed and Wolper then received the entire private film collection, as well as the rights to never-before-released original music written, recorded and filmed by Lennon.

Wolper then contacted the director Andrew Solt, with whom he'd worked on several previous TV documentaries and the feature *This Is Elvis*.

Solt was to say, 'Half of our film is rare footage never seen publicly before. We built the story around the 1971 recording sessions for the *Imagine* album at John's Tittenhurst Park home at Ascot at a time when he was very much on top of the world. It was an especially creative time in his life and we have material no one has seen.'

Some of the footage that Yoko turned over to Wolper and Solt was intended for what Lennon called 'underground films' – art films he and Yoko shot, cut together and screened for university students and art circles in London and New York City. The outtakes, however – what they didn't use – proved all the more fascinating.

'For instance,' says Solt, 'when John and Yoko made the *Imagine* music video, they chose to show very little of John singing on camera. In our film we have five songs from what's considered his creative high point that were shot during the recording session in their studio at their home in Ascot.'

From 1975 until mid-1980, according to Solt, John stopped playing music. 'He said he didn't want to compete, he didn't want to think about his drive to *have* to make music and to try to get a Top Ten hit. So he became a recluse of sorts, a house-husband, taking care of Sean.' However, there are rare home movies from that period and, just two weeks before his death, Yoko had professional filming done in the Dakota Building and walking through Central Park.

Editing on videotape, almost 200 hours of material was cut down to an initial twenty-hour version of the film. A film chronology was created, running to 206 typed pages, listing all the sources obtained by the filmmakers, well over a hundred of them, including the material from the Lennon estate, from every imaginable newsreel library, the BBC, Granada Television, the three American networks, local US and British stations, Visnews, British Movietone, Fox Movietone, Hearst Metrotone, interviews conducted by Dick Cavett, Tom Snyder, Mike

Douglas, material from private collectors, ITN, ITC, ATV and others. Pivotal to the story is Lennon's Aunt Mimi, who gave Andrew Solt an extraordinary seven-hour interview.

Seldom-seen newsreel footage from the Beatles era includes footage of the group in Japan and the Ku Klux Klan demonstrating against a performance in Memphis after Lennon's comment that the Beatles were more famous than Christ. There is also a dynamic debate between John and Yoko and the cartoonist Al Capp, who cynically attacked the Lennons' peace efforts, which took place at the Montreal Bed-In.

The majority of the music in the film is from John's solo career. Solt says, 'Some of our most interesting material is from those solo years and they're the most illuminating in retrospect. About a third of the music will be Beatles tunes. We're trying to focus on the important moments that reflect who John was. For example, when he sings "Help!" He was crying out to the world and people were dancing to it. In retrospect, that kind of moment is essential in telling his personal story. But what is critical for us is *who* John Lennon was, what made him tick. The material that tells the most and answers that question best comes from the period after the Beatles' break up.'

The question had arisen as to why Yoko had held on to John's vast collection of footage for so many years after her husband's death? She said, 'I think it is better that the film is coming out now, when we are able to see John's life in perspective.'

She also commented, 'I believe in the power of truth, and hope that people will get some power from the truth that comes through the film.' She acknowledged, 'I accept whatever view the film takes of my involvement in John's life as being a world's view. In the end, what we are is what we are to the world – nothing less, nothing more. And that's all right.'

Imagine John Lennon Was Dead
A Radio 2 programme broadcast on 9 December 1992, written by Martin Fido.

Imagine – The Motion Picture (album)
The soundtrack to the film, issued on 10 November 1988.

Imagine (musical)

A stage musical presented at the Liverpool Playhouse from 15 July to 22 August 1992 with Mark McGann portraying John. He had played John in the telemovie *John and Yoko: A Love Story* in 1985.

Imagine (single)

The lead track on the album of the same name that was issued in October 1971. The song was to become John's most famous post-Beatles track. It was also issued as a single and reached No. 3 in the American charts, although it wasn't issued as a single in Britain until 1975, when it reached No. 6 in the charts. After John's murder, when it was reissued, it topped the British charts.

When Andy Peebles interviewed John shortly before the ex-Beatle's death, he told him that Yoko had helped him to create the number. He said, 'A lot of it, the lyric and the concept, came from Yoko, but in those days I was a bit more selfish, a bit more macho, and I omitted to mention her contribution. She's just the wife and you don't put her name on it, right?'

He was also to say, 'The song was originally inspired by Yoko's book *Grapefruit*. In it are lots of pieces saying imagine this, imagine that. Yoko actually helped a lot with the lyrics, but I wasn't man enough to let her have credit for it. I was still selfish enough and unaware enough to sort of take her contribution without acknowledging it. I was still full of wanting my own space after being in a room with the guys all the time, having to share everything.'

Initially, although a spiritual song, it did upset religious groups with it's opening line 'Imagine there's no heaven'. John was to say, 'If you can imagine a world at peace, with no denominations of religion – not without religion, but without this "my God is bigger than your God" thing – then it can be true.'

In 1972 he was to comment, ' "Imagine" was a sincere statement. It was Working Class Hero with chocolate on. I was trying to think of it in terms of children.'

One cynical reader wrote to a magazine, 'Imagine John Lennon with no possessions.'

On National Poetry Day 1999, the BBC announced the results of a major poll to determine Britain's favourite song lyric. 'Imagine' won it. As a result, EMI decided to re-release it. A spokesman for the Parlophone label said: 'The release is down to the incredible response we've had from the public following the poll, asking whether it would be available again.'

An enhanced CD single was issued in Britain on 13 December 1999, which reached No. 3 in the charts. The CD also contained the tracks 'Happy Xmas (War Is Over)' and 'Give Peace A Chance', three numbers considered relevant for the new millennium.

I'm a Loser

A number penned by John and recorded by the Beatles on 14 August 1964. At one time it was being considered as a single, but instead was included on the *Beatles For Sale* album. The version recorded live on the *Top Gear* radio show was included on the Beatles' *Live At The BBC* CDs, issued in November 1994. John was later to comment, 'Part of me suspects I'm a loser and part of me thinks I'm God almighty.' It was also obvious that the influence of Bob Dylan was now affecting his songs and he said, 'Instead of projecting myself into a situation, I would try to express what I felt about myself. I think it was Dylan who helped me realise that.'

I'm Happy Just To Be With You

A song that John wrote for George Harrison to sing in the film *A Hard Day's Night*.

He was to comment, rather ungenerously, 'I could never have sung it myself.'

He also said, 'I wrote this for George to sing. I'm always reading how Paul and I used to make him invisible or keep him out, but it isn't true. I encouraged him like mad.'

The Beatles recorded the number on Sunday 1 March 1964, the first occasion they had spent Sunday in a recording studio.

I'm In Love

Song written by John in July 1963, which was recorded by the Fourmost in October of that year.

I'm Losing You

A track on John's November 1980 album *Double Fantasy*. The number originally began life under the title 'Stranger's Room' and he made a rough demo of it late in 1978. In 1980 he cut a polished demo of the number, now called 'I'm Losing You', while he was in Bermuda.

The composition was probably inspired by his feelings of estrangement from Yoko. While he was in Bermuda she visited him only once, briefly. His attempts to contact her at the office in the Dakota Building in New York were frustrated and he was to say, 'It's a song about the past, but I actually started writing it when I called from Bermuda and I couldn't get through to Yoko. I was just mad as hell, feeling lost and separate. But it's also a description of the separation period in the early seventies when I physically couldn't get through.'

He was also to say, 'But, getting a bit distant from it, it is expressing the losing you, of the eighteen months lost – losing one's mother, losing one's everything, losing everything you've ever lost in that song.'

Rick Nielsen and Bun E Carlos of Cheap Trick were brought in on the session when the track was recorded for the *Double Fantasy* album and Lennon told them, 'That was great. It sounds like the Plastic Ono Band.' However, when the album was released, the Cheap Trick contribution had been replaced by that of session men duplicating their parts.

I'm Losing You (promotional video)

In 1998 'I'm Losing You' was one of the tracks from *The John Lennon Anthology*, which was used in the promotion of the CD anthology and featured members of Cheap Trick and animated images based on John's line drawings. The video featured Rick Nielsen and Bun E Carlos of Cheap Trick and the bass guitarist Tony Levin of King Crimson, who all originally played on the track with John in 1980. This was the first time all three had met since then. Levin said, 'Amazingly, after eighteen years, we all remembered our parts on the song.' David Spafford animated John's drawings. The video made its debut on VHI on 3 December 1998. Yoko liked the promo and commented, 'It brings out John's playfulness. I'm very pleased.'

I'm Only Sleeping

Recorded on 27 and 29 April and 5 and 6 May 1966 and included on the *Revolver* album.

I'm So Tired

One of the songs John wrote at Rishikesh when he had Yoko on his mind, although he was still married to Cynthia. As a result he had difficulty sleeping and was to comment, 'I couldn't sleep. I'm meditating all day and couldn't sleep at night.' He completed the number on his 28th birthday and began recording it on Tuesday 8 October 1968 at EMI's Abbey Road studios. The number was included as a track on *The Beatles* double album. He was to say that 'I'm So Tired' was one of his favourite tracks.

I'm Stepping Out

First track recorded for the *Double Fantasy* sessions. Despite being credited to John and Yoko, it's obviously an autobiographical piece by John. It tells the story of a househusband fed up with looking after the kids and pets at home and watching endless repeats on TV. He wants to go out and let his hair down – and is stepping out, although he promises to be back sometime in the early hours of the morning! A number once again begun in Bermuda in 1977 when it was at the demo stage and eventually included on the posthumous *Milk and Honey* album.

It was issued as a single in America with Yoko's 'Sleepless Nights' on the flip on Thursday 15 March 1984.

I'm the Greatest

One of several songs John penned and made home recordings of in December 1971. A few months later he rehearsed and recorded the number, but abandoned it.

When Ringo Starr asked his three former Beatles colleagues to provide him with songs for his new album, John dug out 'I'm the Greatest' and rewrote it to suit Ringo. He then flew to California with Yoko and the two entered the studio on Tuesday 13 March 1973. George Harrison was also there and, as a result, John, George and Ringo all played together on the track, with Klaus Voormann and Billy Preston.

These two musicians had been considered as replacements for Paul when the group had toyed with the idea of continuing playing together after Paul's legal action had brought about the official break-up of the Beatles. As a result, when it was discovered that they'd all been recording together, rumours began to fly about a Beatles reunion.

The recording of the number took eighteen minutes and Ringo's record producer Richard Perry commented 'Just like that: no planning. The three ex-Beatles recorded one of John's songs. Everyone in the room was just gleaming.'

The song was featured on the album *Ringo,* issued in December 1973 on Apple PCTC 252. It was also included on Ringo's *Blast From Your Past* album, issued on Apple PCS 7170 in December 1975.

Immigrant, The

A number written by the hit songwriter and recording artist Neil Sedaka. Sedaka, son of a Brooklyn taxi driver, had over twenty chart hits, including 'Oh! Carol'; 'Stairway To Heaven'; 'Calendar Girl' and 'Happy Birthday, Sweet Sixteen', although the Beatles never included one of his songs in their early repertoire. However, Sedaka was to perform in Liverpool for the first time in the late 1960s and has fond memories of the city. John inspired him to write 'The Immigrant'. Sedaka comments, 'I wrote my song "The Immigrant" about John Lennon's trouble in getting his green card in America. I still have the tape of the show on which we appeared together and, you know, John was so pleased.'

In Gratitude

Following John's death, Yoko prepared a message that was aimed at all the people who were affected by the tragedy. She called the letter 'In Gratitude'. It read:

I thank you for your letters, telegrams and thoughts. They have come from all over the world, including every part of America, Europe, Asia and Africa. This was a consolation to me, since both John and I believed in brother and sister-hood that goes beyond race, colour and creed. They have come from all walks of life, including from those who are in prison. The kind letters from prisons especially warmed my heart.

I thank you for sending your checks to Spirit Foundation. It came in fifty cents, one dollars, five dollars, and has now reached 100 thousand dollars in total. John and I kept the Spirit Foundation staff to the minimum: John, I and a lawyer friend. All three of us, naturally, were unpaid. All expenses were paid out of John's and my own pockets. Since there is no reason to change this good system now or ever in the future, your money, every penny of it plus the interest it generates will go straight to the people in need at the end of the year. In order to maintain the simple and effective operation, Spirit Foundation has not and will not authorise or participate in any outside activity or merchandising.

I thank you for your concern for people who are making money on John's name after his death. There are some of you who feel guilty about receiving paychecks for the Lennon articles you have written for the media. Do not feel guilty. People who wish to do business in a small scale in tribute to John, using his name but in good taste: you have my blessings. Remember, John was a man with a great sense of humour and understanding. 'Whatever gets you through your life,' he would say. He would have felt better that you had a nice meal on him than if you had wallowed in guilt. Spend well for your children and loved ones. If there is any left, give to the ones who are in need. Do not ask for my authorisation of your venture, though, since it will be unfair to give to one and not to the others. Individuals and corporations who wish to exploit John's name in a large scale: I ask your voluntary act to report to me of your intentions and plans, respecting the feelings and legal rights of his family, and make arrangements to satisfy them.

I thank you for your feeling of anger for John's death. I share your anger. I am angry at it myself for not having been able to protect John. I am angry at myself and at all of us for allowing our society to fall apart to this extent. The only 'revenge' that would mean anything to us, is to turn society around in time, to one that is based on love and trust as John felt it could be. The only solace is to show that it could be done, that we could create a world of peace on earth for each other and for our children.

If all of us just loved and cared for one person each. That is all it takes. Love breeds love. Maybe then, we will be able to prevent each other from going insane. Maybe then, we will be able to prevent each other from being violent, as violence is in our hearts and not in the weapons. Guilt is not in the one who pulls the trigger, but in each of us who allows it.

When John fell right beside me, I felt like we were in a guerrilla war, not knowing who or where the enemy was. I kept telling my staff, who were hiding razors and newspaper articles from me, to show me everything: every telegram, every letter and every message. I was in the dark. I had to know. I saw the death photo. John looked peaceful, like in the back of the *Imagine* cover. Are you trying to tell me something, John? I saw the photo where he signed the autograph. It was flashed on the TV again and again. Somehow that photo was harder for me to look at than the death photo. John was in a hurry that afternoon. He did not have to give his autograph but he did, while the man watched him, the man who was to betray John later. I looked at the photo. I noticed that it was the photograph shown on TV where John's head was bent forward, obviously to sign his name. But it was a strange posture for John to show. Then I realised that he was signing for the gate of heaven.

John and I believed that we were one mind taking two bodies at this time 'for convenience, *and* it's more fun,' as he put it. Lately, we were calling ourselves 'the group,' because of the recording. 'I like both of you,' he used to tease me. For the past five years, I was working downstairs in my office during the day, and John, upstairs in the apartment. Now I am still downstairs and he is in the big upstairs.

I felt that I owed this letter to you. This may not answer all your questions but it is the best I can do now. This is also in place of giving interviews, personal appearances, and private talks which many of you have asked for. I would like to have some time to myself.

Remember, there's nothing you can do that can't be done. Imagine.

Love,
Yoko, Jan 11'81
New York City.

In His Own Write (book)

John's work was originally published in *Mersey Beat* under the pseudonym 'Beatcomber'. Three of the original items were used in his first published book. John was to say, 'Some journalist who was hanging round the Beatles came to me and I ended up showing him the stuff. They said, "Write a book" and that's how the first one came about, and the second was your follow-up. Then I forgot about it.'

The journalist in question was Michael Braun, who was travelling with the Beatles, gathering material for his fly-on-the-wall book *Love Me Do: The Beatles' Progress*. He discussed John's work with Tom Maschler of Jonathan Cape, who approached John with a book-publishing contract.

The first edition sold out completely on the day of publication, Monday 23 March 1964. John promoted the book in TV interviews including BBC TV's *Tonight* that evening and on BBC TV's *Line-Up*, and was fêted at the Foyle's Literary Luncheon on 23 April 1964.

The book was announced in *Mersey Beat* two months prior to publication and George Harrison commented on the book in a *Mersey Beat* item in February 1964, saying, 'The "with-it" people will get the gags and there are some great ones.'

In His Own Write comprises 57 items: fifteen mini-stories, eight poems, five other items, three play scenes and twenty-six drawings.

Robert Freeman designed the book and the cover features one of his photographs of John, smiling and wearing a coat and cap. John also wrote a brief biography for the book, which he titled 'About the Awful'. There was also an introduction by Paul McCartney. Paul talks of his first meeting with John at St Peter's Church fête, mentioning that John was drunk and saying that they were both twelve. Actually, Paul had just turned fifteen and John was sixteen.

The first tale is called 'Partly Dave', and concerns a salesman who rises in the morning, breakfasts with Betty, his wife, then catches a bus to work. The black conductor Basuboo gives Dave some advice before kicking him off the bus.

'No Flies on Frank' relates how Frank awakens on the morning of his wife Marian's 32nd birthday to discover his penis has grown an extra twelve inches. In a state of depression,

Frank goes downstairs and tells his wife. Although she tells him he's not to blame, he beats her to death with the head of his penis. After a few weeks her body is covered in flies, which puts Frank off his food, so he puts her in a sack and takes her to her mother's house. But Marian's mother slams the door in Frank's face and he has to return home with the body.

'Good Dog Nigel' is a happy dog, urinating on a lamppost, barking, wagging his tail – until he suddenly hears a message that he will be killed at three o'clock.

'At the Denis' tells how an elderly woman visits Denis the dentist with toothache. Instead of extracting one tooth he tells her he will take them all out and give her false teeth, which will make her look younger. She is flattered and agrees to his suggestion.

'The Growth on Eric Hearble' is a tale in which Eric wakes up one day to discover a growth on his head, which actually calls out to him. Eric ignores it, but that night it introduces itself as 'Scab' and the two become great friends. Unfortunately Eric is fired because his boss now regards him as a 'cripple'.

'The Wrestling Dog' relates how Perry, the lord mayor of a small island, holds a feast each year at harvest time. For the entertainment of his people at his latest feast he has hired a wrestling dog, although the tale ends with the statement, 'Who would fight this wondrous beast? I wouldn't for a kick off.'

'Randolf's Party' is set on Christmas Day and Randolph is alone, with only a Christmas card from his father to keep him company. As the lonely soul begins to decorate his Christmas tree, there is a knock on the door and a group of his friends arrive, giving greetings. They then jump on him and beat him to death, yelling that they never liked him.

'The Famous Five Through Woenow Abbey' is a parody of the popular Enid Blyton books. The group, together with their dog, travel to Woenow Abbey, but they are warned by a mysterious stranger not to go inside. That night they set off for the abbey and meet the stranger again. They overpower him and ask him what the secret of the abbey is. He tells them they can beat him but he'll never reveal the secret.

'Sad Michael' is the tale of a street evangelist who wakes up one morning feeling very sad. After his wife gives him his lunch he sets off to his soapbox. Later in the day a policeman approaches and bids him good evening, but Michael doesn't respond because he's deaf and dumb. However, when the copper asks him about his wife, Michael tells him to shut up. Realising he can now speak, he wonders what he'll do with all his books for the deaf and dumb.

'I Wandered' is a fifteen-line poem, obviously inspired by William Wordsworth's line 'I wander'd lonely as a cloud' from 'The Daffodils'.

'A Letter' is a simple letter from a fan wondering why more photographs and articles about her favourite group haven't become available.

'Scene Three Act One' is a playlet in which a capitalist named Fatty is negotiating with a union representative, Scruddy Taddpill, in order to avert a strike. Scruddy prefers to insult Fatty and they are interrupted by Mammy, who plops a large bundle on Fatty's desk and eats it, telling Fatty that it is his daughter. Fatty says he has never been married.

'Treasure Ivan' is a parody of Robert Louis Stevenson's *Treasure Island*. It's interesting to note that Long John and the Silver Men was one name mooted for the Beatles and it was suggested that John used the name John Silver on his Johnny Gentle tour of Scotland, although he denied it. This time the character is called Large John Saliver, who is overheard plotting mutiny by Jack Hawkins, a 32-year-old midget.

'All Abord Speeching' is a plotless attempt at presenting a 'school lesson' in three parts.

'The Fingletoad Resort of Teddiviscious' is also without a plot and is written as three television surveys parodying the sort of questions asked in such polls.

'Alec Speaking' is a poem in three parts in which a teacher is giving a lesson to a hostile classroom.

'Liddypool' is the adaptation of a 'Beatcomber' column John wrote for *Mersey Beat* under the title 'Around and About'.

'You Might Well Arsk' is a series of questions with scrambled names such as Prevelant ze Gaute, Docker Adenoid, Seldom Loyled, Harassed MacMillion, the Duke of Edincalvert, Priceless Margarine and Bony Armstrove (referring to President Charles de Gaulle), Doctor Adenauer, Selwyn Lloyd, Harold McMillan, the Duke of Edinburgh, Princess Margaret and her former husband Tony Armstrong-Jones, now Lord Snowdon.

'Nicely Nicely Clive' is a tale in which Roger is preparing to get married to Anne, who is confined to her wheelchair. Her father arrives and gets rid of Roger. The Clive referred to is a minor character who actually has a complete name – Clive Barrow.

'Neville Club' is the name of a seamy dive in which the narrator is appalled at the hedonism of its members, who smoke hashish and dance naked. The narrator attempts to leave and is stopped by the doorman who asks him if he is friend or foe.

'The Moldy Moldy Man' is an eight-line poem about a humble man who is mouldy.

'On Safairy With Whide Hunter' is another story from *Mersey Beat*'s 'Beatcomber' column relating the adventures of Jumble Jim and his faithful servant Otumba.

'I Sat Belonely' another poem, this time about a fat man who sits alone by a tree and hears a woman singing. He calls out for her to show herself, but she doesn't and he falls asleep, only to wake up and see a singing pig.

'Henry and Harry' is a tale of father and son. Harry wants Henry to take over the family business, but Henry is not interested and wants to become a golfer. He attempts to get a job playing golf, but is unsuccessful and returns home to join the family firm only to discover that his mother is burying his father.

'Deaf Ted, Danoota (and Me)' is a poem about a group of people who clobber bad guys, and it entreats the reader to look out for the heroes.

'A Surprise for Little Bobby' is a tale about a man who receives a hook for his amputated hand on his 39th birthday. However, the hook is for a left hand and Bobby has his right hand missing, so he chops of his left hand and fixes on the hook, hoping that he'll get another hook for his right hand the following year.

'Halibut Return' tells of a couple who have been parted for fourteen years because of a war. When Halibut returns from war he arrives with a present for Rosebeen – a dead slave.

'Unhappy Frank' is a poem about Frank, who is unhappy because he has to take care of his mother and continually clean the house. He decides to get rid of both his mother and the house and move to another country.

'On This Churly Morn' is the longest poem in the book.

When he rhymes 'Ive' with 'skive', is this a reference to his friend Ivan Vaughan, known as Ive? The book has various references, which could relate to his childhood friends. The name Nigel could refer to his friend Nigel Walley, who also sought a career as a golfer, as the son in 'Henry and Harry' did.

'Victor Triumphs Again and Mrs Weatherby Learns A Lesson' is a tale set in the small village of Squirmly on the Slug, where Mrs Weatherby spreads vile rumours about Victor Hardly, accusing him of holding black masses and desecrating the church cemetery. A group of villagers set up an ambush for Victor, but although they wait for several hours, he doesn't turn up.

'I Remember Arnold' is the final tale in the book and was actually the very first of John's stories to appear in *Mersey Beat*, where it originally appeared as a 'Beatcomber' column on Thursday 17 August 1961.

John was pleased with the reviews, commenting, 'To my amazement the reviewers liked it.' He also admitted, 'I really didn't think the book would even get reviewed by the book reviewers – maybe in the record columns as a new "single" by one of the Beatles. I didn't think people would accept the book like they did. To tell you the truth they took the book more seriously than I did myself. It just began as a laugh for me.'

London's *Times Literary Supplement* commented on the poems and short stories in the work:

They are remarkable; they are a world away from the underdeveloped language of the songs [hovering] between Joyce, Lewis Carroll ... with decorations ... part Thurber. They are also very funny ... the nonsense runs on, words and images prompting one another in a chain of pure fantasy.

The book is beautifully designed. It is worth the attention of anyone who fears for the impoverishment of the English language and British imagination ... humorists have done more to preserve and enrich these assets than most serious critics allow. Theirs is arguably our liveliest stream of 'experimental writing' and Mr. Lennon shows himself well equipped to take it farther. He must write a great deal more.

Tom Wolfe wrote in *Book Week*, 'This is nonsense writing, but one has only to review the literature of nonsense to see how well Lennon has brought it off. While some of his homonyms are gratuitous word play, many others have not only double meaning but a double edge.'

In his book *The Literary Lennon* – a scholarly work on all of John's writings up to the time of publication and published in the USA by Pierian Press in 1983 – Dr James Sauceda writes,

Certainly the most stylistically interesting review came from *Mersey Beat* (the Liverpool periodical in which John's work was first published). In fact, *Mersey Beat* was ahead of everyone else in heralding John Lennon's first book. Nearly two months before publication of *In His Own Write*, an article appeared in *Mersey Beat* entitled 'Beatcomber In Book Form' – as an advance notice of the book.

The *Mersey Beat* review appeared on March 26 1964. It reveals [*Mersey Beat*'s editor] Bill Harry's ability to parody the rhythm and look of Lennon literature.

The review in *Mersey Beat* read:

Paul and Robert and Jonathan and Fleming and Humbug (Baylout Ump) Lester on paper said by Charles Dickens and crew Ump, bound up by Clay Pidge Ump of bung Ho, suffy have assembungled with John Lennings to pollute this book about Harold and Arnold and Eric Hearble and Nigel and Partly Dave and Old Grumbly Pumbles and all etc.

Arfing about Nigel etc has lots of pidgers by John what drawed them all, he did already.

And 'Treasure Ivan' is a parable what had Long John Saliva and Blind Jew and Small Jack Hawkins.

Dear John Lennings, I say, congrastulations on begating your book what hast three stories from the Mersey Beat with Whide Hunter and Kakky Hargreaves and Liddypool.

Conceive some more books and let's have some more stuff for the *Mersey Beat*.

In My Life: The John Lennon File

A ten-part series, broadcast twice weekly by MTV from Monday 19 May 1986.

In My Life (play)

A stage play directed by Slim Stewart Parry and Jon Keats, which was presented at the Liverpool Playhouse from 19 to 31 August 1996. Subtitled 'The Concert John Lennon Never Gave', it featured fifteen songs. Keats was also the actor who portrayed John in the production and he was backed by a band called Instant Karma!. Keats came down with acute laryngitis and at some performances Tim Brown replaced him. Keats had portrayed John six years earlier in the stage production of *Imagine*.

In My Life (single)

One of John's favourite songs, which was originally inspired by his memories of Liverpool. The nostalgic, autobiographical piece was written in 1965 when John was living at Kenwood and he commented, 'I used to write upstairs where I had about ten Brunell tape recorders all linked up. I could never make a rock-and-roll record, but I could make some far-out stuff on it. I wrote it upstairs. That was one where I wrote the lyrics first and then sang it. That was usually the case with things like "In My Life" and "Universe" and some of the ones that stand out a bit.'

The early drafts were the simple memory of a bus journey from John's home in Menlove Avenue into Liverpool city centre, beginning with Penny Lane and listing the main streets and landmarks on the journey.

'It was the first song I wrote that was consciously about my life,' he said – but he was to alter the lyrics and change the direction of the song.

He said, 'I had a complete set of lyrics after struggling with a journalistic version of a trip from home to downtown on a bus naming every sight.'

The number was recorded the same year on Monday 18 October and originally appeared on the *Rubber Soul* album. It was later included on the compilations *The Beatles 1962–1966* and *Love Songs*.

In 1970, John was to say of this number, 'In the early days [the producer] George Martin would translate for us. In "In My Life" there's an Elizabethan piano solo. He would do things like that.'

John said that he liked Jose Feliciano's version of the number.

George Harrison also liked the number and rearranged it for his own interpretive performance on his 1974 Dark Horse tour.

Incantation

A song John co-wrote with Roy Cicala at New York's Record Plant studio on 15 July 1974. The number was never recorded, although the copyright was registered on 15 November of that year.

In His Own Write (stage play)

The American dramatist Adrienne Kennedy decided to write a play based on John Lennon's published books *In His Own Write* and *A Spaniard in the Works*, published by Jonathan Cape in March 1964, and was put in touch with Victor Spinetti, who told her that John's permission would be required before she could go ahead.

Spinetti approached John, who liked the idea, and both he and Spinetti went off to Morocco to work on a script. This was adapted for a one-act play co-credited to John Lennon, Victor Spinetti and Adrienne Kennedy.

The play was submitted to the National Theatre by its literary director, Kenneth Tynan. The National was then based at the Old Vic and Spinetti approached Sir Laurence Olivier, who ran the theatre, who told him to go ahead. John then had a meeting with Olivier, who told him that if the play went ahead he'd be faced with a number of business decisions regarding film and record rights. John told him, 'Don't you have people that you pay to talk about these kind of things who can talk to the people that I pay to talk about these kind of things!'

John was consulted and Sir Laurence Olivier approved the project. Spinetti and Kennedy then co-wrote the play, adapting some of the ideas contained in the books to portray a character called Me and the development of Me's ideas.

The play itself had one performance in 1967 under the title *Scene Three Act One* and was revised for a West End opening the following year. Ronald Pickup portrayed the lead character.

The initial performance took place on 18 June and was one of three one-act plays presented at the National that night.

John and Yoko arrived fifteen minutes late in a Rolls-Royce and alighted before a large crowd of press and reporters. It was only their second public outing and they were holding hands. The cameramen were shouting, 'Where's your wife, then, John?' 'I don't know' was all he could muster.

They caused disruption to the other play when they arrived and they didn't go backstage after John's play had ended.

Spinetti was to say that the play was about 'any of us growing up and the things that made us aware' – and referred to comic books, going to church, school or the cinema, the effects of radio and television in the home and so on. He said that John told him that the play took him back to his childhood.

It received negative reviews. The drama critic Irving Wardle wrote,

> The second half of the programme consists of *In his Own Write* adapted from John Lennon's two books of subcultural word games and cartoons. Victor Spinetti has assembled Lennon's unconnected pieces into a montage of working class provincial upbringing. We go into fantasies of boys' comics and Sherlock Holmes, a burlesque Hamlet, nonsense sermons and launching ceremonies, nightmares and quarrels with the inert family grouped inert round the television set and giving voice to feeble sounds of good cheer at Xmas and blinkered parental advice ... what it leaves you with is a soporific flow of mindless punning that is closer to Prof. Stanley Unwin than to Joyce.

The *Queen* magazine reviewer wrote: '*In His Own Write* is adapted from John Lennon's nonsense verse and shows that he is best employed as a Beatle.'

In His Own Write (stage show)

A one-man show starring Gareth Williams, which ran for a short season at the Lyric Studio, Hammersmith, London, in January 1982. Based on the books *In His Own Write* and *A Spaniard in the Works*, the show featured Williams reciting poems from the books, acting out sketches and singing John Lennon songs.

In His Own Write: The Lennon Play (the book)

The book is the script of the West End production and was published in Britain by Jonathan Cape and in America by Simon & Schuster in 1968 in an illustrated 36-page hardback edition. The author's credits were listed as Adrienne Kennedy, Victor Spinetti, John Lennon, and the cover featured the left profile of a bespectacled face, presumably John's, with a comic mouth painted over it and the title and author's names written in white script down the side.

In My Life: Lennon Remembered

A ten-part BBC Radio 1 series, produced by Kevin Howlett and presented by Simon Mayo, which commenced broadcasting on 6 October 1990.

The first programme was called 'Remember' and concerned John's childhood and family life, with interviews with Paul McCartney, Julia Baird and Vivian Janov. Songs included 'Mother' and 'Beautiful Boy (Darling Boy)'.

Part 2 on 13 October was called 'Rock and Roll Music' and included songs such as 'Twist and Shout' and 'Blue Suede Shoes'.

Part 3 on 20 October was called 'Help!' and dealt with the pressures of Beatlemania and Brian Epstein's death. Songs included 'A Hard Day's Night' and 'I'm So Tired'.

Part 4 on 27 October was 'In His Own Write And Draw', and concerned John's books, had him reading some of his poetry and performing numbers such as 'Lucy in the Sky with Diamonds' and 'I Am the Walrus'.

Part 5 on 3 November was 'Tomorrow Never Knows', which concerned the Beatles' pioneering studio innovations with songs such as 'I'm Only Sleeping' and 'Strawberry Fields Forever'.

Part 6 on 10 November was called 'The Two of Us' and focused on the Lennon and McCartney partnership, with songs such as 'A Day In The Life' and 'How Do You Sleep?'.

Part 7 on 17 November was 'With A Little Help From My Friends', which explored his relationships with fellow Beatles and other musicians, with songs such as 'Fame' and 'Whatever Gets You Thru the Night'.

Part 8 on 24 November was 'Give Peace A Chance' and concerned the peace events, Bed-Ins and 'bagism' with numbers such as 'Revolution' and 'Imagine'.

Part 9 on 1 December was 'Woman' and centred on his relationships with women – Cynthia, Yoko and May Pang, with 'Girl' and 'Woman is the Nigger of the World'.

Part 10 on 8 December was 'Mind Games' and spotlighted John's search for meaning and spiritual happiness through drugs, alcohol, meditation and therapy. Songs included 'Sexy Sadie' and 'Cold Turkey'.

Inn on the Park

Luxury London hotel in Hamilton Place, close to Park Lane, where John and Yoko lived for a short time in 1969 while Tittenhurst Park was undergoing extensive renovations. When it was Yoko's 37th birthday John booked them into the hotel again and had the entire suite filled with red roses as a surprise.

When John and Yoko decided to undergo primal therapy and had the psychiatrist Dr Arthur Janov (its inventor) fly into Britain at their request, he advised them to stay in separate hotel suites from each other and to isolate themselves from everything and everyone. John stayed at the Inn on the Park and Yoko moved into a rival hotel nearby.

Innes, Neil

A former member of the Bonzo Dog Doo-Dah Band, born in Danbury, Essex, on 9 December 1944.

He portrayed Ron Nasty, the John figure, in The Rutles lampoon. Innes, an extremely talented musician and songwriter, initially penned 'It Must Be Love' for a Rutles sketch in a TV show by Eric Idle. It proved so popular that it was decided to film an entire Beatles lampoon with the Rutles' career closely paralleling that of the Beatles. Initially it was called *All You Need Is Cash* and was first broadcast in America on NBC TV in March 1978. The British screening took place on BBC 2 on 27 March 1978. When it was issued on video in 1983, it simply became *The Rutles*.

The music in the production had an authentic Beatles atmosphere to it. In addition to composing the music and writing the lyrics, Innes produced the album, played guitar and keyboards and sang.

A Rutles album was issued and the tracks were a brilliant parody of actual Beatles music. The numbers penned by Innes were: 'It Must Be Love', 'Ouch', 'Living in Hope', 'Love Life', 'Nevertheless', 'Good Times Roll', 'Doubleback Alley', 'Cheese and Onions', 'Another Day', 'Piggy in the Middle' and 'Let's Be Natural'.

Innes has become a popular figure at Beatles conventions.

Instant Karma (promo)

Apple produced a promotional film, which consisted of various clips featuring the Lennons. Tony Blackburn introduced this on the 5 February, 1970 edition of *Top Of The Pops*. The Plastic Ono Band appeared on *Top Of The Pops* twice that month, performing the number live for shows that were broadcast on 12 February and 19 February. In the first show, introduced by Jimmy Saville, Yoko wore a blindfold and sat down while holding up signs reading 'Smile' and 'Peace.' In the second, Yoko was also wearing a blindfold, but this time was knitting.

Instant Karma (single)

A song that was written, recorded and mixed in one day and issued ten days later. John was to comment, 'I wrote it for breakfast, recorded it for lunch, and we're putting it out for dinner.'

When he woke up during the morning of 27 January 1970, John had the idea for the song in his head. At the side of his bed was a notepad, which he kept for just such a purpose, and he immediately began jotting down the verses of the song. Then he went downstairs to his sun room and began to compose on his piano. He next phoned Apple and asked them to contact George Harrison and other specific musicians to join him at Abbey Road in the early evening to record the number.

John was also aware that Phil Spector was in London at the time. He suggested that as an 'audition', Spector could prove his contribution as a producer to John by recording 'Instant Karma!' in one night.

On his way to the recording, John spotted a piano in the window of a shop, stopped the car, ordered the piano to be delivered immediately to the recording studio and continued on his journey.

At Abbey Road studios, John began recording with George Harrison on guitar, Klaus Voormann on bass and Alan White on drums. A rhythm track had been laid down by the time Phil Spector arrived. He then took control and produced some innovative ideas.

During the course of the recording, Billy Preston was sent down to Hatchetts Club in Piccadilly to round up a number of clubgoers to sing on the chorus. George Harrison conducted the chorus, which included Allen Klein.

The number began with a three-note introduction on piano, which harked back to Barrett Strong's 'Some Other Guy', which John used to play at the Cavern.

Spector then invited them into the control room to listen to the playback. John was so pleased with the result that Spector not only got the job of mixing and editing the 'Get Back' tapes, but was appointed Apple A&R man. He went on to produce John's records for the next two years. As soon as he heard the playback, John said, 'It was fantastic! It sounded like there were fifty people playing.'

The number was issued on Apple APPLE S 1003 on 6 February 1970, with Yoko's 'Who Has Seen the Wind' on the flip, and was credited to Lennon/Ono with the Plastic Ono Band. John provided vocals and played guitar and electric piano; Yoko was on vocals; George Harrison was on guitar and grand piano; Klaus Voormann was on bass guitar and electric piano; Alan White was on drums and grand piano; Billy Preston was on organ and Mal Evans provided clapping and chimes.

John performed 'Instant Karma!' on the BBC TV programme *Top of the Pops* on 11 February 1970. He played piano and sang a new vocal over a backing tape. He was joined by White, Voormann and Mal Evans, who all mimed, while Yoko sat on a chair, blindfolded, holding up cards with various slogans written on them, such as 'Smile', 'Peace', 'Hope'. John wore an armband with the slogan 'People For Peace'. It was the first time for four years that a member of the Beatles had appeared on *Top of the Pops*. John recorded two shows. In the second, screened the following week, Yoko is seen sitting behind John knitting.

John was also to perform the number at the One To One

concert at Madison Square Garden in New York on 30 August 1972.

Describing the song, he said, ' "Instant Karma!" is about action and reaction. Whenever you do something, whatever it is, there's a reaction to it. Even if you cough, you cough germs out all over the place. If you cough love out, out goes love. That's what "Instant Karma!" is – it's a great step forward.

'The greatest artists always come round to simplicity. It took Picasso sixty years to go through the whole bit and learn to paint like a child. I hope to record and write songs like an adult child.'

On another occasion he remarked, 'It just came to me. Everybody was going on about karma, especially in the sixties. But it occurred to me that karma is instant as well as it influences your past life and your future life.'

He added, 'Also, I'm fascinated by commercials and promotions as an art form. I enjoy them. So the idea of "Instant Karma!" was like the idea of instant coffee, presenting something in a new form.'

The single was issued ten days after it was recorded and reached No. 5 in the *New Musical Express* charts in Britain. It also became the first solo single from a member of the Beatles to sell a million in America, where it reached No. 3 in the charts after being issued on Apple 1818 on 20 February 1970.

However, the American release contained a different Spector mix from the British one – a mix that hadn't been approved by John. At the end of the recording session, Spector had been dissatisfied and asked John if he could take the tapes back to America and overdub violins on it. John refused. However, Spector went ahead. Although he handed over the original tape to EMI, he remixed the tape that had been sent to Capitol in America.

The number was included on the album compilations *Shaved Fish* in 1975 and *The John Lennon Collection* in 1982.

International Feminist Planning Conference

An event that took place at Harvard Divinity School, Cambridge, Massachusetts, on Sunday 3 June 1973. It was presented by the National Organization for Women and Yoko had been invited to perform before the 350 delegates.

John accompanied Yoko to the conference and while there they gave an interview to Danny Schechter of a local Boston radio station, WBCN-FM. In the interview John discussed how living with Yoko had given him a grasp of the aims of the feminist movement, the formation of his and Yoko's conceptual country, Nutopia, and news of the battle with the immigration department for a green card. Yoko discussed what she had learned at the conference.

Interview with a Legend: John Lennon with Tom Snyder on The Tomorrow Show
A video of the NBC television show of 9 December 1975, issued by Karl Video Corporation in America in the summer of 1981. It also included additional material such as an interview with Lisa Robinson, a journalist who had interviewed John and Jack Douglas, producer of *Double Fantasy*.

Intuition
A love song by John included on his *Mind Games* album.

Irish Families' Arms and Origins
A book by Edward Maclysaght, which was published in 1957.

John used an extract from the book in the booklet enclosed with his *Walls And Bridges* album. It read, 'No one of the name Lennon has distinguished himself in political, military or cultural life in Ireland (or for that matter in England either).' Beneath the quote, John had written: 'Oh, yeah? John Lennon.'

A sequel to the *Irish Families* book, also by Edward Maclysaght, was published by the Irish Academia Press, entitled *More Irish Families*. It contained a seven-line entry on John.

Irish Tapes, The
A political documentary produced and directed by John Reilly and Stefan Moore. The production was a video film with a pro-IRA slant and was supported financially by John and Yoko who were behind the campaign for the IRA after Bloody Sunday. On 12 November 1971, John had also recorded a demo disc of his number 'Luck Of The Irish' and he gave this version of the song to Reilly and Moore to be used on the soundtrack of the film.

Isaacson, Michael
A friend and fellow student of John's throughout his schooldays, who was at Dovedale Primary, Quarry Bank School and the Liverpool College of Art at the same time as John.

Isolation
A track on the *Plastic Ono Band* album expressing John's feelings of loneliness and how he and Yoko had been vilified and ridiculed. It was recorded late in 1970.

It's Alright (I See Rainbows)
An album by Yoko issued in America on Monday 29 November and in the UK on 10 December 1982. On the track 'Never Say Goodbye', John is heard shouting.

It's Johnny's Birthday
A number written by George Harrison to celebrate John's thirtieth birthday. It was included on the *All Things Must Pass* triple album issued in November 1970.

Apart from George, Mal Evans and Eddie Klein performed on the track.

Surprisingly enough, the tune was so similar to that of the Eurovision song 'Congratulations', written by Bill Martin and Phil Coulter, that the two songwriters claimed royalties – and received them!

It's Only Love
Number penned by John at Weybridge, although he was to say, 'That's the one song I really hate of mine. Terrible lyrics.' It was recorded on 15 June 1965 and included on the *Help!* album. The original title of the number was 'That's a Nice Hat'. The record producer George Martin was later to record it with his orchestra under that name.

It's So Hard
A song featured on the *Imagine* album, which was recorded in July 1971. John played guitar and was backed by Klaus Voormann on bass with Jim Gordon on drums. Phil Spector had overdubbed the legendary sax player King Curtis in New York

and John was thrilled. Sadly, Curtis was stabbed to death only a month later.

John performed the number, backed by Elephant's Memory, when he appeared on *The David Frost Show* in New York on 13 January 1972 and also performed it on *The Mike Douglas Show* the following month. Elephant's Memory were also his backing band when he included the song in his repertoire for the One To One concert in August 1972. The album *Live in New York City*, released in February 1986, featured the live track of 'It's So Hard', with Stan Bronstein providing the sax work.

It Won't Be Long

In addition to writing the song, John took over on lead vocals, which were double-tracked when the number was featured on the first track of the *With the Beatles* album, issued in November 1963. The track was recorded on Tuesday 30 July 1963 at Abbey Road studio.

As the songs that John and Paul wrote individually were always credited to Lennon and McCartney by common agreement, one of the ways of discovering who actually wrote the number was by realising that the one who wrote the song generally took over on lead vocals.

John was to say, 'It was the song with the so-called Aeolian cadences, the same as the Mahler symphony, at the end. I don't know what the hell it was about.'

I've Got a Feeling

One of John's unfinished lyrics to a number called 'Everybody Had a Hard Year'. It was mixed with an unfinished McCartney song called 'I've Got a Feeling' and was taped on the roof of the Apple Building in Savile Row. It was the last Lennon and McCartney collaboration and was included on the *Let It Be* album.

Jacaranda Club

A coffee club first opened in 1958 and situated in Slater Street, Liverpool, which was frequented by a group of art students including John Lennon, Stuart Sutcliffe, Bill Harry and Rod Murray. Stuart and Rod painted some murals in the basement.

John and Stuart had a group at the time and the club owner, Allan Williams, co-presented a rock 'n' roll extravaganza at Liverpool stadium headlined by Gene Vincent, but featuring a lot of local groups. Stuart asked Williams if he could get them any work. As he was arranging auditions for Larry Parnes at the nearby Wyvern Club with some of Liverpool's top bands, he invited them along. As a result they were booked to back Johnny Gentle on a short Scottish tour. Since the resident steel band at the club, the Royal Caribbean Steel Band, had left to perform elsewhere, Williams asked the group if they could make some appearances in the small basement cellar, which they did during May and June in 1960.

In the Jacaranda, shortly after the Beatles had returned from their first trip to Germany, Bill Harry had been discussing his plans for a music paper with John and commissioned John to write a feature on the Beatles for his first issue.

Jackdaw

A species of bird (*Corvus monedula*) that belongs to the crow family.

A rather startling claim was put forward by the *Sunday Mirror* on 1 June 1986 under the headline: LENNON HAS COME BACK AS A JACKDAW! CYNTHIA'S AMAZING CLAIM. Apparently, in her new mansion home in Penrith, Cumbria, Cynthia Lennon found a dead jackdaw wrapped in old newspapers dated 1956 behind the fireplace. The bird was perfectly preserved and she placed it on top of the fridge in her kitchen. She confided to the journalist Annette Witheridge, 'John told him [Julian] that if there was life after death he would prove it by sending a feather as a sign. When Julian saw the jackdaw he was really shaken ... it's as if John is trying to get in touch with us.'

The feather incident had been strengthened in Cynthia's mind by another incident concerning an Indian headdress, which John had given to Julian. It began when Lynne Buckley, a housewife, and her husband Gary attempted to sell a Native American headdress to an American buyer for £4,500. They claimed that her first husband Jeremiah had been given the item when he once worked at Cynthia's home in Ruthin, North Wales. Cynthia, as trustee of Julian's property, said, 'I didn't realise it was missing until I heard that someone wanted to sell it.' She fought a court case and won it on Julian's birthday.

'I gave it [the headdress] to him before his first major concert at the Royal Albert Hall, because he was so nervous,' she said. 'It seemed to work – the show was a great success.'

Jackley, Nat

Veteran Scottish comedian, dubbed 'the rubber man' because of his ability to create facial and neck contortions.

He was one of the guest artists who joined the Beatles on their *Magical Mystery Tour* and John personally directed the scene in which Jackley chased a group of bikini-clad girls around a swimming pool. Unfortunately, this was one of the scenes that ended up on the cutting-room floor.

Jackley was 79 years old when he died in September 1988.

Jam

A Dutch television show broadcast on the TROS network on 29 March 1969. Robbie Dale, a Radio Caroline disc jockey, conducted the interview with John and Yoko in their suite at the Amsterdam Hilton. He began by asking John and Yoko if they had chosen Amsterdam because it was geographically at the centre of Europe. They were bemused. He also suggested that they were in the city because of a peace organisation based there called Provo. John told him, 'We both are using the colour white and both are pro peace.'

John told Dale that he hadn't been in Amsterdam since 1964 but he'd read about Provo's activities. Dale then made a gaffe when he asked John whether he'd write simple songs again such as 'Do You Love Me'. John pointed out that he'd never written that song. (It was a Motown number originally recorded by the Contours and then turned into a beat number by the Liverpool band Faron's Flamingos, but providing hits for Brian Poole and the Tremeloes and the Dave Clark Five.)

Jamrag

A number included on the *Sometime in New York City* album. This was actually recorded at the June 1971 concert at the Fillmore East, New York, when John and Yoko performed with Frank Zappa and the Mothers of Invention. Zappa had been recording the show for a planned double album and gave John a set of the tapes the next day. John included some of the tracks on his *Sometime in New York* album. However he wrongly attributed the credit for this number to Lennon/Ono. It was actually a Frank Zappa song.

Zappa first used the theme played at the beginning of the number on his album *Lumpy Gravy,* in the track 'Lumpy Gravy II'. The theme was then elaborated on in Zappa's song 'King Kong', which is found on his *Uncle Meat* album.

Janov, Dr Arthur

One of John's friends, travelling through the States, came across a recently published book called *The Primal Scream* by the American psychiatrist Arthur Janov, who had theorised that all neuroses stemmed from a lack of parental love which resulted in a primal scream between the ages of five and seven. His therapy was to encourage the patient to scream at his absent parents in an attempt to exorcise their ghosts.

The friend posted a copy to John at Tittenhurst Park. Both John and Yoko were so excited by the book that they wrote letters the same night to Janov, inviting him to try his therapy on them. Janov agreed to come if they faithfully followed his instructions and he included a list that directed that they stop smoking, drinking and taking drugs. Twenty-four hours before his arrival they were to isolate themselves in separate rooms and wait for him. There had to be no television, radio or telephone and nothing to read.

When Janov arrived he went straight to John's room, closed the curtain and made John lie spread-eagled on the floor while he told him to concentrate on unhappy childhood memories. 'Feel that, stay with it,' he kept repeating. After two hours he went into Yoko's room.

This particular system he called pre-primal, the breaking down of reserves in order for the patient to be able to 'open up'. After a week he then instructed them that they must find themselves suites in different hotels. John moved into the Inn on the Park and Yoko into a nearby hotel and Janov visited them each day for a three-hour session.

John was to say, 'I was never really wanted when I was a child. The only reason I am a star is because of my repressions. The only reason I went for that goal is that I wanted to say, "Now, Mummy, will you love me?"'

After the sessions, which resulted in both John and Yoko crying for an entire two-week period, Janov returned to the states with the assurance that they would attend his Primal Therapy Institute and enrol for a proper course. They travelled to Los Angeles and stayed with Phil Spector, who lived near to the institute. The two of them attended group therapy sessions for two half-days per week over a period of four months.

After four months, although the therapy hadn't been completed, they both boarded a plane to London, feeling that they had benefited from the course. John was to say, 'Janov showed me how to feel my own fear and pain. Therefore, I can handle it better than I could before, that's all.'

Therapy is generally a lengthy process, and four months is a very short time in which to expect results. Yet the primal therapy was undoubtedly of immense benefit to John and led him to compose the songs he recorded for his *John Lennon/Plastic Ono Band* album in 1970, which is often referred to as 'the Primal Scream album'.

Jarlett, Dorothy

The Lennons' housekeeper at Kenwood, who lived locally. She was initially hired to look after Julian (at a wage some sources say was £10 per week, while others quote £20), but she soon began to take on all the household chores, ranging from cooking and cleaning to checking the fan mail – at the same rate of pay.

John and Cynthia called her Dot and, due to the informality of the household, John insisted she refer to them by their first names and she often took meals with the rest of the family.

Her husband Bernard used to pick her up each evening and John was amused by his first name and was to call one of the Kenwood kittens Bernard.

When Cynthia was on holiday in Greece, Yoko visited Kenwood, John's house in Weybridge, and stayed overnight. Dot informed Cynthia's mother, Lillian Powell. John heard about it and flew into a rage, telling her, 'What goes on in my house is my business. You are here as my housekeeper, and you have no right to tell tales behind my back about anything that goes on here.' Then he told her she was sacked and she ran out of the room, crying.

Dot was later to ask John's friend Pete Shotton to intercede on her behalf to see if John would reinstate her. Since he hadn't been able to find a suitable replacement John agreed – on condition that Yoko would also agree. However, Yoko refused and Dot was not rehired.

Jasper, Sir John

Character played by John in the 'What a Night' sketch in the first half of *The Beatles Christmas Show*, presented at the Finsbury Park Astoria, London, from Tuesday 24 December 1963 to Saturday 11 January 1964.

Peter Yolland, who had been presenting annual pantomimes for several years, produced the show and he wanted to introduce some theatrical elements into it rather than merely present a string of musical acts.

Yolland devised a short melodrama in which Sir John Jasper, dressed in a top hat and long black cloak, appeared brandishing a whip, while twirling a false moustache. He tied the heroine, Ermyntrude (George Harrison), to the railway lines as the snow fell (Ringo sprinkled paper over the actors) until all was saved by the arrival of Fearless Paul (McCartney) the Signalman.

Jealous Guy

John adapted this number from a song he'd previously written in India in 1968 called 'Child of Nature'. It was featured on the album *Imagine*. John himself was a 'jealous guy' and is reputed to have insisted on Yoko making a list of all her former lovers. After John's death, Roxy Music had a chart-topping version of the song. A twelve-inch version was released in Britain on Monday November 18 1985 with 'Going Down On Love' and 'Oh Yoko'.

Jenkins, Arthur Jr

A percussionist who was brought into John's 1980 sessions for the *Double Fantasy* album when another musician who'd been booked couldn't make it.

Jerry Lewis Labor Day Telethon

An annual American show hosted by the comedian Jerry Lewis to raise money to help the fight against muscular dystrophy. John and Yoko, supported by Elephant's Memory, appeared on the show on Wednesday 6 September 1972. They performed 'Imagine', 'Now or Never' and 'Give Peace a Chance'.

Jesus Christ

John first began to attend Sunday School at St Peter's Church, Woolton, at the age of eight and his Aunt Mimi was to comment, 'Religion was never rammed down his throat, but he certainly believed in God, all through his childhood.'

His friends who attended Dovedale Primary School with him remember that at the age of ten John drew a picture of Jesus, which was exhibited in the school hall.

John was very aware of the teachings of Jesus Christ. At the time of his Bed-Ins he said, 'We are all Christ – and we are all Hitler. We want Christ to win. We're all trying to make Christ's message contemporary. What would he have done if he had advertisements, records, films, TV and newspapers? Christ made miracles to tell his message. Well, the miracle today is communications, so let's use it.'

When Paul was sixteen and John eighteen, they both decided that they'd write a musical about Jesus Christ, but nothing came of it.

During his career, John mentioned Jesus in various interviews. At one time he said, 'I believe Jesus was right, Buddha was right, and all of those people are right. They're all saying the same thing, and I believe it. I believe what Jesus actually said, the basic things he laid down about love and goodness, and not what people claim he said.' He also commented, 'If Jesus being more popular means more control, I don't want that. I'd sooner they'd all follow us, even if it's just to dance and sing for the rest of their lives. If they took more interest in what Jesus, or any of them, said, if they did that, we'd all be there with them.'

When John did use communications to get a message across – such as his belief that the Beatles were more famous in the modern world, in some instances, than Jesus – there was a terrible outcry. He was also censured when he used the word 'Christ' in the song 'The Ballad of John and Yoko'. The line 'Christ, you know it ain't easy' caused an uproar in various places. Also, in his song 'God', John used the line 'I don't believe in Jesus'.

John originally wanted both Christ and Hitler to be represented on the *Sergeant Pepper* album sleeve, but his suggestions were vetoed.

On 3 December 1969 Tim Rice and Andrew Lloyd Webber asked John to play Christ in their new musical *Jesus Christ Superstar*, but changed their minds the next day.

During his trip to Canada in 1969, John was once again asked about the furore that his statements about Christ had created. He said, 'I think I said that the Beatles have more influence on young people than Jesus Christ. Yes, I still think it. Kids are influenced more by us than Jesus. Christ, some ministers even stood up and agreed with it. It was another piece of truth that the fascist Christians picked on. I'm all for Christ, I'm very big on Christ. I've always fancied him. He was right.

'As he said in his book, you'll get knocked if you follow my ways. He was so right about that. We got knocked. But I'm all for him. I'm always saying his name, I use it in songs, and I talk about him.'

In 1970 a religious musical called *Jesus Christ* was scheduled to make its debut at St Paul's cathedral. John was offered the role of Jesus and suggested that he'd accept the part if Yoko could appear as Mary Magdalene. Negotiations fell through and neither of them appeared in the production.

JJ

A song John composed on acoustic guitar in September 1971 within a few days of moving into the St Regis Hotel in New York. He later used the tune when he wrote 'Angela' for his *Sometime in New York City* album.

Jodorowsky, Alexandro

A Chilean filmmaker. His film *El Topo (The Mole)* was being screened at the old Elgin Theater, New York, in December 1970. Yoko made a visit to inspect the theatre, which was shortly to screen some avant-garde John and Yoko movies in a film festival.

When she saw *El Topo* she was so impressed she brought John along to view this strange, ambiguous, mystical film about a messianic gunfighter, which was full of graphic violence, but mentally stimulating. The couple met the director and agreed to finance his next film, *The Magic Mountain*.

John also talked Allen Klein into purchasing the distribution rights to the surrealistic epic and Klein obtained *El Topo* for ABKCO Films and it became a big 'midnight movie' cult film when he booked it throughout American college campuses.

In some quarters, Jodorowsky was being hailed as a genius as he wrote, directed and starred in the film, in addition to composing the soundtrack music.

John obtained the rights to the movie soundtrack and *El Topo* was issued on Apple SWAO 3388 on 27 December 1972.

John and Yoko: The Bed-In

A video released on 3 December 1990 to commemorate the tenth anniversary of John's death. It was issued in Britain by Picture Music International on MDV 991 2613. It contained footage of their May/June 1969 Bed-In for peace at Montreal and featured their meeting with Timothy Leary, the confrontation with Al Capp and John's telephone conversations with Berkeley students. Also included were the Yoko songs 'Remember Love' and 'Who Has Seen the Wind' and John's solo acoustic guitar version of 'Because'.

John and Yoko: A Love Story

John J McMahon, president of Carson Productions, the TV production company owned by Johnny Carson, allegedly took eight months before he was allowed a meeting with Yoko Ono in order to pitch the idea of this 150-minute telemovie to her. He was to say, 'I'd tried to get to her through a couple of friends. And I'd written a long letter about what I wanted to do. And she didn't want to have a meeting.' Yoko's assistant Elliott Mintz was to say that the only reason she agreed to a meeting was because she'd heard that some other company was intending to film an unauthorised version.

The film cost $5 million to produce, with locations in London and New York, and took two years to make, during which time there were two title changes and two scriptwriters.

The original scriptwriter was Ed Hulme, but he was sacked because Yoko didn't like his script, which she felt concentrated too much on the sensational aspects of the love affair. Sandor Stern, who also directed, replaced him.

NBC TV premiered the movie on American television on Monday December 2 1985, to tie in with the fifth anniversary of John's murder.

A Liverpool actor, 24-year-old Mark McGann, portrayed John, and Kim Miyori, who had appeared regularly in the TV series *St Elsewhere*, portrayed Yoko. (McGann was to play John in the *Imagine* musical at Liverpool Playhouse in 1992.)

Ralph Walsh featured as Ringo Starr with Peter Capaldi as George Harrison and Kenneth Price as Paul McCartney.

The film included around thirty numbers by John, the Beatles and Yoko.

Stern, who had directed movies such as *The Amityville Horror* and *Fast Break,* read up on all the books, magazine articles and newspaper articles on John he could find and then spent three days with Yoko, eight hours each day, checking out all the research with her and also to receive her input.

Discussing the movie, McGann commented, 'It was important to tell the story as it actually happened, particularly for British viewers. While Lennon was living in the US with Yoko, his UK fans were being told of his activities through second-hand media and didn't really know what was happening. As a result, a lot of hostility from this country was directed at Yoko but in the US, they were public figures.

'The movie is a little glossy in places but I don't think it needed to be any nearer the knuckle. It's really a celebration of an amazing relationship – a relationship that was important to millions. It presents the facts and will tell Lennon's UK fans just why John and Yoko finally left this country.'

When it was issued in Britain on home video on 21 March 1988, it was retitled *John and Yoko: The Complete Story*. SVS Films released it on home video in America on 21 December 1989. The company also issued home videos of *Live in New York City* and *Imagine* at the same time.

John and Yoko Mobile Political Plastic Ono Band Fun Show

Title of a projected 1972 tour by John and Yoko, which never came off.

John, Elton

Born Reginald Kenneth Dwight in Pinner, Middlesex on 25 March 1947, he changed his name to Elton John in October 1967, a combination of Elton Dean's and John Baldry's forenames.

Elton had teamed up with the lyricist Bernie Taupin and the two were eventually signed by Dick James, the Beatles' publisher, who issued Elton's debut album *Empty Sky* on his own DJM record label. Interestingly enough, Alistair Taylor, the Beatles' former office manager at Apple, promoted the album. When James heard that Allen Klein had fired Taylor, he hired him as promotions man for DJM Records.

Tony King first introduced Elton to John Lennon. King was a former song plugger at DJM who joined Apple soon after the company was being slowly wound down.

In July 1974 Elton invited John to join him at the Caribou

recording studios in Colorado where he was recording a version of 'Lucy in the Sky with Diamonds', the first time he'd decided to issue a single that hadn't been written by himself and Bernie Taupin.

John turned up at the session and then agreed to play guitar under the credit, 'the reggae guitars of Dr Winston O'Boogie'. During the session at the Caribou Ranch, Elton also recorded 'One Day at a Time' from the *Mind Games* album, which became the flip side of the single when it was issued. In Britain the single was released on DJM DJS 340 on 15 November 1974, and reached No. 3 in the charts. In America it was issued on 18 November 1974 on MCA 40344 and topped the charts for two weeks.

In August 1974, when Lennon was recording his *Walls and Bridges* album in New York, he invited Elton to join him on the 'Whatever Gets You Thru the Night' track. Elton played piano and organ and also supplied some 'oohs and ahhs' in the backing vocals as well as joining him on backing vocals for the 'Surprise Surprise (Sweet Bird of Paradise)' track. Of his relationship with John at that time, he said, 'I've never met anyone so inspiring. You just instantly fall in love with him when you meet him. I was just knocked out that he would even go into a studio with me – I'm that much of a fan.'

At the studios, Elton told John that 'Whatever Gets You Thru the Night' would be his first American No. 1 single as a solo artist. John told him he didn't think it would, so Elton made him promise that if it did reach the top he'd appear in concert with him. John agreed.

Although 'Whatever Gets You Thru the Night' wasn't a major success in Britain, reaching only No. 24, it did, as Elton predicted, become John's first solo American chart-topper. As a result, he agreed to appear with Elton at his Thanksgiving concert at Madison Square Garden on 28 November 1974, dropping in to see Elton in concert in Boston beforehand.

On the night of the Madison Square Garden concert, Elton announced, 'As it's Thanksgiving, we thought we'd give you a special present. So here's something to be thankful for ...' And John appeared on stage. They performed three numbers together. Originally, Elton had wanted John to sing 'Imagine', but John declined, wanting to perform some rockier numbers instead – 'Whatever Gets You Thru the Night', 'I Saw Her Standing There' and 'Lucy in the Sky with Diamonds'.

Kiki Dee, who was also appearing on the tour, commented, 'Lennon was so nervous, he asked Davey Johnstone to string his guitar for him, which I thought was quite sweet.'

After the show, John joined Elton at a party held at the Hotel Pierre.

The Madison Square Garden concert had been recorded and Elton used the track 'I Saw Her Standing There' as the flip side of his single 'Philadelphia Freedom', which gave him his second No. 1 hit in a row, following 'Lucy in the Sky with Diamonds'. The friendship between the two stars grew and Elton, who often gave his friends nicknames (he called Rod Stewart 'Phyllis'), referred to John as 'Carol'.

In 1980 Elton decided to sign with Geffen Records because John was on the label and said, 'Lennon and I are both on Geffen now. So we may do an album together one day. I'd love that.' Sadly, it never came to pass.

Elton's friendship with John grew in strength and he became Sean Lennon's godfather, frequently dropping into the Dakota Building. During his visits to see John, Yoko and Sean at the Dakota, Elton had become aware of the large wardrobes they had, which were crammed with clothes. With this in mind, on John's fortieth birthday, Elton sent him a card, which read:

Imagine six apartments
It isn't hard to do.
One is full of fur coats
The other's full of shoes.

Two years after John's death, Elton recorded a tribute to his friend called 'Empty Garden (Hey Hey Johnny)', which was included on his *Jump Up* album and also issued as a single. Yoko and Sean attended a Madison Square Garden concert to thank him publicly for the tribute. Elton also recorded a second tribute to John, 'The Man Who Never Died', which was the B-side of his 'Nikita' single.

Elton John actually guested on recordings by three ex-members of the Beatles. He performed piano on 'Devil's Radio' and 'Wreck of the Hesperus' and electric piano on 'Cloud Nine' on George Harrison's album *Cloud Nine* and played piano on the track 'Snookeroo', which he'd written with Bernie Taupin, for Ringo Starr's album *Goodnight Vienna*.

John John (Let's Hope for Peace)

A number by Yoko originally included on the *Wedding Album*. She also performed it at the *Toronto Rock 'n' Roll Revival* concert and it's the last track on the album *The Plastic Ono Band – Live Peace In Toronto 1969*. On the Toronto track Yoko is heard over the feedback guitars of John, Eric Clapton and Klaus Voormann. At the end of the number they placed their guitars against their amplifiers and the feedback sound continued as they walked to the centre of the stage, lit cigarettes and then walked off again. Mal Evans then walked on to the stage and turned the amplifiers off one by one.

John Lennon: A Real Live Fairytale

A book written and illustrated by Marica Huyette between 1975 and 1976. It contained fifty surrealistic drawings, together with background text on the story behind the illustrations.

The book was published by Hidden Studio in a limited edition as a large paperback with two colour plates.

John Lennon and the Rock 'n' roll Circus

A forty-eight-page book of photographs by Michael Randolph of John Lennon's appearance during the filming of *The Rolling Stones Rock 'n' Roll Circus* in December 1968. Published in 1993 by Tracks.

John Lennon (book)

A 1982 biography by Carole Lyn Corbin, commissioned by the New York publisher Franklyn Watts as part of their 'Impact Biographies' series, which also included Marie Curie, Adolf Hitler, Eleanor Roosevelt and Anwar Sadat.

Written for young readers in a similar manner to the British publisher Hamish Hamilton's 'Profiles' series.

John Lennon (book)

Book by Tony Bradman, published in Britain by Hamish Hamilton in 1985. It is one of a series of 'Profiles' books, written with young readers in mind. Simplified biographies of famous people. Other subjects in the series included Paul McCartney, Winston Churchill, Helen Keller and Martin Luther King.

A slim 64-page hardback book, illustrated with several fine black ink drawings by Karen Heywood.

John Lennon (book)

A book of photographs by Dezo Hoffman, published in Britain by Columbus Books in 1985.

The photographs in the selection were taken between 1962 and 1970, but mainly from the 1963–4 period. The book contains an introduction by Norman Jopling, a former *Record Mirror* journalist who was an assistant to Hoffman for several years.

A number of photographs appear in print for the first time and the publication date tied in with what would have been John's 45th birthday. The date of publication coincided with an exhibition of photographs from the book at the Cuts Gallery in Kensington Church Street, London.

John once described Hoffman as 'the most inventive photographer I ever came across'. Interestingly enough, Hoffman didn't take the first photographs in the book. They are a strip of Polyfotos originally taken in 9 October 1944 when John was four years old, which Dezo had bought from John's Aunt Mimi.

Following the photographic collection there is further text, entitled 'Captions', providing background information to most of the individual shots.

Dezo also took photographs of the Beatles continually during 1962 and 1963 until an incident at Twickenham Studios soured the relationship. John had taken exception to one of Dezo's pics of him, which had been printed in *Tit Bits*, magazine and publicly berated Dezo about it.

Hoffman told Jopling, 'I felt so humiliated in front of all those people that I couldn't even answer him. I just turned my back on him and walked out. And I obviously finished with the Beatles also.

'In my imagination I had thought of myself as a father figure to them, and I couldn't believe that John could talk to me as if I were a six-year-old kid.' He later added, 'Even today, I still think the break was my fault, that I was wrong in turning my back on him and walking away, but I had been hurt at being treated like a young boy.'

In the early 70s Dezo was in New York on an assignment and received a call from John inviting him to visit him at his apartment. Dezo commented, 'I'm really glad I went to see him, because we made up our very good friendship. He kissed me when we parted.'

The book was published in America in 1986 by McGraw-Hill under the title *The Faces of John Lennon*. The 162-page book includes over 150 photographs of John, featuring pictures of him with Laurence Olivier, Tommy Steele, Morecambe and Wise, Ed Sullivan and Muhammad Ali. He is pictured on stage, at television shows and in Britain, Paris and America.

John Lennon (book)
Slim hardback book by William Ruhlmann, published by Springmark in March 1993. The 96-page book included a colour poster and 100 photographs.

John Lennon (book)
A Chelsea House paperback in their 'Pop Culture Legends' series, published in 1994. Written by Bruce W Conard, it is aimed at the younger reader and contains a basic biography with chronology, selective bibliography and discography.

John Lennon (book)
A book in the Spanish language by Miguel Martinez and Vicente Escudero, published by Jucar in November 1994. At 240 pages in length, it contained twenty monochrome photos. There was a nine-chapter biography, thirty of John's solo lyrics and various appendices, which included a discography, an A–Z, bibliography of Spanish books, filmography, videography and list of magazines.

John Lennon – the Beatle Years
A Bag One edition of a litho set of John's lyrics, restricted to 1,000 copies and issued in 1995.

John Lennon Boxed Set, The
A special eight-album set of all of John's official album releases from *Live Peace In Toronto* to *Shaved Fish*, which was issued by Parlophone on Monday June 15 1981.

John Lennon the Cartoonist

A television special screened by Arte, a French/German TV channel on 25 July 1995. The one-hour documentary included interviews with Rod Murray and Yoko Ono.

John Lennon Collection, The

A seventeen-track compilation album issued in Britain by EMI Records on 15 November 1982 on EMTV 37. The television-advertised album reached the No. 1 position in the British charts, remaining at the top for five weeks, selling a million copies in Britain in a month.

It was released in the US on Monday November 8 1982.

With the exception of 'Cold Turkey', all of John's British solo singles are included, together with 'Love', 'Jealous Guy' and six tracks from the Geffen Records *Double Fantasy* album and three singles issued on the Geffen label. John David Kalodner compiled the album, with the aid of Yoko Ono and David Geffen.

The cover sleeve featured two previously unpublished shots of John by Annie Leibowitz, taken in December 1980.

The tracks on the album are: Side One: 'Give Peace a Chance'; 'Instant Karma!'; 'Power to the People', 'Whatever Gets You Thru the Night'; 'No. 9 Dream'; 'Mind Games'; 'Love'; 'Happy Xmas (War Is Over)'. Side Two: 'Imagine'; 'Jealous Guy'; 'Stand By Me'; '(Just Like) Starting Over'; 'Woman'; 'I'm Losing You'; 'Beautiful Boy (Darling Boy)'; 'Watching the Wheels'; 'Dear Yoko'.

The album was issued in America on Geffen Records GHSP 2023 on 10 November 1982, where it reached No. 33 in the charts.

Seven years after the album release, the CD version was issued. It included two bonus tracks, 'Cold Turkey' and 'Stand By Me'. A twelve-page insert booklet featured three colour shots of John taken in December 1980 at the Dakota Building by Annie Leibovitz.

The CD version was issued in Britain in November 1990. The American CD was delayed until 6 February 1991 because the US version of 'No. 9 Dream' had been shortened by two minutes and the release was delayed in order to include a full version of it.

The compilation was deleted in September 1997 and replaced with *Lennon Legend. The John Lennon Collection* had sold 1.8 million copies in Britain alone, 350,000 of which were on CD.

John Lennon Conversations

A book by the California medium Linda Deer Domnitz, published by Coleman Publishing in March 1984. Domnitz says she began spiritual conversations with John four days after his death, which continued for a 24-month period, during which she took over 1,000 pages of notes. In the 'conversations' there were messages to Paul McCartney, George Harrison, Ringo Starr and Yoko Ono. There were also fifteen full-colour, channelled paintings by the artist Susan Rowe, which were also available as postcards. Audiotapes of the book were also available.

John Lennon – A Day on the Radio

A radio special broadcast by WGCL Cleveland on Sunday 11 December 1983. It was actually the Scott Muni interview from 13 February 1975 that had originally been broadcast on the New York Station WNEW.

John Lennon Days

A 32-page booklet, published in Japan by Bag Arts Inc in 1992. It was basically the catalogue for an exhibition of John's artwork and memorabilia, held in Tokyo between December 1992 and January 1993. It also contained reproductions of pages from the *Daily Howl,* caricatures, postcards and the manuscript of the lyrics to *Lucy in the Sky with Diamonds.*

John Lennon: Death of a Dream

An American paperback written by George Carpozi Jr and published in New York by Manor Books in 1980. The publication was put together virtually overnight to take advantage of the public interest in John following his death. It contains a photo insert section with approximately two dozen pictures, quite poorly reproduced.

The blurb reads, 'This is the first, biggest, and fastest-selling book on the life and death of John Lennon ... a monumental publishing effort to produce the story of the Gentle Beatle's phenomenal career, reports every detail about his murder, and makes a penetrating study of his crazed assassin.'

At the time Carpozi was a *New York Post* journalist who specialised in crime stories and had written over seventy books, most of them about true-life murders.

Carpozi has concentrated on the sensational elements of the killing, in true crime-reporter style, while most of the information about the Beatles is taken from a previously published Manor paperback by Martin Grove, *Beatles Madness*.

Book One, *A Heinous Crime*, concerns itself solely with the murder. Book Two, *His Legacy*, is the basic Beatles history with details of films and record releases, and it ends with a chapter entitled 'The Fifth Beatle', an interview with the disc jockey Murray the K. Book Three, *Last Words*, covers the aftermath of the tragedy and the various tributes.

John Lennon Drive

One of four Liverpool streets named in honour of the Beatles, the others being Ringo Starr Close, Paul McCartney Way and George Harrison Close.

For some years a number of Beatles friends and fans had been attempting to persuade the local council to pay tribute to the group by naming streets after them. Disc jockey Bob Wooler had even written to the Lord Mayor of Liverpool about the proposal.

However, the council were not interested and claimed that such a practice had been abused in the past. Following John's death, more positive approaches were made to the council's Highways Committee to enable the local builders, Wimpey Homes, to name four streets after the Beatles in one of the new estates they were building.

Once again the idea was turned down. Eddie Porter and Jeff Gilbert then formed the Beatles Street Campaign and together with members of Cavern Mecca, they carried mock street signs to another meeting of the Highways Committee.

The committee finally voted 10 to 9 in favour of the idea and the decision was ratified by the full city council on Friday 17 July 1981, although one councilor opposed, saying, 'The only member of the Beatles I would honour would be George McCartney.'

The estate with the Beatles street names is in Liverpool 6 and the first homes were opened on Friday 27 November 1981 at a ceremony attended by then Minister for the Environment, Michael Heseltine, MP, Sir Trevor Jones, MP, councilor Derek Hatton and Joseph Dwyer, head of Wimpey Homes. Three further blocks of flats have since been added to the estate. Their names are Epstein Mews, Apple Court and Cavern Court.

John Lennon Family Album, The

A book by Nishi Fumiya Saimasru, first issued by FLY Communications in Japan in 1982 in a limited edition of 1,000 (even so, Yoko attempted unsuccessfully to stop the publication of the book) and published in America by Chronicle Books in 1990. Saimasru was employed over a three-year period by the Lennons and the Japanese photographer was literally their personal photographer from 1976 to 1979. Of his photographs, Saimasru was to comment, 'The kind of love that begins with the family can help us to value others. If people can feel the warmth of family love in this collection of photographs, I'll be happy.'

Most of the photographs are of John and Sean together in Japan. A number also feature Yoko and there are shots at the traditional birthday parties for Sean held in the Tavern on the Green in New York. There are also a handful of shots of John with his first son Julian.

John Lennon – The Final Days

A two-hour documentary on the E! Entertainment Channel in USA, broadcast on Sunday 11 October 1998. Fred Seaman provided a video of John and Sean together; there was the background to the *Double Fantasy* sessions and the story of John's assassination.

John Lennon 4 Ever

A book by Conrad Snell, published in America by Crown Summit Books in 1981. It is one of a plethora of paperbacks published in the States just after John's death. Without illustrations to brighten it up, the book relies mainly on text, which is not without its share of inaccuracies.

John Lennon: Gimme Some Truth: The Complete John Lennon Songbook

A book by Thomas Rehwagen, published in Germany by Pendragon Verlag in September 1990. In addition to the lyrics to John's songs, published in both English and German, there was the text of an interview John gave to the radio station WNEW-FM in September 1974, a discography and a filmography.

John Lennon: Give Me Some Truth

A television documentary screened on BBC2 on Sunday 13 February 2000. It was originally scheduled to be shown at 11.30 p.m., but the previous programme, a snooker match, overran and the documentary began at midnight. It included unseen footage from the Lennon archives of the recording of the *Imagine* album at Tittenhurst Park. As the blurb said, 'A camera captured the events as Lennon, Yoko Ono and a gathering of musicians and friends worked on the album that was to become a legend.'

John Lennon in Heaven – Crossing the Borderlines of Being

A book published in 1994 by Pan Publishing. Its author, Linda Keen, relates how a dream in 1986 while she was on holiday in the Swiss Alps led to a six-year journey between the physical and nonphysical worlds, where she was guided through the different layers of Heaven by John Lennon and learned of his various past lives. The spirits of Freddie and Julia Lennon (John's parents) and Brian Epstein were among the many encountered by John and the author relates many discussions with John from subjects ranging from the Gulf War to his own assassin.

John Lennon: An Illustrated Biography

A ten-chapter amble through John's life, from his birth to his death, illustrated with 45 photographs and aimed at the young reader. The book was published in Britain by Hodder & Stoughton in 1983 and issued as a paperback later the same year by Coronet.

The author, Richard Wooton, had previously written books on Elvis Presley and Country Music. It's a straightforward enough retelling of John's life and career, although a number of mistakes do crop up – the author wrongly states that Stuart Sutcliffe and Astrid Kirchherr were married.

John Lennon In His Own Words

One of a series of books published by Omnibus Press, which collated quotes from celebrities. Others in the series included *The Beatles In Their Own Words* and *Paul McCartney In His Own Words*. This entry in the series was compiled by Barry Miles and published in 1980.

Miles also compiled the book of Beatles quotes.

Much of this book consists of photographs: there are nearly 120 of them, a great number taken from newspaper clippings.

There are no credits for the photographs, which come from a number of sources. Most of the quotes have been gathered from interviews John conducted with such people as Jann Wenner and have been assembled in chronological order in a year-by-year sequence.

John Lennon In His Own Write

A one-hour radio special syndicated throughout America by Westwood One during the week of 8 December 1986. It consisted of excerpts from interviews, which had been conducted with John from 1962 until 1980.

John Lennon's Honeymoon

A forty-minute documentary by the Dutch station KRO, which was originally transmitted on Wednesday 19 November 1969. The documentary was woven around John and Yoko's week-long Bed-In at the Amsterdam Hilton. The show was later aired in numerous countries around the world.

John Lennon: A Journey in the Life

A ninety-minute television documentary produced by David Wolf and directed by Ken Howard, which appeared on BBC television in the *Everyman* series on Friday December 6 1985. Howard had approached Julian Lennon to play his father, but Julian refused – and also turned down Howard's request for an interview. He said, 'I don't want to be known just as a shadow of my father.' Cynthia Lennon also declined to co-operate in the making of the programme, and, of the three ex-Beatles, only Paul McCartney bothered to reply to Howard's request with the note, 'I wish you well. But it's all too painful for us to contribute at the moment.' However, Yoko Ono gave the programme her blessing and even provided Howard with some rare home-movie footage.

The film of John playing with Sean was included in the programme, although Julian wasn't even mentioned. This infuriated Cynthia, who called the documentary a 'travesty of the truth'. In a *Daily Mail* interview she said, 'The programme makers should be ashamed because by leaving Julian out, they are denying his existence and his birthright. I'm desperately hurt for Julian. Why show Sean and ignore my son?' She also objected to the portrayal by Bernard Hill, then forty years old, of John as a moronic depressive and she added, 'It was only after his marriage to Yoko that he became unhappy. You only have to look at pictures of him before he was killed. He looked dead before he died.'

The programme was described as 'a re-creation of John's spiritual, physical and music journey through life'.

Nine-year-old Benji Lawrence played John as a boy and Tim McEvoy portrayed a fifteen-year-old Lennon.

A version edited down to sixty minutes was transmitted in America on PBS (Public Broadcasting Service) on 26 November 1986.

Immediately after the BBC broadcast, a fifteen-minute interview with Yoko Ono, conducted by Andy Peebles at the Dakota Building, was screened, under the title *Yoko Ono: My Journey After John*.

John Lennon: Live in New York City

An album and video released in America on Friday 24 January 1986. It was issued in Britain on 24 February. The album and video were recorded at the One-To-One concert at Madison Square Garden on 30 August 1972. A CD was also issued in Britain on Monday 28 April 1986.

John Lennon: The Man, the Memory

A three-hour special broadcast on the RKO Radio network in December 1980.

This was from the final interview that John did while he was promoting the *Double Fantasy* album. The RKO interview took place from 2–5 p.m. on Monday afternoon, 8 December, in John and Yoko's Dakota Building apartment.

Dave Sholin interviewed the couple. Also present were Ron Hummel, an engineer for KFRC in San Francisco; Laurie Kaye, a scriptwriter; and Bert Keane, the national promotion director of Warner Bros Records. John was killed less than six hours later.

The interview had been intended for an RKO Valentine's Day Special but a three-hour special *John Lennon: The Man, the Memory* was broadcast on Sunday 14 December. The interview originally began with questions to Yoko, as John hadn't yet arrived. She discussed marriage, relationships between men and women, the breakdown of the family system, love, trust and commitment, her own marriage, politics, her background and education and other similar topics, also introducing comments on various tracks from the *Double Fantasy* album.

She was asked what her feelings were when she first heard the songs. She said that John had been in Bermuda relaxing with Sean and she was taking care of business in New York, but that John began phoning her all the time and singing the songs and asking her opinion on them.

When John arrived Sholin asked them about their typical day. John said, 'When we're not doing records and being up late, I get up about six, go to the kitchen, get a cup of coffee, cough a little, have a cigarette, papers arrive at seven. Sean gets up seven twenty, twenty-five. I oversee his breakfast. I don't cook any more. But I make sure I know what he's eating …' And he continued to discuss a typical day in extensive detail.

He was asked about Sean and commented, 'I don't know whether it's because he was born on the same day as me, which that in itself is quite strange. He was born on October 9th, which I was, so we're almost like twins.' He then began to describe their relationship and the amount of time he spent with his son.

He admitted he neglected his first son, Julian: 'And I kind of regret it, you know, because he's seventeen. You know, my other son by my first marriage is seventeen. I don't remember seeing him as a child. You know, it was the height of the Beatle thing so

I was working all the time. And I never considered what I was doing to him. I didn't even count it. The mother was at home. I was away.' He then began discussing the state of society at that moment, and then talked of Yoko's relationship with her daughter Kyoko.

Because he was going back into the studio to work on his first album for five years, he had to explain to Sean why he was no longer around the house with him all the time, saying, 'It makes me happy to do the music. And I might have more fun with you if I'm happier, right?' He also revealed that, because he felt guilty about leaving Sean while he recorded the album, he had a picture of him pinned in the studio. The conversation continued to cover the subject of parenthood in relation to Sean.

John then mentioned that they went into the studio to cut 22 tracks, but cut it down to 14, explaining, 'They were all dialogue songs, meaning that we were writing as if it were a play,' and we were two characters in it.' John looked on the album as a play and the songs as the diaries of how they felt.

John was asked how he felt about meeting and talking to people and playing music again after a five-year absence. He said, 'I like to be liked. I don't like to offend people. I would like to be a happy, contented person.'

He then talked about his early relationship with Paul McCartney and Yoko, describing how he first met Yoko.

Yoko then began to discuss her own work, specifically *Approximate Infinite Universe*. Then 'Woman is the Nigger of the World' was mentioned. John said, 'That was banned – "Woman is the Nigger of the World" – because of the word "nigger". Now I had Ebony and Jet both say they're not offended and we went down there with [the comedian] Dick Gregory just in case there were any questions there.' John then went on to discuss *Double Fantasy* in more detail.

He brought up the fact that he was forty years old and continued: 'I want to talk to the people my age. I'm happy if the young people like it and I'm happy if the old people like it. But I'm still talking to guys and gals that have been through what we went through together – the sixties group that survived.'

The talk then covered opinions about history, politics, religion and the nature of power.

Next John discussed various music trends from MOR to

disco. Yoko then told him that they had to be off to the studio and John ended by mentioning the Beatles.

John Lennon Memorial Service

A Liverpool tribute to John, which took place in the huge piazza in front of St George's Hall and opposite the Empire Theatre where the Beatles had appeared on several occasions. The memorial service, organised by a Liverpool promoter, Sam Leach, was held on 14 December 1980. More than 50,000 people of all ages gathered to pay their respects and the Lord Mayor of Liverpool made a speech, and he was followed by a number of other speakers.

Taped messages from Gerry Marsden, former leader of Gerry and the Pacemakers, and David Shepherd, then the Bishop of Liverpool, were played over the loudspeakers.

David Arnold, chaplain to Liverpool Polytechnic, also spoke at the service and asked, 'Which do you think is the most powerful, a bullet or a song? I tell you that a song is, because a bullet can kill one man, but a song can bring a thousand people to life.'

Allan Williams of the Jacaranda Club was among the participants and at 7 a.m. there was a ten-minute silent vigil at the request of Yoko.

John Lennon, My Brother

A book written by Julia Baird (John's half-sister) with Geoffrey Giuliano, published in Britain by Grafton Books in 1988.

When John's mother Julia left her son in the care of her sister Mimi Smith, she went to live with another man and bore him two children, Julia and Jacqui. Little was heard about the two sisters until the 80s, when Julia published her reminiscences in the *Liverpool Echo* and in a limited-edition book. A Beatles scribe, Geoffrey Giuliano, approached her because he wished to collaborate on a fuller story and this book is the result.

After such books as Albert Goldman's iconoclastic biography, it was refreshing to read something positive about John again, particularly something relatively new, which fleshed out some additional personal details of his early family life. The book was also illustrated with a number of family photographs, published for the first time, of John's father, mother, grandmother, aunts, uncles and cousins.

It's interesting to note that Julia doesn't have a high regard for the male side of John's family (Freddie and his brothers) and the reader senses she was never particularly sympathetic to Yoko.

Paul McCartney has contributed a preface to the book, which also contains a Lennon family tree and a Lennon chronology.

John Lennon 1940–1980

A Hungarian book by Koltay Gabor, published by Zenemukiado of Budapest. The 186-page publication contains over 80 illustrations, including several of John's cartoons from his two books, the lyrics to 26 songs (eight of which were actually composed by Paul McCartney), a filmography, discography and text in the Hungarian language.

John Lennon 1940–1980

Also known as *The Front Page News Book*. Published by ESE California in 1981, the book was compiled by Ernest E Schworck.

The large-size publication, printed in both paperback and hardback editions, was a 90-page compilation of headlines, covers and news stories selected from 100 newspapers from around the world depicting their coverage of John's murder on their editions of 9 and 10 December 1980.

John Lennon 1940-1980

A book published in Paris by Artefact in 1980 and compiled by Har van Fulpen with the aid of the Beatles Fan Club of Amsterdam.

The book includes excerpts from the *Playboy* magazine interview; the lyrics to 'Strawberry Fields Forever', 'Lucy in the Sky with Diamonds', 'Across the Universe', 'Ballad of John and Yoko', 'Happy Xmas (War Is Over)' and 'Give Peace a Chance'; a chronology; and an album discography.

There are 36 monochrome photographs, most of them covering a full page. Other illustrations include the covers of the British popular papers the *Daily Mirror*, *Sun*, *Daily Star*, *Daily Mail* and *Daily Express* of Wednesday 10 December 1980.

The headlines were: 'DEATH OF A HERO' (*Daily Mirror*); 'THEY LOVED HIM, YEAH, YEAH, YEAH' (*Sun*); 'THE MAN WHO SHOT

LENNON' (*Daily Express*); 'JOHN LENNON R.I.P.' (*Daily Star*) and 'THE KILLER AUTOGRAPH' (*Daily Mail*).

There are also reproductions of a 'War is Over' leaflet, a 'War is Over' American street sign and a letter John and Yoko wrote to *Melody Maker* on 13 December 1971.

John Lennon: 1940–1980

Of all the biographies issued within twelve months of John's death, this was arguably the best. Published by Fontana paperbacks in 1981, it was written by Ray Connolly, a journalist who had interviewed John on several occasions.

In the winter of 1980, Connolly was due to fly to New York to interview him. Yoko called him on the afternoon of 8 December to confirm it. At 5.30 the following morning he received a telephone call informing him of the tragic news of John's murder. Connolly then wrote the obituary for London's *Evening Standard*. (John had said to him in December 1970, 'Have you written my obituary yet? I'd love to read it when you do.')

The book is literate and informative and contains many anecdotes. It displays none of the haste evident in many of the books, which were rushed out to satisfy public demand for information about John following his death.

The biography is in twelve chapters spread over three sections: 'Liverpool', 'The World' and 'New York'.

In his foreword, Connolly acknowledges that he had to draw 'upon the work of other journalists and upon the memories of the principal characters and their accounts of their lives as told to me and to other writers'.

There are sixty photographs collected by a picture researcher, John Spencer. They include: John dressed as a rocker at the *Magical Mystery Tour* party; eating an apple at the Apple boutique opening; handing Michael X a bag of hair for him to auction; campaigning for a posthumous pardon for James Hanratty; with Elton John at Madison Square Garden; and being leaped upon by a fan on stage in Rome.

One of the most intriguing photographs shows John and Yoko standing among some of their possessions at Tittenhurst Park and a large, framed photograph of 'three virgins' is to be seen in the background – three naked people in full frontal pose. Most people assumed that the shot of John and Yoko naked, featured on the *Two Virgins* sleeve, was taken using a delayed-action device – apparently there was a third 'virgin' around to take the picture.

John Lennon: One To One
Video issued in Britain by BMG on tape: BMG 791 138 and laserdisc: BMG 781 138 on 16 November 1992.

Filmed at the One-To-One concert at Madison Square Garden in New York on 30 August 1972, it is similar to the 1986 video issued by PMI: *John Lennon – Live in New York City*.

However, *John Lennon: One To One*, runs for only forty minutes and contains only ten tracks, in contrast to PMI's fourteen-track video. Only seven of the tracks feature John; the other three are 'Summertime' by Stevie Wonder and 'Somewhere' and 'Reverend Lee' by Roberta Flack.

The tracks by John and Yoko are: 'Come Together', 'Instant Karma!', 'Sisters O Sisters', 'Cold Turkey', 'Hound Dog', 'Give Peace a Chance' and 'Imagine'.

John Lennon Peace Forest
A project organised by the Jewish National Fund. The agency specialises in planting trees to create a new forest in Israel and occasionally a forest is named in the memory of a great person, such as President John F Kennedy. On Israel's Arbor Day in January 1981 it was announced that a forest would be dedicated to John and the initial planting took place.

The forest is being planted in the Safad-Moran region of the Galilee, where prophets and intellectual mystics once walked and are now buried. It will be dedicated when the minimum of 10,000 trees have been bought by subscribers, who can buy a tree for $5. The executive director of the Jewish National Fund said, 'We established this forest because we sincerely thought John Lennon worthy of being memorialised.'

By 1990, John's fans had bought more than 2,500 trees for the living memorial. A stone marker had also been placed at the site with the words to 'Imagine' on it.

John Lennon: A Personal Pictorial Diary
A small 110-page illustrated booklet by Warren Tabath, published by a New York firm, Sportmatic Ltd, in January 1981.

It was designed with newsagent sales in mind rather than through bookseller outlets and is little more than a pictorial essay.

John Lennon (planetoid)

A planetoid named in honour of John. It is planetoid 4147, one of the basalt fragments from the planetoid Vesta, following a crash with another asteroid.

John Lennon/Plastic Ono Band (album)

A bleak album inspired by John's course of primal therapy, which enabled him to lay down a lot of the ghosts of his formative years in a stark, honest confessional, which is undoubtedly a most remarkable album. John's pain of his rejection in his youth by mother and father is among the themes explored.

The psychiatrist Dr Arthur Janov had treated John and Yoko for three weeks in London in March 1970 and the couple had then travelled to Los Angeles for a further five months of treatment from April to August. It was during this period that John wrote most of the songs for the album.

Commenting on the treatment, he said, 'In the therapy you really feel every painful moment of your life. It's excruciating. You are forced to realise your own pain, the kind that makes you wake up afraid with your heart pounding.' He also said of the therapy, 'It was the most important thing that happened to me besides meeting Yoko and being born.'

John began recording the LP at EMI's Abbey Road Studios in September 1970 and completed it in four weeks. Backing him on the album were Ringo Starr, Klaus Voormann and Billy Preston. It was released on 11 December 1970 in both the UK and USA. The British release was on Apple PCS 7124 and the American on Apple SW 3372. The production credits ran: John Lennon, Yoko Ono and Phil Spector.

The tracks were: Side One: 'Mother', 'Hold On', 'I Found Out', 'Working Class Hero', 'Isolation'; Side Two: 'Remember', 'Love', 'Well Well Well', 'Look At Me', 'God' and 'My Mummy's Dead'.

The BBC banned any play of 'Working Class Hero' because the word 'fuck' was used twice, and, when the lyrics to the song were contained in the inner sleeve, EMI insisted that those two occurrences of the word be replaced by asterisks, otherwise they'd refuse to handle the album. They got their way, although Apple inserted the words 'omitted at the insistence of EMI'.

John Lennon/Plastic Ono Band, often referred to as 'the Primal Scream album', reached No. 13 in the *New Musical Express* charts

The cover was a peaceful pastoral scene of John and Yoko reposing beneath a tree in the countryside, taken by Dan Richter. The reverse side of the sleeve featured a photograph of John taken when he was five years old and a pupil at Dovedale Primary School.

Yoko released a companion volume at the same time called *Yoko Ono/Plastic Ono Band*.

John Lennon/Plastic Ono Band (ballet)

A ballet set to the music of John Lennon/Plastic Ono Band opened at Sadler's Wells Theatre in London on Friday, 24 April 1987. The choreography was by Christopher Bruce.

John Lennon: Rock 'n' Roll Never Forgets

An American radio special produced by Westwood One. It was syndicated to a number of American radio stations between Friday 17 and Sunday 19 September 1982. The programme featured an interview with Elliot Mintz.

John Lennon's Secret

A book by David Stuart Ryan, published by Kosmik Press in 1982. Despite the title, there is no secret to reveal.

In company with Ray Connolly's book *John Lennon: 1940–1980*, this is a sincere attempt to produce a biography of John that delves a little deeper into the man than the rash of superficial paperbacks that appeared in the weeks and months following his death.

The author spent some time in Liverpool and New York researching his material and obtaining first-hand information from friends and associates of John, including Bob Wooler and Clive Epstein. He also had access to the manuscript of an unpublished book by the late Freddie Lennon, John's father.

The independently produced book contains a poster and cover illustration based on an Annie Leibovitz photograph.

With this is a note, which states, 'The front cover pictures John Lennon on the last day of his life.'

There are 32 full-page photographs, a list of John's compositions, a bibliography, a section discussing 22 of John's songs in detail and a Lennon family tree.

The 24 chapters cover John's life more closely than previous publications, although there are few surprises. The depiction of John's childhood is highly readable, the author covering the group in much the same was as Philip Norman did in *Shout!*. The influence of Norman's book is evident in the alleged description of Britain Epstein's first visit to the Cavern: 'From the moment the furtive figure of Brian Epstein saw the black leather clad shape of the sardonic, joking, superior Lennon, he was fixated.'

Norman's wild contention in *Shout!* that Brian fell in love with John at that moment and, as a result, signed the Beatles, has been reiterated by several authors, but is a particularly tiresome fabrication.

John Lennon – the Solo Years

A Bag One edition of a litho set of John's lyrics, restricted to 1,000 copies and issued in 1995.

John Lennon: Sometime in New York City

A Genesis publication containing photographs of the last ten years of John's life by Bob Gruen and a text of interviews with John and Yoko. The images range from the album *Sometime in New York City* until *Double Fantasy*. Priced at £275 on publication, there were 3,500 copies of the 236-page book, the first 2,500 of which were signed by Yoko and Gruen.

John Lennon Story, The

The earliest paperback biography of John, written by George Tremlett and issued in Britain by Futura Publications in 1976.

The book was one of a series of over a dozen pop biographies compiled by Tremlett, which also included *The Paul McCartney Story*.

Tremlett was a highly active journalist in the 60s, specialising in pop music in partnership with his wife, Jane.

A meticulous researcher, Tremlett visited Liverpool in the

early 60s, where he bought various items of Beatles memorabilia, including photographs and contracts. In 1982 he put his huge files of rock material up for sale when he abandoned journalism for politics.

The book sports a cover by the popular artist Achilleos depicting John in three aspects of his life.

Tremlett's series of paperbacks for Futura were always worth reading for their store of anecdotes, collected during interviews with friends, relatives or associates of the various stars he wrote about. He even interviewed the local tradesmen who provided the Lennons with their supplies when they lived in Weybridge.

The book begins with an account of the 50s scene in Liverpool, following the skiffle boom. It details the interest in rock 'n' roll and the cult of the teenager – manifesting itself in tribal style with gatherings of youngsters such as the Teddy Boys – then describes the evolution of the Mersey scene itself with its myriad bands. John's biography then unfolds with a portrayal of his father Freddie, the death of his mother Julia, his childhood escapades, time at Quarry Bank School, the formation of the Quarry Men and his meeting Paul.

His life story is documented over the next 105 pages, when we reach 1974 and Tremlett's summation of John's life and career. He commented, 'In financial terms, Lennon is almost certainly one of the wealthiest artists the world has ever known, with a fortune comparable to Picasso.'

Picasso was reputed to be worth a hundred million pounds. As John had complained only five years previously that he was down to his last fifty thousand, it might be supposed that the 70s had brought him more wealth than the entire decade of the 60s!

The 54-page chronology that follows is packed full of interesting background details and trivia:

- 15/2/65, John Lennon passes his driving test;
- 17/8/66, at a press conference Lennon says he is in favour of Americans going to Canada to avoid being conscripted for Vietnam: 'If a man doesn't feel like fighting, he should have the right not to go into the army';
- 25/1/67, thieves try to steal Lennon's Mini Cooper from outside Epstein's home in Belgravia – and are foiled by an anti-thief device;

- 26/7/68, John Lennon spends the day at McCartney's house finishing 'Hey Jude'.

There are sixteen pages of photographs, which include the Beatles at the *Mersey Beat* awards; the opening of the Apple boutique; with Pierre the Clown at Apple; and a shot of John and Yoko on stage at the Lyceum. Tremlett's attempt to find a publisher for a Beatles chronology had been unsuccessful, as had his plans to place books on George Harrison and Ringo Starr.

John Lennon: Summer of 1980

A photo book published by Perigree, which was put together by Yoko and features the work of eight different photographers. There were no captions, except some lines from songs from the *Double Fantasy* album.

John Lennon (train)

Name of a Pullman train which began service from Liverpool's Lime Street Station to London's Euston Station in 1987. A competition took place in the *Liverpool Echo* to name a train after a famous person. There were lots of entries citing John and his name was eventually chosen. A nameplate was to be unveiled for the occasion and the person who'd won the *Echo* competition was invited to unveil it. The person was Madeleine Schatz from Freehold, New Jersey, who had moved to Liverpool two years before.

Charlie Lennon attended the unveiling and said, 'All fans will be able to see this great tribute to John for years to come.'

John's Aunt Mimi was too ill to attend, even though she was thrilled at the tribute, and more delighted with it than with many of the other tributes that had been made. Her message during the opening ceremony was, 'This is wonderful. At last we read some good news about John. Sadly, I cannot be there to see the train, due to illness.' She also explained, 'The train meant more because of the memories. Being with John as a boy, [I know] he would love it all – the stations, the travelling. How he would be excited just watching out the window. They would go to the family in Scotland each summer, most times with Uncle George. John would point to everything – houses, cattle, sheep, the lakes. He loved trains; that's why this means so much to me.'

John Lennon: Vicendo Canrando, Racconti & Lennonsense

A book in Italian containing both of John's books, *In His Own Write* and *A Spaniard in the Works*. Published by Arcana Editrice SRL, the 170-page book had a twelve-page introduction by Antonio Taormina.

John Lennon Video Collection, The

An eighty-minute, nineteen-track collection of John's solo videos, which featured similar cover art to *The John Lennon Collection* (audio), released ten years previously. Compiled by Martin Smith and issued by Picture Music International on MVN 4910343 on 5 October 1992, the first 10,000 copies were shrink-wrapped with a free copy of a two-track CD single 'Instant Karma!' c/w 'Oh My Love'. The video was released in America on 6 April 1993.

It featured all of John's major releases in chronological order from 1969 to 1980, and his posthumous singles up to 'Jealous Guy'. Sixteen of the tracks had been previously unreleased. 'Give Peace a Chance' featured coverage from the Lennons' Bed-In; 'Cold Turkey' was edited by John and Yoko; 'Instant Karma!' featured footage of his second live appearance on *Top of the Pops*; 'Power to the People' had clips of John and Yoko on a peace march and of the mass demonstrations in Tiananmen Square; 'Happy Xmas (War Is Over)' featured new footage with the Harlem Community Choir; 'Mind Games' showed archive footage of John and Yoko; 'Whatever Gets You Thru the Night' featured animations of John's drawings; 'No. 9 Dream' had archive footage of John and Yoko. Then there were 'Stand By Me' and 'Slippin' and Slidin''; footage from John's appearance on *The Old Grey Whistle Test*; 'Imagine', taken from the original *Imagine* film of 1971; '(Just Like) Starting Over', a new video clip produced by Yoko. The next four were all contemporary video clips – 'Woman', 'Nobody Told Me', 'Borrowed Time' and 'I'm Steppin' Out'. 'Jealous Guy' was taken from the 1988 documentary *Imagine – John Lennon*. 'Grow Old With Me' featured an original promotional film and 'Imagine' was a live version taken from John's appearance at the tribute to Lew

Grade in 1975. An audio clip of 'Watching the Wheels' was played over the closing credits.

The video reached No. 26 in the *Billboard* Top 40 Music Video Charts.

John Lennon, Young Rock Star

Book by Laurence Santrey published by Troll Associates of New Jersey in 1990. It's basically a children's book, 48 pages in length in large print with illustrations by Eileen Beier.

John Lennon: Zeichnungen, Performance, Film (book)

Edited by Wulf Herzogenrath and Dorothee Hansen and originally published in Germany in August 1995 by Cantz Verlag. The book was originally conceived as a catalogue for an exhibition of John's work held at the Kunsthalle, Bremen, Germany. It features an introduction by Yoko Ono and features John's artwork presented in chronological order, drawings from the 1950s to the 1970s, together with information on the films he made with Yoko

John Ono Lennon, Volume 2, 1967–1980

The second volume (see *John Winston Lennon* below) of Ray Coleman's exhaustive biography. He'd begun researching the work six months after John's murder. He managed to obtain Yoko's co-operation in the venture and sent her the manuscript of his second volume. She then phoned him with some corrections and suggestions. In addition to covering John's life from 1967 the volume included a chronology of those years and the lyrics to his songs of that period.

John Sinclair

A track on the *Sometime in New York City* album in which John is featured playing slide guitar and singing solo. The number was written in protest against the imprisonment of Sinclair for possession of a tiny amount of marijuana. John's every movement and action was being monitored by the FBI at this time and one of the FBI reports read that the track would 'probably sell a million ... but it is lacking Lennon's usual standards'.

John – Two Years On
A programme broadcast by London Broadcasting Company (LBC) on Wednesday 8 December 1982. It looked at the events in the period since John's death.

John Winston Lennon, Volume 1, 1940–1966
The first volume of Ray Coleman's biography first published in Britain in 1984 by Sidgwick & Jackson. Coleman first met John in Liverpool in 1962. He was invited up to Liverpool to meet the Beatles and although he didn't write a feature article about them, he wrote about five paragraphs, which pleased Brian Epstein and stood him in good stead.

Coleman became close to the Beatles during the 1960s as editor of the music publications *Disc* and then *Melody Maker*, and used to visit John at his home in Weybridge. When he decided to write a biography of John he decided it was important to enlist the co-operation of Cynthia Lennon and Yoko Ono. He spent four years on research, interviewed 100 people and produced a 600-page work, initially published in two volumes. Cynthia co-operated with him on the initial volume, putting Coleman in touch with many people she knew. She also embarked on a nine-day tour of America with him to promote the book. He dedicated the first volume to Julian Lennon.

Johnny and the Moondogs
The name John, Paul and George adopted in October 1959 when they entered the Carroll Levis talent competition at the Empire Theatre, Liverpool.

The three had noticed an advertisement in the *Liverpool Echo* that Mr Starmaker Carroll Levis was bringing *The Carroll Levis Discovery Show* up north. The finals were to be held at the Hippodrome Theatre, Manchester, and there were to be some heats, one of which was to take place at the Empire Theatre, Liverpool.

John, Paul and George needed a name when applying for an audition and thought up the Moondogs. Then, since John was the titular head of the group, changed it to Johnny and the Moondogs. There were a number of acts from the northwest appearing at the Liverpool heats including, according to some reports, Billy Fury.

Some reports also indicated that a group called the Gladiators won. Other sources report that the winners were a duo called Rikki and Dane (Allan Clark and Graham Nash, who were to become leaders of the Hollies).

Johnny and the Moondogs, however, definitely came third. This meant they were entitled to appear in the finals in Manchester. It was to be their first appearance outside of Liverpool. Buddy Holly particularly influenced the trio at the time and during their appearance they sang 'It's So Easy' and 'Think It Over'. John was up front singing, with no guitar. Paul and George were standing behind him playing guitars and supplying the sound of 'Ba ba ba'.

At the end of the show each act was required to reappear and perform a few bars so that the audience's applause could be measured.

However, Johnny and the Moondogs were so short of money that they couldn't afford overnight accommodation at a hotel. So they had to set off to the station to catch the last train home before the finale and missed the opportunity of being judged.

Soon afterwards they came up with the name the Silver Beetles.

Joko Films Ltd

A company established by John and Yoko on Thursday 6 January 1972.

Jones, Brian

A founder member of the Rolling Stones, born in Cheltenham on 26 February 1944. Jones was the most musically talented member of the band and, at the time, the one the girls all screamed over. Their manager, Andrew Loog Oldham, realised the value of having the group write their own material, just as Lennon and McCartney did, and created the Jagger–Richards team to write the songs.

This shifted the power in the group, placing Jones more in the background. As a result he became more reliant on drugs. One evening John found him crying in the Ad Lib Club. He told John, 'They're destroying me. I started the fucking band and now they keep trying to squeeze me out. It's all Jagger–Richards this, Jagger–Richards that. They won't even listen to my songs any more.'

John knew how talented Jones was on virtually any instrument – he'd even picked up the sitar far more quickly than George Harrison had, and played it on the Rolling Stones' single 'Paint It Black'. John told him, 'Look, I get sick of Paul sometimes, of the way he's forever trying to dominate me. You have to stand up to these egomaniacs; you can't just get smashed out of your box. Look, how about if I ask you to play sax or something on some Beatle records? That'd make them all sit up and take notice, won't it?'

Jones began to become even more depressed when his girl-friend Anita Pallenberg slept with both Keith Richards and Mick Jagger. The drink and drugs began to affect his physical appearance and he became hollow-eyed. John said, 'From being brilliant he became the kind of person you dread ringing you up. He was in a lot of pain but I was going through so much myself that it seemed there was nothing I could do to help him.'

John brought him in to play oboe on 'Baby You're a Rich Man' and saxophone on 'You Know My Name (Look Up the Number)'.

On Thursday 3 July 1969 he was found dead in the swimming pool of his home. He was 25 years old.

Journaal

A daily television news programme in the Netherlands. On Tuesday 25 March 1969 the show featured the arrival of John and Yoko for their Bed-In at the Amsterdam Hilton.

Juke Box Jury

John recorded his one and only appearance on *Juke Box Jury* without his fellow Beatles on Saturday 22 June 1963. The BBC TV show was a popular programme, hosted by the disc jockey David Jacobs, in which a panel of celebrities commented on a selection of new record releases, deciding which would be a hit and which a miss. John's fellow panellists were Katie Boyle, Bruce Prochnik, an actor, and Caroline Maudling, an actress.

The records judged by the panel were: 'Southend', Cleo Laine; 'So Much In Love', the Tymes; 'Devil in Disguise', Elvis Presley;

'The Click Song', Miriam Makeba; 'On Top Of Spaghetti', Tom Glaser; 'Flamenco', Russ Conway; 'First Quarrel', Paul and Paula; and 'Don't Ever Let Me Down', Julie Grant. Three other songs reviewed were edited out: through lack of time: 'Lies', Johnny Sandon and the Remo Four; 'Too Late To Worry', Richard Anthony; and 'Just One Look', Doris Troy.

The other members of the Beatles had travelled to Wales earlier that day for the evening's performance at the Town Hall in Abergavenny. Immediately after his television appearance John rushed to Battersea Heliport and flew to the gig by helicopter.

The programme was transmitted on Saturday 29 June 1963 and John's comments about Elvis Presley upset a lot of Presley fans. He was critical about 'Devil in Disguise' and referred to Elvis as 'today's Bing Crosby', suggesting that he return to using rock 'n' roll material.

All four Beatles appeared on a special edition of the show, filmed from the stage of the Liverpool Empire on Saturday 7 December 1963. It was said that the viewing audience for this edition of *Juke Box Jury* was 23 million.

Julia

Song John wrote in tribute to his mother. He also mentioned Ocean Child in the lyrics, which is a reference to Yoko. It was a completely solo performance by John, recorded on 13 October 1968 and included on *The Beatles* double album.

Just Because

A hit for Lloyd Price in April 1957, when John was only sixteen. When he recorded the number for his *Rock 'n' Roll* album on Phil Spector's suggestion, John said, 'Remember this? I must have been thirteen when this came out? Or was it fourteen? Or was it twenty-two? I could have been twelve, actually.'

(Just Like) Starting Over

A track on the *Double Fantasy* album. The sound of a Japanese wishing bell preceded the track, which began life in 1979 as a demo disc recorded in the Dakota Building and called 'My Life'. He developed the number during his sojourn in Bermuda the following year.

John said he'd been inspired by a country song and this is possibly 'Starting Over Again', which topped the country charts in May 1980. Sung by Dolly Parton, it was penned by Donna Summer and relates the tale of a middle-aged couple who decided to get a divorce. John's theme was slightly different. It told of a middle-aged couple who wished to rekindle the flame of their early romance.

John commented, 'It was really called "Starting Over" but, while we were making it, people kept putting things out with the same title. There was a country-and-western hit called "Starting Over", so I added "(Just Like)" at the last minute.'

There was a line – 'It's time to spread our wings' – that John at one time considered scratching in case people thought it referred to Paul McCartney.

There was an air of nostalgia about the track with touches of Elvis Presley and Roy Orbison – and discussing it, John referred to himself as Elvis Orbison.

It was released as a single with Yoko's 'Kiss Kiss Kiss' on the flip. The UK release was on Friday 24 October and the US release on Monday 27 October 1980.

Just William
Generic name given to series of books about a mischievous boy called William, and to the first collection of stories in 1922, which made the name of the author, Richmal Crompton. As a boy John loved reading the books and probably identified with the character as he got up to mischief with his own gang of pals in the Woolton area of Liverpool. Richmal Crompton was one of the original names on the list the Beatles prepared for the *Sergeant Pepper* sleeve, although the author did not appear in the final tableau. It's fairly certain that it was John who placed the name on the initial list.

Kee, Jenny

Australian girl with Italian mother and Cantonese father who slept with John at the Sheraton Hotel in Kings Cross, Sydney, in June 1964. She smuggled her way into the hotel and when John spotted her dressed in a tartan suit and black mod boots he said, 'Would you like to come to a party?'

When they went to bed the first thing she removed were her contact lenses. 'What are those?' asked John.

Jenny was to say their lovemaking 'went on all night' and by the next day she'd decided she wanted to move to England. She heard noises of screams and giggles from another Beatle and a girl next door and John told her, 'He's with a Qantas hostess.'

She did move to England and met John again one night at the Speakeasy club. John was with his wife Cynthia, but when he saw Jenny he whispered two words in her ear: 'Contact lenses.'

Kelly, Frieda

Kelly was born in Ireland on 14 July 1945, and her family moved to Liverpool when she was thirteen. She was a Beatles fan who became their longest-lasting fan club secretary, taking over the position from her friend Bobbie Brown, the first secretary, in 1963.

However if it hadn't been for the intervention of John Lennon, the story might have been entirely different. Kelly joined Brian Epstein's staff at the NEMS shop in Whitechapel in 1962 as a shorthand typist. The following year she had a mishap in the office that resulted in thirty of Brian's letters being erased from a Dictaphone machine.

Brian was furious and sacked her on the spot. Fortunately for Frieda, John Lennon was with Brian at the time and made him see the funny side of things, with the result that Frieda was reinstated and went on to run their official fan club.

Keltner, Jim

An American drummer engaged by John as one of his regular sidemen in the early 70s. When he planned to tour America (a project that never came off), John intended to go on the road with Klaus Voormann, Yoko Ono, Eric Clapton and Keltner.

When two interviewers, Peter McCabe and Robert D Schonfeld, asked him if his choice of Keltner was any reflection on Ringo Starr's drumming, John told them, 'Oh, no, I love his drumming. I think Keltner is technically a bit better, but Ringo is still one of the best drummers in rock.'

Keltner was the drummer and percussionist on the albums *Imagine*, *Sometime in New York City*, *Mind Games*, *Walls and Bridges* and *Rock 'n' Roll*. In addition to playing drums on the single 'Happy Xmas (War Is Over)', he also played sleigh bells. Keltner was also the drummer on the 'Whatever Gets You Thru the Night' single.

Keltner performed as co-drummer with Ringo Starr on the Concert for Bangladesh and backed John and Yoko on their One-To-One concert.

John was not the only former Beatle to employ Keltner on recording sessions. He played drums on George Harrison's albums *Living in the Material World*, *Dark Horse* and *Extra Texture*. On George's promotional film for 'This Song', a track from the $33\frac{1}{3}$, album which was issued as a single, George staged a mock trial in which he handled his own defence – and Keltner appeared as the judge. Ringo also used Keltner on his albums *Ringo*, *Ringo's Rotogravure* and *Goodnight Vienna*.

Kennedy, Adrienne

An Afro-American playwright, born in 1931, who had the idea of writing a play based on John's two books. She originally gave the play to Tom Maschler, managing director of Jonathan Cape, who published the books. Maschler then passed it on to Victor Spinetti, who next showed it to Kenneth Tynan at the National Theatre. Victor Spinetti helped her to complete *The Lennon Play: In His Own Write,* and both of them received initial writer credit. Then Lennon went on holiday with Spinetti to Morocco on 29 December 1967 and he then came in on the project, receiving a writer credit. Kennedy's name was taken off the project, the excuse being that she wasn't a member of the Writers' Guild of Great Britain, but lengthy meetings were to take place at Apple and her name was reinstated, with credit going to all three. The play was presented at the Old Vic in June 1968 in a brief and critically unfavourable run.

Kenwood

Name of the 27-room mock-Tudor house in Weybridge, the 'stockbroker belt', in Surrey, one hour south of London, in the fashionable St George's Estate, where John bought a house in July 1964 on the advice of his accountant.

John paid £20,000 for Kenwood and coughed up another £40,000 for renovations. He engaged a decorator, Ken Partridge, to redesign the house and builders were working on the premises for months while John, Cynthia and Julian lived in one of the attic rooms. He also had a swimming pool built at a cost of £20,000. Originally, he'd wanted a mirrored surface at the bottom of the pool, but accepted a design of a gigantic eye painted at the bottom. He nicknamed the machine that cleaned the pool 'Percy'.

At the time he told the press, 'Weybridge won't do at all. I'm just stopping at it, like a bus stop.'

Apart from John, Julian and Cynthia, there was a small staff, which included a housekeeper, Dorothy Jarlett, and a chauffeur, Les Anthony. Eventually, Cynthia's mother Lil settled in the house with them.

Among the personal memorabilia and possessions John had at Weybridge were his first Rickenbacker guitar, which he'd bought in Germany on hire purchase; two pictures by Stuart Sutcliffe; a lump of stone which he'd been told was prehistoric – which he didn't believe; a stone frog, which he placed in the fireplace near the TV set because he liked looking at it; and a jukebox with 48 records, such as 'Some Other Guy' by the Big Three and 'Be-Bop-A-Lula'.

In his den, or playroom, he had a fruit machine, a pin table and a game table, a model race track – and four car number plates pinned to the wall. He had a large record collection covering a wide range of musical genres from classical to modern jazz – including odd items such as records by the Singing Postman. He had a studio, which had five tape recorders, a bath full of plants, a mellotron, a Farfisa organ and twelve guitars.

He owned three cars, had a pet cat named Mimi, a suit of armour called Sydney, a room full of model racing cars, a fruit machine, a gorilla suit (he told the journalist Maureen Cleave, 'I thought I might pop it on in the summer and drive around in the Ferrari'), a large bible he'd bought in Chester, a huge altar crucifix, a pair of crutches (a present from George Harrison) and five television sets.

He had books by Swift, Tennyson, Huxley, Tolstoy and Oscar Wilde. Other samples of his reading matter included *Little Women*, all the William books by Richmal Crompton, *Forty-One Years in India* by Field Marshal Lord Roberts and *Curiosities of Natural History* by Francis T Buckland.

His music room was at the top of the house. One wall housed a bank of tape machines, another an organ and piano (John had a Broadwood and a Bechstein piano at Weybridge) and a third a mellotron. There was a garden at the back of the house over-looking the hill and a terrace edged by a stone wall, six feet high in places. John used to sit on part of the wall he called his 'thinking place' to meditate.

The idyllic family home became the setting of marital conflict in 1968 when Cynthia arrived home from a holiday in Greece with Jennie Boyd and Alexis Mardas to discover Yoko in her home. The previous evening the pair had made a tape that became the *Two Virgins* album, then climbed into bed and made love. When Cynthia arrived, even though she was 'shattered, not angry', she suggested that John join them for dinner in London. He said no. Fifteen minutes later she left. Cynthia returned three days later and Yoko had gone, but the marriage was over.

After a holiday in Italy, Cynthia and her mother confronted John and Yoko at Kenwood and John suggested that Cynthia, Julian and her mother return to Kenwood while he and Yoko moved into Ringo's flat in Montague Square.

King, Ben E

Famous lead singer with the Drifters, whose first major hit was 'Save the Last Dance For Me'. He also found success as a solo artist and topped the charts with numbers such as 'Spanish Harlem' and 'Stand By Me'.

Both John and Julian Lennon have recorded 'Stand By Me'. John had sent King messages saying that he loved his versions of songs and King later discovered that when John recorded 'Stand By Me' he'd wanted King to come in and record it with him – but King had been on tour at the time.

For his *Rough Edge* album, King recorded John's 'Come Together'. He also recorded 'Don't Let Me Down'.

When King met Julian he told him, 'Your father was not only a fabulous artist within the industry but he was also a marvellous and well-respected songwriter. And I want you to know that.'

King, Stephen

Bestselling author who rose to fame with his first novel *Carrie*. His books are mainly horror tales and over two dozen of his works have been filmed. Stanley Kubrick filmed his novel *The Shining*. King said that the inspiration for the title came from the John Lennon/Plastic Ono Band single 'Instant Karma!'. The author was impressed by the line 'We all shine on' and decided to call the novel *The Shine*. However, he changed it to *The Shining* when he discovered that the word 'shine' was a derogatory word for Negro in America.

King's novel *Misery* told about how an author was plagued by an obsessive fan. King himself became the subject of a stalker called Steven Lightfoot. Lightfoot parked a van near King's house with a sign that read, 'Photos prove it's Stephen King, not Mark David Chapman, getting John Lennon's autograph'. Lightfoot became convinced that King shot Lennon and became so intense that the author had to obtain a court order to keep him away from his house.

King, Tony

A British public relations man, who originally worked for George Martin and later became general manager of the Apple label in America. He moved to America and John hired him to advise on his *Mind Games* album. When John was in Los Angeles during his 'lost weekend', May Pang asserts that he became uncontrollably drunk and had to be hustled into a car by Phil Spector and a bodyguard. They took him to the house where he and May were staying, which was the home of Lou Adler, a record producer. John was taken struggling into the bedroom.

Spector and the bodyguard came downstairs and told May that John was under control. Then she heard the sounds of breaking glass and John staggered to the top of the stairs shouting 'Yoko! You slant-eyed bitch, you wanted to get rid of me.' And he charged at May, who fled from the house. She phoned Tony King because John liked him, and asked him to come to the house. King arrived and John collapsed in his arms and began to cry. They took him back inside the house and noticed that all Adler's platinum albums had been smashed and John had also thrown an antique chair out of the window.

King also took John to Las Vegas to see Fats Domino, who was appearing at the Flamingo Hotel. Domino came over to John and said, 'Ooh, I'm really honoured to meet you.' John replied, 'No, you're the man I've come to see. You shouldn't be honoured to meet me. I should be honoured to meet you.'

Kirkwood, JR
The Liverpool registrar who presided over the wedding of Alfred ('Freddie') Lennon and Julia Stanley, John's parents.

Kirchherr, Astrid
A blonde German girl with elfin features who became engaged to the early Beatles' bass guitarist, Stuart Sutcliffe.

Astrid was born in the Altona suburb of Hamburg in 1938 and began to study dress design at the Meister Schule. While there she changed her course from dress design to photography and joined a class run by Rheinhardt Wolf, who felt she had such potential as a photographer that he hired her as his assistant.

During this time she met Klaus Voormann, who became her boyfriend. Klaus then moved into the attic room in the house at Eimsbutler Strasse where Astrid lived with her mother Nielsa.

One night they had an argument and Klaus drifted into the St Pauli district and was attracted by the sound of Rory Storm and the Hurricanes at the Kaiserkeller. He went inside the club and became even more impressed by the group that followed the Hurricanes: the Beatles. Two days later he brought Astrid and other friends along to see them.

Astrid began taking photographs of the group, one of which became the first of her pictures to be published and was featured on the front page of *Mersey Beat* in July 1961 with the story of the Beatles recording in Hamburg – a picture that Brian Epstein, the Beatles' manager, couldn't have failed to miss. After the photo session she took the Beatles home to meet her mum and have some tea. At the time there was some difficulty in communication as Astrid could barely speak English. She began to seek help from Klaus in conversations between them and Klaus soon coached her in the new language.

Astrid and Stuart fell in love. Astrid's mother showed concern when she found out about the conditions in which Stuart and the other boys were living at the Bambi Kino and invited Stuart to take residence in the attic that Klaus had now vacated. Two months after they met, in late November 1960, Astrid and Stuart became engaged, buying each other a ring in the German fashion.

While the other members of the Beatles returned to Liverpool in December 1960, Stuart opted to remain in Hamburg with Astrid. She soon began to influence his style of dress, making clothes for him, including a collarless jacket in the Pierre Cardin style. Astrid also wore leather clothes and Stuart began to wear leather too, although the fact that the other members of the Beatles began to wear leather was due to the fact that the waiters at the clubs they worked in usually wore leather jackets.

Astrid also changed Stuart's hairstyle, combing it forward in a style then popular in France. She had also styled Klaus's hair like that. Another friend, Jurgen Vollmer, was later to style John's and Paul's hair in a similar fashion when they visited him in Paris. Pete Best didn't adopt the style because he wasn't asked to.

On the Beatles' second visit to the Top Ten Club in the Reeperbahn, Stuart had returned to Liverpool and then set off again for Hamburg a few weeks before the group's arrival. The Beatles were to back Tony Sheridan. At the club, Astrid and her friends continued to watch the band, and, whenever Astrid arrived, Stuart would sing to her. This irked Paul and one night there was a fracas on stage.

Peter Best recalls, 'Stu would look at Astrid when she was in the audience and play to her. He was madly in love with the girl, so what was wrong with that? He took some gentle banter from us, but Paul kept winding him up. On this particular night Astrid was there and Paul said something. I don't actually know what the remark was because Paul was playing piano on the other side of the drum rostrum. Stu took his bass off and it wasn't with a view to giving it to anyone. He put it down and the next thing, the two were swinging at one another.

'When it happened, the audience seemed bewildered, obviously thinking, Hang on, this isn't "*mach schau*", this is really happening. Astrid was horrified.' ('*Mach schau*' means 'make show', and this was a reference to a club owner who had urged the Beatles to do this after he had seen the stage style of another performer. See **Beatles**.)

Stuart was to leave the Beatles and remain in Hamburg. Having been unsuccessful in his application to rejoin Liverpool College of Art to do an art teacher's diploma course, he studied under Eduardo Paolozzi in Hamburg, turning out an impressive body of work.

Together with Astrid he visited Liverpool. When Stuart's sister Pauline saw Astrid she thought she looked like an angel. She commented, 'We were quite stunned by her. She was like nothing we'd ever seen before, ever. She arrived with one orchid in her hand for my mother – and she didn't always wear trousers: she sometimes wore skirts and what we now call opaque stockings and little Italian shoes … She had such wonderful features. She looked elfin and utterly feminine, even when she was wearing black leather pants.'

Back in Hamburg, Stuart continued to dedicate himself to his painting, although he preferred to work in the attic room, just as, in Liverpool, he often worked in the Percy Street flat rather than in the college. One day he fell down the narrow attic stairs and injured his head, which caused concern for Nielsa Kirchherr. From that point on he began to suffer excruciating headaches and bouts of blindness and, despite visits to doctors, no trace of the cause of the problem was found. When Astrid and Stuart visited Liverpool at Christmas 1961, his friends noticed how frail and pale he looked. Paul's brother Mike McCartney said, 'When I met him in a jazz club when he was home on holiday a few weeks ago he said he had a feeling that something was going to happen to him when he went back to Hamburg. He was obviously worried and nervous.'

In February 1962 Stuart collapsed during his class at art college. He was taken home, but never returned. Nielsa suggested he move from the attic and nursed him in her bedroom downstairs and special treatments such as massage under water were undertaken, but the headaches and blackouts continued. Astrid remembered Stuart asking her mother to have him buried in a white coffin. On 10 April 1962 Astrid's mother phoned her at work to ask her to come home straight away. Stuart had collapsed and an ambulance had been called for. He died in Astrid's arms on the way to hospital.

The Beatles were due to fly into Hamburg to appear at the Star Club. John, Paul and Pete arrived first as George had been ill. He was to follow on another flight with Brian Epstein and Millie Sutcliffe.

Astrid was waiting at the airport to tell them the devastating news.

After Stuart's death she became desolate with grief. She was to say, 'It was John who saved me. He convinced me that I shouldn't behave like a widow. "Make up your mind," he said. "You either live or die, you can't be in the middle." '

A few years later, when John and Cynthia took a belated honeymoon in Paris and booked into the George Cinque Hotel, they received a note from Astrid saying she was in Paris with a girlfriend. They called her up, arranged to meet and enjoyed a wild night out in the artists' quarter of the city. They drank so much wine they staggered back to Astrid's lodgings for coffee, but began to drink even more wine and weren't in any state to return to the George Cinque, so all four crawled into the narrow bed together and fell asleep.

Over the next few years Astrid was to meet up with the Beatles on a number of occasions. She went to Liverpool to take photographs of the city, the Cavern and various groups there, and her photographs were to form the basis of a book, *Liverpool Days*, published by Genesis Publications in 1994.

Astrid also visited the Beatles on the set of *A Hard Day's Night*, and on Sunday 26 June 1966 was one of the group of friends who dropped by to see them when they appeared at the Ernst Merck Halle in Hamburg. On that occasion she presented John with some of Stuart's letters.

Five years after Stuart's death Astrid married Gibson Kemp, the Liverpool drummer who had replaced Ringo Starr in Rory Storm and the Hurricanes, but the marriage ended after seven years.

Astrid did not make a career for herself in photography, nor did she exploit her close relationship with the Beatles. Over the years, as their success grew, many newspapers used her photographs without acknowledging credit or paying a fee. At times she worked as a cleaner and even became a dancer in a lesbian bar.

She married for a second time, to a Bavarian businessman called Fink, but that also proved unsuccessful. For a time she ran a hotel on the German–Danish border for Klaus Voormann, but was forced to quit in 1991 and had to return to Hamburg penniless, with nowhere to live. A friend offered her a flat and that was when she worked as a cleaner.

Fortunately, she was approached to become consultant on *Backbeat*, a British film about her love affair with Stuart, and was reputed to have been paid £100,000.

Their romance was immortalised in the film, which was released in 1994, with Astrid portrayed by the American actress Sheryl Lee. Most of the people associated with the Beatles during the period covered by the movie believe it is as much fiction as fact and gives a glossy, overromanticised view of a genuine love story but one that seemed to be on the wane at the time of Stuart's death.

Much of the publicity surrounding *Backbeat* seems to suggest that Stuart and John were naïve and unsophisticated when they went to Hamburg. The film synopsis describes them as Teddy Boys (John may have been, but Stuart certainly wasn't). The synopsis also has John saying to Stuart that Astrid was out of his league. This suggests that Stuart had never been with a girl like Astrid before. On the contrary, Stuart attended Liverpool College of Art – and Astrid attended the Hamburg equivalent. While Stuart was at art college he went out with a number of attractive girls and the art college girls in Liverpool were as much into the arts and culture as Astrid was.

Other interviews surrounding the *Backbeat* release made out that the uncultivated young lads knew nothing about art and culture and people like Jean Cocteau. Nothing could be further from the truth in Stuart and John's case. Stuart was a dedicated artist and knew far more about painting than his new friends in Hamburg. At Liverpool College of Art, their group of friends continually discussed the Beat Generation, San Franciscan poets and the Angry Young Men, and watched films by Jean Cocteau, Salvador Dali and Luis Bunel at the college film shows, while Paul and George were at Liverpool Institute and Pete at Liverpool Collegiate, acknowledged as the city's two premier grammar schools. The urge to illustrate them as uncultured, semiliterate, working-class yobs who were transformed culturally by the young 'Exis' (Existentialists) in Hamburg is one more fiction in the Beatles' history.

In the late 1980s, Astrid also gained a manager, Ulf Kruger. Ulf has managed to gain recognition for Astrid's work and ensured that she is paid her rightful due for any pictures reproduced. She has also become a highly popular figure at Beatles conventions around the world and has published a number of books of her early photographic work.

Kiss Kiss Kiss
Number penned by Yoko Ono which was included on the *Double Fantasy* album and was also issued as the flip side of the '(Just Like) Starting Over' single.

KHJ-AM
A Los Angeles radio station, which was a Top 40 station with four million listeners. During a week in which they were holding a 'Superstar Guest DJ Week', John appeared live on the station's breakfast show from 6 a.m. to 8 a.m. on Friday 27 September 1974. It was during his promotion of the *Walls and Bridges* album and he played a 58-second spot for the album and also read out commercials. Some were for Tobias Casuals sportswear and for a Tower Records plug he said, 'You'll find thousands of your favourite LPs and tapes and a few drunk pop stars.' John performed his task as guest DJ alone and he also announced the

station's phone number, 520-1974, to enable listeners to ask him questions and request songs. The audience mostly comprised teenagers and he had requests from boys asking for Beatles numbers and asking him questions about guitars and his song lyrics. One girl proposed to him over the phone and he said, 'Sure, give me a green card.' When answering the phone calls he used various pseudonyms including Dr Winston O'Boogie, John F Lennon, Fred Zimmerman and Richard Nixon. When he used the name Doris Day a woman caller announced, 'Rock Hudson is on the line.' After he'd played 'Surprise, Surprise' he said, 'Close your legs, Elton – it was very high.'

Klein, Allen

A music publisher and artists' manager, born in Newark, New Jersey, on 18 December 1931. Klein was the son of a poor Jewish butcher and when his mother died of cancer when he was only two years old he was placed in a Hebrew orphanage, along with two of his three elder sisters because his father couldn't run the business and take care of the family at the same time. Klein was in the orphanage for ten years before he was returned to his father.

After a brief spell in the army he worked for a newspaper distributor in New Jersey while attending evening classes in accounting at Upsala College. He then audited for the company handling Bobby Darin's account. Darin was attending a party held in his honour by Capitol Records when Klein strolled up to him and gave him a cheque for $100,000. Darin said, 'What's this for?' and Klein said, 'For nothing.' He'd found a six-figure discrepancy in the audit and got Capitol Records to give him a cheque for the money.

Darin fired his accountants and hired Klein, who then resigned from the company and set up his own business and also launched his own music-publishing companies. He became manager to Sam Cooke and Bobby Vinton and later represented many artists, including Herman's Hermits, the Animals, the Dave Clark Five and the Rolling Stones.

Klein and his wife Betty created the Allen and Betty Klein Corporation, known as ABKCO, which was based at 1700 Broadway, New York. His talent for squeezing royalty payments from record companies earned him the tag 'the Robin Hood of Pop'.

One New York federal district court found him guilty on ten counts of failing to file employees' withholding taxes. He gained control of Cameo Parkway Records, but stockholders accused him of impropriety and sued him. The New York Stock Exchange suspended trading on the company and he was investigated. By that time he had fifty lawsuits and the IRS (Internal Revenue Service) was also after him for failure to file tax records.

Eric Easton and Andrew Loog Oldham, managers of the Rolling Stones, asked him to renegotiate the group's Decca contract. He did so, gaining an advance of royalties of $1,250,000 and in the process also getting rid of Easton and Oldham and taking over the management of the Stones himself. Klein had by then set his mind on getting the Beatles, whom he regarded as the greatest rock 'n' roll group in the world. At one time Mick Jagger introduced him to John, who told Klein that he didn't want to end up broke 'like Mickey Rooney'.

Klein saw his opportunity to move in after John had given an interview to the editor of *Disc* magazine, Ray Coleman, which followed information from an Apple accountant, Stephen Maltz, that the company was in dire financial straits. John told Coleman, 'Apple's losing money every week … if it carries on like this, all of us will be broke in the next six months.' This was an exaggeration, as the royalties John was earning from song-writing and records would have assured him of financial security.

Klein managed to obtain John's telephone number from Derek Taylor. He phoned him and arranged to meet John, together with Yoko, at the Harlequin Room at the Dorchester Hotel in London on Tuesday 28 January 1969. Klein knew how to play John and showed off his knowledge of the Beatles' music, played on his own background as an orphan, comparing it to John's early life, and he poured on the flattery.

John was completely taken in by Klein's background and commented, 'He was an orphan – he never had his parents. His mother died when he was a kid and he's as neurotic as me or any other person that's got no parents. He's a capitalist, but that's all. That's his worst sin. I think that's a bad enough sin, but that's it.'

Klein had also researched Yoko's background and was careful to include her in all aspects of his conversation, and even promised to set up a major exhibition of her work in America, which resulted in John saying later, 'We had him because Klein was the only one Yoko liked.'

Yoko was also to say, 'On personal terms I have nothing against him. He's an orphan, and I would never discredit him for just that reason. He's a guy who's made good from that sort of start, and it's a big thing.'

Following the Dorchester meeting, John sent a note to Sir Joseph Lockwood, then chairman of EMI: 'Dear Sir Joe, From now on Allen Klein handles all my stuff!' When Klein did have a meeting with Lockwood, he was so abrasive that Lockwood threw him out of his office.

Klein told the *Daily Telegraph* on Friday 21 March 1969 that he would receive 20 per cent of all monies collected by Apple other than under their existing recording contracts, though he would still receive 20 per cent of any increase he negotiated on those contract figures.

On Saturday September 20 1969 the *Daily Telegraph* reported that Klein had renegotiated the Beatles' existing contracts with EMI in the USA, Canada and Mexico, subject to their recording a minimum of two albums a year until 1976. 'If they do, all new albums will earn them 58 cents each during the next three years and 72 cents to 1972. This compares with around 6 cents per album before 1966 and 39 cents in 1966/69. Reissues of the earliest recordings will now attract a 56-cent royalty per record until 1972 and 72 cents after that.'

John said, 'I wanted him as my manager. I introduced him to the other three. But if Paul is trying to suggest that I was rushing them and pushing him down their throats, this is a wrong impression.

'I thought that Paul would agree with us in the end after he had seen the benefit of Klein's work. I would have liked him to have agreed with us before the ABKCO agreement was signed, but I thought he was being unreasonable towards the other three of us, and knew that in the last resort his signature was not necessary.'

Klein liked to generate a tough image and his Christmas card for 1969 read, 'Yea, though I walk through the Valley of the Shadow of Death, I will fear no evil, because I'm the biggest bastard in the valley.'

He immediately became involved in a number of complicated manoeuvres. At the time, John Eastman, brother of Linda McCartney, had been negotiating to buy NEMS, which represented the Beatles' management company and deducted commission from their royalties (they were entitled to take 25 per cent of the Beatles' record royalties for a further nine years). Eastman was just about to acquire the company for £1 million and EMI was prepared to lend them the entire amount as an advance against royalties. When Klein met the four Beatles on Wednesday January 29 he advised them not to buy NEMS until he had the opportunity of examining John's financial affairs. George and Ringo supported him and also asked him to examine their finances. A frustrated Paul walked out on the meeting.

This delay and the entry of Klein on to the scene lost them control of NEMS at the moment when Eastman had virtually acquired it. Another company, Triumph Investments, a City merchant bank, had offered £1 million for NEMS, but Clive Epstein felt that he was honour-bound to let the Beatles take over the company. Leonard Richenberg of Triumph Investments, who had made the original offer, had originally approached Clive about acquiring NEMS.

The delay caused by Klein's wishing to study the Beatles' accounts led Eastman to make a wrong move. He wrote to Clive Epstein and part of his letter read, 'As you know Mr Allen Klein is doing an audit of the Beatles' affairs vis-à-vis NEMS and Nemperor Holdings Ltd. When this has been completed I suggest we meet to discuss the results of Mr Klein's audit as well as the propriety of the negotiations surrounding the nine-year agreement between EMI, the Beatles and NEMS.'

This letter infuriated Epstein, who replied, 'Before any meeting takes place, please be good enough to let me know precisely what you mean by the phrase "the propriety of the negotiations surrounding the nine-year agreement between EMI, the Beatles and NEMS".'

It was unfortunate that he sent the note because it probably lost them control of NEMS, although what he pointed out was accurate. The contract with Brian Epstein and the Beatles was about to lapse and Brian was afraid that they wouldn't sign another with him – and Paul McCartney had actually said they didn't intend to re-sign with Brian – without telling them Epstein renegotiated a new contract with EMI, which would give his company 25 per cent of the royalties for the next nine years, even though his contract with them had expired.

Klein then began to boast that he could obtain NEMS for the Beatles 'for nothing' on the strength of money owed to them on back payments. Tired of waiting, with the deadline he had given them now past, Clive sold NEMS to Triumph on 17 February 1969.

Klein then went to see Richenberg, confident that he could get them to relinquish the 25 per cent of the Beatles' earnings, saying that NEMS owed the Beatles arrears stretching as far back as 1966, and he would forget these in exchange for Triumph's dropping the percentage. Richenberg threw him out of his office.

A total of £1.3 million in royalty payments was due to be paid by EMI. Under the terms of the contract they now had to pay it to Triumph, who would deduct their 25 per cent and give the Beatles the rest. On the other hand, the Beatles demanded EMI pay them direct. In a dilemma, Sir Joseph Lockwood froze the money. Eventually, a deal was arranged in which the Beatles paid Triumph £800,000, plus a quarter of the £1.3 million that EMI was holding. As the Beatles themselves still owned 10 per cent of NEMS, Triumph would buy that off them in exchange for £500,000 of the bank's stock.

The Beatles were now free of NEMS.

They next tried to wrest control of Northern Songs. Lew Grade was trying to acquire the company on behalf of ATV and he was the former agent of Dick James, who owned 23 per cent of the company. The balance of power lay in the hands of a consortium of City investors who were apprehensive of Klein's reputation. He assured them he would have nothing to do with the running of Northern Songs and they finally agreed to support the Beatles in gaining control of the company. Then John Lennon made objections that the consortium would possibly interfere in the company, saying, 'I'm sick of being fucked about by men in suits sitting on their fat arses in the City.' The consortium immediately sold their shares to Grade; the Beatles then lost control of their songs for good.

On Thursday 8 May 1969 John, George and Ringo signed a

management contract with Klein. Klein had demanded 25 per cent of their earnings, which they were willing to give, but Paul prevented them from doing this, suggesting that he receive only 20 per cent of income that he actually generated on their behalf. Even though Paul was not a signatory to the contract, they all agreed on his suggestion.

Klein then went into Apple Corps in what became known as his 'reign of terror' and virtually reduced the company to a royalty-collecting agency. All the staff who were qualified or who Klein considered might pose a threat to him were ousted. They included Ron Kass and Peter Asher of Apple's record division, which had sold 16 million records on the label and was a successful venture. Klein replaced the experienced Kass with Jack Oliver, an assistant with no experience. Alistair Taylor, the general manager who had been with the Beatles from the beginning, was ejected, along with Dennis O'Dell, head of Apple Films, and Brian Lewis, head of the contracts department.

Klein's plan was to sack anyone with any influence who he thought would come between him and the Beatles – and that meant every executive with the company. Two of the Beatles' closest associates were Neil Aspinall and Peter Brown, who were both directors of the company. It was a formality at the annual general meeting that all directors resigned and they were then re-elected. When the AGM came and they resigned, they weren't re-elected. However, the Beatles found they couldn't function without them and they were reinstated.

Klein did, however, renegotiate their royalty deal with EMI Records. He was in a strong position to do this as their EMI recording deal was coming to an end.

He was to claim that he had increased their earnings during the first eighteen months of management to the tune of £9 million. This was true – but a great deal of money had come from the sale of their shares of Northern Songs to ATV, and Brian Epstein had been responsible for their having the shares.

When John received an offer to go to Toronto and quickly form a band with Klaus Voormann, Eric Clapton and Andy White, he was delighted. On his return he told Paul he was through with the Beatles. 'I'm leaving the group. I've had enough. I want a divorce, like my divorce from Cynthia,' he told Paul. But Paul didn't think he was serious and regarded it as a similar event to when George had left the group during the recording of *Let It Be*.

However, things came to a head as a result of *Let it Be*. The numerous tapes, originally recorded under the title of 'Get Back', were in a mess and no one felt inclined to make the effort to turn them into a workable album. Klein brought in Phil Spector.

When Paul heard an acetate of the album he was stunned to listen to what Spector had done to his number 'The Long and Winding Road'. He had steeped it in his 'wall of sound', with a violin and horn section and a choir. Paul was horrified. He attempted to contact Spector but couldn't get hold of him, so he sent a note to Klein demanding that his original version of the number be restored. Klein ignored him and the version Paul hated was included on the album. This was the final straw. When it came to someone taking control of his music, Paul realised he couldn't go on.

He received legal advice that pointed out that the only way he could rid himself of Klein would be by taking legal action against him and against his fellow Beatles.

Reluctantly, he set the wheels in motion and the Beatles as a partnership was dissolved.

In 1971 Klein was to say, 'The Beatles have not been prejudiced by my dealings. They have greatly benefited. The assets of the Beatles partnership are in no way in jeopardy.'

Linda McCartney was to say, 'Klein will get his in the end.'

With hindsight one can see the irony of John's words apropos of Klein in 1969: 'He knew all about us and our music. I knew right away he was the man for us.' Ironic because by 1973, when Klein's contract ended, the romance was over.

The official expiry date of the contract between John, George and Ringo and Allen Klein was Saturday 31 March 1973 and Klein made the statement that his company ABKCO was 'cutting its links with Apple and with the former Beatles John Lennon, George Harrison and Ringo Starr on Monday April 2 1973'.

On Sunday 1 April 1973 John, George and Ringo announced that they had split from Klein. Five days later, on Friday 6 April, John Fielding interviewed John and Yoko for London Weekend Television's *Weekend World* programme. When asked why the three ex-Beatles had decided to shed Klein, John replied, 'There are many reasons why we finally gave him the push, although I don't want to go into the details of it. Let's say possibly Paul's suspicions were right ... and the time was right.'

Fielding pointed out that Klein's contract was up for renewal. John answered, 'The contract expired I think in February, and we were extending it at first on a monthly basis and then finally on a two-week basis, and then finally we pushed the boat out.'

Fielding asked John when he had finally decided that Klein wasn't the man for them and John replied, 'Well, you're concluding that I thought he was something. My position has always been a "devil and the deep-blue sea", and at that time I do whatever I feel is right. Although I haven't been particularly happy personally for quite a long time with the situation, I didn't want to make any quick moves and I wanted to see if maybe something would work out.'

In June of 1973 Allen Klein sued John and Apple for $508,000.

The final settlement, which rid the Beatles of Klein, was for more than $4 million.

There was litigation between George Harrison and Allen Klein over the number 'He's So Fine'. In New York in November 1990, Judge Richard Owen gave his decision. He said that ABKCO would own the song for the world, except for the USA, UK and Canada, where Harrison would own it. Harrison would pay Klein $270,020.

The litigation for copyright infringement over George's composition 'My Sweet Lord' began in February 1971 and was instigated by Bright Tunes Music Ltd, who said that the 1963 Chiffons hit 'He's So Fine' had been plagiarised by George's song. Klein was representing George at the time. Klein was later dismissed, but in 1973 had bought Bright Tunes after George had been found guilty, but before damages were determined. Klein received lower damages than he anticipated because the court felt that Klein's act was a breach of duty to his former client.

Also, in February 1971, Klein was convicted on ten counts of 'unlawfully failing to make and file return of Federal income taxes and FICA taxes withheld from employees wages'.

Klein was also jailed for two months for tax evasion in May

1979 – this related to income he'd taken from illegal sales of the album *The Concert for Bangladesh*.

Knight, Curtis

American musician, half black, half Blackfoot Indian, who was reared on a reservation. He first met John while he was touring Britain with Jimi Hendrix and commented, 'I felt that John was someone of tremendous magnitude.' He was also to point out, 'Not many of John's fans realise it, but he was partially responsible for getting Hendrix to appear at the Monterey Pop Festival. The Beatles are actually the ones who suggested to the selection committee that Jimi be asked to perform.'

He was finally able to appear on stage with John in 1971. He commented, 'Like John, I am the type of creative person who is plugged into what is happening around me. In my mind I must have gone through some of the same things he did. I was upset by the killings at Kent State [University], and by what went down at Attica State Prison.

'I sat down and wrote a tune and called it "Attica". This song reflected my inner feelings, and though I was not able to do anything directly, it was a means to an end that allowed me to bare my soul.'

Pointing out that he and John were writing about the same subject simultaneously, he added, 'This was just one of those strange coincidences that sometimes take place. Like John, I've believed in making statements through my music. This way there is always a chance you'll get the attention of people. It was my idea to donate the proceeds from my record to benefit the victims of Attica. In addition, I organised a benefit concert at the Apollo Theatre in Harlem and decided it would be nice to get John and Yoko to participate.'

Knight called the Dakota Building and spoke to the Lennons, who immediately agreed to participate. 'I'm absolutely positive that this was the first time any of the Beatles had ever performed at the Apollo, which is an historical landmark in an all-black neighbourhood,' he said. 'The Lennons didn't get paid for their appearance. Instead they donated their share of that night's earnings to the inmates.

'It was the only time I shared a dressing room with a Beatle. Yoko was there as well as John, and we had a lot in common to talk about.'

John and Yoko were so moved by Knight's song about Attica that they sent him an acetate copy of their version of 'Attica', which they were still in the process of writing.

Knowland, Nick

A cinematographer Yoko approached to work on the film *Rape*. At the time she was pregnant and he was called to meet John and Yoko in her hospital room, which the Lennons were using as an office. They even had an editing machine in the room. Knowland then went on to work on other films for the couple, including *Apotheosis*, *Bed Peace Montreal* and *Imagine*.

Kosh, John

When Yoko was in hospital following her miscarriage, one of her visitors was the graphic designer John Kosh, who was currently working at the Royal Opera House. She suggested that he design a book that would include some of the most vitriolic of the hate mail she'd been receiving. Kosh saw that the letters were spiteful and ludicrous, saying, 'She was being blamed for World War Two and the death of British soldiers.'

She also asked him to design the Aspen Arts Box for the Aspen Arts Society in America. It was a cardboard box of works by several artists. A recording of the baby's final heartbeats represented John and Yoko.

When John and Yoko planned their *Wedding Album*, John contacted Kosh, who was now one of Apple's art directors. John explained that they wanted to include a piece of cake. Kosh persuaded them that they had to settle for a photograph. They also wanted some photos from the wedding itself, a copy of the marriage certificate and a doily.

Kosh said, 'I suggested they include a jigsaw puzzle of the *Two Virgins* picture, where the piece with John's cock fit where Yoko's vagina was and the piece with her vagina fit where John's cock should be. EMI refused to approve it.'

Kosh was later to design the *Let It Be* album package and three album sleeves for Ringo Starr.

Kraft, Dean

A man who claims to have suddenly developed psychic powers in 1976. Yoko, who was interested in numerous aspects of the psychic world, became his first celebrity client when she arranged for him to visit her in the Dakota Building in New York.

He recalled that she invited him into her large kitchen and told him she had been suffering from severe fatigue. She sat on a chair and he began the laying-on-of-hands routine. Yoko said she felt intense energy moving into her and began to feel very strong, with her physical rigidity beginning to ease. Yoko then invited him to meet John in the apartment and he arrived with Harry Nilsson.

Yoko told him that John didn't really believe that Kraft could help Yoko physically, that it was all psychological. So, to challenge John's scepticism, Kraft decided on a demonstration.

He recalled, 'Yoko kept a dish filled with candies, and I asked everyone to be quiet while I sat near it and concentrated. I focused on four separate candies and psychokinetically moved them toward me until each dropped over the side of the dish on the table. The candies moved toward my outstretched fingers, then scattered to every corner of the room. Everyone was gasping. John attempted to repeat my demonstration, trying to move the candy by staring at it and moving his hands, but he had no luck. John decided to book regular sessions for himself. After I treated him, he described feelings of light-headedness, euphoria and great relaxation.'

Kramer, Billy J.

A Liverpool singer who had several major hits in the early to mid-60s with Lennon & McCartney numbers. He also topped the British charts with the Mort Shuman/John Leslie MacFarland number 'Little Children'.

Billy, whose real name was William Ashton, was a popular local singer fronting a group called the Coasters. Brian Epstein, who already managed the Beatles and Gerry & the Pacemakers, paid Billy's manager, a pensioner called Ted Knibbs, a nominal fee to transfer the management.

The Coasters refused to turn professional so Brian secured the services of a Manchester group called the Dakotas to back him. Although the partnership seemed a success on the surface, Billy didn't get on with his new musicians.

He recalls how he originally came by the 'J' in his name.

Shortly after signing with Epstein, he was asked to call in at the Nems offices. Brian was present with John Lennon. Billy was asked how he would like a 'J' added to his name. 'It was John's idea,' said Epstein, 'He thought it made the name flow better.'

Billy agreed to the suggestion, but asked, 'What do I tell people if they ask me what the "J" stands for?'

'John has suggested Julian,' said Epstein.

However, Billy considered that the name sounded effeminate and decided to keep it quiet, unaware of John's secret marriage to Cynthia and the fact that he had a son called Julian.

Kushi

A macrobiotic master. John became interested in Kushi's macrobiotic dishes and bought tapes of Kushi and his recipes, together with cookery books, a steamer and a wok to prepare the macrobiotic dishes.

Lady Mitchell Hall

A concert hall at Cambridge University, England, that was the setting for John and Yoko's first public performance together on Sunday 2 March 1969 before an audience of approximately 500 people.

Yoko had been invited to perform an avant-garde jazz concert and the organisers hadn't realised that John would accompany her. They asked her if she would be bringing a band and she said yes, but didn't tell them that John would also be performing.

John was to say, 'The people were looking and saying, "Is it? Is it?" I just had a guitar and an amp, and that was the first time I'd played just pure feedback. The audience was very weird: they were all these sort of intellectual artsy-fartsies from Cambridge, and they were uptight because the rock-and-roll guy was there.'

Yoko emerged on stage and began singing in her free-form style – yells, groans, screams, piercing shrieks, while behind her, way back, almost in the darkness, John produced a series of feedback sounds from his guitar.

Towards the end of the performance two other musicians joined them, John Tchikai on saxophone and John Stevens on percussion.

Tchikai said he'd played the first part of the concert with European and South African free-jazz musicians. Before the concert John and Yoko had arrived and asked them if they would play with him. He and John Stevens agreed.

Tchikai commented, 'So the A-side of the John Lennon LP *Unfinished Music No. 2: Life with the Lions* was created. The song "Cambridge 1969" was influenced by Yoko Ono. It wasn't what you expect of a Beatle, but we were jazz musicians and this was Yoko Ono's way of music. The first part, Ono and Lennon played alone, John Lennon played the feedback guitar and Yoko Ono sang.'

The concert was recorded and issued as Side One of their *Unfinished Music No. 2: Life with the Lions* album, under the title *Cambridge 1969*. The side lasted for 26 minutes and 30 seconds.

L'assassinat de John Lennon
A French-language book by Pierre Merle, published by Fleuve Noir in 1993. The book is divided into four sections. The first covers the events in New York on 8 December 1980. The second comprises a portrait of John. The third poses the question: was the killer manipulated by the CIA? And the final section asks: was his killer a fool or a psychopath?

Last will and testament
John signed his last will and testament on Monday 12 November 1979. It was apparently vague and unstructured. Yoko Ono was the only heir named in the will and received half of his estate outright. Regarding the other half, the will stated, 'I give, devise and bequeath all the rest, residue and remainder of my estate, wheresoever situate, to the Trustees under a Trust Agreement dated November 12, 1979, which I signed with my wife, Yoko Ono, and Eli Garber as trustees.'

The will concluded, 'In witness whereof, I have subscribed and sealed and do publish and declare these presents, as and for my Last Will and Testament, this 12th day of November, 1979.'

Eli Garber was his accountant at the time.

The will was filed at the Manhattan surrogate court. It basically meant that half his estate would go to Yoko and the remainder into a trust fund for Sean set up by both John and Yoko.

The will also showed some of John's assets, which included

luxury apartments, a number of mansions, a 62-foot yacht, a twin-engine plane and a 25 per cent interest in Apple Records. The properties in the Dakota Building in New York were estimated at $1.5 million, the seven-bedroomed house in Palm Beach, Florida, at $700,000, the house in Cold Spring Harbor, Long Island, at $450,000 and dairy farms in upstate New York at $1 million.

Early in 1980, a British newspaper reported that John was on a fantastic spending spree. 'He acts like he owns Fort Knox,' it said, and related how, four years before, he had bought an apartment in the Dakota Building and now had six, totalling fifty rooms, which together took up five floors of the block.

Maintenance alone cost $40,000 a month. John had also bought a huge mansion overlooking the Atlantic in Palm Beach at $750,000 nine months before, and they also had a mansion on Long Island, NY, costing $850,000, an expensive Mercedes car, and twenty rooms at the Dakota Building full of furs, valued at several million dollars.

Lawson Memorial Hospital

A hospital in Golspie, Inverness-shire, Scotland. John, Yoko, Kyoko and Julian were taken there on Tuesday 1 July 1969, following an accident.

After their Canadian trip, John and Yoko decided to go on holiday to Scotland with their respective children to enjoy some privacy after the recent hectic events of the previous months. They decided to visit some of John's relatives in Edinburgh. Although John had several cars and employed Les Anthony as a full-time chauffeur, Yoko insisted that they drive up the M6 themselves in a hired white Austin Mini, stopping over at cheap bed-and-breakfast accommodations.

John hadn't driven a car in years, being used to chauffeur-driven vehicles. After a spell in Edinburgh, they visited John's relatives at the Sutherland family croft in Sangobay, near Durness. When they set off again, the short-sighted John, while driving around Loch Eborall, saw a car approaching. He panicked and unfortunately lost control of the car and it crashed into a ditch.

They were taken to the Lawson General Hospital, which was 25 miles away from the scene of the accident. At the hospital

John had to have seventeen stitches in his chin while Yoko was suffering from concussion and a fractured back. The children escaped with only minor cuts and bruises.

They were released from the hospital on Sunday 6 July and chartered a jet to return to London.

John and Yoko later bought their crashed Mini and had it erected on a concrete plinth in the grounds of Tittenhurst Park, like a piece of modern sculpture.

Leary, Timothy

A major figure in the American counterculture of the 1960s. The former Harvard professor, who advocated the taking of LSD, created the famous 1960s saying 'Turn on, tune in and drop out.' John first discovered the author in March 1966 when he visited the Indica Bookshop in Mason's Yard, London, looking for a book on Nietzsche. He noticed Leary's book *The Psychedelic Experience,* co-written with Richard Alpert, which was based on the *Egyptian Book of the Dead,* and sat down to read it. The book inspired him to write *Tomorrow Never Knows.*

Leary also visited John and Yoko when they were at the Queen Elizabeth Hotel in Montreal and was one of the celebrities heard on the recording of 'Give Peace A Chance'. John was asked if he'd write a campaign song for Leary, who was about to enter politics. Leary's campaign slogan at the time was 'come together'.

When Leary was on the run from the FBI, John sent him $5,000 via the Black Panthers, but Leary never received it.

He was jailed for possession of marijuana and wrote an auto-biography, *Flashbacks*. He died of prostate cancer in May 1996 and his remains were among those of 24 other people, including Gene Roddenberry (who created *Star Trek*), whose ashes were sent into orbit in April 1997 aboard Spain's *Pegasus* rocket.

Leave My Kitten Alone

A composition penned by Little Willie John in 1959 and popularised by Johnny Preston in his 1961 cover version. The Beatles included this song in their early repertoire and used to perform it at the Cavern.

The group recorded the song on 14 August 1964 but seemed dissatisfied with the five takes and the song wasn't mixed and was never released, although EMI actually announced in July 1982 that it would be released as a single before Christmas that year.

John is lead vocalist on the song, which has remained in the EMI vaults. There was the likelihood of it finally being issued as a Beatles single in 1981, but the plans were dropped following John's murder, although a bootleg version appeared in 1983.

Le Bourget

A French airport near Paris. John and Yoko flew there from Gibraltar shortly after they were married. Journalists were waiting for the couple and John told them, 'We got married in Gibraltar because we tried to get married everywhere else first. I set out to get married on the car ferry and we would have arrived in France married. But they wouldn't do it. We were no more successful with cruise ships. We tried embassies. But three weeks' residence in Germany, or two weeks in France, was required. Gibraltar was a bit small for us to move about for a honeymoon. The wedding was quiet and British.'

Legacy of John Lennon: Charming or Harming a Generation, The

Published simultaneously in both hardback and paperback editions in the US in 1983 by the Nashville publishers Thomas Nelson, this is another of the Revd David A Noebel's anti-Beatles books. *Communism, Hypnotism & The Beatles* and *The Beatles: A Study In Sex, Drugs And Revolution* also revealed his obsession with John's comments in 1966 that 'Christianity will go. It will vanish and shrink … we're more popular than Jesus now.'

The publishers advertised the book, commenting,

> David Noebel's extensive research reveals direct and deliberate encouragement in rock music for young people to abandon biblical morality and embrace sexual perversion and promiscuity, drug abuse, Satan worship, rebellion against society, and violence. Noebel offers page after page of quotes from religious writers, secular commentators, and rock entertainers themselves to support his contention that rock music is a blatant attempt to brainwash its followers with anti-Christian propaganda.

Leibowitz, Annie

A major American rock photographer who began to work professionally in the field in 1969 following a course at the Art Institute in San Francisco. She became chief photographer for the prestigious *Rolling Stone* magazine and her first front-cover contribution to that publication was a portrait of John.

This was taken as part of an assignment to provide shots for the famous Jann Wenner two-part *Working Class Hero* interview in 1970. Of that initial session, she commented, 'It was the first time I had met a legend and it was at the beginning of my career. John was a real person and he seemed to make an effort at being a human, totally in control of the situation. Working with him broke all my fears and barriers. He provided a precedent for the way in which I have interpreted people since.'

Annie was the last person to take photographs of John. This was on Monday 8 December 1980 as part of another *Rolling Stone* assignment. The photographs were taken inside the Lennons' own apartments in the Dakota Building, one of the rare occasions on which John and Yoko allowed a photographer into their private world.

Her portfolio of photographs from this session and the ones taken the previous Wednesday, 3 December, were featured in the 22 January issue of *Rolling Stone* with a front cover of John crouched naked over Yoko, kissing her on the cheek.

Of this now famous picture, Annie commented, 'I promised John that this would be the cover. It was taken a few hours before he died.'

Annie's photographs of John are to be found in several publications, including *Shooting Stars: The Rolling Stone Book of Portraits*, *The Ballad of John and Yoko*, *Lennon Remembers* and *One Day at a Time*.

Lennons: A Family Album, The

A documentary on the Fox Family channel in their *Famous Families* series, screened in 1999. It included Yoko being interviewed in the Dakota Building and also featured John's two sons, although Julian is mainly seen in interview clips from the previous decade.

Lennon: A Journey Through John Lennon's Life and Times in Words and Music

A 128-page book by John Robertson, published by Omnibus Press in 1995. Robertson was also the author of *The Art and Music of John Lennon,* also published by Omnibus Press. The name was a pseudonym for Peter Doggett, editor of *Record Collector* magazine. The book is basically a chronology and is well illustrated with photographs throughout.

Lennon, Alfred

One of the most maligned figures in the John Lennon story, frequently accused in various biographies of deserting his young son, which wasn't actually the case. When an opportunity came to present his case to the Beatles' biographer Hunter Davies, Davies discovered that his manuscript was to some extent vetoed and John's Aunt Mimi wouldn't allow Davies to present Freddie's own version of events.

John's father was born at 57 Copperfield Street, Toxteth, Liverpool, on 14 December 1912, one of five brothers. There was also a sister. He was actually the fourth surviving son of Jack and Mary 'Polly' Lennon and had to initially wear irons on his legs because he was afflicted with rickets. As a result, his legs were four inches shorter than they should have been, resulting in his short stature – he was only five foot four when fully grown.

When he was seven years old his father died and his mother couldn't afford to keep such a large family, and she had no choice but to place two of her children in the Bluecoat Orphanage. Freddie and his sister Edith were the two children taken from the family. Although the Bluecoat provided Freddie with a good education, he became very homesick and looked forward to the holiday periods when he was allowed to visit his family home.

At the age of fourteen he went to a show at the Liverpool Empire with his elder brother Stanley. It was a children's event featuring Will Murray's Gang and after the show Murray invited people who had children with any talent to visit him backstage. Freddie went and auditioned, impressed Murray by playing 'We All Like To Be Beside the Seaside' on the piano, and signed up to join the show. He then travelled to Glasgow with them. However, he was still under the care of the orphanage and within days they brought him back to Liverpool and he was berated in front of the entire school. His dreams of being on the stage scuppered, he remained at the orphanage until he was fifteen.

A week after he left and returned to the family home, he met a fourteen-year-old called Julia Stanley while he was walking in Sefton Park one Sunday afternoon. She was sitting on a bench. He offered her a Woodbine (a cheap cigarette), which she refused, although she couldn't hide the fact that he amused her. He asked her why she kept coming out with bursts of laughter and she told him that he looked ridiculous in the bowler hat perched on his head. He then took it off and threw it into the lake.

The two began to talk and arranged to meet at the cinema the next day. In following months they would walk in the park, with Julia wheeling the pram containing young Stanley Parkes, her sister Elizabeth's son. They were both free spirits and laughed when talking of the conservative attitudes of Julia's sister Mimi and Freddie's brother Sydney.

His show-business aspirations now only a dream, he sought a career to which many a Liverpool lad had turned, that of the sea, and applied for a job as a bell boy on a ship. He managed to find a position in March 1930 on a Cunard passenger liner, SS *Montrose*. After each voyage he would see Julia again. She hadn't found any other serious boyfriends, although she never replied to any of the many letters he sent to her during his various voyages. The relationship continued over the next eight years, although it had become apparent that George 'Pop' Stanley, Julia's father, disapproved of Freddie because he had aspirations of her marrying someone of a higher status in life.

Such a long time had passed that Julia challenged Freddie to put up the banns, even though he was unemployed. Neither of them informed their family of the plans, although, on the day before the wedding, Freddie told his mother because he needed his dole money to pay the registrar. Polly didn't believe him. Julia never told her family and they were married on Saturday 3 December 1938 at Mount Pleasant Registry Office (where John and Cynthia were to marry many years later). Freddie's witness hadn't turned up and so he contacted his brother Sydney, who took time off work, and then invited them to the Big House pub for some food and drink.

The couple spent that evening at the cinema and then Julia went back to her parents' home in Berkeley Street while Freddie set off for Copperfield Street and they both informed their parents that night.

The couple had nowhere to stay together on the night of their marriage and Freddie then had to go to sea again for a number of weeks. On his return he found Julia waiting for him at the docks and she was delighted to tell him that they now had a home.

With the encouragement of his wife Anne, 'Pops' Stanley had accepted the fact that his daughter was now married and sought a way to help them. Since his other daughters had left home, he moved from the Berkeley Street flat into a two-bedroom terrace house at 9 Newcastle Road, Wavertree, which was big enough to accommodate himself and his wife and Julia and her new husband.

Registered with the Merchant Navy, Freddie was on call to sail on various voyages. It was after he'd been home during January 1940 that Julia found she was pregnant.

At the time of John's birth, Freddie was aboard the *Empress of Canada* on a voyage that lasted from 30 July to 1 November and was unable to be present at the hospital. It was Freddie who chose the name John in honour of his father (even though his father was more popularly known as Jack) and Julia decided on the second name, Winston.

Because of the war, Freddie was required to undertake longer and more frequent trips to sea and between 1 August 1940 and 13 January 1944 he was able to spend only three months at home in Liverpool. Even when he was on leave he had to under-take duties as a 'fire watcher'.

As a merchant seaman, he had no choice but to 'do his duty', and this in no way meant that he was deserting his wife and child as some Beatles chroniclers have presumed.

When John was two, Julia's sister Mimi suggested that she move to Woolton into a cottage owned by her husband George. For Mimi, who doted on John, this would be an opportunity for her nephew to be quite close to her. It was this move that possibly led to the parting of the ways between Julia and

Freddie. They had now been together for sixteen years, but Julia had never been out for evenings on her own. While Freddie was away at sea she was in the same house as her parents and such a thing as going for a night out by herself would have been frowned upon.

Julia began to frequent the local pubs, which were popular with members of the armed forces.

When Freddie came home after his next voyage and found that they'd moved to the cottage, he also discovered that Julia now drank. She hadn't previously drunk alcohol and he was concerned, particularly when he found she'd been going out to pubs at night, although she told him she liked going only for the singing and dancing and not the drink. When he wasn't on call as a 'fire watcher', he went to the pubs with her, although she turned down his suggestion of getting Mimi as a babysitter because she didn't want Mimi to know she went out drinking.

When they did go out, Freddie couldn't dance and had to sit around while Julia danced with other men. Having tasted the excitement of pub life, she began to get bored when she and Freddie had to spend the evening at home. By 1943 Julia was going out every night of the week. It was around that time that her mother Anne died and 'Pop' moved in with relatives, which meant that Julia could move back into 9 Newcastle Road. She continued to go out every night, made possible because one of her near neighbours was willing to babysit regularly. As he was away so often, Freddie gave up trying to persuade her to stay in and told her to go out and enjoy herself while he was at sea.

Freddie then obtained a berth on the *Berengaria*, sailing to New York, and had been promoted to chief steward. On arriving in New York he had to wait for some weeks for the next berth and then was told that the ship had already got a chief steward. He reluctantly signed on as assistant chief steward in the belief that the ship was going back to England, but then discovered it was sailing to the Middle East. When he complained he was told that he was unable to sign off the ship without a doctor's note and the only other thing open to him would be to miss the boat – although this could land him in serious trouble.

He did miss the boat and was taken into custody by immigration officers and interned on Ellis Island. He asked the British consulate to inform his wife what had happened, but they didn't and Julia had no idea of the situation and found herself in financial difficulties because Freddie's wages had ceased.

The consul offered him the opportunity of sailing to the Far East on a boat called the *Sammex*, which would prevent him from being charged with desertion. However, this move proved to be disastrous. He was given a bottle of whisky by a crew member and when they arrived in North Africa he was arrested, along with other members of the crew, by army Redcaps. The crew had discovered an excess of whisky, beer and cigarettes on board and had made use of the extra. They were charged with 'stealing by finding' and sentenced to three months in an army prison. By the time the proper documentation had come through, there were only nine days of the prison sentence left, but Freddie found the army prison a nightmare. On release he managed to find a berth home on the *Monarch of Bermuda*.

He landed in Liverpool for the first time in eighteen months. When he arrived at 9 Newcastle Road he found there were lodgers there, who told him that Julia was out and wouldn't be back until midnight. They said she went dancing every night. When Julia arrived the first thing she told him was that she was pregnant. Julia told him that she'd been seeing a man, a soldier, but he had raped her. Freddie was furious and demanded to know who the man was. Julia refused to tell him.

Freddie then found that the lodger had details about the soldier and set out with his brother Charlie to find the man, who was billeted in Cheshire. The officer in charge summoned the soldier and left him in a room with Freddie. His name was 'Taffy' Williams and he said he was madly in love with Julia and wanted to marry her if Freddie would give her a divorce. He denied that he'd raped her.

Freddie, Charlie and Williams set off to Newcastle Road to see Julia and when Williams said that he loved her and would stick by her she laughed in his face and told him to get lost. When Mimi heard she came and berated Julia, who seemed to be treating the matter lightly. When Pop Stanley arrived he made no bones about it: the baby would have to go up for adoption or he'd throw Julia out of the house. Although Mimi was childless he wouldn't let her have anything to do with the child because he didn't want any members of the family involved.

A few days before Christmas Freddie was given a berth on the *Dominion Monarch* and set sail. When he returned Julia had gone to Elmswood, a Salvation Army hostel, to have the baby. Freddie told her that despite Pop Stanley's ultimatum he was willing to keep the baby if she wished, and they could bring it up as their own. But she seemed too afraid of her father and told Freddie not to mention it again.

(It was on 19 June 1945 that she eventually gave birth to a baby girl and named her Victoria Elizabeth – and the baby was adopted.)

When Freddie came home from sea in March 1946 and arrived at Newcastle Road he found that Pop Stanley had moved back in and Julia was with another man, Bobby Dykins. Stanley had taken Freddie's name off the rent book and had it transferred to his name. Freddie threw Dykins out and said that Pop Stanley had to move out the next day. However, Julia declared she was going to live with Dykins and she moved out, taking John with her. Freddie's brother Stanley urged him to go to a solicitor and notices were placed in the local papers that he wouldn't be responsible for her debts.

He couldn't refuse any further offers of voyages and two weeks later had to set sail on the *Queen Mary*. Before the ship set off he received a call from Mimi Stanley, who told him to come to her house immediately. He said he couldn't, because he had to accept the ship assignment or be in trouble from the Merchant Navy. She told him that John was unhappy with Julia and Dykins and had walked all the way to her house in Woolton. She put him on the phone. Freddie promised him he would return in a couple of weeks' time and told him to stay with his Aunt Mimi.

Julia and Dykins had moved back into Newcastle Road, but Dykins had told her that this time he wasn't prepared to bring up another man's child.

When Freddie arrived back at Mimi's she told him that Julia had been neglecting John. Freddie decided to take John for a brief holiday in Blackpool at his friend Billy Hall's house, while he decided what to do. He sent John to his brother Sydney while he went to Southampton with a friend to help him sell nylons on the black market. Sydney and his wife Madge were childless and wanted to adopt John. When Freddie returned he took John back to Blackpool and discussed emigrating to New Zealand.

On Saturday 22 June 1946 Julia, together with Bobby Dykins, turned up at the Halls' house, saying they'd tracked him down via the post office. She said she wanted John back and turned down Freddie's suggestion that they try to patch up the marriage. John was asked who he'd like to stay with and he took his father's hand and said he wanted to stay with him, but, when Julia began to walk down the street, John ran after her, so Freddie collected John's things and they were handed to Dykins.

The next day Freddie set off for Southampton. Until 13 December 1947 he sailed on several voyages on the *Almanzora*. In 1948 he was on board the *Andes*, which set sail for Argentina. While on his second trip there, the local police, called 'the vigilantes', raided a café-bar and arrested twenty to thirty sailors, including Freddie. After a few days in a cell he was told he was going to be executed. They had seen his identity card, which had his signature 'A. Lennon' and immediately below that the name of his next of kin, 'John Lennon'. There was a wanted notice for a man called John Alennon, accused of murder. Fortunately, after a great deal of explanations, Freddie was set free.

He continued on various voyages, with his brother Sydney keeping him up to date on what was happening in Liverpool and telling him that there was no possibility that he and Julia could get back together.

When he landed in Tilbury Docks in London in December 1949 he was on a pub crawl with some friends when they broke a shop window and Freddie grabbed a mannequin. His friends disappeared and he was taken by the police and, in court, sentenced to six months' imprisonment. When he was released he found he wasn't allowed a berth on a ship again because of the prison record.

Mimi, who was now rearing John, wrote to him saying he had lost all chance of ever obtaining custody of John because of his sentence and should go to New Zealand and put his past life behind him. Disillusioned, he took a job as a kitchen porter and began to drift from lowly job to lowly job over the years.

He received a clipping from his brother Sydney with the news of Julia's death, but it was too late to go to Liverpool and pay his respects.

Over the years, as the Beatles came into prominence, Freddie was aware of John's success but kept a low profile. Then his younger brother Charlie told him that the papers were running stories about his having abandoned John when he was a baby and asked him what he was going to do about it. Freddie decided to do nothing about it and went to work at a hotel in Bognor Regis. He received a letter from Sydney telling him to keep out of John's life. He felt that Sydney was still riled at not being able to adopt John.

With stories still vilifying him as a deserting father figure and a headline in the *Daily Express* reading 'BEATLE'S DAD WASHES DISHES AT GREYHOUND HOTEL IN HAMPTON COURT', he approached the *Daily Sketch* who, within a matter of days, had arranged for him to meet John on the set of *A Hard Day's Night*. First, he met Brian Epstein, who led him to a room in which all four Beatles were present. Paul, Ringo and George then left him alone with John.

John was wary of him at first, asking him what it was he wanted. When Freddie told him he didn't want anything, he just wanted to let him know that the stories the papers were running about him weren't true, John said he vaguely remembered him from Blackpool. After ten minutes they shook hands and the meeting was over.

John had asked him to leave his address and he then sent a note to the Greyhound, which read, 'Dear Alf, Fred, Dad, Pater, Father, Whatever ... ' and enclosed with it was £30.

The press still pursued Freddie so he decided to sell his story to *Tit Bits* magazine, for which he received £250. This enabled him to have his first holiday since he was a schoolboy.

While he was working at Shepperton an agent from Liverpool called Tony Cartwright, who'd read the *Tit Bits* feature, approached him. After a few meetings Cartwright suggested he become Freddie's manager and talked him into making a record.

They co-wrote 'That's My Life', basically an autobiographical tale of Freddie's life, which was issued by Pye Records on the Piccadilly label in December 1965.

Piccadilly issued a press handout, which read:

Fifty-three-year-old Freddie Lennon, father of John, has made his first record. It is entitled *That's My Life (My Love And My Home)*.

Mr Lennon has been an entertainer in an amateur capacity for most of his life. He comes from a musical family, for his father was one of the original Kentucky Minstrels, and taught him to sing when he was young.

Most of Freddie's childhood was spent in an orphanage, for he was born into a large family and in those difficult times parents could not afford to feed so many children. At the orphanage, Freddie always took a major part in concerts, played his harmonica to the other children and generally showed an inclination towards the stage. He once sang at a theatre but the orphanage authorities were dismayed at the thought of one of their boys going on to the stage, so Freddie's early dreams were quickly dampened.

After leaving the orphanage at the age of 15, Freddie worked in an office, but the call of the sea was strong, and he joined his first ship as a bell boy at the age of 16. He stayed at sea for 25 years and travelled the world.

Freddie was always connected with entertainment on board ship, and has acted as compere, produced numerous concerts, sang in New York clubs and even conducted an orchestra in Lisbon. He has many interesting stories to relate about his adventures at sea.

At the age of 25 Freddie married, and his son John was born three years later. He was the only child.

When he left the sea 12 years ago, Freddie took a job as a waiter, and later worked in holiday camps at northern resorts. He came to live in London seven years ago. Over the years, Freddie was always interested in songwriting, but he never took it seriously. Six months ago he met Tony Cartwright, who is now his manager. Together they wrote *That's My Life (My Love And My Home)* – a story about Freddie's life. The song was taken to a music publisher, accepted and recorded.

The song received a great deal of airplay and entered the charts at No. 37. Then, without explanation, it disappeared from the charts the following week. Tony and Freddie received no co-operation at Pye when they went there to ask what had happened. A secretary told them that Brian Epstein had blocked the record and it had been withdrawn. Furious, Tony and Freddie went to John's house to see if he could help, but when he saw Tony with his father he thought they were there to cause trouble and said, 'Fuck off,' and slammed the door shut in their faces.

They returned to Pye the following week to see if the secretary could provide them with a written statement about the record's withdrawal, but found she had been promoted and sent to Los Angeles.

They later discovered that John had bought a copy of his father's record and played it regularly – and Julian, John's first son, was always requesting his parents to 'put on Granddad's song'.

When Fred began to work at the Toby Jug Hotel at Tolworth in Surrey he met a young student who was working there during the holidays. The two were to fall in love, despite the disparity in their ages: the girl, Pauline, was only 18 and Freddie was 56.

It was 1967 and Charlie Lennon, furious when he heard that John had slammed the door in Freddie's face, sent a letter to John admonishing him. He told him that he should forget the lies told about his father and listen to Freddie's side of the story. Charlie wrote that it was not Freddie's fault that the marriage had broken up, that he had come home from sea to find his wife pregnant by another man, but he forgave her, and then she ended up walking out on him and taking John with him. John had not heard this before, as his Aunt Mimi had always been careful to portray Freddie as a villain.

During the first week in August 1967 John sent a letter to the Greyhound Hotel, saying that he would meet him on his return from India.

In the meantime he had suggested to the Beatles' biographer Hunter Davies that he see his father and get his side of the story. He did, but John's Aunt Mimi vetoed it and Freddie was once again portrayed as the villain. John admitted in 1971 that he had allowed his Aunt Mimi to have her own version of the events in the authorised biography, rather than Freddie's own story.

John sent his chauffeur to pick Freddie up and drive him to Kenwood, the house in Weybridge. When John saw him he hugged him and told him that they should forget the past.

On 5 January 1968, John told the *Daily Mirror* that he had ended the feud with his father: 'From now on I hope we'll be in close contact all the time … '

John invited him to move into Kenwood, but it was obvious that Freddie found it rather isolated with the nearest pub being a mile away, so John arranged for him to move into a flat in Kew with a weekly allowance of £10.

Freddie had told John about Pauline and he invited them both up to Weybridge for a weekend. While they were there Cynthia suggested they give Pauline a job as a mother's help, babysitting and such for her keep and a modest wage, and she moved into Kenwood at the end of October 1967.

After a few months, Pauline's mother began to voice her opposition to their relationship and Pauline then moved into the Kew flat with Freddie. She was two months pregnant when a summons was served on them. Her mother had applied to make her a ward of court and the newspapers homed in on the story. With all the stress and tension, Pauline suffered a miscarriage. Freddie and Pauline then decided to move out of the public eye and found a one-bedroom flat in Brighton, for which John agreed to pay. In June 1968 Pauline found she was pregnant again and John agreed to fund them on a three-week trip to Gretna Green in Scotland, where they were married. They returned to Brighton and their first son, David Henry, was born in February 1969. By that time John had bought them a house in Brighton in which to live, but he stopped communicating once their son was born.

Almost two years elapsed without contact and Freddie wrote to him suggesting a meeting. John, who had recently undergone primal therapy – a form of treatment developed by the American psychiatrist Dr Arthur Janov – answered immediately and they were invited to Tittenhurst Park on Friday 9 October 1970. They were asked to wait and then John and Yoko came up to them and John began a tirade, venting his anger and frustration and telling them he was cutting off the money. He then threw them out of the house. He told Freddie to get out of his life. Yoko gave a lecture to them on parental responsibility and John showed no interest in his half-brother, who was becoming frightened at the sound of John's harsh voice. More ominous was John's threat that he would have his father murdered. It was the last time father and son ever saw each other.

Within a few days of their return home they received a letter from John's lawyer giving them notice to quit and demanding that they sign a deed of assignment to transfer the property back to John. His National Insurance card had also been returned and not one stamp had been paid in three years.

Frightened of the death threat they had received from John, they went to a solicitor and made a statement, which would be made public if Freddie were to disappear or die an unnatural death.

Allen Klein's legal representative then contacted them and eventually agreed to lending them £500, which would be recouped when the house was sold. They signed a stipulation that they had to hand over the statement they'd given the solicitor so that it could be destroyed, and also to hand over the signed agreement transferring ownership of the house back to John.

The couple and their child moved to another property in Brighton and a second son, Robin, was born in October 1973.

Freddie then developed cancer of the stomach, which was found to be terminal. Pauline contacted Apple, who got in touch with John, who called the doctor and was informed that there was no chance of recovery. John called the hospital and had a lengthy phone call with Freddie. That afternoon a huge bouquet arrived in the ward with the message 'To Dad – Get well soon – With much love from John, Yoko and Sean.'

Freddie died on Thursday 1 April 1976.

John phoned Pauline and offered to pay all the funeral expenses, but Pauline declined the offer. She was later to use the manuscript that Freddie had been writing to complete his story, *Daddy, Come Home*, which was published in 1991.

Lennon: A Tribute

A major concert held in John's memory at the Pier Head, Liverpool on Saturday 5 May 1990. Yoko requested that the proceeds be donated to the Greening of the World John Lennon Scholarship Fund and the Spirit Foundation UK. Tickets for the three-hour concert were £25. The actual price of a ticket was £5, but built into the cost was a £20 'voluntary' donation. One fan actually negotiated a refund of £20 because he didn't want to donate the money!

Two former Beatles donated video clips, which were screened during the concert, along with an oral message. They were Paul McCartney with 'P.S. Love Me Do' (a medley of 'Love Me Do' and 'P.S. I Love You'), filmed at a Tokyo concert in March 1990, and Ringo with 'I Call Your Name', which he'd recently recorded in Los Angeles. George Harrison refused to have anything to do with the event.

The artists appearing live were Al Green, the Christians, Joe Cocker, Lenny Kravitz, Kylie Minogue, Natalie Cole, Wet Wet Wet, the Moody Blues, Lou Reed, Terence Trent D'Arby, Randy Travis, Cyndi Lauper, Deacon Blue, Lou Gramm, Dave Stewart, Ray Charles, Dave Edmunds, Hall and Oates and Roberta Flack.

It seemed disgraceful that only one Liverpool band were allowed to appear: they were the Christians, who said they felt they were the 'token Scousers'. As someone commented, 'It would seem the acts were chosen for their appeal to the American market and Liverpool used as a backdrop for the setting.'

The audience of 15,000 saw some highlights, with Joe Cocker performing 'Isolation', Dave Edmunds with 'A Day In The Life' and 'Strawberry Fields Forever', Hall and Oates with 'Don't Let Me Down' and 'Julia', Lenny Kravitz with 'Cold Turkey', Cyndi Lauper with 'Working Class Hero', Lou Reed with 'Mother' and 'Jealous Guy', Randy Travis with 'Nowhere Man' and Wet Wet Wet with 'I Feel Fine'.

A number of the original Mersey bands who had played together with the Beatles in the original Liverpool venues were refused the opportunity of participating, so they set up their own John Lennon tribute at the Philharmonic Hall. In fact Liverpool set up a number of events during that weekend. Apart from the Mersey Cats tribute concert (see below) there was an alternative John Lennon concert aboard the *Royal Iris*. There was also a John Lennon art exhibition at a local school, inspired by John's art. And there was a twelve-hour John Lennon convention at the Adelphi Hotel, organised by Cavern City Tours. This included guests, including William Pobjoy, former headmaster at Quarry Bank School. There was also a five-hour event set around Cavern Walks and the Cavern Club to support Alder Hey Children's Hospital's 75th-birthday appeal. This featured local personalities from TV and radio, such as the comic Stan Boardman, the cast of the TV soap opera *Brookside* and football stars from Liverpool and Everton football clubs.

The original Mersey Beat bands who had been refused the opportunity of performing at the Pier Head tribute held their own concert at the Philharmonic Hall. This was sponsored by Mersey Cats, an organisation of the original groups who had formed in January 1989 to perform free at concerts to raise money for the seriously ill and handicapped children of Merseyside.

They called their concert *Imagine ... The Sixties*. The event was compered by two Radio Merseyside disc jockeys, Billy Butler and Wally Scott. The bands were eight of the original Mersey bands who had played with the Beatles during their Liverpool heyday. The Big Three and Friends weren't actually the original legendary Big Three, but a group fronted by Faron of Faron's Flamingos, with Brian Griffiths, who had flown in from Canada, and Howie Casey.

The bill toppers were the Pete Best Band, who began with 'I'll Get You' and ended with 'Twist and Shout'. Other performances included Earl Preston and the TT's with Slowdown and 'Send Me Some Lovin''; Ethne Brown with 'Imagine'; Beryl Marsden with 'Boys' and 'I Know'; the Fourmost with 'Hello Little Girl'; Sonny Webb and the Cascades with '(Just Like) Starting Over'; Karl Terry and the Cruisers with 'Ain't That a Shame' and 'Shake, Rattle and Roll' and Geoff Nugent's Undertakers with 'Money' and 'Just a Little Bit'. Gerry Marsden was encouraged to come on stage from his position in the audience and lead the singing with 'You'll Never Walk Alone'.

This was probably the best John Lennon tribute of the night.

The Pier Head show was broadcast live on the ITV network that evening and was broadcast in America on 8 December 1990.

A ninety-minute video of the concert, entitled *Lennon – A Tribute*, was released on Pickwick PVL2160 on Monday 15 April 1991.

Lennon (A Tribute to John Lennon)

A television tribute syndicated in America by LBS Communications Inc. on the tenth anniversary of John's death.

Hosted by Michael Douglas, the tribute mainly comprised video clips by various artists performing John's songs, together with excerpts from the Liverpool Pier Head concert of May 1990. The video clips included Sean Lennon with 'Dear Prudence', Elton John with 'Imagine', Michael Jackson with 'Come Together', Billy Joel with 'Back in the USSR', a Paul McCartney medley, Ringo Starr with 'I Call Your Name' and Ray Charles with 'Let it Be'. Clips from the Liverpool concert included Cyndi Lauper with 'Working Class Hero', Randy Travis with 'Nowhere Man', Al Green with 'Power To The People', Hall and Oates with 'Don't Let Me Down', Joe Cocker with 'Isolation', Wet Wet Wet with 'I Feel Fine' and the Christians with 'Revolution'.

Lennon (CDs)

A four-CD boxed set, released in Britain on Parlophone CDS 79 5220 2 on Tuesday 30 October 1990, with many of the tracks appearing on CD for the first time. The set included tracks from every one of his albums from *Live Peace in Toronto* in 1969 to *Milk and Honey* in 1984. The 73-track set was issued to celebrate what would have been John's fiftieth birthday. The set was released in America in July 1991.

The track listing is: 'Give Peace A Chance', 'Blue Suede Shoes', 'Money (That's What I Want)', 'Dizzy Miss Lizzy', 'Yer Blues', 'Cold Turkey', 'Instant Karma!', 'Mother', 'Hold On', 'I Found Out', 'Working Class Hero', 'Isolation', 'Remember', 'Love', 'Well Well Well', 'Look At Me', 'God', 'My Mummy's Dead', 'Power to the People', 'Well (Baby Please Don't Go)', 'Imagine', 'Crippled Inside', 'Jealous Guy', 'It's So Hard', 'Gimme Some Truth', 'Oh My Love', 'How Do You Sleep?', 'Oh Yoko!', 'Happy Xmas (War Is Over)', 'Woman is the Nigger of the World', 'New York City', 'John Sinclair', 'Come Together', 'Hound Dog', 'Mind Games', 'Aisumasen (I'm Sorry)', 'One Day (At a Time)', 'Intuition', 'Out of the Blue', 'Whatever Gets You Thru the Night', 'Going Down on Love', 'Old Dirt Road', 'Bless You', 'Scared', 'No. 9 Dream', 'Surprise Surprise (Sweet Bird of Paradox)', 'Steel and Glass', 'Nobody Loves You (When You're Down and Out)', 'Stand By Me', 'Ain't That a Shame', 'Do You Want to Dance', 'Sweet Little Sixteen', 'Slippin' and Slidin'', 'Angel Baby', 'Just Because', 'Whatever Gets You Thru

the Night' (live version), 'Lucy in the Sky with Diamonds', 'I
Saw Her Standing There', '(Just Like) Starting Over', 'Cleanup
Time', 'I'm Losing You', 'Beautiful Boy (Darling Boy)',
'Watching the Wheels', 'Woman', 'Dear Yoko', 'I'm Stepping
Out', 'I Don't Wanna Face It', 'Nobody Told Me', 'Borrowed
Time', '(Forgive Me) My Little Flower Princess', 'Every Man
Has a Woman Who Loves Him', 'Grow Old With Me'.

Lennon, Charles

John's uncle, born on 25 November 1926. When he was young
he used to play piano and harmonica. With his brother Freddie
(John's father, Alfred Lennon) he used to sing Italian songs
before World War Two with Freddie's wife Julia (John's mother)
playing banjo.

When Julia Lennon was having a child by a Welsh soldier,
Taffy Williams, while still married to Freddie, Charlie went
along with Freddie to consult the soldier, who was billeted in
Cheshire. They brought him back to confront Julia and Williams
told her he loved her. She laughed in his face and called him 'a
bloody fool'. Charlie went to make a cup of tea and then Julia
told Williams to leave and Freddie and Charlie went for a drink
with him.

Years later, when Freddie was no longer a seaman, Charlie
worked with him in the Barn Restaurant at Solihull. He was
present when their brother Sydney sent a clipping from the
Liverpool Echo reporting on Julia's death. Charlie had told him
that while Freddie was at sea, several people had visited
Copperfield Street while Charlie was still there, asking for
Freddie to give Julia a divorce and offering him £500 if he would
do so – but Charlie told them to get lost.

A despondent Freddie left Solihull and set off for London,
although he kept in touch with Charlie by phone.

Around Christmas 1963 several press people were contacting
Freddie, having discovered he was John's father. He didn't know
what to do and went up to see Charlie, who was still working at
the Barn. Charlie told him, 'The papers are running stories that
you abandoned him as a baby. What the hell are you going to do
about it?'

In an effort to clear his name, Freddie approached one of the
papers that had previously contacted him. A meeting with John

was arranged and Freddie presented his side of the story. Then Freddie was approached by Tony Cartwright, who became his manager, and they wrote a song together about Freddie's life. However, Cartwright said they needed some money to be able to get a flat and a car and they approached Charlie, who lent them £200.

In 1967 Charlie heard that John had slammed the door in his father's face and became angry. He wrote to John, putting forward Freddie's case, how it wasn't his fault that the marriage had broken up, how he came home from sea to find his wife pregnant by another man, how he forgave her and took her back and how she still walked out on him and placed John with his auntie.

In the letter he explained that there were two sides to every story and that he should forget everything his aunts had told him about his parents and see Freddie to get the truth. When Freddie sent him a note of consolation after Brian Epstein's death, John then wrote back to him at the Greyhound Hotel, where he worked, and the two got on together.

Charlie was also invited to visit John at this Weybridge home and John once told him, 'Uncle Charlie, whenever you're confronted by the press you have two left feet and a stub of an arm.'

After the deaths of both Freddie and John, Charlie decided to move back to Liverpool.

In 1989, he wrote a number called 'Ships of the Mersey' and a tape of the song was played on Radio Merseyside.

Lennon, Cynthia

Cynthia was born Cynthia Powell in Blackpool on 10 September 1939 and grew up in Hoylake. She had two elder brothers, Tony and Charles. Her father was a commercial traveller for the General Electric Company.

Cynthia's parents lived in Liverpool until the outbreak of World War Two. They then moved to the Wirral, living in a semidetached house in Hoylake. She attended the Junior Art School in Gambier Terrace, Liverpool, from the age of twelve.

She was to say, 'I had a fabulous childhood, very gentle and quiet with lots of love. There were no ruffles until I was seventeen, when my father died. After that it was all change.'

She enrolled at Liverpool College of Art when she was eighteen. (It's interesting to note that Cynthia's father died when she was seventeen, John's mother died when he was seventeen and Julian's father died when he was seventeen.)

Cynthia said she was apprehensive of John when she first noticed him. In fact she went so far as to say he initially frightened her to death. They were both on the intermediate course and one of the classes they were both enrolled in was the study of lettering, which they attended for one hour twice a week. John would arrive late, sit behind her and borrow her equipment, and every day she would find something missing – a paintbrush, a ruler.

Cynthia considered that he was scruffy, dressed like a Teddy Boy and kept disrupting the lessons.

It was a discussion about glasses that brought her to John's attention. Students were testing each other's eyesight when it was discovered that John and Cynthia had almost identical vision. It helped to break the ice between them.

During a dance at the end of term she had what she described as 'a painful and beautiful experience' – and it was the beginning of eight years with John. He asked her to dance, but she was very tense. Then he asked her out and she didn't know what to say and blurted out, 'I'm awfully sorry – I'm engaged to this fellow from Hoylake.'

'I didn't ask you to marry me,' said John.

It didn't end there: John and some of his friends were off to the art college pub, Ye Cracke, for a drink and John invited Cynthia and her friend Phyllis McKenzie to join them.

John and Cynthia got tipsy and they went to the Gambier Terrace flat and made love.

From that time on they were virtually inseparable. They used to sneak off to the pictures together, cinemas like the Palais De Luxe in Lime Street, or sit together for hours in coffee bars.

Over a period of time she found John to be possessive and jealous, always accusing her of not loving him enough or of being unfaithful, and he'd often break into rages. Although she was terrified of him, she was completely under his spell.

Because of John's obsession with Brigitte Bardot, he encouraged Cynthia to style herself on the French sex kitten. Her hair became blonde; she began to wear tight black sweaters and short skirts with high heels and black fishnet stockings and suspenders. She also decided not to wear her glasses any more.

She began accompanying him to gigs with his group, the Quarry Men, at venues such as the Casbah Club and the Jacaranda, and in 1960 he told her they had been booked to appear in Hamburg.

Cynthia was apprehensive about his trip to Germany, wondering whether he'd become involved with 'beautiful blonde German girls', but he began to write to her every day, scrawling on the envelope, 'Postman postman don't be slow, I'm in love with Cyn, so go man go.'

She was also upset because they hadn't been parted over such a long distance since the romance began. However, she was assured by the number of letters she received, which told of John's life in Hamburg in detail, including his complaints about the filthy quarters they lived in and having to wash up in the cinema toilets. He also gave her lists of records to buy in Liverpool and asked her to listen to them, write down the words and post them off to him.

In the meantime, Cynthia's mother had moved to Canada at the invitation of Cynthia's cousin and his wife, who had emigrated with their baby. They'd asked her to become the baby's nanny while they were studying over there.

On the Beatles' next trip to Hamburg, Cynthia and Paul McCartney's girlfriend Dot Rhone travelled over to join them for two weeks. Cynthia stayed with Astrid Kirchherr at 42 Eimsbutteler Strasse and Dot stayed with Paul on Rosa Hoffmann's houseboat.

There was an incident while the Beatles were on stage and John noticed a drunken man approach Cynthia as if he was going to paw her. He laid down his guitar, jumped off the stage, picked up a bottle and hit the man over the head with it. John then realised what he had done but the man, with blood pouring down his face, said, 'I'm so sorry I was annoying you.' Relieved, John said, 'Well, then, don't do it again.' And he went back on stage.

Of the moment Cynthia told John she was pregnant, John said, 'I was a bit shocked when she told me but I said, "Yes, we'll have to get married." I didn't fight it.'

John's half-sister, Julia Baird, recalls a family discussion about the pregnancy, which obviously drew parallels with Julia Lennon's becoming pregnant with her first daughter. She said, 'I do remember John being told that he didn't have to marry Cynthia, who'd become pregnant. So here another family baby was being called into question. If John had shown any doubt, I think the family might well have closed ranks around him. But John's certain reply was, "I'm going to marry Cynthia." Of course he did – she was beautiful. They both had wit and, as artists, shared a common, creative talent.'

They married at Mount Pleasant Register Office on Thursday 23 August 1962, with Brian Epstein as best man. Also in attendance were Paul McCartney and George Harrison, although the new Beatles drummer Ringo Starr hadn't been informed. The witnesses were Cynthia's brother Tony and his wife Margery.

John's Aunt Mimi and other relatives had refused to turn up.

The ceremony was carried out with the continual noise of a pneumatic road drill outside the window and the rain began to pour down as they emerged from the building and Tony and Margery said their goodbyes. The rest of the party ran down Mount Pleasant to Reece's Restaurant in Clayton Square, where Brian was to treat them to a wedding breakfast. When they arrived they were too late to beat the lunchtime crowds of office workers as they ate a set lunch comprising soup, chicken and trifle. The premises were unlicensed and the couple were toasted in water. That night John joined the Beatles on a gig at the Riverpark Ballroom, Chester, on bill with the Remo Four.

Fortunately, Brian had offered the newly married couple the use of his private flat as a wedding present and they moved into Falkner Street. John had commented, 'I was in the first apartment I'd ever had that wasn't shared by fourteen other students – girls and guys at the art school ... Brian Epstein gave us his secret little apartment that he had in Liverpool to keep his sexual liaisons separate from his home life.'

The Beatles continued their work and were booked almost every night, which left Cynthia by herself for a great deal of the time. In September 1962, when the Beatles were in London recording at Abbey Road, Cynthia began losing blood and thought she was having a miscarriage. Her friend Phyllis McKenzie took her to see a doctor, who told her to go home immediately and stay in bed, as she may lose the child. Cynthia stayed in bed for three days. When a concerned John returned, she suggested that they visit Mimi to prevent any bad blood continuing. Mimi welcomed them with open arms and insisted that, since Cynthia was pregnant and shouldn't be left alone in a flat, they should both move into Mendips, her semidetached house, with her.

Cynthia was out shopping in Penny Lane with Phyllis McKenzie when her pains began and was rushed to Sefton General Hospital's maternity ward in a taxi. There was some difficulty at the birth because the baby's umbilical chord was wrapped around his neck. Julian was born at 7.45 a.m. on Monday 8 April 1963.

Cynthia was then able to apply for a private room and moved in there, and a week later John arrived. He was delighted, saying, 'Who's a clever little Miss Powell, then?' and 'Who's going to be a famous little rocker like his dad, then?' John then surprised her by saying that he needed a break after all the touring and recording and wanted to know if she'd object if he went on a short holiday to Spain with Brian Epstein. It was an unexpected request, but she agreed.

When he returned mother and child were out of hospital and they went and registered the baby's birth. John continued with his tours and Cynthia had the burden of concealing her marriage and, if asked if she was married to John, said she'd never heard of him, that her name was Phyllis McKenzie.

Cynthia's mother Lillian had returned from Canada and moved back to Hoylake, where Cynthia and Julian joined her. When John returned from another tour they had a belated honeymoon in Paris, staying at the Georges Cinque Hotel. While there, they met up with their Hamburg friend, Astrid Kirchherr.

On her return, John set off to join the Beatles for further appearances, while Cynthia began to be besieged by the press, who had finally discovered the secret of the marriage and the birth of Julian. With the newspapers revealing the story, John was then able to become more visible as a family man and began looking for premises in London. His photographer friend, Bob Freeman, recommended an apartment where he lived at Emperor's Gate in Kensington and the Lennons moved in.

It was on the top floor of the building and there was no lift, so

Cynthia had to traipse up six flights of stairs with both Julian
and the shopping every time she went out. Also, with there being
only one door, when fans discovered the address, Cynthia felt
trapped as the stairs became full of fans demanding autographs.
When John tried to get into the flat the fans would swamp him
and he told Cynthia they'd have to get out of the flat before he
was killed.

Cynthia accompanied John when the Beatles made their first
trip to America in February 1964. One incident occurred that
was to be typical of Cynthia's position as part of the Beatles'
entourage. While they were in Miami she left the hotel to go
shopping and on her return the security guard refused to let her
back in. She told him who she was but he refused to believe her.
Cynthia had a tendency to display her natural timidity in these
situations and it took a group of Beatles fans, who *did* know
who she was, to make the guard accept the fact.

Cynthia was like the Candide of the Beatles story, carried
along by events, without any way of controlling them; she was
the one to be left on the railway platform as the train drew out
of Euston Station bound for Bangor; Cynthia did not have the
sophistication or confidence of a Pattie Boyd or a Jane Asher,
nor the determination of Maureen Starkey, and she would prove
no match for the unyielding stubbornness of Yoko Ono.

With Emperor's Gate proving so unsuitable, John bought a
house in then fashionable Weybridge in July 1964 and they lived
in the small staff flat at the top of it for the first nine months
while workmen followed the plans of an interior designer –
plans that meant the virtual stripping out and rebuilding of the
interior.

She was surprised to discover that a Cynthia Lennon Fan
Club had been formed and began to receive lots of letters aimed
at her personally.

Aware that beautiful girls always surrounded the Beatles,
Cynthia tried to boost her confidence by having plastic surgery
on her nose. When she was lying in bed at the London Clinic,
she received a card from John, along with a bouquet of red
roses: 'To Cyn, a nose by any other name. Love from John and
Julian.'

Cynthia believes that LSD initially caused the beginning of the
end of their marriage. When Cynthia and John had gone to

dinner along with George and Pattie to the house of their London dentist in Bayswater, their coffee had been spiked with the stuff. It was a frightening experience for Cynthia, but John became more and more inclined to take the drug and experienced more than 1,000 LSD trips. Because of his use of the drug, she felt John was drifting away from her and ignoring her. In order to capture his attention, she tried an LSD pill with him, but the experience was so horrible that she knew she couldn't take it again and began to feel that their marriage was in difficulty.

Their future seemed encapsulated in an incident that happened when the Beatles and their entourage set off to see the Maharishi Mahesh Yogi in Bangor. At Euston Station a policeman prevented her joining the rest of the party and she was in tears as she saw the train departing and John poked his head out of the window looking for her as it sped away into the distance.

Explaining her tears, in her autobiography she wrote, 'What nobody could possibly understand was that my tears were not because I had missed that stupid train but they were expressing my heartfelt sadness. I know that when I missed that train it was synonymous with all my premonitions for the future. I just knew in my heart as I watched all the people that I loved fading into the hazy distance, that it was to be my future.'

She next accompanied John to Rishikesh to undertake a course of meditation at the Maharishi's ashram. With her and John in the same room, meditation, a solitary exercise, proved difficult at first. She was to write, 'The ideal solution we found was to have our own separate rooms and do our own thing. I think it was at this particular point that John and I began to go our separate ways, not necessarily mentally but physically.'

Cynthia actually loved the idyll in Rishikesh and was sad to leave. She also felt that meditation had been very good for John and had weaned him off LSD.

By that time Yoko Ono had entered the picture. She had been sending letters to the house requesting John's help in promoting her book *Grapefruit*, and Cynthia's housekeeper, Dorothy Jarlett, told her that Yoko had been to the house on several occasions trying to see John.

At the time Cynthia became depressed and as he was spending so much time in the studio John suggested she go on holiday for a few weeks with Jenny Boyd, Donovan, Gypsy Dave and Alexis Mardas. After two weeks they returned home and Cynthia arrived at Kenwood with Jenny and Alexis to propose that John join them for dinner – they'd had lunch in Rome and thought dinner in London would be a fitting end to the day.

When they arrived Cynthia found that her housekeeper, Dot, was not around and discovered John and Yoko in dressing gowns. She felt as if the floor had given away beneath her. Confused, she asked John if he'd come out to dinner and he told her, 'No thanks.' She left with her friends and stayed the night at their town house, in the knowledge that Julian was with Dot. Although Jenny and Alexis shared the house, they weren't lovers. Cynthia and Alexis ended up in bed together that night.

A few days later she returned to Kenwood. Yoko had gone and John said he'd been bored with Yoko and asked Cynthia to move back in with him. After a few days he had to fly to New York with Paul to promote Apple and Cynthia wanted to go with him, but he said he'd be too busy with the promoting and then had more recording to do. He suggested she go on holiday again. Cynthia then left for Italy with her mother and Julian.

During the second week Alexis Mardas appeared and told her that John wanted a divorce and was going to take Julian away from her. Alexis said he'd be a witness to her adultery.

Negotiations took place and John capitulated and agreed to Cynthia's divorcing him and citing his adultery.

In August 1968 she sued John for divorce, citing Yoko Ono. The divorce was finally granted on 8 November 1968. On 1 August 1970 she married an Italian hotelier, Roberto Bassanini, at Kensington Register Office, with Julian as a pageboy. Among the guests at the ceremony were Twiggy and her husband, Justin de Villeneuve.

In 1978 Cynthia talked about the settlement of £100,000 she received on her divorce in 1968. She said, 'It seemed an awful lot at the time, but, looked at in retrospect, it wasn't really that much. It wasn't enough to keep me and my son Julian in the style to which we had become accustomed. I should have asked for a lot more.

'As it was, I had bad financial advice. I invested the money in what I was told were secure shares. But they weren't – and I lost an awful lot.'

The settlement wasn't a vast amount in relation to what John earned: it was approximately what he could earn in a month – and nowhere near the generous settlement Ringo, for instance, made on Maureen following their divorce.

Cynthia had married at 22 and undergone an acrimonious divorce at 28. Her marriage to Roberto Bassanini was two years later, when she was thirty, and during the same year, ironically, she saw the film *Thirty Is a Dangerous Age, Cynthia*. She was to say of this marriage, 'It lasted three years, and then I was on my own for two. I went back to my roots.'

Cynthia then returned to Hoylake, settled Julian in school and found a cottage in North Wales similar to ones she used to go to in her childhood, where she could paint and draw. It was a family home in Ruthin where she and Julian lived for seven years. In 1976 she married John Twist, a down-to-earth engineer from Lancashire. Their marriage ended in 1981. A bistro they had opened lasted only twelve months.

Then she and Julian moved to Wiltshire. Cynthia said, 'My mother was living with me then. She'd just had a stroke and she wasn't doing too well. My eldest brother lived in Wiltshire and quite honestly I needed a bit of assistance from someone close to me.

'I had to go to America for an exhibition of my work in Long Island.' The exhibition comprised a collection of ink-and-wash drawings by Cynthia of the Beatles in early Liverpool days.

For some time they lived in a cottage in North Wales, but sold up and bought a bungalow near Dublin for £36,000.

Cynthia commented, 'The move was for tax reasons. As I have only about a tenth of the original settlement left, I must protect it.'

In 1977 Cynthia said, 'John is an extremely tender person – or rather he's capable of tenderness. This tough, bitter side he has is a kind of protection. I feel sad for him because a lot of people seem to get satisfaction out of hurting him. When I wrote about our marriage break-up in a women's magazine, I had no intention of hurting him. I'm only sorry that with all his wealth and with all his fame, he doesn't appear to be happy. One thing I really wish for him is happiness.'

Following her third marriage, Cynthia changed her name back to Lennon by deed poll.

In December 1984 she moved back up north to a sandstone Georgian building in a village near Penrith, Cumbria, in the Lake District. After three failed marriages she had a new partner, a Liverpudlian called Jim Christie, but commented, 'I will not marry again.' She and Jim had been together for three years, since 1982, but had known each other for a decade. He was now her business manager. The two of them had been staying with friends in Cumbria and Cynthia said, 'We weren't actually looking for a house. We just fell in love with it overnight – when we moved in four months ago it didn't even have a bathroom or kitchen.'

She signed with Granada TV and began appearing regularly on a Friday night programme called *Weekend*.

She was to say, 'The strangest thing is that, throughout the Beatle years, I went about totally unrecognised. Yet since I've been appearing regularly on TV, people recognise me all the time.'

She designed clothes for Jeff Banks of Warehouse and also designed for the Cantona textile firm. Her abstract prints were made up into dresses, tunics, skirts, shirts and headscarves and sold through Banks's fifteen Warehouse shops in March 1985. Banks said, 'I'd met Cynthia a few times in the 1960s. Then about three years ago I met her again through a mutual friend in America. She showed me her designs – and I thought they were great.'

Cynthia commented, 'Obviously my name has something to do with all this. But if I'd been approached just to put my name on something I hadn't created, that wouldn't have been the same at all. Still, it's a name I have worked hard for one way and another.'

Over the years Cynthia dabbled in many projects, designing textiles, paperware, clothes, duvets and perfume. She was commissioned by the Scottish Rites Children's Hospital in Atlanta and by Cavern Walks to design various works of art.

She also ran restaurants. The first was Oliver's Restaurant in Ruthin with her third husband John Twist, although they later changed its name to the Manor House. Then she ran Bunter's on the Isle of Man with her lover Jim Christie. She also became a partner in Lennon's at 13/14 Upper St Martin's Lane, Covent Garden, in London's West End, which opened in 1989, but within a year she became disenchanted with the venture and sold her stake to Ali Jalali.

At the time, she discussed her abilities as a cook, saying that her mother taught her. 'When I was a child she would teach me everything she knew about cooking. She was a real northern cook.' Her mother, Lillian, had died a few years before.

'John was nothing like that,' she said. 'Throughout our years together he never cooked. The only dish he made was Rice Krispies with a sliced banana on top.'

She recalled when she used to take John to the house in Hoylake: 'We were penniless students. I'd met John in Liverpool when I was eighteen, John was seventeen. I remember thinking he was a little crazy, but he was just fighting the world.

'We couldn't afford to eat, so I'd take him home at weekends. My mother loved entertaining and she'd do her famous fry-ups – eggs, chips, beans and bacon – for breakfast, with a roast for lunch. John would eat everything and clear his plate. He'd say nothing but just eat, which I suppose is the best compliment of all.' She also said, 'I used to buy him cigarettes – he was always broke.'

When Cynthia removed herself from Lennon's, the West-End restaurant she had a stake in, she took out adverts in newspapers:

CYNTHIA LENNON
is looking for people to market an environmentally conscious herbal based skin care and fragrance collection, flexible hours, excellent earning and career structure. Shape your new career today contact Jean Phipps on – 051 [xxx xxxx].

In 1991, on Thursday 29 August, at Christie's, Cynthia, despite having described previous sales of Beatles items as 'indecent', auctioned off mementoes of her marriage to John, saying, 'I've had them for thirty years now. So I think it would be nice for someone else to enjoy them.'

A few years before, Cynthia had said of the auctioning of Lennon memorabilia, 'This whole industry has grown on the back of someone who has died. It is sick. It is like taking the pennies off the eyes of a dead man.'

She now said that her memories were intact but the past was

over and it was time for a change. Cynthia was 51 at the time and said, 'Do I want to be wheeled on to television programmes in a wheelchair at seventy, discussing the Beatles and John? I just can't face it.'

The auction raised $100,000. Among the items were letters from John. One, from August 1965, asks about his two-year-old son Julian: 'I can't wait to see him again … I miss him much more than I've ever done before – I think it's been a slow process my feeling like a real father! He doesn't see enough of me as it is, and I really want him to know and love me, and miss me like I seem to be missing both of you so much … I really feel like crying – it's stupid – and I'm choking up now as I'm writing … I love you very much.' There were also an acetate of 'Lucy in the Sky with Diamonds', their address book – with Yoko Ono's number crossed out – and a *Yellow Submarine* proposal with a notation from Brian Epstein written on it: 'This is one idea that Paul worked out with the writer – I like it very much.' There were awards, too, that had been won by John, including an Ivor Novello Award for 'She Loves You'. Also going under the hammer were antique furniture from Kenwood, the birth certificate John had to get to go to Hamburg in 1960 and the couple's divorce papers.

One particular item depicted how much John had loved Cynthia. It was an eight-page Christmas card he'd sent her in 1958. There is a cover drawing of an unshaven John looking lovingly into her eyes. Part of the card reads, 'Dear Cyn, I love you … I love you like guitars … you are wonderful. I adore you. I want you. I need you, don't go I love you. All I want for Christmas is you – so post early.'

Cynthia made her recording debut in 1996 with a cover version of Mary Hopkin's Apple Records hit 'Those Were the Days', and also filmed a video of herself performing the number at various Liverpool Beatles haunts. The same year she appeared on stage as part of the bill of *A Little Help From Their Friends*, along with the Quarry Men, the Merseybeats, Denny Laine, Twinkle and the Silver Beatles.

In 1999 Cynthia had a London exhibition of her works, along with that of her friend Phyllis McKenzie.

Despite the length of time she and Jim Christie lived together, they parted, arguably about the fact that he didn't like her utilising her association with John. She now lives in Normandy.

Lennon, David Henry

First son of Alfred ('Freddie') and Pauline Lennon, born in Brighton in February 1969.

Freddie Lennon lavished love and attention on David – his second son – taking advantage of this new chance at fatherhood and able to provide David with the devotion that he'd never been able to give John. Perhaps subconsciously aware of this, John began to withdraw his attention. Pauline mentioned that, after David's birth, John stopped writing to them and he showed no interest at all in his half-brother.

On Friday 19 October 1970, Fred and Pauline embarked on a two-hour drive from Brighton to Tittenhurst Park with the eighteen-month-old David. The meeting was a trouble-fraught one and John verbally attacked Freddie. He and Yoko had recently been undertaking primal therapy at Dr Arthur Janov's clinic, and all his hostility for his parents was unleashed, which ruined the intention of having John get to properly meet his half-brother for the first time.

When the *People* newspaper traced him in June 1997, he was still living in Brighton, East Sussex, with his mother and brother Robin. He was 28 years old and worked as a computer programmer. He commented, 'I used to get bothered by people asking about John. Now I just want to get on with my own life and be known as myself.'

Lennon/Goldman: The Making of a Bestseller

An eighty-minute television documentary screened by Channel 4 in Britain in December 1988. It concerned the biography of John Lennon, which Goldman was writing, and, although he originally agreed to participate, Goldman pulled out at the last minute saying, 'You'll put me on trial in this film and I don't see why I should be judged by anybody.' Sixteen people were interviewed for the film, including Fred Seaman, AJ Weberman, Howard Smith, David Peel, Robert Christgau, Dave Marsh, Mike McCartney and Bill Harry. Simon Napier-Bell originally agreed to be interviewed, but declined when he was offered only £100, and a friend of Yoko's, Sam Green, said he agreed to be interviewed by Goldman only because of blackmail – Goldman had got his assistant drunk and he had revealed stories about Green which he didn't wish included in Goldman's book. One interviewee was a person called Luciano, who says he was Sam Havatoy's lover and had once seen John Lennon 'nude – uncut and all'.

Lennon: His Last Last Interview, His Greatest Music

A four-hour special broadcast in the US by Unistar, the radio network, on the tenth anniversary of John's death. The special also used extensive excerpts from the 8 December 1980 RKO Radio interview it acquired when it bought RKO Radio in 1985.

Lennon, Jack

The paternal grandfather John never knew, born in 1855. Jack and his brother were born in Country Fermanagh, Northern Ireland. Their father, John Lennon, a ship's cook, and mother Elizabeth Lennon, née Morris, emigrated to America with their two sons. Jack Lennon for a time joined Andrew Roberton's Kentucky Minstrels, touring extensively across the United States, and in later years married an American girl. Jack's brother was ordained a priest and his ministry was in Wallasey, Cheshire.

Jack returned to Liverpool with his American wife, who died in childbirth. He became a shipping clerk and settled in a terraced house at 27 Copperfield Street. The former minstrel also began to entertain in local pubs. He then employed Mary Maguire, known as Polly, as his housekeeper and they were later married. She gave birth to eight children, six of whom survived. There were five boys and one girl.

Jack died of a liver disease in 1921.

Lennon, John

John's mother Julia had been in labour for thirty hours and the doctors were about to perform a caesarean section, but this proved unnecessary and at 6.30 p.m. on Wednesday 9 October 1940 John Winston Lennon was born at Oxford Street Maternity Hospital in Liverpool. His father Alfred 'Freddie' Lennon was at sea at the time, but the baby's first name was chosen in honour of his paternal grandfather and his middle name as a tribute to Winston Churchill, due to the war raging at the time. Fortunately, the bombing of Liverpool had ceased two weeks before the birth and didn't resume until 16 October.

His mother lived with his grandparents at 9 Newcastle Road, Wavertree, a home also shared with his father Freddie in between voyages. As it was wartime, John's father was at sea although, due to unfortunate circumstances, shortly after John's birth he failed to board his ship at New York and his wages were stopped, causing financial problems for Julia.

When Julia's sister, Mimi Smith, offered Julia and John accommodation in a cottage at 120a Allerton Road, Julia moved in. This situation caused problems, however, and was probably the cause of the breakdown of Julia's marriage. Free of her parents' influence and with her husband at sea, Julia began to go to pubs every night and enjoyed singing, dancing and drinking. She began to go with other men, became pregnant by a soldier, and gave birth to a baby girl. Julia then went to live with another lover, Bobbie Dykins, and Freddie placed John temporarily with his elder brother Sydney. Freddie then took John up to Blackpool and planned to emigrate to New Zealand with his son. Julia turned up with Bobbie Dykins and demanded John back. The heartbreaking decision to be with either his father or his mother was left to the five-year-old child, who immediately decided he wanted to remain with his daddy, but when his mother began to walk down the street, he ran after her. Freddie agreed to let him go, unaware that Julia didn't actually want to rear her son and was putting him into the hands of her sister Mimi.

Mimi's household at 261 Menlove Avenue in the suburb of Woolton was a fine semi-detached house, far removed from the types of dwellings in poverty-stricken areas of Liverpool. John lived a comfortable and pleasant childhood, far different from the concept of a 'working class hero' in a Liverpool slum which some writers have depicted. Mimi's husband Uncle George doted on him and was a contrast to the disciplinarian aunt who, while being strict with him, nevertheless loved John with a passion.

The area of Woolton had parks and fields such as Calderstones Park, the Black Woods and Strawberry Fields, and was an idyllic area of the city. John, with his passion for *Just William* books, had his own similar gang of friends who had lots of fun locally and often got up to mischief. These included Ivan Vaughan, Pete Shotton and Nigel Walley.

In addition, John enjoyed a good family life and the Stanley family was a close-knit one. Julia was one of five sisters who, apart from Mimi, were Elizabeth, Anne and Harriet. While Julia was not present in John's early life, as she was rearing two daughters, John's aunts and his cousins were frequent visitors and he enjoyed a degree of family life which also contrasted with the image that his childhood was full of anger and angst. One of his closest friends was his cousin Leila, and when his Aunt Elizabeth moved to Edinburgh, his cousin Stanley used to come to Liverpool and collect John each summer until he was 15 to enjoy pleasant holidays in Scotland at his aunt and uncle's country home in Durness.

John was always cared for, and wanted for nothing. He had numerous aunts, uncles and cousins to afford him the taste of life inside a large family unit, a beautiful house with caring guardians, lots of friends and regular holidays in the beautiful Scottish countryside. He was also someone who didn't get into as many fights, and wasn't as tough, as previous chroniclers have routinely made out. He had a strong personality and an acerbic wit, which intimidated many people, but when it came to fights John would rather run away than stand his ground, which he did on many an occasion.

In his youth John could be described as a mischievous scamp, and he wasn't averse to a bit of bullying, if he could get away with it. He used to get up to pranks such as pulling girls' knickers down, and was expelled from Mosspits Primary School when he was five-and-a-half for bullying a girl. He next attended Dovedale Road Primary School and eventually enrolled at Quarry Bank High School in September 1952. This was a fine school where pupils could gain high academic qualifications; John's close friend Rod Davis went on to Oxford University. The school had also been the home of several prominent Members of Parliament, including Peter Shore.

John, however, was more interested in playing pranks with his mate Pete Shotton than academic pursuits. Even at that time John believed he was a genius and his talent at writing and drawing was evident in the creative exercise books which were an indication of his potential. Despite a report which read,

'Hopeless. Rather a clown in class,' headmaster Mr Pobjoy saw John's potential as an artist and recommended to his Aunt Mimi that he apply to the Liverpool College of Art. In the meantime, John had renewed acquaintances with his mother, who lived only a short bus ride away, and he began to frequent her house regularly. Julia was as free-spirited as John and indulged him and taught him music on her banjo. While Mimi frowned on his guitar playing, Julia encouraged it, and when John formed his own skiffle group, the Quarry Men, they often rehearsed at Julia's house.

His friend Ivan Vaughan was attending Liverpool Institute and brought his new friend Paul McCartney to meet John when the Quarry Men performed at Woolton Parish Church Garden Fête.

John continued his eccentric behaviour at Liverpool College of Art, but began to gather a number of friends there – Tony Carricker, Geoff Mohammed, Cynthia Powell, Helen Anderson, Stuart Sutcliffe, Rod Murray, Bill Harry, Rod Jones and several others. He was to marry Cynthia, Stuart was to become one of his closest friends and join the Beatles, and Bill was to launch the magazine *Mersey Beat* and promote the group locally. The group – at this stage called The Silver Beetles – also began to play at the college dances.

They made some appearances at a local coffee bar, the Jacaranda, and the owner Allan Williams arranged for them to appear in Hamburg, Germany. On their return to Liverpool they astounded local audiences with their new dynamism – and their black-leather look. They began appearing regularly at the Cavern club and in the pages of *Mersey Beat*, came to the attention of record store manager Brian Epstein, who signed them up and they were on their way to fame and fortune.

The persistent rumours that there was a sexual relationship between Epstein and John are untrue. This myth began when a gay friend of Brian's told a journalist that Brian fell in love with John when he first saw him at the Cavern. Brian became a champion of the Beatles, determined that they would become the biggest act in the world, but he also had to suffer many harsh insults from John, particularly over the fact that he was Jewish and homosexual. John always had the innate ability to home in on a person's weak points and exploit them.

There are conflicting reports as to how John coped with the news of Stuart Sutcliffe's death when the group arrived in Hamburg in April 1962. Stuart had left the group the year previously, but John had remained in touch by letter. Some said he greeted the news stoically, others that he cried. The truth is that John always had a problem dealing with grief. He just didn't know how to react, whether it be with hysterical laughter or tears.

When Cynthia told John she was pregnant in 1962, his immediate reaction was that they should get married. In the north of England in particular, in those days, it was regarded as a matter of honour that a person marry a girl if she became pregnant. There was such stigma attached to anyone who had a child out of wedlock that the usual thing was to walk up the steps to the altar – or, in this case, the local registry office. John's son was named Julian, in honour of John's mother, but it was a case of like father like son, because John did not take a great interest in spending time with Julian. Apart from being so busy with the Beatles, by the time they finished touring and began their studio years he was into drugs such as LSD. Cynthia was treated as the typical northern housewife, expected to stay at home and look after the kids and cook the meals.

When Yoko Ono entered John's life in 1966 he was at first, according to witnesses, not really interested and considered her something of a pest. But she set about netting him with a fanatical determination. He became intrigued with her book *Grapefruit* (from which the word 'Imagine' really seeped into his conscious mind) and began to take an interest in the avant-garde. While Cynthia was on holiday he invited Yoko over, made an experimental record with her during the night and the two of them ended up in bed together. The next morning he told his friend Pete Shotton that he was really in love for the first time and was going to give up everything for Yoko. When Cynthia returned, John made a half-hearted effort at reconciliation, but then sent her on another holiday and her fate was sealed.

John's friend Pete Shotton, who had been so close to him throughout his life, became surplus to requirement in Yoko's book. This began a trend of John dropping old friends, who wondered if it was at Yoko's behest. Yoko seemed to want total devotion, with no room for anyone else. This was to continue for the rest of John's life, with, at times, Yoko preventing Julian, Paul McCartney, Mick Jagger and many other friends from contacting John.

The talent John had displayed as songwriter and musician with the Beatles altered with the emergence of Yoko. John Lennon, as an artist in his own right, virtually ceased to exist and everything became a collaboration with Yoko – and was normally led by her. John was critical of the film *A Hard Day's Night*, but many would have found it far more entertaining than *Self-Portrait*, a slow-motion studio film of his penis becoming erect. He was also critical of his songs such as 'Strawberry Fields Forever', but critics regard it as far more enduring than the half-baked political stance of *Sometime In New York City*.

The *Two Virgins* album was John's first post-Beatles project. The cover was a photograph of him and Yoko naked. Asked if he expected a reaction, he said, 'Yeah, well, I expected some noise about it. But I didn't expect as much as we got. I'm sure Yoko didn't expect it. I'd always wanted to produce Yoko's music even before we were lovers.'

He explained, 'It all started with the producing kick the Beatles got into. Paul was producing Mary Hopkins and George worked with Jackie Lomax [former singer with Scouse band The Undertakers], so I decided to produce a record with Yoko. I was in India meditating on the Yoko album and how to present it. One day I just suddenly thought the best way was to have Yoko naked on the cover. I wrote and told her, and I got some static on the other end. She wasn't too keen.' He said he had to talk her into the idea.

John and Yoko were married in Gibraltar on March 20, 1969, and settled down in a huge estate, Tittenhurst Park, in Ascot. John loved it and didn't really want to leave, but Yoko needed to pursue her desire to have custody of her daughter Kyoko, who had been brought up throughout her life by her ex-husband Tony Cox. Yoko's natural mother's need to be with her child was no doubt exacerbated by the fact that she had a number of miscarriages throughout her life. So they went to New York and never returned to England.

However, John came to love New York with a passion and the couple moved into the Dakota Building. They wanted a baby and, with the help of an acupuncturist who aided them in detoxing their bodies, they were rewarded with a son, Sean. It is claimed that before Yoko agreed to have a baby she came to an arrangement with John that he would take over the mother role while she ran their business interests. So for nearly five years he became a househusband, doting on his son, and giving him the affection he never gave to his first son Julian.

It is not true, however, that during these years he abandoned music completely. In fact, during this time he created a large volume of work on demo discs, which he recorded at the Dakota.

Shortly before his death, John had been enthusiastic about his return to the music scene after an almost five-year hiatus. His new album *Double Fantasy* was attracting attention and he had granted a number of interviews including ones to the BBC and *Playboy* magazine.

Talking to the reporting team from *Playboy*, he said, 'We're either going to live or we're going to die. If we're dead, we're going to have to deal with that; if we're alive, we're going to have to deal with being alive. So worrying about whether Wall Street, or the apocalypse is going to come in the form of the great beast is not going to do us any good day-to-day.'

John was shot dead by obsessed fan Mark Chapman in New York on 8 December 1980 in the entrance to the Dakota Building. At the moment of his death, in his birthplace of Liverpool it was actually December 9, due to the time difference. He'd always said that the number nine had been a major feature throughout his life.

John Lennon was cremated at the Frank Campbell mortuary on the east side of Manhattan and his ashes were scattered in Central Park.

Lennon II, John Ono

Yoko and John's unborn baby son. Yoko had been rushed to Queen Charlotte's Maternity Hospital in London on 7 November 1968 soon after the couple had been arrested at the Montague Square apartment on a drugs charge. The nursing staff feared the 35-year-old Yoko might have problems with the birth and, on 21 November 1968, she heard from the doctors that she would lose the baby. John had a tape recorder delivered to their room and with the aid of a stethoscopic microphone recorded the unborn baby's heartbeat shortly before he died.

As the foetus was mature enough to require a death certificate under British law, John called the child John Ono Lennon II. A tiny coffin was made and the baby was buried at a secret location.

Lennon, Julia

John's mother, also known as 'Judy', was born March 12 1914, one of the five daughters of George Ernest 'Pop' Stanley and Annie Millward.

Only five foot two tall, she was a vivacious redhead and called Juliet by her family.

Julia was brought up in the Stanley household at Berkeley Street, Toxteth, and was, to all intents, the black sheep of the family. The Stanley sisters were strong, practical women, but Julia turned out to be rebellious, fun-loving and headstrong.

She was taught to play the banjo and piano by her grandfather, William Stanley, a solicitor's clerk.

Julia was only fourteen when she met Alfred 'Freddie' Lennon, then fifteen, in Sefton Park and the two began a lengthy courtship, disapproved of by Julia's family. Ten years later they were married, on Julia's suggestion.

Freddie was to say, 'One day she said to me, "Let's go and get married." ' Although he was on the dole at the time, the two were wed at Mount Pleasant Register Office on 3 December 1938. They hadn't informed their families and after spending the evening in the Trocadero cinema they went to their respective homes, Freddie to Copperfield Street and Julia to Berkeley Street. Julia, who was 24 at the time, had described herself on the marriage certificate as a cinema usherette, because of her love of the silver screen. Freddie then set sail on one of the numerous voyages he would undertake over the coming years. He was at sea when their son John was born.

Julia underwent thirty hours of labour and the doctors were on the point of preparing for a caesarean section when the baby boy was born. The caesarean became unnecessary.

At 6.30 p.m. on 9 October 1940 Julia's sister Mimi phoned, and was told, 'Mrs Lennon has just had a boy.' Mimi said, 'He was born with blond hair and I remember he weighed seven and a half pounds.'

When Freddie was chief steward on a ship that docked at New

York, he expected to be in the same position on a return trip. But he found the next ship already had a chief steward, and, after signing on in a lesser position, discovered that the boat was sailing to the Middle East. He missed the sailing and was interred, which resulted in his pay being stopped, leaving Julia short of money. He had a series of mishaps, having to take a ship to Africa, then being accused of stealing and incarcerated in an army prison camp before he eventually made his way home.

Soon after Julia and Freddie had married, Annie and Pop Stanley had moved to 9 Newcastle Road in Wavertree and invited the newlyweds to live with them. While Freddie was away on one of his voyages, Mimi Smith invited her sister Julia to bring herself and John to live in a cottage owned by her husband George, so that John could be near to her.

Free of the watchful eye of her parents, with her husband at sea, and careful not to let Mimi know what she was up to, Julia began going out to local pubs each night and began drinking regularly for the first time. She enjoyed dancing and happily built up a social life for herself. When Freddie returned from sea he was horrified to see she now drank and was disturbed to find she was addicted to pub life. While he was away on another voyage she went out with a soldier, Taffy Williams, and became pregnant by him.

Shocked at the discovery, Freddie nonetheless suggested they bring up the baby as their own, but Pop Stanley insisted that the baby girl, whom Julia named Victoria Elizabeth, be given up for adoption. The baby was born at Elmswood, a Salvation Army hostel, on 19 June 1945 and adopted by a Norwegian sailor. Julia was never to see her daughter again.

Returning to Newcastle Road after another voyage, Freddie found that Julia was going out with another man, John 'Bobbie' Dykins. He threw Dykins out of the house, but Julia then packed her things and left, saying she was going to live with her new lover.

The couple had met at the café where Julia had been working and the two began to live in a one-bedroom flat in Gateacre. Her sister Mimi declared that Julia was no longer a fit mother and demanded she hand John over to her. When Julia refused, Mimi brought a social worker along to the flat, but the social worker said that John should remain with his mother. Another social worker inspected the flat and realised that not only did John have no room of his own, but didn't even have a bed to himself, either. The five-year-old had to share the double bed with his mother and his mother's boyfriend.

John then went to live with Mimi.

At this point there is a conflict between the version given by Freddie Lennon and those of Mimi Smith. According to Freddie, when Julia left him for Dykins, Freddie placed John temporarily with Mimi while he went to Blackpool to do some dealing with Billy Hall, a friend of his. He then placed John for a while with his elder brother Sydney and his wife Madge, who wanted to adopt the little boy. There seems to be some evidence that this actually took place.

Freddie then took John up to Blackpool with him and, while there, discussed the idea of the two of them emigrating to New Zealand. Julia then turned up with Bobbie Dykins, having traced Freddie through the Post Office. Julia said that she and Dykins were looking for a new place to live and wanted John to come back to her. They decided to let the five-year-old child make the decision regarding whom he wanted to live with. When asked he said he wanted to stay with his daddy. Then, when Julia began to walk down the street, John ran after her. Freddie decided to let John return with Julia to Liverpool, little knowing that when they arrived there they would immediately place John in the hands of his Aunt Mimi as Dykins refused to bring up another man's child.

Julia and Bobbie never married, but they lived together as husband and wife and on 5 March 1947 she gave birth to their first child, a seven-and-a-half-pound baby girl they named Julia. They were still living at 9 Newcastle Road, but in 1949 Pop Stanley died and the owner of the house put the property up for sale. Julia had become pregnant again so the council moved them into Blomfield Road on the Springfield Estate. Dykins and Julia had a second daughter, Jacqui, born on 26 October 1949.

There was a good deal of closeness in family life among the five sisters and their seven children.

One of them, Leila, daughter of John's Aunt Harriet, remembers Julia as being a vivacious woman whom people would stop to look at in the street. She was a person with a great personality and sense of humour.

Blomfield Road wasn't such a great distance from Menlove Avenue, where John was now living with his Aunt Mimi, and from the age of thirteen he began to visit frequently and often stayed overnight.

Julia had a mother-of-pearl banjo, which had belonged to her grandfather, and she often played it and taught John to play his first ever tune on the instrument: 'That'll be the Day'. He recalled, 'My mother taught it to me on the banjo, sitting there with endless patience until I managed to work out all the chords. She was a perfectionist. She made me go right through it over and over again until I had it right. I remember her slowing down the record so that I could scribble out the words. First hearing Buddy [Holly] absolutely knocked me for a loop. And to think it was my own mother who was turning me on to it all.'

Julia bought John a guitar for £10 and took a great interest in his skiffle group, even acting as wardrobe mistress for them, buying coloured shirts at the open-air market for them to wear. John said, 'I used to be able to borrow a guitar at first, before I had my own. My mother bought it from a mail-order firm and it had a label on the inside, which said, "Guaranteed not to split". I suppose it was a bit crummy, by I played it for a long time and got in a lot of practice.' He added, 'My mother taught me quite a bit, my first lessons really. Most of our stuff then in the early days was just twelve-bar boogies, nothing fancy.'

Once, his mother came to Mimi's house after allegedly being beaten by Dykins. John recalled, 'My mother came one day to see us in a black coat with her face bleeding. She'd had some sort of accident. I couldn't face it. I thought, That's me mother in there, bleeding. I went out into the garden. I loved her, but I didn't want to get involved. I suppose I was a moral coward. I wanted to hide all feelings.'

The Quarry Men rehearsed frequently in Blomfield Road and everyone was charmed by Julia's friendliness and personality.

John's friend Pete Shotton was enchanted by her and said she had the same sense of humour as John. He recalled how she would wear a pair of spectacles without any glass in them and begin talking to neighbours, then suddenly she would push a finger through the missing lens to rub her eye. He said that when he first met her she was wearing a pair of old woollen knickers on her head.

He recalled the occasion: 'When John introduced me by name, she fluttered up to me and extended her hand. "Oh, this is Pete, is it? John's told me so much about you!" Rather than shake my own proffered hand, Julia began stroking my hips. "Ooh, what lovely slim hips you have," she giggled.'

Paul McCartney said, 'I always thought of Julia as being an exceptionally beautiful woman. She was very, very nice to us all. John just adored her, not simply because she was his mum but because she was such a high-spirited lady.'

Paul recalled how Julia had taught John how to play the banjo and added, 'She was always teaching us new tunes. I remember two in particular, "Ramona" and, oddly enough, "Wedding Bells Are Breaking Up That Old Gang of Mine". Much later, during the Beatles years, John and I often tried to write songs with that same feeling to them. "Here, There and Everywhere" was one we wrote along those lines.

'Julia was lively and heaps of fun and way ahead of her time. Not too many blokes had mothers as progressive as she was.'

On 15 July 1958 Julia decided to set out to Mimi's house, which she did at least once a week. John was at Bromfield Road with Bobbie Dykins, Jacqui was in bed and little Julia was playing in the garden.

Julia was chatting with Mimi until ten o'clock in the evening and then left to cross Menlove Avenue to the bus stop. Mimi generally walked to the bus stop with her, but decided not to that night. As she came out of the garden gate she met Nigel Walley, John's friend, who had come looking for him. They stopped to talk for a moment and then she stepped to cross to the central reservation when a car crashed into her, sending her hurtling into the air. She died instantly. A police officer who was late for duty and who was also driving without a licence had been speeding along the road. He was an inexperienced driver and when he saw Julia he put his foot on the accelerator instead of the brake.

Julia was only 44.

When Julia died, John's Aunt Mimi said, 'He just went to his room into a shell.'

John was to recall the incident in detail years later, saying, 'An hour or so after it happened a copper came to the door to let us know about the accident. It was awful, like some dreadful film where they ask you if you're the victim's son and all that. Well, I was, and I can tell you it was absolutely the worst night of my entire life.

'I lost my mother twice. Once as a child of five and then again at seventeen. It made me very, very bitter inside. I had just begun to re-establish a relationship with her when she was killed. We'd caught up on so much in just a few short years. We could communicate. We got on. Deep down inside, I thought, Sod it! I've no real responsibilities to anyone now.

'Anyway, Bobbie and I got a cab over to Sefton General Hospital, where she was lying dead. I remember rabbiting on hysterically to the cabbie all the way there. Of course, there was no way I could ever bear to look at her. Bobbie went in to see her for a few minutes, but it turned out to be too much for the poor sod and he finally broke down in my arms out in the lobby. I couldn't seem to cry, not then anyway. I suppose I was just frozen inside.'

When he left the hospital, John returned to Menlove Avenue and began playing his guitar. Then, later that night, he walked down the road to the house of his former girlfriend, Barbara Baker. They walked to a nearby park and he started to cry and she placed her arms around him. She was to say, 'We just stood there, crying our eyes out, the pair of us.'

John never got over his mother's death and recorded songs such as 'Julia' and 'Mother' about her. He was finally able to externalise some of his feelings when he underwent primal therapy under the American psychiatrist Dr Arthur Janov, and also in recording his album *John Lennon/Plastic Ono Band*. He also named his son Julian after her.

Lennon, Julian

John Charles Julian Lennon was born in Sefton General Hospital, Liverpool, at 7.45 a.m. on Monday April 8 1963. He was named John after his father, Charles after his mother Cynthia's father and Julian after John's mother Julia.

Years later, John was to say, quite unkindly, 'He was born out of a whisky bottle on a Saturday night.' This infuriated Cynthia, who commented, 'He told *Playboy* magazine, "Julian was born out of a bottle of whiskey on a Saturday night." John was with Yoko Ono then but I was still offended and so was Julian. It was so untrue. I could tell that John said it to impress the interviewer but it still hurt. For a start we didn't even drink whisky in those days, but the worst part was the implied denial of our love. We were very much in love and very happy – Julian truly was a love child.'

Julian had jaundice when he was born and the umbilical cord was around his neck. When John eventually came round to the hospital to see him, he said, 'Who's going to be a famous little rocker like his father, then?'

The marriage and the birth of Julian had to be kept secret on the orders of Brian Epstein, who believed that the news would damage the Beatles. As a result, Cynthia moved to Trinity Road, Hoylake, to be with her mother and Julian was christened at Hoylake Parish Church.

When the news of the marriage and the existence of Julian finally appeared in the press, John found them all a place to live in at Emperor's Gate in West Kensington, London. They then moved to Weybridge, Surrey, where Julian was educated at Heath House School. He recalls, 'I was trundled home from school and came walking up with one of my watercolour paintings. It was just a bunch of stars and this blonde girl I knew at school. And Dad said, "What's this?" I said, "It's Lucy in the sky with diamonds." ' As a result, John penned a number using that title for the *Sergeant Pepper* album.

Another of Julian's drawings gained fame when it was used as the sleeve of the Beatles' 1967 Christmas record 'Christmas Time Is Here Again'.

In November 1968, Julian's parents were divorced.

John still had access to his son and he was to join him on a few occasions. One was during the filming of *The Rolling Stones' Rock and Roll Circus* and another time was when he was taken on a trip to Scotland, along with Yoko's daughter Kyoko.

After the divorce, Julian lived with his mother in Cheshire and began attending school at Kingsmead in Hoylake. He and a fellow pupil, Justin Clayton, formed a rock 'n' roll group. At their debut performance at the school Julian played a Les Paul copy guitar, which had been given to him by his father at Christmas when he was eleven. He played in two different groups while at Hoylake, appearing at school dances and playing rhythm guitar. His gym master at Hoylake taught him how to play. When his mother married her third husband, John Twist, they began living in a large sixteenth-century house in Ruthin. He began to attend school in Ruthin, but continued his friendship with Justin.

At the time Julian was studying for his O-levels at Ruthin School, but was hoping to go to an art college in Wrexham to do a foundation course. He'd known that his father had attended Liverpool College of Art and John was pleased when Julian told him he wanted to follow in his footsteps. Julian said that he loved John's drawings and they were the sorts of art that interested him. Julian failed all his O-levels, just like his father.

Then came the period that changed his life: John went off with Yoko and Julian's parents got a divorce. Paul McCartney was concerned at the time and drove over to Weybridge to see Cynthia and Julian. On the way there he made up a song to cheer Julian up. He began idly singing 'Hey, Jules' while he was driving. He commented, 'And then I thought a better name was Jude. A bit more country-and-western for me.' The song ended up as 'Hey Jude', but Julian had been the inspiration.

Julian recalls that when he first met Yoko he thought she was a witch in a miniskirt. Each Friday a chauffeur-driven car would take him to Tittenhurst Park to see his father. Initially, he was scared of Yoko and didn't know what to make of her.

When *Walls and Bridges* was released in October 1974, it included a track called 'Ya Ya' on which John had Julian play the drums. At Christmas 1974 Julian received an electric guitar from his father, with a plaque that read 'To Julian, Happy Christmas'.

After a gap of years in which he hadn't seen his father, Cynthia phoned John in America and asked him if he remembered he had a son in England.

Cynthia and Julian then flew over to America and stayed at the Beverly Hilton Hotel. Cynthia remained in the hotel while Julian went out each day with John and Yoko. After that he was invited to make the occasional trip to America to keep in touch with John. John also threw a party aboard a boat near his Long Beach mansion for Julian's seventeenth birthday.

Julian was to say, 'He was like a real dad, you know? I mean, he was the boss. He got heavy on occasion, so I didn't shoot my mouth off a hell of a lot. I was very quiet. We used to sit down with guitars and mess around, playing old blues and rock.'

In 1979, when he was only sixteen, Julian admitted that he had only recently come to appreciate his father, saying that when his parents split up he didn't realise what was happening and he certainly didn't miss his father. It wasn't until a few years later that he realised how fond he was of him and what he meant to him. Until that time there had hardly been any contact between them, but then they began to phone each other. He didn't see John for three years but then, when they became closer, they began to chat on the phone and Julian would spend part of his holidays with him at the Dakota Building in New York. He began to love going to New York and having talks with his father, saying, 'He advises me on how to cope with problems in life, and what to do as I grow up. He's a very important figure in my life.'

He was also to say, 'When I'm in New York, we go out quite a lot together, round some of the art galleries or to his house at Long Island. When we stay in, we have musical jam sessions together, singing our latest songs to each other or talking about art.'

When he was seventeen he continued jamming with Justin and there were rumours of band names such as the Lennon Drops, but they existed only in press copy.

On the night John was killed, Julian was living in the attic of their house and he was woken up when a chimney fell through. He went back to sleep. He later learned it occurred at the exact moment of his dad's death. Cynthia was in London at the time and when Julian went downstairs, his stepdad John Twist was there, but the curtains were drawn. When Julian pushed them open, it seemed as if there were hundreds of people outside. Cynthia had told Twist not to say anything until she got back. But Julian kept asking him what was going on and in the end Twist told him. Julian burst into tears.

Julian flew to New York and stayed at the Dakota, and there were strict instructions that Cynthia was not allowed to accompany him. Yoko didn't see him for four days. He said, 'I think she thought I'd just gone over there after Dad's money. One thing is for sure: I haven't got much of it.'

In the summer of 1981 Julian was fined £40 for setting fire to thirty government-owned wooden stakes during a drunken party in a Welsh forest.

The young man moved from Wales, parting from his girl-friend Sally Hudson, and began to enjoy the club life in London – but he was rather naïve. In December 1981 the paparazzi photographer Richard Young took a photograph of a girl pointing a gun at Julian's head in L'Escargot club. Julian was wearing a woman's wig and a dress for the cabaret at the club. This caused some controversy and was called 'a sick joke'.

Julian was to explain that it was a harmless prank. He'd been in a cabaret with Karen O'Connor, daughter of the singer Des O'Connor, and he was dressed as a charlady. They were asked to pose for a photograph using props. She'd used a toy gun to shoot at a basket of toy snakes in her act and one of the photographers said she should pose as a James Bond girl. Julian was to say, 'I didn't know the gun was there until I saw the papers the next day. When I read what was written I just felt, Oh, no, not again. The gun was just a toy. I never gave it a second thought.'

At the time, he was being managed by a man called Tariq Siddiqi, who owned a clothing shop in the West End. Julian had been living in his flat, but on 16 April he disappeared, leaving a note: 'I need a break. The pressure is getting too heavy.'

The same year he commented, 'Yoko decided to give me a hundred dollars a week some time ago, but it is not mine by right. The papers say I'm heir to a fortune worth millions but Yoko has total control over everything. I will get half the trust-fund cash when I'm twenty-five. The other half goes to Sean. I have a lawyer who is battling to see what else I'm entitled to.'

Tariq Siddiqi then said that Julian owed him large sums for recording equipment, musical instruments and clothes that he'd bought to launch Julian's musical career, and announced, 'I have got a writ from the High Court. But I hope this business can be settled in a friendly way.'

By 1982 Julian had acquired the image of a playboy, frequented nightclubs and had a series of girlfriends. His partic-ular favourites included Tramps and Stringfellow's. In fact, his nineteenth-birthday party took place at Stringfellow's and press coverage included photographs of models such as Sian Adley-Jones stripping to the waist.

At one time his name was linked with Stephanie LaMotta. She

said that she was the person who talked Julian into becoming a skinhead. LaMotta commented, 'The first time I saw him I had to ask him why he was so shy. He told me who he was and that he was still suffering from the loss of his dad. Since then we've become close friends, like a brother and sister. I even got him to cut his hair and get rid of those large glasses. The change was unbelievable.' LaMotta cut her first record and said, 'When I did the record he calmed me down. He came down to the studio and held my hand and kissed me all over my face. Afterwards I wrote a song and he asked to sing it with me. It worked out so well we're putting it out as a single. I call it "A Song For Jules", which is what I call him.'

After his break-up with Stephanie he lived for some time with the topless model Debbie Boyland, and then another girlfriend was Kate Lotto, whom he lived with after meeting her in Tramps, a fashionable club, in 1981. At the time he was living on £53 a week from his trust fund and said he'd been reduced to taking a modelling job to make ends meet.

He was to comment, 'I really believe that our relationship is very similar to that of my dad's with Yoko. Obviously, sex is important in any relationship, but it can't be everything. There has to be more. Kate and I are best friends as well as lovers and that for me is what makes it work.'

Kate was to sell her story to the *Daily Mirror* in January 1982 in a feature headed 'JULIAN'S BLONDE'. Within two months he was hitting the headlines for dating another blonde, with the *Sunday Mirror* reporting, 'This beautiful blonde is the new girl in Julian Lennon's life. Model Jordana has been wined and dined by Julian since they met at a London nightclub ...'

He also continued to enjoy the nightclub scene. One girlfriend said he was 'trying on his father's fame' – even to the extent of wearing rimless glasses and trying to look like John. As a teenager, he was prey to London's nightlife.

He was to say, 'I wasn't taken seriously because I was always seen hanging around nightclubs. Maybe people thought I was just messing around to get publicity – and money.'

As for his musical influences, he commented, 'As a child I'd grown up on "Sugar Sugar" by the Archies and all that stuff but I later realised the significance of the Beatles and their songs.'

He also said, 'I decided I wanted to learn to play the piano when I was thirteen or fourteen. I had one lesson with this old and very strict German teacher. If I played anything wrong he would whack me across the hands. So I thought, I'm not having any of this. Playing the piano is supposed to be enjoyable.

'So that was my first and last lesson. I decided I'd learn naturally by playing along to my favourite records.'

In 1982 he was interviewed in the national press and commented, 'Yoko has suggested I'm like a spoiled brat. I obviously wouldn't agree with that. She says she's given me things – musical equipment and money – but it's not true.'

The same year he agreed to a series of articles appearing in the *News of the World* in January in which he claimed that his father had offered him marijuana when he was only twelve years old.

In September 1983 he sent a tape of his songs to Tony Stratton-Smith, head of Charisma Records, and was signed to the label. Ahmet Ertegun also signed him to Atlantic Records in the US. In October 1983 Charisma sent him to the Manoir de Valotte, a French château near Nevers, to work for three months writing songs and making demo discs.

In January 1984, on the advice of Ray Coleman, he requested that the producer Phil Ramone work with him on his first album. Between February and August 1984 the album was recorded in various studios in New York and at Muscle Shoals Sound in Alabama. His long-time friend Justin Clayton joined him.

Valotte was released on Friday 19 October 1984 and he had written all but one of the songs. Apart from lead vocal he also played bass guitar, keyboards, electronic drums and percussion. The famed movie director Sam Peckinpah produced video promos of two of the tracks: 'Valotte' and 'Too Late for Goodbyes'. Julian and Peckinpah were also to collaborate on a one-hour TV special, but Peckinpah died before it could be made.

In January 1985 the album was certified gold and the title-track single entered the Top Ten; by March the album was certified platinum and 'Too Late For Goodbyes' became the second Top Ten single entry from the album. 'Too Late For Goodbyes' reached No. 6 in Britain and 'Valotte' reached No. 9 in the US.

March was also the month Julian set out on his first concert tour, which was a complete sell-out. From 8–10 April he played the Beacon Theater, New York City. On stage he was backed by Justin Clayton on guitar, Carlos Morales on guitar, Carmine Rojas on bass guitar, Chuck Kentis on keyboards, Frank Elmo on saxophone and Alan Childs on drums. He began his first American tour on Sunday 24 March 1985 in San Antonio, Texas, ending the US leg in Hawaii on 10 May, before continuing on to Australia and Japan.

Late in 1985 MCA Home Video released *Stand By Me: A Portrait of Julian Lennon in America*. It was a 58-minute documentary of Julian, produced and directed by Martin Lewis. It was set around his first tour and included him performing 'Let Me Be', 'Well', 'I Don't Know', 'OK For You', 'On The Phone', 'Lonely', 'Say You're Wrong', 'Valotte', 'Big Mama', 'Jesse', 'Day Tripper', 'Space', 'Stand By Me' and 'Too Late For Goodbyes'.

In an interview in February 1985, when he was 21, Julian revealed that sometimes Yoko's attitude upset him. He said, 'I think the worst thing that happened was when someone who worked for her and my dad came over to England and gave me a guitar that had belonged to Dad.

'It was a beautiful custom-made instrument with a dragon design in mother-of-pearl and the name "Lennon" in gold on the top.

'I wrote a couple of songs on it and it meant a lot to me. So I called Yoko to say thank you.

'As soon as I phoned her she said, "What guitar?" When I described it, she said, "Why have you got it? Who gave it to you?"

'She was really angry and she claimed the guitar had been stolen. The next thing I knew, she sent over a security guy to take the guitar away from me.

'I had to go to New York to sign a paper saying I had nothing to do with the guy who had given me the guitar. It was all shock horror.

'Maybe the guitar was something special to her ... but it was special to me as well.'

Julian also revealed that Yoko actually practised arguing, saying, 'I once told her that I was becoming better at arguing and that I'd learned to put my thoughts across more clearly.

'She said, "Maybe you should hang around me because nobody has ever beaten me in an argument – and I practise."

'I thought she was joking. But she said, "You have an argument with me now about anything and I'll win." '

From 1983 to 1986 Julian lived with the glamour model Debbie Boyland. The affair ended when she sold their story to the *News of the World*. It appeared as a double-page spread on 9 February 1986 under the strap line 'WORLD EXCLUSIVE' and a headline proclaiming, 'PAGE 3 MODEL TELLS OF HER HEARTBREAK LIFE WITH SON OF BEATLE LEGEND JOHN.' Julian had been in America at the time and there were rumours that he was going out with another girl, which prompted Boyland to make her revelations. A photograph of Julian with a singer called Fiona was published. Julian said that he hadn't been unfaithful during his American trip, but her approach to the media resulted in their split.

Julian said, 'It really angered me, because Debbie didn't even bother phoning me to check out these rumours.'

Another cause of the split was the fact that he felt she was jealous of his need to make music. Whenever he went upstairs in their house to play music, she'd go into a sulk. He said, 'It got so bad that I'd have to give up my music for weeks on end just to placate her.'

In 1986, he admitted that he'd originally wanted a career as an actor, but says that music led him astray. 'I used to hang out with kids who played music at school, and they convinced me it was the thing to do.'

He also said, 'When my dad and mum split up, I still communicated with Dad a lot. I'd even play him songs over the phone, and he'd comment on them. And whenever I saw him, we'd play together.'

On Thursday 9 January 1986 Julian received a Grammy nomination as Best New Artist and the following month was voted No. 1 New Male Singer in a *Rolling Stone* readers' poll. Monday 3 March 1986 saw the release of 'Stick Around', the first single from his second album, and his promo video included cameo appearances from Michael J Fox, Joe Piscopo and Jami Gertz. The album *The Secret Value of Daydreaming* was released on Sunday 16 March 1986. Produced by Phil Ramone, it was recorded at Compass Point Studios in the Bahamas and mixed at the Hit Factory, New York. On Monday 12 May 1986 he played the Royal Albert Hall, and in April 1986 he began his second world tour with a series of European concerts. His second album was certified gold in May and the same month he began his second North American tour and then appeared in Canada, Hawaii and Japan. Julian then took a sabbatical for a year and in 1987 left Britain for tax reasons following a farewell party at Stringfellow's nightclub on Friday 13 February and settled for a time in Montreux, Switzerland, to begin writing further material.

In 1988 he returned to America and bought a former US Army radar station in the Santa Monica Mountains near Los Angeles. His new home had thirteen-inch concrete walls and he paid up to $2 million for it – although he was able to sell it at a later date at a profit.

In July 1998, the British music magazine *Q* featured an article headed 'LENNON VS. LENNON', comparing the two Lennon boys. It said that Julian's legacy was £2,400 a year plus a £50,000 inheritance and that after years of legal activity and negotiation he stood to get around £20 million, while Sean would get £250 million. It pointed out that Julian paid £47,000 to buy some of his father's old clothes at auction while Sean had the pick of his father's belongings. Julian was to comment, 'Being John Lennon's son has come close to destroying me.'

He went into the Johnny Yuma recording studio in Burbank, California, with his producer Patrick Leonard. His first single from the new album, 'Now You're In Heaven', was released on Friday 24 February 1989. It was co-written with the guitarist John Curry. His third album *Mr Jordan*, was issued on 10 March 1989. It featured ten new compositions, three penned by Julian, five by Julian and Curry, and one each by Julian and Justin Clayton, and Julian and Pat Leonard. In addition to his backing band, guest artists included Peter Frampton, Fiona, Marilyn Martin, Fee Waybill and Timothy B Schmidt.

In 1989 he began a tour in June to promote *Mr Jordan*, which hadn't been doing very well. He said, 'It's been a very slow start. Part of the problem may have been that it's been three years since my last album. I was having a lot of business problems. I felt really pressured and pushed while making my last album, and I felt my business people weren't making the right decisions on my behalf. I've spent the last few years getting control of the situation – with a lot of arguing and fighting to become the person who has the final say. *Mr Jordan* is one hundred per cent more reflective than my first two albums were. It's my baby completely.'

In 1989 Julian was a partner in Columbus on Broadway, a restaurant in New York. It is interesting to note his fascination with opening restaurants – similar to his mother, who was involved in running at least three. At another time he wanted to open restaurants in Los Angeles called Revolution – which would be similar to the Hard Rock Café, with rock 'n' roll memorabilia – and he also became part owner of a café/bar in Monte Carlo.

Saturday 28 September 1991 saw the release of his fourth solo album *Help Yourself*. In the US the first single release was 'Listen', while in England it was 'Saltwater'. George Harrison played slide guitar on the 'Saltwater' track. The album was produced by Bob Ezrin and recorded in California, with some of Julian's regular music friends such as Justin Clayton and John McCurry. Apart from vocals, Julian performed on guitars, keyboards, mandolin, percussion, bass and drum programming. Julian co-wrote eleven of the twelve songs on the album.

Julian's single, 'Salt Water', was a Top Ten and a No. 1 hit around the world, except in America. Julian felt its lack of success Stateside was because of certain people at Atlantic Records. It took him five years to get out of the contract and out of the management he was with. During that time he travelled around Europe, meeting friends, and was writing, painting and sculpting and into photography.

He bumped into Bob Rose, who co-produced his fifth album with him.

It was called *Photograph Smile* and was issued in America on 23 February 1999 on MCA's Fuel 2000 label. While on a promotional tour in Australia in October 1998 Julian said of Yoko, 'I think she meddles too much in other people's business. I think she has raped and pillaged the Lennon family, not only the name. She has done extremely nasty things and it's not like she hasn't got enough.'

Ono responded, 'I don't know where he is getting those ideas, but one of the constant things I have to deal with, especially having been associated with John in his lifetime, and even today, are the myths.'

Commenting on Sean's album, *Into the Sun*, Julian said, 'I like it, it's interesting. We have different inspirations. You can tell he likes Nirvana and was brought up in a different lifestyle. He knows he's comfortable for the rest of his life. It's not like he feels a hunger, but he's talented.'

When *Photograph Smile* was issued in England at the same time as Sean's album, there was praise from certain critics who were saying that Sean was the real artist because of the avant-garde nature of his work. Julian believed that Yoko was using her money to squash his career in England.

In an interview with Ken Sharp for *Beatlefan*, Julian said he had documentation of letters signed by Yoko. 'There were letters which she wrote to major publications, one of which is a licensee from one of the major music papers over there, that basically stated that if Sean was not seen as the shining light, as the genius, and I wasn't put in the place of the useless has-been, then, and this was a veiled threat basically, either she would buy up all the publications, which she could probably afford to do, or she would bury this guy's career.'

He also revealed, 'With some of the labels that we were tied in with the distribution deal, which was the same as Sean, she had a lot of power and a lot of say-so. I mean, she's got a lot of shares in certain companies, which have control over labels we were working with.'

Julian also disclosed that Yoko arranged for Sean's album to be released at the same time as his and for his album to be dropped from the priority lists, which it was. He felt that there was manipulation going on and said that Yoko would like it to be seen in the books of history and the film footage that she and Sean are the only Lennon family alive.

Julian also mentioned that on the Beatles *Anthology* radio programme, 'Mum [Cynthia] and I are nowhere to be seen. Not even approached. Weren't even talked to. And that happens with anything and everything to do with the Beatles or Dad because Yoko has everything, has all of it, has the rights to his name, his likeness, you name it. So there's not much we can do in that respect. But the one thing she'll never have is the blood and the talent of the Lennons.'

In an interview in *Look* magazine in August 1998, he commented, 'I'm the thorn in Yoko's side. She would prefer me to just shut up and disappear.'

He also said, 'A lot of Dad's things were sold at auction without me even being asked – I had to buy the Afghan coat he wore in the Beatles.'

In a 1999 interview he said of Ono, 'I think she meddles too much in other people's business. I think she has raped and pillaged the Lennon family, not only the name. She has done extremely nasty things and it's not like she hasn't got enough. One circumstance was when Mum and Dad were together; he bought his half-sister, Julia, and her family a house to live in. Because in those days you didn't think in terms of suing people or taking things away, the house was never changed out of Dad's name. As soon as Dad passed away, Yoko went and took their home, the home that had been given them by him, and gave it away to charity with no compensation for them. Then there's me having to buy back memorabilia with his money so his family, myself, and my kids, can see where they came from, which is sad. The way she handles the estate and his memory is bad.'

August 1998 is when Julian conducted a number of interviews in which he finally revealed what he really thought about his father. He told the *Independent*: 'John Lennon was my biological father, but he left me when I was five years old and I may have seen him ten times in my life after that.' The headline to his *Daily Mail* interview was 'MY FATHER IGNORED ME FOR FIVE YEARS. I NOW KNOW HE'D NO LOVE FOR ME AT ALL.'

Julian announced that he was leaving the music business, then changed his mind and founded his own record label, Music From Another Room. 'I Don't Wanna Know', a single from *Photograph Smile*, was issued and Julian made various appearances in concerts in Germany and Italy and at a Prince's Trust concert in Hyde Park, London.

Following a holiday abroad over Christmas 1999 and New Year 2000 he began recording a new album in a London studio in April 2000.

There have been several books about Julian, all published in the eighties. They include: *Julian Lennon* by Yolande Flesch (Running Press Publishers, 1985); *Julian Lennon: A Biography* by Kalia Lulow; *John Lennon/Julian Lennon* by Nancie S Martin (Avon Books *Avon Superstars* series 1986); *Julian Lennon!* by Mark Bego (St Martin's Press, 1986); *Julian Lennon* by DL Maberg (Library Binding Publications, 1986); *Center*

Stage: Julian Lennon by William Sanfred and Cecil Green (Crestwood House, 1986).

Lennon Legacy: Two Generations of Music, The

Title of an entire evening devoted to John on the American cable station Showtime on Friday 14 March 1986. It included the television premier of *John Lennon: Live in New York City* and also included clips from the Montreal Bed-In and excerpts from the film *Imagine*.

Lennon Legend – The Very Best of John Lennon

A double album (also available on CD – CDPP 037 and cassette) issued in the UK on Monday 27 October 1997 on Parlophone 724382195429. It was issued in the US by Capitol on Tuesday 24 February 1998 and followed by a limited release of 5,000 copies of a vinyl version on 10 March. It was said to replace *The John Lennon Collection,* which had already been deleted in the US by Capitol on 27 December 1997.

The set, which was issued as a CD, cassette or double album, was supported by a £50,000 press campaign. The compilation contained twenty songs from throughout John's career. They were: 'Imagine', 'Instant Karma!', 'Mother' (single edit), 'Jealous Guy', 'Power to the People', 'Cold Turkey', 'Love', 'Mind Games', 'Whatever Gets You Thru the Night', 'No. 9 Dream', 'Stand By Me', '(Just Like) Starting Over', 'Woman', 'Beautiful Boy (Darling Boy)', 'Watching the Wheels', 'Nobody Told Me', 'Borrowed Time', 'Working Class Hero', 'Happy Xmas (War Is Over)' and 'Give Peace A Chance'. Included was a twenty-page booklet with some rare photographs taken by Spud Murphy, a former photographer from *Sounds,* the British music paper, who visited John and Yoko at Tittenhurst Park in 1971. There was also a selection of shots from the Apple archives. All tracks on the album had been digitally reworked.

Lennon, Mary

John's paternal grandmother. She was born Mary Maguire in Liverpool of Irish ancestry and was hired as a housekeeper by Jack Lennon after his first wife had died. He called her Polly. Jack and Polly were married and Polly gave birth to eight children, six of whom survived. The two babies lost at birth had been baptised Roman Catholics owing to the fact that Jack was a Catholic. However, Polly ensured that her other six children were christened Protestants.

She couldn't read or write, but was said to be very witty and was reputed to be psychic.

They lived in a terraced house in the Toxteth district of Liverpool, in an area referred to as Dickens Land because the various streets were named after characters in novels by Charles Dickens. Their house was situated at 27 Copperfield Street. When her husband died, Polly did not have the financial resources to keep the family together and had to place two of the children, Alfred and Edith, in the Bluecoat School, an orphanage. She died on 30 January 1949.

Lennon, Pauline

At the age of eighteen, Pauline Jones, a student at Exeter University, took a holiday job at the Toby Jug Hotel in Esher, where she met and fell in love with a man over twice her age, Alfred 'Freddie' Lennon. Despite an age gap of 35 years, Pauline, who had recently lost her father, found Lennon an extraordinary man with a wicked sense of humour. He asked if he could call her Polly after his mother, because he said Pauline reminded him of her.

They began to go on walks in the surrounding countryside together and he told her that John Lennon was his son. Not knowing much about the Beatles or John, she felt that it was unkind of John to ignore his father. Freddie told her not to judge him because John had believed that he had deserted him as a child and had turned up only when he was famous. He told Pauline that he had loved John's mother Julia deeply and would have still been with her if she hadn't left him for another man.

Pauline returned to Exeter University and began dating boys of her own age, but found she couldn't forget Freddie.

During the Easter holidays she returned to the Toby Jug to see him and Freddie proposed to her, although she didn't take him seriously. She told her mother, Jean, about the relationship, and Jean expressed some concern. When she met Freddie, she told him that, because of the death of Pauline's father two years before, 'I have to be both mother and father to her now. And that's why I just can't agree to her continuing with such an unsuitable relationship.'

Fred was earning only £10 a week at the time and wasn't in a position to get married. Pauline talked him into giving up his job at the Toby Jug in order to find work near the university. However, he was unable to get a job and began sleeping rough in the area around the university and the two quarrelled. When Pauline returned from a lecture she found that Freddie had left her a note:

> My dearest Polly. It is quite obvious that one in my hopeless plight has absolutely no right to entertain the idea of marriage to a girl who has her whole life and career ahead of her. I love you Polly with all my heart, but I now know there can be no future for us together ...
>
> PS I shall be working at the Greyhound Hotel, Hampton Court should you wish to contact me.

When Pauline read the note, she caught a bus to London, went to the Greyhound Hotel and the two vowed to stay together. She then had to tell her mother, who declared, 'I'm not prepared to allow you to see him any longer, so you'd better find a way of breaking it off.'

Pauline then took a temporary job in Paris looking after two children, but decided to return home and see Fred. She hadn't been paid, had no money and approached the British Consulate, who repatriated her.

Fred was reconciled with John, who bought him a house near Kew for £15,000 and arranged for Apple to give him an allowance of £30 a week.

Fred asked if Pauline could work at Kenwood as secretary to John and Cynthia. She worked there for a few months, typing out letters, looking after Julian, but there was not enough for her to do. Cynthia remarked, 'She was as much at a loss about knowing what to do as we were.'

Pauline's mother was furious about Freddie's plans to marry her daughter and made her a ward of court. The couple then decided to get married in Scotland. John asked Pauline to leave Kenwood. He did, however, sweeten the dismissal with a promise to pay the money to cover the court action brought about by her mother. He would also underwrite the costs of the three weeks they needed to spend in

Edinburgh to establish residence in order to be eligible to be married in Scotland.

Of her short term at Kenwood, Pauline commented, 'My impression of John was that he was totally withdrawn into himself when he was at home – unsmiling, cold and unapproachable. He seemed high-strung and tense, yet expressed nothing of himself to the household. His thoughts and feelings appeared tightly guarded.'

John then bought the couple a house in Brighton for £6,500 and their two sons were born there. David Henry Lennon on 26 February 1969 and Robin Francis Lennon on 22 October 1973.

John's attitude was unpredictable. Freddie and Pauline were invited along to Tittenhurst Park to show their firstborn to John. When they arrived he was in a rage, insulted them and told them to leave. It was alleged that John's changed attitude was caused by his recent course of primal therapy (see **Janov, Dr Arthur**), which directed his feelings of anger towards his parents.

A week later Freddie and Pauline were contacted by Apple, who told them they had to leave their house, which had been put in their name for tax purposes, but John now wished to repossess it. They left.

John never met his half-brother Robin.

When Freddie died, Pauline retained the manuscript of his unpublished autobiography and in a woman's magazine claimed that she still contacted Freddie's spirit at séances.

John contacted her and offered to pay for all the funeral costs, but Pauline turned his offer down.

She later remarried and became Mrs Pauline Stone.

Pauline used the original Freddie Lennon manuscript to pen *Daddy Come Home: The True Story of John Lennon and His Father*, which was published in Britain by Angus & Robertson in 1990.

Lennon (play)

A play conceived, written and directed by Bob Eaton, who was artistic director of the Everyman Theatre in Liverpool, where the production made its debut in 1981. Eaton, who was born in Chesterfield, Derbyshire, was to comment, 'I went to the local grammar school and, like millions of others, formed a beat group, under the influence of the Beatles, called the Invaders. I studied drama at Manchester University and worked as a director, writer and actor in many northern theatres.' He became artistic director of the Everyman at the beginning of 1981 and *Lennon* was his first production.

The Everyman had formerly been the Hope Hall Cinema. It was situated in Hope Street, as were the two cathedrals and Liverpool College of Art. It was converted into a theatre and called the Everyman in the 1960s and became a popular cultural centre on Merseyside and encouraged local poets and playwrights. In 1974 it held the world premiere of Willy Russell's *John, Paul, George, Ringo and Bert* for a six-week run before its move to London's West End. On Wednesday 28 October 1981 it presented the musical play *Lennon*.

He also travelled to New York in 1982 to direct the show in the off-Broadway Entermedia Theater, where it received an enthusiastic reception during its nine-week run.

The Entermedia was on 2nd Avenue and 12th Street. David Patrick Kelly portrayed the younger Lennon while Robert LuPone played the elder. There was a cast of seven in the two-and-a-half-hour production, five males and two females, playing a variety of roles. Mitch Weissman, who was associated with the *Beatlemania* stage show, supervised the music. Sid and Stanley Bernstein produced *Lennon* in association with Abe Margolis and Dennis Paget.

Lennon Remembers

The first gritty, no-holds-barred book about the life of a member of the Beatles, published in 1971 and based on lengthy interviews conducted by the *Rolling Stone* publisher Jann Wenner, which were originally published in the magazine as a two-part series entitled 'Working Class Hero'.

The book was issued in America by the magazine's book-publishing arm, Straight Arrow Books and reprinted as a paperback the same year by New American Library. It was published in Britain in 1972 by Talmy Franklin under the title *Lennon Remembers: The Frankest Beatle Reveals All*, which Penguin Books brought out in a paperback version in 1973 containing sixty photographs and a cover painting by Philip Castle. Penguin reprinted the book in 1980. It was published in Germany in 1973 and 1980 under the title *John Lennon*

Erinnert Sich, and a further edition entitled *Lennon Über Lennon – Abschied Von Den Beatles* in a translation by Niko Hansen was published by Rowohlt Taschenbuch in 1981. It was issued in Spain by Ayuso/Akal Editions in 1975 under the title *Lennon Recuerda* and a Japanese edition was published by Soshisha in 1972.

The interview took place soon after the release of the *John Lennon/Plastic Ono Band* album.

Lennon was particularly upset that Wenner published the interviews in book form without consulting him.

In the series of interviews, John is abrasive, rude, angry and – at times – virtually inarticulate. The series also proved to be very controversial, perhaps because he destroyed so many myths.

John describes tours as being like the film *Fellini's Satyricon*: he tells of orgies, visits to brothels, aides securing drugs, and groupies. Some Beatles enthusiasts were appalled that he had turned on long-time friends such as Neil Aspinall and Derek Taylor, but his criticisms were aimed at a number of people, most notably, Paul McCartney. He dismissed the musical products of his former friends and associates, commenting on George Harrison's album *All Things Must Pass*: 'I think it's all right ... I wouldn't play that kind of music but I wouldn't want to hurt George's feelings.' And of Paul's *Paul McCartney* album: 'I thought [it] was rubbish.' Even his former idol Bob Dylan doesn't escape unscathed. John mentions Dylan's latest album, *New Morning*: 'It wasn't much ... I haven't been a Dylan follower since he stopped rocking.'

John discussed a wide range of topics: his attitude towards people with physical disabilities; primal therapy; George Martin; Phil Spector; the Beatles break-up; the Maharishi; Apple; the MBEs; LSD and Yoko – covering all aspects of his career. He mentions that, among his own songs, his personal favourites are: 'I Am The Walrus', 'Strawberry Fields Forever', 'Help!' and 'In My Life'.

Lennon, Robin

The second son of Freddie and Pauline Lennon.

Robin was due to be born on 9 October 1973, John's birthday, but the pregnancy was a long one and he was born on 22 October.

He never had any association with John and continued to live with his mother in Brighton, following Freddie's death.

In June 1997 he was tracked down at his home in Brighton by a reporter from the *People* tabloid, who reported that the 23-year-old was unemployed. A neighbour reported: 'You won't see Robin out a lot. He lived away for a while but moved back in with his mother a few months ago. He seems a nice lad but I think he is quite shy.'

Lennon, Sean Taro Ono

John's second son was born by caesarean section on Thursday 9 October 1975 at 2 a.m. in New York Hospital, New York. He weighed 8 pounds 10 ounces. John was to say, 'I feel higher than the Empire State Building.' He was also pleased that Sean had been born on the same date as he had – under his lucky number nine. It was a high point in the lives of John and Yoko, since she'd suffered three previous miscarriages in their attempts to have a child. When his second son was born John at one time considered naming him George Washington United States of America Citizen Lennon.

It was suggested that Yoko had made a pact with John that if she bore him a child there would have to be a role-reversal: he would have to spend the time looking after the child while she took care of the business. Apparently he agreed to this and entered his five-year period as a househusband.

John was to say, 'He didn't come out of my belly but, by God, I made his bones, because I've attended to every meal, and to how he sleeps, and to the fact that he swims like a fish. That's because I took him to the "Y". I took him to the ocean. He's my biggest pride.'

John began making special drawings for Sean, had photographs taken every single day of the first year of his life by his photographer friend Bob Gruen, in addition to taking hundreds of Polaroid photographs himself. John doted on his son, as if in some atonement for the guilt of neglecting his first child.

During those years John devoted himself completely to Sean's upbringing and would rise at six o'clock in the morning to plan Sean's meals, with the two of them having breakfast at seven thirty – and by ten o'clock John was planning the next meal. It was while the two were on holiday in Bermuda that John decided to resume his musical career.

After John's death Sean was educated at Swiss boarding schools.

Sean made his singing debut at the age of eight on a new Yoko Ono album, *Every Man Has a Woman*.

When Sean was thirteen he appeared in the Michael Jackson video *Moonwalker*. He attended Columbia University and majored in anthropology. In 1988 he was interviewed for the documentary *Imagine: John Lennon*, and three years later, together with Yoko and Lenny Kravitz, organised a recording of 'Give Peace a Chance' as a protest against the Gulf War. He also appeared on Kravitz's album 'Mama Said'.

Sean was interested in the New York indie-rock scene, took up the guitar and piano and formed a rock trio, IMA, who were featured on Yoko's 1995 album *Rising* and backed her on tour. *Ima* means 'now' in Japanese.

He met his girlfriend Yuka Honda when she and her fellow Cibo Matto band-mate, Miho Hatori, remixed Yoko's 'Talking to the Universe' EP. Sean fell in love with Yuka and toured with Cibo Matto.

Sean's influences around this time were the Beastie Boys, Beck and Cibo Matto and he was thrilled when one Beastie Boy, Adam Yauch – who had heard his songs and really liked them – asked him to record for the Boys' label. The result was Sean's debut CD *Into the Sun*, on Grand Royal Records, produced by Yuka Honda, in the spring of 1998.

Sean was to say, '*Into the Sun* was inspired by my girlfriend Yuka. It's about the most important relationship in my life. It's about the beginning of a new relationship and about growing to understand one another. It's about sharing everything with somebody, and the risks involved. It's about overcoming fears of intimacy, about learning to trust each other. It's about the happiness of being in love and the craziness that goes with it. It's about exploring new things and new ideas. It's about growing up a little bit and getting my shit together.

'I met Yuka Honda and Miho Hatori of Cibo Matto after they remixed "Talking to the Universe" for my mum's EP. We loved what they did and wanted to meet them. During a rehearsal in New York for a Yoko tour, they stopped by. We immediately hit it off. That night we all jammed at my studio. It was magic.'

Yuka then asked him to sit in at a Cibo Matto show, and then they asked him to go on tour with them as a bass player. Sean also went on to tour America, Europe and Japan with Yoko.

When the album was released he was interviewed by the *New Yorker* magazine and told them that he believed his father had been assassinated by the American government.

There were thirteen tracks on Sean's debut album: 'Mystery Juice', 'Into the Sun', 'Home', 'Bathtub', 'One Night', 'Spaceship', 'Photosynthesis', 'Queue', 'Two Fine Lovers', 'Part One Of The Cowboy Trilogy', 'Wasted', 'Breeze' and 'Sean's Theme.'

In 1999 he told *The Times*: 'A lot of kids from our generation don't know Beatles music at all, which is cool, it's old, and there's more important music now. Hip-hop is more important than the '60s.'

Lennon, Sidney

One of John's uncles. An ambitious young man, he worked hard in a men's outfitters in Liverpool and rose to the top in the business. Sidney was also rather conservative and frowned on his brother Freddie's rebellious attitude and anti-conventional way of life. He pointed out that Freddie had been given a good education at the Bluecoat School, but had wasted it.

On the day he married Julia, Freddie phoned Sidney and asked him to be a witness. Sidney took some time off work, met Freddie and told him that he was in no position to get married. Julia and a friend arrived and, following the brief ceremony, Sidney took them all to a local pub and bought them lunch.

Sidney emigrated to Ontario, Canada, in 1967. When contacted for an interview for the *Detroit Free Press* following John's death in 1980, he was 72 years old. He claimed that he and his wife looked after John in their home in Liverpool for about nine months when John was four, shortly before John's mother, Julia, placed her son in the care of his Aunt Mimi.

Lennon Tapes, The (book)

A team from BBC Radio 1 travelled to New York to interview John and Yoko while they were recording the *Double Fantasy* album at the Hit Factory. The team comprised an executive producer, Doreen Davies, a producer, Paul Williams, and the disc jockey Andy Peebles.

On Saturday, 6 December 1980, they began what they believed would be a half-hour interview about the making of the album – to their delight this became a three-hour chat in which John talked about his entire life and career.

The team arrived back in Britain on 9 December to learn that he had been murdered. Some short excerpts from the interview were broadcast that day and the entire tapes were broadcast in five parts beginning on 18 January 1981.

This slim volume, published by BBC Publications in 1981, is the transcript of those broadcasts – its publishing royalties were donated to charity. There is a colour photograph of John and Yoko at the Hit Factory on the back cover, and the contents comprise a foreword by Paul Williams, an introduction by Andy Peebles and the 88-page interview.

The topics and personalities John discusses include memories of early BBC recordings; his meeting with Yoko at the Indica Gallery; the making of *How I Won The War*; *Two Virgins*; the film *Rape*; Bagism; *The Ballad of John and Yoko*; *Live Peace in Toronto*; the Lyceum concert; *Double Fantasy*; feminism; Liverpool College of Art; Elton John; David Bowie and Phil Spector and the *Rock 'n' Roll* album.

There were two versions of the book published in Japan that year – *All That John Lennon 1940–1980: You Said Goodbye But We Say Hello*, translated by Ikezawa Natuki and published by Chukoron-sha, and *Last Message*, published by Kodan-sha. A Spanish edition, *John Lennon La Ultima Conversacion*, was published by Ultramar Editores, and a German edition, *Lennon Uber Lennon – Leben In Amerika*, translated by Wolfgang Doebeling, was published by Rowohl Taschenbuch, while the American edition was published by Dell.

Lennon's Women – The Naked Truth

A two-part special broadcast on TV Fox in the US on Monday 17 and Tuesday 18 October 1988.

Let It Be (album)

The final Beatles album release, the production of which was an unhappy affair for all concerned. Their producer, George

Martin, was to comment, 'Right from the beginning everything about *Let It Be* seemed to be out of sync with what we had done before. It was not at all a happy recording experience. It was a time when relations between the Beatles were at their lowest ebb.'

Martin was also to say, 'The idea for *Let It be* was a brilliant one, and I think it was Paul's. The original idea was that we should record an album of new material and rehearse it, then perform it before a live audience for the very first time – on record and film. In other words make a live album of new material, which no one had ever done before.'

As it was, that concept didn't work out. Although they spent a great deal of time rehearsing the numbers, resulting in numerous versions of different tracks, they could not agree on a venue. For a British venue they needed a large auditorium, but it was winter. The Roundhouse in Camden was also suggested, as was the Tunisian desert!

John was to say, 'Someone mentioned the Colosseum in Rome, and I think originally Paul might have suggested a bloody boat in the middle of the ocean. As for me, I was rapidly warming up to the idea of an asylum.'

Martin also observed, 'In order to get things together, Paul would try to get everybody organised and would be rather over-bossy, which the other boys would dislike. But it was the only way of getting together. John would go wafting away with Yoko. George would say he wouldn't be coming in the following day. It was just a general disintegration – disenchantment if you like.'

Paul criticised George's playing and George walked out, not returning until three days later, and the concept of performing live was reduced to a famous performance on the roof of the Apple Building in Savile Row.

Altogether around 30 hours of music and 96 hours of film had resulted from the extended sessions.

They'd originally intended calling the album *Get Back*, but the release was delayed. There were so many takes of the various songs that the Beatles just couldn't face going through all the tapes to select what they considered were the best versions, so they hired a producer, Glyn Johns, to do it. However, John and George weren't happy with the result and both of them decided to let Phil Spector remix the tapes and take over the production. However, instead of portraying the Beatles without all the studio sweetening – as was originally intended – Spector did the opposite and added an orchestra and a female choir to four of the tracks – 'Across the Universe', 'I Me Mine', 'Let It Be' and 'The Long and Winding Road'. Paul was furious with the alterations to 'The Long And Winding Road', which he'd intended as a simple production. He wrote to Allen Klein requesting his original version be used, but Klein didn't bother replying and went ahead with the Spector version. This was one of the main reasons why Paul went forward with the dissolution – because his music was now being interfered with.

The delay in the release was also caused by the fact that Paul wanted his solo album, *McCartney*, to be released, but there had been disagreements about its conflicting with the release date of the new album, and Ringo was sent to see Paul – who threw him out of his house.

The participation of Spector has always remained controversial. Glyn Johns considered Spector had ruined the album. George Martin said, 'I thought the orchestral work on it was totally uncharacteristic. We had established a particular style of music over the years – generally overlaid music on most Beatles tracks – and I felt that what Phil Spector had done was not only uncharacteristic, but wrong.' He summed up, 'I was totally disappointed with what happened to *Let It Be*.'

Paul was to say, 'The best version was before anyone got hold of it: Glyn Johns's early mixes were great but they were very spartan; it would be one of the hippest records going if they brought it out. But before it had all its raw edges off it, that was one of the best Beatles albums because it was a bit avant-garde. I loved it.'

Owing to the delays, the Beatles recorded another album in between – *Abbey Road*.

Let It Be was eventually released in the UK on 8 May 1970 and in the US on 18 May of that year, topping the charts in both countries.

John's compositions on the album were: 'Dig A Pony', 'Across the Universe' and 'One After 909'. John and Paul co-wrote 'I've Got a Feeling'.

Let Me Count The Ways

A number penned by Yoko and inspired by the relationship between the poets Robert Browning and Elizabeth Barrett. It was included on the *Milk And Honey: A Heart Play* album which was released in 1984. Yoko was to say, 'One early morning in the summer of 1980, I woke up with "Let Me Count The Ways" ringing in my head. I called John, who was in Bermuda, and played it over the phone. I asked, "How do you like it?" He said, "I really like it. It's beautiful." I said, "How about you writing one with a Robert Browning line, and we'll have portraits of us as Elizabeth and Robert on the cover?" (This needs a little explaining. John and I always thought, among many other things, that we were maybe the reincarnation of Robert and Liz. So he immediately knew what I was talking about.) We then discussed the *Double Fantasy* cover and thought that it should be two portraits, one of Elizabeth and the other of Robert, only the faces would be ours. John thought we should look very prim and proper with just our hands coming out of the painting and holding in the middle, the funny touch. We both laughed. He said, "OK then, just tell downstairs (our office) to send me the collection of Robert Browning and let's see what happens." I didn't need to send anything to Bermuda, though, because John called me the same afternoon, and said, "Hey, you won't believe this!" He then explained that he'd been watching a fifties film about a baseball player on TV, and in the film he'd seen the girlfriend send a poem by Robert Browning called "Grow Old Beside Me". "Can you believe that?" he asked. "So, anyway, this is my version." Then he proudly played the song over the phone. That's how our two songs happened.'

Let Me Take You Down

A book about John's assassin Mark Chapman, written by Jack Jones and first published in America by Villiard Books in 1992. Virgin Books published the British edition in 1993.

The author corresponded with and visited Chapman in Attica Prison for five years from 1986, before producing the book. In the meantime, his exclusive stories, photographs and interviews with Chapman were translated and circulated throughout the world on the eve of the tenth anniversary of John's murder.

Photographs of a happy, smiling Chapman from early childhood are also contained in the book, which documents the
killer's life in detail.

The reader is left with the uncomfortable suspicion that
Chapman is receiving the fame he craved when he murdered
John and can imagine the pleasure he felt when this book of his
life was published. With the high-profile television interviews
the murderer has given he has, over a period of time, become
something of a celebrity and, no matter how journalists or TV
interviewers chastise him for his crime, the resultant publicity is
akin to rewarding him for the deed.

Levy, Morris

Record company executive who was one of the early business
figures behind the rock 'n' roll boom. A former nightclub owner,
he struck up a partnership with the disc jockey Alan Freed and
formed Roulette Records. At one time he copyrighted the term
'rock 'n' roll', but a court established that the term had passed
into public domain.

When John penned 'Come Together', which was included on
the *Abbey Road* album, he paid tribute to Chuck Berry's 1956
hit 'You Can't Catch Me' and had even included a line that
was identical to one in the Berry song: 'Here comes old flat
top'.

Levy, who published Berry's music, wasn't impressed and was
prepared to sue for infringement of copyright. An out-of-court
agreement was made, which included the promise that John
would record three songs from Levy's publishing company, Big
Seven, including 'You Can't Catch Me'.

When *Walls and Bridges* was issued and the three songs
hadn't been included, Levy was furious that John had gone back
on his word. In an effort to sort it all out, John and his lawyer
Harold Seider met Levy at the publisher's own establishment,
Club Cavallero, on 8 October 1974.

Seider offered Levy $200,000 compensation, but was turned
down. Levy then explained an idea of his concerning a mail-
order record company he owned called Adam VIII. He said they
could issue a rock 'n' roll album by John on TV-advertised mail
order and make a fortune. He said he'd studied the Beatles'
contract with Capitol and discovered that there was a clause

that allowed Apple to release products on mail order without Capitol's permission.

John was excited about the idea and agreed. There were further meetings at Club Cavallero and the album was recorded. When John met Levy at the club on 1 November 1974 he sent around to the Record Plant and a messenger delivered tapes of the entire album on two reels of 7½ r.p.m. tape, which John gave to Levy.

Levy and Seider then began to work out the money to be made. He found that, when all deductions were made, John would only receive 23 cents an album, compared with the 60 cents' royalty he received from Capitol. Seider delayed any further talks with the excuse that they couldn't approach EMI (who had worldwide rights to Beatles products) at the current time owing to complicated negotiations regarding the Beatles' contract.

Then Capitol Records talked John out of honouring the mail-order deal. Seider visited Levy to tell him that Capitol was to release John's *Rock 'n' Roll* album in March and that he should drop his mail-order idea.

Levy was furious at being double-crossed a second time and decided to rush-release the album and pre-empt the Capitol LP. Adam VIII began advertising their album, called *Roots – John Lennon Sings The Great Rock & Roll Hits*, on television in New York on 8 February 1975. Capitol not only brought forward their release to February, but informed everyone associated with Levy's album – advertising agencies, album manufacturers, television stations, etc. – that they would be sued by Capitol if they associated with the mail-order release. The album was killed stone dead and sold only 1,500 copies.

Levy then sued John for $42,000,000. The first court case was declared a mistrial and the second took place in January 1976. Both parties were found guilty of infringement but Levy suffered the heavier penalties and also had to make a settlement to John of $144,700.

Levy died of cancer on 21 May 1990 at his home in Gwent, New York. He was 62 years old.

Lewis, Jerry

An American comedian. He first rose to fame as part of the Dean Martin/Jerry Lewis comedy team. He then went on to make several popular comedies as a solo star, including *The Nutty Professor* and *Cinderfella*.

Lewis also began to hold an annual telethon to raise money for muscular dystrophy. John and Yoko, together with Elephant's Memory, appeared on *The Jerry Lewis Labor Day Telethon* on 6 September 1972.

John and Yoko's appearance on the show drew criticism from the radical left, who felt that, because it came so shortly after their One-To-One concert, the couple were appearing in charity shows to curry favour with the establishment to gain a green card for John. There was also a reaction against the way Lewis paraded the victims of the disease on the show, which many regarded as being in bad taste.

John performed 'Imagine' and was followed by Yoko introducing one of her new compositions, 'It's Now Or Never'. They finished the set with a version of 'Give Peace a Chance', which John announced as – 'This is reggae, baby, like they do it in Jamaica.'

This was the last time that John and Yoko appeared together performing on a stage.

John was to comment, 'Jerry is one of our favourite comedians.'

Ringo Starr was to appear on the telethon in 1979 and Paul McCartney donated a film clip of 'Getting Closer' to the show.

Lewis, Jerry Lee

An influential rock 'n' roll singer/keyboards player who became one of several early influences on John's group the Quarry Men, who performed a number of his songs, including 'Whole Lotta Shakin' Goin' On', 'High School Confidential', 'Mean Woman Blues' and 'Fools Like Me'.

John's hero worship of the early American stars never faded and during his 'lost weekend' in Los Angeles, one of his friends, Elliott Mintz, arranged for John to see Jerry Lee Lewis perform at the Roxy Club in Hollywood. John had never seen Jerry Lee Lewis perform live before and said, 'I only had three childhood idols, Elvis, Carl Perkins and Jerry Lee, and I haven't seen any live. Let's go!' Mintz commented, 'He was as excited as a child going to the circus. Jerry did all his tunes, lifted his foot and put it on the piano keys, and it was thrilling.'

After the show Mintz took an inebriated John backstage and

introduced him to the blond-haired rocker. John dropped to his knees and began kissing Lewis's shoes. Jerry Lee put his hand on John's shoulder and said, 'Now, now, son, no need for that, that's fine, son, just fine.'

Lewis's

One of Liverpool's main department stores, situated at the corner of Ranelagh Street and Renshaw Street in the city centre.

The corner entrance doors opposite the Adelphi Hotel were a favourite rendezvous for courting couples. This was where John would often arrange to meet Cynthia during the early days of their romance.

However, such meetings were not without their degree of embarrassment for Cynthia, who, to please John, would dress with an emphasis on what she called 'oomph'. She was to describe her new look as 'long blonde hair, tight black sweaters, tight short skirts, high-heeled pointed shoes, and to add the final touch, black fishnet stockings and suspenders'.

In her autobiography, she was to say, '… the only trouble with an outfit like that was that on many an occasion, when I had arranged to meet my beloved in Liverpool outside Lewis's store directly underneath the then controversial statue of a nude man, or outside Central Station or whatever, John would invariably turn up late and I was forever in danger of being picked up by the most unsavoury characters that Liverpool could offer.'

Incidentally, the statue of the well-endowed naked man was by the eminent sculptor Jacob Epstein.

The Beatles actually made a single appearance at the department store on 28 November 1962, when they were booked for a staff dance, held on the top floor of the building.

L'Express

A French magazine. In March 1970 the publication included an interview with John, in which he discussed the Beatles' MBEs. He said that he accepted the honour only because Brian Epstein wanted him to and also because of the other members of the Beatles. He mentioned that the Palace allowed them to dress informally, so they didn't have to wear morning suits, that he was too nervous to bring Cynthia along, that he smoked pot in the loo and the Queen was prettier in person.

John had made up the part about smoking marijuana in the Palace, an example of his humour, although it was taken seriously. As a result, for years writers have perpetuated the myth that the Beatles smoked pot when they were at Buckingham Palace.

When he'd been asked about the Beatles' future, he'd said, 'The Beatles are dead – long live the Beatles. People ask what's happened to us. If we never record together again, well, that's bad luck. If we do, it'll be great.'

Life Begins at Forty

John began composing 'Life Begins at Forty', and made a home demo of the song, accompanying himself with acoustic guitar and drum machine.

It was one of four new songs he'd written, which he intended to offer Ringo Starr for his forthcoming album. The song itself was a present to himself and Ringo on their respective fortieth birthdays – John's in October and Ringo's in July 1981.

When Ringo visited him at the Dakota Building on Monday 5 November 1979, John gave him a demo of the song.

The number had a country music style, which would have suited Ringo, and John announced that the performance of the song was coming from 'the Dakota country-and-western club'. Using a country accent, he sang, 'Age is just a state of mind.'

The number was aired in the radio series *The Lost Lennon Tapes*.

Life Without Lennon

A BBC radio show broadcast between 1 and 1.59 p.m. on Saturday 14 January 1984. The programme was based on an interview conducted with Yoko in Tokyo by Andy Peebles.

Lindsay, John V

The Mayor of New York when John was involved in his battle with the immigration authorities. Lindsay wrote letters to the immigration service and also testified on John's behalf. Together with that of his deputy mayor, Edward Morrison, and the future mayor, Ed Koch, his influence was beneficial to John's case and all three insisted that he be allowed to stay in New York as he was 'a cultural asset to the city'.

Lindsay was to say, 'It's true. I was responsible as much as any human being in helping him stay. You recall, he wasn't very popular because of the drug thing. He was way down at that time.'

Lindsay, Mark
British actor who was originally hired to play John in the TV movie *Imagine: The Story of John and Yoko*. One week after he was cast for the role, it was discovered that his real name was Mark Lindsay Chapman and he was sacked. NBC and Carson productions issued a brief statement: 'Although purely a coincidence, we feel it is in the best interest of this project that another actor be cast as John Lennon.' Mark McGann was then hired.

The executive producer, John McMahon, said, 'I feel very badly for him because it's not his fault, but it would be bad form. I mean would you do the love story of John F Kennedy and Jackie Onassis with an actor named Lee Harvey Oswald playing Jack Kennedy? [The studio] plans to find another part soon for [Lindsay/Chapman] because we all feel very badly about this.'

Lindsay said, 'I have no malice toward anybody at all. I am trying to keep a reasonable head on it. Of course I'm disappointed. I'm only human after all. The last thing I'd want to do would be to rake up bad memories for Yoko.'

McGann said, 'I was very, very sad for the bloke. I hadn't even thought about screen-testing for the show before I read about what happened to him.'

In 1986, Lindsay appeared in two TV movies, *Assassin* and *The Annihilator*.

Lisson Gallery
Situated at 68 Bell Street, Marylebone, London NW1.

John provided the finance for Yoko Ono to hold her *Half-A-Wind Show* at the Gallery from 11 October until 14 November 1967. He didn't attend the opening and wished to remain anonymous, although the exhibition was subtitled 'Yoko Plus Me', a reference to John's sponsorship. John was also mentioned several times in the exhibition catalogue.

In one section containing her notes on the show, Yoko wrote, 'When *Hammer A Nail* painting was exhibited at Indica Gallery, a person came and asked if it was all right to hammer a nail in the painting. I said it was all right if he pays five shillings. Instead of paying the five shillings he asked if it was all right for him to hammer an imaginary nail in. That was John Lennon. I thought, So I met a guy who plays the same game I played. This time John suggested how about selling the other half of my half-a-matter objects in bottles. It was such a beautiful idea I decided to use it even though it was not mine.'

The exhibition was also referred to as *Half-A-Memory Show* in the programme, whose cover sported a thin line within a ruled frame with the words 'Have you seen a horizon lately?'

Yoko was as enigmatic as ever and her notes included such observations as 'I think of this show as an elephant's tail' and 'Life is only half a game. Molecules are always at the verge of half disappearing and half emerging.'

The initial section of the exhibition was entitled 'Environments'.

The first item was *The Stone – Laundromat of the Mind*, designed and produced by Tony Cox, Yoko's husband. Yoko was to describe it as 'a square room in which all sides including the ceiling were made of Japanese Shoji paper, or the equivalent. Strong lights were lined up between the Shoji ceiling and the real ceiling of the gallery so when you were inside the room, you felt the lights coming through the ceiling. The lights were on a circulating dimmer that would light up the room and then darken it in a certain rhythm that made one feel as though one was going through day and night. Speakers were set up outside the four corners of the room and the same music came through each speaker except that there was a slight time gap between the speakers so that when you were in the room, you felt as though you were sitting in the middle of different time zones.

'One was asked to first fill out a questionnaire [re: *Grapefruit*] and take off one's shoes to enter the room in a black bag. Everything about the room was white, including the lights through the ceiling, and gave people incredible highs while they went through the experience of sitting in there while the room went from brightness to darkness many times in an hour and while they listened to the music, which was just thousands of crickets singing over and over again. It was like living many, many lives in one hour, or being thrown out in the universe where there's only white light. When this show was put on in New York in 1966 for the first time, multimedia light shows were not quite on their way, and it created excitement just from that point of view. The Zen minimalist aspect of the show still held its ground even after the whole world was into multimedia.'

The next item was called *The Blue Room*. Yoko commented, 'This was an all-white room. One was supposed to stay in the room until the room became blue. There were other aspects of the room that worked to expand your sensory perception. For instance, while you were sitting in it, you would notice that the floor had a little sign saying, "this is the ceiling". You would notice that there was a sign on the window-sill that said, "this is 1,000 feet long", and you would notice a little sign on the wall that said, "you are not here" or "this is not here". "You are here" was John's answer to my "Not Here" signs.'

The next item was *Backyard*. Says Yoko, '*Backyard* was a small lot in which a tiny hole, more like something a mouse would like to hide in, was dug. There was a sign pointing out to the hole saying it was a hole for the clouds to drop from the sky. Also, orders were taken to have the same hole dug in people's own backyards.'

The next section of the exhibition was called 'Objects'. There were Yoko Ono Machines, designed and produced by Alexis Apple. Yoko was to describe them: 'Cry machine – this was a coin machine that drops water when you put money in it and cries for you.

'Mad telephone – this was a three-piece phone set. Only one phone rang and could be dialled from. The second phone only let you listen to the other party. The third phone was to talk into. You had to have three phones to complete the conversation. But the phones were all in different corners of the room so it was very hard to keep up the conversation. A pretty frantic affair!

'Switch place – it was a little electric bulb attached to your under- or over-pants or a T-shirt, that lit up by a remote-control switch which was held by another person. The person with the remote control could light up the bulb whenever he/she would like to send an "I Love You" message from wherever. Imagine you were at a chic cocktail party or something and your pants suddenly lit up! I liked this idea so much that I was going to elaborate on it.'

In fact, Yoko explained this in a note in the brochure:

The switch piece is meant to be mass-produced. By using this switch, you can dispense with a large part of language communication. Instead of shouting to your husband who is in the bath that the dinner is ready, you can turn on the light in the bathroom from the kitchen. Instead of calling your wife and telling her that you are coming home, you can just turn the light in her room from 500 miles away and she will know that you are on your way home, etc., etc. I would have a whole room of lights, like a light flower garden, and see which friends are tuning in.

Commenting on Item D, the final piece in the 'Objects' section, Yoko said, 'Mind telephone – this was a telephone to talk into and it would simply play back what you had said. It worked like this: "I don't like you." "I don't like you." "I don't love you." "I love you." Elaborate talk received an elaborate answer, et cetera. Maybe that's how life is. Just listening to ourselves.'

The next section was 'Air Bottles', credited to John Lennon and Yoko Ono. Yoko's description was, 'There were beautifully empty bottles of different sizes on which labels were put, saying Half-A-Chair, etc. Some small bottles contained half of large objects. Large bottles sometimes contained half of small objects. They were just chosen arbitrarily.'

The next item was entitled *Three Spoons* and there were four spoons on a pedestal that had a sign saying 'Three Spoons'.

This was followed by a three-part exhibit called *Exit*. Yoko was to say, 'Exit b) exit which was in an impossible place to reach.

'Exit c) exit which was really small so you had to bend to go out from. This was done in the tradition of the Japanese Tea House exit – namely, you had to bend and go through it to humble yourself. It was also done in the style of *Alice In Wonderland*: an exit that led to a beautiful English Garden from which you could only peek through until your body became the right size (smaller). It was also done in accordance with the European medieval heritage of a long hall exit you had to crawl through to get out. In medieval Europe it was set up in that way for defence purposes so one would know whether the person passing the exit was armed or not and also it would be easier for the Lords to have the person's head chopped off when you passed my exit but you faced a dead end from which you had to come out using your wits. Of course in the end, you would come out to the lot in the backyard. After the trauma of going through the exit, the lot looked like the beautiful English garden Alice saw through the hole.'

The next item was called *Pawns*. Yoko commented, 'This was the white chess set. All pawns were white. Therefore, in playing the game, one had to remember and/or convince the opposition which of the white pawns belonged to whom. That was more in keeping with the life situation than in the usual chess game.'

The following piece was the *Hammer-A-Nail Painting*, featured at the Indica Gallery exhibition.

The next item was entitled *Windflute for John*. Yoko said, 'This was just a piece of wood. (A very nice one, though. It looked like it travelled a long way until it finally ended up on Brighton Beach where I had found it.) Wood becomes a flute when it's loved.'

The last two items were called *Mind Object*, which Yoko described as 'a) a stethoscope, a needle and a white ball – mix them well in your mind and make an object, b) a beautiful cup – not to be appreciated until it's broken.'

Listen To These Pictures: Photographs of John Lennon

A 112-page book by Bob Gruen, published in the US by William Morrow & Co. in 1985. It comprised 135 black-and-white photographs taken between 1971 and 1980, the last shots being taken two days before John's death. There is an introduction by Yoko, a first-person text by Gruen and among the other celebrities' pictures in the book are those of Elton John, Mick Jagger, Andy Warhol and Allen Klein.

Literary Lennon, The

A book by Dr James Sauceda, published by Pierian Press in 1983. It provides the most scholarly and detailed study of a much-neglected aspect of John's genius – his ability with words.

Subtitled 'The First Study of All the Major and Minor Writings of John Lennon', the book is true to its title in unearthing items ranging from John's review of *The Goon Show Scripts* to his sketch for the musical revue *Oh, Calcutta!*.

In his introduction the author writes of how his life was changed one day in Pickwick's bookstore in Hollywood when he picked up a copy of James Joyce's *Finnegans Wake*. This eventually led to his writing a doctoral dissertation on the book at USC in 1977. Three years later, in the same bookstore, he came across a passage of work which he mistook for Joyce but discovered that it was a piece by John.

Sauceda commented, 'Like millions of others, I knew he was simply "the best", meaning the best musical poet, the best rock artist, the best personality; I was stone-cold ignorant of the literary Lennon.'

He then set out to track down further examples of John's work, a task of research that proved difficult but exciting. The result is this seven-chapter book, which is divided into three sections. Part One covers John's major works; Part Two his minor works; and Part Three his future ones.

The first chapter deals with the critical reaction to *In His Own Write*, followed by a chapter analysing the book. The third chapter deals with the reviews of *A Spaniard in the Works*, followed by an analysis of it. Chapter Five covers John's early work, from childhood to his *Mersey Beat* contributions and Chapter Six reviews his work between 1963 and 1979. The final chapter discusses *The Lennon Play: In His Own Write* and suggests directions for future research.

Dr Sauceda not only attempts a thorough analysis of John's writings, but seeks to understand how his mind worked when he wrote his stories and poems, revealing many little-known facts about John's life.

Little Child

A song John co-wrote with Paul for Ringo. John played the mouth organ and Paul played piano and the track was included on the *Meet the Beatles* album.

Little Prince, the

An enchanting, mystical story by the French writer Antoine de Saint-Exupéry. It became a cult classic in the 1950s, influencing a variety of celebrities, including the actor James Dean. John and Yoko appreciated the innocence, love and wisdom shown by the Little Prince as he arrived on Earth from another world. They claimed that a phrase from the book, 'The essential is invisible to the eye', led them to create 'bagism'.

'The Little Prince' was made into a big-budget film in 1974, but much has been lost in the transition from a slim volume, with a simple message and much charm, to a brash, full-colour motion picture.

Liverpool College of Art

Situated in Hope Street, the street that has a cathedral at each end.

John entered the art college at the age of sixteen in September 1957. After he had failed all his O-levels at Quarry Bank School, his Aunt Mimi had a meeting with the school headmaster, William Pobjoy, to discuss John's options. Pobjoy suggested that since he appeared to have artistic talent, he should seek a place at the art college. Mimi agreed and Pobjoy wrote a letter to the college, which led to an interview with the college principal, Mr Stevenson, which John passed, although he wasn't eligible for a grant during the first year, which meant that Mimi would have to support him, which she agreed to do.

He started life at the school, dressed in Teddy Boy gear and began the intermediate course. This was a course in which all the basics were taught: composition, life drawing and so on. Among the friends John made in his class were Geoff Mohammed, Tony Carricker, Ann Mason and Helen Anderson. One of his first girlfriends at the college was Thelma Pickles. Other members of his intermediate class included Carol Balfour, Jeff Cane, John Wild, Peter Williams, Gill Taylor, Marcia Coleman, Ann Preece, Violet Upton, Diane Molyneux, Ann Curtis and Sheila Jones. Ann Mason was to spend two hours painting a picture of John in March 1958.

John gained a reputation for disrupting classes and was turned down for the painting class. While the intermediate course continued, in place of the painting class he took lettering, in which there were approximately a dozen students in the class including Cynthia Powell, Phyllis McKenzie and Jonathan Hague. Cynthia had joined the lettering class in her second year at the college.

John mixed with various groups of friends in the college. After Bill Harry introduced him to Stuart Sutcliffe, John, Sutcliffe, Harry and Rod Murray were often mixing together socially at parties and local pubs, at coffee bars such as the Jacaranda and in students' flats. First Rod and Stuart had accommodation in nearby Percy Street and then they moved to Gambier Terrace, where lots of gatherings between them took place.

The group also used to go to the nearby Liverpool University, where subsidised drinks could be had at the students' bar, and they went to various university events such as poetry reading and also took part in the annual Panto Day. This was an event for local charities in which the university students collected money in tins and had floats on the backs of lorries, which paraded in the city centre. Some members of the art college such as John, Stuart, Bill and Rod, participated, as well as members of Liverpool Institute, such as Paul McCartney and George Harrison.

John was known to go to the toilets in Lime Street Station where, inside a cubicle, he'd jimmy open his collection box and spend the money on beer.

Ye Cracke in Rice Street was regarded as the local pub. This is where John and Cynthia decided they were in love and from where they then went on to the Gambier Terrace flat to consummate it. This is where Stuart Sutcliffe's father often dropped in to have a drink with Arthur Ballard, one of the tutors, who was a great help to John, Stuart and Bill Harry and who actually prevented John and Bill from being expelled. Arthur attempted to get both John and Bill into the new graphic arts department. Bill was accepted but the teacher, Roy Sharp, rejected John because of his reputation for disruptive behaviour.

Another pub they frequented was the Philharmonic, further along Hope Street.

John was always having a laugh in classes, particularly when a teacher was out of the room – and often got up to high jinks in the life classes, sitting in the lap of the nude model June Furlong, for example.

The Students' Union organised dances in the college canteen, mainly booking local jazz bands such as the Merseysippi. Stuart and Bill Harry were among the organisers, with Bill designing the tickets and collecting them at the door. They obviously booked John's group, referred to as the college band. Stuart and Bill were on the Students' Union committee, along with Alan Swerdlow and Rod Jones, who were also their friends. Alan took part in a college production of the pantomime *Cinderella*, in which he and John were the Ugly Sisters – John wore June Furlong's corset. Alan was also to take photographs of the Beatles at the Odd Spot club later on and was commissioned to design a Beatles Fan Club night ticket and advert by Brian Epstein.

Rod Jones shared the Gambier Terrace flat with Stuart and Rod Murray – where John virtually moved in, although he wasn't an official tenant. Since they were booked at the college dances they asked Stuart and Bill if they could get them some PA equipment and Bill and Stuart proposed and seconded that the Union pay for amplification equipment, which 'the college band' could use. They never returned it and its loss was thought to be the reason why Stuart was rejected for the ATD (art teacher's diploma) course.

John's fashions changed from the early days he was at the college. His initial Teddy Boy style of dress is what first drew Harry's attention to him. He noticed him striding past in the canteen in his Teddy Boy gear and noticed that all the other students were dressed in turtleneck sweaters and duffle coats – making John the 'outsider' or the unconventional one. He later began to adopt a more bohemian style although he was never to actually conform.

As Paul and George were in the building next door, they frequently came into the college canteen at lunchtimes and also used to rehearse in the college life rooms during breaks.

In 1984 Yoko and Sean visited the college and donated £10,000 and a number of John's drawings to it. During the trip Yoko was given a copy of John's college report from 1958 to 1960 during which time he had failed two intermediate exams. A teacher had written, 'Give up your guitar, otherwise you will never pass your exams.'

Liverpool Institute

A grammar school adjoining Liverpool College of Art, in Mount Street, Liverpool. It was founded in 1825 as a Mechanics

Institute, and was officially opened as a school on 15 September 1837.

Charles Dickens lectured there in 1844 and famous pupils have included Sir Charles Lamb, Lord Mersey and Sir Henry Enfield. In 1890 one half of the school became an art college and brick walls were built to separate the two buildings internally. The institute changed from a fee-paying school to a grammar school in 1944, making it the oldest grammar school in Liverpool. The school motto was '*Non nobis solum, sed toti mundo nati*', which means 'Not for ourselves alone but for the good of all the world'.

Paul entered the school when he passed his 11-plus examinations. One of the tutors was Alfred Smith, brother of George Smith, who was married to John's Aunt Mimi.

In the summer of 1957 Paul took two O-level exams and passed in Spanish, but failed in Latin. He took six further subjects in order to move up into the sixth form in 1958. He passed in five and seemed to have a penchant for languages – apart from Spanish, he also has an O-level in German and French.

When John, Paul and George were finally in a group together, following their appearances at the Casbah Club, the two Institute boys used to sneak into the art college at lunchtime to rehearse in the life rooms.

When the Silver Beetles had the opportunity of touring Scotland for two weeks as a backing band for Johnny Gentle, Paul was still in the midst of his studies for his GCE exams. He preferred to be on the road, told his father he was going on two weeks' holiday and went on the tour, neglecting his studies, which resulted in his passing only one further O-level.

After the institute had been closed for a number of years, Paul eventually successfully campaigned for it to be turned into a fame school: the Liverpool Institute of Performing Arts, known as LIPA.

Lives of John Lennon, The

A controversial biography published in 1988. Despite the fact that Albert Goldman spent six years writing the 420,000-word tome, it contains a great number of inaccuracies and not a few fantasies.

Goldman, following the success of his notorious iconoclastic biography of Elvis Presley, received an advance rumoured to be one million dollars. For such a huge amount he had to produce something that would be as commercial and as iconoclastic about John as his Elvis book was about the King. The problem was that John's life had been something of an open book and people were aware of his drug taking, his love life and so on.

The FBI with all its vast resources had tried to blacken John's name, but couldn't come up with anything. Also, a great number of John's friends, including Mike McCartney and Bill Harry, refused offers of interviews and would not co-operate, suspecting what type of book it would be.

Paul McCartney and Elton John asked people to boycott the book and Cynthia Lennon called Goldman a vulture. Julian Lennon described it as 'crap, lies and untruths – the whole thing is just sickening'.

Lockwood, Sir Joseph
The chairman of EMI Records in Britain from 1954 to 1974, throughout the Beatles years. The group met him on numerous occasions and when John and Yoko had been 'busted' while at Ringo's Montague Square flat, John phoned Lockwood from Marylebone Police Station to ask his advice. He was told to plead guilty.

When John finally decided to take on Allen Klein as his manager, he sent a message to Lockwood in January 1969 saying, 'Dear Sir Joe, from now on Allen Klein handles all my things.'

Lockwood also prevented the use of John's selection of Mahatma Gandhi on the *Sergeant Pepper* tableau and when he heard that a picture of the naked John and Yoko were to be used on the *Two Virgins* album cover he said, 'If you must have a naked man on the cover, why didn't you use Paul instead?'

He once said, 'I can stand only so much pop music. But I'll always listen to the Beatles. They are the best.'

He died on 6 March 1991 at the age of 86.

London Arts Gallery
Situated at 22 New Bond Street, London, it was the venue for the first exhibition of John Lennon's 'erotic' lithographs.

In 1968, Anthony Fawcett, assistant to John and Yoko, initially suggested to John that he try his hand at lithographic art. Together with Ed Newman he introduced John to a method using specially treated litho paper. John eventually passed over a number of sketches he had made of himself and Yoko on their honeymoon, walking in Paris, with scenes of the wedding ceremony.

Fawcett and Newman selected four of the drawings, had prints made by the Curwen Studio and presented them to John in the Apple offices. Fawcett had intended to talk John into producing a portfolio of lithos, but John was so impressed with the samples that he immediately said he would be compiling a portfolio and already had a name for it – Bag One.

It was agreed that Newman would co-publish with Bag Productions.

Ted Lapidus, the French clothes designer, was approached to design a special leather bag to enclose the prints. The bag was made in Italy and was in stylish white leather, complete with zips, handles and lock. The words 'Bag One' were imprinted on one side of the bag, together with John's signature. John personally signed each one of the three thousand prints, which had been printed by Curwen Press.

John had presented Fawcett and Newman with twelve images for the set, half of them from his original sketches of the marriage and honeymoon, half of them erotic drawings portraying oral sex and Yoko masturbating. Asked why he had featured so much oral sex in the drawings, John replied, 'I like it.'

The press release issued by the London Arts Group read,

The London Arts Group, with fine art galleries in London, New York and Detroit, will stage the world premiere of Beatle John Lennon's first portfolio of original lithographs on Wednesday, January 14, at the London Arts Gallery, 22 New Bond Street, London. The exhibition will continue through Saturday, January 31.

Lennon, who lately has been receiving world-wide publicity for his peace efforts, is turning to a new artistic career. The images in the album are based on his wedding to Yoko Ono and detail the intimate and erotic scenes from their honeymoon. Shrouded in surrealist imagining,

Lennon's art speaks of life and reality, not mere pornography. The portfolio, containing 14 images, is an edition of 300, packaged in a white portfolio bag, and published by Consolidated Fine Arts. This exhibition is part of a series to be seen at the London Art Gallery this year; others include Pierre Alechinsky (February 18–March 18), Roberto Matta and Julian Stanczal.

The police raided the gallery on 16 January and seized eight prints for possible prosecution, the offending parts on the prints were then covered in black tape. The summons stated that the gallery had 'exhibited to public view eight indecent prints to the annoyance of passengers, contrary to Section 54 (11) of the Metropolitan Police Act, 1839, and the third schedule of the Criminal Justice Act 1967'.

At the Magistrates' Court, Detective Inspector Patrick Luff of the Central Office, New Scotland Yard, told how he saw about forty people viewing prints: 'I saw no display of annoyance from the younger age group, but one gentleman was clearly annoyed.'

The exhibition reopened the same afternoon. The eight prints were eventually returned and the resulting publicity ensured that the exhibition was a huge success. There were three thousand prints at £40 each or £550 a set. Of the 300 sets for sale, 296 were sold. They brought in £159,000 gross, out of which John received £35,000.

The president of the London Arts Group, which had galleries in London, Detroit and New York, was Eugene Schuster. He was unperturbed by the police action and said that the prints would next be exhibited in their gallery in Detroit, where he said he could foresee no arrests or confiscations taking place. 'If they can let *I Am Curious Yellow* [an erotic film] pass, how can they object to this?' he commented. He said he planned to open the exhibition without a prior showing to the Detroit Police Censorship Board, commenting, 'Good or bad is up to the critics. It's not for the police to say.'

The premises later became the site for a costume jeweller's.

Long Black Train

A song John used to sing with the Quarry Men. It was actually a version of the number 'Streamline Train', popular with skiffle groups. There was a record of the song issued by the Ken Colyer Band in 1958 and another by the Vipers in 1957. The Quarry Men used to perform the Vipers' version, although John didn't have the lyrics for the song so he made up some of his own and also changed the song's title to 'Long Black Train'.

Long John and the Silver Men

A name suggested to John, Paul and George by Casey Jones, leader of Mersey Beat group Cass and the Cassanovas, soon after John had decided to dispense with the Quarry Men title.

Cass didn't like the name the Beetles and told them they should have the name of the group leader up front. This was the fashion in those days with bands such as Cliff Richard and the Shadows. The group didn't like the suggestion, but retained the word 'silver' and called themselves the Silver Beetles.

The name is, of course, derived from the character Long John Silver in Robert Louis Stevenson's *Treasure Island*. It is in keeping with the style of names of some Liverpool groups at the time – Al Quentin and the Rock Pounders, Ahab and his Lot, Johnny Autumn and the Fall Guys and so on.

In his first book *In His Own Write*, John penned a story called 'Treasure Ivan', which featured a character called Large John Saliver.

Look At Me

John wrote this ballad in 1968 during his sojourn at Rishikesh. It was a number similar to 'Julia' and he considered recording the ballad for *The Beatles* double album, but didn't. He eventually recorded it in 1970 and it was included on the *John Lennon/Plastic Ono Band* album.

Looking Through a Glass Onion

A stage play based on John's life which opened in London's West End at the Criterion Theatre, Piccadilly, in October 1993 after touring Australia for two years. There was an after-show party at Planet Hollywood following the premiere, attended by Anjelica Huston, Jerry Hall and Koo Stark. It was produced by Michael White, responsible for the hit musical *Crazy For You*, and starred the British-born Australian actor John Waters, who was backed by a live band. Waters had written the play and the show featured him speaking the words of Lennon, reflecting on John's life and playing Beatles songs and moments from John's solo career. White had spent a year clearing the rights to songs owned by Yoko Ono, Paul McCartney and Michael Jackson.

He also released a CD album of the show, *Looking Through a Glass Onion – John Lennon In Word and Music,* issued on Polydor 5214562 in 1993.

Loop De Loop
A single by Harry Nilsson, with 'Don't Forget Me' on the flip, issued on RCA PB 10139 in December 1974. John produced both sides.

Lord, Take This Makeup Off Me
A parody of Bob Dylan. The track was included in the *Lost Lennon Tapes* series and on a CD included with a Swedish edition of *A Spaniard in the Works,* published in 1998.

Losing You
Number John originally recorded in 1980. Rick Nielsen and Bun E Carlos of Cheap Trick and Tony Levin of King Crimson backed John on the track. When the song was included on the *John Lennon Anthology* box set in 1998, the three musicians gathered again to make a video of it. The director, Dead Karr, filmed this in a Los Angeles studio on 2 November. A number of John's line drawings were animated by David Spafford and interacted with the musicians as the drawings floated through the video. The clip was first screened on VH1 on 3 December 1998.

Lost Lennon Tapes, The
A series broadcast in America by the Westwood One radio network from Monday 18 January 1988. Yoko had opened her vaults of John's material for the series, which was written and produced by Stephen Peeples; a later contributor was Lorre Crimi. The host of the series was Elliot Mintz, who had listened to nearly 300 hours of tapes prior to selecting material for the series. He opened the series on the first day with a three-hour introductory programme. The original series was set to run for one year. The intention had been to draw mainly from the 800

hours of tapes that John had recorded from the early 1960s right up to the time of his death and were basically known as 'the Dakota Archives', which Yoko had allowed to become available. However the series was extended and lasted for four years, ending in the spring of 1992. The wealth of material included studio out-takes, home demos, alternative mixes and live performances, although fans felt that, by stretching the series too long, it eventually lost its way and the original focus was lost. Towards the latter part of the series it was virtually a Beatles history: there were four shows on Brian Epstein, three shows on Beatles films, shows on the Beatles in Hamburg – even a programme on Paul McCartney's Russian album.

Lost weekend

The description John gave to the fifteen months he spent away from Yoko, in the company of May Pang, mainly in Los Angeles, between the autumn of 1973 and the beginning of 1975.

The Lost Weekend was the title of a book and film. The 1945 film starred Ray Milland and depicted two days in the life of a dipsomaniac. The association between the title and the fortunes of an alcoholic are obviously attached to the name John gave to this short period of his life.

John himself was to compare it to his days in Hamburg, referring to the LA sojourn as 'one long booze-up, tasty birds, good rock 'n' roll and a little mindless violence on the side'. Yoko had arranged for John to take May Pang as his lover and then suggested that he take May to Los Angeles and spend some time away from her, giving both of them some space. Yoko herself has never admitted that she encouraged John and May to be lovers and, when talking about the period to Ray Coleman, told him, 'It wasn't surprising that we should separate for a while. It turned out to be the best thing that could happen.'

During the lost weekend John was encouraged by May to explore his roots in rock and roll, resulting in his asking Phil Spector to produce his *Rock 'n' Roll* album. He gathered together a number of musicians, but the recording sessions proved to be chaotic, with drink and drugs in abundance and Spector shooting off a gun and absconding with the master tapes.

While in a drunken stupor, John promised Harry Nilsson that he'd produce an album for him. He then rented a beach house because 'it was the thing to do'. He had the musicians living in the house with him – Harry Nilsson, Ringo Starr, Jim Keltner, Klaus Voormann and Keith Moon. He said, 'We'd go into the recording studio, bottles out. Everyone was falling on the floor. So I ran away to New York with the Harry tapes. I didn't steal them. I said, "Harry, you've gotta leave me alone to finish this. I'm supposed to be producing it." He followed me to New York. I finally had to say, "Harry, get the hell out, I want to finish this record." '

While in New York with May he also recorded the *Walls and Bridges* album. Much of the publicity of the period concentrated on his drunken excesses at the Troubadour club.

The period began to come to an end on 28 November 1974, when John appeared on stage at Madison Square Garden with Elton John. Yoko was in the audience. She sent him a single white gardenia with the message 'Good luck, love Yoko'. They then met in the dressing room after the show. John said, 'There was silence: everything went silent and time stood still. We were just sort of looking at each other. Somebody said we looked very much like two people in love although this wasn't the signal for us to get back together. We didn't do that until months later on. It was very weird but it was a great night.'

John then spent Christmas with May and his son Julian, visiting Disneyland in California. Back in New York, John and May were in an apartment formerly occupied by Greta Garbo. In January 1975 John suddenly told May, 'Yoko has allowed me to come home to her now. I'm going to pack a few things.' He met Yoko for tea at the Plaza Hotel and told Yoko, 'This is like I never left. I'm happy to be back. Let's tell the world we're proud that our trial separation was totally unsuccessful. In fact it was a failure.'

Commenting on the lost weekend in the *Imagine: John Lennon* documentary film, Elliot Mintz was to say, 'The lost weekend was a combination of a remarkable party, an exercise into the depths of foolishness, and I think John's last effort to assert his manhood. It was his departure from his youth, to becoming a man, to wanting to be with Yoko, to having a child. Some people have bachelor parties – John had a lost weekend.'

Love

A song John had first written and made a home tape recording of during the July/August period in 1970. It was a simple love song inspired by Yoko, which he began recording in the studio during the *John Lennon/Plastic Ono Band* sessions in late September 1970. On the recording, Phil Spector played piano.

Apart from appearing as Track Two on Side Two of the album, 'Love' was issued as a single in Britain on Parlophone R 6059 on 15 November 1982, with 'Give Me Some Truth' on the flip. The remixed track was issued to promote the new *The John Lennon Collection* album, on which it appeared.

The single reached No. 27 in the British charts and John considered it to be as good as anything he'd written for the Beatles.

Love! Eternal John Lennon

A two-hour Japanese television special transmitted by Fuji Television on 4 November 1980, in celebration of John's fiftieth birthday. It included clips of Japanese Lennon fans and Japanese musicians playing his compositions. There were also clips from the Liverpool tribute in May and a tape of Yoko talking about John.

Love: John Lennon Forever

A ten-track tribute album issued in Japan in December 1992. It was then released in Britain on the Denon label.

Love Letter from John and Yoko to People Who Ask Us What, When and Why, A

On 27 May 1979 the Sunday editions of the *New York Times* and *Los Angeles Times* printed an advertisement booked by John and Yoko headed 'A LOVE LETTER FROM JOHN AND YOKO TO PEOPLE WHO ASK US WHAT, WHEN AND WHY'. The advertisement also appeared the same day in newspapers in London and Tokyo. Each of the advertisements cost them $18,000. They were also to take out the same ad in the trade publication *Record World*.

John and Yoko were always conscious of the media and their power as a means of communication. Despite their access to the press, they occasionally paid for advertisements to convey a message they wished to get across. Their 'War Is Over' campaign, with its huge display posters, is an example of how they utilised advertising. Another example occurred on John's fortieth birthday, when Yoko hired a plane to fly past the Dakota Building in New York with the message, 'SEAN AND YOKO LOVE YOU'.

On 8 November 1968 John and Yoko took out advertisements in the music press in support of the Peace Ship, an independent radio station aboard a ship in the Middle East, which attempted to advocate peace between the Israelis and Arabs.

However 'A Love Letter …' remains their most famous advertisement. It read,

The past ten years we noticed everything we wished came true in its own time, good or bad, one way or the other. We kept telling each other that, one of these days, we would have to get organised and wish for only good things. Then our baby arrived! We were overjoyed and at the same time felt very responsible.

Now our wishes would also affect him. We felt it was time for us to stop discussing and do something about our wishing process. The Spring Cleaning of our minds! It was a lot of work. We kept finding things in those old closets in our minds that we hadn't realised were still there, things we wished we hadn't found. As we did our cleaning, we also started to notice many wrong things in our house: there was a shelf which should never have been there in the first place, a painting we grew to dislike, and there were the two dingy rooms which became light and breezy when we broke the walls between them.

We started to love the plants, which one of us originally thought were robbing the air from us! We began to enjoy the drum beat of the city which used to annoy us. We made a lot of mistakes and still do.

In the past we spent a lot of energy in trying to get something we thought we wanted, wondered why we didn't get it, only to find out that one or both of us didn't really want it.

One day, we received a sudden rain of chocolates from

people around the world. 'Hey, what's this! We're not eating sugar stuff, are we? Who's wishing it?' We both laughed. We discovered that when two of us wished in unison, it happened faster. As the Good Book says – Where two are gathered together – It's true. Two is plenty. A Newclear seed.

More and more we are starting to wish and pray. The things we have tried to achieve in the past by flashing a V sign, we try now through wishing. We are not doing this because it is simpler. Wishing is more effective than waving flags. It works. It's like magic. Magic is simple. Magic is real. The secret of it is to know that it is simple, and not to kill it with an elaborate ritual which is a sign of insecurity.

When somebody is angry with us, we draw a halo around his or her head in our minds. Does the person stop being angry then? Well, we don't know! We know, though, that when we draw a halo around a person, suddenly the person starts to look like an angel to us. This helps us feel warm toward the person, reminds us that everyone has goodness inside, and that all people who come to us are angels in disguise, carrying messages and gifts to us from the Universe. Magic is logical. Try it sometime.

We still have a long way to go. It seems the more we get into cleaning, the faster the wishing and receiving process gets. The house is getting very comfortable now. Sean is beautiful. The plants are growing. The cats are purring. The town is shining, sun, rain, or snow. We live in a beautiful universe. We are thankful every day for the plentifulness of our life. This is not a euphemism. We understand that we, the city, the country, the earth are facing very hard times, and there is panic in the air. Still the sun is shining and we are here together, and there is love between us, our city, the country, the earth. If two people like us can do what we are doing with our lives, any miracle is possible! It's true we can do with a few big miracles now … The thing is to recognise them when they come to you and be thankful. First they come in a small way, in everyday life, then they come in rivers, and in oceans. It's going to be all right! The future of the earth is up to all of us.

Many people are sending us vibes every day in letters, telegrams, taps on the gate, or just flowers and nice thoughts. We thank them all and appreciate them for respecting our quiet space, which we need. Thank you for all the love you send us. We feel it every day. We love you, too. We know you are concerned about us. This is nice. That's why you want to know what we are doing. That's why everybody is asking us What, When and Why. We understand. Well, this is what we've been doing. We hope that you have the same quiet space in your mind to make your own wishes come true.

If you think of us next time, remember, our silence is a silence of love and not of indifference. Remember, we are writing in the sky instead of on paper – that's our song. Lift your eyes and look up in the sky. There's our message. Lift your eyes again and look around you, and you will see that you are walking in the sky, which extends to the ground. We are all part of the sky, more so than of the ground. Remember, we love you.

John and Yoko Ono.
May 27, 1979
New York City
P.S. We noticed that three angels were looking over our shoulders when we wrote this!

Love Me Do

The Beatles' first single, written in 1958, mainly by Paul, but with some assistance from John, who said, 'Paul wrote the main structure of this when he was sixteen or even earlier. I think I had something to do with the middle.' Recalling the recording of the number, Paul told *Playboy* magazine, 'I was very nervous, I remember. John was supposed to sing the lead, but they changed their minds and asked me to sing lead at the last minute, because they wanted John to play harmonica. Until then, we hadn't rehearsed with a harmonica. George Martin started arranging it on the spot. It was very nerve-racking.'

It has been alleged that Brian Epstein bought 10,000 copies of the single for his NEMS store, an accusation he always denied. This seems to be another of the myths. Owing to the structure of the charts in those days, it wouldn't have made any difference if he'd bought 100 or 10,000. The charts were made up of lists from a limited number of 'chart shops' in different parts of the country. If, for instance, the chart compiler phoned NEMS in Whitechapel asking for their best-selling records of the week, the list of Top Ten records would simply be given, from one to ten, but not in the amounts sold. Therefore, if the most popular record in NEMS sold eighty copies that week, it would be placed at No. 1. So Epstein wouldn't have needed to buy 10,000 copies of the record to get that placing in his own store. He would have no effect on records sold in other stores, so why would he have to buy such an amount? Also, a single retailer buying that unprecedented amount of a particular record would soon come to the attention of the chart compilers, who would render it null and void. The '10,000 records' story is an unlikely one.

Lowe, John Charles

John Lowe was born in West Derby, Liverpool, in April 1942 and began taking piano lessons at the age of six. Nicknamed 'Duff', he attended the same school as Paul McCartney, the Liverpool Institute. When they were ten years old, prior to starting at the institute, both Duff and Paul failed their audition for the Liverpool Cathedral choir, although Duff was successful six months later.

Paul, George Harrison and Duff were all in different forms at the institute, but began to get to know each other when the forms coincided and they began to do subjects together such as art and music. One day, while walking across the school yard, Paul asked him if he could play the beginning of 'Mean Woman Blues', which he did, so Paul invited him to his house in Forthlin Road, where he was introduced to John Lennon. The Quarry Men at that time comprised Rod Davis on banjo, Pete Shotton on washboard, Eric Griffiths on guitar, Len Garry on tea-chest bass and John and Paul. A few weeks after Duff joined as a pianist in January 1958, George Harrison became a member. Lowe appeared at a number of gigs with them but left the band in January 1959.

The sixteen-year-old Duff lived in West Derby, which meant he had to take two bus journeys to team up with the other members. They'd rehearse on Sundays and perform on whatever Saturday gigs they could get. He says he can't remember them playing skiffle numbers as their repertoire was based on the music of Gene Vincent, Chuck Berry and Buddy Holly.

Lowe suspected that John felt that the group didn't need a pianist and recalls there were difficulties at gigs because of having to tune the pianos at the different venues they played. Most of the venues had pianos and he doesn't remember a time when he didn't have to join them for the lack of an instrument.

Jeans weren't regarded as a respectable form of attire at the time and Duff remembers how John would lend him a pair of jeans. He'd put them on at home, but they'd be hidden under his other clothes in order that his parents wouldn't see them.

He also recorded with the others at Percy Phillips's studio in Kensington where they performed 'That'll Be The Day' and 'In Spite Of All the Danger'.

Lowe thinks that it was Paul who organised their visit to 53 Kensington and remembers the studio as being like a domestic dining room with 'a big table that had some instruments on it'. There was a piano at one side of the room and a single microphone.

Duff finally got fed up with the hour-long journey from West Derby. His girlfriend was complaining about the time he spent rehearsing and he had his A-levels to get on with, so he quit the group He was later to join a country-and-western band, Hobo Rick and the City Slickers.

In 1975 he moved to Ashton, near Bristol, where he worked in the investment business. He found a copy of the Quarry Men recording in a linen cupboard and spoke to Sotheby's to assess what it was worth. Paul McCartney heard about it and they did a deal, with Paul buying the acetate from him.

In the 1991 he teamed up with Mike Wilsh, former member of the Four Pennies, to form the Pennies. He then decided to make a CD under the name of the Quarry Men, with Pennies' members John Ozoroff on guitar, Charles Hart on lead vocal, Richie Gould on bass – and Rod Davis, former Quarry Man, on rhythm. It was called *Open For Engagements* and featured a tribute to John Lennon called 'John Winston'. He then left the Pennies and met up with former members of the Quarry Men and joined the revived band.

LSD

Lysergic acid diethylamide, a drug discovered by accident in 1943 by a Swiss biochemist, Albert Hofmann.

The chemical was then used in tests on volunteers at certain American universities, some of the research being financed by the CIA.

The chemical, nicknamed 'acid', is hallucinogenic and acts directly on the brain, causing vivid visions and heightened awareness of colours, sounds and textures, and it creates what are known as 'trips'. People can have good or bad trips. Bad trips are nightmarish and can affect a person's sanity. This is why a person taking acid for the first time should have someone who has experienced LSD with them to guide them through the trip.

LSD alters people's perceptions and there have been a number of deaths when people have jumped out of windows believing they could fly.

Dr Timothy Leary, a Harvard professor, believed that the drug could be of great benefit if handled the right way, enhancing man's perception and awareness and heralding a new state of consciousness.

In January 1966, John and Cynthia and George and his wife Pattie were invited to dinner by a dentist who was a friend of George's. John had described him as 'a middle-class London swinger, you know the sort of people George hangs around with'.

They touched on many subjects during the conversation that evening, including the topic of drugs, and the dentist then told them that he'd spiked their coffee with LSD, a drug they'd never experienced before.

They didn't believe him and said they were leaving to visit the Ad Lib Club in London's West End. The dentist advised them not to leave because of the effect of the drug but they ignored him and set off in George's black Mini, with its black windows.

John commented, 'When we got to the club we thought it was on fire. When we finally got into the lift, we all thought there was a fire, but there was just a little red light. We were all screaming ... we were all hot and hysterical.

'George somehow or other managed to drive us home ... we were going about ten miles an hour, but it seemed like a thousand and Pattie was saying, "Let's jump out and play football." I did some drawings of four faces saying, "We all agree with you!" I gave them to Ringo. I did a lot of drawing that night.

And then George's house seemed to be just like a big submarine. I was driving it; they all went to bed.'

The second time John experienced LSD was at a party in Hollywood. Guests included members of the American group the Byrds, Ringo Starr, George Harrison and the actor Peter Fonda.

Fonda kept saying, 'I know what it's like to be dead,' and John used the experience of that night, together with Fonda's phrase, for the number 'She Said, She Said', which appeared on the *Revolver* album.

John was now sold on LSD and over the years claims to have taken over a thousand trips. He took acid on only one studio session, however, and this proved disastrous.

He said, 'I suddenly got so scared on the mike. I thought I felt ill, and I thought I was going to crack. I said I must get some air. They all took me upstairs on the roof and George Martin was looking at me funny, and then it dawned on me that I must have taken some acid. I said, "Well I can't go on, you'll have to do it and I'll just stay and watch." You know I got very nervous just watching them all. They had all been very kind and they carried on making the record.'

When John wrote 'Lucy in the Sky with Diamonds', everyone assumed that it was a clever reference to LSD: *L*ucy, *S*ky, *D*iamonds. John explained that his son Julian came home from school one day with a drawing of one of his school friends. John asked him who it was and he said, 'Lucy in the sky with diamonds,' which inspired John to go on from there.

John was to comment, 'I had many bad trips. Jesus Christ, I stopped taking it because of that. I just couldn't stand it.'

Luck of the Irish

One of two tracks on the *Sometime in New York City* album with reference to the contemporary Irish problems. Yoko also contributes to the lyrics, which are a rather naïve comment on an extremely complex situation, with lines such as 'Let's walk over rainbows like leprechauns'. 'Why are the English there anyway?' John asks.

John sang 'Luck of the Irish' at a demonstration organised by the Transport Workers' Union in New York on 5 February 1972, a week after the incident known as 'Bloody Sunday'.

There were around 5,000 protesters outside the New York offices of the BOAC airline on 44th Street and John also made a speech.

Rushing from the demonstration to their Bank Street apartment, John hurriedly dictated a press statement, referring to himself in the third person. It read,

> Today at Forty-fourth and Fifth Avenue, outside the BOAC building, there was a demonstration in protest against the internment and killing of Irish people in the civil rights movement. Present among many people – five or six thousand – were senators and congressmen, also John and Yoko, Jerry Rubin and Stew Albert. John and Yoko sang *Luck of the Irish*, the proceeds of which they announced would be donated to the Irish civil rights movement.
>
> The police were particularly co-operative as most of them were Irish. The meeting was a great meeting and it got lots of media coverage. The weather was freezing cold. The Lennons looked like refugees – John hadn't shaved for a few days, and Yoko was wrapped up like an Eskimo. At first they went 'round unrecognised, but finally they were announced.
>
> The people joined in singing with the Lennons and great applause and shouting was heard, especially on such lines as 'Why are the English there anyway?' and 'The bastards commit genocide'.
>
> The whole thing was a success, there was no violence, and if you hear otherwise it's a lie.
>
> The mood of the crowd was a happy one under the circumstances, considering we were all there to show our sympathy for the thirteen people who were mercilessly shot down by the British imperialists.
>
> The purpose of the meeting was to show solidarity with the people who are going to march tomorrow in Northern Ireland. Representatives of the IRA spoke, including some secret leaders who had flown in especially for the meeting, considering its importance to try to awaken the American–Irish who are rather middle-class.
>
> We wish to stress that the song by the pop stars was not the important part of the meeting, but the gathering of the

people and the sincerity with which they gathered, and their friendly spirit, was.

The speeches were mainly a denunciation of the British in Ireland, telling them to get out because they had no right there. Also there were lots of words spoken about the fact that the Protestant northerners had been shipped over by the English in the nineteenth century to colonise the North. It was decided that a referendum by the whole of Ireland, including Eire, should decide what country they belong to.

Before John and Yoko sang, Lennon made a short speech about his Irish ancestry, and the main thing he said was, 'My name is Lennon and you can guess the rest,' which got a great round of applause from the people.

And he stressed the fact of his Liverpool upbringing, an area eighty per cent dominated by Irish descent. Lennon reminded the crowd that in England, Liverpool is called 'the capital of Ireland'.

An interviewer later asked John whether his support of the IRA conflicted with his anti-violence views.

He said, 'I don't know how I feel about them, because I understand why they're doing it and if it's a choice between the IRA and the British Army, I'm with the IRA. But if it's a choice between violence and non-violence, I'm with non-violence. So it's a very delicate line.

'Our backing of the Irish people is done really through the Irish Civil Rights, which is not the IRA.'

John and Yoko had originally written the song in October 1971 and made a home demo recording on 12 November. John first performed it in public at the Cristler Arena in Ann Arbor, Michigan, in December 1971 and next performed it on *The David Frost Show* on 13 January 1972.

In February 2000, Yoko denied that John had ever directly funded or supported the Irish Republican Army. 'My husband did not give money to the IRA,' she said. 'He gave money when there were people who asked for it, people who needed it. He thought this money was to be used for children, orphans or women who needed it.' Yoko was responding to UK Sunday newspaper reports that M15 files contained references to Lennon giving money to the IRA.

Lucy In The Sky With Diamonds

A number recorded on 1/2 March 1967 and included on the *Sgt Pepper* album. John felt the song was badly recorded, and swore to his dying day that it had nothing to do with LSD. A version was included on the Beatles *Anthology 2* CD.

John claimed that the images were from *Alice In Wonderland*. 'It was Alice in the boat. She is buying an egg and it turns into Humpty Dumpty. The woman in the shop turns into a sheep and the next minute they are rowing in a rowing boat somewhere, and I was visualising that.' Referring to the initials of the title, he said, 'It was purely unconscious that it came out to be LSD. Until somebody pointed it out, I never even thought of it. I mean, who would ever bother to look at the initials of a title? It's not an acid song. The imagery was Alice in the boat. And also the image of this female who would come and save me – this secret love that was going to come one day.'

The song was also partly inspired by a drawing Julian sketched at school then took home to show John. Ringo commented, 'I've seen the drawing which Julian made. A real kid's drawing with floating people. It didn't have anything to do with LSD.' Paul was also to state, 'I was with John when Julian let us see his drawing. John asked him what it was, and Julian said it was a girl called Lucy in the sky with diamonds. You could virtually hear John thinking, "Hey, that's a good title for a song." But as usual it was misunderstood.'

In 1974 anthropologist Don Johanson discovered the remains of a 3.5 million year old ape-woman in Ethiopia. He named her Lucy after *Lucy In the Sky with Diamonds*, and at the celebration party on the evening of the discovery, the song was played continuously.

Lust, Virginia

A New York actress who was featured in John and Yoko's film *Fly*, shot in an attic in the Bowery at a session lasting a day and a half.

There were actually nineteen auditions held before Lust was chosen – all of the other girls turned out to be ticklish!

It has been suggested that Lust was sedated to enable her to lie still for interminably long periods while flies were filmed crawling over her naked body by a macro lens.

Virginia's nude form was intimately explored in this short film, originally three-quarters of an hour long but pruned to nineteen minutes.

The camera tracks a fly crawling around her toes and moving up her legs, into her public hair and examining her vagina. Different flies were used as the exploration continued over her body, moving from her abdomen to her breasts and to her face.

Lynn, Dr Stephen

A doctor at Roosevelt Hospital who made the primary examination of John's body. He found there was no pulse, no respiration and no brain waves, and concluded that John had died before reaching the hospital. Lynn was to comment that no one could have sustained the type of wounds John had suffered for any length of time. He announced the official time of death as 11.15 p.m.

Lynne, Jeff

Producer of 'Free As a Bird' and 'Real Love' for *The Beatles Anthology*. Lynne had originally been a member of the Idle Race and then the Move, and then led the Electric Light Orchestra, a band John referred to as 'the sons of the Beatles'. While he was working on his debut album at Advision studios in London the engineer at Abbey Road phoned the engineer doing the Lynne session to ask if they would like to see the Beatles working on their new album. It was 10 October 1968 and Lynne met John for the first time when he heard the recording of 'The Glass Onion'. The ELO became a very successful outfit and the Beatles' influence was obvious. Lynne also became a record producer and worked with George Harrison on his album *Cloud Nine* in 1987. It was George Harrison who asked Lynne to work with them on John's demo discs to provide the first new Beatles singles for more than fourteen years. The three remaining Beatles felt that George Martin's hearing was not as good as it was and, allied with the fact that Martin was also working on the *Beatles Anthology* series itself, agreed to engage Lynne.

Lynton, Rod

A session musician invited to John's Ascot Studios in Tittenhurst Park in the autumn of 1971 to work on the 'How Do You Sleep?' track on the *Imagine* album.

Lynton commented, 'I was phoned from Apple and asked to bring down some rhythm guitarists. So I took down some friends of mine. Ted Durner of Wishbone Ash, Andrew Cresswell-Davies of Stackridge and John Tout, who played piano with Renaissance.

'John played vibes, but the rest of us made up a rhythm section. His studio adjoined the kitchen, but he also had a separate control room with some of the finest equipment I had ever seen.

'There were never more than eight of us in the studio at the same time. He had Klaus Voormann playing bass, Alan White on drums, Nicky Hopkins on piano, George Harrison on slide guitar and John Barnham on harmonium.

'When we weren't wanted for one particular song, we just sat it out in the kitchen at a long pine table down the middle of the room, stacked high with chicken, ham, tongue and salad. You just helped yourself if you felt a bit hungry.

'We all had the run of the house when we weren't working. In between some numbers we played billiards in John's library. He had a full-size billiards table in there with thousands of books lining one huge wall from floor to ceiling.

'It really shook me up when we started recording "How Do You Sleep?" because I had grown up admiring the Beatles and there I was standing there playing rhythm guitar, and I heard John's voice coming over the speakers, putting down Paul.

'That really pulled me up with a jolt. Until that moment, I don't think it had really sunk in that I was playing with John, who had always been my idol.

'When I first started to play, Yoko came round the room, sat on the floor opposite me, looking very intense, and I was worried at first because I thought she didn't like me.

'She was just sitting there, staring at me, but I learned afterwards that Yoko does that. She sits thinking very deeply and it can be unnerving if you have never seen her do it before because her eyes are so intense.

McCartney, Paul

James Paul McCartney was born at Walton Hospital in Liverpool on 18 June 1942. His father was Jim McCartney and his mother's name was Mary Patricia. His brother Mike was born on 7 January 1944.

Paul's mother died on 31 October 1956 of cancer of the breast. It was a traumatic event in his life. John Lennon was also to suffer the death of a beloved mother when in his teens, and Paul was to say, 'He lost his mum when he was seventeen. That was one of the things that brought John and me very close together. It was a bond between us, quite a big one. We came together professionally afterwards. And, as we became a writing team, I think it helped our intimacy and our trust in each other. Eventually, we were pretty good mates – until the Beatles split up and Yoko came into it.'

In September 1953 Paul enrolled at Liverpool Institute, one of the city's most prestigious grammar schools. One of his institute friends, Ivan Vaughan, was to introduce him to John Lennon. The historic meeting took place at the Woolton (St Peter's) Parish Church garden fête on Saturday 6 July 1957 when Paul saw John's group the Quarry Men perform. Writing about the meeting in his introduction to John's book, *In His Own Write*, Paul described himself as a fat schoolboy and said that John was drunk.

In October 1961, when John received £100 from his Aunt Elizabeth as a 21st-birthday present, John and Paul went on a holiday to Paris. While there they were given a stylish haircut by Jurgen Vollmer, which became the basis for the famous Beatles moptop. On their return they stopped off in London and bought Cuban-heeled boots from Anello & Davide, which was also to start a fashion trend.

Paul had numerous girlfriends, but his main romance had been with a pretty blonde girl from Liverpool called Dot Rhone. When Dot found herself pregnant, she and Paul were to get married, but she had a miscarriage. Dot accompanied Cynthia on a trip to Hamburg to stay with John and Paul. Soon after, Paul broke up the romance.

On 18 June 1963, when Paul's 21st-birthday party was held at his Auntie Gin's house, there was a nasty incident during which John Lennon viciously beat up a disc jockey, Bob Wooler. This was due to a remark Wooler made about John's recent holiday in Spain with Brian Epstein, in which he alluded to a 'honeymoon'. John took violent exception to the suggestion that he and Epstein were having an affair.

Paul met the actress Jane Asher on 9 May 1963 following a concert at the Royal Albert Hall and the two were to live together for almost five years. On 8 December 1964 Paul announced that he planned to marry Asher. In April 1965 he bought a Victorian house in Cavendish Avenue in St John's Wood for him and Jane to live in.

During that month he also sent a message to the Campaign for Nuclear Disarmament, stating, 'I agree with CND. They should ban all bombs. Bombs are no good to anyone. We might as well ban the bomb as be blown up by it.'

Because of his association with Jane, he gave her brother Peter Asher, a member of the duo, Peter and Gordon, some Lennon and McCartney numbers to record, including one, 'Woman', that he wrote using the pseudonym Bernard Webb.

Jane encouraged Paul to buy a farm in Scotland as a retreat for the two of them.

The effect of Jane and her family on Paul was a positive one, leading him to a further appreciation of the arts, particularly the theatre. Paul began making avant-garde movies (a few years before the John and Yoko ones) and also became the first member of the Beatles to involve himself in experimental music with his 1967 *Carnival of Light* avant-garde psychedelic event. He was also the member who tried to keep the group together following the death of Brian Epstein with projects such as *Magical Mystery Tour*. When it was screened on British television in December 1967 it received a hammering from the critics. Paul said, 'We goofed, really. My dad brought the bad news into me this morning like the figure of doom. Perhaps the newspapers are right – perhaps we're right. We'll have to wait and see.'

However, he persevered with the concept of *Sergeant Pepper's Lonely Hearts Club Band* and even managed to get the group to record the *Abbey Road* album after the *Get Back* project became bogged down.

In April 1968 he wrote 'Thingumybob' as a theme tune for a television series and he was also to compose some music for the soundtrack of the feature film *The Family Way*.

On 20 July 1968 Jane Asher announced on the TV programme *Dee Time* that her romance with Paul was over.

It was while he was at the Bag o' Nails club in Kingly Street, London, that he first met Linda Eastman and in December 1968 his romance with her became public.

Paul married Linda at Eastman Register Office in London on 12 March 1969. Paul's brother Mike was best man, Linda's daughter Heather was bridesmaid and Peter Brown and Mal Evans were witnesses. None of the other Beatles had been invited, since Paul had already started litigation to dissolve the group.

Paul adopted Linda's daughter Heather and the couple had three children together, Mary, Stella and James.

The Lennon and McCartney songwriting partnership became the most famous in the world. They started writing together in the late 1950s, but by the time they were successful on record, they mainly wrote their own numbers in their individual styles. They had agreed that every song they wrote would be credited to Lennon and McCartney, even if one of them had no input. This arrangement came to an end when Paul allegedly refused to record 'Cold Turkey'. John then decided to credit it under his own name.

Many people believe that the Lennon and McCartney credit meant the two of them collaborated on most of the Beatles' hits, but this is not so. As writers, they had very different musical tastes. When Paul recorded 'When I'm 64' for the *Sergeant Pepper* album, for instance, the producer George Martin commented, 'It was a pastiche, a kind of send-up of the old stuff. Paul always had that sneaking regard for the old rutti-tutti music.' Commenting on it, John said, 'I would never even dream of writing a song like that.'

Martin was also to observe, 'John sneered at a lot of things, but that was part of the collaboration between the two of them. They tended to be rivals. Their collaboration as songwriters was never Rodgers and Hart, it was always more Gilbert and Sullivan. If John did something, Paul would wish he'd thought of it and go away and try to do something better and vice versa. It was a very healthy spirit of competition.'

In April 1970 Paul announced he would no longer record with the Beatles and his solo album *McCartney* was issued; it topped the American charts and reached No. 2 in Britain in May 1970.

Paul said, 'We all have to ask each other's permission before any of us does anything without the other three. My own record nearly didn't come out because [Allen] Klein and some of the others thought it would be too near to the date of the next Beatles album. I had to get George, who's a director of Apple, to authorise its release for me. We're all talking about peace and love but really we're not feeling peaceful at all.'

On 10 April 1970 Paul announced that he had left the Beatles and said the reason was 'personal, business and musical differences'. A few days later it was reported that Paul had formed a new company, McCartney Productions Ltd, and he'd also bought the film rights to the Rupert the Bear cartoon character.

On 31 December 1970 Paul began High Court proceedings to end the Beatles' partnership by issuing a writ, which declared that the partnership 'The Beatles & Co.', formed in April 1967, should be dissolved, and a receiver appointed to wind up the company. He had begun proceedings because of advice from his legal representative, John Eastman, his brother-in-law, that it would be the only way he could break away from Allen Klein, who had been appointed manager of Apple's affairs in spite of Paul's protests.

Paul had originally wanted Eastman & Eastman, his in-laws'

family law firm, to represent Apple, but the other members of the group disagreed. Paul, however, felt very strongly about Klein. There were many decisions, apart from financial ones, that upset Paul. Klein, for instance, brought in Phil Spector to remix the *Let It Be* tapes. This interfered with the artistic control the Beatles had over their own product. It was most obvious in Paul's case when Spector completely altered the atmosphere of 'The Long and Winding Road' by adding lush strings and a choir – the usual Phil Spector 'wall of sound'. In other words, he was imposing his own particular style over Paul's music, without Paul having any say in the matter.

There had also been some jockeying regarding the leadership of the group, according to Apple's Peter Brown. He felt that John had wanted to take back leadership of the group, abetted by Yoko, and if he couldn't achieve it he was prepared to destroy the group. Brown commented, 'McCartney was placed in an impossible position. John wanted to go in another direction and McCartney couldn't follow him because there was Yoko in the middle and Yoko didn't want them to continue. Yoko wanted John for herself. And she was very single-minded.'

The legal partnership as it stood had originally been set up in April 1967. In 1969 John had privately announced that he would not work with the Beatles again and was annoyed when Paul made a public statement in a newspaper in April 1970 to the effect that the Beatles had ceased to exist as a group. In an interview with *Rolling Stone* magazine in December 1970, John said that Paul's attempts to dominate the group had led to its break-up. He said that all the other members of the Beatles had 'got fed up of being sidemen for Paul'.

The writ eventually issued by Paul read, 'A declaration that the partnership business carried out by the plaintiff and the defendants under the name of "The Beatles and Co." and constituted by a deed of partnership dated April 19 1967, and made between the parties hereto, ought to be dissolved and that accordingly the same be dissolved.'

During the course of the case in the Chancery Division, Paul was able to point out how Klein had tried to cause discontent and had told him over the phone, 'You know why John's angry with you? It's because you came off better than he did on *Let It Be*.' Klein also said to him, 'The real trouble is Yoko. She's the one with ambition.' Paul said on a future occasion, 'I often wonder what John would have said if he had heard that remark.'

The reasons put forward for the dissolution were: '(1) The Beatles had long since ceased to perform together as a group, so the whole purpose of the partnership had gone. (2) In 1969, Mr McCartney's partners, in the teeth of his opposition and in breach of the partnership deal, had appointed Mr Klein's company ABKCO Industries Ltd as the partnership's exclusive business managers. (3) Mr McCartney had never been given audited accounts in the four years since the partnership was formed.'

When Paul and Linda attended court on 18 February 1971, counsel pointed out that Allan Klein's company had drawn approximately £1,500,000 commission from the group and that in 1970 the Beatles had an income of around £4,000,000. Morris Finer QC, appearing for John, George, Ringo and Apple Corps Ltd, said that they were all opposing Paul's application because the group was on the verge of bankruptcy until Klein took them over.

Paul's debut solo single, 'Another Day', (co-written with Linda) reached No. 5 in America and No. 2 in Britain. Paul's next album, *Ram*, topped the British charts and reached No. 2 in America in June 1971.

Paul commented, 'Linda was very present all the way through. We've been writing many more songs together and we're developing as a harmony team.'

Later that year his new single, 'Back Seat of My Car', reached No. 39 in the British charts while 'Uncle Albert/Admiral Haley', released only in the US, topped the American chart.

After the Beatles' break-up, John sent an undated six-page letter to Paul, which was an attack on both Paul and Linda. The letter was in reply to one Paul had written to him requesting that he stop making bitter remarks about him. John wrote, 'I hope you realise what you and my "kind and unselfish" friends laid on Yoko and me since we've been together.'

In reply to Linda, he wrote; 'I don't resent your husband. I'm sorry for him. I know the Beatles are quite nice people – I'm one of them. They're also just as big bastards as anyone else – so get off your high horse.' He added, 'Do you really think most of today's art came about because of the Beatles? I don't believe you're that insane. Didn't we always say we were part of the movement – not all of it? Of course we changed the world – but try and follow it through – get off your gold disc and fly!'

In November 1971 Paul launched his new group Wings. Which comprised himself and Linda with Denny Laine on guitar and vocals and Denny Seiwell on drums. Their debut album, *Wildlife*, was issued and reached No. 11 in the UK and No. 10 in the US.

Early the next year Henry McCullough had been added to the group on guitar and vocals and they began touring colleges and universities in Britain, beginning with Nottingham University on 8 February. It was Paul's first live appearance in five years. Linda said, 'Eric Clapton once said that he would like to play from the back of a caravan, but he never got around to doing it. Well – we have! We've no manager or agents – just we five and the roadies. We're just a gang of musicians touring around.'

Their new single, 'Give Ireland Back to the Irish', reached No. 16 in Britain and No. 21 in the US. The record was banned both by the BBC and the IBA. In June the new single, 'Mary Had a Little Lamb', reached No. 9 in the UK and 28 in the US. Paul said, ' "Mary Had a Little Lamb" wasn't a great record, but the funny thing about that is we've got a whole new audience of eight-year-olds and five- to six-year-olds – like Pete Townshend's daughter.'

The group then made their concert debut at Chateauvillon in France on 19 July 1972 at the beginning of a seven-week European tour. In August Paul, Linda and Denny Laine were arrested in Gothenburg, Sweden, for possessing drugs after admitting that they had smoked cannabis, which had been sent to them through the post from England. All three were ordered to pay £800. Several months later, on 8 March 1973, Paul was charged with growing cannabis on his farm at Campbeltown, Scotland, and fined £100. He said, 'I must admit I did expect it to be worse.'

The BBC also banned another of Wings' records, the single 'Hi Hi Hi', in January 1973 because it was claimed to be promoting drug use. A spokesman said, 'We thought the record unfit for broadcasting because of the lyric.' It reached No. 5 in the UK charts. On 18 March Paul and Linda appeared with Wings at a special show at the Hard Rock Café in London to raise funds for Release, the charity that aided drug users.

In April Wings' next single, 'My Love', reached No. 9 in the UK and their next album, *Red Rose Speedway*, topped the American charts and reached No. 5 in the UK. The group then began a British tour in May. On 10 May the TV special *James Paul McCartney* was screened in Britain. In June 'My Love' topped the American charts. Paul then composed a theme song for the new James Bond film *Live and Let Die*, and his single of the same name reached No. 2 in the American charts, although Brenda Arnau covered the number on the actual movie soundtrack.

Wings also began a British tour on 11 May. Paul was to say, 'The way we tour now, it seems easier. It's not actually more organised, but we get days off every now and then, so it's quite good. It hasn't ground me into the ground, anyway.'

In August 1973 Denny Seiwell and Henry McCullough left the group and during the same month Paul, Linda and Denny Laine flew to Lagos in Nigeria to begin recording *Band on the Run*. While they were there muggers attacked Paul and Linda. They held a knife to Paul's throat and Linda cried, 'Don't kill him!' The muggers took his wallet and shoulder bag and Linda's bag then ran into the night.

In December the single 'Helen Wheels' reached No. 10 in the US and No. 12 in Britain and their album *Band on the Run* went on to top the charts on both sides of the Atlantic.

In March 1974 the single 'Jet' reached No. 7 in both the US and UK charts. The single 'Band on the Run' reached No. 3 in the UK in August 1974. Between June and August Paul, Linda, Denny and the new Wings members, Jimmy McCulloch and Geoff Britton, recorded in Nashville. 'Walking in the Park with Eloise' was released in October. This was a number Paul's father had written and Paul produced a number of Nashville musicians recording it under the name the Country Hams. On 18 November Paul and Linda joined Rod Stewart and the Faces at the Odeon, Lewisham, to perform 'Mine For Me'.

In December the single 'Junior's Farm' reached No. 3 in the US and No. 16 in the UK.

February 1975 saw Joe English replace Britton on drums and in June the single 'Listen To What the Man Said' topped the US charts and reached No. 6 in Britain. The album *Venus and Mars* also topped the charts on both sides of the Atlantic.

On 9 September Wings began a ten-country world tour during which they appeared before two million people. In October the single 'Letting Go' reached No. 39 in the US and No. 4 in the UK. December saw the first record by Paul McCartney that failed to reach the British charts, 'Venus and Mars Rock Show', although it reached No. 12 in the US.

In April 1976 the album *Wings at the Speed of Sound* topped the American charts and reached No. 2 in Britain. In May 'Silly Love Songs' reached No. 2 in Britain and the Wings tour finally reached the States, where it was called 'Wings Over America'. In September the single 'Let 'Em In' reached No. 2 in Britain and No. 3 in America. Later that month, on 25 September, they played a special concert in St Mark's Square, Venice. The tour ended at the Empire Pool, Wembley, on 21 December.

At the beginning of 1977 the album *Wings Over America* topped the American charts and reached No. 8 in Britain. In March the single 'Maybe I'm Amazed' reached No. 10 in America and 28 in Britain. In April, *Thrillington*, an album comprising an orchestral interpretation of *Ram*, was released and in November both McCulloch and English left Wings and the group continued as a trio. 'Mull of Kintyre' was issued in December and the single, co-written by Paul and Denny Laine, became one of Britain's biggest-selling singles of all time.

April 1978 saw the single 'With a Little Luck' topping the US charts and reaching No. 5 in Britain, while the album *London Town* reached No. 2 in the US and No. 4 in the UK. In July the single 'I've Had Enough' reached No. 25 in the US and No. 42 in the UK and during that month Wings once again became a five-piece, with the inclusion of Laurence Juber on guitar and vocals and Steve Holly on drums. The year ended with the compilation album *Wings' Greatest Hits* reaching No. 5 in the UK and 29 in the US.

The TV special *Wings Over the World* was screened in the USA on 16 March 1979 and in May the single 'Goodnight Tonight' reached No. 5 in both the US and UK charts. In June the single 'Old Siam Sir' reached No. 35 in the UK while the album *Back to the Egg* reached No. 6 in Britain and No. 8 in America. The following month the single 'Getting Closer' reached No. 20 in America.

Paul wrote the song 'Haven't We Met Somewhere Before?' for

the movie *Heaven Can Wait*, but it was rejected and featured in the film *Rock 'n' Roll High School* instead. In September the single 'Getting Closer' reached No. 60 in the UK. During that month Wings appeared on stage at the Odeon, Hammersmith, with the Crickets. This was part of the annual Buddy Holly Week, which Paul had organised following his acquisition of the Buddy Holly music catalogue. October saw the single 'Arrow Through Me' reach No. 29 in the US while in Britain Paul was awarded a medal cast in rhodium after being declared the most successful composer of all time. Wings ended the year at the Odeon, Hammersmith, on 19 December as part of *The Concert for the People of Kampuchea*.

Paul had tried to patch things up with John and when he was in New York he phoned John to offer him an indemnity he was seeking for a clause in one of the Apple contracts. Paul said, 'But there was so much suspicion, even though I came bearing the olive branch.' When Paul asked for the meeting, John said, 'What for? What do you really want?'

When Paul, George and Ringo flew into New York specially to have a meeting with John at the Plaza Hotel to sort out some problems, John wouldn't turn up, even though the Dakota Building where he lived was only five hundred yards away. He'd had his tarot cards read and was told the portents weren't right. George lost his temper, phoned John and said, 'Take those fucking shades off and come over here, you!' John sent a balloon instead with the message 'Listen to the balloon'.

Paul did manage to visit the Dakota because he wanted to see John's son Sean. Yoko Ono shouted at him, 'Don't touch the baby – he doesn't know you!'

At another time he went round to the Dakota with his guitar to see John, just as he'd done so many times in the early days. Lennon refused to allow him into the apartments, sending a message on the intercom: 'You can't just drop in on people in New York like you did in Liverpool. The old days are over.'

When John was murdered Paul received several death threats and hired two 24-hour security guards.

Soon after the murder Paul received the news via a phone call. He telephoned Yoko, and then went into the studio. While he was rushing to the studio a reporter caught him to ask what he thought of John's death. He said the first thing that came into his head: 'It's a drag, isn't it?' It was a quote that went around the world and brought criticism down on to his head.

'If I had known John was going to die, I would not have been as stand-offish as I was. When John started slagging me off, I was not prepared to say "you're quite right". I am human. Nobody would sit there and be called an Engelbert Humperdinck as I was, and say, "Oh, fine, I think you're right." I just turned round and said, "Piss off." Had I known it was going to be that final – and quick – I wouldn't have said it.

'John was not the big working-class hero he liked to make out. He was the least working-class of the Beatles. He was the poshest, but he did have rather a tough upbringing.'

In the aftermath of John's death, the former Beatle was almost canonised by the public. Books and plays not only lionised John, but also tended to demean Paul. Paul's major part in the later days of the Beatles when he virtually kept the group together, working and recording, were forgotten and he was unjustly pictured as almost a second-string player to John.

January 1980 saw Paul's first solo single under his own name since 1971. Called 'Wonderful Christmastime', it reached No. 6 in the UK. Wings were due to tour Japan that month but Paul was arrested at Tokyo Airport and jailed for possession of marijuana. After nearly ten days in jail he was extradited.

In May his single 'Coming Up' topped the US charts and reached No. 2 in Britain. The album *McCartney II* reached No. 1 in Britain and No. 3 in America in June and the following month the single 'Waterfalls' reached No. 9 in the UK. September saw the release of a limited-edition twelve-inch single, 'Temporary Secretary', but it failed to chart.

On 24 October *The Guinness Book of Records* presented Paul with a rhodium disc as the best-selling songwriter and recording artist of all time. The following month the film *Rockshow*, a documentary of Wings' American tour of 1978, was premiered in New York.

February 1981 saw the release of an album, *McCartney Interview*, which was deleted on the actual day of release but nevertheless managed to reach No. 34 in the UK charts and No. 158 in the US.

On 3 March Paul appeared on the Radio 4 programme *Desert*

Island Discs and later that month attended Ringo and Barbara's wedding.

April 1982 saw 'Ebony And Ivory' top both the British and American charts. It was a number about racial harmony that Paul had written specially as a duet for himself and Stevie Wonder. That month Paul became the first ex-Beatle to receive an entry in the prestigious *Who's Who*. His *Tug of War* album topped the charts on both sides of the Atlantic in May and included contributions from Stevie Wonder, Eric Stewart, Ringo Starr and Carl Perkins.

In August his single 'Take It Away' reached No. 15 in Britain and No. 10 in America. October saw his 'Tug of War' single reach No. 53 in both Britain and America. 'This Girl of Mine', a duet with Michael Jackson, reached No. 2 in the US and No. 8 in Britain.

During an interview in 1982 Paul said, 'John said to me a year before he died, "Be careful what you wish for – it might just come true." That's the way I look at it. I wished for this success and I got it. I'm happy with it. Having asked for it and having worked for it, you can't turn round when they give you the first prize and say, "No, I'll just have a bun instead, thank you." '

In an interview in 1983 Paul said he still hadn't got over John's death. He also was concerned that people may have misunderstood his comments when he was quoted on camera in London the day after John's death. He'd said, 'It's a drag, isn't it?' He said he couldn't think of anything to say at the time, but people have thought that his comment was cynical or unfeeling.

On November 1983 another single he recorded with Michael Jackson, 'Say Say Say', topped the American charts and reached No. 2 in the UK.

January 1984 saw Paul top the British charts with the single 'Pipes of Peace' while 'So Bad' reached No. 23 in America. On Saturday 9 June Paul appeared on the first edition of Michael Aspel's new chat show *Aspel and Company*, discussing his songs and their inspiration and also promoting his forthcoming Buddy Holly Week.

In October the single 'No More Lonely Nights' reached No. 2 in the British charts and later reached No. 6 in America. The soundtrack song 'Give My Regards to Broad Street' was issued, but Paul's feature film of that name wasn't a success.

In November 1984 Paul received the Freedom of the City of Liverpool in a ceremony held at Picton Library.

The following month his 'We All Stand Together' reached No. 3 in the British charts. Credited to Paul McCartney and the Frog Chorus, it was a song featured in a short animated pilot film for the cartoon character Rupert the Bear.

In July 1985 Paul appeared on the *Live Aid* concert and in December his single 'Spies Like Us', featured in the film of the same name, reached No. 37 in the UK charts and was later to reach No. 7 in the US.

In August 1986 his single 'Press' reached No. 21 in the US and No. 25 in the UK. The following month his album *Press To Play* reached No. 8 in the UK and No. 30 in the US. His single 'Stranglehold' reached only No. 81 in the US in November.

In November 1987 the compilation album *All the Best!* reached No. 2 in the UK and in December the CD single 'Once Upon a Long Ago' reached No. 30 in Britain. The year 1988 saw *All the Best!* reach No. 62 in the US.

On 27 February 1988 Paul performed at the San Remo Festival in Italy with his new band, who, apart from himself, comprised Linda on keyboards, Hamish Stuart on guitar and bass, Chris Whitten on drums, Gary Barnacle on saxophone and Andrew Chater on violin. On 24 June he was presented with the Silver Clef Award for Outstanding Achievement in the World of British Music. On 28 July he received the title of Honorary Doctorate from the University of Sussex. In August he appealed to fans to boycott Albert Goldman's recently published *The Lives Of John Lennon*. In November Paul produced 'Let the Children Play', donating the profits to the Children In Need charity.

In May 1989 his single 'My Brave Face' was released and reached No. 25 in the US charts and 5 June saw the release of his album *Flowers in the Dirt*, which was to top the British charts and reach No. 21 in the US.

The following month his new single 'This One' reached No. 18 in the UK and No. 94 in the US. Paul and his group then embarked on their 'Get Back' world tour, which stretched from 28 September 1989 to 29 July 1990. His single 'Figure of Eight' was issued in November 1989 and reached No. 92 in the US; and another single, 'Put It There', was issued in February 1990

– it reached No 32 in the UK. 'Bulldog' was the next single, which reached No. 29 in the UK.

At the Grammy Awards on Wednesday 21 February 1990 Paul was presented with a Lifetime Achievement Award.

The live-action concert compilation album *Tripping the Live Fantastic* reached No. 17 in the UK and No. 24 in the US while the final release that year, the single 'All My Trials', reached No. 35 in the UK.

Paul began 1991 performing on the MTV special *Unplugged* and an album, *Unplugged (The Official Bootleg)*, was issued and reached No. 14 in the US charts. On 27 June the Royal Liverpool Philharmonic Orchestra performed Paul's *Liverpool Oratorio* at the city's Anglican Cathedral. The *Get Back* movie, a film of Paul's world tour filmed by Richard Lester, was premiered in September. There was a limited-edition release of *Choba B CCCP (The Russian Album)*, which reached No. 63 in the UK charts. The album *Paul McCartney's Liverpool Oratorio Conducted by Carl Davis* reached No. 177 in the US charts.

The year 1992 saw the fulfilment of a dream Paul had when work began on his old school Liverpool Institute to transform it into LIPA, the Liverpool Institute of Performing Arts, a project that Paul conceived and brought to fruition.

At the beginning of 1993 his single 'Hope of Deliverance' reached No. 18 in the UK and No. 83 in the US. 'Off the Ground' reached No. 5 in the UK and 17 in the US and Paul began another world tour in March. In November *Paul is Live!* reached No. 34 in the UK and No. 78 in the US.

In 1994 Paul attended the ceremony that inducted John Lennon into the Rock 'n' Roll Hall of fame as a solo artist. After the ceremony Paul went to the Dakota Building and sat up talking and drinking tea with Yoko. George Harrison and Neil Aspinall had approached Yoko about obtaining some demo discs of John's, which they could re-record to make new Beatles singles. Yoko played Paul three songs – 'Grow Old With Me,' 'Free As a Bird' and 'Real Love'. Paul liked 'Free As a Bird' immediately. He wasn't keen on 'Grow Old With Me'.

Paul's CD *The Fireman*, which contained no credits in his name, was issued and in May 1995 a thirteen-part radio series called *Oobu Joobu* was devoted to his music. In 1995 the Beatles' *Anthology* packages were released.

LIPA opened early in 1997 and the Queen attended the school on 7 June. On 11 March 1997 Paul went to Buckingham Palace to be knighted Sir Paul McCartney by the Queen.

His single 'Young Boy' reached No. 19 in the UK and his album *Flaming Pie* reached the No. 2 spot in the US. The single 'The World Tonight' reached No. 23 in the UK and No. 64 in the US. On 14 October Paul's symphonic poem *Standing Stone* was performed at the Royal Albert Hall. The album went to No. 34 in the UK and No. 194 in the US.

Tragically, on 17 April 1998, Linda died at the McCartneys' family ranch in Arizona. She had fought a two-and-a-half-year battle with cancer, but it had spread rapidly to her liver. Paul was to say, 'I lost my girlfriend, lover, wife and the mother of my children.'

On Monday 15 March 1999 Paul was inducted as a solo artist in the Rock 'n' Roll Hall of Fame. He said, 'This is a brilliant night for me but it's sad too. I would have liked my baby to be with me. She wanted this.'

On Saturday 10 April Paul appeared on *A Concert For Linda* at the Royal Albert Hall, along with a host of artists including Elvis Costello, Tom Jones, the Pretenders, Marianne Faithfull, Sinead O'Connor and George Michael.

During the year Paul also emerged as a painter by holding his first exhibition of his own paintings at the Kunstforum Lyz art gallery in Hamburg, Germany. Paul was dismayed at the news in June that his 30-year love affair with Linda would be the subject of a four-hour television mini-series. His spokesman said, 'What man would want to see the memory of his beloved wife cheapened like this?'

On 18 September Paul performed six numbers from his forthcoming rock 'n' roll tribute album *Run Devil Run* at the PETA Awards in Hollywood. The album was released in the UK on 4 October and in the US the following day. It had been recorded in just two weeks at Abbey Road studios and the fifteen tracks included three McCartney originals. The album was basically a tribute to his rock 'n' roll mentors of the 1950s and comprised tracks previously recorded by Elvis Presley, Gene Vincent, Carl Perkins, Fats Domino and Little Richard. The tracks were 'Blue Jean Bop', 'She Said Yeah', 'All Shook Up', 'Run Devil Run', 'No Other Baby', 'Lonesome Town', 'Try Not To Cry', 'Movie

Magg', 'Brown Eyed Handsome Man', 'What It Is', 'Coquette',
'I Got Stung', 'Honey Hush', 'Shake a Hand', 'Party.' It reached
No. 27 in the US.

On Saturday 16 October, Paul's *Working Classical:
Orchestral and Chamber Music by Paul McCartney* was
presented at the Philharmonic Hall in Liverpool, with a
performance by the Royal Philharmonic Orchestra. (It was also
released as a fourteen-track album and was screened in April
2000.)

On 6 November 1999 he appeared on BBC2's late-night TV
music show *Later with Jools Holland*. On 13 November he
appeared with Lulu on BBC TV's *National Lottery Red Alert*
show and performed 'Brown Eyed Handsome Man', 'No Other
Baby' and 'Let's Have A Party'. On 3 December he had a full
one-hour spot on *Parkinson*. Michael Parkinson had appeared
on the cover of Paul's *Band on the Run* album many years before
and Paul had told him that he would return the favour by
appearing on his chat show.

He ended the millennium with the highly publicised appearance at the Cavern Club in Liverpool on 14 December. This was
televised and also appeared on the Internet. During his performance Paul played 'Blue Jean Bop', 'Brown Eyed Handsome
Man', 'What It Is', 'Party', 'All Shook Up', 'Lonesome Tears',
'20 Flight Rock' and 'I Saw Her Standing There'.

On 15 March 2000 Paul confirmed his romance with 32-year-
old Heather Mills, a model-turned-activist who devoted herself
to running a charitable foundation for disabled people after
losing part of one leg below the knee in a road accident in 1993.
Paul was to say, 'Yes, we're very good friends. She's a very
impressive woman. We are an item.' He was also to add, 'We've
done charity work together and we've grown close. We have
been on holiday together and that's it.'

On 6 March 2000 Paul inducted James Taylor into the Rock
'n' Roll Hall of Fame. He announced that his next major project
would be a Paul McCartney solo anthology and he was
employing his son-in-law, Alistair Donald, to work on it.

MacDougall, Doug

A former FBI agent who was engaged to act as Sean Lennon's
bodyguard and Yoko's security adviser in February 1980. The

security-conscious MacDougall became alarmed when Yoko gave an interview to the *Daily News* in September 1980 detailing John and Yoko's studio schedule and also mentioning the route they took to and from the studio each day.

He was concerned at the implications and requested a meeting with Yoko on 25 September. At the meeting he suggested that, since more and more fans seemed to be gathering outside the Dakota Building following the news of John's recording activities, the couple should have an armed guard with them when they went to the studio. Yoko rejected the idea. He then suggested that a guard should at least escort them to and from their limousine. She also rejected the request and he was fired. MacDougall told Fred Seaman that the *Daily News* interview was 'an open invitation to every wacko in the country to come after them'.

On 8 December he phoned the Dakota and arranged a meeting with Yoko for the following day to discuss security again. It was too late: John was killed later that day; but MacDougall offered his services to Yoko and was rehired.

It was MacDougall who took John's body to the crematorium and, when he returned to the Dakota with a parcelled package, Seaman asked what he was carrying and MacDougall told him, 'That was once the greatest rock-and-roll musician in the world.'

After Yoko had originally turned down his advice about security, she now turned to the other extreme and ordered him to arrange for Sean to be accompanied by four armed guards wherever he went. MacDougall voiced his opinion that it was a ridiculous idea and he was fired again.

He moved to Long Island, where he retired.

McDowell, Steve

An art dealer from Seattle who, together with Ken Kinnear, manager of a group called Heart, bought four Bag One sets at a cost of $300,000 and arranged for them to become part of a touring exhibition in a hundred American cities. One-twelfth of the admission price was donated to the Spirit Foundation. The lithographs proved too much for the police department at Providence, Long Island (see **Bag One**) and they closed the exhibition when it opened in their jurisdiction.

McGann, Mark

A Liverpool actor and former member of the group Mojo Filter, who has portrayed John on a number of occasions. His very first role was at the Everyman Theatre in Liverpool when he appeared as John in the original version of the musical *Lennon,* and it was the beginning of his full-time acting career. He also appeared in the show when it toured the provinces and remained with the musical when it opened at the Astoria Theatre in London.

McGann auditioned for the three-hour American made-for-TV movie *John and Yoko: A Love Story*, and was originally turned down because he was considered to be too young. The actor selected was dropped when it was discovered his real name was Mark Chapman (the name of John's killer) and McGann was given the part.

McGann said, 'I wept when I got the role. It's almost spiritual the way John Lennon has become intertwined in my life. I broke into the business playing John, and I grew up in Liverpool just a few miles from where he was born. Like John, I was a real rebel at school, and I taught myself to play guitar.'

He was 24 at the time – and so was the Californian actress Kim Miyori, who co-starred as Yoko. Miyori had previously been a regular on the TV series *St Elsewhere*.

McGann commented, 'They didn't want a lookalike or a copycat. I think if you choose a double, the whole image can disintegrate the moment you open your mouth.' He acknowledged that he had a lot of help and advice from people in Liverpool, including Lennon's Uncle Charlie and the disc jockey Bob Wooler.

He also said, 'I have been preparing for this role for five years. I was always top of the list for the part, but they thought I was too young to play him. They didn't even test me the first time.'

During the final stages of shooting the film, McGann visited Yoko at the Dakota Building in September 1985. Yoko told the American tabloid, the *Star*: 'When [Sean] heard Mark's voice, it sounded so much like his dad that he freaked out.' Sean added, 'He looks like Dad with his glasses on and sounds like him.'

McGann was also to say, 'I grew up to really like John Lennon. I think he was the most human of the geniuses. I mean, people could associate with John because he washed his linen in public so often and he made so many obvious mistakes. But he *was* a genius.'

A real-life romance was sparked off between McGann and Miyori during the filming and the two got married.

Continuing his thoughts regarding his portrayal, he was to say, 'I decided to show Lennon warts and all: a man capable of snapping at any moment into an aggressive mood but also a man of great compassion. It was only in his later years that he learned humility – that was when he finally found happiness.

'Lennon never made any excuses but was always suffering great emotional pain. He was not a born leader but thought his grabbing a leadership role would give him the attention he desperately needed.'

McGough, Thelma

Shortly before John began his affair with Cynthia, he had been dating a sixteen-year-old art student, Thelma Pickles, who had been introduced to him by another student, Helen Anderson.

He called her 'Thel' and they were 'going steady' for six months before the romance just fizzled out.

They were both rebels in the way they dressed and had several things in common, including the fact that Thelma's father had deserted her when she was a child.

She was able to stand up to him during his moods, which he appreciated, and at one time in Ye Cracke pub when he began shouting at her, she told him, 'Don't take it out on me just because your mother's dead!'

Thelma described to the writer Ray Coleman how it felt when she and John were sixteen. 'We were always being told what we couldn't do. He and I had a rebellious streak, so it was awful. We couldn't wait to grow up and tell everyone to get lost. Mimi hated his tight trousers and my mother hated my black stockings. It was a horrible time to be young!'

She was also to say, 'John had a complete disrespect for everything, but he always had an audience around him.'

Thelma was dated by Paul McCartney for a while and eventually married Roger McGough, one of Liverpool's premier poets, who was also a member of the popular and successful trio the Scaffold. They were later divorced. Thelma left Liverpool and moved to London to enjoy a successful career in television and was one of the producers of Cilla Black's *Blind Date* series at London Weekend Television. She later moved to New Zealand.

McKenna, Stephen

The actor/musician who portrayed John in the television movie *The Birth of the Beatles*.

McKenzie, Phyllis

Phyllis first knew John when she attended St Peter's Church, Woolton, and her father had lived in a flat in the same house as John's grandparents, the Stanleys. She was also present at St Peter's fête when John and Paul met for the first time, and she knew John at Liverpool College of Art.

Cynthia Powell first met Phyllis McKenzie at the Junior College of Art in Gambier Terrace. When they both attended Liverpool College of Art they became the best of friends. There were a number of lessons in the Intermediate Course which students could opt for and Cynthia and Phyllis chose to attend the lettering class twice a week. Among the dozen or so students present in the lessons were John and his friend Jonathan Hague.

Phyllis accompanied Cynthia when John first invited her to join him for a drink at Ye Cracke pub.

Phyllis had known John since he first enrolled at the college because they both lived in the Woolton area and used to travel on the same bus, the No. 72, each morning. They often chatted, with John sometimes offering to pay her fare.

When Cynthia began to stay overnight at Gambier Terrace with John she used to tell her mother that she was staying with Phyllis.

In April 1963, when Cynthia was expecting Julian, Phyllis decided to stay with her until the baby was born. She was woken in the middle of the night when Cynthia yelled out that the baby was imminent and they phoned for an ambulance. Phyllis accompanied Cynthia to Sefton General Hospital dressed only in a nightie, dressing gown and slippers, with her hair in curlers. Once Cynthia was admitted, Phyllis was told she couldn't stay and wouldn't be given a lift back home in an ambulance.

Without any money on her person she set off on a long walk of several miles, dressed only in her nightclothes. After she'd travelled about two miles, a taxi driver took pity on her, saying,

'Hey, love, I don't think it's advisable to walk round the streets of Liverpool at this time of night dressed like that, do you?' and agreed to take her the rest of the way home.

Following Julian's birth, Cynthia initially attempted to keep her identity secret and, when people asked her if she was Cynthia Lennon, she denied it and said her name was Phyllis McKenzie.

Cynthia's friendship with Phyllis continued throughout the years and it was Phyllis who introduced Cynthia to her third husband, John Twist.

The two women had a joint exhibition of their work in 1999. It took place in June and July at the KDK Gallery in Portobello Road and the exhibition was called *Lennon and McKenzie,* although her married name is Fearon.

McClain, James

An ex-convict who became a Pentecostal minister having become a born-again Christian during his spell in Lewisburg Prison for bank robbery.

He became John's bodyguard during the last few months of John's life. As a security guard at the Hit Factory, the studio where John was recording *Double Fantasy*, he was asked to become bodyguard for John and Yoko. He asked if he could guard them round the clock, but John said he'd be required only at the studio. McClain commented, 'If only I had been there, maybe I could have helped.'

McClain cut a gospel album and said, '[John] doesn't know how much he helped me. He left a big impact on me as far as songwriting is concerned. He found out I was a musician and I sang him a few bars of gospel.'

John told James he liked his voice and looked forward to hearing his record.

MacLaine, Shirley

Actress who appeared with John and Yoko on *The Dick Cavett Show* on Friday 5 May 1972, which was transmitted on 11 May. Then, in 1973, John, Yoko and Shirley planned to work together on a musical about the Watergate scandal. However, owing to their recording commitments when working on the *Mind Games* album, they scrapped the idea.

McLuhan, Marshall

Canadian communication specialist. A renowned authority on the media, he's noted for his books *Understanding Media* and *The Medium Is the Message*.

When he was a professor at the Department of Culture and Technology, University of Toronto, McLuhan (1911–80) invited John to visit him on Saturday 20 December 1969 to participate in an interview being filmed by CBS Television. John and McLuhan spent 45 minutes discussing a variety of subjects ranging from peace to music as the cameras whirled.

'Language is a form of organised stutter. Literally, you chop your sounds into bits in order to talk. Now, when you sing, you don't stutter, so singing is a way of stretching language into long, harmonious patterns and cycles. How do you think about language in songs?' asked McLuhan.

John replied, 'Language and song to me, apart from being pure vibrations, is just like trying to describe a dream. And because we don't have telepathy, we try to describe the dream to each other, to verify to each other what we know, what we believe to be inside each other. And the stuttering is right – because we can't say it. No matter how you say it, it's never how you want to say it.'

As John left, McLuhan escorted him to the door with the words, 'These portals have been honoured by your presence.'

The lecturer/author died in 1980.

McMillan, Keith

Originally a dancer with the Royal Ballet, McMillan became a professional photographer. His first contact with John came when Anthony Fawcett, with whom he'd worked previously on art assignments, called him to take photographs for the Acorn Catalogue being compiled for the National Sculpture Exhibition at Coventry Cathedral.

He was then commissioned to take pictures of the actual event. McMillan also took the official photographs for the *You Are Here* exhibition.

Madison Square Garden

The scene of John's final appearance on a public stage – in this case before an audience of 20,000 people. It took place on

Thanksgiving Day, 28 November 1974. John had promised
Elton John that if 'Whatever Gets You Thru the Night' reached
No. 1 in the charts he would appear on one of Elton's shows.
When the record topped the American charts on 16 November,
John lived up to his promise. On stage he joined Elton to
perform 'Whatever Gets You Thru the Night', 'Lucy in the Sky
with Diamonds' and the Beatles song written by Paul, 'I Saw
Her Standing There'. When he played it, John dedicated it 'to an
old estranged fiancé of mine called Paul'.

John had also been estranged from Yoko at the time, but she
attended the Madison Square Garden concert and, during the
after-show party at the Pierre Hotel, they began their reconciliation.

Madman

A song written by John that was recorded by the Beatles in
January 1969 during the *Get Back* sessions.

Magazines

Over the years there have been numerous magazines devoted to
John. Among them is *John,* a 68-page magazine published in
America by SMH.

A few editions which came out in 1964 were devoted entirely
to John, with articles such as 'Where to see John in person' and
'Win a letter from John'. However, most of the magazines
devoted to John were published following his death.

John Lennon: A Man Who Cared was issued by Paradise
Press in the USA and comprised material from the book *The
Beatles, The Fabulous Story of John, Paul, George and Ringo,*
with additional material updating the story by Chris Rowley.
John Lennon: A Melody Maker Tribute was one of several
British publications issued within weeks of John's death. It
contained 100 photographs, ten of them in colour. The main
text comprised 'Life and times of John Lennon' by Ray
Coleman, Melody Maker's editor-in-chief; a bibliography, 'I
Remember John' by Tony Barrow, the Beatles' former PR man,
'The music' by Patrick Humphries, a discography, 'The early
days' by Bill Harry and 'In His Own Write', a selection of
quotes. An interesting innovation is the reproduction of the
original typewritten captions from the picture agencies, which

accompanied certain shots. Also reproduced are several of the messages John sent to the *Melody Maker* over the years, including a postcard to Ray Coleman. Typical of John's humour, it read, 'Dear Ted, Having a wonderful. The weather is quite. Wish you were. The food is. So are we. See you when we get. Ours truly. Them Beatles.'

John Lennon, All You Need Is Love is an American tribute magazine issued by Mar-Jam Publishing containing a history of John's life and the Beatles' career plus discography, quotes and lots of colour photographs. *John Lennon & The Beatles: A Loving Tribute* was issued by 16 magazine and included a number of Beatles articles originally published in the 1960s, together with lots of photographs and a poster.

John Lennon & The Beatles: A Special Tribute was an American magazine published by Harris Publications at the beginning of 1981 shortly after John's murder. It contains over 100 monochrome photographs and eleven colour pictures. There are several pages documenting the events surrounding John's death but the main section of the magazine is a basic story of the Beatles' career, simple, straightforward and lacking in any great detail. There are one or two minor mistakes such as the reference to Jim McCartney's band as 'a black ragtime band' and the attribution of George Harrison's activities in 1968 to Paul McCartney. Apart from that it offers nothing new and is more a tribute to the Beatles' career as a whole then to John's in particular.

John Lennon: Beatles Memory Book is another tribute magazine from Harris Publications of New York, issued early in 1981 and containing eleven colour photograph and 67 monochrome pictures. Oddly different from its sister magazine, *John Lennon: Beatles Memory Book* has a curious piece entitled 'Unforgettable moments with John Lennon', which begins with a dialogue with God, in near-hysterical, emotional style. For example: 'She's strong, my Yoko. But weak like I am weak. She needs me, God. Needs me near her. Sean needs me. Maybe, God … maybe even the world needs me. But you took me away. Why, God? Why, before I was ready? If only I could have said just one more time, "I love you Yoko for now and for always and into all eternity. From everlasting to eternity." '

The article is coarse at times and then goes into a first-person account with the author of the piece, implying that he was a close friends of John's. But there is no credit. In fact, none of the article writers are named, although several pieces are written in the first person. There is a lengthy piece by a fan, 'We will canonize him with our love; one, two, three, four!!!', a general article about the Beatles; 'Beatlemania England 1962', a sketchy piece on their early career; 'Beatlemania USA' concerning the American success; 'The break-up of the Beatles' and 'On his Own with Yoko Ono'.

John Lennon Im Spiegel der Weltpresse was a Continental publication featuring 92 pages of newspaper cuttings on John's death from Britain, America, Switzerland, Germany, Austria, Belgium, France and Holland.

John Lennon: The Life & the Legend was a lavish colour magazine produced by the staff of the *Sunday Times* magazine with over 100 photographs, most of them in colour and a number printed as large double-page spreads.

The Dream is Over relates the events leading to John's death. This is followed by a series of two-page photographs covering each year of the Beatles' career from 1962.

Twist & Shout: The Early Days and the Beatles Years is a tribute penned by the Beatles' official biographer Hunter Davis, who also contributed John's obituary to *The Times* newspaper.

In My Life ... A Personal File is a selection of photographs of the memorabilia Hunter Davis picked up when he was writing the authorised biography. They include a Polyfoto strip of John when he was five years old, John's handwritten lyrics to a number of songs and several personal photographs from the Hamburg days.

Sometime in New York City: Lennon After the Beatles is a précis of his career, mainly in America, by Michael Watts.

Gimme Some Truth: The Thoughts of John Lennon is a collection of quotes; *Thank You Very Much and I Hope I've Passed the Audition* is a selection of twenty of John's best works, a personal choice by Paul Gambaccini, the Radio 1 disc jockey; and *Some Days in the Life,* a chronology by Mark Lewisohn.

John Lennon Tribute is a magazine published by Woodhill Press, New York, in 1980. It contains more than a dozen colour pictures, including reproductions of film posters, and more than ninety monochrome photographs, among which are reproductions of album sleeves. There are a series of short, sketchy articles: 'The Beatles: the early years', 'The birth of Beatlemania', 'The Beatles: the golden years' and 'The break up and aftermath'. There is only one writer's credit. The last item in the book is 'The final melody' by George Carpozi Jr, the story of John's death.

John Lennon: Working Class Hero is a handsome British tribute magazine that does not have the publisher or printer credited. However, it is believed to have been produced by the *New Musical Express* as Tony Tyler and Roy Carr (authors of *The Beatles: An Illustrated Record* and *NME* staffers) are the only contributors. Twelve large colour pictures and seventy black-and-white photographs are printed on good-quality paper. The main feature, 'John Lennon 1940–1980', has been penned by Tony Tyler and the other contribution 'John Lennon: a chronology' by Roy Carr. The contents are completed with the lyrics to 'Working Class Hero' and 'God'.

Lennon Photo Special was an American picture magazine issued by Sunshine Publication. The tribute magazine included a sixteen-page colour section.

Magical Misery Tour

A National Lampoon comedy album, a spoof on John and Yoko, issued on 2 September 1972, performed by Tony Hedron.

Magical Mystery Tour (album)

With only six numbers, the UK release on 8 December 1967 was issued on two EPs, together with a booklet. The American release was an album issued on 27 November 1967 and included their 1967 singles. The British version contained the tracks 'Magical Mystery Tour', 'The Fool on the Hill', 'Your Mother Should Know', 'Flying', 'I Am the Walrus' and 'Blue Jay Way'. John penned 'I Am the Walrus'. The track listing of the American album was: 'Magical Mystery Tour', 'The Fool on the Hill', 'Flying', 'Blue Jay Way', 'Your Mother Should Know', 'I Am the Walrus', 'Hello Goodbye', 'Strawberry Fields Forever', 'Penny Lane', 'Baby You're a Rich Man' and 'All You Need Is Love'.

Maharishi Song, The

John had put a lot of store by his expectation of what transcendental meditation and the influence of the Maharishi Mahesh

Yogi could do for him. He felt betrayed by the events at Rishikesh, which resulted in his writing and home recording a song in May 1968 called 'The Maharishi Song', which expressed the sense of betrayal he felt.

Mailer, Norman

Born 1923, a prominent contemporary American writer whose works include the novels *The Naked and the Dead* and *The American Dream*. He was one of the many celebrities who spoke up for John during the hearing at the Immigration and Naturalization Service Building in New York on 27 July 1976 when John was finally granted his green card.

When he took the stand, Mailer, who described John as 'one of the greatest artists in the Western world', said he appreciated John's talent and stated that it would be a pity if America lost it: 'We lost TS Eliot to England and only got Auden back.'

Following John's death, Mailer told *Rolling Stone* magazine, 'We have lost a genius of the spirit.'

He also commented, 'The killing of John Lennon altered everything. Like fifty million other people, I cared about Lennon.'

Make Love, Not War

A home demo John recorded in December 1970. John never completed the number, but he was later to use the melody to compose 'Mind Games'. It was included in the *Lost Lennon Tapes* series and on a CD issued with a Swedish edition of *A Spaniard in the Works,* published in 1998.

Malik, Michael Abdul

One-time pimp who also acted as a strong-arm rent collector for the notorious slum landlord Peter Rachman. Malik called himself Michael X and referred to himself as 'the most powerful black man in Europe'.

John and Yoko first met him in 1969 and supported his community centre for black culture, which he called the Black House, situated in Holloway, north London.

On 4 February 1970, after cutting their hair short, John and Yoko arranged a press call on the roof of the Black House, where they presented Michael X with plastic bags containing their hair. In exchange he gave them a pair of bloodstained boxing trunks, previously worn by Muhammad Ali, which they could auction in aid of their peace campaign. John and Yoko weren't popular with the British press at that time and no coverage appeared.

The Black House was mysteriously burned down. Malik was arrested for demanding money with menaces and stealing a paltry £5 from a businessman. He'd already been 'inside' for three years on a previous charge. John and Yoko provided bail in January 1971, but Malik jumped it and fled the country, moving to Trinidad.

John and Yoko visited him in Port of Spain in April 1971 and also arranged for Apple to pay him £30,000 advance for a book, which he never wrote.

Malik began another commune, which he also called the Black House. It suffered the same fate as the first, burning in a mysterious fire in February 1972. Police investigating the arson discovered two bodies buried in shallow graves: one was Joseph Skerett; the other was a white woman, Gale Ann Benson.

Malik was convicted of plotting her murder and was sentenced to be hanged.

John Lennon paid for a lawyer, William Kunstler, to fly to Trinidad to defend Malik. John also wrote to the authorities to plead for Malik's life. He wrote a statement and sent it to his friends, the media, politicians – even royalty – writing, 'We urge you to do what you can for this human being. Every time we turn our backs on someone who needs help we take a step backwards in time. Please help save a life.'

Lennon spent money on three appeals, to no avail. Michael X was hanged in Port of Spain on 16 May 1975.

Many years later a bizarre 'conspiracy theory' arose in America. This was the scenario: Gale Ann Benson, divorced wife of Jonathan Benson, a film director, met Hakim Jamal, an American activist, at the Black House. They became lovers and she changed her name to Hale Kimga, an anagram of Gale and Hakim.

The couple travelled to Morocco together and then to Paris, where they set up home together, and it was rumoured they were involved in a ménage-à-trois with the actress Jean Seberg.

The two then travelled first to Guyana and then to Trinidad, where she got to know Michael X more intimately. Jamal left her behind when he went on a trip to America and Benson and X became lovers in the Black House, fourteen miles from Port of Spain. She assumed the role of white-woman slave to her black master.

After the fire her body and that of Skerett were found. She had been knifed and buried alive.

Six months later Jamal was found murdered in his hometown of Boston, Massachusetts. On 8 September 1979, Jean Seberg's decomposed body was found wrapped in a blanket in the back of her car in Paris. The following year John Lennon was murdered.

The conspiracy theorists alleged that Jamal, Seberg and Lennon had been murdered as a revenge for the killing of Benson, who had a powerful family background. Her father was said to be Captain Leonard Plugge, former Tory MP for Chatham, who eventually died in California at the age of 91 in 1981.

Interestingly enough, it was revealed only in the late 80s that the real father of Gale was Jack Bouvier, making Gale the half-sister of Jackie Kennedy.

The conspiracy theory, of course, doesn't hold up when analysed. John's death had no connection with the Benson killing, and nor did Jean Seberg's.

Seberg was an American actress who first came to fame in the film *St Joan*, but ended up spending most of her life in France where she starred in such films as *Bonjour Tristesse* and *Breathless*. She married the author Romain Gary, but in the 60s, during a trip to America, associated with members of the Black Panther movement. The FBI sought to discredit her and spread the rumour that the child she was expecting was the result of an affair with a Black Panther member. This caused her such anxiety that the baby died at birth. It was white. She had the body sent to her home town to be exhibited in a glass coffin so that everyone could see its true colour.

Her ex-husband said that every year, on the anniversary of the miscarriage, she tried to commit suicide. She succeeded and when her body was found in her Renault she had taken an overdose of barbiturates and had left a suicide note: 'I can't live any longer with my nerves.'

Manchester, Melissa

An American singer, born in 1951, whose hits include 'Midnight Blue', 'Don't Cry Out Loud' and 'You Should Hear How She Talks About You'. Manchester portrayed Yoko Ono in *National Lampoon's Magical Misery Tour* parody.

Man of the Decade

Associated Television commissioned a documentary featuring the personal choice of 'man of the decade' from three figures – the author Mary McCarthy, the broadcaster Alistair Cooke and the anthropologist Dr Desmond Morris. The ATV brief was that each of the three should make a choice and prepare a twenty-minute documentary. The three segments were then to be presented as a sixty-minute programme called *Man of the Decade*.

McCarthy chose Ho Chi Minh. Cooke selected John F Kennedy and Morris opted for John Lennon.

The Desmond Morris interview was filmed at Tittenhurst Park on Tuesday 2 December 1969 and the interview was to be supplemented with stock film of the Beatles and John, which John helped Morris to select when they both viewed clips at a Soho viewing theatre. The film material used included scenes from *A Hard Day's Night* and *Help!*; performances of 'Some Other Guy', 'If I Fell', 'I'm Down' and 'Something'; and news clips of the Marylebone Magistrates' Court appearance in November 1968, of the Bed-Ins in Amsterdam and Montreal and the arrival of the Beatles at Kennedy Airport in February 1964.

ATV screened the documentary nationally at 10.30 p.m. on Tuesday 30 December 1969 with John's section being broadcast last at 11.10 p.m.

During the interview, John commented, 'Not many people are noticing all the good that came out of the last ten years. The moratorium and the vast gathering of people in Woodstock – the biggest mass of people ever gathered together for anything other than war. The good thing that came out of the sixties was this vast, peaceful movement.' He also said, 'The sixties were just waking up in the morning. We haven't even got to dinnertime yet. And I can't wait! I can't wait, I'm so glad to be around.'

Mansfield, Jayne

A pneumatic blonde promoted by Hollywood as another Marilyn Monroe, and most famous among rock fans for her performance in *The Girl Can't Help It*.

May Mann, in her biography *Jayne Mansfield*, claimed that on the Beatles' first American tour John Lennon mentioned that the one film star he wanted to see was Jayne Mansfield. A rendezvous between the star and the group took place at the Whisky-a-Go-Go on Sunset Strip. Mann further claims that John was annoyed when Mansfield brought her husband along and said, 'I just wanted to be alone with Jayne. I've dreamed about it.'

Other sources suggest that it was Paul, not John, who made the original request. Perhaps May Mann got the two mixed up because the famous photograph of the meeting at the Whisky pictures Jayne and John sitting together.

However, Mann's interpretation of events were different from that of someone who actually witnessed them: the journalist Chris Hutchins.

In fact, when the Beatles were staying at the Hollywood suburb of Bel Air it was Jayne, dressed in a mauve catsuit, who dropped in to see them. John was the only member of the group present and she tugged his hair and squealed, 'Is this real?' to which John replied, dropping his eyes to her most famous features, 'Well, are those real?' 'There's one way to find out,' she said.

Hutchins was with John at the time and reports that John offered to make cocktails. Out of the sight of Jayne and a male friend she'd brought along, he poured gin, vodka, red wine and various liqueurs into a mixer – and then peed into it.

Jayne then asked her male friend to read the tarot cards for her and John. He began to read them, and then dropped them with horror, exclaiming, 'My God, this is terrible. I see an awful ending to all this.' John was furious and threw the two of them out.

He then suggested to Hutchins that they join Paul, George and Ringo at the Whisky-a-Go-Go.

After they'd arrived, Jayne Mansfield suddenly entered and squeezed her way into the middle of them, allowing cameramen to take photographs. George was angry and threw a Scotch and

Coke at a photographer, but an ice cube hit another actress, Mamie van Doren, in the face. The Beatles then got up to leave and before they departed John leaned over and told Mansfield about the secret ingredient he'd added to the cocktail he'd made her.

Mansfield was decapitated in a road accident two years later. John remembered the tarot reading and was alarmed. He was then obsessed with numerology and, in particular, the number nine. He told Hutchins, 'Jayne was born on 19 April and she died on 29 June. April is the fourth month and June is the sixth. Add them together and you get ten. I was born on 9 October, the ninth day of the tenth month. She died two months after her birthday, which means I'm going to die on a day with a nine in it, in December.'

Man Who Shot John Lennon, The

A British television documentary produced by Kevin Sims and screened on both sides of the Atlantic in February 1987. The subject was Lennon's assassin, Mark Chapman, and the killer gave Sims permission to interview him in Rikers Island Prison. Although he refused to be filmed, Chapman's voice is heard on the soundtrack.

Many Rivers to Cross

A song written by the Jamaican artist Jimmy Cliff. John decided to include the number on *Pussy Cats,* the album he produced for Harry Nilsson at Record Plant West in Los Angeles in April 1974. John's string arrangement for the number was to inspire him when he composed 'No. 9 Dream'.

During the summer of 1976, John made his own home demo recording of the song acoustically, accompanied by a drum machine.

Mao Tse-Tung

The Communist Chinese leader more commonly referred to as Chairman Mao, who ruled China from World War Two until his death in 1976.

Mao, together with John Lennon and President John F Kennedy, was one of three prominent figures to be selected by the BBC for their television documentary *Man of the Decade.*

John also had a daring mock-up photograph made of a naked Chairman Mao dancing with an equally naked President Richard Nixon for display on the sleeve of his *Sometime in New York City* album. This led one irate American to write to the Immigration and Naturalization Service to protest at John's application for a green card, saying that the album cover was 'obscene and grossly slanderous to the President'.

March of Dimes, The

An American charity organisation. In April 1974 John had returned to New York with May Pang and the couple were staying at the Pierre hotel on 5th Avenue. A March of Dimes benefit concert was held in Central Park on Sunday 28 April 1974. John and Harry Nilsson turned up at the rally and made a brief stage appearance, joined by the New York disc jockey Cousin Brucie, who asked him for information on the current activities of the other ex-Beatles. John and Harry signed autographs and did a short song-and-dance stint.

Margaret, Princess

The sister of Queen Elizabeth II provided a royal presence at the premieres of Beatles films and attended several of their receptions. However, when she arrived at a cocktail party, John heard her make a remark about how she'd been inconvenienced by Beatles fans on her arrival. John responded by saying to someone, 'I didn't know why she'd bothered to turn up if our bloody fans were a nuisance to her. I didn't say it to her directly, but I'm sure she overheard me. I just hope I hadn't misheard her.'

John also none-too-fondly referred to her as Priceless Margarine.

Margo

Surname unknown. A German girl who was reputedly dated by John in Hamburg. George Tremlett in *The John Lennon Story* quotes a musician named Tony Dangerfield who was in Hamburg at the time.

He said, 'John used to go round with a big fat chick called Margo, who used to go everywhere with him. He pulled her out of the audience one night – all the English musicians had

German chicks. It was like a colony of English yobbos and German chicks.'

Martin, George

The Beatles' recording manager was born in London in 1926 and entered the Guildhall School of Music when he was 21, following a three-year stint in the Fleet Air Arm. He began to work for Parlophone Records under Oscar Preuss and then became head of the label when Preuss retired in 1955.

When Brian Epstein was unable to obtain a recording contract for the Beatles, John Lennon told him, 'Right, try Embassy.' This was a joke referring to a record label run by Woolworth's. It really looked as if Epstein would not be able to obtain a contract, since EMI, Pye and virtually every other record label in the country had turned them down. It was only by a fluke that he was put on to George Martin at Parlophone, but even then he had such difficulty getting hold of Martin and would actually cry with rage when his calls weren't returned and threatened to withdraw EMI's labels from his stores.

Martin agreed to sign the group, but the percentage deal was incredibly low, even derisory.

The label itself handled few pop artists and mainly concentrated on classical music, jazz, middle-of-the-road and comedy records. Martin had recorded people such as the Goons, Bernard Cribbins, the *Beyond the Fringe* revue and Flanders and Swann. Ron Richards recorded the few pop stars on the label such as Shane Fenton and Peter Gadd.

When the Beatles went to London to do their first recording audition on Wednesday 6 June 1962 it was Richards who was down as their recording manager and took over the session. Chris Neal, one of the engineers, commenting on the impression the Beatles made when they arrived, said, 'I remember George Martin taking a quick look at them and going down to the canteen to have a cup of tea.'

When the Beatles were performing 'Love Me Do', the chief engineer, Norman Smith, was impressed by this original song and told Neal to go down to the canteen and get Martin, who then returned and took over the session. When the Beatles arrived for their recording session on Tuesday 4 September

1962, Richards rehearsed them during the afternoon and George Martin took over the session in the evening. Ringo Starr had now replaced Pete Best, but Norman Smith was to comment, 'I've a feeling that Paul wasn't too happy with Ringo's drumming, and felt that it could be better. He didn't make too good a job of it.' Ron Richards commented, 'We [he and George Martin] weren't happy with the drum sound on the original "Love Me Do" so I booked Andy White for the remake.'

Richards was the sole producer of the session and it's interesting to wonder whether he would have continued recording them had it not been for Neal bringing Martin up from the canteen that time. After all, on the original sheets he was down as their producer and, since he was the man who usually produced the rock 'n' roll acts for Parlophone, it would have been natural for him to have taken them over. One wonders what he felt at losing the chance to continue producing the act that became the most popular group in the world.

George Martin really came into his own in what became known as 'the studio years', when the Beatles stopped touring. He admitted that prior to that time, any A&R man would have been able to do what he did.

The Beatles developed a rapport with Martin and after some lengthy recording sessions George suggested that they take a holiday as a break and John and Cynthia joined him and his wife Judy at St Moritz for a skiing holiday. Cynthia was to comment, 'George was a true gentleman and Judy a perfect lady. George's quiet manner, and shy humour and tall elegant stature reminded me a great deal of Prince Philip and if you had the pleasure of sitting next to Judy in a restaurant, her voice would ring out more queenly than the Queen.'

John always felt that Martin gave more attention to Paul's songs than his own. Martin was to admit to Ray Coleman, 'That's probably true, but that's because Paul was more interested. John's irritation was a little unfair. John's songs got a great deal of attention, but possibly what he meant was that they never got the attention to detail that he thought they needed. So they didn't quite work out the way he wanted them. But they worked out the way I wanted them.'

Martin thought that he could as it were get inside John's brain to find out what he actually wanted. Yet John was still to say that George was 'always more like a Paul McCartney producer than for my music'.

John was to write a humorous sleeve note to Martin's orchestral album of Beatles hits, beginning, 'George Martin is a tall man. He is also a musician with short hair.' He ended with a little poem, which he said should be sung to the tune of 'Old MacDonald Had a Farm':

> *Good George Martin is our friend*
> *Buddy Pal and Mate*
> *Buy this record and he'll send*
> *A dog for your front gate.*

When the Beatles were in the studio overdubbing voices on one of the *Sergeant Pepper* tracks, Martin was concerned about how John looked and called over the intercom, 'What's the matter, John? Aren't you feeling very well?' John told him, 'I don't know. I'm feeling very strange.'

Martin took him outside into the fresh air, on to the roof of No. 2 studio. As there was a sheer drop of ninety feet to the ground, he told him, 'Don't go to near the edge – there's no rail there, John.' They walked around for a while and then went downstairs.

John had said that he never took LSD when he was due to go into the studio and on this occasion had taken what he thought were uppers. Describing the incident, John said, 'I suddenly got so scared on the mike. I thought I felt ill, and I thought I was going to crack. I said I must get some air. They all took me upstairs on the roof and George Martin was looking at me funny, and then it dawned on me I must have taken acid. I said, "Well, I can't go on – you'll have to do it and I'll just stay and watch."'

John verbally attacked a number of his former friends when Jann Wenner interviewed him at length for *Rolling Stone* magazine and he expressed the feeling that he preferred Phil Spector to produce him, saying of George Martin, 'He's more Paul's style of music than mine.'

He was also to say, 'You see, for quite a few of our albums – like the Beatles' double album – George Martin didn't really produce it. I don't know whether this is scandalous, but he didn't. In the early days. I can remember what George Martin did.'

When the Beatles split up he had another go at George, saying, 'Who does he think he is anyway? What songs has he ever written?'

He was able to apologise for these remarks when he had dinner with Martin in Los Angeles in 1971, saying 'I'm sorry, George. I didn't really mean those things about you and all the others. I was smashed out of my mind when I was speaking.'

Regarding the situation with recording numbers by Paul and John, Martin explained that Paul would sit with him and asked him what he planned to do with his song and would go over it all, virtually note by note. George would have to explain everything to him and Paul would query things and make suggestions. Martin said that John was vague: 'He would talk in metaphors about his ideas. I'd have to get inside his brain to find out what he wanted. It would be more of a psychological approach.'

Examples of this included 'Being for the Benefit of Mr Kite' and 'Strawberry Fields Forever'.

John told him that 'Being for the Benefit of Mr Kite' was about a fairground and he wanted George to 'get the feeling of the sawdust and the feel of the ring'. Then Martin would have to figure out how to translate that into sound.

John told George that he wanted the middle section of the songs to have music, which would swirl up and around. Martin had the musical knowledge and technical expertise to work out how certain things could be achieved, whereas John had no idea. In this case, Martin told him, 'What we'll do is to slow the whole thing down by a half. You play the tune twice as slow and an octave down, and I'll do my runs as fast as I can, but an octave down as well. Then, when we double the tape speed, it'll come out all nice and smooth and very swirly.'

Despite this, John still didn't feel it had come out right and Martin then got together recordings of Victorian steam organs, then cut the tapes into pieces a foot long until he had about sixty of them; then they were flung into the air, picked up in any order and stuck back together again.

With 'Strawberry Fields Forever', John told him that he'd like him to do the score and use a few cellos and a bit of brass – and that was his sole instruction.

Martin said that John always disliked the sound of his own voice, yet Martin felt it was one of the best voices he'd ever heard.

When it came to recording 'Tomorrow Never Knows', John wanted to sound like a Dalai Lama singing on a hilltop, so Martin put his voice through a loudspeaker and rotated it.

As for the work John did after the Beatles split, Martin says he liked *Imagine* and would have loved to produce it, but he didn't like *Double Fantasy*: 'He hadn't been in the studios for a long time, and it shows. It's not vintage Lennon, not the greatest stuff he ever did.'

When contrasting the two Beatle songwriters, George commented, 'Paul's songs will last longer than John's because they get more to the average man, to the heart strings, than John's did.'

He was also to say, 'John was the rebel, the Dylan of the group, and much more of a word man than Paul. Paul learned about words from John.'

Marylebone Magistrates' Court

Situated at 181 Marylebone Road. On 19 October 1968 John and Yoko made their first court appearance here following the drug bust at their Montague Square maisonette the previous day. They were remanded on bail until 28 November 1968.

At their second appearance John pleaded guilty to possessing cannabis resin. His lawyer Martin Polden pointed out that John's music had provided pleasure for millions and asked for leniency, saying, 'An ounce and a half of compassion was not too much to ask.' The charge of wilful obstruction was dropped and John was fined £150 plus 20 guineas (£21) costs.

A photograph of the couple being pressed in by the crowd of three hundred people and surrounded by policemen as they were outside the courthouse on their first appearance there was featured on the sleeve of their *Unfinished Music No. 2: Life With the Lions* album.

John attributed Yoko's miscarriage to the drugs bust. Hours after the original arrest she was taken to St Charlotte's Maternity Hospital and given blood transfusions. John stayed with her in her room, but she miscarried on 21 November. *The Times* announced, 'Yoko Ono, the Japanese artist and friend of

John Lennon and the Beatles, has had a miscarriage in Queen Charlotte's Maternity Hospital. Mr Lennon has said he was the father.'

Maschler, Tom

The managing director of the publishing house Jonathan Cape at the time the company published *In His Own Write* and *A Spaniard in the Works*. John's writings came to his attention in 1964 after Maschler had commissioned a writer called Michael Braun to prepare a book on the British pop scene. Braun showed him some of John's writings and Maschler decided to contact John and publish his works. He continued to associate with John over the years, visiting him in his Emperor's Gate flat and at Kenwood, and stayed in touch until John was divorced from Cynthia. It was Maschler who passed on Adrienne Kennedy's play, based on John's books, to Victor Spinetti, and he also attended the first night of the show. He discussed the play with John and said that John was disappointed in it. He said that John liked Kennedy and was flattered that she'd wanted to turn his books into a play.

Mason, Ann

A student at Liverpool College of Art, who shared the same lessons as John. There was no romantic involvement, as she was the girlfriend of John's mate Geoff Mohammed. However, they were friends and in March 1958 John posed for two hours for an oil painting of himself by Ann that, in later years, was to be featured in several exhibitions. Prior to becoming Mohammed's girlfriend, she had gone out for a brief period with Stuart Sutcliffe.

MBE

There was a formal announcement on 11 June 1965 that the Beatles would each be made an MBE. The initials stand for Member (of the Order of the) British Empire.

However, John, who in some ways was antiestablishment, made it known that he was not entirely happy with receiving the award. When he'd originally seen the brown envelope with 'On Her Majesty's Service' written on it, he said he thought he was being called up.

When he discovered what it was he recalled that his first
instinct was to turn it down. When Brian Epstein phoned him to
discuss it and he told him his feelings, Brian said that he had to
accept the honour. John knew that, if he spurned it, it would do
incalculable damage to the group. Later, he was to comment,
'Taking the MBE was a sell-out for me.'

Once he'd decided to comply with his manager's request, John
began giving out his quotes to the press: 'I thought people got
these things for driving tanks, winning wars.' But when some
protesters began sending their medals back to the Palace, John
became annoyed and said that, while army officers got their
awards for killing people, 'We got ours for entertaining. On
balance, I'd say we deserve ours more.'

The day the Beatles were to be presented with their MBEs,
newspapers ran headlines proclaiming 'BEATLEMANIA AT BUCK
HOUSE' and when the group arrived in their black Rolls Royce,
pandemonium raged outside, but perfect decorum reigned
inside.

The groups for the investiture were then formed into the
Orders of Knighthood, with the MBEs, the lowest, coming last.
Other categories included CBEs and OBEs. There were eighty
MBEs awarded that particular day and all participants were
ushered into an anteroom for briefing.

Everyone in the room was obviously interested in the Beatles.
Robert Dougall, a noted BBC broadcaster who was also to be
presented, described them as 'four slim young men in dark
lounge suits and dark ties. Nothing flamboyant about their
dress, although Ringo Starr's suit had eight buttons down the
front and George Harrison's tailor had given him epaulettes and
buttoned pockets. There they stood, all very well behaved, with
their longish hair and pale green faces.'

Dougall joined the queue of fellow MBEs asking for autographs: 'They signed away as nice as pie.' Paul McCartney
declared the Palace to be a 'keen pad' and John Lennon said he
liked the carpets and especially the staff. He had expected them
to be dukes and things but, 'They are all just fellers.'

They were all briefed by Lt Col. Eric Penn, Comptroller from
the Lord Chamberlain's office.

At Christmas he took his MBE medal down to his Aunt
Mimi's bungalow in Poole, Dorset, and told her she could keep

it. She placed it on her sideboard beneath a picture of John taken by Astrid Kirchherr, but later placed it on top of her television set.

One day he sent his chauffeur, Les Anthony, to collect it from her. Anthony told Mimi, 'Mr Lennon said would you lend him the MBE medal for a while.' Mimi told him, 'Yes, but tell him, don't forget it's mine and I want it back.' John had it wrapped up in brown paper and sent to the Queen at Buckingham Palace with the message, 'I am returning this MBE in protest against Britain's involvement in the Nigeria–Biafra thing, against our support of America in Vietnam and against 'Cold Turkey' slipping down the chart. With love, John Lennon. Bag Productions, 3 Savile Row, London W1.' He also sent similar letters to the Prime Minister and to the secretary of the Central Chancery.

His Aunt Mimi was furious at the deception and told John so in no uncertain terms, accusing him of insulting the Queen. 'He broke my heart over that,' she said. 'And also, he didn't tell me first why that medal was being taken away.'

John was later to regret that he'd added the facetious remark about 'Cold Turkey' in the letter, and despite the fact that he'd returned the medal he retained the honour because it could not be renounced once it had been accepted. Paul, George and Ringo, on the other hand, had no regrets in accepting their awards.

Mean Mr Mustard

Song recorded for the *Abbey Road* album on 24, 25 and 29 July 1969. It had originally been considered for *The Beatles* double album and had been recorded, along with 'Sun King' as one song called 'Here Comes the Sun King'. John had based the story on a newspaper item that he'd read.

In Robert Stigwood's film version of *Sergeant Pepper's Lonely Hearts Club Band,* the comedian Frankie Howerd portrayed Mr Mustard. George Martin had the task of recording the character's two robot assistants singing the song. Martin considered the original a 'quick and throwaway number' and decided to slow the song down 'and make it a bit more groovy'. To make the singers sound like androids he used an instrument called a Vocoder, which makes the human voice sound robotic.

Mean Woman Blues

One of the songs that John sang when he was performing with the Quarry Men. It had been recorded by his idol Elvis Presley and featured in his 1957 movie *Loving You*. Jerry Lee Lewis also recorded the song, originally penned by Claude DeMetrius, and Roy Orbison had a hit with it in 1963.

Meat City

The final track on the *Mind Games* album, which was originally developed from a boogie-style song which John had originally called 'Shoeshine'. A contemporary American poster depicting a cartoon figure of a mother pig and her baby being taken to 'Meat City' may have inspired him. Although the bulk of the album is his eulogy to America, at the tail end of the song he sings, 'Well I'm going to China to see for myself.'

Performing in China was one of John's ambitions and in 1972 he said, 'I shall go there. I will take the opportunity to try to see Mao. If he is ill or dead or refuses to see me, too bad. But if I go there I want to meet people who are doing something important.'

Apparently, it was said that if you played the tune backwards you could hear a mysterious voice between the verses say, 'Fuck a pig.'

Medeiros, Michael

Gardener employed by John and Yoko to attend to the plants in their various Dakota Building apartments and offices. John referred to him as Mike Tree because he couldn't remember his surname.

Following John's death, Medeiros continued in Yoko's employ until 1982, when he began to work as a videotape editor.

He documented his experiences as John and Yoko's gardener in a feature called *Barefoot In Nutopia* in the *Marin Independent Journal* in December 1991.

Mekas, Jonas

The Lithuanian-born former film critic of the *Village Voice*. Mekas was a friend of Yoko's and when Yoko wanted to return to New York to live he invited her to produce a series of films which he would show at the Elgin Theater, where he was currently working. This resulted in the three-evening festival of John and Yoko's films there.

When John and Yoko moved into the St Regis Hotel, she began inviting her old friends from the New York arts world, including Mekas, who was now running the Anthology Film Archives, specialising in avant-garde films. One day the pair arrived unannounced at Mekas's office and he introduced them to Steve Gebhardt, one of his employees. They hired Gebhardt on the spot to work with them on their projected movies. They also had Mekas direct one of the scenes for their *Imagine* film.

Melly, George

Jazz singer, born in Liverpool on 17 August 1926.

He introduced the Beatles on stage at the Royal Albert Hall on Thursday 18 April 1963 for the BBC radio show *Swinging Sound '63*. Describing the occasion, he remembers, 'I went to introduce the Beatles, but I never got any further than "Ladies and Gentlemen ..." An enormous wall of pre-pubescent screaming arose from the Royal Albert Hall and I had to mouth "The Beatles" and get out. That night, I was absolutely sure that our [jazz musicians'] days as popular musicians, in the broadest sense, were over. In fact, they were already over and it was to be the Beatles all the way.'

George and John had met on several occasions, although they nearly came to blows once at a publisher's party over George's review of *In His Own Write*.

Melly had written a favourable review of John's book in the *Observer*. He approached John to mention it to him. They were both drunk at the time and a heated discussion began, with John telling Melly that he hated the fact that he came from a trad jazz background because such groups had blocked the Beatles and other local groups from appearing at the Cavern. He then began calling Melly one of the 'blockers'.

George tried to change the subject by mentioning his review. John said he hadn't read it. George told him that he enjoyed it and that he detected the influence of James Joyce. John became aggressive and said he didn't know who Joyce was.

Melly then said that black singers had influenced them both. This infuriated John further.

Commenting on the heated discussion, Melly said, 'It nearly came to a fight. I'm glad it didn't because he would certainly have won.'

George also appeared on the *Parkinson* television chat show with John and Yoko. Melly was to tell Ray Coleman, 'They irritated me with their 'bagism' and the fact that they were very rich and constantly making humble gestures. If only the acorns had done some good or the bagism had persuaded people to be peaceful. But it just irritated most people. I felt it wasn't very useful.'

When Derek Taylor was involved with WEA Records he struck up a friendship with Melly and promoted the singer on the label. During a trip to Los Angeles with Derek, George was staying in a bungalow at Hollywood's Chateau Marmont hotel when John arrived with some friends in a state of inebriation. Melly and John then spent a night reminiscing about Liverpool and discussing a Liverpool wrestler called Jackie Pye. This particular wrestler was known as Dirty Jackie Pye and he had a reputation for pressing his finger against his nose and flicking snot at the referee.

When Melly was in New York with Derek Taylor, staying at the Algonquin Hotel during the promotion of one of his books, they received a visit from a drunken John and Harry Nilsson and John and Melly once again almost came to blows. At 2 o' clock in the morning John called Melly's female press agent demanding sex. She told him, 'I'm asleep. Go away!'

Melly penned three autobiographical books: *Owning Up, Rum, Bum and Concertina* and *Scouse Mouse*.

George was to pen John's obituary for *Punch* magazine on 12 December 1980. In the obituary, he wrote: 'He was not ashamed to show that he had a penis and that he loved his wife, but his lasting value is in his music both before and after the Beatles broke up.'

Mendips

The name of the semidetached house where John went to live with his Aunt Mimi and Uncle George in 1945. It was named after the Welsh hills.

Situated at 251 Menlove Avenue in the suburb of Woolton, three miles from Liverpool city centre, it was a pleasant house, built in the 30s, with leaded windows and a porch in which John spent many hours practising with his guitar.

It overlooked the busy Menlove Avenue and the house, with its small garden, was where John lived until he shared a flat temporarily in Gambier Terrace with Rod Murray and Stuart Sutcliffe.

After John and Cynthia were married, while Cynthia was expecting Julian, Mimi invited her to move into the house with her. Her husband George had died some years previously. Although Mimi Smith seemed quite content in Mendips, John bought her a luxury bungalow near Bournemouth in 1965 and she moved south.

John asked her not to sell Mendips because he couldn't bear the thought of his childhood home in the hands of someone else, but Mimi disagreed, feeling that a house shouldn't be left empty. He tried to persuade her to spend six months of each year at Mendips and the rest of the year in Poole, but she felt that any break must be a clean one and the house was sold to a doctor.

Over the years it has become something of a shrine and a special sign had to be erected outside the house: 'OFFICIAL NOTICE. PRIVATE. NO ADMISSION. MERSEYSIDE COUNTY COUNCIL.'

In 2000 a special blue plaque was displayed outside the house.

Menlove Avenue (album)

Posthumous album released in America on Monday 27 October 1986 on Capitol SJ-12533 and in Britain on Monday 3 November 1986 on PCS 7308. The ten-track LP comprised previously unreleased tracks that were chosen and assembled by Yoko Ono, who also contributed a brief sleeve note.

The album was named after 251 Menlove Avenue, the Liverpool address where John was reared, and the track listing comprised: Side One: 'Here We Go Again', 'Rock 'n' Roll People', 'Angel Baby', 'Since My Baby Left Me', 'To Know Her Is To Love Her'. Side Two: 'Steel and Glass', 'Scared', 'Old Dirt Road', 'Nobody Loves You (When You're Down and Out)', 'Bless You'.

The tracks on Side One were all recorded in New York and Los Angeles in 1973–74 during sessions for the *Rock 'n' Roll* album, but weren't included on that record. They include the Lennon/Spector composition 'Here We Go Again' and 'Rock 'n'

Roll People', a song given by John to Johnny Winter. 'Angel Baby' briefly appeared on an album called *Roots,* which was withdrawn after a few weeks owing to legal action. All tracks, with the exception of the Phil Spector production 'To Know Her Is To Love Her', were produced and arranged by John and recorded at A&M Studios, Los Angeles, and the Record Plant, New York.

Side Two features alternative versions of songs written for the *Walls and Bridges* album. The tracks were all produced and arranged by John and recorded live at the Record Plant in New York City in 1974. The musicians were Lennon (guitar/piano), Jim Keltner (drums), Jesse Ed Davis (guitar) and Klaus Voormann (bass).

Other than the three cover versions, John wrote all of the songs on the album, and co-wrote the lyrics of 'Old Dirt Road' with Harry Nilsson.

Andy Warhol designed the album cover.

The album was issued in Britain in the CD format on Monday 13 April 1987.

Menlove Avenue didn't receive a particularly pleasing reception from critics and the reviewer in *USA Today* wrote, 'The pickings among Lennon's unreleased music are getting so slim you can almost hear Beatle John muttering "rubbish". Can Yoko Ono fail to see the disservice to the artist?'

Mersey Beat

The publication that chronicled and promoted the Beatles' early rise to fame. When John Lennon, Stuart Sutcliffe, Bill Harry and Rod Murray had gone to see the Beat poet Royston Ellis at Liverpool University, they got together at a favourite watering hole called Ye Cracke.

The discussion ranged over the fact that many of the young poets seemed to copy the San Francisco poets and that popular culture seemed to be dominated by an American influence. It was felt that the Liverpool 8 area was an exciting cultural place and they even likened it to what they'd heard about Greenwich Village in New York. There was also talk of the negative publicity 'Beatniks' were receiving in the national press. Harry suggested that they should do something positive to promote their own ideas, that creatively it would be best to express themselves via their own surroundings rather than copying people from a different environment. He suggested they call themselves 'the Dissenters' and begin to make Liverpool famous: John with his music, Stuart and Rod with their painting and Bill with his writing.

At the time Bill had been editing the University rag publication *Pantosphinx* and had also been working on a music publication for the local music store Frank Hessy's.

He began to plan the publication in 1960 and its format began to take shape. Instead of a magazine he opted for a newspaper, which he originally intended to become a 'what's on' of all musical activity in Liverpool. He'd been switched on to Elvis Presley by a friend at art college, John Ashcroft, and had begun listening to Buddy Holly records at a friend's house. With his coverage of local concerts for *Frank Comments*, the Hessy publication, and the fact that he attended Saturday night dances at places such as Wilson Hall in Garston, he began to realise that something unique was happening on Merseyside, but few people recognised it. He wrote a letter to the *Daily Mail* saying that what was happening in Liverpool was like New Orleans at the turn of the century, but with rock 'n' roll instead of jazz. He received no reply and began to gather information on everything happening locally, filling the details in little red pocket notebooks, which he always carried around.

In May 1960, when the Beatles were appearing at the Jacaranda, he met his girlfriend, Virginia Sowry, who agreed to work on the publication with him. A friend, Dick Matthews, introduced them to a civil servant, Jim Anderson, who agreed to lend them the £50 needed to start the publication.

A tiny attic office was found at 81a Renshaw Street and Virginia became the only full-time member of staff. Bill continued to live on the grant he received from the art college after being awarded a Senior City Art Scholarship.

The group he was most familiar with were now calling themselves the Beatles. They'd been regarded as the 'art college' group and were the ones he was going to promote most in the publication; that he stuck to this resolve was proven by the fact that a local compere, Bob Wooler, said that other groups were upset by the amount of coverage the Beatles were getting and the publication should be retitled *The Mersey Beatle*!

In the early hours of one morning, Bill had been trying to think of a name for the publication. He began to think of the area he would cover and pictured a policeman walking across a map of Merseyside covering the Wirral, up to Southport and nearby towns such as Warrington, Widnes and St Helens. The name *Mersey Beat* popped into his mind, based on a policeman's beat and nothing to do with music. This was similar to the origin of the Beatles' name, which also wasn't using a musical term but had been based on that of an insect, like Buddy Holly's group the Crickets.

When Bill and John used to sit together and drink at Ye Cracke, Bill had once asked him to show him some poetry. Bill was impressed by it because it was a rustic poem which had a typically English feel to it and wasn't like the Beat poems that everyone else was copying. He commissioned John to write a piece about the Beatles, which he could use in the first issue. John gave him an untitled piece he'd written on two sheets of paper. Bill decided to use it in its entirety, without changing a single word. He also made up a caption for it: 'On the Dubious Origin of Beatles, Translated from the John Lennon'.

It was published in the first issue, dated 5 July 1961 and read:

Once upon a time there were three little boys called John, George and Paul, by name christened. They decided to get together because they were the getting together type. When they were together they wondered what for after all, what for? So all of a sudden they grew guitars and formed a noise. Funnily enough, no one was interested, least of all the three little men. So-o-o-o on discovering a fourth little even littler man called Stuart Sutcliffe running about them they said, quote 'Sonny get a bass guitar and you will be alright' and he did but he wasn't alright because he couldn't play it. So they sat on him with comfort 'til he could play. Still there was no beat, and a kindly old man said, quote 'Thou hast not drums!' We had no drums! They coffed. So a series of drums came and went and came.

Suddenly, in Scotland, touring with Johnny Gentle, the group (called the Beatles) discovered they had not a very nice sound – because they had no amplifiers. They got some. Many people ask what are Beatles? Ugh. Beatles, how did the name arrive? So we will tell you. It came in a vision – a man appeared on a flaming pie and said unto them 'From this day on you are Beatles with an "A".' 'Thank you, Mister Man,' they said, thanking him.

And then a man with a beard cut off said – will you go to Germany (Hamburg) and play mighty rock for the peasants for money? And we said we would play mighty anything for money.

But before we could go we had to grow a drummer. So we grew one in West Derby in a club called Some Casbah and his trouble was Pete Best. We called 'Hello, Pete, come off to Germany!' 'Yes!' Zooooom. After a few months, Peter and Paul (who is called McArtrey, son of Jim McArtrey, his father) lit a Kino (cinema) and the German police said 'Bad Beatles, you must go home and light your English cinemas.' Zooooom, half a group. But even before this, the Gestapo had taken my friend little George Harrison (of Speke) away because he was only twelve and too young to vote in Germany; but after two months he grew eighteen and the Gestapoes said 'you can come.' So suddenly all back in Liverpool Village where many groups playing in grey suits and Jim said 'Why have you no grey suits?' 'We don't like them, Jim' we said speaking to Jim. After playing in the clubs a bit, everyone said 'go to Germany!' so we are. Zooooom. Stuart gone. Zoom zoom John (of Woolton) George (of Speke) Peter and Paul zoom zoom. All of them gone.

Thank you club members, from John and George (that are friends).

(It's interesting to note that John gave Paul's surname as McArtrey – and as a result this spelling was used on the cover of Issue No. 13 when the Beatles topped the poll.)

John was thrilled that his piece had been printed in its entirety and came round to the *Mersey Beat* office and gave Bill Harry virtually everything he had written: around 250 items including stories, poems and drawings to use as he saw fit.

Bill decided to use the items as a column. He liked the small funny column by 'Beachcomber' in the *Daily Express* and decided to run the pieces under the name 'Beatcomber'.

The first of John's poems was called 'I Remember Arnold' and it appeared in the issue dated 17 August 1961:

I remember Kakky Hargreaves
As if 'twer Yestermorn'
Kakky, Kakky Hargreaves
Son of Mr Vaughan.

He used to be so grundie
On him little bike
Riding on a Sundie
Funny little tyke

Yes, I remember Kathy Hairbream
As if 'twer yesterday
Kathy, Kathy Hairbeam
Son of Mr May
Arriving at the station
Always dead on time
For his destination
Now he's dead on line
(Meaning he's been got by a train or something)

And so we growt and bimply
Till the end of time

Humpty dumpty bumply
Son of Harry Lime.

Bumledy Hubledy Humbley
Bumbley Tum. (Thank you)

John always liked to slip in some reference to people he knew and 'Son of Mr Vaughan' is obviously Ivan Vaughan, his childhood friend, who introduced him to Paul.

The next 'Beatcomber' was 'Around and About', which appeared in the 14 September 1961 issue. Part of the piece was a lampoon on the *Mersey Beat* entertainments listing.

Another 'Beatcomber' poem was 'Small Stan':

Once upon a Tom there was a small little Stan,
who was very small.
'You are very small Stan,' they said.

'I am only little,' replied Stan answering,
feeling very small.
Who could blame him, for Stan was only small?

'You must be small Stan,'
people were oft heard to cry,
noticing how extremely small Stan was in fact.
But being small (Stan was small) had its condensations.
Who else but Stan (the small) could wear all those small
clothes?

Stan was highly regarded by everyone
(for Stan was small and little).
However, one day Stan saw an adverse in the
Mersey Bean for 'club you quickly grow your boots.'
So on that very day Small Stan (by name called)
Purchased a pair of the very same.
So now when Stan passes by, folks say 'Is not that small
Stan
Wearing a pair of those clubs you quickly grow you
boots?'

And it is.

Another 'Beatcomber' item was 'On Safairy with Whide Hunter', which John was to later use in his first book *In His Own Write*, with a few alterations. Harry was aware that John's inspirations included not only Lewis Carroll, but Stanley Unwin, a radio personality known for his 'fractured English'. Unwin would come out with a monologue that was nonsensical, yet people were still able to pick up the gist of it. An example of John using 'fractured English' in 'On Safairy with Whide Hunter' was the line 'they reached a cleaner in the jumble and set up cramp', which is, quite simply, 'they reached a clearing in the jungle and set up camp'. At its simplest, this form merely replaces one word with a similar-sounding one. For instance, 'in the early owls of the morecambe' is 'in the early hours of the morning'. What would make this nonsensical to some people is the fact that they wouldn't be aware that Morecambe is a seaside resort near Liverpool where a lot of Merseyside people went for sunny weekends.

Owing to the success of *Mersey Beat*, an entire floor in the same building was rented, but unfortunately, during the move, all of John's works were lost. When Bill and Virginia told John at the Blue Angel club one night he cried on Virginia's shoulder.

John was so eager to see his zany writings in print that he also took out equally zany classified ads, which cost him 4d (four old pennies – a smidgen over 1.5 pence) a word. He'd often come into the *Mersey Beat* office and count out his pennies to see exactly how many words he could afford to put in.

In the issue dated 17 August 1961 he placed five classifieds:

HOT LIPS, missed you Friday, RED NOSE.

RED NOSE, missed you Friday, HOT LIPS.

ACCRINGTON welcomes HOT LIPS and RED NOSE.

Whistling Jock Lennon wishes to contact HOT NOSE.

RED   SCUNTHORPE   wishes   to   jock   HOT ACCRINGTON.

The adverts were mixed up among the various other classifieds, spoofing the messages found in the classifieds columns of various provincial newspapers such as the *Liverpool Echo*.

His next series appeared in the 14 September issue:

HEAR BOB WOOLER SING with the Beatles at Aintree Institute.

HEAR BOB BEATLES at the Woolerstute.

WANTED! Talented rock for newly formed.

They satirised the classified ads which a local disc jockey, Bob Wooler, placed in the *Liverpool Echo* advertising groups. His final set of ads appeared in the 14 December issue:

Happy XMAS – JURGEN.

Hello from Norman Lennon Vollmer.

FROLICHE FUSSBODEN – Herr Vollmer.

GOOD MORNING Jurgrow, from George.

These latter classifieds were aimed at Jurgen Vollmer, a photographer friend from Germany who had taken shots of the Beatles in Hamburg, which were published in *Mersey Beat*. John had also taken out a subscription to *Mersey Beat* as a present for him.

Mersey Beat was also to publish other poems by John such as 'The Tales of Hermit Fred' and 'The Land of the Lunapots' and was to print details of his *Daily Howl* contents.

Merv Griffin Show, The

A CBS-TV show. John recorded an interview for it with Martin Ogronsky on Tuesday 25 May 1965 at Cannes shortly before he and Cynthia left to visit the film festival there. The interview was included in the show a week later –Tuesday 1 June 1965.

Michelle

Song generally attributed to Paul, although John was to say, 'This was written by both of us. I wrote the middle with him.' John was also to comment, 'Paul and I were staying somewhere, and he walked in and hummed the first few bars with the words, then he says, "Where do I go from here?" I'd been listening to the blues singer Nina Simone, who did something like "I lo-o-ove you" in the middle of one of her songs, and that made me think of the middle eight for "Michelle" – "I love you, I love you, I lo-o-ove you." '

Midnight Angel

Documentary about Stuart Sutcliffe in Hamburg, produced by Granada Television and screened on 13 May 1990 as part of the *Celebration* arts series.

Mike Douglas Show, The

Mike Douglas was an Emmy award-winning talk show host with his popular daily afternoon shows transmitted from the WBC (Westinghouse Broadcasting Corporation) studios in Philadelphia. In 1972 John and Yoko were invited to be his co-hosts for an entire week, a total of five afternoon shows, which included guests selected by Douglas and John and Yoko.

John and Yoko began taping the programmes on Monday 31 January 1972. During that morning Douglas held a press conference in which Yoko said, 'We tried to show that we're working to change the world, not with dollars, but with love. We're not just freaks shouting and screaming about it, but we're thinking in terms of balancing life – changing it gradually through our daily lifestyle. We're saying to older people, let's work it together, because we have to work it together.'

The shows were transmitted two weeks later between 4.30 and 6 p.m. daily.

Monday 14 February 1972 featured the guests Ralph Nader, an attorney, Louise Nye, a comedian, and the gospel-rock group the Chambers Brothers. 'Michelle' was the show intro and John told Douglas that he had written the middle eight of the song.

John and Yoko, together with the Plastic Ono Band, performed 'It's So Hard'. Douglas chatted with John and Yoko, discussing how they met. Yoko introduced two of the ongoing events that would be taking place throughout the week. The first of these was a blank canvas on which guests and members of the audience would sign their names, which could then be auctioned. 'Put your name on it, Yoko – make it worth a dime more,' said John. The second was a broken cup that would be mended piece by piece over the following five days. John and Yoko, together with Douglas and Nye, began to phone strangers from around the country telling them they loved them.

Tuesday 15 February 1972 featured the US Surgeon General Dr Jesse Steinfield, the radical activist Jerry Rubin, the actress and filmmaker Barbara Loden, and a folk duo, Yellow Pearl. Mike Douglas announced the show intro, 'With a Little Help From My Friends' and 'Oh My Love', an excerpt from the *Imagine* film, was shown. John and Yoko with the Plastic Ono Band and Elephant's Memory performed 'Midsummer New York'. John discussed the Beatles and Elvis, calling Presley 'the Coca-Cola of singers'.

Wednesday 16 February 1972 had the guests Joseph Blatchford, head of Action Corps for Peace, a macrobiotic-food expert, Hilary Redleaf, and a computer scientist, David Rosenboom – plus Chuck Berry. John and Yoko performed 'O Sisters O Sisters' and a clip from the *Imagine* film, 'Crippled Inside', was screened. John, Yoko, the Plastic Ono Band and Elephant's Memory then joined Chuck Berry in performing 'Memphis Tennessee' and 'Johnny B Goode'. There was also a macrobiotic-cookery demonstration by Hilary Redleaf. Rosenboom attempted to use biofeedback to incorporate John and Yoko's alpha brain waves into music.

Thursday 17 February 1972 featured the guests Vivien Reed, an actress and singer, who sang 'Everybody's Talkin'' and 'His Eye Is On the Sparrow', the Ace Trucking Co., who performed a comedy routine, Bobby Seale, the president of the Black Panther Party, Marsha Martin, president of the student body, and Donald Williams, a medical student who discussed sickle-cell anaemia. John, the Plastic Ono Band and Elephant's Memory performed 'Imagine'. And a clip of 'Mrs Lennon' from the *Imagine* film was shown. John also discussed his childhood.

Friday 18 February 1972 had as guests George Carlin, a comedian, Rena Uviller, an attorney, and Dr Gary E Schwartz, a Harvard University researcher. John and Yoko also took questions from the audience and then performed 'Luck of the Irish', which was censored because of its sensitive content vis-à-vis the Ulster situation. A clip of 'How' from the *Imagine* film was shown. Yoko performed a Japanese song and Mike Douglas sang 'Thanks to John and Yoko'. John engaged in a Q&A session with the audience and, when asked about his attack on Paul McCartney in the song 'How Do You Sleep?' said, 'If I can't have a fight with my best friend, I don't know who I can have a fight with.'

During the week there were several revelations from John and Yoko as they discussed various subjects, including their marriage, how they met and John's musical influences. Yoko performed a number of her happenings, including 'Mend Piece', in which a smashed china cup was glued together, and 'Love Calls', in which numbers from the phone book were dialled at random and the recipient was told, 'I love you, please pass this message on.'

Yoko was to make an appearance on *The Mike Douglas Show*, backed by Elephant's Memory, when she performed *Shirankatta* on Friday 19 April 1974.

In 1998 Rhino Home Video issued *The Mike Douglas Show with John Lennon and Yoko Ono*. This was a deluxe package set with five 73-minute VHS tapes and a 48-page hard-bound book which featured previously unpublished photographs taken by the show's official photographer Michael Leshnov. It also included a new Q&A with Mike Douglas and excerpts from a February 1972 press conference with John, Yoko and Jerry Rubin discussing the show.

Milk and Honey: A Heart Play (album)

Posthumous album issued in America on Friday January 20 and in Britain on Monday January 23 1984, shortly after the third anniversary of John's death. It included six of John's songs, recorded as demos shortly prior to the recording of the *Double Fantasy* album. The rest of the album contained numbers by Yoko Ono, which, with the exception of 'Let Me Count The Ways', were all recorded after John's death.

The songs by John are: 'I'm Stepping Out', 'I Don't Wanna Face It', 'Nobody Told Me', 'Borrowed Time', '(Forgive Me) My Little Flower Princess', 'Grow Old With Me'.

The numbers by Yoko are: 'Sleepless Night', 'Don't Be Scared', 'O Sanity', 'Your Hands', 'Let Me Count the Ways', 'You're the One'.

All the tracks on *Milk and Honey* were credited to John and Yoko as co-writers. The colour photograph on the cover was taken at the same sessions as the ones for the *Double Fantasy* album.

Milk and Honey (Video)

A 26-minute video special produced by Ono Video and first screened by MTV in America on Sunday 3 June 1984.

Robert Christgau, the *Village Voice* music critic, interviewed Yoko Ono and the six-year-old Sean and there are music segments and vintage film clips. The music clips include 'Borrowed Time' and 'Grow Old With Me' and clips include home-movie shots of Sean, some Beatles footage and previously unreleased footage from the *Imagine* sessions.

When Christgau said to Sean, 'You're a kid,' Sean told him that he was a fifty-year-old midget and Christgau had been misinformed. Other clips included 'Let Me Count the Ways' and 'Stepping Out' and there were brief clips of a home movie of Yoko as a child, the Lennons in a Jacuzzi and walking in Central Park.

Mind Games (album)

The album that followed the heavily slated *Sometime in New York City*.

The lead track, 'Mind Games', which gave the album its title, was inspired by the book of the same name by Robert Masters and Jean Houston.

The sleeve was designed by John and featured a small full-length figure of himself, with Yoko's profile lying across the horizon like a mountain range. The packaging contained a small booklet of information concerning John and Yoko's conceptual Utopia: Nutopia. The couple declared that their imaginary kingdom should have its flag displayed at the United Nations. The flag was a plain white one, and the 'Nutopian International Anthem' on the album consisted of several seconds of silence.

The album was recorded in August 1973 at the Record Plant in New York and was issued in America on 2 November 1973 on Apple SW 3414 and in Britain on 16 November on Apple PCS 7165. It entered the American charts on 24 November 1973, and reached No. 9, with a chart life of eighteen weeks. It entered the British charts on 4 December and eventually reached the position of No. 9.

Mind Games was the first of John's albums that he produced himself and, ironically, it features a couple of love songs about Yoko – yet by the time the album was issued the couple were estranged and John had begun his affair with May Pang.

The credits read, 'John Lennon (with the Plastic U.F.Ono Band)'. John had gathered together some of the leading New York session musicians to join him in the studio. They included Ken Archer on piano, organ and mellotron; David Spinozza on guitar, Gordon Edwards on bass guitar, Jim Keltner on drums, Michael Breckner on saxophone and Sneaky Pete Kleinow on pedal steel guitar. John also took the opportunity of using one of his pseudonyms on the album – Dr Winston O'Boogie.

The tracks were: Side One: 'Mind Games', 'Tight A$', 'Aisumasen (I'm Sorry)', 'One Day (At a Time)', 'Bring On the Lucie (Freda Peeple)', 'The Nutopian International Anthem'; Side Two: 'Invitation', 'Out of the Blue', 'Only People', 'I Know', 'You Are Here' and 'Meat City'.

Mind Games (Single)

A single by John that was issued in Britain on Apple R 5994 on 16 November 1973. It reached No. 19 in the British charts. It was issued in America on Apple 1868 on 29 October 1973 and reached No. 18 in the charts.

The flip side was another composition by John, 'Meat City', and both tracks were included on the *Mind Games* album.

The number was recorded at New York's Record Plant in August 1973 and it became the only single issued by John that year.

In December 1970, John made a number of home demos, one of which was called 'Make Love Not War'. This particular number, which he'd envisaged as a song to stand alongside 'Give Peace a Chance', was never finished at the time. John was later to use the basic melody to compose 'Mind Games'.

A book called *Mind Games* by Robert Masters and Jean Houston inspired the lyrics. This was an instruction book of exercises that were devised to enhance consciousness-raising. John read it and commented, 'I have read three important and revolutionary books in the last three years: Yoko Ono's *Grapefruit,* Arthur Janov's *Primal Scream* and now *Mind Games*. I suggest you read and experience them!'

In some ways he intended to present the ideas to a larger audience as his lyrics were basically a précis of the book's theme.

John was to say, 'That was a fun track because the voice is in stereo and the seeming orchestra on it is just me playing three notes with slide guitar. And the middle eight is reggae. Trying to explain to American musicians what reggae was in 1973 was pretty hard.'

Mintz, Elliott

A disc jockey and journalist who interviewed John and Yoko for the first time on Saturday 9 October 1971. This was during their exhibition at the Everson Museum.

Shortly before their eighteen-month separation, John and Yoko spoke of their future plans in an interview with Mintz on Monday 16 April 1973, with John commenting, 'Nineteen seventy-three is our year. The whole ball game changes now. Yoko is becoming herself again.' Mintz then interviewed John on Thursday 1 January 1976 for *Earth News*, a radio news service. The sixty-minute interview revolved around the difficulties Yoko had with the birth of Sean and their thoughts about parenthood.

He was around at the time of John's 'lost weekend' and was to comment, 'He was a miserable drunk. One brandy Alexander [a drink made with cream and sweet liqueurs] and he was absolutely delightful. Two was OK. Three, and he started snarling.'

Mintz later became a close friend of John and after John's death became a paid employee of Yoko. He was technical assistant to the NBC TV biopic *John and Yoko: A Love Story* and the narrator on the *Lost Lennon Tapes* radio series.

Mirror Mirror (On the Wall)
A song John originally wrote and demoed during the summer of 1977, when he was in Japan. That demo was unfortunately destroyed, but he cut another version in the Dakota Building late in 1977, which he taped while playing piano. The song had lines such as 'I look in the mirror and nobody's there' and 'I keep on staring, is it me?'

This is one of the songs John intended to use in the planned Broadway musical *The Ballad of John and Yoko*. The recording was first aired on Show 20 of *The Lost Lennon Tapes* radio broadcast.

Misery
A song penned by John with a little help from Paul. While they were on tour with Helen Shapiro, they offered it to her, but her recording manager turned it down. Singer Kenny Lynch, who used to sit next to John on the coach, said, 'I like it. I'll sing that and I've got a session on Thursday.' Lynch took his version of the song to Dick James' office and played it to the band, but John didn't like it, basically because of the guitarist Bert Weedon. John said, 'Who's that?' Lynch told him, 'It's Bert Weedon, he's supposed to be good.' John said, 'It's awful, I'm not letting it out with that on.' Dick James then intervened, saying, 'Oh, I quite like it. What's wrong with it? Bert Weedon's very good.'

The record, however, was not a success.

Miyori, Kim
The actress who starred as Yoko in the 1985 NBC telemovie *John and Yoko – A Love Story*.

When given the role, she said, 'I have been studying her, reading about her, and it seems to me she's been treated unfairly. She has this dragon-lady image and yet from what I've heard, she is nothing like that. The film people said she is surprisingly ordinary and nice. Hopefully I'll be able to get this across in the film.'

When asked what she thought of Yoko's music, Miyori said, 'Well, the early stuff, the very avant-garde stuff, was a little too esoteric for me. I think perhaps if I listened to more of it and could understand the purpose behind it, then I might appreciate it more.'

Towards the end of the production, Miyori and Mark McGann were invited to join Yoko at the Dakota Building. Kim said, 'I found her to be a very, very gentle lady. Very hospitable. She's got a sense of humour. She is very intelligent, very insightful, very determined. I was not disappointed in any way when I met her. Yoko is a very creative, competitive woman. Paul McCartney probably described her best when he said she is completely determined to be herself.'

Miyori was born in Santa Monica, California, and began her career as a dancer, performing in such musicals as *South Pacific*, *Brigadoon*, *The King and I* and *Gigi*. She then appeared on Broadway and in the films *Grease* and *Sergeant Pepper's Lonely Hearts Club Band* before co-starring as Dr Wendy Armstrong in the TV series *St Elsewhere* from 1982 to 1984.

She married Mark McGann, her co-star in *John and Yoko – A Love Story*.

Mohammed, Geoff

Born in Manchester of an Indian father and French/Italian mother, he became one of John's closest friends at Liverpool College of Art.

At a class Christmas party in 1958 Geoff had been trying to interest John in Cynthia Powell (who was to become Lennon's wife), saying, 'Cynthia likes you, you know.' John danced with her and asked if she'd like to come to a party the next day, but she told him she was engaged to a boy in Hoylake. 'I didn't ask you to marry me,' he said.

At one time John and Geoff went on a drunken spree and brought a number of the souvenirs they'd pinched into the college canteen, including signposts, posters and street name-plates.

Geoff was later expelled from the college.

Monday Night Football

An American television sports programme on ABC TV. On 9 December 1974 John went to the Los Angeles coliseum to watch a game between the Los Angeles Rams and the LA Redskins. During the intermission the famed American sports reporter Howard Cosell, who was hosting *Monday Night Football*, said, 'Now, I've got a most familiar figure and face. For all of you across the country, here with me now, of the original Beatles, Mr John Lennon.'

When Cosell asked him his opinion of American football, he said, 'It's an amazing event and sight – it makes rock concerts look like tea parties.

'The first thing I heard when I got in was the playing of a Beatles tune, "Yesterday", which cheered me up no end.'

When asked if the Beatles would ever get back together again, he said, 'You never know, you never know. I mean, it's always in the wind. If it looked like this, it might be worth doing, right?' He was referring to the huge crowd at the game.

Howard said, 'You did spend the weekend with Ringo.'

John said, 'Yeah, and I promised him I'd mention his album, out now. And I said I wouldn't mention my own, which is out now too, forget it.'

John then went back to his seat.

Money (That's What I Want)

Song written by Berry Gordy and Janie Bradford, which was originally a chart hit for Barrett Strong in 1959. The Beatles included it in their repertoire in 1960, with John on lead vocals, and performed it during their Decca recording audition. It was the last track on the *With the Beatles* album and the last of three Motown covers John sang on the album. It was also included on the EP *All My Loving*, the album *Rock 'n' Roll Music* and the American release of *The Beatles Second Album*. John also performed it in Toronto and it appears on the *Live Peace in Toronto* album.

34 Montague Square

This was a ground-floor basement maisonette in London's West End. Ringo Starr took out a lease on the premises early in 1965.

Soon after moving in he married Maureen Cox and the two settled in a new house, Sunny Heights, in Weybridge.

Ringo decided to keep the lease on the Montague Square premises and sublet it to various friends, including Jimi Hendrix with his manager, Chas Chandler, and the author William Burroughs. Lilian Powell, Cynthia Lennon's mother, also lived there in 1967.

When the John and Yoko affair began and John became estranged from his wife Cynthia, they asked Ringo if they could move into his flat. He agreed and the couple moved into Montague Square in July 1968.

It was here that they took the shot of themselves naked for the cover of the *Two Virgins* album. Tony Bramwell was present and set up the cameras. It was alleged that he then rushed away before they took their clothes off and John took the photograph by delayed action. However, in a photograph taken of John and Yoko when they initially moved into Tittenhurst Park there is a large photograph in the background from that session clearly showing three naked people.

John had been given a tip-off by a journalist that the police would be raiding the Montague Square maisonette on 18 October 1968. Pete Shotton apparently arrived to find John vacuuming the floor. He told him, 'You know what those cunts are like. They'll bust you if the fucking dog smells something in the rug. They'll Hoover up all the minuscule bits and put them under a microscope and bust you.'

At 11.30 that morning, the police raided the premises, led by Detective Sergeant Norman Pilcher of the Scotland Yard Drug Enforcement Squad. Six policemen and one policewoman accompanied him. They used two dogs – black and golden retrievers which were trained to sniff out marijuana. The police claimed to have discovered 27.3 grains of cannabis in an envelope in a suitcase and a further 191.8 grains in a binocular case.

The police spent more than an hour with the two of them, who were then first accused of being in possession of cannabis resin and then of obstructing the police in the execution of a search warrant. The pair were then taken in two separate cars to Marylebone Lane Police Station. Yoko left first, dressed in a short fur jacket and black slacks, accompanied by a woman police officer. John left next, wearing a Chinese-style, hip-length black jacket and black bell-bottoms.

John was to say of the raid, 'So all of a sudden, like, there is this knock on the door and a woman's voice outside and I look around and there's this policeman standing in the window wanting to be let in. We'd been in bed and our lower regions were uncovered, like. Yoko ran into the bathroom to get dressed with her head poking out so they wouldn't think she was hiding anything. And then I said, "Ring the lawyer, quick," but she went and rang Apple – I'll never know why. So then they got us for obstruction, which was ridiculous because we only wanted to get our clothes on.'

Paul McCartney had gone to Marylebone Lane Police Station to enquire about John. He then placed a call to Sir Joseph Lockwood, chairman of EMI, to ask him if he could use his influence to help John and Yoko. Lockwood agreed to call the station and advise John. When Lockwood phoned him, John answered, 'Hello! This is Sergeant Lennon. Can I help you?'

The couple were then charged and bailed to appear at Marylebone Magistrates' Court the next day.

Owing to this particular drug bust John was to have a battle with the American immigration authorities when he wanted to settle in New York.

It's interesting to consider whether John was actually framed. Pilcher was later arrested and jailed for planting drugs on people. He had sought to make a reputation for himself by targeting celebrities. At one time he had raided Keith Richards's Redland country house. Pattie and George Harrison had been there along with Mick Jagger, Marianne Faithfull and Robert Fraser, and heroin and LSD had been in use. When Marianne Faithfull entered naked after having a bath and draped herself in a fur rug, George and Pattie left. The premises were immediately raided.

It was suggested that Pilcher had waited until George and Pattie had left because he was apprehensive about arresting them because of the influence of Brian Epstein and his lawyer David Jacobs. However, at the time of his raid on Montague Square, both of them were now dead.

After the tip-off John had, it is said, ensured that not a grain of marijuana was left on the premises, even to the extent of washing the bowl that the marijuana had been kept in. John always maintained that he had been framed, but agreed to plead guilty when told that, if he did so, charges against Yoko, who was pregnant at the time, would be dropped.

In February 1969, owing to the charges levelled against John and Yoko, the landlords of the premises, Brymon Estates, sought an injunction against Ringo to prevent 'illegal, immoral or improper' use of the flat. They were successful and Ringo had to sell the lease. In the meantime, he allowed the couple to move into his own home, Sunny Heights in Weybridge, until they bought their premises at Tittenhurst Park.

Morris, Lord 'Ronnie'

The man who managed Tittenhurst Park, the estate in Ascot, Berkshire, for John. In 1969 John presented him with his own personal diary as a Christmas present. Bearing the printed words 'Diary, John Lennon' on the plain white shiny cover, it was a one-year diary that contained intimate details of his life with Yoko. A few years later, Morris went to work in the Merchant Navy, so he entrusted the diary to a friend for safekeeping. Sadly, she didn't keep it safe and threw it on to a rubbish tip on the Isle of Wight. In 1993 Morris was to comment, 'I read the diary cover to cover, perhaps three times. There was an entry for each day – around four inches of writing for each entry.'

Mosspits Lane Infants School

The first kindergarten attended by John, situated in Mosspits Lane, Wavertree, Liverpool L15. John was enrolled in the primary school on 12 November 1945 and was still living at Newcastle Road at the time. The five-year-old boy apparently bullied a young neighbour, Polly Hipshaw, who also attended the school. In April 1946 John was expelled for his disruptive behaviour and on 6 May was enrolled at Dovedale Road Junior School.

Mother

A track on his *John Lennon/Plastic Ono Band* album. After undergoing primal therapy John attempted to exorcise the deep and possibly buried feelings of rejection he'd suffered in early life through the absence of both mother and father. Funereal bells open the track, which led John to comment, 'It's a church bell which I slowed down to 33, so it's really like a horror movie and that was like the death knell of the mother/father Freudian trip.'

Pauline Lennon was to use the line 'Daddy come home' from 'Mother' as the title of her book about Freddie Lennon.

Motown Records

John recorded three Motown covers on the *With the Beatles* album and admitted that Smokey Robinson had been one of his songwriting influences. When they mentioned their appreciation of Motown, the Motown boss Berry Gordy Jr commented, 'We are very honoured the Beatles should have said what they did. They're creating the same kind of music as we are and we're part of the same stream.' When Brian Epstein held a party for the Four Tops when he booked them for his Saville Theatre John was heard to say to Larry Payton, 'Tell me something, man: when you cats go into the studio, what does the drummer beat on to get that backbeat? You use a bloody *tree* or something?'

Mount Nelson Hotel

A hotel in Cape Town, South Africa, where John stayed between the dates Friday 23 and Tuesday 27 May 1980. He booked in using the name of his astrologer, John Green, and began sending messages and telegrams to friends. He then travelled to Germany and Spain.

64 Mount Pleasant, Liverpool

Site of a former Georgian Town House, which had become the Mount Pleasant Register Office, where both Freddie and Julia Lennon and John and Cynthia Lennon were married.

Freddie and Julia were wed on 3 December 1938 and that morning Freddie set off for the Eagle public house in Paradise Street, looking for one of his mates to stand as a witness. No one he knew turned up and, in desperation, he phoned up his brother Sydney at work in a local men's outfitters. Sydney agreed to meet him outside the Adelphi Hotel and the two of them hung around until 12.30 p.m. when Julia turned up, accompanied by a friend. They then left for the register office and the short ceremony. Sydney then treated them to lunch and some drinks at the Big House, a pub adjacent to the Adelphi.

The marriage of John and Cynthia took place on Thursday 23 August 1962. After Brian Epstein had been informed that John had proposed to the pregnant Cynthia, he arranged for a special licence. Brian also sent a car to pick up Cynthia at her Garmoyle Street flat. She arrived to find her brother Tony and his wife Marjorie, Brian, John, Paul and George. Ringo, who had recently joined the group, was not invited.

Cynthia wore a purple and black check two-piece suit, a white frilly high-necked blouse, which had been a present from Astrid Kirchherr, black shoes and a handbag. Brian wore a pin-striped suit and John, Paul and George wore black suits, white shirts and black ties.

When they were ushered into the room where the ceremony was to take place, Cynthia observed how dour the registrar looked and also noticed, through a window, a workman in the yard of the building next door holding a pneumatic drill. As soon as the three-minute service began the workman started up the drill and the noise was deafening. John was to claim that he hadn't heard a word that was said during the ceremony. Cynthia, commenting on the noise of the drill in her autobiography *A Twist of Lennon*, observed, 'John had not only gained a headache, he had gained a wife and the promise of a child in only eight months – possibly a bigger headache.'

John was to comment, 'I went in the day before to tell Mimi. I said Cyn was having a baby, we were getting married tomorrow, did she want to come? She just let out a groan. There was a drill going on all the time outside the register office. I couldn't hear a word the bloke was saying. Then we went across the road and had a chicken dinner. It was all a laugh.'

The witnesses, James Paul McCartney and Marjorie Joyce Powell, signed the certificate and as the party emerged into Mount Pleasant the heavens burst and it poured with rain as they ran down the hill towards Reece's Restaurant and their wedding breakfast.

In the 70s the building became the offices of the Merseyside Racial Equality Council.

Mourning of John Lennon, The

A 235-page book by Anthony Elliott, a research fellow in political science at the University of Melbourne in Australia. The

University of California Press published it in April 1999. The author describes it as a 'metabiography' that aims to 'dip into our collective imaginings of Lennon and sift through them for what they can tell us about contemporary society, to loop biography and culture around politics in its broadest sense'.

Move Over Ms L

This was a number that John had originally demoed in June 1974 and then recorded on Monday 15 July 1974 at the Record Plant studios in New York City during rehearsals for the *Walls and Bridges* album. However, he was dissatisfied with the recording and didn't use it on the album, although he was to record it again in October 1974.

John had completed the song after he'd left Yoko and was living with May Pang, and it was a dig at Yoko, who had once called herself Mrs Lennon in a song.

'Move Over Ms L' eventually became the flip side of 'Stand By Me', issued as a single in America in March 1975 and in Britain the following month.

John also gave the number to Keith Moon to use on his debut album *Two Sides of the Moon*, which was also issued in America in March 1975 and in Britain in May of that year.

The song was featured as the first track of Side Two of Moon's album and the former Beatles road manager Mal Evans was one of the album's producers.

Mr Holland's Opus

A 1996 film starring Richard Dreyfuss which shows the reaction to John's death by a composer-teacher and his son. There are also performances of some of John's songs. The soundtrack album, *Mr Holland's Opus: A Symphony of Life*, was issued on Polydor Records and contained two tracks by John: 'Imagine' and 'Beautiful Boy (Darling Boy)'. There was also a track, 'Cole's Son', by Julian Lennon. This was specially recorded for the soundtrack and written by Julian, Justin Clayton and Michael Kamen.

Mr Moonlight

Song written by Roy Lee Johnson, which was originally recorded by Dr Feelgood and the Interns in 1962. John selected the number for inclusion in the Beatles' early repertoire, performing it at venues such as the Cavern in 1962. The group recorded the number on 18 October 1964 and it was included on the *Beatles For Sale* album and the American EP *4 By The Beatles*. A live version is also to be found on the Star Club recordings while another version of the song was also included on the *Anthology 1* CDs.

Mucho Mungo

A song that John originally began composing between the *Rock 'n' Roll* album sessions. He'd initially intended to give it to Jesse Ed Davis. When Harry Nilsson asked him to produce the *Pussy Cats* album, Harry was also short of a few songs and asked John for some new material. John decided to use 'Mucho Mungo', although Nilsson wanted it segued with another track, 'Mt Etna'.

John was stuck on the bridge of the number and Harry said, 'I have a bridge that needs the rest of a song!' Nilsson could barely remember it, but it included the words 'Mount Etna, Mount Etna'.

John also made his own acoustic version.

Muni, Scott

A leading American disc jockey. One of the main New York DJs, he covered the Beatles' arrival at JF Kennedy Airport on 7 February 1964. At the time he worked for WABC and the station's name was changed to W-A-Beatles-C for that day. At one time Ringo Starr fainted during an interview he was doing with Muni for the station.

Muni conducted several further interviews with the Beatles, but then left the field of radio to open a rock club in New York.

In 1966 Muni returned to radio and joined the station WOR-FM, which changed its name to WNEW-FM in 1967.

When John moved to New York, Muni interviewed him on a number of occasions and John granted him a lengthy interview late in 1971.

When John turned up at WNEW-FM on 8 September 1974, he was interviewed by the DJ David Elsas and expressed his disappointment that he didn't meet up with Muni while he was at the station that day. When he finished his afternoon spot on the programme, John told Elsas, 'Maybe next time, I'll come and sit around with Scott a bit. I'll be back some day. Who knows when? Only the Shadow knows.'

On Thursday 13 February 1975, John strolled into his studio unexpectedly with an advance copy of his *Rock 'n' Roll* album and Muni completed a ninety-minute programme with him. The broadcast was later repeated on WGCI, a radio station in Cleveland, on Sunday 11 December 1983 under the title *John Lennon – A Day on the Radio*.

Munro, John

The incumbent Canadian Minister for Health in 1969 when John and Yoko visited the country. Following their meeting with Prime Minister Pierre Trudeau, the duo went for a conference with Munro and members of his department and the press. Among the topics for discussion were the generation gap and the use of soft drugs.

Murray, Rod

Born in the West Derby area of Liverpool, Murray enrolled at Liverpool College of Art in 1958. He befriended Stuart Sutcliffe and eventually invited Stuart to share a flat he rented at 8 Gambier Terrace. John Lennon also began staying at the flat on a regular basis.

John, Stu, Rod and Bill Harry used to get together on a regular basis and on one occasion Harry suggested they called themselves 'The Dissenters' in an effort to use their talents to make Liverpool famous.

When John needed a bass guitarist for his group, he offered the job to both Rod and Stu, without telling either one about the other. Rod began to make a bass guitar, but Stu sold a painting and was able to buy a guitar on hire purchase. This was how he, and not Rod, become a Beatle.

After the Beatles left for Germany, Rod found he couldn't afford the rent on the flat by himself and moved out. Among the items he took with him were copies of some early John Lennon manuscripts, which he was to sell at auction many years later.

Rod later became a lecturer at a prominent London art college, and has now retired.

Music International

A BBC2 television series. John was interviewed for the programme on Monday 2 August 1965.

My Life

A number that John recorded as an acoustic-guitar demo at the Dakota Building in New York in late 1978. John reworked the piece the following year into another song, 'Don't Be Crazy', which was later used to become the middle part of '(Just Like) Starting Over'. The song was featured in the *Lost Lennon Tapes* series and also included in a CD published with John's *A Spaniard in the Works*, in Sweden in 1998.

My Mummy's Dead

Final track on the primal therapy-inspired *John Lennon/ Plastic Ono Band* album. The brief song utilises the tune from the nursery rhyme 'Three Blind Mice' and John compared the song to a haiku poem (a Japanese three-line, seventeen-syllable poem) commenting, 'Obviously, when you get rid of a whole section of illusion in your mind you're left with great precision. Yoko was showing me some of these haikus in the original.'

Nasties, the

The name John gave to the Auslander Polizei, the Aliens Police, in Germany who had the power to deport members of British groups if there were any misdemeanours.

The Beatles' first trip to Hamburg was cut short because 'the nasties', acting on a complaint that members of the group had tried to burn down the Bambi Cinema, deported Paul and Pete Best.

The Aliens Police later allowed the group to return to the city.

National Sculpture Exhibition, The

In 1968, this was a major event in the British contemporary-sculpture calendar. The organisers included Fabio Barraclough and Anthony Fawcett. Yoko asked Fawcett if she and John could contribute to the exhibition. He in turn asked Barraclough, who then raised the matter at a committee meeting.

Barraclough told them that they could take part in the exhibition but would not be mentioned in the catalogue. The couple decided to design and print a catalogue of their own, which would describe their exhibit. Keith McMillan took a photograph of the pair crouching behind a long table on which were two plant pots. The unusual perspective produced a visual that looked as if John and Yoko were growing out of the pots. This photo was used as the cover of the catalogue. The inside was a simple design. On one page was John's statement, 'This is what happens when two clouds meet.' Opposite was Yoko's statement, 'This is what happens when two clouds meet (the piece is John's idea but it was so good that I stole it).' The back cover contained a brief commentary by Fawcett.

Yoko described their sculpture to Fawcett as 'Two acorns planted in the ground, one facing to the east, the other to the west. The acorns will symbolise our meeting and love for each other and also the uniting and growth of our two cultures.'

John also ordered a silver-plated plaque containing the engraved words, 'John by Yoko Ono. Yoko by John Lennon. Sometime in May 1968.' A final touch was a wrought-iron garden seat that John wanted placed over the acorns to enable viewers to sit down and contemplate the work.

However, when the couple arrived at Coventry Cathedral (see **Acorns**) on 15 June 1968, with the sculpture, the cathedral's Canon Stephen Verney refused to allow their exhibit to be displayed on cathedral grounds with the other works. He objected to the fact that they were having an extramarital relationship and refused to allow their acorns to be planted on consecrated ground. Yoko began a long argument with the priest following a remark he made intimating that the acorns were not art. She insisted he phone a number of prominent sculptors for their opinion on the work. They unsuccessfully attempted to contact Henry Moore. The canon then allowed them to plant their exhibit on a patch of lawn adjacent to the cathedral, but refused to allow them to hand out their catalogues.

The acorns were duly laid, the plaques put in place and the garden seat set down – resulting in a massive photo session that gave the exhibition its largest dose of publicity.

Within a week of the opening, an intruder had dug up the acorns in the middle of the night. John and Yoko planted a second pair, but this time engaged a security service to watch over the exhibit 24 hours a day until the close of the exhibition.

Nationwide

A British current-affairs programme originally televised by the BBC five nights a week. On Tuesday 21 December 1982 the programme featured an interview with Yoko recorded inside the Dakota Building's apartments. She was with Sean and the interview was on the theme of Christmas and the many happy Yuletides they had spent together in the apartment. Yoko recalled a time when John bought forty separate presents for Sean and how much he enjoyed seeing Sean opening each one. The six-minute interview had been carried out by Tom Brooke at the Dakota Building on Wednesday 8 December 1982.

Never Say Goodbye

A Yoko Ono single issued in Britain on Tuesday January 25 1983. John is briefly heard shouting on the track. The flip side was called 'Loneliness'.

Newby, Chas

Bass guitarist who played with the Beatles. Newby was originally a member of Pete Best's group, the Blackjacks, who replaced the Quarry Men as resident band at the Casbah Club. The group were about to disband in 1960 as Newby was about to enter college and another member, Ken Brown, was leaving for London. The Beatles then offered Pete Best the job of drummer.

While in Hamburg in November, Stuart Sutcliffe was on the verge of leaving and they wrote to Newby offering him the job as their permanent bass guitarist. He wrote back turning their offer down, but agreed to play with them over the Christmas season. When they returned from Hamburg in December 1960, Stuart Sutcliffe had remained in Germany and Best was able to accept Newby's offer of joining them for four appearances while he was on holiday from college. John Lennon again offered him the job on a permanent basis, but Newby turned him down, preferring to continue his studies. He was later to say he never regretted his decision and was to become a teacher at Droitwich High School in Worcestershire.

It's interesting to note that several writers of books about the Beatles seem to feel that John insisted on Stuart's being bass guitarist with the group, despite protests. This doesn't seem to be the case. Not only had he offered Newby Stuart's job with the group, but previously, when he originally sought a bass guitarist, he offered the position to both Rod Murray and Stuart Sutcliffe, without informing either that it was a case of first come, first served – whoever came up with a bass guitar became a member of the band.

9 Newcastle Road

A two-bedroom terraced house in the Wavertree area of Liverpool. It was the cause of some controversy in 1981 when an estate agent advertised it as John's birthplace, offering it for sale at a hugely inflated price.

John's Aunt Mimi said that it was her parents' home where John had spent a couple of months when he was a baby. This was actually the Stanley home. George and Annie Stanley had originally lived in Huskisson Street and their first two children, a boy and a girl, died before their third birthdays. They then had five healthy daughters: Mary Elizabeth, Elizabeth, Ann Georgina, Julia and Harriet. The family then moved on to the house in Newcastle Road.

New York City

The Beatles originally arrived in New York together in February 1964 and their first experience of the USA must have been exhilarating with the fervour of the fans and the onset of Beatlemania there.

John was to fall in love with the city and, together with Yoko, packed most of his possessions from Tittenhurst Park and moved over to New York in August 1971, initially settling in the St Regis Hotel.

John was thirty years old at the time and remained in New York for the rest of his life, buying apartments in the Dakota Building, which he made his home and where he remained a virtual recluse for five years while rearing Sean.

John was to say, 'If I'd lived in Roman times I'd have lived in Rome. Where else? Today, America is the Roman Empire and New York is Rome itself.'

John also explained, 'I think for me it has to do with Liverpool. There's the same quality of energy, of vitality in both cities. New York is at my speed. It's a twenty-four-hours-a-day city; it's going on around you all the time, so much so that you almost stop noticing it ... I like New York because they have no time for the niceties of life. They're like me in this. They're naturally aggressive; they don't believe in wasting time.'

New York also took John to its heart and, when the federal authorities were attempting to deport him, the city's mayor, John Lindsay, spoke up for John. A later mayor, Ed Koch, was also supportive of John and after John's death he agreed to rename part of Central Park as Strawberry Fields.

John found New York vibrant and exciting and soon got to know the people, initially coming under the influence of the political activists who inspired his political album *Sometime in New York City*. Eventually he got to know the ordinary New Yorkers whom he met on the streets during the daily round of his life.

New York City (song)
Similar to his 1969 composition *The Ballad of New York City*, being a diary of recent events in his life. He describes his concert with Frank Zappa, his meeting with a street musician, David Peel, his visit to Max's Kansas City Club, the Attica Benefit at the Apollo, his delight at being able to walk around the city, which he then refers to as 'bass ass city'.

He was to comment, 'In New York I could walk around, where I still couldn't walk around in London.'

The song was included on his album *Sometime in New York City*.

Night Ride
A late-night BBC radio show that was broadcast live between the hours of 12.05 and 2 a.m. The show was recorded at Broadcasting House in London and John and Yoko appeared on the programme following their telerecording of *The Rolling Stones Rock 'n' Roll Circus* on Wednesday 11 December 1968.

The disc jockey John Peel hosted the interview with John and Yoko, who discussed their new album, *Two Virgins*.

Nilsson, Harry
The man John Lennon called 'my favourite American group' was born Harry Edward Nilsson III in Brooklyn, New York City, on 15 June 1941. When his parents separated he moved to Los Angeles with his mother and was to end up working at a computer centre for a bank. He had aspirations of becoming a

musician and songwriter and made his album debut on the Tower label, a subsidiary of Capitol Records.

His first album for RCA was *Pandemonium Shadow Show* in 1967. The LP came to the attention of Derek Taylor, particularly the track 'You Can't Do That', which featured a medley of Beatles numbers. Taylor arranged for the Beatles to hear the album.

They were so enthusiastic about Harry that they asked Brian Epstein if he would manage him, but Harry had had bad experiences with his previous manager and decided he wanted to manage himself.

Harry then received a phone call from John Lennon, who said, 'Harry, you're fantastic, man. You're great.'

Harry said, 'Jeez, you're not so bad yourself. Who is this really?' 'John Lennon,' said John. Harry said, '*The?*' and John said, 'Yeah. I just called to say you're great, that's all.'

Nilsson's two biggest hits were 'Everybody's Talking', and 'Without You'. His recording of 'Everybody's Talking' was chosen as the theme song for the film *Midnight Cowboy* and earned Harry his first Grammy award.

He recalled how he discovered 'Without You'. He was at a friend's house in Laurel Canyon playing records one night and heard one that he thought was a Lennon song. The next day he phoned his friend about the number saying, 'I think it's Lennon and it could be a Beatles album.' He discovered it was actually a track on an Apple album by Badfinger. He bought the album and then phoned his producer Richard Perry and told him he wanted to record the song.

The song, which had been penned by Pete Ham and Tom Evans of Badfinger, became his biggest hit and earned him another Grammy.

He recorded around nineteen albums, with his bestselling one being *Nilsson Schmilsson*, which included the 'Without You' track. His 'Son of Schmilsson' featured George Harrison and Ringo Starr as guest musicians. He also penned songs that were recorded by numerous people, including 'Without Her' by Herb Alpert and 'Ten Little Indians' by the Yardbirds.

John Lennon also acted as recording manager for his *Pussy Cats* album.

When John decided to record Nilsson, Peter Lawford's old

house in Santa Monica was rented and Ringo Starr and Keith Moon also participated in the recording, during which Nilsson had an ulcerated throat. John and Harry wrote some numbers together, including 'Old Dirt Road' and 'Mucho Mungo/Mt Etna', and, by all accounts, the album was recorded when all participants were enjoying a rip-roaring spree on alcohol.

This all took place in 1974 during John's 'lost weekend' in Los Angeles. The notorious Troubadour incident occurred at this time (see **Troubadour**).

Harry and John had stopped at Tower Records and Harry had bought a copy of his current favourite record 'I Can't Stand the Rain' by Ann Peebles. Harry tried to force the record on John, who kept saying, 'Well, here's my favourite records. I'll give you favourite records. Give me twenty of those.' They returned to their limousine, which was fitted with a record player, and Harry began playing the Ann Peebles single. John got fed up of it and threw it out of the window. So Harry grabbed John's records and threw them out of the window as they were driving down Sunset Strip. They then went on to the Troubadour club, where they began singing 'I Can't Stand The Rain' at their table. Other patrons, such as Jack Haley Jr and Peter Lawford, kept telling them to keep quiet. When the Smothers Brothers came on, the pair continued their disruptive antics and were thrown out.

Following the period of his 'lost weekend' with John, Nilsson met and married Una O'Keefe and the couple were to have six children together and live in Bel Air. He'd had a son, Zak, from his previous marriage. In the latter half of the 1980s he referred to himself as a retired musician and went into partnership with the author Terry Southern in a company called Hawkeye Entertainment. He decided to move with his family to Upper Nyack, New York, because he wanted his children educated in the east. However, problems with the company saw him return to Bel Air to take a more active role in the company. Hawkeye began to do well and Harry saw the success of the company as a form of security for his family. Then disaster struck. He discovered that there was only $300 in his current account. A trusted assistant had disappeared with all his money, together with all the finances of Hawkeye. The FBI finally arrested the woman concerned and she was jailed, but she never revealed the location of the money. Referring to the effect it would have on his children, he said, 'She stole their future.'

On the night of 8 December 1980 Nilsson was in the studio working. During a break in the recording he began to write a letter to John thanking him for mentioning his name in his interview in the latest issue of *Playboy*. He then heard the devastating news of John's death.

Within a few months, Nilsson began to support the National Coalition to Ban Handguns.

He eventually managed to pay off the bankruptcy and the film director Terry Gilliam asked him to record the song 'How About You' for his movie *The Fisher King*. It was Nilsson's last release.

On St Valentine's Day in 1993 he suffered a massive heart attack. While recovering he decided to begin his autobiography and record a new album. The album was completed a week before his death, but his autobiography was never finished. At 2.30 a.m. on 15 January 1994 he woke up with terrible breathing problems. His heart gave out and he died at his home in Agoura Hills, Los Angeles. He was 52.

Harry had completed a new album, *Lost and Found*, only three days before, and his last public performance was when he joined Ringo's All Starr Band on stage at Las Vegas in 1992.

Ringo Starr played on his posthumously released 1995 album *The Harry Nilsson Anthology*.

There was a 1994 tribute album called *For the Love of Harry*, and *Personal Best: The Harry Nilsson Anthology* was issued in 1995.

Nine

Nine was John's favourite number and several songs have reflected this: 'No. 9 Dream', 'Revolution No. 9' and 'One After 909', the last being written at 9 Newcastle Road, Liverpool, his grandfather's house.

John was born on 9 October and killed on 9 December (at least it was 9 December in Britain, making allowances for the time change). Numerous important events in his life took place on the 9th: Brian Epstein saw the Beatles for the first time on 9 November; the Beatles' EMI contract was confirmed on 9 May; the Beatles made their *Ed Sullivan Show* debut on 9 February; John appeared solo on Peter Cook and Dudley Moore's *Not*

Only ... But Also TV show on 9 January; John first met Yoko on 9 November; the Beatles' partnership was officially dissolved on 9 January; John and Yoko's son Sean was born on 9 October; and when John was shot (in Liverpool it had turned 9 December), he was rushed to Roosevelt Hospital – on 9th Avenue. John had once predicted that he would die on the ninth day of the month, and, indeed, nine plays a part in a slightly less direct way in that he was shot on 72nd Street (7 + 2 = 9) and declared dead at 11.07 (1 + 1 + 7 = 9).

Other combinations of numbers that added up to nine digits also intrigued him. He travelled on the number 72 bus to art college; he and Yoko had an apartment on West 72nd Street; their original Dakota Building apartment number was 72.

1975 Lennon Interview, The
The writer Lavinia Van Driver set out to print a series of booklets transcribing legendary Beatles interviews. This sixteen-page illustrated transcript of the *Old Grey Whistle Test* programme, in which John was interviewed by Bob Harris, was published in a limited edition by Donkey Productions in 1984. The author's name sounds like that of a character from one of John's books.

No Bed for Beatle John
A song conceived by Yoko shortly before her miscarriage. She was admitted to Queen Charlotte's Hospital, London, early in November 1968 and John remained with her. When there was a shortage of spare beds in the hospital, John elected to sleep next to Yoko on an air mattress on the floor, an action that inspired her to write the song.

They recorded the number together on a portable tape machine and performed it in the manner of a Gregorian chant. Basically, it was just John and Yoko reading press reports of their activities.

The piece was included on their *Unfinished Music No. 2: Life With the Lions* album and Yoko performed it on stage at the Lady Mitchell Hall, Cambridge, on 2 March, 1969 with backing from John on guitar, John Tchikai on sax and John Stevens on percussion. The number also found its way on to the flexi-disc issued with the 1969 spring/summer edition of the American arts magazine *Aspen*.

Nobody Loves You When You're Down and Out

A track on the *Walls and Bridges* album, written at a time when John was estranged from Yoko and felt his career was at a low ebb. The title was probably inspired by the Jimmie Cox blues number 'Nobody Knows You When You're Down and Out', which Eric Clapton had included on his Derek and the Dominoes album *Layla and Assorted Love Songs*.

John felt it expressed that particular period of his life and he could visualise it as a song for Frank Sinatra in the mood of 'The Wee Small Hours of the Morning'.

John recorded it in August 1974. He was to say, 'I had been sitting on the song because I knew I would ruin it if I tried to record it at the time I wrote it. My head wasn't together to deal with it so I just kept it in my pocket.'

Nobody Told Me

Track on the *Milk and Honey* album, which John had possibly originally considered offering to Ringo. It became the first single from the album to be issued when it was released in America on Friday 6 January 1984 with Yoko's 'O Sanity' on the flip. It was issued in Britain on 9 January. It was re-released on Saturday 15 June 1985, on Polydor POSP 700, and earned a BMI (British Music Industry) award.

No. 9 Dream

A number John recorded in August 1974 for the *Walls and Bridges* album. Some sources claim that May Pang was the song's inspiration, and May can be heard singing John's name in the chorus, yet other sources claim that it was a message to Yoko during their separation and was composed on the 9th day of the month in which he wrote it.

The number nine had a special significance for both John and Yoko (see **Nine**).

He was living with May Pang at the time and awoke to tell her that he'd dreamed of two women who were saying his name. They were obviously May and Yoko. He also heard a refrain with gobbledegook words: 'Ah! Bowakawa pousse, pousse.'

John plays acoustic guitar on the track, using the pseudonym Dr Dream, and Eddie Mottau also plays an acoustic guitar.

Klaus Voormann plays bass, Jim Keltner is on drums, Nicky Hopkins plays electric piano and Ken Ascher the clarinet, while the backing vocalists, under the name the 44th Street Fairies, are May Pang, Lori Burton and Joey Dambra.

The song, which was originally called 'So Long', became the second single issued from the *Walls and Bridges* album. It was released in Britain on Apple R 6003 on 31 January 1975, and reached No. 23. It was released in America on Apple 1878 on 16 December 1974 and reached, appropriately, No. 9 in the charts.

The flip side was another composition by John called 'What You Got'.

'No. 9 Dream' was also included on the *Shaved Fish* compilation.

Nordoff-Robbins Music Therapy

A show-business charity that raises money for people recovering from debilitating illnesses. Their 22nd Silver Clef Luncheon and Awards was held in London on Friday 20 June 1997 at the Inter Continental hotel. Yoko and Sean were in attendance as there was a posthumous award presented to John for 'outstanding contribution to the British music industry and world peace'. Yoko received the award on behalf of John and said, 'There was a time when the message John and I were giving out was not getting through, but things have changed. In those days, probably twenty per cent of people believed in world peace, and the rest believed in military glory. Now it's the other way around. It's a blessing to be around and see how things turned out. I only wish John was here to witness it too.'

During the luncheon a statue of John was auctioned off for £23,000. HMV and their executive Stuart McAllister, who donated it to the charity, had commissioned the bronze statue by the artist Mo Farquharson. The four-foot statue showed John in his familiar New York City T-shirt, jeans and sunglasses.

No Reply

A composition by John that the Beatles originally recorded as a demo at their EMI studio session on Wednesday 3 June 1964. The demo was given to Tommy Quickly, one of Brian Epstein's signings, for release as his next single on 7 August. He quickly recorded the song, but it was never released. The Beatles then made a more complete recording of the song during their Wednesday 30 September recording session, with George Martin playing piano.

The song was considered as a single, but was instead included as a track on the *Beatles For Sale* album. The track was also included on the *Beatles For Sale* EP and the American *Beatles '65* album.

John was to comment, ' "No Reply" was the one where Dick James said, "That's the first complete song you've written where it resolves itself." You know, with a complete story. It was sort of my version of "Silhouettes".'

In fact, the Little Diamonds' hit record 'Silhouettes' proved to be the inspiration for 'No Reply'. As John was to point out, 'I had that image of walking down the street and seeing her silhouetted in the window and not answering the phone, although I never called a girl on the phone in my life. Phones weren't part of the English child's life.'

Norwegian Wood (This Bird Has Flown)

The song began life as 'This Bird Has Flown', but John changed the name and kept the original as a subtitle. The number concerned one of John's extramarital affairs and he said, 'I was very careful and paranoid because I didn't want my wife, Cynthia, to know that there really was something going on outside of the household.' He must have enjoyed the subterfuge as he wrote most of it in a hotel room he shared with Cynthia in January 1965 when the couple were on a skiing holiday in St Moritz with George Martin and his girlfriend Judy Lockhart-Smith. He completed the number at Kenwood.

The track was used on the *Rubber Soul* album. The ambiguous lyrics are strongly poetic and were composed at a time when John was strongly influenced by the work of Bob Dylan, resulting in what was to become one of John's own personal favourites of all the songs he had written.

George Harrison played sitar, an Indian instrument given prominence for the first time on a Western pop record.

John also explained, 'I was trying to write about an affair without letting my wife know I was writing about an affair, so it was very gobbledegook. I was sort of writing from my experience: girls, flats, things like that.'

The introspective autobiographical number allegedly concerned an incident when John spent the night at a girl's flat. 'Norwegian Wood' referred to the style of decoration, popular in the mid-60s of having natural-finish pine used in house decor, and was obviously part of his description of the girl's flat.

Subsequent information seems to point to a brief affair rather than a one-night stand with a woman possessing a dominant personality, possibly a journalist. John was to say, 'That's why it's gobbledegook. I wanted to get the affair out of my head and on to paper, but not in a way that Cyn would suspect what I was really on about. Yes, I was hiding this love away, but I was also getting it off my chest right under everyone's nose, which I find exciting.'

Not Only ... But Also

A satirical television showcase series for Peter Cook and Dudley Moore, which was broadcast on BBC2.

John was a special guest of Pete and Dud on the very first edition of their show, which he recorded at 8.30 p.m. on Sunday, 29 November 1964 at Television Centre's Studio One in London before an audience.

This edition of *Not Only ... But Also* was broadcast on 9 January 1965. John appeared in a surrealistic film sequence and also read some of his poetry, together with Dudley Moore and Norman Rossington, the Liverpool actor who had appeared as one of the Beatles' road managers, Norm, in *A Hard Day's Night.*

The programme provided John with prestige promotion for his newly published book, *In His Own Write.* He read out the biography of himself that he'd written for the book, 'About the Awful', and Rossington recited 'Good Dog Nigel' and 'The Wrestling Dog'. John, Moore and Rossington recited the next excerpt 'All Abord Speeching' while Rossington and Moore were to read 'Unhappy Frank'.

Dudley Moore's biographer, Barbara Paskin, was to recall: 'The first programme went out under the title *The Moore Show Starring Not Only Dudley Moore But Also Peter Cook and John Lennon.* In one sketch, filmed on Wimbledon Common, they did a take-off of the sometimes mannered style of BBC's *Monitor,* during which John Lennon was seen in slow motion swinging on the children's swings. Dudley was pushing him, but eventually he pushed so hard that John's contact lenses fell out and were lost in the grass. Joe McGrath had to stop filming while everyone searched frantically among the tall blades. "Luckily," he said, "John had another pair on him, because we never found the first ones."

'John Lennon was paid only fifteen pounds for his appearance on the programme – not even enough to cover his lost contact lenses – but he relished every minute of working with Peter and Dudley.'

'At the end of the show,' McGrath recalled, 'we all went for a Chinese meal at the restaurant round the corner, and John, who was very sombre by the end of dinner, suddenly got up and sat on top of the table and said quite seriously to the boys, "I really dig what you're all doing." '

In their 1966 Christmas edition of the show they had John appear as their special guest in a sketch filmed outside a public convenience in Broadwick Street, London, on Sunday 27 November 1966. John appeared for 51 seconds in the sketch, dressed in a commissionaire's uniform. As Dan, the doorman to a trendy club, he pockets a £5 backhander from Cook, playing Hiram J Pipesucker, an American TV presenter. John stands outside the loo, which had a MEMBERS ONLY sign placed outside it. He is also wearing his granny glasses, which he would now wear more frequently in public.

The programme was screened by the BBC on Boxing Day, Monday 26 December, at 9 p.m. and repeated on Tuesday 7 February 1967 at 9.05 p.m.

Earlier in the same programme, Pete and Dud, together with Dud's trio and an orchestra, performed 'LS Bumble Bee'. This number was recorded and a single issued in Britain on Decca F12551 on 27 January 1967 with 'Bee Side' as the B-side!

It was a release that was to gain the stature of a mystery disc for some years as the word on the grapevine was that John Lennon was involved in the number, either as writer or one of the vocalists.

This was due to some fans saying they recognised John's voice on the record. There was also the suspicion by some record collectors that John was making an attempt to comment about LSD on the disc. The rumour gained momentum because the song was included on some Beatles bootleg releases, thus confusing fans still further.

The rumours were unfounded: the song was solely written and performed by Peter Cook and Dudley Moore.

Not a Second Time

A song penned by John, which the Beatles recorded on Wednesday 11 September 1963 and included on the *With the Beatles* album. It was said that John had been influenced by Arthur Alexander when he wrote the song and it has also been suggested that it was one of the first numbers he composed on a piano, rather than on guitar, as was usual at the time.

John's voice was double-tracked and the number was highlighted by the critic William Mann in his famous analysis of the Beatles' music in *The Times* in 1963.

His comment about this particular number read,

> ... harmonic interest is typical of their quicker songs too, and one gets the impression that they think simultaneously of harmony and melody, so firmly are the major tonic sevenths and ninths built into their tunes, and the flat submediant key switches, so natural in the Aeolian cadence at the end of *Not A Second Time* (The chord progression that ends Mahler's *Song Of The Earth*) ...

An incredulous John, when asked to comment on the review, remarked, 'Really, it was chords, just like any other chords.'

Now and Then

Jeff Lynne reported that this song, or one called 'Miss You', was one of the demos mooted for a third single by Paul, George and Ringo. It was the fourth demo that Yoko had passed on to Paul. Lynne recalls working on a backing track for it one afternoon, but the so-called 'Threetles' – the remaining Beatles – didn't finish it. He says, 'It didn't have all the lyrics.'

Nowhere Man

Recorded at Abbey Road on 21 and 22 October 1965 and included on the *Rubber Soul* album. The inspiration came to John in Weybridge during a period when he had a writer's block.

In the famous interview he did for *Playboy* magazine, he was to say, 'I'd spent five hours that morning trying to write a song that was meaningful and good, and I finally gave up and lay down. Then "Nowhere Man" came, words and music, the whole damn thing, as I lay down.'

Now or Never

This single by Yoko Ono and Elephant's Memory, with 'Move Over Fast' on the flip, was released in the United States only by Apple on Monday November 13 1972.

Nudity

There was much controversy when John and Yoko posed full frontal for the front cover of their *Two Virgins* album. John wasn't always so liberal about the exposure of the naked form. When he arrived at the American poet Allen Ginsberg's 39th-birthday party on 3 April 1965 with Cynthia and George and Pattie Harrison, he was embarrassed to see that Ginsberg was naked. The poet was prancing around with a pair of his shorts on his head and a sign reading 'DO NOT DISTURB' on his penis. John immediately left with his companions saying, 'You don't do that in front of the birds.'

John had certainly shed any such inhibitions by August 1969 when he and Yoko made a film called *Self-Portrait*, which consisted entirely of a slow-motion view of John's uncircumcised penis as it rose from a flaccid state to erection. When Tony Cox had filmed John and Yoko's daughter Kyoko having a bath together, he showed the film during a custody hearing in Texas (see **Cox, Anthony**), but the judge pointed out that Cox had had no previous objections to nudity, having been arrested on one occasion for appearing nude in public.

John also used to walk around the Dakota Building apartment in the nude. Photographs of him and Yoko in the nude, allegedly found in a dustbin, were published in the American soft-porn magazine *Swank* in 1983. Shortly before John died, on Wednesday December 3 1979, a *Rolling Stone* photographer, Annie Leibowitz, took a number of photographs of John in the nude, clinging to a clothed Yoko, which were later used in the magazine.

Number One

Title of Yoko Ono's first movie short. A five-minute film in slow motion of a match being struck. The film was shown as part of the festival of avant-garde films in the 1965 Fluxfilm Programme in New York, along with Yoko's *Number Four* film, which showed close-ups of twelve naked bottoms.

Nutopia

Imaginary country created by John and Yoko, although the concept is typical of a Yoko inspiration. The couple created Nutopia during 1973 when John was experiencing difficulties with the immigration authorities in the USA, who wanted to deport him. He included the 'Nutopian International Anthem' on his *Mind Games* album, although it comprised just three seconds of silence.

He said that Nutopia should be allowed to become a member of the United Nations. There was a sheet of information about Nutopia in the *Mind Games* album sleeve, in which he invited people to pledge their allegiance to this state, which did not have any boundaries or passports. It read, in part,

> We announce the birth of a conceptual country, NUTOPIA. Citizenship of the country can be obtained by declaration of your awareness of NUTOPIA. NUTOPIA has no land, no boundaries, no passports, only people. NUTOPIA has no laws other than cosmic. All people of NUTOPIA are ambassadors of the country. As two ambassadors of NUTOPIA, we ask for diplomatic immunity and recognition in the United Nations of our country and its people.

'Citizenship of the country can be obtained by declaration of your awareness of Nutopia,' he wrote. John even hung up a plaque reading 'NUTOPIAN EMBASSY' outside the door to his apartment.

The conceptual country was first announced to the public at a press conference John and Yoko held at the New York American Bar Association, during which they both waved the Nutopian flag – white tissues!

Nutopian National Anthem

A brief three seconds of silence to be found at the end of the first half of the *Mind Games* album.

Nutter, David

Brother of Tommy Nutter, the Savile Row tailor who made the Lennons' wedding suits. He was also godfather to their son Sean.

David was a photographer who was frequently commissioned to take photographs of John and Yoko on behalf of Apple, including shots of them at EMI studios signing with Allen Klein, and around the Apple building.

One of his most important sessions was the John and Yoko wedding, of which he commented, 'I got this James Bond-type phone call asking me to pack my bags and camera and catch the first plane to Gibraltar. No names were given and I had to try to guess who it was. I had one camera and one lens and when I found out it was for John I was as nervous as hell.'

Together with Peter Brown, Nutter became an official witness to the ceremony. He was also taken with them to Paris in a private jet. He was racked with worry as he hadn't any money on him and didn't know how he'd get back to London – but he was offered a lift in the private plane.

Nutter was also upset with what he regarded as John and Yoko's purloining of the copyright of the wedding photographs, for which he had never been paid and which, in fact, cost him money because he was never even reimbursed for his expenses.

After John, Yoko, Julian and Kyoko were involved in their car crash (see **Lawson Memorial Hospital**) in Scotland, it was Nutter who was asked to pick them up in Golspie.

He maintained his relationship with John, meeting him in New York when he was with May Pang, and he was also present backstage when John and Yoko were united at Madison Square Garden. John also took Nutter to see Sean at the Dakota Building. During the meeting, Yoko said she wanted Nutter to take photographs on her behalf. After John had died she asked him to photograph the cover of her own album. It was called *Season of Glass* and the sleeve pictures a bloodstained pair of spectacles. It was controversial and received criticism as being in bad taste.

Nutter said that, when Yoko asked him if he would do the album cover, she brought out a pair of bloodstained glasses. He didn't think it in the best of taste, but told her he could take the photograph in the room they were in. He suggested putting the glasses by the window and employing a 28mm wide-angle lens using available light. She said she'd call him herself in a couple of days, but never did. 'She did it herself in her own way. I just felt a little bit used,' he said.

Nutter, Tommy

A roommate of Peter Brown. Brown was then an Apple executive, who backed him financially when he opened a Savile Row shop. His first customers were John and Yoko, who immediately ordered half a dozen suits each. On their visits, the couple used to walk around the shop naked. Nutter commented, 'I didn't find it particularly attractive, I must say. So that was quite embarrassing, really – in front of other people in the middle of the shop.'

Nutter also made suits for the Beatles and their entourage and three of his suits are featured on the *Abbey Road* sleeve. He died at the age of 49 in August 1992 of an AIDS-related disease.

O'Donnell, Lucy

Arguably, the inspiration behind the famous *Sergeant Pepper* song 'Lucy in the Sky with Diamonds'. Despite the many journalistic reports that maintained that the song was inspired by LSD, citing the initials of the song as proving their point, John always insisted that the inspiration and imagery came from a painting his son Julian brought home from school one day. Julian showed his artwork to his parents and John asked him what the painting was supposed to represent. 'It's Lucy in the sky with diamonds,' Julian said.

Lucy O'Donnell was in the same class as Julian at Heath House infants' school in Weybridge in 1967 and Julian had invited her to his birthday parties. The girl was the daughter of a journalist and later became a nursery nurse. The school was run by two old women and has since closed down and been demolished

She recalled, 'I can remember Julian's face clearly and I can remember another boy called Mickey. But I can't remember anyone else. We used to sit alongside each other in proper old-fashioned desks. Julian and I were a couple of little menaces from what I've been told.' Lucy later went on to become a nursery school teacher in Weybrdge.

Her claim to be the Lucy who inspired the song was challenged in 1986 in the *Daily Express*, which reported that a 24-year-old freelance art director in the film business called Lucinda Richardson had been the little girl who inspired the story. In the newspaper she said, 'It was a long time ago, but, yes, I'm the Lucy that Julian Lennon drew a picture of. I don't really remember anything much at all about that period, but Julian and I used to play together a lot in the Heath House school in Weybridge.'

O Sanity
The closing track on the *Milk and Honey* album, composed by Yoko Ono.

Oh, Calcutta!
Oh, Calcutta! was a controversial stage show consisting of fifteen sketches devised by the late Kenneth Tynan and directed by Jacques Levy.

Tynan has gone down in history as the first person to utter a particular four-letter word on British television. The event occurred in October 1965 when Tynan was literary manager of the National Theatre. He was appearing on the satirical show *BBC 3* and was being interviewed by Robert Robinson, who asked him if he would be likely to agree to sexual intercourse being performed on stage.

Tynan replied, 'I think so, certainly. I think there are very few rational people in this world to whom the word "fuck" is particularly diabolical or revolting or totally forbidden. I think that anything that can be printed or said can also be seen.'

The show was a live one and the utterance produced shock waves, newspaper headlines, letters from the TV watchdog Mary Whitehouse, then secretary of the National Viewers' and Listeners' Association, and the comment from Robert Robinson, 'I think he was up the pole to use that word.'

Oh, Calcutta! was a sexual stage romp with full frontal nudes and risqué sketches from fifteen contributors, including the playwright Samuel Beckett and the cartoonist Jules Feiffer. There was also a sketch based on a three-line 'premise' by John Lennon, inspired by his early masturbatory activities when, together with some other boys from Quarry Bank School, including his best mate Pete Shotton, they would indulge in group masturbation in which they would voice the names of sexy film stars.

John invariably chose Brigitte Bardot, although on one occasion he shouted out the name Winston Churchill.

Tynan penned a sketch based on the incident called 'Four In Hand', which featured four seated actors with their backs to the audience who simulate masturbation while they chat to the strains of the *William Tell* overture.

John was to say, 'I met Tynan a few times around and about and he just said, "I'm getting all these different people to write something erotic. Will you do it?" And I told him that if I come up with something I'd do it and if I don't, I don't. So I came up with two or three lines which was the masturbation scene. It was a great childhood thing. Everybody's been masturbating and trying to think of something sexy and somebody'd shout, "Winston Churchill!" in the middle of it and break down. So I just wrote that down on a paper and told him to put whichever names in that suited the hero and they did it. I've never seen it.'

The contributors were also asked to provide a brief biography to be included in the printed programme and John submitted: 'Born October 9, 1940. Lived. Met Yoko 1966!'

The Lennon-inspired sketch was presented as follows:

Four chairs with their backs to the audience. Facing them is a large projection screen divided into four sections, one for each chair. Three men are waiting impatiently and then a doorbell rings.
No. 1: 'There he is now. I told you he'd make it.' (He opens door.)

George enters, wearing a fedora.

George: 'Sorry I'm late, fellas.'
No. 1: 'If you're going to join the group, George, you have to remember we always start on time.'
No. 2: 'We don't like people breakin' the rules, George.'
George: 'I already said, "I'm sorry." '
No. 3: 'Look, we gonna talk, or we gonna jerk off?'
No. 1: 'OK, let's get started. This is your seat, George. Now this' (he points to the screen) 'is a new kind of machine, a telepathic thought transmitter. Whatever you think about flashes on the screen. Now the rules of the

game are this: all of us think of things to jerk off to – until somebody comes, and the first guy who comes has to stop everybody else from coming. Got it?'
No. 1: 'All right. Let's give it a try. Whatever comes to mind, George.'

No. 1 goes to his seat and George sits between No. 2 and No. 3 while rhythmic music starts and images begin to flash on the screens. The men's arms start moving rhythmically in front of them. The screens facing No. 1, No. 2 and No. 3 show Hollywood and *Playboy*-type pin-ups. George's screen remains blank. Screens 1, 2 and 3 are all flashing pictures of beautiful women. Suddenly we hear the strains of the William Tell Overture and during a crash of cymbals a picture of the Lone Ranger flashes on George's screen.

All screens go blank and all four men stop masturbating.

No. 3: 'What the fuck was that?'
No. 1: 'What are ya tryin' to do, George?'
George: 'What's wrong?'
No. 2: (rising and adjusting pants): 'I told you not to invite outsiders.'
George: 'I'm sorry, fellas, it's the first thing that came into my mind.'
No. 2: 'We haven't had a vacancy in six months, George! Harvey only left because he got a divorce.'
No. 3: 'How'd you like a silver bullet up your ass!'
No. 1 (walking up to George): 'You sure you're all right, George?'
George: 'I'm fine, thanks.'
No. 1: 'All right, let's try again.' (They all sit down.) 'And cut the horse shit, George.'

The music starts again and the images which flash are more explicit than before, close shots of breasts and bottoms. The four screens begin to form a composite picture and George is dutifully collaborating. At the height of the rhythm the screen facing No. 1 shows a nude model's head, screen No. 2 shows her breasts, screen facing No. 3 her legs. Pause. The image of the model is almost complete. Suddenly the strains of the *William Tell Overture* are heard and another image of the Lone Ranger appears on George's screen.

George: 'A-a-a-ah!' He rises as the screen continues to flash the Lone Ranger and sweeps his arm and the Lone Ranger appears on the other screens. No. 1, No. 2 and No. 3 lose their concentration and give up the contest.
George (turning to leave): 'See you next week, fellas.'
No. 1: 'Get the fuck outta here!'

Sound of four gunshots as each remaining screen blanks out.

Oh My Love

A poignant song, which Yoko co-wrote with John soon after she miscarried on 21 November 1968. The number is a tragic anthem for the child, in which she expressed her feelings in words such as 'You had a very strong heartbeat, but that's gone now', and 'Probably we'll forget about you, but whoever you were, you were an angel'.

Early in December, John set music to Yoko's lyrics and three demos were made, two with John playing guitar and singing.

The song surfaced two years later on the *Imagine* album and it was the only track on the LP to be credited Lennon/Ono.

Recorded in July 1971, it featured John on piano, George Harrison on guitar, Klaus Voormann on bass, Alan White on drums and Tibetan cymbals and Nicky Hopkins on electric piano.

Oh Yoko

A song that John wrote in celebration of his love for and marriage to Yoko. He first began making home demos of the song in December 1970 when he composed a version on piano that was rather dirge-like in tone. When he made some further demos in May 1971 he performed the number using a guitar and the melody became more uplifting. The number was then recorded in the studio in July 1971 as part of the *Imagine* album sessions, produced by Phil Spector.

On the track, John played guitar and mouth organ and was supported by Nicky Hopkins on piano, Klaus Voormann on bass, Alan White on drums and Rod Lynton and Andy Davis on acoustic guitars.

'Oh Yoko' was featured on the *Imagine* album. Following the release of the 'Imagine' single in America, it was suggested that 'Oh Yoko' become the second single from the album to be issued in the US. John rejected the idea because he felt that a love song from a husband to his wife didn't fit in with the macho image he wished to maintain.

He was later to tell *Playboy* magazine, 'It was a very popular track. Everybody wanted it as a single, but I was sort of shy and embarrassed, maybe because it didn't represent my image of myself of the tough, hard-biting rock 'n' roller with the acid tongue.'

Old Dirt Road

A song that John and Harry Nilsson wrote together while recording the *Pussy Cats* album. John was to include it on his *Walls and Bridges* album, with Harry singing backing vocals. Harry himself went on to record it for his 1980 album *Flash Harry*.

The two of them decided to write a song and John said, 'Harry, what's a good American expression?' Harry said, 'It's like trying to shovel smoke with a pitchfork in the wind.'

John said, 'Now you're cooking! Carry on.' Some lawyers then came in to discuss some matters with John, who told Harry, 'Just finish it, do your own thing.' Harry continued working on the piano, then John joined him and the two of them finished the song.

They also wrote another one called 'Here You Are (You Are Here)', but they never recorded it.

When John recorded the number, crediting himself as Revd Thumbs Ghurkin, he had Nicky Hopkins on piano, Ken Ascher on electric piano and Jesse Ed Davis on guitar.

Old Grey Whistle Test, The

When John was promoting his *Rock 'n' Roll* album, he agreed to an interview with *The Old Grey Whistle Test*, a BBC2 programme hosted by Bob Harris, although he insisted that

Harris fly to America and conduct the interview in New York because he was afraid of leaving the country in case he had problems with the immigration authorities on re-entry.

Billed as 'A John Lennon Special', it was broadcast between 8.10 and 8.59 p.m. on 18 April 1975.

Harris had pointed out that he felt New York was a 'tense' city. John said, 'To me it's no tenser than Liverpool or London was. On the street in Liverpool, unless you were in the suburbs, you had to walk close to the wall, and to get to the Cavern – for those of you who remember all that – it was no easy matter, even at lunchtimes, sometimes. It's a tense place. And Glasgow and Newcastle … London had it. When I first got to London, it was pretty nerve-racking. We were all putting on the "We're from Liverpool and we're tough" bit, but there were some hard nuts down in London.'

They discussed the music scene in New York and the difference between the American and British charts. John said, 'That's what I'm finding out to my detriment. So what I did was, I had a person at my office keep sending me the Top Ten from England because I have to find out what's going on, don't I? But, I mean, if I'm fighting "If" by Telly Savalas, well I've got a long battle.'

When asked if he missed England, John said, 'Yeah. I try not to. I had somebody bring me some Chocolate Olivers; it's little things you miss, like black pudding, you know, and the Chocolate Olivers. I don't allow myself to miss it that much because then I couldn't carry on fighting about my green card, and I'm gonna win that one first. I keep telling myself, "I'll be there." It'll take another eighteen months to get the card, maybe two years; it's gonna be there, it ain't going nowhere.'

Harris asked him if it was the fact that he might be unable to gain re-entry to America that prevented him from returning to England.

John said, 'Yeah. Nobody's said that in too many words. Nobody wrote a piece of paper … apart from every now and then they say, "You've got thirty days to leave." I know that, if I went, they wouldn't let me back in. I'd have a hell of a job getting back in. I mean, I was having a hell of a job coming in and out as it was. So does Paul, so does Mick, so does George. I mean, all the time when they want to come in here, they have to get on their knees six months in advance. I got sick of that, you know, so I wanted to stay.'

He discussed the green card. 'The situation is I'm still appealing. Like every now and then they'll say, "You've got thirty days to get out." Then my lawyer will appeal, and we'll go up to another court. It'll just go on for ever.

'[The author] Terry Southern put it well. He says it keeps the conservatives happy that they're doing something about me, and what I represent, and it keeps the liberals happy because I haven't actually been thrown out, so everybody's happy.'

John also discussed depression. He said, 'I was in a trough for *Help!*, but you can't see it. I'm singing "Help!" for a kick-off, and it was less noticeable, because you're protected by the image of the power of the Beatles. Now, when it happens, I'm on my own; it's easier to get sniped, so I've been in a trough, so I'm out of it, I'm coming out of it ... whoopee! I'll go around for the rest of my life in this business, so I don't get too serious about it. I only worry about what's happening to me.'

Next he mentioned the trouble at the Troubadour Club in Los Angeles (see **Smothers Brothers** and **Troubadour Club**). 'I got drunk and shouted. It was the first night I drank Brandy Alexanders, which is brandy and milk, folks, and I was with Harry Nilsson, who didn't quite get as much coverage as me, the bum!

'He really encouraged me. I usually have somebody there to say, "OK, Lennon, shut up!", and I take it, but I didn't have anybody around me to say "shut up" so I just went on and on. But there was some girl who claimed I hit her and all. She just wanted some money. I had to pay her off because I thought it would harm [the fight with] immigration.'

Harris brought up the subject of the Beatles re-forming and asked John if he thought it was a good idea.

John commented, 'Now that's another point altogether, whether it would be a good idea or not. You see, it's strange, 'cause at one period when they're asking me, I say, "No, never. What the hell! Go back? No, not me."

'Then it came to the period when I thought, Oh, why not, if we feel like making a record or doing something? Everyone always envisages the stage show. To me, if we work together it ought to be in the studio again.

'When I'm saying that, then I turn the paper and George is saying, "Not me", it's never got to a position when each one of us have wanted to do it at the same time. I've worked with Ringo. I've worked with Ringo and George. I haven't worked with Paul because we had a more difficult time, but now we're pretty close.

'The other question is, would it be worth it? If we wanted to do it, then it would be worth it. If we got in the studio together and thought, We turn each other on … again, then it would be worth it, and sod the critics. They've got nothing to do with it. The music is the music. If we make a piece that we think was worthwhile, it goes out, but it's pie in the sky.

'I jammed with Paul; I did actually play with Paul. We did a lot of stuff in LA, but there was fifty other people playing. They were all just watching me and Paul.'

John was then asked if he regretted writing 'How Do You Sleep?'.

'No. Someone said the other day it's about me.' He did say that he regretted there was so much talk about Paul that they missed the song. 'It was a good track; he lived through it. The only thing that mattered was how he and I feel about those things.'

He then discussed his *Rock 'n' Roll* album and the recording of it, with Phil Spector running off with the tapes (see **Instant Karma!**). 'He's a mysterious man. Phil works in such mysterious ways,' said John.

They next discussed the *Sergeant Pepper* recording and he mentioned he was putting together a television special and that when he got his green card he would return to England.

'You bet. I've got family in England,' he said. 'Hello, Julian, hello, Auntie Mimi!'

John ended the interview by saying, 'Hello, England. Keep sending those Chocolate Olivers. Keep your chin up.'

The programme was also screened on 30 September 1975 and 11 October 1980.

Oldman, Gary

John's housemaster and chemistry teacher at Quarry Bank School. He noted, as John slipped down from the A-stream class to the twentieth position in the C-stream, the absolute bottom, that John simply didn't have any desire to get on.

One After 909

Recorded during the Apple rooftop session on 30 January 1969, and included on the *Let It Be* album. John had originally written the track in 1957 and attempts were made to record it originally in March 1963 when it was considered as a single. That version remained unreleased until it was included on the *Anthology 1* CDs.

One of the Boys

Another of John's home demo tapes, recorded late in 1977, which never made it into the recording studio environment, but which was to turn up several years later in Show No. 81 of *The Lost Lennon Tapes* radio series.

There was much humour in the ironic lyrics in which John noted the fact that although he was growing older he was still one of the boys.

One Day at a Time (book)

A book by Anthony Fawcett, first published in America by Grove Press in 1976. Fawcett, an Oxford graduate who became an art critic, first met John at the Arts Laboratory. He became John and Yoko's personal assistant for two years, organising some of their artistic ventures. We can also thank him for suggesting and encouraging the famous Bag One erotic lithographs.

Fawcett explains in his introduction: 'This book is about the growth of the artist John Lennon, a poet, a primitive musician, and certainly a practical dreamer.'

The creative work of the duo is explored with sympathetic insight: the National Sculpture Exhibition; Yoko's early conceptual 'happenings' in London; Exhibition No. 2 at the Indica Gallery; the *Two Virgins* album; the John and Yoko films; the *In His Own Write* book and erotic lithographs. In addition, the story takes in John and Yoko's personal and musical life from their first meeting until they had settled in New York. There is also a short chronology and a discography.

The book contains over 200 photographs, taken by ten different photographers, including Bob Gruen, Annie Leibowitz, Chuck Pulin and Ethan Russell. Various events are portrayed in a series of photographs, affording us a more intimate knowledge of specific experiences such as the acorn planting at Coventry Cathedral; the *You Are Here* exhibitions; the Gibraltar wedding; the Montreal Bed-in; the Apple office and the One-To-One concert. There are also reproductions of some of the less sensational erotic lithographs and a photograph of a wall painting John created in a friend's house in 1967.

The book was published in Britain the following year by New English Library and in Japan in 1978 by Shinko Music in a translation by D Eguchi, J Harrison and H Sawa. In 1979 a German edition, translated by Hannelore Zander, was published by Gustav Lubbe.

A revised edition was published in America by Grove Press and in Britain by New English Library in 1980, with the subtitle *John Lennon 1940–1980*.

The publishers commented, 'For this reprint it was decided to leave the text in the present tense, but to update the chronological sequence and the discography.' There is a quote on the title page from Yoko: 'John loved and prayed for the human race. Please do the same for him.' Fawcett added a two-page item, 'Epilogue: the Last Four Years', filling in details of John's activities in the years since the original edition was published.

One Who Writes the Lyrics For Elton John, The

A book of Bernie Taupin's lyrics illustrated by guest artists in the style of *The Beatles Illustrated Lyrics*.

John contributed a collage illustrating the song 'Benny and The Jets'. Among the many images in John's picture are girls' legs, the head of Andy Warhol, two naked girls in stockings and suspenders and a pair of motorbikes.

Only People

A track from the *Mind Games* album, its title coming from a phrase that is quoted on the album sleeve by Yoko: 'Only people can change the world.'

Ono, Eisuke

Yoko's father. Eisuke had begun a career as a concert pianist when he fell in love with Isoko Yasuda. He was 29 years old, she was 21. Her family was a prominent one in Japan and there were objections to the couple getting married because of his profession. Eisuke was also a Christian, while Isoko was a Buddhist. However, the family agreed to the match on condition that Eisuke forsake the piano and join the banking fraternity. The marriage was permitted and Eisuke gave up his musical career and joined the Yokohama Specie Bank.

Eisuke left Tokyo two weeks before Yoko was born, to work in the San Francisco branch of the bank, and Yoko didn't meet her father until she was three years old. She met him again on a trip to New York when she was seven years old and her father was now working in the Manhattan branch of the bank.

As the tensions grew between Japan and America, Eisuke left the United States for a position in a branch of the bank in Hanoi. At the time Japan had been engaged in a lengthy war with China. After the fall of Hanoi to the Allies, Eisuke was jailed for more than a year. On his release he was included on a list of 1,500 'Class B' war criminals, which rendered him unemployable. However, when an American administration moved into Japan they realised that, in order to rebuild the country, they would need the professional men and Eisuke was allowed to return to banking and joined the Bank of Tokyo.

Yoko confessed she had an unhappy childhood because of the barriers both her parents placed between themselves and their daughter. Even though she lived in her parents' home, if she wanted to see her father she had to make an appointment through his secretary at the bank.

When Yoko wanted to marry the pianist Toshi Ichiyanagi, her parents objected and said that such a match would bring dishonour to the family. Yoko pointed out that her parents had undergone a similar experience. They explained to her that Eisuke had given up his profession as a concert pianist to marry and they threatened to disinherit her if the marriage went ahead. Yoko left home.

In 1971, Yoko and John went to visit her parents in Japan. Eisuke was now 57 years old and had retired from banking. The family now lived in Fujisawa, 35 miles from Tokyo.

Ono, Isoko

Yoko's mother, whose maiden name was Isoko Yasuda, was the youngest of eight children. She was the granddaughter of one of

Japan's richest merchant princes. Isoko married Eisuke Ono, eight years her senior, although she was a Buddhist and he was a Christian. The marriage was allowed to take place on the understanding that Eisuke forsake his career as a concert pianist to join the family bank.

Isoko was involved in her social life and left the raising of her daughter Yoko to servants. Throughout her life Yoko's relationship with her parents was formal.

When Yoko was two and a half years old, her mother took her to America to join her father, who had taken a position in a bank in San Francisco two weeks before Yoko's birth.

When Yoko brought the penniless pianist Toshi Ichiyanagi home to meet her parents, Isoko made her husband tell Yoko that Ichiyanagi was an unsuitable suitor, although they eventually agreed to the marriage.

After the Onos had retired and settled back in Japan, Yoko brought her third husband, John Lennon, to meet them. Isoko was to tell the press what they talked about. 'Most of the time it was about Yoko's brother and sister, but we also talked about her home in England. It sounds beautiful. We would love to go there, but I'm afraid we are too old.'

She died at the age of 88 on 23 January 1999. Yoko attended her funeral in Tokyo.

Ono, Keisuke
Yoko's younger brother born in December 1936.

Ono Music Limited
A music-publishing company formed by John and Yoko in July 1970, mainly to publish material by Yoko.

Ono, Setsuko
Yoko's younger sister born in December 1941.

Ono, Shinya
One of Yoko's cousins who was a shop steward in the Los Angeles branch of the Teamsters Union. In 1980, at the age of 42, Shinya had become involved in a strike by Japanese–American workers in Los Angeles and San Francisco, protesting against three major Japanese food-importing companies who had given their workers

rises only of three per cent, well below inflation, over a period of three years. White workers were paid more money for the same work.

Shinya worked for Japan Foods Corporation, the largest of the three companies, and he approached Yoko for support. Both John and Yoko offered to make a public statement on behalf of the workers and Shinya pointed out to the strikers that Yoko supported them because she was Japanese and John because he understood the situation. He said, 'She had sympathy, he had empathy.'

The statement that John and Yoko gave to the workers, which was then issued to the media, said,

> We are with you in spirit. Both of us are subjected to prejudice and abuse as an Oriental family in the Western world.
>
> In this beautiful country where democracy is the very foundation of its constitution, it is sad that we have to still fight for equal rights and equal pay for the citizens.
>
> Boycott it must be, if it is the only way to bring justice and restore the dignity of the constitution for the sake of all citizens of the U.S. and their children.
>
> Peace and love,
>
> John Lennon and Yoko Ono.
>
> New York City, December, 1980

They also told Shinya that they would be prepared to travel to San Francisco for any march or rally on behalf of the workers. Shinya told them that a march had been organised during the week of 8 December, so John, Yoko and Sean obtained their plane tickets to fly out. Unfortunately, fate intervened tragically, and John was shot dead before the event.

Ono, Yoko

Yoko was born on 18 February 1933. Her name means 'ocean child'. It is interesting to note that she was born in the Year of the Bird, which is guided by the number nine (this was John Lennon's magical figure. The numbers in the day of her birth also add up to nine.)

Yoko's father Eisuke was a former concert pianist who had

given up his profession to become a banker, in order to marry Isoko Yasuda.

Isoko loved her social life and rarely bothered with her daughter. As Eisuke was so busy at the bank, the servants of the household raised Yoko. In fact, Yoko did not even meet her father until 1936 when she was three years old and first taken to America.

Yoko and her mother returned to Tokyo in 1937, the year Yoko's brother Keisuke was born. Their mother took them both to America in 1940. The following year Isoko was pregnant with Yoko's sister Setsuko and the family once again returned to Japan.

Despite the apparent aloofness of her parents towards her, Yoko admitted that they were supportive and although her father was absent from her early life most of the time, when he was with her he doted on her. He was also thrilled when, after the war, she became the first female student to major in philosophy at Gakushuin University. By that time Eisuke was working in a bank in New York and the family moved to America and settled in Scarsdale. At the age of 19 Yoko became a summer student at Harvard University and then entered Sarah Lawrence College where she studied for three years.

Yoko met Toshi Ichiyanagi, a young composer, and married him – much to the annoyance of her parents. The couple moved into 11 Chambers Street, a loft in Manhattan's Lower west side and Yoko became involved in New York's art scene.

According to friends, Yoko was the dominant partner in the relationship and proved demanding and ambitious. She also had several affairs, and eventually the two decided to split, with Toshi returning to Japan early in 1961. The following year Yoko's parents talked her into returning to Tokyo and she moved into a high-rise apartment with Toshi. Yoko was extremely unhappy at the time, and kept trying to jump out of the window. Several times Toshi had to restrain her, but she eventually took an overdose of pills and was taken to a hospital for the mentally disturbed, where she was heavily sedated.

In the meantime, Tony Cox, a New Yorker who had heard about Yoko and was intrigued by her, left New York and arrived in Tokyo. He attended the hospital, pretending to be her American physician and found that she was so heavily drugged she could hardly talk. He made the hospital staff cease giving her such a high dosage of sedatives, and eventually arranged for her to leave the hospital and return to her apartment. For a time he lived with Yoko and Toshi in a ménage-à-trois, until Yoko became pregnant by him. She divorced Toshi and rapidly married Cox. Their daughter Kyoko Chan was born in Tokyo on 8 August 1963. An artist who knew them at the time said that Cox acted like Yoko's servant and did whatever she told him. Yoko also mentioned to the artist that she liked younger men. The relationship, to all intents, seemed fraught. Cox was to report one incident in which Yoko broke a bottle and pressed it against his throat, keeping him captive in a bathtub for nearly an hour.

During her period in Tokyo Yoko paid for the publication of her book *Grapefruit*. Tony Cox returned to New York with Kyoko, and Yoko followed in November 1964. She then became involved in the avant-garde scene as a member of a group collectively known as Fluxus.

During this time she conceived a number of her conceptual 'happenings,' including 'Cut Piece' in which an audience snipped her clothes off with scissors and 'Stone Piece' (which later became 'Bagism') in which two people would get inside a bag and either take their clothes off and put them on again or remain motionless.

It has been reported that in 1966 Yoko and Cox were so short of money they were looking for sponsors and discussed the Beatles. One friend of theirs even said that at the time Yoko said that she'd like to marry John Lennon. When they received an invitation to appear at a symposium in London, this provided the opportunity they needed.

Tony Cox was a very good hustler and he managed to talk the owner of a large flat in Hanover Place to let them live there rent-free. But despite his gift of the gab, he still seemed awed by Yoko. Barry Miles, a member of the London art scene at the time, says that Cox was cowed by her and did what he was told.

Miles, along with John Dunbar and Peter Asher, ran the Indica Gallery in Masons Yard. Yoko managed to talk them into allowing her to have an exhibition there. The golden-tongued Cox even talked a rival gallery owner into paying for the catalogue!

Apparently, although John Lennon and Paul McCartney regularly attended exhibitions at the gallery, Yoko spoke to John Dunbar several times requesting that he ensure that John turned up. Dunbar phoned John and told him about Yoko's 'Bag Piece', saying she climbed into a bag with a friend and 'either fucked or didn't fuck.' This intrigued John, who said he'd come along.

John turned up to the preview of 'Unfinished Paintings And Objects By Yoko Ono' on 9 November 1966. He picked up an item labelled 'Box Of Smiles' and when he opened the lid saw his own face reflected in a mirror, causing him to smile. He climbed up a ladder to look at an exhibit and when he climbed down Yoko was there and handed him a card that said 'Breathe'. John stuck out his tongue and began to pant. Dunbar then came up and introduced them.

John then noticed an exhibit which read *Hammer a Nail In*. He asked if he could do so, but Yoko objected saying that she wanted the canvas to be without nails for the opening night the next evening. Eventually, though, she conceded, saying, 'It will cost you five shillings.'

John answered, 'I'll give you an imaginary five shillings and hammer an imaginary nail in.'

On the way out, he noticed an apple on a pedestal with a price tag of £200. He picked up the apple, bit it and put it back on the pedestal.

Yoko was to say, 'I had a very poetic piece – a fresh apple on a stand. He grabbed the apple and bit into it. I thought, How dare he? That's my work. I was totally livid. He noticed and went, "Hee-hee" sheepishly and put the apple back on the stand.'

John's later version of these events and his description of the rapport he established with Yoko during the exhibition differs from that of some witnesses at the time, including John's chauffeur Les Anthony, who says that John didn't pay much attention to Yoko and that she ran into the street after him.

Yoko's assertion that she didn't even know who the Beatles were at this time can be disproved, not only by the fact that several of her friends said she'd set her cap at John Lennon and looked to the Beatles for funding, but because weeks before the Indica Exhibition she had approached Paul McCartney to ask for some Lennon and McCartney manuscripts for a 50th birthday gift to John Cage, and Paul had referred her to John.

By the following year Yoko began to appear frequently in the press due to her conceptual events. One that caused some controversy was a film called *Bottoms* which featured the naked behinds of 365 people. In June of that year Yoko and Tony went to Belgium and were arrested for dancing naked in public.

In the meantime, Yoko was pursuing her plan to contact John Lennon and sent a copy of *Grapefruit* to Abbey Road studio while the Beatles were recording there. She had John's telephone number and began calling him. She told him she wanted to hold an exhibition at the Lisson Gallery but needed a sponsor. John agreed to let her have £5,000 to mount the show. It was called 'Half Wind Show' and subtitled 'Yoko and Me', which referred to John, who wished to remain anonymous. He didn't even attend the exhibition.

Yoko then began phoning John's home in Weybridge, and even started turning up on the doorstep unannounced. Once, when John and Cynthia weren't at home she talked housekeeper Dorothy Jarlett into letting her make a phone call and the next day said she was coming round as she'd left her ring by the phone. Another time she got into the Rolls Royce when John and Cynthia were leaving the studio. Cynthia was to ask John what was going on and he told her that Yoko was just crackers and a weirdo who just wanted money for her 'avant-garde bullshit.'

By January 1968 tensions between Yoko and Tony had increased to the extent that the couple temporarily split up, with Cox and Kyoko moving into a Hanover Square flat and Yoko into a set of rooms in a nearby hotel.

In May, when Cynthia was on holiday in Greece with friends, John phoned Yoko and invited her round to the house in Weybridge. Cox was in the South of France with Kyoko at the time. She arrived to find John and his friend Pete Shotton both stoned. Shotton soon went to bed. John took Yoko into his small studio in the attic and played her some tapes which he said were for a song he was creating for the next Beatles album, which he called 'Revolution No. 9'. She and John then began to work on the tapes together (which were to become the experimental album *Two Virgins*) and then went to bed and made love.

When Shotton got up that morning, John told him that he had fallen in love and was willing to give up everything for Yoko. Cynthia arrived back from holiday in the company of Jenny

Boyd and Alexis Mardas and was startled to see John wearing a robe sitting with Yoko, who was wearing one of Cynthia's kimonos. John just said, 'Oh, hi.'

As Cynthia had had breakfast in Athens and lunch in Rome that day, she'd thought it would be nice to cap it with dinner in London and when she suggested to John that they go out to dinner, he just said 'No thanks.'

Yoko smiled at Cynthia with what she later described as 'a very positive, confident look'.

Cynthia was to say, 'Well, obviously, John fell in love with Yoko. I think it all built up from the death of Brian [Epstein]. I think it built up from the change in the Beatles' role. They stopped performing and all they were doing was recording. Their lives were becoming very insular and not exciting enough ... Yoko arrived and they were on the same wavelength mentally. And she was just the right woman for him at the time.'

John was to recall, 'My marriage to Cyn was not unhappy. But it was just a normal marital state where nothing happened and which we continued to sustain. You sustain it until you meet somebody who suddenly sets you alight. With Yoko I really knew love for the first time. Our attraction was a mental one, but it happened physically too. Both are essential in the union – but I never thought I would marry again.'

Cynthia stayed away for a few days and when she returned, John was alone, as Yoko had returned to Cox and Kyoko. John implied that his marriage with Cynthia would continue, but he said she couldn't accompany him on his trip to New York with Paul to promote Apple as he'd be too busy. He suggested she go on holiday again and she went to Italy. The marriage was now over, and John sent Alexis Mardas to Italy to tell Cynthia he was going to divorce her.

He then began to be seen openly with Yoko and involve himself in her conceptual ventures, the first of which took place early in June 1968 and was an exhibition of acorns at the National Sculpture Exhibition at Coventry Cathedral. Initially, they were refused permission to put their exhibit in the main exhibition. Apple's Peter Brown commented, 'Yoko turned into a sputtering little volcano of rage. She launched into a red-faced harangue, insisting that all the leading sculptors in England be telephoned to testify to the validity of her acorn idea.'

On 18 June the couple appeared together to attend the stage production of John's *In His Own Write* at the Old Vic and reporters insisted on asking him repeatedly, 'Where's your wife, John?'

When Tony Cox returned from another trip to France he was concerned about the turn of events. When they'd made plans for her to see John in order to get funding for her work, he hadn't anticipated that they'd fall in love. He told her that he was willing to divorce her if she signed an agreement giving him fifty per cent of what she received from John.

Dan Richter, a friend of both Tony and Yoko, told journalist Jerry Hopkins, 'Tony felt as if he'd been screwed. He'd encouraged Yoko to see John. He thought it was great. But when he felt he was losing her, he insisted on the agreement. She was close to Tony, and she owed him a lot. He got her out of the mental hospital, he kept her going, raised money for her shows, got them airline tickets to London, went after all the publicity, found backers for her films, borrowed money from banks, all of it. She came to realise in a way that everything she did was him. She felt she owed him. She felt she owed him her thanks.'

Yoko then signed the contract and Richter witnessed it.

On 1 July John staged his own exhibition which he named 'You Are Here' and subtitled 'To Yoko From John, With Love.' On 22 August Cynthia sued for divorce. Whilst Cynthia and Julian moved back into Weybridge, John and Yoko stayed for a short time at Ringo's home and then moved into Ringo's flat at 34 Montague Square, London W1.

On 18 October 1968 the flat was raided by police officers, led by a Sergeant Pilcher, who said they discovered 219 grains of cannabis resin on the premises. John insisted that it had been planted but agreed to plead guilty to keep Yoko, who was pregnant at the time, from having to go through a trial. However, by pleading guilty, John was to find the offence caused him great problems in the future when he attempted to gain a green card in America. Pilcher, who was responsible for finding the cannabis, was later jailed for planting evidence on others.

Cynthia obtained her divorce on 8 November. At this time Yoko had complications in her pregnancy and had to be admitted to Queen Charlotte's Maternity Hospital for a few days. John stayed with her, camping in a sleeping bag.

November 11 saw the first of the John and Yoko record collaborations, *Unfinished Music No. 1: Two Virgins*. This record was to cause great controversy due to the fact that John and Yoko appear completely nude on the cover of the album. Yoko claimed that the nudity was John's idea and was to comment, 'I suppose he just thought it would be effective. He took the picture himself, with an automatic camera. It's nice. The picture isn't lewd or anything like that. Basically we are both very shy and square people. We'd be the first to be embarrassed if anyone were to invite us to a nude party.' Yet despite talk of an automatic camera, photograph No. 16 in Ray Connolly's book *John Lennon 1940–1980* clearly shows John and Yoko at Tittenhurst Park with a large framed picture of *three* naked virgins.

Sadly, Yoko miscarried on November 21 and it is believed that this came about due to the continuing stress caused by the arrest.

One major problem that John's fellow Beatles experienced was that John insisted on having Yoko at the Beatles recording sessions. This broke a long-standing agreement that none of them would bring wives or girlfriends to recording sessions.

Yoko has said she was always quietly sitting in a corner of the studio because she didn't want to disturb the others. She said, 'John just wanted me to be with him, and if I wouldn't have accompanied him to the studio, he probably wouldn't have even taken part in the sessions. And albums such as *Abbey Road* or the "White Album" probably would not even have existed.'

Following a road accident in Scotland on 1 July, Yoko ordered Harrods to deliver a double bed to the Olympic Studios in Barnes where the Beatles were recording. She lay in the bed for days on end with a microphone near to her mouth to enable her to make comments while the Beatles were recording.

Even George Martin was annoyed at her presence and was later to say, 'That was a bit difficult to deal with. Suddenly she would appear in the control room. Nobody would say anything to me. I wasn't even introduced to her; she would just sit there. And her influence would be felt. To begin with, everyone was *irritated* by her.'

One observer said that Yoko clung to John 'as if she had been surgically attached'. He added that Yoko knew nothing about music, but kept offering her opinion. Ringo said to John,

'Listen, John, does Yoko have to be there all the time?' John replied, 'You just don't understand. It's different with Yoko and me.'

Some years later Paul was to comment, 'Yoko has since told me that if for any reason she ever sat remotely nearer to me than John, then he would give her hell when he got home.'

On 12 December John appeared on the *Rolling Stones Rock 'n' Roll Circus*. The Stones had invited John to perform, but the omnipresent Yoko had to be part of the deal and this was to be the way it was in all of John's future ventures for the rest of his life. They next appeared in public together on 18 December when they both appeared in a huge white bag at the Alchemical Wedding at the Royal Albert Hall. Yoko said that 'bagism' was inspired by the book *The Little Prince* and its theme, which was: 'The essential is invisible to the eye.'

In January 1969 John and Yoko had meetings with Allen Klein with the view to Klein managing the Beatles. Part of John's decision was tied to the fact that Klein flattered Yoko and promised to organise an exhibition of her work in America. On 2 February Yoko and Tony Cox's divorce was ratified in the Virgin Islands, but it upset Cox because John's lawyers had obtained settlement terms that he wasn't happy with. The court had also granted custody of Kyoko to Yoko, even though Tony had brought her up all of her life.

Klein was appointed Beatles manager, despite the objections of Paul. Klein began a clean-out at Apple, sacking nearly everybody he could. This might have provided some gratification for Yoko as the Apple staff had apparently treated her very badly and had made racist remarks about her. Peter Brown was to write, 'The hostility poured out. To her face they were sarcastic and cold; behind her back they called her the "Jap Flavour of the Month" and made jokes about her vagina being slanted like her eyes.'

However, it was also said that Yoko treated the Apple staff as if they were her servants. One of them reported that Yoko had said, 'There's only rich men and rich men's chauffeurs in this life. John is a rich man and anyone who works for him is his chauffeur. That's how it is.'

John and Yoko then appeared at an experimental concert in Cambridge on March 2.

When Paul and Linda were married on March 12, John and Yoko didn't want to be upstaged and desperately attempted to arrange an immediate marriage themselves. Unable to get married aboard a ship and finding they'd have to wait weeks in either Germany or France, John and Yoko were told they could get hitched straight away in Gibraltar and the marriage took place on March 20, with Yoko commenting, 'We're going to stage many happenings, and this marriage is just one of them.' This was followed immediately by a 'Bed-In for Peace' at the Amsterdam Hilton, with John saying, 'Just suppose we had wanted to go to Capri for a secret honeymoon, like Jackie Kennedy had. The press would have been bound to find out. So we thought we might as well do something constructive with the publicity.'

The Beatles' American fan club sent out a memo to all the area secretaries about the wedding: 'Please try to understand that we should at least give Yoko the same chance we are going to be giving Linda and that Maureen and Patti got! I know this news is shocking, but if it will make John happy, we should all be very enthused too.'

John and Yoko continued to keep a high profile and appeared on *The Eamonn Andrews Show* on April 3, during which they persuaded Andrews to climb into a white bag with them.

On 22 April John changed his name by deed poll to John Ono Lennon and on 26 May the couple began a ten-day bed-in at the Queen Elizabeth Hotel in Montreal. A few days later on 30 May the new Beatles single 'The Ballad Of John and Yoko' was released, and went to the top of the British charts.

The couple continued with their joint artistic ventures, beginning with a film called *Rape,* then announcing 'Nuts for Peace' by sending acorns to world leaders with requests that they plant them for peace. They also suggested that the world leaders could hold their peace talks inside a giant bag.

On 5 May John and Yoko bought Tittenhurst Park, a huge mansion in Ascot, and a few days later their new album *Unfinished Music No. 2: Life With The Lions* was released. During the course of the year they also produced further avant-garde films such as *Self Portrait,* and in September the couple set off for Toronto for the Rock 'n' Roll Revival Concert. John was to say, 'I can't remember when I had such a good time. We did all the old things from the Cavern days in Liverpool. Yoko, who you can say was playing bag, was holding a piece of paper with the words to the songs in front of me. But then she suddenly disappeared into her bag in the middle of the performance and I had to make them up because it's so long since I sang them that I've forgotten most of them. It didn't seem to matter.'

In October 'Cold Turkey' by John Lennon and the Plastic Ono Band was released, in addition to *The Wedding Album*, and in November an album called *Live Peace In Toronto* was issued. On 15 December John and Yoko appeared at a concert at the Lyceum in London for the United Nations Children's Fund, and flew off to Toronto again the next day. During the month they also flew to Aalborn in Denmark to join Tony Cox, his new wife Melinda, and Kyoko.

John and Yoko announced 1970 as 'Year One'. They had their hair cut short and donated the trimmings to Michael Abdul Malik. In January John's erotic lithographs were displayed and during the year the couple became interested in Primal Therapy. On 29 March Yoko announced that she was pregnant again. After spending months in Primal Therapy, John and Yoko created two albums, *John Lennon/Plastic Ono Band* and *Yoko Ono/Plastic Ono Band*. In March of 1971 they visited Japan where John met Yoko's parents for the first time, and in June they joined Frank Zappa and the Mothers of Invention in a performance at the Fillmore East in New York. George Harrison invited John to appear on the Concert For Bangladesh but because he declined to give Yoko a spot on the concert, there was an argument and John didn't appear. In August John and Yoko decided they'd settle in New York permanently, despite the problems John had with the immigration authorities. Initially they became involved with a number of activists such as Abbie Hoffman and Jerry Rubin, appearing at benefits for John Sinclair and for the prisoners at Attica State, and in various protest marches. The two also co-hosted TV's *The Mike Douglas Show*, appeared on *The Dick Cavett Show* and released the album *Sometime in New York City*. They also appeared at the 'One to One' concert and John co-produced Yoko's album *Approximately Infinite Universe*, for which she was backed by Elephant's Memory.

In October 1973 John split from Yoko for 18 months, and left for Los Angeles with a new lover, May Pang. He was to call this period his 'lost weekend'. On 28 November 1974 he appeared on stage at Madison Square Garden with Elton John, and Yoko was present in the audience. In March of the following year John moved back into the Dakota with Yoko and when the two appeared at the Grammy Awards, with John agreeing to be a presenter, he said, 'I thought it would be a good opportunity to kill two birds with one stone. A – to show that sometimes I'm sober and B – that I was back with my wife and that everything was back to normal.'

When Yoko once again became pregnant at the age of 42, she agreed to go ahead with the birth if she and John changed roles. She would become the breadwinner and he the full time mother. 'I must confess I had not wanted a baby. I wanted an abortion, but John would not hear of it,' she told journalist Barbara Graustark.

After her three previous miscarriages, Yoko gave birth to her son Sean Ono Lennon on 9 October 1975, which was also John's 35th birthday. When Yoko went into convulsions during labour the surgeon said to John, 'I've always wanted to shake your hand.' John said, 'Fuck off and save Yoko's life.'

This was the period when John became a real househusband, virtually retired from music (apart from creating some home demos at the Dakota) while Yoko became the businesswoman. In five years she quadrupled their fortune. John also continued his affair with May Pang for approximately 18 months after Sean was born.

During 1977 the Lennon's spent four months in Japan, where they were to return during the summer of 1979. In February 1979 Yoko hired Fred Seaman to be John's personal assistant and he became very close to John for the remainder of his short life. He was to comment about Yoko in January 1980: 'Yoko's behaviour became increasingly weird and was accompanied by a marked deterioration in her physical appearance. Her face was haggard, her eyes glassy, and she began to spend much of her time in the bathroom making loud snorting noises, frequently followed by frightful retching. I realised she was strung out on heroin. On the rare occasions John met Yoko, they circled each other wearily; John would harangue Yoko about her vampire hours and her dishevelled zombie-like appearance.'

Yoko suggested John take a sailing trip to Bermuda in June 1980. Once there, he sent for Sean and his nanny and his assistant Fred Seaman. Seaman had given tapes of new groups such as the Pretenders, Madness, the B52s and Lena Lovitz to John (he called her Lenny Loveritch). He began listening to them in Bermuda and asked Fred to take him to a disco. It was the first time he'd been to one since London. Whilst there he heard the B52s' 'Rock Lobster' and told Fred, 'Jesus, get the axe. And call Mother. She's finally made it. They do her to a t!' John then began writing songs.

Around that time there were several rumours that Yoko was about to divorce John and she was seen frequently with the art dealer Sam Green, with whom she spent a weekend at the end of July. When John decided to record again, Yoko wanted half of the album to comprise her own compositions and the plan to divorce John was dropped.

During the recording sessions, when Yoko kept fluffing her lines, John was reported to have turned to her angrily and shouted, 'Remember the bridge on the River Kwai, you fuck!'

Then came the tragic day, 8 December, when John was assassinated. When the police interviewed Yoko their notes read: (Yoko:) 'Went to Record Plant. Stayed until about 10.30. We wanted to go to restaurant but did not. We came back. We normally go into the gate but did not. Got out, walked past gate. John was walking past the door, he was walking faster. I heard shots. I heard shots. He walked to door upstairs. Said, "I'm shot." I followed him. He was standing but staggering. I told him to lie down. Sometimes he was ahead, sometimes I was. I saw a male by the watchman's box. It was dark and night. He nodded at me – dark greyish clothing. Male, white. He was not small.'

At Roosevelt Hospital, when Yoko was told that John was dead, she said, 'Do you mean that he is sleeping?' When she returned to the Dakota in the company of David Geffen, the record company head who had released *Double Fantasy*, she asked her music manager Rich De Palma to inform John's Aunt Mimi, his son Julian and Paul McCartney of John's death. Elliot Mintz arrived to comfort Yoko and she told him that she had decided to have John cremated at Hartsdale Mortuary.

In the early hours of the morning they received a call from a man in Los Angeles who said that he was flying to New York to finish the job Chapman started. The police caught him at Los Angeles airport and he told them, 'I'm gonna get Yoko Ono.'

Yoko then wrote out a public announcement, requesting that John be remembered by a silent vigil. She wrote:

There is no funeral for John. Later in the week we will set the time for a silent vigil to pray for his soul. We invite you to participate from wherever you are at the time. We thank you for the many flowers sent to John. But in the future, instead of flowers, please consider sending donations in his name to the Spirit Foundation Inc., which is John's personal charitable foundation. He would have appreciated it very much. John loved and prayed for the human race. Please pray the same for him. Love, Yoko & Sean.

On 10 December Yoko released another statement:

I told Sean what happened. I showed him the picture of his father on the cover of the paper and explained the situation. I took Sean to the spot where John lay after he was shot. Sean wanted to know why the person shot John if he liked John. I explained that he was probably a confused person. Sean said we should find out if he was confused or if he really had meant to kill John. I said that was up to the court. He asked what court – a tennis court or a basketball court? That's how Sean used to talk with his father. They were buddies. John would have been proud of Sean if he had heard this. Sean cried later. He also said, "Now Daddy is part of God. I guess when you die you become much more bigger because you're part of everything."

I don't have much more to add to Sean's statement. The silent vigil will take place December 14th at 2pm for ten minutes.

Our thoughts will be with you.

Love, Yoko and Sean.

On January 11 1981 Yoko issued a statement headed 'In Gratitude.' She said that for three months after John's death she could eat only chocolate cake and mushrooms and stayed in bed for most of the time.

In March Yoko began working on her solo album, but the musicians, most of whom had performed on *Double Fantasy* refused to take directions from her. She then hired Phil Spector, but this also didn't work out and she took over the production herself. She called it *Season Of Glass* and it was released on June 8 with a sleeve which pictured John's blood-stained glasses and a track which opened with the sound of gunshots.

In the meantime she had changed the name of their music publishing company from 'Lenono Music' to 'Ono Music By Yoko'. Yoko then became embroiled in a court case with Jack Douglas, who had received no royalties for *Double Fantasy*. In August 1981 she sent out a letter regarding her plans for a Strawberry Fields area in Central Park.

On October 9 of that year she announced, 'October 9 has been proclaimed as International World Peace Day by the Foundation for World Peace. This was endorsed immediately by many organisations around the world. Keep wishing. Wishing is magic. Imagine all the people living life in Peace. Hope and love, Yoko Ono Lennon.'

Over succeeding years Yoko released various albums containing John's works and a number of albums and singles of her own. She published John's book *Skywriting By Word Of Mouth,* and opened up her archives for projects such as the *Imagine: John Lennon* feature film and *The Lost Lennon Tapes* radio series. She also had exhibitions of her own work in different parts of the world, including an exhibition of a dozen John/Yoko films, and selections of her artwork at Riverside Studios in London in March 1990. A few months later, in May, she introduced the tribute concert to John at the Pier Head in Liverpool. A four-CD compilation of previously unreleased material under the title *Lennon* was issued in October 1990 and Yoko accepted a lifetime achievement award on behalf of John at the Grammy Awards in February 1991. Her own CD box set *Onobox* was issued in March 1992.

Yoko also continued with her conceptual happenings and in October 1994 plastered the town of Langenhagen, Germany with 70,000 posters of naked bottoms.

Yoko called a Polydor executive on Monday January 23 1984 to arrange for her and Sean to visit Liverpool. They arrived on Merseyside the next day. She said, 'Sean has never seen

Liverpool and as this is John's birthplace, it is obvious that he had always wanted to come here. It will be an emotional visit, how emotional we can't tell until we have been there. Sean is very excited at seeing his father's birthplace.' Yoko mentioned that Sean had been asking if he could visit Liverpool since the age of three. They went to Strawberry Fields, Menlove Avenue, Penny Lane, Quarry Bank School and the Pier Head. They also visited Mimi who was in Rock Ferry in the Wirral with her sister Anne, due to her illness. Yoko and Sean then went to the Adelphi Hotel for a rest.

In March 1995 an unusual event occurred. Yoko and Sean joined Paul and Linda McCartney, their daughters Heather, Stella and Mary and son James in producing a record together at Paul's home studio. It was a composition by Yoko called 'Hiroshima, It's Always A Beautiful Sky' and she was lead vocalist. Yoko was later to comment, 'Montague and Capulet coming back together was beautiful. It was a healing for our families to come together in this way. That feeling was very special.' Sean was to comment, 'It's the result of our reconciliation after 20 years of bitterness and feuding bullshit. Here were these people who had never actually played together actually making music. It was incredible working with Paul.'

In a December 1998 interview, Yoko said, 'John had a very mature side and that is what kept the Beatles going. He was the leader and he was protective. He was always concerned about Ringo. And he was protective of George. John could see that George was becoming a good songwriter and tried to bring that on. That was something that Paul didn't appreciate.'

Yoko is the executrix of John Lennon's estate, which implies that she makes every effort to maintain John's memory and reputation. Any such position also requires that one doesn't bring the name into disrepute. It could be said that in some ways her position has proved controversial. She allowed John's music, for instance, to be used for TV commercials, something the other members of the Beatles refused to do and which upset his fans. John's son Julian has also considered some of Yoko's actions in licensing and exhibiting 'tacky', and that they have demeaned his father. In November 1993 Yoko organised an exhibition called 'Family Blood Objects' in which she had bronze casts of John's bullet-ridden bloodstained shirt at

$25,000 per cast and replicas of his shattered glasses for $18,000.

In December 1996 Yoko allowed a John Lennon watch to be marketed – only, instead of having a portrait of John, it depicted his bare buttocks. She also took to colouring John's black and white artwork herself.

Yoko's closest aide is Sam Havadtoy, who has been a part of Yoko's life longer than John was. There has always been ambiguity about their relationship although at various times papers have hinted at a marriage.

Open Your Box

The B-side to 'Power to the People', also known as 'Hirake', was credited to Yoko Ono and the Plastic Ono Band. Philip Brodie, then managing director of EMI Records, objected to the original lyrics, saying that they were 'distasteful' and insisting that they be changed. The track then had to be re-recorded.

A spokesman for Apple commented, 'The original lyrics said, "open your trousers, open your skirt, open your legs and open your thighs". The last words in each case, with the consent of John and Yoko, have now been changed to "houses, church, lakes and eyes".'

Apple also claimed that John and Yoko didn't object to the record being censored.

The record was originally due to be released on Friday 5 March 1971, but Yoko had to go into Abbey Road Studios to re-record the vocals on the day before and the record was issued in Britain on Monday 8 March. When 'Power to the People' was issued in America on Monday 22 March, 'Touch Me' had replaced 'Open Your Box' as the flip side.

The reason for the American ban, according to John, was because of the word 'box'. He was to tell the radio interviewer Andy Peebles, ' "Box" in America means something to do with the female anatomy below the waist.'

Other Side of Lennon, The

A Lennon biography, written by the author of *The Marilyn Scandal* and published in Britain in 1990 by Sidgwick & Jackson.

Sandra Shevey interviewed John and Yoko for four and a half hours at the Greenwich Village flat at the beginning of the 70s.

John discussed 'the pain of being a Beatle', living with Cynthia and Yoko, his politics and his music.

When Shevey rediscovered her interview in the 80s, she decided to use it as the basis for a book and set about tracking down and interviewing various people who knew Lennon both in Britain and America. The interviews provide interesting anecdotal background and among the people the author interviewed were Nat Weiss, David Nutter, Eleanor Bron, Virginia Harry, Al Brodax, John Junkin, Walter Shenson, Sid Bernstein and Alan Livingstone.

Generally, Shevey seems unsympathetic towards her subject and reveals nothing startlingly new, although few books about John have contained so many inaccuracies.

Out Of The Blue

Another love song to Yoko featured on the *Mind Games* album.

Oxford Street Maternity Hospital

Situated in Oxford Street, Liverpool, the hospital where John was born in the old main building at 6.30 p.m. on Wednesday 9 October 1940. He had blond hair and weighed seven and a half pounds. His mother Julia was 27 years old and the baby was overdue. She'd been in labour for thirty hours and the medical staff were planning a caesarean operation, but he was born naturally.

Julia's sister, Mimi Smith, received a phone call from the hospital: 'Mrs Lennon has just had a boy.' She ran two miles to Oxford Street.

She recounted, 'There was shrapnel falling and gunfire and when there was a lull I ran into the hospital ward and there was this beautiful little baby. But they had this rough blanket around him and I said immediately, "Take this blanket off his face, it's too rough." '

Her report of the birth may have been slightly blurred over the passage of 25 years when biographers began asking her to recollect events of that night because she claimed that John had been born in the middle of an air raid. The Luftwaffe had been bombing Liverpool in September and the last Luftwaffe raid over Merseyside took place on the night of 22 September. The bombardment didn't resume until 16 October.

This is verified by the *Liverpool Echo* of that date. As the raids took place during the weeks before and after John was born, she can be forgiven for confusing the events, because it was a week before the new baby was brought home and Mimi visited him there every evening and doubtless experienced the turmoil of the air raids. In hindsight, writers claim that at one time a bomb fell directly outside the hospital and, at another, the baby was placed underneath the bed.

Notice of John's birth appeared in the *Liverpool Echo* on Saturday 12 October. It read,

LENNON – October 9, in hospital to JULIA (nee Stanley), wife of ALFRED LENNON, Merchant Navy (at sea), a son – 9 Newcastle Road.

The hospital closed its doors for the very last time on 3 March 1995.

Palmer, Tony

Journalist, author and documentary filmmaker who directed the TV series *All My Loving* and *Cream's Last Concert*. In November 1969 he was asked by John and Yoko to write their biography. He said, 'I was a little sceptical at first but eventually agreed to do it. The catch did not come until I was about to leave. John just popped in the one snag: the proof had to be with the publishers the following Monday. It was then Tuesday.'

Incredibly, Palmer managed to write 75,000 words in a week and rushed the manuscript to the Lennons. Initially they approved it, then Yoko changed her mind and rejected it because she said 'the stars were no longer propitiously aligned'.

Pang, May

John's lover, born in New York of Chinese parents. In 1969, one year after leaving New York City Community College, May Pang became a receptionist at ABKCO Industries (formed by Allen Klein and his wife Betty), where she first met John and Yoko in late 1970. She was then asked to aid John and Yoko during the production of the films *Up Your Legs Forever* and *Fly*. As with ABKCO, she had a myriad duties. For *Up Your Legs Forever* (one of John and Yoko's avant-garde films) she had to phone hundreds of members of New York's arts élite to ask them to display their naked legs. For *Fly*, she had to find a girl who would lie naked for days while flies crawled all over her body. She then became the couple's secretary and general factotum, working for them for three years.

One day in August 1973 Yoko took May aside and told her that she and John were growing apart and suggested that she go to bed with John. 'He likes you a lot,' said Yoko. May was stunned: she said she couldn't possibly sleep with John, who was her employer; but Yoko kept pressing her, saying she was 22 years old and didn't have a boyfriend and that the arrangement would suit everyone.

One of May's duties was to accompany John to the recording studio and, following their next trip there, John told her, 'I'm going to come home with you tonight.' She refused and they were dropped off at their respective destinations. The following night John repeated his desire to go back home with her and once again she refused. The third time he asked, he'd sent the limousine away and they had to share a cab and he insisted on seeing her home. Then he persisted in going up to her room with her and told her that Yoko had told him that she'd fixed it for the two of them to become lovers. They finally went to bed together that night.

From that time on they began their affair with John teaching the sexually inexperienced girl various intense erotic practices. When Yoko told them she was going away for a week to attend a feminist conference in Chicago, John and May began dating openly and on Yoko's return she suggested that the two of them go to Los Angeles for a while.

John had turned 33 when he flew to Los Angeles with May for the period that was later described as his 'lost weekend'. She was now his mistress. They arrived at Los Angeles airport in October 1973 and were met by John's friend Elliot Mintz. John and May initially stayed in the apartment owned by Harold Seider, John's lawyer, but John was to virtually wreck it during a drunken spree. They were then lent a house in Stone Canyon Road, Bel Air, by the record producer Lou Adler.

May also continued to act as John's secretary and helped to organise some of his West Coast recording projects. She was credited as production co-ordinator on the *Rock 'n' Roll* and *Walls and Bridges* albums.

Throughout the entire affair, they had to report all their activities to Yoko and people such as Mintz were also keeping Yoko up to date. Yoko was initially phoning John twice a day, but the calls increased to six a day. After one of them May asked what Yoko was saying. John said she'd just been to a store and told him what she had bought. Another time John told her that Yoko was going out with someone else but wouldn't tell him who it was (the person was a musician, David Spinozza).

However, it also proved a nightmarish time for her because John was involved in many drunken sprees and seemed out of control at times. In one incident he misinterpreted something May said and attempted to strangle her. He seemed to be succeeding until his friend Harry Nilsson pulled him off.

John decided to return to New York and finish off Harry Nilsson's album *Pussy Cats*, which he had been producing. Together with May he settled down in a penthouse at 434 East 52nd Street on Sutton Place – for $750 – a month and even prepared a spare room so that John's first son Julian could visit them there. It was May who had suggested that he see Julian on a more regular basis and, now he wasn't with Yoko, he was able to contact many friends and relatives with whom Yoko had prevented him from being in touch. He resumed regular calls to his Aunt Mimi and got in touch with other members of his family in England, including his half-sister Julia. By December 1974 John was refusing to accept Yoko's calls and he and May were thinking of buying a house.

John had an appointment with Yoko in January 1975, but he didn't return home that night. When May phoned the next morning Yoko wouldn't let her speak to John, saying he was asleep and exhausted after a hypnotic session. She said John was being hypnotised to cure him of his smoking habit. Two more days passed and May still couldn't contact John.

On the Monday they'd had a joint appointment with a dentist and, when May turned up, John was there. There were bags under his red-rimmed eyes and he seemed dazed. After he'd seen the dentist, May took him to their apartment, thinking he was acting like a zombie. He then told her that Yoko had said she would allow him to go back to her. May discovered that the hypnotic sessions were similar to primal therapy (see **Janov, Dr**

Arthur) and she believed that John had been brainwashed. He then said that Yoko knew he still loved May and that she'd allow him to continue seeing her, that Yoko could be the wife and May the mistress.

Yoko then issued a statement saying their separation had failed and they were back together. John's lawyer arranged that May could keep her job within the Apple organisation at a salary of around £10,000 a year and she continued seeing John. When Sean was born John stopped seeing her for two months and then they met again and continued lovemaking.

When Cynthia Lennon (John's first wife) had contacted John to point out that he was ignoring their son Julian, John arranged to travel to Los Angeles again and meet him there. As Julian was still a child, Cynthia had to accompany him. Yoko, not happy at the idea that Cynthia would be there, instructed May to accompany John on the trip. Although Cynthia was supposed to remain in the hotel and not join John, Julian and May, when it came to visiting Disneyland, Julian wouldn't go without his mother, so she joined them on their visit.

She was also invited to a dinner party at the home of Mal Evans's girlfriend Frances Hughes. While there Cynthia made a chance remark that she'd always wanted another child by John. John took this the wrong way and felt it was an invitation for them to get back together and phoned Yoko about it, saying this confirmed Yoko's suspicions that Cynthia was trying to win him back. At this time Yoko was so worried about John being in Cynthia's presence that she was phoning him up to 23 times a day.

When John returned to Yoko, May resettled in New York, where she later became professional manager of United Artists Music.

She was having dinner at a girlfriend's house when the news of John's murder came over the radio. She started screaming and didn't stop for a long time.

Following John's death, she became friendly with Cynthia Lennon and accompanied her on some Beatles conventions.

Her book *Loving You – The Untold Story*, written in collaboration with Henry Edwards, was published in 1983.

May married the record producer Tony Visconti, Mary Hopkins' ex-husband, on Saturday 25 February 1989.

Paperback Writer

A song mainly written by Paul, but John said he helped with the lyrics.

Parkes, Stanley

One of John's elder cousins, born in 1933, the son of Elizabeth 'Mater' Stanley and Charles Parkes. He was seven years older than John, and as a youth used to take him regularly to the cinema, for haircuts and on trips to the park. When Stanley's mother remarried the family moved to Scotland and Stanley used to travel down to London and bring John up to Scotland on the bus. Stanley commented, 'John, cousin Leila and I were very close. From Edinburgh we would bundle into the car and head up to the family croft at Durness. That went on from about the time John was nine years old until he was about 16, and he loved his holidays up there."

They kept in touch throughout the 60s and John bought Stanley a garage, but when John moved to New York there was little contact. However, John did send occasional letters and notes, the last one reading, 'Come on man, send me a postcard! Life is short. Love and Happy New Year. John.'

Parkinson

Parkinson was a popular British BBC TV chat show, hosted by the former journalist Michael Parkinson, which ran for more than a decade. John and Yoko appeared as special guests on the show's fifth edition on Saturday 17 July 1971, which was filmed that afternoon at the BBC Television Centre in Wood Lane, London, ostensibly to discuss Yoko's book *Grapefruit*.

John and Yoko had coaxed an agreement from Parkinson that, if he mentioned the Beatles, he'd have to conduct the rest of the interview from the inside of a black bag!

As they arrived on stage, the Harry Stoneham Five played 'Help!'.

The interview lasted for eighteen minutes, with Parkinson initially admitting that he found Yoko's book incomprehensible.

Here is a transcript of part of the interview:

Parkinson: You've made a film about a fly crawling up a woman's body, you've made your famous *Bottoms* film and there's also been a film made of your penis, isn't there, John?

John: That was a joke really. I made a film called *Self Portrait*, you know, and at that time I was a bit of a prick. (Yoko then read extracts from her book and Parkinson asked about the hostility they'd received from the British press.)

John: The British press actually called her ugly. I've never seen that about any woman or man, even if the person is ugly. You don't normally say that in the papers. She's not ugly, and if she were you wouldn't be so mean! They even say 'attractive' about the most awful-looking people to be kind ...

Parkinson: Recently, another reason for people taking a dislike to you is because you're known, again through the newspapers, as the woman who broke up the Beatles.

John: But that's not true! Listen, I tell ya, people on the streets and kids do not dislike us ... It's the media; I'm telling ya. We go on the streets and the lorry drivers wave. 'Hello, John, hello, Yoko', all that jazz, and I judge it by that. My records still sell well. Her records sell all right.

Parkinson: Did Yoko's presence put tension on the group?

John: The tension was already there you see ... after Brian died.

(Then John suggests that Parkinson get inside the black bag.)

Parkinson: What do you want me in the black bag for, John?

John: Because, then it's total communication if you're in the black bag. Are you going to do that? And then we'll talk about the Beatles.

(Parkinson then crawls inside the black bag and conducts the interview from within it.)

John: Imagine if a coloured guy, or a black guy, went for a job, or that anybody who went for a job at the BBC had to wear a bag, then they wouldn't know what colour people were, and there'd be no prejudice for a kick-off.

Parkinson (beginning to gasp for air): I'll tell you what, they'd fritter away 'cause it's red hot inside this bag! Why did you break up? What were the real reasons?

Yoko: The Beatles are four very talented young men and they're four very strong people, so I don't think I could have tried even to break them up.

John: We broke ourselves up, you know.

(When Parkinson, still inside the black bag, hears that John and Yoko are lighting up a cigarette he shouts:)

Parkinson: I smoke too!

John: When we was twenty-eight or twenty-nine, it began to be, 'What's the goal? You know. We've made it!' We'd become more talented and George began to write more songs. He was lucky to have a track on an album. The personalities have developed. They were a bit stifled in the Beatles. Between us now, we sell ten times more records than the Beatles did. Individually, if you add them all together we're doing far better than we were then.'

(Parkinson is then allowed out of the black bag, fussing about his hair.)

John: Your hair's fine.

Parkinson: One thing, it proves it's not a wig!

John: I never wanted them to slide down and sort of make comebacks and things like that. I said, when I was twenty in the Beatles, that, 'I'm not going to be singing "She Loves You" when I'm thirty! Well, I was thirty this year and I didn't force it to happen. It just happened naturally. I guessed that by the time I was thirty I would have just grown out of it. And I have, you know ...

This interview, for which the couple received a fee of £100, which they asked to be donated to the *Oz* Obscenity Fund, was John's last on a British television show.

Immediately after the interview, the singer Marion Montgomery performed John's song 'Love', backed by the Harry Stoneham Five.

Among the many viewers, were Paul and Linda McCartney, who were watching the show at their home in Cavendish Avenue.

Later guests on *Parkinson* were Ringo and Barbara Starkey, who appeared on the show on Saturday 12 December 1981. Parkinson was also one of the figures featured on Paul's *Band on the Run* album sleeve.

Partridge, Ken

An interior designer whom John hired to redesign Kenwood in Weybridge. He had originally been recommended to Brian Epstein by Epstein's lawyer David Jacobs and, when John noticed what he had done to Brian's apartment at Whadden House, he gave the designer a completely free hand, against Cynthia's wishes. The work began on 17 August 1964 and continued for nine months, and John, Cynthia and Julian were confined to a tiny attic part of their new home. Partridge was later commissioned to decorate Brian Epstein's Surrey mansion. The lavish and expensive designs weren't really suited to the lifestyle they wanted and the family used only a few of the many rooms.

Passover Plot, The

A controversial book by HJ Schonfield. John had read the book and had been impressed by its contents. He brought it up during his interview with Maureen Cleave on 4 March 1966. This was what led to the controversial quotes, initially ignored when they appeared in London's *Evening Standard,* but creating a furore when they appeared in the American teen zine *Datebook* – 'I don't know what will go first – rock 'n' roll or Christianity.'

John was to say, 'I can't express myself very well, that's my whole trouble. I was just saying, in my illiterate way, what I gleaned from HJ Schonfield's book, *The Passover Plot.* It was about how Christ's message had been garbled by disciples and twisted for various selfish reasons by those who followed, to the point where it lost its validity for many today.'

Peace for Christmas

The title of a special charity concert held at London's Lyceum Ballroom in Wellington Street, off the Strand on Monday 15 December 1969 in aid of UNICEF, the United Nations children's charity.

The concert had been reported in the press earlier that month, with claims that the Plastic Ono Band would be appearing. At the time of the announcements John hadn't even been invited to appear, but commented, 'We got back from holiday and kept reading we'd agreed to do it. Anyway, because of the way the public was a bit conned about it, I knew we'd only get the finger pointed at us if we said no. So we'll do it anyway, because it's a good thing and it's in aid of UNICEF.'

John also decided that the concert was a suitable occasion on which to launch John and Yoko's 'War Is Over' campaign and they appeared on stage with what was to be called the Plastic Ono Supergroup, which had been organised within a 48-hour period. Apart from John and Yoko, the supergroup comprised George Harrison (joining John on stage for the first time since 1966), Eric Clapton, Keith Moon, Klaus Voormann, Alan White, Larry 'Legs' Smith, Billy Preston, Bobby Keys, Jim Gordon and the Delaney and Bonnie Band.

Other acts on the bill were the Rascals, the Hot Chocolate Band, Jimmy Cliff, Black Velvet, the Pioneers, Ram Jam Holder, Blue Mink, the TV celebrities Simon Dee and Hughie Green and the actor Richard Harris. The DJ Emperor Rosko acted as compere.

The supergroup had had only brief rehearsals and was the last act to appear that evening. As it turned out, the group simply performed two numbers. The first was 'Cold Turkey', John's latest single, which he announced to the audience with the words, 'We'd like to do a number. This song's about pain.'

John was dressed in a white suit and, as he finished the number, Yoko, who had been sprawled at his feet hidden in a huge white bag, emerged, dressed also in a white suit. She then dominated the next number, which lasted a full twenty minutes. Yoko stood up, took hold of the microphone and shouted, 'John, I love you,' then turned to the audience and screamed, 'You killed Hanratty, you murderers.' Then the band launched into her number 'Don't Worry Kyoko', during which Yoko wailed and screamed. At the end of the number, as the band left the stage, the audience responded only in a shocked silence.

Later, discussing the attitude of the audience, John commented, 'It's only to be expected that some people were disappointed. We play *1984* music. I don't know what they want. I'm trying to get it across that the Plastic Ono Band plays the unexpected. It could be anything. It could be "Blue Suede Shoes" or Beethoven's ninth!

'People should expect something from the Stones or the

Beatles, but with Plastic Ono anything goes. I don't do variety shows any more. I stopped that when I was with the Beatles.'

Reviewing the concert in the *New Musical Express*, the journalist Alan Smith commented, 'Without wishing to be offensive, the physical result was that it gave me one of the worst headaches I've suffered since I don't-know-when.'

The gig was the first official concert appearance John had made in Britain without the Beatles. Part of the show was filmed by Movietone News and the entire concert was recorded by Geoff Emerick, with the aid of two engineers, Peter Bown and John Kurdlander, and eventually included on the double album *Sometime in New York City* in June 1972.

Peace at Last

A book subtitled *The After-Death Experience of John Lennon*. It was written by the clairaudient Jason Leen and published by Illumination Arts Publishing Company in 1989.

Leen maintains that he first encountered John three days after his death and in early March 1981 John asked him to write a book based on the months they had been in contact.

It alleges that when John was shot he sped through a tunnel and heard someone call his name. It was his mother Julia, who told him, 'Oh, John, I have been with you every day for years – if only you could have known. I was to be Mother to you now that I couldn't be on earth.'

The book tells of radiant geometric energy forms, vast legions of stellar beings, entities radiating weaves of crystalline energy. John has come to dwell in an environment full of globes of energy, angelic choruses and great halls and temples.

Peace of Mind

According to Ian MacDonald, author of *Revolution in the Head,* John wrote this number and it was taped around the time the Beatles recorded 'All You Need Is Love', but it was never released.

Peace Ship

A radio station that called for peace in the Arab–Israeli conflict. John and Yoko took out advertisements in support of the ship on 8 November 1968.

Pederson, Ingrid

John Lennon's long-lost half-sister, whom he was fated never to know.

During the period that Freddie Lennon was away from his wife Julia and son John during his pursuit of a career at sea, he literally deserted them both and at one time wrote to Julia giving his blessing for her to date other men.

While working as a waitress in a tearoom in Penny Lane she met a Welsh artillery officer called Taffy Williams from Moreton, Wirral. They had a six-month affair and she became pregnant with his child. The baby was born Victoria Elizabeth Lennon on 19 June 1945 at Elmwood, a Salvation Army Hostel in North Mossley Hill Road, Liverpool.

Williams offered to stay with Julia and bring up the child, but refused to take on John as well. He left her and his name was never entered on the child's birth certificate.

Julia had to reveal her parlous state to her father George Stanley at the end of 1944. He was furious and insisted the baby be adopted.

Julia had also been working as a cinema usherette and developed a friendship with Margaret Mary Pederson, who had married a Norwegian sailor, Peder Pederson, the previous year.

Margaret couldn't have children and, when they heard about the adoption, they jumped at the chance and the Salvation Army arranged for the adoption through their own agency.

They renamed the baby Lillian Ingrid Maria Pederson and for eleven years they lived at 86 The Northern Road, Crosby, L25.

John was unaware of the existence of his half-sister until 1964, when his Aunt Harriet told him about her. John's cousin Stanley Parkes commented, 'He did everything in his power to find her. He wanted to make her part of the family and look after her.'

The daughter was also unaware of the existence of her half-brother until 1966. She never contacted him because she did not wish to upset her adoptive mother. She was to say that she was aware that John had tried to search for her.

In August 1998 she finally revealed her secret, five weeks after the death of her adoptive mother, saying, 'I kept this secret for the sake of my mum. But now she's dead I want to find my real family.'

At the time Ingrid was 53 years old, working as a clerk in a maternity hospital and living in Chandlers Ford, near Eastleigh.

When the story first appeared in the *Sun* in Britain on 15 August 1998, she said, 'Now at last I can admit who I am – the little sis John loved but could never find. I kept all this secret for the sake of my mum.'

Peel, David

A Puerto Rican from Brooklyn (real name David Rosario), who was a street musician in Greenwich Village when he first met John and Yoko in June 1971.

Peel had recorded one of his songs for Elektra Records, 'Have a Marijuana', which sold 75,000 copies. With his band, the Lower East Side, who performed with banjos and fiddles, he sang a series of anarchic songs, condemning police brutality, praising pot, ridiculing establishment figures and damning the war in Vietnam.

Howard Smith of *Village Voice*, together with his girlfriend Sarah Kernochan, had been showing John and Yoko around Greenwich Village on 3 June. They convinced the pair that they should abandon the limousine in which they always drove around and explore the village on foot. It's said that the very first meeting between Peel and John took place in the Limbo Shop, St Mark's Place, while John and Yoko were shopping for clothes. Peel appeared, went up to John and shook hands, saying, 'Hello, my name is David Peel. I work for Elektra Records.' They chatted for a while.

A few days later, Smith engineered another meeting by taking John and Yoko to Washington Square. Peel and his street musicians performed in Washington Square each weekend and always drew large crowds. John and Yoko watched him and were tickled pink when he played 'The Pope Smokes Dope'.

Peel was delighted to hear of the two celebrities in his audience. He said, 'I was shook up. No famous people ever come to see me play. I'm a Beatles freak. I had been brainwashed. I was into that "All You Need Is Love" thing – peace, no matter which way you get it.'

A week later Jerry Rubin – an American radical who had the ear of the Lennons – called Peel and said that John and Yoko wanted him to go to the East Village. Peel brought his guitar with him and they met by the Fillmore East. He said, 'How you doin'?' and started singing 'The Pope Smokes Dope'. John began singing with him, then Yoko, and as they walked down Second Avenue about fifty people joined them and began singing. The police came and told them they had to stop, possibly concerned for the safety of John and Yoko in such a growing crowd. John was delighted – it gave him street credibility. He was to say, 'We got moved on by the police. It was all very wonderful.'

Peel was so thrilled by the experience that he wrote a song called 'The Ballad of John and Yoko', and was invited to the Bank Street studio to play it for them. He then became a regular visitor to Bank Street, where he joined the pair for macrobiotic meals, and John decided that he would record him.

John said, 'We loved his music, and his spirit, and his philosophy of the street. That's why we decided to make a record with him. People say, "Oh, Peel, he can't sing, and he can't play." But David Peel is a natural, and some of his melodies are good.'

John had also written a song about the event, which he called 'New York City', and included on the *Sometime in New York City* album.

John and Yoko recorded Peel's album *The Pope Smokes Dope* in April 1972. Peel commented, 'At Apple the secretaries called me "a fate worse than death". There was no way the album was gonna sell, you know. And Paul [McCartney] got peeved about it. But I didn't care.'

As for the recording of the album, Peel said that John proved to be an excellent producer. 'He had that Phil Spector Wall of Sound down pat, with everything exaggerated.'

The Pope Smokes Dope wasn't issued in Britain. It was released in America on 17 April 1972 on Apple SW 3391. All of the numbers, with the exception of 'The Ballad of New York City', which was written by John and Yoko, were written by Peel.

Tracks were: Side One: 'I'm A Runaway', 'Everybody's Smoking Marijuana', 'F Is Not A Dirty Word', 'The Hippie from New York City', 'McDonald's Farm', 'The Ballad of New York City'; Side Two: 'The Ballad of Bob Dylan', 'The Chicago Conspiracy', 'The Hip Generation', 'I'm Gonna Start Another Riot', 'The Birth Control Blues', 'The Pope Smokes Dope'.

Because of the nature of the songs, there was limited radio

promotion. In an attempt to achieve further radio play, two special promotional singles for disc jockeys were issued – 'F Is Not a Dirty Word' and 'The Ballad of New York City', which was issued on 29 April, and 'Hippie from New York City' and 'The Ballad of Bob Dylan', which was issued on 16 June.

For a time, John and Yoko invited Peel to join them on a number of events. He performed at their John Sinclair rally (see **Sinclair, John**) in Ann Arbor, although he was booed during his performance and commented, 'The place is screaming mad and I'm enjoying every bit of it, because, being on the streets, we're conditioned to the boos. It's all the same to me.' He also joined them on their David Frost and Dick Cavett television appearances and on their Madison Square Garden One-To-One concert.

As it became obvious that John wouldn't be able to tour and, because of the problems relating to his obtaining a green card, Peel saw less of him. He then launched his own record label, Orange Records, and among his releases were 'Bring Back the Beatles' in 1977 and 'John Lennon for President' in 1980. He also occasionally called his band the Lower East Side Ono Band.

Peel continued to perform in New York, moving into small bars, and also began appearing at Beatles conventions on the east coast. In 1987 he issued his own sixty-minute video, *David Peel – Rock 'n' Roll Outlaw*, on which he included a monologue and musical tribute to John.

By the early 90s Peel had begun recording for another label, Helter Skelter Records, based in Rome, and his first project was an album, *Missing in America*, dealing with subjects such as John's murder, AIDS, the homeless and the JF Kennedy assassination.

Peggy Sue

Buddy Holly was one of the Beatles' seminal influences. John recorded this version of the Holly hit on his *Rock 'n' Roll* album. The Quarry Men began performing it in 1957, the year of its original release, with John on lead vocals.

Perdomo, Jose

The doorman who was on duty at the Dakota Building in New York on the night that John was killed. Perdomo said that he felt terrible about having chatted with Lennon's killer while he was waiting for John to come home that night. He asked to be transferred to inside duty after the murder. At one time it was rumoured that he was writing a book about his Dakota experiences with a professional editor, Jo Isenberg.

Perrin, Les
One of the premier music public-relations men in Britain during the 1960s, who included the Rolling Stones among his clients. When John began to feel that no one at Apple loved Yoko and when he began to imagine that everyone around him hated her, he dispensed with the services of Apple's publicist Derek Taylor and employed Perrin to promote himself and Yoko.

Pickup, Ronald
British actor, born in Chester, near Merseyside, who spent a great deal of his youth in the Liverpool area.

He was selected to appear as Me, a character based on John Lennon, in the stage version of *In His Own Write,* which was staged at the Old Vic in June 1968.

Me was the leading character, an antiestablishment figure developed from the material in John's two books. Born on 9 October 1940, Me has the same birthdate as John and is an adolescent who has been influenced by the media, comics and various heroes.

Pickup was able to assume a Scouse accent in the role and recalled that John and Yoko came along to see them when they were rehearsing in an old warehouse. The director Victor Spinetti also took him up to Abbey Road to see John, who was working on the sound effects for the show.

Pilcher, Detective Sergeant Norman
Police officer who was responsible for the drug bust that caused so many problems for John when he attempted to obtain his American green card.

When John and Yoko were staying at Ringo Starr's Montague Square flat, a friendly journalist informed them that there was the possibility of a drugs raid on the premises. John and Yoko had the place cleaned and made sure there were no drugs to be found. Two weeks after the warning, Detective Sergeant Pilcher raided them on 18 October 1968.

Pilcher claimed that an ounce and a half (42.5 grams) of marijuana was found on the premises. John said, 'The thing was a set-up.'

He was later to comment, 'Some of the pop stars had dope in their houses, and some didn't. It didn't matter to him. He planted it. That's what he did to me. He said, "If you cop a plea, I won't get you for obstruction, and I'll let your missus go." '

John agreed to plead guilty if Yoko, who was pregnant at the time, was left out of it.

The police withdrew their charges against Yoko.

At Marylebone Magistrates' Court on 28 November 1968 John was fined £150 with £21 costs and the charge of 'an offence of moral turpitude' was placed on his record, which is what caused him so much difficulty in obtaining a visa for the United States.

Pilcher did attempt to focus on pop stars and raided the Pheasantry in March 1969, trying to capture Eric Clapton on a drug charge, but Clapton wasn't present. The same month Pilcher raided Mick Jagger and Marianne Faithfull's Chelsea house.

On 2 March 1969, the day of Paul and Linda McCartney's wedding, Pilcher raided George and Pattie Harrison's bungalow, Kinfauns, in Esher, Surrey. Although George admitted there were some seeds on the coffee table, he denied all knowledge of a block of hash that Pilcher alleged was found in a cupboard by a police dog.

George said, 'I'm a tidy sort of bloke – I put records in the record rack, tea in the caddy and pot in the pot box. That was the biggest block of hash I'd ever seen.'

Pilcher was eventually jailed for two years on Wednesday 8 November 1972 for 'conspiracy to pervert the course of justice' after being convicted of planting evidence in other cases.

Pill

A song with drugs as its theme, which John wrote and recorded in January 1972 when he was composing numbers for the *Sometime in New York City* album. John made a home demo of the song on his cassette recorder, backed by acoustic guitar, and it mainly comprised a repetition of the words 'you need a special pill to keep you on the line'.

John obviously considered the song wasn't worth pursuing and never performed it in a recording studio.

The demo was eventually aired on *The Lost Lennon Tapes* radio series.

Piper Seminole
Type of small private plane which John and Yoko bought for Sean's fifth birthday at a cost of $150,000. The plane was housed at an airport in Farmingdale, Long Island, and a pilot was hired to fly it.

Placa de John Lennon
A new town square in Barcelona, Spain, which was named in honour of John in May 1993. The square was designated with a brass plaque and a large commemorative record with the words '*Doneu una oportunitat a la pau*', which is the Catalan translation of 'Give peace a chance'.

Plastic Ono Band
The Plastic Ono Band was never intended to be a full-time group, just a concept in which John and Yoko would invite other musicians to join them in recording or live performances.

John was to tell the Radio One disc jockey Andy Peebles, 'Plastic Ono Band was a concept of Yoko's, which is an imaginary band. The first advert was a photograph of some pieces of plastic with a tape recorder and a TV in it. And her idea was a completely robot pop group.'

They were to be launched with a party for the release of the single 'Give Peace a Chance', but John and Yoko had been involved in a car accident in Scotland (see **Lawson Memorial Hospital**) and weren't able to attend the press launch. John said, 'All the press came to meet the band, and the band was on stage, which was just a machine with a camera pointing at them, showing them on stage themselves. So the Plastic Ono Band is a conceptual band that never was. There never had been any members in it, and the advert said, "You are the Plastic Ono Band". So I just want to clear that: it wasn't the re-forming of a new band like Wings or a Hollies, or whatever, where you have a name and you belong to it. There's never been anybody in the band. There are no members.'

A postcard was sent to the press inviting them to the event. It read:

> John and Yoko and Apple Records invite you to join them on Thursday this week, July 3rd to meet the Plastic Ono Band in Chelsea Town Hall, Kings Road.
>
> The Band's first release 'Give Peace A Chance' (on the other side 'Remember Love'), recorded in Montreal, will be performed by the Band and a splendid time is guaranteed for all.
>
> 'Give Peace A Chance' is to be released on Friday, July 4th and it couldn't happen at a better time to a nicer record.
>
> The time: 5.30 p.m.
> The place: Chelsea Town Hall, 169/183 Kings Road
> The date: Thursday July 3rd
> RSVP: Derek Taylor, Apple, Regent 8232.

When John and Yoko received an invitation to appear at a rock 'n' roll festival in Toronto he suddenly had a desire to get a small group together and perform.

The Plastic Ono Band appeared at the event, called *The Toronto Rock 'n' Roll Revival*, in Canada on Saturday 13 September 1969. Discussing how he came to be part of the Toronto event, the bass guitarist Klaus Voormann revealed that he received a phone call at 8 p.m. It was Terry Doran, George Harrison's personal assistant, who told him, 'John and Yoko are going to do a concert in Canada. There's a plane leaving in two hours – be on it.' Klaus, together with the drummer Alan White, rushed to the airport. They waited a long time. No one turned up. So they went home. The next day at 3 p.m. the phone rang again. Doran told him, 'It's all on again – go to the airport.' So he went and waited. Doran had been trying to locate Eric Clapton and finally got him in late evening. Eric had been in bed and wasn't answering the phone. They all met at the airport: Clapton, White, Voormann and John and Yoko.

Continuing with his thoughts on the Toronto trip, Voormann said, 'Apparently John had met some people on his last visit when he did "Give Peace a Chance" who suddenly phoned and asked him to appear at the concert. He said he couldn't because he didn't have a band. They said, "Of course you can, don't worry." So he phoned round everyone he knew and liked working with to see if they were free.

'When John phoned, I was really quite excited and very pleased. It sounded like such a good idea – even though none of us had ever played together on stage before. On the plane going over, we tried to vaguely rehearse. We picked out chords on the guitar – which you couldn't hear because we had no place to plug in – and of course Alan didn't have his drums on the plane with him. So really when we walked out on the stage it was a glorified jam session. John had stood in the dressing room – which was admittedly rather tatty – beforehand saying, "What am I doing here? I could have gone to Brighton." After all it was rather a long way to go for one concert. But the feeling when we all got out on stage and started playing together was truly fantastic.'

When discussing the band in *Disc & Music Echo* in November 1969, Klaus Voormann said,

John is really quite vague about it at the moment. So far there hasn't been any trouble with the recording sessions. Eric and I have always managed to be free when we're required for sessions and it really is a matter of a last-minute phone call from John. Nobody ever plans sessions months ahead. You see, the great thing is, we have no contract to say we are a group. We are just friends playing together. And that is such a marvellous way to work. There's no pressure on us and because of that, much better things get done. In fact, the first thing ever to come out as the Ono band was very nearly a ridiculous jam session we all did at the studios one day when everyone was just fiddling about. I don't know whether John wants to make anything permanent out of it. He didn't set it up with the idea that 'this is a band'. And the last thing anyone wants to see is something like this take on such a steady fixed position that it might split up the Beatles. This way, John can do what he wants to within the confines of the Beatles. Just as he can do his films and his peace thing, just as Paul can record Mary Hopkin and George can record Billy Preston or Jackie Lomax. As things are at the moment, each one of us – John, Eric or myself – are free to do anything we want.

The number 'What's the New Mary Jane', which had been recorded on 14 August 1968 for *The Beatles* double album but not used, was considered as a new Plastic Ono Band single, but John recorded 'Cold Turkey' on 15 September 1969 instead. He'd first offered the number to the Beatles but Paul had allegedly refused to record it, so John decided to issue it as a Plastic Ono Band single.

Further releases included the album *The Plastic Ono Band – Live Peace in Toronto 1969*, which was issued on 12 December 1969; the single 'Instant Karma!' c/w 'Who Has Seen The Wind', which was issued on 6 February 1970; the *John Lennon/Plastic Ono Band* album, which was issued on 11 December 1970; and 'Power to the People' c/w 'Open Your Box', which was issued on 12 March 1971. The single continued the tradition of having a Yoko Ono number on the flip side.

'God Save Us' c/w 'Do the Oz' by the Elastic Oz Band was issued on 16 July 1971; *Imagine*, the album credited to John Lennon and the Plastic Ono Band, with the Flux Fiddlers, was issued on 8 October 1971. The album *Sometime in New York City* saw Side One credited to John and Yoko/Plastic Ono Band with Elephant's Memory plus Invisible Strings and Side Two to the Plastic Ono Supergroup and the Plastic Ono Mothers, and was issued on 15 September 1972. The single 'Happy Xmas (War Is Over)' c/w 'Listen, The Snow Is Falling' was credited to John and Yoko/Plastic Ono Band with the Harlem Community Choir and issued on 24 November 1972. The album *Mind Games* was credited to John Lennon (with the Plastic U.F.Ono Band) and issued on 16 November 1973. The single 'Whatever Gets You Thru the Night', credited to John Lennon with the Plastic Ono Nuclear Band, was issued on 4 October 1974 with the flip side 'Beef Jerky' credited to John Lennon with the Plastic Ono Nuclear Band/Little Big Horns and Booker Table and the Maître D's.

Finally, *Walls and Bridges* was credited to John Lennon (with the Plastic Ono Nuclear Band) and issued on 4 October 1974.

After that, John returned to crediting the work solely in his own name.

Plastic Ono Band – Live Peace in Toronto 1969

Album of the performance by the Plastic Ono Band at the *Rock 'n' Roll Revival* concert, held at the Varsity Stadium, Toronto, on 13 September 1969. Apart from John and Yoko, the other members performing as the Plastic Ono Band were Eric Clapton on lead guitar, Klaus Voormann on bass guitar and Alan White on drums.

Side One of the album featured John performing three rock 'n' roll classics he'd previously recorded with the Beatles, plus two of his own compositions. Side Two comprised two lengthy tracks by Yoko, the first four minutes and twenty seconds in length, the second a full twelve minutes long.

The track listing was: Side One: 'Blue Suede Shoes', 'Money', 'Dizzy Miss Lizzy', 'Yer Blues', 'Cold Turkey', 'Give Peace a Chance'; Side Two: 'Don't Worry Kyoko (Mummy's Only Looking For Her Hand In The Snow)' and 'John John (Let's Hope for Peace)'.

The album was issued in Britain on Apple CORE 2001 on 12 December 1969, but failed to reach the Top 30. It was issued in America on Apple SW 3362 on the same day and reached No. 10 in the charts.

John Kosh designed the album sleeves. Initial purchasers of the album received a bonus – a John and Yoko calendar for 1970, which included songs and poems by John and Yoko, mainly selected from the books *In His Own Write*, *A Spaniard in the Works* and *Grapefruit*.

Playboy Interview John Lennon and Yoko Ono, The (book)

A book originally published by Playboy Press in America and New English Library in Britain in 1981 and republished in America by Berkley Books in 1982. A Japanese version was issued by Sheisha Publishing Co. and a French version called *Les Beatles, Yoko Ono et Moi*, in a translation by Francesca Dandolo, was issued by Editions Generique.

Playboy magazine had been granted the first interview with John for almost five years following his period as a recluse. However, *Newsweek* magazine pipped them to the post with Barbara Graustark's interview (later printed in *Strawberry Fields Forever: John Lennon Remembers*).

David Sheff took three weeks to tape the interviews in September 1980, filling almost twenty hours of taped conversations. He eventually wrote a 20,000-word interview piece for *Playboy*, which proved to be too long for the magazine. An edited version appeared in the issue for January 1981 (coincidentally, with Ringo Starr's wife Barbara Bach on the cover), although it was on the news-stands in early December and was read by John and Yoko on 7 December, the eve of his killing.

There was such an abundance of material on the tapes that over 60,000 words were gathered by Sheff to present in book form.

In the book, John discusses many subjects ranging from his 'lost weekend' period on the west coast and the well-publicised drunkenness at the Troubadour Club to his guilt feelings over his and Yoko's attempts to take Kyoko away from her father. His relationship with Yoko is probed, as is his memory regarding the songs he personally wrote under the Lennon/McCartney banner. He discusses feminism, early influences, being a father and the merits of the individual members of the Beatles. Yoko, of course, also has her say.

The book is illustrated with an eight-page photo insert.

Playground Psychotics

An album by Frank Zappa, issued on Rykodisc RCD 10557/58 in October 1992. The album included part of the recordings made at the Fillmore East when John and Yoko joined Zappa and the Mothers of Invention on stage.

In his sleeve notes, Zappa writes,

Some of you might have heard another version of this material on the John and Yoko album *Sometime in New York City*. When they sat in with us that night we were in the process of recording the *Live at The Fillmore East, June 1971* album, and all of this insanity was captured on tape. After the show, John and I agreed we would each put out our own version of the performance and I gave him a copy of the 16-track master tape. Here is our version – a substantially different mix from what they released.

Zappa changed some of the titles of the songs, listing them as 'Well, Say Please', 'Aaawk, Scumbag' and 'A Small Eternity with Yoko Ono'. He also edited the encore screams.

The tracks recorded with John and Yoko on Disc One of the double album were tracks 22 up to and including 26. Track 22 was 'Well', a 4-minute-43-second version of a number penned by Walter Ward. Track 23 was 'Say Please', a 57-second number with lyrics and music by John, Yoko and Zappa. Track 24 was 'Aaawk', a 2-minute-59-second number with words and music by John, Yoko and Zappa. Track 25 was 'Scumbag', a 5-minute-54-second number with words and music by John, Yoko, Zappa and Kay Lan. Track 26 was 'A Small Eternity with Yoko', a 6-minute-11-second track with words and music by John and Yoko.

Please Don't Ever Change
A number John produced during a session at New York's Record Plant studio on Monday 29 April 1974, with Mick Jagger on lead vocals.

Please Mr Postman
A number penned by Dobbin, Garrett, Garman and Brianbert, which was recorded by the Motown act the Marvelettes. John tackled the lead vocal on the Beatles version of the song, which was recorded on 30 July 1963 and included on the *With the Beatles* album.

Please Please Me (single)
Penned by John, who said that it was his song completely. He was 'trying to do a Roy Orbison' and wrote it in the bedroom of his house in Menlove Avenue. Apart from the inspiration from an Orbison number he'd recently heard, he was also inspired by a Bing Crosby song and said, 'I was always intrigued by the words of "Please Lend Your Little Ears to My Pleas" – a Bing Crosby song. I was always intrigued by the double-use of the word "please". So it was a combination of Bing Crosby and Roy Orbison.'

The Beatles included the number in their repertoire from 1962 to 1964 and first recorded it on 11 September 1962.

The original recording session didn't go down too well as the producer, George Martin, considered that particular version to be too slow and insisted that they record 'How Do You Do It' as their second single. When they demurred he promised them that, if they recorded 'How Do You Do It', they could record another version of 'Please Please Me'. They recorded 'How Do You Do It', but didn't put much effort into it. Martin had told them that the song should be much faster and the group took his advice and recorded their new version on 26 November 1962. Martin was to say, 'I listened. It was great. I told them what beginning and what ending to put on it, and they went into Number Two studio to record. It went beautifully. The whole session was a joy. At the end of it, I pressed the intercom button in the control room and said, "Gentlemen, you've just made your first number-one record." '

The record was released in Britain on 11 February 1963 and topped the charts on 22 February. It was indeed the Beatles' first No. 1 hit.

Capitol Records were offered the record for the American market, but rejected it. Vee Jay Records then issued it on 25 February 1963, but it failed to make any impact. Vee Jay reissued it on 30 January 1964 and it reached No. 3 in the US charts. Vee Jay issued it for a third time on 10 August 1964, but it failed to chart.

Please Please Me (album)

The Beatles' debut album was recorded live on a two-track machine in a marathon recording session lasting just under ten hours on Monday 11 February 1963. The album was released in Britain on 22 March of that year.

Capitol Records refused to release it in America and it was eventually issued on Vee Jay Records as *Introducing the Beatles*, sans the tracks 'Please Please Me' and 'Ask Me Why'. The Beatles' producer, George Martin, said that all they basically did in this lengthy recording session was to repeat their Cavern Club performance.

Discussing the album in *Playboy* magazine, John commented, 'We were just writing songs à la Everly Brothers, à la Buddy Holly, pop songs with no more thought of them than that – to create a sound. And the words were almost irrelevant.' John penned 'Please Please Me', 'Do You Want To Know a Secret?' and 'There's a Place', and co-wrote 'I Saw Her Standing There', 'Misery', 'Ask Me Why', 'Love Me Do' and 'P.S. I Love You' with Paul.

Pobjoy, William Edward

The retired headmaster of Quarry Bank Grammar School. He succeeded ER Taylor and was 35 years old when he took over the headship, which was during the fifth year John Lennon had attended the school, in 1957.

He revealed that 'John was a very talented lad, but from junior school he had taken a delight in mischief. Things were different in those days, and I remember one of the remarks on his report was a complaint from a teacher about John, who had been caught gambling on the cricket field during a house match. Cricket was taken very seriously in those days. I remember that the last thing written on his final report was that he could go far.'

John's friend Pete Shotton contradicts this and says, 'For Mr Pobjoy to claim that he took a special interest in John's development is patently ridiculous. He probably wouldn't have recognised John if he'd passed him on the street. Mr Pobjoy scrawled at the bottom of his last report card, "This boy is bound to fail." '

The actual wording on Mr Pobjoy's reference was, '... he has been a trouble spot for many years in discipline, but has somewhat mended his ways. Requires the sanction of "losing a job" to keep him on the rails. But I believe he is not beyond redemption and he could really turn out a fairly reasonable adult who might go far.' (By 'losing a job', Pobjoy presumably meant that John would need to experience the salutary lesson of getting the sack to make him address his indiscipline.)

Pobjoy was also to say, 'John didn't come my way until I'd been there [Quarry Bank] a month. Eventually he was brought to me as headmaster as a last resort. On that first and one occasion I gave him three strokes of the cane, which was the ordinary thing to do in those days.'

He added, 'When I did cane him on that one occasion, apart from the usual, "This is going to hurt me more than it hurts you", I reasoned with him. But it did not make a lot of difference with John.'

On the other hand, Pete Shotton alleges that the caning incident did not occur. Describing a meeting with Pobjoy following a suspension, he says he told him, 'Well, sir, you told my mother and John's aunt that you tried caning us, and when that didn't work you decided to suspend us from school. But, sir, you never caned us at all!'

He mentioned that Pobjoy was visibly shaken when he told him this.

In an effort to determine what John might be best at, the headmaster asked him what his interests were, in order of priority. John told him, 'Salmon fishing, writing poetry, painting, drawing, poster design and skiffle.'

Pobjoy had been informed of John's misbehaviour and considered he had only two options in dealing with it. One was that he could put John on daily report. This meant that the subject master would write a note about John's behaviour each day and John would have to take it to the headmaster, in order that the headmaster could determine whether John was misbehaving. This strategy enjoyed little success. The other option was to discuss the matter with his guardian, Mimi Smith, which Pobjoy did on a number of occasions.

There is no doubt that the headmaster aided John in securing a place at the art college.

John's Aunt Mimi was called to Quarry Bank for another meeting with Pobjoy. She commented, 'Mr Pobjoy said to me, "Mrs Smith, this boy is an artist, he's a bohemian. If I can get him into the art college, are you prepared to keep him for the next twelve months?" '

She was, and Pobjoy wrote to the principal of the art college on 17 July, the last day of term, requesting that he consider admitting John. As a result John was able to enter Liverpool College of Art without taking an examination.

Pobjoy has also admitted, 'I never thought that Lennon would do anything with his life. He just seemed a total failure. It was obvious that he was a bright lad but he just didn't want to make the effort.'

Polden, Martin

John's defence counsel at Marylebone Court, London, on Thursday 28 November 1968 when John was fined £150 with 20 guineas (£21) costs after pleading guilty to possessing cannabis. Roger Frisby, the prosecutor, accepted Yoko's plea of not guilty. Polden commented '[John] is a public figure, but he stands before you in a private capacity. I hope by accepting that he did make efforts to cleanse himself that you will see the charge in its true perspective.'

Polythene Pam

In early interviews, when commenting on this particular song, John was quoted as saying, 'I wrote this one in India and when I recorded it I used a thick Liverpool accent because it was supposed to be about a mythical Liverpool scrubber dressed up in her jackboots and kilt.'

This has turned out to be a typical Lennon smokescreen. While he undoubtedly wrote the song during his sojourn at Rishikesh, he later revealed that the inspiration for it was based on two separate females.

One was a Liverpool girl who was a Beatles fan. She'd begun attending their local gigs when she was only fourteen in 1961. When they were on gigs out of town they would often give her a lift back home in their van. The girl was nicknamed Polythene Pat at the time because she ate polythene. She had a friend who worked in a polythene factory who used to supply her with the material, which she would then tie into a knot and eat. Her name is Pat Dawson (née Hodgett).

The other inspiration occurred on 8 August 1963 when the Beatles were appearing on the Channel Island of Guernsey. The poet Royston Ellis, who had met the Beatles in Liverpool in 1960, was working on the island at the time, and he and his girl-friend Stephanie invited John back to their flat to stay the night. They'd brought a girl to meet John and she wore polythene. 'She did,' said John, when recalling the origin of the song. 'She didn't wear jackboots or kilts. I just sort of elaborated. Perverted sex in a polythene bag. I was looking for something to write about.'

The girl was reputedly a bondage queen.

The number was originally considered for *The Beatles* double album, but ended up on the *Abbey Road* album as part of a medley. It was initially recorded on Friday 25 July 1969 and on the album it was linked to a number of songs that blended into each other and was preceded by 'You Never Give Me Your Money', 'Sun King' and 'Mr Mustard'. It was followed by a number by Paul called 'She Came In Through the Bathroom Window'. The song by John was 1.08 minutes long while Paul's number was 1:52 minutes in length.

Pop Music Legends: John Lennon

A 128-page book by Bruce W Conord, published by Chelsea House in 1994.

Postage stamps

Numerous countries have issued postage stamps to commemorate John and they have become major collectors' items, not only for philatelists but for the average Lennon fan.

The Maldive Islands issued a 70-laari stamp of John on Thursday May 15 1986.

On 14 April 1988, West Germany issued a set of official stamps, depicting Buddy Holly, Elvis Presley, Jim Morrison and John Lennon. The multicoloured stamps were available for only 180 days from their date of issue.

Gibraltar issued a set of four John Lennon stamps in 1991. The 20p featured him with a tallow flower in his eye. The 30p was an early black-and-white picture. The 40p was a photograph of him wearing coloured glasses. The $1 stamp was a picture of John and Yoko on the runway of Gibraltar airport.

St Vincent issued a souvenir set of nine stamps featuring portraits of John, valued at $1 each.

Antigua and Barbados issued a stamp with a basic portrait of John featured on it and the entire mintage sold out within a week. On the first day of issue, there were queues outside the post offices of people wearing Beatles outfits and carrying guitars. The country's Postmaster Agneta Bleau said the mintage was such a success that they would plan another one.

Azerbaijan issued the first official postage stamp of John to be used in a former Soviet Republic, and received thousands of requests from abroad. The issue of the stamp proved to be front-page news in the local newspapers. The Pacific nation of Palau issued a Lennon stamp as the second issue of a series of universal legends, and the country's Postmaster was able to announce, 'They have passed Elvis in popularity and have become the fastest seller.'

Tanzania issued Lennon stamps in 1995, each one a distinct image of John from different periods of his life. Other countries that have issued John Lennon stamps include Nicaragua, Ghana, Guyana and Mali.

On Friday 8 December 1995 the Inter-Governmental Philatelic Corp. premiered an eight-nation John Lennon series of stamps, known as 'John Lennon World Postal Salute' at a special ceremony at the Hard Rock Café in New York. At the time it was one of the world's biggest postal tributes with an issue of 100,000 stamps from Nicaragua, Guyana, Azerbaijan, Antigua/ Baruba, Palau, Ghana, Mali and the Maldives. Attending the ceremony were Billy J Kramer, Peter Noone and Mary Wilson of the Supremes.

Power to the People

Written immediately after John's interview with Tariq Ali. John was becoming politically aware, and radical viewpoints intrigued him. He began to wear military garb, which gave both him and Yoko the appearance of revolutionaries sporting berets and army jackets with sergeant's stripes.

Tariq Ali was to say, 'John rang me up one day after the interview and said, "Look, I was so excited by the things we talked about that I've written this song for the movement, so you can sing it when you march."

'I said, "This is great!"

'He said, "Well, do you want to hear it?"

'I said, "What do you mean, over the phone?"

'He said, "Well, I won't sing it: I'll just read you the words."

'So he did, and said, "What do you think?"

'I said, "I think it's fine and I'm sure lots of people will be singing it on demonstrations." '

John's initial attempts at recording the single at the end of January 1971 were unsuccessful. The original recording, which included Bobby Keys on sax and a chorus of female gospel singers, didn't work out. A second attempt was also considered unsatisfactory and Phil Spector was brought in to produce it in early February.

Lots of echo was added to Bobby Keys's sax work and Spector turned the small gospel group into a fully fledged choir led by Rosetta Hightower.

An American release of the single pictured John giving a clenched-fist salute while wearing a tin helmet with a Japanese slogan painted on it. The single was issued in Britain on Apple R5892 on Monday 6 March 1972 with 'Open Your Box' as the flip.

'Open Your Box', penned by Yoko and recorded by Yoko Ono and the Plastic Ono Band, originally proved to be too hot for the record company executives, who regarded some of the lyrics as suggestive. They insisted that John and Yoko change various words, and they did this.

The American release on 22 March on Apple 1830 featured 'Touch Me' as the flip.

The single reached No. 7 in the British charts and No. 8 in the States and was to sell over a million copies.

The song was included on the *Shaved Fish* album and John and Yoko performed it on stage at the John Sinclair Benefit in 1971 (see **Sinclair, John**).

In later years, John expressed his disappointment at the song. Discussing it with David Sheff during his *Playboy* interviews, John said, 'It didn't really come off. I was not thinking clearly about it. It was written in the state of being asleep and wanting to be loved by Tariq Ali and his ilk.'

Preludin

A type of German slimming pill. It was readily available in the pharmacy shops in Hamburg when the Beatles arrived there in 1960. Containing high amphetamine content, the tablets could act as pep pills if the recommended dose were exceeded. Several of the tablets, when swallowed, would produce a pretty good high. Together with a similar tablet called Captogen, the 'Prellies' were a common pep pill for British musicians in Hamburg.

John was well known for his use of the tablets and on the wall of photographs behind the Star Club bar was a picture of John, together with a blow-up of a Preludin packet and the words, 'JOHN LENNON, KING OF PRELO'.

Presley, Elvis

Presley was one of the major seminal influences on the young John, causing his Aunt Mimi to say, 'It was Elvis Presley, Elvis Presley, Elvis Presley. In the end I said, "Elvis Presley's all very well, John, but I don't want him for breakfast, dinner and tea." '

During their early career, the Beatles included in their repertoire several of the tracks Elvis had recorded. John performed 'Hound Dog', 'Jailhouse Rock', 'Blue Suede Shoes' and 'I'm

Gonna Sit Right Down and Cry (Over You)', while Paul performed 'All Shook Up', 'Blue Moon of Kentucky' and 'That's All Right (Mama)'. Stuart Sutcliffe performed 'Love Me Tender'.

While in Las Vegas, Presley issued a statement on the arrival of the Beatles in the States: 'If there's nothing but catfish in the market not many will come and buy. If there are several kinds of fish it draws a bigger crowd and that's good for show business.'

When John heard this, he said, 'I'll have a pint of what Elvis is on, please.'

On their appearance on *The Ed Sullivan Show*, the Beatles' press agent Brian Somerville handed them a telegram:

CONGRATULATIONS ON YOUR APPEARANCE ON THE ED SULLIVAN SHOW AND YOUR VISIT TO AMERICA STOP WE HOPE YOUR ENGAGEMENT WILL BE A SUCCESSFUL ONE AND YOUR VISIT PLEASANT STOP GIVE OUR BEST TO MR SULLIVAN STOP SINCERELY ELVIS AND THE COLONEL.

Sullivan read out the congratulatory telegram on the show. However, Presley's manager, Colonel Tom Parker, had sent this and Presley didn't know anything about it.

The historic meeting between the Beatles and Elvis Presley took place during the evening of Friday 27 August 1965 and had been arranged by Chris Hutchins, a journalist with the *New Musical Express*.

It had been agreed that the meeting could go ahead after they made a deal with Hutchins that there would be no pictures, no taping and no leaking of any details in advance.

John had told the Beatles' PR man, Tony Barrow, 'If we do go to Elvis, I'd prefer it to be just the five of us, not even Brian, not even you. If both sides start lining up teams of supporters it will be like a contest to see who can field the most players.'

However, since Colonel Parker would be present, then Brian Epstein would have to be there. Since Presley would have his minders – the Memphis Mafia – with him, the Beatles' road managers Neil Aspinall and Mal Evans had to be there. As Hutchins was invited, Tony Barrow had to be there to keep an eye on him.

'Let's stop there or it'll get out of control,' said John.

Hutchins joined Brian Epstein and Presley's manager Colonel Tom Parker in a car driven by Tom Diskin and they drove to the house at 2850 Benedict Canyon, where the Beatles were staying. Neil Aspinall, Mal Evans and Tony Barrow then got into a limousine driven by Alf Bicknell and they drove to Elvis's house at 565 Perugia Way in Bel Air, arriving after 10 o'clock in the evening.

Elvis was standing in the doorway as their limousine pulled up, wearing a red shirt and pale-grey trousers. They were all ushered inside to an enormous circular room where around twenty more people were gathered – road managers, their wives, girlfriends and children. They included the Memphis Mafia of Joe Esposito, Marty Lacker, Billy Smith, Jerry Schilling, Alan Fortas and Sonny West. The room was bathed in red and blue light.

Pricilla Presley joined them. She had her black hair styled in a bouffant and was wearing a sequinned minidress.

When he saw Elvis, John put on an Inspector Clouseau voice, saying 'Oh, zere you are!'

The Beatles were invited to sit on a large settee with Elvis, although everyone seemed nervous and no one spoke. Finally, Elvis said, 'If you guys are just gonna sit there and stare at me, I'm going to bed. Let's call it a night, right, Cilla? I didn't mean for this to be like the subjects calling on the King. I just thought we'd sit and talk about music and maybe jam a little'

That broke the silence.

John told him, 'When the fans went for you, you were up there all alone. With us, it's four against everybody and we can draw support from each other.'

The Colonel and Joe Esposito had set up a roulette wheel and Epstein joined them. Aspinall and Evans drifted over to the bar and started to chat with the Memphis Mafia.

After some conversation, Elvis decided they should have a jam and electric guitars were produced and plugged into amplifiers. Elvis took up the bass guitar; John and George were on rhythm and Paul was on piano.

'Sorry there's no drum kit for you – we left that back in Memphis,' Elvis said to Ringo.

'That's OK,' Ringo said. 'I'd rather play pool.'

John drifted into his Inspector Clouseau voice again, saying, 'Zis is ze way it should be ... ze small 'omely gathering wiz a few friends and a leetle music.'

They began playing along to Elvis records on the jukebox, and Elvis also led them on 'I Feel Fine'.

John asked Elvis, 'Why do you do all these soft-centred ballads nowadays? What happened to the good old rock 'n' roll? When are you doing the next film? How long is it since you were in Memphis?'

Elvis said, 'Listen, just because I'm stuck with some movie soundtracks doesn't mean I can't do rock 'n' roll no more. I might just get around to cutting a few sides and knocking you off the top. But I'm making movies at a million bucks a time and one of them – I won't say which one – took only fifteen days to complete.'

John said, 'Well, we've got an hour to spare now. Let's make an epic together.'

It was obvious that Presley was getting tense about Lennon's remarks and the staunchly patriotic singer was aware of John's anti-Vietnam war stance.

Hutchins, who had been creeping to the bathroom to take notes, heard Elvis go over to West and Fortas and say, 'Someone ought to talk to the FBI about that sonovabitch.'

The meeting had lasted for three hours and, as they were about to leave, the Colonel handed everyone a set of Elvis's albums as a souvenir.

At the front door Elvis said, 'Don't forget to come and see us again in Memphis if you're ever in Tennessee.'

Despite the edgy aspect of his personal conversations with Elvis, the next day John told the press, 'There's only one person in the United States of America that we ever wanted to meet – not that he wanted to meet us! And we met him last night. We can't tell you how we felt. We just idolised him so much. The only person we wanted to meet in the USA was Elvis Presley. We can't tell you what a thrill that was.'

A few months after his meeting with the Beatles, Elvis issued a statement, probably at the urging of the Colonel:

People have said my absence from personal appearances has given the Beatles their big opportunities. I know nothing about that. As for the Beatles, all I can say is – more power to them. I have watched all their television appearances over here. I don't think I should say what I feel about them. It wouldn't be fair to fellow entertainers.

I'll say the Beatles have got what it takes and in great abundance and that they've been given a heck of a vote of confidence. I'm sorry, but I have to be diplomatic and I'm honest about it. They are entertainers like myself and I guess they're as dedicated as the rest of us. Which, in the long run, is all that matters. I wish them luck.

When John read it, he said, 'I'm not sure who's the biggest bullshitter – him, or me!'

Chris Hutchins was to say, 'It was a splendid house in Bel Air, but the meeting was tense. John Lennon didn't want to be there; Paul was never the diplomat; George looked bored; and Ringo played snooker with the Memphis Mafia. "Be sure to tell the fans they had a great night together," the Colonel called to me as we got in the limousine for the drive back to the LA house the Beatles had rented. "Tell 'em the truth – it was crap," said John Lennon.

'Elvis was always pleasant but never forgot that I was the one who took the Beatles to his house for the meeting from which he ended up hating "the Beatle that bit" – John Lennon.'

When Brian Epstein died in 1967, a message from Elvis was delivered offering 'deepest condolences on the loss of a good friend to you and all of us'. It was obvious that it was really the diplomatic Colonel who had sent it.

Elvis began to believe that the Beatles were anti-American and would have a detrimental effect on the youth of America. He began to concentrate on listening to the lyrics of every Beatles record that was released, studying them to detect if they contained any anti-American propaganda.

He believed they included coded messages in their lyrics and was convinced – as were many people, in truth – that 'Lucy in the Sky with Diamonds' was about LSD.

When discussing the sleeve of the *Sergeant Pepper* album, Paul had said, 'We want all our heroes together here. If we believe this is a very special album for us, we should have a lot of people who are special to us on the sleeve with us.'

Elvis noticed he wasn't represented, but he did spot the figure of Karl Marx, which seemed proof enough to him that the Beatles had leanings towards communism.

When the Charles Manson murders took place on 9 and 10 August 1969, Elvis was to note the Beatles-inspired messages at the crime scenes – the bloody words 'Helter Skelter' and 'Death to Pigs'. His suspicions seemed justified when, at Manson's trial, Manson admitted that he'd been inspired by *The Beatles* (the 'White Album'), which he believed had contained secret messages to him.

Elvis told President Nixon on 21 December 1970 in the Oval office, 'The Beatles, I think, are kind of anti-American. They came over here, made a lot of money, and then went back to England. And they said some anti-American stuff when they got back.'

On New Year's Day 1970 Elvis visited the FBI offices in Washington to pursue his grudge against John. J Edgar Hoover ordered a confidential report on Elvis's visit to the FBI HQ. It was prepared by MA Jones and sent to Hoover on 4 January 1971. Part of the report read, 'Presley indicated that he is of the opinion that the Beatles laid the groundwork for many of the problems we are having with young people with their filthy, unkempt appearances and suggestive music while entertaining in this country during the early and middle 1960s.'

Hoover read the report and immediately wrote to Elvis thanking him. He then ordered a review of all FBI files concerning John Lennon.

At a press conference in Atlanta, Georgia, in 1965, when asked, 'What do you think of Elvis Presley?' John answered, 'We liked his early stuff, but he's got a bit middle-aged, hasn't he?'

On Saturday 13 August 1977, from the Hotel Okura in Tokyo, when he heard of Elvis's death John issued a short statement: 'Nothing really affected me until Elvis.'

At a press conference at the same hotel on Tuesday 4 October 1977, when he was asked about the death of the King, John replied, 'Elvis died when he went into the army. Up until he joined the army, I thought it was beautiful music, and Elvis was for me and my generation what the Beatles were to the sixties. I basically became a musician because of Elvis Presley. I never did concerts to influence people. I did them for many reasons, and since 1966 I have not performed for money, only charity.'

People's Almanac, The

An American book published in 1975 and compiled by the writer Irving Wallace and his son David Wallechinsky.

The publication, which was a bestseller, gathered lists of facts and opinions on a variety of subjects. One section was called 'Exclusive Symposium on Utopia'. The authors had sent a series of questions to nine famous individuals to poll their opinions on their personal visions of Utopia.

The individuals petitioned included the designer Buckmister Fuller Jr, the singer Eartha Kitt, the author Monty Hall, the child psychologist and paediatrician Dr Benjamin Spock, the sociologist Desmond Morris and John Lennon.

John completed a questionnaire whose brief queries concerned distribution of goods, education, family life and such. John's replies, in the main, comprised one or two words. To the question 'How would a government be organised?' he replied, 'Toss a coin.'

Production

John acted as record producer on a number of projects. They included the single 'You've Got To Hide Your Love Away' by the Silkie; the album *Yoko Ono/Plastic Ono Band*; the single 'God Save Us/Do the Oz' by Bill Elliot and the Elastic Oz Band; the album *Fly*, with Yoko Ono and The Plastic Ono Band; the album *The Pope Smokes Dope* by David Peel and the Lower East Side; the album *Elephant's Memory* by Elephant's Memory; the album *Approximate Infinite Universe* by Yoko Ono; and the album *Pussy Cats* by Harry Nilsson.

Pseudonyms

John loved to make up wacky names, which is apparent in his books *In His Own Write* and *A Spaniard in the Works*.

The first time the Beatles used pseudonyms was in 1960 on their short tour of Scotland. Paul called himself Paul Ramon (which, it is said, was the inspiration many years later for the American band, the Ramones). George called himself Carl Harrison and Stuart Sutcliffe adopted the name Stu de Stijl. It was reported that John called himself Johnny Silver, but he denied this.

Once he'd become internationally famous, John often used the alias John Green when travelling, but his most frequent use of the pseudonym was in recording credits.

For the record 'Scared' he used the name Mel Torment, an obvious 'fractured English' variation of Mel Tormé.

John O'Cean, which he used for his contribution to Yoko Ono's 1973 *Feeling the Space* album, when he played guitar on the tracks 'She Hits Back' and 'Woman Power', was obviously inspired by the English translation of her name: Ocean Child.

Dr Winston O'Boogie was used on the *Mind Games* album; and, on his following LP *Walls and Bridges,* some printed comments by Dr Winston O'Boogie were to appear, and John did a mock interview with himself for *Interview* magazine, using that name.

He liked using his real middle name, Winston. On his 'Steel and Glass' track he was credited as Mr Winston O'Reggae, and another of his variations was Dr Winston and Booker Table and The Maitre D's, an obvious pun on Booker T and The MGs, and he used this name on the 'Beef Jerky' track on the *Walls and Bridges* album.

Reverend Thumbs Ghurkin was used on his song, 'Old Dirt Road' and Reverend Fred Ghurkin was another example of his fascination with the title 'Reverend', this time one of his pseudonyms on the *Walls and Bridges* album. He was also to use this name when he travelled abroad with Yoko, booking into some hotels as the Reverend Fred and Ada Ghurkin.

Captain Kundalini was the name he credited himself with on the track 'What You Got' on his 1974 album *Walls and Bridges*. Kundalini is an Eastern term referring to the latent power personified by an invisible serpent within the human body. Its arousal and journey through the spine is said to spark off transcendental awareness or cosmic consciousness.

Dr Dream was the pseudonym he used on the track 'No. 9 Dream' on the *Walls and Bridges* album.

Dwarf McDougal was the name John used for the track 'Nobody Loves You When You're Down and Out' on the *Walls and Bridges* album. John's pseudonyms were not necessarily arbitrary choices. Some of them were created as in-jokes. In this case, the 'Dwarf' probably relates to the name of Bob Dylan's publishing company and 'McDougal' is the name of a street in

Greenwich Village which saw the birth of the US folk music scene.

Public Ear, The

A BBC radio series broadcast on the Light Programme (which became Radio 2).

George and Ringo had appeared on the show in January 1964 and the edition broadcast on Sunday 22 March 1964 at 3 p.m. provided John with a good plug for his book *In His Own Write*. This particular Beatles contribution was recorded at Twickenham Studios on Wednesday 18 March and had George assuming a posh accent while he discussed *In His Own Write*: 'It's a laugh-a-minute with John Lennon. Some of you might have found it a bit difficult to understand because, you see, it's in a sort of funny lingo … I don't really know how you could describe it but it's sort of rubbish! Maybe that's one way.'

George then talked about the book with Ringo and John. John then read one of his pieces from the book, 'Alec Speaking'.

Pussy Cats

An album recorded by Harry Nilsson and produced by John. John recalled that when he was in a drunken stupor he promised Harry Nilsson that he'd produce his new album for him. Because of recent large hotel bills, John decided it would make financial sense to lease a house for himself and his friends for the period covering the recording sessions. He rented a big old house on the Santa Monica beach, No. 625 Pacific Coast Highway, where Marilyn Monroe had held her trysts with Jack and Bobby Kennedy.

He commented, 'I thought, Get them all in one house and they'll behave themselves.' This didn't quite work out. With people such as Lennon, Nilsson, Keith Moon and Ringo in the same house, they were boozing and having fun all the time and drinking while recording. In a BBC radio interview in 1980, John said, 'So I ran away to New York with the "Harry Tapes". I didn't steal them. I said, "Harry, get the hell out, I want to finish this record!" '

Recording began at the Record Plant West in April 1974, although Harry had written only four songs for the album. John gave him a number called 'Mucho Mungo', and numerous musicians joined them in the studio, where various other tracks emerged from a series of jam sessions. The basic line-up comprised Nilsson, Starr, Moon, Klaus Voormann and Jim Keltner, although other musicians included Jesse Ed Davis (guitar), Danny Kootch (guitar), Sneaky Pete (pedal steel guitar), Bobby Keys (sax) and Ken Ascher (piano).

Derek Taylor, who penned the sleeve notes, wrote, 'Most of what Harry and John said and did was bloody funny and sometimes terrifying. They have been living a vampire timetable recently ... they are madmen in tandem.'

Pussy Cats was issued in America on RCA CPL 1-0570 on 19 August 1974 and in Britain on RCA APL 1-0570 on 30 August 1974. The tracks were: Side One: 'Many Rivers to Cross', 'Subterranean Homesick Blues', 'Don't Forget Me', 'All My Life', 'Old Forgotten Soldier'; Side Two: 'Save the Last Dance for Me', 'Mucho Mungo/Mt Etna', 'Loop De Loop', 'Black Sails', '(We're Gonna) Rock Around the Clock'.

The opening track, 'Many Rivers To Cross', was a Jimmy Cliff number and the songs written by Nilsson were 'Don't Forget Me', 'All My Life', 'Old Forgotten Soldier' and 'Black Sails'. John's composition 'Mucho Mungo' was segued into a folk number 'Mt Etna', which had been adapted by Nilsson. 'Subterranean Homesick Blues' was the Bob Dylan song and the Drifters' hit 'Save the Last Dance For Me' was played at a very slow pace.

Edsel Records issued a CD version of the album in Britain in 1992 and a digitally remastered version was issued in America by BMG's Buddha midline label on June 15 1999. This release included five previously unreleased bonus tracks.

Quarry Bank School

A school in Harthill Road, Allerton, Liverpool L18. It was founded in 1922. The first headmaster, ironically, was a George Harrison. Former pupils had included the Labour ministers Peter Shore and Bill Rodgers; later pupils included the horror writer Clive Barker and Douglas Bradley (Pinhead in the *Hellraiser* movies). The most famous pupil was undoubtedly John Lennon, who began to attend Quarry Bank in 1952, five years after it had become a grammar school. The school motto was: *Ex hoc metallo uirtutem.*

When he enrolled at the school in September 1952 he recalled, 'I looked at all the hundreds of new kids and thought, Christ, I'll have to fight my way through all this lot.'

His academic record was not one he could be proud of and he was noted for the antics he took part in with his best friend, Pete Shotton. His third-year report read: 'Hopeless. Rather a clown in class. A shocking report. He is wasting other pupils' time.'

An incoming headmaster, William Pobjoy, reputedly took an interest in the rebellious pupil and, although his exam results were disastrous, John was able to find a place at Liverpool College of Art, with Pobjoy's recommendation. It was while at Quarry Bank that John formed his first outfit, the Quarry Men.

He left in 1957, having failed the O-level examinations that he sat for in June 1957.

With the demise of grammar schools and the advent of the comprehensive, the name was changed to Calderstones Community Comprehensive School – Quarry Bank Wing.

Quarry Men

The Quarry Men originally formed in late September 1956, originally without a name. They initially comprised John Lennon, his friend Pete Shotton – who'd constructed a tea-chest bass using an old broom handle and a piece of string – and Bill Smith on washboard. Eric Griffiths next joined them on guitar. Rod Davis then came in on banjo followed by Colin Hanton on drums. However, by October 1956 they dispensed with Smith's services because he never seemed to turn up for rehearsals, and replaced him with Len Garry. Occasionally, another friend, Ivan Vaughan, would stand in on tea-chest bass.

There is some dispute as to whether the initial name, albeit for only a week or so, was the Black Jacks. Rod Davis and Len Garry remember the name; Pete Shotton disagrees, although Nigel Walley recalls the name the Black Jacks was used for a very short time. That name was said to have been inspired by their stage outfits, which were simply black jeans and white shirts. Pete also says he formed the group with John, while Eric Griffiths disputes this, saying that both he and John went to a guitar teacher in Hunts Cross with the intention of learning to play and then forming a group – although they had only one or two lessons.

Shotton says he named the group the Quarry Men because of the school song, which contained the words 'Quarrymen, strong before our birth, straining each muscle and sinew'.

Lonnie Donegan was their inspiration and they began with a repertoire of skiffle songs such as 'Rock Island Line', 'Puttin' On the Style', 'Cumberland Gap', and 'Maggie May'. They were soon also including Elvis Presley numbers such as 'Blue Moon of Kentucky', 'All Shook Up', 'I'm Left, You're Right, She's Gone' and 'Baby Let's Play House', in addition to numbers such as 'Come Go With Me'.

There was only one microphone and, as it was John's group, he was the one who got it.

They learned the words to songs by listening to them on the radio and scribbling down the words, or going into a record booth and writing out the words until they got thrown out of the record store.

Using this method often resulted in wrong words being used. Commenting on this system of learning songs, Davis says, 'John would fill in the missing words and that's how we got the bit about the penitentiary in "Come Go With Me", which scanned and fitted in with the themes of skiffle songs. I remember his rewriting "Streamline Train" as "Long Black Train", but he didn't make lyrics up on the hoof.'

The group initially played at friends' parties and in skiffle contests, and, when Nigel was appointed manager by John, he arranged their gig at Lee Park Golf Club, which led to their first Cavern booking on 7 August 1957. Nigel also confirms that the name was always split into two words – Quarry Men – and not as later writers put it, as one word (the group's business card, drums and local adverts at the time, as well as the photograph at the village fête clearly show Quarry Men as two words).

The group appeared at the Empire Theatre, Liverpool, on Sunday 9 June 1957 in the heat of a talent show called *TV Star Search* hosted by Carroll Levis, but were unsuccessful. Later that same month they appeared at a street party in Roseberry Street. This took place on Saturday 22 June and came by way of Colin Hanton's friend Charles Roberts, whose mother Marjorie organised the event. The group performed on the back of a lorry and later had to flee into the Roberts's house when some thugs threatened to beat them up – and they were specifically threatening to John.

Their most important date took place at St Peter's Parish Church, Woolton, garden fête on Saturday 6 July 1957 when Ivan Vaughan brought Paul McCartney along to meet John. Although McCartney had been asked to join the group, when they made their Cavern debut on Wednesday 7 August, Paul was away at camp. The Cavern at this time was strictly a jazz club and skiffle groups were often booked as support acts on the understanding that rock 'n' roll was banned. However, following a performance of 'Come Go With Me', John decided to introduce some Elvis Presley numbers and performed 'Hound Dog' and 'Blue Suede Shoes', which upset the club owner, Alan

Sytner, who sent the Quarry Men a note on stage stating, 'Cut out the bloody rock!'

At a Quarry Men booking at New Clubmoor Hall on Friday 18 October, Paul McCartney made his debut with the band. They comprised John on rhythm guitar, Len Garry on tea-chest bass, Eric Griffiths on guitar and Colin Hanton on drums – and, since the venue had a piano, they invited John 'Duff' Lowe to join them (Pete Shotton and Rod Davis had left the group by this time).

Their manager Nigel Walley had arranged the booking. Nigel had suggested that they all wear large check shirts to project a country-and-western image, while John and Paul were to wear white coats. This was to be the first time that John and Paul appeared on stage together, with Paul playing a Zenith guitar and singing on numbers such as 'Twenty Flight Rock', 'Long Tall Sally' and 'Be-Bop-A-Lula'. Paul was due to play a guitar solo called 'Guitar Boogie'. This would have been difficult for him as, being left-handed, he'd had to string his instrument for a left-handed player, but the plectrum guard remained affixed above the sixth string, which caused problems. Halfway through playing the instrumental, Paul began to make mistakes and John brought the number to a halt, saying, 'He's our new boy. He'll be all right given time.'

A series of gigs at Wilson Hall in Garston followed, a venue run by a popular promoter called Charlie McBain, who also booked the group at New Clubmoor Hall.

Paul's second gig with the Quarry Men took place at Wilson Hall, Garston, on Thursday 7 November 1957.

On November 16 they appeared at the Stanley Abattoir Social Club and returned to New Clubmoor Hall on Saturday 23 November.

Another Saturday evening booking at Wilson Hall followed on 7 December. The group began their performance with Paul singing 'Twenty Flight Rock' and John followed with 'That'll Be the Day'. Their first session went well and Paul was able to cope on his 'Guitar Boogie' solo. Their second set went well and they were ready to leave, although they were apprehensive that two local toughs, Rodney Johnson and George Wilson, might be seeking them out. They all left to catch buses to their individual destinations and John and Pete went together, carrying the tea-chest bass. They were heading towards the bus stop when they noticed Johnson and Wilson, so they left the tea chest in the road and jumped on a bus. To their horror they found that the two toughs had also run after the bus and caught it at the next stop. They were mainly after John, but came on the top deck and began to hit Pete. John ran downstairs and the two lads ran after him and jumped off the bus. Pete went down expecting to see John battling with them on the pavement, but John had hidden himself away on the lower deck and escaped their attention. The tea-chest bass had remained at the side of the road for days and became weather-beaten, but Ivan Vaughan and Len Garry retrieved it and Ivan repaired it.

The Quarry Men began 1958 with a further appearance at New Clubmoor Hall on Friday 10 January. They had one further gig that month, a return to the Cavern Club on Friday 24 January. On Thursday 6 February they appeared at Wilson Hall, where George Harrison, then fourteen years old, was invited along to watch them.

Thursday 13 March saw the opening of the Morgue, a tiny cellar club in Broadgreen, run by Alan Caldwell, later to become the legendary Rory Storm. This was the night it was said that George played 'Raunchy' for them, a brief audition which resulted in his joining the band. They were to make a couple of appearances at the venue. Their final date of the year came through George as they were booked to appear at the wedding reception for George's brother Harry and his bride Irene McCann and performed at the Harrison household at 25 Upton Green, Speke, on Saturday 20 December.

During the summer of 1958 they made a record at a small recording studio at 53 Kensington in Liverpool, run by Percy Phillips. Johnny Guitar and Paul Murphy of Rory Storm's band had gone there earlier to record the number 'Butterfly'. John, Paul, George, John Lowe and Colin Hanton were the Quarry Men appearing at the session during which they recorded two numbers, 'That'll Be the Day', the Buddy Holly number, with John on lead vocal, and 'In Spite of All the Danger', a song written by Paul and George, and credited as such, although Paul was later to state that it was really his composition. They clubbed together to buy a single two-sided shellac disc and Phillips wiped the tape over afterwards.

That one copy ended up in the hands of Lowe, who kept it for decades. Paul bought it from Lowe in 1981 and commented, 'It says on the label that it was me and George but I think it was written by me, and George played the guitar solo. It was my song. It's very similar to an Elvis song.

'I remember we went down on the bus with our instruments and waited in the little room outside while somebody else made their demo, and then it was our turn. We just went into the room, hardly saw the engineer because he was next door in a control booth. We ran through it very quickly and it was all over.

'John did "That'll Be the Day", which was one of our stage numbers. George played the opening guitar notes and I harmonised with John singing lead.'

Their first gig of the new year was also via the Harrisons with the Quarry Men being booked at Wilson Hall on Thursday 1 January 1959 by George's father Harry for a party in aid of the Speke Bus Depot Social Club. The Bus Depot party was supposed to lead to a series of gigs at the Pavilion Theatre as Harrison Snr had talked the manager of the theatre into coming along to listen to them. They got drunk in the interval, had a disastrous show in the second half and blew their chances of appearing at the Pavilion. After an argument on the bus home, a frustrated Colin Hanton left the group, never to return.

The Quarry Men appeared at Woolton Village Club in Allerton Road on Saturday 24 January 1959 and no other official dates are listed for the band until the end of August of that year. It appears that the Quarry Men had actually disbanded, the members going their own ways. George Harrison was to join another group, the Les Stewart Quartet, who had a residency at Lowlands Club in the West Derby area of Liverpool, while John and Paul met, usually at Paul's house in Forthlin Road, to write songs together.

It was a stroke of luck that revived the group. The Les Stewart Quartet was offered a residency at a new West Derby club, the Casbah, due to open on Saturday 29 August 1959. Les Stewart, irked that his guitarist, Ken Brown, had been missing rehearsals to help with the decoration of the new club, suddenly decided not to accept the residency. Brown and George left the group and George asked Mona Best, who was running the Casbah, if they could have the Saturday evening residency if he brought along two of his musician mates. She agreed. George contacted John and Paul and a new four-piece Quarry Men made their debut at the Casbah on Saturday 29 August.

They continued with their Saturday evening appearances until 10 October, when Brown couldn't perform with them owing to some illness, but still received part of their appearance fee. They argued with Mona Best and abandoned their residency and ejected Brown.

As a trio they changed their name to Johnny and the Moondogs for some appearances at the Empire Theatre in yet another Carroll Levis talent competition, passed a heat and appeared at the Hippodrome Theatre, Manchester, on Sunday 15 November, although they had to leave before the end of the show to catch their last train to Liverpool.

Stuart Sutcliffe joined the group in January 1960. They were now a quartet comprising John, Paul, George and Stuart, sans drummer. They appeared at a number of art college dances on Saturday evenings, supporting jazz bands such as the Merseysippi, but began to experiment with a number of different names, including the Beatals, the Silver Beats, the Silver Beetles, the Silver Beatles and, finally, on the eve of their Hamburg season, the Beatles.

The Quarry Men, as a name, no longer existed.

Thirty-seven years after the original formation, two original members of the Quarry Men, John Lowe and Rod Davis, teamed up in 1993 and funded the album *Open for Engagements*, which was released on 1 August 1994 on Kewbank Records KBCD 111. They were billed as the Quarry Men featuring John 'Duff' Lowe and Rod Davis. The other members were John Ozoroff on lead guitar and vocals, Charles Hart on drums and Ritchie Gould on bass. The album tracks were: 'Dizzy Miss Lizzy', 'History', 'Thumbin' a Ride', 'Come Go With Me', 'In the Right Place', 'Twenty Flight Rock', 'John Winston', 'Shinto', 'Misty Eyes', 'Tryin' To Get To You', 'Mean Woman Blues', 'Tanya', 'That'll Be the Day', 'The Cycle Song' and 'A Life of Sleep'.

In January 1997, when the new Cavern Club celebrated the fortieth birthday of the opening of the original club, the former members of the Quarry Men were all invited, together with John

Lowe. In the evening they were persuaded to perform four numbers with the Lennon lookalike Gary Gibson.

Rod Davis commented, 'I hadn't been in touch with the others for forty years. We hadn't been invited to play. I just went along for the free drink, but I put an old tea chest and washboard in the boot of my car, just in case. In the event, we did play together for the first time in four decades.'

This led to their appearance at the fortieth anniversary of the St Peter's Church fête on Saturday 5 July 1997.

The fete's previous Rose Queen, Sally Wright, was in attendance to crown the present Rose Queen, and lorry driver Doug Chadwick, drove the Quarry Men around.

The personnel comprised Pete Shotton on washboard, Colin Hanton on drums, Eric Griffiths on guitar, Len Garry on teachest bass and Rod Davis on banjo. John Lowe was there but they wouldn't let him play because they said he was a Quarry Man at a later date. The group performed 'Rock Island Line', 'Maggie May', 'Cumberland Gap', 'Baby Let's Play House', 'Twenty Flight Rock', 'Come Go With Me' and 'Worried Man Blues'.

The occasion saw messages of good will from Yoko Ono, Cynthia Lennon, George Martin, Tony Blair, the Queen and Paul McCartney.

Three thousand people attended the event. Pete Shotton sang 'Imagine' in the evening at the church hall and it was the first time he'd ever sung solo.

The show was recorded and issued on a fifteen-track CD in mid-November 1997 under the title *John Lennon's Original Quarry Men Get Back Together*.

Queen Charlotte's Maternity Hospital

Hospital in Goldhawk Road, Hammersmith, London. Yoko attended for a blood transfusion early in November 1968. It was established that she was pregnant. The baby was due in February 1969, but Yoko had to enter the hospital on 7 November. John insisted on being with her and moved into her room during her three-week stay, sleeping in a sleeping bag on the floor.

A Conservative MP, Captain Henry Kirby, objected to John's being allowed to stay in the hospital, but the Minister of Health told him that it was not unusual for the hospital to 'allow a prospective father to attend confinement and be present at the delivery, unless asked to leave by a doctor'.

While in the hospital, John made a number of recordings, including ones of the six-month-old foetus's heartbeat, which was subsequently included on the album *Unfinished Music No. 2: Life With the Lions*.

Nurses had been concerned about the 35-year-old Yoko's pregnancy and on 21 November she miscarried. John and Yoko had named the foetus John Ono Lennon II and buried it at a secret location.

Queen Elizabeth Hotel

Also known as Hotel Reine-Elizabeth. Situated in Dorchester Boulevard West in Montreal, Quebec, it became the site for John and Yoko's second and final Bed-In, between Monday 26 May and Monday 2 June 1969.

Since John and Yoko couldn't obtain visas for America they had considered the Bahamas as the setting for their next Bed-In. However, on arriving at the Caribbean island, they deemed it wasn't suitable after all and decided to travel to Canada. This would enable them to be close enough to the United States to be interviewed by US radio stations.

They flew into Toronto Airport where the immigration authorities detained John for almost four hours. They finally agreed to allow him a provisional visa, which granted him the short stay. John and Yoko moved on to Quebec and arrived at the Queen Elizabeth at midnight with their entourage.

Derek Taylor was along to co-ordinate the media and a film crew was also in attendance as John and Yoko planned a feature film of the Bed-In, tentatively titled *The Way It Is*. The film was never shown, although material from it was utilised and eventually used in the home video release *John And Yoko: The Bed-In*.

During the event to promote their peace campaign, they stayed in Room 1742 on the 19th floor, surrounded by record players, film equipment, seven phones and handwritten notices with messages such as 'Bag Peace', 'Peace Now' and 'Bed Peace'.

It was a busy and fruitful time during which Derek Taylor estimated that they dealt with 150 press people daily and called more than 350 radio stations in America.

John was to comment, 'The whole effect of our Bed-In has made people talk about peace. We're trying to interest young people into doing something for peace. But it must be done by nonviolent means – otherwise, there can only be chaos. We're saying to the young people – and they have always been the hippest ones – we're telling them to get the message across to the squares. A lot of young people have been ignoring the squares when they should be helping them. The whole scene has become too serious and too intellectual.'

From their bed they engaged in talk and debate with AM and FM stations in Canada and the United States. At one point the announcer at KPFA in Berkeley, California, asked John for advice on behalf of students at Berkeley University who were in conflict with the police at a demonstration at the People's Park. John had a direct hook-up with the students and advised them: 'There's no cause worth losing your life for; there isn't any path worth getting shot for, and you can do better by moving on to another city.'

He was concerned about the students being involved in violence and suggested, 'Don't move about if it aggravates the pigs, and don't get hassled by the cops, and don't play their games. I know it's hard – Christ, you know it ain't easy, you know how hard it can be, man, so what? Everything's hard – it's better to have it hard than not to have it at all!'

There were numerous visitors, including Richard Brown of Capitol Records, Canada, a local pop singer, Tony Roman, and a string of celebrities and media people. The telephone was also busy and among the numerous callers were Norman Mailer, Bob Dylan and Allen Ginsberg.

One unpleasant episode occurred when Al Capp, the American cartoonist, interviewed the couple and was decidedly aggressive and hostile. Derek Taylor was particularly upset by his rudeness and during one heated exchange when Capp turned to Yoko and said, 'As for you, Madam Nhu', a furious Taylor jumped up and ordered Capp out of the room. John placated him, saying, 'He's our guest, Derek.'

The radio interviews were so widely broadcast that the suite became inundated with letters, both for and against the peace campaign. One housewife, Else Zinke from Hamilton, Ontario, wrote: 'If I had your money, I would stay in bed too. It so happens, I often do not get enough sleep because it takes many hours of hard work just to make ends meet. So go ahead, enjoy your twelve hours in bed, with room service no doubt. When I was a few years younger than you are now, a war was all around me. It was even noisier than the music you used to play and most deadly.'

A letter from Swami Vishnu Devcananda read, 'I am glad to hear that you are near Montreal now and also that you are interested in the peace movement. I will be very happy to see you personally and discuss our Yoga Peace Movement and Yoga World Brotherhood convention to be held here in the Laurentian Mountains where we have a Yoga camp.' The swami paid a visit to the suite and gave a demonstration of breathing techniques that he claimed could help a person to live to be 100 years old.

John and Yoko's peace efforts always proved controversial, but did manage to garner positive comment from some publications.

Don Bourbon, in his column in the Quebec newspaper the *Lachute Watchman*, wrote, 'John Lennon has often been compared to Christ, a thought that turns some Christians off immediately. Yet in terms of popularity, message and significance, there is an obvious comparison to be made. What he was striving for was the conversion of men and women towards a way of life based on love and brotherhood between all men and all nations. What kind of people are we to react in such a gross manner? Are we going to string him up and nail him to a cross between two robbers!'

Probably the most significant event of the Bed-In was the recording of the peace anthem, 'Give Peace a Chance', which took place on the evening of Saturday 31 May. The room was crowded with approximately fifty people. They included a camera crew, a sound engineer in charge of the portable four-track Nagra tape machine, various members of the hotel staff, the disc jockey Roger Scott, who thumped on a table to keep time, the comedian Tommy Smothers, who continued playing two basic chords on an acoustic guitar, the British singer Petula Clark, the black American comedian Dick Gregory, members of the Canadian chapter of the Radha Krishna Temple, Timothy Leary and his wife Rosemary, and the former crooner Rabbi Abraham L Feinberg.

When the gathered throng completed the recording, John said, 'Beautiful.'

Queen Elizabeth II

John and Yoko intended to travel on this luxurious ship to New York, where they planned to stage a Bed-In. They had made arrangements to sail from Southampton to New York via Le Havre on Monday 19 May 1969 and had invited Derek Taylor and his wife Joan to join them. With their 27 items of luggage, they arrived accompanied by an entourage that also included Kyoko Cox, Anthony Fawcett and a two-man film crew. They were teaming up on the voyage with Ringo Starr and Peter Sellers.

Ringo and his wife Maureen had brought along their sons Zak and Jason; Peter Sellers was with his wife Miranda; and their party also comprised the *Magic Christian* author, Terry Southern, and the filmmakers Dennis O'Dell, Joe McGrath and Tony Palmer. Palmer was on the trip to film a documentary on Sellers.

As John and Yoko handed in their passports the immigration officials informed them that their application for a visa had been turned down because of John's drugs conviction. The trip therefore had to be postponed, although, hoping that the visa permission might arrive at any time, they had made tentative plans to join the vessel from a helicopter.

John was so excited about his course of primal therapy, which began in April 1970, that he considered hiring the *QE2* to promote it. Arthur Janov – author of *The Primal Scream* – was to comment, 'John was really taken with primal therapy. He wanted to rent the *QE2* and have us sail around the world doing primal therapy; he wanted to buy an island and found a primal nation. He was pretty serious. I put the kibosh on it.'

Question Why, The

A BBC1 series on religion televised in the 'God slot' early on Sunday evenings, with Malcolm Muggeridge in the chair.

John and Yoko appeared on the show on Sunday 7 December 1969, which was broadcast live from Studio E of Lime Grove Studios in London between 6.15 and 6.50 p.m.

The subject of the debate was 'Evil' and among those also

taking part were the Revd Christopher Neil-Smith, David Cooper, General Sir John Hackett, Paul Zeal, Canon Edward Carpenter, Gerald Cohen and Henry Cecil.

Early in the discussion, John described himself as 'a Christian and whatever else is going – a Buddhist as well'.

He continued: 'I think the way I and my crowd, whoever they are, think – in terms of God being a source of power, like Battersea Power Station, or like electricity, and that he just *is*.'

During the debate John revealed that he was not 'over-shocked' by the recent Manson killings in America, commenting, 'It is only today's news, it happened last week and every day, and how can we be shocked by it when the whole system is geared to that kind of thing.

'The people are brought up to be like that. They are brought up to be evil or wicked, or whatever the definition is.

'I think we are all potentially divine, and I think we are all potentially the devil. It is very hard for all of us to be good.'

Quotations

During both his career with the Beatles and in his solo years, John was quoted on numerous occasions and, of course, did literally hundreds of interviews. He was noted for his pithy comments, acid wit, acerbic remarks, Scouse humour and occasional recourse to some home-spun philosophy. Here are just some of the quotes attributed to him over the years:

On the early Beatles career, he commented, 'From our earliest days in Liverpool, George and I on the one hand, Paul on the other, had different musical tastes. Paul preferred "pop type" music and we preferred what is now called "underground". This may have led to arguments, particularly between Paul and George, but the contrasts in our tastes I am sure did more good than harm, musically speaking, and contributed towards our success.'

When appearing at the Royal Command Performance he said, 'On this next number I want you all to join in. Would those in the cheap seats clap your hands. The rest of you can rattle your jewellery.'

When discussing the adulation he received, he said, 'When I feel my head start to swell I look at Ringo – then I know perfectly well we're not supermen.'

Talking about the Beatles' manager, Brian Epstein, he commented, 'He and Paul had some kind of collusion to keep me straight because I kept spoiling the image. My little rebellion was to have my tie loose, with the top button of the shirt undone. But Paul would always put things straight.'

He was to say, 'I get my spasms of being intellectual. I read about politics but I don't think I'd vote for anyone: no messages from any phoney politicians are coming through me.'

Of Liverpool he commented, 'It was a port – that means it was less hick than somewhere in the English Midlands.'

On 11 February 1964 John was interviewed in Washington by the disc jockey Carroll James. James asked John who his influences were. 'Small Blind Johnny,' said John. 'Small Blind Johnny?' asked James. 'Oh yes, he played with big deaf Arthur,' John answered. James then said, 'John, they call you the chief Beatle …' John said, 'Carroll, I don't call you names!' James then said, 'Excluding America and England, what are your favourite countries you've visited.' John said, 'Excluding America and England, what's left?'

Commenting on being made an MBE (Member of the British Empire) by the Queen, he said, 'It was hypocritical of me to accept it. We did a lot of selling out then.'

When the Apple venture was launched, he said, 'The aim isn't to put a stack of gold teeth in the bank. It's more of a trick to see if we can get artistic freedom within a business structure.'

He was later to say, 'Apple was a manifestation of our collective naïveté. We got conned on the subtlest and bluntest level. We didn't get approached by the best artists – we got all the bums.'

One of his most famous quotes was to cause the Beatles problems in America: 'Christianity will go. It will vanish and shrink. We're more popular than Jesus now.' Although a couple of sentences taken out of the context of a lengthy interview did tend to cause the wrong impression in America.

Discussing his break-up with the Maharishi Mahesh Yogi, he said 'No ethnic bastard's gonna get no golden apples outta me.'

On his personal philosophy, he said, 'The main thing is not to think of the future or the past. The main thing is to just get on with now.'

He also said, 'If the Beatles or the sixties had a message, it was to learn to swim. Period. And once you learn to swim, swim.'

Philosophically, he said, 'If art were to redeem man, it could do so only by saving him from the seriousness of life and restoring him to an unexpected boyishness.'

In June 1965, on receiving notice of his MBE, he said, 'When my envelope arrived marked "OHMS" [On Her Majesty's Service] I thought I was being called up. I shall stick it on the wall or make it into a belt.'

When he went solo he said, 'I'm opening a door for John Lennon – not for music, or for the Beatles or for a movement or for anything. I present myself to as broad a scope as I can.'

When an Italian asked John if he knew who Shakespeare was, he replied, 'Certainly. He was English like me. But come to think of it, I don't think he sold any records.'

John once said, 'My music is about love and peace. But what's wrong with the people in the world? Are they all bloody deaf?'

When John received his MBE from the Queen, he was to say, 'She was just like a mum to us. She was so very sweet. She really put us at our ease.'

During a trip to Toronto in 1966 he commented on the number of young Americans who went to Canada to avoid being conscripted for Vietnam, saying, 'If a man doesn't feel like fighting, he should have a right not to go into the army.'

On 17 November 1973, John told the *Daily Express*, 'I'm a survivor. My instinct is to survive and I came through everything … Beatlemania … the Maharishi … therapy … American immigration. It's all water off a duck's back and I put it down to experience.'

When John was asked, 'What time do you get up in the morning?' he replied, 'Two o'clock in the afternoon.'

In a *Melody Maker* interview on 27 May 1967 John confirmed that the Beatles' touring days were over. He said, 'No more tours, no more mop-tops. We could never hear ourselves playing properly. Anyway, what more could we do after playing to 56,000 people? What next? More fame? More money? We were travelling all over the world – and couldn't move outside our hotel.'

In the *Imagine: John Lennon* movie, John is heard to say, 'I always was a rebel, but on the other hand I wanna be loved and accepted by all facets of society and not be this "loud-mouth lunatic, poet, musician", but I cannot be what I'm not.' He also made an antidrug comment: 'It's no good us preaching at people and saying don't take them, because that doesn't work. But if people take any notice of what we say, we say we've been through the drug scene, man, and there's nothing like being straight.' He also said, 'I still believe in love, peace, I still believe in positive thinking. I consider that my work won't be finished until I'm dead and buried and I hope that's a long, long time.'

In 1980 John said, 'Didn't the Beatles give everything on God's earth for ten years?'

Another example of John's philosophy: 'The main thing is not to think of the future or the past. The main thing is just to get on with it now.'

When asked how he wrote his books *In His Own Write* and *A Spaniard in the Works*, he said, 'I just put things down on sheets of paper and stuff them in my pockets. When I have enough, I have a book.'

In 1973, commenting on success, he said, 'Success is something I can take or leave. But I suppose you have to take it before you can decide to leave it.'

Expressing his dissatisfaction about his recording work he said, 'I'm unhappy with every record the Beatles ever made. There isn't one of them that I wouldn't remake, including all my individual ones. I used to think we were the best group in the world, but I heard "Lucy in the Sky with Diamonds" on radio again, and I thought it was abysmal.'

Of the individual Beatles, he was to say, 'None of us would have made it alone because Paul wasn't quite strong enough, I didn't have enough girl appeal, George was too quiet, and Ringo was the drummer. But we thought everyone should be able to dig at least one of us, and that's how it turned out.'

John wasn't interested in the analysis of the Beatles' music by critics: 'Theory is for the critic or the audience. The experience is for the artist and for the audience that isn't theorising about it. That's what is valid. For me criticism doesn't exist. It affects me if you say what a terrible song I've written in the way it would if you say you don't like my suit. I think one note is as complex as anything, but I can't spend my whole life explaining that to critics who want complex musical harmonies, tonal cadences and all that crap.'

At one time John talked of pop stars who had died prematurely, commenting, 'I have always hated the cult followings for people like Buddy Holly or Jim Reeves, or whoever, because there is something unhealthy about it.'

John often talked about living to a ripe old age, but he also said, 'I believe in life after death. Through meditation and drugs I've been aware of the soul, and know that God is a world power we can all tap. It's no good blaming God for war, because we can either use the H-bomb for cheap lighting power or as a bomb.'

Rain

At the end of this track, recorded in April 1966, the vocal is turned backwards and John sings 'Rain, when the rain comes they run and hide their heads.'

Commenting on this, the record producer George Martin was to say, 'It was just an in-joke. The Beatles weren't quite sure what to do at that point, so I took out a bit of John's voice from earlier on and played it backwards. They all thought it was marvellous – it had a sort of unexpectedly Easter sound. So we kept it in. We often like to do things like that for a giggle, particularly as they so often work out.'

John contradicts this and claims to have discovered the sound by accident. He said he had returned home from the studio, stoned, and incorrectly threaded a 7½-inch rough mix on to the tape machine.

Martin remained adamant that it was his idea and says he fitted the backwards vocal on deliberately when John was out having lunch.

It was arguably John's attempt at trying to re-create the LSD experience that prompted him to suggest that the entire number be taped in reverse, but Martin restrained that enthusiasm and restricted it to the last 25 seconds of the track.

The song, penned by John, was issued as the flip side of 'Paperback Writer' in June 1966.

It was included on *Past Masters Volume II*.

Rape

In November 1968 John and Yoko launched one of their most ambitious ventures, the 72-minute mini-feature called *Rape*. It starred Eva Majlata, a 21-year-old Hungarian actress who couldn't speak English. In the movie she cannot escape the prying attentions of the camera, which follows her around the streets of London, through a park, allowing her no privacy and almost causing her to walk into the path of a truck. She attempts to escape in a taxi, but is still followed. She is eventually cornered in an apartment from which she apparently cannot escape and her tearful pleas to the camera remain ignored.

Initially, when the camera first spots her walking through a London cemetery, she is not disturbed. She even attempts to obtain a light for her cigarette from the cameraman, to no avail. Her attempts to communicate in Italian and German are ignored. In fact, the camera follows her dispassionately throughout until she is angry, then frightened and eventually, when trapped inside the apartment like a caged animal, begins to cry, her German pleas tinged with hysteria, and she attempts and fails to open the apartment door. Distressed, she makes a phone call in which she is yelling about her passport.

Rape was shot while John and Yoko were at Queen Charlotte's Hospital following Yoko's miscarriage. The cameraman was Nick Knowland, who worked on most of John and Yoko's productions, and he shot the film with one sound assistant. At the premiere, Yoko issued a statement that included the comment, 'Nick is a gentleman, who prefers eating clouds and floating pies to shooting *Rape*. Nevertheless, it was shot.'

The film received its world premiere on Austrian television on 31 March 1969. John and Yoko completed their Bed-In in Amsterdam to fly to Vienna, where they held a press conference for *Rape* from the inside of a white bag at the Hotel Sacher. That year the film was also shown at the Montreux Television Festival and the Mannheim Film Festival. It was entered in the *Hors Concours* section of the Montreux Television Festival by Austrian TV and was screened on 25 April 1969.

Following the Austrian Television broadcast John and Yoko held a press conference in the public room at the elegant Hotel Sacher, having decorated the room with notices carrying slogans such as 'I LOVE JOHN', 'I LOVE YOKO', 'BAGISM', 'GROW YOUR

HAIR, STAY IN BED'. They took the bed cover from their bed and turned it into a white sack. John said, 'We came down the elevator in the bag and we went in and we got comfortable, and they were all ushered in.'

John commented, 'We are showing how all of us are exposed and under pressure in our contemporary world. This isn't just about the Beatles. What is happening to this girl on the screen is happening in Biafra, Vietnam, everywhere.'

The Austrian journalists were bemused at conducting an interview with a large white bag on a low table. John said, 'It was a very strange scene, because they'd never seen us before or heard – Vienna is a pretty square place. A few people were saying, "C'mon, get out of the bag." And we wouldn't let 'em see us. They all stood back, saying, "Is it really John and Yoko?" and "What are you wearing and why are you doing this?" We said, "This is total communication without prejudice." It was just great! They asked us to sing, and we sang a few numbers. Yoko was singing a Japanese folk song, very nicely, just very straight we did it. And they never did see us.'

At Montreux the viewing rooms were full at the beginning of the film, but scores of people walked out before the end. The following evening, John and Yoko held a press conference in which Yoko described *Rape* as 'a symbolic film about exposure in this world'. She added, 'Everyone today is exposed, to the world, to each other.'

John was asked why, if the film was a genuine situation, the girl hadn't simply smashed the camera. John replied, 'She thought of everything, but stopped at that. Everybody seems to have a basic respect for machinery.'

The theme of the relentless, clinical camera lens, 'raping' the privacy of individuals or groups for the entertainment of the viewing public intrigued the critic Willie Frischauer. He wrote in London's *Evening Standard*, 'This film does for the age of television what Franz Kafka's *The Trial* did for the age of totalitarianism.'

In her note for the film at the time, Yoko wrote, 'A cameraman will chase a girl on a street with a camera persistently until he corners her in an alley and, if possible, until she is in a falling position. The cameraman will be taking a risk of offending the girl as the girl is somebody he picks up arbitrarily on the street. May chase boys and men as well.'

When the premiere took place she'd also prepared some programme notes:

Violence is a sad wind that, if channelled carefully, could bring seeds, chairs and things pleasant to us. We go on eating and feeding frustration every day, lick lollipops and stay being peeping toms dreaming of becoming Jack The Ripper.
This film was shot by our cameraman, Nick, while we were in hospital. Nick is a gentleman, who prefers eating clouds and floating pies to shooting *Rape*. Nevertheless it was shot. And as John says: 'A is for parrot, which we can plainly see.'

The film is also known as Film No. 6 and was the third film John and Yoko collaborated on.

Rape Part Two
A sequel to John and Yoko's 1968 film *Rape,* made at the end of 1969. John is credited as a sound engineer and also cited as providing the music, although only a brief excerpt from the number 'Radio Play', lasting a few seconds, was used at the end of the film.
Shot with a hand-held camera, the film once again presented the audience as voyeur, but was mainly shot in a darkened room. It was 77 minutes long with the final 45 minutes being filmed in that darkened room. The only dialogue spoken was German.

Ready, Steady, Goes Live!
Cathy McGowan interviewed John and George live for the programme at its Wembley Studios location on 16 April 1965. The two were discussing the latest Beatles release, 'Ticket to Ride'.

Ready Teddy
A rock 'n' roll hit for Little Richard. During the Beatles years, it was Paul McCartney who generally sang the little Richard songs. When John was recording his *Rock 'n' Roll* album he recorded 'Ready Teddy' as part of a Little Richard medley, along with 'Rip It Up'. The track began with 'Rip It Up' and then segued into 'Ready Teddy'.

Real Love

A number that had begun life in 1977 as a song called 'Real Life'. John used some of the material from the song in others, placing a full verse and lyrics into a song called 'I'm Stepping Out' and using part of the melody in 'Watching the Wheels'. John next used the basic tune for 'Real Love', changing the title in 1978. He'd intended it as one of several new songs to be included in a proposed Broadway musical *The Ballad of John and Yoko*. It was an acoustic ballad and John made several demo recordings of the number, one of which was used on the soundtrack album of *Imagine: John Lennon* in 1988.

John rewrote the number again in 1980, changing the title to 'Boys and Girls'.

When the three remaining Beatles wanted to work on a recording with John in 1996 for their Anthology project, Yoko gave them three demo tapes, including 'Free As a Bird', which became a single, and 'Real Love', which became the second new Beatles single to be released.

Unlike 'Free As a Bird', for which Paul and George had to complete the lyrics, John had finished all the lyrics to 'Real Love'. The number was recorded at Paul's studio, the Mill, and Paul played a stand-up bass that had once belonged to Bill Black, Elvis Presley's bass player.

Paul commented, 'It was good fun doing it. Unlike "Free As a Bird", it had all the words and music and we were more like sidemen to John, which was joyful, and I think we did a good job.'

A press release stated, 'The surviving Beatles decided to use as little state-of-the-art equipment as possible, to give a timeless Beatles feel to the single. To enhance this effect, Paul McCartney used a stand-up double bass originally owned by Elvis Presley's bassist, the late Bill Black. Both Paul and George used six-string acoustic guitars to augment the electric instruments and Ringo used his Ludwig drum kit. The result is a *bona fide* Beatles single with ageless appeal.'

Radio One didn't include it on their play list, stating, 'We have played "Real Love" a few times, but no, it's not on the play list.'

Paul wrote an article about the Radio One ban in the *Daily Mirror* on Saturday 9 March in which he said, 'Is Radio One as important as it was? As Ringo said to me about all this, who needs Radio One when you've got all the independent stations?'

In a poll, 91 per cent of *Mirror* readers voted in favour of hearing the new single on the radio.

'Real Love' was released on Monday 4 March 1996, reached No. 4 in the *Music Week* chart and was in the Top Ten for a fortnight. It was also issued as the lead track on the *Anthology 2* CDs.

Real Love (Drawings for Sean)

A book published in America by Random House Children's Publishing in June 1999. It comprised forty drawings John made for Sean to help him to read when his son was three years old.

Reflections and Poetry

A record issued in America in June 1988 by Silhouette Music which included excerpts from the RKO Radio interview that John gave on the day he died, together with tapes from the mid-1960s of John reading some of his poems

Release

A BBC2 television series. On Thursday 6 June 1968, John, together with Victor Spinetti, was interviewed at EMI Studios for this arts programme in which the forthcoming stage presentation of *In His Own Write* was discussed. John also had the opportunity of voicing some of his opinions about politics. The recording took place at 5 p.m. and Peter Lewis interviewed the two.

The recordings were broadcast on Saturday, 22 June between 10.05 and 10.45 p.m.

Remember

A track on the *John Lennon/Plastic Ono Band* album in which John reminisces about his past. He includes a refrain from a children's song about Guy Fawkes Night, the traditional Bonfire Night in Britain: 'Remember, remember the fifth of November.'

Remembering John

An MTV tribute transmitted on Saturday 8 December 1984.

Remembering John

A fifty-minute programme broadcast on the American TV *Late Show* on Friday 7 October 1988. It included interviews with Cynthia Lennon, Yoko Ono, May Pang, Julia Baird, Peter Brown, Sid Bernstein, Bruce Morrow, Elliot Mintz, Geraldo Rivera and Albert Goldman.

Remembering Lennon: Ten Years Later

An American ABC radio special, broadcast on the tenth anniversary of John's death. The show was four hours in length and was hosted by Graham Nash.

Remember Love

The flip side of the first Plastic Ono Band single, issued on Apple 13 on 4 July 1969. It was recorded in June 1969 after John and Yoko had returned from Canada. They recorded it in their home studio with Yoko on vocals and John playing acoustic guitar.

Revolution

Track on *Past Masters Volume 11*, originally recorded on 10, 11 and 12 July 1968. After Paul and George had resisted John's wish to have 'Revolution' as a Beatles A-side because they said it was too slow, he persuaded them to re-record the number. This version was considerably faster than the original 'Revolution 1'.

Revolution 1

The first number to be taped for *The Beatles* double album, recorded on 30 and 31 May and 4 and 21 June 1968. It was among eleven numbers written by John in India and originally considered as the next Beatles single. In addition to the Beatles, other musicians on the track were Derek Watkins and Freddy Clayton on trumpets and Don Lang, Rex Morris, J Power and Bill Povey on trombones. John argued for it to be the Beatles' next single but both Paul and George objected, saying it was too slow – although Paul was concerned about its political implications. John said that they could do it again at a faster pace, but it was issued as the flip side of 'Hey Jude' on 26 August 1968.

The 30 May version was a basic backing of the number, which was ten minutes in length. The first four minutes of it were used for 'Revolution 1'. The last six were used in the production of 'Revolution 9'.

John's friend Pete Shotton was to observe, 'Paul made little effort to mask his distaste for a few of John's more way-out compositions, specifically "Revolution" and "Revolution 9". "Revolution", however, meant more to John at the time than any song he'd written in years, and he was determined that it should appear as the A-side of the Beatles' debut release on their soon-to-be-launched Apple Records. Apart from marking a return to the high-adrenalin, no-frills rock 'n' roll that had always remained his first musical love, "Revolution" was the first Beatles song to constitute an explicitly political statement – which in turn is precisely why Paul felt so wary about it. Non-political to the core, he would have much preferred the Beatles to steer clear of such "heavy" topics.'

On the version of the track included on the album, John declares himself against violence, saying, 'Count me out.' On the faster, B-side version, however, he says, 'Count me in.'

He was to say, 'The underground left only picked up on the version that said, "count me out". The original version, which ends up on the LP, said, "count me in" too; I put in both because I wasn't sure. On the version released as a single I said, "When you talk about destruction you can count me out." I didn't want to get killed.'

Criticism came from the underground press in both the US and the UK – from the *Village Voice* in America and *Black Dwarf* in Britain. Robert Christgau in the *Village Voice* wrote, 'It is puritanical to expect musicians, or anyone else, to hew to the proper line. But it is reasonable to request that they not go out of their way to oppose it. Lennon has, and it takes much of the pleasure out of their music for me.'

In response to the attacks on 'Revolution' in *Black Dwarf*, John wrote,

> I don't worry about what you, the left, the middle, the right or any fucking boys' club think. I'm not that bourgeois. I'm not only up against the establishment but you too. I'll tell you what's wrong with the world: people – so do you want to destroy them? Until you/we change our heads – there's no chance. Tell me of one successful revolution.

Who fucked up communism, Christianity, capitalism,
Buddhism, etc.? Sick heads, and nothing else.

'Revolution 1' was the first of two versions of the number to
be recorded: the other was around ten minutes in length. John
also decided to record a faster version in July 1968 (see above).

Beatles fans around the world were furious when Nike paid
Capitol Records $25,000 to use the number in a $7 million
series of television commercials in March 1987. For years,
permission to allow Lennon and McCartney numbers to be used
in commercials had been refused. It was said that Yoko had
agreed to its use and comments she made at the time seemed to
support this, yet the three surviving Beatles and Yoko, through
Apple, sued Nike and its ad agency, Capitol Records and EMI
Records, claiming that Nike was using the Beatles' 'persona and
goodwill' in its ads without permission. Capitol claimed that
Yoko Ono had insisted that Nike use the Beatles version.

When Nike featured the number in their commercials, Jon
Wiener wrote a history of the song for *New Republic* magazine,
detailing the controversy the song had aroused when it was originally released. He called Yoko asking for a statement for his
article and she told him, 'John's songs should not be part of a
cult of glorified martyrdom. They should be enjoyed by kids
today. This ad is a way to communicate John's song to them, to
make it part of their lives instead of a relic of the distant past.
Sports shoes are part of a fitness consciousness that is actually
better for your body than some of the things we were doing in
the 60s.'

However, Wiener was to complete his piece by writing,
'Maybe there's no reason to object to turning some pop songs
into commercials – they didn't say anything in particular, and
were written to make money in the first place ... But the
Revolution ad is different. The song had a meaning that Nike
destroyed.'

New Republic wanted to reproduce the lyrics of the song with
the article, but were refused permission on the grounds that it
would offend Nike.

Wiener commented, 'They said that before they'd grant us
permission, they wanted to read the piece, because they didn't
want the piece to be critical of Nike. So we sent it to them.'

Nike decided that the article was offensive to Nike and permission was refused.

Wiener than said, 'So now you can't quote John Lennon any more if it offends Nike or Michael Jackson, which is pretty horrifying.'

Admitting that it had received letters of complaint, Nike issued a statement:

They say Revolution was about social and political change in the '60s. They feel it's a mortal sin to use it in advertising. We tend to think there's a fitness revolution. The gimmick isn't that we used a Beatles song. The gimmick is that this is the song that describes what's going on – a 'Revolution in Motion'.

Beatles fans were incensed by the commercial, leading to the *New York Post*'s banner headline 'BEATLE FANS BUGGED BY COMMERCIALS'. *Time* magazine featured an article on the controversy headlined 'WANNA BUY A REVOLUTION?' It quoted different executives of advertising companies who were either for or against its use. John Doig of Ogilvy & Mather said he remembered the days of the anti-Vietnam demonstrations with 'bloody police truncheons coming down and "Revolution" playing in the background – what that song is saying is a damned sight more important than flogging running shoes.'

James Taylor, who had been in the studios when the Beatles were recording the number, said, 'For me and my generation that song I watched John Lennon creating at the Abbey Road Studios was an honest statement about social change, really coming out and revealing how he felt. It was the truth – but now it refers to a running shoe.' (Incidentally, other celebrities present during 'Revolution' recording sessions included Twiggy, Lulu and Davy Jones of the Monkees).

US singer John Fogerty, formerly the vocalist with Creedence Clearwater Revival, was to comment, 'I was one of the people who reacted violently the first time I saw the Nike commercial. I think I was in a hotel room somewhere, and I was jumping up and down! I was real pissed off. Goddammit, I was mad, you know, because when John Lennon wrote that song, he wasn't doing it for the money. And to be using it for any corporate thing. It made me angry.'

George Harrison said, 'If it's allowed to happen, every Beatles song ever recorded is going to be advertising women's underwear and sausages. We've got to put a stop to it in order to set a precedent. Otherwise, it's going to be a free-for-all. It's one thing if you're dead, but we're still around! They don't have any respect for the fact that we wrote and recorded those songs, and it was our lives.'

Paul McCartney said, 'What has happened is some people have used it without the right to use it. People who haven't got the right have been giving away the right. But the most difficult question is whether you should use songs for commercials. I haven't made up my mind. Generally, I don't like it, particularly with the Beatles stuff. When twenty more years have passed, maybe we'll move into the realm where it's OK to do it.'

The Thompson Twins did a cover version of the number in 1986.

Revolution 9

A collage of sounds, which utilised the second half of the original recordings of 'Revolution 1'. Recording originally began on Thursday 30 May 1968 under the title of 'Revolution' and was a version almost ten minutes in length. Recording continued the next day, although six minutes were to be taken from the number and later used as a basis for 'Revolution 9'. 'Revolution' continued to be recorded on Tuesday 4 June and on Monday 10 June, in the absence of the other members of the Beatles, John spent three hours at Abbey Road creating sound effects for 'Revolution 9'. He continued with his recording experiments for the number on 11 and 20 June. On Thursday 20 June, most of the recording of 'Revolution 9' was completed, mainly by John and Yoko, although in the evening George Harrison joined him to chant 'the Watusi ... the Twist ... Eldorado' and such. During that day John had found some sound-check tapes in which an engineer had kept repeating the words 'number nine'. These were actually from some examination tapes for the Royal Academy of Music that had been stored at Abbey Road.

It began with a snippet of an unreleased Paul McCartney song, 'I Will', then the EMI test tape repeating the words 'number nine' over and over. The number was basically an avant-garde experiment and contained tape loops, feedback, screams, vocal overdubs, voice filters, tape distortions and various sound effects. Occasionally the voice of John would intone words, such as 'Take this, brother, may it serve you well' and 'Dream sweet dreams for me', with radio noises and the honking of car horns included.

It was a musical montage from John and Yoko, without the other Beatles. Paul McCartney was in New York while it was being recorded and Ringo and George said only a few words, which were included in the mix. They were all unhappy about its inclusion on *The Beatles* double album and George Martin express a forcible opinion that it should be excluded.

Admitting that the experimental recording was done under Yoko's influence, John said, 'Once I heard her stuff – not just the screeching and the howling but her sort of words pieces and talking and breathing and all this strange stuff – I thought, My God! I got intrigued, so I wanted to do one.'

Martin and John also did tape loops on a two-track recorder from a sports sound-effects record. And there was the sound of banging water glasses from the first version of 'Revolution'. There was a monologue from Yoko that had been recorded on a cassette tape recorder and John made a vocal track. Martin transformed all the noises to sixteen tracks, under John's direction.

Pete Shotton said some of the noises were produced at an evening he spent with John in May 1968. He commented, 'We shared a piece of LSD, smoked a few joints, and idly amused ourselves with John's network of Brunell tape recorders. We opened the windows to the spring air and were shouting out whatever came into our heads at the uncomprehending trees while the tapes rolled in the room behind us. I, for one, had no inkling that this particular evening's lark was destined to be captured for posterity.'

John was to say, 'I thought I was painting in sound a picture of revolution, but I made a mistake, you know. The mistake was that it was anti-revolution.'

When the album was released and people obsessed with the 'Paul is dead' affair looked for 'clues', they declared that at the point where the voice repeats 'number nine', it then sounds like 'turn me on, dead man' if you play it backwards.

At 8 minutes 15 seconds 'Revolution 9' is the longest track ever released by the Beatles. The New York magazine *Village Voice* once voted it the most unpopular Beatles track ever recorded.

Lennon was to say, 'This is the music of the future. You can forget all the rest of the shit we've done – this is it! Everybody will be making this stuff one day – you don't even have to know how to play a musical instrument to do it!'

Revolver

The Beatles' seventh album. They considered calling it *Abracadabra* until they found that another band had used that title for an album. Other titles considered and rejected were *Beatles On Safari*, *Bubble & Squeak*, *Free Wheelin' Beatles* and *Magic Circles*. The cover sported a Grammy-award-winning design by Klaus Voormann, although Pete Shotton was to say that the idea for the sleeve was originally conceived at John's house, Kenwood, in Weybridge.

He said, 'John, Paul and I devoted an evening to sifting through an enormous pile of newspapers and magazines for pictures of the Beatles, after which we cut out the faces and glued them all together. Our handiwork was later superimposed on to a line drawing by Klaus Voormann.'

The album was recorded between 6 April and 21 June 1966 and released in Britain on 5 August 1966. The American album was issued on 8 August 1966, minus three tracks by John – 'I'm Only Sleeping', 'And Your Bird Can Sing' and 'Doctor Robert'. The compositions penned by John were 'I'm Only Sleeping', 'She Said She Said', 'And Your Bird Can Sing', 'Doctor Robert' and 'Tomorrow Never Knows'. The only contribution to a number by Paul was slight. Commenting on 'Yellow Submarine', John called it Paul's baby and said that he and Donovan helped with the lyrics, but it was Paul's idea, it was based on his inspiration, and it was his title.

Richter, Dan

Richter first made the acquaintance of Yoko and Tony Cox (her first husband) in Japan and became associated with them again when they moved into an apartment across the hall to him at 25 Hanover Gate Mansion in London in 1967, while he was in

Britain appearing in Stanley Kubrick's *2001: A Space Odyssey* as the principal ape in the 'Dawn of Man' sequence.

Yoko employed Richter as her personal assistant, and, when she began bringing John along to the Hanover Gate apartment, introduced them to each other. As a result, Richter became personal assistant to John and Yoko for a time. When the couple bought Tittenhurst Park, Richter, his wife Jill and their children Sasla and Misha moved into the estate to supervise the extensive reconstruction work ordered by the Lennons.

Richter was also involved in John and Yoko's attempts to gain custody of Kyoko and worked as their assistant on the *Plastic Ono Band* album. Commenting on the album, Richter said, 'John succeeded in using his power to walk the tightrope between pop and art. He accomplished something he had never previously done. It was a watershed.'

Rip It Up

During the Beatles' early gigs, it was Paul McCartney who performed the Little Richard numbers. It was John's turn to sing lead on 'Rip It Up' when he recorded his *Rock 'n' Roll* album. He included it in a medley in which he segued the number with Richard's 'Ready Teddy', which he recorded in October 1974.

Rivera, Geraldo

An American television celebrity. His reports on Willowbrook School for WABC-TVs *Eyewitness News* in 1972 led him to approach John and Yoko to appear in a special charity performance in aid of the school. This was called the One To One concert and took place at Madison Square Gardens, New York on 30 August 1972.

Robinson, Smokey

Singer/songwriter/record producer who began his career as lead singer with Smokey Robinson and the Miracles in 1957. The Beatles included a version of his number 'Slow Down' in their early repertoire. They also recorded his song 'You Really Got a Hold On Me' and George Harrison wrote a song, 'Pure Smokey', which he included on his *33⅓* album.

Referring to the Beatles, he was to say, 'Some of the greatest songs ever done were done by these guys, John Lennon and Paul

McCartney.' One of John's numbers to be inspired by Robinson was 'All I've Got To Do'.

Rock 'n' Roll

Album issued in February 1975. The UK release was on Apple PCS 7169. The LP reached No. 6 in both the US and UK charts.

The tracks were: 'Be-Bop-A-Lula', 'Stand By Me', 'Ready Teddy/Rip It Up', 'You Can't Catch Me', 'Ain't That a Shame', 'Do You Want to Dance', 'Sweet Little Sixteen', 'Slippin' and Slidin'', 'Peggy Sue', 'Bring It On Home to Me/Send Me Some Lovin'', 'Bony Moronie', 'Ya Ya', 'Just Because'.

Rock and Roll Hall of Fame

Leading figures in the American music industry launched the Rock and Roll Hall of Fame in 1983. The aim was to recognise contributions from those who had a significant impact on the evolution, development and perpetuation of rock and roll by inducting them into the Hall of Fame. The Beatles were inducted in 1988, and John Lennon as an individual in 1994. Paul McCartney and George Martin were inducted in 1999.

John was officially inducted as a solo artist at a ceremony held at New York's Waldorf-Astoria hotel on 19 January 1994. The dinner banquet was held in the gala ballroom of the hotel and there was an audience of 600 producers, record executives, broadcasters, artists and critics who had voted for the eight acts to be inducted that day. The other artists were the Animals, the Band, the Grateful Dead, Rod Stewart, Bob Marley, Elton John and Duane Eddy.

As the Beatles had already been inducted as a group, John became only the second performer inducted both as a solo artist and also as a member of a group – the first being Clyde McPhatter, former lead singer with the Drifters.

Paul and Linda, who had special vegetarian dinners prepared for them, joined a table with Eric Clapton, John F Kennedy Jnr, Yoko Ono and Sean Lennon. Julian wasn't present and Cynthia Lennon said he hadn't been invited.

Paul gave the induction, which Yoko accepted on John's behalf. On stage he read a letter he called 'Dear John', part of which was as follows:

I remember when we first met. It was a beautiful summer day. I saw you on stage and you were singing 'Come Go With Me' by the Del Vikings. But you didn't know the words so you made them up: 'Come go with me, to the penitentiary ...' It's not in the lyrics.

I remember writing our first songs together. We used to go to my dad's house. And we used to smoke Typhoo tea with this pipe that my dad kept in a drawer. It didn't do much for us, but it got us on the road.

I remember the visits to your mum's house – Julia, who was a very handsome woman, a very beautiful woman. She had long red hair, and she played a ukulele. I'd never seen a woman who could do that. I remember having to tell you the guitar chords because you used to play the ukulele chords.

On your twenty-first birthday you got a hundred pounds off one of your rich relatives up in Edinburgh. So we decided we'd go to Spain. We got as far as Paris and ... eventually got our hair cut by a fellow called Jurgen and that ended up being the Beatle haircut.

I remember introducing you to my schoolmate, George, and him getting into the group by playing 'Raunchy' on the top deck of the bus ... and when we met Ringo, he was a seasoned professional, but the beard had to go.

A bloke called Larry Parnes gave us our first tour. I remember we all changed our names. I changed mine to Paul Ramone, George became Carl Harrison. And although people think John didn't change his name, I seemed to remember he was Long John Silver for the duration of the tour.

And then came New York City, where we met up with Phil Spector, the Ronettes, the Supremes, our heroes, our heroines. And then later in LA, we met up with Elvis Presley for one great evening on his home territory. He was the first person I ever saw with a remote control.

And then later, Ed Sullivan. We'd wanted to be famous. Now we were getting *really* famous. I mean, imagine meeting Mitzi Gaynor in Miami.

And later, recording at Abbey Road. I remember doing the vocals to 'Kansas City', but I couldn't quite get it. John came down from the control room. He took me to one side and he said, 'You can do it. You know, you just gotta *scream,* leave the top of your head!' Thank you for that.

I remember writing, 'A Day In the Life' with him. And the little look we gave each other as we wrote the line, 'I'd love to turn you on.' We kind of knew what we were doing – sneaky little looks. After that, there was this girl called Yoko. I set up a couple of recording machines. They stayed up all night and they recorded 'Two Virgins'. You photographed the cover yourselves. I had nothing to do with *that.*

And then there were the phone calls ... after all our business shit we had gone through, actually getting back together and communicating once again. And the joy, as you told me, how you were baking bread now and playing with your little baby, Sean. That was great for me because it gave me something to hold on to.

So now, years on, here we are, all these people, here we are assembled to thank you for everything that you mean to all of us. This letter comes with love from your friend, Paul. John Lennon, you made it. Tonight, you're in the Rock and Roll Hall Of Fame.

God bless ya.

Paul then introduced Yoko, whom he hugged and kissed, and Sean.

Ono commented, 'I'd like to thank Paul for being here tonight. I think John would have been very pleased. It's really grand, Paul, thank you.'

Both Paul and Yoko held a press conference following the event in which Paul said, 'It's a privilege to come along and do this. John, no matter what people thought of him from minute to minute, was a very, very beautiful person. And it's an honour to be able to do this with Yoko and Sean. It's just a lot of fun and it's a privilege, because he was some serious dude.'

Asked whether the writing of his 'Dear John' letter was difficult, he replied, 'It was wonderful. It wasn't hard at all. I mean, the thing is, you must remember, I'm a number-one John Lennon fan and I love him to this day. I always did love him. Even when we were bitching and going through our problems, which we all went through ... and even though Yoko and I, you know, for a long time were bitching at each other –'

Yoko interrupted to say, 'I didn't know that.'

Paul smiled. 'Hmm. Maybe we weren't bitching at each other ... But we still know that the man we're talking about tonight, the man who's been honoured tonight, was a seriously incredible dude.'

When asked how she thought John would have felt about being inducted, Yoko answered, 'I think that it especially meant something to him that his solo effort was honoured because, as you know, there were trials and tribulations. It was not very easy for him in his solo efforts. And he passed away even before *Double Fantasy* went to number one. I wish he had known that. I wish he can see us here, too. And I wish he could have received it himself. Because he would have been very proud.'

Paul then said, 'He would have loved it. You know, the terrible thought going through my head as all this stuff's going on here tonight and everyone's being reverential, John would have been the guy in the crowd heckling.'

'And being kicked out, maybe,' Yoko suggested.

'Yeah, man,' said Paul, 'he probably would have been kicked out of here tonight. That's the kind of guy he was. And we love him sincerely and he's a beautiful man and always will be.'

During the press conference Paul had announced that the three surviving Beatles were going to record together the following month and Yoko said, 'Give the three of them a chance.'

Reporting on the event, *Rolling Stone* magazine commented, 'Quite simply, there is no single figure more important in the history of rock & roll than John Lennon.'

Incidentally, it was during his trip to New York for the induction ceremony that Paul visited Yoko at the Dakota Building, where she gave him four of John's home demos: 'Free As A Bird', 'Real Love', 'Grow Old With Me' and 'Now And Then'.

Rock and Roll People

John originally made a home demo tape of this song in May 1973, intending it for his *Mind Games* album. He attempted to record the number on Wednesday 4 July 1973 during the *Mind Games* sessions, but decided to drop the number from the LP and gave it to Johnny Winter to record instead. Winter released it on his album *John Dawson Winter III* and also included a live version on his concert album *Johnny Winter Captured Live.*

One of John's versions of the song was finally issued on the *Menlove Avenue* album in 1986.

Rock Around the Clock

The song, first used on the soundtrack of the film *The Blackboard Jungle,* helped to launch rock 'n' roll around the world. As a result, a feature film based on this iconic track and also called *Rock Around the Clock* was rush-released. It starred Bill Haley and the Comets, whose version of the song first made an impact on the British charts in 1955. The screening of the film in Britain caused riots in the cinemas and headlines in the press.

To the young John Lennon, it was a movie he couldn't miss. 'I went to see it and was most surprised: nobody was screaming, nobody was dancing. I mean, I had read that everybody danced in the aisles. It must have all been done before I went. I was all set to tear up the seats too but nobody joined in.'

Rock Island Line

A traditional American railroad song which became a major hit on both sides of the Atlantic for Britain's 'king of skiffle', Lonnie Donegan.

The singer was born Tony Donegan in Glasgow on 29 April 1931 and adopted the name Lonnie in tribute to one of his heroes, Lonnie Johnson, the blues singer.

The track was issued in Britain on Decca F 10647 and reached No. 8 in January 1956. It was issued in America on London 1650, and reached No. 8 in March of that year.

Donegan's version of the record is what sparked off the British skiffle boom and Donegan was one of John's seminal influences. Although, at the age of sixteen, John didn't have enough money to buy records, he purchased a 78-r.p.m. version of 'Rock Island Line'. He played the song until it was nearly worn out – then sold it to Rod Davis, a friend who was to join him in his first skiffle group, the Quarry Men.

John began to perform the number as soon as the skiffle group began performing locally.

In August 1972, John performed 'Rock Island Line' with Elephant's Memory while they were rehearsing for the One-To-

One concert in New York. He also made a home demo tape of the number, performing on electric guitar, during his househusband period at the Dakota Building. This was the version featured in *The Lost Lennon Tapes* radio series.

Rock Peace

In August 1969 it was announced that 'Rock Peace', an instrumental by the Plastic Ono Band, would be released as a follow-up to 'Give Peace a Chance'. The single never appeared and there is no evidence that it was ever actually recorded. The second Plastic Ono Band disc, 'Cold Turkey', was issued several weeks later in October.

Rollin, Betty

A former classmate of Yoko's who had attended the Sarah Lawrence School with her. Rollin was to become a senior editor of *Look* magazine and, immediately after Yoko's miscarriage, she invited Rollin to interview her and John.

Rollin was to write, 'Yoko is bossy too. She is bossy with the people in the Beatles' Apple office, and they resent it. And she is bossy with us. "Say it this way," she shrieked once, trying to dictate the story to her specifications.'

Rollin spent a few days in their company, beginning at Queen's Charlotte's Maternity Hospital and continuing at Kenwood, the house in Weybridge, Surrey. On the final day she spent with them, Rollin accidentally spilled some sugar on the tablecloth and was berated by Yoko for it. Yoko then began telling her how her mother had ignored her when she was a child and how her parents had disowned her when she'd married 'beneath' her. Rollin then asked her about her daughter Kyoko and wondered how she felt about being apart from her. She mentioned that perhaps Yoko was doing to Kyoko what her parents had done to her.

After the article had been published in *Look* magazine it was then sold on to a major British newspaper and Yoko was incensed by the article and its reference to her being 'bossy'.

Rolling Stone

Influential American music magazine. John appeared on the front cover of the debut issue on 18 September 1968, in a portrait taken during the filming of *How I Won the War*. He granted one of his longest ever interviews to Jonathan Cott, which appeared in the 23 November 1968 issue. The longest interview of all took place on 8 December 1970, when the magazine's editor, Jann Wenner, interviewed John. The interview was published in two parts in 1971 and then appeared in book form under the title *Lennon Remembers*. John had never given his permission for this and was furious with Wenner because of it. His next *Rolling Stone* interview was with Pete Hamill and took place in February 1976.

Rolling Stones' Rock 'n' Roll Circus, The

A fifty-minute television special filmed in colour, with the £50,000 production costs financed by the Rolling Stones. It was taped at Stonebridge Park studios in London and filming began on Wednesday 11 December 1968 and stretched into the following morning. However, the special was not screened as planned. There were several rumours as to why the project was shelved. Some said it was because the Stones were upstaged by the Who, who played 'A Quick One (While He's Away)'. Others said it was because of the hammering the Beatles special, *Magical Mystery Tour*, received from the critics.

Michael Lindsay Hogg directed it, three weeks before he began filming *Let It Be*. The cameraman, Tony Richmond, who also worked on the Beatles documentary with him, assisted.

As the title suggested, the musical special had a circus theme and Sir Robert Fossett's Circus provided a number of acts, including a tiger, midgets and a fire-eater. A number of the musicians also wore circus outfits, with Mick Jagger as the ringmaster. Incidentally, Brigitte Bardot had originally been offered the role of ring mistress, but was contractually unable to accept.

It was decided also to feature a relatively new band and Mick Jagger turned down Led Zeppelin in favour of Jethro Tull. They had also decided to create a one-off group with musicians from different bands fronted by Steve Winwood. A few days before shooting began Winwood said he couldn't do it because he was ill. Jagger then phoned Paul McCartney, but he wasn't free to do it. He next asked John Lennon, who agreed. Then John asked Eric Clapton to join him, along with Keith Richards, who agreed to play bass, and Mitch Mitchell of the Jimi Hendrix Experience, who agreed to play drums. John called his supergroup the Dirty Macs.

An arena had been set up to resemble a circus ring with a costumed audience surrounding it.

John, playing rhythm guitar, performed 'Yer Blues' with his backing musicians. Then Yoko Ono and the French violinist Ivry Gitlis joined them for 'Boogie Whole Lotta Yoko', which was later called 'Her Blues'.

John was dressed as a juggler and Yoko as a witch. John had also brought his son Julian along that day.

The Stones performed 'You Can't Always Get What You Want' and 'Sympathy for the Devil'.

The cast credits read,

> The Rolling Stones' Rock 'n' Roll Circus Starring ... Ian Anderson. Eric Clapton. Roger Daltrey. John Entwhistle. Marianne Faithfull. Mick Jagger. Brian Jones. John Lennon. Julian Lennon. Mitch Mitchell. Keith Moon. Yoko Ono. Anita Pallenberg. Keith Richards. Pete Townshend. Charlie Watts. Bill Wyman.

The Who opened the show and Keith Moon had put water on his drum kit to produce a spectacular effect. Marianne Faithfull then sang 'Sister Morphine'. When John's supergroup began to perform, Yoko was on the stage in front of them in a black bag, from which she emerged.

Glyn Johns and Jimmy Miller recorded the entire show on a mobile four-track machine and the intention was to issue it as a soundtrack album with proceeds being donated to charity. That, too, was never released.

The photographer Mike Randolph took the production stills, which were eventually published in the book *The Rolling Stones' Rock 'n' Roll Circus*, published by Faber & Faber in 1991.

Allen Klein was to acquire the rights to the film and, on Monday 14 October 1996, ABKCO Video and Records eventually released it on video, laserdisc and CD. Polygram also issued it in the UK at the same time. The video was 65 minutes in length.

Rood Wit Blauw

A Dutch television show screened by the Vara network in the Netherlands on Wednesday 15 January 1969, featuring a full forty minutes of interviews with John and Yoko. It was filmed in a dentist's waiting room in Knightsbridge, London, on Wednesday 20 November 1968. Bram de Swoon interviewed Yoko Ono while John was having treatment from the dentist. When John entered the room twenty minutes later, de Swoon also interviewed him.

Roosevelt Hospital

The hospital situated on 69th Street and Ninth Avenue, New York, where John was taken after he was shot.

When police officers Steve Spiro and Peter Cullen received a report on their radio that shots had been fired outside the Dakota Building, they were only two blocks away and arrived in less than a minute, followed by a second patrol car with officers Bill Gamble and James Moran.

While Spiro and Cullen were dealing with the assassin, Gamble and Moran assessed the situation. There was blood gushing from John's chest, which was forming a pool under his body, and they knew that it would be too late to call an ambulance, so they took him in their arms and put him across the back seat of their car and set out for Roosevelt Hospital – St Luke's Medical Center – which was only half a mile away. Moran leaned over the back seat and asked John, 'Are you sure you're John Lennon.'

John said, 'Yeah.'

Gamble asked, 'How do you feel?'

'I'm in pain,' John said. They were the last words he ever spoke.

Behind them Yoko was in another police car, driven by Officer Anthony Palma, crying, 'Tell me it isn't true! John is not shot. Please tell me that.'

Officer Moran had radioed an alert and there was a rolling stretcher waiting at the entrance of Roosevelt's emergency section. The drive had taken less than three minutes.

The two policemen lifted John out of the car and placed him on the stretcher. The hospital staff then rolled it into the emergency room.

Dr Stephen Lynn, the medical director of the emergency

room, made his examination and found no pulse, no respiration, no brain waves and believed he'd died before reaching hospital. He said, 'I'm pretty certain he was dead at the time of his arrival. Yet we weren't prepared to give up on him.'

He was also to comment, 'It wasn't possible to resuscitate him by any means. He'd lost three to four quarts of blood, about eighty per cent of his blood volume.'

Dr Lynn was to say that no one could have lived for more than a few minutes with such wounds, although they tried extremely hard to revive him.

The surgeons finally had to give up and Lynn gave the official time of death as 11.07 p.m., although Yoko was told it was 11.15 p.m.

Yoko approached Lynn asking, 'Where's my husband? I want to be with my husband. He would want me to be with him.'

Lynn told her, 'We have very bad news. Unfortunately, in spite of massive efforts, your husband is dead. There was no suffering at the end.'

A crying Yoko said, 'Are you saying he's sleeping?'

Yoko left the hospital with David Geffen (creator of Geffen Records) and returned home around midnight.

At 12.10 a.m. Lynn conducted a press meeting in a room adjacent to the emergency room.

He announced, 'John Lennon was brought to the emergency room of St Luke's Roosevelt Hospital this evening, shortly before 11 p.m. He was dead on arrival. Extensive resuscitative efforts were made, but in spite of transfusions and many procedures, he could not be resuscitated. He had multiple gunshot wounds in his body. I don't know exactly how many bullets there were. I'm certain that he was dead at the moment that the first shots hit his body.'

He was asked, 'Did you tell Yoko that Mr Lennon was dead? What did she say?'

Lynn answered, 'I did tell his wife that he was dead. She was most distraught at the time and found it quite hard to accept. She is no longer in the hospital.'

Roots

TV-advertised album that was withdrawn from sale. When John originally composed the song 'Come Together', the opening two lines, 'Here come old flat top/He come grooving up slowly', were taken from a Chuck Berry number 'You Can't Catch Me', which was obviously a tribute to one of his seminal influences. However, the publishing company, which owned the right to 'You Can't Catch Me', was Big Seven Music, owned by Morris Levy, who filed a lawsuit for alleged copyright infringement.

Although John denied the charges he didn't want to become involved in a lengthy court case, and in October 1973 decided to make an out-of-court settlement. Part of the settlement was an agreement that John would record three songs from the Big Seven catalogue ('Angel Baby', 'Ya Ya' and 'You Can't Catch Me') on his next album. He began working on the album, which was to comprise some of his favourite rock 'n' roll classics, using the working title *Oldies But Mouldies*.

The sessions took place at the Record Plant West in Los Angeles and John engaged Phil Spector as producer. However, the recording sessions were to deteriorate into farce, with drink and drugs being freely available, resulting in chaos. After two months Spector then vanished, taking all the tapes with him. John couldn't get hold of the tapes and didn't want to start on a new album, so in the meantime he became a producer himself and worked with Harry Nilsson on *Pussy Cats*.

Later in the year, John returned to New York and began planning his *Walls And Bridges* album. Just before he began work on it, he received the Spector tapes, which Capitol had paid Spector $90,000 to obtain. When John listened to the tracks he found that only four out of the nine tracks were usable. They were 'Bony Moronie', 'Just Because', 'Sweet Sixteen' and 'You Can't Catch Me'. He didn't want to complete the *Rock 'N' Roll* album at that time, and went ahead with *Walls And Bridges*.

When *Walls And Bridges* was released, Morris Levy had expected the three promised Big Seven numbers to be on it. However, all he found was a truncated version of 'Ya Ya' at the end. Several meetings were arranged to discuss the situation and although John tried to explain the fiasco regarding the *Rock 'N' Roll* sessions, Levy wasn't satisfied. So, in an effort to placate him, John handed over a rough mix of the album.

Levy, who had a company called Adam VIII, had once suggested to John that they could mail order an album through

TV advertising. At the time John said it was an interesting idea that would be all right as long as Levy obtained permission from John's recording company.

On 8 February, 1975, Levy issued an album *John Lennon Sings The Great Rock & Roll Hits,* subtitled *Roots.* This was advertised on American TV and the record sleeve bore the words, 'Produced from master recordings owned by, and with permission of, John Lennon and Apple Records Inc.'

John himself ordered a copy of the record – it took three weeks to reach him. He disliked the photograph of himself on the cover, which had been taken in 1968. Capitol Records were furious as they were planning to release the *Rock 'n' Roll* album in April. They immediately rush-released the LP, which was issued in America on 17 February and in Britain on 21 February, 1975.

Both sides issued lawsuits and a court case ensued with Judge Griesa presiding. Capitol Records claimed that *Roots* had affected the sale of *Rock 'n' Roll.* The judge awarded Big Seven Music $6,795 for breach of contract, but also awarded John $109,700 in lost royalties, together with an additional $35,000 for the damage inflicted on his artistic reputation.

In fact, only 2,500 copies of *Roots* had been pressed.

The tracks on the album were: Side One: 'Be-Bop-A-Lula', 'Ain't That A Shame', 'Stand By Me', 'Sweet Little Sixteen', 'Rip It Up', 'Angel Baby', 'Do You Want To Dance', 'You Can't Catch Me'. Side Two: 'Bony Moronie', 'Peggy Sue', 'Bring It On Home To Me', 'Slippin' And Slidin''. 'Be My Baby', 'Ya Ya', 'Just Because'.

Royal Isis

A yacht that John bought from Tyler Conley. He took possession of the 64-foot vessel on 1 May 1980 and spent the following month learning how to sail it. It was moored at Long Island, New York.

Rubber Soul (story)

Title of a short story in the paperback book *Melancholy Elephants,* by the science fiction writer Spider Robinson. In the tale, Paul McCartney freezes John Lennon and brings him back to life twenty years later.

Rubber Soul (album)

The Beatles' fifth album. It was recorded at Abbey Road between 12 October and 11 November 1963 and released in the UK on 3 December 1965.

The American version, released on 6 December 1965, contained ten tracks from the UK album and two tracks from the British *Help!* album. The pressure was on John and Paul, with a little help from George, to come up with a complete album of original songs in only four weeks. Their recording engineer, Norman Smith, was to comment, 'With *Rubber Soul*, the clash between John and Paul was becoming obvious. Also, George was having to put up with an awful lot from Paul. We now had the luxury of four-track recording, so George would put his solo on afterwards. But as far as Paul was concerned, George could do no right – Paul was absolutely finicky.'

John said that Paul had come up with the title for the album. At one time they had considered calling it *The Magic Circle*. John's compositions were 'Norwegian Wood (This Bird Has Flown)', 'Nowhere Man', 'Girl' and 'Run For Your Life'. His collaborations with Paul were 'Drive My Car', 'The Word', 'What Goes On', 'In My Life' and 'Wait'.

Rundgren, Todd

A guitarist from Philadelphia who formed the Nazz in 1968 before making a number of solo albums such as *Runt* and *Runt, The Ballad of Todd Rundgren*. He recorded 'Strawberry Fields Forever' on his 1978 album *Faithful*.

John called him Turd Runtgreen and Sodd Runtlestuntle following a short feud between them conducted in the pages of the British music weekly *Melody Maker*. In the 14 September 1974 issue, Rundgren began the attack with a tirade laced with four-letter words, represented coyly as strings of asterisks by the paper: 'Lennon ain't no revolutionary. He's a f****** idiot. Shouting about revolution and acting like a ****. It just makes people feel uncomfortable.'

John sent a lengthy reply to the criticism headed 'An Opened Lettuce To Sodd Runtlestuntle (from Dr Winston O'Boogie)', which was printed in the 28 September issue. John answered several points with comments such as 'I never hit a waitress in the Troubadour. I did act like an ass, I was too drunk. So shoot me!' And perhaps he got to the nub of the matter when he wrote, 'I think that the real reason you're mad at me is because I didn't know who you were at the Rainbow (LA). Remember that time you came in with Wolfman Jack? When I found out later, I was cursing, cause I wanted to tell you how good you were. (I'd heard you on the radio.)'

In the issue of *Melody Maker* published on Saturday 9 November 1974 a letter from Rundgren concluded: 'First, I would like to extend my apologies to John Lennon for the extreme nature of my remarks. I am often reputed to be over-critical, and my comments do not reflect my personal respect for him. I would like to dissipate the idea that I am involved in a feud with anyone, as our prime interest, I'm sure, is the same, that being a little honest communication. Thank you.'

Rundgren went on to produce records by a number of major artists, including Patti Smith, Grand Funk Railroad and Hall and Oates. In 1989 he composed the music and lyrics to Joe Papp's off-Broadway production of *Up Against It,* the screenplay originally written by Joe Orton for the Beatles' projected third feature film.

The cover of the 1982 album *Swing To the Right,* by Rundgren's group Utopia, featured a cover that pictured a group of youngsters gathered around a disc jockey at a burning of Beatles albums in the Southern States, following John's 'Jesus' remarks. In the original photograph, a boy in the foreground is holding up a Beatles album prior to tossing it on to the bonfire. The Beatles sleeve has been replaced on the photograph by one of Rundgren's albums.

In 1992 Todd became one of the members of Ringo Starr and His All Starr Band, who began an American and European Tour in June 1992.

Run for Your Life
Recorded on 12 October 1965, the first song to be recorded for the *Rubber Soul* album and the disc's last track. John was to say, 'I always hated that one. It was one I knocked off just to write a song, and it was phoney.' John was to admit that the line 'I'd rather see you dead, little girl, than be with another man' came from the blues standard 'Baby, Let's Play House', which was recorded by Elvis Presley in 1955.

Oddly enough, the song was banned in the 1990s by a Canadian golden oldies station. Female listeners had complained about the line.

Russell, Bertrand

British philosopher and pacifist. He died on 2 February 1970, at the age of 97.

In 1969 when John was involved in his peace campaign, he wrote a letter to Russell asking for his help. Russell replied, congratulating him on the way he was using the media to present his views on peace and also for his stance on Vietnam and Biafra.

Commenting on John's decision to send his MBE back to the Queen, Russell wrote to him: 'Whatever abuse you have suffered in the press as a result of this, I am confident that your remarks will have caused a very large number of people to think again about these wars.'

Ryan, Robert

Veteran Hollywood actor, star of films such as *Bad Day at Black Rock*, *The Tall Men*, *The Proud Ones*, *The Professionals*, *The Dirty Dozen* and *The Wild Bunch*.

On 20 May 1972, together with several other celebrities, he joined John and Yoko on a candlelit vigil and procession for peace in Washington, DC.

In April the following year they rented his apartment, No. 72, on the seventh floor of the Dakota Building. When John and Yoko moved into the apartment they reputedly held a seance and contacted Ryan's wife, who'd died recently. Yoko then got in touch with the Ryans' daughter, Lisa, to tell her how her mother was progressing on 'the other side', but the gesture wasn't appreciated.

Several months after they moved in, Robert Ryan died of cancer and the Lennons bought the apartment from the executors of his estate.

Rykodisc

An American label specialising in rarities. They released a Yoko Ono box set, *Onobox*, in 1990, and on 3 June 1997 they issued the entire John and Yoko catalogue, together with the remainder of Yoko's solo recordings, on compact disc. They were all digitally remastered by George Marino and Rob Stevens. Each disc contained several bonus tracks, selected by Yoko, many of them from private, never-before-heard tapes. All of the original art from each of the albums was presented intact, including the nude cover on *Unfinished Music No. 1: Two Virgins*. The bonus track on the disc is Yoko's 'Remember Love'. *Unfinished Music No. 2: Life With the Lions* contains two bonus tracks, 'Song for John' and 'Mulberry'. *Wedding Album* contained four extra tracks, 'Who Has Seen the Wind', 'Listen', 'The Snow Is Falling' and 'Don't Worry Kyoko'. The final disc in the initial set of four releases was *Yoko Ono/Plastic Ono Band*, Yoko's first solo album, which was issued as a companion album to John's *John Lennon/Plastic Ono Band*. Bonus tracks include a previously unreleased studio version of 'Open Your Box', plus 'Something More Abstract' and 'The South Wind'. On 22 July 1997 Rykodisc issued Yoko's last three Apple albums, *Fly*, *Approximately Infinite Universe* and *Feeling the Space*, together with *A Story*, which had previously been available only as part of the *Onobox*. On 26 August 1997 Rykodisc released the solo albums Yoko issued after John's death – *Season of Glass*, *It's Alright* and *Starpeace*.

Saimaru, Nishi

A Japanese photographer who was employed as John's personal
assistant in 1975. His duties included shopping and ensuring
that John never ran out of items such as his favourite cigarettes,
Gitanes, and, crucially, marijuana. He also took instructions
from Yoko.

Nishi left the couple's employ in 1979 to get married and was
replaced by Fred Seaman. In 1991 he published his book of
photographs *The John Lennon Family Album*.

Sally and Billy

John originally wrote and taped this song for a rough home
demo at Tittenhurst Park in December 1970. Several years later,
he returned to the number during the summer of 1976 at the
Dakota Building in New York and made another demo using
piano and drum machine.

A narrative song, it tells the story of a beautiful girl named
Sally who sits in a café reading books. Billy is a singer. They are
both hoping that Jesus will show them what to do with their lives.

Salute to Sir Lew Grade – The Master Showman

This was a TV tribute to the British TV mogul Sir Lew Grade.
Despite the fact that Grade's company, ATV, had defeated John

and Paul in their attempt to gain control of Northern Songs, the Beatles' publishing company, the genial cigar-smoking impresario was able to talk Paul into filming a TV special for him, *James Paul McCartney*, which was screened in 1973. This is generally acknowledged to be due to the fact that there had been a legal challenge to Paul's co-writing with Linda, his wife, as Grade's company now owned the rights to the Beatles' songs.

Grade was also able to talk John into appearing in this television special for the same reasons. Earlier that year there had been a publishing dispute about John and Yoko co-sharing songwriting credits. To settle the matter, without taking legal steps, it was agreed that John would appear in this Grade tribute.

The event was videotaped in the Grand Ballroom of the Hilton Hotel in New York on Friday 18 April 1975.

John wore round dark glasses and a red boiler suit, came on with an acoustic guitar and performed live versions of two of the tracks from his *Rock 'n' Roll* album, 'Slippin' and Slidin'' and 'Stand By Me', followed by 'Imagine'. He also made the members of his backing group, whom he called Etcetera, wear masks with the image of a face on the back of their heads. This created the illusion of their having two faces. Was this John's way of saying that Sir Lew was two-faced? Apparently so: when he was asked about the masks, he said, 'It was a sardonic reference to my feelings on Lew Grade's personality.'

The eight-piece backing group were also wearing matching red boiler suits. The real name of the group was BOMF (BOMF standing for Brothers Of Mother Fuckers). The show proved to be John's final live appearance before an audience.

Hosting the show was the comedian Dave Allen, and other artists appearing included Tom Jones, Julie Andrews and Peter Sellers. At the end of the show, John appeared dressed in blue shirt and white trousers, also wearing a cap and scarf, to take a bow with the rest of the artists.

The 52-minute show was videotaped and screened in America on 13 June 1975 and in Britain on 20 June.

Grade died in December 1998.

Sanders, Peter

The artist who, in 1964, drew the figures for the series of cartoons for television based on the Beatles' songs.

Sanders drew numerous sketch studies of John. He noted such observations as: 'pulls funny faces, especially after giving orders, which he immediately wipes off; John never sits, he slouches; John moves with fast, jerky, almost aggressive movements; when facing front he uses a sly, sideways look to talk to somebody' and 'John, especially when delivering important lines, really looks the leader. Feet apart, hands on hips, chin up, looking down his nose with a slightly mocking expression.'

John used to enjoy watching repeats of the cartoon series when he lived in New York.

Saturday Night Live

A major American NBC TV comedy show, which almost led to a John and Paul TV reunion. Paul was visiting John and Yoko at the Dakota Building in New York on Saturday 24 April 1976. During the evening John had wanted to watch *Saturday Night Live* because Raquel Welch and John Sebastian were among the guests. The show featured what was known as Lorne Michaels' 'Beatles Reunion' offer.

During the show, its producer made a tempting offer: 'Hi, I'm Lorne Michaels, the producer of *Saturday Night*. Right now, we're being seen by approximately 22 million viewers, but please allow me, if I may, to address myself to four very special people – John, Paul, George and Ringo, the Beatles. Lately, there have been a lot of rumours to the effect that the four of you might be getting back together. That would be great. In my book, the Beatles are the best thing that ever happened to music. It goes deeper than that: you're not just a musical group, you're a part of us; we grew up with you. It's for this reason that I'm inviting you to come on our show. Now, we've heard and read a lot about personality and legal conflicts that might prevent you guys from reuniting – that's none of my business. You guys will have to handle that. But it's also been said that no one has yet come up with enough money to satisfy you. Well, if it's money you want, there's no problem there. The National Broadcasting Company authorises me to offer you a cheque for three thousand dollars. Here, can you get a close-up of this?'

Michaels then held up a cheque to the camera, which was made payable to the Beatles.

He continued, 'As you can see, verifiably, a cheque made out to you ... the Beatles for three thousand dollars. All you have to do is sing three Beatles tunes. "She Loves You, yeah, yeah, yeah" – that's a thousand dollars right there. You know the words, and it'll be easy. Like I said, this cheque is made out to the Beatles. You divide it any way you want. If you want to give Ringo less that's up to you. I'd rather not get involved. I'm sincere about this. If it helps you to reach a decision to reunite, well, it's a worthwhile investment. You have agents. You know where I can be reached. Just think about it. OK? Thank you.'

Recalling the occasion, John said, 'Paul was visiting us at our place in the Dakota with Linda. He and I were watching it and we went, "Ha-ha, wouldn't it be funny if we went down?" And we almost went down to the studio, just as a gag. We nearly got into the cab, but we were actually too tired.'

Michaels again made an appeal on the show on Saturday 2 October 1976. He said, 'Hi, I'm Lorne Michaels. Several months ago I made a bona-fide offer of three thousand dollars to the Beatles to perform on *Saturday Night Live*. For months there was no response and then, about two weeks ago, I got a long-distance phone call from Eric Idle, tonight's host, in London saying that if I would let him come over and host the show, he would bring the Beatles with him. Well, in my excitement, I agreed and foolishly sent him the cheque for three thousand dollars. You see, he said the Beatles wanted the money in advance so that they could buy some new clothes to wear on the show. Well, when I met Eric at the airport last Monday, I noticed that he was alone. So I said, "Where are they? I mean the Beatles." He said, "Well their new clothes weren't ready yet, so they were going to catch a later flight." I still didn't think anything was wrong, until yesterday, when a telegram arrived saying, "Can't come now. Ringo's pants too long ... Stop. Please send more money for alterations. Stop. Signed the Beatles." When I showed the telegram to Eric, he said he would call London immediately and did, and convinced John, Paul, George and Ringo to send over a film instead. Well, twenty minutes ago, the film arrived from England. I just saw it and it's ... quite good, only it's not the Beatles, it's the Rutles. Evidently, Eric had a bad phone connection to London and, well, anyway ... it's halfway through the show and Eric's already spent the three thousand dollars, so, ladies and gentlemen, here are the Rutles.'

When VH-1 screened a TV movie *Two Of Us* in February 2000 concerning a meeting between John and Paul at the Dakota, *Saturday Night Live* immediately came up with a parody. They showed John and Paul getting together again years after the Beatles have disbanded, with plans to open a fried chicken restaurant. John then brings in Yoko, and she starts telling them that they should sell Taritaki Friend Chicken. Paul then decides to leave, complaining about Yoko and her 'bloody avant garde' chicken recipes, and shouting, 'I'm going vegetarian!'

However they resolve their dispute and get together in opening a restaurant where a customer shouts out, "Hey McCartney, you tard, where's my coleslaw?"

Scared

A track on the *Walls and Bridges* album which opens with the sound of a howling wolf, said to describe John's gloom at being parted from Yoko, and his increasing intimations of mortality. His use of the phrase 'no bell, book or candle' probably comes from one of his favourite Shakespearean phrases, one that appeared in *King John*: 'Bell, book and candle shall not drive me back'. He also borrowed from Bob Dylan with the line 'like a rolling stone'.

John was to comment, 'I was terrified when I wrote it, if you can't tell. It was the whole separation from Yoko, thinking I lost the one thing I knew I needed. You know, I think Mick Jagger took the song and turned it into "Miss You". When I was in the studio, the engineer said, "This is a hit song if you just do it faster." He was right because "Miss You" is a fast version of my song. I like Mick's record better. I have no ill feelings about it. It could have been subconscious on Mick's part or conscious. Music is everybody's possession. It's only music publishers who think that people own it.'

Scene and Heard

A Radio 1 magazine programme. John and Yoko were interviewed for the show at Apple by John Bellan on Thursday 6 February 1969.

Scene Three Act One

See also *In His Own Write* (stage play).

A one-act play co-credited to John Lennon, Victor Spinetti

and Adrienne Kennedy. The American dramatist Adrienne Kennedy had decided to write a play based on John Lennon's published books *In His Own Write* and *A Spaniard in the Works*. She was put in touch with Victor Spinetti, who told her that John's permission would be required before she could go ahead. Spinetti approached John, who liked the idea, and both he and Spinetti went off to Morocco to work on a script.

The play was submitted to the National Theatre by its literary director, Kenneth Tynan. The National was then based at the Old Vic and Spinetti approached Sir Laurence Olivier, who ran the theatre, who told him to go ahead. Spinetti and Kennedy then co-wrote the play, adapting some of the ideas contained in John's books to portray a character called 'Me' and the development of Me's ideas.

The play itself had one performance in 1967 and was revised for a West End opening the following year. Ronald Pickup portrayed the lead character.

Scumbag

A song that arose out of an onstage jam session when John and Yoko appeared with Frank Zappa and the Mothers of Invention at the Fillmore East in New York on the evening of 6 June 1971. During the performance John urged the audience to join him in repeating the word 'scumbag', while the Mothers of Invention backed him instrumentally.

The entire show had been recorded and was to take up one half of John's double-album *Sometime in New York City* the following year. 'Scumbag' was included on the album and was the only song that John and Yoko gave Zappa co-composing credit for.

Seale, Bobby

A co-founder and chairman of the Black Panther Party.

Seale visited the Lennons in their Bank Street apartment in Greenwich Village on two occasions. During his visits he told them of the humanitarian programmes the party was involved in, such as People for Musical Research and Free Breakfast for Children. John and Yoko were particularly interested in the efforts to provide children with proper nutrition and contributed to the programme.

Seale was also an effective orator and roused the audience at the John Sinclair Ten for Two rally, when he took the stage and told them, 'The greatest form of pollution on the face of this earth is the bullets and bombs falling on the bodies of the Vietnamese.' He also said, 'The only solution to pollution is a people's humane revolution.'

John and Yoko invited Seale to be one of their guests when they co-hosted *The Mike Douglas Show* for a week in February 1972. Seale arrived with two guests of his own: one was a young student who discussed a national conference for black students, and the other was a medical student who discussed sickle-cell anaemia. John then introduced Seale, who discussed some of the Black Panther programmes such as the community health clinics and free food, shoes, clothing and transport initiatives.

John then interviewed Seale, asking him what the philosophy of the Panthers was. Seale told him, 'Our philosophy is what we call intercommunalism. We're not nationalists. We don't believe in nationalism. Nationhood has always been hooked up to superiority. It's akin to racism.'

He mentioned that when the Black Panther Party began five years previously the media had tried to sabotage it by intimating that it was violent. 'They said the Black Panther Party picked up guns to go into the white community and kill white people. We've been here five years. We've never done that. That was never our intention. Our intention was to defend ourselves against unjust, brutalising, racist attacks on black people in the black community – attacks by police and other racists.' He pointed out that their method of defence was by the organisation of their programmes to fight poverty.

Seaman, Fred

The son of the concert pianist Eugene Seaman. In February 1979, when Nishi Saimaru, the previous assistant to John and Yoko, decided to return to Japan, Seaman took his place. His duties included running errands, doing office work for John and Yoko, answering fan mail and picking up marijuana. Yoko said his duties were 'to do a little shopping and cook John brown rice'.

In his interview with the DJ Andy Peebles two days before his death, John said that Seaman had introduced him to new music – the B52s, Madness and the Pretenders.

Seaman kept daily journals until John's murder and these proved to be a major source for Albert Goldman's iconoclastic biography *The Lives of John Lennon.*

Seaman had his own book *The Last Days of John Lennon* published in America by Citadel in 1990 (a book that Cynthia Lennon said she found 'fascinating'). Throughout his book, Seaman sees Yoko as the wicked witch, declaring, 'She would scare him with ominous psychic predictions and mystical mumbo-jumbo.' He claims she was turbulent, spiteful and selfish and says that she ordered the placenta of her son Sean to be frozen so she could eat it for its rejuvenating properties.

In August 1982 there were reports that Seaman had parted company from Yoko under a 'mutual agreement'. He had actually been fired in January. Then the *New York Daily News* reported that Yoko had information that a number of items had been stolen from the Dakota Building apartments and had decided to make an inventory. Detective Lieutenant Robert Gibbons said, 'She then came to us and an investigation was begun.' He then said that the police had recovered stolen material in Seaman's apartment and in a warehouse.

After John's death Seaman was arrested on Tuesday 28 September 1982 for stealing various items from the Dakota apartment, including John's personal diaries covering the years 1975–79. He said he hoped to deliver the diaries to Julian.

A report said he'd been arrested for the theft of letters, paintings, electronic equipment and unreleased tapes. Virtually all of the stolen property, including thousands of dollars' worth of recording equipment, was recovered.

He pleaded guilty to grand larceny and was sentenced to five years' probation in July 1983. All of the diaries, with the exception of the one for 1980, were returned to Yoko. Judge Jeffrey Atlas honoured a request by Yoko that Seaman not be jailed. She said his punishment will be 'having to live with his conscience'. The judge ordered Seaman not to reveal their contents under threat of a seven-year jail sentence.

After the hearing, Seaman commented, 'I did not take them for profit. There are aspects of this case which have not been revealed.'

Springing to Seaman's defence, *Double Fantasy*'s co-producer, Jack Douglas, revealed that John loved having Seaman around, that he hired him as his assistant and used to give him things. He says, 'He probably made a couple of mistakes. But what he got nailed for was really off the wall.'

Douglas says that John used to get a lot of things sent to him – everything from boom boxes to cassette machines – and not just one: many times there'd be two or three of them. Companies would keep sending things to John in the hope that he would use them.

Douglas revealed, 'He told Fred one day, "Take that," he says. "Go in the room, Fred, and take whatever you want, man, you can have it." And Fred went in and took stuff and he brought it home and it was practical stuff he could use but Yoko had somebody always keeping an inventory of everything that was in the room.' Douglas explained that Seaman never signed the stuff out because John kept telling him, 'Keep it. Take it. I don't want that crap.'

'As a result, Seaman got arrested because there was stuff missing which they found at his house and they matched the serial numbers, so he was charged with grand larceny.'

In 1997, while appearing at Beatle conventions in the US, Seaman told audiences that Yoko Ono and Sam Havadtoy were married in Hungary in 1981, but had kept the marriage a secret so as not to lessen 'Yoko's image of the grieving widow'. He also revealed that he was writing a book about Yoko called *Black Widow*.

Britain's *Mail on Sunday* revealed in its 5 December 1999 issue that Seaman's own personal diaries were discovered after their disappearance in a burglary. It was said that Yoko Ono had bought the two diaries in good faith from a person who said they found them in a garbage dump in east Harlem.

Among the revelations in the diaries, Seaman related that Yoko didn't like John being with old friends from his Beatles days and that she generally 'protected' him from outsiders. As a result, John didn't call Mick Jagger after the Rolling Stones' leader dropped by and left a note at the Dakota Building. Yoko also gave Seaman instructions about Elton John, telling him, 'If Elton calls again, say we're not interested.' It was the same regarding John's own son Julian after Yoko said he'd 'badgered'

John for money to buy a motorbike. Seaman wrote, 'She told me not to put Julian through to John again but to make sure all calls went to her.'

When Seaman first went to work for John at the Dakota he said that over the front gate was an Indian head carved in stone surrounded by the digits 1, 8, 8, and 1. He said that the digits represented the years in which the Dakota was built. As a result of his experiences with the Lennons he said that after a few years working for them he saw the number in a different light: 'Eight plus one is nine, the highest number, denoting change and spirituality; if you add 99 to 1881, you get 1980 – the year in which John Lennon was struck down by a hail of bullets in this very spot.' Yoko's obsession with numerology had obviously influenced him, as had John's obsession with the number nine (see **Nine**).

Season of Glass

A Yoko Ono album released in the USA on Geffen GHS 2004 on 8 June 1981 and in Britain on Geffen K 99164 on 12 June. It is an album in which Yoko professed to express her grief at John's murder. She described it as a form of psychological diary for her.

The album came in for some criticism regarding what people considered a lack of taste. The cover featured a photograph of John's blood-covered spectacles placed beside a glass half filled with water. The background is the New York skyline and the shot was taken from a window of Yoko's apartment in the Dakota Building. One song, 'No, No, No', starts with four gunshots and ends with an ambulance siren. At another point on the album Yoko screams, 'You bastards – we had *everything*!' Critics said the inclusion of the spectacles and gunshots was appalling.

Yoko answered, saying they were both statements about the murder. 'John would have understood and approved of everything. He would have gone much further.' She said, 'Well, there was a dead body, you know.'

Another sentiment Yoko voices on the album is, 'My body's so empty, the world's so empty without you.' She said she wanted the world to be reminded of what happened.

The tracks on the album were: Side One: 'Goodbye Sadness', 'Mindweaver', 'A Little Story', 'Even When You're Far Away', 'Nobody Sees Me Like You Do', 'Turn of the Wheel',

'Dogtown', 'Silver Horse'; Side Two: 'I Don't Know Why', 'Extension 33', 'No, No, No', 'Will You Touch Me', 'She Gets Down On Her Knees', 'Toyboat', 'Mother of the Universe'.

'A Little Story' was by the five-year-old Sean Ono Lennon.

The album reached No. 49 in the *Billboard* chart.

Sedaka, Neil

The American singer/songwriter whose hits include 'Calendar Girl', 'Oh Carol', 'Breaking Up Is Hard To Do' and 'Sweet Sixteen'. He dedicated his single 'The Immigrant' to John.

Sefton General Hospital

Situated in Smithdown Road, Liverpool L15, it was the hospital Julia Lennon was taken to on Tuesday 15 July 1958 after she'd been knocked down by a car in Menlove Avenue. She died in the ambulance on the way. Sadly, her common-law husband John Dykins was also to die in the same hospital following a road accident (see **Dykins, John**).

Julian Lennon was born here at 7.45 a.m. on Monday 8 April 1963. After Cynthia had experienced labour pains while she'd been shopping, she asked her best friend Phyllis McKenzie to stay overnight with her in Mendips. Cynthia cried out in pain once she'd gone to bed and Phyllis phoned for an ambulance. The two girls were taken to Sefton General Hospital dressed only in their nightdresses, protected from the cold by their dressing gowns.

Describing the birth, Cynthia was to write, 'He was beautiful. The reason for the difficulty during Julian's birth was because the umbilical chord was wrapped around his neck; he arrived into this world an awful yellow colour. Apart from that he was perfect, just perfect.'

John, who had been touring, arrived at Sefton General a week later. By this time, Cynthia, who had initially been placed in a public ward, had been moved into a private room costing 25 shillings (£1.25) a day. When John arrived he was delighted and exclaimed, 'Who's going to be a famous little rocker like his dad, then?'

Seider, Harold

When John and Yoko dealt with Allen Klein in New York, they enjoyed the services of the ABKCO legal counsel Harold Seider.

It was Seider who arranged for them to move into Robert Ryan's apartment in the Dakota Building.

Seider resigned from his post as chief corporate counsel of ABKCO in 1971 and became vice-president of United Artists Record Management. When John fired Klein he offered Seider the job as his manager. Seider turned down the position but agreed to act as the Lennons' adviser or counsellor in their business affairs, after receiving permission from United Artists to work for John part time. They engaged him on 1 April 1973.

Seider then hired accountants and lawyers for the Lennons. He also made John get his financial affairs in order. Previously John sent all his bills to Klein to be paid and literally millions of dollars had been wasted. Seider made him sign every cheque each month, which made John realise how much money he'd actually squandered in the past – and he almost became a skinflint, querying every item. John was also told that his financially unproductive businesses – such as Joko Productions – had to go.

It was Seider whom the publisher Morris Levy contacted when he wanted to meet John personally to discuss the *Rock 'n' Roll* tapes (see **Berry, Chuck**). John had said, 'Harold Seider told me that Morris wasn't too happy about the situation, about me not doing the songs or whatever I was supposed to do for that agreement we had made and he wasn't too happy about "Ya Ya" on *Walls and Bridges*.'

Self Portrait

One of John and Yoko's avant-garde movies, and one that generated a wealth of controversy, because the entire film was focused on John's uncircumcised penis, which was to rise from a flaccid to an erect state in slow motion. Initially it was a fifteen-minute sequence in slow-motion, using high-speed film and the completed movie was 42-minutes in length.

John commented, 'My prick, that's all you saw for a long time. No movement, but it dribbled at the end. That was accidental. The idea was for it to slowly rise and fall, but it didn't.'

Initially, John found it difficult to raise an erection because of the film crew, even when Yoko struck some erotic poses for him. It took a copy of *Playboy* magazine to bring about the desired effect.

Self Portrait was made in August 1969 and received its world premiere at the newly opened Institute of Contemporary Arts a few weeks later, on 10 September. It also received a screening at the New Cinema Club, London.

The background sounds included birds, planes and passing cars.

The programme notes explained: 'The result is translucent and hypnotic and mystifying. The combination of slow motion and outdoor sound is perfectly balanced, thus neutralising the awareness of its technology.'

Sellers, Peter

British comic genius, born in 1925. John was always a fan, particularly during the days when Sellers was a member of the Goons. Sellers also recorded for George Martin, who had hits with his album *Songs For Swinging Sellers* and singles such as 'Goodness Gracious Me'. Sellers was later to record three Beatles numbers in comically deadpan fashion; 'Help!', 'A Hard Day's Night' and 'She Loves You'. Although recorded in 1965, 'She Loves You' wasn't released until 1981, the year after Sellers had died of a heart attack.

Sellers became a friend of the Beatles and appeared on their Granada TV special *The Music Of Lennon & McCartney*. In it he performed his version of 'A Hard Day's Night', recited in Shakespearean fashion while he was dressed in a Richard III-style costume. This was issued as a single on Parlophone E 5393 and reached No 14 in the UK charts. Sellers also made a film with Ringo called *The Magic Christian*.

At one time John wanted to buy Sellers' house, Brookfield, but Sellers sold it to Ringo for less than John had offered because he'd promised it to him first.

An example of how John and Sellers shared the same bizarre sense of humour is apparent from the tape of a conversation made when Peter Sellers dropped in to Apple.

Lennon: 'Now, what do you think about mock Tudor shit-houses in Weybridge and places like that?'

Ringo: 'I don't mind them being in Weybridge – it's just when they try and put them in London, they get in the way of the traffic.'

Lennon: 'I'll never forget it ... Pull up a star's seat. We've been lucky enough this evening to secure the talents of Mr. Peter Sellers here, who is going to give us Number Three.'

Sellers: 'Number Three, folks, Number Three.'

Lennon: 'How about that, folks? That was Number Three from Peter Sellers. Now on to the next round.'

Sellers: 'And there's more where that came from.'

Lennon: 'If I ask him really nicely he'll probably do Number Five.'

Sellers: 'Yes, I might.'

Lennon: 'Over to you Peter.'

Ringo: 'He is doing Number Five.'

Sellers: 'I can't count that far these days. I used to be able to.'

Lennon: 'Do you remember when I gave you that grass in Piccadilly?'

Sellers: 'Really stoned me out of my mind, really. Acapulco Gold, wasn't it? Fantastic.'

Lennon: 'Exactly.'

Sellers; 'Sorry I'm not holding any right now.'

Lennon: 'We can't get it.'

Sellers: 'Oh, yeah?'

Lennon: 'I've given up, you know – as stated by Unter Damn Yer.' [Hunter Davies]

Sellers: 'Well, I'm sorry about that, fellas, but I, you know, if I'd known I was going to see you, of course, I would have had some on me. Because I know you love it and dig chewing that thing.'

McCartney: 'Got you, Pete. You got it? Can you dig it?'

Sellers: Oh, yes. God, I can dig it.'

Lennon: 'Do you want to make the scene in the gents lavatory?'

Sellers: 'That's a groove.'

Lennon: 'Way out.'

Sellers: 'Exit?'

Lennon: 'Just don't leave the meddles lying around, you know. We've got a bad reputation.'

Send Me Some Lovin'

A number which was originally a hit for Sam Cooke, and was penned by Cooke and Lloyd Price. John recorded in September 1971 for the soundtrack of his film *Clock*. He recorded it again during sessions in March 1972 for his *Sometime In New York City* album. He also recorded it in a medley with another Cooke number 'Bring it On Home To Me' during his *Rock 'n' Roll Sessions* with Phil Spector in October 1974.

Sergeant Pepper's Lonely Hearts Club Band

The album was made between 6 December 1966 and 3 April 1967 and took more than 700 hours to record. It was released in the UK on 1 June 1967 and in the States one day later. John penned 'Lucy In The Sky With Diamonds', 'Being For The Benefit Of Mr Kite' and 'Good Morning, Good Morning'. His main collaboration with Paul was on 'A Day In The Life', in which parts of two different songs by John and Paul were merged.

Commenting on the album, John was to say, '*Sgt Pepper* is called the first concept album, but it doesn't go anywhere. All my contributions to the album have absolutely nothing to do with this idea of Sergeant Pepper and his band, but it works because we said it worked, and that's how the album appeared. But it was not as put-together as it sounds, except for Sgt Pepper introducing Billy Shears and the so-called reprise. Every other song could have been on any other album.'

He was even more critical in his 1980 *Playboy* interview, complaining about his recordings; 'You play me those tracks and I want to remake every damn one of them. I heard "Lucy In The Sky With Diamonds" last night. It's abysmal, you know? The track is just terrible. I mean, it's a great track, a great song, but it isn't a great track because it wasn't made right.' He added, 'I feel I could remake every fucking one of them better, but that's the artistic trip, isn't it? That's why you keep going, always trying to make that next one the best.'

Sergeant Pepper's Lonely Hearts Club Band (sleeve)

It is generally assumed that the figures on the famous cover of the *Sergeant Pepper* album were the Beatles' heroes, personally chosen by the group. This isn't actually the case. The majority of the selections were made by Robert Fraser, Peter Blake and Jann Haworth. It was said that each member of the Beatles was asked to write down a list of ten figures they would like to see on the sleeve. Ringo didn't choose any; George chose mainly religious figures; and a number of John and Paul's selections were rejected.

Paul McCartney, for instance, included Brigitte Bardot on his list and even made her the most prominent figure in a sketch he drew of the proposed cover. She was left off the sleeve. Perhaps this is because Peter Blake had been given a waxwork figure of Diana Dors from Madame Tussaud's and considered that one such glamorous sex bomb was enough.

We can assume that John chose Stuart Sutcliffe, his late friend and former member of the Beatles. He also chose Albert Stubbins, a footballer for Liverpool FC, whom he never knew but decided to include because he'd been a favourite of his father. And he chose Edgar Allen Poe – the famous American writer of gothic horror tales such as 'The Fall of the House of Usher' and 'The Murders in the Rue Morgue' – and Leo Gorcey, leader of the Bowery Boys, a popular screen comedy gang. However, Gorcey wanted a payment of £500, so his image, already prepared and part of the tableau, was taken down and he lost his place in posterity. Another Bowery Boy, Huntz Hall, remained on the set, so it is likely he was also a choice of John's. John was also very influenced by the writer Aldous Huxley and no doubt included his name on his list. He chose the poet, playwright and wit Oscar Wilde and the author Lewis Carroll, who were also early influences on his writing. As a child he loved the adventures of a character called William Brown in a series of books of stories by Richmal Crompton that began with *Just William* in 1922, so he had Crompton's name on his list – but Crompton did not appear on the finished sleeve.

Two of John's other choices, Adolf Hitler and Jesus Christ, were also rejected for fear they would cause controversy. When Sir Joseph Lockwood, chairman of EMI, turned up at the photographer's studio to see the tableau he rejected the figure of Mahatma Gandhi as India was a strong market for EMI and he didn't wish to offend anyone. Perhaps Gandhi was part of George Harrison's list of spiritual gurus. Other rejected figures were René Magritte, Alfred Jarry, the Marquis de Sade, Nietzsche and Lord Buckley.

Serve Yourself

A song that John wrote and made a home demo tape of early in 1980. This was basically an attack on Bob Dylan, who had become a born-again Christian, and John was in full vitriolic form, making several different takes of the song, some of which have found their way on to bootleg albums. It was also a parody of Dylan's own song 'Gotta Serve Somebody'. John recorded another version in October 1980 and a final version was recorded at the Dakota Building in New York in November 1980.

The diatribe also rails about various sacred cows, political and religious, bringing in Christ, Buddha, Mohammed and Krishna.

In 1985 the track appeared on *Yin and Yang*, a bootleg Lennon album. It's believed to be taken from one of the tapes that Fred Seaman took and eventually had to return to Yoko (see **Seaman, Fred**).

When the bootleg was issued, *Melody Maker* contacted Sam Havadtoy (John and Yoko's designer) to ask him about it and he was surprised to hear of its release. When asked if the song would be released officially, he said, 'You know how it is when an artist records an LP: he always writes and records more songs than will be on the record. So there are several other songs in the archives; maybe when the time comes to make a documentary on John's life then they'll be released.'

One of the versions was also aired on Show 14 of *The Lost Lennon Tapes* radio series.

Sexy Sadie

The idyll at Rishikesh and faith in the Maharishi came tumbling down when Alexis Mardas, John's Greek friend who was also known as 'Magic Alex', suggested to the Beatles that their spiritual guru was carnally interested in several of the women at the ashram.

John was to say, 'When George started thinking it might be true, I thought, well, it must be true because if George is doubting him, there must be something in it. So we went to see the Maharishi. The whole gang of us the next day charged down to his hut, his bungalow, his very rich-looking bungalow in the mountains.

'I was the spokesman and as usual when the dirty work came I actually had to be the leader. Wherever the scene was, when it came to the nitty gritty, I had to do the speaking, and I said, "We're leaving." He asked why and all that shit and I said,

"Well, if you're so cosmic, you'll know why," because he was always intimating that he did miracles, you know.'

As they were preparing to leave, John began to write a song about the Maharishi, pouring all his despair at being let down into the number – 'Maharishi, you little twat/Who the fuck do you think you are?/Oh you cunt'.

He'd called the number, 'Maharishi What Have You Done, You Made A Fool Of Everyone.' On returning to England he rewrote the number and, after receiving some legal advice, decided to call the song 'Sexy Sadie'.

A demo was made at the end of May at George's bungalow Kinfauns in Esher, Surrey, when the Beatles taped a number of demo recordings for their forthcoming double album.

The group began recording the song on Friday 19 July 1968 for their *The Beatles* double album, also known as the 'White Album'. The session began at 7.30 p.m. and John sang lead and played a Gibson acoustic guitar on the track. The group spent Wednesday 24 July recording further takes of 'Sexy Sadie', but John was still dissatisfied and a second remake was recorded on Tuesday 13 August.

Shades of a Personality

The title of one of the proposed projects submitted as a possible third Beatles film. Scripted by Owen Holder, the screenplay concerned one central character with four personalities, enabling all four Beatles to portray the same person.

The group was originally to begin filming with director Michelangelo Antonioni in Spain in September 1967, but the project fell through. The *New Musical Express* had reported earlier, 'John Lennon will play the part of the man himself, while the three other Beatles will portray each of the facets of his split personality: the dreamer, the human being and the man as perceived by the outside world.'

Shapiro, Helen

British singer, born in Bethnal Green, east London, on 28 September 1946. She reached No. 3 in the British charts with 'Don't Treat Me Like a Child' in 1961 at the age of fourteen and swiftly followed with two chart-toppers, 'You Don't Know' and 'Walkin' Back To Happiness'.

Richard Lester directed her first film, *It's Trad, Dad!*, and the Beatles were booked to appear on her first headlining tour.

Shapiro said she had a crush on John Lennon. 'I really fell for him. He always made me a cup of tea and a lot of fuss. But alas, as I was fifteen at the time, John always regarded me as a kid sister.

'Yes, they supported me on my tour. We all travelled by bus and used to sing Beach Boys songs together, with John taking the lead.'

She recalled one time on the touring coach when she was reading an article headlined 'Is HELEN SHAPIRO A HAS-BEEN AT 16?' Shapiro said, 'That hurt me enormously, especially because I was so young. But I do remember John Lennon peering over my shoulder, reading the headline and saying that the person who wrote it was an idiot.' She added, 'He was twenty-one and saw me as a younger sister – though I had the most amazing crush on him. It was only later that we found out he was, in fact, married to Cynthia. He kept it a real secret.'

Shaved Fish (Collectable Lennon)

A compilation album of previously released recordings produced by John and Phil Spector which John had issued to celebrate the birth of his son Sean earlier in the month and his own 35th birthday. John himself supervised the selection. It was to be his last release for some years as he intended to devote the rest of the decade to rearing Sean personally.

The album was issued in both Britain and the US on 24 October 1975. The British release was on Apple PCS 7173 and the American on Apple SW 3421.

The majority of the tracks were the A-sides of his American singles, a number of which had previously been unavailable on albums.

The track listing was: Side One: 'Give Peace a Chance', 'Cold Turkey', 'Instant Karma! (We All Shine On)', 'Power to the People', 'Mother' and 'Woman is the Nigger of the World'; Side Two: 'Imagine', 'Whatever Gets You Thru the Night', 'Mind Games', 'No. 9 Dream', 'Happy Xmas (War Is Over)' and 'Give Peace a Chance'.

The version of 'Give Peace a Chance' that opens the album is the track originally issued as a single. The version that closes the album is from a live recording of the One-To-One concert.

The sleeve, designed by Roy Kohara, contains illustrations to each of the songs by Michael Bryant.

The album reached No. 9 in the British charts following its release in 1975. In America it reached No. 12 in *Billboard*, No. 19 in *Cash Box* and No. 21 in *Record World*.

After John's death, sales of his albums that were still available rose to the extent that *Shaved Fish* re-entered the British charts and reached No. 7.

She Loves You

Song penned by John and Paul in a Newcastle hotel room on 26 June 1963 while they were on tour. It topped the British charts for four weeks but once again was given the thumbs-down in America by both Capitol Records and Vee Jay Records. It was eventually issued as a single there by Swan records on 13 September 1963 and topped the charts for two weeks.

John was to say, 'The woo woo was taken from the Isley Brothers "Twist and Shout", which we stuck into everything – "From Me To You", "She Loves You", they all had that woo woo.'

She Said, She Said

When the Beatles were attending a party in the Hollywood Hills in August 1965, during their American tour, there were various guests, including Dave Crosby and Jim McGuinn of the Byrds and the film actor Peter Fonda. The group had taken LSD for the second time and were approached by Fonda, who kept whispering, 'I know what it's like to be dead, man.'

John said they didn't really want to listen to him, particularly as he kept on repeating the same thing over and over again. John commented, 'We were saying, "For Christ's sake, shut up, we don't care, we don't want to know," and he kept saying it.'

John remembered this when he'd assembled home-taping equipment at his home in Weybridge and he made a demo tape of a song in March 1966, which he tentatively called 'He Said, He Said'.

John, accompanying himself on acoustic guitar, mainly kept repeating the phrase. He was later to refine the song and the Beatles recorded it during a single session on Tuesday 21 June 1966. At the beginning of the session, John still hadn't decided on a title for the song, but finally plumped for 'She Said, She Said'.

The line 'You're making me feel like I've never been born' was originally 'You're making me feel like my trousers are torn'.

The track was recorded on 21 June 1966 and included on the *Revolver* album.

Sheff, David

A young journalist commissioned by G Barry Golson, *Playboy* magazine's executive editor, to conduct a *Playboy* interview with John Lennon in 1980.

The Boston-born Sheff had to submit his time and place of birth to enable Yoko to check his horoscope before she granted him permission for the series of interviews to take place.

Sheff spent three weeks with John and Yoko from 8 September 1980 during which he taped over 24 hours of material. The edited interview appeared in the issue of *Playboy* dated January 1981 and issued in America the day before John was killed.

A fuller version of the tapes' contents was published in the form of a 193-page paperback by Playboy Press in America in 1981 and by New English Library in England during the same year, under the title *The Playboy Interviews with John Lennon and Yoko Ono*.

In the March 1984 issue of *Playboy*, Sheff and his wife Victoria contributed an article called 'THE BETRAYAL OF JOHN LENNON', which told the sad account of how virtually anyone associated with Lennon's inner circle ripped off and stole from Yoko in a number of ways following John's murder.

She's a Friend of Dorothy

One of John's home demo discs, which was never developed into a proper studio recording. The number, penned by John in 1980, was included in the 81st episode of *The Lost Lennon Tapes* radio series.

Shevey, Sandra

The Other Side of Lennon was a book written by Sandra Shevey, first published in Britain by Sidgwick and Jackson in 1990.

Shevey is an American writer who became a permanent British resident and is the author of an international bestseller about Marilyn Monroe called *The Marilyn Scandal*.

In 1972 Shevey, whose articles had appeared in publications such as the *New York Times*, *Harper's Bazaar* and *Ladies' Home Journal*, interviewed John and Yoko at their Greenwich Village apartment.

Following John's death, Shevey rediscovered her interview and decided to write a book, during the course of which she interviewed a number of Lennon's friends, fellow musicians, girlfriends and various other people who knew him. They included Robert Whitaker, Vic Lewis, Eleanor Bron, William Pobjoy, Walter Shenson, Nik Knowland, Kenny Lynch, Jack Douglas and Bill and Virginia Harry.

The Other Side of Lennon comes to a number of conclusions about John, many of them uncomplimentary. However most of them cannot be taken seriously, as the conclusions have been drawn from completely inaccurate information.

For instance, Shevey attempts to prove that John is a 'poor lyricist' and begins by citing three songs. As if to consolidate her opinion that John was a racist, she writes about the number 'Get Back': 'The original, unedited "Don't Want No Pakistanis" is a nasty, trite piece of racism against both coloured minorities and Common Market countries. Its ethos is National Front, with Lennon tossing in a tagline about "the Common Market being too common for me. Ha, ha." '

She then writes, 'Did anyone ever consider why Lennon, at the height of Beatlemania, felt compelled to publish songs under a pseudonym to see if they could sell? Can you imagine Tim Rice doing it? And yet this is precisely the case with *Woman*, published under the pen-name of Bernard Webb. The song, recorded by Peter and Gordon, reached Number 23 in the charts.'

To consolidate her analysis of John's songwriting, she writes, 'Many of the people and places Lennon sang about nostalgically were actually very painful experiences, which he did not want to gift-wrap. The song *Penny Lane*, for instance, a nostalgic bit of English whimsy about bus shelters, barber's shops, a nurse selling poppies and an eccentric banker, is nothing but an advert for British tourism. It had no reality for Lennon ... and for

whom the Liverpool Penny Lane district was a grim reminder of
his mother's desertion.'

It is incredible that an author researching and writing about
John Lennon didn't know that John had no part in any of the
above songs that she credited him with writing. All three were
written solely by Paul McCartney and it was Paul who used the
pseudonym Bernard Webb for 'Woman', the song he gave Peter
and Gordon.

John himself was to write a song called 'Woman' several years
later, but it has no association with the song Shevey cites.

Incidentally, when commenting on John, Shevey said, 'I do
still like him but it's like saying you like Hitler. He was a vastly
overrated, arrogant little guttersnipe.'

Shoeshine

An uncompleted number John wrote at the St Regis Hotel in
New York soon after he moved in there in September 1972. He
was later to use some of the lyrics in his 1973 composition
'Meat City'.

Short, Don

A *Daily Mirror* show-business columnist of the 60s who tracked
the Beatles all round the world in search of a good story.
Although he covered the entire pop music scene, he seemed
particularly partial to three subjects: the Beatles, Miss World
contests and location filming of James Bond epics. In fact he
went on to write a book about the Miss World contests, in addition to ghosting Britt Eckland's bestseller *True Britt*. He left the
Mirror to form his own highly successful freelance agency, Solo.

When John took his second LSD trip in Hollywood he later
commented, 'There was a reporter, Don Short. We were in the
garden; it was only our second [LSD trip] and we still didn't
know anything about doing it in a nice place and keeping it
cool.'

Then they spotted Short and thought, How do we act?

John added, 'We were terrified waiting for him to go, and he
wondered why we couldn't come over. Neil [Aspinall], who had
never had acid either, had taken it and he would have to play
road manager. We said, "Go get rid of Don Short," and he didn't
know what to do.'

Anthony Fawcett in his book *One Day at a Time* relates how, when Apple was being planned at Wimpole Street, John and Yoko, Paul and Neil Aspinall were in a room drinking coffee and checking the proofs of the Beatles' biography when Short appeared in the doorway with his photographer.

John and Paul, both apparently horrified at the unannounced intrusion, muttered in unison, 'Get 'im out.'

'Just a quick photo, boys,' he pleaded, while his photographer took aim.

'And what's all this big business you're getting into?' Short asked, and John shouted at him, 'Get out, we're not telling you anything.'

Nevertheless, the very next day a complete page of the *Daily Mirror* carried a story, 'THE BIG BUSINESS BEATLES', with a large byline for Don Short.

A few days after John's death, a week-long series of articles on him began on 11 December in the *Sun* tabloid under the byline 'By Don Short – The Man Who Shared His Secrets'.

The series was syndicated and a small excerpt entitled 'The Lighter Side of John Lennon' was contained in the 1981 book published by Proteus, *A Tribute to John Lennon 1940–1980*.

John also mentions Don Short in his book, *A Spaniard in the Works*. In January 1987, Short placed a handwritten draft of *A Spaniard in the Works* in an auction. He said that, during a dinner at a country inn, 'John disappeared into the loo and emerged nearly an hour later clutching a torn white envelope and two brown disposal bags. He explained that it was the start of "a great new book". John thrust the pages into my hand and said, "Here, Don, they're yours. Flog them if ever you go broke."'

Shotton, Pete

John's childhood friend, whose association with him spanned almost thirty years.

The pair first met when they attended the same Sunday school and Shotton's last meeting with John was at the Dakota in New York in 1976. His memories of their long-term friendship were the basis of *In My Life*, Shotton's autobiography, written in collaboration with Nicholas Schaffner, which was published in 1983 and is full of intriguing anecdotes.

Shotton was born on 4 August 1941 and reared at 83 Vale Road, Woolton, close by where John lived in Menlove Avenue. His mother Bessie worked for Gallop Poll and his father George was a draftsman. Pete had an elder brother and sister, Ernest and Jean, and a younger brother, David.

At the age of six, Pete met John when they attended Sunday school in the area. Shotton led a small gang of local boys, including Ivan Vaughan and Nigel Walley, who also lived in Vale Road, and when the friendship between Pete and John blossomed, the two became inseparable, apart from one or two occasions when they fought as a result of John's sometimes overbearing sense of superiority and acidic wit. John dubbed them 'Shennon and Lotton' and their association became even closer in 1952 when they both passed a scholarship to Quarry Bank High School and were placed in the same class in Woolton House. This brought the two closer together as their other friends began to attend different schools – Ivan to the Liverpool Institute and Nigel to the Bluecoat School. The two decided to become blood brothers, but failed in their attempts to draw blood when they used a blunt knife on their wrists, which resulted only in a red weal.

Bessie Shotton considered that John was a bad influence on her son while John's Aunt Mimi felt the same about 'that Shotton'.

Shotton's recollections in his autobiography linger over the early sexual adventures of the pair, with coarse language capturing the adolescent fumbling of their initial incursions into sex. He describes the mutual masturbation sessions they indulged in during their first year at Quarry Bank, conjuring up erotic images of female film stars and shouting out their names as they approached climax – this particular incident was later immortalised in Kenneth Tynan's revue, *Oh, Calcutta!*.

The two also indulged in all sorts of mischief at Quarry Bank, resulting in at least one suspension.

Shotton attributes John's initial awareness of music to his mother Julia. When John visited her home, he'd listen to records on her gramophone – and Julia would buy John records he particularly liked.

When John decided to form his skiffle group he asked Shotton to join, and Pete became washboard player with the group. He was a bit apprehensive at first as John had also brought in Pete's arch-enemy Bill Smith. Initial rehearsals took place in the corrugated air-raid shelter in Shotton's back garden and in the bathroom of Julia Lennon's house in Blomfield Road. Smith failed to turn up at rehearsals, was always on the brink of fighting with Pete and eventually just disappeared with their tea-chest bass, so Pete and John took an afternoon off school and broke into Smith's house to recover it.

Pete never felt comfortable as a member of the skiffle group and often told John of his misgivings. During an open-air party in the Toxteth area John and Pete got drunk on beer and John picked up the washboard and broke it over Pete's head, telling him that his problem about being in the group was now over.

Both youths failed their O-level exams, but John managed to secure a place at Liverpool College of Art, while Pete became a cadet at Liverpool Police College. On graduation he became a policeman patrolling the Garston area, but quit the force nine months later and went into partnership with the owner of the Old Dutch Café near Penny Lane, and then married his girlfriend Beth in March 1963. The café was at 316 Smithdown Road and was an all-night establishment frequented by taxi drivers. The Beatles used to drop in there after gigs for bacon sandwiches.

During one of John's trips to Liverpool he discovered that Pete was unhappy at the Dutch and insisted on providing him with £2,000 to start up his own business. Pete also revealed that at the same time, Brian Epstein offered him the post as his personal assistant, but he turned it down.

Pete had originally attempted to open a betting shop, without success, and spent most of the £2,000. At Christmas 1964 he and Beth were staying with his sister Jean and her husband Frank at Fareham and discovered that there was a supermarket for sale in Hayling Island for £20,000 – and by Easter 1965 John had bought it for him, forming a company on 18 March called Hayling Supermarkets Ltd with John, George Harrison and Pete as directors. As the supermarket was only an hour's drive from John's new home in Weybridge, Pete used to visit him regularly at weekends.

When the Beatles launched their Apple empire, John asked Shotton to come and work for them as a director. Pete arranged for his mother to move south and take over the running of the supermarket and his wife Beth and son Matthew remained in Hayling Island while he sought a London flat. For a time he ran the Apple Boutique, but the venture wasn't a success and in 1968 he told John he was quitting. As a result he became John's personal assistant for a time. His relationship with Yoko became strained and, after being asked to clean up the Montague Square flat where the couple was staying, he resigned.

By the beginning of the 1990s Shotton had become a businessman in the Poole area of Dorset. He opened an American-style restaurant, Fatty Arbuckle's, in 1994 and was soon running a string of restaurants of that name. In 1998 he sold the chain for millions and retired. Pete lives in Southampton.

His first wife died of cancer when she was 35 and he's been married twice since.

Following the celebration to mark the fortieth anniversary of the Cavern Club, in which original members of the Quarry Men performed together for the first time in forty years, Pete rejoined the band, which began to perform regularly at Beatles conventions and has been booked to appear in venues as far away as Cuba, Las Vegas and Canada.

Sidie Man

Nickname given to John by the more arty section of the young German fans who began to attend the Beatles' shows at the Kaiserkeller club during their initial Hamburg trip in 1960.

John gave this set the nickname 'Exis' because they reminded him of the French Existentialists. The Exis also called Paul 'the Baby' and George 'the Beautiful One'.

Silver, Johnny

A name John was purported to have used during a brief period when the Silver Beatles adopted pseudonyms in an attempt to glamorise their image, perhaps inspired by the Larry Parnes method of creating a new name for each of his discoveries, such as Johnny Gentle, with whom the Silver Beatles were to tour.

Hunter Davies, in the Beatles' authorised biography, mentions that John denied he used the name Johnny Silver, although the other members of the group claimed that he did.

The reports that he'd used the name irritated John and, when he saw it mentioned again in the book *The Beatles: An Illustrated Record*, he sent a note and a clipping to the publishers:

> Please tell our pals Roy Carr and Tony Tyler that unlike wot is writ in their Beatle book, I was never ... repeat never known as Johnny Silver. I always preferred my own name. See enclosed rare item from the files ... (possibly the first review of Beatles ever). Set the (Illustrated) Record straight, or forever hold your penis!
>
> There was an occasion when a guy introduced me as Long John and the Silvermen ... in the days of old when they didn't like the world Beatle!! I'm actually serious about this ... it gets my TIT!
>
> Bonnie Jock Lennon.

The clipping came from the *Heswall and Neston News and Advertiser* and had been given to John by Millie Sutcliffe when Bill Harry had taken him round to visit her. The clipping read:

'ROCK' GROUP AT NESTON INSTITUTE
A Liverpool rhythm group 'The Beatles', made their debut at Neston Institute on Thursday night when north-west promoter Mr Les Dodd, presented three-and-a-half hours of rock 'n' roll.

The five-strong group, which had been pulling in capacity houses on Merseyside, comprises three guitars, bass and drums.

John Lennon, the leader, plays one of three rhythm guitars, the other guitarists being Paul Ramon and Carl Harrison. Stuart DaStael plays the bass and the drummer is Thomas Moore. They all sing, either together or as soloists.

Recently they returned from a Scottish tour, starring Johnny Gentle, and are looking forward to a return visit in a month's time.

Among the theatres they had played at are the Hippodrome, Manchester; the Empire, Liverpool and the Pavilion, Aintree.

Long John and the Silver Men was actually a name suggested to them by Casey Valance, leader of Cass and the Cassanovas, primarily because it was fashionable at the time to have a solo name placed in front of a group name.

Simon Dee Show, The

A London Weekend Television show hosted by the former pirate radio disc jockey Simon Dee. John and Yoko, together with Michael X (Michael Abdul Malik), recorded for the programme on February 8 1970 for a show broadcast the following day.

Since My Baby Left Me

A song penned by Arthur Crudup, which was recorded by Elvis Presley at Sun Records. John recorded the song in 1973 with Phil Spector during his *Rock 'n' Roll* album sessions. It didn't appear on the album, but was included on the posthumous *Menlove Avenue* album in 1986.

Sinclair, John

A leading radical in America during the 60s. A Beat poet, Sinclair became Minister of Information for the White Panthers when they formed in October 1968, and was also the manager of the group the MC5. An undercover policewoman managed to entice him into giving her two joints of marijuana and, as a result, he was sentenced to ten years in prison. John and Yoko first heard about him after he'd been in prison for over two years. They were shown Ed Sanders' poem 'The Entrapment Of John Sinclair' and Jerry Rubin talked them into appearing at a Free John Sinclair rally. As John hadn't appeared in public for some time, the concert aroused a great deal of attention and, because of John's involvement, Stevie Wonder volunteered to appear. The concert was officially called *Two For Ten* (two joints, ten year sentence) and took place over seven hours at the Chrysler Stadium, Ann Arbor on December 10/11, 1971.

Poet Allen Ginsberg improvised a song and John Sinclair's new band, Up, performed 'Jailhouse Rock' and 'Nadine'. Various speakers appeared, including Ed Sanders, and Stevie Wonder received a tremendous reception for his performance of 'For Once In My Life'. Other musicians included Commander Cody, Phil Ochs and Bob Seeger. John was supposed to appear at 2a.m. but didn't. At 3a.m. David Peel came on stage. The audience, waiting in anticipation for John, booed Peel, but he sang 'John Lennon Yoko Ono New York City Are Your People'.

John was terrified of going on stage again, but eventually plucked up the courage and went on to announce, 'We came here tonight to say that apathy isn't it. And that we can all do something. So Flower Power didn't work. So what! We start again!' Then, to the accompaniment of an acoustic guitar, he sang 'Attica State', followed by 'Luck Of The Irish'. Yoko performed 'Sisters, O Sisters' and John sang a song specially written for the occasion, 'John Sinclair'. The audience was disappointed at hearing four unfamiliar songs after waiting so long, but 55 hours after John and Yoko left the stage, Sinclair was freed.

Together with his wife Leni, Sinclair then visited John and Yoko in New York. Sinclair talked about jukebox music, John about his guitar. Leni and Yoko discussed food co-ops and travelling kitchens. Then John outlined his plans for a tour which would go from town to town picking up local bands. 'I just want to be a musician and transmit some love back to the people,' he said. 'That's what attracts me most, getting to play with a band again. It will be the regular scene, but without the capitalism. We'll pay for the halls and the people will pay to get in but we'll leave our share of the money in the town where it can do the most good.'

The song 'John Sinclair' was included on the *Sometime In New York City* album. John had arranged for the benefit concert to be filmed, but instead of having proceeds from the film donated to various agreed charities, had Yoko donate the money to women's groups, which made Sinclair feel cheated. Talking about John and Yoko's *War Is Over* peace campaign, Sinclair said, 'You are going to sound awfully fucking stupid trying to tell the heroic Vietnamese people that "The war is over if you want it," while they are being burned and bombed and blown out of their pitiful little huts and fields.'

Sisters O Sisters
A number recorded and performed by Yoko, which was included on the *Sometime in New York City* album. She sang it on the *Ten For Two* concert appearance in Ann Arbor,

Michigan, the Apollo Theater, Harlem, for the Attica State benefit, on *The David Frost Show* on 13 January 1972, on *The Mike Douglas Show* the following month and at the One-To-One concert in August 1972.

Skywriting By Word of Mouth

In an interview with the writer David Sheff for *Playboy* magazine, John told him about his work on this book, which he said began in 1976. Discussing the fact that he'd virtually given up music to concentrate on being a househusband, he said, 'I got frantic in one period that I was supposed to be creating things, so I sat down and wrote about two hundred pages of mad stuff – *In His Own Write*-ish. It's there in a box, but it isn't right. Some of it's funny, but it's not right enough.'

It appeared in 1986 in a volume of writings compiled by Yoko.

In a radio interview, Yoko commented, 'The book is a collection of writing that have never been published before. He's talking about his life and what happened in the United States, with immigration and all that. He's very, very articulate and also outspoken as usual. I wish I could be that outspoken, but nobody can in this age. He just did it and it's very refreshing in that sense, to show people that you can do it, you can have that courage to say outright what you think.'

John recorded readings from the book on to tape. However, these were stolen from the Dakota Building shortly after John's death. Yoko promised that, if the tapes were ever returned, she would release them officially.

Tony Barrow, former press agent to the Beatles, reviewed the book for *Stage and Television Today*, commenting,

> I would have been strongly tempted to question the authenticity of at least a portion of these John Lennon essays if his second wife, Yoko Ono, a figure of absolute credibility and total integrity, was not the reliable and personal force behind their somewhat belated publication.

He added, 'Not much on this *Skywriting By Word of Mouth* falls precisely or even comfortably into a Lennonesque category I recognise.'

One controversial aspect of the book is the colourisation of John's artwork on the cover. When she was asked why she added watercolour to some of John's finished drawings (she also did them on greetings cards), Yoko said, 'I got involved when a book publisher wanted to add colour to John's art. They had done a cover, and coloured it, and I told them it's almost sacrilege to do that. I could understand why they wanted colour, so I decided to do the colouring, because I'd been close to John.'

The first section of the book, with four items, is called 'The Ballad of John and Yoko'. This is followed by 'Two Virgins' and 'An Alphabet'. 'Skywriting By Word of Mouth' follows, with over two dozen short stories, and there is an afterword by Yoko.

Sleepless Night
A Yoko Ono track on the album *Milk and Honey*.

Slick, Earl
An American guitarist who worked with John on the *Double Fantasy* album.

Slick also played on David Bowie's *Young Americans* album, which featured John on some of the tracks. He told *Starzone*, the David Bowie magazine, that he wasn't present when John attended the Bowie session, saying, 'We played on the same songs, but we were never in the studio at the same time. The funny thing is that, when I worked with Lennon on *Double Fantasy*, he swore blind that he knew me from working on those sessions! Unless my memory is worse than I think it is, we were never in the studio together. I don't think I'd forget that.'

He also remarked on his working with John for the *Double Fantasy* album. 'That was amazing. It's still a hard one to talk about. It's very strange how it affects you. John was so easygoing. John, just like David Bowie, wanted what you could do, gave you the room to do it and got what they wanted not by intimidating everyone around them.'

During an interview with *Guitar World* in July 1985, he said that at first he felt out of place at the *Double Fantasy* sessions because, 'I was the only guy who could not read music, but the guys – Hughie McCracken, Tom Levin and Andy Newmark – were so great. It was cool. I did one or two solos live, the others were overdubbed. And 'Milk And Honey' was recorded at the same time. But when we recorded *Double Fantasy* he [John] was just a guy in a studio wanting to have fun and play, which is exactly what we did for two-and-a-half months. Yoko had input on her songs, and I also later did her solo album, *Season Of Glass*. A lot of people have a rough time working with Yoko but I loved working with her.'

Slippin' and Slidin'
The flip side of Little Richard's 1956 hit 'Long Tall Sally'. John included the track on his *Rock 'n' Roll* album and was to comment, 'It was a song I knew. It was easier to do songs that I knew than trying to learn something from scratch.' He was also to perform it on the TV special *Salute to Sir Lew – The Master Showman*.

Slow Down
John's cover of the Larry Williams number, recorded on 1 and 4 June 1963. It was included on the *Past Masters* CDs. Another version, recorded for the *Pop Go The Beatles* radio series, was included on the *Beatles Live At The BBC* CDs.

Smile
One of the earliest of John and Yoko's film collaborations, also known as Film No. 5, which they produced in August 1968.

The idea was originally Yoko's. She wanted a film of John's face smiling and said it would be available 'for people who'd like to have the film on their wall as a light-portrait'.

Smile was shot with a high-speed camera able to take 30,000 frames per minute, in the garden at Kenwood. It is, indeed, a shot of John smiling, with natural background sounds of birds on the soundtrack.

He was to describe it as 'a symbol of today smiling – that's what I am, whatever that means. I don't mind if people go to the film just to see me smiling because it's not that harmful. The idea of the film won't really be dug for another fifty or sixty years.'

Yoko commented, 'Last year, I said I'd like to make a smile film which included a smiling-face snap of every single human being in the world. But that had obvious technical difficulties and it was very likely that the plan would have remained as one of my beautiful never-nevers.

'This year, I started off thinking of making films that were meant to be shown in a hundred years' time, i.e. taking different city views, hoping that most of the buildings in them would be demolished by the time the film was released; shooting an ordinary woman with her full gear – knowing that in a hundred years' time, she'd look extraordinary, et cetera, et cetera. It's to apply the process of making vintage wine to filmmaking. This, in practice, would mean that, as a filmmaker, you don't really have to make a film any more but just put your name (that is, if you so wish) on any film and store it. Storing would then become the main endeavour of a filmmaker. But then, the idea started to get too conceptual. That's the trouble with all my strawberries. They tend to evaporate and I find myself lying on the floor doing nothing.

'One afternoon, John and I went out in the garden and shot Film No. 5 – the *Smile* film – and *Two Virgins*. They were done in a spirit of home movies. In both films we were mainly concerned about the vibrations the films send out – the kind that was between us.

'But, with Film No. 5, a lot of planning, working and talking out things had preceded the afternoon. For instance, I had thought of making Film No. 5 into *Dr Zhivago* and let it go on for four hours with an intermission and all that, but later decided to stick to a more commercial length of about an hour; eight-millimetre copies of the film are also available for people who'd like to have the film on their wall as a light-portrait. Also, we'll store some copies for the next century.

'They say that in the corner of the world there is a man who sits and spends his life in sending good vibrations to the world, and when a star twinkles, we are only catching the twinkle that was sent a thousand light years ago, et cetera.

'Imagine a painting that smiles just once in a billion years. John's ghostly smile in Film No. 5 might just communicate in a hundred years' time, or maybe, the way things are rolling, it may communicate much earlier than that. I think all the doors are just ready to open now. One light knock should do. It's just that there are still a minority group in the world who are afraid of the doorless world to come. They're just not sure how they can cope with it. But most of us know that doors are just figments of our imagination. The good thing is, though, that law of nature that once you know, you can never unknow things, so the doors are going to disappear pretty rapidly, I think.

'Some critic recently commented on us, John and I, as being lollipop artists who are preoccupied with blowing soap bubbles for ever. I thought that was beautiful. There's a lot you can do with blowing soap bubbles. Maybe the future USA should decide their presidency by having a soap-bubble contest. Blowing soap bubbles could be used as a form of swearing. Some day the whole world can make it its occupation to blow soap bubbles.

'There wasn't any point in just making love, secretly and everything. We had to make a film, which had the same vibrations as making love. A smile for everyone. That's us.'

It was originally a three-minute film, which was slowed down for public screening to last for 52 minutes.

Smile was premiered at the Chicago Film Festival in December, 1968, together with *Two Virgins*, and was one of the films shown during the *An Evening with John and Yoko* film event at the New Cinema Club, London, in September 1969.

A newspaper report of a London screening read, 'A 52-minute film showing Beatle John Lennon breaking slowly into a smile attracted few viewers in London's Trafalgar Square. Most people walked past the giant screen outside St. Martin in the Fields church without noticing the Lennon smile above them. The film, called *Smile,* and another, called *Two Virgins,* featuring Lennon and his Japanese wife Yoko Ono smiling at each other, were shown as part of a charity drive called *Focus on Famine*.

Smith, Bill

One of several friends of John at Quarry Bank School. When John first decided to form a skiffle group in 1956, the two original members were he and Pete Shotton. The next person asked to join was a fellow classmate, Bill Smith, who played tea-chest bass. However, he was with the group for only a matter of weeks as he rarely turned up at rehearsals and had to be replaced by Len Garry.

Smith, George

John's uncle was a father figure in his early life. George was a dairyman, like his father and grandfather, and delivered milk from a horse-drawn float in the Woolton Village area.

George had been courting Mimi Stanley for ten years and they were finally married on 15 September 1939, when she was 33 years old. He was called into service, but discharged three years later and went to work in an aircraft factory in Speke. The couple moved into the semidetached house known as Mendips in Menlove Avenue.

George's ambition had been to become an architect, but this dream came to an end when he was expelled from school and entered his father's dairy business.

He was particularly fond of John and when the boy was four and a half years old taught him to read by reciting the headlines from the *Liverpool Echo* to him. He also taught John how to draw and paint and bought him his first mouth organ.

John's Aunt Mimi was to say, 'My husband George adored John just as though he was his own son. And like all dads he spoiled him. Sometimes when John had done something wrong and I sent him up to his room, I'd find George creeping upstairs with the *Beano*, John's favourite comic, and a bar of chocolate.'

When John was fourteen he was away on holiday at Durness, Scotland, with his Aunt Elizabeth. At Mendips, George suddenly began to vomit blood and was rushed to Sefton General Hospital where he died of a haemorrhage. John wasn't told immediately. When he arrived home a few days later and asked for his Uncle George, Mimi told him the tragic news. John went upstairs. He was to say, 'Then my cousin Leila arrived and she came upstairs as well. We both had hysterics. We just laughed and laughed. I felt very guilty afterwards.'

George was 52 when he died on 5 June 1955 and he left his wife £2,000.

Smith, Howard

A journalist who wrote the 'Scenes' column in the New York magazine *Village Voice*. Yoko contacted Smith by phone in December 1970 as she believed he would make a good guide for John in New York when they eventually moved there. John and Yoko were at Ronnie Hawkins's farm in Canada at the time and Yoko suggested that he come up and meet John. Smith, who also hosted his own radio show on WPLJ, agreed on condition he could interview John for his show. Yoko agreed and Smith travelled to the farm and taped a two-and-a-half-hour interview.

He next heard from Yoko in November 1970, when she told him they'd be arriving in New York. The couple booked into the Regency Hotel on Park Avenue and Smith immediately began escorting them to all the right places, introducing them to fashionable eateries such as Max's Kansas City, recommending places where they should shop and taking them to Washington Square to see the street singer David Peel.

Smith invited John on to his radio show on 6 June 1971. John, affecting a German accent, said, 'This is WPLJ, playing your favourite tunes; this is Edgar Hoover here. I'd like to do your room.'

One listener, puzzled by the announcement, phoned in and asked, 'You'd like to do my room? What colour would you like to paint it?'

John said, 'No, no. I'm gonna Hoover it.'

In the afternoon Smith was set to interview Frank Zappa and mentioned it to John, who said he'd always wanted to meet him. Smith said he would take John and Yoko with him and they went along to No. 1 Fifth Avenue, where Zappa was staying.

During the meeting it was suggested that John and Yoko join Zappa and his band on stage at the Fillmore East that night – or, more precisely, at 2 p.m. the following morning. After they left the meeting, Smith stayed with them to ensure that John, who was now becoming nervous at the thought, would actually turn up at the theatre.

When Yoko issued her album *Fly,* John joined her on Howard's radio show, praising the LP and comparing Yoko to Little Richard.

Smith, Mary Elizabeth

Born in 1906, she was the aunt who reared John, and was affectionately known as Aunt Mimi. She was one of Julia Stanley's four sisters.

She left home at the age of nineteen to become a resident trainee nurse at Woolton convalescent hospital and eventually became a nursing sister in charge of a ward full of mentally handicapped patients. Later, she became a private secretary to a local businessman.

Mimi was 33 when she married George Smith, a dairy farmer, on 15 September 1939, but the couple had no children of their own and Mimi insisted that Julia let her take care of John, as she believed that Julia was neglecting him. Julia agreed and John went to live with his aunt from the age of five.

Yet she was to say that it wasn't true that he was that age when he came to her. 'I brought him up from a few weeks old until he was twenty-one,' she asserted. 'My husband George adored John just as though he was his own son.

'All this talk about John's hard upbringing in a Liverpool slum is a fantasy. He wasn't pampered but he had the best of everything we could provide.'

She said, 'To tell you the truth, when he was born I nearly went off me nut! A boy! Because we were all girls.'

Recalling when she rushed to the hospital on 9 October 1940 and saw John for the first time, she said, 'Do you believe in fate? Because I knew the moment I saw John in that hospital that I was the one to be his mother, not Julia. Does that sound awful? It isn't really, because Julia accepted it as something perfectly natural. She used to say, "You're his real mother. All I did was give birth." '

It was Mimi who chose the name John and Julia who chose the name Winston. Julia was feeling patriotic and gave him the middle name of Winston after Winston Churchill, then Britain's wartime leader.

She enjoyed rearing him and recalled how she used to send him off to bed with a panda under one arm and a teddy bear under the other. She said he sang himself to sleep every night.

'We so enjoyed having him – they were the best years of my life bringing him up.'

Mimi took care of him, although she was very strict, particularly when her husband died and she had to raise John on her own. Although she bought him his first guitar, she told him, 'The guitar's all right as a hobby, but you'll never make a living out of it.'

She was to say, 'I would sometimes rant and rave at him, but deep down he knew I loved him and that he loved me. We were very close.'

On the historic day that John met Paul at the St Peter's Church fête, Mimi couldn't find John. So she went along to the fête by herself. When there she met some of her sisters and other members of the family. It wasn't until John actually went on stage that she knew he was even taking part in the fête.

She was to say, 'I was having a cup of tea in the refreshment tent. Suddenly, in the midst of everything, came this – this eruption of noise. Everyone had drained away from where I stood, in the field next door. And there on the stage I saw them, John and that Shotton.

'John saw me standing there with my mouth open. He started to make words up about me in the song he was singing. He sang, "Mimi's coming down the path." '

Of his years with Mimi, John commented, 'I never forgave my auntie for not treating me like a genius. It was obvious to me. I was different. I used to tell her not to throw my poetry out because she would regret it when I was famous – but she still threw it out.'

However, it was Mimi who bought him his first proper guitar, following a £10 mail-order guitar he'd bought after seeing it in a *Reveille* advertisement. He'd been badgering her so often that she recalled, 'I thought I would teach him a lesson by getting him one. I thought that the novelty would wear off soon, and he would forget about it. So one Saturday we went down to Hessy's shop in Liverpool, and I bought him one there. It cost me fourteen pounds. *Fourteen pounds!* That was a lot of money in those days. I begrudged paying it on a guitar for him, but I thought that if it keeps him quiet, then there's no harm done. He would even stand in front of his bedroom mirror with the guitar pretending to be that man Elvis Presley.'

Mimi admitted that she didn't approve of Paul or George when she first saw them. When he talked about his group, she was to comment, 'I did everything I could to talk John out of it. I thought he was daft. Stick to art, I told him. But he was right – although I still say he would have made a big success in art even if he hadn't made quite as much money. Any time I tried to reason with him, or when I got annoyed with him, he'd just answer in that nonsense talk of his and it made me laugh so I always lost the argument. He does that with interviewers, too.'

She was also to say, 'When he lived with me, he was always very considerate. When he first got mixed up in the beat business in Liverpool he was out in cafés till all hours. Finally I told him that no boy of mine was going to hang around cafés late at night, and he was never very late after that.'

When the Beatles became successful, John bought her a bungalow for £25,000 – Harbour View, at 126 Panorama Road,

Poole, Dorset – on 3 August 1965, where she remained for the rest of her life. The bungalow was situated in Sandbanks, an exclusive peninsula at Poole Harbour, and John said it was 'the most beautiful place I have ever seen'.

Mimi was to say, 'I never wanted to move. John made me. He came to love the place.'

She said, 'Before I moved here, when I lived in Liverpool, sometimes there would be fifty girls outside the house. Of course, I couldn't just let them stay out there, so I'd bring them in for tea. And you know they'd pinch the cups for souvenirs. Then, one afternoon after I'd moved here, two young American girls pulled up in a big car and started taking pictures. When I asked them what they wanted, they said, "We've come to look over Johnny's house." What a cheek! I shouted, "This is not a museum," and I sent them on their way. Sometimes, even today, when the boats pass on the harbour, I hear a man say over the loudspeaker, "And here lives the aunt of Beatle John Lennon." If I'm out in the back garden, he says, "There she is now!" I guess there's nothing I can do about it, though. They think I'm someone special.'

Once, when she visited John at Apple, she voiced her dismay at the cover of the *Two Virgins* album with its nude photos of John and Yoko, telling him, 'It would have been all right, John, but you're both so ugly. Why don't you get somebody attractive on the cover if you've got to have somebody naked?'

In fact, she was quite upset by the *Two Virgins* cover and commented, 'He's been a naughty boy and the public doesn't like it, and he's sorry for it. Now he wants sympathy. That's why he's come out with those fantastic stories about an unhappy childhood. It's true that his mother wasn't there and there was no father around, but my husband and I gave him a wonderful home. Why, John even had a pony when he was a little boy. He certainly didn't come from a slum.'

When the Beatles broke up she said, 'I don't know what all this business between John and Paul is about. But I don't dare ask John. I did ring Paul about it, and he told me things would straighten up. The boys have been friends so long. I remember them coming home from school together on their bikes, begging biscuits. I'm sure they'll get back together again. This is just a phase they're passing through.'

She also commented, 'She's responsible for all this. Yoko. She's changed him. I'm sure Yoko and Linda [McCartney] are behind John and Paul's break-up. Cynthia was such a nice girl. When she and John were in art college, she'd come to my house and say, "Oh, Mimi, what am I going to do about John?" She'd sit there until he came home. She really chased him. He'd walk up the road and back until she got tired of waiting and went home. I think he was afraid of her.'

Mimi told Alanna Nash, a Beatles fan who visited her in 1971, 'The boys had talent, yes, but they had a lot of luck too. When they first played me "Love Me Do" I didn't think much of it.'

Mimi lived alone, except for a housekeeper, Mrs Bailey.

In 1979 she discussed John: 'He rings up and announced, "Hi, it's Father Christmas here." He's the same old jokey John. He really seems much more settled and happy now than he used to be. He'll be doing something, just you wait and see, something that will surprise everyone. I only hope he doesn't go pouncing on stage any more. He's nearly forty now and if he went back on stage he'd be doing exactly what he was doing at nineteen. You must go on. When he phones now he wants to talk about Sean [his second son], about when he was a little boy himself. When he phoned the other night he was talking about the time I wrapped him in a blanket because it was cold and I brought him downstairs. He can't have been more than five then. He just amazes me with the things he remembers.'

In 1982, all the people selling Lennon memorabilia – T-shirts, badges and so on – irked her and she said, 'They're making a mockery of his memory. I feel he is still with me. I have the memory of those wonderful phone calls from the person the public never really knew.'

She was also to say, 'Every time John does something bad and gets his picture in the papers, he rings me up to smooth me over. A big present arrives every time he's been naughty.' She also had a habit of taking John's pictures off the wall if she felt he had done something of which she disapproved.

When the *Imagine* film came out in 1989 she said, 'Maybe now those people who've been bringing these books out will see the real John and not the one they made up in some terrible books.'

When John was in Japan he sent some postcards to Mimi. One read, 'Mimi: Are up in mountains, really very nice. Love John, Yoko and Sean.' She said, 'You'd think he could have written a bit more than that, wouldn't you?' The next card read, 'Still up in mountains. Here is the number in case you wanna give us a call. Love Da-da, mom-ma and Sean-chan.'

She said, 'That really is typical of him. He gives me some telephone number in the middle of the Japanese mountains, I don't know where, and expects me to call him. I don't know what time it will be there, whether he'll be in or anything. If he wants to talk to me, he can jolly well call me.'

John kept in continual touch with Mimi and he'd spend two hours a week on the phone talking to her. Recalling his phone call on Friday 5 December 1980, Mimi said, 'He rang and said he was looking out of a window in New York, looking at the docks and ships and wondering whether any of them were going to Liverpool. It made him homesick. He was coming home. He was coming here to Poole, Dorset, and going to Liverpool.' She said that the night before he was murdered he told her once again that he would be coming over to Britain and would be going to Liverpool.

She was in bed listening to the radio when she heard the mention of John's name. She didn't actually hear what the announcer was saying, but had a feeling of dread. Then the phone rang and it was Neil Aspinall, one of John's oldest friends and a former Beatles road manager, with the dreadful news. This was followed by a call from her nephew Michael. Soon after, the press gathered outside her door.

She said that when she heard the news she was in a trance and didn't know what she was doing. She suddenly realised she had a pair of scissors in her hand and had been cutting her hair off in grief.

In the 1980s she was in poor health and was attended by a nurse every day. At one time she had to go and stay with her sister, Anne Caldwaller, in Rock Ferry, but returned to Poole in 1985.

In November 1980, to celebrate the release of *Double Fantasy*, John sent Mimi a silver box from Cartier's with a pearl necklace and matching brooch. The message engraved on the box read, 'Double Fantasy – Christmas 1980 – NYC – John and

Yoko.' Mimi then rang John at the Dakota Building and said, 'You're daft!' John laughed, saying, 'Go on, Mimi, spoil yourself. Just for a change.'

Mimi died at her home at the age of 88 on Friday 6 December 1991 and Yoko, Sean and Cynthia attended her cremation at Poole Crematorium in Dorset on Thursday 12 December, while Paul, George and Ringo sent bouquets. The message on Paul's wreath read, 'Dear Mimi, it's great to know you in life. You were an exceptional woman, and loved by many of us. God bless, Paul, Linda and children.'

There were thirty mourners, who also included John's half-sisters Julie and Jacqueline.

The property was bought in 1994 and the bungalow was knocked down and replaced with a new luxury home.

Smothers Brothers, The

Popular American comedy duo who had their own television series, *The Smothers Brothers Comedy Hour*, which was launched in 1967. The brothers had frequent problems with CBS due to the controversial nature of the sketches and the network finally pulled the plug on their show in June 1969.

Tommy Smothers was one of the celebrities John recruited for his backing choir on 'Give Peace a Chance', recorded in a Montreal hotel bedroom. Tommy was also interested in appearing in a film with Ringo Starr in 1969 called *Captain Blood,* but nothing came of it.

In March 1974 at the Troubadour club in Los Angeles, the Smothers Brothers were attempting a comeback after their TV series had been so abruptly cancelled – and there was a lot of sympathy for the duo. On their opening night, John Lennon turned up with May Pang and Harry Nilsson. He had consumed too many potent Brandy Alexanders and began to heckle the act, shouting out to one of the brothers, 'Dickie, you're an asshole.' Some scuffles and ugly scenes followed.

John was later to admit that he'd always liked Tommy, but he considered Dickie was 'a wimp'.

Solt, Andrew

Director of *Imagine: John Lennon*. Solt also co-wrote the script with Sam Egan and the two also co-authored the book of the same title. Solt was a producer, director and writer for television and films, and his work included *This Is Elvis, Heroes of Rock and Roll* and the Emmy-award-winning *Cousteau: Mississippi*. In 1991 he bought the rights to all 1,087 hours of *The Ed Sullivan Show,* which included all of the Beatles' appearances.

When Yoko Ono proposed the idea of the film to the producer David L Wolper, she opened her complete archives of rare film footage, photographs and writings. Solt and Egan sifted through two boxcars full of material and also approached Lennon's family and friends for new interviews.

Solt had originally extended an invitation to Lennon in 1978 when he offered the host position on the TV special *Heroes of Rock 'n' Roll* to the former Beatle. John didn't do the show, but Solt felt a connection nonetheless.

It was while he was completing work on the documentary *This Is Elvis* that he heard of John's death. He said, 'While we were finishing *Elvis*, we talked about what a tragedy Lennon's death was, and what a potent story it would be to tell.' For six years Solt had tried to put the Lennon film in motion, at one point trying to bring in Wolper, but Yoko resisted. Finally, it was Yoko herself who approached Wolper in 1986 and Solt was hired to write and direct. Solt also produced and directed *Gimme Some Truth*, which was released in 2000.

Song for John

A medley of three Yoko compositions, which Yoko recorded in November 1968. The song included parts of 'Let's Go On Flying', 'Snow Is Falling All the Time' and 'Don't Worry Kyoko'. It was one of the tracks issued on the flexi-disc by *Aspen* magazine in 1969.

She also recorded a version of the number for her *Approximately Infinite Universe* album in November 1972.

Songwriting

Most people believe that the songs of Lennon and McCartney were genuine collaborations between the two. Although a large number of early songs were co-written, with each of them contributing a bit more or less than the other on particular songs, the majority of the later numbers were individual compositions, although, as agreed at the beginning of the partnership, they always went under the Lennon and McCartney banner. John was to say, 'We only ever wrote together because in the early days it was fun and later on convenient. But our best songs were always written alone.'

Originally, it was mooted that the name be McCartney and Lennon. There was always a rivalry between the two and often a battle to get as many numbers on an official release as possible – with the third songwriter, George Harrison, usually the loser. Generally, although it was not always the case, the one who wrote the songs took over on lead vocal.

They agreed that everything they wrote together or individually should go on co-composer credit and the two would share all earnings equally, even on songs written 100 per cent by only one of them.

When Paul composed music for the film *The Family Way*, John was to say, 'I copped money for *The Family Way*, the film music that Paul wrote, when I was out of the country filming *How I Won the War*. I said, "You'd better keep that." He said, "Don't be soft." It's the concept. We inspired each other so much in the early days. We write how we write now because of each other.'

John also commented on their occasional collaborations when he discussed 'A Day In the Life', a track from the *Sergeant Pepper* album: 'Well, it was a peak. Paul and I were definitely working together; especially on "A Day In the Life" – that was real. The way we wrote a lot of the time: you'd write the good bit, the part that was easy, like "I read the news today" or whatever it was; then, when you got stuck or whenever it got hard, instead of carrying on, you just drop it. Then we would meet each other, and I would sing half, and he would be inspired to write the next bit and vice versa. He was a bit shy about it because I think he thought it's already a good song.

'Sometimes we wouldn't let each other interfere with a song either, because you tend to be a bit lax with someone else's stuff – you experiment a bit. So we were doing it in his room with the piano. He said, "Should we do this?" "Yeah, let's do that." But *Pepper* was a peak all right.'

John usually felt that Paul's songs were more lightweight than his own compositions. He was say, 'My contribution to Paul's songs was always to add a little bluesy edge to them. He provided a lightness, an optimism, while I would always go for the sadness, the discords, the bluesy notes.'

On another occasion he said, 'Yoko and I once signed a guy's violin in Spain after he played us "Yesterday". He couldn't understand that I didn't write the song. But I guess he couldn't have gone from table to table playing "I Am The Walrus".'

The rivalry between them was probably deeper than many people realise. John said, 'In the early days the majority of singles were mine. Only when I became self-conscious and inhibited did Paul start dominating the group a little too much for my liking.'

This rivalry must have also spilled over to the recording of the songs, with John commenting, 'Usually we'd spend hours doing little detailed cleaning-ups of Paul's songs, but when it came to mine, especially if it was a great song like "Strawberry Fields Forever" or "Across the Universe", somehow this atmosphere of looseness and casualness and experimentation would creep in: subconscious sabotage.'

The songwriting partnership was doomed when Paul refused to record John's song 'Cold Turkey' as a Beatles number. As a result, John issued it as a Plastic Ono Band single and decided to drop the Lennon and McCartney credit and issue it solely credited to himself.

His resentment flared up when he composed 'How Do You Sleep?', which was an attack on Paul's songwriting capabilities, with a reference to 'Yesterday' as the only decent song he wrote and a comparison between it and one of Paul's solo ventures, 'Another Day'.

South Ocean Boulevard

Area in West Palm Beach, Florida, where John and Yoko bought a neo-Spanish beachside mansion on 28 January 1980 from a Mr and Mrs Jock McLean for almost a million dollars. The house had seven bedrooms, two swimming pools and a hundred and fifty feet of beach front.

The Lennons spent their eleventh anniversary in the house on 20 March 1980 – John bought Yoko a diamond heart and 500 fresh gardenias, and Yoko bought him a vintage Rolls-Royce.

Spacek, Sissy

American film actress who starred in movies such as *Coalminer's Daughter*, *Carrie* and *Missing*.

Before she was a film star, Spacek tried her hand at singing and, in 1969, under the name Rainbo, she issued a single on which she was critical of the full-frontal nude shot of John and Yoko on the *Two Virgins* album. The single was entitled 'John, You Went Too Far This Time' and was coupled with 'C'mon, Teach Me To Love'. The single was issued on Roulette 7030.

Spaniard in the Works, A

John's second book, published by Jonathan Cape in 1965. It was designed by Robert Freeman and included illustrations by John. The title is a typical pun by John on 'A Spanner in the Works' and relates to the title story about a Spanish handyman.

The book continued in the vein of 'In His Own Write' and there were fifty-six items in it including fifteen mini-stories, six poems and thirty-eight drawings, including some self-portraits and two Beatles portraits. The contents included:

- 'A Spaniard in the Works', a mini story about Jesus El Pifco, who emigrates from Spain to the Highlands to work as a handyman for a Scottish laird. He falls for the laird's chambermaid and marries her. The groom's mother phones from Barcelona to advise them she is travelling to Scotland to visit the newlyweds. When they tell the employer he says, 'You're all fired!'
- 'The Fat Budgie', a poem about a bird called Jeffrey. The yellow budgie's owner recalls his own Uncle Arthur, who ate so many budgies that he died. The man then begins to force-feed his pet by stuffing him with eggs and toast.
- 'Snore Wife and Some Several Dwarts', an obvious parody on 'Snow White and the Seven Dwarfs'. In John's story the eight Dwarts arrive home from working in the diamond mine to find Snore Wife sleeping in Grumpy's bed. In the meantime, the Wicked Queen is looking into her magic mirror in her castle and is observed by Miss Craddock. The Dwarts accept Snore Wife into their household and a few days later a woman tries to sell poisoned apples to Snore White. The woman is really the Wicked Queen and Miss Craddock turns out to be a handsome prince who eats both the Wicked Queen and the mirror, then moves in with the Dwarts, although he doesn't marry Snore Wife.

- 'The Singularge Experience of Miss Anne Duffield', a tale set in London in 1892. Shamrock Womlbs and Doctored Whopper discover that Mr Oxo Whitney has escaped from prison. Whitney turns up at their door and Womlbs proceeds to beat him to a pulp. A prostitute, Mary Atkins, and her pimp, Sydney Aspinall (typical of John's humour – a name check for their road manager Neil Aspinall?), next enter the scene, and Mary is killed by Jack the Ripper, who is taking revenge on prostitutes for giving him a venereal disease. Whopper fixes breakfast for Womlbs the next morning, but finds the master detective has disappeared. He turns up again a week later in a dishevelled state and explains to Whopper what has happened to him, but Whopper can't recall a word he'd said.

- 'The Faulty Bagnose', another poem. It's a rather muddled piece, which is basically a religious sermon from a preacher. One of the lines is 'Give us thisbe our daily tit' – which could be another hidden joke by John as he played Thisbe in a short sketch based on *A Midsummer Night's Dream* in the *Around the Beatles* TV special.

- 'We Must Not Forget … The General Erection', a satire on the 1964 British General Election, written as a newspaper editorial. The first line is typical of John's style of writing: 'Azue orl gnome, Harrassed Wilsod …', which basically translates from the Lennon to: 'As you all know, Harold Wilson …' The piece talks of the Labour Party coming back into power, mentions the backing of the trade unions and the disappointment in the election results by Sir Alec Douglas-Home, the former Prime Minister. All of this is written in the typical Lennon mangled and fractured English with names such as Sir Alice Doubtless-Whom.

- 'Benjamin Distasteful', obviously another political satire in which the Prime Minister Benjamin wants to end one war and start another.

- 'The Wumberlog (or The Magic Dog)', John's longest poem, running to 121 lines. A boy is heartbroken at the death of his Uncle Joe and a Magic Dog appears and leads him to an enchanted boat. He is joined on his journey by a heavily feathered bird, the Wumberlog, and they arrive at a place where dead people still live. The boy is reunited with his uncle and they share a grave together.

- 'Araminta Ditch', is a woman who can't stop laughing. From the moment she wakes up she begins to laugh, which proves embarrassing for her boyfriend Fred and his family. Her neighbour Mrs Cambsby feels she'll go mad if Araminta doesn't stop laughing, and other neighbours feel the same. Eventually she seeks help from the Reverend Lionel Hughes, but no one can help her and she continues her perpetual laughing – although everyone else dies before her and she leads a long life before she laughs herself to death.

- 'Cassandle', a parody of a *Daily Mirror* columnist of the time who used the pseudonym Cassandra. John has his columnist attack the Beatles and mention himself fifteen times in a short item, indicating his high self-esteem.

- 'The National Health Cow' moves to a farm where a cow is relieved when a lad comes to milk her as she hasn't been milked for days. After asking her why she's been ignored, he kills her with a brick.

- 'Silly Norman', a lengthy poem. In it a character called Norman is ready to partake of his favourite snack, choco-late cookies and tea, when he discovers there is no water in the tap – he is unaware that the pipes are frozen. He goes outside and discovers there are no houses anywhere and he believes that God has destroyed the world. His mother arrives and he tells her the world has been destroyed, but she informs him that no one has ever lived near to them. They go inside, discover the tap is now on and decide to have their tea.

- 'Mr Boris Morris', a tale of a man who crashes posh parties and takes compromising photographs of the guests. He accomplishes this at the Oriental party hosted by Miss Pearl Staines, but when he does the same at the Hunt Ball, one of the guests shoots him in the face. He looks into the mirror and wonders how he'll fix 'this blob of mine'.

- 'Bernice's Sheep', a 25-line poem in which Bernice spends her days slaughtering cows but seeks comfort in protecting her sheep.

- 'Last Will And Testicle' is, as its title implies, about the reading of a will. The benefactor of Reginald Bunker-Harquart's will is little thirteen-year-old Elsie, who has to be entombed in a box until her 21st birthday. Old Nanny Harriette boxes Elsie in the garden and charges people admission to see her. On the eve of Elsie's 21st birthday, Nanny brings the box inside to warm it by the fire, but it ignites and Elsie is incinerated.

- 'Our Dad' is the final poem, 72 lines in length. This concerns a father who realises he's not wanted by his family, so he packs his bags and leaves. His sons then begin to search for any valuables he has left behind, seize his money and pension book and then plan a party.

- 'I Believe, Boot …' is another of John's attacks on religion and takes the form of a television debate between a cleric and Mr Wabooba. An argument ensures in which Wabooba calls the cleric 'a Christian imperialist'.

John appeared on a number of radio programmes to promote the book. Discussing his writing on the BBC's *World of Books*, he said, 'I'm selfish about what I write, or big-headed about it. Once I've written it I like it and the publishers sometimes say, "Should we leave this out or change that?" And I fight like mad because, once I've done it, I like to keep it. But I always write it straight off. I might add things when I go over it, before it's published, but I seldom take anything out, so it's spontaneous.' He also referred to two of his influences during his writing of the book: Sir Arthur Conan Doyle, creator of Sherlock Holmes, whose influence can be detected in 'The Singularge Experience of Miss Anne Duffield', and Lewis Carroll. John said, 'I always admit to that because I love *Alice['s Adventures] In Wonderland* and *Through The Looking Glass*, but I didn't even know he'd written anything else, I was that ignorant. I just had it as a birthday present as a child and I liked it.'

Commenting on the reviewers who had said his inspirations were people like Edward Lear and James Thurber, John said, 'I deny it because I'm ignorant of it. Lear I'd never heard of. Well, I'd heard the name obviously somewhere but we didn't do him at school. The only classic or very highbrow anything I read at school or knew of is Chaucer. I might have read a bit of Chaucer at school because I think they do that. And so I bought all the books they said it was like. I bought one book on Edward Lear, I bought *Finnegan's Wake*, Chaucer, and I couldn't see any resemblance to any of them.'

John maintained that he hadn't read James Joyce prior to critics maintaining that the Irish writer inspired him. He must have been livid with John Wain's review of *A Spaniard in the Works* in *New Republic*, when Wain wrote, 'The first thing any literate person will notice on reading through Mr. Lennon's book is that it all comes out of one source, namely the later work of James Joyce. Not only the determination to communicate almost exclusively in puns, but the equally determined smutty, blasphemous and subversive tone, are Joycean.'

John also lampooned Cassandra of the *Daily Mirror* and said, 'I did it mainly because he knocked us. We get a lot of knocking, which we don't mind. We don't want everyone to love us; if somebody doesn't like us they're entitled to but we have no defence against people like that writing about us in newspapers, because we can't say anything back ... And this is just my way of having a go back. It was just a sort of personal joke amongst ourselves. I'm definitely planning on Bernard Levin for the next one.'

In 1998 the Swedish publisher Bakhall republished the book, which contained John's work in both English and Swedish. The cover photos had been taken during John's trip to Sweden in July 1984 and a bonus CD containing five previously unreleased songs by John was included. The CD was 24 minutes long and was authorised by Yoko.

They were five numbers from the *Lost Lennon Tapes* radio series, interspersed with clips taken from an interview with John and Yoko in 1980. The songs were 'My Life', 'Dear John', 'Lord Take This Makeup Off Me', 'Make Love Not War' and 'Here We Go Again'.

The initial print of 500 sold out and the reprint did not contain the CD.

Spector, Phil

The man whom the writer Tom Wolfe described as 'the tycoon of teen'. He was born in the Bronx, New York, on 24 December 1940 and wrote and produced the No. 1 hit 'To Know Him Is To Love Him' when he was only sixteen.

Spector then went on to record artists such as the Crystals and the Ronettes and produced a string of hits, including 'He's a Rebel', 'Then He Kissed Me', 'Be My Baby' and 'Baby I Love You'. He was to develop a lush style of recording that was described as his 'wall of sound', and received further acclaim for his classic album *A Christmas Gift To You*. When Andrew Loog Oldham, one of the managers of the Rolling Stones, booked the Ronettes to tour with the Stones in Britain, Spector flew out with them from New York to London on 24 January 1964, despite his phobia about flying. While in London he was a guest on TV shows such as *Ready, Steady, Go!* and *Juke Box Jury*. When the impresario Tony Hall threw a party for the Ronettes at his house in Mayfair, the Beatles asked if they could attend.

John, George and Ringo turned up and met Spector for the first time. They asked his advice about their coming trip to New York and also asked him to fly out with them. He agreed. When they actually arrived in New York the Beatles were apprehensive and asked Spector to lead them off the plane. Discussing the trip with Jann Wenner of *Rolling Stone* magazine in 1969, Spector said, 'It was a lot of fun. It was probably the only time I flew that I wasn't afraid, because I knew they weren't going to get killed in a plane.' He also said, 'John Lennon was with his first wife, he was very quiet. Paul asked a lot of questions. George was wonderful.'

In 1969 when John had begun to make solo recordings, beginning with 'Cold Turkey', he decided he just wanted to go ahead and perform in the studio and not have the task of producing a record himself. The intricacies and the technical work of producing didn't interest him and he was looking for someone to produce his new number, 'Instant Karma!'. It was Allen Klein who suggested Spector to him. This was immediately acceptable to John, who had once said, 'If we ever used anybody besides George Martin, it would be Phil.'

A friend of Spector was to comment, 'Phil needed that association with Lennon and the Beatles ... He thought he couldn't possibly fail if John Lennon was with him. He didn't particularly want the association, but he needed it.'

Phil arrived in London, sharing a room at the Inn on the Park with his promotions man, Peter Bennett, and accompanied by his bodyguard, George Brand.

When John gathered with his Plastic Ono Band – George Harrison, Klaus Voormann and Alan White – at Abbey Road Studios, Spector kept them waiting for an hour, one of the tricks he usually pulled to establish his power. John was delighted with the finished production but Spector wasn't. He told John he wanted to take the tape back to Los Angeles and add strings to it. John said no: he was satisfied with the number as it was.

However, without John's permission or knowledge, Spector went ahead and remixed the record for its release in America. It became his biggest solo single to date reaching No. 3 in the US and selling one million copies in America alone.

As a result of its success John and Allen Klein asked Phil if he could do something with the *Let It Be* tapes and they would allow him carte blanche. Early in 1970 Spector arrived and settled into the basement studio at Apple in Savile Row. There were thirty hours of unmixed recording tape, which he had to assemble into a credible album. The tapes had been the result of Paul McCartney's desire for them to 'get back to their roots', but the recording sessions had been fraught with tensions and none of the Beatles really wanted to get involved in sorting out so many hours of recording. George Martin didn't want to begin mixing the tapes, which then sat on a shelf at Apple, and John was to comment about the task of putting it all in shape, 'I really couldn't stand it.'

Throughout February and March, Spector sat in the Apple basement trying to find some ways of turning the chaos into a salvageable album. Only one song from the sessions had been previously rescued when George Martin had produced 'Let It Be' in a form suitable for release.

Spector decided to produce some lush overdubbing using strings and choirs. George Harrison attended some of the sessions and was so impressed he talked Phil into producing his solo album.

When he had completed the task, Phil sent an acetate to each member of the Beatles.

Paul McCartney was repulsed by what Phil had done to his number 'The Long and Winding Road', which Paul had recorded with only an acoustic guitar, having aimed for simplicity in the recording. Phil had added strings, harps and background singers; Paul was incensed and ordered Allen Klein and Phil to jettison the 'wall-of-sound' version and replace it with his original. He was ignored and the Spector version appeared on the album. Paul was able to use this as an example in his court case for the dissolution of the Beatles, that there had been a conspiracy to 'ruin my career artistically'.

Paul wasn't the only person to be unhappy at the way Spector had stamped his own influence on the Beatles' album. A reviewer in *Rolling Stone* magazine, John Mendelsohn, wrote that Spector had 'whipped out his orchestra and choir and proceeded to turn several of the rough gems of the best Beatles album in ages into costume jewellery'.

When George Martin also criticised the production, Spector told Richard Williams, a journalist, 'It was no favour to me to give me George Martin's job because I don't consider him in my league. He's an arranger, that's all. As far as "Let it Be", he had left it in deplorable condition, and it was not satisfactory to any of them. They did not want it out as it was. So John said, "Let Phil do it," and I said, "Fine." Then I said, "Would anybody like to get involved in it, work on it with me?" "No." They didn't care. But they did have the right to say, "We don't want it out," and they didn't say that.'

Within two weeks it had sold over two million copies in America, establishing a record in sales up to that time. With sales of four million worldwide, it outsold several of the previous Beatles albums.

When it won a Grammy award for the best original score in a motion picture, it was Paul McCartney who picked up the award, which hadn't ruined his career artistically after all.

In May of that year Spector went into the studios with George Harrison and over a six-month period produced the three-album set *All Things Must Pass*. The album was released in November 1970 and became the No. 1 album in both the UK and US within two weeks. The first single issued, 'My Sweet Lord', also topped the charts and the follow-up, 'What Is Life?', reached No. 9.

Ten days later, John's *John Lennon/Plastic Ono Band* album which had also been produced by Spector, was released. The album was unique in the naked honesty expressed by a rock performer and nothing like it had ever been released before. John exposed his inner feelings following a course in primal therapy (see **Janov, Dr Arthur**) and screamed and cried in anger on a harrowing and emotional album. It reached No. 6 in the charts in December, but has since increased in reputation as the years go by.

Spector was made head of A&R at Apple Records and he also produced 'Tell The Truth', a number by Eric Clapton and his band, Derek and the Dominoes. Clapton didn't like what Phil had done to the number and refused to release it.

In the meantime, Spector continued his association with John and produced 'Power To the People', which reached No. 11 in the charts.

For Apple he brought his wife, Ronnie Spector, former singer with the Ronettes, to record a number penned by George Harrison called 'Try Some, Buy Some', although it didn't chart. Phil also produced the *Concert for Bangladesh* album.

He next produced John's chart-topping classic, the *Imagine* album and, with John having moved to New York, then produced 'Happy Xmas (War Is Over)'. Unfortunately, John was coming under the influence of political dissenters such as Jerry Rubin and Abbie Hoffman and his next album, *Sometime In New York City*, sold only 164,000 copies. Phil's contribution was to co-produce, with John and Yoko, the parts of the album recorded live at the Fillmore East, with Frank Zappa and the Mothers of Invention, although he is credited on the sleeve with co-producing both sides of the album.

The association between John and Phil ended temporarily and Phil moved to Los Angeles. Then, in October 1973, John arrived in LA with May Pang during his separation from Yoko. He approached Spector and said that he wanted to record an album of old rock 'n' roll numbers and would leave the production completely in Phil's hands.

In a clever move, Spector paid for the sessions himself, effectively taking control away from John, Apple and Capitol Records. However the sessions at A&M Studios turned into a nightmare for all concerned. There was tension in the studios, with both Phil and John getting completely drunk and out of hand. On one occasion, John was so drunk that Phil and his bodyguard, George Brand, had to take him home and bind his wrists and ankles to prevent him from hurting himself. As they left John shouted 'Jew bastard!' at Spector.

A witness to the sessions said, 'Phil had to handcuff John because John would have killed himself ... John would sleep at Phil's house and Phil would have to lock the door on him when he'd get too crazy. But when he woke up and it was all over, it was kind of like, you know, "Thanks a lot for doing that".'

Studio equipment was damaged, there were reports of people defecating in hallways and A&M ordered Spector out. He moved to the Record Plant in LA. A few days later, a frustrated Spector pulled out a gun and fired it into the studio ceiling. John said, 'Phil, if you're gonna kill me, kill me. But don't fuck with me ears. I need them.'

Spector was also in the middle of a custody hearing and asked John to come into the court with him as a character reference. But, when Ronnie Spector came into the courtroom, Phil let off such a stream of obscenities that John left the courtroom and was never to be in the same room as Spector again. John then found that he couldn't get hold of the tapes. Spector claimed that they were his property and he'd taken them from the studio. Spector refused to see John each time he came round trying to obtain the tapes.

Then Spector was involved in a road accident and suffered multiple head and body injuries, serious enough to warrant surgery. When John went around trying to get his tapes again, he was told, 'Mr Spector died in an accident.'

Frustrated, John decided to abandon the tapes and let Capitol handle things. He left for New York.

Capitol Records was able to arrange a deal with Spector in June 1974 and paid him $94,000 for the tapes. However, John found most of the tapes unsatisfactory and only five of the unremixed tracks were eventually used on John's *Rock 'n' Roll* album.

John never forgave Spector for what had happened and, when John was murdered, Spector wanted to atone in some way and went to see Yoko. As a result he testified on her behalf in her case against Jack Douglas, co-producer of the *Double Fantasy* album (see **Douglas, Jack**). She then hired him to produce her *Season of Glass* album, but told him to finish halfway through: she wanted to produce the rest herself because it was too personal. She later gave Spector one of John's guitars.

Spinetti, Victor

Welsh actor who appeared in *A Hard Day's Night, Help!* and *Magical Mystery Tour,* all at the invitation of the Beatles. The group first visited him backstage when he was appearing in the play *Oh, What A Lovely War!* They asked him to be in their debut film, and when they were making *Magical Mystery Tour* they asked him to take on the part of the courier. However, he was appearing in a West End play at the time and couldn't appear, although he told them he could make time to film during the day. John sent him part of the script and said, 'Well, this is as far as we've got, come and make something up.' Victor said he could do the drill sergeant he'd played in *Oh! What A Lovely War* and John said, 'Okay. Great!'

He also arranged to work on the stage play based on *In His Own Write* for the National Theatre, and John took him to Morocco to work on it. After a party, both of them became ill after smoking hashish. John was still feeling bad the following day and Victor looked after him, feeding him headache powders. The Rolling Stones arrived at the hotel and Brian Jones was also feeling ill. Victor offered him one of the headache powders and Brian immediately lined it out and snorted it in the hotel lobby.

They had even planned to make a film of the play and the two of them went up to Liverpool to look at the locations. Although John was very keen at the time, once he got remarried he was too preoccupied to go ahead with it.

Victor was able to relate some of his anecdotes about John and the Beatles when he launched his own one-man theatre show *Thoughts From A Very Private Diary* in 1989. The show was staged at the Donmar Warehouse Theatre in Covent Garden and ran from 27 February – 1 April.

Spinozza, David

A guitarist who performed on the *Mind Games* album. It is believed that Yoko was going out with him when John was with May Pang on his 'lost weekend'. He is probably the person hinted at in the song 'Bless You' when John sings 'Bless you wherever you are / Holding her now ...'

Spirit Foundation

A charitable organisation set up by John and Yoko, which officially came into existence in December 1978. Allegedly, the couple said they intended to 'tithe' their money and give away 10 per cent each year to charitable causes. However, from the time it was set up in 1978 with $100,000, according to Internal Revenue Service accounts, by the end of 1979, only one contribution had been made – to the Salvation Army for a sum of $10,000.

Following John's death, Yoko made a statement: 'John loved and prayed for the human race. Please do the same for him.' And she said that, instead of sending flowers, 'Please consider sending donations to Spirit Foundation Inc., which is John's personal charitable foundation. He would have appreciated it very much.' She also gave the address of the foundation as: One Battery Park Plaza, New York, NY 10004.

Thousands of people contributed donations in memory of John and it was this money that Yoko distributed to various causes.

On 8 December 1981, Yoko issued a statement about the Spirit Foundation:

I think of John's death as a war casualty. It is the war between the sane and the insane. All his life, John had fought the insanity within us and of the world. Ironically, he was killed by an act of insanity at the time he was enjoying the sanest moment of his life.

Through the warm letters of support I received after John's death, I have learned that there are many beautiful people in the world leading good lives and enjoying good thoughts and good deeds. Though they are not mentioned in the press for their quiet contributions, they are the true silent heroes holding the sky up for us through these turbulent times. The Spirit Foundation received many gifts from such people.

To date, $285,829 have been received by the Spirit Foundation this year. The monies were donated to the following organisations:

Harlem Interfaith Counselling Service – $20,000
East Harlem Family Health Service – $20,000

Hale House – $20,000
Covenant House – $20,000
Phoenix House – $20,000
Society For The Prevention Of Cruelty To Children – $20,000
New York Foundling hospital – $20,000
St Barnabas House – $20,000
Police Athletic League (PAL) – $10,000
American Civil Liberties Union (ACLU) – $10,000
Amnesty International – $10,000

In addition to the above contributions, we have donated $50,000 to various disarmament groups, anonymously, so that we would not be pressed to become politically involved with them.

The remaining $35,000 have been set aside for a project of musical exchange between the people of the western hemisphere and those behind iron curtains and countries controlled by dictatorships.

The support we have received for the Spirit Foundation has given me great hope for the future. 'Think globally and act locally' is our motto. Let's not waste John's death. Please let John's death become a springboard for finally bringing sanity and peace to the world, for ourselves and our children.

Thank you.

In 1982 she said she no longer wished fans to send donations to the Spirit Foundation because she didn't want it becoming a bureaucracy feeding professional money raisers. 'If you have $2 to send to Spirit Foundation, I appreciate the intent, but please give that $2 to some-body near you who needs it. We should think globally but work locally. If we all do that, the whole world will be fine.'

Sport, Speed and Illustrated

From the age of seven, while still at Dovedale Primary School, John began to work on a series of books with this title, adding 'Edited and illustrated by JW Lennon'.

The books contained cutout pictures of soccer players and film stars which he'd pasted in among the various poems, cartoons, short stories and serials which he had composed.

Stand By Me

Song written by Ben E King, Jerry Leiber, Mike Stoller and Ollie Jones, which King first issued as a single in April 1981.

The song went on to become something of a standard in soul and C&W circles. John recorded it for his *Rock 'n' Roll* album and, in a bid to boost sales of the album, it was issued as a single in America on Apple 1881 on 10 March 1975 with 'Move Over Ms L' on the flip. The record was issued in Britain on Apple R6005 on 18 April.

The flip side was a number that John had written for Keith Moon's debut album *Two Sides of the Moon,* which was also issued in America in March 1975 and in Britain in May. Mal Evans was one of the album's producers.

The single reached No. 20 in the American charts and No. 27 in the British. It didn't chart when it was reissued in Britain on 17 April 1981.

Julian Lennon was also to record the song

Stanley, Annie

Relatively little is known about John's maternal grandmother, compared with the information available on her husband and other close relatives.

Annie (née Millward) was the daughter of John Millward, a solicitor's clerk. *Up the Beatles Tree,* a brief ancestral history of Beatles members, points out: 'Millward is another combination of Old English words meaning a miller. It is not common as a surname in the southern counties but is found in the name of John le Milleward in a list of landowners in Huntingdonshire as early as 1279.'

Annie married George Ernest Stanley in 1906 and the couple's first two children, a boy and a girl, both died before reaching the age of three. She then gave birth to five healthy daughters: Mary Elizabeth, Elizabeth, Anne Georgina, Julia and Harriet.

Stanley, Anne Georgina

Another of John's aunts, who was nicknamed 'Nanny'.

She was the third daughter of George and Annie Stanley and was born in 1912.

A civil servant, she waited until she was in her mid-30s before marrying Sidney Caldwaller. They had one son, Michael, and, as soon as he was born, Nanny declared that she wouldn't have any more children.

Stanley, Elizabeth

One of the five daughters of George and Annie Stanley, John's aunt.

She was known as 'Mater' and, when her son Stanley was born, she decided she couldn't cope with rearing him. Although he was only a few weeks old, she placed him into the hands of her mother, Annie, to bring up until he was old enough to go away to boarding school. This was obviously an upbringing not dissimilar to that of his cousin John.

Stan was the only child conceived during her first marriage to Charles Parkes, a naval architect and marine surveyor. After his death she moved to Scotland in 1940 and married Robert Hugh Sutherland, commonly known as 'Bertie', an Edinburgh dentist, but she had no further children.

Bertie's family had a croft in Durness at the northernmost tip of Scotland where he, Mater and Stanley would spend the summer months. From the ages of nine to sixteen, John spent several weeks there each year among the lochs and hills. Stan was sent down to Liverpool to collect John each summer.

John had been staying at their home in June 1955 when George Smith, his Aunt Mimi's husband, died. He was also visiting Mater in July 1968 with Yoko, Julian and Kyoko, when he was involved in a car accident.

On John's 21st birthday in 1961, Mater sent her nephew £100, causing Paul McCartney to declare, 'My God, you must have a rich aunt.'

Elizabeth died of cancer in 1974.

Stanley, George Ernest

John's grandfather, born in Liverpool in 1874, the son of William Henry Stanley and Eliza Jane Gildea.

His father was a solicitor's clerk and part-time musician. George spent most of his life at sea and worked for the Glasgow and Liverpool Salvage Company, often involved in raising submarines from the sea bottom. He later worked as an insurance investigator for the company, but his early life took him away from home so often that his wife Annie Millward, whom he married in 1906, took care of the family of five daughters, turning it into a matriarchal household.

Their first two children, a boy and a girl, died before their third birthdays. They then saw the birth of five daughters between 1906 and 1916.

Originally the family lived in Huskisson Street in the Liverpool 8 district but, after Annie had died in 1932, George moved to 9 Newcastle Road in the Wavertree area and the daughters lived at home until they were married.

When Julia married Freddie Lennon, she remained in Newcastle Road while her husband was away at sea, but soon began going out with other men. When she gave birth to a daughter at the age of thirty in 1944, 'Pop' Stanley, as he was now known in the family, made her put the child up for adoption. When Julia began to live with John Dykins, they moved into a one-bedroomed flat in the Gateacre area with her son John. The social services were not happy about the fact that John had to share their bedroom, so they all moved back to Newcastle Road and lived there until Pop died in 1949.

Pop was very fond of his grandson John and used to take him for walks. One day they decided to go for a walk to New Brighton, but on the way John complained that his new shoes were hurting. Pop told him, 'We can't have that.' He then took them off and threw them in the river because he didn't want them pinching John's feet.

Four of his five daughters weren't referred to by their first names. They had pet names. Elizabeth was called Mater, allegedly because her son Stanley went to a public school and that was what he called her. Mary was called Mimi; Anne was called Nanny and Harriet was called Harrie. Julia remained as Julia, although she was sometimes referred to as Judy.

Starr, Freddie

Starr was a leading British comedian who was one of the handful of Mersey Beat singers who achieved success and maintained high public profiles. When he joined Howie Casey and the Seniors they became the first Liverpool group to sign a recording contract with a major British record label.

He appeared on many bills with the Beatles and led several of his own bands on Merseyside, including Freddie and the Delmonts and Freddie Starr and the Midnighters.

A few days after John's death, Freddie mentioned to a British national newspaper that he'd heard some unreleased tapes by John Lennon in Lennon's former home at Tittenhurst Park, now owned by Ringo Starr.

When the newspaper checked, John Hemingway, one of Ringo's aides, denied that there were any Lennon tapes at the mansion. When the paper got back to Freddie with the news he told them that he'd not only seen the tapes, but had actually played them.

He then commented, 'When I went back to Tittenhurst the other night, after John's death, the tapes were gone and somebody said they had been sent to America.'

Starr, Ringo

The Beatles' drummer was born Richard Starkey on 7 June 1940. His mother and father were Elsie and Richard Starkey and they lived in Madryn Street in the Dingle area of Liverpool.

Throughout his early years, Ritchie (as he was known) suffered from ill health, which was to seriously affect his education. From the age of six, when he was diagnosed with a ruptured appendix, he was subject to several operations and at one time slipped into a coma. His parents divorced and his mother married Harry Graves, whom Ritchie referred to as his 'stepladder'. The youth was hospitalised again with chronic pleurisy in 1953 and suffered lung complications, which kept him in hospital until 1955.

It was while working as a trainee joiner that he joined the Eddie Clayton Skiffle Group and in March 1959 he became a member of one of Liverpool's leading groups, Rory Storm and the Hurricanes. They were to top the bill over the Beatles at the Kaiserkeller club in Hamburg in October 1960, and, during the short season there, Ringo drummed on a record with John, Paul and George.

He left the Hurricanes briefly to join Tony Sheridan's band in Hamburg, but returned to the Hurricanes and another Butlin's holiday camp season. He had decided to hang up his drumsticks and become an apprentice at the end of 1962. Before the season was even midway through, however, he'd received two offers, both involving more money than he'd been earning with the Hurricanes. He decided to opt for the bigger offer – that made by Brian Epstein on behalf of the Beatles.

The group had already been voted No. 1 in the *Mersey Beat* polls and Ringo felt a little nervous about joining a group that had found success with someone else in the drum seat. That person happened to be the handsome Pete Best, whom the local girls regarded as the best-looking Beatle. In those days pop stars were expected to be handsome.

Ringo shaved off his beard and rid himself of the silver streak in his hair, but still didn't think of himself as a Beatle. When he was a member of Rory Storm and the Hurricanes, conventional good looks hadn't mattered – but the Beatles' front line comprised three good-looking guitarists. However, Ringo's personality soon began to win the fans over.

Ringo joined the Beatles in August 1962. On the night he made his Cavern debut there was a great deal of protest from fans of the former drummer, Pete Best. Brian Epstein had to be escorted by a bodyguard and George Harrison received a black eye in the scuffles as the Best fans loudly chanted their hero's name. However, the hostility didn't last too long: that very night, when the group finished their set, Ringo was cheered and applauded.

Ringo really came into his own when the Beatles toured America. Among American fans, for a time, he became the most popular member of the group and there were numerous tribute records about him, including 'Ringo For President'. On each of the Beatles' albums Ringo was given his own vocal spot, but he spread his wings, not only as a musician and singer, but also as an actor.

The first inkling that he was a natural actor came with a brief appearance in BBC One's *The Mersey Sound*, in which he acted out the part of a hairdressing salon owner. Other sketches followed on various TV shows such as *Blackpool Night Out*.

Then, in 1964, *A Hard Day's Night* brought reviews that suggested he had the potential to become a fine movie comedian.

Badgered by Paul's 'grandfather', played by Wilfred Brambell, Ringo gained the audience's sympathy. He stole the film during a number of sequences in which he wanders off by himself to the tune of 'Ringo's Theme', an orchestral arrangement by the George Martin Orchestra. He wanders the London streets only to be spotted and pursued by a group of fans. He dodges into a shop, waits for the girls to go by, then emerges dressed in an old mac and peaked cap.

Ringo then nearly gets turfed out into the murky waters of a canal when an old tyre knocks him over. A nine-year-old boy claims his 'hoop' and the two exchange words. They begin a friendly chat until the boy's mother calls him. Ringo walks on and enters a pub called, appropriately, the Liverpool Arms. He orders a lager and a sandwich, but isn't too pleased with the state of the latter. He moves around awkwardly and upsets some of the pub games, which a number of hefty workmen are playing. Putting on a bold front, he picks up some darts and throws them at the board. Unfortunately, the first finds it way into a cheese sandwich, the second into a pint of beer and the third into the pub's parrot. Ringo is thrown out and encounters a policeman who has been keeping an eye on him for some time.

Ringo continues his stroll, noticing workmen who've been digging holes in the road. He spots a girl attempting to cross some puddles and lays down his mac for her in true Sir Walter Raleigh style. She smiles, steps on the coat – and then disappears from sight. The puddles had gathered in holes dug by the workmen! One of the men tries to help her, and then a young man comes along, thinks the workman is trying to accost his girl and it looks as if trouble is brewing. Ringo skips off – straight into the arms of a policeman. He's taken to the local cop shop, where he is rescued by his fellow Beatles.

On the eve of the Beatles' world tour on Wednesday 3 June 1964, Ringo collapsed during a photo session and was diagnosed with tonsillitis and pharyngitis and a substitute drummer, Jimmy Nicol, was used on a number of early dates.

In the Beatles' second film, *Help!*, Ringo was given what amounted to the leading role. Unable to take a sacred ring off his finger, he is stalked by an Eastern sect intent on sacrificing him. The other Beatles spend most of their time protecting him from the cult while also attempting to remove the ring from his finger.

In his personal life he had married his Liverpool girlfriend, Maureen Cox, on Thursday 11 February 1965. The couple had three children. Zak was born on 13 September 1965, Jason on 19 August 1967 and Lee on 11 November 1970.

In 1968 he was offered his first film role in a non-Beatles movie, *Candy*, an updating of Voltaire's *Candide*. The movie was scripted by Buck Henry from the rather risqué comic novel by Terry Southern and Mason Hoffenberg, which had originally been printed in Paris by the Olympia Press. When it was eventually published in the United States it became a bestseller. Other stars who appeared in the film included Marlon Brando, Richard Burton and James Coburn.

Ringo played the part of Emmanuel, a Mexican gardener who attempts to seduce Candy Christian. The comparatively unknown Swedish actress Ewa Aulin starred in the title role.

Someone has spilled whisky on Candy's dress so she takes it off and begins to sponge it. Emmanuel enters the room and grabs her, attempting to make love to her on a pool table. Her father arrives and the gardener is thrown out. His pride hurt, Emmanuel complains to his relatives, and this ill-assorted group of Mexicans pursue Candy and her father to the airport on motorbikes. One of Emmanuel's kinfolk hurls a bolas, which splits open the head of Candy's father.

Apart from a brief appearance at the end of the movie, Ringo takes no further part in the film. Though much publicised, his part was little more than a cameo role with only a few lines of the 'Dis is no good' variety – wearing a suitably lusty leer on his mustachioed face as he tries to seduce Candy.

Terry Southern was also the author of *The Magic Christian* on which Ringo's second solo movie was based (no wonder Ringo's *Goodnight Vienna* album sleeve included the phrase 'buy a Terry Southern book'). While he had appeared for only about ten minutes in *Candy*, he was given the co-starring role with Peter Sellers in this British movie, filmed in colour and released in 1969. The film's score was by Ken Thorne, while the theme song, 'Come And Get It', was written by Paul McCartney and performed by the Apple band, Badfinger.

Peter Sellers appeared as Sir Guy Grand, Ringo played his adopted son Youngman Grand and guest stars included Richard Attenborough, Laurence Harvey, Christopher Lee, Spike Milligan, Roman Polanski and Raquel Welch.

Although one reviewer wrote, 'Ringo Starr continues to exploit the melancholy wanderer's role he made his own in *A Hard Day's Night*,' Ringo didn't really have much to get his teeth into. His part had been specially written for the film (the character he played wasn't in the original book) and his role was mainly that of an observer, watching the various stunts that Sellers sets up.

The film received its royal world premiere on 12 December 1969 at the Odeon, Kensington, in the presence of Princess Margaret. Also in attendance were John and Yoko, sporting 'WHO KILLED HANRATTY?' signs.

In April 1970 Ringo's solo album *Sentimental Journey*, produced by George Martin, contained a selection of golden oldies. He said, 'I did it for me mum.' Arrangers included Elmer Bernstein, Quincy Jones, Johnny Dankworth, Les Reed and the Bee Gees. Later that year, in October, his next album, *Beaucoups Of Blues*, reached No. 65 in the US charts. He made the album in Nashville and commissioned some of the leading country-music writers to pen songs for him. Pete Drake was the producer and Scotty Moore the engineer. Ringo was supported by a number of country musicians, including the Jordanaires, Jerry Reed and Charles Daniels. The title track reached No. 87 in the US charts the following month.

In August 1971 he appeared on *The Concert for Bangladesh*.

Ringo's next film was a spaghetti western, written by Tony Anthony, who also played the lead. Allen Klein set up Ringo's appearance. Klein also appeared in the movie, along with Beatles' assistant Mal Evans.

Ringo played a baddie called Candy and, as usual with Italian westerns, the location was Spain. Filming took place between June and August 1971. Although Ringo wrote some music for the film, his soundtrack was never used. The song 'Blindman', which he'd intended to be the main tune, ended up as the flip side of 'Back Off Boogaloo'.

The film did not receive the international distribution of his previous movies. It opened in Rome on 15 November 1971 and received its US premier in Chicago on 12 January 1972. Later that year it received a limited showing in Britain.

The *Monthly Film Bulletin* commented, 'There are some nice ideas here and there, notably the spectacle of the fifty girls twittering through the desert in their nighties and being rounded up like a herd of cattle, and of Ringo Starr tethered to a locomotive and hung with cowbells lest he move without alerting the Blindman.'

200 Motels saw Ringo in a dual role, portraying both Larry the Dwarf and Frank Zappa. The film was released in 1971. Ringo arrived on the set with a beard, but he cut most of it off, just leaving a goatee, for his part as Zappa. The movie was premiered in New York on 10 November 1971 but never received proper distribution in Britain.

In November 1972 he appeared as Uncle Ernie on the Lou Reizner album of the Who's rock opera *Tommy*.

Ringo made his directorial debut with *Born To Boogie*, filmed between March and April 1972 and premiered on 18 December 1972 at the Oscar Cinema in London. The film was made entirely on location, mainly at a T Rex concert at the Empire Pool, Wembley.

In 1972 the pop superstar Marc Bolan was a friend of the then 32-year-old Ringo. The scenes of 'T Rextacy' that had accompanied Bolan's concerts had impressed the former Beatle. He decided to record the atmosphere on film. Elton John, Keith Moon and Ringo himself made cameo appearances.

George Melly, writing in the UK daily, the *Observer*, commented, 'The film is directed and in part filmed by Ringo Starr. The incidental humour is drawn from the nursery surrealist world of the "Magical Mystery Tour", but lacks that famous disaster's pretensions. Nuns, one bearded, take tea, a dwarf gnaws ravenously at a car's offside mirror. Simple oral-fixation, but the music goes like the clappers.'

Weekend of a Champion was a Roman Polanski documentary filmed in 1970 to celebrate Jackie Stewart's winning the 29th Monte Carlo Grand Prix. Ringo appears in a scene showing Stewart and his friends at a celebratory party.

In 1972, Ringo acted as producer for a strange project that was filmed between August and October and premiered two years later in Atlanta, Georgia, on 19 April. The movie was a horror spoof originally called *Count Downe*, but altered to *Son of Dracula* for its limited release by Apple. Ringo starred as 200-year-old Merlin the Magician and the title role went to Harry Nilsson as Count Downe.

Commenting on the movie, Ringo said, '*Son of Dracula* has a great premise, which is that Dracula takes the cure and marries the girl. I'm using all the elements, the Wolfman, Frankenstein, Merlin, just the whole gang. It's like a nonmusical nonhorror, noncomedy – or it's a horror-horror, musical-musical, comedy-comedy.' He mentioned the casting of Harry Nilsson: 'The freaky thing was that I asked him to do it without knowing that he'd done a Drac photograph for the cover of the album I'd been playing on with him. So it seemed right.'

That'll Be the Day was one of the best British musicals ever made, although the soundtrack consisted of American rock numbers from artists of the late 1950s such as Little Richard, Bobby Vee, Dion, the Everly Brothers and Jerry Lee Lewis – a selection chosen by Keith Moon and Neil Aspinall.

The script was by the Liverpool writer Ray Connelly, who had interviewed the Beatles on a number of occasions.

The story concerns a youth growing up in the late 1950s and early 1960s who turns to music. It provided Ringo with what is arguably his finest screen performance. It's a relatively brief role and Ringo spent only ten days filming, but the character of Mike, a Teddy Boy who works in a fairground, suited him ideally.

The lead character is Jim Maclaine, played by David Essex. The story begins in 1958 in a town where Jim lives with his mother. The boy's father had deserted the family when Jim was a small boy but Jim still recalls how his father used to take him out for walks in the park. In some ways, these scenes are reminiscent of the early life of John Lennon.

Jim eventually leaves home and finds work in a fairground, where he meets Mike, a Jack the Lad with greased hair and sideburns. The two share a flat, date girls together and become firm friends. While at a holiday camp they watch a rock band called Stormy Tempest and the Typhoons (which must have brought back memories for Ringo of his days at Butlin's holiday camp with Rory Storm and the Hurricanes). Tempest was portrayed by the late Billy Fury, who was in the same class at school as Ringo; his drummer in the film was Keith Moon.

At the fairground, Jim notices Mike having an argument with a youth. Mike has fiddled the boy out of his change on one of the amusement rides. Later that evening the youth and his friends beat Mike up badly, an assault witnessed by Jim. Instead of helping his friend, Jim runs away.

The film was premiered on 12 April 1973 and was successful enough to spawn a sequel, *Stardust*, in 1975, in which Ringo was once again offered the part of Mike. For some reason Ringo turned down the part, even though the role was much meatier than in the first film. Adam Faith stepped in and received critical acclaim for the role.

In April 1973 Ringo's single, 'Photograph', co-written with George Harrison, topped the American charts and reached No. 8 in Britain. His album, *Ringo*, produced by Richard Perry, reached No. 2 in America and No. 7 in Britain. It included a number written for Ringo by John Lennon, 'I'm the Greatest'. He was also aided by a number of talented musicians on the album, including Paul McCartney, George Harrison and John Lennon.

January 1974 saw him top the charts in America with 'You're Sixteen', which reached No. 3 in Britain. In April he reached No. 5 in the States with the single 'Oh My My', and his album *Goodnight Vienna* reached No. 8 in America and No. 30 in Britain in December.

January 1975 saw him enter the US charts, reaching No. 6 with 'Only You' and reaching No. 28 in Britain. His 'No No Song' reached No. 3 in the US in April. His single 'It's All Down To Goodnight Vienna' reached No. 31 in America.

Ringo and Maureen were divorced on 1 July 1973 and Ringo immediately gave Maureen a £500,000 settlement before moving to Monte Carlo to become a tax exile. He set up home there with the American model Nancy Andrews, who had been named in his divorce. He'd visit Loews Casino four evenings week and the casino manager commented, 'He's well known around Monte Carlo and people treat him very much as a star, which is something he seems to enjoy. He is exactly like someone who has spent years working extremely hard to build up a business and become a multimillionaire, who is now sitting back, enjoying the fruits of success. When he walks around Monte Carlo now people notice him and point him out, but they don't go rushing up to him for autographs like they used to. Let's face it, he's hardly a sexy young pop star any more, is he?'

Andrews left him and Ringo had a succession of glamorous girlfriends, including the singer Lynsey de Paul. He admitted, 'Well, I'm a jet-setter. Whatever anyone may think and whoever puts it down, I am on planes half the year going different places. And, in people's eyes, Monte Carlo is a jet-set scene. Los Angeles is a jet-set scene. London – swinging London, not that it swings any more. Amsterdam, you know. It's a crazy kind of a world. Wherever I go it's a swinging place, man.'

For a time Ringo had even launched his own record label, Ring O Records, although it didn't suit his playboy lifestyle. He said, 'Then I realised that to run the company you've got to be in the company. You've got to come to the office every day, which I did. And you've got to go and have all those meetings, which I hated, because you'd have all these meetings and nothing would happen. You usually have meetings to decide about the next meeting. So I did tend to leave it alone – and then I just decided I didn't want it no more.'

Ringo's next film venture was taking a guest role as the Pope in Ken Russell's *Lisztomania*, released in 1975. A critic commented, 'Perhaps Russell's most audacious piece of *Lisztomania* casting is that of former Beatle Ringo Starr as the Pope. He visits Liszt (now an Abbé) in his monastic cell to tell him that Wagner has become possessed by the Prince of Darkness and orders Liszt to use his God-given musical powers to exorcise the devil in Wagner's soul.'

In December 1975 Ringo's greatest-hits album, *Blast From Your Past*, reached No. 30 in the US charts.

October 1976 saw his album *Photogravure* reach No. 28 in the US while a single from the album, 'A Dose of Rock 'n' Roll', reached No. 26 in the US charts.

In 1976, Robbie Robertson's the Band made their farewell performance at San Francisco's famous Winterland ballroom. The event was filmed as *The Last Waltz* by Martin Scorsese and Ringo joined Bob Dylan and Ron Wood to accompany the Band on their rendition of 'I Shall Be Released'.

In 1977 *Sextette*, Mae West's last film, provided another cameo role for Ringo. The legendary actress played Marlo Manners, an American sex goddess. Ringo appeared as Laslo Karozny, a European movie director and one of Marlo's ex-husbands.

February 1977 saw Ringo's single 'Hey Baby' reach No. 71 in the US charts, with his album *Ringo the 4th* reaching No. 162 in America in October. In December of that year he appeared as a guest on the album *Scouse the Mouse*.

A TV special, *Ringo*, was first screened in America by NBC on

26 April 1978, shortly before his *Bad Boy* album release. The film was a loose adaptation of Mark Twain's *The Prince and the Pauper*, about a prince and a commoner who change places.

It begins with George Harrison telling a press conference about two babies born at the very same moment in Britain. 'Remarkably, both children, though born of different parents, look exactly alike.' One of the children was brought to America; the other remained in Britain and achieved fame as Ringo Starr.

Ringo is in a car with four girls. A motorcycle escort takes him past screaming fans. We hear him singing 'Back Off Boogaloo'.

George points out that fortune didn't smile on the other baby, who became known as Ognir Rats. We see Ognir selling maps outside Hollywood stars' homes. Some nuns ask him if he has maps to the homes of Jill St John, Susan St James and Peter, Paul and Mary. Then a carload of blonde surfers call him a 'nerd' and run over his sandwich board. He daydreams about success, then sets off for home, climbing into his room by ladder. His father (Art Carney), a 'cruel, vicious, mean' man, comes in and takes all his money off him, not even leaving him enough to take his girlfriend on a date that night.

Meanwhile, Ringo is in the studio playing drums. He takes a break and his manager Marty (John Ritter) tells him of the satellite concert, a forty-city tour, autographs to sign, and the pressure is evident. Ringo says he needs some time to himself. Granted a few minutes' break, he goes to the door and notices Ognir in the street. He calls him over and they begin to chat. To the tune of 'Yellow Submarine' they enter a fantasy sequence peopled by dancers in golden costumes.

Ringo talks Ognir into changing places with him and then sets off for Hollywood Boulevard, where he pays a youth a fistful of dollars in exchange for the loan of his car. Ognir's girlfriend Markene (Carrie Fisher) spots Ringo and gets into the car. He sings 'You're Sixteen' to a scene that combines live action and animation. Ognir's father sees them parked in the car, mistakes Ringo for Ognir and hauls him out, accusing him of stealing the vehicle. He locks him in his room and then phones the police. While in the room, Ringo watches *The Mike Douglas Show* on TV and sees Ognir make a mess of it, knocking down a table, chairs and a mike and tapping away at the cymbal when he's supposed to play a number.

'He's going to ruin my reputation,' wails Ringo. He then crawls out of the window but a policewoman (Angie Dickinson) is waiting for him and he's dragged off to the cop shop.

At the police station, two cops argue about the photographs Ringo's just had taken, which gives him the opportunity to escape. He bumps into Markene and tells her they must go to the concert. They rummage in some trashcans and he puts on a disguise.

Meanwhile, Marty has brought along a hypnotist (Vincent Price) to examine his client. The doctor puts Ognir into a trance and he imagines he is in a Hall of Fame with such stars as Roy Orbison, Jerry Lee Lewis, Chuck Berry, Elvis, Buddy Holly and Hank Williams. In a smoky tunnel, illuminated with laser light, Ognir sings 'With a Little Help From My Friends' and comes out of the trance believing he is Ringo. He goes on to the stage, but the hypnotist makes an unconscious gesture, which brings him out of the trance, and he becomes Ognir again. The real Ringo arrives with Markene to save the day and he goes on stage to perform 'Heart On My Sleeve' and 'Hard Times'. The screen then darkens until a single star is illuminated. Ringo, dressed in white, walks on and sings 'A Man Like Me'. Backstage all is well and Ringo offers Ognir a job as his road manager.

In May 1978 Ringo's album *Bad Boy* reached No. 129 in the US charts.

The following year he featured in the Who's documentary *The Kids Are Alright*. The movie covered the group's fifteen-year career and Ringo once again appeared with his close friend Keith Moon.

Ringo also had a serious stomach operation in Monte Carlo after collapsing with intestinal pains. 'They cut me to pieces and took away five feet of gut,' he said. This occurred in April 1979 after he'd collapsed in a coma. When told he was lucky to be alive, and remembering the number of his friends who had now died, including Keith Moon, Marc Bolan and Mal Evans, he said, 'I won't go to funerals because I don't believe in them. I totally believe your soul has gone by the time you get in the limo. She or he's up there or wherever it is. I'm sure … I can't wait to go half the time.'

Ringo then featured in the prehistoric comedy *Caveman*, in which he starred with Barbara Bach. Ringo commented, 'It's right that people forget that since the break-up ten years ago I have had a very good career on my own, and not only as a recording artist. As an actor, people only really think about *Help!* and *A Hard Day's Night.* I've never starred in a movie before: I've just done parts ... and as for lessons in acting, I think I have had the best lessons by working with the best craftsmen, like Peter Sellers and Richard Burton – people like that. Practical experience is a thousand times better than any class. They all taught me a hell of a lot!'

Filming began in 1980 and *Caveman* was released in 1981.

Ringo played Atouk, who is thrown out of a prehistoric tribe because of his lust for the chief's woman Lana, played by Barbara Bach.

Caveman was played for laughs, tosses any attempt at historical accuracy out of the window and pokes gentle fun at *One Million Years BC* and *2001: A Space Odyssey* and is set one zillion years ago! As Lana, Barbara Bach looks rather like Raquel Welch in *One Million Years BC.* Ringo, however, is nothing like John Richardson's macho Tumak in that film.

In May 1980 he and Barbara Bach were in a road accident when his Mercedes rolled over and over on the A3 in Kingston, Surrey. The car demolished three lampposts and Ringo was thrown clear, although Bach was trapped in the car. Fortunately, they both suffered only minor cuts and bruises. He promptly asked Barbara to marry him. She had recently posed nude for *Playboy* magazine and was to say, 'I'm incredibly happy now. I had always secretly believed in Prince Charming, if ever he came riding up on his charger. And Richard came. We'll get married, and that's it ... happily ever after, all the rest. So now I'm into fairy tales.'

Ringo was completely devastated by the news of John's murder. As soon as he heard of the shooting he cut short his holiday in the Bahamas and, together with Barbara Bach, flew to New York, feeling a need to be with Yoko. When he arrived at the Dakota Building his car was unable to enter the forecourt because of the thousands of fans blocking the entrance, so he had to make his way on foot. People were pulling his clothing, asking for autographs, which shook him badly and he refused to give a statement to reporters.

Inside the Dakota he was told that Yoko would prefer to see

him without Barbara, but Ringo wouldn't have this. He told the aide, 'Please tell her that we both want to see her.' They were then both admitted.

Following John's death he returned to live in England after six years abroad, obviously worried about the security of his family and himself. He said, 'Afterwards, I did have several threats to my own life, and I had to have guards with me. I hated it.'

Incidentally, he'd recently had a tattoo of a star and a moon on his left arm and Barbara had an identical one tattooed on her thigh.

At 10 p.m. on Tuesday 31 March 1981 Ringo appeared on *Barbara Walters Special*, an ABC TV chat show in America, to promote the film *Caveman*. Barbara accompanied him and during the interview Ringo mentioned that they would be getting married later that year. Asked about the Beatles, he commented, 'We used to call John the wit, Paul pleasantly insincere and George the mystic.'

His explanation for the Beatles' break-up was that they had each begun to form their own ideas about what they should be doing. He discussed John's death and mentioned how happy John and Yoko had been and of his trip to the Dakota following John's murder. 'When we came I didn't need to hear people telling me how much they loved the Beatles or any of that when we'd just lost John, because I wasn't there to see a Beatle. I was there to see my friend, not relating to this band.' He also mentioned that he believed John was 'up there with Jimi Hendrix and Elvis and all the rest of them'.

Ringo and Barbara were married on 27 April 1981. That year they were also involved in another car accident. Ringo woke up in hospital and a nurse was offering him a cup of tea. 'That's England for you. Tea cures everything,' he said.

In November of that year his album *Stop and Smell the Roses*, to which Paul McCartney and George Harrison contributed, reached No. 98 in the American charts. The following month Ringo's single 'Wrack My Brain' reached No. 38 in the US.

Ringo's next appearance was in a short, *The Cooler*. When he recorded his album *Stop and Smell the Roses*, Paul McCartney wrote and produced the numbers 'Private Property' and 'Attention', and produced the number 'Sure To Tell', which had been written by Carl Perkins, Quinton Claunch and William

Cantrell. It was Paul's idea to make a video of these three songs to use as a promotional video for the album. It worked out as an eleven-minute 'surrealist musical', directed by Godley and Crème, and it was entered in the Short Subject category at the Cannes Film Festival on 24 May 1982.

Ringo played a habitual escapee who at the beginning of the film is caught and thrown into the 'cooler', a special solitary-confinement cell. As his mental state deteriorates, he fantasises about his situation and his ambiguous relationship with the camp commandant, played by his wife Barbara Bach. Paul McCartney appeared three times in the film, as a prisoner, as Ringo's cowboy father and as the double-bass player in a country-and-western band. Linda McCartney played a guard.

Ringo and Barbara then appeared together in the American three-part TV miniseries *Princess Daisy*, based on the bestselling novel by Judith Krantz. Ringo and Barbara were the Valerians, a successful dress-design couple. The married pair in the film have a hidden secret – they are both gay.

In October 1984 Ringo narrated the children's television series *Thomas the Tank Engine and Friends*. He was to say, 'It's just mind-blowing that Thomas is so big in this day and age. It used to be "Look, there's Ringo!" in the street. Now it's "Look, there's Thomas!" Would you believe there's hordes of screaming three-year-olds outside the house?'

Ringo and Barbara also appeared in Paul McCartney's film, *Give My Regards To Broad Street*. His album *Old Wave* was turned down in both Britain and America and was released only in Canada.

July 1985 saw Ringo become the first ex-Beatle grandfather when his son Zak and Zak's wife Sarah had a daughter, Tatia Jayne.

In December, along with George Harrison, he appeared on an all-star band in a television tribute to Carl Perkins.

In February 1988 Ringo appeared in George Harrison's video, *When We Were Fab*. This was the year in which it was revealed that both Ringo and Barbara had been suffering severe drink problems and the two booked themselves into a clinic in Tucson, Arizona, to dry out.

Ringo's version of 'When You Wish Upon a Star' was issued on a Walt Disney compilation album, *Stay Awake*, in January

1989 and in April Rhino Records issued *Starrstruck: Ringo's Best 1976–83*, which contained a previously unreleased track 'Can't Fight Lightning'.

In June he returned to the touring circuit when he formed his first All-Starr Band with Dr John, Billy Preston, Joe Walsh, Rick Danko, Levon Helm, Nils Lofgren, Jim Keltner and Clarence Clemons.

Early in 1990 he recorded a video of the song 'I Call Your Name' for showing at the John Lennon tribute concert in Liverpool on 5 May of that year. His record 'You Never Know' was, in November 1991, included on the soundtrack of the movie *Curly Sue*.

The year 1992 saw Ringo embark on a world tour, during which he appeared at the Empire Theatre, Liverpool, on 6 July. In April 1993 he formed a backing band called the New Maroons and in September *Volume Two: Live from Montreux*, an album of the All-Starr Band tour from the previous years, was issued on Rykodisc.

1995 saw him together with Paul McCartney and George Harrison working on the Beatles' *Anthology*, which was to include new recording sessions for 'Free As A Bird' and 'Real Love'. He also recorded 'Lay Down Your Arms' with Stevie Nicks for the Nilsson tribute album *For The Love Of Harry*. In July he began another tour with a different line-up of the All-Starr band, which included his son Zak on drums. Other members included Billy Preston, Felix Cavaliere, Mark Farner, Randy Bachman and John Entwistle. He then curtailed the tour due to the fact that his daughter Lee had a brain tumour. Fortunately, surgery in September of that year was successful. However, sadly Ringo's former wife Maureen had passed away several months earlier. She died in December 1994, having contracted leukaemia following complications in a transplant operation.

Ringo's 1997 All-Starr Band was an all-British line-up with Peter Frampton, David Mason, Gary Brooker and Jack Bruce. In 1998 his album *Vertical Man* reached No. 61 in the US charts. His tour during the year also reached Europe, although he only did one British date, at the Shepherd's Bush Empire in London on August 21. He then went on to a series of concerts in Germany in September. In 1999 he continued touring with the

All-Starr Band in a tenth anniversary tour with Todd Rundgren, Gary Brooker, Jack Bruce, Simon Kirke and Timmy Cappello.

Steel and Glass

A song penned by John in 1974 that was a veiled attack on Allen Klein and refers to the building that housed Klein's company, ABKCO, a 41-storey steel-and-glass tower situated at 1700 Broadway. Allen Klein is not referred to by name and John had been careful to ensure that the lyrics did not contain anything libellous, although there are a number of clues. When Klein first approached John about management of the Beatles, he emphasised how alike they were in that both were reared without their mothers, which may explain John's line, 'Your mother left you when you were small'. This was a very cruel remark, as Klein's mother had died of cancer.

John kept up the pretence that the song wasn't to do with any specific person and at one time even claimed it was about himself. Also, when interviewed by Andy Warhol's magazine *Interview,* he was asked the identity of the person referred to as 'your friend and mine' in the song and commented, 'I can tell you who it isn't about, for instance: it's not about Jackie Kennedy, Mort Sahl, Sammy Davis, Bette Midler ... Eartha Kitt, it's not about her either.' The track was included on the *Walls and Bridges* album.

There are similarities to 'How Do You Sleep?', John's veiled attack on Paul, and he later described 'Steel and Glass' as 'a son of "How Do You Sleep?" '

A different version of the song was included on the posthumous *Menlove Avenue* album that contained some further venomous words that he'd left off the *Walls and Bridges* album.

Stefanelli, Joe

This actor provided the voice of John for the sequence in the film *Forrest Gump*, where John appears on *The Dick Cavett Show* with Gump. Stefanelli is a member of the Los Angeles-based Beatles tribute band, the Moptops. In the Paramount Television miniseries *I Elvis*, there is a scene in which Elvis meets the Beatles – who were played by the Moptops. When Paramount was looking for a Lennon lookalike for the Gump movie, Stefanelli's agent contacted them and he got the part. Originally he was to appear as John in the scene and was made up to appear as John did in September 1971. He said, 'They duplicated everything – the same brand of shirt, the same cigarettes he had in his shirt pocket. They even made that necklace that he was wearing at the time.'

Then it was decided to use actual footage of John from the original show instead and only Stefanelli's voice was used. He commented, 'It doesn't quite match John's mouth, but it's close.'

St Peter's Church garden fête

An annual garden fête was organised on behalf of St Peter's Parish Church of Church Road, Woolton, Liverpool L25, where John and his mates had attended Sunday school. Pete Shotton's mother had arranged for the Quarry Men to be booked for the event on Saturday 6 July 1957.

The leaflets promoting the fête read,

Woolton Parish church
GARDEN FETE
And
Crowning of Rose Queen
Saturday, July 6th, 1957
To be opened at 3 p.m. by Dr. Thelwell Jones
Procession at 2 p.m.
Liverpool Police Dogs Display
Fancy Dress Parade
Sideshows, Refreshments
Band Of The Cheshire Yeomanry
The Quarry Men Skiffle Group
Adults 6d. children 3d. or by Programme
GRAND DANCE
At 6 p.m. in the Church Hall
GEORGE EDWARDS' BAND
THE QUARRY MEN SKIFFLE GROUP
Tickets 2/- [2 shillings, now 10 pence]

At 2 p.m. five flatbed lorries set out from Church Road, with the Quarry Men aboard the last one, a coal lorry. On another truck, sitting in a chair under a flower-bedecked trellis, was thirteen-year-old Sally Wright, the Rose Queen, dressed in a white lace gown with a train of pink velvet. The 25-man Band of the Cheshire Yeomanry led the procession as it entered Allerton Road, then Woolton Street, King's Drive, Hunt's Cross Avenue and back to Church Road. Accompanying the procession on foot were Brownies, Cubs and morris dancers.

Shortly before 3 p.m. they arrived at St Peter's church field and the procession ended, while the Yeomanry Band entered the field and continued to entertain the crowd. The Quarry Men stored their equipment in the Scouts' hut and began to wander round the various stalls. After the crowning of the Rose Queen, there was a fancy-dress competition.

At 4.15 p.m. the Quarry Men lugged their equipment on to the stage, which was slightly under three feet high and was twenty-five feet wide by fifteen feet deep. Their line-up that day comprised John Lennon on guitar, Eric Griffiths on guitar, Len Garry on tea-chest bass, Pete Shotton on washboard, Rod Davis on banjo and Colin Hanton on drums.

John's Aunt Mimi and two of her sisters were having a cup of tea in the white refreshment tent in the upper field. She recalled, 'Suddenly, in the midst of everything, came this – this eruption of noise. Everyone had drained away from where I stood, into the field next door. And there on the stage I saw them: John and that Shotton.

'John saw me standing there with my mouth open. He started making up words about me in the song he was singing. "Mimi's coming," he sang. "Oh, oh! Mimi's coming down the path." '

Ivan Vaughan, John's close childhood friend, attended Liverpool Institute and had befriended Paul McCartney. Vaughan felt that Paul should meet John and invited him along to see the Quarry Men at the fête – with the enticement that it was a good place to meet girls. He was to say of Paul, 'I knew this was a great fellow. I only ever brought along great fellows to meet John.'

They had been playing for about ten minutes when Paul McCartney arrived on his bike, his guitar strapped to his back. Hoping to pick up a girl, he was dressed in a white sports jacket and black drainpipe trousers. He spotted Ivan Vaughan and they went up to listen to the Quarry Men as they played 'Come Go With Me', which had been a hit for the Dell Vikings. John didn't know all the words to the song, but made some of them up, which he did quite often. They finished playing at around 5 p.m. and made way for the military band, which was followed by the police-dog display. Shortly after 6 p.m. the Quarry Men took to the stage again, the last outdoor performance of the day.

At around 6.15 p.m. one of John's classmates from Quarry Bank, Geoff Rhind, took a photograph.

He was to say, 'I knew all the Quarry Bank School boys, but this was the first time I'd seen them play. I remember it being extremely loud although they had only one mike and one amp for the vocals. We weren't used to things being so loud in those days.

'My mother had bought me a camera for my birthday, a black plastic Kodak Comet 5. I was very shy, but I really wanted to get a picture of them, so I pushed my way through the crowd. I just took one shot. That's all you did back then.'

In addition to the historic photo taken by Rhind, the performance was also recorded by another youth, Bob Molyneux.

He was to comment, 'I didn't even know that the Quarry Men were going to be playing. I went along in the afternoon because I belonged to the church and the youth club, same as John Lennon did, and this was our big event for the year. All the stalls for the fête were laid out in the field behind the church and the Quarry Men were effectively just one attraction among all those stalls. You could walk right past ... or stop and listen if you wanted to.'

He was also to say, 'I noticed that my friend Rod Davis was playing the banjo with them, and that they had one of those double-basses made out of a tea chest with a broom handle stuck on to it and a length of rope stretched out. They had a washboard too, which you played by scraping it with a thimble. I didn't pay much more attention than that, except that I made a note to come back in the evening and tape-record them, because I enjoyed making tapes.'

The Quarry Men finished their performance at around 6.40 p.m. and carried their equipment over Church Road to St Peter's church hall. A few minutes later, Paul and Ivan entered, with Paul leaving his bike by the church hall wall. Ivan then took Paul to where the group were gathered and introduced him. There didn't seem to be much rapport between Paul and the group, so after a few minutes he began to play 'Twenty Flight Rock' on his guitar. He followed with 'Be-Bop-A-Lula' and finished with a Little Richard medley.

The performance lasted about six minutes and had focused John's attention. They began to talk and Paul showed John how to play 'Twenty Flight Rock' and then offered to write out the lyrics to 'Twenty Flight Rock' and 'Be-Bop-A-Lula' for him. Then he showed John and Eric how to tune their guitars. At around 7 p.m. Paul said his goodbyes and left.

Remembering the occasion, Paul commented, 'I showed him a few more chords he didn't know. Then I left. I felt I'd made a good impression.'

John was to say, 'I half thought to myself, He's as good as me. I'd been kingpin up to then. Now I thought, If I take him on, what will happen? It went through my head that I'd have to keep him in line if I let him join.'

Paul's musical ability had impressed John. Pete Shotton recalled, 'Once Paul had gone, John asked what I thought of him. I said I liked him and John asked what I would think about having him in the group. I said it was OK with me, if John wanted him in and if Paul was keen to join.'

The Grand Dance began at 8 p.m. with the George Edwards Band opening and closing the proceedings. The Quarry Men played two half-hour sets, one from 8.45 p.m. the other from 10 p.m.

Bob Molyneux had turned up at the Grand Dance to record the event and comments, 'Half the music at the dance was the George Edwards Band. They were an old-fashioned dance group, doing quicksteps and foxtrots and waltzes. Useless really. The youngsters wanted to get jiving, you see. The Quarry Men were very well received.

'There was no special lighting, so it was very dim in there. My first priority was just to get plugged in to the nearest power socket, which was in an adjoining room, so I had to run an extension lead through.

'I had this Grundig TKB tape recorder, heavy, but just about portable. It had cost me 82 guineas [£84.10], which was a lot of money then, so very few 16-year-olds had anything like it.

'I didn't have to get any permission, just walked in and did it. I don't think they even noticed me, it was so dark. I had to keep my leads near the wall so the dancers wouldn't trip over it. I positioned myself about fifteen yards back from the stage, and held the mike up in my hand. I got them doing "Baby Let's Play House", which was an Elvis Presley thing, and "Puttin' On the Style", which was Lonnie Donegan's number one at the time. My arm kept getting tired, so I didn't record everything.'

John was sixteen at the time and Paul had turned fifteen two weeks before.

A few weeks after the fête Pete Shotton saw Paul riding his bike along Menlove Avenue and asked him if he'd like to join the group. Paul thought about it, said, 'Oh, all right' – and then cycled off home.

St Regis Hotel

The hotel John and Yoko moved into when they arrived in New York on Tuesday 31 August 1971, having already stayed at the hotel during previous visits. They took up residence in rooms 1701, 1702 and 1703 on the twelfth floor. They'd originally moved to New York to continue with Yoko's efforts to gain the custody of her daughter Kyoko.

John was to say, 'Yoko and I were forever coming and going to New York, so finally we decided it would be cheaper and more functional to actually live here.'

While at the hotel they were able to continue their filming of *Imagine* and were able to include a number of celebrities who were staying at the hotel in it – Fred Astaire, Jack Palance and Dick Cavett. They also began shooting their avant-garde film *Clock* in the hotel.

When he moved into the hotel, John said, 'I'm going to have a jukebox of just Elvis records.'

Strawberry Fields

A Salvation Army orphanage situated in Beaconsfield Road, Liverpool L25, where the young John Lennon used to play in its environs. There was originally a large Victorian mansion on the site, but that was knocked down and replaced by a modern building. Together with his mates Pete Shotton and Nigel Walley, John used to visit the annual fêtes, which took place in the grounds of Strawberry Fields in the summer.

The several acres of grounds were well wooded and ideal for John and his mates to play in. The garden fêtes enabled them to sell lemonade bottles for a penny each. They later admitted to a habit of stealing items from stalls during those bittersweet days, which resounded to the throb of the Salvation Army band.

His Aunt Mimi recalled, 'There was something about the place that always fascinated John. He could see it from his window, and he loved going to the garden party they had each year. He used to hear the Salvation Army band, and he would pull me along, saying, "Hurry up, Mimi – we're going to be late!" '

The memories provided his inspiration for 'Strawberry Fields Forever'. Commenting on the number, Paul McCartney said that Strawberry Fields 'was the place right opposite John's house where he used to go and play in the garden kind of thing, so it was a kind of magical childhood place for him. We transformed it into the sort of psychedelic dream, so it was everybody's magical childhood place, instead of just ours.'

John was to say, 'Strawberry Fields is a real place ... I moved in with my auntie, who lived in the suburbs in a nice semide-tached place with a small garden and doctors and lawyers and that ilk living around – not the poor slummy kind of image that was projected in all the Beatles stories ... Near that home was Strawberry Fields, a house near a boys' reformatory where I used to go to garden parties as a kid with my friends Nigel and Pete. We would go there and hang out and sell lemonade bottles for a penny. We always had fun at Strawberry Fields. Also that's where I got the name. But I used it as an image, "Strawberry Fields Forever".'

John was later to name a boat after the place and his Aunt Mimi was to buy a tree to be planted in Strawberry Fields in memory of John.

Strawberry Fields Forever

In 1966 John and Paul each wrote a song about childhood days in Liverpool. They were to be part of a concept double-album based on the memories of a day in the life of Liverpool children.

John composed 'Strawberry Fields Forever', Paul penned 'Penny Lane'. 'Strawberry Fields Forever' was originally called 'Calderstones Park'.

As it turned out, further ideas were developed and the album eventually became *Sergeant Pepper's Lonely Hearts Club Band*, *sans* the two Liverpool childhood tracks.

There were a couple of variations of the number. The initial one was almost a heavy-rock number. John asked the producer George Martin to include strings or brass on another version. On listening to the different tracks John told Martin he liked the beginning of the first one and the end of the second one and asked him to join them together.

George explained that they were not only in different keys but also in different tempos. John told him to just go ahead and fix it.

Martin recalled, 'He never professed to know anything about recording. He was the least technical of the Beatles. He had a profound faith in my ability to cope with such problems, a faith which was sometimes misplaced, as I certainly felt it was on this occasion.

'He had presented me with an almost impossible task. But I had to have a go. I listened to the two versions again, and suddenly realised that with a bit of luck I might get away with it, because, with the way that the keys were arranged, the slower version was a semitone flat compared with the faster one.

'I thought, If I can speed up the one, and slow down the other, I can get the pitches the same. And with any luck the tempos will be sufficiently close not to be noticeable. I did just that, on a variable-control tape machine, selecting precisely the right spot to make the cut, to join them as nearly perfectly as possible. That is how "Strawberry Fields" was issued, and that it how it remains today – two recordings.'

There are a couple of puzzles on the track. Just after John has sung 'Let me take you down' there is a noise like Morse code which, when translated, are two letters: J and L. At the end of the record John mutters 'cranberry sauce', but fans looking for clues in the 'Paul is dead' craze suggested that John was saying, 'I buried Paul.'

Paul was to comment, 'That wasn't "I buried Paul" at the end of "Strawberry Fields Forever" at all: that was John's humour. John would say something totally out of synch like "cranberry sauce". If you didn't realise that John's apt to say "cranberry sauce" when he feels like it, then you start to hear a funny little word and you think, Ah-ha!'

Strawberry Fields, of course, has a strong meaning in relation to John's childhood as it was close to Mendips, the house he lived in with his Aunt Mimi.

He was to say about Strawberry Fields (the orphanage, that is), 'It was an old Victorian house converted for Salvation Army orphans, and as a kid I used to go to their garden party with my friends Ivan, Nigel and Pete. We'd all go up there and hang out and sell lemonade bottles for a penny and we always had fun at Strawberry Fields. Apparently, it used to be a farm that made strawberries or whatever. I don't know. But I just took the name as an image – 'Strawberry Fields Forever' – it had nothing to do with the Salvation Army.'

John originally composed the number during the six-week period he was making *How I Won The War* in Almeria, Spain. The four-minute, five-second number was not issued as a single until 17 February 1967, when it was released in Britain on Parlophone R5570 as a double-A-side with 'Penny Lane'.

John plays lead guitar, harpsichord and solo vocal. Paul is on bass guitar, piano, bongos and flute. George Harrison plays lead guitar and timpani while Ringo is on drums, Mal Evans on tambourine and Philip Jones on alto trumpet, and there are two cellos and two horns.

Despite almost half a million sales during the first week of its release, the single became the first Beatles release since 'Love Me Do' not to make the top of the British charts.

It reached No. 2 and was held off from the top spot by Engelbert Humperdinck with 'Release Me'. However, the number did top the American charts after it was issued there on 13 February 1967 on Capitol 5810.

In the film *Sergeant Pepper's Lonely Hearts Club Band,* Sandy Farina sang the song. She sings it during a tender moment between herself and Peter Frampton. George Martin thought he had to soften it and add strings to make it more of a romantic song.

Strawberry Fields Forever: John Lennon Remembered

A paperback book published in America by Delilah/Bantam in 1980, written by Vic Garbarini, Brian Cullman and Barbara Graustark. It was one of the first books issued as a tribute to

John within a short time of his murder and sported photographs by Jack Mitchell on the front and back of its cover and included a photo insert with over two dozen photographs.

In some ways it is three short books in one. Dave March contributes the introduction, which is followed by six chapters. The first, 'The Dream is Over', reports the news of John's murder. 'Seven Days in December' details the events leading up to the assassination. 'Some Time in NYC' is the story of John and Yoko's love affair with New York. 'All The Lonely People: The Early Years' describes John's life in Liverpool and his career as a Beatle. 'Strawberry Fields' covers part of the Beatles' story and their music, and includes a great many quotes from John. 'The Plastic Ono Band' concerns John's solo career.

The next section of the book, 'Two Virgins', contains the text of the *Newsweek* magazine interview conducted by Barbara Graustark. The third and final section of the book, 'Liverpool to New York: 1940–1980', is a chronology.

Strichweise Lennon
A German film about John's art, first screened in 1995.

SunDance
A cultural and political magazine published in 1972 by Running Dog Incorporated of Fillmore Street, San Francisco.

It was edited by Kenneth Kelley and Craig Pyes, two hippie journalists who had intended to launch a rival publication to *Rolling Stone* magazine. A benefit was held to raise money for the new project in December 1971 and John participated by acting as one of the auctioneers at the event.

The American radical Jerry Rubin then took Pyes along to the Bank Street apartment to meet John and Yoko. During the meeting John voiced his anger at the book *Lennon Remembers,* which had been published by Jann Wenner of *Rolling Stone* without John's permission. John said he felt ripped off by it.

When they discussed *SunDance* John told him, 'If you get something started, let me know.' He said he hoped *SunDance* would put *Rolling Stone* out of business.

Before he left, Pyes asked John if he'd be willing to write a column for the new magazine. John said he'd already been asked to write a column for *Esquire* magazine, which had a circulation of ten million. 'Yes, but *Esquire* is completely owned by pigs. We've got to build up our own media. How are you going to break *Rolling Stone* without co-operation?'

John said he'd write the column.

The first issue of *SunDance* was published in April 1972. A cover blurb mentioned 'John and Yoko on Women' and the masthead announced a regular column from John and Yoko entitled 'Imagine'.

The couple's first contribution was actually called 'It's Never Too Late to Start from the Start'. The subject was feminism and was mainly written by Yoko, although the three-page feature was illustrated with line drawings by John.

The second issue was published in June and mainly concerned the political content in their *Sometime in New York City* album, in which they wrote, 'To us, it is a direct descendant of Yoko's early peace events and *Grapefruit* (pre-John), and also John's satire in *A Spaniard in the Works*.'

The third issue contained instructions by Yoko on how couples could get on with each other better, couched in her *Grapefruit* style.

The magazine was losing money and Pyes approached John and Yoko for help. He told them, 'Look, we're desperate, our cover story on Nixon and the Mafia just has to come out. Can you give us anything?'

John and Yoko weren't too pleased at being asked to fork over money after they'd already helped the magazine by donating a regular column for free, but they gave the magazine $5,000 – although it was too late to save *SunDance* and there was no fourth issue.

Sunday Bloody Sunday

One of two songs on the *Sometime in New York City* album that refer to the presence of British troops in Northern Ireland.

Although John held a romanticised view of Ireland and was descended from Irish stock via his paternal grandfather, he had no real grasp of the Irish problem. Liverpool did have a large Irish community, but they were far removed from the pleasant suburban neighbourhood where John was reared.

He recorded 'Sunday Bloody Sunday' for the album in March 1972 and it referred to events in Londonderry, Northern

Ireland, on 30 January of that year. During a civil rights march in Londonderry's Bogside area, which turned into a riot, British paratroopers opened fire. Thirteen men were killed. A reporter noticed more than a hundred youths hurling sticks and iron bars at the soldiers, which caused a running battle. Shots were fired. A number of witnesses claimed that the initial shots were fired by a Loyalist sniper and the army chief, Major-General Robert Ford, commented, 'There is absolutely no doubt that the Parachute Battalion opened up only after they were fired on.' He agreed with witnesses and said that the dead 'might not have all been killed by our troops'.

Opposition MPs described the event as 'Bloody Sunday'.

The IRA began an immediate policy of killing as many British troops as possible. John's support of the IRA waned as the bombings, massacres and killing of soldiers and civilians escalated.

John sang lead vocal on the track, with Yoko assisting on the chorus.

John had received some flak for seemingly supporting a terrorist organisation, so he explained to the music paper *Sounds* on 2 September 1972, 'Our backing of the Irish people is done through the Irish Civil Rights, which is not the IRA. Although I condemn any violence, if two people are fighting, I'm probably gonna be on one side or the other even though I'm against violence.'

Sun King

Song featured on the *Abbey Road* album. John originally called it 'Los Paranoias'. It was also called 'Here Comes the Sun King!' but that name was shortened to avoid confusion with George Harrison's 'Here Comes The Sun'.

It includes some nonsense lyrics, including Spanish-sounding words that didn't exist, and opens with a variety of sounds, including bird whistles and cowbells. Additional instruments used include John on maracas, Paul on harmonium, Ringo on bongos and George Martin on organ.

Superstars in Film Concert

A 1971 film by Peter Clifton, which included footage of John and Yoko, the Animals, Donovan, Ten Years After, Arthur Brown and the Rolling Stones.

Surprise, Surprise (Sweet Bird of Paradox)

A song featured on the *Walls and Bridges* album, issued in America in September 1974 and in Britain the following month. John first made home tapes of the number in June of that year and recorded it in August. Nicky Hopkins backed him on piano, Ken Ascher on clavinet, Jim Keltner on drums, with Elton John on backing vocals.

Some sources say that May Pang was the inspiration, others that the song was about Yoko. Although John was living with May Pang at the time he wrote the song, he was allegedly eager to be reunited with Yoko and had called her in January 1974 asking if he could return. She told him he wasn't ready at that time.

It has also been pointed out that Paradox was the name of a restaurant in Greenwich Village where Yoko worked in the 60s.

On the other hand, May Pang states the song was definitely written with her in mind at the beginning of their affair and says she cried when John first played the song to her. A musical inspiration was said to be the Diamonds' hit 'Little Darlin''

Elton John provided some vocal harmony on the track.

Sutcliffe, Stuart Fergusson Victor

Stuart was born at Simpson Memorial Maternity Pavilion in Edinburgh, Scotland, on 23 June 1940. His father was Charles Fergusson Sutcliffe and his mother, Martha, was more familiarly known as Millie. Stuart's sister Joyce was born in 1942 followed by another sister, Pauline, in 1944.

Because of the war, Charles was detailed to work at the Camel Laird munitions factory in Birkenhead and the family moved down to a council house in the Liverpool suburb of Huyton. Stuart was to join the choir at St Gabriel's in Huyton and became the head chorister. Together with his sisters he also had weekly piano lessons for a year, although, by all accounts, the tutor gave Stuart's parents false reports of his progress and she was sacked.

In September 1951 Stuart attended Prescot Grammar School. At the age of sixteen, in 1956, he became an intermediate student at the Liverpool College of Art. As his home was several miles from the college and outside the area allocated for the local grants, he couldn't obtain a maintenance grant.

One of the first students he formed a friendship with was Rod Murray, a youth from the West Derby area of Liverpool. Both students decided to share a flat together closer to the college, although initially their parents wouldn't allow them to stay there overnight. They later moved into other premises at 9 Percy Street.

Owing to Stuart's growing reputation as a brilliant student, another student, Bill Harry, sought him out as a friend and introduced him to a friend of his, John Lennon. They were all in different classes but used to get together socially in the college canteen, in the local pub, Ye Cracke, and at parties and social gatherings.

Stuart became passionate about painting and was regarded by one of their lecturers, Arthur Ballard, as the most talented student at the college. Because of Stuart's frequent reluctance to attend classes, Ballard even visited him at his Percy Street flat to provide him with tuition. Ballard's influence is evident in their shared love of the work of the Russian-born French painter Nicolas de Staël. It was also at the flat that Stu (as he was known) and Bill Harry spent many hours discussing the future, metaphysics and the work of mystics such as the Danish religious philosopher, Søren Kierkegaard, books such as those published by the Olympia Press, the San Francisco poets, the Angry Young Men and individual works such as *Catcher in The Rye* (JD Salinger), *On the Road* (Jack Kerouac) and Albert Camus' *The Outsider*. The two even planned to work on a book about Liverpool, with text by Harry and illustrations by Stuart. John was also invited to contribute. Owing to the initial lack of a grant, Stuart had to be financed by his mother.

During one of their Percy Street sessions, Stuart mentioned that he liked the new jacket Bill had bought with his first wage packet from working at a demolition site in Birkenhead during the school holidays. Bill offered Stu the jacket in exchange for a portrait of himself. 'What style would you like it in?' asked Stuart. 'Van Gogh,' said Harry and Stuart completed the work in one sitting.

Both Stuart and Harry were members of the Students' Union committee at the college. John had mentioned a group he led and it was decided to book them for college dances supporting bills topped by bands such as the Merseysippi Jazz Band. Two other members of his group, Paul McCartney and George Harrison, were students of Liverpool Institute, a building that was adjacent to the college. They would come into the college canteen at lunchtimes and also rehearse in the college life rooms (a life room was a huge area where students drew from live nude models).

John had sought a bass guitarist for his group and he offered the job to both Rod Murray and Stuart, without telling either that he'd asked them both. John figured that whoever managed to possess a bass guitar first would get the job.

The two impecunious students couldn't afford to buy one, but Rod got to work on actually making a bass guitar himself.

In the meantime, Stuart had entered one of his paintings in the biennial John Moores Exhibition, which took place at Liverpool's Walker Art Gallery between 17 November 1959 and 17 January 1960. He submitted a work called *Summer Painting*, which was actually only one half of a very large canvas he'd worked on, the other half of which had been lost when Stuart and Rod moved into a new flat in Gambier Terrace. Despite there being over 2,000 entries, Stuart's work was accepted and, when the exhibition opened, John Moores himself bought Stuart's painting for the princely sum of £65.

Stuart was then able to obtain a Hofner President guitar at Frank Hessy's shop in Liverpool on hire purchase, with his mother as guarantor. Contrary to legend, Stuart did not use his exhibition money to buy the guitar outright: he paid only a deposit on it. (Later, while he was in Germany he kept reminding his mother that she had to keep up the payments on his behalf.)

But for Stuart's good fortune at the John Moores Exhibition, Murray could have ended up as the Beatles' bass player.

By this time Stuart's family had moved into Liverpool, with Millie and the two girls settling at 37 Aigburth Drive while Charles, now a merchant seaman, was now away most times on various voyages. Millie used to visit the Gambier Terrace flat to pick up Stuart's clothing, which she cleaned for him each week.

Stuart had always been interested in both music and art and he was particularly enthusiastic about Elvis Presley. As well as taking the piano lessons, he'd attempted to play acoustic guitar Spanish style, with an instrument his father had bought for him following a sea trip. With his new guitar he began to practise to Elvis Presley records on his tiny record player. He also had another student, David May, teach him how to play the Eddie Cochran number 'C'mon Everybody'. May, who was later to join a group called the Silhouettes, offered to teach Stuart to play, if Stuart would allow him to measure his guitar in order that May could build one of his own.

Stuart had also begun to develop a style of appearance that made him stand out: a particular hairstyle, winkle-picker shoes and dark glasses. The inspiration for the dark glasses came from Zbigniew Cybulski, a charismatic actor known as the polish James Dean. Bill Harry ran the college film society and mainly booked continental films including Saldavor Dali and Luis Bunuel's *L'Age D'Or* and Jean Cocteau's *Orphée*. He also booked Andrzej Wajda's film *Generation*, which starred Cybulski.

Now a member of the group, who were appearing at art school dances, Stuart got together with Bill Harry at a Students' Union committee meeting to propose and second that union funds be used to buy a PA system which the group could use. This was agreed, but the equipment was never returned to the college and it is alleged that this is one of the reasons why Stuart was rejected when he later reapplied at the college for an art teacher's diploma course.

The late 1950s saw the establishment of a coffee bar culture and the group of students – John, Stuart, Bill and Rod – used to frequent a coffee bar called the Jacaranda in Slater Street. Its owner, Allan Williams, had presented a pop concert at Liverpool Stadium in conjunction with the London impresario Larry Parnes. Topping the bill was Gene Vincent, but there were a number of local groups in support including Rory Storm and the Hurricanes, Derry and the Seniors and Cass and the Cassanovas. John and Stuart attended the event, which proved to be a local success. Parnes was also impressed by the local groups and asked Williams to set up an audition with some local bands whom he could use as backing outfits to his solo singers.

Stuart approached Williams, asking why he hadn't booked his group at the stadium, and Williams said they could attend the audition. Stuart had been useful to Williams as he'd helped to paint some floats for a Williams promotion at St George's Hall and also painted some murals in the club basement, along with Murray.

The audition took place at another of Williams's clubs, the Wyvern in Seel Street, on 10 May 1960. The other groups on the bill were Cass and the Cassanovas, Derry and the Seniors, Gerry and the Pacemakers and Cliff Roberts and the Rockers. By that time John's group had changed their name to the Silver Beetles.

Rory Storm turned up, but not to perform. He was the lead singer with his group and didn't want his own band to become the backing outfit for another singer.

When it was the turn of the Silver Beetles to perform, their drummer Tommy Moore hadn't arrived. Johnny Hutchinson, drummer with Cass and the Cassanovas agreed to sit in with them. They began their set, then Moore arrived and finished the set with them. Parnes booked the Silver Beetles, Derry and the Seniors and Cass and the Cassanovas to back his artists on tour.

This particular audition sparked off another Beatles legend – that Stu was entirely hopeless on bass guitar and couldn't play at all. Although he wasn't expert on his instrument, he could play and an accusation to the contrary by Williams in his book *The Man Who Gave The Beatles Away* has grown out of all proportion until virtually everyone who writes about Stuart says he was a hopeless musician.

Williams alleged that, because Stuart couldn't play, he turned his back to Parnes and, in fact, generally played with his back to the audience. Williams alleged that this was the reason they weren't chosen as Billy Fury's backing group. In fact, *no one* was chosen as Fury's backing group – even Cass and the Cassanovas, reckoned to be the best group in Liverpool at the time. Yet three of the bands were chosen to back Parnes's artists. When Parnes heard what Williams had alleged, he said it was completely untrue and that he had no worries about Stu. His only objection was to the drummer, Moore. Not only had he been late, but he also dressed differently from the other members and, at 26, was far older than the others.

However, Williams's mud had stuck. Even Paul McCartney, many years later, was to say, 'The problem with Stu was that he couldn't play bass guitar. We had to turn him away in photographs because he'd be doing F-sharp and we'd be holding G.' Initially, all the local musicians were self-taught and in various stages of ability. Paul himself made a hash of it at the New Clubmoor Hall on 18 October 1959 when he attempted to play lead guitar. He played an abominable version of 'Guitar Boogie' and ended his one and only stint at playing lead.

Stuart's playing was nowhere near as bad as people have been led to believe from writers who have used Williams's book as the source. Stuart was only an adequate musician, it's true, but he had presence and charisma on stage.

It is also untrue that he played with his back to audiences or was instructed to turn his back when photographs were taken. The photographs actually taken at the Wyvern audition show Stuart facing the camera and playing his instrument – an image that contradicts Williams's assertion. Photographs of Stuart on stage at the Top Ten Club in Hamburg also show him performing while facing the audience.

There seemed to be no complaints about Stuart's ability in the group while they were playing in Liverpool and Hamburg. While the Beatles were performing at the Indra, Stuart was even placed in a group with Howie Casey to play at the Kaiserkeller. Many of the young 'Exis' who were drawn to the Beatles rated Stuart as their most popular member. (The 'Exis' were young German fans who began to attend the Beatles' shows at the Kaiserkeller. John gave them the nickname 'Exis' because they reminded him of the French Existentialists.)

Stu was called 'the James Dean of St Pauli' and his solo turn, 'Love Me Tender', was one of the highlights of their act in Germany. He didn't play with John, Paul and George when they backed Lu Walters of the Hurricanes on a recording of 'Summertime' because Lu was a bass guitarist himself and the three Beatles had been asked to participate only because of their vocal harmonies. He didn't perform on their recordings with Bert Kaempfert because he'd already decided to leave the band. Yet, even when he left the group, he still hankered to play occasionally and joined a German band for a time.

Rather than look to Williams's book, which many contend is more fiction than fact, it would be wiser to accept an actual witness to Stuart's many performances in Hamburg. Klaus Voormann was inspired by Stuart and became a bass guitarist himself. He was to say, 'He was a really great bass player, a very basic bass player, completely different, so basic that you could say he was at the time my favourite bass player but primitive. But, of all the people or groups and when we saw groups later, he was my favourite bass player.' In fact, it was Stuart who first began to show Klaus the basics of playing bass guitar.

Stuart's sister Pauline was to tell Bill Harry that Stuart thought himself a better musician than history remembers him. She says it was relative to how good or bad they all were at the time: 'I don't think he was as outstandingly bad as he's been described,' she said, 'because none of them were excellent, were they, until they went to Hamburg and started to play?' She believes that the way Stuart stood as he performed was 'a piece of stylistic staging on Stuart's part, nothing to do with shyness'. She added, 'I think that was a very well-thought-out, planned stage strategy – and it worked, didn't it? George was better, Paul was better, but nothing like the musicians they became. I mean, they were just more competent, but according to Stuart's letters and conversations with him he thought he was progressing quite well and loved it and thought he was quite innovative as a bass player. He thought himself good enough to do session work after he left them and – I've got letters – he was asked to be in other groups.'

When the Beatles arrived in Hamburg they found they were to play at a small club called the Indra in the Grosse Freiheit. The Liverpool band Derry and the Seniors, the first Liverpool group to travel to Hamburg, were performing at the Kaiserkeller. Derry Wilkie was a showman and his performance on stage was proving so popular at the club that its owner, Bruno Koschmider, told the Beatles that they must also 'Mach Shau' ('make show').

The interest generated by the Seniors was such that Koschmider decided to stop having a jukebox in the interval and turned Derry and the Seniors into two groups by taking their sax player, Howie Casey, and pianist, Stan Foster, and teaming them up with Stuart and a German modern-jazz drummer.

The Seniors' season at the club ended and another Liverpool group, Rory Storm and the Hurricanes, became the bill toppers, with the Beatles having also moved to the Kaiserkeller, because the Indra had had to close down owing to complaints about the noise.

In October 1960 a young German student, Klaus Voormann, was attracted to the sounds emanating from the club and entered the Kaiserkeller to watch Rory Storm and the Hurricanes. He was even more fascinated when the Beatles took to the stage. A few days later he returned and during the interval approached John. He mentioned that he had designed a record sleeve for 'Walk, Don't Run' by the Ventures. John referred him to Stuart. A few days later Klaus entered the club again, this time accompanied by his girlfriend, Astrid Kirchherr, and a friend, Jurgen Vollmer.

Soon, their whole set of friends, now tagged 'the Exis', began to frequent the Kaiserkeller and Kirchherr asked the Beatles if she could photograph them. She met them at Der Dom in the local fairground and took what were to become famous pictures before inviting them out for a Chinese meal.

The Exis were particularly drawn to Stuart, bedecked with dark glasses, coming to the forefront to perform 'Love Me Tender'.

He was to write 'The girl thought that I was the most handsome of the lot. Here I was, feeling the most insipid working member of the group, being told how much superior I looked – this alongside the great Romeo John Lennon, and his two stalwarts Paul and George: the Casanovas of Hamburg!' (No mention here, though, of Pete Best, who was generally recognised to be the most handsome member of the group.)

A fortnight after they first met, Astrid bought him a chocolate heart and they soon began to date. Initially there was some embarrassment owing to the presence of Klaus, but he soon realised what was happening and moved out of the Kirchherr house in Altona, leaving the field open to Stuart, who became the new lodger.

In November Astrid told her mother that she was going to marry Stuart.

During this period, Stuart's influence was to have an effect on the group. Not only had he taken to wearing black leather, but he had a Pierre Cardin-style collarless suit and Astrid changed his hairstyle into what was later to become a style association with the Beatles' moptop.

Some signs actually indicated that Stuart wanted to leave the Beatles at this stage. As a result Pete Best contacted Chas Newby, the former bassist with his group the Blackjacks, by letter. Newby replied in a letter dated 29 November 1960 that he could not come over to Hamburg and join them as a permanent member, although he would be free during the Christmas period and would be willing to play with them then for a limited time – which he did, for four appearances in Liverpool.

The Beatles' term in Hamburg was coming to an end. They had secured work in a new club, the Top Ten, much to the annoyance of Koschmider and in contravention of their contract with him. The police then decided to take action against George for being under age and deported him. Stuart and Astrid accompanied him to the railway station. Paul and Pete were the next to go: locked up by the police for allegedly trying to burn down Koschmider's cinema, they were then escorted by the police to the airport.

While the police investigated the alleged arson, they also arrested Stuart, who was locked up in a cell for over six hours with no food or drink before being set free after the police were satisfied with his statement.

Only John and Stuart remained. John opted to return to Liverpool while Stuart remained in Hamburg.

For their initial gigs in Liverpool, the Beatles recruited Chas Newby, who refused John's further offer to him to replace Stuart as a permanent member of the band. Until Stuart returned, Paul took over on bass, playing his Lucky 7 guitar upside down and backwards.

George had refused to become their bass guitarist and he wrote to Stuart in Hamburg, 'Come home sooner, as if we get a new bass player for the time being, it will be crummy, as he will have to learn everything. It's no good with Paul playing bass, we've decided, that is if he had some kind of bass and amp to play on!'

George, acknowledged as a talented guitarist, wouldn't be requesting Stuart to rejoin the group if Stuart was unable to play and as hopeless as writers in hindsight maintain.

Stuart did return to Liverpool in late February and then returned to Hamburg ahead of the others, early in March, prior to their season at the Top Ten Club. The group members were unsure about his position with them as Paul had now taken up the bass. Stuart had also put in his application for the ATD (art teacher's diploma) course at Liverpool College of Art, beginning in September.

Astrid remembers him as being quieter than the other members of the group and also said that he was sensitive. Stuart would portray a different side to various people, depending on his moods. Some would find him introspective, almost introverted, others gregarious. Gerry Marsden regarded him as 'a very quiet, nice guy ... Maybe too quiet to the stage of boring.'

Stuart had teamed up with the Beatles to play again at the Top Ten, but arguably his heart wasn't really in it any more. He and Astrid had become engaged and, unable to return to Liverpool College of Art, he'd enrolled at the State High School of Art Instruction in Hamburg. Initially, while waiting for approval for a grant, he worked in Gustaf Seitz's Sculpture Department and was then able to join a class under the tuition of Eduardo Paolozzi, who'd actually arranged the grant for Stuart. He then embarked on a remarkable volume of work.

While they were at the Top Ten they also backed Tony Sheridan. Because they considered this would result in having too many guitarists in the group, Paul played piano.

Pete Best recalled an incident on stage between Stuart and Paul. Stuart would look at Astrid in the audience and although the other members of the group made some light-hearted banter about it, Paul kept winding Stuart up. Best says, 'On this particular night Astrid was there and Paul said something. I don't actually know what the remark was because Paul was playing piano on the other side of the drum rostrum. Stu took his bass off and it wasn't with a view to giving it to anyone. He put it down and, the next thing, the two of them were swinging at one another.' The other members of the band had to intervene.

When the Beatles backed Tony Sheridan on record Stuart attended the sessions but didn't play as he'd decided to leave the group. The Beatles returned to Liverpool and Stuart remained in Hamburg, now a full-time student.

John and Stuart used to write letters to each other. Once John wrote to Stuart,

I remember a time when Everybody I loved hated me
Because I hated them. So what, so what, so Fucking what.
I remember a time when Belly buttons were knee high
When only shitting was dirty and everything else Clean
and beautiful. I can't remember anything Without a

sadness So deep that it hardly Becomes known to me. So
deep that its tears leave me a spectator Of my own
stupidity. And so I go rambling on With a hey nonny
nonno no.

Stuart also began work on a novel about John, which he
called *Spotlight On Johnny*. This actually ran to 27 handwritten
pages and was basically a biography of John and Stuart. He
wrote,

With John it was different as I said he was unlucky. Given
the breaks that other people had he would have been all
right. As it was he brooded trying to find the answer. He
was born old. He'd dried up before his time. He wilted,
because he knew that someday he would wilt anyhow.

This description is also obviously a self portrait: 'He was
obviously suffering from nervous tension and probably high
blood pressure. This left him suffering from dizziness and
headaches ... when he stood up he complained of a black-out
and tremendous headaches.'

The manuscript was sold at auction at Sotheby's Rock 'N'
Roll Memorabilia sale on Thursday 1 September 1983.

In the meantime, in Liverpool, Rod Murray had been evicted
from the Gambier Terrace flat. He'd claimed to Stu's mother
that both Stu and John hadn't paid their fair share of the rent.
Mrs Sutcliffe settled some money on him and hired a van to
collect Stuart's belongings. She was to recall that writers later on
wrote fanciful stories about Stuart sleeping in a white coffin in
Gambier Terrace, which was a ridiculous tale: he had a camp
bed, which was among the items she collected. She also took a
chest of drawers, which were full of John Lennon's clothes and
other items – her husband threw it out when he discovered who
it belonged to. A number of John's paintings had also been left
outside the flat and Johnny Byrne, who lived downstairs, took
them as fuel and burned them.

The work Stuart was creating in Hamburg was considerable
and he was in a masterclass with students from various countries. Eduardo Paolozzi wrote, 'One of my best students. He is
working very hard and with high intelligence.'

However, as in Liverpool, he began to work more and more outside the actual college, painting frenetically in the attic of the Kirchherrs' house.

Millie Stucliffe, who kept Bill Harry informed of all Stuart's activities in Hamburg, phoned him to say that she was very concerned because Stuart had had an accident and had fallen down the stairs leading from the attic at the Kirchherrs' house. Following the accident he had begun to experience headaches, nausea and occasional bouts of blindness. He began to be depressed; he wouldn't eat. Mrs Sutcliffe became extremely worried.

Astrid's mother, Nielsa Kirchherr, was to say that when Stuart had fallen down the narrow attic stairs in her house, he had bumped his head severely. The severe headaches were so intense that he began to visit a doctor in Hamburg in February 1962. X-rays were taken, but they revealed nothing. Another doctor, Peter Hommelhoff, examined Stuart in June 1961 and found he had a shadow on the entrance of his lung – although it wasn't TB or cancer – and he also had gastritis. On a visit to Liverpool he visited a consultant at Sefton General Hospital, who also confessed he could not find anything wrong. Stuart was to refer to him as a quack.

In January 1962 he collapsed during art class and Astrid was called from work to take him home. Dr Hommelhoff was summoned, although he still couldn't find anything wrong with Stuart and recommended that he relax more, have massages and a course of hydrotherapy at the local hospital.

In February Stuart visited Liverpool again. He was wearing a velvet Pierre Cardin-style suit when he took his little sister, Pauline, down to the Cavern to see the Beatles. The next day Pauline told her mother, 'Those Beatles hate Stuart. Especially Paul McCartney. They were saying, "Oh, you're wearing your sister's suit, Stuart." They always made Stuart out as a softie, but it was the other way around. Stuart had a strong character and in the important things John abided by what Stuart said.'

Back in Hamburg the mysterious illness became worse and the bouts of temporary blindness became more frequent.

On Tuesday 10 April 1962 Nielsa Kirchherr heard a scream and noises from the attic. She rushed up to discover Stuart on the floor in convulsions and called for Dr Hommelhoff. The two of them carried Stuart downstairs and Hommelhoff voiced his concern that Stuart had a cerebral haemorrhage. He phoned the Heidbert Hospital, which had a neurological clinic, for Stuart to be taken there in the afternoon.

Mrs Kirchherr sent a telegram to Millie Sutcliffe saying Stuart was seriously ill, and Astrid rushed through the lunchtime traffic to reach home. Stuart died in Astrid's arms on the way to the hospital at 4.45 p.m. Mrs Kirchherr then sent another telegram to Millie informing her of her son's death – and this telegram arrived before the first, which informed her that he was ill.

Millie took the lunchtime flight from Manchester Airport to Hamburg on 12 April. John, Paul and Pete had already left for their Star Club appearance and hadn't heard of Stuart's death. George had been delayed by a bout of German measles and Brian Epstein had waited with him. When he received news of Stuart's death, Epstein took Millie to the airport and sat next to her on the plane.

Astrid had been at the airport to meet John, Paul and Pete and tell them the dreadful news. John strode forward towards Astrid first and asked her where Stuart was. She told him and he found it difficult to express himself.

Millie went to the morgue and made the formal identification of her son's body. She returned with the coffin to Liverpool. Dressed in a suit made by Astrid, Stuart was buried in grave No. 552 at Huyton Cemetery in Blue Bell Lane.

Although both Millie Sutcliffe and Nielsa Kirchherr attribute Stuart's death to the fall he had down the attic steps at the Eimsbuttler Strasse house, another myth has been created, owing to Allan Williams's book *The Man Who Gave The Beatles Away*. Not only did he create the nonsense about Stuart always performing with his back to the audience and not being able to play the bass, but also said that a fight outside Litherland Town Hall caused Stuart's death.

He wrote,

It was on such a night that Stuart Sutcliffe received the injuries which I believe hastened his death a couple of years later. Stuart was attacked outside Litherland Town Hall, where the Beatles played regularly, and was kicked in the head by a local thug. From then on he complained to me often of severe headaches. Just before he died the pain was so severe and constant he feared for his sanity. I am firmly convinced that if it hadn't been for the toe of a brute's boot at Litherland, Stuart would be with us now – as one of the best-known painters in the world.

The Beatles' very first appearance at Litherland Town Hall took place on 27 December 1960, after they had severed their relationship with Williams. Stuart was still in Hamburg. He returned to Liverpool for a few weeks in February 1961 and then returned to Hamburg. No incident as Williams described ever took place outside Litherland Town Hall. Stuart was also in Hamburg, not Liverpool, when his headaches began, so he wouldn't have been complaining to Williams about them then.

Pete Best was a member of the band from August 1960 until Stuart left and was present at every gig Stuart performed with the Beatles during that time, and confirms that no such incident as Williams described ever took place.

Philip Norman perpetuated the myth in his book *Shout*, where he stated that after Stuart's death Mrs Sutcliffe remembered a night three years before when Stuart had been kicked in the head in a scuffle outside Litherland Town Hall. Norman's interview with Mrs Sutcliffe had been arranged by Bill Harry and Millie made no such assertion. She continued to maintain that the head injury was caused by the attic fall. Also, three years prior to his death, Stuart had never appeared at Litherland Town Hall. Philip Norman's piece of fiction has been taken up by others.

In the film *Backbeat* Stuart was depicted as being beaten by a group of thugs outside a club. In Albert Goldman's book *The Lives of John Lennon* he asserts that John kicked Stuart in the head in Hamburg.

Returning to Pete Best, he recalls that the only incident in which Stuart was involved in a fight while he was a member of the Beatles took place at Lathom Hall, Seaforth. Although they appeared there for the first time on 14 May 1960, it is unlikely to have been on that date, as Neil Aspinall recalls the event and, since he didn't become associated with the group until early in 1961, it couldn't have been that date. Their last performance at Lathom Hall took place on 25 February 1961, George

Harrison's birthday, and this seems the most likely date, as Stuart had returned to Liverpool from Hamburg at the time.

Aspinall recalled, 'At Lathom Hall ... two troublemakers followed Stu Sutcliffe into the dressing room muttering things like "Get your hair cut, girl!" John and Pete saw this and went after them. A fight broke out and John broke his little finger ... It set crooked and never straightened.'

Another witness was Pete Best, who has recalled the incident in detail:

> When Stu came back there was an incident at Lathom Hall. Lathom was reputed to be a tough gig. While we were on stage there was a gang of lads who picked on Stu.
>
> When we'd done our session and come off, we changed, which didn't take an awful lot of time because we basically played in what we stood up in. Stu went out, followed by John and myself.
>
> These lads staged a fight with Stu after picking on him. We got to know about it because some people ran back to the side of the stage where we had come from and said, 'Stu's getting the living daylights knocked out of him.'
>
> So John and I dashed out. We threw a couple of punches, sorted things out and pulled Stu back in again ... When people talk of Stu being beaten up, I think it stems from this incident. I don't remember Stu getting to the stage where he had his head kicked in, as some legends say, alleging that his caused his fatal brain haemorrhage.
>
> For as long as I was with the band I can only remember two incidents when fists were thrown and Stu was involved. The Lathom Hall incident aside, the other occasion was at the Top Ten Club, and that was between Paul and Stu.

There you have it. The only time Stuart was involved in a fracas outside a Liverpool ballroom was a time when he had no head injury at all. This is not the only evidence concerning the cause of death.

Stuart died of a cerebral haemorrhage, which is bleeding into the brain, in Stuart's case bleeding into the right ventricle. In the case of a fight in Liverpool being the cause, that was too long a period before his death: no head traumas that cause cerebral bleeding or death could take place that long after such an injury.

John Willett, in his 1967 book *Art In a City*, wrote,

> Probably no recent Liverpool painter has worked with anything like this intensity, and the range, variety and colour of his last few months' work made a very strong impression when they were shown at the Walker Art Gallery in May 1964. He was an outstanding loss to Liverpool and quite possibly to English painting. Over and above the merit of his pictures he has a special significance as somebody whose burning creativity switched from art to pop music and then back again. He showed the way.

Millie Sutcliffe decided to spend the rest of her life attempting to gain recognition for her son's work and arranged a memorial exhibition at the Walker Art Gallery in Liverpool in 1964 and over the years several other small-scale exhibitions were organised.

Bill Harry had kept in touch with Millie after Stuart's death (and indeed kept in touch with her in all succeeding years until she died), and knew how disappointed she was in the fact that she had never heard from any members of the Beatles following Stuart's demise.

Harry decided to rectify that on Sunday 8 November 1964. The Beatles were appearing at the Empire, Liverpool, and he went along in the afternoon and spent the day with them. After their last show he suggested to John that they drop in on Mrs Sutcliffe. John agreed and, along with Bill, his wife Virginia and Pete Shotton and his wife Beth, visited her at her home in Aigburth. She was delighted and showed them Stuart's work, which was on the walls, stacked in the halls and under the beds. She gave John a copy of *How to Draw Horses*, which he'd lent to Stu some years before, and also gave him a clipping from a local newspaper of the first mention of the Beatles in print. She then asked John and Bill to take their pick of Stuart's work. John selected a blue abstract oil painting and Bill picked a red collage.

Millie's husband Charles died in 1966 and she decided to move to Sevenoaks in Kent. She died on 8 December 1983.

A few months before she died she was able to see the one-man show, *Stu*, which was presented at the Bromley Little Theatre, Bromley, from 21 to 24 September 1983. Jeremy Stockwell and Hugh O'Neill wrote it. Twenty-one-year-old Paul Almond, a graduate from Bristol University, acted the part of Stuart. Millie told Bill Harry, 'He bore a slight resemblance to Stuart – he was superb.'

Stockwell and O'Neill wrote,

Stu is an attempt to portray the complex nature of a unique individual and a highly original artist who, despite his tragically early death, also informed much of popular culture since the sixties trough his relationship with, and impact on, its foremost innovators. Sutcliffe's life and death embodies many of the romantic notions of art and artists which still persist in popular mythology, while the genuinely tragic nature of the wasted talent and unfulfilled potential that his death signifies transcends commonplace cliché to become a tangible and poignant reality.

Stockwell went on to say, 'Sutcliffe was a brilliant talent and really was the first link between rock 'n' roll and art. He had this aura about him. He had the kind of style that summed up a generation, really. His story is fascinating, if not a sad one – that's why we wrote the play.'

The hour-long production was split into twelve scenes, each preceded by slides indicating its locale. There were also slides of Stu's work from each period.

- Scene 1: Hamburg, April 1962, just before his death.
- Scene 2: Liverpool, early in 1959. Stu and Bill Harry are sitting in Ye Cracke pub and are joined by John Lennon.
- Scene 3: Ye Cracke a few months later; John asks Stu to join his group.
- Scene 4: Hamburg, June 1961. Stu is painting and is joined by his fiancée Astrid Kirchherr.
- Scene 5: Liverpool, 1959. Stu has sold a painting at the John Moores Exhibition and buys a guitar.
- Scene 6: Hamburg, April 1961. Stu is once again at his easel, telling Astrid about the Beatles.

- Scene 7: Liverpool, June 1960. Stu returns home with a head injury and tells his mother how he has been attacked.
- Scene 8: Hamburg, December 1961. Stu is tired, has constant headaches, but confides to Astrid that he is looking forward to returning home to Liverpool at Christmas to see his mother and sisters.
- Scene 9: Hamburg, September 1960. Stu is in a club with Astrid and Klaus Voormann, watching the Beatles perform.
- Scene 10: April, 1962. Stu tells both his mother and the audience of his experiences, and of his hopes and aspirations.
- Scene 11: April, 1962. Stu finishes playing 'Love Me Tender' in Germany, has a row with Paul, takes his guitar and leaves.
- Scene 12: Hamburg, April, 1962. Stu talks to Astrid as he sketches; he listens to the imaginary voice of John reading a letter Stu has sent him discussing Hamburg and the career of the Beatles: 'Today, Litherland Town Hall, tomorrow the world!' He gives a shout of pain and the play ends to the sound of the Hamburg version of the Beatles performing 'Twist and Shout'.

Millie was delighted with the play, although she pointed out the inaccuracy of Scene 7.

The year 1990 saw an atmospheric monochrome drama called *Midnight Angel*, produced by Granada television, which depicted Stuart's days in Hamburg.

Huge interest was aroused when the film *Backbeat* was released. The movie was premiered in April 1994, directed by Iain Softley and starred Stephen Dorff as Stuart, Sheryl Lee as Astrid and Ian Hart as John. Despite the fact that Astrid Kirchherr was hired as an adviser – as the story basically concerned her romance with Stuart – it is a flawed film and far from accurate, beginning with the fictitious 'fight' in Liverpool.

It also implied that John had a crush on Astrid, which is not so. Apart from his relationship with Cynthia, John had more than his fair share of girls in Hamburg and it was reported that at times he actually resented her. Jurgen Vollmer, who was witness to the romance, also contests the accuracy of the movie.

However, it did succeed in bringing Stuart's part in the Beatles story to an international audience.

The official synopsis of *Backbeat* reads:

At a church fête in Woolton, Liverpool, in 1957, 15-year-old guitarist Paul McCartney successfully auditioned for a skiffle group, the Quarry Men, which also featured a young John Lennon. In the next few months, two more recruits were added, a lead guitarist, George Harrison and an art school friend of Lennon's, Stuart Sutcliffe. Briefly known as Johnny And The Moondogs, the group re-christened themselves the Silver Beetles, touring Scotland early in 1960, as support act to Johnny Gentle. Shortly afterwards, Pete Best, a full-time drummer, joined the group, which by now had settled on a permanent name – THE BEATLES.

Liverpool, a great grey seaport city, is still recovering from the ravages of wartime bombing. In a shabby nightclub, a young singer is trying valiantly to make herself heard above the unwelcome accompaniment of a mischievous pair of Teddy Boys. John Lennon (Ian Hart) and his best friend Stuart Sutcliffe (Stephen Dorff) are doing what comes naturally – upsetting the status quo.

The boys' high-spirited performance is not going down well with a group of sailors, who take exception to their flippancy. After an exchange of insults, John and Stuart make their escape, but find themselves trapped in an alley. The sailors give them a savage beating, kicking Stuart repeatedly.

Stuart is a talented painter, but is not yet ready to commit himself to a career in art. When he sells his first painting to a wealthy collector he uses the money to buy a bass guitar. He's not much of a musician, but he's burning with enthusiasm – the opportunity to spend a few months rocking in Hamburg with John and the band is irresistible.

So, after a wearying ferry journey, the Beatles arrive in Hamburg: John, Stuart, Paul McCartney (Gary Bakewell), young George Harrison (Chris O'Neill) and Pete Best (Scott Williams). Five relative innocents at large in St Pauli, sin capital of Europe. Their sleeping accommodation is

more like the Black Hole of Calcutta, but the teeming deca-
dence of their surroundings soon distracts them. Besides,
their first gigs in the seedy Kaiserkeller bring the promise of
... girls.

With their raw musical energy fronted by John's surreal
and intense irreverence and with Stuart, the super-cool
personification of rock 'n' roll style luring the female fans,
the Beatles start to acquire a loyal local following. One
night, a young artist and musician, Klaus Voormann (Kai
Wiesinger), visits the club. He is immediately won over by
the freshness and vitality of the English group, which he
describes enthusiastically to his long-time girlfriend, Astrid
Kirchherr (Sheryl Lee). A beautiful young blonde photographer, dressed always in black, she is a leading light of
Hamburg's Existentialist scene.

Klaus takes her to the Reeperbahn to see this new
phenomenon, particularly the cool young bass player who
looks like James Dean. When Stuart catches sight of Astrid
in the audience, their mutual attraction is immediate and
total.

Astrid takes the group to the Existentialist Bar Enfer.
Paul, George and Pete feel uncomfortable in this bizarre
environment and John rails against the pretentiousness of
it all – 'It's all dick!' Stuart, however, only has eyes for
Astrid, and John, hurt and jealous, flies into a blind rage
and stalks out.

Lying in bed, troubled and awake, when an elated Stuart
returns, John warns his friend that Astrid is out of his
league, but Stuart asks him to give her a chance. He
convinces John that Astrid should be allowed to photograph the group and, on an old truck in a deserted fairground, she takes the picture which epitomises the Beatles'
Hamburg years.

Gradually Stuart is drawn into Astrid's life. He visits her
house, he meets her friends and he discovers a new world
where sexual distinctions are blurred and where art
dictates the rules. The other members of the band indulge
Stuart's obsession, but their patience is sorely tried when a
record producer visits the club just as Stuart is performing
an un-Beatle-like version of 'Love Me Tender', as a tribute

to Astrid. The mystified producer departs hurriedly and the tensions within the group erupt into bitter recriminations. Paul suggests that they cannot afford to carry Stuart, but John threatens to quit if his friend is allowed to leave. Stuart, meanwhile, is spending more and more time with Astrid, revelling in the new experience she shares with him, but showing the first, disturbing signs of mental turmoil and illness.

The band's fortunes take a turn for the better, when the record producer returns to the Kaiserkeller to catch their act and offers them the opportunity to record a backing track. They leap at this chance of a first small step on the ladder to stardom – all except Stuart, who dares not admit that he has promised to spend the day with Astrid. John is furious when Stuart feigns illness in the morning and refuses to join them.

And so, while the Beatles cut their first record – as backing singers on Tony Sheridan's version of 'My Bonnie Lies Over the Ocean', Astrid is taking pictures of Stuart on the banks of the Elbe. Gradually, he is coming to realise that he hasn't the driving musical ambitions of the rest of the group – he tagged along purely out of loyalty to John.

The Beatles, with Paul now on bass, throw themselves wholeheartedly into their recordings of rusty old standards, while across town, in Astrid's stylish bedroom, the lovers fall into each other's arms.

Their idyll is shattered, however, by the unexpected arrival of Klaus at her apartment. Sadly, the young German realises that by bringing his new friend into Astrid's life, he has lost her, perhaps for ever. Stuart's life has changed, too. His admission that he has moved in with Astrid brings only mockery from John. But there is good news: the Beatles have been booked into the more prestigious Top Ten Club – and they are top of the bill.

Stuart is deliriously happy. He and Astrid are in love and he is painting again. John comes to visit and Astrid challenges him about his attitude. She would like to be his friend, but finds his perpetual anger too much of a barrier. Suddenly, she accuses him of being jealous of her relationship with Stuart. This bombshell is just sinking in, when there is a thunderous knocking at the door. The police have come to deport the Beatles, who have been working without proper papers.

Stuart is back in Liverpool, but his heart remains in Hamburg. He confesses to John that he has to return, whether the band goes or not. He has hardly painted a thing since leaving and he has been offered the chance to apply to the Hamburg art school with Scottish teacher Eduardo Paolozzi. John realises that he is losing Stuart to Astrid and Hamburg, just as the Beatles are starting to make an impact in the music business.

Now that George has reached his 18th birthday, the band is free to head back across the North Sea, where Astrid is waiting for Stuart. He throws himself into his painting, becoming accepted by her Exi friends. Astrid cuts Stuart's hair in the mop-top style she has been developing with Klaus and John is horrified when he turns up to play at the Top Ten with his new look. Astrid is in the audience and Stuart has difficulty concentrating on the music. Tempers flare and Stuart leaves the stage as Paul and John begin to argue.

In the morning, John tries to convince Stuart that he should stay with the group, that Astrid is only a passing fling. He reminds Stuart that she dropped Klaus for him readily enough. Stuart reacts by throwing a punch at him and their repressed anger and frustration boils over into a fight in the street.

Stuart's affair with Astrid increases in intensity. He is painting like a madman, often through the night, fuelled by amphetamines and a sense that time is against him. He is living and loving at a furious pace and it begins to take its toll. At a party, high on 'speed', he collapses while attempting to limbo-dance. A doctor diagnoses an old head injury and warns him to slow down, to lay off the amphetamines, but he takes little notice. Outwardly, his life is taking wing – Astrid has agreed to marry him and he has been accepted by the Hamburg Art College – but his health is deteriorating rapidly.

John's girlfriend, Cynthia Powell (Jennifer Ehle), comes to Hamburg to visit them. She confides to Astrid how she intends to marry John and have his babies and, as the two couples spend a relaxed and peaceful night on a lonely beach, John at last seems more at ease with Astrid. He admits to her that he might have fallen in love with her himself, if she hadn't fallen for his best friend. John makes a last attempt to entice Stuart back to the group, but even the prospect of international success with the Beatles is not enough to persuade him.

Stuart plays one last time with the band and makes his peace with John and Paul. The Beatles return to England without him, unaware of how ill he has become. He suffers uncontrollable fits of rage, even picking a fight with the innocent Klaus, and attacking his paintings in bouts of savage, pain-racked frenzy.

The Cavern club's first shrill strains of Beatlemania are still echoing in their ears, as the mop-topped band makes a triumphal return to Hamburg. A sombre, devastated Astrid is at the airport to greet them. Stuart is dead, struck down by a massive brain haemorrhage, only hours before their arrival.

At a sell-out gig at the Star club, Astrid is in the audience as John announces a song 'for absent friends' and softly croons the opening bars of 'Love me Tender'. The puzzled fans are beginning to grow restless, when the band changes gear and launches into a raw, driving version of 'Twist And Shout'. As the Beatles rock the rafters, Astrid turns and silently slips away.

It would be unreasonable for biopics to aim for 100 per cent accuracy, since they are a medium that condenses a person's life into about ninety minutes of screen time. They also need a basic formula that engages the interest. Not only did the opening of the film, with John and Stuart being beaten outside a club, never happen, but the type of club and the people in it are nothing like the clubs and occupants they would have encountered in Liverpool at the time. It was totally untypical and seems pure fantasy to people who were actually around.

John wouldn't consider Astrid as out of Stuart's league as there were similar, stunning girls they both knew at Liverpool College of Art. No record producer saw them at the Kaiserkeller.

This was put in to imply that Stuart was no good as a musician, further consolidating an unfair assessment of his ability. No record producer returned to the Kaiserkeller to ask them to record a backing track. This refers to their appearance at another club, the Top Ten, the following year on their second trip to Hamburg when they were actually backing Tony Sheridan – and it was Sheridan whom the producer came to see. Stuart didn't feign illness to miss out on the recording: he had already decided to leave the group.

When Klaus finds Stuart and Astrid in the apartment together, this also gives a false picture. Astrid lived in a house with her mother in Altona and, once Stuart and Astrid were going together, Astrid's mother agreed to Stuart's becoming a lodger in the house because of the poor conditions at the Kaiserkeller – this happened on their first trip.

It's then said that they are bill toppers at the Top Ten Club, but they were the backing band to Sheridan. Then the police come knocking at the door and they are deported, because they haven't got the correct papers. This happened on their first trip, but not as suggested. George was deported first because he was under age; Pete and Paul were deported later because they were accused of arson; John left soon after and Stuart remained in Hamburg. Yet the film has Stuart back in Liverpool, 'but his heart remains in Hamburg', when he actually *did* remain in Hamburg!

The next chestnut is John trying to talk Stuart into rejoining the band, yet while Stuart was still a member he had offered Stuart's position to Chas Newby, who turned it down. The implication that John fancied Astrid is also wrong. One is then led to the assumption that his death was the result of the fictitious fight at the beginning of the film when, in truth, his head injury was actually caused by the fall down the stairs at Astrid's house in Hamburg.

However, the film sparked off interest in his art, resulting in a paperback, *Backbeat*, by Pauline Sutcliffe and Alan Clayson, published by Pan, and a limited-edition book, *Stuart,* also co-written by Pauline, this time with Kay Williams, and published by Genesis. There was also a Genesis reproduction of one of Stuart's sketchbooks entitled *Stuart – The Life & Art of Stuart Sutcliffe.* Various international exhibitions were also arranged.

From the time of his first painting shown at the John Moores Exhibition in 1959, his other exhibitions have included: Walker Art Gallery, 1964, a major retrospective; one-man shows at the Neptune Gallery, Liverpool University and Bluecoat Gallery, all in Liverpool between 1965 and 1967; the *Art In a City* exhibition at the ICA, London, in 1967; a one-man show at the Room, Greenwich, in 1972; the *Art of the Beatles* exhibition at the Walker Art Gallery, Liverpool, in 1984; the Art of the Beatles tour of Japan between 1987 and 1988; the *Art of the Beatles* exhibition in Cologne, Germany, in 1988; one-man show at Sotheby's, London, and the Barbizon Gallery, Glasgow, Bluecoat Gallery, Liverpool, and BBK Gallery in Cologne in 1990; mixed exhibition at the Bluecoat Gallery, Liverpool; a one-man show in Japan in 1994; and a one-man show at Govinda Gallery, Washington, USA, in 1994.

Swank

A sex magazine that in 1983 announced it would publish nude photographs of John and Yoko in its October issue. It said that the photographs had been discovered in a dustbin. Yoko immediately took legal action.

This could probably be traced to Gary Westcoatt who, earlier that year, was attempting to sell fifty slides of John and Yoko in various nude poses to different magazines. When he broke up with his girlfriend, she took the slides with her. In May of that year Westcoatt set fire to the house where the girl and her new boyfriend were living. He was arrested by the New Orleans police, who verified that the slides were of the Lennons and that they had been stolen. Westcoatt confirmed that the slides had been found in a dustbin in New York.

Sweet Little Sixteen

Chuck Berry was one of John's idols and he was to comment, 'When I hear good rock, the calibre of Chuck Berry, I just fall apart. I have no other interest in life. The world could be ending and I couldn't care.' John recorded this number with Phil Spector for his *Rock 'n' Roll* album.

Tannebaum, Allan

One of the last photographers to take shots of John and Yoko. At the time he was working on music assignments for the *SoHo News* and took the shots ten days before John was murdered. He noted that the couple had been out of the public eye for some time and commented, 'But they were working on their album *Double Fantasy* and they were talking to the press for the first time in years.' He said that talking to John was 'like talking to someone you'd known all your life. While I was photographing John and Yoko, I knew these pictures would be something special.'

The shots were of John and Yoko in the nude and were originally intended for the *Double Fantasy* album cover. The shots disappeared and Tannebaum said that a worker of Yoko's had stolen them from the Dakota Building.

Two magazines then began publishing the shots. *Swank* magazine issued them under the title 'John and Yoko's Secret Porno Pix' and *High Society* published them under the title 'Beatle Sex Mania'.

Tannebaum sued both magazines, claiming $500,000, saying that their use of the photographs had caused his reputation as an internationally recognised photojournalist to be harmed.

The shots were from two separate sessions Tannebaum took

of John and Yoko. He visited the Dakota on November 30, 1980, to show John and Yoko some photos from one of his sessions. Lennon was pleased, telling him, 'You know what I like about these? You really show how beautiful Yoko is'. Five photos from the session were used in the book *Summer of 1980*.

Tarbuck, Jimmy

A noted Liverpool comedian. Tarbuck attended Dovedale Primary School at the same time as John, and remembers how the eight-year-old youth stood out from the rest of the young pupils with his offbeat behaviour and aggressive manner. He also recalls going on a school camping trip with John to the Isle of Man, a trip organised by their teacher Fred Bolt.

In his book *In My Life,* Pete Shotton recalled an anecdote concerning Tarbuck who, he says, was known as the 'terror of Woolton' because of his bullying tactics. He claimed that Tarbuck once challenged John for squinting at him and began to choke him with his school scarf. Shotton intervened to tell Tarbuck that John wasn't deliberately squinting at him – 'When he looks at anything without his glasses, he has to kind of squint to see it better.' When Tarbuck confirmed that this was so, he left John alone.

Jimmy comments, 'I read in a book that I'd been a school bully at Dovecote Primary and hit Lennon. They were never my best friends, but I don't recall that incident. In those days I was just a cheeky schoolkid, a mischievous lad who got into a few problems – but that's life.'

He also made a further comment about John at Dovedale: 'He later became a pacifist, but he did not mind a playground fight.'

When John was at Quarry Bank Jimmy was at Rose Lane School. Eric Griffiths, who played guitar with the Quarry Men, relates that John met Tarbuck in Penny Lane and Jimmy said, 'What are you looking at?' At the time, with John being short-sighted, he stared at people in an effort to recognise them. Paul explained to Jimmy that John was short-sighted and there was no trouble.

Jimmy became a successful comedian locally and, when the Beatles rose to popularity, he was able to appeal to a wider audience, wearing collarless jackets on stage and telling jokes about pop groups at a time when a Liverpool accent was in fashion.

An appearance on *Sunday Night at the London Palladium* launched him into the big time and he moved to London, where he often went on pub crawls with John. On the subject of Beatlemania, he says, 'There were a lot of us who shone in the Beatles' reflection. Everyone who came out of Liverpool then came with a golden spoon.'

Jimmy, who was awarded an OBE (Order of the British Empire) in 1994, lives in Surrey with his wife Pauline, whom he married when he was eighteen. They have three children, Cheryl, Liza and James. Jimmy was often called the 'chubby funster' and has a gap in his teeth, which was caused when he hit his teeth on a bar in the swimming pool at school and refused to have a brace.

Tavener, John

A classical composer, born in 1934, who recorded for Apple. Ringo Starr originally spotted him in 1968 when he performed his composition *The Whale* with the London Sinfonietta. He was then signed to Apple and recorded *The Whale* at the Church of St John the Evangelist in Islington. Following its release in 1970 he produced a second Apple album the following year, *Celtic Requiem*. Ringo was later to rerelease *The Whale* on his Ring O'Records.

Tavener observed the relationship with John and Yoko, recalling, 'I remember Yoko coming into the Indica Gallery one day, wearing a mink coat and saying "I've landed myself a Beatle." That shocked me. I was surprised at her materialism.'

Recalling the couple in Apple days, Tavener says, 'I remember they turned up in a gigantic white Rolls and they'd brought their own macrobiotic food. At that time I was using tapes, doing very experimental things. I think they'd heard about me, and we played tapes to each other all evening. John was a very nice, simple man.'

Tavener was to receive a knighthood.

Ten For Two (concert)

A political rally, also known as the 'Free John Sinclair' rally, which was held at the Chrysler Arena, Ann Arbor, Michigan, on 10 and 11 December 1971.

Sinclair, who had been jailed for ten years for selling two joints to an undercover policewoman, was the focus of a determined movement to free him. Peter Andrews had organised a rally in which there were to be speeches by members of the Chicago Seven – Jerry Rubin, Rennie Davis, Dave Dellinger and Bobby Seale, with music by Phil Ochs. Andrews and the other rally organisers were concerned that they might get a poor turnout at the 15,000-seater arena. Then Jerry Rubin talked John and Yoko into appearing. To make sure that people believed the news that John would be performing in concert in America for the first time since the Beatles' last appearance at Candlestick Park, San Francisco, fifteen years before, John and Yoko made a tape for radio stations to play. Within hours of its broadcast, the arena was completely sold out.

Andrews received a call from Stevie Wonder, who had also heard the tape, offering his services. He decided not to advertise the fact, but to leave Wonder's appearance as a bonus surprise for the audience.

The rally began with the poet Allen Ginsberg embarking on a half-hour chanting marathon, before improvising a poem about Sinclair. He was followed by Sinclair's band, Up, who performed 'Jailhouse Rock'. For their second number they added their own politicised lyrics to Chuck Berry's 'Nadine'.

The rock poet Ed Sanders took the stage next and was followed by Bob Seeger. Bobby Seale then gave a speech and was cheered when he said, 'The greatest form of pollution on the face of this earth is the bullets and bombs falling on the bodies of the Vietnamese.'

The folk singer Phil Ochs took to the stage to sing a song about Nixon, which must also have been noted by the FBI agents who were in the audience primarily to report on John Lennon's movements. Rennie David then discussed Vietnam and was followed by Dave Dellinger. A musical break came next with Archie Shepp playing avant-garde jazz, followed by a country rock performance from Commander Cody.

John Sinclair's mother addressed the audience and was followed by Jerry Rubin. A telephone hook-up from John Sinclair in jail to his wife and daughter was broadcast over the PA system.

Stevie Wonder appeared and after he'd performed 'For Once In My Life', gave a brief speech about Nixon and his Vice President, Spiro Agnew.

The crowd had been waiting for John to appear and at the time specified: 2 a.m., there was no sign. At 3 a.m. David Peel took to the stage to sing 'John Lennon Yoko Ono New York City Are Your People' and a song about Bob Dylan and was booed virtually throughout his performance.

Finally, at 4 a.m., seven hours after the concert had begun, John and Yoko appeared to rousing cheers. John said, 'We came here to show and to say to all of you that apathy isn't it, that we can do something. OK, so flower power didn't work. So what? We start again.' He received another outburst of cheering and then began to play four numbers that were completely new to the audience: 'John Sinclair', Yoko's 'Sisters O Sisters', 'Luck of the Irish' and 'Attica State'. The guitarists Leslie Bacon and David Peel, with Jerry Rubin as percussionist, backed John and Yoko.

John and Yoko had the entire concert filmed on 16mm and the edited version of the film was entitled *Ten For Two,* referring to the ten-year sentence of Sinclair for selling two joints.

Commenting about the rally in the *East Village Other*, Jerry Rubin wrote that it was 'not a rock concert; it was not a teach-in. It was some beautiful new combination of rock and political event, some new form of mass celebration and affirmation.'

Ten For Two (film)

A movie, owned by Yoko Ono, of John's 1971 concert in aid of the political activist John Sinclair. Steve Gebhardt directed it.

The concert took place at the Chrysler Arena in Ann Arbor, Michigan, on 10 and 11 December 1971. John and Yoko financed the filming of the event on 16mm film. They decided to call it *Ten For Two* after a line in John's song 'John Sinclair', which he performed at the concert. (Sinclair had been jailed for ten years for selling two joints to an undercover policewoman: *ten* years for *two* joints.) They saw a rough cut of the film and editing was completed in May 1972. However, owing to the problems John was experiencing in his struggle against deportation, it was initially decided not to release the film. It was actually premiered in December the following year in Ann Arbor but wasn't given a full American release until 1 April 1989.

John and Yoko are seen with acoustic performances of 'Attica State', 'The Luck of the Irish', 'Sisters O Sisters' and 'John

Sinclair'. Also included in the film are appearances by Bobby Searle, Allen Ginsberg, Jerry Rubin and David Dellinger.

Tennessee

A tribute to the American dramatist Tennessee Williams. John wrote it in January 1975 after reading Williams's play, *A Streetcar Named Desire*. John made a home demo of the number on which he played piano. He made a further, much more polished, home demo tape in the summer of the following year, in which he added further references to Williams's plays.

The song was later to undergo some title changes – to 'Memories' and 'Howling at the Moon'. Part of the 'Memories' version was incorporated into 'Watching the Wheels' on the *Double Fantasy* album.

Incidentally, John used to sing lead vocals on a number called 'Tennessee', penned by Carl Perkins, when he led the Quarry Men.

Testimony

An interview CD released in Britain by Magnum Force in November 1990. Issued on the tenth anniversary of John's death, it contains 75 minutes of an interview conducted with John at the New York offices of Geffen Records on the morning of 8 December 1980. The interviewer was the disc jockey Bob Miles and the original interview lasted for an hour and a half.

John discussed many topics, including the album *Double Fantasy* and his first meeting with Yoko. He also discussed his first meeting with Paul, his thoughts about his first son, Julian, his plans for the future and the five years he spent looking after his second son, Sean. Ironically, on the eve of his death he was to say, 'My work won't be finished until I'm dead and buried – and I hope that's a long, long time off. The 80s is like we've got a new chance.' He also said, 'You have to give thanks to God, or whatever is up there, for the fact that we all survived the tremendous upheaval of the whole world. The map's changed, and we're all going into an unknown future, but we're still all here. While there's life there's hope.'

Commenting on his meeting with Paul, he said, 'Paul met me on the first day I did "Be-Bop-A-Lula" live on stage. A mutual friend brought him to see my group, called the Quarry Men, and we met and talked after the show. I saw he had talent – he was playing guitar backstage, doing "Twenty Flight Rock" by Eddie Cochran. I turned round to him right then and said "Do you want to join the group?" George came through Paul, Ringo came through George, although I had a say in where they came from, but the person I actually picked as my partner, who I recognised had talent and I could get on with, was Paul. Twelve or however many years later, I met Yoko and I had the same feeling, but in a different field, so as a talent scout I think I've done pretty damned well!'

Thank You Girl

Song recorded on 5 and 13 March 1963. It was issued in Britain as the flip side of 'From Me to You' on 11 April 1963 and John was to comment, ' "Thank You Girl" was one of our efforts at writing a single that didn't work. So it became a B-side.'

It was released as a single in America by Vee Jay no fewer than three times. It failed to chart when it was originally issued as the B-side of 'From Me To You' on 27 May 1963 and was then issued as the flip side of 'Do You Want to Know a Secret?' on 23 March 1964 and enjoyed modest success, reaching No. 35 in the charts. It was issued again on 10 August 1964, without success. The song was co-written by John and Paul and John referred to it as 'just a silly song we knocked off'. A version was included on the *Past Masters* CDs.

That'll Be the Day

The famous Buddy Holly hit, which Holly wrote after hearing John Wayne repeatedly utter the phrase 'That'll be the day' in the film *The Searchers*.

It was the first song that John could play to his own satisfaction and his mother Julia originally taught him the chords.

John was to recall the time in an interview, 'My mother taught it to me on the banjo, sitting there with endless patience until I managed to work out all the chords. She was a perfectionist. She made me go through it over and over again until I had it right. I remember her slowing down the record so that I could scribble out the words. First hearing Buddy absolutely knocked me for a loop. And to think it was my own mother who was turning me on to it all.'

When the Quarry Men made a home recording in the summer of 1958, the two numbers they cut were 'That'll Be the Day' and 'In Spite of All the Danger'. John sang lead vocals on 'That'll Be the Day'.

He also recorded it many years later during the October 1974 sessions of rock 'n' roll numbers, but the track wasn't used.

That's My Life (My Love and My Home)

Title of a single by Freddie Lennon, father of John, issued by Pye Records on their Piccadilly label in Britain on 31 December 1965 with 'The Next Time You Feel Important' on the flip, a former hit for Vera Lynn.

When Freddie Lennon was discovered working in a hotel, Tony Cartwright, a Liverpool agent based in London, who also worked as Tom Jones's road manager, approached him with the suggestion that he become his manager. The two of them collaborated on an autobiographical song 'That's My Life (My Love And My Home)'.

Present at the recording session was Tom Jones's manager Gordon Mills, the music publisher Don Agnes and the musical director Alan Tew. Freddie was backed by a Midlands group called the Loving Kind (Noel Redding, later to become bassist with the Jimi Hendrix Experience, was a member). They were supplemented by a dozen or so session men, with vocal backing provided by the Ladybirds, a female vocal trio who were formerly members of the Vernons Girls.

Freddie was invited to Amsterdam to sing the number on a live Dutch television show, which proved to be a success for him. The single, which entered the radio charts, had completely sold out of most stores on its first day and seemed poised to hit the charts. Then the record appeared to vanish. Freddie and Cartwright approached Pye Records to find out what happened, but their enquiries went unanswered until a sympathetic secretary told them that Brian Epstein had had the record blocked. At 11 p.m. one evening in February 1966, Freddie and Tony turned up at John's house to find out what had happened, but John refused to let them enter.

John had actually conspired with Epstein to have the record blocked, although he had bought a copy himself and played it constantly at home and was amused by it. Julian also loved the record and kept asking his mother to 'put on Granddad's song'.

Tony and Freddie then went to Pye Records to see the secretary again as they intended to sue – but discovered she had been promoted and sent to America. Tom Jones, on his return from the States, said that he'd been told during a visit to Los Angeles that Freddie's record had been withdrawn without an explanation.

It was the one and only record that Freddie Lennon made.

There's a Place

An introspective song by John from the group's early career that disproves the popular theory that he began composing introspective numbers only after discovering Bob Dylan. The song was included on their *Please Please Me* album recorded on 11 February 1963. It was the first song taped during their mammoth recording session. Originally, 'Tip of My Tongue' was the number scheduled for that spot, but George Martin did not think the arrangement was strong enough. It was issued by Tollie in America as the flip side of 'Twist and Shout' and reached No. 2 in the charts following its release on 2 March 1964, although it never reached the Top 40 when it was reissued by Vee Jay on 10 August 1964. John was to comment, ' "There's a Place" was my attempt at a sort of Motown, black thing.'

They Died Too Young: John Lennon

A miniature sized book by Tim Stockdale, published by Paragon. The 73-page book contained sixteen colour pictures. It was one of a series of books about celebrities who had died prematurely, and others in the series included works on Jimi Hendrix, Elvis Presley, Jim Morrison and Marc Bolan.

Thisbe

A character in Shakespeare's *A Midsummer Night's Dream*.

When the Beatles starred in the Jack Good TV production *Around the Beatles,* they performed a short excerpt from the play in which John took the part of Thisbe. Paul portrayed Pyramus, Ringo was Lion and George appeared as Moonshine.

The special was first screened in Britain on 6 May 1964.

This Boy

A number composed by John that was recorded on 17 October 1963. It was issued as the flip side of 'I Want To Hold Your Hand' in the UK and as a track on Capitol's *Meet the Beatles* album in the US. The number was also included in their concert repertoire during 1963 and 1964, was performed at their 13 October 1963 London Palladium show and also on their *Ed Sullivan Show* debut on 9 February 1964. John was to comment that it was 'just my attempt at writing one of those three-part harmony/Smokey Robinson songs. Nothing in the lyrics; just a sound and harmony.' George Harrison was also to observe, 'If you listen to the middle-eight of "This Boy", it was John trying to do Smokey.'

John was also to say, 'There was a period when I thought I didn't write melodies, that Paul wrote those and I just wrote straight, shouting rock 'n' roll. But of course, when I think of some of my own songs – "In My Life", or some of the early stuff, "This Boy" – I was writing melody with the best of them.'

In fact, when William Mann, the music critic of *The Times* in London, reviewed the number, he wrote that the song contained 'chains of pandiatonic clusters'.

George Martin composed an instrumental version of the number for *A Hard Day's Night,* which was recorded under the title 'Ringo's Theme'.

A version of the number was also included on the *Past Masters* CDs.

This Is Not Here

A big-scale exhibition of Yoko Ono's works, presented by the Everson Museum of Art in Syracuse, New York. The museum had spent $100,000 on the exhibition, bolstered by an additional $70,000 donated by John.

The exhibition was timed to open on John's 31st birthday, Saturday 9 October 1971 and lasted until 27 October. The event was taped and later screened as *John and Yoko in Syracuse, New York* on American television on 11 May 1972.

John was also represented in the exhibition, along with a smattering of New York artists, pop celebrities and journalists. Bob Dylan sent a copy of his album *Nashville Skyline* in a fish tank; George Harrison sent a milk bottle; and Ringo Starr entered a green plastic rubbish bag filled with water and the tag, 'This sponge was caught off the Libyan coast, taken to Kalymos Island and prepared. It is filled with British water. When it dries it will be a sponge caught off the Libyan coast, taken to Kalymos Island and prepared and filled with water from another land.' John included a piece called Napoleon's Bladder, which was a pink mass inside a clear plastic bag.

On the ground floor there were various Yoko items, including *Portrait of John Lennon As a Young Cloud,* and *Lennon Tour* tickets. On the museum's second level, reached by ascending a spiral staircase, there were a number of Yoko's past works such as her *Eternal Clock* and all-white chess set. Another exhibit was called *Iced Tea.* It was a gigantic block of ice in the shape of the letter T, which was allowed to melt.

Over 8,000 fans turned up on the first day, almost causing a riot and breaking a number of the exhibits.

The guests at the opening included Ringo Starr and his wife Maureen, Phil Spector, Allen Klein, Andy Warhol, Bob Dylan, Dick Cavett, John Cage, Dennis Hopper, Spike Milligan, Jack Nicholson and Frank Zappa.

John presented the guests with a silver zodiac necklace.

John and Yoko also produced a seven-minute film of the exhibition and called it *The Museum of Modern Art Show.*

John's birthday was celebrated later that evening in a local hotel. Eric Clapton, Allen Ginsberg, Klaus Voormann, Jim Keltner, Mal Evans and Neil Aspinall were among the guests.

365 Days of Sean

John and Yoko took special pains to document their lives together and amassed a great collection of tapes, film and photographs.

In the summer of 1976 John announced that he would be publishing a book called *365 Days of Sean.* He had been so thoroughly engrossed in every aspect of the baby Sean's life – and had begun taking snaps of his son every day, almost from the moment of birth – that both he and Yoko discussed the publication of the book. It was to comprise a selection of photographs of Sean taken each day during the first twelve months of his life.

Although there had been an announcement, the book was never published.

Incidentally, the couple was intrigued by the fact that there were 365 days in the year – and that was the exact number of bare bottoms presented by Yoko in her *Bottoms* film. It was also the precise number of helium-filled balloons released by John for his *You Are Here* exhibition.

Three Stigmata of Palmer Eldritch, The

A controversial science-fiction novel written in 1964 by the brilliant sci-fi author Philip K Dick, who died in 1982.

Members of an overcrowded Earth are forcibly transported as settlers to planets with hostile environments. Living within protective domes, they take drugs such as Can-D and Chew-Z, which transport them to exotic dream worlds.

John Lennon was so impressed with the book that he intended to buy the film rights and make a movie of it.

John never got around to it, but Dick became a posthumous 'cult' figure and his complex novels were filmed for the first time in the 80s – and included *Blade Runner* and *Total Recall*.

Ticket To Ride

The Beatles' first single release of 1965. John once described it as the forerunner of heavy metal and was to comment, 'It was pretty fucking heavy for then, if you go and look what other people were making.' It was recorded on 18 February 1965 and also included on the soundtrack album *Help!*

In an interview in 1965, he was to comment, 'Now Ticket to Ride was three-quarters mine and Paul changed it a bit. He said let's alter the tune. It is not as commercial as most of our singles because it wasn't written as a single. It was intended to be in the film [*Help!*]. It was the first time a single was released that wasn't brought into the studio for that purpose.'

Tight A$

A rockabilly-style tune, which John featured on his *Mind Games* album. Sneaky Pete Kleinow, a former member of the Flying Burrito Brothers, played the steel guitar.

Tittenhurst Park

A Georgian mansion in an estate of 70 hilly acres of heath and groves in Sunningdale, Berkshire, which John bought for

£150,000. It had seven main bedrooms, three reception rooms, large kitchen regions and extensive staff quarters in addition to several guest cottages.

The 300-year-old house's grounds also contained oriental trees, which the local council protected, plus a farm and a lodge at the entrance gates. John bought the house in 1969 and moved in during August. On Yoko Ono's suggestion, he created an artificial lake with rubber lining to prevent the water from running away. There was a notice on the front door stating 'THIS IS NOT HERE' and another notice further down on the door 'PLEASE GO ROUND TO THE SIDE'.

After the Lennons moved permanently to America, Ringo Starr bought the mansion on 9 September 1973 (John's magical number nine again) within two weeks of John's having put it on the market. Ringo, Maureen and their three children moved into the mansion almost immediately. Additions to the building had been a swimming pool, sauna and snooker room. The eight track-recording studio (formerly a private chapel) where John had recorded the *Imagine* album was renamed Startling Studio and Ringo made it available for public hire.

Ringo sold the property in 1979 to Sheikh Zayed bin Sultan al-Nahyan, ruler of Abu Dhabi, for $9 million. The sheikh then spent $72 million renovating it. Every room in the house was gutted and rebuilt and there was a new steel-domed swimming pool connected by a tunnel. The centrepiece of one room was a $100,000 chandelier. Next to the mansion he built a three-storey mosque.

Wall paintings, which had been done by John, were removed, as 'they didn't fit in'.

Today (radio)

A BBC radio programme on the Home Service (now Radio 4), which aired an interview with John to tie in with the release of his second book, *A Spaniard in the Works*.

John recorded the interview for the programme with Tim Matthews on Wednesday 16 June 1965, which was then broadcast twice on Monday 21 June – initially at 7.15 and again at 8.15. This was in the days when items were often repeated an hour later. In addition to the interview, John also read two verses from his *A Spaniard in the Works* story 'The National Health Cow'.

At the time *Today* was broadcast, the Beatles were appearing on their short European tour.

Today (TV)

A Thames Television chat show. On Tuesday 1 April 1969, John and Yoko were guests on the programme, which was hosted by Eamonn Andrews from Studio Four in Television House, Kingsway, London. The show was live and broadcast from 6.04 to 6.30 p.m.

The couple discussed the ventures they were currently involved in such as acorns for peace and bagism and even encouraged Andrews to crawl into a large white bag with them.

The other guests, Yehudi Menuhin, Jack Benny and Rolf Harris, were visibly uncomfortable with the Lennons' behaviour and the audience was not very supportive, indicating that the British public at the time were not quite sympathetic to the John–Yoko relationship and their current exploits.

To Know Her is To Love Her

A Phil Spector composition, originally known as *To Know Him is To Love Him,* which was a major hit in 1958 for Spector's group the Teddy Bears. The Beatles frequently covered the number and John recorded it in Los Angeles during his *Rock 'n' Roll* album sessions with Spector. The track was eventually released in 1986 on the *Menlove Avenue* compilation.

John originally sang the number during the Decca recording auditions on 1 January 1962 and also performed it during the Beatles' Star Club appearance in December 1962 when Adrian Barber recorded the band, and the track is to be found on various compilations of the Star Club tapes.

During the October and November recording sessions in Los Angeles in 1973, Spector arranged a version of the number for John to record called 'To Know Her is To Love Her'.

Tomorrow Never Knows

A number John described as his first psychedelic song. This was during the period after he'd experienced LSD and was interested in Eastern mysticism and, in particular, the *Egyptian Book of the Dead*. George Martin was to comment, 'John wanted his voice to sound like a Dalai Lama on the top of a hill. He wanted it very sort of atmospheric. We laid down the track with Ringo on drums and a tamboura drone, and I put John's voice through a Leslie speaker to make a weird noise. For the background we've got all these tape loops and I got tape machines from all over the building at EMI; in fact, we used sixteen.' It was the last track on the *Revolver* album.

John had originally called the song 'The Void'. Discussing it, he said, 'With "Tomorrow Never Knows" I had imagined in my head that in the background you would have thousands of monks chanting. It was impractical of course and we did something different. I should have tried to get nearer to my original idea because that was what I really wanted.'

The first title was dropped and it was Ringo who suggested the phrase 'Tomorrow Never Knows'. John sings solo vocal on the track and was involved in ideas of experimental recording at the time. He used tape machines playing at different speeds, tape loops and backward-running tapes to produce an unusual and slightly psychedelic sound.

'Tomorrow Never Knows' was recorded on 6, 7 and 22 April 1966. It was the first track to be recorded for the *Revolver* album. Take 1 of the studio session was eventually issued on the Anthology 2 CDs.

Tomorrow Show, The

An American television show hosted by Tom Snyder. John taped the show on Tuesday 8 April 1975 and it was transmitted on Monday 28 April. The entire fifty-minute show was devoted to John and the main topic of discussion was his immigration wrangle with the US authorities.

Snyder discussed the initial impact of the Beatles in America in 1964, recalling when he saw them in Philadelphia the following year, 'So much screaming and carrying on.' He asked John, 'Did this bother you at all while you were doing these concerts, that people couldn't hear your music and that all they could hear was themselves screaming?'

John said, 'It got a little boring. It was great when it first happened: when you first come on, all you got was "wah!"; but then it became lip-synching, miming, sometimes things would break down and no one would know … It wasn't doing the music any good.'

Snyder said, 'As I recall there were fan clubs or clubs of followers for each of the individuals in the organisations –'

John interrupted, 'Well, it was mainly a "Beatle Club", but they fanned it out a little just to keep a –'

Snyder interrupted him, 'Now, I'm just wondering just how unified any group can be when the audience have certain favourites. Maybe they like Paul more than they like John …'

John laughed. 'That's true,' he said.

Snyder continued, 'I just wondered if it's awfully difficult to be friends. And do you really care about whether or not you're friends when you are a group such as the Beatles, or whether you are the Rolling stones or whatever?'

John replied, 'We didn't break up because we weren't friends. We just broke up out of sheer boredom, you know, and boredom creates tension.'

Snyder said, 'How can you get bored doing what you did?'

John replied, 'Because it wasn't going anywhere, you know. We'd stopped touring and we'd just sort of say, "Time to make an album". You know, go into the studio, the same four of us, looking at each other and be playing the same licks –'

Snyder interrupted, 'In those silly haircuts.'

John said, 'Those silly haircuts that you have now. [Points to Snyder's hair.] If you notice, he's got his now.'

Snyder then went on to ask John about the Bed-Ins.

John said, 'What we virtually had was a seven-day press conference in bed. The first day they fought at the door to get in, thinking there was something sexy going on.'

Snyder said, 'Like sensuous?'

John said, 'That was the word I was looking for, and they found two people talking about peace. Reporters always have about five minutes with you, ten minutes with you. We'd let them ask anything for as long as they wanted for seven days, and all the time we just kept on plugging peace.'

Snyder then asked about the problems celebrities have regarding their privacy.

John said, 'I can walk down the street and somebody'd say, "Hi, John" or "How's your immigration?" They don't hassle me. I might sign one autograph – I don't get hassled. I actually went through that period when I couldn't go anywhere. We go and eat, we go to the movies, and we go wherever we want but if we decide to go and eat, it's cool. We're probably less recognisable than you.'

Snyder then began to ask John about the situation with drugs in the music business.

John told him, 'There's as much dope in the music business as there is in virtually every other business now. Dope is so out in the open that you can go anywhere and it's there. There's no underground movement of people taking dope. The most extraordinary straight people are taking dope, including cocaine, anywhere and at any time. If you want it, you can have it.'

John then mentioned his drugs bust in London, which led to his problems with the immigration people, and said he'd brought his attorney, Leon Wildes, whom he then introduced.

Wildes explained the background and history of the attempts to deport John: 'We understand that a series of memoranda led from the Attorney General all the way down to the district director for New York, and that the action he took was not as a result of John's immigration status, but rather with the intention of preventing John from exercising constitutionally protected rights.'

John explained why he wanted to live in America and replied to Snyder's query about why he put up with such hassle, 'Because I'd like to live in the land of the free, Tom. And if it was up to John Doe on the street, he either doesn't care about it, or would be glad to have an old Beatle living here. I like to be here, because this is where the music came from, which is my whole life and got me where I am today. I love the place. I'd like to be here.'

John also discussed various music topics, including rock music history, black music, rock musicians and drugs and the dissolution of the Beatles.

NBC repeated the show on 9 December 1980. For the rebroadcast special guests included the journalist Lisa Robinson and Jack Douglas, producer of *Double Fantasy*. Starbox Home Video released the programme on video in 1983.

Tonight

A BBC TV current affairs and arts programme on which John first appeared on 23 March 1964, the day of publication of his first book *In His Own Write*.

Tonight was broadcast live from Lime Grove Studios in London from 7 to 7.35 p.m. The show's presenter Cliff Michelmore read extracts from the book, as did the *Tonight* regulars Derek Hart and Kenneth Allsop.

Allsop also conducted a four-minute interview with John and asked him why he didn't put some of his wordplay, as contained in *In His Own Write*, into some of his songs.

On 18 June 1965 John appeared on the final broadcast of the series, the 1,825th show. He was promoting his latest book *A Spaniard in the Works* and read excerpts from 'Wumberlog (Or The Magic Dog)' and 'We Must Not Forget the General Erection'. He discussed the writing of his books, his approach to writing poetry and what it was like being a Beatle.

Too Many Cooks

In May 1974, while in Los Angeles, John produced a track with Mick Jagger singing the soul and R&B number 'Too Many Cooks'. The event occurred at the Record Plant West one Sunday morning with John supervising the session and Jagger singing. The musicians backing him were Harry Nilsson, Billy Preston, Bobby Keys, Jack Bruce, Geoff Lawrence and Jim Keltner.

When asked about the number for the BBC radio series *In My Life*, Jagger said, 'I don't even know what happened to the tape.'

The tape had actually become part of John Lennon's archives, but had never been released for contractual reasons, although the recording was played in its entirety on *The Lost Lennon Tapes* radio series.

Topes, Spiggy

The satirical magazine *Private Eye*, launched in London in the early 60s during the 'satire boom', often referred to celebrities by comic pseudonyms when they sniped at them within their pages.

In the latter part of the 60s, once John and Yoko became lovers and partners, *Private Eye* often ridiculed them. Initially *Private Eye* began lampooning Yoko, calling her Yoko Hana, beginning in August 1968 with an item which started, 'We've started to make lots of films together. There's this one of him sitting in a chair picking his nose. Every so often he gives a little gurk'. In the stories that were obviously sniping at John, they referred to him as Spiggy Topes and to Yoko as Okay Yoni.

An example is the story they ran when John was supporting the defendants in the *Oz* trial. *Private Eye* wrote,

> Len Trott, member of the Acting Editorial Board of *Wozz*: 'I would like to say a word about Comrade Topes, who is supplying the bread to pay for the legal expenses incurred at the trial. A lot of people have put Spiggy down in the past at being nothing but a half-witted pop singer with too much money, which frankly may be true, in part, but since yesterday, when his cheque came in, you have to hand it to him, to my mind, that he is prepared to stand up and be counted on behalf of international socialism.'

John was very amused by the story.

Toronto Rock & Roll Revival Show

An open-air concert held at the Variety Stadium of the University of Toronto in Ontario, Canada, on Saturday 13 September 1969. A local company called Brower Walker promoted the event.

One of the two promoters was 23-year-old John Brower, a local man who had travelled to California to become a rock musician, but who'd recently returned to Canada with his wife and child. He was broke at the time and borrowed money to promote the concert. He became concerned when only 800 tickets were sold.

With Little Richard, Fats Domino, Gene Vincent, Chuck Berry, Bo Diddley, Jerry Lee Lewis (he pulled out at the last minute), the Doors, Chicago and Alice Cooper set to appear, the inadequate ticket sales meant that the promoters would be in serious financial straits. It was suggested that Brower call John in England and invite him to compere the show. Brower managed to contact John and discuss the event with him and was surprised when John turned down the job, but said, 'The only way we could come is if we could play.'

John had only a few days to set it all up and contacted his friend Klaus Voormann, the former Manfred Mann bass player, and Alan White, the former drummer with Alan Price. They both agreed immediately. With John playing rhythm guitar, he wanted Eric Clapton to join them on lead guitar, but couldn't get hold of him.

Terry Doran, George Harrison's personal assistant, tried to get hold of Clapton at his home several times, to no avail. Everyone believed the guitarist was out clubbing it somewhere.

The plane was due to take off at 10 a.m. and, by 9.30 p.m., most of the party had gathered at the airport and checked in. John and Yoko then phoned Mal Evans to say it was all off because they hadn't reached Eric. Then Terry informed them that he'd managed to contact Eric, who had agreed to join them on the trip. Doran had sent a telegram to Clapton's house and his gardener woke him up. It seemed that he'd been at home all the time. He'd gone to bed at 11 p.m. the previous evening and hadn't heard the telephone.

Eric couldn't make it for the 10 a.m. plane, so they rebooked for 3.15 p.m., which was fortunate for Doran, who discovered he'd left his passport at home.

Booked for the flight were John, Yoko, Eric, Alan, Klaus, John and Yoko's assistant Anthony Fawcett, Doran and Dan and Jill Richter, who had been filming John and Yoko's activities and were asked to make a permanent record of the Toronto concert.

They had asked for first-class seats on the flight, but only three were available, so John, Yoko and Eric sat up front. As none of the musicians had played together before they walked down to the back of the Boeing 707 and began to rehearse at the rear of the plane, using amplified guitars. The five of them worked out all of the songs and ran through them, finally settling on eight numbers.

On arrival they had an initial difficulty getting through customs because Yoko hadn't been vaccinated.

The stadium was a complete sell-out with its 27,000 capacity. When Brower had received confirmation from John he'd phoned the radio stations to inform them of the Plastic Ono Band appearance, but the stations hadn't believed him. He then contacted Apple again and taped Anthony Fawcett reciting a list of the people who were coming. The stations then made the announcements and there was a rush for tickets.

The stage where the artists were to appear was a twelve-foot (3.5-metre) dais in the middle of the pitch, facing the arena where the audience were. When John and his fellow musicians settled backstage they plugged into one small amp and began running through the numbers.

Allan Klein had also flown over to organise a special filming of the event, in addition to the Richters' video tape.

John hadn't appeared on stage for three years, apart from his Cambridge appearance backing Yoko, and he was particularly nervous. He said, 'I just threw up for hours until I went on.'

At midnight, the compere, Kim Fowley, went on stage to announce the Plastic Ono Band. He arranged for all the lights to be turned down and asked everyone to strike a match. John, Yoko, Eric, Alan and Klaus came on stage for their forty-minute set and John announced, 'We're just going to do numbers we know, as we've never played together before.'

They began with 'Blue Suede Shoes', 'Money', 'Dizzy Miss Lizzie' and 'Yer Blues'. Then John said, 'Never done this number before – best of luck,' and the band performed 'Cold Turkey', which had never been played in public before. Then, before the last number 'Give Peace a Chance', he said, 'This is what we came for really, so sing along.' And the audience sang along with 'Give Peace a Chance'. Then John said, 'Now Yoko is going to do her thing all over you.'

During John's performance she had been on stage inside a white bag, howling. She then sang 'Don't Worry Kyoko' and 'Oh John (Let's Hope For Peace)'. The last number was thirteen minutes long. As it ended the guitarists all placed their guitars against the speakers of their amps and walked to the back of the stage, leaving their guitars to produce a feedback effect. Mal Evans then switched off the amps. Evans was to comment that Gene Vincent had stood next to him during the Plastic Ono set with tears in his eyes and said, 'It's marvellous; it's fantastic, man.'

There was a ten-minute press conference during which he described their performance as '1980s music' and then the party crammed into four cars for a two-hour drive to the estate of a Canadian millionaire, Mr Eaton.

John was to comment, 'I can't remember when I had such a good time. We did all the old things from the Cavern days in Liverpool. Yoko, who you could say was playing bag, was holding a piece of paper with the words to the song in front of me. But she suddenly disappeared into her bag in the middle of the performance and I had to make them up because it's so long since I sang them that I've forgotten most of them. It didn't seem to matter.'

The performance had been taped and John was delighted with the result, commenting 'I don't care who I have to play with, but I'm going back to playing on stage.'

Two months later the album of the event, *Live Peace in Toronto*, was issued. There were problems, however, with the official film of the event. DA Pennebaker's *Sweet Toronto*, John refused permission for the use of the Plastic Ono Band performance. As a result it was issued under the name *Keep On Rockin'*, although the sequence with John's performance was eventually issued on home video in 1989.

Toy Boy

Second longest of all John Lennon's published poems, comprising eight stanzas and 80 lines. It was published on page 68 of the December 1985 issue of the American magazine *McCalls* and, surprisingly, was not even trailered on the cover. The poem was illustrated with a specially commissioned colour photograph by Robert Freeman, taken at John's house in Weybridge, in which he is sitting against a wall with his arm around a giant toy panda.

The poem begins from the point of view of a group of toys in a young boy's bedroom. They gather together to discuss whether the boy is actually alive.

Ralph the Elephant is in charge of the debate in which a rocking horse and Sydney the Shoe testify in the boy's favour. Ralph doesn't accept their observations and demands a vote. The other toys refuse, saying that there will be adequate proof in the morning because, if the boy is alive, that's when he'll wake up.

The clock alarm rings at 8 a.m. and the toys all freeze. We now see things from the boy's point of view and he begins to wonder whether the toys are alive. He comes to the conclusion that they are and tells his parents.

They take him to a psychiatrist who, pronounces that the boy is insane.

The poem ends with the words, 'There you are.'

'Toy Boy' was originally written for a proposed third book of poetry and prose, which the publisher Jonathan Cape had contracted John to write as a follow-up to *In His Own Write* and *A Spaniard in the Works*. The piece was the only item completed for the project at the time of the deadline, which was set for the summer of 1964, so plans for the book were abandoned.

Toy Boy, The

A bootleg album issued by Bag Records 5069. Tracks on Side One were: 'As Time Goes By', 'I Saw Her Standing There', 'Whatever Gets You Thru the Night', 'Move Over Ms L', 'Angel Baby', 'I Found Out', 'Happy Xmas (War is Over)', 'Nutopian International Anthem' (long version), 'Give Peace a Chance'; Side Two: 'I'm The Greatest', 'Be My Baby', 'Yer Blues', 'Do the Oz', 'What a Shame Mary Jane Had a Pain at the Party', 'As Time Goes By 2', 'Startin' Over (Postscript)' and 'Good Night'.

There were two packages issued of this album: one featured gold lettering on a white cover and contained a booklet; the other featured a colour photograph on a blue background.

Tributes

John's death stuck a chord with people throughout the entire world and many people considered it as traumatic as the news of the assassination of President John F Kennedy.

Among the thousands of people who publicly voiced their tributes were:

- Paul McCartney: 'John was a great man. His death is a cruel and bitter blow. I really loved the guy. He was one of the best. He will be sadly missed by the whole world. John will be remembered for his contribution to art, music and world peace. I can't tell you how much it hurts to lose him.'
- George Harrison: 'After all we went through together I had and still have great love and respect for him. I am shocked and stunned. It is such a waste of life. I can't believe it's happened.'
- Ringo Starr: 'Even though he was always treated in the press as a cynical put-down artist, John had the biggest heart of all of us. He was so up, so happy lately – he blew me away, he was so happy.'

- President Jimmy Carter: 'I know that I speak for millions of Americans when I say that I am saddened by his death, and distressed by the senseless manner of it. It is especially poignant that John Lennon has died by violence, though he had long campaigned for peace.'
- Cynthia Lennon: 'I would like to say how terribly upset we are at the sudden and tragic death of John Lennon. I have always had the deepest affection for John since the divorce and have always encouraged his relationship with Julian, which I thought was for the best. He was looking to his father for guidance. Julian was hoping to see his father after Christmas. We don't know what will happen now.'
- George Martin: 'He was a true original. His zany sense of humour could elevate the meanest of spirits. He will be sadly missed.'
- Dick James, the Beatles' publisher: 'There'll never be another songwriter like John Lennon. He and Paul McCartney were the greatest team of the century.'
- Andy Peebles, broadcaster: 'I am absolutely shattered. The Beatles were more to me than anything else in the world.'
- Arthur Ballard, John's art college tutor: 'I think his death is more significant that that of a leading politician. Like Michelangelo has never been forgotten, neither will John Lennon.'
- Jeff Lynne: 'Lennon was the greatest influence on my life and probably on anyone else's as well. He was my idol. He was the one person I always wanted to meet. What can you say? It's terrible. Absolutely terrible.'
- Mick Jagger: 'This is an awful moment for his family and millions of fans and friends. I knew him for eighteen years, but I don't want to make a casual remark now.'
- Cilla Black: 'I don't believe it. I thought it was some sort of sick joke. Now I'm shattered. I owe everything to John. He committed himself one hundred per cent to the music business.'
- Billy J Kramer: 'I am completely shattered. I owe everything to John Lennon. It was John who brought Brian Epstein to a club in Liverpool to see me and the band.'
- Gerry Marsden: 'John had an unbelievable talent and a fantastic, if at times eccentric, sense of humour.'

- The former British Prime Minister Harold Wilson: 'It was a great shock to my wife and myself when we heard he was dead. In an area where there was great social deprivation and juvenile unemployment, the Beatles did more to keep kids off the streets than all the forces of law and order put together. He gave the kids something to think about.'
- Sammy Davis Jr: 'His loss is a real tragedy to the millions who loved him and his compositions.'
- Elton John: 'I'm so shocked I don't want to say anything at all.'
- Cliff Richard: 'There are only a few people who could really be called rock-and-roll greats. John Lennon was one of them. We shall miss him for a long time.'
- Pete Townshend of the Who: 'I'm too upset to talk about it. I can't find words to express how I feel.'
- The composer/conductor Leonard Bernstein, a Dakota Building neighbour: 'We're all in a state of shock. His music will live as long as the music of Bach, Beethoven, or Brahms has lived.'
- The American comedian Milton Berle: 'I thought his musical compositions were giantlike in nature.'
- New York Governor Hugh L Carey sent a telegram to Yoko: 'John Lennon was a man who stood for peace and non-violence and love and kindness. Your husband has been struck down under conditions that are tragic and are, frankly, sorrowful in our society.'
- Bruce Springsteen, who told the audience before a concert appearance: 'It is a hard night to come out and play when so much has been lost. The first song I ever learned was a record called "Twist and Shout" and if it wasn't for John Lennon, we'd all be in a different place tonight.'

Tribute to John Lennon, 1940–1980, A

A small, hard-bound volume, published on both sides of the Atlantic by Proetus Books in 1981. Edited by Lyn Belanger, Michael Brecher, Jo Kearns, Nicolas Locke and Mike Shatkin, it contains a collection of almost forty tributes selected from newspaper and magazines – most of them America, a few British, which include 'This Is All About the John Lennon I Lost', by Denny Boys; '"Yesterday"' Mourning Before Sunrise', by

Richard Roberts; 'How John Was Overwhelmed by Life and Death', by Phil Sutcliffe; 'They Loved Him, Yeah, Yeah, Yeah', by Leon Taylor; 'Lennon Remembered for More than Music', by Russ Christian; 'Within His Music', by Richard Dyer; 'The Lighter Side of John', by Don Short; 'Lennon: Always Up Front', by Tony Kornheiser and Tom Zito; 'Intellectual John: Social Revolutionary', by Clive Barnes; 'Everyone Should Speak Lennon's Language', by Rabbi Marcus Kramer; 'John Lennon: No Secret Interior, Just Integrity', by Robert Hilburn; 'A Lot of People Were Crying', by Al Carter; 'The Surreal Genius of Rock', by Ray Connolly; 'John Lennon's Music Will Never Die', by John Murray; and 'The Promise is Gone', by Ellen Goodman.

The majority of items are written in a highly emotive style, indicating the impact Lennon had on the lives of so many people of his generation. At times, the style begins to overwhelm, so it is not advisable to read the book at one sitting.

A number of valid points are made, including the fact that, as was the case with the death of JF Kennedy, most people remember where and what they were doing when they first heard the news of John's killing. Most writers also agreed that, because of his death, he will never grow old in people's minds.

There are sixteen full-page photographs and a jacket illustration by JP Tibbles, printed on quality tinted paper.

All royalties from the book were distributed equally between the Spirit Foundation and the Handgun Control Inc group.

Tribute recordings

Following John's death there were a number of recordings made by a wide range of artists, fans and superstars alike. Over the years tribute discs continued to be released, together with dedication songs and cover versions that have been specially dedicated to John.

Some of the tribute records are:

- 'All Those Years Ago', George Harrison's own tribute to John. A unique record, it also features Paul McCartney and Ringo Starr. The three ex-Beatles teamed up to record the track, which is also included on George's *Somewhere in England* album. It was the only tribute record to hit the Top Ten and reached No. 2 in the American charts. It was issued on Dark Horse DRC 49725 on 11 May 1981. In Britain it was released on Dark Horse 3K 17807 and reached No. 13 in the charts.

- 'Scandinavian Skies', a tribute song to John by Billy Joel, included on his *The Nylon Curtain* album, issued on 20 September 1982.
- 'A Love That Lasts Forever (A Tribute To John Lennon)', a 1982 tribute from Brant Mewborn, one of the editors of *Rolling Stone* magazine, who sings and composed the music to the single. There is also the credit, 'Lyrics compiled by Brant Mewborn from songs by John Lennon and Lennon-McCartney', as the songs consist of 21 lines from various numbers by John.
- 'Dear John' by the Italian band Cavern was issued in Autostop AUT CD 50194 with 'Fast' on the flip, in 1994.
- 'The Dream Is Over' was written and sung by David Faircloth and produced by Robby Robertson. The single was issued in the States on Nugget Records, NST 8005.
- 'Elegy For the Walrus' by Sid Bradley was a limited-edition acetate sent to American radio stations.
- 'Empty Garden (Hey Hey Johnny)' was Elton John's own tribute to his friend, and featured on his *Jump Up* album, issued in 1982 on Rocket Records, HISPD 127. The song was composed by Elton and Bernie Taupin. It was later issued as a single on Rocket XPRES 77. The single reached No. 51 in the British charts. When Elton performed the number at Madison Square Garden in August 1982 Yoko and Sean joined him on stage.
- 'For a Rocker', by Jackson Browne, with 'Lawyers in Love' on the flip side was released on Asylum 96-0268-1 in 1983.
- 'Not Now John' was a tribute by Pink Floyd, although it wasn't issued until 21 March 1983.
- 'Moonlight Shadow', a tribute by Mike Oldfield, was issued on 6 May 1983.
- 'For the Walrus (Tribute To JL)' was a single by Sando, issued on the first anniversary of John's death.
- *Homenaje A John Lennon* was an Argentinean album of tribute songs recorded by various artists.
- 'I Did It For You' was recorded by the band Full Circle on Mother Records in America.

- 'Imagine, A Tribute To John' was an American record by Glass Onion, issued on Onion Records UR 2317A/B. Originally recorded on 9 December 1980 by a group of fans comprising Charles F Rosenay III (vocals), Mike Streeto (drums), Dean Falcone (bass), Steve Harris (keyboards) and Miles Standish (additional instruments).
- 'Imagine John' by the Beatles Revival Band, with 'John, a Tribute to a Hero' on the flip, issued on Dance Street DST 1140-8 in 1993.
- 'It Was Nice To Know You, John' was issued in America on Tapestry TR005. This single was produced and sung by the 50s singles idol Bobby Vinton and written by Vinton and his son Robbie.
- 'John' was recorded within 24 hours of Lennon's murder, a tribute disc issued in America on Sun 1160 by Baxter, Baxter & Baxter (brothers Rick, Mark and Duncan). Produced by Shelby Singleton Jr and written by Stephen Kilgore, Virginia Fielder and B Castleman. 'A Hard Day's Night', 'Yesterday', 'I'll Follow the Sun', 'Ticket To Ride', 'Can't Buy Me Love', 'Imagine' and 'Tell Me Why' are mentioned in the lyrics.
- 'John Lennon Pt. 1/Pt. 2'. This record of interviews and songs was sponsored by an American Presbyterian organisation, with a spiritual slant, and was issued by a radio station on MA 1869. Each side contains five minutes of music and dialogue taken from a radio series called *What's It All About?* The single, by Bill Huie, was originally issued to radio stations.
- 'John Lennon Remembered' was an unusual tribute single issued in America on Marigold MP 705. It consisted of a completely blank A-side, lasting for ten minutes. The flip side was 'Lookin' Back', by Rich Dodson.
- 'John Lennon's Guitar', a record by Barclay James Harvest, coupled with 'Welcome to the Show', was issued on Polydor 841 751-2 in 1990. It was a number about the band playing John's guitar at Abbey Road.
- 'John Would Agree' was an American tribute single written and sung by Bob Farnsworth.
- 'The Legend of Lennon (In Memory of John Lennon)' was written, sung and produced by John Gill and issued in the US on Sunlite Records 81001.

- 'Life Is Real (Song for Lennon)'. This was a song by the British group Queen, written by their lead singer Freddie Mercury, and included on their April 1982 album *Hot Space* on EMI EMA 797.
- 'Live With Love' was an American single dedicated 'to the living spirit of John Lennon', and issued by Crescent Records on the first anniversary of John's death. The A-side, 'Live With Love', was written by Ross and Holly Hoffman and sung by a sixteen-year-old girl, Daphne Latham. The B-side was John's self-penned song from the *Revolver* album, 'Tomorrow Never Knows', sung by Dawn Thompson.
- 'Much Missed Man' was a single issued in Britain on the Mayfield records label, MA 103, on 29 January 1982. Joe Flannery, a Liverpudlian who was active as a group manager in the Mersey Beat years, was in contact with John by phone a few weeks before the murder. When he heard the tragic news he wrote a poem, which was put to music by a fellow Liverpudlian, Peter Wynne, and sung on the record by a local singer, Phil Boardman.
- 'Nobody Knows' was sung by Billy Squire and featured on his album *Don't Say No*, issued on Capitol 12146.
- 'Rest In Peace' was an American single by Juan Hernandez.
- 'Song for John' was a tribute by Bridget St John, released on *Road Goes On Forever* RGF CD 026.
- 'Tomorrow Never Knows' by Phil Collins had just been recorded at the time of John's death. As a tribute, he placed 'Over the Rainbow' on the flip side. It was released in 1981.
- 'To You Yoko: A Tribute To John' was issued on the Rota Doi label by A Tint Of Darkness. This American single was written by FL Pittman, LC Coney and C Rupert.
- 'Voices in the Sky (A Tribute to John)' was a track from the album *I Remember Love (And Rock & Roll)* by Joey Welz. Welz was formerly keyboard player with Bill Haley and the Comets and in the sleeve notes he mentions that he once jammed with the Beatles at Hamburg's Star Club. The single was issued in America on Music City Records 5008.
- 'We Won't Say Goodbye, John' was an American single written, produced and sung by Irene Koster. One of the

many backing singers in the chorus of the record is Peter Noone, former leader of Herman's Hermits. The proceeds of the record were donated to the Spirit Foundation.

The 1985 album *Private Audition* by Heart was mostly about John's death. The band's Ann Wilson commented, 'Nance [her sister, also in the band] and I were so floored by his death that we almost couldn't function. All we wanted to do was write about that. The songs were real melancholy. It was what we felt. It was nice for us but I guess it was a real drag for people to listen to.'

Trocadero Cinema

Formerly situated in Camden Street, Liverpool L13, it was once a major city-centre cinema, but it suffered the fate of 95 per cent of Liverpool's cinemas – closure due to shrinking audiences in the television age.

'The Troc' as it was affectionately called, was Julia Lennon's favourite cinema. When she and Freddie were married in 1938 they spent their honeymoon evening in the cinema and, when the show ended for the night, Julia returned to her parents' home in Toxteth while Freddie went back to his lodgings.

The cinema's name was changed to the Gaumont in the 1950s and in 1964 was the setting for a reception for *Ferry 'Cross The Mersey,* which Gerry Marsden attended as guest of honour. Pat Delaney, the Cavern's famous doorman, once mimed on stage there to Al Jolson records prior to a trailer for the film 'Jolson Sings Again'.

Troubadour, The

Club in Los Angeles which was to witness John making a disgraceful public exhibition of himself during his eight-month 'lost weekend', when he was parted from Yoko and living with May Pang.

On one Saturday night in January 1974 he had gone to a restaurant, Lost On Larabee, with May Pang, Jim Keltner and his wife Cynthia and Jesse Ed Davis and his girlfriend. After drinking several Brandy Alexanders (a drink made with cream and sweet liqueurs, which they nicknamed 'milk shakes') he went to the toilet and looked through a supply cabinet, where he found a Kotex sanitary towel. He returned to the table with it on his head.

The group then departed after the restaurant manager suggested they leave because they were too boisterous. They then travelled the few blocks to the Troubadour, with John still sporting the sanitary towel on his head.

It was alleged that he said to a waitress, 'Do you know who I am?'

'Yeah, you're an asshole with a Kotex on,' she replied.

However, May Pang claims that it was Jesse Ed Davis who was hassling the waitress and that she was too busy with drink orders to take any notice and didn't say anything.

Ann Peebles, then riding the charts with 'I Can't Stand the Rain', was performing. John made so much trouble and was shouting obscenities at the stage that the Troubadour manager asked him to leave.

When they returned to their apartment, John was so drunk that he smashed Davis over the head with a Coke bottle. They thought he'd been killed and the police were called. Davis was all right and had recovered, so one of the cops asked John, 'Do you think the Beatles will ever get back together again?' John's reply is – maybe thankfully – not recorded.

The worst incident, however, took place on 13 March 1974.

At around midnight John and May, accompanied by Harry Nilsson, entered the club and were seated in the VIP section, along with celebrities such as Peter Lawford.

John was drinking Brandy Alexanders again. Both he and Nilsson were drunk and they began singing 'I Can't Stand the Rain'.

The act that night was the Smothers Brothers, who had once had a TV series, which had been cancelled, and they were trying to make a comeback. When they came on stage they received a tremendous ovation, but John and Harry kept shouting and heckling and interrupting their act.

John shouted out, 'Hey! Smothers Brothers, fuck a cow!'

Lawford told him to shut up.

Ken Fitz, manager of the Smothers Brothers, went over to the table and took John by the shoulder. John knocked over the table as he hit Fitz and he also threw a punch at a waitress called Naomi. She said later, 'It's not the pain that hurts: it's finding out that one of your idols is a real asshole.'

Peter Lawford and a group of waiters swept forward and hustled the trio out of the club. There were some photographers and more scuffles took place. A female photographer shouted out, 'He hit me, he hit me', and took out a lawsuit accusing John of striking her.

The next day Harry Nilsson sent out bunches of flowers and notes of apology with the message, 'From John. With love and tears,' to the club's manager, the Smothers Brothers, Ken Fitz, Peter Lawford and some other celebrities who were in the VIP lounge.

Trudeau, Pierre

At a historic meeting in Ottawa at 11 a.m. on Monday 22 December 1969, John and Yoko had a private audience with Pierre Trudeau, the Prime Minister of Canada. When John had been working on his acorns-for-peace idea (see **Acorns**), he'd commented that he would like to meet the Canadian premier and present him with an acorn.

Trudeau heard of this and commented, 'I don't know about acorns, but if he's around I'd like to meet him. He's a good poet.'

John was in Canada at the time and arrangements were made for the meeting, with an agreement that there would be no advance publicity. John wore a cape over his Pierre Cardin suit when he left to meet the Prime Minister at his office.

They talked together for 51 minutes, covering many subjects. Trudeau described his visit to China and asked John many questions concerning the peace movement, contemporary youth, the Beatles and John's books and poetry.

After the meeting, John said, 'Trudeau was interested in us because he thought we might represent some sort of youth faction. We spent about fifty minutes together, which was longer than he had spent with any head of state, which was the great glory of the time.' He later added, 'If there were more leaders like Mr Trudeau, the world would have peace ... you don't know how lucky you are in Canada.'

Along with Golda Meir, Trudeau was one of the two world leaders to plant acorns.

Tsukai Ningen-Den

A Japanese children's programme broadcast on NHK TV. The English translation is *Dashing Life Stories*. On Monday 20 April

1992 the programme devoted 43 minutes to John's life through photographs and archive material, together with video footage of John, Yoko and Sean visiting Japan in August 1978.

Twenty Flight Rock
A hit for Eddie Cochran, this was the number to which the fifteen-year-old Paul McCartney knew all the words, impressing John Lennon when they first met at St Peter's Church fête in Woolton.

24 Hours
A BBC One TV current affairs programme, which devoted the entire show on 15 December 1969 to a documentary on John and Yoko, introducing much new material.

The documentary was called *The World of John and Yoko* and shooting covered a five-day period, beginning on Tuesday 2 December at Tittenhurst Park when John was filmed being interviewed by Desmond Morris for the programme *Man of the Decade*.

The following day the crew returned to Tittenhurst Park and filmed John and Yoko in bed. Then they filmed the couple in the bathroom and John watching a clip of the Beatles playing 'Some Other Guy' on his home movie screen. They then followed the couple in their Rolls-Royce on their way to Apple, accompanied by their PA, Anthony Fawcett.

At the Apple offices they were filmed conducting their business, telephoning and being interviewed by people such as Alan Smith of the *New Musical Express* and the disc jockey Stuart Henry. An argument between John and the American journalist Gloria Emerson was also captured on film.

The third day of shooting found the team filming a Plastic Ono recording session at Abbey Road and on Friday 5 December, the *24 Hours* team followed the couple's Rolls-Royce to the village of Lavenham in Suffolk, where John and Yoko were filming their *Apotheosis* movie. The final day of shooting on Saturday 6 December took place at the Bull Hotel, Long Melford, where John and Yoko were staying.

The fifty-minute documentary was screened on *24 Hours* between 10.30 and 11.05 on Monday 15 December, with David Dimbleby introducing it.

During the same evening the Plastic Ono Supergroup were performing their *Peace for Christmas* concert at the Lyceum Ballroom in the Strand.

The five-day shoot comprised a great deal of footage on numerous different locations. They included the recording studio, office, hotel, bedroom, bathroom, car, etc. John and Yoko allowed this highly personal footage to be taken only on a contractual agreement, which resulted in the BBC handing all the footage over to John and Yoko, together with full rights to use it as they saw fit. Yoko was able to use a number of the clips in the 1988 film *Imagine: John Lennon*.

20/20

An American television programme. The 4 December 1992 edition featured the first television interview with John's killer, conducted by Barbara Walters, one of the premier celebrity interviewers on American television. The criminologist James Fox was to comment that John's killer resented John's celebrity and wished for celebrity himself. The programme certainly added to that theory and the killer had already conducted newspaper interviews from prison, had been the subject of a cover story in *People* magazine and appeared in a British TV documentary in 1988.

Walters was to say, 'It isn't that he is having his fifteen minutes of fame. He's had his time of horror. He's not going to suddenly get a motion picture contract, nor will this help him in any sense go free. He's not up for parole for eight years.'

The assassin was to comment, 'John Lennon fell into a very deep hole. A hole that was so deep inside of me that I thought by killing him, I would acquire his fame.'

He told Walters that he had turned to Satan to gain the strength to shoot John and described the assassination itself. He then made a plea to Yoko: 'Please understand, Yoko: I wasn't killing a real person – I killed an image; I killed an album cover. I'm sorry. And I mean that. I'm sorry.'

Walters claimed that the interview gave an insight into the killer's mind, commenting, 'He had never done an interview. Nobody knew why he had committed this horrible crime.' Walters also reported that the killer had undergone an exorcism in prison, with the help of a priest standing outside the prison walls.

Twist of Lennon, A

Cynthia Lennon's autobiography, first published in Britain by WH Allen in 1978.

John didn't want to see this book published and attempted legal action to prevent it, which is odd, because it is an honest, positive work, not a kiss-and-tell book, and John was aware that Cynthia was a loving person with no rancour in her.

Although subtitled 'Her First-Hand Story of That Incredible Phenomenon – The Beatles', it is mainly about Cynthia's own odyssey through life, which makes it that much more interesting.

Judging by the account, Cynthia was an innocent tossed about by events. We can always remember Cynthia as the one left behind on the railway platform as the Beatles chugged off to Bangor, or being refused entrance to hotels by policemen who didn't believe she was Mrs Lennon.

It's a courageous autobiography because she reveals herself as vulnerable and unworldly. Cynthia seems eternally grateful: grateful for her marriage in the first place; grateful for being allowed to tag along. She never complained when she had to give birth to Julian with no moral support, and then had to spend the next critical months trying to elude the press and maintain the secrecy of her marriage.

Cynthia remained the traditional North of England housewife, subservient to her husband and aware of her maternal responsibilities. She'd try to look like Brigitte Bardot to please him, wither beneath his acerbic wit, yet end up feeling the guilty one.

After describing the shoddy treatment she received, she ends her story with only complimentary things to say about John and Yoko. She gives us a thanks-for-the-memory finish when we expected some anger at her treatment: no rancour, no vitriol, no fury – only sadness.

It had been felt by friends associated with Lennon that if Cynthia had stood up to John when the Yoko affair began, instead of just walking away, the marriage would probably have survived and John may have just taken Yoko as a temporary mistress.

Considering the circumstances, she is remarkably tolerant of Yoko. Cynthia was a wife in love with her husband who had another woman intrude in her life and take her husband away, yet she relates that her instincts told her that Yoko was 'the one' for John as soon as she saw her and that with Yoko 'John found his soul mate'. She even writes, 'I understood their love. I knew I couldn't fight the unity of mind and body they had with each other.'

The marriage started to go wrong when John began to dabble with psychedelic drugs – and to try to heal the schism she agreed to take LSD herself, but it proved horrendous to her. It seems she lost her spirit after that.

Following her divorce, Cynthia married Roberto Bassanini in 1970 and later married a businessman, John Twist, whom she also divorced. According to tradition, her name remained that of her last husband – Cynthia Twist. However, it was John himself who told Cynthia that she must use the Lennon surname as she wished and, since she never stopped loving John, it seems appropriate – but that explains the pun in the book's title.

Ultimately, the book is sad. Cynthia was a spectator during the heyday of the world's greatest musical phenomenon when she could have been a participant. She remained a spectator, on the periphery, afraid to take her rightful place in the drama.

Cynthia has included a number of her own poems in the book, together with twelve of her own black-and-white drawings to illustrate various anecdotes. There are also fourteen photographs in an insert.

Cynthia mentioned on occasions that she intended writing another book about the relationship, but she never did. It would have been interesting to have some in-depth accounts of how John actually treated her; his attitude towards Julian; how she felt about his not spending time with Julian; why she didn't fight to keep her husband when Yoko appeared on the scene, and so on.

A Japanese version, *Sugao No John Lennon,* in a translation by D Eguchi, was published by Shinko Music in 1979 and an American edition by Avon Books was published in 1980.

Twist and Shout

A number originally penned by Bert Russell and Phil Medley and first recorded by Phil Spector's Top Notes. The Isley Brothers later recorded it, in a much more dynamic version, and it provided them with their first chart hit, reaching No. 17 in the US charts in June 1962.

This was another belting rocker from the Beatles' early career and it was recorded as the final number of their lengthy *Please Please Me* album recording session on 11 February 1963. John was to comment, 'I couldn't sing the damn thing. I was just screaming.' George Martin was to say, 'There was one number which always caused a furore in the Cavern – "Twist and Shout". John absolutely screamed it. God alone knows what he did to his larynx each time he performed it, because he made a sound rather like tearing flesh. That had to be right on the first take, because I knew perfectly well that if we had to do it a second time it would never be as good.'

The Beatles included the number in their repertoire from 1962 to 1965, although John was to say, 'I hate singing "Twist and Shout" when there's a coloured artist on the bill. It doesn't seem right, you know. It seems to be their music, and I feel sort of embarrassed. Makes me curl up. They can do these songs better than us.'

The Beatles' version of the song was used on the soundtrack of the 1988 film *Ferris Bueller's Day Off*, causing it to chart again.

Two Minutes Silence

This 'song' is exactly what its title describes. It's included on the *Life With The Lions* album.

Two Mrs Lennons, The

A seventeen-minute report which was included in the CBS TV show *60 Minutes* in Sunday 2 October 1988. The current affairs programme presented interviews with both Cynthia Lennon and Yoko Ono.

Two Of Us

A made-for-TV movie written by Mark Stanfield and directed by Michael Lindsay-Hogg, first screened on VH1 on 1 February 2000.

The movie starred Jared Harris, son of the actor Richard Harris, as John Lennon and Aidan Quinn as Paul McCartney, in a fictional account of their meeting on the evening of Saturday

24 April 1976, when Paul visited the Dakota Building in New York to see John.

A meeting actually took place on that date. Paul and Linda were in America as their album *Wings at the Speed of Sound* had just topped the US charts. They both dropped in to see John and Yoko at the Dakota and John was watching *Saturday Night Live*, on which Lorne Michaels made his 'Beatles reunion' offer, which John and Paul were almost tempted to take him up on (see *Saturday Night Live*).

The movie is a fictional account of that meeting, although it is speculative, leaving out the presence of Yoko and Linda and lasting a full day rather than the evening.

The two characters discuss many topics ranging from a Beatles reunion to their families to their songwriting. They smoke and joke, sit at the piano and play 'Tumbling Tumbleweeds', disguise themselves and stroll through the park. Back at the Dakota they watch *Saturday Night Live* and are about to take up Michaels's offer when Yoko arrives and Paul says his farewells.

Two Virgins

Together with *Smile*, the first joint movie venture for John and Yoko, shot on 16mm film.

They hired a film crew to shoot a head-and-shoulders shot of each of them against an identical background. The film super-imposed their faces, which merged and then separated and ended with the couple settling in an embrace.

The 21-minute film was shot in the garden at Kenwood in early August 1968 and screened at the Chicago Film Festival in December of that year.

The soundtrack comprised music from their *Two Virgins* tapes.

Commenting on the filming, Yoko was to say, 'One afternoon John and I went out in the garden and shot Film No. 5 – the *Smile* film – and *Two Virgins*. They were done in a spirit of home movies. In both films, we were mainly concerned about the vibrations the films send out – the kind that was between us.

'Imagine a painting that smiles just once in a billion years. John's ghostly smile in Film No. 5 might just communicate in a hundred years' time, or maybe, the way things are rolling, it may communicate much earlier than that. I think all the doors are just ready to open now. One light knock should do. It's just that there are still a minority group in the world who are afraid of the doorless world to come.'

This was also, of course, the title of John's 1968 debut solo album, *Unfinished Music No 1 – Two Virgins*.

Tynan, Kenneth

At the invitation of Laurence Olivier, Tynan became the artistic director of the National Theatre in 1962. On 16 April 1968 he wrote to John Lennon:

'Dear John L,

You know that idea of yours for my erotic revue – the masturbation contest? Could you possibly be bothered to jot it down on paper? I am trying to get the whole script in written form as soon as possible.'

John replied, 'You know the idea, four fellows wanking – giving each other images – descriptions – it should be ad-libbed anyway – they should even really wank which could be great.'

UFO Connection

A science-fiction comic magazine from the Marvel Comics group published in the Marvel Premier series and dated Winter 1978. The magazine featured a three-page article called 'John Lennon's Close Encounter', which described his sighting of a UFO on 23 August 1974. This was regarded as a 'close encounter of the first kind' as John, together with friends, witnessed the object from the Dakota Building in New York where John was then residing.

John also referred to this unusual experience on the sleeve of his *Walls and Bridges* album, with the message, 'On 23 August 1974 at 9 o'clock I saw a UFO'.

The event occurred when he was sitting in his living room and noticed some strange lights. He then walked over to the balcony and spotted the flying saucer. He could see it clearly floating slowly between buildings. One of his assistants joined him on the balcony and started taking photographs.

He then phoned the police to ask them if anyone had reported a flying saucer and they told him he was the third person to contact them about it.

He then called the *Daily News* and they told him they'd received five calls about the sighting. He phoned Bob Gruen, the photographer, and asked him to come over and develop the film but, unfortunately, it was blank.

May Pang, who was with John at the time, has a slightly different recollection. She says that she and John had just ordered some pizzas and he decided to step out on to the terrace. There were no windows facing them, so John stepped outside without anything on. May was in the bedroom when she heard John calling her. She walked out and saw a large circular object in the sky. She said, 'It was shaped like a flattened cone and on the top was a large, brilliant red light, not pulsating as on any of the aircraft we'd seen heading for landing at nearby Newark Airport. When it came a little closer we could make out a row or circle of white lights that ran around the entire rim of the craft – and they were also flashing on an off. We did take a couple of pictures, but they turned out unexposed.'

She also said that John reported it to the New York *Daily News* in the hope that they would confirm his sighting – and they did.

John was to say, 'I went to the window, just dreaming around in my usual poetic frame of mind ... hovering over the building, no more than a hundred feet away was this thing with ordinary electric light bulbs flashing on and off round the bottom, one nonblinking red light on top ... What the Nixon is that?'

Ugly George

Assumed name of a roving reporter for a New York subscription channel, Manhattan Cable, who used to trek around the area with his camera enticing girls to strip off their clothes for him to film for his late-night show.

On Friday 24 September 1976 he spotted John and Yoko in a restaurant and approached them. He filmed a brief interview in which he asked John, 'How much of that dialogue that you wrote as part of the Beatles in the sixties and today is associated with sex?' John told him that the reference to 'fish and finger pie' in 'Penny Lane' was 'an old colloquial Liverpool saying for frigging'.

When Ugly George asked him about Manhattan Cable's new policy of cutting down on the sexual content on the channel, John said, 'Tits and arse is good here, they should show more!'

Unfinished Music No. 1: Two Virgins

John and Yoko's first collaboration on record, which they recorded at John's Weybridge home on 20 May 1968, when

Cynthia Lennon was on holiday in Greece. It was also his first recording venture without the other three Beatles.

Pete Shotton was in the house at the time, but he remained downstairs when the couple went into John's home studio to record. John had been using the studio to experiment with sounds for some time. He and Yoko began recording what was to be their debut album together, which contained sounds of a piano tinkling, recordings of birds outside the window, fragments of conversation – e.g. John in a Lancashire accent saying, 'It's just me, Hilda, I'm home for tea' – Yoko's screams and so on.

John commented, 'We started the album at midnight and finished it at dawn. Then we made love.'

If critics were to hammer the musical content and what they considered a load of rubbish, the actual album sleeve itself was to create a furore.

It comprised a full-frontal shot of John and Yoko stark naked, and the back cover was a rear view of the same subject. Yoko said that the idea of the nude shot came from John – although Yoko herself had used the same idea for publicity purposes when she and her husband Tony Cox were photographed together in the nude and the photographs were used in magazines.

Yoko said, 'I suppose he just thought it would be effective. He took the picture himself with an automatic camera. It's nice. The picture isn't lewd or anything like that. Basically we are both very shy and square people. We'd be the first to be embarrassed if anyone were to invite us to a nude party.'

The photographs were taken in the basement of Ringo's flat in Montague Square, London, where the couple were staying, in October 1968.

In fact, it's likely that a photographer was present. Some uncropped photographs from the session exist which show a third naked figure, a young man with a beard. It's possible that the 'third virgin' was an Apple employee named Tony Bramwell, who often took photographs on the company's behalf.

When John sent the photos to Peter Brown at Apple, he initially thought it was a joke. Then John called confirming that he wanted the photos used on the sleeve, saying, 'I want people to be shocked.'

Paul was particularly appalled with the pictures and was very unhappy about their being used, although he was talked into writing a brief, but cryptic, caption for the cover: 'When two great saints meet it is a humble experience. The long battles to prove he was a saint.'

EMI refused to have anything to do with such a cover and John and Yoko requested a meeting with its chairman, Sir Joseph Lockwood. He agreed to EMI's pressing the album, but would not have his company involved in distributing it. He also looked at the photo and said, 'If you must have a naked man on the cover, why didn't you use Paul instead?'

A small British label, Track Records, agreed to handle the album, but they wrapped it in a brown paper bag to escape being prosecuted under the Obscene Publications Act. This still didn't prevent most record shops from refusing to stock it and no publications would accept advertisements for it, with the result that it sold only 5,000 copies and never entered the charts.

In America Capitol Records also refused to be associated with the album and it was issued on an obscure label called Tetragrammaton, although the customs officers in New Jersey impounded 30,000 copies of the LP and an obscenity trial was conducted in Newark – which the record company lost. However, when the album was issued in the States on Tuesday 11 November 1969 it entered the charts on Sunday 8 February 1970. It remained in the charts for eight weeks, although the highest position it reached was only 124, with sales of 25,000 copies. Although distributed by Tetragrammaton, it had the catalogue number Apple T 5001.

John and Yoko had said that they'd felt like Adam and Eve in the picture, but they couldn't have expected such a hostile reception to their venture, which was particularly vitriolic in Britain.

Answering criticism, John commented, 'If people can't face up to the fact of other people being naked or smoking pot, or whatever they want to do, then we're never going to get anywhere. People have got to become aware that it's none of their business, and that being nude is not obscene. Being ourselves is what's important.'

He added, 'We were both a bit embarrassed when we peeled off for the picture, so I took it myself with a delayed-action shutter. The picture was to prove that we are not a couple of demented freaks, that we are not deformed in any way and that our minds are healthy. If we can make society accept these kind of things without offence, without sniggering, then we shall be achieving our purpose.'

The album tracks were: 'Two Virgins No. 1', 'Together', 'Two Virgins No. 2', 'Two Virgins No. 3', 'Two Virgins No. 4', 'Two Virgins No. 5', 'Two Virgins No. 6', 'Hushabye, Hushabye', 'Two Virgins No. 7', 'Two Virgins No. 8', 'Two Virgins No. 9' and 'Two Virgins No. 10'.

In Britain the album was released on Track 613012 on 29 November 1968.

Unfinished Music No. 1: An Unauthorized Companion to Year One of the Lost Lennon Tapes

A look at the first fifty shows in the *Lost Lennon Tapes* radio series in a 109-page book by LRE King, published by Storyteller Productions in a limited edition of 1,000 copies in December 1990. LRE King (Ellery King?) seems to be a pseudonym for a researcher and historian of Beatles bootlegs, whose previous discography books include *Do You Want To Know A Secret?*, *Fixing a Hole* and *Help!*

Unfinished Music No. 2: Life With the Lions

John and Yoko's second album and first release on a new experimental label from Apple called Zapple (this was one of only two releases on Zapple).

Produced by John and Yoko, it was issued in Britain on 9 May 1969 on Zapple 01. The cover, a photograph by Susan Wood, shows John and Yoko looking despondent in Room No. 1 of the Second West Ward at Queen Charlotte's Hospital, London, following the miscarriage of their child. Yoko is seen propped up in bed and John is lying in a sleeping bag on the floor next to her.

The reverse side of the sleeve featured a contrasting picture also portraying their torment at the time. The photograph was taken by a *Daily Mirror* photographer and shows John protecting Yoko amid a crowd outside Marylebone Magistrates' Court on 29 October 1968, following their marijuana drug bust.

The album sold only 5,000 copies.

Side One was recorded live at Lady Mitchell Hall in

Cambridge on 2 March 1969. In addition to John and Yoko there are John Tchikai on saxophone and John Stevens on percussion. The side runs for 26 minutes and 30 seconds and is entitled 'Cambridge 1969'. It contains the tracks 'Song for John', 'Cambridge 1969', 'Let's Go On Flying', 'Snow is Falling All the Time' and 'Mummy's Only Looking For Her Hand In the Snow'.

John recorded Side Two on portable recording equipment in November 1968 while staying at Yoko's bedside at Queen Charlotte's Hospital. 'No Bed For Beatle John' consists of John and Yoko singing out stories from the newspapers, which reported on their recent exploits. 'Baby's Heartbeat' was a few seconds' recording of the unborn baby's heartbeat in Yoko's womb, the sound of which John extended to a length of five minutes in his home studio. 'Two Minutes Silence' was exactly that – a gimmick that had previously been used by John Cale. 'Radio Play' was a twelve-minute track with the sound of someone fiddling with the dials of a radio while John and Yoko make phone calls in the background.

The album was issued in America on Zapple ST 3357 on 26 May 1969, entered the US charts on 28 June 1969 and reached No. 174 in the Top 200 chart, remaining in the charts for eight weeks.

Commenting on the LP, John said, '... the album was part of a series that will go on for the rest of our lives. We'd like to be able to produce them as quickly as newspapers and television can. It will be a constant autobiography of our life together.'

Unfinished Music No. 4

Another projected Zapple album from John and Yoko.

At the time it was announced, in November 1969, John commented: 'One side is laughing, the other side is whispering.'

The album was never completed.

Up Your Legs Forever

A film made by John and Yoko in a dance studio near the Lincoln Center, New York, in December 1970. Also called Film No. 12.

The concept was basically Yoko's and was similar in theme to her *Bottoms* film. The couple decided to ask a few hundred people, including a number of celebrities, to donate their legs for peace. Over 365 members of New York's art scene participated, including the film producer DA Pennebaker, the poet Allen Ginsberg, the painter Andy Warhol, the *Rolling Stone* proprietor Jann Wenner, the film actor George Segal and the artist Larry Rivers. Other participants included Henry Geldzahler, Shirley Clarke, Jack Smith, Taylor Mead, Paul Krassner, Jonas Mekas and David Johansen.

Mekas was to say, 'The thing that shocked me when I saw the film was how ugly, abnormal, distorted, crooked, uneven, sickly most of the legs were. Now the world can see on what legs the whole of New York art, intellect and culture rest. What a document for future historians!'

The completed film ran for 75 minutes and comprised a string of shots of people's legs with the camera climbing from their feet right up to the top of the thigh, ending before reaching the genitals. The soundtrack comprised dialogue recorded during the filming and John played bottleneck guitar while Yoko improvised in a bluesy style, singing 'Up Your Legs Forever'.

John recited the film's credits following a brief scene in which he and Yoko exposed their bare buttocks to the camera.

In her programme notes, Yoko wrote, 'The camera work of the film should constantly go up, up, up, non-stop. Collect 367 pairs of legs and just go up the legs (from toes to the end of thighs) pair after pair and go on up until you run through the whole 367.'

The film was screened at the Elgin Theater, New York, that same month on a bill with *Fly*.

Vallee, Jean François

A French television interviewer who was to interview John on two occasions. The first time was on Tuesday 14 December 1971 when he interviewed John, Yoko and Jerry Rubin at the Lennons' Greenwich Village flat. The interview was for the French television show *Pop 2* and was transmitted in January 1972. His second interview with the couple took place on 18 March 1975 on behalf of the French television programme *Un Jour Futur.*

Valley View Farm

An upstate New York dairy farm, which John and Yoko bought in 1978. This was actually only one of four farms in Delaware County near to the Catskill Mountains that they bought that year, along with a thousand head of prize Holstein Friesian cattle. The purchases were generally regarded as motivated by a desire to avoid a cripplingly high tax bill.

Vaughan, Ivan

An important figure in John's early life, born in Liverpool on 18 June 1942 – the same day as Paul McCartney, another of his close friends. Vaughan was the son of a policeman who had been killed in the war. His mother was a shorthand typist who became a school dinner lady to be more at home with her three kids.

Ivan had originally attended Dovedale Primary School with John, but later he enrolled at Liverpool Institute while John went to Quarry Bank.

At Liverpool Institute he was in the same class as Len Garry, whom he introduced to John, who then seconded him into the Quarry Men. When Ivan and Len wanted to miss the gymnastic sessions at school, which they hated, Ivan would get them both to say, 'Spasms, sir, spasms', which was enough to allow the games teacher to excuse them. Len noted that Ivan was particularly good at Latin and Greek, but in 1955 they were split into two different classes, with Ivan taking up classics.

Ivan lived in Vale Road, near to John's house, Mendips, and Ivan's house was called Vega; in fact their gardens backed on to each other. Ivan had rigged up a rope between a tree in his garden and one in John's. He looped a tin can on a string to it and would send John written messages, such as 'Hello'. When Len Garry asked if he hadn't anything more adventurous to say than 'Hello', Ivan said he couldn't think of anything else, but it was the novelty of the contraption that mattered.

When John formed the Quarry Men he invited Ivan to join them and he made a tea-chest bass on which he painted the legend 'IVE THE JIVE, THE ACE ON THE BASS'. He alternated on the instrument with Nigel Walley, but then Len Garry replaced both of them as tea-chest bassist.

Ivan had been one of John's closest friends since they were little children and was one of the 'gang of four', along with John, Pete Shotton and Nigel Walley. He shared John's interest in the Goons and was arguably as madcap as John and a very eccentric character – he painted his name in letters three foot high on the façade of his house when his mother was out one day – although he was also described as 'bookish'.

He also indulged in his strange antics at Liverpool Institute. Pupils had to wear regulation black shoes but Ivan arrived at school one day having painted them with canary-yellow paint.

A fellow student, Peter Sissons, was to comment, 'John Lennon was a highly original character, but in my opinion, much of the outrageousness and unpredictability he displayed later in life came from Ivan Vaughan and not the other way round.'

It was Ivan Vaughan who was responsible for introducing Paul McCartney to John. He was a schoolmate of Paul's at Liverpool Institute and, noting Paul's interest in rock 'n' roll music, thought John and he might get on together. Ivan always introduced people he considered were interesting to John. He told Paul that his friend was appearing with his skiffle group at St Peter's parish fête on 8 July 1958 and invited him along. Paul was reticent at first, but Ivan enticed him with promises that it was a great place to pick up girls.

Paul arrived on his bike, his guitar strapped on his back, and met Ivan in the field and they both went over to watch the Quarry Men, then drifted around the various stalls. Later, Ivan took Paul into the village hall, where the group were to play that evening, and introduced Paul to John and the other members of the group. There wasn't much rapport at first, but Paul began to play some numbers on his guitar, which perked John's interest and resulted in Paul's becoming a member of the Quarry Men.

Once the Beatles had achieved success, John continued to keep in touch with some old friends and often invited Ivan and his wife Jan to visit him at home in Weybridge. Ivan was also present at the *Sergeant Pepper* recording sessions. At the time he noted a change in John's attitude to people and commented, 'Even a couple of years ago the old animosities were still there: refusing to talk to anybody, being rude, slamming the door. Now he's just as likely to say to people, "Come in. Sit down." '

When Ivan and his wife Jan visited Paul at Apple's Wimpole Street office one day, Paul, aware that Jan taught French, asked her if she could help him with the lyrics to a song he was writing. He asked if she could suggest something to rhyme with 'Michelle' and she said '*ma belle*', telling him it meant 'my beauty'. She was then able to put some words into French for Paul, which he used in the song, 'Michelle'.

When projects for Apple were discussed, it was John who came up with the idea of an Apple school. He felt that the Beatles' children and those of Apple employees should have an alternative to the traditional system of education that he had hated so much as a child. He wanted a school to be launched with about twenty children, including Julian Lennon, Zak Starkey, Derek Taylor's children and so on. He suggested that Ivan be appointed head of the school. At the time Ivan was earning a living as an educational psychiatrist, but was persuaded to give up his job to join the project. Fortunately, he requested a deposit of £10,000, which he received, because Neil Aspinall and Pete Shotton talked Apple out of the idea as they felt it would be too expensive to run.

During the 1970s Ivan was struck with Parkinson's disease, for which there is no known cure. He decided to battle against the disease, becoming a guinea pig in the use of new drugs and mercilessly banging his limbs against solid objects when they refused to respond.

His remarkable and courageous struggle came to the attention of Jonathan Miller, who produced a television documentary on him, simply called 'Ivan' and screened in the *Horizon* series on BBC2 on Monday 3 December 1984. Ivan was 43 at the time. Paul allowed the use of his song 'Blackbird' free of charge. Paul invited Ivan to spend Christmas 1984 with the McCartneys at their home in Sussex. He kept in touch with his friend until he died.

Commenting on the documentary, Ivan said, 'I decided to make my illness my hobby. Not as something useful. Not to help thousands. Just selfishly, to find out all I could about it and its implications. I wanted to explore it, to play with it, and even to laugh about it.'

His book *Ivan – Living With Parkinson's Disease*, was published by Macmillan in 1986.

Ivan initially lost touch when John moved to New York permanently. Then, in September 1980 he phoned the Dakota Building asking for John. He was asked to prove who he was. Ivan explained that he'd written 'Jive with Ive, the ace on the bass' on his bass, and John came on the phone. When Ivan mentioned his disease, John sent him some books, including Arthur Janov's *Primal Scream*.

When Ivan died in 1994 his death touched Paul so deeply that he began to write poetry for the first time since he was a child.

Vollmer, Jurgen

At the time of the Beatles' first trip to Hamburg in 1960, Jurgen was a student at Hamburg's Institute of Fashion. Astrid Kirchherr was a pupil of Professor Reinhardt Wolf studying photography. She asked Jurgen if he would model for her.

Through her he met Wolf, who had decided to give up teaching to become a full-time photographer and required an assistant. Jurgen got the job, even though he'd never taken a picture himself. Through Astrid he also got to know Klaus Voormann and when the Beatles moved from playing at the Indra to the Kaiserkeller, Jurgen was one of the friends invited by Klaus to watch the group at the club. It was during this period that Jurgen became friendly with the Beatles.

Jurgen's father had been a professional army officer who had died on the Russian Front shortly after his son's birth. When Jurgen began to attend the Hamburg college, he became friendly with Klaus and Astrid, who were dating each other. At 17, Jurgen was five years younger than the other two. He made the acquaintance of the Beatles, and said John was, 'The obvious leader of the group ... a typical rocker ... a Brando type.' He was initially fascinated by John, but felt he was totally menacing and didn't go near him. Later he said that he found John, 'was actually a softie.'

The Liverpool band and the German Exis (existentialists) formed a close relationship and both Astrid and Jurgen took photographs of the Beatles, which the group brought back to Liverpool to give to Bill Harry to be published in *Mersey Beat*. The photographs were impressive, containing a mood and atmosphere unlike any rock photographs published elsewhere in Britain. They are generally regarded as a unique record of that early Hamburg trip and were reprinted in various American magazines over the years.

The photographs that Jurgen took were mainly from a session at the Top Ten Club in the Reeperbahn in 1961. He didn't want to take photographs of the group while they were actually performing in front of an audience in case some of the audience took offence, so he arranged for the pictures to be taken one afternoon when the club was closed. Since few people had flashes on their cameras at the time, he directed the club lights towards the stage and put the members of the group closer together than they'd normally have been when they played.

The Beatles had been sleeping above the club and when they came down John was still half-asleep and wasn't wearing his leather jacket. Jurgen asked him to go back and put it on, which John did reluctantly. He then got them to perform and began to take photographs from different angles. Later that same afternoon he took them to a run down area of the town and took some further photographs, including the one which was later to be used as the cover of the *Rock 'n' Roll* album. Altogether, Jurgen took ten rolls of film of the Beatles that day. When he showed John the enlargements of the shots he'd taken, John said, 'Thank God you made me wear my leather jacket.'

In 1961, Jurgen moved to Paris and when John received a 21st birthday gift of money from his Aunt Elizabeth, he used the cash to enable both Paul and himself to travel to the French capital where they contacted Jurgen. Of this particular trip, Jurgen remarked, 'I gave both of them their first Beatles haircut in my hotel room on the Left Bank. John wanted a corduroy jacket like mine and a sweater with cut-off sleeves like I wore, which was collarless and vest-like.' Jurgen took them to a flea-market and John bought a green corduroy jacket. This seems to indicate that the Pierre Cardin collarless look, which they were to adopt for a short time, had their origins in the influence of Jurgen.

However, the origins of the Beatles' moptop haircut may well have been the dual influence of Astrid Kirchherr and Jurgen. Although Astrid had shaped Stuart Sutcliffe's hair, it was Jurgen who, during the Paris trip, shaped John and Paul's hair into the new style. 'I gave them the haircut,' he claims. 'It was their idea to have it the same as mine. They left Paris, and never brushed their hair back again. That's the real story of the haircut. Don't let anyone tell you different.' And in an interview, when George Harrison was asked how the Beatles haircut came about, he said, 'I only brushed my hair forward after John and Paul came back from Paris.'

Jurgen felt that both John and Paul looked like rough rockers at the time and when he brought his girlfriend to see them she refused to sit with them. Jurgen told them that he had two mattresses and he could put them up on the floor to sleep. He asked the concierge – he was living in a hotel at the time – if he could have John and Paul stay and she refused. That night he tried to smuggle them in, but she caught them and told them to leave. As they passed her at the door, John said 'I didn't like the service anyway, Madame,' and turned to Paul and said, 'Shall we try the Ritz?' They ended up in Montmartre.

John Lennon paid for a subscription to *Mersey Beat* for

Jurgen and even took out some classified ads in which he mentioned his photographer friend: They said, 'Happy XMAS Jurgen', 'Hello from Norman Lennon Vollmer', 'FROLICHE FUSSBODEN Her Vollmer' and 'GOOD MORNING Jurgrow, from George'.

The Beatles regarded Jurgen as a good friend, but when they became famous he was embarrassed about seeing them. They were such celebrated people that he had feelings of inadequacy. When they arrived in Paris in January 1964 to appear at the Olympia, George called him and invited him to their hotel. However, Jurgen didn't have the nerve to go and see them there. Then George contacted him again and asked him to come to the stage door of the theatre and they'd let him in. However, the security guards wouldn't admit him. When George phoned the next day, Jurgen explained what had happened and George said he could join them and they would all go to the Olympia together. However, Jurgen put the phone down because he knew he was too intimidated to join them. He reflects, 'It's weird: in Hamburg, these guys looked up to me, they wanted my haircut, my clothes, my ideas about books. And then suddenly they were the stars and I felt like a cockroach.'

When John arrived in Paris for a few days on his way to Spain to appear in *How I Won the War*, he called Jurgen up once again and invited him round. Jurgen was still nervous about meeting his famous friend and had to drink several glasses of wine before finding the courage to visit. He was nervous and flustered when he arrived, but later settled down and realised that the John he was seeing was still the John he knew in Hamburg and they both enjoyed each other's company. Jurgen took him around to the flea market, then out to a café and, when they couldn't find a cab, Jurgen suggested they catch a bus. John said he hadn't travelled by bus for years, but Jurgen talked him into it.

The next time Jurgen saw John was in 1975, when John had split from Yoko. May Pang contacted him on John's behalf and Klaus Voormann, who was playing on the *Rock 'N' Roll* album John was recording at the time, also came to see him. Jurgen met John in the recording studio and John asked him to design the layout of the album, so he designed a fold-out cover. However, the bootleg album *Roots* was issued and *Rock 'N' Roll* had to be rush-released, so was issued without Jurgen's original design, but with Jurgen's Hamburg photograph of John on the cover.

In 1981 Jurgen had a book of his photographs published in Paris and New York. Among them were the pictures he took of the Beatles in Hamburg. The Paris edition was published by Editions de Nesle and the American by Google Plex Books. Entitled *Rock 'n' Roll Times,* the book is divided into two parts. The second part consists of Jurgen's photographs of Paris youngsters, bearing intriguing captions of rock 'n' roll songs to describe them. The first section contains his shots of the Beatles in Hamburg, and John wrote in his short introduction to the book, 'Jurgen Vollmer was the first photographer to capture the beauty and spirit of the Beatles. We tried very hard to find someone with his touch after we returned from Hamburg ... nobody could.' The cover of the book features a shot Jurgen took of John in the doorway of a building in the seafront area of Hamburg. Two blurred figures pass by – Paul McCartney and Stuart Sutcliffe. Fourteen years after it was taken, John was to select that shot as the cover of his *Rock 'n' Roll* album. Jurgen moved to New York where he became a professional photographer and other collections of his work published in book form include *Nureyev In Paris, Sex Appeal* and *African Roots.*

Vollmer later moved to Los Angeles, and among the celebrities he photographed were Madonna, Arnold Schwarzenegger, John Travolta, Sylvester Stallone and John Mellencamp.

In 1997 Genesis issued a lavish limited edition book of his work called *From Hamburg To Hollywood.* Another collection, under the title *Rockers,* was published by Edition Oehril in 2000. This also included his Hamburg pictures of the Beatles.

Voor de Vuist Weg

A Dutch television programme on the AVRO network, which conducted a live interview with Freddie Lennon on 21 January 1966. Freddie also sang his autobiographical song 'That's My Life'.

Voormann, Klaus

Born Manfred Klaus Voormann in Berlin before World War Two, the son of a doctor. The family escaped to the western part of Germany when the Russians entered the country, but Klaus returned to Berlin when he was nineteen to study classic arts. He had a friend who then took him to Hamburg to study at art school. While at art college he met Astrid Kirchherr and found they had a lot in common – the same tastes in art, a love of jazz – and she became his girlfriend.

Voormann first saw the Beatles appearing at Hamburg's Kaiserkeller club in 1960.

Fascinated by rock 'n' roll, he drifted into the St Pauli district following an argument with Kirchherr and was drawn to the sound of Rory Storm and the Hurricanes playing at the Kaiserkeller. He'd heard jazz bands before and had been to jazz concerts, but had never heard a rock 'n' roll group. He went inside and was strongly impressed by the raw rock 'n' roll being performed by the Beatles.

In particular the one who impressed him was Stuart Sutcliffe, who he thought was the leader of the group. He came on first with his collar up, wearing sunglasses, and Voormann recalls, 'He looked so fantastic. Nobody looked like that on the streets of Hamburg. It was a shock for me to see.'

After their set he approached John Lennon and attempted to strike up a conversation about the design of album covers. He showed him a cover he'd done for the Ventures' *Walk Don't Run*. John pointed to Stuart Sutcliffe, the group's bass guitarist and said, 'Go to Stuart; he's the arty one.' Klaus returned to the club the following evening, then brought Kirchherr along and soon all their friends were visiting the Kaiserkeller to see the Beatles.

Sutcliffe intrigued Voormann – and he also fascinated Astrid. Klaus's girlfriend then began her love affair with Sutcliffe, which lasted until his death in 1962. The influence of the Beatles, and Stuart in particular, inspired Klaus to become a musician and he decided on Stuart's instrument, the bass guitar, and he actually bought Stuart's bass instrument. He went to England for Stuart's funeral and liked the country so much he decided to stay.

When he was in London he received a call from Gibson Kemp, a Liverpool musician, who asked him if he knew any good bass players as he was going to Hamburg. Three days later he was a member of the group. He'd teamed up with two Liverpool musicians, Gibson and Paddy Chambers, to form Paddy, Klaus and Gibson, who were later signed by Brian Epstein. Kemp went on to marry Astrid. The group disbanded and Klaus became a member of the hit group Manfred Mann.

In the meantime John Lennon called up Klaus and invited him to design the cover for their next album, which was later called *Revolver*. John told him he would be completely free to utilise any design idea he had, saying, 'If it's no good, we're not going to take it.' Klaus worked on around fifteen different ideas and liked the one with the four band members' heads best.

He took the designs to them while the Beatles were in the studio and they told him *they* liked the heads idea best, too, and asked him to go ahead with it. It was the design for which he received a Grammy Award. He was paid £50.

As a result he designed some further sleeves for artists including the Bee Gees and Jackie Lomax.

He was also to design twelve lithographs for the album booklet accompanying Ringo Starr's *Ringo* album in 1973.

When Paul took his action to disband the Beatles, John, George and Ringo considered continuing with the group, using another name, the Ladders, and replacing Paul with Klaus. There was even a press release to that effect, but it was withdrawn and a denial made soon after.

In September 1969, John and Yoko received an invitation to appear at a rock 'n' roll festival in Toronto and they asked Klaus to become their bass guitarist. Apart from the Toronto Rock 'n' Roll Festival, Klaus performed with them at their Lyceum appearance in December 1969.

He was a member of the Plastic Ono Band and appeared on the various singles and albums – and also on a number of other Lennon recordings after John had decided to drop the Plastic Ono Band name.

Klaus performed on the singles 'Cold Turkey', 'Instant Karma!', 'Power To the People', 'God Save Us' and 'Whatever Gets You Thru the Night' and the albums *The Plastic Ono Band – Live Peace in Toronto 1969*, *John Lennon/Plastic Ono Band*, *Imagine*, Record Two of *Sometime In New York City* and *Walls and Bridges*. He also performed on the Record Plant sessions of the *Rock 'n' Roll* album in New York.

He continued performing with groups as bass guitarist and was with Dr John's band in 1979.

Klaus then became a record producer and returned to Germany, producing 'Da Da Da', which became a hit for Trio in

1984. Once settled in Germany, he decided to give up being a musician and return to graphic art. He also wanted to spend some time with his family as he had two children.

In June 1995 he was contacted by Neil Aspinall, one of John's oldest friends and a former Beatles road manager, who invited him to submit ideas for the Beatles' *Anthology* package. His concept was accepted and Klaus decided to work in collaboration with a Munich-based graphic artist, Alfons Kiefer.

Klaus also worked for six years on oil paintings and sketches re-creating the Beatles' early days in Hamburg. His work, together with photographs by Astrid Kirchherr, was published in a limited-edition book *Hamburg Days*, issued by Genesis Publications in 1999.

Walking On Thin Ice (promotional film)

The promotional film of the record. It depicted John and Yoko's naked bodies, pictured from the waist up while making love. The film was screened at the Ritz Disco in New York in 1981 and was, bizarrely, also available on a local pay TV station in New York City.

Walking On Thin Ice (single)

This was the track that John was mixing on the night he died. The flip side, 'It Happened', was originally recorded in 1973 during the *Feeling The Space* session. The record opens with some dialogue from John and Yoko recorded on 26 November 1980.

The single was issued in America on Geffen GEF-49683, two months after John's murder, and in the UK on Friday 20 February 1981. The picture sleeve depicted stars in the sky and the dedication 'For John'. John played lead guitar and keyboards on the session. In her sleeve notes, Yoko recalls John telling her, 'Yoko, you paid your dues, and you produced a top ten record. Don't let them kick you around anymore.' She ended by writing, 'Getting this together after what happened was hard. But I knew John would not rest his mind if I hadn't. I hope you like it, John. I did my best.'

Walley, Nigel

One of John's childhood friends, whom John often referred to as 'Whalloggs'. Walley was born in Woolton, Liverpool, on 30 June 1941, and lived in Vale Road, to the rear of where John lived in Menlove Avenue and in the same road as another friend, Ivan Vaughan. When John formed his group the Quarry Men, Nigel was invited to play tea-chest bass, although he says he played it only occasionally, with Ivan Vaughan being the main bass player.

At the time Nigel was an apprentice golf professional at Lee Park Golf Club, and sadly was deterred from playing tea-chest bass for good by an unsavoury incident. Having finished a gig one night, the band travelled home by bus, and when they got off they were approached by two aggressive local youths, Rod and Willo, who threatened to beat them up. Everyone fled, leaving the tea-chest bass in the road.

The group needed someone to get the gigs sorted out and promote them. No one really wanted to do it, but John asked Nigel, who then set about getting them work. He placed a card in the window of a Woolton sweet shop at 2d per week, took small ads in the *Liverpool Echo* and the *Daily Post* and even had professional cards printed. The name on it was 'Quarry Men', he says, 'and the correct name is two separate words, not one, as people these days seem to think.'

His printed card read:

COUNTRY. WESTERN. ROCK 'N' ROLL. SKIFFLE
THE QUARRY MEN
OPEN FOR ENGAGEMENTS

When the Quarry Men were deciding on their repertoire, Nigel says, 'They picked out records by Buddy Holly, Bill Haley and popular rock 'n' roll numbers of the time. Elvis Presley's "Heartbreak Hotel" was a number John was particularly struck on. We saw Buddy Holly live with the Crickets when he appeared on the Liverpool Empire. It was one of the highlights of my life.

'We picked the tunes from records that were readily available in the shops. That story about Liverpool groups getting their repertoires from records brought in by merchant seamen is a myth, although lots of Liverpool men went to sea. Pete Shotton's brother Ernie was in the navy.'

Nigel used to go round to John's house and ask his Aunt Mimi, 'Where's John?' 'Where do you think? In his bedroom, playing his guitar' was the standard response. Nigel would go up and sit on the bed while John would be playing. 'He'd write a song in a few minutes,' said Nigel. 'I didn't think much of it at the time.'

Lee Park Golf Club was an exclusive Jewish club. One of the members was Dr Sytner, whose son Alan ran the Cavern Club, which was then a jazz venue that occasionally booked local skiffle groups as supports. Nigel asked Dr Sytner if he could persuade Alan to book the Quarry Men at the Cavern. He was told that they'd have to see the group before they could be booked and he suggested they perform at the golf club first. If they were any good, then Alan would book them at his club.

They were told that, as the appearance would be something of an audition, they wouldn't be paid. However, they would have all the drink that they wanted plus a slap-up meal, and the hat would be passed around. When they completed their performance they did have lots of drink, a hearty meal – and the hat, when passed around, brought them more money than they'd ever received from a gig before. Not only that, Alan Sytner liked the group and booked them at the Cavern.

They appeared there on 7 August 1957, although John was to upset Sytner when they did appear, by singing Elvis Presley numbers at a time when rock 'n' roll was barred from the club (see **Beatles**).

Although Nigel acted as their manager, when he didn't actually perform with them on tea-chest bass, Paul McCartney got understandably upset and said that he should take a reduced fee.

In 1958, 15 July proved to be a traumatic night for Nigel. He'd dropped around to Mendips house to see if John was at home, and found he was out. John's mother Julia was at the gate talking to her sister Mimi Smith. Nigel then walked along Menlove Avenue with Julia, having a chat, then continued on his way while Julia crossed the road. Hearing the squeal of brakes, he turned to see Julia's body being tossed into the air as a car crashed into her. Julia, tragically, was killed.

The off-duty policeman, Eric Clague, who was driving was sent to trial and Nigel was called as a witness. The inquest established that Clague was driving without a licence, but he still escaped with a reprimand and a period of suspension from duty. This verdict so angered John's Aunt Mimi that she shouted 'Murderer!'

Nigel had to cease managing the group when his family moved from Vale Road to New Brighton as he now lived too far away from them to manage the band. He then left Liverpool in 1961 when he qualified as a professional golfer and found work in a hotel complex in Semmering, Austria. He never returned to Liverpool, apart from occasional visits.

He was invited round to see John when he lived in Kensington as John still liked to keep in touch with the friends who knew him before he became famous as a Beatle. Nigel also visited John on several occasions at his Kenwood house.

Nigel has enjoyed a successful and happy career in the golf world after finally settling down at Wrotham Heath Golf club in Borough Green, Kent.

Walls and Bridges

In the summer of 1974 John returned to New York City with May Pang and began recording at the Record Plant between June and August. The result was his fourth solo album proper *Walls and Bridges,* the title inspired by a phrase he'd heard on television. The LP hit the No. 1 spot in the American charts on 16 November – at the same time that a single from the album, 'Whatever Gets You Thru the Night', brought John his first chart-topper in the singles chart since leaving the Beatles.

The musicians he gathered about him included Jim Keltner on drums, Jesse Ed Davis on guitar, Eddie Mottau on acoustic guitar, Klaus Voormann on bass and Nicky Hopkins, Elton John and Ken Ascher on keyboards. The New York Philharmonic Orchestra, conducted by Ken Ascher, was featured on several tracks. The album was credited to John Lennon (with the Plastic Ono Nuclear Band).

The songs on the album were: Side One: 'Going Down On Love', 'Whatever Gets You Thru the Night', 'Old Dirt Road', 'What You Got', 'Bless You', 'Scared'; Side Two: 'No. 9 Dream', 'Surprise, Surprise (Sweet Bird of Paradox)', 'Steel and Glass', 'Beef Jerky', 'Nobody Loves You (When You're Down And Out)', 'Ya Ya'.

The album was issued in America on Apple SW 3416 on 26 September 1974, and topped the charts for one week, achieving a million sales and a Gold Disc within ten days of release. It was issued in Britain on Apple PCTC 253 on Friday 4 October 1974, and reached No. 5.

Roy Kohara designed the album sleeve, which comprised a number of photographs of John, together with some of John's very early school paintings. Five of John's school paintings from 1952 were also included in a booklet of lyrics that came with the album.

John was to use a number of pseudonyms for himself when he played guitar, acoustic guitar and piano on various tracks.

Some time later he was to comment, 'Musically, my mind was just a clutter. It was apparent on *Walls and Bridges*, which was the work of a semi-sick craftsman. There was no inspiration and it gave an aura of misery.'

Warhol, Andy

When John and Yoko first arrived in New York City they met Warhol. John was to say to Yoko, 'Do you think he's gonna do us? I think he's gonna do us. Well, we should ask him.' Then John changed his mind and said, 'No, we shouldn't ask. He's an artist – he has to get the inspiration so we'll wait and see if he asks us.'

Paul Morrissey, Warhol's colleague, said that Warhol wasn't interested in John and Yoko. He commented, 'Andy thought Lennon was a pest – a leech – and worse, he was a professional grouch, an uninteresting, nasty person. A smart ass.'

Warhol never asked and never painted a picture of John and Yoko. However, the relationship couldn't have been as bad as Morrissey implied. Yoko was to say, 'Andy visited me at home and he noticed on a wall five photographs of Sean, each representing a year of his life. Andy wanted to know why the photographs stopped when Sean was five years old. I told him that it was John's project and when John died it stopped.

'I'll finish the project if you want,' Andy said. 'I'll paint Sean every year.' Warhol took Polaroid shots for the continuation of the project, but his plans were cut short by his own sudden death at the age of 59 following unexplained complications after a gall bladder operation.

After John's death Yoko asked Warhol to design the cover of *Menlove Avenue*, the last album of John's studio tracks that she was to issue, and he did so.

Yoko gave the eulogy at Warhol's funeral service in New York's St Patrick's Cathedral. Thousands attended the one-hour memorial mass.

War is Over

These three simple words were the official slogan that John and Yoko devised at the end of their year of peace activities. They launched the 'War Is Over' campaign on 15 December 1969 by buying billboard and poster space in twelve cities around the world, including London, New York, Hollywood, Toronto, Paris, Rome, Berlin, Athens and Tokyo. The huge signs read, 'WAR IS OVER – IF YOU WANT IT – HAPPY CHRISTMAS, JOHN AND YOKO'.

John was to say, 'Henry Ford knew how to sell cars by advertising. I'm selling peace, and Yoko and I are just one big advertising campaign. It may make people laugh, but it may make them think, too. Really, we're Mr and Mrs Peace.'

The signs were placed in the most prominent areas of the cities such as Times Square in New York, Sunset Strip in Hollywood and Shaftesbury Avenue in London, in the language of the country in which they were displayed: 'E FINITA LA GUERRA!' in Rome and 'DER KRIEG IST AUS!' in Berlin.

On the same day John and Yoko performed at a *War Is Over* benefit concert for UNICEF at the Lyceum, London, appearing on stage with a 'War Is Over' billboard as a backdrop.

During a press conference in London to discuss the campaign John was asked if he really believed it would contribute to world peace.

He said, 'It's like asking Mr Coca-Cola, "Do you really believe your advertisements are contributing to selling Coca-Cola?" It certainly does contribute. We believe in advertising. On a David Frost programme the other night, we saw this firm making adverts against racialism [sic]. The adverts weren't too good, but the idea was. We thought we'd invented the idea, of course, but somebody had thought of it. It's a very good idea to advertise for peace against racialism. You must advertise. That's what everybody else does.'

A few months later, during another interview, John was to comment, 'You've got power. All we have to do is remember that: we've all got the power. That's why we said, "War is over if you want it." '

John and Yoko utilised the slogan once more at Christmas 1971 when they recorded the Christmas song, 'Happy Xmas (War Is Over)', which featured a chorus of the Harlem Community Choir singing 'War is over, if you want it'.

Commenting on the poster campaign to Jann Wenner of *Rolling Stone* magazine, John said, 'We got a big response. The people that got in touch with us understood what a great event it was apart from the message itself.'

Yoko repeated the campaign on Tuesday 1 December 1998 by placing messages in Times Square, New York City, which read 'WAR IS OVER! IF YOU WANT IT ... HAPPY CHRISTMAS FROM JOHN AND YOKO.' She then commented, 'This is a billboard event John and I did twenty-nine years ago, in Christmas of 1969. At the time it created good vibrations around the world and gave people strength. The message is "We can do it", and it's still valid. If one billion people in the world would think peace – we're gonna get it. You may think, Well, how are we going to get one billion people to think? Isn't this something we should leave to the politicians who have the power to do these things?

'Well, politicians cannot do anything without your support. We are the power. Visualise the domino effect and just start thinking positive, that we are all together in this. For the holiday season, I wanted this to be a gift to you from John and I. Stand in front of the billboard. Take photos of yourself, your friends and family. Send them out so the message will circulate. Above all, have fun.'

Yoko's belief in the positive effect of peace seemed to take a battering when she learned that John's killer, Mark Chapman, would be due for parole at the end of the year 2000. Her horror of violence was also awakened when George Harrison was attacked and almost murdered at Christmas 1999.

Early in 2000 she made a statement to the *Independent* newspaper: 'Unlike in the Sixties when it was easier to live our idealism, our recent history shows how we live in very different times. Knowing that our close friend and his family have been subjected to a violent incident, I am naturally most concerned about the safety of Julian and Sean.

'I am of course concerned for my safety as well and the safety of many of our friends who are also in the limelight.'

Watching Rainbows
A number John wrote at the beginning of 1969.

We're All Water
A track written and performed by Yoko on the *Sometime in New York City* album.

Watching the Wheels
A song featured as the first track on Side Two on the *Double Fantasy* album. The autobiographical ballad evolved from a demo song called 'Watching the Flowers Grow'. When John was in Bermuda in 1980 he began developing the number, composing once again on piano. Fred Seaman, John's assistant, said he watched John enter a sort of trance when he began working on the song. John later explained to him that, by clearing his mind, he seemed to pick inspiration out of the air.

'Watching the Wheels' was also inspired by the outside reaction to his absence from the music scene while he spent his time rearing Sean.

During this time John had been content just sitting 'watching shadows on the wall'. It was his own life, his own choice, yet the press kept requesting his return from the apparent musical inactivity. In 1978 *New Musical Express* had headlined 'WHERE THE HELL ARE YOU, JOHN LENNON?' and other musicians were puzzled by his abandonment of the music scene.

John answered them in an interview in *Newsweek* magazine: 'I couldn't believe it. They were acting like mothers-in-law,' he said.

On a trip to Japan he told the press, 'We've basically decided, without a great decision, to be with our baby as much as we can until we feel we can take the time off to indulge ourselves creating things outside the family. Maybe when he's three, four or five then we'll think about creating something else other than the child.'

He also discussed the song in a *Rolling Stone* interview: 'The whole universe is a wheel, right? Wheels go round and round. They're my own wheels mainly. Watching myself is like watching everybody else. And I watch myself through my child too. The hardest part is facing yourself. It's easier to shout about *Revolution* and *Power To The People* than it is to look at yourself and try to find out what's real inside you and what isn't.'

The number became the third single from the album and was issued in America on Geffen Records 49695 on 13 March 1981 with Yoko's 'Yes, I'm Your Angel' on the flip. It reached No. 10 in the *Billboard* chart. In Britain it was issued on Geffen Records K 79207 on 27 March 1981 and reached No. 27 in the *New Musical Express* chart.

The song was also coupled with 'Beautiful Boy' and issued as a single in America on Geffen Records GGEF 0415 on 4 November 1981.

Waters, John

Musician, born in London in 1948. In 1969 he appeared in the Australian version of *Hair* and later appeared in the film *Breaker Morant* and then played Pontius Pilate in *Jesus Christ Superstar*. Waters portrayed John in his touring play *Looking Through a Glass Onion*, which reached London's West End at the Criterion Theatre in 1994.

The play moved through John's life in a chronological style with Waters voicing John talking about his life, interspersed with performances of the songs. He talked about the loss of John's mother prior to singing 'Julia'. Other songs, spaced out among the dialogue, included 'Nowhere Man', 'Strawberry Fields', 'Glass Onion', 'Sexy Sadie', 'Imagine', and 'Beautiful Boy'.

Watkins, Peter

A British film director with a cult following. His movies include *Performance*, starring Paul Jones and Anita Pallenberg, a sci-fi rock story, and *Panic in Needle Park*, another film set in the near future.

His most controversial work was *The War Game*, a film he produced for BBC TV showing the effects of a nuclear holocaust on London. It was felt to be too horrific for showing on television and has been screened at a number of independent cinemas since it was made in the mid-60s. His sequel was called *The Peace Game* (a.k.a. *The Gladiators*).

John acknowledged that it was a letter from Watkins that finally persuaded him to work actively for his peace campaign. The lengthy missive covered aspects of media manipulation and pointed out that John and Yoko, as prominent media figures, had a responsibility that they should use to advocate peace in the world.

He concluded with the challenge, 'What are you going to do about it?'

The letter had a profound effect on John, who, three weeks after he received it, decided to go ahead with Watkins's suggestion by launching his first bed-in.

We All Shine On

Book by Paul Du Noyer, published in Britain by Carlton Books in May 1997. It basically covers stories behind the songs that John wrote between 1970 and 1980. It is illustrated with ninety colour and monochrome photographs and contains a brief chronology and discography.

Weberman, AJ

A leading member of the Rock Liberation Front, a New York-based organisation that campaigned against the commercialisation of rock music.

Weberman was also the person who invented 'garbology', the practice of studying people's garbage in order to gain insights about their private lives. He began this when he started ransacking the garbage at Bob Dylan's house in McDougal Street, seeking to analyse it and understand Dylan more. He concluded that Dylan was a heroin addict and created the Dylan Liberation Front with the aim of getting him to reject drugs and to take an active interest in radical politics again. His campaign verged on persecution and he even picketed Dylan's house with signs reading 'SLUM LANDLORD'.

John was annoyed at the attacks on Dylan. Together with Yoko, he wrote a letter to *Village Voice* attacking Weberman's persecution of Dylan. They asked him to publicly apologise to Dylan for the malicious slander he'd spread over the past year: 'It's time we defended and loved each other, and saved our anger for the true enemy, whose ignorance and greed destroys our planet,' the letter went on.

When Dylan's new single, 'George Jackson', was issued, Weberley praised it and said, 'I'm never going to harass him or his family again.'

John and Yoko invited Weberman around to their Bank Street apartment and also joined the Rock Liberation Front. In December 1971, Weberman organised a demonstration outside Capitol Records in protest at the company's failure to release the *Concert for Bangladesh* album. There were signs with slogans such as 'PAKISTANIS STARVE BECAUSE OF CAPITOL'S GREED.'

Two people appeared at the demonstration wearing bags and many people believed that they were John and Yoko. Steve Gebhardt was there filming at their request and Weberman announced, 'John and Yoko are the newest members of the Rock Liberation Front, a group dedicated to exposing hip capitalist counterculture rip-offs and politicising rock music and rock artists.'

Weberman also began a campaign against Allen Klein after *New York* magazine accused Klein of pocketing some of the *Bangladesh* receipts. He organised a Rock Liberation Front demonstration with banners proclaiming 'KLEIN THE SWINE', and occupied Klein's offices, in addition to ensuring that a number of magazines, including *Rolling Stone, Variety* and *Village Voice*, printed the anti-Klein charges.

Weberman was later to say that the demonstration convinced John and Yoko that Klein was ripping the two of them off and they were to fire Klein a year later and sue him.

Wedding Album

When John and Yoko began to document their activities on film and record, *Wedding Album* was one development to take advantage of the growing archives. The couple had intended to issue material soon after each event, to capture the flavour of instant news. However, there were numerous delays on this package, which was released eight months later than planned.

It was issued in America on 20 October 1969 on Apple SMAX 3361, and spent three weeks at the lower end of the Top 200, reaching its highest position of No. 178. It was issued in Britain on 7 November 1969 on Apple SAPCOR 11, but made no impact on the charts.

The souvenir itself was impressively packaged in a box. This contained the album, a photocopy of their marriage certificate, a photograph of a slice of wedding cake, a book of press clippings about the couple's activities, a plastic bag with the tag 'Bagism', a cartoon strip of the wedding drawn by John and a strip of 'passport' photos.

John Kosh designed the package and there was a selection of pictures by various photographers, including Richard DiLello, John and Yoko, Nico Koster, David Nutter, John Kelly and Mlle Daniau.

The A-side of the record comprised 22 minutes and 38 seconds of recordings called 'John and Yoko'. On Tuesday 22 April 1969, John and Yoko had gone along to Abbey Road studios for an evening session that lasted from 11 p.m. to 3.45 a.m., to record the 'John and Yoko' side. They recorded a few seconds of each other's heartbeat using a special stethoscope-shaped microphone.

The heartbeats were superimposed on a tape and then made into a loop, which was to last for more then twenty minutes and on which John and Yoko called out each other's name repeatedly, shouting out 'John', 'Yoko', whispering, crying, wailing and expressing the names in various vocal ways.

The second side of the album was called 'Amsterdam' and comprised 24 minutes and 54 seconds of recordings, with Yoko improvising on a number she called 'John, Let's Hope for Peace'. Strumming on acoustic guitar, John next sings 'Goodbye Amsterdam Goodbye'. John also plays guitar when he and Yoko sing 'Bed Peace' and John also sings a small fraction of the song 'Goodnight'. In between the songs are excerpts from the cassette that had been documenting their Amsterdam Bed-In. These included the couple conducting a press interview from their bed. There is the sound of John ordering tea and brown toast from room service and there's also an interview about the peace campaign, which had been taped in London on their return from Amsterdam.

Weekend World

A London Weekend Television current affairs programme. On Friday 6 April 1973 John and Yoko videotaped an interview for the show with John Fielding in Los Angeles. The main subject of the interview was the recent split with Allen Klein. The interview lasted ten minutes and was transmitted in the LWT area on Sunday 8 April. It began with Fielding asking, 'Can you tell me what happened with Allen Klein? Why did you and the other two decide finally to get rid of him?'

> John: 'There are many reasons why we finally gave him the push, although I don't want to go into the details of it. Let's say possibly Paul's suspicions were right ... and the time was right.'
> Fielding: 'His contract was coming up for renewal anyway ... wasn't it?'
> John: 'The contract expired I think in February, and we were extending it at first on a monthly basis and then finally on a two-week basis, and then finally we pushed the boat out.'
> Fielding: 'When did you personally decide that Klein probably wasn't the man you thought he was?'
> John: 'Well, you're concluding that I thought he was something. My position has always been a "Devil and deep-blue sea", and at that time I do whatever I feel is right. Although I haven't been particularly happy personally for quite a long time with the situation, I didn't want to make any quick moves and I wanted to see if maybe something would work out.'

When asked if Klein's being out of the picture would enhance the chances of the Beatles' getting back together again, John replied, 'With or without the present situation, the chances are practically nil! Although I hate to say "definitely" to anything, because, every time, I change my mind. But I don't have a feeling about it and I don't think any of the others really do. If any of you actually remember when we were together, everybody talked about it as though it was wonderful all the time. All the press and all the people, all saying how great and how wonderful ... but it wasn't like that at all! And imagine *if* they did get together, what kind of scrutiny would they be under? Nothing could fit the dream people had of them. So forget it, you know – it's ludicrous.'

There was some further discussion before John ended by

waving at the camera and saying, 'Hello, Aunt Mimi, how are you? We're OK! We're eating well, and I haven't given up my British citizenship. I just want to live here, that's all.'

Weiss, Milton
A Californian psychiatrist who attempted to analyse John in 1974 but gave up in despair, commenting, 'If I was doing this as a job, I'd have to send him two bills – one for each personality!'

Well (Baby Please Don't Go)
The song with which John opened his performance at the Fillmore East in New York on 6 June 1971, backed by Yoko and Frank Zappa and the Mothers of Invention.

After the main part of the concert featuring Zappa and his group, John came on stage as the encore to the show. He carried an electric guitar and Yoko carried a bag. After announcing the number as 'a song we used to do in the Cavern in Liverpool', he began performing 'Well (Baby Please Don't Go)' accompanied by Zappa and the Mothers, with Yoko howling alongside.

The number had originally been written by Walter Ward and recorded by the Olympic, an R&B quartet from Los Angeles, in 1958, and was the flip side to their 'Western Movies' single. The Beatles began playing the song in 1960, with John on lead vocals, and included it in their repertoire until 1962.

The following month, during the *Imagine* sessions, he cut a studio version of the song, which included a sax break by Bobby Keyes, although he didn't issue it as the flip side of a single, as he'd originally intended.

The live version of the song, lasting 3 minutes, 38 seconds, and appeared on the *Sometime in New York City* album.

Well Well Well
John recorded a home demo of this number in August 1970. It featured John on acoustic guitar and included the line 'She looked so beautiful I could wee', which was later changed to 'She looked so beautiful I could eat her'.

'Well Well Well' was included on the *John Lennon/Plastic Ono Band* album, issued on 11 December 1970. It was the third track on Side Two and featured John, Ringo Starr and Klaus Voormann on a number produced and mixed by Phil Spector.

We Love You

A Rolling Stones single issued in Britain on Decca F 12654 on August 1967 and in America on London 905 on 28 August, with 'Dandelion' as the flip. On 18 May of that year, at Olympic Studios in Barnes, John and Paul McCartney provided backing vocals on the record and John can clearly be heard singing 'We love you'.

Wenner, Jan

Founder of *Rolling Stone* magazine. He interviewed John on 8 December 1970 and published the lengthy 30,000-word interview over the Thursday 21 January and Wednesday 3 February 1971 issues. In the interview John insults virtually everyone he knows ranging from Apple friends such as Derek Taylor and Neil Aspinall to the Rolling Stones and his fellow Beatles. Wenner adapted the interview into book form, published as *Lennon Remembers,* which infuriated John because he had never given his permission and hadn't been consulted.

West, Mae

Legendary Hollywood star, famous for her overt sexuality and double-entendre one-liners. The blonde, buxom actress was born in 1892 and appeared in a stream of movies, including *She Done Him Wrong, I'm No Angel* and *My Little Chickadee.*

West was one of the characters the Beatles included on their *Sergeant Pepper's Lonely Hearts Club Band* album sleeve. When researcher Wendy Hanson originally contacted West for her permission to include an image of her in the tableau, West refused, with the words, 'What would I be doing in a Lonely Hearts Club Band?' The Beatles wrote her a personal letter and she then agreed to be included on the sleeve.

John once asked his aide, Elliot Mintz, to obtain Mae's autograph for him. As she signed the autograph, she asked, 'Now, what's this fella's last name?'

Ringo Starr was to appear with her in the last film she ever made, *Sextette,* in 1977 and at one time she considered engaging the former Beatles aide Derek Taylor to handle her public relations, but changed her mind.

The flamboyant star died in Los Angeles on 22 November 1980, following a stroke.

Whatever Gets You Thru the Night

A song that John wrote in 1974 after hearing the title line in a TV show concerning alcoholism.

He recorded the number in August 1974 for his *Walls and Bridges* album and Elton John joined him on the track, playing piano and singing along with John.

John had invited Elton to play piano and provide backing vocals on any of the tracks that he particularly liked. He played Elton some tapes of the new songs he'd written and was surprised when he selected 'Whatever Gets You Thru the Night'. This was John's least favourite of the numbers he'd written. John still had reservations about the number but Elton assured him that it was a very commercial offering and was so convinced it could make it to the top that he challenged John, saying that, if the number topped the charts, John should appear on a show with him. John agreed.

The record was released as a single with 'Beef Jerky' on the flip, credited to John Lennon with the Plastic Ono Nuclear Band. The musicians featured on the track were Elton John on organ and piano, Jim Keltner on drums, Eddie Mottau on acoustic guitar, Jesse Ed Davis on guitar, Ken Ascher on clavinet, Klaus Voormann on bass, Arthur Jenkins on percussion and Bobby Keyes on tenor saxophone. John played guitar, but credited himself as Hon. John S John Johnson.

The single was issued in America on Apple 1874 on 23 September 1974 and reached No. 1 in the charts there on 16 November, becoming John's first No. 1 solo single since the Beatles' break-up. As a result of the record's success, John fulfilled the promise he'd made to Elton by appearing on his Madison Square Garden concert in October.

'Whatever Gets You Thru the Night' was issued in Britain on Apple R5998 on 4 October 1974, but didn't fare so well as it did in the American charts, reaching only No. 24.

Commenting on the number, John was later to say, 'That was a novelty record. It's the only one I've done since I left the Beatles to get to number one. We didn't get a good take on the musicians, but I quite like the words. It was more commercial than, say, "Imagine", but in my opinion "Imagine" should have been number one and "Whatever Gets You Thru the Night" should have been number thirty-nine. It just doesn't make sense. Who knows?'

Whatever Gets You Thru the Night (promo)

John produced this film, shot on a sunny afternoon in New York City on 16mm colour film. John wandered around New York dressed completely in black – black hat, coat, trousers, shoes – filming anything that crossed his path. One clip featured the exterior of the Beacon Theater, which was featuring the musical *Sergeant Pepper's Lonely Hearts Club Band*, and John homed in on a part of the poster reading 'John Lennon & Paul McCartney'. He is seen in Central Park, filmed in Times Square and filmed many of the people he met, including truck drivers and street beggars. He is also seen entering the doors of Tiffany & Co., the famous jewellers, and is seen emerging eating a hot dog – a reference to *Breakfast at Tiffany's*?

Whatever Happened To ...

One of several home demo numbers John taped during the closing months of 1977. He never developed it into a full-scale recording.

What Goes On

A song credited to John, Paul and Ringo. John was to say, 'This was a very early song of mine, but Ringo and Paul wrote a new middle eight together when we recorded it.' It was the first track on the second side of the *Rubber Soul* album and was recorded on 4 November 1965.

What's The New Mary Jane

John claimed he wrote the number with Alexis Mardas, even though it is copyrighted to Lennon/McCartney. He began recording it on Wednesday 14 August 1968. The number was originally destined for *The Beatles* double album, but was left off and unreleased officially until the *Anthology 3* CDs in October 1996. However, two bootleg versions of the song had been available for years. One was 6 minutes and 35 seconds in length, the other 7 minutes and 7 seconds – and both were issued under the title 'What a Shame Mary Jane Had a Pain at the Party'.

The only Beatles performing on the number were John and George, with John as the solo vocalist. On Thursday 11

September 1969, since the Beatles still hadn't put it out, he went to the Abbey Road studios and asked for stereo mixes of the previous recording. He then had them put on a 7½-inch spool and took it away. John wanted the song released and even considered issuing it as a Plastic Ono Band single. On Wednesday 26 November 1969 the Beatles recorded new overdubs of the number, intending it to become the flip side of 'You Know My Name (Look Up the Number)', but the planned single wasn't released.

As 'Mary Jane' is a slang term for marijuana there were naturally the suggestions that it was a drugs song.

What You Got

A song written by John in the style of Carl Perkins, of which he originally made a home demo in June 1974. It was another of the numbers in which he was pleading for a reconciliation with Yoko, noticeable in lines such as 'give me one more chance' and 'you don't know what you got until you lose it'.

He recorded the number in August 1974 during the *Walls and Bridges* album sessions and it was included on the album. John plays guitar using the pseudonym Kaptain Kundalini and other musicians include Ken Ascher on clavinet, Nicky Hopkins on piano, Klaus Voormann on bass and Jim Keltner on drums.

The song was also issued as the flip side of the 'No. 9 Dream' single.

When A Boy Meets A Girl

An unreleased song that John composed in the autumn of 1970 when he made a home demo of it, accompanying himself on acoustic guitar. It was one of the compositions he began working on following his primal therapy and was considered but rejected for the *John Lennon/Plastic Ono Band* album. In all, John cut two composing demos of the song, which was finally aired in public on *The Lost Lennon Tapes* series.

When I Get Home

A song that John wrote for the soundtrack album *A Hard Day's Night,* recorded by the Beatles on 2 June 1964. He was to say, 'That's me again, another Wilson Pickett, Motown sound, a four-in-the-bar cowbell song.'

Where It's At

A BBC Radio 1 show. On 25 November 1967 Kenny Everett interviewed John for the programme. John was to discuss his song 'I Am The Walrus', which Everett then played. As it turned out, it was the last time the record was played on BBC radio for a number of years because the BBC then decided to ban it because of the mention of the word 'knickers'.

White, Alan

A drummer, born in Pelton, County Durham, on 14 June 1949. Terry Doran, head of Apple Publishing and later George Harrison's personal assistant, had seen White play and told John he was a good drummer and should get him in his band. John agreed, even though he'd never heard him play – although some reports say John had spotted White playing in a London club. When John decided to fly to Toronto to appear in the *Rock 'n' Roll Revival* concert he phoned White and asked him to become part of the Plastic Ono Band. The different members hadn't played together before and had to rehearse on the plane to Canada. White also appeared as a member of the Plastic Ono Supergroup at the Lyceum Ballroom, the Strand, London, on 15 December 1969.

He appeared on the album *The Plastic Ono Band – Live Peace in Toronto 1969* and on the single 'Instant Karma'.

Recalling the *Imagine* sessions, he said it was recorded with a live vocal and live piano, drums and bass. All the musicians were playing in a studio and filming was taking place at the same time. White had a cameraman around his feet pointing a lens up at him.

As a result of his association with John, White became an established drummer and joined the band Yes in 1972. He was also in demand for recording sessions with artists such as George Harrison, Joe Cocker and Alan Price.

White, Carol

British actress who rose to fame in the mid-1960s with the starring role in a TV play about the plight of the homeless called *Cathy Come Home*. She appeared in several other films, notably *Poor Cow*, before moving to America, where she remained during the 1970s. She returned to Britain at the beginning of the 1980s with her third husband Mike Arnold and in November 1982 her autobiography *Carol Comes Home* was published.

In it she related how she first met John in a Chelsea boutique. She was having a chat with him when Yoko, who had been trying on a black minidress, came up, ignored her and said to John, 'Well, what do you think of it?' John said, 'Not a lot,' and she retorted, 'You never like anything,' and stormed back to the changing room.

White admitted that she didn't like Yoko. She was biased by the fact that she preferred John's first wife, Cynthia.

She died in 1991 at the age of 47.

Why Is John Lennon Wearing a Shirt?

A one-woman play by Clair Dowie. It opened at the Oval House Theatre in London in January 1991. The play related the thoughts of a fourteen-year-old girl who identified with Lennon.

Wiener, Jon

History professor of the University of California whose researches for a book on John Lennon uncovered previously unreleased material about the attempt to have John deported from America. Wiener had spent 14 years trying to compel the FBI to release its file on John Lennon to him. He eventually received a 300-page dossier – even then, ten pages were still withheld. He also received $204,000 compensation for his legal expenses.

Under the American Freedom of Information Act, Wiener was able to study, in 1983, FBI and Immigration files which had previously been unavailable to the public. He discovered that former President Richard Nixon supported a campaign to discredit John and have him deported before the Republican conference in 1972.

The President actually believed that John's activities in America could cost him the election. John was involved with a number of American radicals at the time and was being used to gain publicity for various causes such as that of freeing John Sinclair. Nixon was told that John could be used to spearhead a mass anti-Nixon demonstration before the Miami Convention.

The late Edgar J. Hoover, head of the FBI, had been instructed to obtain evidence against John that could lead to his arrest on drug charges and subsequent deportation proceedings. As a result, John's New York apartment was bugged and the FBI sent reports of John's daily activities to the CIA, the Secret Service and Bob Haldeman, presidential aide to Nixon.

Wiener discovered that the FBI harassed and followed Lennon over a period of several years and schemed to arrest him on drug charges so he could be easily deported. Agents monitored his public appearances, kept tabs on his private life and built a massive file on him.

He published a critically acclaimed book of his researches, *Come Together: John Lennon In His Time* in 1984 and a follow-up book *Gimme Some Truth* was published in 2000.

On 18 February 2000 Professor Wiener won a 17-year legal battle with the FBI to see ten documents about John Lennon that originated in Britain and revealed that the MI5 and MI6 intercepted his phone calls and letters while John lived at Tittenhurst Park in Britain in the late 1960s and also bugged his home. Papers relating to this were passed over to the FBI when John was fighting the Immigration authorities in America.

Wiener had already received most of the FBI files on John, but took on the FBI again in order to obtain the final files which they had refused to hand over. The FBI issued a statement; 'If they were US documents, we would release them. They are not a threat to national security. Their release would be damaging not because of content but because it would undermine the trust and faith that the foreign service involved has in our intelligence service to keep documents secret.

'They [the British] don't want these pages released because they show Lennon was being monitored in ways that may now prove to be embarrassing.'

Wiener added wryly, 'This is not national security information. It is 30-year-old reports on the political activities of a dead rock star.'

Wildes, Leon

A New York immigration attorney who was hired by John and Yoko to represent them in their dispute with the immigration authorities in the US. When the authorities were moving to separate their cases and assign them to different judges, Wildes had them dress in identical black suits, white shirts and black ties, advising them to hold hands throughout the hearing to show they were a pair and shouldn't be separated.

On 23 March 1973, Yoko's application for permanent residency in the States was granted, but John's was rejected. He had 60 days in which to leave the country. Wildes was granted an extension on appeal. He joined John on the NBC TV programme *Tomorrow,* hosted by Tom Snyder, on 28 April 1975, when they discussed the progress of John's case for obtaining his green card.

Wildes fought the courts on John's behalf for three years, eventually winning a federal court decision which now prevents anyone being deported for a minor violation committed outside the United States.

Williams, Larry

One of John's seminal influences, and an American artist who influenced many of the Mersey Beat groups, dozens of whom performed his songs, including Howie Casey and the Seniors, the Swinging Blue Jeans and the Escorts. Williams, who was born on 10 May 1935, had begun his musical career as a session pianist with Lloyd Price before branching out as a recording artist and composer in his own right.

John was to take over on lead vocals when the Beatles recorded three of his numbers: 'Slow Down', 'Bad Boy' and 'Dizzy Miss Lizzie'.

John was also to record 'Bonie Moronie' on his *Rock 'n' Roll* album.

Tragically, Williams died of self-inflicted gunshot wounds on 7 January 1980.

Williams, Paul

A senior producer of BBC's Radio 1, who was responsible for setting up the famous John Lennon–Andy Peebles interview. Originally, he and Peebles, together with the executive producer, Doreen Davies, had planned to travel to America to interview David Bowie, a project that was subsequently broadcast on 5 January 1981.

Arrangements were made for them to meet John and Yoko at the Hit Factory on 6 December 1980 and the interview continued for a total of three hours, with Paul and Andy carrying on their conversations with John and Yoko over dinner.

The pair were naturally horrified when they arrived back in London on the morning of 9 December to be informed of John's murder. They spent the day editing excerpts from the interview, which were broadcast immediately. They then arranged for the full five-part series to be broadcast on Sundays from 18 January 1981. The broadcasts have been aired on several other occasions.

Will the Real Mr Sellers ...

A BBC television documentary about Peter Sellers. It was directed by Tony Palmer and produced by Denis O'Dell. The 50-minute programme was broadcast on Thursday 18 December 1969 between 9.10 and 10 p.m.

Footage from the feature film *The Magic Christian* was used, along with some taken at the party held at Les Ambassadeurs club in London to celebrate the end of filming on Sunday 4 May 1969. The Beatles were present at the party and Paul was among the celebrities interviewed, while John was to be seen standing in the background.

Winston's Walk

One of John's early compositions, along with 'One After 909', which he wrote in Paul McCartney's Forthlin Road house in Liverpool. 'Winston's Walk' was an instrumental and John included it in the repertoire of the Quarry Men, but it was never recorded. The title most likely referred to John himself, as his middle name was Winston.

Winter, Johnny

His album *John Dawson Winter*, released on 25 November 1974, included John's song 'Rock 'n' Roll People'.

Winters, Shelley

Blonde movie star who graduated from glamour-girl roles to dramatic parts and eventually settled down to character and cameo appearances. Her films include *Lolita* and *Alfie*.

She was one of the famous neighbours of the Lennons in the Dakota Building in New York. Following John's murder she began to wear disguises whenever she ventured out of the building.

'I wear a wig and dark glasses and am driven around in a little Toyota, so I don't look like a movie star,' she said.

With the Beatles

The Beatles' second album, recorded between 18 July and 23 October 1963, was released in the UK on 22 November 1963. It went to No. 1 in the charts, replacing the *Please Please Me* album. *With the Beatles* was also only the second album in British chart history to sell a million copies in the UK, the first being the *South Pacific* soundtrack. The American release was called *Meet the Beatles*, and excluded five of the tracks on the original album and replaced them with three others. John wrote 'It Won't Be Long', 'All I've Got To Do' and 'Not a Second Time'. His collaborations with Paul were 'Little Child', 'Hold Me Tight' and 'I Wanna Be Your Man'.

Woman

The haunting, evocative love song obviously inspired by Yoko that was originally featured on the *Double Fantasy* album. In the context of the album, John described it as 'the Beatles track' and 'an 80s version of "Girl".'

When recording it, John described the number to his backing musicians as being 'early Motown/Beatles '64. It's for your mother or your sister, anyone of the female race. That's who you're singing to.' He saw it as an updated version of the track 'Girl' from the *Rubber Soul* album. When issued as a single, following John's death, it topped the charts in Britain.

Discussing the song in a BBC interview, he said, 'It sounds a bit like "Girl" and a bit Beatle-y, but I do like it.' He went on to observe, 'I'm supposed to be macho. Butch Cassidy or something and tough Lennon with the leather jacket and swearing. And I really am just as romantic as the next guy, and I always was. It's sort of an eighties version of "Girl" to me. I call this one the Beatle track.'

He added, 'It suddenly sort of hit me about what women represent to us, not as the sex object or the mother, but just their contribution. That's why you hear the muttering at the beginning "For the other half of the sky", which is Chairman Mao's famous statement. That it is the other half. All this thing about man, woman, man, woman is a joke. Without each other there ain't nothing.

'It was a different viewpoint of what I'd felt about woman and I can't express it better than I said in the song.'

Following John's death, it was issued in America on 5 January 1981 on Geffen GEF 49644 and in Britain on 16 January on Geffen K 79195. It became a chart-topper on both sides of the Atlantic, first entering the British charts at No. 3 and reaching No. 1 the following week on 7 February, simultaneously with the album *Double Fantasy,* which reached the top of the album charts.

The single was among the shoal of releases in the wake of the tragedy and there was a blitz of John's material issued, producing a chart domination that hadn't been seen since the initial impact of the Beatles in America in 1964.

John's posthumous hit singles within a short period of time included three No. 1's: '(Just Like) Starting Over', 'Woman' and 'Imagine', in addition to hits with 'Give Peace a Chance', 'Happy Xmas (War Is Over)' and three Top 20 albums.

There were also two Beatles albums in the chart at that time, as well as the single featuring John's duet with Elton John on 'I Saw Her Standing There'.

'Woman' went on to win several awards, including a Grammy and an Ivor Novello Award.

The backing musicians were session men from New York and included Tony Levin on bass, Arthur Jenkins on percussion, George Small on piano, Earl Slick and Hugh McCracken on guitars and Andy Newmark on drums. The flip side was Yoko Ono's 'Beautiful Boys'.

Incidentally, Paul McCartney had written a song called 'Woman', some years previously, which had been recorded by Peter and Gordon.

Woman Is the Nigger of the World

Under Yoko's tutelage, John became interested in the feminist movement. He was intrigued by something Yoko said during an interview in *Nova* magazine, published in March 1969: 'woman is the nigger of the world'.

John remembered the words and recorded a song of the same name on the album *Sometime in New York City.*

John was to say, 'It was actually the first women's liberation song that went out. It was before Helen Reddy's "I Am Woman".'

He added, 'It was talked about. It got the message across. The whole story is the title, the lyrics are just a fill-in. I felt the lyrics didn't live up to Yoko's title.'

The song made its debut on *The Dick Cavett Show*, recorded on Friday 5 May 1972 and transmitted on Thursday 11 May.

The executives at ABC TV initially wanted to cut the number from the broadcast, but Cavett insisted it be used. As a result he was allowed to record an explanation of why he felt the song had to be included, which was broadcast prior to the transmission.

It was reasoned that the use of the word 'nigger' could cause offence. John then gained the support of Ron Dellums, chairman of the Congressional Black Caucus, who issued a statement that was read out on the Cavett show. 'If you define "nigger" as someone whose lifestyle is defined by others, whose opportunities are defined by others, whose role in society is defined by others, the good news is you don't have to be black to be a nigger in this society. Most of the people in America are niggers.'

Owing to a dispute over copyright, the single wasn't issued in Britain

It was released in the United States only on Monday 24 April 1972, with Yoko's 'Sisters O Sisters' on the flip. Despite its lack of airplay because so many radio stations refused to play it, the record reached No. 57 in the *Billboard* chart.

John was to comment, 'It was banned in America because you couldn't say "nigger".'

He also said, 'It's such a beautiful statement. What she was saying is true. Woman still is the nigger. You can talk about blacks, you can talk about Jews, you can talk about the Third World, you can talk about everything but underlying the whole thing, under the whole crust of it, is the women and beneath them the children.'

Woman Power

One of the numbers penned by Yoko, which she recorded in April 1973 for her *Feeling the Space* album.

The song was issued as the A-side of a Yoko single, released in America on Apple 1867 on 24 September 1973. John played guitar on the track.

The single, produced by Yoko, also featured her singing another of her compositions, 'Men, Men, Men' on the flip side. This was a satirical number on which John appeared at the end in the role of a henpecked husband. One of the lines in the song went: 'J-O-H-N-N-Y, God's little gift to a woman'._

Wonder, Stevie

Born Steveland Judkins on 13 May 1950, in Saginaw, Michigan, Stevie Wonder was blind from birth. As a Motown recording artist, he first came to the attention of the Beatles with his single 'Fingertips'.

In 1971 he recorded a version of a Lennon and McCartney song, 'We Can Work It Out', which reached No. 13 in the American charts and No. 27 in the British. Paul mainly wrote the song, although John was said to have contributed to its middle section.

Wonder joined the bill of the John Sinclair rally on 11/12 December 1971. He heard on the radio that John and Yoko would be performing at the rally and phoned up offering his services. He ended his performance singing 'For Once In My Life', then gave a speech attacking the incumbent President Richard Nixon and his Vice President Spiro Agnew.

Wonder was also one of the artists to offer their services when John and Yoko appeared at the One-To-One concert at Madison Square Garden in New York on 30 August 1972. During the finale, John and Stevie led the cast in singing a reggae version of 'Give Peace a Chance', with John shouting, 'No more war' and Stevie singing, 'Oh baby, say it again!'

Stevie also wrote a letter in support of John for the hearing of his application for a green card.

In 1982, Stevie recorded a hit single with Paul McCartney, 'Ebony and Ivory'.

Wonsaponatime

A 21-track CD issued in a three-part fold-out digipack with a sixteen-page booklet on Monday 2 November 1998. The CD contained highlights from the *John Lennon Anthology* set, omitting spoken intros. The booklet contained lyrics and personnel credits, plus an introduction by Yoko.

Discussing the selection of the material, Yoko said, 'It was hard work making those choices. I wanted to give a fair representation of all the material on the box set, but it's nearly impossible to present an edited version of nearly a hundred tracks, all of which are very special. I hope people will see this as a taste of the *Anthology*. It's being released not only as something that John's fans can enjoy and celebrate, but hopefully as an introduction to his music and thoughts for a new generation of people as well.'

The tracks were: 'I'm Losing You', 'Working Class Hero', 'God', 'How Do You Sleep?', 'Imagine', 'Baby Please Don't Go', 'Oh My Love', 'God Save Oz', 'I Found Out', 'Woman Is the Nigger of the World', 'A Kiss Is Just a Kiss', 'Be-Bop-A-Lula', 'Rip It Up/Ready Teddy', 'What You Got', 'Nobody Loves You When You're Down and Out', 'I Don't Wanna Face It', 'Real Love', 'Only You', 'Grow Old With Me', 'Sean's "In the Sky" ' and 'Serve Yourself'.

Woodstock

The most famous rock festival of them all, which took place on 15 August 1969 in Sullivan County, New York, over a three-day period, attracting half a million people.

The star-studded festival featured many major names, including Jimi Hendrix and the Who. The organisers had attempted to book the Beatles and had written to John Lennon offering to pay whatever sum of money the Beatles demanded to appear. John wrote back saying that the Beatles wouldn't be able to attend, but he offered to perform himself, together with the Plastic Ono Band.

The promoter, Michael Lang, decided to turn down the offer.

Wooler, Bob

The Cavern disc jockey who was an early Beatles champion and helped them to obtain several of their early major local gigs.

When the Beatles had their first official meeting with Brian Epstein in his office, they brought Bob along to observe and advise them. When Brian asked who he was, John told him Bob was his father.

At Paul's 21st birthday party on 18 June 1963, which was attended by various musicians including the Shadows, the Fourmost, the Scaffold and Billy J Kramer, John savagely beat Bob up. Allegedly, Wooler had asked, 'How was the honeymoon, John?' This referred to the fact that John and Brian Epstein had gone on a brief holiday to Spain together in April. John, who had been drinking heavily with Pete Shotton, was furious and knocked Wooler to the ground and began kicking and punching him. Brian Epstein drove Wooler to hospital.

When asked to resolve the matter by apologising to Wooler, John was unrepentant and refused, saying, 'He called me a queer, so I battered his bloody ribs in.' The story leaked and there were a number of press enquiries. Press officer Tony Barrow prepared an apologetic statement, which appeared on the back page of the *Daily Mirror* in a story by Don Short, headed *Beatle In Brawl - Sorry I Socked You*. Barrow had quoted John as saying, 'Bob is the last person in the world I want to have a fight with. I can only hope he realises I was too far gone to know what I was doing.' Brian Epstein instructed his solicitor Rex Makin to make a settlement to Wooler, and he was paid compensation of £200.

Wooler also received a telegram, which read: MR BOB WOOLER FLAT 8 CANNING STREET LIVERPOOL 1 REALLY SORRY BOB TERRIBLY WORRIED TO REALISE WHAT I HAD DONE STOP WHAT MORE CAN I SAY JOHN LENNON

Woolton House

When students entered Quarry Bank School in Liverpool they were divided into houses that were named after the part of the city in which they lived. John, Peter Shotton and Rod Davis were among the pupils in Woolton House.

Words and Music of John Lennon, The

A one-hour BBC Radio One programme, produced by Kevin Howlett, which was broadcast on Sunday 8 December 1985 and repeated on Saturday 6 December 1986.

Working Class Hero

John had revealed to *Rolling Stone*'s boss, Jann Wenner, that he hoped this song would become an anthem for 'the workers'. It was a track from the *John Lennon/Plastic Ono Band* album and, once again, EMI censored the swearwords on the printed lyrics on the album sleeve.

Owing to the simple acoustic nature of the track, reviewers described it as 'Dylanesque', which annoyed John, who was tired of the comparisons made on a number of his songs, and he pointed out that solo acoustic recordings were a part of folk music long before Dylan recorded 'Blowing in the Wind'.

He commented, 'Anybody that sings with a guitar and sings about something heavy would tend to sound like Dylan. The only folk music I know is stuff about miners up in Newcastle, or Dylan. So in that way I've been influenced, but it doesn't sound like Dylan to me.'

Working Class Hero (film)

A 60-minute film directed by John and Yoko in 1971. The film was not released, although portions of it were included in the 1988 film *Imagine: John Lennon*.

Working Class Hero: A Tribute to John Lennon

A tribute album issued in America on Hollywood HR-62015-2 on 10 October 1995. Tracks included 'I Found Out' by the Red Hot Chilli Peppers; 'Working Class Hero' by the Screaming Trees; 'How Do You Sleep?' by the Magnificent Bastards; 'Cold Turkey' by Cheap Trick; 'Power to the People' by the Minus 5; 'Nobody Told Me' by Flaming Lips; 'Isolation' by Sponge; 'Steel and Glass' by Candlebox; 'Instant Karma' by Toad the Wet Sprocket; 'Well Well Well' by Super 8; 'I Don't Wanna Be a Soldier' by Mad Season; 'Jealous Guy' by Ed Roland of Collective Soul; 'Crippled Inside' by Blues Traveler; 'Grow Old With Me' by Mary Chapin Carpenter and 'Mind Games' by George Clinton.

The gatefold sleeve included three photographs of John and there was a booklet with lyrics of each song and a text by David Sheff. Half of the royalties of the album went to a fund set up by the Humane Society to finance the spaying and neutering of cats and dogs.

World of Books, The

BBC radio programme broadcast on the Home Service (now Radio 4). John's interview in which he discussed his new book *A*

Spaniard in the Works, was recorded on 16 June 1965 and broadcast on the show on 3 July that year, nine days after publication of the book.

World of John and Yoko, The
The title of a 35-minute documentary screened on the BBC *24 Hours* programme on 15 December 1970.

WRKO
An American radio station which conducted one of the last interviews with John before his death, when he was promoting the *Double Fantasy* album. Yoko, of course, was also present at the interview, in which John was asked why he'd decided to return to the recording scene.

He said, 'We feel like this is just the start now, this is the "first" album. I know we worked together before, we even made albums together before; we feel like this is the first album. I feel like nothing happened before today. I was possessed by this rock 'n' roll "devil".'

He told of the holiday in Bermuda with Sean in which he became inspired to write songs again. He commented, 'I always felt that the best songs were the ones that came to you. I do have the ability – if you ask me to write a song for a movie or something, I can sort of sit down and make a song. I wouldn't be thrilled with it but I can make a song like that ... I call it "craftsmanship" but I like it to be inspirational – from the spirit. Being with Sean and switching off from the business allowed that channel to be free for a bit. It was switched off and, when I switched it on again, zap! – all this stuff came through. We did enough material for the second album and now we're talking about the third album; so we're full of vim and vigour!'

Discussing Sean, John said, 'He was born on October 9, which I was, so we're almost like twins. If he doesn't see me for a few days or if I'm really, really busy and I just get a glimpse of him or if I'm feeling depressed, without him even seeing me, he sort of picks up on it and he starts getting that way. Something will make me depressed and there's no way I can deal with it and then he'll get a cold or trap his finger in the door. So now I have more reason to stay healthy and bright. I think it's better for him to see me as I am; if I'm grumpy, I'm grumpy. I don't kowtow to him.'

Then he mentioned an incident between himself and Sean.

'I hadn't been in the studio for five years or whatever, so he's used to me being around all the time. I was always a homebody. I started to work and he started seeing a bit less of me. One day we were sort of lying down on the bed together, maybe watching some cartoon or whatever, and he just sat up and said, "You know what I want to be when I grow up?" I said, "No, what's that?" He looked me right in the eye and said, "Just a daddy." I said, "You mean you don't like me when I'm working?" He said, "Right." '

John then explained to him that making records made him happy and therefore he was a better daddy because of it.

Discussing his public image, John said, 'I was most uncomfortable when I didn't feel that I was being myself ... when I'd have to smile when I didn't want to smile ... it became like being a politician ... I like to be liked. I don't like to offend people. I would like to be a happy, contented person. I don't want to have to sell my soul again, as it were, to have a hit record. I've discovered that I can live without it and I'm not going to come back in and create a persona who would not be myself.'

He also discussed Paul McCartney. 'Paul and I developed in public, as it were. We had a little rehearsal in private but mainly we devoted our abilities in public ... but then it got to be format and sort of not the pleasure that it was. The person who I actually picked as my partner, who I recognised had talent and I could get on with, was Paul.'

Discussing his 'lost weekend' away from Yoko he said, 'I really, really wanted to be with her, needed to be with her and could not literally survive without her as a functioning human being. I just went to pieces and I just realised that I needed her so much. I realised that I needed her more than she needed me and I always thought that the boot was on the other foot.'

He also revealed how reluctant he'd been to get involved with Yoko's avant-garde projects in the late 1960s. 'Some of the ideas she wanted both of us to do then – I must say that I was more "square" then than I am now in a way – I wish we'd done, because now other people have done them.'

John continued to dwell on his partnership with Yoko. 'I wouldn't enjoy just putting an album out by myself, having to do things by myself. I didn't want to work with another guy even. We're presenting ourselves as a couple and to work with your best friend is a joy. I don't intend to stop it.

John went on to describe how, during the recording of *Sometime in New York City*, he and Yoko joked about how making the album was like publishing a newspaper, and they were trying to rush it 'into print'.

Consequently, John and Yoko did not deliberate on clarity of tracks, overdubbing or harmonies.

'I started feeling down about that record – it was a mistake. We tried to say something about love and peace and we got into so much trouble. Politics were in the air in those days – you couldn't avoid it. We wanted to be right there down on the front line. Our intentions were good.

'I still believe in love, peace; I still believe in positive thinking. I'm not always positive but, when I am, I try to project it. We're going into an unknown future.'

John discussed several other topics during the interview, including providing a clarification of some of the lyrics to 'Imagine' and the fact that all achievements eventually begin as an idea in someone's mind.

Poignantly, with John's new confidence and optimism for the future, he was to say that his work wouldn't be finished 'until I'm dead and buried – and I hope that's a long, long time'.

Ya Ya

A number John originally sang and recorded on his *Walls and Bridges* album, issued in October 1974.

Morris Robinson, Clarence Lewis and Lee Dorsey penned the song. John's son Julian was eleven at the time of the recording and sat on drums for an impromptu session, which is why John credits himself as 'Dad' on the track listing.

'Ya Ya' is the last track on the album and is only 1 minute and 3 seconds long. John originally included it as a sop to the publisher Morris Levy because of a dispute that resulted from John's having admitted that he based his number 'Come Together' on Chuck Berry's 'You Can't Catch Me', published by Levy.

John was to comment, 'It was a contractual obligation to Morris Levy. It was a humiliation and I regret having to be in that position, but I did it. That's the way it turned out. Julian was playing the drums and I just left on the piano and sang "Ya ya".'

Levy was still not satisfied, despite the royalties, and John then recorded the number again with studio musicians for his *Rock 'n' Roll* album, issued in February 1975.

The term 'Ya Ya' referred to a boy- or girlfriend in the original song that gave the ex-boxer-turned-singer Lee Dorsey a million-seller in 1961. It was also a British hit for Petula Clark, reaching

No. 14 in the charts in the same year, and by now called 'Ya Ya Twist'.

Year One
Title given by John to the year 1970.

As from January of that year he decided that he and Yoko would devote the ensuing twelve months to their peace campaign and make it 'Year One for Peace'.

John mentioned that a Canadian friend had come up with the idea that the New Year should not be called AD 1970. 'Everyone who is into peace and awareness will regard the New Year as Year One AP – for After Peace. All of our letters and calendars from now on will use this method,' he said.

John was also to write, 'We believe that the last decade was the end of the old machine crumbling to pieces. And we think we can get it together, with your help. We have great hopes for the New Year.'

Ye Cracke
A public house in Rice Street, Liverpool L1. It was the nearest pub to the Liverpool College of Art. During a college party, John went across to Cynthia Powell and asked her for a dance. Cynthia, who had a crush on John but was too nervous to admit it, panicked and said, 'I'm awfully sorry, but I'm engaged to a fellow in Hoylake.' Annoyed, John snapped, 'I didn't ask you to marry me.' When the dance was over, John invited Cynthia to Ye Cracke for a drink and later that evening he took her to the Gambier Terrace flat and they made love for the first time.

Arthur Ballard, one of the college lecturers, used to tutor some of his pupils in the 'War Office', a tiny room in the college so named because it had regularly been used to discuss the events of the Crimean War as they occurred.

Once when they were standing outside the pub one lunchtime, drinks in hand, John and Cynthia spotted the actor John Gregson (a Liverpool-born British film star whose most popular film was *Genevieve*). John desperately looked around for something unusual for the actor to sign. He spotted an old boot and asked Gregson to autograph it. The actor was amused by the gesture and signed it across the stitching.

The painter and poet Adrian Henri remembered one incident

at Ye Cracke during which John was lying on the floor miming swimming movements. A barmaid told him to stop and he said, 'I can't stop, or I'll drown!'

John and Stuart Sutcliffe also used to discuss art and artists, with Sutcliffe filling John in with the background to art movements of the early twentieth century such as the Dada school.

Bill Harry and John also used to have long conversations together in their favourite seat, beneath an etching of *The Death of Nelson*. Bill once told John that he'd heard he wrote poetry and asked if he could see some. At first embarrassed, because he liked to maintain his macho image, John then produced a sample. It was a piece of rustic wit, which Harry found both amusing and charming. He was particularly pleased to note it was in the English tradition of comic humour, in contrast to the Beat poetry of San Francisco which so many British poets were copying. Harry remembered this when he commissioned John to write a piece about the origin of the Beatles for his magazine, *Mersey Beat*.

When Lennon, Sutcliffe, Rod Murray and Harry used to chat in the evenings, Harry suggested that the four of them call themselves the Dissenters and attempt to make Liverpool famous: John with his music, Stuart and Rod with their paintings and Bill with his writing.

Yellow Submarine (album)

At the time *Yellow Submarine* was being made, the Beatles weren't too enthusiastic about the venture. Initially they had believed that making the film would terminate their United Artists film contract, but this wasn't so – the contract applied only to their live appearances and not animated images. They were to warm to the venture only later on, owing to its critical success. Therefore, when it came to providing songs for it, they didn't exert much effort and the resulting album comprised only six Beatles numbers, with the rest of the album made up of George Martin orchestrations.

The album was issued in the UK on 17 January 1969 and reached No. 3 in the charts (*The Beatles*, the so-called 'White' album, was still in the No. 1 position) and issued in the US on 13 January 1969, reaching No. 2. John's contributions were 'Hey Bulldog' and 'All You Need Is Love'.

Yer Blues

During a period of almost two months at the Maharishi's ashram in Rishikesh, India, John and Paul wrote almost thirty new songs. Among those composed by John during this period was 'Yer Blues'.

The Beatles recorded the number on Wednesday 14 August 1968 for *The Beatles* double album. Later the same year, during the filming of *The Rolling Stones Rock 'n' Roll Circus* on 10 and 11 December, John also performed this parody of the British blues boom, with backing from Eric Clapton on guitar, Keith Richard on bass and Mitch Mitchell on drums. John's name for this particular line-up was Winston Legthigh and the Dirty Macs.

John performed the number live on 13 September 1969 at the *Toronto Rock 'n' Roll Revival* festival, backed by the Plastic Ono Band – Eric Clapton, guitar, Klaus Voormann, bass guitar, Alan White, drums. The performance was recorded and issued in December 1969 as *The Plastic Ono Band – Live Peace In Toronto 1969*.

Ying-Tong Song, The

John was a fan of the Goons and bought this 78-r.p.m. record when it was issued on Decca F10780 in 1956. John, ever delighted by unusual names, would have been amused when he discovered that Maurice Ponke and his Orchestre Fromage backed the Goons. He purchased the record with money he received for his sixteenth birthday.

Yoko Ono: A Life After John

A fifteen-minute BBC programme broadcast on Friday 6 December 1985 and based on an interview which Andy Peebles conducted with Yoko at the Dakota Building apartments. It was transmitted immediately after the *Everyman* programme 'John Lennon: A Journey In His Life' which starred Bernard Hill.

Yoko Ono, Arias and Objects

A paperback penned by Barbara Haskell and John Hanhardt and published in America in 1991 by Peregrine Smith Books.

The book covers Yoko Ono's artistic works from the 60s to

the present day. Hanhardt was curator of film and video at the Whitney Museum of American Art and Haskell was curator of painting and sculpture there.

Complete with rare photographs, illuminating illustrations and insightful text, it affords the reader a unique opportunity to appreciate Yoko's work.

Reproductions of posters, newspaper clippings and quotes from Yoko about her work offer a solid background, particularly to her early work in New York with the Fluxus group. There is also a section of the book that presents a number of her works, including *Cloud Piece*, which was John's inspiration for 'Imagine'; the performing work *Cut Piece* and *Music of the Mind*, which includes a piece John and Yoko performed in 1972.

Yoko Ono (biography)

An unauthorised biography by Jerry Hopkins, contributor to *Rolling Stone* and author of books such as the Jim Morrison biography *No One Gets Out of Here Alive*, *Bowie* and *Elvis, The Final Years*. Yoko refused to be interviewed for the book, possibly because she had co-operated with interviews for Peter Brown's *The Love You Make*, which turned out to be a 'kiss-and-tell' account, rather than a book about the 1960s, which Brown had assured interviewees it would be.

The main 'revelation' seemed to be the contention that Yoko had set her sights on getting John's wealth to fund her art and knew all about him when she held her exhibition at the Indica Gallery. Hopkins presents it as a calculated and planned move by Yoko and her husband Tony Cox to ensnare John.

Allan Kaprow, a 'happenings' artist who used to sail with Tony Cox and Yoko in Cox's father's boat, recalled an incident in 1966. 'One day Tony was skippering the boat and Yoko told me she had a close interest in the Beatles. She said she had seen them in Japan. My memory was very clear. She said, half laughingly, "I'd like to marry John Lennon." '

Hopkins was to say 'This story is confirmed by others who knew Yoko in New York, although it is unlikely that she actually saw the Beatles in Japan, since they didn't appear there during the period of her residence. Possibly she saw them on television or, just as likely, on American television during the summer of 1966.'

The book was published in the US by Macmillan and in the UK by Sidgwick & Jackson in 1987, with a blurb that begins, 'Black widow, dragon lady, Mrs John Lennon, the woman who broke up the Beatles, millionairess, philanthropist, avant-garde artist, pop superstar – who is the real Yoko Ono?'

Yoko Ono/Plastic Ono Band

An album Yoko recorded at the same time as John was recording his *John Lennon/Plastic Ono Band* album. Both had undergone primal therapy and each album was their inspiration from it. Produced by John and Yoko, the album was issued on 11 December 1970, the same date as John's album. In the UK it was issued on Apple SAPCOR 17 and in the US on Apple SW 3373. The tracks were: Side One: 'Why', 'Why Not?', 'Greenfield Morning I Pushed An Empty Baby Carriage all Over The City'; Side Two: 'AOS', 'Touch Me', 'Paper Shoes'.

Yoko Ono: Then and Now

An American documentary, made in 1983. It was produced, written and narrated by Barbara Graustark. It was screened in Britain on the ITV network on Saturday 8 December 1984 between 11.46 p.m. and 12.28 a.m. The documentary presented Yoko as a major artist and included clips of her early 'happenings' such as *Cut Piece* and the film *Bottoms*.

There were snatches of the Lennons' home movies, together with newsreel footage, an excerpt from *The Mike Douglas Show*, clips from *Imagine* and promos of Yoko's 'Walking On Thin Ice' and 'Goodbye Sadness'. Yoko was interviewed and was seen recording an album. Paul and Linda McCartney were also featured, talking about John and Yoko. Polygram Video/Media Entertainment issued the home video on 14 October 1984.

Yoko Ono's Response

A radio programme whose full title was *Westwood One Special Report: Yoko Ono's Response*. Elliot Mintz hosted it and the sixty-minute interview was Yoko's answer to the many allegations put forward by Albert Goldman in his recently published book *The Lives of John Lennon*. Radio stations syndicated it across America on 14 September 1988.

Yoko: The Film Maker

A feature article written by Henry Edwards, which was published in *Crawdaddy* magazine on 27 August 1971.

Yorke, Anne

Australian photographer based in Toronto who teamed up on several occasions with the Canadian rock journalist Ritchie Yorke. Anne covered the Lennons' Canadian Peace Trip in December 1969 and a selection of her photographs of that particular tour are featured in the Anthony Fawcett book *One Day at a Time*.

Yorke, Ritchie

Australian-born, Canadian-based journalist, who became closely involved with John and Yoko's activities during 1969 and 1970, having initially interviewed John about his 'War Is Over' campaign for the *Toronto Globe and Mail*. At one time he literally became a peace envoy for John when he travelled to several countries around the world, including Italy, Australia and Japan promoting the 'War Is Over' campaign. When in Hong Kong, together with the singer Ronnie Hawkins, he went to the border of the People's Republic of China with the slogans and almost caused an international incident.

John had requested that Yorke 'dig the dirt' about Allen Klein and he compiled a dossier of information based on his enquiries with various people. John asked him to bring it over to Denmark for him to see – he'd gone to a farmhouse in the Jutland region to visit Tony Cox and Kyoko.

Yorke arranged for John and Yoko to stay at Hawkins's ranch while they were in Canada and he also arranged the famous meeting between John and Yoko and the Canadian Prime Minister, Pierre Trudeau.

Another idea of Yorke's was to hold a John and Yoko peace festival at Mosport Park in Toronto and make it the world's biggest ever rock festival. It was to be organised by the Brower and Walker agency, but logistical and organisational problems meant it never happened.

Yorke also wrote several features on John for *Rolling Stone* magazine.

You Are Here

Title of John's first art exhibition, which opened at the Robert Fraser Gallery, Duke Street, Mayfair, London W1, on 1 July 1968. The show was dedicated: 'To Yoko from John, With Love'.

John and Yoko stepped outside the gallery and released 365 helium-filled white balloons, each of which had a note attached which read, 'You are here – please write to John Lennon, c/o the Robert Fraser Gallery'.

John mentioned that the inspiration came to him when he remembered the delight he'd felt on discovering a balloon with a note attached when he was a child. There were a number of replies, but they were mainly attacks on his relationship with Yoko. John's art adviser, Anthony Fawcett, commented, 'Replies came in by the hundreds, objecting to John's upcoming divorce from Cynthia, his association with Yoko, his wealth, his long hair and his presumption at stepping into the preserve of art.'

One of his main exhibits was a huge white circular canvas in the centre of which John had written 'You are here.' There were also a number of collection boxes for charities such as the Sons of the Divine Providence and the National Canine Defence League. John had also left a hat on which he'd written, 'For the artist. Thank you', which people began to fill with coins.

Some students from Hornsey College of Art sent along a rusty old bike with the note, 'This exhibit was inadvertently left out' – and John promptly included it in the exhibition.

You Are Here (slogan)

Seen on a badge John wore in 1968. While he was appearing on *The David Frost Show,* Frost asked him about the badge and he said, 'People read it and suddenly realise it's true. Yes, I'm here, they think. So are these other people. We're all here together. And that's where the vibrations start being exchanged. Good and bad ones according to who is sending out and how they feel.'

You Are Here (song)

John based the title of the song on the conceptual exhibition he staged in London in 1968. John begins the song with the word 'nine', which was his special number. This was a song in which he considers the meeting of East and West, as reflected in his romance with Yoko, which he saw as bringing together the cities of Liverpool and Tokyo. He began recording the song in August 1973 and it was included on the *Mind Games* album.

You Can't Catch Me

A song penned and recorded by Chuck Berry. John included part of the number as a tribute to Berry on his song 'Come Together', basically by beginning the number with some lines from Berry's song. He'd always acknowledged Berry as a seminal influence and commented, 'Chuck Berry's lyrics were intelligent. In the fifties, when people were singing about virtually nothing, he was writing social comment, songs with an incredible metre to the lyrics, which influenced Dylan, me, and many other people.' As a result of 'Come Together', Morris Levy, the publisher, sued him. A deal he made to solve the problem was to record a couple of Berry numbers on forthcoming albums and he included 'You Can't Catch Me' on his *Rock 'n' Roll* album.

You Can't Do That

A song penned by John on which he sang lead vocals, with harmony backing by Paul and George. The backing track was recorded at the Pathe Marconi Studios in Paris on 29 January 1964 and the vocals recorded at Abbey Road on 25 February and 22 May 1964. The number was included on the *A Hard Day's Night* album. Of all the tracks on the LP, this was the one John was proudest of and he played lead guitar on it with his newly acquired Rickenbacker. George played twelve-string guitar for the first time on a Beatles recording. It was a blues-influenced, R&B style number. John was later to admit that he had been partly inspired by Wilson Pickett (the Soul singer who was to have a hit with 'Hey Jude' in 1969). It's a number with some aggression in which John tells his girl that if he catches her talking to another boy he'll leave her straight away.

John was later to say in an interview in *Melody Maker*, 'I find it a drag to play rhythm guitar all the time. I like to work out something interesting to play. The best example is what I did on "You Can't Do That". There wasn't really a lead guitarist and a rhythm guitarist on that because rhythm guitar is too thin for records.'

'You Can't Do That' was issued as the flipside of 'Can't Buy

Me Love', released on 20 March 1964 in the UK and on 16 March 1964 in the US. It was also included on *Rock 'N' Roll*. In November 1995 it was included on the *Anthology 1* CDs.

You Know My Name (Look Up the Number)
A song John initially began composing in November 1966 when he recorded it as a home demo. The Beatles made recordings for the backing track of the song on 17 May and 7 and 8 June of the following year, with Brian Jones of the Rolling Stones contributing a saxophone solo at the invitation of Paul. However, as John hadn't finished writing the lyrics, the track was not completed until 30 April 1969 when John and Paul completed the vocals.

The track was finally issued as the flip side of the 'Let It Be' single on 6 March 1970.

It was included on *Past Masters Volume II*.

Young Justice
An American comic series published by DC Comics. The February 1999 issue featured a fictional story inspired by John's murder.

You Really Got a Hold On Me
A song written by Smokey Robinson for the Miracles, which the Beatles included on their *With the Beatles* album. John was lead vocalist on the number when the Beatles recorded it on Thursday 18 July 1963. Discussing the Beatles' version in 1964, he told the interviewer Valerie Wilmer, 'Oh, God, I can't stand that now! I never like any cover we do, though at that time it was really a vogue cover. No one in England had heard of the Miracles then. But it always embarrasses me – it's me trying to do a coloured voice and I can't do it.'

You Saved My Soul
John recorded a home demo tape of this number in November 1980. With its autobiographical, self-analytical lyric, it relates how Yoko saved John from a suicide attempt in New York. It was a time when they were on the West Side of the city and John went to throw himself out of an apartment window, but was prevented from doing so by Yoko.

The number was one of the many home demos by John that were broadcast during *The Lost Lennon Tapes* series.

Young Americans

A David Bowie album issued on RCA JB 10320 in June 1975. John appeared on two tracks, with his own 'Across the Universe' number and with 'Fame', which he co-wrote with Bowie and Carlos Alomar.

Young Lennon

Script by Ray Connelly for a projected film from Warner Brothers. Connelly, who had scripted the acclaimed British rock movies *That'll Be the Day* and *Stardust,* completed a screenplay that, arguably, could have become a major rock movie. The film concentrated on John's early years and closed when he began to play at the Cavern. Instead, Yoko and Warners then did a deal in which Yoko offered access to her archives and *Imagine* was made instead.

Young Lennon, The

A 174-page book in the Spanish language by Jordi Sierra i Farra, published by Ediciones SM in February 1995.

You're Gonna Lose That Girl

A composition by John that was recorded on Friday 19 February 1965 and included on the soundtrack album *Help!* The song was recorded in the afternoon and was the last track recorded for the album before the group flew off to the Bahamas for the filming of the movie.

Your Mother Wouldn't Like It

A programme on the London station Capital Radio. John recorded an interview for the show with the disc jockey Nicky Horne by transatlantic phone on Tuesday 9 April 1974. The interview was transmitted the next evening between 9 and 10.59 p.m.

You've Got to Hide Your Love Away

The Bob Dylan influence was apparent in this number, as John explained: 'This was written in my Dylan days for the film,

Help! When I was a teenager I used to write poetry, but I was always trying to hide my real feelings.

'I was in Kenwood [the house in Weybridge] and I would just be songwriting and so every day I would attempt to write a song and it's one of those that you sort of sing a bit sadly to yourself, "Here I stand, hand in hand ..." '

The track was featured on the *Help!* album and was also given to the Silkie to record as a single. The Silkie were a folk group from Hull University, comprising Sylvia Tatler (vocals), Mike Ramsden (guitar/vocals), Ivor Aylesbury (guitar/vocals) and Kevin Cunningham (double bass). They had been signed by Brian Epstein.

Since the Silkie were part of the same NEMS stable, on the urging of Brian Epstein, John and Paul decided to co-produce the single for the group, with Paul playing guitar and George Harrison making an appearance on tambourine. With its Dylanesque flavour, the number was an ideal song for the Silkie, who were very influenced by Dylan's work and later recorded an album of his compositions.

The song was issued in the UK on 10 September 1965 on Fontana TF 600 and in the States on 20 September on Fontana 1525.

The flip side was entitled 'City Winds'. The disc was a minor hit in Britain, entering the *New Musical Express* charts at No. 20 for a single week, providing the Silkie with their only chart hit.

The Beatles' version of the number was recorded on the afternoon of Thursday 18 February at Abbey Road's Studio Two. An additional musician was brought in to join them on the track – a flautist, John Scott. Apart from Andy White performing as drummer on 'Love Me Do', this was the first time the Beatles had brought in an extra musician on one of their recording sessions.

A version without the overdubbed flute was included on the *Anthology 2* CDs.

Zappa, Frank

A singer-guitarist-songwriter, born in Baltimore on 21 December 1940. Zappa was founder of the Mothers of Invention and noted for his satires of popular culture, an example of which was his album *We're Only In It for the Money*, which lampooned the Beatles' *Sergeant Pepper* sleeve.

Zappa was to come to John's defence during the outcry over John's remarks about Christianity following the publication of the Maureen Cleave interview in the London *Evening Standard* (see **Cleave, Maureen**). Zappa stated publicly that he considered that John was right in what he had said.

For a time Zappa lived in London, where he wrote and starred in the film *200 Motels*, in which Ringo Starr also appeared in the role of Frank Zappa.

On Zappa's political comments, John had said, 'We appreciate Zappa's intellectual struggle to get through to people.'

On 6 June 1971, John and Yoko had been appearing on Howard Smith's talk show on WPLJ. Smith, who was also a writer of the 'Voices' column in the *Village Voice*, heard that John admired Zappa and took him round to meet him at the hotel at No. 1 Fifth Avenue, where he was staying with the Mothers of Invention. John was to say, 'I expected sort of a grubby maniac with naked women all over the place. The first